Short Story Criticism

Guide to Gale Literary Criticism Series

For criticism on	Consult these Gale series
Authors now living or who died after December 31, 1999	*CONTEMPORARY LITERARY CRITICISM (CLC)*
Authors who died between 1900 and 1999	*TWENTIETH-CENTURY LITERARY CRITICISM (TCLC)*
Authors who died between 1800 and 1899	*NINETEENTH-CENTURY LITERATURE CRITICISM (NCLC)*
Authors who died between 1400 and 1799	*LITERATURE CRITICISM FROM 1400 TO 1800 (LC)* *SHAKESPEAREAN CRITICISM (SC)*
Authors who died before 1400	*CLASSICAL AND MEDIEVAL LITERATURE CRITICISM (CMLC)*
Authors of books for children and young adults	*CHILDREN'S LITERATURE REVIEW (CLR)*
Dramatists	*DRAMA CRITICISM (DC)*
Poets	*POETRY CRITICISM (PC)*
Short story writers	*SHORT STORY CRITICISM (SSC)*
Black writers of the past two hundred years	*BLACK LITERATURE CRITICISM (BLC)* *BLACK LITERATURE CRITICISM SUPPLEMENT (BLCS)*
Hispanic writers of the late nineteenth and twentieth centuries	*HISPANIC LITERATURE CRITICISM (HLC)* *HISPANIC LITERATURE CRITICISM SUPPLEMENT (HLCS)*
Native North American writers and orators of the eighteenth, nineteenth, and twentieth centuries	*NATIVE NORTH AMERICAN LITERATURE (NNAL)*
Major authors from the Renaissance to the present	*WORLD LITERATURE CRITICISM, 1500 TO THE PRESENT (WLC)* *WORLD LITERATURE CRITICISM SUPPLEMENT (WLCS)*

ISSN 0895-9439

Volume 55

Short Story Criticism

Criticism of the
Works of Short Fiction Writers

Lynn M. Zott
Project Editor

GALE®

THOMSON
★
GALE

Detroit • New York • San Diego • San Francisco • Cleveland • New Haven, Conn. • Waterville, Maine • London • Munich

THOMSON
✦
GALE
™

Short Story Criticism, Vol. 55

Project Editor
Lynn M. Zott

Editorial
Jenny Cromie, Kathy D. Darrow, Justin Karr,
Julie Keppen, Ellen McGeagh

Research
Nicodemus Ford, Sarah Genik, Tamara C. Nott,
Tracie A. Richardson

Permissions
Shalice Shah-Caldwell

Imaging and Multimedia
Dean Dauphinais, Lezlie Light, Dan Newell

Product Design
Michael Logusz

Composition and Electronic Capture
Gary Leach

Manufacturing
Stacy L. Melson

LIBRARY OF CONGRESS CATALOG CARD NUMBER 88-641014

ISBN 0-7876-5955-X
ISSN 0895-9439

Contents

Preface vii

Acknowledgments ix

Literary Criticism Series Advisory Board xi

Preface

*S*hort Story Criticism (*SSC*) presents significant criticism of the world's greatest short story writers and provides supplementary biographical and bibliographical materials to guide the interested reader to a greater understanding of the authors of short fiction. This series was developed in response to suggestions from librarians serving high school, college, and public library patrons, who had noted a considerable number of requests for critical material on short story writers. Although major short story writers are covered in such Gale series as *Contemporary Literary Criticism* (*CLC*), *Twentieth-Century Literary Criticism* (*TCLC*), *Nineteenth-Century Literature Criticism* (*NCLC*), and *Literature Criticism from 1400 to 1800* (*LC*), librarians perceived the need for a series devoted solely to writers of the short story genre.

Scope of the Series

SSC is designed to serve as an introduction to major short story writers of all eras and nationalities. Since these authors have inspired a great deal of relevant critical material, *SSC* is necessarily selective, and the editors have chosen the most important published criticism to aid readers and students in their research.

Approximately four to six entries are included in each volume, and each entry presents a historical survey of critical response to an author's work or to a single, widely-studied work. The length of an entry is intended to reflect the amount of critical attention the author—or, in the case of a single-work entry, the work—has received from critics writing in English and from foreign critics in translation. Every attempt has been made to identify and include the most significant essays on each author's work. In order to provide these important critical pieces, the editors sometimes reprint essays that have appeared elsewhere in Gale's Literary Criticism Series. Such duplication, however, never exceeds twenty percent of an *SSC* volume.

Organization of the Book

An *SSC* entry consists of the following elements:

- The **Author Heading** cites the name under which the author most commonly wrote, followed by birth and death dates. Also located here are any name variations under which an author wrote, including transliterated forms for authors whose native languages use nonroman alphabets. If the author wrote consistently under a pseudonym, the pseudonym will be listed in the author heading and the author's actual name given in parentheses on the first line of the biographical and critical introduction. Uncertain birth or death dates are indicated by question marks. Single-work entries are preceded by the title of the work and its date of publication.

- The **Introduction** contains background information that introduces the reader to the author and the critical debates surrounding his or her work.

- A **Portrait of the Author** is included when available.

- The list of **Principal Works** is ordered chronologically by date of first publication and lists the most important works by the author. The first section comprises short story collections, novellas, and novella collections. The second section gives information on other major works by the author. For foreign authors, the editors have provided original foreign-language publication information and have selected what are considered the best and most complete English-language editions of their works.

- Reprinted **Criticism** is arranged chronologically in each entry to provide a useful perspective on changes in critical evaluation over time. All short story, novella, and collection titles by the author featured in the entry are printed in boldface type. The critic's name and the date of composition or publication of the critical work are given at the beginning of each piece of criticism. Unsigned criticism is preceded by the title of the source in which it appeared. Footnotes are reprinted at the end of each essay or excerpt. In the case of excerpted criticism, only those footnotes that pertain to the excerpted texts are included.

- Critical essays are prefaced by brief **Annotations** explicating each piece.

- A complete **Bibliographical Citation** of the original essay or book precedes each piece of criticism.

- An annotated bibliography of **Further Reading** appears at the end of each entry and suggests resources for additional study. In some cases, significant essays for which the editors could not obtain reprint rights are included here. Boxed material following the further reading list provides references to other biographical and critical sources on the author in series published by Gale.

Indexes

A **Cumulative Author Index** lists all of the authors that appear in a wide variety of reference sources published by the Gale Group, including *SSC*. A complete list of these sources is found facing the first page of the Author Index. The index also includes birth and death dates and cross references between pseudonyms and actual names.

A **Cumulative Nationality Index** lists all authors featured in *SSC* by nationality, followed by the number of the *SSC* volume in which their entry appears.

An alphabetical **Title Index** lists all short story, novella, and collection titles contained in the *SSC* volume in which it appears. Titles of short story collections, separately published novellas, and novella collections are printed in italics, while titles of individual short stories are printed in roman type with quotation marks. Each title is followed by the author's last name and corresponding volume and page numbers where commentary on the work is located. English-language translations of original foreign-language titles are cross-referenced to the foreign titles so that all references to discussion of a work are combined in one listing.

In response to numerous suggestions from librarians, Gale also produces an annual paperbound edition of the *SSC* cumulative title index. This annual cumulation, which alphabetically lists all titles reviewed in the series, is available to all customers. Additional copies of this index are available upon request. Librarians and patrons will welcome this separate index; it saves shelf space, is easy to use, and is recyclable upon receipt of the next edition.

Citing *Short Story Criticism*

When writing papers, students who quote directly from any volume in the Literature Criticism Series may use the following general format to footnote reprinted criticism. The first example pertains to material drawn from periodicals, the second to material reprinted from books.

Henry James, Jr., "Honoré de Balzac," *The Galaxy* 20 (December 1875), 814-36; reprinted in *Short Story Criticism,* vol. 5, ed. Thomas Votteler (Detroit: The Gale Group), 8-11.

Linda W. Wagner, "The Years of the Locust," *Ellen Glasgow: Beyond Convention* (University of Texas Press, 1982), 50-70; reprinted and excerpted in *Short Story Criticism,* vol. 34, ed. Anna Nesbitt Sheets (Farmington Hills, Mich.: The Gale Group), 80-82.

Suggestions are Welcome

Readers who wish to suggest new features, topics, or authors to appear in future volumes, or who have other suggestions or comments are cordially invited to call, write, or fax the Project Editor:

Project Editor, Literary Criticism Series
The Gale Group
27500 Drake Road
Farmington Hills, MI 48331-3535
1-800-347-4253 (GALE)
Fax: 248-699-8054

Acknowledgments

The editors wish to thank the copyright holders of the excerpted criticism included in this volume and the permissions managers of many book and magazine publishing companies for assisting us in securing reproduction rights. We are also grateful to the staffs of the Detroit Public Library, the Library of Congress, the University of Detroit Mercy Library, Wayne State University Purdy/Kresge Library Complex, and the University of Michigan Libraries for making their resources available to us. Following is a list of the copyright holders who have granted us permission to reproduce material in this volume of *SSC*. Every effort has been made to trace copyright, but if omissions have been made, please let us know.

PHOTOGRAPHS APPEARING IN *SSC*, VOLUME 55, WERE RECEIVED FROM THE FOLLOWING SOURCES:

Literary Criticism Series Advisory Board

The members of the Gale Group Literary Criticism Series Advisory Board—reference librarians and subject specialists from public, academic, and school library systems—represent a cross-section of our customer base and offer a variety of informed perspectives on both the presentation and content of our literature criticism products. Advisory board members assess and define such quality issues as the relevance, currency, and usefulness of the author coverage, critical content, and literary topics included in our series; evaluate the layout, presentation, and general quality of our printed volumes; provide feedback on the criteria used for selecting authors and topics covered in our series; provide suggestions for potential enhancements to our series; identify any gaps in our coverage of authors or literary topics, recommending authors or topics for inclusion; analyze the appropriateness of our content and presentation for various user audiences, such as high school students, undergraduates, graduate students, librarians, and educators; and offer feedback on any proposed changes/ enhancements to our series. We wish to thank the following advisors for their advice throughout the year.

Donald Barthelme
1931-1989

(Also wrote under the pseudonym of Lily McNeil) American short story writer, novelist, essayist, and children's author.

The following entry provides an overview of Barthelme's short fiction works. For additional information on his short fiction career, see *SSC,* Volume 2.

INTRODUCTION

A preeminent writer of experimental fiction, Barthelme created stories that are both humorous and unsettling by juxtaposing incongruous elements of contemporary language and culture. He typically structured a piece of short fiction in the form of a verbal collage by assembling disparate fragments of information, conversation, narrative, and wordplay and by detailing contemporary settings in which objects and abstract ideas proliferate and threaten to overwhelm his characters. Barthelme's writing is characterized by the absence of plot and character development, disjointed syntax and dialogue, parodies of technical, mass media, and intellectual jargon and clichés. His work contains allusions to philosophy, psychology, and various forms of art and popular culture. Barthelme entertained such themes as the ability of language to accurately convey thought and emotion, the function of art and the role of the artist in society, the complications of sexuality, the frailty and transience of human relationships, and the fragmentary nature of reality.

BIOGRAPHICAL INFORMATION

Barthelme was born in Philadelphia, Pennsylvania and raised in Houston, Texas, where his father became established as an innovative architect. While sharing his father's respect for visual art and architecture, Barthelme developed a strong interest in literature. After serving as editor for a literary journal published by the University of Texas and as a journalist and a museum director, Barthelme traveled to New York City in the early 1960s and edited *Locations,* a short-lived arts and literary journal. His first stories were published in literary periodicals during the early 1960s. A prolific writer, several of his stories appeared in the *New Yorker.* In his later years, he divided his time between New York City and a teaching position in the creative writing program at the University of Houston. He died of cancer in 1989.

MAJOR WORKS OF SHORT FICTION

Believing that traditional forms and structures of art and literature are inadequate for addressing the peculiar needs and concerns of the modern world, Barthelme endeavored to promote new and inventive approaches. Rather than creating traditional, linear fictional forms that provide commentary on life by conveying meaning and values that readers expect and are prepared to find, Barthelme viewed each of his stories as an individual object. In his early stories, many of which originally appeared in the *New Yorker* and were subsequently collected in the books *Come Back, Dr. Caligari* (1964) and *Unspeakable Practices, Unnatural Acts* (1968), Barthelme blended parodies of such media as advertising, comic books, and television shows with puns, non sequiturs, and disjointed dialogue and narrative. The publication of *City Life* (1970) solidified Barthelme's reputation as a major figure in contemporary literature. The stories in this collection exhibit such characteristic Barthelme devices as black humor, deadpan narrative tones, and experiments with syntax, punctuation, illustrations, and typography. In several stories Barthelme explored themes relating to art, including the positive and negative effects of irony, anxieties faced by artists who find traditional artistic approaches to life to be outmoded, and individuals whose search for meaning is complicated by a superabundance of objects, ideas, and random and incomprehensible events. Irony, anxiety, and sorrow are important motifs in the stories collected in *Sadness* (1972). The stories collected in *Great Days* (1979) and *Overnight to Many Distant Cities* (1983) feature several new elements along with Barthelme's various characteristic techniques and concerns. For instance, *Overnight to Many Distant Cities* is composed of stories juxtaposed with brief, dreamlike monologues. While some critics have faulted this collection for Barthelme's idiosyncratic use of literary devices, others note the presence of hope in many of the pieces as well as an uncharacteristic willingness by Barthelme to confront and reflect emotions. *Sixty Stories* (1981) and *Forty Stories* (1987) collect pieces from all phases of Barthelme's career.

CRITICAL RECEPTION

The unconventional nature of Barthelme's work has provoked extensive critical debate. His detractors perceive in his work a destructive impulse to subvert language and culture and an emphasis on despair and irrationalism. These critics claim that he offers no remedies for the ills of contemporary life that he documents and that he refuses to convey order, firm values, and meaning. On the other hand, Barthelme enjoys widespread critical acclaim and is particularly praised as a stylist who offers vital and regenerative qualities to literature. There have been several commentators who have noted parallels between Barthelme's stories and those of Franz Kafka and Jorge Luis Borges. They assert that like Kafka, Barthelme presents a surreal, irrational world in which the anxieties of his characters are amplified, and that he experiments with form like Borges to create fantastic and ironic scenarios that blur distinctions between the real and the imaginary. Some critics regard Barthelme as an insightful satirist who exposes pretentious ideas that purport to answer life's mysteries.

PRINCIPAL WORKS

Short Fiction

Come Back, Dr. Caligari 1964
Unspeakable Practices, Unnatural Acts 1968
City Life 1970
Sadness 1972
Amateurs 1976
Great Days 1979
Sixty Stories 1981
Overnight to Many Distant Cities 1983
Forty Stories 1987

The Teachings of Don B.: The Satires, Parodies, Fables, Illustrated Stories, and Plays of Donald Barthelme 1992

Other Major Works

Snow White (novel) 1967
The Slightly Irregular Fire Engine; or, The Hithering, Thithering Djinn (children's book) 1971
Guilty Pleasures (satirical essays) 1974
The Dead Father (novel) 1975
Paradise (novel) 1986
Sam's Bar (novel) 1987
The King (novel) 1990
Not-Knowing: The Essays and Interviews of Donald Barthelme (essays) 1997

CRITICISM

Morris Dickstein (essay date 1977)

SOURCE: Dickstein, Morris. "Fiction at the Crossroads." In *Critical Essays on Donald Barthelme,* edited by Richard F. Patteson, pp. 59-69. New York: G. K. Hall & Co., 1992.

[*In the following essay, originally published in 1977, Dickstein regards Barthelme's* City Life *as the apotheosis of fictional experimentation and ingenuity and compares it to other innovative fictional works of the late 1960s.*]

When two publishers in 1962 brought out overlapping collections of the work of the Argentine writer Jorge Luis Borges it was an important event for American readers, but few could have anticipated the impact it would have on our fiction. His work hardly fit into any traditional niche. The short story, even in the hands of Chekhov and Joyce, had always been the most conservative of all literary genres, the most tied to nineteenth-century conventions of incident and character, the least given to formal or technical innovation. Borges' stories hardly seemed to be stories at all; some of the best masqueraded as essays, laborious researches about nonexistent countries, ingenious commentaries on nonexistent books, mingled fantastically with the most out-of-the-way knowledge of real countries and real books. Where the traditional story took for granted the difference between the solid world out there and the imaginary world that tried to imitate it, Borges willfully confounded them. His stories were "fictions," original creations, less reflections than subversive interrogations of reality. They were also "labyrinths" which, like Kafka's writing, dressed out their mystery in a guise of earnest lucidity and matter-of-factness.

Today there is not much life in the old kind of story, though some good ones and many bad ones continue to be written. This sort of well-crafted object, which used to be the staple of dozens of now-defunct magazines, became so moribund in the sixties that it will now probably experience a mild resurgence, since changes in culture often proceed like swings of the pendulum. But the publication in 1975 of anthologies like *Superfiction* by Joe David Bellamy and *Statements* by members of the Fiction Collective confirms that our younger and more talented fiction writers have by no means abandoned the experimental impulse, though it may sometimes take them in wayward and even fruitless directions. Like so much of what emerged from the sixties, fiction today is a lesson in the uses of liberation. Whatever the results (and I intend to stress their current limitations), they remain inherently superior to a return to the old stringent molds, which conservative pundits are always ready to reimpose.

The progress of American fiction in the 1960s conjoined two different but related insurgencies against the constraints of traditional form, and against the cautious realism and psychological inwardness that had been dominant since the second world war. The first rebellion gave rise to big, eclectic books like John Barth's *The Sot-Weed Factor*, Heller's *Catch-22*, and Pynchon's *V.*, as well as ribald free-form tirades like Mailer's *Why Are We In Vietnam?* and Roth's *Portnoy's Complaint*. In all these books the grand raw materials of history, politics, literary tradition, and personal identity were transposed into fantasy, black or obscene humor, and apocalyptic personal expression. . . .

These writers did not so much cease to be realists as seek grotesque or hilarious (but accurate) equivalents for realities that were themselves fantastic. *Catch-22* not only did not lie about war, it scarcely even exaggerated. Portnoy is not fair to his mother but he is true to her, even as he caricatures and mythicizes her. These writers took advantage of the decline of censorship and of the constricting demands of formal neatness and realistic verisimilitude to broaden the range of fictional possibility, to discover new literary ancestors—Céline, Henry Miller, Nabokov, Genet—and to claim their legacy.

In the last three years of the sixties, however, culminating in the publication of Donald Barthelme's *City Life* (1970), but to some extent continuing right to the present day, a second insurgency came to the fore. Between 1967 and 1970 American fiction, following its Latin American counterpart, entered a new and more unexpected phase, which was also a more deliberately experimental one. For convenience we can call this the Borgesian phase, though Borges has not been the only model for the short, sometimes dazzlingly short, and multi-layered fiction that is involved. (Interestingly, Borges' example served to release the influence of others, including his own master, Kafka, and even such different writers as Beckett and Robbe-Grillet.)

In just these three years there were many significant collections of this new short fiction, including Barthelme's ***Unspeakable Practices, Unnatural Acts*** (the mock melo-

drama of the title is typical of him), Barth's *Lost in the Funhouse* (Barth's funhouse is the original American equivalent of Borges' labyrinth), William H. Gass's *In the Heart of the Heart of the Country*, Robert Coover's *Pricksongs & Descants* (subtitled "Fictions"), plus many of the impacted, truncated melodramas in Leonard Michaels' *Going Places* and some of the stories in Vonnegut's *Welcome to the Monkey House* (his novels were even more to the point). But the last of them, Barthelme's ***City Life,*** was more audacious and more successful than any of the other volumes, a book that went beyond experimental ingenuity to find new ways of connecting fiction with feeling. I'd like to use it as my positive pole in examining the uses of liberation in fiction, and I'll play it off against a larger number of other works, including some by Barthelme, which (to my mind) take experiment and liberation down less rewarding paths.

The collections I've listed all had a great deal in common, yet no two are alike. All tended to eliminate (or use ironically) the realistic matrix in which most works of fiction are embedded—the life-like quality that gives them credibility and coherence, the thematic explicitness that gives them the gratifying feel of significance. "We like books," Barthelme once wrote, "that have a lot of *dreck* in them, matter which presents itself as not wholly relevant (or indeed, at all relevant) but which, carefully attended to, can supply a kind of 'sense' of what is going on."[1] But these writers sometimes pay a heavy price for excising or satirizing this dross, which is rarely dross in good fiction anyway. They fall into inaccessibility, abstraction, or mere cleverness, substituting the *dreck* of literary self-consciousness for that of popular realism.

Coover and Barth, for example, seem overwhelmed by their own freedom, by the writer's power to invent a scene, a character, a world, to choose which word and which sentence he will set down next. Take Coover's maniacally brilliant and finally oppressive story "The Babysitter" (in *Pricksongs & Descants*), an elaborate set of variations on a few deliberately banal and melodramatic characters and plot possibilities, all merging into one another, all going off at once—a fiction-making machine run amok with its own powers, threatening to blow up in our faces, or blow our minds.

Several of Barth's stories in *Lost in the Funhouse* do comparable things in a more playful and self-ironical way. The title piece, for example, interweaves a sharp-minded yet pedantic commentary on fictional technique between the lines of a story that can't quite get itself written. In "Title" and "Life-Story," Barth can already subject this very manner of formal self-consciousness to a weary and ambivalent parody, which in turn gives the stories another layer of the same self-consciousness they criticize. Barth's fictions make the case against themselves neatly: "Another story about writing a story! Another regressus in infinitum! Who doesn't prefer art that at least overtly imitates something other than its own processes? That doesn't continually proclaim 'Don't forget I'm an artifice!'?"[2] At times the formalism and literary preciosity that were routed from the novel during the sixties seem to have returned with a vengeance in the new short fiction.

Self-consciousness has always been a key element in modern art, however, and in fiction (as Robert Alter has demonstrated anew in *Partial Magic*) it has a long ancestry that goes back beyond modernism to Diderot, Sterne, and Cervantes, a tradition that sometimes makes nineteenth-century realism look like a mere episode. (Fortunately we also have Erich Auerbach's book *Mimesis* to demonstrate the long and complex history of the realist method.) E. M. Forster once said that it's intrinsic to the artist to experiment with his medium, but in the twentieth century we've often seen how the spiral of self-consciousness can reach a point of diminishing returns. This happens when artists mimic other artists without fully appropriating them, or when they make their concerns as artists their exclusive subject. We need to hold fast to the distinction, often hard to apply, between experiment for its own sake, out of touch with any lived reality, and experiments that create genuinely new ways of seeing. The fiction of the sixties shows how the once-subversive gestures of modernism can themselves become tiresome conventions (as Barth suggests but can't seem to evade); but it also indicates, quite to the contrary, that only now that the towering first generation of modernists has been safely interred in literary history have our young writers been willing to resume the risks of the modernist program, which is nothing if not experimental and avant-garde.

I'd like to examine Barthelme's achievement in *City Life* and elsewhere to show what experimental writing has only recently been able to do without becoming self-indulgent or imitative. . . . Barthelme's earlier books, which were as intransigently original as *City Life,* were mostly notable for what they did *not* do, for the kinds of coherence they refused to supply, for their discontinuities and even incongruities, which mixed abstract ideas with pop allusions, political figures with fairy-tale characters, pedantically precise facts with wild generalities and exaggerations, and so on. They aimed to cut the reader off, to keep him guessing and thinking, to make him angry. His novel *Snow White* (1967) was a book that adamantly refused to go anywhere at all. Without benefit of plot, characters, or even much of the sober-zany humor of the stories in his first book, **Come Back, Dr. Caligari** (1964), the novel mainly limited itself to fragmentary take-offs on a huge variety of rhetorical styles and verbal trash. It was a minor-league version of what Ezra Pound saw in *Ulysses,* a species of encyclopedic satire; the book was all language, and at least on first acquaintance it seemed certain that the language was just not good enough to carry it.

Subsequent readings of *Snow White* have given me much more pleasure; though the book doesn't work as a whole, it has grown with time. It's still too detached, too satirical and fragmentary, but the author's really dry and wicked wit has worn surprisingly well. But it's finally too much of a book about itself and crippled by the absence of a

subject. Its detachment is deliberate, but it leaves a void that language and satire can't entirely fill. By the book's whimsical discontinuities, by a certain deadpan mechanical quality, by a whole range of Brechtian alienation devices, Barthelme was deliberately blocking the debased and facile kinds of identification that we readers make in traditional fiction, yet he found little to substitute. . . . Taking a cue, I suspect, from Godard's films, Barthelme eliminated most of the dross of primitive storytelling so that the *dreck* of contemporary culture could more devastatingly display itself. He tried to remain, as he said, "on the leading edge of this trash phenomenon,"[3] but the project was too plainly negative, and despite his wit he nearly foundered in the swill.

In his next book, *Unspeakable Practices, Unnatural Acts,* Barthelme still proclaimed that "fragments are the only forms I trust," but the fragments began insidiously to cohere, into point fables like **"The Balloon"** and **"The Police Band,"** into surreal and indirect political commentary, such as **"The President"** and **"Robert Kennedy Saved from Drowning."** Like Vonnegut and Pynchon, whom he somewhat resembles—indeed, like Dickens and Kafka—Barthelme discovered that fantasy and caricature could serve maliciously to heighten reality as well to block it out, that fiction could, by symbolism and indirection, recover the world that it had long since abandoned to the journalists and historians.

"The President" is part Swift, part Kafka, part surrealist playlet; its hero is "only forty-eight inches high at the shoulder," a graduate of City College, a "tiny, strange, and brilliant man."[4] He is like no president we've ever had, but his spooky presence tells us something about all of them. (In a similar way, when Pynchon and Vonnegut take on the Southern California scene, or the Eichmann case, or the Dresden bombings, they refract these topical subjects through a very personal imaginative medium, but without losing touch.)

In the Kennedy story Barthelme tried neither to explain Kennedy nor to give a credible portrait of him, but rather to thicken him into an enigma—he is called K. throughout—to find symbolic equivalents for his image, and for our fascination. Authentic facts—how he frequently changed shirts each day—mingle with astonishing inventions, such as Kennedy's capable discourse as [to] the literary criticism of Georges Poulet. The result is neither "about" Kennedy nor an exercise in Barthelme's technique, but a weird mélange of the two. The example of Borges may have made such an interrogation of reality possible, but Barthelme's handling of it is wholly original.

In *City Life* Barthelme for better or worse abjured topical occasions for literary and personal ones. The public immediacies of politics and war give way to Borgesian meditation on books, writers, and ideas. Barthelme was exploring his loyalties as an artist, and even his stylistic virtuosity, though toned down, served him well. There were a few stretches of mere verbal display or experiment for experiment's sake (an unreadable piece of Joycean gobbledygook called **"Bone Bubbles"** was the main offender).

Most of the stories move in an entirely different direction. At a time when some of Barthelme's contemporaries were trying hard to leave personal experience behind in hot pursuit of technical innovation, the pleasure of *City Life* came from seeing Barthelme break through to new areas of feeling with no loss of rhetorical verve. Without falling back to direct emotional statement or personal psychology, he learned to write fables whose ironies, far from blocking our emotions, make more complex demands upon them.

"Views of My Father Weeping" at once mimics a style of personal narrative, pays tribute to a whole body of literature in which such narrative abounds—it's written in the style of 1910 translations from the Russian—and interweaves two strands of action more successfully than Barthelme had ever done before. The speaker's father has been run down and killed by an aristocrat, but it is his father whom he repeatedly sees weeping: these alternating actions create between them a field of significance, an atmosphere rich in implicit emotion, while the author himself remains cool, detached, tantalizingly elusive. (The story concludes, staggeringly, on the word "etc.," as if to say, you've heard all this before, fill in the blanks. The text of *Snow White* included an actual questionnaire addressed to the reader.)

Following Borges (and Cervantes, for that matter), Barthelme discovered anew how crucially books mediate our access to our deepest experience, and he brings to his "discussions" of literature his own large reserves of fervor and ambiguity. Few passages in the book are more vivid than the retelling of a Tolstoy story in **"At the Tolstoy Museum"** or the paraphrase of Kierkegaard's theory of irony in **"Kierkegaard Unfair to Schlegel."** In each story the narrator, who may or may not be Barthelme, feels fascinated and alarmed by the strange, imposing figure he is confronting, by the book he is bringing to life. Tolstoy's story, he says, "is written in a very simple style. It is said to originate in a folk tale. There is a version of it in St. Augustine. I was incredibly depressed by reading this story. Its beauty. Distance."[5]

Most of Barthelme's story, however, is not about Tolstoy's work but about a museum full of huge pictures, clothing, and other supposed effects of Tolstoy—the book provides large illustrations of them—all of which are the absurdly displaced objects of the speaker's ambivalence toward Tolstoy, his nostalgia for Tolstoy's kind of writing. (The story begins with an echo of Psalm 137, a poem of exile and loss.) Tolstoy is after all the greatest of the realists, and his work is the immense anti-type to Barthelme's own mode of fantasy and irony. Yet the story that Barthelme chooses to retell, **"The Three Holy Men,"** is a small religious parable about three hermits and the strange but authentic way that they too pray. Moreover, his account of its atmosphere is eerily exact: "Its beauty. Distance."[6] Though most realistic in detail, the parable as a whole is cool in tone, integral, moving but untouchable—in short, very much like Barthelme's own tone. Tolstoy and Barthelme, opposites, rearrange themselves, and our conventional expectations

are disoriented. Traditional parable and contemporary fable meet, as if to arrange a joint subversion of realism in the cause of reality.

One could give a comparable account of the Kierkegaard story, which raises different issues, or of **"The Phantom of the Opera's Friend,"** which, besides being wonderfully funny, further develops Barthelme's rich involvement with melodrama, conventional realism, and kitsch, his longing, like Barth's, to be a more traditional kind of writer. (The book's illustrations, half absurdly old-fashioned, half surreal, betray the same secret wish.)

Should the Phantom of the Opera leave his sumptuous underground quarters to take up a respectable life in the "real" world? Will the "hot meat of romance" be "cooled by the dull gravy of common sense"? Does the narrator deserve a more conventional friend, from the world of Henry James perhaps, "with whom one could be seen abroad. With whom one could exchange country weekends, on our respective estates!"?[7] Will the angels in **"On Angels"** recover from the death of God and find new employment to replace their lapsed duties of adoration? Tuning in next week will not answer any of these questions, but Barthelme raises them in a way that gives a new wrinkle to the possible uses of pop material for serious purposes in fiction (mingled, in his case, with flotsam and jetsam of the most arcane intellectuality). Along with so many other of our new writers, Barthelme relegates the cultural hierarchies of the fifties to a memory. Learning to appreciate his best stories, we also learn to read in a new way, savoring them for their mock-serious humor, their imaginative weight, and their profound urbanity.

I've hardly done justice to the great variousness of *City Life,* or to the design of the book, which beautifully complements its substance. One story that must be mentioned is **"Brain Damage,"** which has no story at all but is a superb justification of Barthelme's fragmentary and surrealist method—he brings to mind the painter Magritte as much as he does any writer. It is one of the best pieces of non-sequential fictional prose I've ever read, a series of brilliant but unrelated narrative fragments—Barthelme could have been a fine conventional novelist—that finally cohere around the single inspired metaphor of the title.

The quality and character of Barthelme's work in the late sixties, and its frequent appearance in a glossy, above-ground periodical like *The New Yorker,* helped experimental fiction come of age in this country and released a flood that has continued to swell, though aside from *Gravity's Rainbow* it has yet to roar. In this, his best book, there's very little about city life but much that adds to our imaginative life and the life of our feelings. . . . *Snow White* and a later collection called *Sadness* have shown that Barthelme is not always strong in this way. More than fiction must have been involved when a character in *Snow White* made the following speech: "After a life rich in emotional defeats, I have looked around for other modes of misery, other roads to destruction. Now I limit myself to listening to what people say, and thinking what pamby it is, what they say. My nourishment is refined from the ongoing circus of the mind in motion. Give me the odd linguistic trip, stutter and fall, and I will be content."[8]

Barthelme comes out of all his books as a complex and enigmatic person, one who has seen many things, but *Snow White* was a book of personal withdrawal, dour satire, "the odd linguistic trip." I hope I've been able to indicate how *City Life,* with its new risks and new emotional defeats, represents a quite different sort of fictional victory.

The relative failure of *Chimera*[9] underlines the limitations of nostalgia as a solution to the dilemmas of experimental fiction. Nostalgia really does take the writer backward rather than forward. Traditional stories, however conscious they may make us of the writer's "creative contradictions," in themselves provide no instrument of creative breakthrough unless the writer experiences them in a new way. Barthelme's *Snow White,* though circumscribed by its linguistic and satirical rigor, was a much more successful book, for in its purity of intention it breaks more drastically with its traditional source. Where Barth's style is mock-dainty, or chatty and low, a lesson in the art of sinking in fiction, Barthelme's language is a model of planned incongruity. Like some of the New York poets, whose playfully surreal styles have similar roots, Barthelme has a background in the visual arts; he edited art journals, did the design for *Fiction* magazine, and illustrated many of his own stories, including a children's book. All his books are attractive objects, informed by an easy elegance and urbanity, and his fictional method is similar to his visual one. Barthelme the designer is principally a collector, who does bizarre collages of nineteenth-century engravings, the effect of which is neither wholly satiric, antiquarian, nor camp, but poised in a vacant eerie zone between nostalgia and irony, mad and mod. Barthelme the writer is also a connoisseur of other people's styles, not so much literary as sub-literary ones—the punishment corner of language, where curious things happen—from Victorian kitsch to modern pop, from professional jargon and journalistic formula to the capacious regions of contemporary cliché. His puckish feeling for other people's oddities of style is what makes *Guilty Pleasures,* his 1974 collection of fables and parodies, such an engaging book. The trash of inert language is his meat and drink. *Snow White* is a book about language, a collage of styles bleached and truncated into one pure and rigorous style of its own. Its fairy-tale subject is a hollow sham, the eye of a word-storm, the common theme of an anthology of ways of not saying anything. Its purity of purpose is cold and bracing: a good book for writers to read, like a verbal purge; or like ordinary-language philosophy, always sharpening the tools. But the book suits the theory of the new fiction a little too well: its surface is rarely ruffled, let alone subverted, by any actuality.

Snow White is an extreme case. Dominated by an austere, bookish wit and a negative appetite for verbal trash, it is a work of severe ironic distance. The perfection of Bar-

thelme's method, now so widely and ineptly imitated, comes in half a dozen stories of *Unspeakable Practices, Unnatural Acts* and nearly everything in its successor, *City Life,* still the most brilliant collection of experimental fiction these last years have produced. In stories like **"Brain Damage," "At the Tolstoy Museum,"** and **"Robert Kennedy Saved from Drowning,"** as I tried to show earlier, the cool mode heats up electrically, and experimental writing proceeds from critique to creation. Where *Snow White* is a clearing of the ground, these stories construct a new fictional reality. They show what even *Snow White* made clear; that Barthelme is no mere collector, but a writer who juxtaposes strange forms and fragments in a way that creates new form and releases new meanings. Where *Snow White* is mainly an ironic book, *City Life* is also an impassioned one. *Snow White* is more sophisticated and condescending but it is experientially vacuous; *City Life* gives free play to that other side of Barthelme's temperament, the melancholy nostalgia for traditional art and old-fashioned feelings, unlike Barth's a nostalgia that animates rather than inhibits him. The longing is hopeless of course—he can't try to be Tolstoy. But he can plumb his ambivalence and make that contribute to the enigma, adding thick shadows to his subject. The Barthian writer escapes from personality; though he babbles about himself incessantly he discovers very little and achieve no deep subjectivity; his self-consciousness tells him that no art, no imagination, is still possible, and the prophecy is self-fulfilling. The Barthelmian writer is scarcely ever present; he loses himself in the oddest, most unpromising subjects—Kierkegaard, Robert Kennedy, angels, the Phantom of the Opera—but the space between passion and irony is filled with new perceptions and connections, self-discoveries, as in all the best fiction. The art is not confessional but it is hauntingly personal, full of mood and mystery, and the author is arrestingly present. Where writers like Wurlitzer, proclaiming the death of feeling, merely betray their own emotional poverty, Barthelme finds new imaginative life in the heart of the contemporary wasteland, in the land of "brain damage," where art shacks up with kitsch and tradition lies down with the New. This art of incongruity brings Barthelme's stories closer to the work of the comic-apocalyptic writers of the early sixties, such as Pynchon, Heller, and Vonnegut—who meet reality halfway, and strike a Faustian bargain—than to the verbal austerities of, say, Gass's fiction, or of his own younger admirers.

Unfortunately Barthelme was unable fully to maintain his creative élan in the early seventies, and his difficulties are symptomatic of the problems of experimental writing during this period. Fiction is one of the few areas of our cultural life where the breakthroughs of the sixties have been sustained, if not carried forward. By the fall of 1973 *Newsweek* could inform its readers that Barthelme had become the greatest influence on our newer writers, but by then it seemed clear that neither the established nor the younger talents had delivered the body of innovative work the late sixties had seemed to promise. Other writers imitated Barthelme's manner rather than his inventive rigor, while he himself fell frequently into shallowness, decadence, and self-imitation. On both sides this resulted not in the kinds of stunning collage and fable that made *City Life* fresh and important but in an epidemic of easy-to-write pastiche or put-on which would have been at home in a college humor magazine of the 1950s.

It was to the credit of Barthelme's next (but weakest) collection of stories, *Sadness* (1972), that he became very conscious of the perils of repetition and self-parody. His main sadness is the fear that he's already said what he has to say: "When one has spoken a lot one has already used up all of the ideas one has. You must change the people you are speaking to so that you appear, to yourself, to be still alive."[10]

It is difficult to keep the public interested. "The public demands new wonders piled on new wonders. Often we don't know where our next marvel is coming from. The supply of strange ideas is not endless. . . . The new volcano we have just placed under contract seems very promising. . . ."[11] The realistic writer, who may take his form for granted, in principle need only find another corner of reality to portray, another "subject" for a novel. If he has the energy he can write a *Comédie Humaine*; this may be why writers like Updike and Joyce Carol Oates are so prolific. But the writer who interrogates and subverts his form at every turn has no such luck. He can run out of new wonders very easily, or stick to a manner that quickly degenerates into mannerisms.

Though it contains a few good stories, *Sadness* is a sad case in point, for it exposes the underside of all the writer's virtues. It shows who the collage method fails when the fragments remains disjunctive, unillumined. It shows how the fascination with cultural trash can devolve into a taste for trivia, lovingly collected but barely transformed. It exposes the merely campy side of Barthelme's interest in melodrama, kitsch, and old-fashioned iconography, or the snobbish side, in which the artist flaunts his cultural status while slumming and loving it. The book even betrays the limitations of Barthelme's most basic virtue, his purity of language and narrative technique, which cleans up too much—psychology, description, interaction—leaving only plastic figures with curious names, leaving elegant surfaces that mesh too well with *The New Yorker*'s waning cult of style.

Barthelme is at his worst where the realistic writer is best: in describing the relations between men and women. Here he retreats entirely into the satiric and ironic mode of *Snow White* but without that book's freshness and wit. (I suspect this accounts for some of the difficulties he had in writing a second novel.) *Sadness* is much too full of the trivial and the inconsequential, the merely decorative or the merely enigmatic. I have no idea why Barthelme regressed in *Sadness* from the passionate fabulistic manner of his two previous books, except for the reasons he himself suggests, but the lesson for experimental fiction is clear enough. The "cool" mode has its limitations, espe-

cially in a period of disengagement and disintegration like our own. When **"Robert Kennedy Saved from Drowning"** (arguably Barthelme's best story) appeared in book form in the late sixties, an otherwise admiring William Gass dismissed it, no doubt in alarm over its topicality. But the story is both fervently engaged and formally daring. Barthelme needs a great subject, an immediate subject, to draw him at least halfway out of his irony and aesthetic detachment. The feverish immediacy of life in the late sixties, the energy and pressure and swirl, which affected all of us, worked their way into his fiction with a fascinating indirection, just as it ruined some writers who tried to devour it too directly. Without that stimulus, without the pull of social ferment and spiritual possibility, Barthelme's work in *Sadness* looks the same but feels listless and remote, sketched rather than imagined.[12]

Notes

1. Donald Barthelme, *Snow White* (New York: Atheneum, 1967), 106.

2. John Barth, *Lost in the Funhouse* (Garden City, N.Y.: Doubleday, 1968), 117.

3. Barthelme, *Snow White*, 97.

4. Donald Barthelme, *Unspeakable Practices, Unnatural Acts* (New York: Farrar, Straus and Giroux, 1968), 147, 150.

5. Donald Barthelme, *City Life* (New York: Farrar, Straus and Giroux, 1970), 47.

6. Barthelme, *City Life*, 47.

7. Barthelme, *City Life*, 103.

8. Barthelme, *Snow White*, 139.

9. [*Ed. note:* In its original form, this section was preceded by a discussion of John Barth.]

10. Donald Barthelme, *Sadness* (New York: Farrar, Straus and Giroux, 1972), 61.

11. Barthelme, *Sadness*, 139.

12. *The Dead Father* (1975), his second novel, is better but not much better. It abandons the satiric language of *Snow White* for the gusto of Rabelaisian catalogues and word-heaps. Only one segment shows Barthelme at his best: an utterly brilliant but entirely tangential text-within-a-text called "A Manual for Sons," which once appeared separately in *The New Yorker.*

Paul Bruss (essay date 1981)

SOURCE: Bruss, Paul. "Barthelme's Short Stories: Ironic Suspensions of Text." In *Victims: Textual Strategies in Recent American Fiction*, pp. 113-29. Lewisburg: Bucknell University Press, 1981.

[*In the following essay, Bruss explores the suspension of self and the roles of narrative style and irony in Barthelme's short fiction.*]

One of Barthelme's early short stories contains this quotation, which is Robert Kennedy's comment on Poulet's analysis of Marivaux:

> The Marivaudian being is, according to Poulet, a pastless futureless man, born anew at every instant. The instants are points which organize themselves into a line, but what is important is the instant, not the line. The Marivaudian being has in a sense no history. Nothing follows from what has gone before. He is constantly surprised. He cannot predict his own reaction to events. He is constantly being *overtaken* by events. A condition of breathlessness and dazzlement surrounds him. In consequence he exists in a certain freshness which seems . . . very desirable.
>
> ([*Unspeakable Practices, Unnatural Acts;* hereafter]
> *UP,* 46)

This passage serves nicely as a touchstone for an introduction to Barthelme's short fiction because it addresses, with remarkable fullness, the matter of the timeless present that generally serves as the fundamental boundary for all human activity. It is true that Barthelme's stories frequently focus upon characters who are profoundly conscious of past achievements and/or of future goals, as if time were a continuum within which they can carefully stage their lives. Nevertheless, because these characters also know the terrible difficulty of trying to substantiate themselves, of verifying their perspectives as real, this consciousness of past and future tends to submerge in the overwhelming pressures of facing up to the present. The characters cannot know themselves in any final, absolute way, and for them, therefore, the question of their existence comes down to whether they possess the courage to acknowledge their insufficiency and, even more than that, whether they possess the vigor and freedom of mind to participate in a full dialogue with the present. In the process of "being *overtaken* by events," the characters have a wonderful opportunity for observing the nature of their own reactions, to perceive the emergence of a texture that is both unanticipated and imaginative, and thus to explore that mode of Marivaudian being which has become the foundation of so much recent art.

In Barthelme's fiction time ultimately surrenders all authority. To some extent this surrender is already present in Nabokov—at least in the sense that, having freed his narrators to explore the bizarre character of their imaginative being, Nabokov develops a narrative texture that appears to be dominated by the succession of time but that finally only recovers the specific mingling of memory and the imagination in the present. As a result of the tricks of both memory and imagination, Nabokov's narrators always have some difficulty in maintaining strong coherence within their conceptions of themselves, particularly when they unleash their Humberts and Kinbotes, but in the end the dialogue of selves that underlies each Nabokovian text does stabilize in the narrators' increasing understanding of themselves.[1] In Barthelme, on the other hand, the narrator generally possesses a more fragile, and sometimes very tenuous, relationship to a conception of self; and thus, al-

ways worried about the character of his identity, but at the same time recognizing that the identity will never cohere, he must engage in deliberate acts of suspension that allow him to come into closer contact with that complex world of the present which surrounds him. The narrator, or the character, who manages to avoid full organization "into a line" (where plural instants of time develop some pattern), gains a genuine, albeit limited (because he will never fully understand it), opportunity for freedom, for fresh personality, for spontaneity—for that "condition of breathlessness and dazzlement" which is crucial to retaining life's intensity. Man's deliberate surrender of authority for himself to the processes of being in which he is "overtaken by events" is for Barthelme, then, the key to the overthrow of time's authority and thus of those psychological obstacles which prevent man from remarking and even relishing the strangeness of whatever surrounds him. Quilty and Shade and even Veen manage this surrender only through the contrivances of narrative stance. In Barthelme, however, this surrender is the possession not only of certain obtrusive narrators, but also of all those characters who have avoided lives of content by maintaining full contact with the marvelous texture of the everyday experience that is theirs by birthright but that is so frequently lost in a misguided determination to establish a web of significance for experience.

Poulet's analysis of Marivaudian being serves as a nice touchstone for Barthelme's fiction because it isolates the fundamental consideration that underlies all of Barthelme's techniques. So often readers of Barthelme tend to dismiss him as a master of the parody, as a writer who is particularly adroit at capturing and mocking the absurd character of contemporary experience, but his ability in creating brief yet effusive forays into the quirks of the present is actually better evidence of his awareness of the impossibility of what has gradually become the post-existential position. For the post-existentialist, vision (even if created and sanctioned by the individual) is virtually a contradiction of itself: regardless of what one may accept as a framework of significance and value, the framework exists on quicksand because it can never contain all the perceptions that impinge on any human consciousness. The post-existentialist, therefore, like Barthelme's resourceful characters, cannot expend himself in anxiety over the consistency of his responses to the environment (as did many of the existentialists) but must, instead, freely indulge himself in the marvelous quiddities of the moment. He may not always regard those quiddities with enthusiasm, but at the very least he must accept as the source of his vitality and energy his contact with what in any ultimate sense represents the unknown but what in the immediate present is an opportunity for the unleashing of his being. Like the beings of Marivaux, Barthelme's characters extend themselves in what amounts to a negative space—negative because the space is not dominated by the characters' categories of thought—and thus come into touch with the deeper structures of their experience. That this is the case becomes even more evident if I now turn my attention to several of Barthelme's stories in which he, by employing a question-and-answer methodology, appears to pursue the reverse, i.e., positive (filled) space.

In **"The Explanation"** the exchanges between Q. (the questioner) and A. (the answerer) seem to be focused upon the desire for a full understanding of life's mysteries. The questioner is from the beginning, however, so overwhelmed by the monumentality of the task that he has great difficulty sticking even to one topic. As he shifts from subject to subject, in fact, from machines to blouses to literary questions to Maoism, the story turns into a rather exciting venture because its lacunae seem to swallow up the questioner's intentions, thus giving the story an unexpected texture in which negative space counts rather heavily. The black square that punctuates the story, apparently at random, probably serves as the best image of this negative space, but in the end all the verbal exchanges in the story (much like the exchanges between Julie and Emma in *The Dead Father* and the dialogues in **Great Days**) accomplish nothing and thus themselves rival the importance of the black square. Toward the middle of the story A. at least gives the reader a hint of what is happening when he comments on the advantage of Q.'s Socratic method: "I realize that [the method] permits many valuable omissions: what kind of day it is, what I'm wearing, what I'm thinking. That's a very considerable advantage, I would say" ([*City Life*; hereafter] *CL,* 73). A.'s comment goes to the heart of the matter, for by allowing the lacunae within and between the bits of conversation to take over the story, Q. has effectively avoided the folly of establishing a model that purports to explain all human experience. Later the shrewd A. seems to figure out what underlies Q.'s method, for during a conversation about madness and purity A. suddenly observes that "the content of right reason is rhetoric."[2] In other words, what A. seems to realize is that any system of understanding is dominated, not by "right reason" or unassailable models of logic, but by the persuasive powers of rhetoric—by the attitudes and assumptions that allow a logic to emerge. In and of itself, of course, rhetoric possesses no sufficient ground. It is merely the means (largely a technique or style) whereby a content is established. In Barthelme's fiction, because there is no category of absolute content, rhetoric—technique and style—lacks its usual function but at the same time becomes all the more important. Near the end of the story Q. rather urbanely points out that "the issues raised here are equivalents. Reasons and conclusions exist although they exist elsewhere, not here" (*CL,* 78). Reasons and conclusions generally reflect the use of an established, consistent rhetoric, and in the absence of such a rhetoric, as in this story of open-ended juxtaposition of questions and answers, there seems nothing to control the exchanges and thus organize the conversation. The exchanges in such a situation can only represent equivalent moments in time. Despite the lack, however, of a traditional rhetoric, one that supports the conventional acts of communication, this story does achieve its own imaginative, even supralogical, rhetorical character.

In **"The Agreement,"** a brilliant tour de force, the answers actually disappear. In the story, which is merely a long series of questions, the questions emerge out of the narrator's paranoia concerning his ability to complete the "task" (which is never specified), and they generate a nearly incredible realization of the anxieties latent in his awareness of the fundamental solipsism that attaches to human consciousness. Consider, for instance, the following sequence:

> Will I deceive myself about the task that is beyond my abilities, telling myself that I have successfully completed it when I have not?
>
> Will others aid in the deception?
>
> Will others unveil the deception?
>
> ([*Amateurs*; hereafter] *A,* 62-63)

This passage clearly addresses the horror of the narrator's inhabiting of a world of hypersensitivity where the personal splitting of hairs has become the modus operandi. Try as he may to establish for himself a stance of some courage and determination, he is always left only with the enervating sense that the assumptions underlying any stance he might choose lack sufficiency. The upshot is that, instead of accepting the limitations that attach to any formulation of experience, he increasingly finds himself the victim of a paranoia that has as its sources both his sense of the "mess" out there and his sense of his own inadequacies before the fundamental dilemmas of contemporary epistemology. As he recites the case, "If I embrace the proposition that, after all, things are not so bad, which is not true, then have I not also embraced a hundred other propositions, kin to the first in that they are also not true? That the Lord is my shepherd, for example?" (*A,* 64). Clearly this narrator desires the positive space of secure, i.e., rationalized, ground, and in its absence, instead of courageously accepting the challenge of Marivaudian being, he finds himself the victim of such nagging anxiety that finally he approaches the necessity of deliberate self-deception. Paranoid about himself, he even finds that he has no choice but to resort to social activities and associations that can convince him of his self-worth. Such deception will, however, depend heavily on "aid" from others, for given the extremity of his paranoia this narrator now requires the corroborating evidence of others in order to recover his pose of esteem. His is obviously a thoroughly unsatisfactory situation. At the very end of the story he may quote at length—and rather wistfully—the twelfth article of his divorce agreement, an agreement that seemingly spells out in detail the "rights, obligations and causes of action arising out of or under this agreement," but even that agreement cannot give him the stability and exactitude that he desires. The divorce agreement, in fact, serves only as another illustration of his inability to rise above his paranoia, to surrender to the world of the present.

If in **"The Explanation"** the avoidance of strict logic and rhetoric makes possible a life of Marivaudian being, **"The Agreement"** points to the difficulty of achieving a separation from logic and rhetoric that will allow one to suspend oneself in the processes of unfolding experience. The first story exposes an eloquence of being; the second story, the failure to achieve the same. In a third story written in the Socratic method, **"The Catechist,"** the difficulty of establishing sufficient appreciation of one's "deeper structures" becomes even more clear. In the story the first-person narrator, himself a priest, encounters another priest who, while holding a text on church doctrine, daily catechizes the first priest about his use of alcohol and his relationship with a woman with dark hair. In order to deflect the catechist's concerns, the first priest alludes to the presence of alternative interpretations within any situation—a theme that causes the catechist to refer to his book, where he finally discovers the response, "*A disappointing experience: the inadequacy of language to express thought. But let the catechist take courage*" ([*Sadness*; hereafter] *S,* 122). Intellectually, prompted by the text on doctrine, the catechist knows the problem of language and thus the corollary inadequacy of any rhetoric that presumes to fill the lacunae within all verbal statements, but there is little sense in the story that this knowledge has profoundly opened him up to experience. Rather, he is still clinging to as much structure as the church can provide. When the first priest proceeds with his "self-defense," in fact, by professing to know nothing even of the theological virtue of love, the catechist immediately refers to several theologians whose views have established the ground for his own experience of that lofty emotion. Unquestionably the catechist requires a stable world of language and meaning that is no longer available to the first priest. In a certain sense what the first priest provides the catechist is an opportunity to come into contact with the deeper character of human experience—that character which lies beyond definitions wedded to doctrine. The catechist, however, fails to open up.

On the other hand, at least once he has given himself up to emotional realities beyond doctrinal limits, the first priest experiences only a compulsion to write inconclusive letters ("one does what one can") or to submit to "analysis terminable and interminable" (*S,* 125). He has surrendered himself to the deeper character of his experience but in the process has lost his comfortable grasp on "reality." When the catechist questions him about his call to the priesthood, for example, the bewildered priest can only admit that he "heard many things. Screams. Suites for unaccompanied cello. I did not hear a call" (*S,* 125). The catechist has failed to appreciate his having been trapped within a theological rhetoric, but the first priest, presumably more perceptive and imaginative, has failed to establish a creative relationship to a new, presumably more open, style that would allow him to accept the character of each moment in time as sufficient in itself. At the end of the story, to be sure, the priest does return to the woman with the dark hair. The woman, however, is married to a psychologist who is engaged in measuring "vanishing points" in an effort "to define precisely the two limiting sensations in the sensory continuum, the upper limit and the lower limit" (*S,* 126). Much in the fashion of this psychologist, who, despite his learned awareness of the limitations of perception and language, tries to quantify what is surely variable

from person to person, the priest still hopes for some understanding and thus fails to surrender fully to the unstable nature of his experience. Instead of embracing from moment to moment a process of being that is inexplicable and thus unpredictable, he—despite his sensitivity—still thinks in terms of defining the limits of his own understanding. He has moved beyond the catechist's dilemma, but he is not yet free.

The most interesting feature of these three stories is that their method virtually contradicts what Barthelme seems to have concluded about human experience. The very posture of questioning, because it entails the construction of answers, frequently prevents the questioner from achieving that final gesture of liberation in which he, having recognized the unavailability of answers, turns his experience into the creative play, not of content, but of mere being.[3] The principals in **"The Explanation,"** because they recognize that there is no explanation, gain such imaginative ground. The principals in **"The Agreement"** and in **"The Catechist,"** on the other hand, display varying degrees of hysteria because they fail to separate themselves entirely from the need for understanding. Even the narrating priest, whom the reader might not initially associate with hysteria, lacks the perspective that would introduce him to a radically new sense of being. What happens in these three stories, of course, generally characterizes the heart of almost all of Barthelme's fiction, where there is never much effective communication or human understanding. Whether I cite *Snow White,* which focuses upon problems of communication among peers, or *The Dead Father,* which focuses upon problems of communication between generations, the difficulty of substituting a new openness for the limited grounds of the past leads to the failure of all the principal characters. Trapped within their own solipsism, these characters know only a profound sense of personal inadequacy when dealing with the world of people about them. In order to broaden my discussion of this sense of inadequacy in Barthelme's fiction, I want to examine briefly four stories in which the husband-wife, the father-son, and the doctor-patient relationships serve almost as paradigms for man's fundamental need for a suspension of self as a means of countering his deeply felt anxieties.

In the first story, entitled **"The Big Broadcast of 1938,"** the principal character, Bloomsbury, manages to retain his hold on reality following a divorce from his wife, Martha, only by sounding off as the rather peculiar owner of a radio station. Repeatedly, and in an incantatory manner, he singles out in his broadcasts, "for special notice, free among all the others, some particular word in the English language, and repeat[s] it in a monotonous voice for as much as fifteen minutes, or a quarter-hour" ([*Come Back, Dr. Caligari*; hereafter] *DC,* 67). On occasion such repetition discloses in a word "new properties, unsuspected qualities," almost as if the repetition were introducing the speaker to a new level of eloquence, but because Bloomsbury has actually intended only to fill up the time with such repetitions he never realizes that new dimension of experience which is rooted in a shrewd appreciation of the function of language in his life. That this is the case becomes more apparent when Bloomsbury devotes himself to a series of radio "announcements" that he directs at his wife. One of these announcements toward the end of the story gets to the heart of the matter: "You [Martha] veiled yourself from me, there were parts I could have and parts I couldn't have. And the rules would change, I remember, in the middle of the game, I could never be sure which parts were allowed and which not" (*DC,* 77). What Bloomsbury wanted in his relationship with Martha was stability, i.e., a stability that matched up with his conception of what a marriage should be. What he fails to realize here, however, is that short of defusing the normal processes of perception and language, stability will always remain an impossible goal. Stability is basically a function of content, and in a world where content is secondary to the actual processes of perception and language, stability cannot serve as the object of a relationship. When a dissatisfied Martha openly took another lover, therefore, the unimaginative Bloomsbury, who required above everything else steadiness in his life, completely fell apart. Having fashioned himself a "reckoner," someone who could tally up the events of life and thus establish its significant quality, he could not deal with a situation that lay beyond his tally sheet. His experience without Martha is hardly much different. By his own reckoning Bloomsbury may have been "an All-American boy," but now, following the collapse of his marriage, he continues to display the All-American failure to acknowledge the fundamental limitations of his childhood patterns of perception and language. Threatened, even cornered, by his recent experience, he resorts to the expedience of concentrating on words like *nevertheless,* or *assimilate, alleviate, authenticate, ameliorate,* or *matriculate*—all words that by virtue of their suggestiveness seem to offer a subtle and imaginative comment on his life—but finally these words fail to enlarge his understanding of that eloquence which lies at the heart of Barthelme's fiction.[4] The story concludes with the termination of Bloomsbury's broadcasting career in the interruption of electrical service as a result of an arrears in his account. His propensity for reckoning has entirely failed him.

In the second story, **"Views of My Father Weeping,"** which serves as a brilliant analogue to *The Dead Father,* the relationship shifts to that of father and son. In the story the son, who has always felt powerless in the presence of his father, sets out to determine the facts of his father's death (the father has been run over by an aristocrat's carriage). From the beginning of the story, however, it is clear that he has had great difficulty establishing a perspective of his father when alive and, now, cannot establish a perspective of him when killed. He cannot, for example, ascertain whether it is his father who was lying in bed weeping or whether it is his father who, by virtue of drinking, was at fault in the carriage accident. The first issue, that of a perspective on his father when alive, explodes only in a series of unrelated images—such as the father wearing "a large hat (straw) on which there are a number of blue and yellow plastic jonquils" (*CL,* 13) or

"peering through an open door into an empty house" (*CL,* 14) or "weeping" in bed (*CL,* 14) or "attending a class in good behavior" (*CL,* 15). Clearly there is no coherence in the images. In fact, the only moment of intensity that the son remembers in his dealings with the father, a moment that presumably might solidify his character, occurs on a hunting trip when, in the absence of "a long list of animals" (*CL,* 13) to shoot at, the two of them "hunkered down behind some rocks, Father and I, he hunkered down behind his rocks and I hunkered down behind my rocks, and we commenced to shooting at each other. That was interesting" (*CL,* 13). It is a strange scene—but not so strange, perhaps, in the absence of a coherent perspective that might bind father and son together. The son and his father are separate, and thus after the father's death the son still feels the difficulty of verifying the nature of his father. He never succeeds. The other issue, that of verifying the father's responsibility for the accident, would appear to reach a similar conclusion, but here the story takes a new turn. The son may establish the identity of the aristocrat's liveryman, but he also finds other witnesses to the event who both affirm and deny the father's blame. Even when the son visits the aristocrat's house, he hears in one moment the liveryman deny any responsibility for the tragedy and in the next a dark-haired girl rebuke the liveryman for being "an absolute bloody liar" (*CL,* 16). The son, like the questioners and catechists, can never get to the heart of the matter, at least in a preconceived sense, for the real problem in this situation is the limitation of all perception and language—a fact that depreciates the value of content and reinforces the importance of developing the ability to suspend oneself continuously in the processes of experience. The story concludes on the simple note of "Etc." and at that point the fundamental question before the reader is whether the son has embraced this principle of suspension.[5] Given the style of the story, one of Barthelme's finest and one narrated by the son, I think it probable that he has. A Bloomsbury he is not.

In the third story, **"The Sandman,"** which is essentially a letter from the narrator to his girl friend's psychiatrist (the Sandman), the importance of suspension in life's processes rather than adherence to a content is unmistakable. In his letter the narrator accuses Dr. Hodder, who has judged Susan to be a voyeur, of allowing "norms" to "skew" his view of Susan's problem (*S,* 92). What is interesting about the accusation, of course, is that the narrator, privy to Barthelme's basic attitudes, recognizes that the reliance upon norms introduces a content that may have little, if any, validity in its application to Susan. Hodder's belief, for example, that Susan might "become an artist and live happily ever after" profoundly troubles the narrator not only because such a belief is a commonly accepted norm for creative people but also because, at least in his eyes, "the paradigmatic artistic experience is that of failure" (*S,* 93). In his view Hodder's juxtaposition of Susan and a happy career as an artist constitutes an incredibly naive and arbitrary formulation of a "content." The narrator, presumably because he is more sensitive to the dilemmas of perception and language, shrewdly recognizes that the artist deals fundamentally in failure because "the actualization [that he seeks in his art] fails to meet, equal, the intuition" with which he initiates his work. For the narrator, Hodder's associating of Susan, or anyone with an imagination as alive as Susan's, with the "content" of an artist is pointless because the artist finally deals not in content but in the processes that surround and support his being—and that resist easy classification and understanding. Distressed by the confusion or, perhaps, the absence of content in her life, Susan may herself have sought Hodder's assistance, but at the same time, as the narrator is quick to point out, she has taken care to avoid the easy content of such "instant gratification as dealt out by so-called encounter or sensitivity groups, nude marathons, or dope" (*S*, 94). Regardless of Hodder's appraisal of her dilemma, therefore, it is clear that her imaginative world lies well beyond a dependence upon his limited formulations. Eventually, in fact, having routinely seduced Hodder (he is himself clearly open to "instant gratification"), she recognizes that he possesses no real solution to the basic doubts that have momentarily diminished her self-confidence. She thus initiates her withdrawal from Hodder, and it is at that point, having patiently waited for Susan to master her own problem, that the narrator writes his letter in order to squelch any further interference in Susan's life that Hodder might be considering. As the narrator remarks about Susan, "Susan is wonderful. *As is.* There are not so many things around to which that word can be accurately applied" (*S*, 95). It is an astute observation. The imaginative being who develops his own technique and style, his own eloquence of being, despite the failure of all content, is genuinely a marvel.

There is another early story that parallels, but with a significant twist, **"The Sandman."** That story, entitled **"Alice,"** is noteworthy not only because of the narrator's general suppression of punctuation (an act that destroys the fragile border between coherence and chaos) but also because of the narrator's indulging of himself in daydreams that center on a desire that compromises his professional ethics. In this story the narrator is the doctor, here an obstetrician, who in the course of his practice falls prey to an overwhelming desire to "fornicate with Alice" (*UP*, 119). The obstetrician is aware of the potential impact of such a relationship upon both his own and Alice's marriages, but influenced by the intellectual atmosphere of the New School he easily manages to regard "'good' and 'bad' as terms with only an emotive meaning" (*UP*, 125). Like the psychiatrist in **"The Sandman,"** the obstetrician with an air of sophistication tries to create a clever game whereby he might calm those moral qualms which hinder the fruition of his desire. Toward the end of the story, however, having already fantasized his release from the bonds of moral perspective, this obstetrician continues to consider such facts of his past experience as his having "followed obediently in the footsteps of my teachers" (*UP*, 126). Obviously, even after long consideration, he is having difficulty overthrowing his deep-seated moral scruples. His fantasies may turn to the crudeness of "chewing" on Alice's breasts, but by the end of the story, with no fruition

of his desire at hand, he has managed only a sensitive examination of his situation—yet an examination that surely surpasses the psychiatrist's rather easy formulations. Here is the obstetrician's appraisal of himself:

> possible attitudes found in books 1) I don't know what's happening to me 2) what does it mean? 3) seized with the deepest sadness, I know not why 4) I am lost, my head whirls, I know not where I am 5) I lose myself 6) I ask you, what have I come to? 7) I no longer know where I am, what is this country? 8) had I fallen from the skies, I could not be more giddy 9) a mixture of pleasure and confusion, that is my state 10) where am I, and when will this end? 11) what shall I do? I do not know where I am

> (*UP*, 127)

Unlike the psychiatrist, the obstetrician does not possess an easy ground for initiating extramarital affairs. No matter what stance he adopts in relation to his desire for Alice, he cannot avoid the terrible sense of violating the moral field of his past experience. The reader who is impatient with his temporizing might even be tempted to accuse him of having allowed himself to be victimized by a rather narrow perspective of human relationships. And yet, particularly if one recalls the nature of Bloomsbury's possessiveness, there is good reason to argue, here, that the obstetrician is in fact very sophisticated in his examination of his personal situation. Indeed, instead of merely violating his past, or instead of merely discounting the significance of a relationship with Alice, he shows a wonderful ability to sustain himself in the very complicated addressing of the contradictions that have surfaced in his feelings. To be sure, he may never resolve the contradictions, and thus he may never fully escape his present confusion, but at least he has come into contact with the fundamental notion that human beings are not simply empty vessels but consciousnesses with peculiar imaginative configurations—configurations nurtured in childhood, sustained in maturity, and thus open to many contradictions. To some extent maturity does open the doctor's fields of moral experience, but finally some of the limits from his past will remain. Having realized this much, the doctor is a privileged character—confused yet eloquent.

The progression from Bloomsbury's life of narrow content to Susan's and even the obstetrician's lives of complex style points finally to the need, in Barthelme's fiction, for an ironic suspension of self. Whereas the son who tries to figure out the nature of his father is only beginning the process of suspension, Susan and the obstetrician have already committed themselves to its necessity. Barthelme's fiction in general reflects the same imaginative suspension, and as a fiction principally of technique and style it remains, at least theoretically, a matter of infinite variation. As an artist, of course, Barthelme may seem to limit the possible variation by his preference for certain stylistic traits. Despite his use of his own peculiar styles, however, his fiction continues to possess a remarkable openness that suggests that his stylistic variations shall know few boundaries. There is no question that style counts very heavily in Barthelme's fiction—witness, here, the final two selections of *City Life.*

"**Brain Damage,**" a story replete with the ominous headlines reminiscent of *Snow White,* on the surface provides an excursion into the cerebral litter of contemporary society—from the promise of ESP to the enthusiasm of the flower culture, from the priesthood of waiters to that of university professors. Throughout the story, however, people are caught up in the confusions of the present, and at the heart of it all is the narrator who works for newspapers "at a time when I was not competent to do so." In Barthelme's world, it should be clear, no one is competent to report content, and thus the reader must not be outraged when the narrator elaborates on his incompetence: "I reported inaccurately. . . . I pretended I knew things I did not know. . . . I misinterpreted. . . . I suppressed. . . . I invented. . . . I faked. . . . I failed to discover the truth. I colored the truth with fancy. I had no respect for truth" (*CL,* 138). At the very point (in its development as a medium) that the newspaper has so much varied content to offer its readers, it has—rather ironically—become a generally unreliable source of information. The narrator knows that any source of information is inadequate, and, aware of the arbitrariness of all truth, he even goes so far as to argue, "Some people feel you should tell the truth, but those people are impious and wrong, and if you listen to what they say, you will be tragically unhappy all your life" (*CL,* 145). The long tradition of attempting to fix truth has in his view resulted in brain damage, and because Americans continue to be prone to the need for establishing "truth," he has come to the second conclusion that "this is the country of brain damage." In the narrator's world there are surely others besides Americans who know the dangers of content, but because the brain damage that originates in the pursuit of content is so widespread and even sustained in those American centers of learning that should avoid such contamination, he is hardly hopeful about the possibility of any real escape from the dilemma: "You can hide under the bed but brain damage is under the bed, and you can hide in the universities but they are the very seat and soul of brain damage" (*CL,* 146). For the narrator there is no escape. He is himself damaged, and in his own writing and howling, in his moans, he may ask repeatedly "WHAT RECOURSE?" but the answer is pale at best: "RHYTHMIC HANDCLAPPING SHOUTING SEXUAL ACTIVITY CONSUMPTION OF FOOD" (*CL,* 141). Even his question, as a question of content, exposes his lack of redress. In the end "**Brain Damage,**" like much of Barthelme's fiction, coheres only at its seams. While each of its fragments continues to unleash a furious comment on life's inanities, the story as a whole tends toward an awesome silence that mirrors the lacunae separating its fragments and thus again reinforces the importance of style.

"**City Life,**" the final story in the volume of the same name, is probably one of the best examples of the substitution of technique for content in all of Barthelme's fiction. In [a previous essay] I have already recounted Charles's description, late in the story, of the artist who manages to wrest something from his canvas only after a long series of seemingly false starts. Generally the story, which hinges on the complex and shifting relationships among Elsa, Ramona, Charles, and Jacques, achieves little more in terms of content than what the artist gains on his canvas. For as it explores the dilemma of men and women launching careers presumably of substance (in business and in law), it is continually pulling back in the face of the principal characters' discovery that the "content" that they have pursued is largely a hoax.[6] Charles, for example, despite his grand intentions, loses his commitment to a promising business career in Cleveland. Elsa, in turn, quits law school in order to satisfy another desire, that of marriage, and Ramona, although continuing her legal education, finally sees the law as a joke that genuinely deserves the affront of her virgin pregnancy. Eventually all of the principal characters find themselves inhabiting a world of contradictory impulses—a world in which even such institutions as racetracks and art galleries merge and thus a world in which the most rigorous of distinctions and categories finally dissipate. Victimized by the loss of the framework that has traditionally supported the acts of civilization, the characters all seem to have misplaced their sources of energy, especially the energy necessary for sustaining a relationship. As Ramona rather succinctly remarks, the world of "**City Life**" is a place where "one couldn't sleep with someone more than four hundred times without being bored" (*CL,* 159).

In this apparent void, to be sure, Moonbelly writes his songs as if there were still something to be said and sung about human experience. Organized as comments upon contemporary life, the songs' very titles reveal Moonbelly's determination to establish some "content" for his existence: "The System Cannot Withstand Close Scrutiny" and "Cities Are Centers of Copulation." The songs, nevertheless, instead of supporting human vitality, tend only to reinforce the emptiness that has reduced the characters of the story to postures of ennui. In the end, in fact, the songs have less imaginative value than the achievement of the artist whose struggles with his canvas results only in a busy quality of surface. In the final section of the story, when Ramona alludes to the fact that the people of the city "are locked in the most exquisite mysterious muck" (*CL,* 166), a muck that "heaves and palpitates" and "is itself the creation of that muck of mucks, human consciousness," there is no longer any question that the pursuit of "content" is, in the context of urban complexity and contradiction, a hopeless venture. Ramona herself, unable to identify the father of her baby (is it Vercingetorix or Moonbelly or Charles?), simply indulges herself in the possibility that she is the chosen one, the vessel of light, the second virgin who will give birth. Such indulging is ludicrous—all the more so when a law student begins to defend her position—but as she herself recognizes, that ludicrousness is all she has: "What was the alternative?" (*CL,* 168). In Ramona the madness that lies near the surface of "**Brain Damage**" finally breaks out. She is the character of unleashed style. If, in the process of playing with the surfaces of her existence, she does end up with a content of flagrant madness, it is a content that is marginal at best. In the city style is everything.

The best example of the eloquence of style, however, is Barthelme's brilliant **"A Shower of Gold."** In this story an artist named Peterson, while considering the possibility of appearing on a TV program suggestively entitled *Who Am I?*, confronts in rapid succession a number of instances of his own negligibility: a president who mutilates his—Peterson's—latest piece of sculpture in order to make him think; a barber-philosopher who insists that "in the end one experiences only oneself"; and a cat-piano player who obfuscates the issue of personal choice by confronting Peterson with the dilemma of whether he chose the cat or the cat chose him. The narrator of the story very cagily blurs the distinctions between dreaming and consciousness, and thus while it is apparent that Peterson wants the freedom to be the artist, it is also evident that the lack of a world that stands at attention, with strong outlines and moral purposes, prevents him from achieving such freedom. As in the two stories that conclude *City Life,* Peterson seems only to enjoy a choice of which brain damage or muck he wishes to associate with, for regardless of whatever achievement he gains as an artist, he remains the victim of an inescapable solipsism. In his own mind he may continue to hope for the circumstances that will allow him to establish his credentials as a man who can dominate the world about him, but those circumstances never arrive. In addition to the intrusions of the president, the barber, and the cat-piano player, his gallery director abuses him by neglecting to display his work and then by suggesting that Peterson might sell more of his work if he were to cut it into two—make the pieces smaller. Circumstances are never propitious, and Peterson is not much of a man. When he makes his TV appearance and there witnesses the humiliation of the other contestants, nevertheless, he rises above his strong sense of failure and manages to turn the absurdity of the situation into a running commentary that the announcer cannot terminate. Significantly the commentary is one of hope: "In this kind of world, . . . absurd if you will, possibilities nevertheless proliferate and escalate all around us and there are opportunities for beginning again" (*DC,* 183). The barber may have earlier reminded Peterson of Pascal's comment that man's condition is so "wretched" that he must be inconsolable, but now an eloquent Peterson, having earlier despaired of achieving the appearance of substance, does Pascal one better by counseling his audience to "turn off your television sets, . . . cash in your life insurance, indulge in a mindless optimism." In the face of brain damage and muck Peterson himself now indulges in what amounts to the act of poetry:

> My mother was a royal virgin . . . and my father a shower of gold. My childhood was pastoral and ener-

getic and rich in experiences which developed my character. As a young man I was noble in reason, infinite in faculty, in form express and admirable, and in apprehension. . . .

> (*DC,* 183)

If with Ramona's announcement of a virgin pregnancy in **"City Life"** there is a strain of pessimism about the ability of the mind to manage its prison of solipsism, in **"A Shower of Gold"** there seems to be some real hope. The narrator may conclude the story by suggesting that in his last comments Peterson "was, in a sense, lying, in a sense he was not," but there can be little doubt that Peterson's new style finally represents a marvelous, perhaps the only marvelous, ground of human experience left to a Barthelmean protagonist.[7]

In a recent story, **"What to Do Next,"** Barthelme expands on the nature of Peterson's experience. In the story the narrator is providing counsel to someone whose life has apparently fallen apart. After citing such instructions as adopting a new attitude, traveling, writing a will, etc., he concludes his counsel by suggesting that the person in distress must become "part of the instructions themselves," thus turning the person (and his style) into a creative act:

> we have specified that everyone who comes to us from this day forward must take twelve hours of you a week, for which they will receive three points credit per semester, and, as well, a silver spoon in the "Heritage" pattern. . . . We are sure you are up to it. Many famous teachers teach courses in themselves; why should you be different, just because you are a wimp and a lame, objectively speaking? Courage. . . . You will be adequate in your new role. See? Your life is saved. The instructions do not make distinctions between those lives which are worth saving and those which are not.

> (*A,* 86)

Here the person who accepts his status as maker, regardless of his stature as a man, becomes the standard for those about him—clearly a distressing situation and yet an astute observation of recent times. In a world that lacks a consistent metaphysical framework, eloquence becomes a matter of developing as much vitality of perception and language as one can.[8] Because no one owns a corner on truth, every person alive, at least theoretically, enjoys a genuine chance of becoming the arbiter of the world in which he lives. In these terms human existence becomes, above everything else, a test of a man's courage to be "adequate" in his own role—and thus to enjoy his own limited yet profound sense of truth.

The madness of **"Brain Damage"** and **"City Life"** seems to conflict with the more confident and optimistic[9] character of **"A Shower of Gold"** and **"What to Do Next,"** but by returning to another story in the Socratic method, **"Ki-**

erkegaard Unfair to Schlegel," I think it is possible to capture the quality that unites all four of these stories and that also makes the emphasis upon individuality in the latter two more palatable. In this story A. seems at first to be interested in establishing how and why Kierkegaard is unfair to Schlegel. Later, however, he acknowledges that he is merely annihilating Kierkegaard "in order to deal with his disapproval" (*CL,* 90) of the character of such lives as A.'s. A. knows that Kierkegaard is in fact fair to Schlegel, but by establishing the reverse he gets himself off the hook of Kierkegaard's argument that religion is necessary for a "reconciliation with actuality." Because A. cannot accept the religious stance, he must subject Kierkegaard to the irony inherent in his own—A.'s—insights into the matter. In reality, nevertheless, as Q. is quick to recognize, what A. is about is merely "the unavoidable tendency of everything particular to emphasize its own particularity" (*CL,* 92). For Barthelme, it appears, the location of any irony, of the contradictions that permeate even the simplest of contemporary experiences, becomes the source of an important grace: as long as man can establish a peculiarity of personal vision, if only in terms of irony, he can warrant himself as vital and still thinking for himself.[10] It is a limited grace, but surely it is its realization that enables such different characters as Ramona and Peterson to achieve their styles of eloquence.

In the context of all these stories that emphasize the suspension of the self in the play of style and irony, it is clear that Barthelme himself continues to layer into his fiction at least a partial content. He may, as in the Socratic-method stories, disparage the deliberate pursuit of content, but in the end—and despite the fragmented character of his stories—he introduces content by way of his thorough exploration of the ironic nature of contemporary man. As the narrator of **"Hiding Man"** at one point implies, there is always a content, for "one believes what one can, follows that vision which most brilliantly exalts and vilifies the world" (*DC,* 35). The precise definition of such vision always remains problematic in Barthelme's fiction, but finally, as yet another narrator (from **"The Party"**) suggests, man must in moments of heightened consciousness reckon with his contents: "Of course we did everything right, insofar as we were able to imagine what 'right' was" (*S,* 62). In Barthelme there is no easy grace that allows his characters to escape the "brain damage" that surrounds and envelops them. At the same time that he stresses man's need for style and irony, however, Barthelme also recognizes man's continuing need for content. This contradiction underlies the genius within all his fiction.

Notes

1. The complex strategies underlying Nabokov's texts are his means of approaching the fringes of human experience in an effort to understand them; in Barthelme the characters are at the fringes, and because there is no perspective that binds the experience together, there is no understanding.

2. John Leland, "Remarks Re-marked: Barthelme, What Curios of Signs!" *Boundary 2* 5(1977): 807, has

pointed out that right reason is "a function of cultural codes and conventions which prescribe our ways of doing, thinking, seeing, being." The codes and the conventions define what is acceptable logic.

3. For further discussion of the relationship between questions and answers, see R. E. Johnson, Jr., "'Bees Barking in the Night': The End and Beginning of Donald Barthelme's Narrative," *Boundary 2* 5(1976): 84.

4. James Rother, "Parafiction: The Adjacent Universe of Barth, Barthelme, Pynchon, and Nabokov," *Boundary 2* 5(1976):26, makes the point that "the trouble with words is that they are at our disposal, . . . and we use one another, dispose of one another, again and again" by manipulating words. Bloomsbury uses his wife through words.

5. Rother, p. 34, suggests that "the one purpose writing can boast at this stage of the game [tradition of fiction] is that of isolating us from our fictions, not sinking us deeper into them. . . . Parafiction invariably takes up where ordinary fiction leaves off, where characters, situations, events no longer attune themselves to climax and dénouement." Because the son in "Views of My Father Weeping" cannot stabilize his "fictions" of his father, whether alive or dead, he has a chance for achieving that openness of attitude at the heart of Barthelme's stories.

6. Claude Lévi-Strauss, "From Cyclical Structure in Myth to Serial Romance in Modern Fiction," trans. Petra Morrison, in *Sociology of Literature and Drama,* ed. Elizabeth and Tom Burns (Baltimore: Penguin, 1973), pp. 212-13, has commented: "Life, dreams, the past carry dislocated images and forms which haunt the writer when chance or some necessity . . . preserves or rediscovers in them the shadowy outline of myth. Nevertheless, the novelist drifts among these floes which the heat of history detaches from the solid formation which it has broken up. He collects these scattered materials and reuses them as they present themselves to him, though not without dimly perceiving that they come from another structure, and will become rarer and rarer as a current different from the one which kept them together bears them away. The decline and fall of the plot was contained within the development of the novel from the beginning and has recently become external to it—since we are witnessing the decline and fall *of* plot after the decline and fall *in* the plot." The collapse of plot is especially evident in a story like "City Life."

7. Johnson, pp. 79, 81, has expanded upon the importance of this new style: "Fictional language . . . offers the only ground for the realization of consciousness. . . . Fictional language is given the task of animating an object or objects which will, in the process, acquire emotional value." Peterson's fictions are the very ground of his being.

8. Leland, p. 809, has pointed out that this eloquence is a function of one's understanding the processes of

perception: "Orders are built up, only to be decomposed in a continual probing of the ordering of orders, an ordering which plays itself out over an essential abyss of non-meaning."

9. Johnson, p. 87, has pointed out that "Barthelme's is no facile optimism; he sees the inescapably destructive character of language as clearly as anyone today using words." I obviously agree with Johnson.

10. For a larger discussion of Barthelme's irony, see Alan Wilde, "Barthelme Unfair to Kierkegaard: Some Thoughts on Modern and Postmodern Irony," *Boundary 2* 5(1976): 45-70.

Lois Gordon (essay date 1981)

SOURCE: Gordon, Lois. "Come Back, Dr. Caligari." In *Donald Barthelme,* pp. 35-61. Boston: Twayne Publishers, 1981.

[*In the following essay, Gordon surveys the dominant thematic concerns of Barthelme's first short story collection,* Come Back, Dr. Caligari.]

The first collection introduces many of Barthelme's themes and landscapes, most prominently the spiritually weary, contemporary world, brainwashed by popular culture and the media (**"Viennese Opera Ball"**), a society of people looking for "the right words" (**"Florence Green"**) and specific scripts with which to duplicate an identity (**"For I'm the Boy," "Big Broadcast," "Hiding Man," "Margins"**). The theme of failed marriage recurs (**"To London and Rome," "Broadcast," "For I'm the Boy," "Will You Tell Me?" "Piano Player"**). Another subject, which Barthelme will pursue, is the problem of using words, because "signs" sometimes "lie" (the remarkable **"Me and Miss Mandible"**). The artist as subject, in his personal and professional life, is the focus of **"Shower of Gold"** and **"Marie,"** two of the volume's best stories which treat, in a consummately humane and wildly parodic fashion, the contradiction of "the absurd" in theory and reality.

I "Florence Green Is 81"

"The aim of literature is the creation of a strange object covered with fur which breaks your heart."

[In **"Florence Green Is 81"**] Barthelme explodes linearity of language and event, and splices characters, in order to capture the disintegration of value in both the contemporary world and individual consciousness. Love, lentils, children, toilets, and Texaco merge as equal priorities in a world only occasionally and peripherally acknowledged as one of war, loneliness, sexual desire, and professional yearning.

Barthelme, in addition, is concerned with the language that defines our world and minds, that conglomeration of catchy and hypnotic slang that swallows both serious and

fashionable subject matter. As he focuses upon the rhythms that compose the contemporary psyche, his language slides in and out of meaning, like—to borrow two details of the story—Mandrake's piano and Joan Graham's gazpacho. Clichés, inadequately understood abstractions, fragments of anachronistic, woolly dreams of contemporary American life, and eminently quotable tidbits ransacked from the literature of the world, are jumbled together and packaged in easy slogans and matchbook and media rhetoric.

Words and more words: such is the junk and value of our lives. As the narrator-writer puts it, in a startlingly honest statement: "We value each other for our remarks"; "on the strength of this remark," he goes on, "love becomes possible." Nevertheless, if he is going to talk to us, and if we are to understand him, author and reader must make their way through the sludge of verbiage that envelops them and "free associate," "brilliantly, brilliantly, to [be] put . . . into the problem."

The "problem" is this: Florence Green, "a small fat girl" of eighty-one, who has 300 million dollars and blue legs, sits before her dinner guests and complains of a toilet that malfunctions. The narrator, a would-be writer (Baskerville), who aspires toward Florence's continuing patronage, is troubled by her mysterious statement: "*I want to go to some other country*" (our first of many askewed associations with T. S. Eliot). As preoccupied with a sexy girl at the dinner table as with Florence's drop-dead statement, the narrator describes the evening (which includes Florence's falling asleep "untidily") in a rambling assemblage of non sequiturs. In the back of his mind is his growing anxiety that he will not impress this arbiter of contemporary taste and values; interspersed, in addition, are his own self-mocking and somewhat self-aggrandizing comments. About Florence Green, who provides, after all, the title of the story, there are only occasional comments: she is rather ridiculous, spoiled, and possibly senile, the matriarch who supports both war and art (really the narrator's two main concerns). At the same time, she is a wonderfully appealing and somewhat enigmatic woman who, despite her enormous vanity and eccentricities (she has a room filled with a cane collection), has driven men to write poetry for her.

Barthelme's particular brand of box-within-box satire on any number of subjects serves not only to equate the trivial and serious (to reflect how everything has become equally meaningless), but also to equate the very identities and activities of his characters. Ultimately, one has an impossible task "characterizing" anyone—and this is perhaps the point. Both Florence and the narrator, for example, prize "uniqueness" and both fear "boredom." The narrator relates how, many years before, Florence vomited upon seeing the atrocities of Buchenwald (in *Life* magazine). Although she didn't know what "*exterminated*" meant, she raced to a resort for solace. Now her life, devoted (at least tonight) to toilet-repair-inflation and recollections of the good old days with her oil-baron husband, is boring, and she would go away. Although war is mentioned in the same breath as vegetables, its reality fills the story. Can it be that Florence will go away (again), because the atrocities of the contemporary world are overbearing? Or is toilet repair overwhelming? Is she bored with her life and guests? Is she bored with the world situation? Or is she simply looking for some new words to say—because words *are* one's identity? ("On the strength of" our remarks, "love becomes possible.") All Barthelme gives us is this: "She is afraid of boring us. She is trying to establish her uniqueness." At this point, let us remark not only on the impossibility of "characterizing" Florence, but on the extraordinary difficulty of understanding what the simple and frequently used words "bored" and "unique" mean.

About Florence's desire to go away—and her earlier escape to a resort—Barthelme, again, refuses to comment. But traditional readers that we are, we trust the narrator's point of view and share his alternating scorn and respect for her. Florence invites moral interpretation, and to prod us on, Barthelme even plants a line from Husserl in the story that fits our bill: Florence has "not grasped the living reality, the essence." Yet, while this might neatly fit within the well-made story (and alienate us from Florence), Barthelme undercuts its authority at once. Indeed, if we impose any such fixed meaning, it is we who will not have grasped the living reality, which is that there is no such thing as *the* living reality, at least attainable through language.

Let us turn to one of many examples. Although Florence appears to attach equal importance to trivial and tragic concerns, so does the narrator. If this were traditional satire, the narrator, who at points enlists our respect, would stand as a foil against Florence. Instead, after drawing us to his side, he reacts in an equally indiscriminate manner to the reality about him. He recurrently qualifies his own positions to the point of contradiction. Thus, if he is the ironic voice, he is ironic about his own irony. As a result, we lack a consistent foil against which to construct a standard or central focal point. If Florence's evasion of reality for the "unique" *seems* a cop-out, the narrator, in his own statements about "uniqueness" and "boredom," evades characterization, as he wavers erratically between integrity and opportunism.

First, he would be *honest* in his writing (presumably an indictment of war). Yet, comparing himself to a psychiatrist's patient, he admits that he would be *manipulative,* striving "mightily to establish" his "uniqueness." He explains, in addition, that he writes to *amuse* and not bore. He then undercuts this with the conjunction "or" which, in context, neither qualifies nor contradicts, which is its function: "Or for fear of boring you: which?" Finally, he admits, "I adopt this ingratiating tone because I can't help myself." What has happened to the fearless antiwar commentator? He then answers a claim that writing should not be discursive by defining it as "portages through the whirlpool country of the mind" and adds, "Mostly I make remarks."

It is almost impossible to organize this mishmash of confessional material. Is the writer honest? playful? a liar? neurotic? confident? condescending? Is he socially committed? One is also dazed trying to figure out whether the narrator is indeed Baskerville and, in any case, if one can trust him. After all, while he is maintaining his integrity, he is also nervously jogging his memory for impressive comments other people might have made at a dinner party. He even admits, with self-mockery, how he has sold out professionally: he edits an interdisciplinary journal (with his left hand!), "The Journal of Tension Reduction," which pampers the contemporary need for self-help information with "learned disputation[s], letters-to-the-editor, anxiety in rats."

Yet this is really only the beginning of our confusion. If both Florence and the narrator are/are not, for example (in traditional "moral" terms), responsible/irresponsible, in their aspirations toward "uniqueness," Barthelme plays with several other levels of irony, so that by the time we finish the story we haven't the slightest idea what self-confrontation, or evasion, or being "committed" and "having integrity" mean. First, it seems as if the speaker mocks and upholds *both* self-knowledge and self-evasion. He says (possibly of himself): "Oh Baskerville! you silly son of a bitch, how can you become a famous writer without first having worried about your life, is it the *right kind* of life, does it have the right people in it, is it *going well*?" Further, the narrator connects and equates introspection with middle-class chic: in Santa Ana, California, "100,350 citizens nestle together in the Balboa blue Pacific evenings worrying about their lives." What *is* the narrator's point of view? Where has our author, Barthelme, disappeared to?

War, toilets, discursiveness, essence, Fleischmann's gin (the antidote to angst: "I favor the establishment of comfort stations providing free Fleischmann's . . . on every street corner"), psychiatrists, writing, and war: where are we? Barthelme tantalizes us with meaning; his story is indeed a "portage" through the "whirlpool country of the mind." By the time one finishes, he has difficulty pinpointing anything or anyone. The final effect is curiously like a Cubist painting, montage, or mobile. No single surface, in terms of character, event, indeed words or their meaning, is fixed. The "colored doctor" at the dinner table (is he Mandrake the Magician and the pianist on Florence's vacation?), is also the proposed colored doctor for a novel. (Does life create art, or is it the other way around?) The doctor (psychiatrist) is the writer's audience, absorbing the author's "fantastications," while acting out his own. The narrator's search for uniqueness is everyone's search for uniqueness; Florence herself writes poems and is their subject; it becomes increasingly more difficult to separate the dancer from the dance, that is, who, during this party, is author, and who is guest. The narrator gets a "promotion" and a "discharge" from his writing school (his "orders"), and words are surely a major "war" Barthelme writes about. Ultimately, the narrator is Baskerville, the soldier, the doctor, the poet, Florence, the sexy Kathleen (whose name is really Joan Graham), Pamela Hansford Johnson, and Onward Christian. We move full circle, patients and writers alike, all looking—in our compulsive search for and belief in the "right word"—for non-boring experience, for "total otherness." Ironically, however, we avoid our true "uniqueness," the total "otherness" we basically are—which could be ours if we would just recoup the instinctive life or those ideas and words that are truly ours, beneath or between all the packaged words and slogans. Unfortunately we remain, in grand philosophical terms, as well as in linguistic and concrete everyday terms, "all involved in a furious pause, a grand parenthesis."

Finally, then, in **"Florence Green,"** there is no center or final resting point. Everything has been refracted by the narrator's uniquely personal perception of experience, all colored by his conflicting public and private values—this necessarily filtered through the limited and yet necessary forms of language. The final object created is indeed all of the story's seeming contradictions and shapes of meaning (which ultimately never coalesce)—Husserl's living reality, an essence which is a general discursiveness—free associations and portages through the whirlpool of the mind, a truly unique work of art, "a strange object covered with fur."

II "WILL YOU TELL ME?"

A number of Barthelme's stories are *tours de force* in linguistic virtuosity, where, although syntax and sentence structure remain traditional, meaning is continuously challenged and widened by juxtapositions of odd, banal, literary, or technical diction; at other points, ordinary language is violated by bizarre and fragmented action. Space and time may be dislocated to reinforce the distortions of traditional language or narrative pattern. Here [in **"Will You Tell Me?"**], in what appears to be a very simply told story, Barthelme outdoes Ionesco and his colorless Mr./Mrs. Smith/Martin people in *The Bald Soprano*. Identities merge; banality and horror are interchangeable; everything is equally meaningful and hence meaningless. Specifically, everyone is everyone else's lover, child, threat, and even nemesis.

III "THE PIANO PLAYER"

Similarly, here [in **"The Piano Player"**] is the typically fashionable and bored suburban couple in an exaggeratedly affluent background. Barthelme exposes the silly hollowness, indeed, the almost grotesque and ghostly quality of the contemporary family. Forms of meaning or structure (i.e., marriage) are present, in language as in life, but details and linguistic variations again prevent anything whole or substantial beneath from finalizing.

The identical and shallow inner and outer worlds of the mother, for example, are concretized, as she pleads that her dreary mental and physical condition (like her children's) will improve if only she can have a fancy car to take her to hobnob with intellectual celebrities: "If you gave me a TR-4, I'd put our ugly children in it and drive away. To Wellfleet. . . . I want to talk to Edmund Wilson." Throughout, Barthelme literalizes metaphor (his trademark), as in the frequently quoted: "You're supposed to be curing a ham," followed by "The ham died."

IV "FOR I'M THE BOY WHOSE ONLY JOY IS LOVING YOU"

"We can discuss . . . the meaning but not the feeling."

[In **"For I'm the Boy Whose Only Joy is Loving You"** the] elegantly named Bloomsbury, accompanied by the also formally named Whittle and Huber, is returning from the aerodrome; his estranged wife, Martha, has just flown the coop. Conversations among the three men draw a bitter (and wildly funny) picture of empty marriage, sex, and even friendship. Once again, these people can articulate anything; what they lack is feeling: "There's little enough rapport between adults" without "clouding" the "issue" with "sentiment," they say.

The story, filled with sardonic manipulations of familiar literature (from *Hamlet*'s "what manner of man is this!" to *The Waste Land*'s "[Tell me] whether she wept when you told her"), is remarkable in style. Barthelme manipulates, for example, two entirely different literary techniques to portray the common emptiness of human relationships—an elegant Jamesian style in which Whittle and Huber figure, and the more earthy Lawrentian lower-class idiom, in which Bloomsbury recites his sexual encounters with both his wife, Martha (who would rather spend the night with words—Mallarmé's), and his lover, Pelly: "An' what a fine young soft young warm young thing you have there Pelly on yer bicycle seat." (Pelly's husband literally prefers bringing his T.V. to bed rather than her.) Not only is contemporary language incapable of communicating feeling, but the old standbys, even the language of fairy tale, are equally disfunctional: "Ah Pelly where do you be goin'?"; his Little Red Riding Hood answers, "T' grandmather's." Regardless of linguistic mask, an emptiness fills all the love nests—for Bloomsbury and Martha, Bloomsbury and Pelly—knock offs, in name alone, of Joyce's Molly, Polly, and Bloom.

The story is very funny, beginning with a takeoff on the *Casablanca*-type airport scenario. The only catch is that Bloomsbury's friends are not sure if they have been "required" or "invited" to come along (as a guard against "privacy" and "thus weeping"). Barthelme focuses on their cold formality and bland self-awareness. Bloomsbury says, his "friends . . . were as men not what he wished them to be," and he adds, "it was [also] very possible . . . that he was not what they wished him to be."

He knows, for example, that they care most about his money and that one has even made a grab for his wife. Whittle and Huber speak with only the *form* of caring; any real feeling is missing: "Customarily . . . ribald," they "nevertheless maintained attitudes of rigorous and complete solemnity as were of course appropriate." Barthelme pushes to an absurd degree our role-playing and the way language reflects our blind adherence to scripts. Can Bloomsbury's friends, for example, still be "family friends" if the family has split up? Whittle sounds like a semanticist and lawyer: "The family exists . . . as a legal entity" "whether or not the family *qua* family endures beyond the physical separation of the partners." Such dialogue is often interrupted by a familiar literary line or a song, which thickens Barthelme's irony and adds to the bitterness of his portrait. Bloomsbury can only say of his friends (from *The Student Prince*): "Golden days . . . in the sunshine of our happy youth."

In one of the most memorable sequences, they question him on the "extinguishment" of his "union," the details of the breakup. In efficient list fashion they say: "It would be interesting I think as well as instructive" to know "at what point the situation of living together became untenable, whether she wept when you told her, whether you wept when she told you . . . whether she had a lover or did not . . . , the disposition of the balance of the furnishings including tableware, linens, light bulbs, . . . the baby if there was [one] . . . in short we'd like to get the feel of the event." To be "instructed" is to get the "feel"; light bulbs are as important as babies.

Huber, who has never married, says he knows the "exquisite pain" of breakup. (He had an affair with a Red Cross worker named Buck Rogers, after which he literally jumped from the Chrysler Building. Again Barthelme literalizes the metaphor: what could be more appropriate after a sad affair? Here, he goes on to admit—and this dislocates meaning—he got "a wonderful view of the city.") Thus, when he is asked, "How would you know . . . you've never been married," his answer is grim: "I may not know about marriage . . . but I know about words." In a final, sardonic touch, Barthelme adds that he was "giggling" as he described his pain. They all comment on life, rather than feel it; forms of language have substituted for experience.

At the end, Barthelme turns whatever "meaning" we may have grasped thus far against us. Up to this point, we think that Bloomsbury has more "feeling" than his friends. Yet when he is asked, "How does it [the breakup] feel," he replies: "What is *it*?" Reflecting on how one is "trained" to confront the inevitabilities (i.e., divorce), Bloomsbury also says (with playful echoes of Husserl): "It was interesting . . . that after so many years one could still be surprised by a flyaway wife" (shades of TWA). And he continues: "Surprise . . . that's the great thing, it keeps the old tissues tense." His response (his language) is so alienating, it is not surprising that with this dramatic move *away from* feeling—his friends move *toward* it, with a vengeance. Now, when they want to know what he feels, he answers (with playful echoes of Gertrude Stein and Wittgenstein): "The question is not what is the feeling but what is the meaning?" They try bribing him and beat him with a cognac bottle and tire iron, at which point he is transfixed by the memory of a Tuesday Weld movie (whose name, like Rock Hudson's, must surely inspire), after which he felt like "a good man." (Media creates identity and morality.) Bloomsbury has obviously had a more intense emotional experience from the movie than from his divorce. But art is short, and life long, and Bloomsbury is now depressed. The two friends, beating him for meaning,

confuse his bloody response with feeling. In fact, what they get is "all sorts of words." Indeed, contrary to the popular saying, one *can* get blood—not feeling—from a stone, a final irony.

V "THE BIG BROADCAST OF 1938"

"Are you tuned in?"

Orson Welles's 1938 radio drama "The War of the Worlds" was so lifelike that people actually took to the streets to protect themselves from what they believed was an extraterrestrial invasion. Barthelme's [**"The Broadcast of 1938"**] pursues the way life is modeled after art, specifically the media—radio, film, magazine romances—and their various forms of soap opera. If life fails—i.e., a marriage collapses—it is due to the failure of script; should the role model for our "parts" age or die (the actor, a "legend," like a god), a new one must be created. The media alone provide our culture heroes, our scripts—our lives. Life is but an arrangement of words to be enacted.

We meet Bloomsbury again, now divorced from Martha. He has given her the house, in exchange for a radio station where, in addition to playing music (he plays "The Star-Spangled Banner" "hundreds of times a day" because of its "finality"), he presents two kinds of talks. The first, for mysterious and private (i.e., creative) reasons, involves his endless repetition of a single word—like "nevertheless." The second involves commercial advertisements, all directed to Martha; these consist of long recollections of their courtship and marriage. They are apparently spoken to woo her back.

One day a "girl or woman" of "indeterminate age," in a long, bright red linen duster, which she takes off to reveal fifties-style toreador pants and an orange sweater (she is also wearing harlequin glasses), visits the studio. After brief verbal sparring, regarding why he is looking at her ("It's my you might say *métier/Milieu/Métier*"), we learn that she was the former president of the Conrad Veidt fan club. Now, however, she laments that Veidt's death has caused the death of a "vital part" or her "imagination." Again they argue about words, discuss their attraction to one another (she's been told she resembles the actress Carmen Lambrosa), and before we know it, the woman is revealed as Martha. (Is she really, or does Bloomsbury simply see all women as Martha?) This Martha does indeed seem wooed by Bloomsbury's ads; she even takes up residence there and sleeps under the piano.

The difficulties of Bloomsbury's marriage are further revealed, and once again the trivial and significant are horrifically and hilariously juxtaposed: their problems in adequately freezing the ice cubes are given as much attention as their sexual incompatibility, unwanted child, and marital infidelities. Ordinary metaphors that one might use about a relationship are literalized—i.e., the proverbial mother-in-law "lay like a sword between us," literally, in the bed.

Interestingly, in the present time of their meeting, they still act out the same problems and hurl the same abuses at each other, mostly over sexuality and language. As the story ends, their roles (or what Barthelme has once again tricked us into believing are their "roles") are reversed. She would "come back" to him (is she more taken with artifice, his ads, than reality?), but he has lost interest (because he now realizes she is his wife, and he can only respond sexually to an illusion of the Hollywood type?).

In the light of this story, Barthelme's title **Come Back, Dr. Caligari** is clarified. What the modern world seems to need, Barthelme implies, referring to the movie *The Cabinet of Dr. Caligari,* is a Caligari, a giver of roles, a programmer of people, whether the roles are mundane or monstrous. Hence, all of the scriptwriting, playacting, and absences of "identity" in these stories.

Specifically in this story, it is doubly ironic that Veidt should have been a kind of Caligari to Martha. First, in the movie, the Veidt character is only a psychotic who imagines himself to be controlled by a legendary figure, Caligari. Second, the legendary status Martha has given Veidt as "handsome and sinister" has been created entirely through celluloid, through Veidt's movie roles. Yet, despite this last irony, Barthelme further implies that for one to function in the everyday world, he needs role models; he must mimic an actor who is himself only an interpretation, a reading of someone else's words.

In such a world, with God thus dead, Bloomsbury (whose name we associate with the literary group) seeks out his own mythology by writing, producing, directing, and acting in his ridiculous radio show. With no ready-made word supply or dialogue (for his role as "husband" or "lover"), he tries to create one. He uses his favorite (chic and utterly hackneyed) words to create a reality: "assimilate," "alleviate," "authenticate," "ameliorate." Barthelme explains: he singled out "for special notice . . . some particular word . . . [and repeated it] in a monotonous voice for as much as fifteen minutes." (And Barthelme adds, to fracture meaning: "*Or* a quarter-hour"—which, of course, is fifteen minutes.) But Bloomsbury's intention in repeating these words remains private; although exposed to the audience, "the word would frequently disclose new properties [and] unsuspected qualities." (Is this true for all writers and their words?)

With no ready-made "action" or "pattern" to his life, Bloomsbury chants his ads. (What better means of creating rituals by which to structure a life?) Perhaps if he repeats sufficiently his recollections of his marriage with Martha, he can create a myth to which she will at least subliminally acquiesce (and then be anesthetized to meaning or content).

What is, of course, odd but amusing is that these commercials—in mock-romantic, narrative style—provide the *form* of life and adventure story, with touches of chivalry, sacrifice, and honor. But their details betray a grotesque reality about their marriage. Although he may act out the Sir Walter Raleigh role, he is in fact an infantalized and castrated male: "I remember the time you went walking without your shoes, . . . I got down on my hands and knees and crawled in front of you. . . . Afterwards you treated me to a raspberry ice, calling for a saucer, which you placed, daintily, at your feet. I still recall . . . the way the raspberry stained my muzzle. . . . We had our evening quarrel. . . . The subject, which had been announced by you at breakfast and posted on the notice board, was *Smallness in the Human Male.*"

This reminds us of Pinter's and Beckett's couples (in plays like *A Slight Ache* and *Happy Days*), but where these writers reveal the terror and pain beneath ordinary word games and daily routines, Barthelme omits any distancing between what his figures seem and are. His people are unique in their abstract weirdness; they blindly and totally live out the *structure* of marriage (life) without demanding any substance. Hence their words have the form of meaning (the substance) but are continuously drifting off into distracting particularizations or amplifications that leave behind their essential, conceptual meaning. An argument is an argument as long as it follows that *form* of discourse. At one point they make freezing ice cubes a cause célèbre; and somewhat reminiscent of Beckett in his sucking stones sequence in *Molloy,* Barthelme devotes two pages to their "procuring," "conceiving," "whelping," "genesis," and "parturition" of ice cubes.

Nevertheless, unlike Pinter and Beckett, Barthelme's final effects are always funny. Appropriately, the story ends with the melodrama suitable to Barthelmean soap opera. Bloomsbury doesn't die; he sort of fades away. His great amatory loss is mirrored by the stoppage of his electrical current. The universe is indeed just: "That was the end of this period of Bloomsbury's, as they say, life."

VI "The Viennese Opera Ball"

That this party [in **"The Viennese Opera Ball"**] at the Waldorf-Astoria (a parody of the annual ball in Vienna) should be called the "Viennese Opera Ball" is just as pretentious as the conversations captured there. There is no dancing, as "Ball" might suggest (although both Lester Lanin and Meyer Davis are presumably playing their very classy music), and even the romantic excesses associated with Viennese opera are totally alien to this group. This "Ball" is just an excuse for a large cocktail party, where Barthelme plays theme and variations upon the silly words and mere rhythms of meaning that dance about the room.

Once again he juxtaposes meaningful and trivial chatter, mouthed by the indistinguishably undistinguished, chic and mod, successful and affluent guests. This he does in a fabulous evocation of radically different subjects and styles—of obstetricians, financiers, fashion writers, anthropologists, and empty-headed models. Paced at top speed, the barrage of wildly disparate subjects assaults the reader—on the techniques and instruments of abortion, the

Jumbo tree and its resemblance to the elegant monkey and bison, the financial status of the American Machine Company, the "*art* rather than *sheer force*" of penile stimulation, Edward Stone's buildings in Islamabad, the size of black bands on both widows' and widowers' calling cards, Abbey Lincoln's stature as a great jazz singer, and so on. Surgery, travel, modeling, mortality, forceps, and freedom: these are one's concerns, and they share equal billing in one's life.

The story is not only funny because of Barthelme's measured juxtapositions, but it is also strangely interesting. In eavesdropping on these chic, contemporary New Yorkers—walking versions of *Fortune,* medical journals, anthropology texts, fashion magazines, biographies, and dictionaries—we must admit (if we are to be honest) we save ourselves time from our own reading. Typical of so many of his stories, this one is weirdly informative, as at the same time, it is thoroughly mocking. Barthelme allows us, in fact, in our greed for information, to identify with his figures—but only briefly, owing to their exaggeration.

Barthelme once again literalizes and/or plays with metaphor: "The devil is not as wicked as people believe, and neither is an Albanian"; "An abortionist [should] empty the uterus before . . . [the patient] has retinitis"; "the members were ruptured artificially and a Spanish windlass applied." Finally, if we look closely at the story, we can discern a few motifs that underlie much of the sludge—on violence, art, force, and mortality. Serious lines emerge from time to time—i.e., Baudelaire's "Mortality is the final evaluator of methods." But if—to Baudelaire—death justifies life in the existential sense, to Barthelme one can never be sure, for he pokes fun (but serious fun) at everything we do and think, including such highfalutin and serious pronouncements. Barthelme, to be sure, is in it for the fun, and humor always wins out. Immediately following Baudelaire's line is: "An important goal is an intact sphincter."

VII "ME AND MISS MANDIBLE"

Structuralist, phenomenologist, and deconstructionist critics alike can have a heyday here [in **"Me and Miss Mandible"**] where, like a master chessman, Barthelme plays out the story's key line: "We read signs as promises" but "some of them are lies." Focusing essentially upon the arbitrariness of *both* "seeming" and "being," he goes beyond the disparity between what appears (in signs) and what is then interpreted (as fact or illusion) in order to show how virtually everything is sometimes true but sometimes false. One's roles and even the tenacity, or veracity, with which they are held, is similarly true/false, real/unreal. The "authority" both behind and presumably inherent within the word, the interpreted act, the relationship, perhaps life itself, is arbitrary. This most playful and imaginative story begins:

> Miss Mandible wants to make love to me but she hesitates because I am *officially* a child; I am, *according to the records,* according to the gradebook on her desk,

according to the card index in the principal's office, eleven years old. There is a *misconception* here, one that I haven't quite managed to get cleared up yet. I am *in fact* thirty-five, I've been in the Army, I am six feet one, I have hair in the appropriate places, my voice is a baritone, I *know* very well what to do with Miss Mandible if she ever makes up her mind.

> (Italics mine)

Our man-child, Joseph, has returned to Horace Greely Elementary School to learn exactly where he went wrong. He was brought up to believe in signs and to believe that the promises of life would materialize: "Everything" in life, he says, "is promised . . . most of all the future." Furthermore, "everything is presented as the result of some knowable process." As a result, he followed all the prescriptive steps; his life was not of his choosing but of following the "clues"—"diplomas, membership cards, campaign buttons, a marriage license, insurance forms, discharge papers, tax returns, Certificates of Merit." But no one prepared him for the fact that "arrangements sometimes slip, . . . errors are made, . . . signs are misread."

His life went awry as he misread two very important signs, the first involving his marriage, the second his career. His wife had "beauty, charm, softness, perfume, cookery," and so, he thought, he "had found love." But his wife, who read in him the same signs that now Miss Mandible and the other girls read (i.e., a woman "would never be bored"), in fact left him "for another man." Too, as an insurance claims adjuster, he followed the company's motto: "Here to Help in Time of Need," but when he awarded a settlement of $165,000 to a claimant who without his aid "lacked the self-love to prize her injury so highly," Henry Goodykind (note his name, as sign) fired him. He failed to understand the double message in his company's motto.

Now he sits in the classroom trying to get to the source of life's "conspiracy," trying to learn the rules of life: "All the mysteries [of life] that perplexed me as an adult have their origins here." His main questions are "Who decides?" and how does one apply those rules to life (specifically in his interpersonal relationships which, as Miss Mandible and her texts assume, alone make the rules relevant)?

What he learns, or at least we do, is that the promises we're given don't always come true, and this is a lesson necessarily learned *after* the fact. "It is the pledges that this place makes to me, pledges that cannot be redeemed, that confuse me later." He learns that all signs (and therefore rules) and the interpretation of them (like all roles) are arbitrary. This he calls the "whimsy of authority" and adds: "I confused authority with life itself."

Meaning, in fact, is locked in *outside* of one's experience—synchronically, rather than diachronically. It is only after the fact, chronologically after his role as soldier, husband, and employee, that he has any perspective on his life. Written in the form of a diary, it is only in the present moment that he can say: "Placed backward in space and time, I am beginning to understand how I went wrong, how we all go wrong."

His present then consists of mysterious signs, which will make sense to him only after he lives through them. Reality can be articulated and placed in the construct of words, sentences, and interpretations, only *after* one has "finished" the experience. The logic that organizes words, like one's so-called comprehension of life, is not necessarily appropriate to the experience; it is a part of it, while not particularly descriptive of it. Any role he plays out, furthermore, will be as arbitrary and "meaningful" as any other he might have chosen. Hence, he can make an easy transition from insurance adjuster to student. As he says: "The distinction between children and adults" is "a specious one. . . . There are only individual egos, crazy for love."

Miss Mandible tries to teach the children how to interpret signs or roles—how to apply their "knowledge" to real life situations. From her text "Making the Processes Meaningful," she is advised that children will enjoy fractions if the subject has social significance. One student mockingly illustrates the inappropriateness of such an approach: when Bobby Vanderbilt "wishes to bust a classmate in the mouth he first asks Miss Mandible to lower the blind, saying that the sun hurts his eyes. When she does so, *bip*!"

While the teacher's text—and the applicability of the logic of common fractions to everyday experience—may be laughable, other "literature," even popular magazines, contains messages or signs which, when interpreted, may or may not lie, but which indeed effect life, and this leads to the very funny conclusion, and Barthelme's ingenious treatment of how "art" or the media create life.

To begin, within this sixth-grade class, with its geography, history, and common fractions, there are numerous signs that lie. Each morning as the students face the American flag, our most obvious, misleading sign—the thirty-five-year-old Gulliver who is perceived as eleven (and who speaks as an eleven-year-old might: "Me and Miss Mandible")—pledges allegiance to both Miss Mandible and Sue Ann; as they all lift their geography books to read, he lifts his clandestine journal. The major sign in the classroom, totally ignored by the authorities, is its atmosphere of "aborted sexuality": the class is "a furnace of love, love, love."

Not only is Miss Mandible confused about which sign to respond to in her student/sex-object, but the narrator has his second eye on eleven-year-old Sue Ann, who actually "reminds him of his wife," just as Miss Mandible seems "like a child." Frankie Randolph, another young girl (note how her name as "sign" misleads) is also attracted to him, and Bobby Vanderbilt, hard at work transferring his libido into peculiar oral imitations of racing cars, is making a record called "Sounds of Sebring."

One day Frankie gives our narrator a copy of *Movie-TV Secrets,* after which the jealous Sue Ann thrusts seventeen more magazines at him, with their variety of infinitely suggestive articles on Liz Taylor, Eddie Fisher, and Debbie Reynolds: "Isn't It Time to Stop Kicking Debbie Around?" "Can Liz Fulfill Herself?" among many others.

Joseph has been examining a rather compromising photo with the caption: "The exclusive photo isn't what it seems." The "facts," it continues, are otherwise. He, however, is not convinced. To him, the picture (the sign) and his interpretation, are one: "I am happy," he says perhaps facetiously, "that the picture is not really what it seems"; "it seems to be nothing less than divorce evidence."

An ad juxtaposes less ambiguous signs, although their connection with "reality" is questionable. "Hip Huggers," or "padded rumps," offer eleven-year-olds "appeal" in their "hips and derrière, both." Realizing the unified message here between picture, caption, and inevitable interpretation, Joseph adds: "If they cannot decipher the language the illustrations leave nothing to the imagination."

What follows is riotous. Amos Darin (because he is prepubescent? because he is stimulated by the ads? because he wishes to be Eddie Fisher?) draws a dirty picture in the cloakroom that is, the narrator says (with the expertise of a thirty-five-year-old), "sad and inaccurate." "It was offered," he continues, "not as a sign of something else but as an act of love in itself." (But this is our narrator's "reading.") This, in turn, is followed by (does it stimulate?) an acting out in the cloakroom of the Fisher-Reynolds-Taylor triangle: "Sue Ann Brownly caught Miss Mandible and me in the cloakroom, during recess, and immediately threw a fit . . . certain now which of us was Debbie, which Eddie, which Liz."

Although he tries to convince the authorities of his responsibility in this act, they continue to read him as an innocent though wayward child who will simply have to see a doctor. As to Miss Mandible, and Barthelme literalizes his metaphors shamelessly, she has been "ruined but fulfilled." Having read him as a thirty-five-year-old healthy male, her "promise had been kept." She indeed now knows "that everything she has been told about life" is "true." At the same time, she "will be charged with contributing to the delinquency of a minor." At the end, preparing to depart, our narrator receives a gift from Bobby Vanderbilt, the recording *Sounds of Sebring*—perhaps to help him in what Bobby still reads as his eleven-year-old peer's confusion amid the mysteries of sex.

VIII "Marie, Marie, Hold On Tight"

Because the pleasure of reading Barthelme lies so much in his wit, one is self-conscious in merely focusing on his "situations." This is particularly true here [in **"Marie, Marie, Hold On Tight"**], where Barthelme mixes a matter of philosophical speculation with an everyday New York happening, and the two transform into an outlandishly comic situation.

The story is this: Pickets, "pursuing their right to demonstrate peaceably under the Constitution," are marching and distributing flyers in front of a church (St. John the Precursor!) and Rockefeller Center. They are met with a few sympathizers and hecklers, and even some bullies who beat them up. What is absolutely hilarious is their cause—or at least the concrete form their cause or "revolt" takes. Barthelme literalizes their rebellion against the inequities of the human condition and the existential plight—in a picket line.

Their placards read: "Man Dies! / The Body is Disgust! / Cogito Ergo Nothing! / Abandon Love!" Their flyers reflect their dissatisfaction and rally to action: *"Why does it have to be that way?"* "What Is To Be Done?" contains, in fact, a "program for the reification of the human condition from the ground up." All of this, by the way, is being televised and "written up" for the "important" magazines.

Barthelme is equally funny as he captures the mentality of the bystanders (i.e., haven't you ever heard of Kierkegaard? some ask). Others, the "innocents"—"possibly from the FBI"—cross the picket line and enter the church. Most of the tourists milling around Rockefeller Plaza, however, are indifferent: "It's a paradigmatic situation . . . exemplifying the distance between the potential knowers holding a commonsense view of the world and what is to be known, which escapes them as they pursue their mundane existences."

Now one may laugh at what seems to be Barthelme's parody of contemporary philosophical dilemmas, but if this sort of subject is not worthy of lofty language and concern, what is? What Barthelme is illustrating is that while content (man's condition) is of utmost significance (like "the absurd" in **"Shower of Gold"**), *any* form its expression takes is inadequate, or inaccurate—indeed ridiculous (although Barthelme is good-humored, rather than mocking toward these people).

Levels of comedy expand—through incongruity of situation and language and through excessive details; these undercut potentially dramatic statements that otherwise might advance the plot (indeed a *reflection* of our absurdity). When the bullies arrive, for example, "dressed in hood jackets . . . [and] tight pants"—and here Barthelme's psychologizing distracts us from our usual associations with delinquents—"they were very obviously . . . from bad environments and broken homes where they had received no love."

If, up to this point, Barthelme has been playful with the demonstrators and non-demonstrators, he shifts gears and concludes on a more serious note. One of the picketers has been physically assaulted; nonetheless, with his head bandaged, he manages to get to the "Playmor Lanes" to deliver his lecture: "What Is To Be Done?" The story concludes: "With good diction and enunciation and in a strong voice" he "was very eloquent." "And eloquence . . . is really all any of us can hope for." If ripeness or readiness was all, at another time in man's history, now—in a bowling alley, pulpit, or just about anywhere—good style is all.

The title of the story (evoking the absence of belief and love in *The Waste Land*) is significant. The speaker has an obviously important and guarded relationship with someone named "Marie." She, it would appear, has painted the placards, which are now fading in the rain, and she remains at home watching this on television. Now, as he passes a restaurant, he is reminded of something she said when at Bloomingdale's they bought her "cerise" bathing suit (the color of *The Waste Land*'s hyacinths). (Is he recalling "And I was frightened," the line that precedes "Marie, Marie, hold on tight"?) Questions of this sort, like his relationship with her, remain enigmatic, although he (and presumably she) are picketing on the "chimera of love." What Barthelme really is doing here, typical of many of his best stories like **"The Balloon"** and **"Indian Uprising,"** is allowing his narrator to verbally focus on one thing—picketing, the human condition—while really concentrating on something else, i.e., Marie.

What we experience in the story (a series of boxes within other boxes) is the difficulty of pinpointing meaning in the narrator, as he tells a story about the dilemma of discerning meaning in life. Nevertheless, it is both a very funny and serious story. As Barthelme writes: "Eloquence . . . is really all any of us can hope for."

IX "Up, Aloft in the Air"

Very much like **"Will You Tell Me?"** [**"Up, Aloft in the Air"**] is another example of Barthelme's technical virtuosity. It abounds in the mockery of cliché, the burlesque of traditional technique, and the literalization of metaphor. Plot is disarrayed; sentences flow with the form of meaning, but non sequiturs intrude upon otherwise potentially logical statements. What we have often is the *form* of meaning, suspended without logical content, or *content* that lacks clear-cut context.

Divided into four sections, the story would seem to be a picaresque adventure—as Flight 309 is forced to land in Cleveland, Akron, Toledo, and Cincinnati, and a would-be macho hero, named Buck (actually, one of Prufrock's descendants) encounters and is himself an example of the lust, infidelity, indifference, and general death-in-life quality in every decadent city he visits. The trivial and tragic are juxtaposed as Buck walks the streets of Akron, equally impressed with suicidal lovers and the shape of skyscrapers, his sweet tooth, the bakery salesgirl, and the sanitation men who clean up the suicides' blood. Note how the word "green" ties all together: "From the top of the Zimmer Building . . . a group of Akron lovers consummated a four-handed suicide leap. . . . *The air*! Buck thought as he watched the tiny figures falling, *this is certainly an air-minded country, America! But I must make myself useful.* He entered a bunshop and purchased a sweet green bun, and dallied with the sweet green girl there, calling her 'poppet' and 'funicular.' Then out into the street again to lean against the warm green façade of the Zimmer Building and watch the workmen scrubbing the crimson sidewalk."

Striking are Barthelme's creations of unusual and expanded metaphors—i.e., "And the great horse of evening trod over the immense scene once and for all"; "Hookers of grog thickened on the table placed there for that purpose." Even the following has its own logic if we literalize "ill-designed": "The citizens of Akron, after their hours at the plant, wrapped themselves in ill-designed love triangles which never contained less than four persons of varying degrees of birth, high, and low and mediocre." Some of Barthelme's most frequently quoted metaphors are found here: "Bravery was everywhere, but not here tonight, for the gods were whistling up their mandarin sleeves in the yellow realms where such matters are decided, for good or ill"; "[Buck] took the hand offered him with its enormous sapphires glowing like a garage."

Barthelme literalizes a wild (green) salad mix(ture) with his "mix" of people, as he simultaneously plays on "grass" and "blanched": at a party where people are dancing, "sensuously, they covered the ground. And then two ruly police gentlemen entered the room, with the guests blanching, and lettuce and romaine and radishes too flying for the exits, which were choked with grass."

He incorporates the cornball language of melodrama to set up content (the structure of meaning) without context. In the midst of some silly instructions of how to deal with "orange and blue flames" in a 707 plane, we read: "And now, Nancy. He held out his arms. She came to him. / 'Yes.' / 'Aren't we?' / 'Yes.' / 'It doesn't matter.' / 'Not to you. But to me. . . .'" One has little idea what they are talking about.

The story is filled with puns: "Former slumwife and former slumspouse alike," enraged with their "progressive" new housing units in Akron, would call the day it all came to pass "Ruesday." Barthelme moves quickly from one literary style or form to another. There is the silly drama involving the local poet, Constantine Cavity who, in his drugstore, holds meetings of the Toledo Medical Society. (The action is continuously disorienting, for we move from the poet to the drugstore, with its "cadenzas of documents," to a long list of doctors present, including Dr. Caligari, Dr. Scholl, and Dr. Il y a, to the condemnation of the poet: "It was claimed that Cavity had dispensed . . . but who can quarrel with Love Root, rightly used? It has saved many a lip.") In another funny sequence—this time, slapstick—Buck goes into the wrong hotel room and finds a beautiful girl in bed and makes a date with her for the next day.

In the midst of all of this are serious undertones, regarding the immorality of apathy. Near the end is an interesting line, reminiscent of Prufrock's "I grow old": "I grow less, rather than more, intimately involved with human beings as I move through world life."

X "MARGINS"

Back in the world of pickets, we meet the black Carl (Carl Maria von Weber), the cultured man whose life, in part spent in jail, is advertised on his sandwich boards, and the white Edward, who tells him that the proper "presentation" on the boards—i.e., the size of the loops in the "g" and "y"—will or will not get him a job, even that of U.S. Vice-President. An implied satire on the possibility of openness between the races, the story ["**Margins**"] really deals with how meaning is divorced from words. "*What is your inner reality?*" Edward repeatedly asks Carl, who replies, "It's mine."

XI "THE JOKER'S GREATEST TRIUMPH"

This ["**The Joker's Greatest Triumph**"] is whimsical in its focus on the comic-strip characters fighting crime in our affluent, consumer society. Everyone has two Batmobiles in his Bat-cave. Although the "tale" involves an encounter with the Joker (whom Bruce analyzes by paraphrasing Mark Schorer's biography of Sinclair Lewis), it focuses on the relationship of Bruce Wayne, Batman, and his friend (lover?) Frederic Brown. (Robin, now at Andover, is having trouble with his French.) Its humor derives both from its quasi-humanization of these cardboard characters in a superchic society, and from its juxtapositions of the ridiculous or fantastic and the banal: "The Batmobile sped down the dark streets of Gotham City toward Gotham Airport"; "I usually prefer Kents . . . but Viceroys are tasty too."

XII "TO LONDON AND ROME"

In this visually and typographically interesting story, ["**To London and Rome**"] Barthelme places the "narrative" on the right side of the page and a gloss on the left. **"To London . . ."** is a satire on contemporary marriage, about people who accumulate things to assure themselves they are alive.

Their purchases, starting with a Necchi sewing machine and including a mistress, a big house, a piano, a Rolls Royce, a race horse, and finally a hospital that treats horses and Viscount jets, is an exercise in pataphysics. The story, in addition, is filled with "pauses" in the gloss which, unlike Pinter's famous pauses (which are always a mask for terror beneath), emphasize the empty silence of the typically respectable, affluent couple, and they, the pauses, are really the subject of the story. The horror we feel in reading this comes from our locating meaning *only* in the lines and pauses, in the absence of anything beneath.

XIII "A SHOWER OF GOLD"

Although this story ["**A Shower of Gold**"] brings back many of the weirdly abstract people of the collection, it is Barthelme's jubilant affirmation of life's possibilities, contradictions, and indefinability. Peterson, a "romantic" sculptor, goes on a television program "Who Am I?" to earn some much-needed money. The program, designed "to discover what people *really are*," is based on each contestant's personal testimony to life's absurdity. But Peterson revolts. Although he accepts the absurd condition, he realizes the contradiction of terms in articulating and embracing it. His final statement, with its echoes of Hamlet and Perseus, lacks Barthelme's typical irony and is unusually lyrical:

Don't be reconciled. Turn off your television sets . . . indulge in a mindless optimism. Visit girls at dusk. Play the guitar. How can you be alienated without first having been connected? Think back and remember how it was. . . . My mother was a royal virgin . . . and my father a shower of gold. My childhood was pastoral and energetic and rich in experiences which developed my character. As a young man I was noble in reason, infinite in faculty, in form express and admirable, and in apprehension. . . .

"Turn off your television sets" and close your texts—is this Barthelme speaking and the underlying message of the story? We live in what Joyce called a "hyper-educated" age, where, today, existential jargon is not only part of everyone's vocabulary, but it is our very identity. Not only are we walking texts of Pascal, Heidegger, Sartre, and the others, but we are the living products of T.V. lingo. Television has, after all, become the contemporary art that popularizes manners and morality, that establishes our ethical and spiritual consciousness.

Barthelme is caustic, as he belittles the cold indifference of the T.V. employee who says to Peterson: "Mr. Peterson, are you absurd? . . . do you encounter your own existence as gratuitous? Do you feel *de trop*? Is there nausea?" The catchwords of modern philosophy follow, as she continues, abstractly: "People today, we feel, are hidden away from themselves, alienated, desperate, living in anguish, despair and bad faith." She could be speaking for mouthwash or corn pads: "Man stands alone in a featureless, anonymous landscape, in fear and trembling and sickness unto death. God is dead. Nothing everywhere. Dread. Estrangement. Finitude." Lest she forget her Ivory soap-slogan mentality, she continues: "We're interested in basics"; and she adds: "*You* may not be interested in absurdity . . . but absurdity is interested in *you*" (echoing patriotic Uncle Sam posters and reversing JFK's "Ask not what your country can do for you . . .").

Peterson goes to his art dealer, who can't sell his work because of the weather. (It is the season for buying boats, not art.) He mouths sympathy with the artist's having to sell himself to television, but he babbles more Pascal and Sartre. You are estranged, he says, "from those possibilities for authentic selfhood that inhere in the present century." To cater to the public taste, he urges, Peterson should saw his sculptures in half: "two little ones would move much, much faster."

Back in his loft Peterson thinks of the President, who has encouraged the arts, and he completes a new sculpture. Suddenly a wildly absurd event *literally* occurs. The President himself runs in and cracks a sledge hammer on the new sculpture, breaking it into several small pieces. As Peterson next tells his barber-confidant about this, the barber, another lay analyst and philosopher (like everyone these days) and the author of four books, all titled *The Decision to Be* (or not to be?), diagnoses Peterson, now in Martin Buber's "I-Thou" terms, cites Pascal and others, and tells Peterson to get out of his solipsism and be more

like the President. Yet, like the dealer, he too scorns the television show as a sellout, totally unaware of how much like it he is: "It [and he] smells of the library."

Two other wildly absurd events then occur, absurd again in the palpable and practical (literal), not theoretical sense—the only "absurd" one can really fathom and articulate. A piano player, who is a living example of a seventeenth-century engraving, arrives (with switchblades) to play a cat piano (made from real cats) and parrot more "pour-soi" philosophy. Three girls from California also barge in to freeload in his loft (since by definition the artist is automatically into the free life), and although they are waiting for their "connection," they too spout Pascal.

Peterson finally goes on the television program, where the emcee resembles the President, and the contestants are attached to polygraphs to test the "validity" of their answers. Following their displays of "bad faith" (scientifically measured), Peterson admits: "The world is absurd . . . I affirm the absurdity." Yet, he continues, "On the other hand, absurdity is itself absurd," and recites the lengthy statement quoted above. Dwelling on the irrational and pursuing through logical discourse the illogical is, of course, ridiculous. One is rather obliged to "indulge in a *mindless* optimism [italics mine]." Most importantly, "absurdity is absurd," because ultimately it affirms the meaninglessness of life. Peterson's answer to all of this is that one must "play."

Attacking all the living-dead in this volume, Barthelme writes: "How can you be alienated without first having been connected? Think back and remember how it was. . . ." Indicting our "socialization," education, and brainwashing by texts and the media, Peterson affirms the human potential for greatness: "My mother was a royal virgin. . . ." Evoking the great classical past, he, in a sense, is not lying as he tells of the time man was connected to a beautiful or humanistic universe, which he truly thought he could comprehend, a time when one's childhood could be rich, when one might grow up to be noble.

Although Peterson is aware that the world has changed, a potential for nobility still remains. Peterson bespeaks a passion for other pleasures still very much alive in today's world—generosity, creativity, integrity, and his own brand of optimism. Lest one forget the conclusion of **"Marie,"** "eloquence" is all.

As much as one might like to end the discussion here, once again nothing ever "finishes" in Barthelme, and we are reminded that words (we are discussing "eloquence," after all)—any words—never truly reflect the texture of reality and one's experience: "Peterson went on and on and although he was, in a sense lying, in a sense he was not." Indeed, one cannot verbalize "mindless optimism," just as one cannot verbalize the absurd. In fact, not only may what one *feels,* in both cases, be similar, but once translated into words, both (emotional) experiences become transformed.

Furthermore, if one tries to utter the unutterable (i.e., Peterson's "eloquence"), his words may connect with associations—i.e., a mythology—that are totally anachronistic to his everyday world. Peterson's words move us because they are (in part) Hamlet's—not even Shakespeare's or Barthelme's, and they evoke a sensibility that is totally divorced from our (from *Peterson's*) contemporary world. We have our Barthelmean boxes-within-boxes once again.

Finally, the story is not only about the artist who must "play" and strive for eloquence. It is also about the urgent need we all have for authority—whether in our barber or President, our media or history and literature of the past, or our own artistic creations. It is about our passionate need for meaning—for some control over the incomprehensibility of life—and how ultimately any answer, even that of the greatest literary artist, must be shaped in sounds, and thus be removed from the very impulse that motivated it, like one's "sense" of the absurd or "mindless optimism."

A final point: if, as Barthelme illustrated in **"Me and Miss Mandible,"** signs do sometimes lie, this extends beyond words to the richest sign of all—life itself. Words are but a microcosm of an infinitely suggestive and fluid reality. Beneath all its humor and levels of irony, **"Shower of Gold"** is both a proud and jubilant affirmation of artistic ambition, as at the same time it conveys the humility of the individual in the face of an endlessly provocative and irreducible reality.

Frank Burch Brown (review date 31 March 1982)

SOURCE: Brown, Frank Burch. Review of *Sixty Stories,* by Donald Barthelme. *Christian Century* (31 March 1982): 385-86.

[*In the following review, Brown views* Sixty Stories *as a welcome overview of Barthelme's work and "gives ample evidence that contemporary writing and stories of this kind defy capsule description."*]

At 50 Donald Barthelme has established himself as a remarkable—and remarkably influential—writer with a seemingly boundless capacity for invention. This representative collection of 60 stories [*Sixty Stories*] provides a welcome overview of his work to date, including an excerpt from the novel *The Dead Father* and five stories not previously available in book form. It also gives ample evidence that contemporary writing and art can be most frustrating at the very points at which they succeed most brilliantly.

More than one critic has called Barthelme's stories "parables"—presumably because the works are short, perplexing and suggestive, verging (one might suppose) on some larger realm of significance. But, as one soon realizes, these opaque little fictions are markedly different from the parables of Jesus or even Kafka. One feels, in fact, that they are the sort of thing a poststructuralist like Derrida would produce if *he* set out to write parables.

Ever ironic, sophisticated, perverse, fantastic and often extremely witty, Barthelme's stories seldom focus on character, plot or other features of traditional narrative. Instead, they seem determined to explore the range of interesting "misreadings" to be derived from intentionally eccentric ways of perusing and rearranging the artifacts—the "texts"—of the modern world. In so doing they envision other, impossible worlds; and they improvise endless permutations of the structures discernible in actual language and everyday perception.

Stories of this kind defy capsule description. It must suffice to note that some of them display as "found objects" certain moments of history, whether actual or invented (e.g., **"Cortes and Montezuma," "Robert Kennedy Saved from Drowning"**). Most of them bring to mind aspects of the current "scene," as in the wonderful account of Hokie Mokie the jazz king. A number play with material borrowed from politics, philosophy, metaphysics and religion. What, he wonders, are angels to do now that God is gone? What if a benign capitalist bought Galveston, Texas? And occasionally Barthelme goes in for genuine satire, the sharpest of which is directed at such things as pop psychoanalysis, commercialized existentialism, religious pieties of all sorts, modern marriage (and divorce), and other banalities of our culture, high and low.

Obviously, then, the world of ordinary experience and thought is related to the worlds of this fiction. But—unlike many of their absurdist and surrealist analogues—Barthelme's fictions are so constructed as to illumine, in the end, very little of that actual human experience or of real human possibility. Indeed, they reflect nothing so much as Barthelme's love of purely linguistic effects. And in this respect the stories in this volume are not parables (or stories) at all.

Yet it is also in just this respect that these pieces remind one of a great deal of contemporary art, including the nonverbal (to which many of Barthelme's stories allude). For it is plain that much of our "high" culture regards everything except the medium itself with disinterest and/or irony, with the result that—as Barthelme himself hints in **"Kierkegaard Unfair to Schlegel"**—even the ironist's medium is purged of most of what can greatly amuse or engage.

It is fascinating, then, to watch Barthelme and others attempt to make more and more out of less and less. The greater their success, the closer they come to an already visible limit. Just once, as Barthelme is creating so much out of so little, one wants to quote for him the words of a nameless character in his story **"Grandmother's House"**: "Having seen all this I then realized what I had not realized before, what had escaped my notice these many years, that not only is less more but that *more is more too*" (his italics). But of course—ironically—he knows that already, while possibly forgetting that less can also be less.

Maurice Couturier and Regis Durand (essay date 1982)

SOURCE: Couturier, Maurice and Durand, Regis. "Barthelme's Code of Transaction." In *Donald Barthelme,* pp. 42-50. London: Methuen, 1982.

[*In the following essay, Couturier and Durand analyze the different forms of transaction and discourse in Barthelme's short fiction.*]

Barthelme's fiction—rather like Beckett's—does point in the direction of a theoretical reconstruction of the self; this is a comic enterprise, however, and is undercut by one of Barthelme's favourite strategies of displacement and defence, his constant irony. His irony is, as we have seen, a generator of fiction, but when applied to the psychological and historical world it becomes part of the complicated game of the troubled subject. A good example of this is his story '**The Sandman**', in *Sadness,* which consists of a letter written by a girl's boyfriend to her analyst. It is a funny letter, which displays Barthelme's thorough knowledge of psychoanalysis but also his ambivalent position towards it.

In '**The Sandman**', the author of the letter writes to explain why he supports his friend's wish to terminate the analysis and buy a piano instead; he proceeds to expose the power game that underlies the process of psychoanalysis. He calls the analyst 'the Sandman' in reference, he says, to the old rhyme ('Sea-sand does the Sandman bring / Sleep to the end of Day / He dusts the children's eyes with sand / And steals their dreams away' (*S,* p. 86); but it is also a reference to Freud's use of the Sandman figure, which he borrowed from E. T. A. Hoffmann's famous tale '**The Sandman**'. The game of allusions and references is carried further when the author uses psychoanalytic literature against the analyst, quoting from articles in professional journals. The boyfriend is in effect challenging the methodology of the analyst—his rigid ego psychology and its underlying norms of behaviour, his desire to 'stabilize' Susan. This, if we bear in mind the author's own unhappy experience at the hands of a righteous 'liberal' analyst, can, of course, be construed as an indictment. The ironic refutation of the reductive practices of the analyst is forceful, and so is the act of love and total acceptance of the other which is put in its place. But the irony is both enhanced and undercut by the fact that in the process the narrator shows considerable analytic knowledge and skill (his observations would place him as a Freudian phenomenologist, not surprisingly for a writer who here and elsewhere quotes from Biswanger, Ehrenzweig, Ricœur and *Phenomenological Psychology*). His interpretations of voyeurism and creativity, in particular, are the standard ones. What comes out of the discussion of the case of Susan is a plea for the integrity of the self against stabilization, violent integration or escapism.

Beyond the anecdote and the little theoretical excursion, there remains a lesson for the artist. The lesson concerns not only creation itself (here, a characteristic way of writing stories) but also a way of being in the world (the characteristic 'Barthelmean' being):

> Let me point out, if it has escaped your notice, that what an artist does, is fail. Any reading of the literature (I mean the theory of artistic creation), however summary, will persuade you instantly that the paradigmatic artistic experience is that of failure. The actualization fails to meet, equal, the intuition.
>
> ([*Sadness*; hereafter] *S,* p. 91)

What the individual is left with is the sense of his own energy, of his existential and intellectual creativity and integrity, with the inevitable ups and downs an uncompromising awareness brings about. But this seemingly self-centred consciousness leads to new developments in Barthelme's work, of a technical as well as of a psychological nature—as can be seen in more recent work, such as *Great Days* (1979).

. . . . .

Apart from its constant inventiveness in the use of language and fictional forms, Barthelme's writing has impressed its readers with the accuracy of the commentary on American life it provides. His work is, indeed, especially in collections such as *City Life* and *Sadness,* a *critique de la vie quotidienne* of urban civilization in the USA. This has been amply documented by critics and by the writer himself, but one particular aspect of it is worth pursuing here: the interactions, the interface in his work between the individual psychology and the social or political element. There is a formulation of this in '**The Sandman**':

> What do you do with a patient who finds the world unsatisfactory? The world *is* unsatisfactory; only a fool would deny it. . . . Susan's perception that America has somehow got hold of the greed ethic and that the greed ethic has turned America into a tidy little hell is not, I think, wrong.
>
> (*S,* p. 93)

This remark, probably because it is formulated by a character whose explicit theme is a critique of strategies of escapism and adjustment, has a liberal modernist ring to it. But, if Barthelme deserves to be called, as he often is, a post-modernist, it is because of the way he captures and presents obliquely aspects of what we might call the *cultural unconscious* of America. We say 'cultural unconscious' not only to avoid the very dubious word 'collective' but also because other concepts, like 'ideology' or 'epistemology', are perhaps too heavy, too formidable for what we have in mind. But it is clearly something of the same nature, the sort of analysis of the forces at work in society as well as in discourse which Jean-François Lyotard and Jean Baudrillard, among others, have been conducting over the last decade.

Barthelme's fictions are crisscrossed by a bewildering circulation of flows and forces: money, speech, affects, information in the form of quotations, clichés and noise (the opposite of information) are caught in a process of continuous symbolic exchange. At times, especially in the early stories, discourse is explicitly translated into monetary terms (either because it is worth so much on the market, say in the media—as in **'A Shower of Gold'**, [**Come Back, Dr. Caligari**] *CBDC*; or more generally because language and speech are a commodity, a currency that can be exchanged against almost anything, as in **'The Balloon'**, [**Unspeakable Practices, Unnatural Acts**; hereafter] *UPUA*). Like money, discourse can suffer devaluation because of bad currency: *dreck,* scraps, clichés, waste. Or else excessive accumulation and acceleration of exchanges can create an inflationary whirlwind, leading to giddiness and panic. Barthelme, in stories such as **'The Rise of Capitalism'** (*S*) or **'Paraguay'**, is a remarkable analyst of the uncharted waters of post-industrial capitalism. What makes him so intuitively accurate, and so close to the more theoretical work of, say, Baudrillard, is that the economic or monetary metaphor or level is always bound up with the psychic element. Discourse, reduced to pure exchange value, stripped of all referentiality, may suddenly regain objectality or use value because of scarcity or unexpected difficulties in the utterance—as in the wonderful scene from **'A Picture History of the War'** quoted earlier—which characterize our retentiveness, the anality and anxiety of our greed ethic. But it is never long before it loses its objecthood and becomes an empty sign system, in the blanks between words, in the aimless repetitions and fruitless rewordings, the disjunction and monotony that characterize the obsessional neurosis of the culture.

In this respect, Donald Barthelme has affinities with William Gaddis, especially with his novel *JR* (1975)—except, of course, that with Gaddis the shattering of codes is more complete, the text becomes purely transactional, and words are only so many particles in a network of flows, totally and instantaneously exchangeable with others: stocks, automobile traffic, TV images, static, scraps of music, and so on. The human voice, like currency, is the vehicle for an infinite exchange-ability, void of all use value, in which exchanges create only additional exchange. The apparent differences in style between the two writers (the extreme length of Gaddis's novel, and its slow accretion over the years, as opposed to Barthelme's short fictions, and their appearance in periodicals, for example) should not conceal the deeper analogies. If there is a real difference, it lies in the fact that Gaddis carries the 'destabilization' of discourse, its decodification, much further. Barthelme—and this is perhaps one of his limitations—shifts his ground quite often, begins again from new positions, falls back on old dispositions. Precisely because his fictions are short, the strategies are more visible—indeed, they sometimes call attention to themselves. This is not necessarily a liability, since it is one of the constitutive aspects of Barthelme's post-modernism, giving his work a contemporary (one could almost say fashionable) self-reflexiveness and sense of the cultural *ambiance*. Besides, the brevity of the

form generates intense situations, humour and the satisfaction (for reader and writer alike) of something having been, as Barthelme puts it, 'completed'.

But the feeling of strategies of manipulation is never very far away. Barthelme is ever the gamester, the master of language games which often carry over into self-parody and to the edge of self-destruction. One of the favourite games is in the form of dialogue. Dialogue here is seldom 'conversational' in the traditional sense; rather, it serves as a generator of fiction: a word, a statement, is offered, tossed about, picked up, played with, and yields a certain amount of free association, self-confession or pure verbal energy. This can be considered the more 'successful' form of 'conversation', when a certain smoothness of rhythm is achieved, a lubrication, a music, as is the case in the voice stories of **Great Days**. But such 'felicitous trularity' is not always so easily achieved. A complicity has to be established, a framework set up. That is why conversations often borrow ritualized forms: the confession, the question-and-answer test, the psychoanalytic session, the interview, and so on. All those situations have in common an informational or therapeutic objective, as well as a power relation more or less explicitly realized. But, most of all, they provide the space and the pretext for a discourse free of the requirements of 'normal' conversation, free to indulge in all its obsessions, repetitions, fantasies and self-defences:

Q: Are you bored with the question-and-answer form?

A: I am bored with it but I realize that it permits many valuable omissions: what kind of day it is, what I'm wearing, what I'm thinking. That's a very considerable advantage, I would say

Q: I believe in it

(**'The Explanation'**, [*City Life*; hereafter] *CL*, p. 80)

Every conversation is a form of mutual aggression and/or of mutual analysis. Sometimes this produces the standard rebellion of the 'analysand' against the 'analyst':

Q: You could interest yourself in these interesting machines. They're hard to understand. They're time-consuming

A: I don't like you

Q: I sensed it

A: These imbecile questions . . .

Q: Inadequately answered . . .

A: . . . imbecile questions leading nowhere . . .

Q: The personal abuse continues

A: . . . that voice, confident and shrill . . .

Q (aside): He has given away his gaiety, and now has nothing

(**'Kierkegaard Unfair to Schlegel'**, *CL*, p. 99)

In the several stories based on a similar pattern, the answerer is a sensitive, depressed person, who believes in the power and confusion of love, against the technocratic order of textbooks of all kinds, against the inquisitorial discourse of psychology, religion or 'science'. **'The Explanation'** is particularly significant in this respect, since it stages the resistance of the 'answerer' to the questioner's technological cant and his attempts to manipulate him. The strategy is that of affects against hyperrationality, of 'madness' against 'the reign of right reason' (the content of which, according to the A figure, is rhetoric):

> Q: I have a number of error messages I'd like to introduce here and I'd like you to study them carefully . . . they're numbered. I'll go over them with you: undefined variable . . . improper use of hierarchy . . . missing operator . . . mixed mode, that one's particularly grave . . . argument of a function is fixed-point . . . improper character in constant . . . improper fixed-point constant . . . improper floating-point constant . . . invalid character transmitted in sub-program statement, that's a bitch . . . no END statement
>
> A: I like them very much
>
> Q: There are hundreds of others, hundreds and hundreds
>
> A: You seem emotionless
>
> Q: That's not true
>
> A: To what do your emotions . . . adhere, if I can put it that way?
>
> **('The Explanation'**, *CL*, p. 79)

Confronted here are two modes of scanning the real and the discourses that attempt to structure it. And, in the comic enunciation of faulty transmission of information, the answerer probably sees, as the reader does, nothing but fantastic possible worlds of fiction, lusciously, parasitically proliferating. But, ultimately, his challenge is not even to the other as agent of organized technocratic power. Rather it is addressed to him, as the end of the quotation makes clear, as an agent and a victim of the tedium of repetition, of the slow death of non-feeling. **'The Catechist'** (in *Sadness*) gives a particularly successful staging of this symbolic situation. A priest who has fallen in love with a woman is being questioned and instructed day after day by a catechist:

> The catechist opens his book. He reads: '*The apathy of the listeners. The judicious catechist copes with the difficulty.*' He closes the book.
>
> I think: Analysis terminable and interminable. I think: Then she will leave the park looking backward over her shoulder.
>
> He says: 'And the guards, what were they doing?' I say: 'Abusing the mothers'
>
> 'You wrote a letter?'
>
> 'Another letter'

> 'Would you say, originally, that you had a vocation? Heard a call?'
>
> 'I heard many things. Screams. Suites for unaccompanied cello. I did not hear a call.'
>
> 'Nevertheless—'
>
> 'Nevertheless I went to the clerical-equipment store and purchased a summer cassock and a winter cassock. . . .'
>
> (*S*, p. 123)

. . . . .

The change that takes place with ***Great Days*** is that the dialogues seem to free themselves of the question-and-answer pattern and become more complex procedures. At the same time, the relations between the two voices are no longer ruled by aggression or investigation principles as in the examples above. Has conversation, then, become, as one of the speakers in ***Great Days*** puts it, a 'nonculminating kind of ultimately affectless activity'? (***GD***, p. 159). Yes, in the sense that play has been substituted for confrontation, analysis and anxiety. As the same speaker says to his partner, 'I respect your various phases. Your sweet, even discourse' (***GD***, p. 159). This is not to say that Barthelme's later stories have become gentle psalmodies of love. If love does figure prominently in them, it is in a somewhat ambiguous way, and always with the peculiar edge of his humour: 'Love, the highest form of human endeavour', but also 'Love which allows us to live together male and female in small grubby apartments that would only hold one sane person, normally' (**'The Leap'**, ***GD***, p. 152).

But that is only one of the reasons why the later stories cannot be termed 'affectless' in any way. Affects, as always, are pervasive. The difference with earlier fictions is that they have become so pervasive that they are now the very object of the language games being played. 'Morning' begins as an exorcism of fear ('Say you're frightened. Admit it—'). **'The Leap'** is a ritual in preparation for the great day, the day 'we make the leap to faith'. **'Great Days'**, similarly, is a ritual review and exorcism of past behaviour leading to the final promise to love and remember:

> —There's a thing the children say
>
> —What do the children say?
>
> —They say: Will you always love me?
>
> —Always
>
> —Will you always remember me?
>
> —Always
>
> (***GD***, pp. 171-2)

But, beyond such apparent 'culminations', a lot of 'nonculminating' activity does go on in the ***Great Days*** texts. In fact, their structural principle is the performative mode. Micro-sequence after micro-sequence, games are played, promises made, inventions, rituals, exorcisms performed. Unidentified voices perform, act. In **'The New Music'**, the two voices 'doing mamma' fall into it like musicians going through a routine number. The texts become the record of the activity of voices; more accurately, they *are* the activities themselves.

Barthelme's success in this new form of experimentation is brilliant: the stories are, one feels, 'purified' of the whimsy and of the sometimes facile post-modernist chic of the earlier collections. They are also purified in the sense that all trace of narrative 'dross' has been removed from them. The surprising fact is that this genuinely innovative technique also remains accessible and enjoyable to the reader. With the precision and insight of the master craftsman, Barthelme has refined and inflected his technique, emphasizing the more creative elements of his earlier work and discarding the rest, and working into it the dynamism of the performative mode. One is reminded of Samuel Beckett's wonderful rebound in *Company* (1980), of his cunning use, once more, of the voice, of what in recent theories has the highest creative potential, the verbal inventiveness, the sense of play and transaction. Such a keen sense of transactions and strategies (will Barthelme ever write a play, one wonders?) radically displaces the question of metafiction. The notion itself always had, it seems, something formalistic and limiting about it. Of course, it is true that one aspect of some of Barthelme's stories does concern itself with the art and the act of telling stories, of performing discursive acts of all kinds. And their modernity certainly has to do with the way the reader finds himself actively enlisted in them, his alertness and creativity being part and parcel of a successful performance of the text, of its being 'completed'. But then this can be said of almost every good writer, even though the modalities, of course, can be widely different. And metafiction, if it is to be successful as such, must carry the self-reflexiveness and the self-performance much further—as, for example, Italo Calvino has done in his recent meta-novel to end all meta-novels, *Se per una notte d'inverno, un viaggiatore* (*If On A Winter's Night A Traveller*, 1981). Clearly, Barthelme's originality and effectiveness do not rest on such brittle notions. His is a genuinely inventive and innovative fiction, for the many reasons we have suggested (and, no doubt, for several others as well).

Larry McCaffery (essay date 1982)

SOURCE: McCaffery, Larry. "Donald Barthelme: The Aesthetics of Trash." In *The Metafictional Muse: The Worlds of Robert Coover, Donald Barthelme, and William H. Gass*, pp. 99-149. Pittsburgh: University of Pittsburgh Press, 1982.

[*In the following excerpt, McCaffery focuses on the "metafictional interests" of Barthelme's short fiction.*]

> The final possibility is to turn ultimacy, exhaustion, paralyzing self-consciousness and the adjective weight of accumulating history . . . to make something new and valid, the essence whereof would be the impossibility of making something new.
>
> —John Barth, "Title"

> After a life rich in emotional defeats, I have looked around for other modes of misery, other roads to destruction. Now I limit myself to listening to what people say, and thinking what pamby it is, what they say. My nourishment is refined from the ongoing circus of the mind in motion. Give me the odd linguistic trip, stutter and fall, and I will be content.
>
> —Donald Barthelme, *Snow White*

On August 31, 1963 the *New Yorker* carried a story entitled **"Player Piano,"** which was written by an almost totally unknown thirty-year-old writer named Donald Barthelme. Although few readers or critics could have anticipated it at the time, the appearance of this brief, surreal story in a magazine as rich in literary heritage as the *New Yorker* must today be regarded as one of the most significant events in recent literary history. Ever since that date, the steady stream of Barthelme's fictions that have appeared in the pages of that magazine has undoubtedly served as a constant source of inspiration to other young experimental writers. Indeed, especially during the late 1960s and early 1970s, Barthelme's work probably had more impact on American innovative fiction than that of any other writer.

Even today, more than fifteen years since his *New Yorker* debut, much of Barthelme's work—particularly his output up through his collection *Sadness*—still seems enormously fresh and vital. Because of his stories' resistance to paraphrasable interpretations, their surreal landscapes, unusual characters, and fragmented, seemingly chaotic style, Barthelme's fictional methods have often been compared to those of surrealist or minimalist painters, pop artists, and such writers as Kafka, Beckett, Ionesco, and Borges. More important to this study, however, is the inward, metafictional quality of his writing, the way he uses his fiction to explore the nature of storytelling and the resources left to language and the fiction-maker. As was true with Coover, Barthelme's metafictional concerns are intimately related to his other thematic interests: the difficulties of expressing a total vision of oneself in a fragmenting universe, the failure of most of our social and linguistic systems, the difficulties of making contact or sustaining relationships with others. But above all, Barthelme has been our society's most consistently brilliant critic of the language process itself and of the symbol-making activity of modern man. And like the work of Coover and William Gass, Barthelme's metafictional examinations of how our symbols and fiction systems operate—or fail to operate—offer direct and revealing insights into the sadness, anxieties, terrors, and boredom of the modern world.

Rather than attempting to examine each of Barthelme's novels and collections of fiction—a repetitious process, as it turns out—this study will first of all make some general observations about his thematic and stylistic approaches and will then examine more closely two representative early works: *Come Back, Dr. Caligari* (1964) and *Snow White* (1967). This approach will emphasize the metafictional continuity of Barthelme's work and will not analyze the relatively unimportant ways his work has evolved during his career. Barthelme's literary methods and major thematic concerns have remained relatively stable over the years and, in fact, his recent works—with the exception of *Great Days* (1979)—seem to be suffering from too much of this very "sameness." For a period in the late 1960s, especially in *City Life* (1970), Barthelme seemed very interested in exploring the possibility of using visual and typographic elements to reinforce certain moods or themes. And, as several critics have suggested, there seems to be a greater sense of acceptance or resignation in Barthelme's recent work, a less rebellious or despairing attitude than we find in the early works.[1] But for the most part Barthelme's metafictional interests have remained remarkably consistent throughout his career.

AN OVERVIEW OF BARTHELME'S FICTIONS

The title of one of Barthelme's best short stories, **"Critique de la Vie Quotidienne,"** offers a good summary of what has always been the principal focus of his fiction: the attractions and frustrations offered by ordinary modern life. As Alan Wilde suggests in his perceptive examination of Barthelme's work, it is this scaled-down range of interests which may be what is most distinctive about his work: "The articulation [is] not of the larger, more dramatic emotions to which modernist fiction is keyed but of an extraordinary range of minor, banal dissatisfactions . . . not anomie or accidie or dread but a muted series of irritations, frustrations, and bafflements."[2] Certainly the reaction of Barthelme's characters to "la vie quotidienne" is easy to summarize, as a few of their remarks pointedly indicate:[3]

> "I was happier before."

> "Like Pascal said: 'The natural misfortune of our mortal and feeble condition is so wretched that when we consider it closely, nothing can console us.'"

> "I've been sorry all my life."

> "I spoke to Sylvia. 'Do you think this is a good life?' The table held apples, books, long-playing records. She looked up. 'No.'"

> "The paradigmatic artistic experience is that of failure. . . . The word *is* unsatisfactory; only a fool would deny it."

Nearly all of Barthelme's work to date has been permeated by this overwhelming sense that life is not as good as we expected it to be—"The world in the evening seems fraught with the absence of promise," says the disgruntled narrator of **"La Critique."** This lack of satisfaction on the part of Barthelme's characters is produced by a series of closely connected personal anxieties which are neatly balanced by Barthelme's own evident artistic anxieties and the anxieties presumably experienced by Barthelme's readers. Indeed, there is a significant relationship in Barthelme's fiction between his *characters*' struggles to stay alive, to make sense of their lives, and to establish meaningful connections with others, and *Barthelme's* own

struggle with the disintegration of fictional forms and the deterioration of language. Often Barthelme's self-conscious, metafictional approach allows these struggles to operate concurrently within the stories (many of his main characters even being surrogate artist figures), the two serving to reinforce or symbolize each other. Meanwhile, we *ourselves* provide a third aspect of this relationship: as we grapple with the elements to organize and make sense of them, we provide an additional sort of analogue or reflection of this struggle with disintegration. The relationship between these personal and metafictional concerns can be seen more clearly in the following schematic listing:

PERSONAL	METAFICTIONAL
Ennui with life's familiarities (both animate and inanimate); ongoing personal fight against the "cocoon of habituation which covers everything if we let it" (*S*, p. 179)	Anticipation of the reader's sense of boredom; need to invent new revitalized literary forms
Sense of personal, political, and social fragmentation	Impulse toward collage, verbal fragmentation, free association, and other methods of juxtaposition to break down familiar sense of order
Inability to sustain relationships with others (especially women)	Inability to rely on literary conventions (linear plots, notions of cause and effect, realistic character development, etc.) which tie things together into a pleasing whole
Sexual frustration and anxiety; sense of impotence and powerlessness in comparison with others	Artistic frustration and anxiety; belief that art is useless and can never effect significant change
Inability to know; impulse to certainty blocked (and mocked) by lies, disguises, simplistic formulas, and the irreducible mystery of life	Refusal to explain or clarify, denial of hidden or "deep meanings" with tendency instead to "stay on the surface"
Inability to communicate with others; frustrating	Suspicion that language has become "drek," so full of "stuffing" and clichés that

PERSONAL	METAFICTIONAL
sense that language blocks or betrays the feelings one wishes to express	meaningful communication with an audience is impossible
Inability to create change in one's condition, a condition made more difficult by one's self-consciousness which serves to paralyze one from spontaneous, possibly liberating, activities	Sense that one must accept language's limits and its trashy condition (hence the "recycling tendency," with clichés and drek being transformed into new objects); self-consciousness making the telling of traditional stories impossible

In Barthelme's fiction, then, the sources of dissatisfaction as well as the means of coping with it are intimately connected for both the artist and the ordinary person. Although the specific manifestations are varied, these parallel struggles often have to do with the attempt to maintain a fresh, vital relationship with either words or women—an obsession which is evident in the works of many other contemporary male metafictionists such as Gass, Coover, Barth, Sukenick, and Federman. Moreover, Barthelme's characters are typically shown not only to be painfully aware of their own personal and sexual inadequacies but, more generally, to be disgruntled or bored with the systems they rely on to deal with their fragmented, meaningless lives. Simply stated, their fundamental problem is twofold: on the one hand, they are bored with their humdrum lives and humdrum relationships with others and are therefore constantly seeking a means of overcoming their rigidly patterned but ultimately inconsequential lives; on the other hand, Barthelme's characters fear any loss of security and are unable fully to open themselves to experience because they find it so confusing, ambiguous, and unstable and because they don't trust the systems at their disposal for coping with it. Paradoxically, then, their very awareness of the dismal realities around them makes it all the more difficult for them to face up to the frightening moment when they must go forth and confront "the new." The narrator of **"Subpoena,"** after being forced to dismantle his "monster-friend" Charles, offers a good summary of these mixed feelings: "Without Charles, without his example, his exemplary quietude, I run the risk of acting, the risk of risk. I must participate, I must leave the house and walk about" ([*Sadness*; hereafter] *S,* p. 116). Even more pointed are the remarks of the narrator of **"The Dolt"** (possibly Barthelme himself) regarding a would-be writer's inability to think of anything to say: "I myself have these problems. Endings are elusive, middles are nowhere to be found, but worst of all is to begin, to begin, to begin" ([*Unspeakable Practices, Unnatural Acts*; hereafter] *UP,* p. 65).

Thus, the question for Barthelme's characters remains: given a reality which is chaotic, and given the fact that the system of signs developed by man to help him deal with reality is inadequate—"Signs are signs and some of them lie," says the narrator of **"Me and Miss Mandible"**—how does one generate enough humanly significant, exciting moments to insure that one is alive? Certainly one cannot rely on any exterior systems to help find assurances and solutions. As Alan Wilde suggests, "In a general way, what Barthelme takes his stand against are pretentions to certainty and the insistence on perfection; large demands and great expectations; dogmatisms and theories of all kinds."[4] Like Coover's characters, then, Barthelme's characters find themselves constantly confronting worn-out systems which fail to operate successfully—systems such as the government, the church, the military, the news media, and a changing series of intellectual systems. (Psychiatry, existentialism, literary criticism, and Freudian psychology are among Barthelme's favorite targets.) Indeed, Barthelme often seems to suggest, perhaps playfully, that the acceptance of any final claims to truth and certainty may result in a deadening of our ability to respond naturally to experience. In "The Photograph" Barthelme suggests precisely this point when he has one scientist suggest to another that they should burn the photographs they have discovered of the human soul:

> "It seems to me to boil down to this: Are we better off *with* souls, or just possibly *without* them?"
>
> "Yes. I see what you mean. You prefer the uncertainty."
>
> "Exactly. It's more creative. Take for example my, ah, arrangement with your wife, Dorothea. Stippled with uncertainty. At moments, we are absolutely *quaking* with nonspecific anxiety. I enjoy it. *Dorothea* enjoys it. The humdrum is defeated. Momentarily, of course."
>
> (*GP*, pp. 158-59)

As Barthelme well knows, any solution to casting off this "cocoon of habituation"—which deadens our responses to art, to other human beings, and to ordinary reality—can only be provisional in nature. But the key for Barthelme, just as it was for Coover, lies in our "keeping the circuits open," in our remaining open to experience sufficiently so that new responses and new systems can be produced to generate the freshness and vitality we all seek. This is the overt subject matter of a number of Barthelme's best fictions, such as **"The Balloon"** and **"Daumier,"** in which Barthelme examines how art can rescue man from the ordinary.

Barthelme's much-analyzed metafiction, **"The Balloon,"** presents a wonderfully deft and amusing allegory about the status of an art object's relationship to both its creator and its public.[5] As with Coover's "The Magic Poker," the narrator of **"The Balloon"** opens his story by describing his creation and then reminding us of his control over it: "The Balloon, beginning at a point on Fourteenth Street, the exact location of which I cannot reveal, expanded northward all one night, while people were sleeping, until it reached the Park. There I stopped it" (*UP*, p. 15). Although we discover in the very last paragraph of the story that this balloon had a specific meaning and served a specific purpose for the narrator—(it is revealed to be "a spontaneous autobiographical disclosure, having to do with the unease I felt at your absence, and with sexual deprivation" (*UP*, p. 21), the narrator apparently does not intend for this private meaning to be apprehended by his audience. Indeed, his main interest seems to be simply to add another interesting object to the landscape of Manhattan. As he explains:

> But it is wrong to speak of "situations," implying sets of circumstances leading to some resolution, some escape of tension; there were no situations, simply the balloon hanging there . . . at that moment there was only *this balloon,* concrete particular, hanging there.
>
> (*UP*, pp. 15-16)

Not surprisingly, the public experiences some initial difficulties in its attempts to analyze the balloon; but eventually the fundamental epistemological uncertainty of the times forces people to take a more practical approach to the balloon's presence:

> There was a certain amount of initial argumentation about the "meaning" of the balloon; this subsided, because we have learned not to insist on meanings, and they are rarely even looked for now, except in cases involving the simplest, safest phenomena.
>
> (*UP*, p. 16)

Rather than seeking external "meanings," the public soon contents itself with using the balloon for its own private uses: "It was agreed that since the meaning of the balloon could never be known absolutely, extended discussion was pointless, or at least less purposeful than the activities of those who, for example, hung green and blue paper lanterns from the warm gray underside, in certain streets, or seized the occasion to write messages on the surface" (*UP*, p. 16). Soon the balloon is also being used much like any other arbitrary coordinate system to assist people in orienting themselves: "People began, in a curious way, to locate themselves in relation to aspects of the balloon: 'I'll be at the place where it dips down into Forty-seventh Street almost to the sidewalk, near the Alamo Chile House" (*UP*, p. 20).

The balloon also serves another function that reveals much about the role that Barthelme believes that art can play for a regimented easily bored public. As the narrator suggests, the balloon offers an archetypal representation of the limitless freedom of the imagination itself:

> It was suggested that what was admired about the balloon was finally this that it was not limited or defined. . . . This ability of the balloon to shift in shape, to change, was very pleasing, especially to people whose lives were rather rigidly patterned, persons to whom change, although desired, was not available. The balloon . . . offered the possibility, in its randomness, of mislocation of the self, in contradistinction to the grid of precise, rectangular pathways under our feet. The amount of specialized training currently needed, and the consequent desirability of long-term commitments, has been occasioned by the steadily growing importance of complex machinery, in virtually all kinds of operations; as this tendency increases, more and more people will turn, in bewildered inadequacy, to solutions for which the balloon may stand as a prototype, or "rough draft."
>
> (*UP*, pp. 20-21)

Like all good art objects, then, the balloon effectively provides a sense of freedom and a moment of distraction from the mundane [. . .] effects of reality. Because its shifting, ambiguous surface allows it to be played with and freely interpreted, the balloon also serves as a reminder of the freedom we all have in confronting experience itself.

In **"Daumier,"** Barthelme explores how the fictional "construction of surrogates" allows a writer to accommodate himself to his unsatisfactory "real" life. The story—which in its labyrinthine structure resembles a miniaturized *Universal Baseball Association*—opens with the writer/narrator Daumier explaining to his wife the nature of the "great dirty villain," the self: "Now, here is the point about the self: it is insatiable. It is always, always hankering. It is what you might call rapacious to a fault. The great flaming mouth to the thing is never going to be stuffed full" (*S*, pp. 163-64). In response to this view of the self, Daumier has decided that the construction of surrogate selves in his fiction will help ease his plight. As he suggests, "The false selves in their clatter and boister and youthful brio will slay and bother and push out and put to all types of trouble the original, authentic self" (*S*, p. 163). In fact, Daumier has already succeeded in creating a fictional Daumier who "is doing very well" because he knows his limits. He doesn't overstep. Desire has been reduced in him to a minimum" (*S*, p. 164). During parts of the story we observe this second Daumier operating in his own fictional setting, transporting a number of lovely young women across the "plains and pampas of consciousness" (*S*, p. 164). After a while the fictional Daumier becomes especially enamored of one particularly attractive woman, a long-legged, kindly lady named Celeste; and, as in *The UBA* and "The Magic Poker," we begin to observe a "real" character becoming obsessed with his own creation. Thus the real Daumier notes at one point, "I then noticed that I had become rather fond—fond to a fault—of a person in the life of my surrogate. It was of course the girl Celeste. My surrogate found her attractive and no less did I; this was a worry. I began to wonder how I could get her out of his life and into my own" (*S*, p. 177).

Sensing that his one fictional construction is not really enough to sate his rapacious self, Daumier next decides to invent another surrogate, "a quiet, thoughtful chap who leads a contemplative life" (*S*, p. 178). This second person provides us with one of the most direct statements available of what Barthelme feels must be done to accommodate oneself to the world. After a lengthy period of self-analysis, he says, "It is easy to be satisfied if you get out of things what inheres in them, but you must look closely, take nothing for granted, let nothing become routine. You must fight against the cocoon of habituation which covers everything if you let it. There are always openings, if you can find them. There is always something to do" (*S*, p. 179). This solution sounds remarkably similar to the advice Henry Waugh gives himself just after he sacrificed Jock Casey: "The circuit wasn't closed, his or any other: there were patterns, but they were shifting and ambiguous and you had a lot of room inside them" (*UBA*, p. 143). At the story's end, the fictional Celeste has entered into the "real" Daumier's life, while he has temporarily packed away his other surrogates until he feels he will need them. Daumier seems well aware that this solution is but a momentary relief from the demands of the self, but nevertheless this projection has provided exactly the sort of imaginative "opening" that frees the ordinary from its tediousness and allows us to go on. The story concludes with Daumier himself rephrasing his surrogate's advice: "The self cannot be escaped, but it can be, with ingenuity and hard work, distracted. There are always openings, if you can find them, there is always something to do" (*S*, p. 183).

Barthelme also knows, however, that the ability of the artist to create a new, vital form of distraction is a self-generating problem, for what is new and fresh today is destined to soon lose these qualities. Often, as in **"The Glass Mountain,"** Barthelme depicts man striving to unlock the new only to discover that what he has produced is merely another cliché. In this story, the artist/narrator seeks to escape from his ugly, hostile surroundings to the magical realm of art; but what he finds is merely more conventions, more clichés: when he finally reaches the end of the search he tells us, "I approached the symbol, with its layer of meaning, but when I touched it, it changed into only a beautiful princess" ([*City Life*; hereafter] *CL*, p. 71). **"The Flight of the Pigeons"** deals with the difficulties of sustaining the new even more directly, as when its narrator says, "Some things appear to be wonders in the beginning, but when you have become familiar with them, are not wonderful at all. . . . Some of us have even thought of folding the show—closing it down" (*S*, p. 139). Clearly this struggle with the new has wide implications for the ordinary man as well as for the artist; indeed, as many other metafictionists have observed (see, for example, John Barth's "Title" in *Lost in the Funhouse*), people's tendency to become tired of the familiar is just as damaging to personal relationships as it is to the artist. Thus we should realize that the narrator's remarks in **"The Party"** apply to us equally as well as they do to the writer: "When one has spoken a lot one has already used up all of the ideas one has. You must change the people you are speaking to so that you appear, to yourself, to be still alive" (*S*, p. 61).

Compounding the difficulties of both the artist and the ordinary individual is the decay of the communication process itself at a time when modern man is becoming increasingly inundated with supposedly meaningful symbols.

"You can't even eat breakfast any more without eating symbols as much as anything else," said William Gass in a recent interview,[6] and Barthelme's fiction constantly examines the various ways that man is betrayed by these very symbols. The main problem facing us all, of course, is the trashy, brutalized condition of language itself which makes our communication process almost completely bog down— hence the "sludge quality" of our language—how it is filled with "stuffing"—which is described more thoroughly in *Snow White*. As a result of his views about language, Barthelme often suggests that language itself may be responsible for the isolation of his characters, their inability to put the pieces of their lives together, and their inability to sustain personal relations. Consequently, ambiguity constantly stalks their lives. They are, quite literally, unable to make sense of their lives or of what is going on around them—though, as the earlier quotation from **"The Party"** suggests, there does seem to be the Beckett-like hope that if they go on, if their *words* go on, things may finally come together. One indication of this self-reflexive interest in the linguistic process is the way these characters so often question each other about the meaning and implication of words, though they are almost never able to come up with any definite conclusions. The failures and dissatisfactions created by these linguistic investigations serve to reflect the larger pattern of failure and dissatisfaction in their lives. Information can be gathered, of course—for example, about Robert Kennedy in **"Robert Kennedy Saved from Drowning"** or about one's father in **"Views of My Father Weeping"**—but final answers or insights are beyond them. This epistemological skepticism, evident in many Barthelme stories, tends to keep our attention focused on the surface of the events. When his characters—or we ourselves—try to gain "deeper" insights or teleological explanations about what has happened, the search inevitably ends futilely with our efforts often being anticipated and directly mocked.

Both **"Robert Kennedy Saved from Drowning"** and **"Views of My Father Weeping"** offer formal critiques of the whole information-gathering process. Each of these stories, which Jerome Klinkowitz has termed "experiments in epistemology," is composed of brief, seemingly unrelated bits of prose which will supposedly provide enough information to clear up the basic mystery of their subjects.[7] **"Views"** opens with a casual introduction of violence: "An aristocrat was riding down the street in his carriage. He ran over my father" (*CL*, p. 3). The rest of the story describes the narrator's frustrating efforts to uncover the meaning of this murder and of his father's character. As Coover does in his cubist stories, Barthelme here takes all the elements of a familiar literary framework—in this case, the stock characters and language of a cheap nineteenth-century melodrama or detective thriller—and manipulates our conventional expectations for his own purposes. Much of the enjoyment of the piece comes from Barthelme's uncanny ability to mimic worn-out style and conventions while totally undermining or trivializing the easy assumptions they make. This mimicry also tends to keep our attention focused on the process of the story unfolding while distancing us from its human reality.

Not surprisingly, the story's narrator finds it difficult to relate the bits of contradictory evidence he uncovers. In fact, he finds even the simplest of statements difficult to make without qualification—he is not even sure that he can identify his father. As he tells us, "Yes, it is possible that it is not my father who sits there in the center of the bed weeping. It may be someone else, the mailman, the man who delivers the groceries, an insurance salesman or tax collector, who knows. However, I must say, it resembles my father" (*CL*, pp. 3-4). While trying to maintain a straightforward method of investigation, the narrator soon discovers that anything he is told is qualified by later considerations. For example, when he questions a witness, he is told that the man in the carriage "looked 'like an aristocrat'"; but this just leads him to consider the fact this description might simply refer to the carriage itself because "any man sitting in a handsome carriage with a driver on the box . . . tends to look like an aristocrat" (*CL*, p. 4). Certainly the old signposts and clichés no longer seem useful to his investigation. When he discovers that the driver's livery was blue and green, for instance, this seems like a substantial clue. But even this proves to be useless because, as he explains, "In these days one often finds a servant aping the more exquisite color combinations affected by his masters. I have even seen them in red trousers although red trousers used to be reserved, by unspoken agreement, for the aristocracy" (*CL*, p. 8).

Finally, when the denouement arrives, the narrator is able to talk with Lars Bang, the driver of the carriage, who explains the death away as a mere accident caused by the father himself. But within one sentence of this "final resolution," contradictory data is added by a dark-haired girl who defiantly announces that "Bang is an absolute bloody liar" (*CL*, p. 17). The story ends with the word "Etc.," an ending which, as Jerome Klinkowitz suggests, "cheats us of the supposedly false satisfaction fiction supplies"[8] and which also suggests that we are familiar enough with the material at hand to continue the story ourselves if we should desire.

Like **"Views of My Father Weeping,"** the **"Robert Kennedy"** story also mocks our traditional epistemological assumptions. Ostensibly the story aims at illuminating the nature of an ambiguous referent—the life of Robert Kennedy—by the usual method of gathering bits of factual and interpretive information. These descriptions are assembled for us, but because the reports are so contradictory and banal, we never gain any real insight into the subject. Once more, much of the information we receive is immediately qualified or contradicted.[9] The story opens with the news that Kennedy "is neither abrupt with nor excessively kind to associates. Or he is both abrupt and kind" (*UP*, p. 33). When Kennedy himself talks, his words are inevitably created out of political clichés—"Obsolete facilities and growing demands have created seemingly in-

soluble difficulties and present methods of dealing with these difficulties offer little prospect of relief"—pure blague—"It's an expedient in terms of how not to destroy a situation which has been a long time gestating, or, again, how *to* break it up if it appears that the situation . . ."—or useless redundancies—"I spend my time sending and receiving messages. Some of these messages are important. Others are not" (*UP*, pp. 36, 41, 33). As Klinkowitz has pointed out, the main thrust of the story is basically that "the conventional epistemology fails,"[10] and this failure is underlined in the last section in which Kennedy is saved by the narrator from drowning. Because of the story's title and because of the dramatic nature of the events, we surely expect a revelation into Kennedy's character at last. But even here Kennedy "retains his mask" and when he emerges from the water, he offers a noncommittal and very *un*revealing cliché: "Thank you" (*UP*, p. 44).

Because of their skepticism and self-consciousness, most of Barthelme's characters react very differently from Coover's inveterate fiction makers to the prospect of a random, absurd universe. In **"See the Moon,"** one of Barthelme's most famous stories, the narrator provides a striking metaphor for the epistemological dilemmas faced by so many Barthelme characters. The story opens with the narrator explaining that he is conducting certain "very important lunar hostility studies"; he goes on to explain that "at night the moon [is] graphed by the screen wire, if you squint. The Sea of Tranquility occupying squares 47 through 108" (*UP*, pp. 151-52). If we consider the relationship that exists between the narrator, the moon, and the porch screen he uses as a personal grid system, we find a nicely defined metaphor for the way Barthelme seems to view man, reality, and the fragile, artificial systems man has devised to help him organize his experience. Like the equally arbitrary grid system developed by Descartes for analytic geometry, the screen is a neatly patterned but artificial system which doesn't give us any clues about the real nature of the moon (Kant's *ding an sich*). Yet the screen is *useful* to the narrator in that it creates a certain temporary order and meaning; like the balloon in **"The Balloon,"** the screen itself remains ambiguous even though it can be used to help us locate ourselves in relation to other objects. [From] the postmodern perspective we can view *all* of our fictional grid systems—including science, mathematics, history, and art—to be, epistemologically speaking, really no different from this porch screen.

The narrator in **"See the Moon"** is therefore representative of most Barthelme characters in that he perceives the world, in Alan Wilde's words, "as a kind of haphazard, endlessly organizable and reorganized playground."[11] Unlike Coover's typical characters, who tend to invent systems and then rely on them too absolutely, Barthelme's characters are often all too aware of the way reality seems determined to resist our efforts to categorize and control it. "See the moon," says the narrator after explaining how his screen porch functions. "It hates us" (*UP*, p. 152). Because of his desire to discover some underlying sense of coherency in the elements of existence, the narrator has pinned objects from his past onto his wall. These objects are "souvenirs" which he hopes "will someday merge, blur—cohere is the word, maybe—into something meaningful. A grand word meaningful" (*UP,* p. 152). Within the story itself, these souvenirs are transformed into the text of words which the narrator produces for us with the same hope of generating some sort of meaning. Before us pass fragments of his past life, anecdotes about his family, his friends, his own experiences, none of which he is able to organize into the neat patterns, supported by explanatory cause-effect relationships, that were available to previous literary generations. Acutely aware of how his self-consciousness about the limitations of our systems hinders his ability to create pleasing, well-rounded wholes, the narrator jealously comments about contemporary painters:

> I wanted to be a painter. . . . You don't know how I envy them. They can pick up a Baby Ruth wrapper on the street, glue it to the canvas (in the right place, of course, there's that), and lo! people crowd about and cry "A real Baby Ruth wrapper, by God, what could be realer than that!" Fantastic metaphysical advantage. You hate them, if you're ambitious.
>
> (*UP,* p. 152)

Unable to connect the pieces together—hence the famous statement, "Fragments are the only form I trust"[12]—this narrator can only wistfully hope that the fragments of his existence will someday mysteriously come together. In the meantime, what frightens him the most is the prospect of initiating his as yet unborn child into this whole process:

> You see, Gog of mine, Gog o' my heart, I'm just trying to give you a little briefing here. I don't want you unpleasantly surprised. I can't stand a startled look. Regard me as a sort of Distant Early Warning System. Here is the world and here are the knowledgeable knowers knowing. What can I tell you? What has been pieced together from the reports of travelers. . . . What can I do for him? I can get him into A.A., I have influence. And make sure no harsh moonlight falls on his new soft head.
>
> (*UP,* pp. 164-65)

What we have been examining thus far has been the "first level" of Barthelme's fiction—the personal struggles of his characters with disintegration and fragmentation. On the second level, however, the reader is usually aware that Barthelme himself is engaged in the same epistemological struggles that plague his characters—struggles that are intimately related to the disintegration of fictional forms and the decay of language itself. Self-conscious about the inadequacies of such fictional conventions as linear sequence, causal explanations, and well-rounded characters, Barthelme finds himself in a difficult position as a writer. As we have already seen in our discussion of **"Robert Kennedy"** and **"Views of My Father,"** Barthelme feels that he cannot offer his readers the easy assurances which lie at the center of most realistic narratives, and he is equally suspicious about the ability of language to probe beneath the surfaces of things. In **"Paraguay,"** for example, Barthelme suggests that the modern experience presents special difficulties to the writer simply because of the sheer quantity of *things* that we are bombarded with:

> The softening of language usually lamented as a falling off from former practice is in fact a clear response to the proliferation of surfaces and stimuli. Imprecise sentences lessen the strain of close tolerances. Silence is also available in the form of white noise.
>
> (*CL,* p. 27)

Faced with both the "proliferation of surfaces and stimuli" and the loss of confidence in our systems' ability to explain and define reality, Barthelme's work is characterized by his refusal to present well-rounded characters, supply easy explanations, or make causal connections. As a result his characters never develop into psychologically convincing people so much as mere linguistic consciousnesses or collections of odd words. Realistic characters and events, suggests Barthelme, are patently false because the elements out of which they are created—words, plot conventions, arbitrary connections—have proven unable to depict faithfully how human beings operate in the world. So, instead, Barthelme contents himself with creating literary fragments, anecdotes, and sketches which he skillfully builds out of the clichés and verbal drek of our contemporary idiom. Barthelme's emphasis on "surface" and on process is further heightened by his manipulation of style and the technological aspects of print on the page which serve to keep the reader aware of the writing itself and to discourage the reader's search for "depth." Wilde summarizes this tendency as follows:

> The use of collage, of fragments, of pictures and black spaces; the sudden irruption of large, capitalized remarks, which may or may not comment on the surrounding text; . . . the constant experimentation with styles, ranging from the severely paratactic to the most involutedly subordinative: all function, of course, to call attention to the fact of writing (or *ecriture,* as we are learning to say), to the medium in which Barthelme and his perceptual field intersect.[13]

Thus like Coover, Gass, and other metafictionists, Barthelme often creates fictions which reflexively examine their own status as artifacts even as they proceed. The point which seems to unify the intentions of all the metafictionists is that there is a close analogy between the author's difficulties in composing and organizing a work of fiction and our own attempts to build the fiction we call our life. It is at this point that the second, reflexive level of Barthelme's fiction intersects with the first and third levels: the point at which personal and literary disintegration serve to mirror and reinforce each other.

As has already been mentioned, this third level in Barthelme's fiction is the role that we ourselves play as we confront the often absurd, seemingly random and meaningless elements in his fictions. Typically these fictions present us with a surreal mixture of the mundane and the peculiar; often the structure employed is fragmentary, with bits of words and visual elements threatening to disassemble completely into noncontiguous puzzles or, as with Kafka, mysteriously appearing to present themselves as ambiguous allegories. Like the "protagonists" of the first two levels—i.e., Barthelme's characters and Barthelme himself—we as readers probably sense that it is up to us to hold the pieces together, to find hidden clues in the elements before us, to create some sense of order and meaning without our responses being too rigidly determined. Like Barthelme's characters, we find ourselves trying to unmask the meaning of symbols and to uncover patterns—and, similarly, our efforts are usually mocked. We may even begin to share their suspicions that any order or meaning to be found is the product primarily of our own fiction-making ability, that Barthelme's stories are "merely" what they first appear to be: wonderfully deft and amusing verbal constructions that show us something of the nature of contemporary living, but which don't really "mean" anything in the way we would expect. Although I do not wish to push the "nonmeaning" aspect of Barthelme's fiction too far,[14] the possibility that many of his fictions can be analyzed as constructions to be encountered as we encounter other objects in the world brings up several crucial points about contemporary innovative fiction.

Like Beckett, Joyce, and Flaubert, Barthelme often seems primarily interested in assembling all possible combinations of words, and in the process he exposes the condition of the current status of our language. Thus like many modern painters—and again like Beckett—his art is reductionary in that he throws away ideas and concentrates instead on the effect of words themselves. Given Barthelme's pessimistic attitudes about the condition of contemporary language, probably the best phrase to describe his fiction is one which he coined himself in *Snow White*: "the leading edge of the trash phenomenon." In the much-quoted passage which produced this phrase, a manufacturer of plastic buffalo humps gives the following speech which reveals what Barthelme's "aesthetics of trash" is all about:

> Now you're probably familiar with the fact that the per-capita production of trash in this country is up from 2.75 pounds per day in 1920 to 4.5 pounds per day in 1965, the last year for which we have figures, and is increasing at the rate of about four percent a year. Now that rate will probably go up, because it's *been* going up, and I hazard that we may very well soon reach a point where it's 100 percent. Now at such a point, you will agree, the question turns from a question of disposing of this 'trash' to a question of appreciating its qualities, because, after all, it's 100 percent, right? And there can no longer be any question of 'disposing' of it, because it's all there is, and we will simply have to learn how to 'dig' it. . . . So that's why we're in humps, right now, more really from a philosophical point of view than because we find them a great moneymaker. They are 'trash,' and what in fact could be more useless or trashlike? It's that we want to be on the leading edge of this trash phenomenon, the everted sphere of the future, and that's why we pay particular

attention, too, to those aspects of language that may be seen as a model of the trash phenomenon.

(*SW*, pp. 97-98)

By building his novels and stories precisely out of "those aspects of language that may be seen as a model of the trash phenomenon," Barthelme reflects the increasing banality and vulgarization that is rapidly becoming 100 percent of our society. Barthelme shares with both Coover and Gass a deep concern for the way in which language has assumed a dead, cliché-ridden character, as is demonstrated in today's mass culture represented by television, newspapers, movies, and supermarket best-sellers. For Barthelme, however, Gass's call for a new poetry of language and Coover's for a revitalization of fictional designs is useless, for the "trash" is "already 100 percent." What is needed, then, is a means of appreciating the trash ("digging it")—an appreciation which Barthelme assists by building new artifacts out of the verbal garbage that he finds around him.

An obvious, but perhaps inexact, analogy that comes immediately to mind would be one between Barthelme's fictions and a painter's collage, which is similarly built out of "found" elements. And, indeed, the analogy with painting in general and with the collage in particular is very useful in understanding the relationship between many of Barthelme's fictions and their "meaning." Up until now, we have been considering Barthelme's fictions primarily as "meaning systems" which indicate, however indirectly, something about current conditions in the world. As our examination of Barthelme's metafictional impulses has already indicated, his fictions can be analyzed as "saying something" about related personal and literary dissatisfactions with the modern world. Barthelme's work also mirrors other specific aspects of the world in much the same way that a painting by El Greco or Rembrandt might indicate something about a particular country's mode of dress, its architecture, or even its system of values. On the other hand, like some of Coover's fictions, Barthelme's works often seem to function mainly as ways of looking at things; in this respect, his fictions are like the paintings by the cubists or the Italian Futurists: they aren't nearly as interesting for what they themselves have to tell us about the world as for presenting different methods of viewing or thinking about it.

Obviously these analogies with painting are inexact and are open to objection. Yet it is interesting that we have come to accept this idea of the art object *as object* in painting—and we have always accepted it in music—but the idea has never really caught on in fiction writing. This probably has to do with the nature of the writer's medium: words seem to always be "pointing" somewhere, to have a referential quality about them that lines and colors or sounds and rhythms do not necessarily possess (William Gass discusses this idea at several points in *Fiction and the Figures of Life*). Many contemporary writers, however, are seeking new means and strategies with which to focus the reader's attention on the book as object. In an important early essay entitled "After Joyce," Barthelme discussed this idea of the work of fiction as a new reality or object in the world, rather than as a comment upon a previously existing reality. Referring to what he terms "the mysterious shift that takes place as soon as one says that art is not about something but *is* something," Barthelme says:

> With Joyce, and to a lesser degree Gertrude Stein, fiction altered its placement in the world in a movement so radical that its consequences have yet to be assimilated. Satisfied with neither the existing world nor the existing literature, Joyce and Stein modify the world by adding to its store of objects the literary object—which is then encountered in the same way as other objects in the world. The question becomes: what is the nature of the new object? Here one can see an immediate result of the shift. Interrogating older works, the question is: what do they say about the world and being in the world? But the literary object is itself "world" and the theoretical advantage is that in asking it questions you are asking questions of the world itself.[15]

Barthelme acknowledges that the point he makes here is hardly new, although it was not usually emphasized by the theme-conscious writers who largely dominated American fiction in the 1930s, 1940s, and 1950s. But this idea lies at the center of innovative fiction of the past ten years, with its emphasis on the writer's obligation not to mirror reality or express something (be they private or social realities), but to *add new objects to the world.*

Let's imagine Barthelme sitting in his Manhattan apartment—his "studio," we'll call it—about to begin building one of these "literary objects." All around him are *words.* Words issue from his radio and television, which drone on tirelessly. Newspapers cover his floor, along with all sorts of popular magazines and obscure, scholarly journals. The bookshelves which line his walls are filled with the works of his favorite authors (Kleist, Kafka, Kierkegaard, William Gass, Walker Percy). Through his open window he can hear people walking down the street exchanging banalities and gossip; words even seem to linger in the air from the incredibly boring, pretentious party he went to the night before. Obviously, he has plenty of material at hand, but how to put it down, how to organize it? As a post-modern metafictionist, Barthelme sees no reason to limit what he can build to what resembles everyday life, a model which will mimic an exterior order. Besides, what with cameras, recording devices, xerox machines, and assembly lines, reality is being reproduced often enough as it is. He is not even sure that there *is* an exterior order; maybe cause and effect, beginnings and endings, and character motivation are just conventions developed by fiction writers. Like many other modern artists, Barthelme is also interested in getting his audience more actively involved in the artistic process; he wants to force their participation, break down the old creator/consumer barriers. So he won't order his stories in a linear way or give them the sort of "finish" his readers expect; he'll even add random elements which the reader may or may not attempt to assimilate, along with other elements ostensibly untransformed

from the real world. One of his intentions is to make the reader create his/her own connections and associations in order to link them up—let them do some of the work. He is finally ready to begin writing:

> We defended the city as best as we could. The arrows of the Comanches came in clouds. The war clubs of the Comanches clattered on the soft, yellow pavements. There were earthworks along the Boulevard Mark Clark and the hedges had been laced with sparkling wire. People were trying to understand. I spoke to Sylvia. "Do you think this is a good life?" The table held apples, books, long-playing records. She looked up. "No." Patrols of paras and volunteers with armbands guarded the tall, flat buildings. We interrogated the captured Comanche. Two of us forced his head back while another poured water into his nostrils. His body jerked, he choked and wept. . . . And! sat there getting drunker and drunker and more in love and more in love. We talked.
>
> "Do you know Fauré's 'Dolly'?"
>
> "Would that be Gabriel Fauré?"
>
> "Then I know it," she said. "May I say that I play it at certain times, when I am sad, or happy, although it requires four hands."

(*UP,* p. 3)

This passage, taken from the opening to **"The Indian Uprising,"** was chosen because it contains much of what is characteristic of Barthelme's fiction: the surrealism, the sense of chaos and fragmentation, the unexpected combination of words, the casual overtones of violence, the sexual despair, the sadness, the banality, the clichés. We might say, "Excellent! Barthelme has created a brilliant symbol of the modern wasteland." But it can also be argued that although we can apply Barthelme's story to the world in this manner—just as we can apply Euclid's geometry to the everyday world—this is not to say that Barthelme's intention is really to make a statement "about the world" (just as Euclid's geometry, so it turns out, is not really "about the world" either). Indeed, the characteristics listed above may be viewed as deriving not from the nature of the world but from the nature of modern language.

To see what this means, we might imagine a sculptor who is building an object which he covers with strips of print from his morning newspaper. Someone who sees this object might say, "Oh, I see—this artist is trying to comment on the United States' involvement in Angola, along with something about dissention on this year's Yankees." But because newsprint is the medium of this artist, it might be argued that although his object does "say" these things, it really shouldn't be analyzed as being "about" them; actually, such an object could probably best be viewed, in the self-referential sense we have been discussing, as being "about" newsprint as a medium. In short, considering the nature of the society from which Barthelme draws his materials (and his "materials" are words, concepts, systems of thought), it shouldn't be surprising that his stories frequently exhibit violence, confusion, utter banality, and cliché, hackneyed thinking. The fact that words are "trashy" and that the rational systems built out of them are full of holes can, in some respects, be seen as being beside the point for Barthelme—though not necessarily for his characters—just as painters have not been kept from using straight lines in their work despite Einstein's discoveries about the curved nature of space. Thus the process involved here can be likened to a "recycling approach" in which the drek of familiar, banal language is charged with a renewed freshness via the mysterious sea-change of art.

At the end of a remarkable piece of metafiction entitled **"Sentence,"** Barthelme observes that both writers and philosophers have had to face the fact that because language is a human system, it therefore has its limitations. This discovery has been "a disappointment, to be sure, but it reminds us that the sentence itself is a manmade object, not the one we wanted of course, but still a construction of man, a structure to be treasured for its weaknesses, as opposed to the strengths of stones" (*CL*, p. 121). This passage, which might serve as a gloss on Wittgenstein, also emphasizes what Barthelme, Coover, and Gass all use as a starting point in their fiction: that stories made of words and sentences can never escape their purely constructed, fictive nature, and that the awareness of this condition, far from being a source of despair for the author, can actually free the writer to take full advantages of the treasures of language—even bankrupt language.

Notes

1. See, for example, Alan Wilde, "Barthelme Unfair to Kierkegaard: Some Thoughts on Modern and Postmodern Irony," *boundary 2* 5 (Fall 1976), 45-70.

2. Ibid., p. 51.

3. The following passages are taken from Donald Barthelme, *City Life* (New York: Farrar, Straus & Giroux, 1970), p. 84; *Come Back, Dr. Caligari* (Boston: Little, Brown, 1964), p. 177; *Sadness* (New York: Farrar, Straus & Giroux, 1974), pp. 9, 93-95; *Unspeakable Practices, Unnatural Acts* (New York: Bantam, 1969), p. 3; henceforth these works will be abbreviated as *CL, CB, S,* and *UP*. Also cited will be *Snow White* (New York: Bantam, 1968) and *Guilty Pleasures* (New York: Farrar, Straus & Giroux, 1974), abbreviated as *SW* and *GP*.

4. Wilde, "Barthelme Unfair to Kierkegaard," p. 56.

5. The fullest critical treatments of "The Balloon" are R. E. Johnson, Jr., "'Bees Barking in the Night': The End and Beginning of Donald Barthelme's Narrative," *boundary 2* 5 (Fall 1976), 71-92; Maurice Couturier, "Barthelme's Uppity Bubble: 'The Balloon,'" *Revue Française d'Etudes Américaines* 8 (1979), 183-201.

6. William H. Gass, in interview with Larry McCaffery.

7. Jerome Klinkowitz, *Literary Disruptions: The Makings of a Post-Contemporary American Fiction* (Urbana: University of Illinois Press, 1975), p. 69.

8. Ibid., p. 72.

9. Thus R. E. Johnson's remark that "almost anything the reader might determine about a Barthelme sentence will be taken away from him by some contrary movement in that sentence or another" (p. 83).

10. Klinkowitz, *Literary Disruptions,* p. 70.

11. Wilde, "Barthelme Unfair to Kierkegaard," p. 52.

12. *UP,* p. 153. This statement has often been quoted as a statement of Barthelme's own aesthetics, something which he objects to in an interview with Jerome Klinkowitz when he says, "No. It's a statement by the character about what he is feeling at that particular moment. I hope that whatever I think about aesthetics would be a shade more complicated than that." (In *The New Fiction,* ed. Joe David Bellamy [Urbana: University of Illinois Press, 1974], p. 53.) John Leland examines the role of fragments and meaningful wholes in Barthelme's fiction in "Remarks Re-marked: Barthelme, What Curios of Signs!" *boundary 2* 5 (Spring 1977), 795-811.

13. Wilde, "Barthelme Unfair to Kierkegaard," p. 52.

14. For a more complete treatment of this issue, see my essay, "Meaning and Non-Meaning in Barthelme's Fictions," *Journal of Aesthetic Education* 13 (1979), 69-80.

15. Donald Barthelme, "After Joyce," *Location* 1 (Summer 1964), 14.

Charles Molesworth (essay date 1982)

SOURCE: Molesworth, Charles. "The Short Story as the Form of Forms." In *Donald Barthelme's Fiction: The Ironist Saved from Drowning,* pp. 10-42. Columbia: University of Missouri Press, 1982.

[*In the following essay, Molesworth examines the defining characteristics of Barthelme's short stories.*]

About fifty years ago, Elizabeth Bowen, in her introduction to the *Faber Book of Modern Short Stories,* compared the short story to the cinema, that other "accelerating" art form. She listed three affinities between the two:

> neither is sponsored by a tradition; both are, accordingly, free; both, still, are self-conscious, show a self-imposed discipline and regard for form; both have, to work on, immense matter—the disoriented romanticism of the age.

Such affinities may not seem very illuminating at first glance and may strike some as the result of an intuition that barely rises above the journalistic. Still, the three points are worth considering, if only as a way to orient Barthelme's talent in terms of this protean genre. Take the last point first: the immensity of matter. This is perhaps the most obvious characteristic of Barthelme's work, its heterogeneous range of subjects, or at least its range of references. The stories in some sense reflect their place of publication, namely the modern magazine. Addressed to an audience with a relatively wide experience of travel, an acute sense of fashion and change, as well as a consciousness formed in part by a purposely pliant cultural context, these stories must constantly widen, shift, and quicken their readers' sense of timely details. In a sense, Barthelme's stories must compete with, even as they ironically comment on, the advertisements and nonfiction "features" that surround them. This calls for a fictional voice that is both coy and disaffected, naively desirous and dispassionately suave, especially in regard to the vagaries of status and the quicksilver tokens of its possessors.

Which leads us to Bowen's characterization of the age's matter: a disoriented romanticism. It's easy to imagine how Barthelme would respond to such a phrase. In fact, one could imagine him writing a brief sketch or story that would revolve around the very inanity such a phrase can lend itself to. Yet it's just the tone of this phrase—an exhaustion that wants to proclaim itself, but that must be on guard against making its very lack the ground for too large a claim—that Barthelme's fiction often explores. For the typical Barthelme character, it is just the variousness of the world that spells defeat, since the variety is both a form of plenitude and the sign of its absence. The realm of brand names, historical allusions, "current events," and fashionable topics exists in a world whose fullness results from the absence of any strong hierarchical sense of values, and the casual randomness of such things both blurs and signals how any appeal to a rigorous, ordering value system would be futile.

The second affinity between the short story and the cinema suggests a similar double truthfulness. Where the immensity of matter is both a fullness and an emptiness, the self-conscious, self-imposed discipline of both forms is also a burden and a possibility. In its earliest days, the cinema turned directly to the stage for its discipline, especially its plots and characters and settings. But before long the new form had developed strict generic limits of its own. The train robbery, the last-minute rescue in the weekly serial, the gothic horror show, the costume drama: in ways large and small the cinematic vocabulary defined itself by following its own successes. At one level this was mere common sense. Chase scenes seemed a natural thing to film, and reenacting past historical epochs obviously satisfied a longing for entertainment and curiosity. The cinema found its own mimetic boundaries, often because it discovered it could create illusions. So, to quote one cynical entrepreneur, "we give 'em what they like, and they like what we give 'em." The short story, especially in its appearances in nineteenth-century magazines, obviously borrowed heavily from the parent form, the realistic novel. Increasingly, short stories began to utilize certain devices that not only worked well, but seemed to be natural extensions of its form, generic limitations turned to advantage. The elliptical opening, reliance on especially accurate dialogue, a

certain use of symbolist concentration on atmosphere, and the surprise ending (refined by Joyce into an epiphany): such things would work less well in an extended narrative. So the short story slowly built up its own tradition, in part supplying what in another context Ezra Pound said "the age demanded," an "accelerated image of its own grimace."

But how much of this discipline was imposed by its creators and how much was a response to audience demands, real or supposed? Everyone knows how hard Joyce had to labor to get *Dubliners* published, and clearly some of the resistance to the stories centered on their structural innovations as well as their bleak moral tone. The trick of writing surprise endings was that they shouldn't be too surprising. By building with care toward the singular epiphanic moment, Joyce obviously challenged the generic limits. The point of all this for Barthelme is that the devices that provided for the short story's self-imposed discipline are turned into a storehouse of parodic motifs. As the would-be short-story writer in **"The Dolt"** says, "I've got the end but I don't have the middle." Indeed, the story inside *this* story, that Edgar, the struggling writer, has produced as part of the National Writing Examination, is a classic parody of the opening of one of those nineteenth-century novels of frustrated romanticism. It is a narrative that could easily be seen as the equivalent of painting by numbers, a rationalized assembly of preplanned parts. But the joke is that it remains essentially a narrative for a novel, not a short story. (The further joke is that Edgar can easily pass the oral part of the Examination, having become so proficient that he prepares for it by reciting the answers and asking his wife to supply the questions. Edgar has, like many of Barthelme's characters, mistaken form for substance.)

The short story's self-imposed discipline also concentrates on singularity of effect (here Poe's theory is the classic articulation), and on a brevity, almost a static sense of character development (here the essays by H. E. Bates and Alberto Moravia, among others, stand out.) This almost lapidary sense of getting just the right effect in the tightest space will undoubtedly put a premium on devices, and on the self-conscious play they usually entail in an ironic age. Each of Barthelme's selections of stories is a veritable catalogue of such devices, which are often parodied and played off against one another. One of the most subversive of these devices is the unreliable narrator. In full-length novels such a device allows the reader slowly to adjust his or her moral and veridical senses, even if, as with *Gulliver's Travels,* such adjustment cannot lead to a final, singular standard. But in the short story the smaller scope makes such unreliability resemble mere prankishness. And the notoriously final sense of the short story's closure also invites a self-conscious use of narrative trickery. Where a strained ending in a novel can obviously harm the overall effect, it does not necessarily ruin it. But in a short story such closure dominates our sense of the story's structure, even its very reason for being written. And where this dominance is too strong, as with many of de Maupassant's and O. Henry's stories, we feel cheated, as if the story is merely an excuse for its ending. Such a feeling can often be caused by a variety of devices in a Barthelme story. Rather than a free, unsponsored tradition, the short story's battery of generic devices can be as bafflingly plentiful, and possibly self-defeating, as that of any other art form.

And so as for the third of Bowen's suggested affinities, that neither the short story or the cinema is sponsored by a tradition, the argument thus far has maintained nearly the opposite. In a strictly limited way, the modern short story doesn't have a clear tradition that extends in any way like the novel's. But again there is a doubleness here. For the very lack of a tradition, seen from a different vantage point, can mean that the short story has open to it a host of traditions. If there is no mainstream to the genre before the popularity of magazine stories that originated in the latter part of the nineteenth century, still there are a dozen or so tributaries that constitute a flood of possible models and sources. Again, like the cinema, the short story's pliancy makes it a veritable devourer of other artistic traditions. Here the figure of Borges is especially germane, as he extended the story into the realm of the "ficciones," impinging on and often incorporating elements of the tale, the philosophical essay, the romantic "fragment," and other popular and familiar forms. For Barthelme, the line between the short story and other genres is, of course, a prancing, erratic, subversive line even when it's most stable. The clearest evidence of this is in his volume, *Guilty Pleasures,* called his "first book of nonfiction." But many of the pieces in this book are easily compared to his stories, and he even tries to categorize them as

> . . . pieces [that] have to do with having one's coat pulled, frequently by five people in six directions. Some are brokeback fables and some are bastard reportage and some are pretexts for the pleasure of cutting up and pasting together pictures, a secret vice gone public.

The last sentence refers to several pieces that use actual photographs and line engravings, with ironic, playful captions, recalling the once popular illustrated tales designed for semiliterate audiences. And by extension it can refer to the use of collage, one of Barthelme's aesthetic devices. But the "six directions" offers the clue to how Barthelme sees the short story, namely as a genre that is overdetermined, as it were, subject to an excess of impulses and obsessions. Somehow, wonderfully, the author manages to avoid having these impulses cancel each other out. Yet the other clues in the above quotation—brokeback, bastard, pretexts—also point toward the hybrid destiny of the genre, as if in trying to vindicate its lineage the short story had first to acknowledge all the illegitimate offspring that preceded it and still haunt its memory.

One family resemblance of a majority of the pieces in *Guilty Pleasures* is the shared source of their parodic material, the mass media. This would include such "byways" as the letters-to-the-editor column and the consumers' bulletin annual. The media are also a source for much of Barthelme's fiction. In a general sense, Barthelme's work can be read as an attack on the false consciousness generated by meretricious sources of information that are accepted as commonplace in the modern, technologized, urban society of mass man. This is, however, to read the stories as more morally pointed than they are intended. But in formal terms, the stories are obviously shaped to a large extent by the fascination of the abomination their author feels when faced with the media. It seems to me the stories are built with a divided consciousness that says first that all the formats of information and narrative are compromised, if not actively corrupt. The possible response is then twofold: either use these available formats since the audience is reachable by no other, or demonstrate by a parodic "de-creation" of the formats that no real binding or altering force is left to the narrative imagination in today's world.

A great many of Barthelme's stories are structured parodically on various fictional formulae and their closely related forms in the other media. This variety of formal structures reflects the absence of clear generic demarcations in modern literature, a fact that has become commonplace, as witness such "new" genres as the nonfiction novel and the new journalism. But formal diversity is such a salient fact of Barthelme's fiction that it has to be interpreted as part of his artistic vision. Consider, for example, the first seven stories in the collection, *Sadness.* The opening story is a first-person narration of a marriage that ends in divorce. The second is a manic third-person monologue, apparently addressed by a mother to her son, an aging child-prodigy. Next comes a story, called **"The Genius,"** made up of nonsequential paragraphs, some only a sentence or two long (the story is structured much like **"Robert Kennedy Saved From Drowning"**). Then there's a story built out of numbered sections, but told in a relatively continuous narrative line, although the line is "split" between two major characters. (Here the characters are an estranged couple, much like the one in the first story.) The fifth story is built on the conceit conveyed by the title, **"A City of Churches"**; a newcomer is instructed in the rather bizarre local piety and is both repelled and entangled by the repressive forces that are symbolized by the several dozen ecclesiastical structures that dominate the city. The sixth story, **"The Party,"** is a first-person monologue concerned with the whacky events and overheard chatter among the guests, as well as with the narrator's not-too-secure relationship with his friend, Francesca, to whom the story is ostensibly addressed. The seventh story concerns the artist Paul Klee, during his service in the German Air Force in March 1916. It is constructed out of two overlapping but partly contradictory accounts, one given by Klee himself and the other drawn from the files of the Secret Police who have the artist under surveillance.

All in all, a very mixed bag, and no two of the stories are related in terms of the effect of their formal structures. Two are told from a first-person point of view, but **"The Party"** is much like a manic letter or plea to Francesca, whereas the first story is told very dispassionately. The two stories that have a split focus are also quite different in effect, as are the two that are made up out of discrete paragraphs (the first using nonnumbered, nonsequential units, the other using numbers and a fairly continuous narrative line). Thematically, some of the stories can be loosely grouped: two deal with divorce or estrangement, two deal with an individual trying to manoeuvre around repressive, institutionalized forces, two have manic narrators (one first-person, the other third) who clearly suffer from paranoia, and so forth. But it is the profusion of formal inventiveness that strikes most forcefully, especially when one glances at the rest of the stories in the collection. These include one that uses line engravings, another that mimics a catechism lesson, yet another that is a letter from the narrator to his girlfriend's analyst. And in many cases the parodied form—the catechism, the letter to the analyst, the secret police files—is both thematically appropriate and at the same time undercut by the narrative.

The story about Paul Klee typifies this dual status of the trustworthiness of the stories' formal dimensions. Entitled **"Engineer-Private Paul Klee Misplaces an Aircraft between Milbertshofen and Cambrai, March 1916,"** thematically the story centers on the artist oppressed by institutionalized structures. An aircraft, one of the three in his care, is "misplaced," and Klee's first reaction is to sketch the loose canvas and rope that had been covering the plane. Eventually he conceals the loss of the plane and apparently goes unpunished. This ending makes a mockery of the Secret Police files, since, though the police are obviously observing him with skill and thoroughness, the discipline or punishment such observation is meant to insure never takes place. Of course part of the story's theme is that the secret files are their own justification for being, regardless of whether they bring about punishment or reward. In fact, the "voice" of the files is in many ways more sensitive, more laden with *Weltschmerz* than is Klee. As the Secret Police say:

> Omnipresence is our goal. We do not even need real omnipresence; hand-in-hand as it were, goes omniscience. And with omniscience and omnipresence, hand-in-hand-in-hand as it were, goes omnipotence. We are a three-sided waltz. However our mood is melancholy. There is a secret sigh that we sigh, secretly. We yearn to be known, acknowledged, admired even. What is the good of omnipotence if nobody knows? However that is a secret, that sorrow. Now we are everywhere.

In some ways this "voice" resembles that of the deranged narrator from some existential novel. The self-deluding consistency and the consistent self-contradiction are played off against an obviously comic distortion of formulaic language ("hand-in-hand-in-hand"). While other parts of the secret files contain the sort of information we might expect (the registration numbers of the aircraft, for example), this passage conveys the tone of existential *angst,* and further back, the conundrums of scholastic theology. Again, at this further remove, the form becomes thematically appropriate, since parodically the Secret Police are the "absent God" that haunts the modern artist. As the story ends, the Secret Police even condone Klee's falsification of the official papers to conceal the missing aircraft, and say,

"We would like to embrace him as a comrade and brother but unfortunately we are not embraceable. We are secret, we exist in the shadows, the pleasure of the comradely/brotherly embrace is one of the pleasures we are denied, in our dismal service." By this time, the Police have begun to sound like the guardian spirit of a romantic knight-errant. Meanwhile, Klee tells his part of the story in rather matter-of-fact, naive language.

Of course, among the manifold ironies of this story, one central element is the presentation of a real-life, historical individual named Paul Klee through a secret file that we presume is entirely Barthelme's invention. Some readers will assume that Klee was a private in the German Air Force during March 1916 and may even have visited the towns of Milbertshofen and Cambrai mentioned in the story. This thread of verisimilitude in some ways violates the principles of realism, which generally militate against using facts about actual, specific people. And thus the device of the secret file is both part of the possibly "real" detail of the story and a sign of its impossible, even surreal, fictiveness. By having the story incorporate the formats of Klee's diary and the police files, otherwise historically reliable sources in most cases, Barthelme playfully undercuts the historicist yearnings for "real" data about "real" famous people. And by parodically reducing Klee's sensibility while increasing that of the Secret Police, Barthelme deflates the theme of those stories about the persecuted, alienated artist. In a sense, the story pretends there is a "real" record behind the stories, the received opinions; at the same time, the story obviously creates fictional records to make its points. Clearly the fictional records are less true than the "imagined" truth about alienated artists and oppressive institutions. The story, then, "de-creates" not only imaginative stories but actual police files (since the only thing "true" about these files is the melancholy self-doubt they record, a quality strictly proscribed in all actual police records).

We can for the moment reduce the formalist play of the story to a few "statements": 1) sentimental notions about alienated artists are often contradicted by the historical record; 2) the historical record is made up out of rhetorical formats that often preclude certain kinds of truth from being recorded; 3) stories, which are free to mix the actual and the imagined, might lay claim to a higher truth than records, but 4) stories, if they are to be at all believable, must acknowledge their own fictiveness, although 5) if all the forms of conveying information are equally suspect, because each in its own way must answer formal demands, then the story, by its very ability to mix and violate other formats, can approach the otherwise fugitive truth. The story, that is to say, will, even more readily than the novel, acknowledge its own formal requirements by the parodic manipulation of the formats of other genres. The short story, for Barthelme, pollutes itself so that it can demystify other genres. Or to put it the other way around, it seeks to demystify other forms because it cannot claim any but a formal truth for itself. For Barthelme the highest success is not if the story strikes us as true, but rather if it shows us how it works.

All this is to apply something like Barthes's "writing degree zero" to Barthelme's playful consciousness of generic forms. For Barthelme, as for Barthes, writing can never be a pure, transparent representation of reality; it must always involve a choice among previously formed models of selection and arrangement. And neither can writing produce totally autonomous structures free of ethical forces and temporal limitations. In a real sense all writing is compromise, an attempt to mediate between apparently pure forms that claim an unequivocal truth, however limited. The short story engraves this compromise into the very lines of its fabrication. Barthes's formulation of these problems has a Marxist-existentialist cast to it, but the terms nevertheless can illumine Barthelme's situation. Barthes says:

> It is under the pressure of History and Tradition that the possible modes of writing for a given writer are established; there is a History of Writing. But this History is dual: at the very moment when general History proposes—or imposes—new problematics of the literary language, writing still remains full of the recollection of previous usage, for language is never innocent: words have a second-order memory which mysteriously persists in the midst of new meanings.[1]

This "second-order memory" often results from the use of a word, or phrase, or general vocabulary in a specific genre. Barthelme takes the generic freedom of the short story, which is also of course a generic limitation, and uses it to attack the "old" meanings. The generic limitation consists in the very absence of a strictly definable generic format, and so for Barthelme the short story is condemned, as it were, to be a parasite of other genres.

Many genres, of course, develop historically with a given outlook or ideology. In fact one well-known definition, proposed by Wellek and Warren in their *Theory of Literature,* says that genre consists of an integration of an inner form (attitude, tone, purpose) and an outer form (structure). But the short story as practised by Barthelme resembles cinema in that it appears to be an empty form that can be filled by various kinds of matter, and so not reducible to a coherent outlook. In cinema we have the newsreel, the training film, the animated short, as well as the feature film, with its full range of generic traditions. And pursuing this a step further we can borrow a notion from an early theorist of film, Sigfried Kracauer, who formulated film's chief aim as "the redemption of physical reality." This is admittedly a vague notion, but adapting it to our purposes we might venture the following: Barthelme uses the short story for the goal of "redeeming fictional consciousness." But for Barthelme, as for Kracauer, the prior act in this redemption is mimesis. By mimicking other forms, rather than by trying to "imitate" the real, by giving the reader the experience of form recaptured by form, Barthelme is, like many filmmakers, partly an archivist. He has an obvious hunger for play and manipulation that takes for its material less character and plot than the formal, one might almost say the technical, aspects of writing. This, of course, is what leads many critics to dismiss his work as trivial, and the charge has a certain substance. The reader of a

Barthelme story is bound to be aware of effects. But whereas other metafictionists create effects of estrangement and disorientation only eventually to re-establish a consistency on some other grounds, Barthelme is open to the charge that he disorients for the sake of disorientation.

But joined with this largely comic disorientation there is a serious sense of a hunger for the fugitive and the ephemeral, that is in turn joined with impulses that may be called archival. Barthelme's work contains an undeniable note of melancholy, and though it doesn't have the grandeur or resonance we find in writers like Borges or Beckett, this sadness still functions as a vital part of the overall effect. This longing for the fugitive, at its strongest, comes from an existential ethos, an awareness that all human desire for permanency remains condemned to frustration, and that to institutionalize means to destroy, though *not* to do so is to face the same result. Genres are institutionalized structures on a small scale. While they represent attempts to preserve that which is undeniably fugitive, genres are fit subjects for black humor. But while they represent attempts to create what Frost called "a momentary stay against confusion," their redemption in and through another structure can be an act of homage as well.

Too much can be made out of the purely formal aspects of Barthelme's work, however. Theoretically there would have to be some ideological content in any work, no matter how ostentatiously or genuinely preoccupied with formal matters it was. This is especially true of narratives, which implicitly tell us how people have come to be the way they are and what their prospects of change and development involve. Again, the comparison with cinema provides a clue. The early cinema, especially in the hands of Eisenstein, Vertov, and the other Russian experimenters, was hailed as a revolutionary art, superbly suited to contain the message of a new social reality. This claim was based on several factors, including the need for cooperative effort in the various stages of filmmaking as well as the revelatory and gripping effect of photographic accuracy combined with the emotional charge of "moving" pictures. A similar ideological intention has been imputed to the short story by one of its masters, Frank O'Connor. For him, the short story is dominated by "the lonely voice"; it is the fiction of "the Little Man." Tracing his notion back to Turgenev's famous remark, "We all came out from under Gogol's 'Overcoat,'" O'Connor goes on to focus on a juxtaposition. O'Connor says:

> What Gogol has done so boldly and brilliantly is to take the mock-heroic character, the absurd little copying clerk, and impose his image over that of the crucified Jesus, so that even while we laugh we are filled with horror at the resemblance.[2]

Of course, Gogol's clerk is far removed from the "new man" of socialist visionaries such as Eisenstein, even assuming Gogol had the benefit of O'Connor's Christological context to enlarge his historical resonance. But the antiheroic figure does find an appropriate home in many modern and contemporary short stories. One reason is that the story allows for little extended sense of chronological development; in a story, character seems given, whereas in a novel it can appear earned or slowly uncovered or shaped by alternating or dialectical forces. And if character is given in the short story, then society, the "other" against which we recognize and evaluate the single character, is equally fixed and unyielding. In simplified Marxist terms, the Little Man may be seen as counterrevolutionary, bringing with him an ideology that posits the impossibility of social change, let alone upheaval.

Barthelme creates many characters who are closely kin with Gogol's clerk. From the narrator, either a precocious eleven-year-old or a stunted thirty-five, who is obsessed with his teacher in **"Me and Miss Mandible,"** to the would-be writer in **"The Dolt,"** to the frustrated speaker in **"And Then"**: All these figures, and many more like them, have difficulty dealing with social forms. Often, as in Gogol, the social forms are agencies of accreditation or certification that make consistent but impossible demands on their increasingly hapless victims. The structure of their stories is often congruent with the exposition of their situation. Very little change is depicted; the inability to act becomes the dominant theme. Origins and apocalyptic conclusions seldom occur. Even **"The Balloon,"** from *Unspeakable Practices,* in which a forty-five-block-long balloon covers Manhattan, raises all sorts of terminal anxieties and catastrophic possibilities, but ends with this sentence:

> Removal of the balloon was easy; trailer trucks carried away the depleted fabric, which is now stored in West Virginia, awaiting some other time of unhappiness, some time, perhaps when we are angry with one another.

The juxtaposition at the end is one between an implied social disaster ("some other time of unhappiness") and a trivial personal feeling ("when we are angry with one another"). Besides Gogol's clerk, Prufrock lingers in the background here, as someone for whom eating a peach and disturbing the universe are commensurate and unthinkable possibilities.

This figure of impotence confronted by bureaucratized reality dramatizes many of the features of a society that has increasingly developed toward what Max Weber called "rationalization"—the employment of carefully chosen means for limited ends. For Weber, the domination that provides the social cohesion that allows means and ends to be mediated exists in three forms—traditional, charismatic, and rational-legal. Barthelme's fiction is clearly dominated by the third of these forms, although it has a faint nostalgia for the first and a skewed enchantment with the second. But a special sense of rational-legal forms constitutes a weird counterpart to the highly self-conscious sense of aesthetic form Barthelme constantly exhibits. Part of the irony in Barthelme comes from just this tension: a highly skilled author is creating especially maladroit characters, that is, a writer enchanted with the manipulation of artistic constructs is constantly showing us people who are baffled and defeated by bureaucratic forms. And, again, it is the very transparency of the short story genre, its openness to other genres, that allows Barthelme access to the greatest range of forms, allusions to form, and formalized behavior.

As O'Connor puts it: "In discussions of the modern novel we have come to talk of it as the novel without a hero. In fact, the short story has never had a hero. What it has instead is a submerged population group." Add to this the feeling that for Barthelme's fiction the submerged population group has been extended to become virtually coterminous with the entire society, and you have a fair sense of what the stories are about. Barthelme's characters, for all their tics and guilts, are like flawed versions of Phillip Reiff's "therapeutic man," people hyperconscious of the mechanisms of repression and neurosis but unable effectively to alter their condition. It is this psychological literacy that also gives them access to the various forms the stories parody. In Barthelme the narrator or main character has always read the current best-seller, has always just finished a course in self-improvement (or has promised himself he will begin soon), has always learned the value of appearances. As I said earlier, the typical character values form over substance, but he is also often defeated by his inability to deal properly with form.

One story that exhibits many of these themes and characteristics is **"At the End of the Mechanical Age,"** from *Amateurs.* Here is the opening section:

> I went to the grocery store to buy some soap. I stood for a long time before the soaps in their attractive boxes, RUB and FAB and TUB and suchlike, I couldn't decide so I closed my eyes and reached out blindly and when I opened my eyes I found her hand in mine.

> Her name was Mrs. Davis, she said, and TUB was best for important cleaning experiences, in her opinion. So we went to lunch at a Mexican restaurant which as it happened she owned, she took me into the kitchen and showed me her stacks of handsome beige tortillas and the steam tables which were shiny-brite. I told her I wasn't very good with women and she said it didn't matter, few men were, and that nothing mattered, now that Jake was gone, but I would do as an interim project and sit down and have a Carta Blanca. So I sat down and had a cool Carta Blanca, God was standing in the basement reading the meters to see how much grace had been used up in the month of June. Grace is electricity, science has found, it is not *like* electricity, it *is* electricity and God was down in the basement reading the meters in His blue jump suit with the flashlight stuck in the back pocket.

> "The mechanical age is drawing to a close," I said to her.

> "Or has already done so," she replied.

> "It was a good age," I said. "I was comfortable in it, relatively. Probably I will not enjoy the age to come quite so much. I don't like its look."

> "One must be fair. We don't know yet what kind of an age the next one will be. Although I feel in my bones

that it will be an age inimical to personal well-being and comfort, and that is what I like, personal well-being and comfort."

"Do you suppose there is something to be done?" I asked her.

"Huddle and cling," said Mrs. Davis. "We can huddle and cling. It will pall, of course, everything palls, in time . . ."

The God here recalls the play by Bruce Jay Friedman, in which the Supreme Being turns out to be a Puerto Rican attendant in a steambath. Barthelme's story is clearly in the absurdist tradition, for this and other reasons. But notice how the details and the run of certain sentences in the story recall other fictional forms. We can hear a quick mocking reference to the woman's magazine story in "nothing mattered, now that Jake was gone"; the tone of the first exchange of dialogue recalls, say, the fiction of John Cheever or John O'Hara, though the actual references don't fit that mode at all. The reference to grace and electricity refers to the sort of surrealism made popular by Vonnegut and Brautigan, while the phrases "interim project" and "the mechanical age" mock the jargon of academic disciplines. The conceit about electricity may have been inspired by the ironic Auden poem, "Petition," in which God is asked to send us "power and light." But the structure of the story has a further and more complex ironic resonance. The narrator and Mrs. Davis eventually marry and then divorce. But before they marry, each sings to the other a "song of great expectations." The somewhat lengthy songs are in fact parodies of a sort of epithalamion, in which an ideal mate, a Jungian *anima,* is described as coming to satisfy the deepest desires of each partner. Further back still is the ecstatic description from the *Song of Songs,* though Barthelme's hymns are thoroughly modern in content. The irony, of course, is that the two characters are not at all comparable to the ideal mates of the songs. But a further irony is generated by the actual wedding itself, which is attended by God, "with just part of his effulgence showing," and the narrator wondering "whether He was planning to bless this makeshift construct with His grace, or not." What we see finally in the story is a parody not only of the epithalamion but also the story of Genesis, and the Miltonic version of Adam and Eve's marriage from *Paradise Lost.* The new age, the post-mechanical epoch, is thus analogously linked with the post-lapsarian world. By implicit comparison the new electronic or cybernetic or post-industrial age (Barthelme doesn't name it in the story) will make the now passing mechanical age look paradisal.

At the end of the story, the narrator is in the same position as when it began, a helpless bystander blindly stabbing at a future over which he has no control but into which his air of knowingness will carry him almost protectively. (Ralph and Maude are the names of the ideal mates in the hymns, and the explanation referred to is Mrs. Davis's disquisition on how marriage is "an institution deeply enmeshed with the mechanical age.")

After the explanation came the divorce.

"Will you be wanting to contest the divorce?" I asked Mrs. Davis.

"I think not," she said calmly, "although I suppose one of us should, for the fun of the thing. An uncontested divorce always seem to me contrary to the spirit of divorce."

"That is true," I said, "I have had the same feeling myself, not infrequently."

After the divorce the child was born. We named him A. F. of L. Davis and sent him to that part of Russia where people live to be one hundred and ten years old. He is living there still, probably, growing in wisdom and beauty. Then we shook hands, Mrs. Davis and I, and she set out Ralphward, and I, Maudeward, the glow of hope not yet extinguished, the fear of pall not yet triumphant, standby generators ensuring the flow of grace to all of God's creatures at the end of the mechanical age.

The joining of hands here signals separation, whereas in the opening paragraph it meant a new joining. Viewed as "generators," the characters are perfect metaphors for the period of transformation from the mechanical to the post-mechanical age, while the modifier "standby" reduces them to the realm of the superfluous. And the mixture of moods, the hope and fear, mimics the similar balance achieved in the famous last lines to *Paradise Lost.* In the largest terms, the story parodies the themes of fin-de-siècle melancholy and the uncertain hopes of the dawning of a new age, both classic literary subjects.

There are at least two ways to formulate the ideological implications of this story's structure. The first is implied in what has been said, namely, an impotent narrator confronts issues beyond his powers, though not his comprehension, and the story leaves him as immobilized by choice as it found him. His is O'Connor's "lonely voice," he is kin to Gogol's clerk, brought up to date with references to contemporarily fashionable details such as casual divorces, ethnic food, and mid-cult versions of historical theories. The second way is to see the structural play in the story as an ideological matrix, in which various versions of historical development and individual responsibility are intermingled.

Viewed in this way, the story's structure becomes a complex of impulses, some of which the author cannot make fully known, since they are so deeply inscribed in not only the original genres but also in their present layering. Take the hymns of praise each partner sings to the other. At one level they are built on the separation of gender and the stability of marriage as an institution that controls otherwise unlimited instincts. Yet the parody of the form suggests that such social controls are no longer effective. The narrator's song to Mrs. Davis paints a portrait of a man "right in the mud with the rest of us," though his mate "will be fainting with glee at the simple touch of his grave immense hand." As for Mrs. Davis's song, she presents a woman with "inhuman sagacity," Adamic powers, the ability to bestow names on things; the irony is that the song uses as its examples of such originating nomenclature a list of tools, including the needle-nose pliers, the rat-tail file, the ball-peen hammer, and so forth. Clearly the gender stereotypes are being reversed: the woman knows all about tools, while the man is charmingly ineffective in practical matters. (Barthelme is also alluding to the biblical notion of fallen man needing to earn his bread through work; at the same time he is mocking the irrelevance of such tools for the coming age.) An analogous irony is generated by the juxtaposition of the historical patterns the story presents, in which a potentially new era is shown to be no more than a repeated moment of transition, so the hope of social and cultural renewal is offset by the dislocations and ennui of the beginning of yet another epoch. The creation myth and epithalamion structures are canceled, as it were, by those of the woman's magazine story, with its emphasis on the normalization, even the rationalization, of matters of desire and self-fulfillment. The spirit of divorce (seen in so many Barthelme stories that it may be his single most recurrent subject) demands contest, and of course the rational-legal systems are meant to control this contest, though their actual function is often to prolong it.

As for the closure of the story, we have already seen how it hovers over the end of one age and the beginning of another. But other details are at issue: the child, for example, is both a symbol of stylized competition, his first name being the initials of the national federation of labor unions, while his place of exile is simultaneously suggestive of conflict (Russia) and serenity (a life expectancy of more than a century). (Recall how the balloon, in the story of that title, is stored in West Virginia. Place is always loaded with cultural significance for Barthelme, having spent much of his time in what was a cultural periphery, Houston, and the last two decades or so at the center, New York City.) Thus the surprise ending of the short-story genre is both enacted and dismissed, as the child's bizarre name and fate erupt in the story's narrative line and at the same time benignly close it. As a totally enclosing structure the story implicitly says that nothing will happen, or to put it more accurately, many different, disruptive events will occur, but the end result will be a sense of stasis. There will be recurrent modes of apocalyptic yearning, to be sure, and some actual historical and social changes will foster anxiety and ennui. But finally, whether the metaphor consists of divinely given grace or humanly engineered electricity, there can be "no exception to general ebb/flow of world juice and its concomitant psychological effects," as Mrs. Davis's explanation of marriage puts it.

Seeing the story as a dismissal of older narrative forms is to see it only from one perspective. The alternative perspective would suggest that by salvaging earlier forms, Barthelme is in fact paying homage to earlier visions. The story, after all, does have a visionary subject matter in the case of the songs of great expectations, although the vision is in no way offered as a ready or even legitimate possibility. Still, old forms are the residue of old dreams. And we might see Barthelme's surreal juxtapositions as attempts to go beyond (or beneath, or outside) the everyday superficial flux of consciousness. Because of his irony, his suspension between or among various opposing stances, at least two governing contexts are possible. First, his method of recycling is "merely" a reflection of the fragmented, disoriented, leveling value systems operating in today's society. Second, his recycling constantly offers to contemporary consciousness the detritus of the past (even the immediate past) on the assumption that the half-remembered visions will serve to keep alive some glimmer of a transcendent belief.

The first of these possibilities is perhaps the more acceptable. By his constant use of fragments, Barthelme would seem to defeat any sense of a transforming or totalizing artistic vision. To say this, however, may mean little more than that Barthelme is no Dante or Tolstoy and doesn't aspire to be. The use of fragments can be defended by saying that the contemporary writer of fiction mistrusts any attempt to totalize. Furthermore, it was the hunger of the modern masters, such as Joyce, Woolf, and Faulkner, to create a total vision that drove them into the recesses of myth and interior consciousness. To deal exclusively with surfaces in the contemporary world is to deal with fragments. And to deal with surfaces in fact constitutes an achievement of sorts, for it means the writer rejects the attractions of transcendent, totalizing systems as versions of mystification. In an interview[3] Barthelme has, however, turned the tables on any assumption that his art is built solely on fragments. The interviewer asks if Barthelme's earlier statement, "Fragments are the only form I trust," represents his aesthetic. The negative answer takes the form of a playful "public recantation" that Barthelme casts in the form of a mock newspaper item in *Women's Wear Daily,* complete with headlines, subheads, datelines. But even without this witty authorial disclaimer, I think the stories do present a vision that is not exclusively one of fragments, although the process of fragmentation—aesthetic, as well as social and psychological—is certainly a significant part of Barthelme's work.

The second alternative, that the recycling of generic matter, even in fragmented or allusive form, consciously offers a set of flawed utopian visions, must be considered. Of course, to offer visions that the containing structure implicitly identifies as partial and hence ineffective, might strike readers as aggressively antiutopian. Here we arrive at an impasse, an impasse that will separate the admirers of Barthelme from those who find his work superficial or affected. In a larger sense, it depends on how we read. Perhaps we use something like Northrop Frye's scheme of literature as always speaking to a vision of a classless society, an ideal community, which the species must always remember and yearn for. In this case, Barthelme will be a truly comic writer whose centripetal structures are an enactment, although one often perversely presented, of the "archetypal function of literature in visualizing the world of desire," as Frye puts it in *Anatomy of Criticism.* But if we come to stories more for a reflection of how we live now, or even more seriously as a criticism of life, Barthelme's playful use of fragments will strike us as irresponsible and ludicrous.

To put the best possible case for Barthelme would be to make something like the following argument. Any artist today, who accepts the demystified sense of a humanist vision that turns away from the comfort of a transcendent system of beliefs and values, must acknowledge the irrational and fragmented social structures that dominate our lives. But such acknowledgment need not turn into a maelstrom of existential *angst*. In fact, we can take some comfort,—albeit limited,—in knowing that humans have at least conceived transcendent schemes as part of their cultural legacy. The problem now is to create an art that disentangles those past visionary schemes from their elements of self-delusion and self-aggrandizement. At the same time, such heroic cultural ideals are not to be achieved easily, no matter if now we feel we are in a privileged position regarding our past illusions. In short, man is most human when he neither ceases to dream, nor takes his dreams at their own valuation.

Any moral formulation can have at least two differing tonal casts to it. Both Hamlet and Falstaff know that desire always outstrips capacity, though one is defeated by this awareness while the other laughs at it. For absurdists, such as Beckett, the formulation might go like this: man deludes himself with both appetite and consciousness, since neither is fully consistent in apprehending the world, and all systematic explanations will eventually fail. Yet man cannot simply stop trying to explain the world systematically, since such a longing for consistency is as inextinguishable as our appetite and our need to know. Barthelme sees this, or something like it, but sees it from a comic vantage point. For him, man, especially mass man, or little man, continuously creates forms that will rationalize his existence. These forms return to defeat him, in large part because they exclude and curtail and delimit his desires and consciousness. But rather than reject these forms as simple encumbrances, man recalls and repeats them because they reassure him that his littleness, his mass identity, is not all he has. Here Freud's *Beyond the Pleasure Principle* is obviously relevant, with its notion that the "repetition compulsion" is based on a desire to return to an earlier, simpler form of existence. I will deal with this notion later on when I discuss Barthelme's irony, especially as his sense of parody involves repetition.

But there is an ideological scheme that illumines Barthelme's comic sense of form as that which must be clung to and yet fought against. This is the sense of seriality that has been formulated by Sartre.[4] Put simply, Sartre's scheme says that men enter the social contract and surrender their individuality in order to achieve a social and historical goal. In modern history especially, this grouping eventually provides each individual with considerable freedom and self-definition. Then, however, as each individual becomes increasingly self-defining, he also tends to lose the earlier sense of collective identity. But instead of thousands, or millions, of distinct individuals, society produces men who are in effect isolated by their very individuation, so that each can no longer see the other as like himself. However, each suffers this same limitation of vision and so in fact does resemble the other; this is serialization, where everyone's longing for a distinct identity has the paradoxical effect of making all men virtual strangers and yet interchangeable. The group identity has been atomized, as it were, and the principles of cohesion and fraternity are dissolved. It is the phenomenon of mass man, but its development is given special clarity by Sartre's explanation of its dialectical formulation.

This strikes me as pertinent in the case of Barthelme, because of his emphasis on social forms that are intended to bridge the gap between individuals but actually only serve to exacerbate the sense of impotence caused by social atomization. Sometimes this ideology is thematically explicit. For example, in stories like **"The Indian Uprising," "Marie, Marie, Hold On Tight,"** and **"The Rise of Capitalism,"** social unrest has become part of the very fabric of modern urban life. But the unhappiness and longing that fuel this unrest are drained off into individualized psychological distortions. And at this level, the unrest becomes reshaped as mere personal quirks and so lacking in any real social import. Take a brief passage from **"The Rise of Capitalism,"** in which the narrator tries to comprehend how social forces and individual identity are related:

> Darkness falls. My neighbor continues to commit suicide, once a fortnight. I have his suicides geared into my schedule because my role is to save him; once I was late and he spent two days unconscious on the floor. But now that I have understood that I have not understood capitalism, perhaps a less equivocal position toward it can be "hammered out." My daughter demands more Mr. Bubble for her bath. The shrimp boats lower their nets. A book called *Humorists of the 18th Century* is published.

The self-conscious and even self-correcting political awareness dribbles away into cliché, mundane demands, routine actions. Even suicide, paradoxically a very self-defining act, has been submitted to a scheduled containment, a rational-legal form that both defuses and prolongs it. It is possible to read the clause "continues to commit suicide, once a fortnight" as simply an exaggerated way of representing someone who contemplates or discusses his suicide often, but who never performs it, so that it has become a "regular occurrence." This is true, and many of Barthelme's bizarre formulations can be traced back to some recognizable, even plausible, mimetic referent. But we are still left with the narrator's "distortion," and it is in this matter-of-fact presentation of otherwise desperate situations that we can see the ideological implications of Barthelme's vision.

The ambiguity I have been describing—the embedding of past forms in the short story as either a submission to fragmented reality or the attempt partially to overcome it at least with the memory of some ideal—can be seen as the dramatization of the serial identity Sartre describes. In Barthelme, the individual longs for some earlier, lost cultural wholeness that is inscribed in older narrative and literary forms, with their idealizations of desire. But the inescapably fragmented social order offers only degraded forms, such as the newspaper, the advertisement, the slogan, the brand name, with which to mediate our longings and anxieties. So by using collage Barthelme can turn to the "form" that contemporary consciousness has developed for itself, and he can as an author suspend his own "affirmation" between sardonic rejection and naive nostalgia.

A digression here. What happens on the larger scale of forms such as older genres and various fictional structures also occurs on the level of the individual sentence. This is part of the very texture of Barthelme's irony; here, a few examples will suffice. Often in Barthelme's stories we run across cliché expressions of the sort that serve readers as an affirmation of shared values. To show what I mean, let me list several sentences, drawn from the pages of five different stories in *Great Days*:

—"Yes, success is everything."

—"Genuine sorrow is gold."

—"Set an example. Be clear."

—". . . Cortes declines because he knows the small pieces of meat are human fingers."

—". . . the unforgiving logic of this art demands we bow to Truth, when we hear it."

Each of these sentences is a cliché, a predictable, recognizable formulation, often of a piece of common wisdom. Even the fourth example, the one least clearly related to what I'm describing, has a very stylized sense to it: the knowing conquistador is obviously wary enough to spot the hideous "native practice," though he must appear insouciant in the face of barbarity. This particular cliché suggests an origin in the movies rather than in spoken axioms, but the effect is the same. This sense of formulaic sentences is counterpointed in Barthelme by the use of surreal and collagist elements, to be sure. But one of the effects of the texture in a Barthelme story comes from this recycling of clichés and common wisdom.[5]

In these local phrases and sentences we get a distinctive mixture of tones, sardonic and naive. Clearly the author is not offering such axioms or "home truths" with the same straightforwardness we would find in a nineteenth-century author. Yet very often the character who utters such axioms is doing so out of a genuine need or belief. And so an ironic resonance is established, whereby some previous, but now clearly outdated, faith—one that used to be called a touching, simple faith—is embedded in a story where it not only doesn't avail the speaker of any immediate or practical result, but also serves to remind us how such faith is now inoperative. By falling back on such axioms, Barthelme's characters show how they desire an ethical, normative measure that will allow them to comprehend

their experience. But such axioms are also part of the Weberian sense of rationalization, that cautious desire to enunciate some meaning for life as a whole that will lend credibility to specific actions. Thus, though these axioms are often uttered to cover moments of an individual's distress or ineptitude, they call up grander schemes of meaning in which vindication on a social or historical scale is at least implicitly invoked. The wisdom, the grand, shared truth has become no more than chatter.

So the irony of the sentence is analogous to that operating on the level of structure. And in each case, the irony is generated by the resonance of the two tones, sardonic rejection and naive nostalgia. But in the stories this particular blend of attitudes produces a language that is virtually toneless. If the short story in Barthelme's hands is best seen as an empty form that encases the fragments of other forms, the same is also true for the "voice" that tells the stories. Another way of putting this is to see Barthelme's style as a pastiche of other styles, most of them "popular," but some more recondite. What we hear then in Barthelme is something like an anonymous voice, or to use a figure from one of the media, that amalgam of voices that confronts us as we turn the selector dial on our radio. This is how such a style is characterized by the Russian critic, M. Baxtin:

> Direct auctorial discourse is not possible in every literary period; not every period commands a style, since style presupposes the presence of authoritative points of view and authoritative, durable social evaluations. Such styleless periods either go the way of stylization or revert to extraliterary forms of narration which command a particular manner of observing and depicting the world. When there is no adequate form for an unmediated expression of an author's intentions, it becomes necessary to refract them through another's speech.[6]

The "extraliterary forms of narration" for Barthelme are the mass media; these, as well as the past forms of literary structure, serve both to conceal and to contain Barthelme's own voice. Pursuing our sense of doubleness one step further, we can say that Barthelme's own voice is both without authoritative force and yet completely in control. Hannah Arendt has suggested that in a modern bureaucratic state, since what happens is a constant shifting and displacement of authority, what we get in effect is "rule by no one." Something like this could well apply to Barthelme's style, with its curious mixture of total transparency and complete depersonalization.

Of course it is not easy to be scientifically precise about such matters, since any sense of style that would really tell us what we wanted to know would have to deal with non-quantifiable elements. Indeed, all sense of style is in large measure comparative. What I'm calling the depersonalized style in Barthelme is so only in relation to the much more affective, more emotionally charged writing of people like Norman Mailer or Joyce Carol Oates. A depersonalized prose similar to Barthelme's is found in Vonnegut or Kosinski, if by depersonalized we mean a relative absence of evaluative modifiers, emotive metaphor, and a firm sense of a subjectivized ego in either the characters or the narrative voice. What makes Barthelme's style distinctive, I would suggest, is its conjunction of a collagist technique with a relatively depersonalized texture. There is little or no intersubjective reality in Barthelme's world, at least certainly not the kind we are used to in conventional fiction. An otherwise interesting typology of fiction such as Dorrit Cohn's *Transparent Minds,* with its sense of fiction as characterized by the representation of states of mind, hardly applies to Barthelme at all.

At the same time we meet, in virtually every Barthelme story, situations and expressions that embody unmistakable emotions, most frequently anxiety, self-doubt, indecisiveness, and anomie. This is the result of Barthelme's carrying the modernist injunction to present rather than to interpret or to express, to "show" rather than to "tell," to something like a *reductio ad absurdum.* Indeed, when looked at closely, what Barthelme's style offers is a world charged with emotion and expressiveness that is constantly undercut, or displaced, or mentioned but not dealt with. Here is the opening paragraph of **"The President,"** from *Unspeakable Practices,* which shows a typical alternation between highly subjective material and a seemingly non-consequential set of surfaces:

> I am not altogether sympathetic to the new President. He is, certainly, a strange fellow (only forty-eight inches high at the shoulder). But is strangeness alone enough? I spoke to Sylvia: "Is strangeness alone enough?" "I love you," Sylvia said. I regarded her with my warm kind eyes. "Your thumb?" I said. One thumb was a fiasco of tiny crusted slashes. "Pop-top beer cans," she said. "He is a *strange fellow,* all right. He has some magic charisma which makes people—" She stopped and began again. "When the band begins to launch into his campaign song, 'Struttin' with Some Barbecue,' I just . . . I can't . . ."

Clearly the scarred thumb mocks what Barthes has called "the effect of the real," the result of small details of observation that hardly advance the narrative line, and indicate only that the contingent world is somehow behind the story, "out there" in the flow of reality. . . . But for now the thing to notice is how the two speaking characters here reveal everything, as it were, yet seem not to hear one another. The emotional openness and critical awareness ("Is strangeness alone enough?") eventually modulate into confusion and aphasia. And the story, and many others like it, makes it apparent that the phrase "warm kind eyes," which is repeated in connection with the narrator's secretary, is a hollow marker, one of those numberless clichés from other stories that Barthelme is constantly recycling. And so what might be expected to serve as certification of the story's verisimilitude (the pop-top cans and the scarred thumb) or its emotional sincerity (the warm kind eyes) creates the opposite effect.

So again there is a sense of duality in Bartheleme's fiction, in this case a sense of the hyperreal merged with the depersonalized. Another way to see this duality is to return once more to the question of genre, and ask what, if any, social compact exists in the case of the short story. I have already suggested that one goal in telling stories in a contemporary idiom may be to keep alive earlier forms of storytelling, a redemption of fictional consciousness. This conclusion has led to speculation about Barthelme's awareness of how readers might recall past visions of communal or group harmony, a nostalgia for some transcendent belief when they confront the fallen and fragmented forms of narration so common in the media. But I have also suggested a different, opposed, readerly disposition, which was built on a notion of the story as a reflection of how we live now, and even as a critique of contemporary society and its values. These two uses of the short story, or implicit understandings of how a story ought to function, when pushed to extremes can be summarized in two terms: storytelling and information. I borrow these terms from Walter Benjamin, whose essay "The Storyteller" explores how the ancient tale is transformed into the modern story. In preliterate society, but extending down to early modern times, the tale had a different epistemological status from that of the modern short story. In part the modern short story is close, in form and detail, to such "true" accounts as we find in newspapers, magazines, and so forth, while at a far remove the tale recalls obviously apocryphal forms such as fairy tales and romance legends. Here is how Benjamin states the distinction:

> The intelligence that comes from afar—whether the spatial kind from foreign countries or the temporal kind of tradition—possessed an authority which gave it validity, even when it was not subject to verification. Information, however, lays claim to prompt verifiability. The prime requirement is that it appear "understandable in itself." Often it is no more exact than the intelligence of earlier centuries was. But while the latter was inclined to borrow from the miraculous, it is indispensible for information to sound plausible. Because of this it proves incompatible with the spirit of storytelling. If the art of storytelling has become rare, the dissemination of information has had a decisive share in this state of affairs.[7]

This characteristic of appearing "understandable in itself" would apply to Barthelme's use of clichés, as well as to the use of brand names and allusions to current events and bits of media consciousness. Barthelme's world is clearly one in which we confront all sorts of things that have only their very ordinariness to make them recognizable. The pop-top can, the A. F. of L., the cool Carta Blanca, all serve as raw bits of information; they tell us the story is contemporary, that we are "in touch" enough to be able to recognize such references, and they suggest the world is swamped by its own flood of contemporaneity.

On the other hand, the bizarre, surreal references, the sudden irruptions of fantasy, and the presence of older forms of consciousness all tell us that the stories are more like ancient tales. The role of the return of the repressed in Barthelme's stories is crucial in this sense. By their very structures the stories imply that the social order and the rational-legal forms are not working. The goal of total secularization has not been achieved. Some authority, not subject to verification, and certainly not localizable, can be appealed to, however faintly. However short the President is in stature, he still "has some magic charisma which makes people—" The dash is crucial here, for it indicates how the knowing Little Man, the possessor of "information," no longer accepts the older forms of social domination and authority, yet at the same time he cannot fully dismiss them.

The stories do two things. First, they introduce us to the contemporary world, or rather reintroduce us, and so acknowledge its familiarity and make it safe. This is achieved largely by the superfluity of contemporary references. Second, they show us that the contemporary world is full of myth and fantasy, in which the structures of rationalization are constantly threatened with the irruption of unsafe and uncontainable instincts and awarenesses. This is achieved largely by the use of surreal collage and the parody of both social and aesthetic forms. This scheme of duality is reductive, however. In the actual reading of the stories at their best, these two functions overlap to such an extent that they virtually reverse themselves. It is the superfluous references to contemporary "junk" that strike us as disorienting, while the half-glimpsed bits of our cultural legacy tend to reassure us that we are, after all, only being entertained, only told a story.

I would venture a tentative bit of literary history here. The "high modernist mode" was built on at least two principles: it distrusted the positivism of the scientific world view that dominated the nineteenth century, and it also distrusted the smug moral certitude it identified with the figure of the Victorian sage. From these two principles flowed several various mediations, from Joyce's use of myth to redeem the everyday, to the rigorous phenomenalism of the imagist movement. But the disinterested Flaubertian "eye" suspended above the confusions of subjectivity, yet accurately recording the data and effects of that subjectivity, was certainly one of the dominant stylistic responses to the modernist dilemma. As Susan Sontag put it, two of the chief elements of modernism are homosexual aesthetic irony and Jewish moral seriousness. Now for Barthelme it is impossible to reduplicate the achievements of the high modernist mode. But neither can he dismiss the principles. (Barthelme speaks in his interview about growing up in the house his father, an architect in the modernist mode, designed: "It was wonderful to live in but strange to see on the Texas prairie.") As a result the emphasis on detachment and the use of collage continue to play a large part in his style. But in the meantime the cultural dislocations of the first two decades of the twentieth century have been followed by the even greater dislocations of the Second World War, the atomic bomb, the Cold War, and so forth. In brief, dislocation has become the order of the day. What had seemed at first like a total decay of cultural and social values had, by 1960, begun to be recontained in a new mode of consciousness. Instead of the leveling of values being perceived as a threat, it is enshrined by Pop Art. Instead of psychological fragmenta-

tion being treated as an affliction, it becomes commodified, with the help of the mass media, as a series of new "life styles." Instead of the new status of women, for example, being felt as a social upheaval, it becomes grist for the mills of the media.

But all this change, this sense of "the tradition of the new," has by now settled into a duality of its own, built out of change and integration, and hence a stable duality. From the vulgarization of a work like Alvin Toffler's *Future Shock,* to the redoubled, circuitized consciousness of McLuhan's *Understanding Media* to the sense of crisis in writers such as Norman O. Brown, what emerges is an awareness that some new consciousness is awaiting its answering form to give it full artistic life. Whatever else this form will express, it must be prepared to accept change, even accelerating change, as just another component of our cultural matrix, without special value or moment. Here the interest in such things as video, conceptual art, environmental art, as well as the quick commodification and exhaustion of these forms, is germane. The answering form that is sometimes suggested—as in the widespread acceptance of the poetry of John Ashbery, for instance (a writer Barthelme praises highly), and the drama of Robert Wilson—is a form that perfectly balances, and hence effectively overcomes, the twin demands of total empathy and total control. And Barthelme can be seen as part of this new sensibility, with his modernist use of collage and his post-modern sense of parody. And I would suggest that it is his use of generic awareness, simultaneously to acknowledge the death of genre and to point the way to its recreation in new terms, that makes him such a successful innovator.

Notes

1. *Writing Degree Zero,* trans., Annette Lavers (New York: Hill and Wang, 1968), p. 16.

2. O'Connor's essay can be found in *Short Story Theories,* ed. Charles May (Athens, Ohio: Ohio University Press, 1976). This collection includes many of the standard essays on the topic, including Poe's, and the ones by Bowen and Jarrell that I also cite.

3. In *The New Fiction: Interviews with Innovative American Writers,* by Joe David Bellamy (Urbana, Ill.: University of Illinois Press, 1974).

4. For a useful exposition, see Fredric Jameson, *Marxism and Form* (Princeton, N.J.: Princeton University Press, 1971), pp. 247-50. Sartre's analysis itself appears in *Critique of Dialectical Reason.*

5. Such wisdom and proverbs are part of what Barthes calls the "cultural code." See *S/Z,* trans. Richard Miller (New York: Hill and Wang, 1974), p. 205. Such wisdom is to be imagined as coming from "an anonymous Book whose best model is doubtless the School Manual."

6. From "Discourse Typology in Prose," in *Readings in Russian Poetics,* ed. A. Matejka and Z. Pomorska (Cambridge, Mass.: M.I.T. Press, 1971), pp. 183-84.

7. *Illuminations,* ed. with an introduction by Hannah Arendt (New York: Schocken, 1969), p. 89.

Wayne B. Stengel (essay date 1985)

SOURCE: Stengel, Wayne B. "The Art Stories." In *The Shape of Art in the Short Stories of Donald Barthelme,* pp. 163-202. Baton Rouge: Louisiana State University Press, 1985.

[*In the following essay, Stengel discusses Barthelme's twelve art stories, which evaluate the role of art and of the artist in contemporary life.*]

[This essay] examines Barthelme stories that describe the place of art in contemporary life. All the stories interpreted here examine the role of the artist and the reaction of the audience when art becomes a massive object in the landscape, a museum piece, or an insurmountable obstacle. Though all twelve stories appear unconcerned about what their art works mean, some ask from what materials contemporary art can be formed; others question whether human beings are the proper subject matter for art, what should be the goals of art, or how the artist may create in a restless, exhausted world. The highly whimsical art objects created raise still other questions about the function and utility of art in a pragmatic world frequently indifferent or hostile to aesthetic considerations.

Art in these stories hardly constitutes mimesis. Rather, as long as an audience believes in their art, the artists represented here seem free to create people or human abstractions that could not in all likelihood exist. The stories imply that the effort to know another human being may well be futile and art as representation of facets of the personality may be a sham. All art in these stories is a poor likeness, a stand-in, or a bodyguard for reality. Yet the stories also acknowledge that the only means to make art in their cynical, confused worlds is through painstaking, repetitive destruction of reality's fallacious signs and symbols. Thus each tale forms its own artistic vision by denying that it is creating art, by redefining the symbolic nature of reality so that the artistic and the symbolic include elements of life that lie within the range of common experience. The narrators of these stories attempt to make art no less exciting but less privileged and exclusive than conventional concepts have allowed. Ironically disdaining all claims for aestheticism, Barthelme's creators insist on a different, more meaningful vision of art than the art objects around them provide. They transcend this art with an art of their own.

To assure this creativity, the artistic narrators encountered in this [essay] regard art as a self-contained object without necessary meaning beyond its surface appearance or assumed reference to a world outside itself. The narrators of these stories construct original, inventive works because they are acutely aware that the modern audience for their works has grown jaded with conventional, predictable artistic experiences and the traditional responses that most works want to elicit. Accordingly, these stories sometimes attempt to involve the reader in the very processes by which they are created.

Turning to the major story in the first block of art stories, **"The Balloon,"** from *City Life* (1970), we discover a story that directly asks what the materials of modern art should be. As critic Richard Schickel has observed, the balloon that suddenly appears over forty-five blocks of Manhattan in this story serves as a metaphor for the problems of modern art and the public's reaction to it.[1] Imitating the style of environmental and conceptual art seen in New York art galleries in the sixties and seventies, the story presents readers with a superficially meaningless, self-referential object, which offers a variety of interpretations to its public. The narrator of the story shapes a work of art rich in sense of play. This playfulness exists in the childlike whim that prompts him to inflate the airy fabric of the balloon over many city blocks, the joyous spontaneity that a seemingly purposeless object produces in spectators who leave the streets and climb onto the balloon, and the comic tension between the obvious form of this enormous toy and its ambiguous content and meaning.

"The Balloon" has no plot and shows no intensification of theme or language as it progresses. The story becomes merely a catalog of public responses to the presence of this huge, rubbery plaything. The clash between the soft, undifferentiated form of the balloon and the hard-edged contours of the city buildings and skyscrapers on which it rests illustrates another of the many conflicts between fluid content and solidified form that appear throughout the story. Similarly, critic Tony Tanner sees Barthelme's balloon as representing a contemporary, abstract art object and its contradictions as embodying the dominance of its form over its content: "But take it as a kind of free-form artistic product, flexible, plastic and ephemeral, and it exemplifies the sort of art which Barthelme and many other American writers are increasingly interested in. It represents an invitation to play, a gesture against patterning, a sportive fantasy floating free above the rigidities of environment; and the invitation and the gesture are more important than the actual material of which the balloon is composed."[2] If the invitations and gestures which the form of the balloon induce in an audience are more important than its content or material, the persona of the story has been canny nonetheless in shaping an art work whose flexibility encourages a wide range of speculation about its contents. This malleability leads Jerome Klinkowitz to a somewhat different view of **"The Balloon"** from Tanner's: "Barthelme appreciates form, but he never allows it to define content."[3]

Not only does the balloon suggest endless play between its form and content, but it prompts a return to a childish sense of play among those who watch it. Realizing that the balloon can never suggest meaning in the limited terms that more respectable works of art do, the narrator describes the sense of gaiety and freedom the balloon generates among members of its audience:

> There was a certain amount of initial argumentation about the "meaning" of the balloon; this subsided, because we have learned not to insist on meanings, and they are rarely even looked for now, except in cases involving the simplest, safest phenomena. It was agreed that since the meaning of the balloon could never be known absolutely, extended discussion was pointless, or at least less purposeful than the activities of those who, for example, hung green and blue paper lanterns from the warm gray underside, in certain streets, or seized the occasion to write messages on the surface, announcing their availability for the performance of unnatural acts, or the availability of acquaintances.[4]

For the narrator, art must be a source of play as well as inspiring play in those who experience it, and such art defies exact interpretation. Yet the narrator does not explain until near the end of the story the mysterious hold an object of pure, purposeless speculation has on many observers below: "This ability of the balloon to shift its shape, to change was very pleasing, especially to people whose lives were rather rigidly patterned, persons to whom change, although desired, was not available. The balloon, for the twenty-two days of its existence, offered the possibility, in its randomness, of mislocation of the self, in contradistinction to the grid of precise, rectangular pathways under our feet" ("**B,**" 21). Thus the narrator offers his view that the appeal of the balloon lies in its perpetual indeterminacy, its ability to lose and consume those individuals who examine it. By extension, the story offers a theory of the appeal of much modern art: its elusiveness and random qualities allow the casual visitor to the gallery as well as the knowledgeable art student to forget momentarily the utilitarian regularity of his own life.

Just as suddenly as the narrator first had the balloon inflated over Manhattan, he turns off its supply of helium, the balloon expires, and the story ends. As in many Barthelme stories developed through play, the protagonist is a mischievous, hiding man who withholds his motives or identity from the reader. Only in the last paragraph of the story does one learn that the narrator has used the balloon to forget his loneliness and his sexual longing for his lover while she was out of the country. With her return he no longer needs his sublimatory toy. Just as this story, an example of modern art in its own right, reaches an arbitrary conclusion, so does the balloon; yet the demise of neither story nor balloon supplies a satisfactory meaning for the tale. The story suggests that though contemporary art may evolve out of a state of longing or deprivation, these specific, documented emotions fail to explain the work or the audience's fascination with it.

This droll tale argues that in a utilitarian world, frequently suspicious of art, many modern art works do not evoke reducible meaning. Rather, the balloon encourages the individual to lose the self in its surfaces, to relish a work's refusal to be interpreted, and to experience not only a continuing sensation of change and process but also an uninhibited sense of play that the intellectual demands of other forms preclude. "**The Balloon**" demonstrates that modern art, germinating in an incidental emotion of the artist, can be constructed from any object, toy, or plaything as long as it causes an audience to participate in a full array of its possibilities.

Critic Jerome Klinkowitz understands the force of the balloon as an art object. In his discussion of Barthelme's early essay, "The Case of the Vanishing Product," in which Barthelme contends that much modern advertising gives "not so much as a clue as to what is being advertised," Klinkowitz concurs that the "very novelty of presentation effaces the product itself."[5] In "**The Balloon**," the narrator creates an artful advertisement that is total wish fulfillment, a complete Rorschach for each observer's fantasies and desires. Like a Goodyear blimp without a message written on its side, the balloon nurtures frustration, awe, and imaginative wonder in its audience because of the advertising slogans it omits. As the narrator slyly acknowledges: "The apparent purposelessness of the balloon was vexing (as was the fact that it was 'there' at all). Had we painted, in great letters, 'LABORATORY TESTS PROVE' or '18% MORE EFFECTIVE' on the sides of the balloon, this difficulty would have been circumvented. But I could not bear to do so" ("**B,**" 18).

Nor does Barthelme add a label to "**The Police Band,**" the first auxiliary story in this category. Here the quality of play remains intact, and the tale does not yield to easy interpretation. In "**The Police Band,**" from *Unspeakable Practices, Unnatural Acts* (1968), the narrator, a former Detroit mailman and jazz musician, is sent to New York as part of the mayor's special police band. The mayor believes that whenever the rage of the city spills into the streets, the police band will go into the conflict and the soothing sound of its jazz will quell the disturbance. In practice, the mayor's plan proves a disaster. The rage of the city remains much too strong for the police band's music to tame. The mayor and his police commissioner are not reelected, and the city's rage remains unchecked by his artistic antidote.

For all its whimsicality, the parable of "**The Police Band**" raises interesting questions not only about the obvious inadequacy of music to appease urban turmoil but also about the impossibility of any art form to conquer the ugliness of reality. The story's playful juxtaposition of anguish and art, of policemen turned into artists, and of force used to beautify, illustrates the jocular intermingling of form and content that these three playful stories see as one of the functions of the contemporary art object.

"**The Police Band**" is also play because it is narrated by an amusing, unnamed critic of society, who joins the band believing that art can briefly transform the despair of reality. Unlike the balloon, however, the police band fails to claim its ghetto audience with the surface of its sounds, to convince them their lives can change or even that the playing of its music can momentarily transcend their cramped existence. The other art object on view, however, the Barthelme story itself, does succeed in reaching a quite different audience. First published in the *New Yorker,* "**The Police Band**" forced its audience of largely affluent, self-consciously sophisticated readers to question what it meant or even if it had meaning.[6] That question defines these stories' concept of the modern art object. "**The Police Band**" exists as an object of endless play, and its audience can well wonder whether the sardonic band member who narrates the story believes his own description of these musicians as representing "a triumph of art over good sense."[7] Art here does thrive on emotion, however, and has little use for good sense. The despondent narrator laments that the city dwellers, like the members of his band, remain angry. Sublimation frequently generates art in these stories, but the tales also demonstrate that one must have a balloon or music to quell one's longing or anger before art will emerge. The police band, though an object of play, differs from the balloon in failing to sublimate the desires of either its maker or its audience. It shares this dual sense of frustrated play with "**The Policemen's Ball,**" the second auxiliary story in this grouping.

"**The Policemen's Ball,**" from *City Life* (1970), depicts forceful, authoritarian policemen attempting to relax at an elaborate dance hall decorated with the theme of Camelot. The art object presented here, a ludicrously prettified social gathering of men and women dedicated to law and order, gives the form of their party an absurdly incongruous content because it contradicts the highly rigid form of these policemen's daily lives. These officers and their wives consistently adapt all their activities to some form of coercion and control. The men turn sex into compliance and submission to their will, and the women see their acquiescence as instrumental in keeping their men fit to protect them from the violence and lawlessness lurking in the streets. Even forms of reason acquire the content of force in this tale. The Pendragon, leader of all the policemen, makes a speech during the ball urging caution in pursuing those who wish to disrupt the law and incite the police: "But I must ask you in the name of force itself to be restrained."[8] Yet long before his words are spoken, whatever pleasure and exuberance the ball might possess have taken on the regimented, military bearing of its dancers.

The minimalist plot of "**The Policemen's Ball**" concerns the efforts of Horace, a young policeman, to use the sexual overtones of this sumptuous event to entice his girl friend, Margot, into his bed. Sex represents protection and control to both Horace and Margot, yet the story insists on the uncertainty and vulnerability of modern life and modern art. The tale most resembles its matched stories on the typology in its reliance on the mysterious, subversive voice that describes the ball and injects its own opinions on it into the narrative. As in "**The Balloon,**" the voice of this hiding man brings the story to an abrupt, artificial conclusion. Consummating their relationship after the ball, Horace and Margot are locked safely in Horace's apartment. Yet as the narrator asserts in the absurdly melodramatic final sen-

tence of the story: "The horrors had moved outside Horace's apartment. Not even policemen and their ladies are safe, the horrors thought. No one is safe. Safety does not exist. Ha ha ha ha ha ha ha ha ha ha ha!"[9]

The failure of the policemen and their ladies to escape their fears in the festivities of this beautiful, completely unmilitary ball or its aftermath parallels the failure of the ghetto residents to be cajoled by the police band. Both reactions show the hostility of the contemporary audience to purely playful art forms and the inability of this art to overcome the tensions of modern life. Yet both tales as examples of modern prose art exert just the sense of play, of the continual flux between form and content, that the police band and the policemen's ball fail to exert on their audiences. Nonetheless, the narrator's laughter at the conclusion of "**The Policemen's Ball**" contains a final irony. The reader can ask if these stories suggest interpretations beyond their sense of play; or, perhaps the nervous, theatrical laughter signifies that the narrator and the horrors themselves are pursued by similar goblins. Regardless, in a world of constant change and process nothing remains inviolable. Yet these stories about enormous sublimatory toys—balloon, band, and ball—provide ways to return art to pleasure while in each case suggesting the fear with which such pleasure is frequently viewed.

If these three stories developed through the process of play ask what forms innovative art might take in the contemporary world, the three tales of knowing or of desiring to know ask why famous human beings or the glorification of humanity have become objects of art. The three tales analyzed here, "**Robert Kennedy Saved from Drowning,**" "**The Genius,**" and "**On Angels,**" examine in exacting detail a charismatic political hero, a famous media-conscious intellectual, and the concept of angels as instruments of God and man, respectively. Each story's technique divides the qualities of its man or idea into specific properties and elements. In each case the resulting assessment forms a collage of contradictory poses and impressions which reveal that even highly public human beings remain unknowable.

However rigorously one attempts to investigate the enigma of the human personality, these tales demonstrate the futility of conclusively defining an individual temperament. Yet the stories that evolve from the effort have the quality of modern art in the jarring, contradictory impressions they render of the surfaces they superficially explore. Art emerges from the effort to know in these portraits of a modern politician, a contemporary intellectual, and a humanized religious image because their sense of incompletion and ellipsis allows the observer to participate in the visions formed. The reader can bring his limited knowledge and imaginative resources to shape a sense of unity and coherence in these pictures where none may actually exist.

The central art story developed through the effort to know, "**Robert Kennedy Saved from Drowning,**" from *Unspeakable Practices, Unnatural Acts* (1968), resembles the central art story developed through play, **"The Balloon."** Both stories take familiar objects, a balloon and the external, well-publicized behavior of Robert Kennedy, and inflate them to grotesque proportions. Through the irregularities and flexibility of the surfaces of the balloon and Kennedy the stories offer these objects as works of art. But whereas **"The Balloon"** asserts that play rather than interpretation should be the fruit of art, **"Robert Kennedy Saved from Drowning"** suggests that a desire to understand the art object might be the goal. **"The Balloon"** consists of the catalog of an audience's spontaneous responses to a huge air-filled toy, while **"Robert Kennedy Saved from Drowning"** seeks to construct a collage of Robert Kennedy's contradictory traits, impulses, and reactions in his role as a political figure. The audience for **"Robert Kennedy Saved from Drowning"** contains all those readers of the story who attempt to do as the narrator does in the last of the story's many short, disconnected segments. There the narrator tries to rescue Kennedy from the sea of publicity that always threatens to submerge him. Throughout the tale he uses his artistic invention to unify as best he can all these discordant snapshots of this awesome man into a complex portrait of a three-dimensional hero.

Simultaneously the story gives the reader all the evidence necessary to pronounce Kennedy a great, selfless humanitarian or to condemn him as a sham, a totally shallow political charlatan. Yet, deferring to the endless mystery of the human personality and the power of modern art to create a wide range of responses in its audience, the story never commits itself to either point of view. The reader sees Kennedy's role as a husband and father and his relations with an administrative assistant, an old friend, a secretary, a former teacher, and the young people who make up a significant part of his growing constituency. Some of these individuals speak of his warmth and compassion, while others emphasize his impulsiveness and sudden unpredictability. We hear Kennedy's own words describing his massive work load, his views on urban transportation, his feelings about the immense crowds that continually follow him, and his responsibilities as a political leader. These hollow, stereotypical responses could be the stock phrases of an insincere fraud trying to give the electorate what it wants to hear. Or they could represent the efforts of a guileless, striving statesman attempting to break free of the clichés of the political jargon expected by the media and the public.

In the twenty-four separate fragments of this story, Kennedy resembles nothing so much as a huge collage, a mosaic of all the paradoxical characteristics that a contemporary leader must possess to succeed. Robert Kennedy embodies so many perspectives and facets that the story suggests even the famous photographer, Karsh of Ottawa, can never find the right pose, the key shot that will capture the real Robert Francis Kennedy. Kennedy emerges as the ultimate art object, and one segment of the story entitled **"Gallery-going"** describes Kennedy, the politician as art object, visiting a modern art gallery.

"Gallery-going"

> K. enters a large gallery on Fifty-seventh Street, in the Fuller Building. His entourage includes several ladies and gentlemen. Works by a geometrist are on show. K. looks at the immense, rather theoretical paintings.
>
> "Well, at least we know he has a ruler."
>
> The group dissolves in laughter. People repeat the remark to one another, laughing.
>
> The artist, who has been standing behind a dealer, regards K. with hatred.[10]

The ironic effect produced here juxtaposes Kennedy, a living, three-dimensional political art object, against a superficially more severe two-dimensional one, the geometrical painting. Since his function as a politician is to draw a satisfied response from his audience, Kennedy jokes about the rigidity of the other art object on view. As expected, his audience approves, establishing that they understand and appreciate his political art. Yet Kennedy, in a different sense from the angry artist standing behind him, frequently uses a hard edge. Conditioned to make sardonic quips to further his image, he disregards taste and sensitivity to please his followers.

As becomes a skilled contemporary politician, the Robert Kennedy of this story reaches for an intellectual element within the voting public. In a concluding segment Kennedy discusses a 1949 study by the French writer Georges Poulet of a character type Poulet identifies in the drama of eighteenth-century French writer Pierre Marivaux.[11] This personality obviously represents Kennedy's own ideal of the totally adaptable political chameleon. As Kennedy relates Poulet's vision of the Marivaudian man:

> The Marivaudian being is, according to Poulet, a pastless, futureless man, born anew at every instant. The instants are points which organize themselves into a line, but what is important is the instant, not the line. The Marivaudian being has in a sense no history. Nothing follows from what has gone before. He is constantly surprised. He cannot predict his own reaction to events. He is constantly being overtaken by events. A condition of breathlessness and dazzlement surrounds him. In consequence he exists in a certain freshness which seems, if I may say so, very desirable.[12]

In choosing the condition of the Marivaudian being as his own goal, Kennedy again invites comparison with works of art. He resembles a pointillist painting, but one in which the arrangement of dots forming the picture becomes less important than the markings themselves. Kennedy's comments suggest that the reader might see each of the twenty-four points of reference of this story as existing without continuum or totality but still having fascination as isolated elements in their own right. In the final fragment of the story, Kennedy nearly drowns in the flood of so many discontinuous points of view. At just this moment the narrator intervenes. Attempting to know Kennedy in some immediate, human, and nonpolitical way, he slips a rope around his waist and throws it into the ocean to save

Kennedy from inundation. Kennedy eventually grasps the narrator's rope, but, emerging from the water with a mask still covering his face, he offers the narrator only an impersonal "thank you."

The story consistently presents a potentially frightening portrait of Robert Kennedy as a pastless, futureless man constantly surprised by his own reactions. This man might well be a political leader without commitment to anyone but himself or to anything but the present moment. Consequently, the tale has divided its critics into those who feel that it indicts Kennedy as a hopeless egomaniac obsessed with his own continually shifting image and those who believe that it offers an elliptical portrait of a deeper, more complex man, which emerges when the reader imaginatively connects the dots—Kennedy's contradictory traits—with other implicit, positive attributes. Critic Neil Schmitz belongs among the former commentators:

> The journalistic profile which seeks to humanize the great man by revealing the trivial and the intimate succeeds only in declaring the one-dimensional enormity of the figure's self-consciousness, an ego that has rigorously stylized behavior into a series of gestures. Yet this same Kennedy, master of the stock response, humorlessly quotes Poulet at the end of the piece on the Marivaudian man "born anew" in each instant of experience constantly "overtaken by events." It is scathing picture of the human surface.[13]

Although the reader may agree with Schmitz that Robert Kennedy develops into a blatantly vapid figure in this story, Schmitz's appraisal does not consider that the tale chooses to define Kennedy almost exclusively through his surface actions, however transparent their one-dimensionality. Therefore, Schmitz fails to calculate the demands of Kennedy's audience, which insists that he control and stereotype his behavior if he wishes to remain a public icon and an art object.

Balancing Schmitz's denunciation of the image of Kennedy in the story, William Stott feels that the final triumph of **"Robert Kennedy Saved from Drowning"** lies ironically in its failure to produce a believable human being from so many mutually exclusive tendencies and attitudes. Stott finds the story a parody of feature article technique which reveals the limitations of journalism to explore the interior life of any human being. Kennedy emerges as a manipulative automaton because any human personality remains, at depth, unknowable, particularly one subjected to such intense scrutiny. But Stott does value the narrator's effort to rescue Kennedy, his desire to know the art object even though it refuses to lower its mask:

> K. can't be explained in a news magazine: his public aspect has too little coherence. K.'s self is exactly what the mock notes and the article that will come from them must leave out—what they can't touch, treat, predict. . . . And Barthelme has saved K.—the K. whom Kafka taught us to recognize as Everyman—and Robert Kennedy and similar public figures, from drowning in the sea of publicity by simply insisting that the sea,

though it has K.'s body, his acts, his words, even certain of his past dreams and thoughts, doesn't have the real man.[14]

Is Kennedy's nature then all surface or all depth? The truth probably lies somewhere between these critical extremes. Still, Schmitz and Stott do not disagree on some of the qualities that make Robert Kennedy, like the balloon, an art object. Both critics see Kennedy as a figure who refuses to explain or give meaning to the world around him. He becomes an aesthetic object because of the fascination his pliable surface has for an audience wary of conventional art, exhausted with literary interpretations and deeper significance. Comparable to the balloon's inability to have a purpose or an advertising function, Kennedy's directly opposite quality, his completely utilitarian goals as a political object, confirms for Stott the extensive interior life the man must possess. These two modern art objects may contain in abundance just those qualities they appear to lack. The seeming uselessness of the balloon disguises the need for the sense of play, spontaneity, and change it prompts, and the total pragmatism of Kennedy's external character may hide the humanity and confusions beneath. Moreover, **"Robert Kennedy Saved from Drowning"** functions as an excellent modern art object itself, a short story which suggests that a famous politician acquires aesthetic force if, following the narrator of the story, the reader attempts to apprehend the collage formed from the elements of Kennedy's personality. Always ending in some degree of futility, this effort nonetheless demonstrates that a human being shares all the intricacy and contradiction of art if the reader allows his own human nature to participate in the mystery of another personality.

Two auxiliary stories, **"The Genius"** and **"On Angels,"** evoke the extreme loneliness and isolation experienced by a man or, in the case of angels, spiritual beings who have become art objects in their society. Unlike **"Robert Kennedy Saved from Drowning,"** these stories encompass the points of view of the genius and various angels. Consequently, both tales lack a narrator who futilely tries to know how the diverse strands of a genius's or several angels' personalities have made them art objects esteemed by their society. In each tale, however, the genius or the angels are filled with self-doubt, and the stories evolve as investigations of the means by which these figures can know themselves and explain their power as art.

Of the two tales, **"The Genius,"** from *Sadness* (1972), shows the greater similarity to the themes and structure of **"Robert Kennedy Saved from Drowning"** and frequently seems merely an extension of that story. In **"The Genius,"** however, the Kennedy parallel appears as an intellectual resembling Marshall McLuhan or Buckminster Fuller, whose ideas, misinterpreted by the oversimplifications of the media, have moved beyond a strictly academic audience and into voguish public acceptance. Similarly, the structures of the two stories are analogous. **"The Genius"** consists of a series of sentences, descriptions, or anecdotal fragments, which portray the genius as a cantankerous, inconsistent man given to arbitrary, moody poses and responses. These elements of the genius's personality form the collage of his character, which makes him an art object both to those individuals who observe his public behavior and to the readers of the story. The chief difference between this story and **"Robert Kennedy Saved from Drowning"** arises in the genius's troubled self-consciousness. Unlike Kennedy's impassivity, this trait causes the genius himself, and not a narrative voice, to doubt, question, and challenge his right to be regarded as a significant thinker and an art object.

Throughout the story the genius's quest for self-knowledge serves as a motif uniting its fragments and demonstrating the artistry of the tale. The elements of this collage include an aphorism from Valéry noting that every man of genius also contains a false man of genius. The genius freely acknowledges that he may be a sham, and immediately following Paul Valéry's remark, he describes the contemporary age as a time of ignorance in which no one knows what others know and no one knows enough. **"The Genius"** depicts a world in which men's and women's efforts to know and their fascination with increasingly higher planes of abstraction, including the concept of genius, have only increased individuals' failures to communicate. Indeed, this struggle has torn and separated people from one another and from themselves. Accordingly, in another fragment the genius speaks of his frustration in attempting to define the sources of his genius. He has no clue as to what makes him a great thinker: "The mystery remains a mystery."[15] If a genius cannot explain genius, the story suggests that the riddle of the human personality may never be solved.

Yet the futility of his task does not prevent the protagonist from seeking an answer. Reminiscent of the segment in **"Robert Kennedy Saved from Drowning"** in which Kennedy, a political art object, confronts another art object in a gallery, **"The Genius"** reveals its hero as an intellectual art object who reads Theodore Dreiser's novel *The Genius* to gain self-awareness. Curious to know whether the florid descriptions of the genius in Dreiser's prose resemble his own demeanor, the genius puts the novel down and walks to a mirror. **"The Genius,"** like **"Robert Kennedy Saved from Drowning,"** functions as an endless plane of mirrors in which the popular idol sees himself reflected in the adulation of his audience. In **"The Genius,"** however, the intellectual savior attempts to search for the causes of his acclaim.

By the conclusion of the story the genius realizes that he will never know his meaning or significance as an artistic phenomenon. Yet in a world of monotonous conformity he understands his hold on the public. He attracts an audience by constantly questioning all the events, data, and circumstances it takes for granted. Without solutions to the problems he poses, the genius as an art object nonetheless allows his public to participate in the possibilities for thought he opens to them. Petulant, gnomic, unable to communicate with other people and frightened of other geniuses,

the genius constitutes a calculated human puzzle whose pieces defy unity or coherence. By attempting to understand how his own fragments might align, this Marivaudian being saves himself from drowning and presents a picture of both his surface and his depths. In the process, the readers of **"The Genius"** are free to construct their own genius from this genius's personal, fragmented self-exploration.

The second auxiliary story, **"On Angels,"** from *City Life* (1970), is Barthelme's most whimsical examination of man's potential to become an art object. If the other two stories in this square demonstrate that politicians such as Robert Kennedy and intellectuals such as McLuhan and Fuller develop many of the qualities of a work of art for a contemporary audience, this tale suggests that any object of man's imaginative speculation assumes some of the qualities of art and that the intense effort to know eventually becomes an artistic endeavor. Specifically, the story investigates the fate of the angels after the presumed death of God, and it poses several questions about their threatened existence. If the omnipotence and assured presence of God have vanished from the earth, what, the tale asks, will happen to His divine messengers and servants? Moreover, if angels appear as men in perfect form, what will become of them once men stop believing in godlike perfection and omniscience? Furthermore, should anyone expect artistic perfection in a world in which men can know so little?

"On Angels" rhetorically dismisses its own doubts by quickly asserting that men will continue to believe in art, perfection, and the human possibilities for attaining these qualities regardless of the existence of God, certainty, or final knowledge. To illustrate its view, the story cites three items from the vast literature on angels. Using Emanuel Swedenborg's study of angels, Gustav Davidson's *Dictionary of Angels,* and "The Psychology of Angels," a contemporary essay by Joseph Lyons, the tale demonstrates the enormous force angels have had on the human imagination.[16] The news of the death of God should have made this literature meaningless, but since men and women will always wonder if they can become more perfect and more beautiful, angels will continue to offer a vision of human perfection that traditional art sometimes neglects. The narrator of this essayistic story thus concedes that much writing about angels is actually writing about human beings in angelic forms.

After surveying the literature on angels, the tale concludes by discussing the angels' attempt to find a new role for themselves following the death of God. Once various suggestions are overruled as unworthy of angelic skill and perfection, one faction of the angels proposes that their new function should be to celebrate their refusal to exist. Not only is this alternative immediately rejected by the other angels as a sign of spiritual pride, but the moral force of this story also makes it immediately unacceptable. The tale insists throughout that the human quest for perfection will never die despite the impossibility of mankind ever knowing whether angels, God, or certainty exists. Consistent with the aesthetic vision that the preceding art stories have taken, angels are perfect Barthelme art objects. Inviting an audience to know their frequently changing shapes and to attempt an understanding of their play of form and content, angels in addition serve as intellectual abstractions that may totally be a product of the artistic imagination. Paralleling angels as an art form, this short story becomes a fitting art object itself. The tale develops as a collage of references, scholarship, and angelic views on some of the human forms angels may acquire. The reader, attempting to know all possibilities for his own aesthetic expression, never discovers whether angels actually exist. Yet in this endless search he can be persuaded of his potential for spiritual perfectibility and angelic form.

Turning now to stories of stasis developed through repetition, we find three tales: the central identity story, **"The Glass Mountain,"** and the two auxiliary stories, "Nothing: A Preliminary Account" and **"Concerning the Bodyguard."** Rather than questioning what contemporary art should be, or if men and women can achieve aesthetic perfection as the past art stories have, these tales examine the artistic process itself. They recognize it as a quest, an endless, repetitive search, which insistently tries to shape some vision or make some statement from the confusions, uncertainties, and contradictions of experience. In these tales art exists as a venture that always ends in some degree of failure because the artist realizes he has been falsely educated to regard many of the misleading signs and symbols of his world as faithfully designating reality. Accordingly, the artist in these stories acts as a translator and interpreter of reality, attempting to lessen the distance between the artistic symbol and the reality it represents, between the claims of art and its actual possibilities in an often debased, ugly world. Art in these stories becomes a catalog of all that contemporary art cannot achieve, thereby enabling the audience to understand what the contemporary artist seeks from the artistic process. These stories represent the struggle of the artist to express a reality greater than his world yet a reality that still does not exclude a pragmatic assessment of his world. Though raising more questions than they can answer, these investigations of the artistic process are never completely nihilistic because they reveal that the conflict between reality, art, and ideas will always continue even though its terms are always changing.

Turning to the typology, we find the central art story, **"The Glass Mountain,"** from *City Life* (1970), developed through Barthelme's sense of repetitive concern. Superficially, it appears to be one of his most straightforward tales. In one hundred numbered statements the story relates the quest of its artist-protagonist to climb a steep glass mountain, which has suddenly risen at the corner of Thirteenth Street and Eighth Avenue. Once again, a Barthelme story presents its readers with an enormous art object, like the balloon or Robert Kennedy. In this instance, however, the reader is encouraged neither to play with the object nor to understand it, but to conquer the mountain

by slowly, painstakingly scaling it. The aesthetic goal to be gained here is not a final prize or reward but the sheer process of accomplishing a very difficult task, even if the odds against completing the climb seem formidable. Many brave knights have tried to scale the mountain, but their dying bodies, groaning in pain, circle its base. Furthermore, the mountain air is bitter cold, and the protagonist has strapped climbing irons to his feet and holds an incongruous tool, a plumber's helper, in each hand. If these physical conditions are not enough to deter the hero, the street below is full of his acquaintances shouting abusive taunts as he inches his way to the summit.

"The Glass Mountain" neatly functions as a metaphor for the plight of the modern artist. Striving to achieve an impossible task, to scale heights others have attempted and failed, the contemporary artist here is a Don Quixote figure. He represents the incurable romantic, who wants to climb the glass mountain to make the world better, not only for himself but for his society. The numbering of each sentence in this story emphasizes the static, repetitive nature of his quest while conveying the numbing despair of the lives of those in the street below. They envy this adventurer because he attempts to do what they cannot: overcome misery through art. As he crawls up the side of the mountain, the narrator describes the city he has left behind. He pictures a world full of senseless violence and fear in which alcoholic, failed artists and drugged teenagers walk on sidewalks caked with dog shit. A vandal wantonly saws down a row of elm trees on a city street as people pass by, nervously observing the incident but doing nothing to stop it.

Consequently, the narrator journeys up the mountain to find artistic values a contemporary audience can still revere. He has heard in a childhood nursery story of a castle of pure gold at the top of the glass mountain. The story says that in a room in the castle tower sits a beautiful, enchanted symbol. Several hundred feet above the city the narrator contemplates his chances for artistic transcendence of the pain and failure of city life. At this point he reconsiders his motives for undertaking this quest. He realizes that though men still need symbols, the harshness of the reality around them should force artists to disenchant the symbol, to bring it down to earth, and to make art more conversant with reality and mankind.

54. It was cold there at 206 feet and when I looked down I was not encouraged.

55. A heap of corpses both of horses and riders ringed the bottom of the mountain, many dying men groaning there.

56. "A weakening of the libidinous interest in reality has recently come to a close." (Anton Ehrenzweig)

57. A few questions thronged into my mind.

58. Does one climb a glass mountain, at considerable personal discomfort, simply to disenchant a symbol?

59. Do today's stronger egos still need symbols?

60. I decided that the answer to these questions was "yes."

61. Otherwise what was I doing there 206 feet above the power-sawed elms, whose white meat I could see from my height?[17]

In examining this passage, critic Alan Wilde sees **"The Glass Mountain"** as a radical effort not only to disenchant the idea of the symbol in Barthelme's storytelling but also as his challenge to the givens of much American popular culture.

> The project of the story, and of others like it, is in fact precisely one of demythifying, or disenchanting—. . . the cultural imperatives (scientific, religious, psychological, governmental, and aesthetic) of the present and the past: of everything, in short, from Batman to the American Dream. As compared with the enchanted symbol, the narrator's acquaintances, shouting throughout the climb a volley of obscene discouragements and standing on the sidewalks below—which the narrator sees with a curiously radiant intensity as "full of dogshit in brilliant colors: ocher, umber, Mars yellow, sienna, viridian, ivory black, rose madder" (**"CL,"** 66)—are pure disenchanted, phenomenal reality, and, so the story implies, all the better for that.[18]

Though Wilde's criticism values the story's intention to deflate the authority of symbols in contemporary narrative, his assessment ignores what the passage in question clearly, unambiguously tells the reader. The narrator may climb the mountain to disenchant the symbol, but he also realizes that contemporary men and women need symbols, if not grandiose ones like the glass mountain. The problem of his quest and of contemporary art is in finding symbols that stimulate the modern imagination without completely falsifying deprived, quotidian existence. Contemporary art must somehow mediate between its former lofty perspectives and a harsh modern world, which makes idealized artistic insights ludicrous. The chorus of street people who revile the mountain climber with their discouragement does, as Wilde says, represent phenomenal reality, yet their lives are depicted as brutal and limited. Only through the eyes of the thoroughly romantic narrator, and not through any vision of the people themselves, does the dog shit lining the streets acquire the rainbow of color of the artist's palette.

Therefore, the story suggests that much of this dilemma in modern art arises in the vision of the artists themselves. Miseducated to believe their endless supply of signs and symbols will still produce the aesthetic responses in contemporary audiences this short-hand has always evoked, many contemporary artists continue to build castles of gold filled with enchanted symbols, regardless of how squalid the conditions of the contemporary world may be. Moreover, the romantic who climbs the glass mountain learns that reality destroys the efforts to discriminate made by artists, literary critics, and semiologists. Consulting *A Dictionary of Literary Terms,* which he carries with him as he climbs, the protagonist finds a distinction made between symbol and sign, which is immediately invalidated by the world around him. The situation explains why contemporary men and women can make so little sense of either their own battered lives or the badly outmoded terminology of literature.

70. In the streets were people concealing their calm behind a facade of vague dread.

71. "The conventional symbol (such as the nightingale, often associated with melancholy), even though it is recognized only through agreement, is not a sign (like the traffic light) because, again, it presumably arouses deep feelings and is regarded as possessing properties beyond what the eye alone sees." (*A Dictionary of Literary Terms.*)

72. A number of nightingales with traffic lights tied to their legs flew past me.[19]

At last the explorer nears the summit and the golden castle containing the enchanted symbol. He dares to disenchant the symbol, to give it new meaning for those trapped in the street below. Approaching the symbol with its many layers of interpretation, he reaches to touch it. To his disgust, his touch transforms the symbol into a beautiful princess. Furious, he throws the princess down the mountain to his vulgar, vengeful friends, who will know what to do with her.

In this conclusion the artist ironically fails both himself and his audience. Searching for an art uncontaminated by his fraudulent literary terms or his overeducated conception of what art should be, this artist wants to reach an audience whose hostile physical environment makes the ethereal symbols of traditional art ridiculous. Yet when the narrator transforms the enchanted symbol into a beautiful princess—a hopelessly commonplace symbol even for people starved for beauty—he becomes enraged at the striking unoriginality of his art. Torn by his conflicting desires to reach his audience and to achieve the high standards he sets for himself, the protagonist can be true to neither goal. Though he is an emissary of art to the people and an interpreter of their artistic reality, the protagonist's soaring standards ironically prevent him from disenchanting the symbol to satisfy his own aesthetics or theirs.

If the narrator's final anger suggests the failure of this artistic process to fulfill either the contemporary artist or his audience, as an art work itself, **"The Glass Mountain"** demonstrates the ability of new forms of art to transcend the limitations and worn conventions of the old. This story, as a parody of the fairy tale, actually adheres to and reveres the romance form it superficially ridicules. The repetitive, static listing of the one hundred steps necessary to disenchant the symbol finally makes the new symbol, however hackneyed, worth attaining. Moreover, this artistic quest becomes an art unto itself. As Alan Wilde states, this distinctive, numbered technique for composing a short story ultimately represents not just an unsuccessful effort to disenchant the narrative symbol but an examination of Barthelme's aesthetic motivations for writing a story in this form: "But what one senses in the best of his work is an effort to use art to overcome art (as the moderns characteristically employ consciousness to move beyond consciousness)—or, better still, an attempt parallel to that in **'The Glass Mountain'** to disenchant the aesthetic, to make of it something not less special but less extraordinary."[20]

This effort to overcome established art forms with less conventional and predictable ones appears also in "Nothing: A Preliminary Account" and **"Concerning the Bodyguard,"** the two auxiliary stories. These tales illustrate the power of the artistic process to shape something—some object, vision, or statement—from the nondescript character, the nothingness, a situation or concept possessed before the artist examined it. Like **"The Glass Mountain,"** both stories are quests that become catalogs of all the ways their particular subject cannot be defined or categorized. Developing through a static sense of repetition, both stories fail to exhaust or limit their subject, thereby suggesting the endless aesthetic possibilities of the art object or artistic conflict each explores.

Of the two stories, "Nothing: A Preliminary Account," from *Guilty Pleasures* (1974), more directly questions the purpose of the artistic process. The tale consists totally of a run-on list of many objects and ideas, which, occupying space, time, or both, refuse to be merely nothing. In this tale nothing represents the emptiness or void in which all art originates and to which most imperfect art, outliving its inspiration only by a few years or decades, returns. Accordingly, the artistic process in this story becomes the effort to make something of permanence from nothing. Nothing also describes the feelings of despair and incompetence that the effort to produce art characteristically evokes in the artist who realizes that anything he makes will fall short of the complete verisimilitude he seeks to depict in it. Yet the tale functions as well as an effort to trap this destructive quality of nothingness, to exorcise and dispel it from the artist's work. Try as he might, however, nothing eludes this list maker. He decides that to capture nothing permanently and rid it from his art he must compose a compilation of everything that nothing is not. Thus this survey forms the story. Nevertheless, before the tale ends the narrator recognizes that, if given eternity to complete his catalog, he could still find items to include in it. If, miraculously, he could finish his inventory, the tabulation itself would remain, and this endless scroll would not be nothing.

Rather than causing the artist to become nihilistic, his growing awareness that nothingness can never be contained within the artistic process only renews his gleeful sense of possibility characteristic of the story's slapdash tone from the beginning. Realizing that the greatest art endures many centuries and his own life will be infinitely short, the narrator rushes through the thought of philosophers from Gorgias to Heidegger, Kierkegaard, and Sartre for their views on nothingness and being. Finally perceiving that his list of contradictory opinions and data will

never be finished, he chooses to see it as a constant beginning, a series of approximations that, even if he could live indefinitely, would still keep him waiting forever for its conclusion. From this perspective, all art and artistic process become a constant correction and reshaping of the partial ideas, philosophies, signs, and symbols that have encouraged men to believe in permanence, conventions, and finite truths.

The story adds to its compendium of thoughts about nothingness such works as Dylan Thomas' "Do not go gentle into that good night" and Samuel Beckett's closing words from *Krapp's* beckoning of death, "Burning to be gone."[21] Yet as his own storytelling time expires, the narrator understands that death is hardly nothing despite the loss it imposes and neither is that art which tries to deny or embrace the sense of death. Nothing in this story represents the void from which all art emerges and to which most art drifts, as well as the feelings of inadequacy artistic effort generates in those who attempt it. In his concluding lines the narrator makes an ecstatic discovery: nothing also signifies the impossible purity and perfection to which all art aspires and fails: "What a wonderful list! How joyous the notion that, try as we may, we cannot do other than fail and fail absolutely and that the task will remain always before us, like a meaning for our lives. Hurry. Quickly."[22] Consequently, "Nothing: A Preliminary Account" asserts the value of the failed artistic product and contends that the static, repetitive artistic process, however fruitless, gives value to the artist's vision. This story attempting to climb its own glass mountain, to disenchant the aesthetic of nothingness, finds that its own repetitive technique reveals that nothing can never be known and, hence, the denial of nothingness, like its affirmation, will always be a source of art.

The second auxiliary story, **"Concerning the Bodyguard,"** from *Great Days* (1979), which shares a box on the typology with **"The Glass Mountain"** and "Nothing: A Preliminary Account," also attempts to disenchant the aesthetic of nothingness. In a series of static, repetitive, unanswered questions, the story examines the relationship of a bodyguard to the wealthy, internationally famous man he watches and protects. The bodyguard serves as a functionary whose only role is to follow, surround, and symbolize another, implicitly superior individual. Therefore, the artistic process of the story becomes the quest to make something of this human nothing, to transform the bodyguard into an art object, a symbol worthy of the esteemed man he represents. Art in this tale quickly takes the role of duplication, reproduction, and repetition. The artistic process or quest here can be likened to an act of substitution in which the bodyguard must assume many of his employer's habits and routines.

Interestingly, the artistic metaphors implicit in **"Concerning the Bodyguard"** develop complexity as the story proceeds. The story is concerned not just with the relationship between a human symbol and the reality he represents but with the quality of art in a repressive, class-conscious society. As the list of its insinuating questions continues, this story becomes a repetitive catalog of the indifference and subtle abuse the arrogant industrialist shows his lower-class, poorly educated bodyguard. The story insistently asks about the bodyguard's low pay, shabby clothing, and poor benefits; and these questions reveal the increasing contempt he feels for the man he follows. Consequently, the bodyguard as a symbol can have only strained relationships to his employer's world. This man's art of replication seems a poor stand-in, a contemptuous, disdainful reproduction of the realities of his society. In **"The Glass Mountain"** the artistic process attempts to disenchant the romantic, elevated symbol and to bring it to the level of the people in the street. In contrast, the artistic process in **"Concerning the Bodyguard"** questions the purpose of art in a society whose symbols must shield and honor a corrupted, callous humanity.

Eventually, **"Concerning the Bodyguard"** envisions a society in which art or artistic symbols can slowly transform the world that first adopted them. The tale, like "Nothing: A Preliminary Account," demonstrates that the concept of nothingness, in its absolute aesthetic purity, can never exist. Consequently, the story and its questions are continually making something from nothing, giving distinctive, individualized life to the emptiness of the bodyguard's symbolic function as another man's double. The reader learns that the bodyguard has a wife and two children in another country far away, that he lives in a cramped efficiency apartment and enjoys pornographic films and magazines. Although the bodyguard appears largely ignorant of politics or of the ways his employer exploits workers all over the world, he grows steadily more resentful of the man's displays of personal power. He has mixed feelings of camaraderie and jealousy for the other bodyguards who surround this magnate. He hears the complaints of his fellow workers that their job is dangerous and boring, and he wonders about the loyalty and reliability of the newest bodyguard in their ranks. The story's questions end with a report that, much to the joy of the general public, the industrialist has been assassinated and presumably the bodyguard, or one of his counterparts, bears some responsibility.

All the story's unceasing, unanswered queries do not actually make us know or understand the bodyguard, but they do present the reader with the man's range of response. Totally shaping the process of the story, these interrogations demonstrate that the art of this tale is all process without results, products, or discoveries, other than the certainty that the symbolic life of narrative dies when the reality it represents becomes abusive and corrupt. The artistic process of the story supplies the goal of the bodyguard's life: to kill through static repetition and negligence the reality that is numbing his existence. With the death of this tyrant the bodyguard no longer serves as a slavish symbol, and art can search for more imaginative, liberating ways to transform reality into symbols. As **"The Glass Mountain"** attempts to move symbolism closer to reality and "Nothing: A Preliminary Account" makes something

from nothingness, **"Concerning the Bodyguard"** says art will follow life indefinitely only if life shows some signs of vitality and humanity.

Approaching the final three stories on the typology, **"At the Tolstoy Museum," "The Falling Dog,"** and **"The Flight of Pigeons from the Palace,"** one can see these art stories as probing one of the central dilemmas of the modern artist: how does one create in a world in which existing works of literature and art seem to dwarf the potential for contemporary expression? These tales examine the plight of the modern artist who attempts to affirm his own creativity while acknowledging that the mastery of a writer such as Tolstoy only accentuates the limitations of his own obsessive images. Complicating his dilemma, the artist senses the flight of the contemporary audience from works that cease to titillate, shock, or amuse it. In **"At the Tolstoy Museum,"** the reader observes that modern art and architecture which only entomb the past. Yet the story also shows the successful effort of its lyrical, inspired narrator to create art in his own style by imaginatively retelling a story from Tolstoy. Similarly, **"The Falling Dog"** reveals an additional source of a sculptor's creativity after he seems to have exhausted his personal storehouse of images. Receptive to the world around him, this contemporary artist allows the objects of his immediate experience to become the objects of his art. A bizarre event in the sculptor's life serves as an object of his playful speculation and offers him limitless possibilities for a new artistic image, a wealth of materials from which it might be composed, and a variety of techniques other artists have used to develop it. His play of mind does not explain the new work of art the sculptor shapes, but it does predict similar associations that the work might elicit in the audience that discovers it. **"The Falling Dog"** demonstrates one means by which reality may jar the artist into new stages of creativity without giving definitive meaning or interpretation to the work that results.

The second auxiliary story, **"The Flight of Pigeons from the Palace,"** focuses on the contemporary audience forever in search of new sensations and experiences. Bored by the traditional values and proven effects of conventional art, this audience forces the artist to turn his work into a literal circus, a freak show filled with absurd, unrelated acts. Consequently, the story consists of a collage of verbal descriptions of each of his performers paired with drawings illustrating and following each novelty he places on view. **"The Flight of Pigeons from the Palace"** reflects the extent to which the contemporary artistic performer feels he must pander to a dwindling public to appease and satisfy it. Lacking confidence in its own skills to transcend the art of the past, the sensibility in each of these three stories crafts a mosaic of words and pictures. These collages demonstrate the powerlessness of many contemporary images, visual as well as written, to evoke an aesthetic response in an audience. Yet a considerable contradiction looms in all three stories. In its audacity and imagination each shows an artist affirming his unique creativity, and a literary artist at that, who flourishes without visualization of his materials when he controls his audience's expectations and not merely reacts to its demands.

Returning to a more complete examination of **"At the Tolstoy Museum,"** the central art story developed through an analysis of its narrator's creative process, the reader finds a story that blends words and drawings. The tale describes an utterly contemporary art object, a modernistic museum containing thirty thousand pictures of Tolstoy. In the story the architectural presence of the museum is juxtaposed with sketches of several pictures within it and with exhibits about Tolstoy on view there. The story serves as a parable on the modern tendency to institutionalize the art and artists of other times and to build mausoleums to honor this deification. In describing the inclination of enthusiasts of contemporary art and contemporary artists themselves to regard great works of other eras as insurmountable art objects, **"At the Tolstoy Museum"** becomes a museum piece itself. If the tale were nothing more than this it would be only an arid essay. But the story records the account of a Sunday visitor to the Tolstoy Museum. This narrator observes several pictures of Tolstoy, accumulates miscellaneous facts about Tolstoy's life from various displays, reads one short story and two of Tolstoy's social pamphlets on exhibit, and reacts to the grotesque architectural modernism of the museum. Above all, he attempts to dispel the sadness that permeates the museum and consumes the response of all the visitors to what they see. This viewer tries to break through the awesome, monumental grief that Tolstoy's majesty induces in writers or other artists, who feel that whatever they might create would be hopelessly inadequate by comparison. The narrator, haunted by these visions of Tolstoy, nevertheless attempts to form an art work of his own from his experience in the museum. Trapped within the aesthetic and architectural constraints of this building and this story, he can frame his art only from an awareness of Tolstoy's genius. In the most important moments of his trip to the museum, the protagonist retells a short story by Tolstoy he finds in the museum's library. Bringing his unique simplicity and feeling to the effort, he affirms his creativity in the process of recasting another man's fable. With this vignette, **"At the Tolstoy Museum"** becomes a metaphor for the way a contemporary artist, momentarily blinded by the brilliance of an earlier writer, nevertheless can use the author's basic materials to transcend them and claim his own art.

Before the narrator emerges from Tolstoy's shadow he describes the quality that proves so overwhelming to an artist trying to discover his own identity. This story begins with a full-page drawing of Tolstoy's grizzled beard and long face that stares imperiously at the reader and the visitors to the museum. The same sketch reappears on the next page, but this time it dwarfs the small figure of Napoleon drawn in the lower left-hand corner. This juxtaposition of images and sizes conveys the ability of the epic artist Tolstoy to overshadow even the sweeping, awesome history of Napoleonic conquest he recreates. As the story momentarily turns to prose descriptions of the museum, the narrator tries to demythologize the reverential status of

Tolstoy generated by the building. He wonders whether the pictures of Tolstoy on one wall might be lowered. Furthermore, he attempts to know and understand Tolstoy by reading unrelated details about his life. Yet all the information the museum provides makes the personality of Tolstoy, like that of Robert Kennedy or the genius, seem an enigma, a series of formidable contradictions. Seeking to unearth the man this modern art museum has entombed, the narrator discovers only a multilayered, infinitely paradoxical human being. Just as the three cantilevered, tilting floors of the futuristic museum seem ready to topple on those who pass before it, so Tolstoy's enormous spiritual and political force shook his world. Yet the beauty of much of his writing suggests a man of considerable aesthetic delicacy. The narrator obviously cannot resolve this conflict between the strength of Tolstoy's social vision, dramatized in the architecture of the museum, and the poetic fragility of his style.

> The entire building, viewed from the street, suggests that it is about to fall on you. This the architects relate to Tolstoy's moral authority.
>
> In the basement of the Tolstoy Museum carpenters uncrated new pictures of Count Leo Tolstoy. The huge crates stencilled FRAGILE in red ink.[23]

Repeatedly, the narrator notes that artists who visit the museum weep profusely at its Tolstoy pictures, exhibits, pamphlets, and stories. Sensing the immense burden this great artist has placed on their own creative powers, they feel Tolstoy's gaze resting on them, like the scrutiny of their fathers or that of any older authority figure. Yet Tolstoy's magnificent artistry, despite its grandeur, has considerable emotional distance from our age and less and less to teach an aspiring contemporary writer. Ironically, the revelatory truth of Tolstoy's social pamphlet proclaiming that children would be better teachers of their elders than the old men who instruct the young is completely lost on these observers of Tolstoy, who are paralyzed by their own grief.

> The guards at the Tolstoy Museum carry buckets in which there are stacks of clean white pocket handkerchiefs. More than any other museum, the Tolstoy Museum induces weeping. Even the bare title of a Tolstoy work, with its burden of love, can induce weeping—for example, the article titled "Who Should Teach Whom to Write, We the Peasant Children or the Peasant Children Us?" Many people stand before this article, weeping. Too, those who are caught by Tolstoy's eyes, in the various portraits, room after room after room, are not unaffected by the experience. It is like, people say, committing a small crime and being discovered at it by your father, who stands in four doorways, looking at you.
>
> ("TM," 45)

Implicit in the misery that an art object like the Tolstoy Museum causes the contemporary imagination lies some respite from its very claustrophobia. Tolstoy relates in another of his social pamphlets on view how men stupefy and sadden themselves when, lionizing past art and artists, they forget that their own opportunities for creativity exist only in the present. Demonstrating Tolstoy's view, the narrator contrasts a single musician playing a trumpet before two children in the plaza of the museum with the 640,086-page Jubilee edition of Tolstoy's collected works for inspection in the building. This musician's skill, though largely unheard and unappreciated, constitutes a means by which a man, creating his own art, frees himself of the past. By contrast, the edition of Tolstoy represents a source of inertia for all potential artists chained to the past, particularly those who would read Tolstoy to charge their own imaginative energies. Thus this museumgoer observes that men sadden and stupefy themselves by looking to the past for their art rather than relying on their own resources for creativity, however modest their talents.

> At the Tolstoy Museum, sadness grasped the 741 Sunday visitors. The Museum was offering a series of lectures on the text "Why Do Men Stupefy Themselves?" The visitors were made sad by these eloquent speakers, who were probably right.
>
> People stared at tiny pictures of Turgenev, Nekrasov, and Fet. These and other small pictures hung alongside extremely large pictures of Count Leo Tolstoy.
>
> In the plaza, a sinister musician played a wood trumpet while two children watched.
>
> We considered the 640,086 pages (Jubilee Edition) of the author's published work. Some people wanted him to go away, but other people were glad we had him. "He has been a lifelong source of inspiration to me," one said.
>
> ("TM," 49)

As acknowledged, the chief lessons that the Tolstoy Museum has to teach a modern audience are exemplified in the narrator's own version of a simple Tolstoy folk tale, which he reads in the museum. The narrator quickly recounts the story of a bishop who discovers three hermits on a desert island. By substituting the Lord's Prayer for their primitive prayer, the bishop believes he has taught these men greater communion with God. The same evening the bishop sees the hermits floating over the ocean. They tell him they have already forgotten his prayer. Aghast at their miracle and his own ignorance, the bishop says that he has nothing to teach them, that their own message reaches God. Concisely and artfully, this story within **"At the Tolstoy Museum"** epitomizes and summarizes the themes of the tale. The hermits in this fable stand in the same relationship to the bishop as the writers who come to his museum stand to Tolstoy, or as the narrator stands in his moving reworking of this parable to Tolstoy's skill in the original. Only by breaking free of the restraints, conventions, and revered teachers of the past and using them or rejecting them as needed can an artist affirm a unique sense of creativity and identity. The agony of influence is endurable if an artist knows when to stop agonizing and how to start reinventing.

In this story the Tolstoy Museum, like the balloon, the gargantuan Robert Kennedy mannequin, or the glass mountain in the other central art stories, represents a huge object, which dominates the landscape and the perceptions of the audience and artists who view it. In certain respects the Tolstoy Museum is the most complete and self-referential art object Barthelme has created because it contains other art objects and comments on relationships between the artifacts housed within. Barthelme critic Jerome Klinkowitz sees a story like **"At the Tolstoy Museum"** as representing Barthelme's effort to develop a new plane of vision for contemporary fiction. Using Barthelme's theory from his 1964 essay "After Joyce,"[24] Klinkowitz recognizes the author's desire to make the short story an environmental, participatory art form, which, like the Tolstoy Museum, envelops the reader's world just as do the rooms in which the reader lives and works:

> "Art is not about something but is something. . . . The reader is not listening to an authoritative account of the world delivered by an expert (Faulkner on Mississippi, Hemingway on the corrida) but bumping into something that is there, like a rock or a refrigerator." More actively, "the reader reconstitutes the work by his active participation, by approaching the object, tapping it, shaking it, holding it to his ear to hear the roaring within. It is characteristic of the object that it does not declare itself all at once, in a rush of pleasant naivete. Joyce enforces the way in which *Finnegans Wake* is to be read. He conceived the reading to be a lifetime project, the book remaining always there, like the landscape surrounding the reader's home or the building bounding the reader's apartment.[25]

Unquestionably, the Tolstoy Museum that the narrator explores in this tale is just such an environment. Though Barthelme may hope the reader returns to this story periodically to puzzle the meanings that its unlimited associations suggest, this story, unlike **"The Balloon,"** does offer certain explicit interpretations or at least definite directives. In **"The Falling Dog,"** however, the first auxiliary story to occupy the final square on the typology with **"At the Tolstoy Museum,"** a sculptor creates an art object that resembles Barthelme's artistic ideal in that it resists meaning or interpretation. Although hardly absorbing his entire physical environment, the dog of the title falls literally into the sculptor's life, and he quickly seizes on this grotesque chance encounter to transform the dog into the latest image for this sculpture. **"The Falling Dog"** addresses itself to the same problem that vexed the narrator of **"At the Tolstoy Museum,"** but it takes the point of view not of an artist so awed by great writers of the past that he inhibits his own capabilities for creativity but of a productive craftsman who has momentarily depleted his mind of images for his art and waits in limbo for an intruding force to stir his creative spirit.

Watching an artist gather images for his own art rather than observing an artist trapped by the images and architecture of other artists produces a unique investigation of the creative process. In **"The Falling Dog"** the sculptor freely adapts the events of his collision with the dog, all he knows about dogs and their roles in past art, and his reservations about sculpting a statue of the falling dog in a verbal collage of the artistic possibilities that his clash with the animal affords. As a carefully composed artifact, **"The Falling Dog"** even more closely resembles Jerome Klinkowitz's view of Barthelme's intention for the perfect art object than does **"At the Tolstoy Museum"**: "The key to Barthelme's new aesthetic for fiction is that the work may stand for itself, that it need not yield to complete explication of something else in the world but may exist as an individual object, something beautiful and surprising and deep. . . . Not just a juggler of fragments, Barthelme is an assembler and constructor of objects."[26]

Accordingly, what little plot **"The Falling Dog"** contains involves the efforts of its protagonist to make an art object from the senseless fall of the dog from a third-story window onto his back. The sculptor tries to yoke all his knowledge and information about dogs and dogs in art into a sculpted aesthetic whole. The story that results explores the confusions, anger, and cunning in this artist's mind and creative process as he sits on the sidewalk, dusts the concrete from his chin, and watches the dog that has quickly jumped off his back and moved several feet down the street. The story captures the extravagant play of mind by which a skillful creator transposes a fantastic moment in his life into potential art. **"The Falling Dog"** thus becomes a story about the creative act of writing its story, and its sculptor, attempting to unify all its pieces into one cohesive falling dog, assembles and constructs a surreal variety of objects before his audience. This assemblage includes lists of puns, clichés, and adages involving dogs, all the artists the sculptor can remember who have painted or made dogs, and all the forms and materials in which they have worked. The resulting montage of phrases, jokes, vignettes, and anecdotes is a collage of variously sculpted language that makes **"The Falling Dog"** a wildly amusing, self-referential art object in which the narrator affirms his unique identity and creativity.

In the process of choosing his images and rejecting those that falsify and distort his intentions, the sculptor invites the reader to participate not in a finished work but in the shaping of his artistic perspective. Unlike **"At the Tolstoy Museum,"** **"The Falling Dog"** uses no pictures to tell its story. Though always searching for the right image, the sculptor discovers that words, used creatively, supply the audience with all the vision necessary to see the falling dog and to appreciate this aesthetic situation. In the final lines of the story, he rushes up to his canine assailant and, clutching the dog in his arms, takes it back to his studio. The sculptor admits that he wonders what the entire episode means. Yet as long as he and his audience respond to the same image, they both can worry about meaning later.

The final auxiliary story sharing a box on the typology with **"At the Tolstoy Museum"** and **"The Falling Dog,"** **"The Flight of Pigeons from the Palace,"** from *Sadness* (1972), concerns the fate of the contemporary creative process, not at the hands of past art or at an artist's own imaginative standards but at the mercy of an easily bored, fickle audience. The tale views traditional art forms and conventional aesthetic effects as elitist, outmoded palace art, which no longer delights the restless contemporary audience. Therefore, like the adventurer climbing the glass mountain, the narrator attempts to disenchant and dethrone the aesthetic of art, to please and excite the pigeons who are rapidly fleeing the palace.

The narrator thus recounts his elaborate devices for reclaiming the dilapidated palazzo, clearing the weeds that have grown around it, and making the art displayed there palatable to a general audience. Before our eyes, the protagonist of the tale turns this amphitheater into cheap summer stock, a continual sideshow that caters to the most obvious vaudeville attractions. He brings onto its stage the Amazing Numbered Man, who exhibits thirty-five demarked, completely movable parts. He hires fools to mumble and wander across the footlights, and he even auditions an enormous explosion. All these performances are described in the narrator's prose and illustrated in witty, detailed ink drawings that only heighten the ridiculousness of the artist's attempt to sate the masses. Once again, a Barthelme story achieves collage effects, juxtaposing words and pictures and suggesting the inability of contemporary language to sustain a modern audience without visual parallels.

Though the narrator believes he must appeal to the lowest common denominator of the contemporary audience for his theatrical tent show to survive, the story also shows him needlessly pandering to his spectators' basest feelings about controversial issues. His vaudeville includes scenes of blatant male chauvinism and, to please all factions, an episode in which a woman murders her husband. In his effort to stay a diminishing audience, the modern artist too often sees his role as combining elements of the burlesque comedian, the carnival barker, and the flimflam man. Frequently, his circus becomes merely an effort to shock or titillate those who watch. Yet despite his audience's demand for the grotesque and the lurid and his willingness to supply these commodities, the show does not succeed. The audience feels so manipulated by this bevy of sensations and sees their own desires so constantly exploited in these vignettes that they give the show only the faintest applause.

The force of this tale rests in its ability to be both joyous and sad, to show the tireless exuberance of this contemporary artist attempting to entice the modern audience back to art with vulgar routines that defy most senses of artistry. The tale portrays the modern artist as a cynical magician, who ironically comes to believe in his own bogus tricks. Yet the real skill of the story emerges in the ability of its collage to ridicule these misguided efforts at a new art form and yet, paradoxically, to produce through its startling juxtapositions and acute self-awareness a new art form all the same. The narrator of **"The Flight of Pigeons from the Palace"** concludes his dilemma with the recognition that the show must and—as long as human invention prevails—will go on:

It is difficult to keep the public interested.

The public demands new wonders piled on new wonders. Often we don't know where our next marvel is coming from.

The supply of strange ideas is not endless. . . . Some things appear to be wonders in the beginning, but when you become familiar with them, are not wonderful at all. . . . Some of us have even thought of folding the show—closing it down. That thought has been gliding through the hallways and rehearsal rooms of the show.

The new volcano we have just placed under contract seems very promising.

[Drawing of an active volcano.][27]

A fascinating tension exists in these Barthelme stories about art and the creative process. The protagonist of each attempts to return his art to its sources of wonder before the contemporary audience, massive social discontent, and the eminence of other artists convinced him to experiment with the play of form and content or collages of pictures and words. Ironically, the narrator of **"The Flight of Pigeons from the Palace,"** though hardly averse to these techniques, uses them to stimulate his own resilient imagination. Critic Jerome Klinkowitz recognizes that the outlandish formal innovation in this and other Barthelme tales, however futuristic in appearance, actually represents the effort of the artist in each to attain a sense of perspective, proportion, and control in his art: "Barthelme's vignettes are, then, not conventional arguments in the dialectics of form, but imaginative volcanoes, radical stopgap measures to save experiences which might otherwise be eroded with our loss of traditional standards. In this sense he is a counterrevolutionary, opposing the new language of technology and manipulation with pleas for old-fashioned interest and imagination."[28]

As Klinkowitz's comments indicate, **"The Flight of Pigeons from the Palace"** shows Barthelme at his most revealing and most contradictory. Forever the juggler of fragments, fully committed to experimentation with the short-story form, Barthelme is also an entertainer and a *New Yorker* writer who inverts, revises, and rearranges our conceptions of art to show us how much we lose by demanding to be entertained, shocked, and amused. Beneath his surreal trappings and collage structures lies a classically conservative sensibility that insists that the world, however torn apart, can be artfully and responsibly put back together again. The artists in **"At the Tolstoy Museum," "The Falling Dog,"** and **"The Flight of Pigeons from the Palace"** affirm unique creativities by giving fragmented worlds surprising aesthetic harmony.

This [essay] logically concludes with the outlines of a theory of art emerging in the twelve stories examined within it. These tales see their works of art as enormous aesthetic objects, which dramatize the endless play of form and content. For an audience to appreciate this art, it must participate in these objects not by examining their internalized meaning but by exploring their contradictory, surprising surfaces. This theory of art divorces the art work from a specific meaning or interpretation. In these stories art is not about something but is something—a toy, object, person, event, performance, landscape, or environment. Freed to be abstract, art can reflect the contours of the world around it and the varied shapes of experience of the audience whose world intersects its own.

Moreover, art in these tales resists the force of the past. Incorporating the immense vision of a writer like Tolstoy or the magnetism of a political leader like Robert Kennedy, these stories attempt to transcend the limitations these figures impose on their narrator's creative possibilities. Thus these tales consciously strive to disenchant the preeminent symbols, to demythologize the totems of past and present. In so doing, the stories transform our previous conceptions of art with an art of their own. This artistry envisions worlds that partake of the imperfections and uncertainties of contemporary life. This art can still be a romantic quest, however, as exemplified by a story like **"The Glass Mountain,"** in which an idealistic knight ascends a treacherous mountain to bring art to the suffering urbanites below. Often, however, these quests become catalogs and lists of all the ways in which conventional art fails the people it seeks to inspire. These tales contend that for too long art has been obsessed with a grandeur of life which seems incongruous with the debilitating quality of much modern experience or with the chaos of events and circumstances that mirrors reality without illuminating it.

Consequently, these tales seek to disenchant this aesthetic of nihilism, to dissect the confusions of contemporary existence without offering final conclusions or interpretations. These stories eventually realize that art substitutes aesthetic effects for the reality it purports to capture; art offers a surrogate life in place of the phenomena it attempts to record. Therefore, contemporary art becomes a ceaseless search for the legitimate, the genuine, and the creative, which yields no definite products or results. Nonetheless, these stories collectively assert that art should be the effort to bring the symbol closer to reality, to make something from nothingness, and to serve and embody that vision of reality which offers a sense of emotional or spiritual transcendence to its audience.

Rather than projecting a sense of defeat or despair, these stories' view of the fallibility of all art instills a sense of joyous determination in their narrators and artists. Art in these tales functions as the unattainable yet perpetually exhilarating object of life, and the four central art stories in this [essay] delight in dramatizing ways by which art may be fleetingly grasped. In **"The Balloon"** the narrator forgets his personal pain by shaping a huge sublimatory toy, which intrigues and frightens its audience with its lack of constructive meaning. Similarly, in **"Robert Kennedy Saved from Drowning"** the narrator as audience rescues Kennedy's personality from submerging in a sea of contradictions. At the same time, this story suggests that men's and women's failures to know themselves or others, coupled with their drive for perfection, have transformed artistic and political celebrities into contemporary art objects. Attempting to question the authority of an accepted artistic symbol, the mountain climber of **"The Glass Mountain"** ironically discovers, not the many-layered symbol he desires but a beautiful princess, whom he throws to the foot of the mountain. This frustration of modern art, torn between the mechanistic symbols of the past and the effort to create an art that functions organically in the present, is vividly illustrated in **"At the Tolstoy Museum."** Here the narrator destroys the anxiety of much contemporary art by realizing he must accept the past. Acting on his conviction, he immediately uses one of Tolstoy's fables to create a lyrical fable of his own.

The balloon, Robert Kennedy, the glass mountain, and the Tolstoy Museum loom awesomely in the landscapes of the artists in each of these stories. Yet by making their environments endless fields of play, each of these artists shapes a new concept of art. Lacking the purity of a Grecian urn or the authority of a scarlet letter, these tales nonetheless form a vision of art less interested in the object itself than in an audience's perceptions of it. In these stories the art work's environment becomes a huge art object designed for the restless, fickle modern audience encouraged to touch, know, scale, and inhabit a world alive to discovery and change.

Notes

1. Richard Schickel, "Freaked Out on Barthelme," *New York Times Magazine,* August 16, 1970, p. 15.

2. Tanner, *City of Words,* 405.

3. Klinkowitz and Behrens, *Life,* 73.

4. Barthelme, "The Balloon," in *Unspeakable Practices, Unnatural Acts,* 16-17, hereinafter cited parenthetically in the text as "B."

5. Klinkowitz and Behrens, *Life,* 73-74.

6. Klinkowitz, "Barthelme: A Checklist," 52.

7. Donald Barthelme, "The Police Band," in *Unspeakable Practices, Unnatural Acts,* 75.

8. Donald Barthelme, "The Policeman's Ball," in *City Life,* 55.

9. *Ibid.,* 56.

10. Donald Barthelme, "Robert Kennedy Saved from Drowning," in *Unspeakable Practices, Unnatural Acts,* 41.

11. James R. Giles, "The 'Marivaudian Being' Drowns His Children: Dehumanization in Donald Barthelme's 'Robert Kennedy Saved from Drowning' and Joyce Carol Oates' *Wonderland,*" *Southern Humanities Review,* IX (Winter, 1975), 63.

12. Barthelme, "Robert Kennedy," 46.

13. Schmitz, "Satire," 112.

14. Stott, "Donald Barthelme and the Death of Fiction," 385.

15. Donald Barthelme, "The Genius," in *Sadness,* 27.

16. Donald Barthelme, "On Angels," in *City Life,* 127-28.

17. Donald Barthelme, "The Glass Mountain," in *City Life,* 61-62.

18. Wilde, "Barthelme Unfair to Kierkegaard," 57.

19. Barthelme, "Mountain," 63.

20. Wilde, "Barthelme Unfair to Kierkegaard," 60.

21. Donald Barthelme, "Nothing: A Preliminary Account," in *Guilty Pleasures* (New York, 1974), 165.

22. *Ibid.*

23. Barthelme, "At the Tolstoy Museum," in *City Life,* 45, hereinafter cited parenthetically in the text as "TM."

24. Barthelme, "After Joyce," 15.

25. Klinkowitz and Behrens, *Life,* 77.

26. *Ibid.,* 80, 76.

27. Donald Barthelme, "The Flight of Pigeons from the Palace," in *Sadness,* 139.

28. Klinkowitz and Behrens, *Life,* 76.

John Domini (essay date winter 1990)

SOURCE: Domini, John. "Donald Barthelme: The Modernist Uprising." *Southwest Review* 75, no. 1 (winter 1990): 95-112.

[In the following essay, Domini explores Barthelme's modern consciousness through an examination of his short stories.]

"Barthelme has managed to place himself," William Gass once declared, "in the center of modern consciousness." Gass of course meant "modern" in the sense of "up to the minute"; he was praising Donald Barthelme for what always strikes one first about this author's highly imaginative and wickedly ironic fiction, namely, its free-wheeling use of contemporary culture in all its kitschy largesse. The majority of his closer critics—Tony Tanner, Wayne B. Stengel, and Larry McCaffery, to name three—have since seconded Gass's judgment, emphasizing what that early reviewer called the author's "need for the new." In general the criticism has stressed how Barthelme revels in the *dreck* of contemporary culture—how he delights in our brokeback and hopelessly modish contemporary language—using the very elements of a civilization mad for superficial values in order to deride it. Robert A. Morace praises the author's "critique of the reductive linguistic democracy of the contemporary American mass culture," (in *Critique*), and Larry McCaffery adds: "Barthelme's stories can thus be viewed as allegorical presentations of the writer attempting to make fictions in an age of literary and linguistic suspicion" (in *The Journal of Aesthetic Education*). By now the point has been developed at book length more than once, perhaps best by Stengel's *The Shape of Art in the Short Stories of Donald Barthelme*.

Yet Gass had the original insight some twenty years ago. His essay, "The Leading Edge of the Trash Phenomenon," was a review of *Unspeakable Practices, Unnatural Acts,* a collection published in 1968. More to the point, what he had to say pertained to work that must be counted as three Barthelme styles ago. The complexly written and showily strange prose of that book and the previous two (*Come Back, Dr. Caligari,* 1964, and *Snow White,* 1966) was supplanted by the simpler address and less rococo imaginings of *City Life* (1970) and *Sadness* (1972), a simplification reflected in the differences between the later titles and the earlier. Indeed the directness of the writing and the explosive abruptness of the visions may make the two early-seventies collections the peak of Barthelme's career to date. But the writer has since moved on, first to the dialogue format originally explored in his novel *The Dead Father* (1975) and dominant in his 1979 collection, *Great Days*. These dialogues, often between nameless protagonists, and never between anything remotely like two developed characters, carry the stories further from the satisfactions of narrative than ever before—indeed, further than in the decade since. His 1981 career retrospective, *60 Stories*, offers occasional revisions of his earlier work, and those revisions, though slight, without exception smooth out the prose and clarify story purpose. His latest efforts demonstrate an amalgam of previous styles, most effective in the scrupulously arranged *Overnight to Many Distant Cities* (1983), but his 1986 novel *Paradise* is by and large a return to accessibility (to hearty sexuality, for that matter) and to storyline.

This brief overview of his career and its changes, then, indicates that Barthelme's "modern consciousness" is in fact chameleonic, and by no means limited to the cultural choices or linguistic bric-a-brac of any one period. On closer examination—in *Sixty Stories,* which stands as the authoritative edition—the contemporanea in the texts seems even less reportage, more art.

In the best of Barthelme's dialogue-stories, **"The New Music,"** for instance, the partners in the colloquoy start by discussing the question, What did you do today?

> —Talked to Happy on the telephone saw the 7 o'clock news did not wash the dishes want to clean up some of this mess?
>
> (*Sixty Stories*)

All nicely late-twentieth century. But the second speaker replies:

> —If one does nothing but listen to the new music, everything else drifts, goes away, frays. Did Odysseus feel this way when he and Diomedes decided to steal Athene's statue from the Trojans, so that they would

become dejected and lose the war? I don't think so, but who is to know what effect the new music of that remote time had on its hearers?

The exchange continues likewise contrapuntally:

> —Or how it compares to the new music of this time?
>
> —One can only conjecture.

Clearly **"The New Music"** is concerned with more than just what we did today. Yet it seems a likely "conjecture" that the story refers not only to Homeric poetry, and to all that its ancient music implies of death and renewal in eternal cycles, but also to an artistic movement much closer to our own time. Barthelme refers, that is, to a central work of twentieth-century Modernism, itself inspired in part by the Greek classics. In the 1979 story, the two speakers spend most of their time discussing their mother, who has recently died. They speak of her familiarly but edgily; they dwell on her repressiveness—on all the things "Momma didn't 'low"—and yet insofar as two faceless voices can show emotion, these two show us something very like guilt ("Yes, I remember Momma, jerking the old nervous system about with her electric *diktats*"). Thus with the early references to Odysseus, and with the characters' ambivalence about hidebound but much-missed Momma, a quiet pattern of allusion emerges. Elsewhere one of the men describes a lit-up theater as "glowing like a coal against the hubris of the city"—a faint but clear echo of Stephen Dedalus, characterizing the moment of catharsis or epiphany (and himself borrowing from Shelley): that moment when "the mind is like a fading coal." Yet another Joycean note is sounded when the two speakers discuss a rather grotesque cemetery, one in which the recorded voices of the dead are played from their graves. Yet this boneyard has been imagined before, by Leopold Bloom at Paddy Dignam's funeral. As Bloom puts it, early on in *Ulysses*: "Have a gramophone at every grave or keep in the house." Talking graves, reinforcing a son's unquiet guilt over a dead mother—we have heard *this* music before as well.

The references are often this subtle. Yet though he may be quiet about it, Barthelme repeatedly complements his up-to-dateness by similar allusive games, rooted in literary history. The glances backward are not to Joyce exclusively, but nearly always to the great Irish author's peers: to the European Modernist movement of the first third of the century.

Undeniably there's a good deal else going on in his work. As John Barth has suggested, literary conventions may wear out, but the best artists in any mode remain inexhaustible. Yet despite the increasing critical attention given his fiction, Barthelme's reliance on the Modernists—his "modern consciousness" of another sort—remains largely undiscussed. Now and again, writers have noted the more obvious references. Even Gore Vidal makes mention of one, as part of his well-known attack on Barthelme and his peers ("American Plastic," from *Matters of Fact and*

Fiction). But no one I've read has seen just how pervasive the allusions are. No one has seen that they operate in stories from every stage of his career, or seen, especially, how the Modernist canon provides emotional resonance and internal coherence for **"The Indian Uprising,"** the 1968 story that may still rank as his greatest. Finally, his echoes from the first third of this century inform the larger purposes of his work, and help define his place in contemporary letters.

In one of the earliest stories, **"For I'm the Boy,"** the author refers more or less explicitly to three Modernist masters. Their purpose, too, seems fairly clear. Barthelme wishes to enhance the drama's essential reticence: to increase—though sportively—what it costs his main character when he has to put his high feelings into words. The story takes place during a drive back from an airport. There the protagonist, Bloomsbury, has bid goodbye once and for all to his ex-wife, Martha. These names alone call to mind a major author and primary text of the earlier period, specifically, Virginia Woolf and *Ulysses* again (indeed, coincidentally or not, in Joyce's novel Bloom exchanges dirty letters with a woman named Martha). And two "friends of the family" are along for Bloomsbury's farewell trip. In the course of the tale's eight pages these friends grill the protagonist more and more closely about how he's feeling. "I may not know about marriage," one says, "but I know about words" (*Sixty Stories*). Meanwhile Bloomsbury suffers flashbacks to the growing coldness between his wife and him, and to his adultery. These flashbacks are done in a shameless parody of Irish brogue, lightly demonstrating the impoverishment of storytelling. Even a race that once lived by blarney is now subject to withering irony:

> Ah Martha coom now to bed there's a darlin' gul. Hump off blatherer I've no yet read me Mallarmé for this evenin'. Ooo Martha dear canna we nooo let the dear lad rest this night? when the telly's already shut doon an' th' man o' the hoose 'as a 'ard on? . . . Martha dear where is yer love for me that we talked about in 19 and 38? in the cemetery by the sea?

Thus murmurs of Valéry—disciple of Mallarmé, author of the signal Modernist poem, "A Cemetery By the Sea"—are added to the Joycean echoes and the blush of Woolf.

Soon after the flashbacks begin, it becomes clear that Bloomsbury's "friends," themselves both separated, expect their companion to share his pain with them. They treat it as their due, they all but demand he open up. "So now . . . ," one friend declares, *give us the feeling.*" Stranger still, Bloomsbury has actually invited these two along, in part to armor himself for the leavetaking, but also—so it begins to seem—as if he wanted their interrogation, their drawing him out. The friends' avidity about seeing Bloomsbury's bruises is a low emotion but certainly familiar. Bloomsbury's own motives however are more complex, rather like an urge to give penance. At story's end Barthelme delivers just such a ritual cleansing, with typical startling exaggeration. The friends stop the car and

work Bloomsbury over, "first with the brandy bottle, then with the tire iron, until at length the hidden feeling emerged, in the form of salt from his eyes and black blood from his ears, and from his mouth, all sorts of words."

In this story the Modern canon, for all the author's joviality, functions nonetheless as a part of the characters' emotional blockage. Even the Woolf reference, though of tertiary relevance, makes the protagonist seem stuffy, on a last-name basis—more aloof than is good for him. And the wife chooses Mallarmé ahead of making love, and our Bloom's Irish Rose now lies buried in cemetery by the sea. The piece may be said to cut these mighty works down to size, as part of a young author's gamely joshing struggle with the tyranny of a previous literary generation; in the story's original version (in *Come Back, Dr. Caligari*), Barthelme toyed with Joyce and Valéry even more extensively. The Moderns, like poor Bloomsbury, at times prized intricate games or rules of decorum over "the hidden feeling."

The great period of *City Life* and *Sadness* produced several stories with Modernist underpinnings. Rather than rummage through several sample references, however, it may be more useful here to point out that this author, a former gallery critic, provides references to the period in all the arts. The title story from the first of these two collections, for instance, features a trombone player named Hector Guimard—not coincidentally, the architect who designed the flowery lamps and Metro stops of *fin de siècle* Paris. Likewise Barthelme's own work is shoved towards the visual. He has claimed in more than one interview that **"Bone Bubbles,"** from *City Life,* is his own addition to the verbal-plastic experiments of Gertrude Stein. And these two books are the only ones in which his more serious collage stories appear (the picture-pieces in his 1974 omnibus, *Guilty Pleasures,* are intended solely for laughs). These intriguing hybrids feature reproductions of etchings and woodcuts, generally nineteenth-century and earlier, alongside whatever drama the author has imagined as a companion. The most provocative was **"Brain Damage,"** also from *City Life*; one wonders why Barthelme didn't include it among the few collages he selected for *Forty Stories,* in 1987.

But in **"Daumier,"** the last piece in *Sadness,* the references are again literary, again to Valéry, and merit closer examination. The story, as Daumier himself cheerfully admits, "maunders"; our narrator wanders into and out of the surreally cowboyish adventures of his imaginary "surrogate," a creature also named Daumier. The purpose is somehow to "distract," somehow to "slay and bother . . . the original, authentic self, which is a dirty great villian." Along the way, the twinned Daumier dramas are saturated with French art and literature, from the eponymous cartoonist and painter to the cracked Dumas plot in which the puppet-self frolics. So this heady surrogate, designed to free us from self-consciousness, soon comes to suggest another such stand-in made for the same reason, namely, M. Teste.

One recalls that Valéry (in discussing Mallarmé), claimed that the contemplation of the self was the root of alienation. Moreover, self-absorption and the subsequent loss of contact with others seemed to Valéry a vexing and paradoxical offshoot of his love for literature, because any thoughts of self first arise from reading, and yet thereafter leave a reader alienated even from his books, lost in solipsism. This conviction led the author to create his M. Teste, at once a paradigm of pure thought and a proof of thought's helplessness. And Barthelme, replacing Valéry's complex and high-flown prose with plain Americanese, has his Daumier create a second surrogate for an interesting reason: "Two are necessary," he explains, "so that no individual surrogate gets the big head." Indeed. Daumier's second dybbuk, moreover, sounds very much like the original Big Head: "I see him as a quiet, thoughtful chap who leads a contemplative-type life." A single page-long paragraph then gives this surrogate its "trial run"—and provides this maundering tale with its essential declarations: "There are always openings, if you can find them. There is always something to do." The sentences are repeated at the story's close.

Here Valéry functions differently, substantially so, from how he and his peers did in **"For I'm the Boy."** The invention of a new Teste-ing device offers escape, discovery, possibility. At one point **"Daumier"** lightly filches the French poet's most famous opening, "The Marquise went out at five o'clock," and the result is a small festival of city life:

DESCRIPTION OF THREE O'CLOCK IN THE AFTERNOON

I left Amelia's place and entered the October afternoon. . . . [S]ome amount of sunglow still warmed the cunning-wrought cobbles of the street. Many citizens both male and female were hurrying hither and thither on errands of importance, each *agitato* step compromising slightly the sheen of the gray fine-troweled sidewalk. Immature citizens in several sizes . . . were engaged in ludic agon with basketballs, the same being hurled against passing vehicles producing an unpredictable rebound.

Here for once the language is toney enough, the insight elaborate enough, to suggest the Gallic. Yet it's Gallic "ludic agon," Gallic *play,* that Barthelme emphasizes. One recalls too—since in this passage the narrator is leaving the apartment of his lover—that M. Teste had a wife, a woman indispensable to him despite all his ratiocinations. This wife had a humanizing effect on Valéry's surrogate, an effect neatly summarized by Edmund Wilson, who explains in *Axel's Castle* that the husband would come to Madame Teste "with relief, appetite, and surprise"—and Madame's first name was Emilie, a close enough approximation of Daumier's Amelia. This woman's amorous ameliorative attentions provide Barthelme's narrator with his own best reliefs and surprises.

Since *Sadness* the Modernist play has continued. *The Dead Father,* a grim and skeletal exercise, succeeds best in those sections that snitch a whiskey or two from *Finnegans Wake.* **"A Manual for Sons,"** the book-within-the-book, slips in and out of colloquial voices, Biblical voices, and essay rhetoric; it equates the Oedipal urge finally with *Wake*'s central theme, original sin: "There is one jealousy that is useful and important, the original jealousy" (**"A Manual"** is reprinted in *Sixty Stories*). Likewise the author of **"A Manual"** has a name with several working parts, Peter Scatterpatter, and towards the novel's end we enter the mind of the soon-to-be-dead father, where the stream of consciousness is choked by weedy *Wake*ish punning. Then four years after *Dead Father,* **"The New Music"** offered its syncopation of Greek mythology and Joycean mother-worship. As for Barthelme's most recent major work, the excellent novel *Paradise,* while the book certainly has Modernist references, in scope and direction it offers a break from the shadows of the century's first third. As such, its consideration may wait till after we are done with **"The Indian Uprising."**

William Gass judged this story the best in its collection, thus granting an imprimatur of sorts. The piece is probably Barthelme's most widely anthologized, and it's often discussed in the criticism. Stengel uses the story as a cornerstone of his concluding insights, and Frederick Karl, in his mammoth *American Fictions: 1940-1980,* devotes as much space to **"Uprising"** as to novels many times its length. In its density, its speed ("I accelerate," a character explains near the start, "and ignore the time signature"), and its tragic yet open-ended resolution, the story stands out in this author's madcap but generally looser *oeuvre.*

At some level at least the story is indeed about an Indian uprising, a Commanche attack on a late-twentieth-century city. By means of this comic juxtaposition Barthelme surreally fixes the story's moment, the Vietnam era, when the urban chic were fascinated particularly with the primitive and disenfranchised. But from the start he enriches this understanding of the society—of the new and now—by using the same native assault as a metaphor for an affair that's breaking up. "The sickness of the quarrel," the narrator confesses, "lay thick in the bed." Our protagonist is older than his beloved, more experienced in romance, but his girlfriend is a willful youngster, an Indian sympathizer. She affects bear-claw necklaces and has an apt name: Sylvia. The uprising in other words refers to an outbreak in the culture, a time when passionate young women strung themselves in sylvan finery, and also suggests a rise of a more intimate kind—stiff and engorged with need—in the love-bed. In the process Barthelme, subtly but with accumulative clout, opposes two views of the good life. He sets the romantic, artistic sensibility, forever on the point of battle or breakdown, against the stodgy but more livable quietude that most of us eventually settle for. All this is done in frantic collage. The protagonist expresses now the romantic view, now the domestic, and in the same way he functions at times as the narrator, and at other times as just another benumbed reader of the latest bulletin from the front. Barthelme may change tone or subject in mid-sentence, folding together B movie clichés ("And I sat there getting drunker and drunker and more in love and more in love") and anguished poetic effects.

With these thematic elements in mind—a diseased and self-devouring social order; an affair between an older man and a freer spirit; and the struggle between dangerous self-expression and unsatisfying sanity—one thinks soon enough of the early T. S. Eliot. And so, the story's opening lines: "We defended the city as best we could. The arrows of the Commanches came in clouds. The war clubs of the Commanches clattered on the soft, yellow pavement." Prufrock's yellow fog, turned deadly. Note too that this time the seepage separates at once into the story's two opposed ideologies: the coulds freeflying yet dangerous, the pavement restful yet cloying.

Prufrock is trapped by the cups, the marmelade, the tea, by "the dooryards and the sprinkled streets." In Barthelme's city the streets are sprinkled more dangerously—hedgehogged with barricades. But these fortifications, described early in the story, contain precisely the sort of thing Eliot's narrator complains about. Here one finds cups and plates, can openers and ashtrays, empty bottles of scotch, wine, cognac, vodka, gin . . . (though it's not a Modernist reference, one thinks as well of the drinker's slang, "dead soldiers"). In his 1981 *Paris Review* interview, Barthelme described this passage about the barricade as "an archeological slice," but the digging here is not simply into Vietnam-era arcana. It's a strip of the narrator's own past, the detritus of his own bereft living room perhaps—his own nerves, as Prufrock would have it, thrown in patterns on a screen. And yet the barricade *is* archeology, it takes in the culture at large, and the story never stops shuttling between private trash and the trashing of a society. Thus the most explicit echo of Prufrock fuses the narrator's biological decay with that of his town:

> There was a sort of muck running in the gutters, yellowish filthy stream suggesting excrement or nervousness, a city that does not know what it has done to deserve baldness, errors, infidelity.

It is not only the narrator's hair that is growing thin, but the tissue of lies by which his city convinces itself that the life it has is worthwhile. With these mournful catalogues, Barthelme is doing precisely what most critics say he is: he's calling attention to the stink that our mass culture prefers to ignore. He's a Jeremiah, brandishing plastic instead of prophecy. But in this case he lays on the post-Modern cool not by means of New-&-Improved media babble, but rather by acknowledging that another complainant was there first. In the same paragraph, his desire for the girl is chilled by still more Prufrockian trash—including some bits and pieces very like the erections of his adversaries:

> But it is you I want now, here in the middle of this Uprising, with the streets yellow and threatening, short, ugly lances with fur at the throat [clearly these invaders have the narrator outnumbered] and inexplicable shell money lying in the grass.

"Son of man / You cannot say, or guess, for you know only / A heap of broken images. . . ." So *The Waste Land* (itself echoing another angry prophet, Ezekiel) comes to

have a place in this Uprising as well, as a compatibly heartsore investigation of urban diaspora. References to Eliot's second great work are as lightly handled as those to "Prufrock," but they squeeze self and society into still more savage shapes.

Hurt by Sylvia's change of heart, about mid-story the narrator goes to a "teacher" named Miss R., yet the only help she can give him is the same reproof as the queenly Chess Player of *Waste Land* II: "You know nothing," Miss R. declares, "you feel nothing, you are locked in a most savage and terrible ignorance. . . ." And as love turns to insults, gestures of oppression are confused with those of love. When the people of the city's ghetto join the Commanche attack instead of resisting, the narrator's forces make two wildly disparate defenses. "We sent more heroin into the ghetto," he explains, "and hyacinths, ordering another hundred thousand of the pale, delicate flowers." Here again the political and personal collide. The passage condenses widely held assumptions of late-sixties urban studies—namely, that those in the black ghetto were the natural allies of revolution, and that therefore the white power structure looked the other way when ghettoites fell prey to drugs—and in so doing combines those assumptions with the love-gift in *Waste Land*'s "Burial of the Dead": "'You gave me hyacinths first a year ago; / They called me the hyacinth girl." The lovers' attempt at a reconciliation, immediately following, comes off likewise folded and spindled. The narrator points to the section of the battle map held by the Commanches—by those with whom his own hyacinth girl sides—and he says, "Your parts are green." That is, punning on the color, he acknowledges Sylvia's youth and relative sexual inexperience (his own parts, not insignificantly, are blue). Her reply? "You gave me heroin first a year ago!" In the wasteland of an unbalanced love, even gentle gestures make us think only of power politics.

The Commanches' ultimate triumph combines both poems, adding to the narrator's loss the resonances of those twinned deaths by water. At story's end, the blue player is taken before the Clemency Committee, whose spokesperson is the ambiguous Miss R.—a triumph of the mermaid, as in "Prufrock," or of the witch, as in *Waste Land*. Facing her, Barthelme's lover also confronts a strange double vision. Outside he sees "rain shattering from a great height the prospects of silence and clear, neat rows of houses in the subdivisions"; inside, he sees only "their savage black eyes, paint, feathers, beads." One recalls of course the apocalyptic rainstorm that ends *The Waste Land*. "Prufrock," however, seems here inverted, for Eliot's man drowns in the waters of a repressive society, very like those neat rows of houses visible outside the Committee Room. Barthelme's narrator, on the other hand, glimpses those houses as a "prospect," something to be longed for when confronted with the painted savagery that his love affair has become.

Such a domestic yearning is rare in this writer's work, which (like his Daumier) generally strives to create new possibilities. Yet this momentary yen for the hearth is part of what makes **"Uprising"** a cultural benchmark, and at the same time spiritual kin to early Eliot. Naked before the Clemency Committee, Barthelme's story confronts its essential duality: freedom versus government, passion versus clarity. Miss R. may be Miss Reality, demanding that all lovers face up—though the suggestion of *misery* certainly seems pertinent as well. Understood in this way, the story's close doesn't invert Prufrock's tragedy but rather carries it forward forty years. As in the poem, Barthelme's narrator must balance private desires against public uproar. In both cases, a man's uprising comes to nothing, powerless against what the story describes as the world's "rushing, ribald whole." Or consider the first word Sylvia speaks, in the opening paragraph. The narrator puts the question that underlies Prufrock's meditations, and that drives every wanderer in *The Waste Land*: "Is this a good life?" The girl responds: "No."

So much for smaller samples, a few exemplary instances of allusion at work. What does this detail reveal of the larger picture? How can we apply it to this author and his place?

Barthelme himself explains a crucial aspect of the fascination that the Modernists have for him in his *Paris Review* interview, an exchange that the interviewer (the critic J. D. O'Hara) claims was carefully edited and reworked. Recalling his father's career as an architect, the author says: "I was exposed to an almost religious crusade, the Modern movement in architecture." And he adds: "we were enveloped in Modernism. The house we lived in, which he'd designed, was Modern and the pictures were Modern and the books were Modern."

Though he goes on to note, judiciously, that the movement didn't amount to much, the crusade image seems telling. The best art made between, say, 1896 ("La Soirée avec M. Teste") and 1939 (*Finnegans Wake*) by and large represents a moral reckoning point for this author. Just as he can rarely handle emotion without first wrapping it in deprecatory wit, so his essential ideas are often cloaked in the priestly robes of our century's most demanding *littérateurs*. That these allusions are often subtle only increases that arcane priestliness. It should be pointed out, for instance, that **"The Indian Uprising"** also contains two explicit references, each quite serious despite their bizarre placement. The first is to Valéry, whom Miss R. names and quotes: "The ardor aroused in men by the beauty of women can only be satisfied by God." The second is made by a Commanche under torture, who adopts the major role from Thomas Mann's *Death in Venice* ("His name, he said, was Gustave Aschenbach"). Thus the story's twinning of love and war takes on two more suggestions of the search for something better, something beyond the world of compromise and decay: a crusade. Modernism offers Barthelme a bedrock ideological seriousness which, while it may be applied in different ways for different stories, cannot be robbed of its ethical force, not even by his otherwise devastating irony.

This grounding in transatlantic artistic values is of course in keeping with Frederick Karl's thesis, who argues in *American Fictions* that American literature in general has been "Europeanized" over the last half-century. Barthelme's particular heros in that older cultural canon, we can here add, helps to situate him more precisely in contemporary letters. His commonality with Eliot or Valéry or Joyce, that is, helps clarify what he shares not only with experts in the short form, like Robert Coover, but also with a lover of excess like William Gaddis; it allows us to see that he has some more unlikely cohorts, names that might not occur to us were it not for the Modernist connection—Cynthia Ozick, for one. Indeed the best theorist of the bunch, William Gass, has claimed: "My view is very old-fashioned, of course; it's just the Symbolist position, really." (Gass was speaking at a 1975 symposium on contemporary fiction, later transcribed in *Shenandoah*.) That position unites these authors, more than tics of style or coincidences of close publication. The larger question, then, is whether Barthelme and his peers must forever play second fiddle to their European forerunners. In their defense, I would point out that a century and a half ago a homegrown group of late-arriving Romantics, beginning with Emerson, went on to earn their own considerable place in literary history.

The Modernist connection also provides a better sense of Barthelme himself, as distinct from his contemporaries. Here the key figure is Samuel Beckett, and the most revealing book is the latest novel, *Paradise*.

Beckett may or may not be a Modernist; critics are divided and after *Murphy* at least his books are stubbornly *sui generis*. Undeniably however he is essential to Donald Barthelme, mentioned time and again as his single greatest inspiration. Of course the younger author has wanted to take his chosen medium beyond the work of his master, as *Malone Dies* took it beyond *Ulysses,* but Barthelme's means have been in large degree precisely the opposite of Beckett's. The expatriate Irishman attempts to rid his work of cultural flotsam and jetsam; he wants nothing that would interfere with isolating the unnameable. Barthelme on the other hand heaps up barricades of sheer stuff. For all the brevity of his individual pieces, they are far more full of color and circumstance, of names and tastes and tidbits, than the older author's grim parings. Those bits, as we've seen, include the breakage and shards left behind by Beckett's own forebears, and thus Barthelme may be seen as more the restorer, the preservationist, than he appears at first glance. If he has gone beyond, he has done so in part by digging back. For all his speed and shocking combinations, his "need for the new," this is an artist with respect for the artifacts of the old, and a restraint about how he handles them.

Yet that would suggest that Barthelme is some sort of museum keeper, that whatever flash he has is secondhand. The latest novel proves otherwise, turning retrospection to rediscovery. The protagonist is Simon, a fiftyish architect recently divorced, who enjoys what one character calls a "male fantasy." For a few months, Simon shares his apartment and bedroom with three young women he met at a lingerie show. Yet the man's good luck generally causes him to think back on his daughter, his marriage, and his vocation. The architect's introspection under the circumstances is in fact something like his creator's response to the possibilities of fiction after 1945: faced with the sundering of old narrative promises, he's gone back to where the breakup began. And this book too has its over-the-shoulder glances, mostly to Kafka. The opening dream sequence suggests "In the Penal Colony," the later dream passages other of the Czech master's fictional nightmares, and the overall situation recalls *The Trial*—a similar urban jungle, in which worldly women throw themselves at a protagonist who's trying to figure out where they've all gone wrong. Yet the book is something new for this author. In particular, the sex is like nothing he's done, the scenes briefly scorching, full of flesh and unabashedly perverse. The novel begins by presenting the *menage* as something Simon has already outgrown ("After the women had gone . . .") and it ends with the laissez-faire spirit of the weekend ("It does feel a bit like Saturday . . ."). Exploring their complex new freedoms, both Simon and one of the women have outside affairs, which he refers to as "frolic and detour," and repeatedly his lovers admit, in one way or another, that their situation doesn't "fit the pattern" of "suppression and domination of female-kind."

It would be a misrepresentation, a bad one, to suggest that the book is a mere soulless romp. Simon starts from heartbreak and his story generates enormous sympathy for the women—powerless and uneducated *"pure skin,"* as one of them says. Yet just as the architect emerges reborn from his brief burial in flesh and economic constraints, so in this novel Barthelme himself may have at last gotten that demanding Modernist monkey off his back. He challenges us to find the harm in sabbatical pleasures ("Everybody always wants somebody to be sorry. Fuck that"); his *Trial* is paradise.

"You're not a father-figure," one of Simon's lovers tell him, more or less defiantly. "That surprise you?" Not at all: bright youth has always had to deny its forebears. For the upstart Barthelme as well, the father remains a stubborn image, in spite of all the times the author has denied the old man or left him in fragments. Likewise the intractable seriousness of Modernism, as it lurks in the novels and stories, is to some extent the ineradicable whisper of Dad. There are personal implications here, considering what Barthelme has said about his own father's training and career. But *Paradise* makes clear he wants no part of surrendering, all Oedipally, to fate. His art exists not to prove us the pawns of Freudian theory, nor of any other uprising put down long before we were born, but rather to sift and reshape the debris of those earlier struggles, scotching this piece of law to that emblem of freedom, this nose off the Emperor's bust to that foldout from the latest issue. Any bedrock moral seriousness, after all, is only so much dirt if lacks application to contemporary surfaces. John Barth has called his brand of Post-modernism "the literature of replenishment"—that is, an attempt to reinvigorate narrative fiction despite the exhaustion of certain conventions and approaches. Donald Barthelme should be understood as, among other things, our replenisher of Modernism. Whatever he has achieved, he's done it not merely by reference and mimicry but by a more vital connection: by his passion for the new in the old, by his insistence that Stephen Dedalus wasn't the last to have an epiphany at seeing a woman's bared thighs. Barthelme by no means stands with the "old artificer" of Dedalus, but he has the genius to recognize the ancient figure, and he has the courage to stay with our resurgent contradictions at every unexpected glimpse.

. . . . .

The above was finished before Donald Barthelme's death this past summer. The facts of a person's passing are, in themselves, generally beside the point; date and disease shrivel to nothing in the face of permanent loss. But there are exceptions, in which the data borrow significance from the man. To begin with, Barthelme was young yet, fifty-eight. Indeed, his forthcoming novel, *The King,* proves that he never lost his invigorating uneasiness with the form; he never cooled his rambunctious relationship with his masters. Secondly, the writer passed away in Houston, and the place too feels appropriate. A cloverleaf'd sprawl, a place of twang and toxins, Houston is just the sort of impossible contemporary city to which this writer dedicated a career. Barthelme's jittery urban vignettes were perfect, absolutely on the money for all their outlandishness. Finally, he succumbed to cancer, his second bout with the disease within the last five years. During that time he completed two novels and a number of short stories; he continued to teach, give readings, and maintain his efforts on behalf of P.E.N. International and other organizations. His last years suggest virtues more old-fashioned than his body of work would lead one to expect.

The King, to be published in the spring of 1990, seems a throwback to the early work. It juggles archaisms like "God wot" with Americanisms like "plumb wore out," and recalls *Snow White*'s dizzying mix of fairytale and feminism. The king of the title is Arthur, the Arthur of Malory, but the book resets the famous disturbances of his reign during the Second World War. It lays classic on classic, the legends of a thousand years ago looming larger and stranger against the "finest hour" of twentieth-century Britain. To be sure, such a setting also allows room for allusion. By and large Barthelme continues to jibe at his fathers: the text interpolates a few half-mad excerpts from Ezra Pound's fascist diatribes.

Arthur himself is another father, firm about regulations no matter how nonsensical. He hasn't made love to his still-young Guinevere in twelve years, because "twenty-four is my absolute upper limit. Always was and always will be." And yet his neglected wife is a "surpassing beauty," a freewheeling outdoorswoman, and a stiletto wit—a worthy Barthelme *femme fatale.* Indeed, the novel offers a small catalogue of this author's star-crossed romantics. The central relationship decays in the midst of general upheaval, and yet Guinevere's succession of knightly lovers offers her little by way of alternative. Sir Launcelot, though something of the book's artist-hero, puts scruples ahead of satisfaction. "I am a foul unworshipful caitiff," he tells Guinevere at one point, "and I must go away now to pray your forgiveness." The queen replies, "You must *go away* to pray my forgiveness?"

The abiding difficulty for men like Launcelot is that they're thinking of other things, of the war or the rules of proper conduct. Such larger concerns, as always with this author, come round eventually to the question of art. When Arthur lectures on "leadership," he uses the metaphor of craftsmen and their tools: "The king's sceptre, the marshal's baton, the conductor's baton, the physician's caduceus, the magician's wand—a stick of some kind, with which one must animate a mass." Not surprisingly, the next sentence mentions a pencil. Yet it's another tool which most animates *The King*—the "stick" that men are born with. Barthelme's portrayals of *la vie passionée* retain the lively ambivalence that has distinguished them from the first, an uncertainty rooted in his twinned perceptions of making art and making love.

Despite these familiarities, however, *The King* lacks an element crucial to nearly everything else the author produced, namely, an urban setting. The new book's anachronisms in general feel bucolic, pastoral: "Music carpets the forest floor . . . !" The rest of Barthelme, on the other hand, carries on what Simon calls, in *Paradise,* "a great argument for cities." Of course the author preferred to make his points by indirection and understatement, but this very restraint allowed Barthelme to concentrate on what was less obvious and more telling. Other excellent talents have described contemporary urban excess, certainly, but most writers tend to emphasize the externals, the neon and the crime statistics. Barthelme on the other hand brought his streets and kitchens to life by heaping on the internals. The first slow moment in **"The Indian Uprising"** is the compendium of the barricade's materials, all household goods and manmade colors: internals, right down to the orange blur at an ashtray's lip. The author's aesthetic exists here in microcosm, in the list's freedom from narrative mechanics and its piquant blush of fading emotion. Nor were these catalogues limited to hard goods; as his dialog-stories proved, Barthelme had the audacity to concoct drama out of *unseen* internals. The interlocutors of **"The New Music,"** for instance, are constructions of pure thought. Their talk purveys much hand-me-down give and take, pitting borrowed irony against nightmares from bygone cultures.

The worst traffic jam a contemporary urbanite has to deal with is the glut between the ears. After a few years of MTV, indeed, anyone might start to think that a woman's over the hill once she turns twenty-five. In this new Babel, the so-called information age, Barthelme's stories offer a workable flow chart; his turning points are those moments when the media-made must somehow bend to fit bedrock humanity. It's an art of accommodation, in which instead of rejecting the matter in which he finds himself, the artist

attempts to identify the few noises that might be lived with comfortably. The process implies a critique, certainly. Yet it's also a philosopher's puzzle, and now and again a dry-eyed intimation that there is yet reason for joy: an argument *for.*

In the still uncollected **"Brain Damage,"** the narrator and an unknown woman on the street for a moment escape "the terrible thing that was about to happen," the brain damage. For a moment, they hum together the cigarette-company jingle, "Me and My Winstons." Is this truly an escape? Truly interpersonal communication—by means of an advertising slogan? Donald Barthelme's brief and energetic career would suggest so. The self doesn't exist, it suggests, unless it's of the moment. The flash and idiocy of the age, moreover, may clothe the artist as easily as suffocate him. At a time when culture could seem beyond the reach of words, when the only modes of discourse could seem either IBM or ICBM, he turned those same hard choices to something witty, well-made, and profound.

Charles Baxter (essay date autumn 1990)

SOURCE: Baxter, Charles. "The Donald Barthelme Blues." *Gettysburg Review* 3, no. 4 (autumn 1990): 713-23.

[*In the following essay, Baxter traces Barthelme's literary development, focusing on his utilization of characters and language.*]

The same day that a friend called with the news that Donald Barthelme had died, a freight train derailed outside Freeland, Michigan. Among the cars that went off the tracks were several chemical tankers, some of which spilled and caught fire. Dow Chemical was (and still is) reluctant to name these chemicals, but one of them was identified as chlorosilene. When chlorosilene catches fire, as it did in this case, it turns into hydrochloric acid. Upon being asked about the physical hazards to neighbors and on-lookers near the fire, a company representative, interviewed on Michigan Public Radio, said, "Well, there's been some physical reactions, yes, certainly. Especially in the area of nausea, vomiting-type thing."

The area of nausea, vomiting-type thing: this area, familiar to us all, where bad taste, hilarity, fake authority, and cliché seem to collide, was Donald Barthelme's special kingdom. "I have a few new marvels here I'd like to discuss with you just briefly," says the chief engineer in **"Report."** "Consider for instance the area of realtime online computer-controlled wish evaporation." Like his creation Hokie Mokie, the King of Jazz, no one could top Barthelme at deadpan riffs like these—these collages built from castoff verbal junk—and imitation was beside the point, because the work was not a compendium of stylistic tics but grew out of—has anyone bothered to say this?—a spiritual enterprise owned up to in the work, a last stay against the forces of wish evaporation. Comedy is partly the art of collage, of planned incongruity—the Three Stooges as brain surgeons, King Kong as an adjunct professor of art history—and Barthelme was a master tailor of these ill-fitting suits in which our culture likes to dress itself. A yoking of the virtuosic-articulate with the flat banal; an effort to preserve wishes, and certain kinds of longings, in the face of clichés; not innocence, but a watchful clarity, even an effort to preserve the monstrousness of Being itself: all these difficult ambitions seemed to be part of the project. The work was a comfort, in the way the blues are a comfort, in its refusal to buy stock in the official Happiness Project, in its loyalty to "inappropriate longings," a phrase whose ironic positive side he particularly valued.

As an undergraduate I was taught that when a writer starts a story, he or she must begin with *a character,* an active, preferably vivid, ideally sympathetic, character. It takes a bit of time to see that stories don't in fact begin with characters, not from here, at least, not from behind this keyboard. They begin with words, one word after another. It seems doltish to point this out, but in Donald Barthelme's fiction, that's where the project begins: with the stress first on the language, the medium, and then on the problem of who owns it. Who does own language? I can evade the question by saying that no one does; it is just out there, part of the culture. But Barthelme did not practice this evasion. In his stories, all kinds of disreputable people claim to own both language and its means of distribution. They invent instant clichés that they want you to buy and use; they want you to join and submit to their formulas. Invariably, they are selling something that can only be sold if they trash up the language first. They are lively practitioners of a black art, these commodifiers, and Barthelme's stories don't mind saying so.

Barthelme's characters inhabit not the prison-house of language, but the prison-house of official cliché—which is not the same thing as saying "Fine" when someone asks how you are but is more a processing of statements into the professional formulas usually called jargon, like the analyst's transformation of Susan's statement (in **"The Sandman"**) that she wants to buy a piano into, "She wishes to terminate the analysis and escape into the piano." The narrator, Susan's boyfriend and a slightly irritable opponent of normative psychotherapy, observes that the analyst is methodologically horse-blindered: "The one thing you cannot consider, by the nature of your training and of the discipline itself, is that she really might want to terminate the analysis and buy a piano."

What *are* the conditions under which we lose the ability to know what we want? And what are the exact words for longing? Most of the words we have are not the words for what we really want. "What we really want in this world, we can't have" (**"The Ed Sullivan Show"**). There is a certain stranded quality to the Barthelme protagonist, sitting in an easy chair at twilight with eleven martinis lined up in soldierly array. A fastidiousness, this is, and a humor

about the shipwrecked condition, the orphaned longings, and something like an investigation of the possibilities inherent in melancholy. The heroes and heroines in this fiction are the not-joiners, the *non serviam* types, like Cecelia in **"A City of Churches,"** who has come to Prester to open a car-rental office. Mr. Phillips guides her around. It turns out that in Prester everyone lives in a church of one kind or another, "the church of their choice." Mr. Phillips asks Cecelia what denomination she is: "Cecelia was silent. The truth was, she wasn't anything." She tells him, however, that she can will her dreams. What dreams? "'Mostly sexual things,' she said. She was not afraid of him." Mr. Phillips admits to a certain discontent with Prester, despite the town's perfection. "I'll dream the Secret," Cecelia says. "You'll be sorry."

Notice the capitalization of the word *secret*. Our secrets might be the last places where we have hidden ourselves away, where we are still upper-case. Susan wants her piano; Cecelia wants her dreams; and the Phantom of the Opera resists the operation that would, as we might say now, *renormalize* him. All any of these heroes would have to do to be renormalized is trade in their desires for rooms furnished with comfortable clichés: nice wing chairs, plastic slipcovers. The Phantom's friend waits, patiently, "until the hot meat of romance is cooled by the dull gravy of common sense once more." That's a long time, if you're loyal to your desires.

The price one pays for being loyal to certain kinds of anomalies is typically melancholy or acedia: more of this later. What Barthelme's fiction asserts is that one of the first loyalties serious people give up in the theater of adulthood is a claim upon what they actually want. Of course, other desires are available, and can be acquired, but they are curious grafts, what other people want you to want— not desires so much as temptations, desires-of-convenience. Barthelme's stories are obviously and constantly about such temptations, which might itself be called the temptation to become unconscious and let others program your yearnings. The stories exude an almost religious seriousness about this subject; although they are not pious, they do move obsessively around ethical-theological quandaries. A good deal of reading about religion is made visible in them. The Barthelmean character is tempted not by ordinary sins but by the ordinary itself. Does God care about adultery? Sins generally? "You think about this staggering concept, the mind of God, and then you think He's sitting around worrying about this guy and this woman at the Beechnut Travelodge? I think not" (*Paradise*).

It wasn't activities like adultery that caught Barthelme's attention, but the inclination to disown one's wishes and to give in to the omnipresence of the Universal Banal. Barthelme was not a snob in this respect; plain common pleasures—food, sex, Fleetwood Mac, John Ford movies, dull days at home—find themselves celebrated (however mildly) in his pages; ordinary pleasures are all right if that is what you really want. But no, the problem is not the banal as such but banality's hope that you will dumbfoundedly join in its program, spend yourself in it: that's the problem. In Barthelme a saint is tempted not by sin but by life in the suburbs: "St. Anthony's major temptation, in terms of his living here, was maybe this: ordinary life" (**"The Temptation of St. Anthony"**). People want to see his apartment; they want to look at the carpet from Kaufman's, and the bedroom. How might a Saint resist the ordinary?

A simple question, calling forth slyly complicated answers. One begins by talking about deserts (where the Saint goes), grottos, the stony home of the grotesque. In a catalogue commentary on a Sherrie Levine exhibit, Barthelme put it this way:

> Where does desire go? Always a traveling salesperson, desire goes hounding off into the trees, frequently, without direction from its putative master or mistress. This is tragic and comic at the same time. I should, in a well-ordered world, marry the intellectual hero my wicked uncle has selected for me. Instead I run off with William of Ockham or Daffy Duck.

William of Ockham or Daffy Duck: yes, the true object of your desire quite often looks and sounds a bit, well, bizarre, and hard to introduce to your wicked uncle. The more bizarre the object, the more Barthelme seems to like it. There is a pleasant sideshow quality, a circus element, to the spectacle of desire. It generates dwarves and witches (*Snow White*), a son manqué (eight feet tall and wearing "a serape woven out of two hundred transistor radios" in **"The Dolt"**), monsters, and impossibly beautiful women. It's as if longing generates out of itself, as Susan Stewart has argued in her book on the subject, narratives of the gigantic and tiny, narratives of altered proportion: there is the dead father, that huge living corpse of origination, being dragged around by the bickering sons; there are the zombies, spouting their death-in-life clichés; there is King Kong, already alluded to, the adjunct professor of art history at Rutgers. Big and little: figures of all sizes and shapes have their moment in the most highly invented sentences grammar and sense permit. This sideshow resides very comfortably, too, in the short story form, a haven, as Frank O'Connor has claimed, for the otherwise disappeared, all the everyone-elses who fall between the cracks of the more official forms, such as the novel and the sonnet.

Sometimes behind this cultivation of the beautiful grotesque, this show-and-tell of the alien wish, a certain weariness is sometimes apparent. One is after all confronted by the banal in the midst of the weird; there is also that terrible moment familiar to all members of the avant-garde when the weird *becomes* the banal. "Some things appear to be wonders in the beginning, but when you become familiar with them, are not wonderful at all. Sometimes a seventy-five-foot highly paid cacodemon will raise only the tiniest *frisson*. Some of us have even thought of folding the show—closing it down" (**"The Flight of Pigeons from the Palace"**).

What is the secret name of this weariness? At first it is called irony, and then acedia.

Under the powerful microscope of post-structuralist Neo-Marxist semiotically-based hyphen-using critical theory, Barthelme's fiction at first seems to be all about cultural junk, verbal junk, "the leading edge of the trash phenomenon," and about the way structures of meaning, let loose from the objects they're supposed to represent, are pasted onto something else (the Campbell's Pork-and-Beans labels on my necktie; Elvis's *Jailhouse Rock* on dinner plates from the Franklin Mint; the Batman label on sandwiches). Words go wild. They are set free from the house of correction and have a party (**"Bone Bubbles"**) or, freed up like a chatty aunt off her medication, go on and on (**"Sentence"**). For a time in the early seventies, Barthelme and John Ashbery seemed to be operating similar circuses in different parts of town. This period included the moment of greatest academic interest in Barthelme's work; critics had much to say about the mechanisms of meaning in the fiction, about the arbitrariness of the sign and the problems of language. The defamiliarization in the work matched the defamiliarization of American social life. But semiotics and fragments are not the essential subjects of these stories. I'm not sure how often it has been noticed that Barthelme's imagery, cast of characters, and preoccupations are drawn from religious sources. Who is the dead father in *The Dead Father*? The father and The Father. In **"City Life,"** Ramona gives birth to Sam; it's a virgin birth. Angels, in their current earthly diminished lives, have their say in **"On Angels."** Kierkegaard is invoked several times. Such maneuvering has an element of travesty in it, a playing-around with the broken relics of religious iconography and meaning-creation; but religion appears so often and with such odd sideways intensity that it signals a persistent curiosity about the Absolute and such of its elements as authenticity (in post-structuralist thinking, a completely discredited category).

In Barthelme's early stories, modern culture is gleefully and relentlessly unmasked: engineers, doctors, politicians, newspapers, television quiz shows, and the plastic assembled-with-glue language they use. There is a certain violence in the ripping off of the masks here, a ferocity that produces a prose poetry (Barthelme probably would have hated the term) of rage and clarity. Lines often-quoted from the first paragraph of **"The Indian Uprising"** hit this note and sustain it: "People were trying to understand. I spoke to Sylvia. 'Do you think this is a good life?' The table held apples, books, long-playing records. She looked up. 'No.'"

These early stories sometimes seem to demonstrate that the serious world is about as well-constructed as a puppet show; it is certainly no more real. All experience gives way to representation. You pull back the pretense: another pretense. Pictures give way to pictures, acts to acts. It's unhinging, the metaphysics of the onion-skin giving way to nothing: the wisps and whiffs of frenzy I hear in *Come Back, Dr. Caligari, Unspeakable Practices, Unnatural Acts,* and *City Life* strike me as sounds made by someone reaching for the irreducibly real but coming up with fistfuls of sand—or an empire of signs, themselves nauseating and revealing of nothing. Knowing—as the Barthelmean narrative knows so well—that this reaching, this frenzy, and this sand are commonplaces in the history of twentieth century spiritual-critical life is no solace. What good is it to know that your metaphysical nausea, which you suffer from daily, has been experienced before and expressed very well by Mallarmé, Sartre, and the others? As the stories themselves say, "No good at all!"

Starting with **"Kierkegaard Unfair to Schlegel,"** in *City Life* and then intermittently throughout the other books, Barthelme seemed to be setting himself a challenge to go beyond this unmasking process—a process that would, if continued indefinitely, have yielded up wacky but tedious self-repeating satires, or exercises in dry malice. The nature of this challenge is not easy to state discursively, but it may be at the center of any life which is simultaneously mindful and bourgeois (if in fact those two categories can be placed next to each other). We can call it, in honor of one of its first diagnosticians, the Chekhov problem, which goes something like this: what does one do, do actively, with one's honest revulsion and disgust with the cruelties, lies, and deceptions of middle-class life? Chekhov's response to this challenge—this is a gross oversimplication—is to show that, hidden under the outward mimes of character there lies the substance of real character, a kind of essence. Something genuine sooner or later will show itself; all we need do is wait, observe, and hold onto those moments when they arrive. In this way, weariness and cynicism are kept at arm's length. Because no character can be wholly co-opted by any system, some particle of the genuine will emerge at some point.

This solution, if one can call it that, was closed to Barthelme almost from the beginning. Either he did not believe in character in this sense (one cannot imagine him using so square a phrase as "real character underneath"), or he had no feel for it as a writer. As a result his characters tend toward allegory and stylization. Exceptions exist, notably in the Bishop stories, but they are few. It is not so much that the characters in Barthelme's fiction are unreal but that they seem more to have been constructed out of pre-existing emotions than out of motivations, a more common writerly starting-point. In any case, without the solution of character, we are back at the original problem of what to do after all the lies have been exposed. And of course we are still enjoying the unreflecting privileges of middle-class life.

This far from trivial problem exists only if you assume that middle-class American life does carry with it a gnawing burden of guilt. I think I could argue that a significant number of the strategies of contemporary American "serious" fiction are maneuvers for dealing with the issue of middle-class guilt. One possibility is to handle it more or less as Chekhov did. Another, also very common, is the strategy of cynicism, enjoying the benefits of middle-class life while holding oneself slightly above it. A third response, almost always characterized as "toughness," has been a part of American culture for at least a century.

Toughness is the obverse side of sentimentality, fighting against and reflecting it all at the same time. It is the poetry of denial. What it refuses to give to character it lavishes on its prose, which typically is highly stylized and self-regarding. The idea is to withhold expressions of human sympathy—because they seem "weak" and because they capitulate to a false order of experience. Hemingway is the great bard of this mode, saying in effect I-may-be-here-but-I'm-not-really-part-of-this-scene. Obviously, cynicism and toughness may be easily combined as strategies. They carry with them a certain feeling for hermit life, for withholding, and for clipped sentences, oracular statements, and derailed ordinary language. However, the toughness mode is crabbed and repetitious, qualities that Barthelme never sought. He invented situations and sentences: I'd like to quote page after page of them, hair-raising for their sheer sound, their surprises and elaborations. Their shine. No: toughness, the metaphysics of the hermit crab, was not enough.

Which returns us to the problem of cynicism, which does not seem an adequate response to the problem of being located inside conflicting desires, of being the very person one does not want to be. Cynicism and its spiritual second-cousin, irony, are regular combatants in Barthelme's stories, but there is something wrong with both of them; the stories work hard to disclose what it is. For one thing, cynicism is hypocritical: it enjoys what it claims to despise. It is happy in its unhappy consciousness. It understands the destructiveness of its own pleasures but does nothing to stop it. It is enlightened about its own moral condition. It will agree to any accusation made against it. World-weariness is its poetry. Growing out of snobbery, its only pleasure is manipulation. Cynicism is irony that has moved into a condition of institutional power; cynicism and power have a tendency to breed each other. But Barthelme's stories—especially the early ones and the novel *Snow White*—typically struggle against institutional cynicism and the language employed in its cause. To use a phrase by the German philosopher Peter Sloterdijk, employed in another context, these are "études in the higher banalities." Far from being an exercise in cynicism, the narrative voice in Barthelme consistently attacks cynicism—the cynicism of official institutional spokespersons. But the weapon that comes most readily to hand is irony, which creates the (as Barthelme might say) *interesting* struggle and tension in his writing.

The nature of the problem, if you simultaneously feel guilty and disgusted by the progress of modern culture, is the temptation to become a snob, to join a like-minded coterie of people with good taste who define themselves by an awareness of all the vulgarities they do not perform. Or you can become a hermit like Saint Anthony, benefiting from the culture while pretending not to live in it. Viewed unsympathetically, this is a central impulse in Modernism, one of its worst errors. Barthelme's fiction never makes this error: it challenges readers but never insults them or pretends to instruct them from an angle higher than their own. It disclaims righteousness. **"The Party"** concludes by asking: "Is it really important to know that this movie is fine, and that one terrible, and to talk intelligently about the difference? Wonderful elegance! No good at all!"

At this point, the really astonishing difficulties of Barthelme's project start to become apparent: exiled from character-drawing, and in the midst of (one might almost say "drowning in") cultural sign-systems, most of which are duplicitous, the Barthelmean narrator must struggle simply in order to find a location, a place to stand and speak that is not so far inside the culture that it replicates its falseness and lies, and not so far outside that it becomes cold, snobby, or self-righteous. This is a problem not just for writers but for anyone who lives in a powerful and culturally dominant country. And it is not an issue that anyone finally "solves." Writers must devise strategies for dealing with it, some of which are more effective than others. Some are distracting—and Barthelme's work is very high, one might almost say intoxicated, with distractions—while also presenting roads and avenues, certain kinds of metaphorical paths for action. And they do so, it has always seemed to me, with a good deal of warmth—as in the ending of **"Daumier,"** where Celeste is in the kitchen, making a *daube,* and the narrator says he will go in to watch her. The story ends with two sentences that, in their quietness, modesty, and precision, have always moved me. "The self cannot be escaped, but it can be, with ingenuity and hard work, distracted. There are always openings, if you can find them, there is always something to do."

One word for this technique is *forbearance.* Starting with the stories in **City Life,** we move onto a thematic ground governed by a feeling where piano music instead of analysis might be possible, where "little dances of suggestion and fear" might be staged: "These dances constitute an invitation of unmistakable import—an invitation which, if accepted, leads down many muddy roads. I accepted. What was the alternative?" (**"City Life"**). Odd, the fastidious articulation of these feelings, their insistence on the possibility of continued action. And beautiful, the playing with children, the turning to childhood, in two late stories, **"Chablis"** and **"The Baby."**

As for religion: can one discard its content and still admire its interest in, perhaps its necessary commitment to, the issue of where one places oneself in relation to one's own experiences? This is exactly the question that arises in two of Barthelme's most interesting stories, **"Kierkegaard Unfair to Schlegel"** and **"January"** (the last story in **Forty Stories** and therefore something of a curtain-speech). In both stories we are in the presence of a ghostly sort of interview, considerably more ghostly in the Kierkegaard story, that gives the sense of an internal quarrel or an interview between two spirit entities.

Characters named Q. and A., question and answer, argue in **"Kierkegaard Unfair to Schlegel,"** with Q. being particularly annoyed by A.'s inability to get enthusiastic about "our machines": "You've withheld your enthusiasm, that's damaging . . ." Something like the problem of cynicism

arises here, the question of spiritual snobbery. A. answers by discussing irony, which he uses in conjunction with political activism:

> I participate. I make demands, sign newspaper advertisements, vote. I make small campaign contributions to the candidate of my choice and turn my irony against the others. But I accomplish nothing. I march, it's ludicrous.

This sense of self-irony leads into a discussion of Kierkegaard and his analysis of irony as a magical power that confers upon its user a "negative freedom." When irony is directed against the whole of existence, the result, says Kierkegaard, is "estrangement and poetry"—a poetry that "opens up a higher actuality, expands and transfigures the imperfect into the perfect, and thereby softens and mitigates the deep pain which would darken and obscure all things." Thus Kierkegaard. Unfortunately, this variety of poetry does not reconcile one to the world but produces an animosity to the world:

> A. But I love my irony.
>
> Q. Does it give you pleasure?
>
> A. A poor . . . a rather unsatisfactory. . . .
>
> Q. The unavoidable tendency of everything particular to emphasize its own particularity.
>
> A. Yes.

If Barthelme were the kind of ironist described by Kierkegaard, the sort who turns his irony upon the "whole of existence," then he would be tracking Beckett in pursuit of an absolute negativity, thinking directed against being itself. Or he would be following William Gass into a principality built out of the toothpicks and straw of words. But though this irony has the virtue of purity, it can in no way account for the pleasures we consciously enjoy in Barthelme's fiction. What is their ultimate source?

Answering this question seems to me the task Barthelme set himself in his novel *Paradise,* published in 1986. If it is about anything, this book is about pleasures, even beatitude: the pleasure of sex and the friendship it can produce; the pleasure of making and building (its protagonist, Simon, is an architect); the pleasure—unbelievable to imagine this in the early books—of improving the world. The tone of this book, in its mixture of fantasy, high comedy, and caring, is close to *blessedness.* Barthelme of course gives his usual warnings about stupid optimism:

> Simon wanted very much to be a hearty, optimistic American, like the President, but on the other hand did not trust hearty, optimistic Americans, like the President. He had considered the possibility that the President . . . was not really hearty and optimistic but rather a gloomy, obsessed man.

Because the fantasy in this story—a single man living with three beautiful women—is so stylized, the imaginative force seems to move from the specific situation to the nature of the lineaments of gratified desire. The book is therefore about happiness. It is as if Barthelme were saying that we must try to imagine happiness. This book is one version of it. Happiness, in these times, may be the last frontier of the imagination, the most difficult challenge of all. But if happiness cannot be imagined, if alienation cannot be balmed at the source, then truly one might as well do nothing, or simply drift toward death. Near the end of *Paradise,* Barthelme argues that our desires inhabit and inspirit us:

> Simon flew to North Carolina to inspect a job he'd done in Winston-Salem, a hospital. The construction was quite good and he found little to complain of. He admired the fenestration, done by his own hand. He spent an agreeable night in a Ramada Inn and flew back the next day. His seatmate was a young German woman on her way to Frankfurt. She was six months pregnant, she said, and her husband, an Army sergeant in Chemical Warfare, had found a new girl friend, was divorcing her. She had spent two years at Benning, loved America, spoke with what seemed to Simon a Texas accent. Her father was dead and her mother operated a candy store in Frankfurt. They talked about pregnancy and delivery, about how much wine she allowed herself, whether aspirin was in fact a danger to the baby, and how both of her brothers-in-law had been born in taxis. She was amazingly cheerful given the circumstances and told him that the Russians were going to attempt to take over Mexico next. We had neglected Mexico, she said.
>
> Over the Atlantic on the long approach to Kennedy Simon saw a hundred miles of garbage in the water, from the air white floating scruff. The water became agitated at points as fish attacked the garbage and Simon turned his mind to compaction. When they landed he kissed the German woman goodbye and told her that although she probably didn't feel very lucky at the moment, she was very lucky.

That's beautiful. The balance is miraculous: everything that is—including abandonment, garbage, ecological decay—is held in equilibrium with what is possible: delivery, compaction. There is always something to do. The style is also beautiful, because of all the hurricanes Barthelme has traveled through in order to formulate this difficult calm. The book ends up radiating not a sense of peacefulness but a sense of high intellectual and spiritual comedy, a form of art characteristic of late middle and old age.

"**January**" concludes Barthelme's final collection, *Forty Stories.* The first month. This piece (*is* it a story? of what sort?) presents an interview with theologian Thomas Brecker, whose dissertation was written in the forties on the subject of acedia:

> The thesis was that acedia is a turning toward something rather than, as it's commonly conceived of, a turning away from something. I argued that acedia is a positive reaction to extraordinary demand, for example, the demand that one embrace the *good news* and become one with the mystical body of Christ. . . . Ace-

dia is often conceived of as a kind of sullenness in the face of existence; I tried to locate its positive features. For example, it precludes certain kinds of madness, crowd mania, it precludes a certain kind of error. You're not an enthusiast and therefore you don't go out and join a lynch mob—rather you languish on a couch with your head in your hands.

Brecker goes on to talk about the healing power of absolution, its ability to create new directions. He thinks about his own death, "I hate to abandon my children," and concludes the story this way:

> The point of my career is perhaps how little I achieved. We speak of someone as having had "a long career" and that's usually taken to be admiring, but what if it's thirty-five years of persistence in error? I don't know what value to place on what I've done, perhaps none at all is right. If I'd done something with soybeans, been able to increase the yield of an acre of soybeans, then I'd know I'd done something. I can't say that.

Barthelme's last collection of stories ends here, in a perfectly serious tone of modesty, not to say humility. "I was trying," Brecker says, "to stake out a position for the uncommitted which still, at the same time, had something to do with religion." It would be incorrect to say that Barthelme, the chronicler of word-nausea, had mellowed into the drabness of total sincerity. What actually seems to have emerged toward the end is both more interesting and more complicated: a kind of tenderness toward existence, isolated from the junk of culture through which it is commonly viewed. Though still surrounded by intellectual defenses, and therefore still enveloped and distracted, these later stories are generous; almost miraculously they transform metaphysical irony into caring watchfulness. Giving up finally *does* turn into giving over. Though it is not typically American to have a second act in one's career, and then a third, and even a fourth, Barthelme had them. And despite what was sometimes said against him, he did not repeat himself, did not endlessly replay the old tricks. He found new tricks, and then, toward the end, discarded most of them. How rare, also, in America, to see writing develop into such variety and generosity! Almost unheard-of. Almost unseen.

Ewing Campbell (essay date fall 1990)

SOURCE: Campbell, Ewing. "Dark Matter: Barthelme's Fantastic, Freudian Subtext in 'The Sandman'." *Studies in Short Fiction* 27, no. 4 (fall 1990): 517-24.

[*In the following essay, Campbell considers the connection between Barthelme's "The Sandman," E. T. A. Hoffmann's tale "The Sandman," and Sigmund Freud's essay "The 'Uncanny.'"*]

In its farewell to Donald Barthelme *The New Yorker* reminded readers that he had been variously defined "as an avant-gardist, a collagist, a minimalist, a Dadaist, an existentialist, and a postmodernist" (22). It is an extensive, but incomplete list, for Rosemary Jackson in her *Fantasy: The Literature of Subversion* places him among the literary fantasists (164). As the embodiment of a literary period—American postmodernism—he was all of the above and more. Responses to his work were intense and often at variance. It was daunting to some, nonsense to others, abstract, concrete, irreverent, wonderful, trivial, each qualifier depending on the humor and sensibilities of those making the judgment, but his fiction was always rich enough and elusive enough to bear the weight of serious inquiry. **"The Sandman,"** an epistolary fiction abounding in arcane references, is no exception. Although its surface text seems simple enough, appropriated and concealed subtexts complicate any detailed discussion to the point of confusion, creating a situation that justifies a compass for keeping us on course. The four points of that compass are the following:

•First, the primary text is a story by Donald Barthelme called **"The Sandman,"** which takes the form of a letter to a lover's psychiatrist. As such it possesses an internal writer, the correspondent, and an internal reader, Dr. Hodder.

•Second, the title of the story recalls E. T. A. Hoffmann's fantastic tale "The Sandman," although the correspondent disingenuously claims he has the sandman of nursery rhyme in mind.

•Third, Hoffmann's tale was interpreted by Sigmund Freud in his essay "The 'Uncanny'" as an Oedipal struggle in which a father-castrator figure destroys the son. This figure appears as two different men with the names of Coppelius and Coppola in different parts of the tale.

•Fourth, Dr. Hodder, as a psychiatrist, would have known Freud's essay, and the correspondent's arcane references reveal his own knowledge of psychological literature, making his awareness of Freud's sandman-castrator equation evident to Hodder, which in turn explains the doctor's annoyance at being called a sandman. It also subjects the letter writer's protestation of innocence to irony.

The invisible presence of Hoffmann's tale and Freud's interpretation addresses Dr. Hodder and us in a dialogue of texts. As Mikhail Bakhtin insists the word, "permeated with the interpretations of others," is never innocent (202).[1] Some, however, are less innocent than others, and Barthelme's fiction is the least innocent of all. In the absence of innocence an elucidation of the story by means of other texts is justifiable because it takes into account the literary space of prior voices, a space analogous to the dark matter of galaxies—present, measurable, but unseen.

In a confrontational voice the letter writer assails psychiatry and indirectly portrays the doctor as a modern extension of Hoffmann's sandman even though the two stories are superficially different. One conveys well-motivated hostility toward a lover's psychiatrist; the other is a tale about a young man's obsessive fear of losing his eyes to the sandman. One of the effects of approaching this story contextually is that such a method reveals the similarity of the two as Oedipal struggles while exposing the complex layers of an assault that uses Freudian interpretation against itself.

Hoffman's tale begins with a series of letters, the first recounting Nathaniel's childhood memories of being sent to bed with a warning that the sandman is coming, a warning always accompanied by the heavy tread of a visitor. Hoffmann's use of folklore occurs when Nathaniel's nurse explains that the sandman throws sand into children's eyes, making those organs jump from their sockets to be gathered up by the sandman and carried away. On occasion after occasion of grotesque fantasy one encounters the severed part as a defining feature of the genre. So it is not surprising to see it in a tale that depends on tradition for much of its effect.

This is significant in the context of Freud's analysis of the tale, which asserts that psychoanalytic experience teaches us fear for one's eyes is a childhood anxiety often retained by adults and morbid concerns about eyes and blindness are manifest fears of castration: "In blinding himself, Oedipus, that mythical law-breaker, was simply carrying out a mitigated form of the punishment of castration—the only punishment that according to the *lex talionis* was fitted for him" (137).

Freud goes on to contend that, in spite of all arguments to the contrary, dreams, myths, and fantasies establish a substitutive relation between the eye and the reproductive organs. Without offering examples other than Oedipus, he writes, "All further doubts are removed when we get the details of their 'castration-complex' from the analyses of neurotic patients, and realize its immense importance in their mental life" (138).

One literary example supporting this contention in graphically violent and sexual scenes is Georges Bataille's *Story of the Eye*. Juxtaposing an eye and a bull testis Bataille explicitly equates the two in the following passage from that novel:

> Thus, two globes of equal size and consistency had suddenly been propelled in opposite directions at once. One, the white ball of the bull, had been thrust into the "pink and dark" cunt that Simone had bared to the crowd; the other, a human eye, had spurted from Granero's head with the same force as a bundle of innards from a belly. This coincidence, tied to death and to a sort of urinary liquefaction of the sky, first brought us back to . . .
>
> (75-76)

The ghastly sight of Granero's dangling eye produces a monorchid image as he is borne away. Another example less esoteric than Bataille's novel is the familiar story of Samson's emasculation and blinding, which lends conviction to the idea.

Nathaniel's childhood fear is powerfully felt, but not enough to negate his voyeuristic attraction to the threat. Resolving to see the sandman the child hides in his father's study and sees Coppelius the lawyer, who calls out while working at the hearth, "Eyes here! Eyes here!" (Hoffmann 6). Nathaniel reveals himself involuntarily and is seized by Coppelius. The father's plea saves the boy's eyes from the glowing coals Coppelius is about to deliver to them, but does not save him from a thorough shaking at the hands of his tormentor or prevent a long illness.

At a later, similar visit from Coppelius the father is killed by an explosion. Freud stresses the intimate connection between the student's anxiety about his eyes and his father's death and Hoffmann is clear about linking Nathaniel's father and Coppelius:

> Good God! as my old father bent down over the fire, how different he looked! His gentle and venerable features seemed to be drawn up by some dreadful convulsive pain into an ugly, repulsive Satanic mask. He looked like Coppelius.
>
> (6)

The father-Coppelius figures represent the two opposites created by the child's ambivalence toward his father: one threatens to blind (castrate) him, the other saves his eyes.

Years later while away at school Nathaniel receives in his room Coppola, an itinerant optician in whom the student sees his old nemesis, now saying, "What! Nee weatherglasses? Nee weatherglasses? 've got foine oyes as well—foine oyes!" (20). He offers spectacles for sale and a telescope, which Nathaniel purchases. The motivation for this act is unclear until we see that it allows him to look across into Professor Spalanzani's house, a second manifestation of voyeurism, to see the professor's strange daughter, Olympia. Obsession follows; his love for Clara at home is forgotten; but he soon discovers the professor and the optician struggling over Olympia, the wooden doll they have contrived to give life to, shaking her eyes out of her head as Coppola carries her off. Spalanzani snatches up her eyeballs from the floor and throws them at Nathaniel, claiming Coppola has stolen them from the student.

Freud proceeds to identify Olympia as the personification of Nathaniel's narcissism so that the struggle between Coppola and Spalanzani over Olympia can be seen as a doubling of the earlier struggle over Nathaniel's eyes by the father-Coppelius figures.

As might be expected, the susceptible Nathaniel enters his second long illness, going mad, crying out, "Fire wheel—fire wheel! Spin round, fire wheel! merrily, merrily! Aha! wooden doll! spin round, pretty wooden doll!" (31). In this condition he attempts to strangle the authority figure of the professor, but the murder is prevented by neighbors.

The second illness is followed by apparent recovery and plans for Clara and Nathaniel to marry. Walking with his betrothed, he agrees to mount the tower of the town hall. She draws his attention to a curious figure coming along the street. Unable to resist the voyeuristic impulse in spite of all that has occurred, Nathaniel gazes through his telescope at the figure. One look through the glass reveals Coppelius and is enough to trigger the third illness of the tale, a new madness in which he attempts to fling his fian-

cée from the tower as he shouts, "Spin round, wooden doll!" (34). Her brother saves her, leaving the raving man above, shrieking, "Spin round, fire wheel! Spin round, fire wheel!" (34). When the people want to go up and overpower the lunatic, Coppelius laughs and says, "Wait a bit; he'll come down of his own accord" (34). And he is right. Catching sight of the lawyer, Nathaniel suddenly shrieks, "Ha! foine oyes! foine oyes!" (34) and throws himself down to the pavement.

According to Freud, the child's repressed death wish against the father finds expression in the father's death, but the full responsibility for the death of the father shifts to Coppelius, thus if not exonerating Nathaniel of all complicity in the death, at least transferring the guilt and providing an object for his hostility, which he actively directs against the authority figure of the lawyer Coppelius and his double, the optician Coppola. "I am resolved to enter the lists against him and revenge my father's death, let the consequences be what they may" (9). However, the solution—which is only a displacement of culpability—is no solution at all, for in the end Nathaniel succumbs to the will of authority. The very presence of Coppelius is sufficient to compel his self-destruction.

Although the three instances of spying seem to invite Freudian attention to voyeurism, to its built-in tensions of attraction and the need to keep a careful distance, and to their roles of introducing the three illnesses, which parallel Coppelius's function of interrupting sexual fulfillment, Freud passes up the opportunity to avail himself of that material and topic.

Before we finish reading the first paragraph of Barthelme's story, we see a request from the letter writer: "Please consider this an 'eyes only' letter' (191). It is the sort of expression—a commonplace of confidential notes, reports, and memoranda and a category of governmental secrecy—we might expect from a correspondent who is writing his lover's psychiatrist, an act that is itself transgressive and a power play. By virtue of the phrase's naturalness it slips through unless we remember it is addressed to the individual most likely to understand the sexual connotations of visual organs in a Freudian context. Still early on—in the second paragraph of the letter—Barthelme's correspondent admits he knows Hodder is irked by his little nickname for him, but insists he means nothing malicious by it:

> I know, for example, that my habit of referring to you as "the sandman" annoys you but let me assure you that I mean nothing unpleasant by it. It is simply a nickname. The reference is to the old rhyme: "Sea-sand does the sandman bring / Sleep to end the day / He dusts the children's eyes with sand / And steals their dreams away." (This is a variant; there are other versions, but this is the one I prefer.)
>
> (191-92)

Some who read the reference to the sandman of rhyme may wish to take this assurance as a reliable disclaimer. However to accept it at face value is to be misled by the correspondent's partial concealment of the appropriated text. He wants the doctor to know what he meant while being able to deny it. Concealing his source, rather than depriving it of interest, works to increase the density and force of that interest through its multivalence. If we frame our reading of the story with Hoffmann's tale and Freud's psychoanalytic text, we can see the letter writer's words are not innocent. They have been inhabited and conditioned by others. This prior conditioning reveals the letter writer's intention of going beyond, or behind, his utterance by means of context. His words would have a meaning quite different from their ironic content were he not writing to a psychiatrist who shares his lover's favors.

For someone initiated into the specialized reading of Freud's "The 'Uncanny'" sandman could never be simply a nickname; for Dr. Hodder it would be an accusation of castrator. The sinister effect of an apparently innocent term depends on the correspondent's ability to convey to the doctor his knowledge of standard psychological texts. Hence the references to Percy's "Toward a Triadic Theory of Meaning," Straus's "Shame as a Historiological Problem," and Ehrenzweig's *The Hidden Order of Art.* They support his arguments, but they also ensure Dr. Hodder's recognition that the allusions are intentional, the denials insincere. Toward that end the letter writer enrolls the chastening trope of irony and the sharp edge of wit to undermine his rival's position.

Barthelme's correspondent locates the origin of his hostility toward the authority of psychiatry in his earlier trusting visits to a Dr. Behring, who blusters indignantly about a civil rights injustice, but fails to act in any way to correct it, demanding instead to know what the writer is going to do about the situation. Barthelme's reworking of this hostility from the Hoffmann text seems clear enough once it is recognized. However his narrator is so convincingly motivated that we may not read Doctors Behring and Hodder as extensions of father/Coppélius and Spalanzani/Coppola, those projections of Nathaniel's ambivalence toward his father.

Although Freud avoids voyeurism as a topic the letter writer explicitly reminds Dr. Hodder that he has diagnosed Susan's openness as voyeurism, "an eroticized expression of curiosity whose chief phenomenological characteristic is the distance maintained between the voyeur and the object" (195). According to this position the tension created by opposing emotions—the desire to draw near and the need to maintain distance—is what the voyeur seeks. Unavoidably we are reminded of Nathaniel's fear of losing his eyes, while at the same time unable to resist the desire to see the very sandman who would steal his eyes away. The correspondent first denies that distance is one of Susan's needs, then suggests that the doctor is actually attempting behavioral modification which will interfere with her sexuality. And interfering with sexual fulfillment is exactly the function of Hoffmann's sandman each time he appears in one of his guises, as Freud points out—separating Nathaniel from his betrothed, destroying Olympia, and

compelling madness and suicide just as the lovers are reconciled and about to marry.

At the end of the epistle Barthelme's correspondent returns to this theme with a telling anecdote after alluding to the doctor's attempts to undermine his relation with Susan by saying he is not supportive enough during her depressions:

> One night we were at her place, about three a.m., and this man called, another lover, quite a well-known musician who is very good, very fast—a good man. He asked Susan "Is he there?" meaning me, and she said "Yes," and he said "What are you doing?" and she said, "What do you think?" and he said, "When will you be finished?" and she said, "Never." Are you, Doctor dear, in a position to appreciate the beauty of this reply, in this context?

> (197-98)

In this context he drops all pretense of innocence, turning to the immediacy of sexuality in his relations with Susan, and declares his commitment to that sexuality without the repression we see in Hoffmann's tale. Unlike Nathaniel he will not yield to authority and self-destruction. The ringing taunt hurled at the psychiatrist is clear: No sandman—neither the good, fast musician, nor Dr. Hodder—is going to interfere with his love and steal his dreams away.

To a crucial extent Barthelme's letter writer is an agent of transformation, attempting to subvert the authority of Dr. Hodder, and a conserver of the *status quo,* seeking to maintain his relationship with Susan. The contradiction parallels Barthelme's successful attempt to conceal superficially his appropriated text, rendering it invisible, while at the same time making it possible to measure its dark presence. The other texts function for the letter writer as commentaries on Dr. Hodder and are useful in his attack on psychiatry, an attack that is not itself completely free from the Freudian myth. For we can hear a little too much protest in the correspondent's defiance to be thoroughly convinced he has thrown off the bonds of the father. This dependence on subtexts is the dialogic imperative insisted on by the principle of prior voices, and in this instance it is essential for a full appreciation of Barthelme's **"The Sandman."**

Notes

1. For additional discussions of the role prior voices play in narrative see also M. M. Bakhtin, *The Dialogic Imagination: Four Essays,* ed. Michael Holquist, trans. Caryl Emerson and Michael Holquist (Austin: U of Texas P, 1981).

Works Cited

Bakhtin, M. M. *Problems of Dostoevsky's Poetics.* Trans. Caryl Emerson. Minneapolis: U of Minnesota P, 1984.

Barthelme, Donald. "The Sandman." *Sixty Stories.* New York: Putnam's, 1981. 191-98.

Bataille, Georges. *Story of the Eye.* Trans. Joachim Neu-groschel. New York: Urizen, 1977.

Freud, Sigmund. "The 'Uncanny.'" *On Creativity and the Unconscious.* Trans. Alix Strachey. New York: Harper Torchbooks-Harper, 1958. 122-61.

Hoffmann, E. T. A. "The Sandman." *The Tales of Hoffmann.* Trans. J. T. Bealby. New York: Heritage, 1943.

Jackson, Rosemary. *Fantasy: The Literature of Subversion.* London: Methuen, 1981.

"The Talk of the Town." *The New Yorker,* 14 August 1989: 22-24.

Stanley Trachtenberg (essay date 1990)

SOURCE: Trachtenberg, Stanley. "Barthelme the Scrivener." In *Understanding Donald Barthelme,* pp. 102-64. Columbia: University of South Carolina Press, 1990.

[*In the following essay, Trachtenberg provides a thematic overview of Barthelme's short fiction.*]

Art, Barthelme insists, cannot *not* think of the world.[1] Accordingly, in his fiction, the function of art and the situation of the artist provides an enabling metaphor by which it becomes possible to come to terms with a resistant and often opaque reality, whose disappointment and confusions are not so much dispelled by language as mediated, or, in the best case, perhaps even confronted by it in such a way as to change, if not the world, then at least the reader's awareness of its possibilities. The stories about art seldom interrogate either its meanings or its effect, other than on the artists themselves and the difficulties they experience in creating it. As an object in the fictive landscape, then, art as art, like the urban settings or the figures that inhabit them in much of Barthelme's fiction, emerges more in outline than in any realized depth.

Calling attention to the situation of Barthelme's artistic narrators, Wayne Stengel points to their insistence on a more meaningful reality than one provided by the art itself. At the same time, Stengel notes, they "regard art as a self-contained object without necessary meaning beyond its surface appearance or assumed reference to a world outside itself."[2] The lack of a recognizable environment does not, as Stengel argues that it does, ask the reader to become involved in the process of the story. Rather, as part of that process, it resists interpretation in favor of re-imagining ordinary reality. In **"How I Write My Songs,"** another of the previously uncollected stories which appeared in *Sixty Stories,* the parody of the creative process revolves around the simplistic explanations the narrator provides of his method and the naïvete of his imitative approach. Despite the copybook account which reduces the art of songwriting to a commercial formula, despite the misspellings ("When I lost my baby / I almost lost my mine") which suggest the writer has little understanding of

the sense and no authentic idea of the feeling behind his traditional lyrics, despite the clichéd sentiment with which he concludes, the elemental force of the lyrics confirms the narrator's conviction that "what may appear to be rather plain or dull on paper becomes quite different when it is a song."[3]

The blankness or opacity, the discontinuities, interruptions, digressions, hesitations, incompleted thoughts, elliptical structure, and uncertain reference of language, all subject the narrative to a compression that both invests it with an intensity and places it seemingly beyond the reach of thematic focus. Just such a focus is given, however, by a comic perspective that, in American fiction at least, reaches back to the nineteenth century example of Herman Melville's "Bartleby the Scrivener." Built around the metaphor of a writer and the public, Melville's elusive parable describes the conflict between an eccentric law copyist and his seemingly obtuse employer. The specific circumstances of the tale are left pretty much untold. Almost childlike, even petulant in his stony refusal to accept either instruction or request, Bartleby offers nothing to account for his behavior. About his past, the lawyer admits, "nothing is ascertainable except from original sources, and in his case, those are very small."[4] In fact, original sources prove inaccessible. This lack of origins does not serve as the animating force of the story by prompting Bartleby to go in search of them. Rather it is a condition deliberately imposed by the scrivener, who will tell the lawyer nothing about himself or even indicate any reasonable objections he might have to such disclosure.

Bartleby's negation, in fact, appears so comprehensive as to convert his protest against meaninglessness into a statement of it. Indifferent as an inanimate object to any claims upon him, Bartleby is, at the same time, immovable as any natural force. His refusal of every suggestion the lawyer makes about employment while continuing to insist that he is not particular (a term which in context thus has significant resonance) suggests the joke with which the appeals for reason are uniformly greeted throughout Melville's fiction. In ironic counterpoint to the bust of Cicero at which he stares and mirroring its vacant, eyeless sockets, Bartleby's eloquent silence is, in fact, universal. His ultimately infectious habit of using the term "prefer" gives the illusion of choice to what proves an insistent if not immiscible condition. His opposition to fate, then, becomes itself the judgment of fate—equally cold and inflexible, ubiquitous, finally imprisoning no less than silently imprisoned. Bartleby, in short, changes from a victim of an indifferent universe to a symbol of its negation.

As with so much else in this puzzling tale, Melville leaves uncertain the lawyer's relation to his clerk; yet this, too, becomes somewhat less intimidating when it is seen in the context of a joke. If Bartleby is unwilling to perform the functions of a scrivener, the lawyer, a self-acknowledged storyteller takes delight in the sound of words and is able to find an element of beauty even in the blankness of walls. Neither in his legal nor his literary manner does the lawyer evidence any interest in originality. He describes himself as a "conveyancer and title hunter" and, in fact, becomes himself a copyist, not only imitating even the characteristic expression Bartleby employs but also echoing for a time the scrivener's withdrawal into self-imposed isolation. In an effort to elude those who, like the landlord of his former offices or the current tenants who persist in holding him accountable for Bartleby's continued occupancy, he reduces his lifestyle to a minimum, consisting chiefly of fugitive visits to the suburbs and, in what can only be the last stages of desperation, to Jersey City and Hoboken.

Despite his smug boast of safety, then, a boast which, it turns out, is mistaken, his pride in his prudence and method, above all, his overblown rhetoric, the lawyer is able, as Bartleby is not, to displace a "doctrine of assumptions" with an awareness of the "noise and heat and joy of the roaring thoroughfares at noon" (128). It is, in fact, precisely this intermingling of classical and commonplace, the punctuation of exaggerated narrative formality with sly hints of self-awareness, deliberately concealed backgrounds, and abruptly transformed characters, that caution against too great a preoccupation with interpreting life and a consequent loss of its more substantial immediacy, even within the framework of literary construction, perhaps within that framework most of all. The resistance of rhetoric to interpretation allows the lawyer elegiacally to commiserate not only with humanity but even with the principle of emptiness that opposes it.[5] Recognizing the inescapability of that confrontation, the lawyer shows as well the tragi-comic possibilities with which, as scrivener, he can mediate with reality. And in telling the story, he settles for a rueful acceptance of the fact that there is no way to make sense of it and that no answers, now or in future, will be forthcoming.

For Barthelme, as for Melville, these limited possibilities remain centered in the object of representation and, in particular, in its distinctive verbal quality rather than in the formal unity of its disparate elements, perhaps most prominent among them, the unnamed but isolating horror and the "domestic associations" without whose humanizing influence, the lawyer is convinced, one is led even to acts of murder, or, more poignantly, in whose absence the indifferent scrivener is seen to waste away. *Sadness,* Barthelme's fourth collection of short stories, seems to mark a shift in emphasis in his work that recognizes in the presence of the commonplace a necessary balance to the nihilistic horrors accompanied in such earlier stories as **"The Policeman's Ball"** (*City Life*) by a hooting chorus of melodramatic laughter. And while maintaining their emotional detachment, the stories additionally seem to find the dilemmas of modern existence less a subject for bemused indifference, or even playful hilarity, than for tense recognition and for exploration of the often parallel difficulties faced by the artist. The sadness of the title, accordingly, refers to the largely domestic anxieties prompted by the exaggerated expectations generated in literary forms and the consequent inability to satisfy those expectations. Such

disappointment leads to the separation of the couple in **"Critique de la Vie Quotidienne,"** which, Barthelme has acknowledged, was salvaged from an earlier attempt at a novel.[6] The narrator and his wife, Wanda, struggle unsuccessfully to cope with the banalities of everyday life and, in particular, with the demands of child-rearing. The results are discouraging. "The world in the evening seems fraught with the absence of promise," the narrator complains, "if you are a married man."[7] The qualification which opposes evening and romance to the daily routine of marriage is crucial and points to an unwillingness to deal with limits. The consequence of such childish self-absorption (the wife sucks her thumb while the narrator yells at their child; he retreats from the marriage in alcoholism and hostility), is envy of the extravagant displays of wealth in their society, mutual antagonism, and a general state of boredom. When the couple is confronted with the limits of mortality by death-masks their child has learned to make at school, the father demands to know the meaning of the knowing look with which the child displays them. "You'll find out," he is warned. The refusal to heed that warning leads to a divorce, whose appearance of civility breaks down into mutual recrimination and an attempt by the wife to shoot her ex-husband. Not even this dramatic expression of buried feeling marks a change in their lives. Following the divorce, Wanda immerses herself in the study of esoteric subjects, the narrator attempts to soothe his own fear of death with the anticipation of a limitless supply of scotch whiskey, and the child is placed, significantly, in an experimental nursery.

The same exhaustion, preoccupation with the trivial, and self-absorption in contemporary culture informs **"The Party,"** which begins with the admission by the narrator that "I went to a party and corrected a pronounciation" ([*Sadness*; hereafter] *S* 57). Unable to distinguish between significant variations of art and influenced by movie cliché expressions of anxiety ("Drums, drums, drums, outside the windows"), the guests are indifferent even to the arrival at the party of the sudden towering figure of King Kong ("Giant hands, black, thick with fur, reaching in through the windows" (*S* 57), a pop-culture icon of brute passion combined with sentimentality. Kong's menace, it turns out, has been acculturated; the ape now teaches art history at a public university, where his interest is in seduction rather than primitive expression of desire.

Like the others in the room, the narrator remains largely passive and pessimistic about his chances to break out of the torpor which envelops his generation with its "emphasis on emotional cost control as well as its insistent, almost annoying lucidity." The annoyance stems from the refusal to confront the problems inherent in ordinary life. "What made us think," the narrator asks rhetorically, "that we would escape things like bankruptcy, alcoholism, being disappointed, having children?" (*S* 62). Though uncomfortable in this environment, in which ambitious people desperate for entertainment reduce experience to word games and in which literary fashion substitutes for felt response ("Now that you have joined us in finding Kafka, and Kleist, too, the awesome figures that we have agreed that they are"), he can only appeal to his companion, Francesca, to take some decisive action which will enable them to leave (*S* 62). Her refusal to leave the party does not indicate contentment with her situation or even a fundamental difference with the narrator's philosophy. In a kind of helpless self-justification that is often exchanged by a couple regretfully agreeing to the necessity of a divorce, he insists, "Of course we did everything right, insofar as we were able to imagine what 'right' was" (*S* 62). In the social climate that continues to make extravagant demands for fulfillment, such efforts prove resistant even to the compelling power of words. "When one has spoken a lot," the narrator is persuaded, "one has already used up all of the ideas one has. You must change the people you are speaking to so that you appear, to yourself, to be still alive" (*S* 61).

Change mistaken for the appearance of vitality also marks the manner in which the narrator attempts to deal with his inability either to understand or meaningfully affect his circumstances and leads to a final appeal to Francesca to reject him so that he may try something else. In the absence of any response from her, the narrator is unable to make one of his own or even to believe any longer that discriminations of value are necessary. "Is it really important to know that this movie is fine, and that one terrible," he concludes hopelessly, "and to talk intelligently about the difference? Wonderful elegance! No good at all!" (*S* 62).

The self-doubt which leads to that final dispiriting assessment is more hopefully resolved in **"The Temptation of Saint Anthony"** by the assertion of value in the sheer phenomenal quality of existence. The story is narrated by one of the members of a local community in which St. Anthony takes up residence. In contrast to his neighbors for whom, he notes waspishly, "everything is hard enough without having to deal with something that is not tangible and clear" (*S* 151), and who consequently find the higher orders of abstraction to be a nuisance, the narrator claims to find them interesting. What he admires chiefly is the marvelous or ineffable which, he contends, in a world of mundanity allows the saint to shine. His sense of decency, to some extent self-congratulatory, misses the point. St. Anthony unexpectedly reveals a fondness for such banal delights as fried foods and department store carpeting and diplomatically adopts an offhand manner designed to make his presence less disturbing to the community. It is these temptations of the commonplace—the attractive quality of things—that he must struggle with. His ascetic refusal to give in to them finally prevents his ability to choose, and, toward the end of his residence in the community, he is heard to say only the word "Or."

When Camilla, an unconventional if provocative young woman of the town, accuses him of attempting some physical intimacy, this lack of definition rather than any truth to the accusation leads St. Anthony to return to the desert. But not without a final, unsettling revelation. Less an es-

cape from the alternatives of ordinary life than an exclusion from them, the saint amusingly confesses to the narrator in the last line of the story that he regarded the temptations as "entertainment."

The refusal to take the whole thing seriously hints at the attitude Barthelme encourages the reader to adopt as well. Though the narrator's response to the saint is sympathetic, his folksy tone and gossipy manner, at odds with his use of sophisticated diction, his pretentious moralizing, and his fondness for the abstract, work against his authority as an authorial surrogate. He is narrowly judgmental about Camilla who, he points out, "went to the Sorbonne and studied some kind of philosophy called 'structure' with somebody named Levy who is supposed to be very famous" (*S* 158). Overly insistent on his indifference to the possibility of the saint's having given in to sexual temptation, and seemingly unaware of the implied condescension in his boast of periodic visits to the saint when he is not vacationing with his wife in Florida, he ironically (and, for the purposes of the story, unknowingly) condemns those people who resent St. Anthony's indifference to the material world and wish he would "go out and get a job, like everybody else." Thus the narrator values St. Anthony for the very qualities of withdrawal the story works to resist. In a deeply human if ambiguous sense, he cannot accept the idea of the ordinary as itself exceptional and yet recognizes that "you have to keep the ordinary motors of life running in the meantime" (*S* 153).

In **"The Sandman,"** the narrator reaches something of the same conclusion. "The best thing to do," he advises, "is just to do ordinary things, read the newspaper, for example, or watch basketball, or wash the dishes" (*S* 95). Sometimes taken as a defense of imagination or art, the story takes the form of a letter to Dr. Hodder, a psychiatrist, who regards the desire of his patient Susan to terminate analysis and buy a piano instead as symptomatic of her illness and so of her need to continue analysis. Normative and aberrant behavior quickly become reversed. Written by Susan's boyfriend, who, like St. Anthony, is confronted by the prospect of seemingly limitless alternatives, the letter acknowledges the hidden impulses that may account for behavior but sees in them an accurate reflection of conditions that may respond more to neglect than to treatment. "What do you do with a patient who finds the world unsatisfactory?" he asks, "The world *is* unsatisfactory; only a fool would deny it" (*S* 95). In contrast, then, to the utopian impulse to which he drily alludes in the repeated song refrain, "The world is waiting for the sunrise," the narrator insists that he is content with Susan "as is," an acceptance of the ability to affect experience, not merely the way we think about it, that is as equally distant from Ramona's reluctant acknowledgment of the world's throbbing sexuality as it is from the psychiatrist's attempt at normative manipulation.

This reductive concern for the ordinary projected in a "muted series of irritation, frustrations, and bafflements" rather than in the more dramatic emotions of existential dread has led the critic Alan Wilde to find in Barthelme's fiction the possibilities for a more dynamic response than that promised solely by the modernist escape to a vision of fictive order.[8] Life in Barthelme's fiction, Wilde concludes, has become less mysterious but more puzzling, by which I take him to mean that it has lost not only its belief in the supernatural but in the ability and even the desire of fiction to convincingly represent that belief. As a result, it preempts the struggle of characters to search for meaning within the text and moves instead from a self-contained world which circumscribes their existence toward an enveloping one that accounts for their reality, in other words, moves from the interior to the surface of a work.

That movement is facilitated by the illustrations which, as in **"At the Tolstoy Museum,"** once again reduce the text to the status of a caption in **"The Flight of Pigeons from the Palace."** The story addresses the ever-increasing demands of the public for sensational performance by the artist and consequently conceives of art as a collection of sideshow exhibits at a circus or an old-fashioned theater bill. "It is difficult to keep the public interested," the narrator explains, and lists among the promised attractions The Prime Rate, Edgar Allan Poe, and The Sale of the Public Library, before concluding with the announcement of a new volcano, pictured with suitable irony in the middle of an eruption. The illustrations include numbered drawings from an anatomy text, statues, groupings of figures in different styles and from different historical eras, as well as mock Renaissance-style perspective drawings which, as R. E. Johnson points out, flatten the illusion by projecting the lines which are superimposed on the central image off the drawing into some infinite point beyond where the picture can be seen to begin or end.[9] What is perhaps most significant about these illustrations, however, is the contrast between the accuracy of the descriptions and the tortured interpretations which the narrator draws from them. Literal representation, Barthelme appears to suggest, is not by itself either immune to or a refuge against the distortions of the imagination.

Art seems to consent to its own destruction in **"Supoena,"** which indirectly addresses the framing conditions that link the narrative to the world in which it exists. The narrator is sent a tax notice from the obscurely sinister "Bureau of Compliance" on a robot or surrogate called Charles he has built to, among other things, "instruct him in complacency." Like the audience demands in **"The Flight of Pigeons from the Palace,"** the tax seems greater than the narrator's ability to pay and forces him to disassemble the robot. The consequences remain ambivalent. Charles's detachment from social conditions and the obligation to take some action to alleviate them serve as an example for the narrator's own posture. Looking at him, the narrator confesses, "I said to myself, 'See, it is possible to live in the world and not change the world'" (*S* 116). Charles thus functions a surrogate not only for the narrator but for fiction itself. In this regard, he suggests a role which balances impersonal objectivity with the need for immersion in the everyday. "Without Charles," the narrator realizes

with alarm, "without his example, his exemplary quietude, I run the risk of acting, the risk of risk. I must participate. I must leave the house and walk about" (*S* 116). Displacing to fiction his obligation to become involved in reality, the narrator not only evades that responsibility but reduces fictive possibilities as well. His desperate cry, then, is not exclusively an expression of repressed emotion or even an appeal for involvement in experience. It is a statement of the ambivalence with which fiction must address the often conflicting requirements of actuality and imagination, the opposing claims of didactic and aesthetic impulses, the demands of form and those of feeling.

The artist-hero of **"Engineer-Private Paul Klee Misplaces an Aircraft between Milbertshofen and Cambrai, March 1916"** provides an indication of how Barthelme hopes to reconcile those demands in his struggle with both his art and the Secret Police. Drafted into the army, Klee has been assigned to escort a train transporting aircraft to various bases across Germany but takes more interest in the life around him. His interior monologues alternate with those of the police, who watch closely to discover what he is doing and learn, as they reveal, his secret, really the secret of his art. This proves to be Klee's concern with the ordinary course of his life: the sale of his drawings, the meaninglessness of the war, the arrangements he makes to meet his lover. In a statement that echoes the process of art described in **"City Life,"** he points out, "There are always unexpected delays, reroutings, backtrackings" (*S* 65), but while concentrating on its details—"He is reading a book of Chinese short stories." "He has removed his boots." "His feet rest twenty-six centimeters from the baggage-car stove."—the police are unable to see their significance (*S* 66). Klee is more concerned with the quality of experience. "These Chinese short stories are slight and lovely," he thinks (*S* 66). When he notices one of the planes unaccountably missing, he decides to alter the manifest (the artist, he observes, is not so different from the forger) and to replace the plane with a drawing. The drawing, however, is not of the plane but of its absence, and it is this absence-as-presence which allows the police to accept, if not fully appreciate, the contradictions they have attempted to monitor. The association of the police with critics is suggested in their final assessment of Klee's achievement:

> We would like to embrace him as a comrade and brother but unfortunately we are not embraceable. We are secret, we exist in the shadows, the pleasure of the comradely/brotherly embrace is one of the pleasures we are denied, in our dismal service.
>
> (*S* 70)

But if criticism is short, art, Klee is aware, like chocolate, meltingly sweet, at once temporary and eternal, goes on forever.

In **"The Catechist,"** art out of the machine emerges in the confession of a 40-year-old priest who has fallen in love with a married woman and who responds to the incantatory and comic catalog of the way hatred of Sundays is expressed in various countries with a contrasting specificity of detail. The strategy of naming and, in particular, of naming absences thus serves as a means not only of calling them into being but of acknowledging their magical existence. It is this existence in all its variousness which prompted the priest's sense of vocation. Asked by the catechist if he initially heard a call, he replies "I heard many things. Screams. Suites for unaccompanied cello" (*S* 125).

In contrast to a postage-sized Old Testament the catechist produces and almost at once replaces in favor of a button on which is printed the word "Love," the priest remembers the picture on a stamp he used to mail a letter to his lover and responds to his superior's dry textbook formula for dealing with apathy with the following recognition: "I think: Analysis terminable and interminable. I think: Then she will leave the park looking backward over her shoulder" (*S* 125). As opposed to the interpretation, it is the perceived instant that stirs the emotion (of the catechist as well as the sinful priest) so that what endures, paradoxically, is the perishable human gesture, whose meaning rests entirely in its transience and its preservation solely in the repetitive form of memory.

"Damier," the concluding story in *Sadness,* reinforces the need to connect the imaginative with the everyday world by examining the attempt to escape not from an unsympathetic public but from the desire, at once limitless and limited, which is to say the authentic configuration of the self. Daumier, the central figure, whose name evokes that of the great nineteenth century French master of caricature, describes himself as a "tourist of the emotions." He projects two fictive alter egos, or surrogates as he calls them. Both, he acknowledges, are designed to permit a distraction of "the original, authentic self, which is a dirty great villain, as can be testified and sworn to by anyone who has every been awake" (*S* 163). In contrast to that self, villainous because insatiable, the surrogates are in principle, satiable, which is to say, can be designed with adventures that are brought to an end. The ambition to structure art in this way proves an example of the narrator's hubris and meets an appropriately ironic fate when the narrator ultimately opens his own world to that of one of his fictive creations.

Arranged in a series of disconnected passages, each of which, like a Victorian novel, is headed by a brief description of its contents or of the action to come, the story leads to levels within fictive levels, complicated even further by allusions to several genres—the western, the historical romance, the domestic comedy, and the story within a story among them. Often these become literalized metaphors. When the original Daumier comments that one of his surrogates rides "the plains and pampas of [his] consciousness," the following scene takes place on just such a location. When he imagines a scene in his mind's eye, he goes on to imagine a mind's neck as well.

There are frequent indications these inventions are to be responded to as pictures rather than as narrative. Along with abrupt shifts, lists, passages of literary quotation, or

mixtures of highly stylized and colloquial diction that interrupt the narrative to confirm its artificiality; the situations themselves, as John Ditsky among others has noted, are self-consciously pictorial, a device Barthelme employs to undermine the authority of plot.[10] Rather than suggest the relation between the various elements of the story, the compositional effect is highly ironic. In one passage, for example, a fictive possibility is translated into a literal situation:

> Two men in horse-riding clothes stood upon a plain, their attitudes indicating close acquaintance or colleagueship. The plain presented in its foreground a heavy yellow oblong salt lick rendered sculptural by the attentions over a period of time of sheep or other salt-loving animals. Two horses in the situation's upper lefthand corner watched the men with nervous horse-gaze.
>
> (*S* 165)

Daumier himself engages in a discussion of this fictive strategy with a friend named Gibbon, who attributes his comparatively untroubled sense of self-worth to his having been raised without the use of irony. Gibbon, however, confesses finally that he doesn't have enough money to pay for the drinks the two men are having and, in fact, can offer only the bizarre alternative of Krishna Socialism as an alternative to fiction as a means of meliorating the anxieties which trouble both men and presumably everyone else as well.

Unlike the satiability of his surrogates, the narrator's claim of impersonality, proves spurious. As in **"The Balloon,"** he intrudes to acknowledge the function of the story as compensatory. Then, literally folding his characters away in tissue paper, he underscores their flatness and their fragility. It is, in fact, one of the surrogates who provides him with a formula that applies to his fictive existence and through it to the enveloping idea of fiction as well. "There are always openings, if you can find them," a second Daumier promises, "there is always something to do" (*S* 179). The promise comes at a time when the original Daumier finds himself at a dead end in his life no less than in his fiction. His romantic attachments seem to last exactly two years; his hope of doing something great "perhaps in the field of popular music, or light entertainment in general" is shadowed by the sense of his own mortality. "You eye the bed, the record-player, the pictures," he thinks, "already making lists of who will take what" (*S* 179).

By plunging the self into comically proliferating openings, Barthelme struggles against what one of the surrogates, perhaps in at least partial self-justification, calls "the cocoon of habituation." At the same time, he exposes the artificiality of the strategy the artist employs in an attempt to separate the story from autobiography. What needs to be remembered is that the strategy Daumier adopts is one of replication rather than novelty, one whose force, as his companion Amelia skeptically seems to be aware, rests, if anything, in a more realistic assessment of possibilities than Daumier is prepared to admit. If the self is to be reassured, or, as Daumier proposes, at least distracted, conviction must come from the energy and movement of the city itself. Barthelme conveys this movement in a descriptive passage that further complicates the narrative's fantastic mingling of plots. Daumier imagines a surrogate and his cowboy band driving a herd of *au-pair* girls into a life of white slavery pursued by Ignatius Loyola and "a band of hard-riding fanatical Jesuits" who hope to rescue the girls. This plot is complicated by the unexplained arrival of a musketeer from a Dumas's novel, who needs help in retrieving the Queen's necklace. An interruption, headed "Description of Three O'Clock in the Afternoon," adds a further level of reality (or unreality). Characteristically, Barthelme combines baroque diction with a specificity of detail in the following extract that needs to be quoted at length:

> Dispersed amidst the hurly and burly of the children were their tenders, shouting. Inmixed with this broil were ordinary denizens of the quarter—shopmen, *rentiers,* churls, sellers of vicious drugs, stum-drinkers, aunties, girls whose jeans had been improved with applique rose blossoms in the cleft of the buttocks, practicers of the priest hustle, and the like. Two officers of the Shore Patrol were hitting an imbecile Sea Scout with long shapely well-modeled nightsticks under the impression that they had jurisdiction. A man was swearing fine-sounding swearwords at a small yellow motorcar of Italian extraction, the same having joined its bumper to another bumper, the two bumpers intertangling like shameless lovers in the act of love. A man in the organic-vegetable hustle stood in the back of a truck praising tomatoes, the same being abulge with tomato-muscle and ablaze with minimum daily requirements. Several members of the madman profession made the air sweet with their imprecating and their moans and the subtle music of the tearing of their hair.
>
> (*S* 168)

Despite the aimlessness, the density, the messiness of the scene, really because of them, a vitality emerges from the very surface of events—the listing rather than dramatization—in a catalog that copies and so reminds, even assures the reader of activity and so creates it into being. At length, Daumier becomes so entranced with his creations that he allows Celeste, one of the *au-pair* girls, to replace his real-life companion Amelia in his affections and literally to enter the world in which he exists. The ontological confusion of levels ends with Daumier anticipating a meal Celeste is about to prepare, which in its wonderful elegance recalls the irrelevance which the narrator of **"The Party"** felt marked the attempt to discriminate among critical values. Though Daumier repeats the reassurance given by his surrogate—"There are always openings, if you can find them. There is always something to do." (*S* 177)—the qualification "if you can find them" suggests he is aware of both the tentative and tenuous nature of such options. Both distancing himself from and embracing his creations, then, he confirms by his act both the need to, and the means by which fiction can, enter the world and the ambiguous condition that results when it does so.

Many of the concerns Barthelme expressed in *Sadness* appear again in his next collection of short stories, *Amateurs,* where they are often subjected to more manic treatment. In **"Our Work and Why We Do It,"** the narrator describes the operations of a publishing house which serves as the center of a series of bizarre, unrelated activities, somewhat resembling the acts in **"The Flight of Pigeons from the Palace."** The owners, William and Rowena, lie naked in bed in the middle of the plant discoursing on the advantages of being bourgeois, which allows William to worry about his plants and his quiches, his property taxes, and, in a stunning incongruity, his sword hilt. The pressmen turn out jobs ranging from matchbook covers to the *Oxford Book of American Grub* and the Detroit telephone book, while awaiting the introduction of new machines which will print underground telephone poles, the smoke on smoked hams, and the figure 5 in gold. "Should we smash the form?" one of the pressmen wonders when a job receives a bad review, then realizes "But it's *our* form" ([*Amateurs*; hereafter] *A* 7).

It is an exchange it is not hard to imagine the author having with himself. In the absence of conventional forms (and perhaps the occasional impulse to smash them), the story serves as a paradigm of Barthelme's work and suggests why he does it. The narrator is unable to end some of his sentences and begins others seemingly in the middle, punctuating both with occasional non sequiturs, lists, and even an obscurely threatening note wrapped around a brick that sails through the window and identifies conditions without indicating the consequences. "And I saw the figure 5 writ in gold," is one of the statements he abruptly introduces. The allusion is to a painting by Charles DeMuth, inspired by William Carlos Williams's Imagist poem "The Great Figure." Though a symbolic homage to the poet, whose name and initials are worked into it, the painting is done in the hard-edge style of the precisionists, a group of artists including Charles Sheeler and Stuart Davis with whom Demuth is commonly grouped and who painted everyday themes and common household objects—grain elevators, barns, silos, factories, ship's turbines—in an attempt to reduce and simplify natural forms to the borderline of abstraction. It is a style that in many ways seems to anticipate Barthelme's own. "Some things don't make sense," the narrator explains of the rush of words that can be seen finally as the subject of the story:

> But that isn't our job, to make sense of things—our job is to kiss the paper with the form or plate, as the case may be, and make sure it's not getting too much ink, and worry about the dot structure of the engravings, or whether a tiny shim is going to work up during the run and split a fountain.
>
> (*A* 5)

The process of the story not its content is what the reader is instructed to pay attention to.

In **"The Captured Woman"** a similarly improbable situation results from the transformation into literal terms of the vocabulary of power and sexual domination commonly used to describe relationships. The narrator and his friends boast of their methods (one uses tranquilizing darts, another a lasso, a third a spell inherited from his great-grandmother; the narrator uses Jack Daniels) and of their success in taming the women they have captured. Like the domestic situations the women have left, these more exotic arrangements after a while come to seem "as ordinary as bread," and, though the narrator feels they are at best temporary, over the course of time they take on a permanence as the women at first subtly and then more aggressively use their supposedly dependent status to gain control of the relationship.

Control operates as the informing principle of **"I Bought a Little City,"** which also literalizes then reverses the wish-fulfillment conditions with which it begins. The city which the narrator buys, Galveston, Texas, is treated as though it were a sports franchise run by a benevolent owner. Starting with some modest urban renewal, he tears down an entire city block and converts it into a park. "I put the people into the Galvez Hotel, which is the nicest hotel in town, right on the seawall," the narrator drawls full of self-satisfaction, "and I made sure that every room had a beautiful view. Those people had wanted to stay at the Galvez Hotel all their lives and never had a chance before because they didn't have the money. They were delighted" (*A* 52). Predictably the satisfaction fades with the problems of relocation and the increasingly arbitrary changes the narrator makes (partly in response to the citizens' requests) in an effort to convert his city into a utopian dream. The result is a fragmented jigsaw puzzle which pleases no one. The attempt to bring order to the city is no more successful and when the narrator is rebuffed by one of the married women who live there he decides to sell it back at a loss. By attempting to be imaginative one can only hurt people, not help them, he concludes. It is a way of playing God, whose more powerful and painful imagination causes him to withdraw from society completely, still tormented by the thought of the wife whose fidelity could not be tempted.

Barthelme reverses that situation in **"You Are as Brave as Vincent van Gogh,"** which deals with the desperate reassurances that attempt to keep an affair from falling apart, and in **"The Agreement," "What to Do Next,"** and more obliquely, in **"At the End of the Mechanical Age,"** all of which seem more nakedly informed by a personal voice struggling with the problem of divorce and its aftermath. In **"The Agreement,"** the divorced speaker, as in a catechism, asks himself a series of searing questions beginning with "Where is my daughter? Why is she there? What crucial error did I make? Was there more than one?" (*A* 61). Concerned as well about social approval (Will the mailman laugh at him? The butcher? The doctor?), he worries about his lover's fidelity and his own competence. The narrator's self-questioning is abruptly ended by a parody of one of the terms of a supposed divorce agreement, covering every possible contingency "from the beginning of the world to the execution of this agreement." Having agreed to the terms of this document, he

finds the loss and dislocation intrude upon his efforts to get on with the painting of his apartment and the beginning of a new life it promises.

"What to Do Next," consists of ostensible instructions for what the narrator ironically terms "starting fresh, as it is called" after a couple has separated. Initially comparing the experiences to the loss of one's dog, he at first advises distractions to help one forget the depression but quickly recognizes that such diversions do little to address the central difficulty: the loss of self-esteem. The narrator traces such "wrenches of the spirit," to the culture which, he recognizes, "makes of us all either machines for assimilating and judging that culture, or uncritical sops who simply sop it up, become it" (*A* 85). The image of separation from one's culture—that of a banged thumb, swollen and red—is, however, no more appealing. His solution, which he compares to "frontier-busting," is to become part of the instructions themselves or in other words to write about the experience just as he himself is doing. Even this strategy is viewed ironically. Along with the instructions the newly authoritative divorcee is required to give a course twelve hours a week to others seeking solace for which the instructor will receive three credits and a silver spoon in the Heritage pattern. "The anthology of yourself which will be used as a text," the narrator hollowly reassures the reader, "is even now being assembled by underpaid researchers in our textbook division" (*S* 86) and underscores the ambivalent irony he directs at these mechanical means for dealing with the pain of loss by concluding the instructions with the words, "Congratulations. I'm sorry" (*S* 86).

Toward the middle of **"At the End of the Mechanical Age,"** the narrator wonders whether the end of the mechanical age, which he equates with the present age of electricity, is simply a metaphor. "We have a duty to understand everything," he is told, at which point the boat, in which he and his companion have been riding out a flood which followed forty days and forty nights of rain, sinks. His companion, Mrs. Davis, had reached out to him in a grocery store and following extravagant promises of idealized romantic fulfillment which both are aware can never be realized, they marry. His ideal had been a woman named Maude, who, as in Barthelme's own fiction, attempts to create things by naming them. Mrs. Davis's fantasy is that of a natty dresser with many credit cards who bears a resemblance to her first husband, Jake. The wedding turns the metaphor into reality with the mechanical nature of the ceremony:

> "And do you, Anne," the minister said, "promise to make whatever mutually satisfactory accommodations necessary to reduce tensions and arrive at whatever previously agreed-upon goals both parties have harmoniously set in the appropriate planning sessions?"
>
> (*A* 181)

The accommodations set the tone of the relationship, and despite the narrator's appeal for the blessing of some Divine Presence, which ironically had been hovering behind everything that has happened, the marriage ends in a divorce which along with "blackouts, brown-outs, temporary dimmings of household illumination" only confirms divine indifference. God, the narrator concludes bitterly, is "interested only in grace—in keeping things humming" (*A* 183). The ending of the story once more combines the compromises demanded by the world and the more abstract truths of metaphor. Neither Mrs. Davis nor the narrator appear discouraged by the need to find happiness without the aid of some supernatural being. Their child goes to live in Russia where, the narrator believes, "He is probably growing in wisdom and beauty." With "the glow of hope not yet extinguished, the fear of pall not yet triumphant" the couple continues to search for an ideal, but only with the aid of standby generators which ensure the flow of grace.

Like the writer in **"The Dolt,"** whose story lacked a middle, the narrator of **"And Then"** struggles with metaphors and with the difficulty of completing his own fiction. "The part of the story that came next was suddenly missing," he begins (*S* 105) and then goes on to imagine a series of increasingly fantastic encounters with a public which appears to him in the form of an obscurely threatening policeman who comically multiplies (or divides) into several more, all with bicycles, demanding that he turn over a harpsichord he had given to his wife as a present. Only by lying, the narrator decides, can he successfully distract this looming presence, and desperately looking for ways to keep his audience interested he becomes lost in his own inventions. The two problems—satisfying the audience and completing his story—thus fuse into one, which he plans to resolve with an extravagant gesture. He will throw chicken livers *flambé* all over the predicament. "That," he concludes hopefully, "will 'open up' the situation successfully. I will resolve these terrible contradictions with flaming chicken parts and then sing the song of how I contrived the ruin of my anaconda" (*A* 112).

As a means of resolving the predicament of both artist and audience, the spontaneous gesture proves a fragile solution in **"The Great Hug,"** a story which returns to the central metaphor of **"The Balloon."** Summoned to console a companion to whom the narrator has given some terminally bad news, the Balloon Man appears like a carnival huckster with an assortment of balloons of all colors and varieties. They range from the Balloon of Not Yet and the Balloon of Sometimes to the Balloon of Perhaps, which the story concludes, is his best balloon. Unwilling to have his picture taken because he "doesn't want the others to steal his moves," the Balloon Man explains "It's all in the gesture—the precise, reunpremeditated right move" (*A* 46). Although the balloons do not lie, the reader is told, the Balloon Man is less straightforward than the Pin Lady, his antagonist, who presents an actuality with which his imaginative creations must ultimately be locked. His balloons, or the stories with which they are associated, at best thus provide only qualified or temporary refuge in dealing with reality. Referring to the scene with which the story begins, the narrator says "When he created our butter-colored balloon, we felt better," then adds thoughtfully, "a little bet-

ter" (*A* 48). Yet the Balloon Man defends with spirit the qualified nature of one's encounter with his product. "Not every balloon can make you happy," the Balloon Man admits, "Not every balloon can trigger glee. *But I insist that these balloon have a right to be heard!*" (*A* 48).

Nearly half of the sixteen stories in *Great Days* take this insistence literally, by concentrating in dialogue form on the sound of language. Barthelme has described this contrapuntal technique as an attempt through the arrangement of words to arrive at new meanings rather than simply providing an altered perspective in which to regard them.[11] In fact, the use exclusively of dialogue as a framing device allows Barthelme to reduce the story to its basic dramatic element eliminating for the most part such narrative elements as plot, description, development, and even climax. Unlike the adversarial debates of **"The Explanation"** or **"Kierkegaard Unfair to Schlegel,"** in *City Life*, or even the more playful story, **"The Reference"** in *Amateurs* (in which the exchange takes place between a stuffy, jargon-spouting prospective employer whose difficulties with social engineering have resulted in "planarchy" and a slangy, jive-talking antagonist whose often meaningless patter evolves into that of an agent's, representing the person for whom the reference is sought), the voices in *Great Days* are more like syncopated duets.

Structured like the classic jazz tune "Momma Don't 'Low," with its refrain and improvisations, **"The New Music"** develops the conversation of two brothers who have difficulty in liberating themselves from the influence of a repressive, largely unfeeling mother. Once again the parallels with an authoritative artistic tradition suggest themselves. Ironically the conversation begins with the admission by one of the brothers of imitation in a surprising context. Asked what he did that day, he replies, "Went to the grocery store and Xeroxed a box of English muffins, two pounds of ground veal and an apple. In flagrant violation of the Copyright Act" ([*Great Days*; hereafter]*GD* 21). Their discussion of the new music is, in actuality, an example of it, touching on both its eclectic quality and its almost syncopated rhythms:

> —If one does nothing but listen to the new music, everything else drifts, goes away, frays. Did Odysseus feel this way when he and Diomedes decided to steal Athene's statue from the Trojans, so that they would become dejected and lose the war? I don't think so, but who is to know what effect the new music of that remote time had on its hearers?
>
> —Or how it compares to the new music of this time?
>
> —One can only conjecture
>
> (*GD* 21-2)

Alternately building on and echoing each other's remarks, the brothers remind each other of all the prohibitions to which they have been subjected and which spill over from their musical interests to their social lives. Their attempt to reassure themselves with brave resolutions ("Get my ocarina tuned, sew a button on my shirt." "Got to air my sleeping bag, scrub up my canteen.") centers around a vision of the utopian city of Pool, which, it turns out, only projects a dated image of itself obtained from movies that seem made of standard film clichés.

Despite the discouragement they feel at the prospect of getting older and the intimidating influence of official statements such as that of *The Hite Report,* a study of female sexuality, the brothers' conversation itself finally proves sustaining, even revitalizing. Like the new music, which has no steady beat ("The new music is drumless, which is brave)." (*GD* 33), the conversation renews itself by accommodating a wide range of subjects from Greek mythology and poetry of the French symbolists to discos and mixed drinks. "The new music," one of the brothers says, "burns things together, like a welder." At the same time, its colloquial rhythms resemble "the new, down-to-earth, think-I'm-gonna-kill-myself music, which unwraps the sky" (*GD* 37). Despite its echo of Shakespearian tragedy in the recognition that "the new music will be there tomorrow and tomorrow and tomorrow," the brothers are convinced, at length, that they can deal with the prospect of things coming to an end and the troubling dreams which are certain to follow by abandoning the prospect of utopian dreams and confining themselves to a new music whose novelty depends, above all, simply on routine maintenance.

Elliptical jazz rhythms also structure the conversation in **"Morning,"** in which two men similarly attempt to confront the terrors of aging and loss as they are brought home in the early light of another day. "Say you're frightened. Admit it," one begins. "I watch my hand aging," the other replies with an unconvincing attempt at casual bravery, "sing a little song" (*GD* 123). The song consists in the main of disconnected riffs which include imitations by one of them of the loneliness in the cry of a wolf and appeals to literary and artistic diversions. "What shall we do? Call up Mowgli? Ask him over? . . . Is Scriabin as smart as he looks?" (*GD* 123).

The two men attempt to comfort themselves with formulaic, singsong repetitions ("One old man alone in a room. Two old men alone in a room. Three old men alone in a room."), by mocking allusions to familiar catchphrases ("Have any of the English residents been murdered?"), and by humorous variations of classic song titles ("They played 'One O'Clock Jump,' 'Two O'Clock Jump,' 'Three O'Clock Jump,' and 'Four O'Clock Jump.'") Without the awareness of them as a strategy, the reassurances prove hollow, remaining abstractions rather than acquiring density. The story ends not with the expected daylight but with darkness and the abandoning of the search for any pleasurable or even satisfying illumination.

A parallel pessimism informs the conversation in **"On the Steps of the Conservatory,"** which describes one woman's rejection by a Conservatory, whose standards remain arbitrary and whose function is never made clear. What is known is only that the Conservatory "is hostile to the new

spirit." Without identifying in explicit terms which institution the Conservatory is identified with (in one sense it parallels the non-permissive momma in **"The New Music"**), its syllabus reveals a traditional concern for image rather than substance. "Christian imagery is taught at the Conservatory, also Islamic imagery and the imagery of Public Safety," Hilda explains to her friend Maggie (*GD* 134). Like everything else, however, even the image of the conservatory itself continues to shift. Initially its staff is described as indifferent to the models, subsequently as sexually involved with them. Even Maggie does not remain a fixed entity, speaking alternately in her own voice, which repeatedly reminds Hilda of her pregnant condition and as a spokeswoman for the conservatory, who delights in pointing out the privileges to which Hilda will never be entitled. The conversation ends with Maggie's suggestion that even her intermittent attempt at consolation, like Hilda's tenuous effort to cope with her rejection, is questionable and that jealousy and envy rather than support underlies the nature of the women's relationship.

The same irony is evident in the abstract conversation of the two unnamed women in **"Great Days,"** which, unlike the dialogues between two women in *The Dead Father* that preceded the story and that it otherwise resembles, was, according to Barthelme, a more concrete experiment in combinations that could keep the reader interested without a strong narrative line on which to lean.[12] In **"Great Days,"** the voices of two women are projected against the menacing background of crime reports that sound like broadcasts on an urban police radio frequency, both repetitive and discontinuous. The women worry about growing older, their fading beauty, their uncertain achievements. They attempt to reassure each other with meaningless sentiments from popular song lyrics or current catch-phrases expressing popular wisdom, while hoping for the childlike renewal associated with rainwashed watercolors. "Control used to be the thing," one of them decides, "Now abandon" (*GD* 166). In part, the voices constitute a parody of Barthelme's reductive style, bouncing off of, though never quite responding to, what one says to the other. Yet the staccato, elliptical rhythm of their conversation is illuminated by the description one of them gives of her own painting style which is marked by her efforts to "get my colors together. Trying to play one off against another. Trying for cancellation" (*GD* 159).

The style is Barthelme's as well, and the effort at cancellation expands into a more general statement that is not directed at any identifiable object or made in response to any specific comment but seems to express Barthelme's view of art: a "nonculminating kind of ultimately affectless activity" one of the women calls it (*GD* 159). Neither focused by some controlling purpose nor generating some precise emotion, it is just that kind of aimless activity the women think of as the great days of their lives filled with concrete if transitory everyday moments of childlike playfulness and enveloping sensory experience. Making mud pies, eating ice cream, singing, they recall, the days were "all perfect and ordinary and perfect" (*GD* 157). The loss of those days occasions in the women as adults an insatiable need for reassurance and a consequent mistrust of the attempt or even the ability either of lovers or friends to provide it.

Reassurance is also sought in **"The Leap,"** a story in which antiphonal responses alternate with shifting tonal modulations and philosophies to make it appear the two voices the reader hears are contesting sides of a single personality. Cheered by "the wine of possibility," one speaker attempts to persuade his companion to make the leap of faith, but only after each has carefully reexamined his conscience and acknowledged the failings it reminds him of. The force of this religious argument is mockingly challenged by the other voice, that of a self-styled double-minded man who wonders whether "He wants us to grovel quite so much?" "I don't think He gives a rap," his friend replies, "But it's traditional" (**GD** 151).

The ludicrous consequences of too strict an observance of tradition is suggested by the doubter's insistence on regarding his sins item by item. His mock humility prompts the first speaker to express a hierarchy of values that proves both arbitrary and comically restrictive in its fine discriminations. "I like people better than plants," he points out, "plants better than animals, paintings better than animals, and music better than animals" (**GD** 147). This list contrasts with a more comprehensive idea of the sublime to which both men enthusiastically subscribe, one that does not discriminate among alternatives but celebrates the rich variety of earthly phenomena, from a glass of water or the joy of looking at "a woman with really red hair" to the beauty of the human voice. In contrast to the evidence of some religious meaning in existence, the men comment on the human creative impulse responsible for the most banal works of art, the childlike regularity of which both men underscore by alternately quoting the lines of Joyce Kilmer's "Trees," along with the typographical appearance of the lines on the page. ("'I think that I shall never see slash A poem lovely as a tree.'")

Rehearsing the torments of the damned as they are typically phrased in sermons, the two men suggest yet another motive for the leap of faith. Here the man who would make the leap seems to take on the posture of his double-minded antagonist. Reminded of the philosophical argument that "purity of heart is to will one thing" he replies, "No. Here I differ with Kierkegaard. Purity of heart is, rather, to will several things, and not know which is the better, truer thing, and to worry about this, forever" (**GD** 151). In its complexity, the statement suggests something of the skepticism or hesitancy that inhibits the will to believe. In its concern and consequent anxieties, it points to the urgency of precisely that need and the correlative desire for reassurance.

The two men agree that the divine plan is artificial in its established forms and suspect as it appears to work itself out in the inability of nations to achieve zero population growth or in such individual acts of self-destruction as sui-cide—a leap away from faith, the first speaker admits—and the impersonal way society deals with it as evidenced by an itemized hospital bill. Nonetheless they acknowledge evidence of the plan can be found in the example of love in all its complexity. "Is it *permitted* to differ with Kierkegaard?" the double-minded man wonders. "Not only permitted," he is assured, "but necessary. If you love him," (**GD** 152).

With this realization of complexity, even in love, the first speaker concludes by sharing his friend's abruptly confessed inability to make the leap of faith or at least his willingness to delay it and so becomes more in need of reassurance than ever. He finds that reassurance in the appreciation of the chaotic but nonetheless sublime quality of concrete experience in its ordinary forms. "A wedding day," he suggests. "A plain day," the double-minded man corrects him, bringing to his uncertainty a measure not only of comfort but of hope.

The broken rhythms of the dialogue stories find an echo not only in the voices of **"The King of Jazz"** but in the art of its central figure, the trombone player Hokie Mokie who, Barthelme has acknowledged, reflects his interest in the legendary jazz musicians of the 1930s, whose skill at improvisation served as a model for the writer's own strategy of renewing familiar material by unexpected placement of emphasis or by introducing elaborate variations of it. "You'd hear some of these guys take a tired old tune like 'Who's Sorry Now?'" Barthelme told one interviewer, "and do the most incredible things with it, make it beautiful, literally make it new. The interest and the drama were in the formal manipulation of the rather slight material."[13] The material in **"The King of Jazz"** recounts the challenge to the newly crowned king, Hokie Mokie, from the Japanese jazz man Hideo Yamaguchi. After an initial performance, Hokie is forced to acknowledge the superiority of Hideo's playing, but in a subsequent encounter Hokie's inspired playing allows him to reclaim his crown, sending Hideo back to Japan with the knowledge of "many years of work and study before me still." Barthelme takes the opportunity to make fun both of the dated critical vocabulary to which the artist's performance is subjected and the exaggerated enthusiasms it generates. Ironically harking back to the categories of modernism, Hokie's playing is described as having "the real epiphanic glow," while Hideo's peculiar way of holding his horn prompts the supposedly knowledgeable observation, "That's frequently the mark of a superior player." Even Hokie's naming of the tune the band will play is greeted with syncophantic adulation: "'Wow'!" everybody said. "'Did you hear that? Hokie Mokie can just knock a fella out, just the way he pronounces a word. What a intonation on that boy! God Almighty!'" (**GD** 56). At length, a description of Hokie's playing yields an improvisation of its own, which parallels the music it attempts to describe and brings together in an ambivalent tone the truly heroic nature of the art and, for Barthelme, the finally inescapable extravagance with which it is greeted. Called upon to identify Hokie's sound, one of the audience supplies the following similes:

"You mean that sound that sounds like the cutting edge of life? That sounds like polar bears crossing Arctic ice pans? That sounds like a herd of musk ox in full flight? That sounds like male walruses diving to the bottom of the sea? That sounds like fumaroles smoking on the slopes of Mt. Katmai? That sounds like the wild turkey walking through the deep, soft forest? That sounds like beavers chewing trees in the Appalachian marsh? . . ."

(GD 59)

The speaker continues to add to the list growing wilder and wilder as he goes on. Unable to end, he is brought to a stop only when he is interrupted by the observation, perhaps meant to shape his own jazzy flights, that Hokie is playing with a mute.

A different sort of performance becomes the subject of **"The Death of Edward Lear,"** whose hero literally transforms the moment of his death into a vibrant and enduring performance with a life of its own. The situation, dreamlike in its associational logic—the displacement of emotion, and the neutralization of time and space—draws its meaning, like dreams, from the intention of the dreamer, that is to say, from the enactment of his desire rather than the revelatory content of images. This is not to suggest that in Barthelme's fiction history has no meaning; it is to say that imagination brings with it its own deceptions or, more accurately, establishes its own myths. The sources of these myths are found in public, or shared, as well as private visions. Lear invites his public to witness his death, which they prepare to attend with all the confusion and excitement that would accompany their spending a day in the country, but from which they come away "agreed that, all in all, it had been a somewhat tedious performance" (*GD* 103). Subsequently repertory companies reenact the death scene, which in the course of time, they modify to portray Lear "shouting, shaking, vibrant with rage." These revivals thus lose sight of the author's intention and, in the process, of his originality and charm. In the whimsical and arbitrary nature of his final acts, the narrator explains, "Mr. Lear had been doing what he had always done and therefore, not doing anything extraordinary. Mr. Lear had transformed the extraordinary into its opposite. He had, in point of fact, created a gentle, genial misunderstanding" (*GD* 103).

In **"Cortes and Montezuma,"** events resist interpretation in part because of the distortions that occur when different civilizations view each other's customs solely from the limited perspective provided by their own. Eating white bread appears just as cannibalistic to the Incan culture as human flesh does to the Spanish. Each regards the other's religious practices as equally perverse. "That the Son should be sacrificed," Montezuma tells Cortes, "seems to me wrong. It seems to me He should be sacrificed *to*" (*GD* 46). Cortes responds by replacing an image of the god Blue Hummingbird with one of the Virgin. In more secular terms, Montezuma defines the role of the ruler in a way that parallels the artist Barthelme describes in stories such as **"The Balloon,"** or, more obliquely, **"The Glass Mountain"**: he prepares dramas that make it easier for both himself and his subjects to face "the prospect of world collapse, the prospect of the world folding in upon itself . . ." (*GD* 47).

It is fiction, however, not the world which threatens to fold in upon itself. Structured in disconnected scenes whose details make them highly visual but which impose strict limits on its own thematic organization, the narrative does not allow the reader to move easily from one episode to the next but rather keeps attention focused on a single action at a time, often as it occurs within a single paragraph. Like the annoying green flies, whose ubiquitous presence is unaccounted for other than as a reminder of a nagging commonplace reality, anachronistic references insistently disrupt the conventional relation between history and invention. "What's he been up to?" Cortes asks in current slang about a member of his expedition while the translator, Dona Marina, walks with one hand tucked inside the belt of her Incan lover, at the back, like a contemporary couple strolling through Greenwich Village. Allusions are made to private detectives, home movies, and to words such as "guillotine," "temperament," "entitlement," "*schnell,*" some of which have yet to be coined, all of which are clearly out of place in the context of Incan culture.

The attempt throughout, then, is to reduce the mythic stature of these figures to a more human if still unfamiliar history, whose sudden and surprising turns are illustrated in the person of Bernal Diaz del Castillo, who, the reader is told, will one day write a *True History of the Conquest of New Spain.* Bernal is pictured as whittling on a piece of mesquite as though passing a long afternoon telling stories on the porch of a southwest country store. Looked at in one way, these incongruous juxtapositions deflate the fabulous element of the narrative; in another they become themselves magically predictive in the sense indicated by the narrator of **"Paraguay"** of that mixture of invention and reality.

This tension, typical of Barthelme's fiction, is not limited to linguistic content but rather works its way out from the center of the story—the intimate treatment of legendary figures whose history has become obscured by the mythic significance, in part slyly internalized, to which it has become attached. The same ominous omens—lightning and rain sweeping off the lake—accompany insignificant events such as the building of a chicken coop as well as those of historical importance such as the murder of the Incan ruler. The mixture of levels is similarly illustrated in the Spaniards' search for treasure, which results in the discovery of mummified animals concealed behind a wall but also yields a "puddle" of gold. Both the sound and the meaning of the word "puddle" suggest the banality of experience. Contextually associated with gold, it becomes invested with a more magical sense.

The literal acceptance of even the most unlikely conjunctions is, perhaps, most forcefully conveyed by the uninflected tone used to describe the exchange between the two political antagonists as a variation of the relation between lovers. Cortes and Montezuma hold hands, exchange useless gifts, spy jealously on one another, finally give way to acts of betrayal and scenes of recrimination. Like the course of events, even the imaginative forms through which the two men attempt to anticipate and so understand them remain outside their control. In a concluding ghostly confrontation, Montezuma reproaches his friend for failing to alter the outcome of a dream which Cortes did not have and which he did not even appear in. "I did what I thought best," Cortes had earlier explained to the Emperor Charles of Spain, "proceeding with gaiety and conscience." It is Montezuma who unaccountably replies, "I am murdered" (*GD* 51). It is the gaiety to which the reader is particularly directed. Without it, as one learns from the two often stand-up-comic voices exchanging questions and replies in **"Kierkegaard Unfair to Schlegel,"** one has nothing with which to face the "imbecile questions," which look for a pattern in life, the unsatisfying answers, and the inescapable fact that things appear to lead nowhere.

All art, the reader can infer, takes as its informing purpose, the attempt to express "the possible plus two," which is found in the example of the 400,000 welded steel artichokes constructed by the artist-hero of **"The Abduction from the Seraglio."** In doing so, however, it must follow the example in that story of the artist's former girlfriend, Constanze, who does not compromise her values by her decision to move in with a wealthy car dealer but who continues to live "in a delicate relation to the real." And though the artist has lost his muse to the attractions held out by the Plymouth Dealer, who updates Mozart's Pasha as a representative (though somewhat less benevolent) of a self-indulgent society, he pronounces this qualified though still ultimately upbeat benediction: "We adventured. That's not bad" (*GD* 95).

Published in 1983, *Overnight to Many Distant Cities,* Barthelme's eighth volume of short fiction is, in many ways, his most innovative collection. Several of Barthelme's familiar themes are easily recognizable, among them the anxieties of urban life, the fragility of domestic arrangements, the transience of romance, the qualities of sadness and beauty that inform the awareness of time, and the moments of perceived vitality that mark as luminous its passage. Yet the 12 stories that make up the volume take on a less ironic, more personal voice than that which typically marks Barthelme's earlier work. These full-length stories are counterpointed by the inclusion of brief (typically no more than 2 or 3 pages), italicized interchapters, which adopt a tone of nuanced sophistication that challenges the conventional relations between the order of things and the order of words, challenges, that is, the different ways in which structure or fictive order is imposed upon the dizzying impact of experience. In one of them, for example, two women, described as gift-wrapped, are initially pictured wearing nothing but web belts to which canteens are attached. The women appear in a succession of situations initially located in the indeterminate space of a performance art work by Yves Klein ("Nowhere—the

middle of it, its exact center").[14] Subsequently the scene shifts to an architectural office where they sit before a pair of drafting tables, a lumberyard in southern Illinois, the composing room of an Akron, Ohio, newspaper, New York City, where they appear first as taxi drivers then as loan officers in a bank, and finally to an archeological dig in the Cameroons. Intermittently the women excite satyr-like young men who "squirm and dance under this treatment, hanging from hooks, while giant eggs, seated in red plush chairs, boil" ([*Overnight to Many Distant Cities*; hereafter] *O* 70). Figures ranging from the Russian artist Vladimir Tatlin in an asbestos tuxedo to Benvenuto Cellini and the French painter Georges de La Tour, both wearing white overalls, appear in the background. The surreal quality of the images (La Tour, who watches the women in a film, is subsequently pictured in the lobby of the theater opening a bag of M& Ms with his teeth) prohibits any interpretation other than to suggest that women, particularly in their nakedness, constitute somewhat troublesome gifts and also breathtaking works of art that are drawn from the most representative kinds of experience.

The sly undercutting of the ideal is directed toward art no less than life in the first interchapter of the volume which envisions a utopian city much like that of Barthelme's earlier story **"Paraguay,"** and begins abruptly with the narrator's remark, "They called for more structure, then . . ." (*O* 9). There is no indication of who has made the request, what kind of structure is required, or even the nature of what has already been built. While the story is filled with a wide range of contemporary allusions, none appear in recognizable contexts or satisfy conventional expectations so that it is not so much another world that is glimpsed as this one slightly out of focus. Clad in red Lego, for example, the city is spread out in the shape of the word FASTIGIUM, which proves to be not its name but a set of letters selected for the elegance of the script. Even the structure which follows the initial request is achieved by the use of materials with surprising characteristics—"big hairy four-by-fours [are nailed] into place with railroad spikes" (*O* 9) while the impermanence of the whole is suggested by specified areas designed to decay and so return in time to open space.

The fluid architectural design serves equally as a paradigm of Barthelme's own fiction in which the elements of fantasy do not so much displace or even alternate with reality as exist side by side with it. In another interchapter, the narrator puts a name in an envelope which, like a children's counting song, he continues to expand until the succession of envelopes and objects stuffed into them includes the Victoria and Albert Museum, the Royal Danish Ballet, boric acid, and the entire history of art. All are compressed into a new blue suit which walks away on its own, an action that suggests something of both the compression and the autonomy of art.

The casual acceptance of the bizarre as part of the ordinary lies at the center of yet another interchapter (reprinted in *Forty Stories,* where it is given the title **"Pepperoni"**) which describes in matter-of-fact terms a daily newspaper in which the editorials have been subcontracted to Texas Instruments, the obituaries to Nabisco, and in which the reporters form a chamber orchestra that plays Haydn in the newsroom. The incongruities that mark the running of the paper are highlighted in the selection as the page-one lead of a story on pepperoni—"a useful and exhaustive guide"—run alongside instructions on "slimming-your-troublesome-thighs" with pictures (*O* 25).

Strangely appealing, obscurely menacing, this anti-utopian world in which the trivial takes so prominent a place blends with the everyday in the concluding interchapter, which describes in surrealistic terms, among other things, the decoration of a Christmas tree and a party which possibly follows at which the guests include both thieves and deans of cathedrals. The setting is a magical forest, alive with sensuality and far from Western civilization. In this fairy-tale world in which inanimate objects come to life women at one point partner themselves with large bronze hares (which may also be Christmas tree ornaments) while the narrator's companion jealously regards the already-beautiful who stand watching with various exotic animals cradled in their arms. Despite the unpredictability of events and the tensions to which they seem to give rise, the narrator insists, "This life is better than any I have lived, previously" (*O* 164). Even the weather, perhaps the most insistent reminder of the unpredictability of human affairs, continues to be splendid. "It is remarkable," the narrator concludes in what finally appears to be the judgment of the volume, "how well human affairs can be managed, with care" (165).

To such tranquility, however, Barthelme seldom fails to append a cautionary qualification chiefly directed at the relationships which describe much of our contemporary domestic arrangements. In one of the interchapters a wife catalogs the history of a marriage while her husband remains absorbed in the idiosyncratic events chronicled in his newspaper, indifferent even to her complaint that a guest he has brought home occupies himself exclusively with eating mashed potatoes in a back room of their apartment. In **"Visitors,"** the initial full-length story of the volume, Bishop, a divorced father, nearing 50, struggles to bring order to a career which includes caring for a teen-aged daughter visiting at his small apartment during the summer. He must also deal with the end of an idyllic affair with a younger woman and with the various uncertainties and incongruities of city life presented in a catalog that establishes the documentary logic of ennumeration Barthelme typically relies on in place of linear development to structure his narrative. Taking a walk down West Broadway, the narrator encounters "citizens parading, plump-faced and bone-faced, lightly clad. A young black boy toting a Board of Education trombone case. A fellow with oddly-cut hair the color of marigolds and a roll of roofing felt over his shoulder" (16). After Bishop gives his daughter a mock lecture on art, the story concludes with an enigmatic scene he witnesses in an apartment across the way of two old ladies who habitually breakfast by candle-

light. Bishop cannot decide whether they are incurably romantic or simply trying to save money on electricity, and the alternate interpretations, which serve as well as a paradigm for the responses the story itself invites, suggest the choices no less than the limits which experience simultaneously holds out.

The disconnection that brings to such unusual circumstances a disturbing sense of the commonplace marks the adventures of the eponymous hero of **"Captain Blood."** "When Captain Blood goes to sea," the story begins, "he locks the doors and windows of his house on Cow Island personally" (*O* 59). Though Blood more exotically keeps marmalade and a spider monkey in his cabin, his pockets are filled with mothballs, and he notes with satisfaction the decorous behavior of his crew. Blood, the buccaneer, is nonetheless plagued by the conventional anxieties of any responsible business entrepreneur. "Should he try another course?" he wonders after a long period during which he is unable to capture any booty, "Another ocean?" (*O* 60). His adventures, which culminate with an unlikely battle in which he first defeats then gallantly frees John Paul Jones, are anchored if not exactly in reality then at least in a more factual illusion by lists that contain a mixture of the prosaic and the spectacular. These include the names of the ships he has captured as well as the value of his prizes. Ultimately there is a description of the Catalonian sardana, a dance which, Blood "frequently dances with his men, in the middle of the ocean, after lunch, to the music of a single silver trumpet" (*O* 65). The image of the trumpet evokes a sense of wonder which the wry qualification "after lunch" makes sure to anchor in the requirements of the everyday.

The mystery that informs the everyday continues to resist explanation for Connors, a free-lance journalist in **"Lightning,"** who is given the assignment of interviewing nine people who had been struck by lightning. Middle-aged, barely scraping by after a brief period of affluence, Connors is nonetheless able to reclaim his journalistic integrity only after his wife leaves him for a racquetball pro. He is himself figuratively struck by lightning when, in the course of his assignment, he meets Edwina, a beautiful black model with whom he falls instantly in love. For Edwina, as for the others Connors interviews, it is the pragmatic rather than dramatic effects of the experience that are significant. One man becomes a Jehovah's Witness, another subsequently joins the Nazi Party, a woman subsequently marries a man she had been seeing for two years, a Trappist monk is able to indulge his passion for rock music, and someone dumb from birth is, after being struck, able to begin speaking fluent French. Missing the underlying fact—the lack of drama for the people who must live their lives as subjects of it—Connor is unable to find a common denominator for these experiences and unsuccessfully attempts to impart to them a religious significance. His story, however, both begins and ends with the transient earthly beauty of Edwina, which his editor, Penfield, calls "approximately fantastic." The self-qualifying terms of the description suggest the inexplicable mixture of the extraordinary and the human imperfection which necessarily limits both our approach to and understanding of it and which consequently locates the value of experience in its surface rather than in some transcendent meaning.

In **"Affection,"** emotional intensity similarly emerges less in contrast to the irritating sameness of domestic routine than as a consequence of it. Harris, the husband in a shaky marriage, his wife Claire, his mistress Sarah, all express the need for affection in repetitive appeals whose self-absorbed demands for fulfillment at length merge into a dreamlike blending of figures and relationships. His complaints of infidelity, of sickness, of sexual inadequacy, of the lack of understanding are greeted with indifference, even boredom, by the fortune teller Madame Olympia, who Harris consults only to hear his own domestic quarrels repeated in the experience of her other clients.

The attempt to rehearse the poverty of one's environment is wittily mocked by a T-shirt Madame Olympia wears on which is printed the ironic legend "Buffalo, City of No Illusions." Like Dr. Whorf, the psychiatrist Sarah consults, Olympia can do little to relieve the misery and estrangement she is told about other than to convert them into clichés. It is the same strategy the story itself employs in a series of melodramatic alternatives intrusively proposed as possibilities for narrative development. "Did they consent to sign it?" an unidentified voice asks without specifying what document needed to be signed or who the signatories were, "Has there been weight loss? . . . Have they been audited?" (*O* 32).

While Harris finds anger and resentment erupting in even the conventional situation of a husband leaving for work in the morning, Claire quotes with approval a statement she attributes to Freud about the need for novelty in order to achieve orgasm. Yet it is the memory of the domestic scene of Sarah nearsightedly groping for toothpaste in the morning that most moves Harris, and Claire finds an enduring object of affection finally in the jazz pianist Sweet Papa Cream Puff who mixes nostalgic reminiscence with barefaced invention. Like the trumpet player Hokie Mokie in Barthelme's earlier **"The King of Jazz,"** Papa Cream Puff is aware of his reputation and of the need to maintain it in the face of youthful challenge. He does so, however, not by inspired performance alone but by studying his opponent, so that he has "two or three situations on the problem" (*O* 33). Responding to the surprising possibilities that, at least in part, emerge as a comic accompaniment to Sweet Papa Cream Puff's playing as well as to the steady brilliance of his performance, Claire joyfully embraces him with sudden and unself-conscious pleasure.

In a final abrupt shift, signaled as is each of the preceding scenes by blank space, the story concludes—or almost concludes—with an insistently repeated "What?" echoing the inability to hear each other that at its start comically counterpoints the efforts of Claire and Harris to prepare dinner. The couple nonetheless achieve an optimistic if not necessarily permanent reconciliation when Harris unex-

pectedly makes some money in the stock market. Like Sweet Papa Cream Puff's boast of having written a piece called "Verklarte Nacht," which he explains innocently means "stormy weather," invention thus makes fun of itself. Conventionally, repeated statement establishes an exclusively linguistic and so artificial environment in which words appear unfamiliar and so strange. Here the repetition parallels the nature of the exchanges between the characters and, in fact, invites the narrative presence directly into the world they inhabit. The triumph of the everyday is startlingly confirmed by the sudden emergence of the narrator for whom, he himself admits, the act of washing the newsprint of the daily paper off his hands constitutes an affirmation of routine through which he can continue to assert his own value.

The spilling over of the framing and fictive levels of narrative into one another—a device which in one form or another Barthelme has employed in stories such as **"The Balloon," "Daumier," "Rebecca,"** or **"On the Deck,"** among the more often noted examples—sends the reader outside the text to its structure for response, that is to say, directs one to the kinds of associations it establishes rather than to the narrative possibilities it invites. The illusion of an imagined world made accessible through the transparency of a narrative voice is further discredited by an unlikely reversal in which all difficulties are resolved by abrupt statement rather than by a sequence of actions consistent with what is known of the characters. It may be that this distortion of reality as much as anything else prompts Harris or the narrator—it is hard to be sure which—to urge Claire, as his last word, to smile. Yet the banal and somewhat artificial affirmation, associated with the posed awareness and fixity exhibited by the subject of a photograph, evokes an affectionate frame in which to regard those insistent if unanswerable questions that continue to provide both a challenge and a reassurance by being asked.

The triumph of ordinary interaction over the uncertainties which prevent any response to experience is confirmed by Thomas, the narrator of **"The Sea of Hesitation,"** who abandons his efforts to change human behavior and takes instead a job processing applications for an office of the city bureaucracy called the Human Effort Administration. He has resolved insofar as possible to let people do what they want to do. Though Thomas acknowledges that "my work is, in many ways, meaningless," (*O* 96), the substitution in this way of process for result, allows him to cope with the demands of his former wife that he help make life more comfortable for her and her current lover, to endure with equanimity the angry letters of a former mistress, and to listen sympathetically to the idiosyncratic interest of a current one who is absorbed in a defense of Robert E. Lee and the Confederate cause.

Like his brother Paul, who is happiest doing work other than that for which his formal training has prepared him and who has to read the daily paper in order to relieve his depression, Thomas struggles with the exaggerations of the present. At the same time, he rejects the preoccupation with the past of his friend Francesca, who is persuaded that in an earlier existence she was one of Balzac's mistresses. Even great writers, Francesca is convinced, suffer moments of doubt and concludes "The seeking after greatness is a sickness . . . It is like greed, only greed has better results" (*O* 101). Neither greatness nor greed finally prove appealing to Thomas, who rejects even truth in favor of volition and the pursuit of possibility. They are achieved, he concludes, finally only in some form of human desire and of love, which allow him to cross the Sea of Hesitation that separates him, as it does so many of Barthelme's characters, from the fulfillment possible only in the society of others. "Some people," Thomas concludes wistfully, after an idyllic description of the urgencies which mark the beginning of an affair, "have forgotten how to want" (*O* 105).

That the goal of human effort is the transient condition of love is suggested as well in **"Terminus,"** which describes the affair between a married man and a younger woman which takes place during the unnamed couple's stay as guests in the Hotel Terminus. Despite the knowledge that the affair must end shortly and the tensions which consequently trouble even the most playful exchanges between the lovers, the joy they take in one another leads the man to behave "as if *something* were possible, still" (*O* 115). The judgment the story makes is more explicitly expressed by the woman who celebrates sensuality even in the acknowledgment of its transience. "*That which exists,*" she reminds him," *is more perfect than that which does not*" (*O* 116).

In the concluding story of **Overnight to Many Distant Cities,** which gives its name to the volume, the narrator assembles what appear to be a series of journal entries which provide a history of his visits to various cities around the world ranging from Stockholm to Taegu, South Korea. The entries consist of anecdotes, commentary, sometimes even accounts of meals he has eaten. In San Antonio the narrator argues for adultery as a normative activity, in Copenhagen he goes shopping with some Hungarian friends who are starved for Western material goods, in Mexico City, as a teenager, he runs away from home, in Berlin he is unsettled by the stares his evident happiness with a companion draws from bystanders. Occasionally the accounts are political—an Israeli journalist explains the complex politics of the Middle East, the Swedish prime minister good-naturedly accounts for the high cost of liquor in his country, the narrator is himself enlisted by a writer from an Iron Curtain country to smuggle some writing to the West.

The absence of connection as well as the relative pointlessness of the notations once again establish Barthelme's compositional principle as that of subtraction. "In London," one of the entries begins, "I met a man who was not in love" (*O* 171). The man's desperate insistence serves only to confirm the narrator's conviction of the value of love even as he acknowledges the frequency of his own

divorces. "Show me a man who has not married a hundred times," he remarks, "and I'll show you a wretch who does not deserve the world" (*O* 174). Finally it is the world or more accurately the people and events he encounters which, with or without meaning or connection, constitute the redeeming fact of existence merely by virtue of their being. Despite the unpredictability of things, underscored by weather bulletins that intermittently punctuate the central action, it is the world even with its minor imperfections (unreliable electricity in Barcelona) that leaves the narrator—and the volume itself—pleasing the Holy Ghost with his praise and in an "ecstasy of admiration for what is" they share a communal meal.

Notes

1. "Not-Knowing," *Georgia Review* 39 (Fall 1985): 522.

2. Wayne B. Stengel, *The Shape of Art in the Short Stories of Donald Barthelme* (Baton Rouge: Louisiana State UP, 1985) 161.

3. *Sixty Stories* (New York: Putnam's, 1981) 420.

4. Herman Melville, "Bartleby the Scrivener," *Selected Tales and Poems,* ed. Richard Chase (New York: Holt, 1964) 92. Further page references will be noted in parentheses.

5. The importance of rhetoric to Melville's story is perceptively examined by Sanford Pinsker, whose suggestive reading in "'Bartleby the Scrivener': Language as Wall," *College Literature* 2 (1975): 17-22 stands out among the unrelenting critical notice the story continues to receive. Pinsker argues that language itself constitutes a wall of rhetoric behind which the lawyer's facile optimism attempts to falsify the dark knowledge of irrationality that Bartleby's enigmatic silence refuses to blink. Though I share Pinsker's view of the importance the story places on dealing with the irrational, I find far more sympathetic Melville's treatment of the lawyer and of the limits implicit in his use of language as well as his self-awareness of the comic possibilities of inflated rhetoric.

6. Quoted in *Anything Can Happen: Interviews with Contemporary American Novelists,* ed. Tom LeClair and Larry McCaffery (Urbana: University of Illinois Press, 1983) 33.

7. "Critique de la Vie Quotidienne," *Sadness* (New York: Farrar, 1972) 3-4. Further references to Barthelme's works discussed in this chapter will be given in the text and indicated by the following abbreviations: *Sadness; S; Amateurs; A; Great Days; GD; Overnight to Many Distant Cities; O.*

8. Alan Wilde, *Horizons of Assent: Modernism, Postmodernism, and the Ironic Imagination* (Baltimore: Johns Hopkins UP, 1981) 170. For the importance of the ordinary to Barthelme as a suspensive value against the hopelessness and outrage, against the sheer intractability of things, I am indebted to Wilde's indispensable study.

9. R. E. Johnson, Jr., "Bees Barking in the Night: The Beginning of Donald Barthelme's Narrative," *Boundary* 2 5 (1977): 78.

10. John M. Ditsky, "'With Ingenuity and Hard Work, Distracted': The Narrative Style of Donald Barthelme," Style 9 (Summer 1975): 394-95.

11. J. D. O'Hara, "Donald Barthelme: The Art of Fiction LXVI" *Paris Review* 80 (1981): 197.

12. O'Hara 197.

13. O'Hara 185.

14. *Overnight to Many Distant Cities* (New York: Putnam's, 1983), 68. Further page references will be noted in parentheses.

Brian McHale and Moshe Ron (essay date summer 1991)

SOURCE: McHale, Brian, and Ron, Moshe. "On Not-Knowing How to Read Barthelme's 'The Indian Uprising.'" *Review of Contemporary Fiction* 11, no. 2 (summer 1991): 50-68.

[*In the following essay, McHale and Ron describe the difficulties of collaborating on a close reading of "The Indian Uprising."*]

The writer is a man who, embarking upon a task, does not know what to do.

—Donald Barthelme, "Not-Knowing"

1

When, early in 1989, the two of us began to collaborate on a project involving Barthelme's story **"The Indian Uprising,"** we both knew and did not know what to do. We knew we wanted to undertake a close reading of **"The Indian Uprising,"** for reasons we could specify: because critics have tended to shy away from fine-grained, continuous analysis of postmodernist texts, with the implication—perhaps inadvertent but in any case, in our view, unjustified—that such texts could not sustain analysis of this kind; and because we aspired (no doubt hubristically) to produce model close readings in the postmodernist paradigm analogous to those produced by Brooks and Warren in the New Critical paradigm. We did not know what such a postmodernist close reading would look like; we only knew, negatively, that it could not take for granted the kinds of assumptions that underwrote New Critical close reading (closure, unity, functionality and intelligibility of every element, etc.), which had been rendered untenable by skeptical reflections on language and meaning. We thought that, between us, we knew quite a lot about **"The Indian Uprising,"** one of us (Ron) having translated it into Hebrew, the other (McHale) having described elements of it in a book on postmodernist fiction. We did not know whether we could reach some joint understanding

about the text which would be acceptable to both of us, or, if we did, how we could shape this joint understanding into a piece of writing.

Our project was not without precedents, but the nearest precedent was minatory rather than encouraging. In his essay called "Not-Knowing," in the context of remarks on "critical imperialism" and the "element of aggression" in certain kinds of critical attention, Barthelme describes a run-in with a close reader:

> A couple of years ago I received a letter from a critic requesting permission to reprint a story of mine as an addendum to the piece he had written about it. He attached a copy of my story he proposed to reproduce, and I was amazed to find that my poor story had sprouted a set of tiny numbers—one to eighty-eight, as I recall—an army of tiny numbers marching over the surface of my poor distracted text. . . . I gave him permission to do what he wished, but I did notice that by a species of literary judo the status of my text had been reduced to that of footnote.[1]

The story in question was **"The Zombies,"** and the close reader was Carl Malmgren, whose essay, "Barthes's *S/Z* and Barthelme's 'The Zombies': A Cacographic Interruption of a Text," appeared in the journal *PTL* (1978). We knew the piece well, McHale, as assistant editor of *PTL,* having had a hand in its publication; we knew it well enough to recognize how Barthelme had shaped the incident to his own rhetorical purposes. Malmgren had, indeed, interpolated index numbers in Barthelme's text—but forty of them, not eighty-eight. More to the point, Barthelme fails to remark on the distinctly unacademic tone of Malmgren's piece, which is so shifty and ironic as to lead one to suspect that this may be less an "application" of Barthes's *S/Z* model of textual commentary to Barthelme's text than a sly parody of Barthes. If there is "literary judo" in Malmgren's essay, it may well be Barthes who has been flipped to the mat, not Barthelme. Indeed, Malmgren's jujitsu strategy here (if that's what it is) bears a good deal of resemblance to Barthelme's own elusive ironies, to the point that this essay might be read as a pastiche of, or even homage to, Barthelme. In that case, perhaps Barthelme's testiness can be seen as a kind of backhanded testimony to the accuracy of Malmgren's pastiche.

In any case, Barthelme's account of the incident served as a warning to us about the risks of critical imperialism, real or perceived. We felt that Malmgren had actually shown considerable restraint in his treatment of Barthelme's text, allowing for a good deal of latitude or "play" in the text and not claiming to have said the last word about it or to have finally mastered it; yet even this degree of critical restraint evidently did not satisfy Barthelme (for whatever reasons). How were we to proceed in the light of this precedent? How were we to leave room for "not-knowing"—the writer's, the text's, our own—while at the same time pursuing our goal of knowing?

2

"We defended the city as best we could."[2] So begins Barthelme's **"The Indian Uprising."** Our problem was, which side were we on? ("'Which side are you on,' I cried, 'after all?'"—the narrator to Sylvia, § 20.) Were we defending the city of narrative intelligibility, asserting the familiar forms of sense-making against the anarchic onslaught of the Comanches of indeterminacy? Or did we identify with the Comanches—were we really, like the "people of the ghetto" and the girls of the narrator's quarter, fifth columnists, proposing forms of intelligibility only in order to explode them, thereby "demonstrating" how the text first invites, then undermines its readers' attempts to make familiar kinds of sense of it? To do the first would be in effect to regress to New Critical reading practices, which would reflect extreme bad faith on our part, in view of all we knew about the untenability of New Critical positions: you can't go home again. But to do the second would be to subject Barthelme's text to what has already become a post-structuralist critical cliché. It would be, in effect, to follow the recipe for poststructuralist reading: set up, as a straw man, some totalizing interpretation (typically, one so naïve that no real reader would ever endorse it), then have the "text" (actually, your own critical discourse interpolated into the text) knock the straw man down. But who would be interested to read such an analysis? Not students, for its pedagogical value is zero; not our fellow critics, for they could follow the recipe as easily as we could, and do the job for themselves.

How to begin?[3] "We propose to begin," we wrote, "reading 'naïvely,' that is, linearly, sentence by sentence and passage by passage in the order that the text offers itself to us, reporting on our experience of reading the unfolding text—the sense we can make of it as it unfolds, the obstacles to sense-making that arise to block our progress." But this was disingenuous. We very early recognized that we could not hope to pursue this "naïve," "linear" reading to the end of the story, for our annotations would proliferate endlessly, finally swamping the text; this, after all, is what Barthes demonstrated with such bravado in *S/Z,* where a meager story spawns hundreds of pages of annotation, and, while this was an effective demonstration the first time around, to repeat it would only be redundant. Moreover, to annotate the "unfolding text" would be unfaithful to what we knew the reader's experience of this text, or any other text, to be like. No reader, however naïve, actually reads "sentence by sentence and passage by passage"; all readers also read "vertically," so to speak, seeking out the familiar underlying structures that the particular text in question shares with others. In other words, in order adequately to capture the reader's experience of even so unconventional a narrative text as **"The Indian Uprising"** we needed to take into account the structuralist insight "that underneath the variety and contingency of the text lie abstract structures which all competent readers presumably 'know' or have in some sense mastered, but which can only be made available for inspection and analysis through a methodological reduction of the text to its underlying structure."

In undertaking this "methodological reduction," we took for our model the actantial analysis practiced by A. J. Greimas.[4] In terms of this model, **"The Indian Uprising"**

may be reduced to the narrative proposition "Subject loses Object," where "Subject" and "Object" represent not characters as such, but roles. The story can be made to yield this abstraction if we agree to match the actantial model against the story's actor personnel roughly as follows:

> Subject = we, I.
>
> Object = city, Sylvia (she, you), and other women.
>
> Anti-Subject = Comanches, Kenneth.
>
> Helper = defenders and barricades, Miss R.? Block?
>
> Opponent = Miss R.? Block?[5]

Where was the profit in submitting the story to such a radical reduction? For us, the profit lay in the insight that this same abstract scheme applied equally to each of the three distinct stories that coexist in **"The Indian Uprising."** It is as if the text were layered, each story occupying a separate "plane" and drawing on a distinct area of the total semantic material of the text, yet each nevertheless conformable to one and the same underlying narrative proposition, "Subject loses Object," and to a parallel (though not identical) distribution of actantial roles.

The three concurrent and parallel stories we proposed to distinguish in the text of **"The Indian Uprising"** were these:

(1) The public-political story. This is the story, named in the title of the text, of violent conflict between Comanche attackers and citizen-defenders for possession of the city. The Subject and his Helpers (i.e., the narrator and his fellow defenders) lose the Object (the city, security, the good things of upper-middle-class urban life) to the Anti-Subject (the Comanches and their allies, including the "ghetto-dwellers" [§ 13], and girls of the narrator's quarter, Sylvia conspicuous among them). We wrote:

> Any historical narrative of a war of liberation or resistance is a potentially relevant context for reading **"The Indian Uprising."** This is because its underlying plot-pattern is capable of being mapped onto that of any of these historical narratives [viz., the Algerian uprising against the French, the Afghan resistance to the Red Army, the Palestinian *intifada*], but also because the text of **"The Indian Uprising"** systematically prevents our making an association with *any one particular* historical context. The text is riddled with deliberate anachronisms from its very first sentences: Comanches besiege what is obviously a late-twentieth-century city; war clubs mingle with zip guns, lances and fire-arrows with helicopter gunships.[6] By conflating such a range of historical conflicts, the text "disqualifies" itself from representing any particular conflict and signals its availability to be read as, in effect, an allegory of historical conflicts of a certain type. Nevertheless, if all wars of national liberation are potentially relevant contexts for reading **"The Indian Uprising,"** two such cases impose themselves on our attention as particularly relevant. One is, of course, the Indian wars themselves, especially in the form in which that conflict has been represented in countless movie Westerns—except that

in Barthelme's version the repressed "natives" return, like America's bad conscience, to reclaim what had been expropriated from them. The other is the war approaching its height of ferocity and divisiveness in the very year (1968) in which Barthelme published **"The Indian Uprising"** in book form, namely, of course, the war in Vietnam. To read **"The Indian Uprising"** as an allegory of the Vietnam War seems not just plausible but irresistible, particularly since the analogies between the Indian wars and the Vietnam War, between Comanches (or Apaches) and Viet Cong, have become a commonplace of discourses about and representations of the Vietnam War.[7]

(2) The erotic-biographical story. This is the parallel story of the narrator's unsatisfactory private (in particular erotic) life, his course of therapy with Miss R., and (presumably) his final breakdown. In transposing the conflict of **"The Indian Uprising"** into a personal and psychological key, the actantial roles are reassigned. Obviously the Subject remains the "I" of the narrator, but the Object of his desire is no longer, as in the public-political narrative, the city (that is, the way of life threatened by the Indian uprising), but a desired woman (Sylvia, who may or may not be identical with "you") or desirable women in general, generic Woman, in fact a series of interchangeable women with whom the narrator has apparently had unsatisfactory, or at any rate unenduring relationships (Nancy, Alice, Eunice, Marianne [§ 9]). The Anti-Subject role is assigned to the narrator's rivals for these women's affections, in particular Kenneth (whose coat Sylvia evidently loves [§ 18]), while the Helper role is ambiguously occupied by the therapist, Miss R. There appear to be four sessions with Miss R. distributed through the text (§ 11, 13, 21, 26). We meet Miss R. for the last time (§ 26) when she strips the narrator of his belt and shoelaces ("Skin," she orders him, i.e., "Strip down"), as one would do when admitting a prisoner to jail—or a patient to a mental institution?—and introduces him to the Clemency Committee. If Miss R.'s course of therapy was meant to save the narrator from his own private demons, it appears to have failed, for at the story's end he comes face-to-face with "savage black eyes, paint, feathers, beads": madness personified?

(3) The cultural-historical story. On this third plane the story of attack and defense is recast in terms of movements in cultural history, the defenders aligning themselves with the values of literary (and more generally aesthetic) modernism, while the attacking Comanches align themselves with what we might call (though Barthelme himself does not) postmodernism. Less explicit than either the public-political or the erotic-biographical stories, the narrative on this plane is conducted in a coded discourse of literary and other allusions, mostly to high-modernist writers (or their Symbolist precursors): T. S. Eliot (*The Waste Land,* possibly other texts as well), Thomas Mann (*Death in Venice*), Valéry, Baudelaire ("Au Lecteur").[8]

What exactly the citizens of this modern city are defending is perhaps suggested by sentences like this one: "Patrols of paras and volunteers with armbands guarded the tall, flat buildings" (§ 2). Why "tall, flat buildings"? This would seem to be an allusion to the steel frame and glass curtain-wall skyscrapers of the modernist International Style, and thus, by extension, to the values of aesthetic modernism in general. Even more intransigent in her defense of modernist values is Miss R., in whose aesthetic credo (§ 21) it is possible to detect an echo of the modernist period's linguistic skepticism and the minimalist poetics of some of its most influential writers. Miss R. endorses "the hard, brown, nutlike word": so did modernist prose stylists like Gertrude Stein and her most apt pupil, Ernest Hemingway. Hemingway's aesthetic of the short, punchy sentence and the hard, brown, nutlike word was partly inspired by a profound skepticism, which he shared with others of his generation, about language itself, a medium which had proven to be all too malleable to the purposes of demagogues and ideologues. The philosophical version of this poetics of linguistic skepticism is identified above all with Wittgenstein, the final proposition of whose *Tractatus Logico-Philosophicus* Miss R. also paraphrases: "I believe our masters and teachers as well as plain citizens should confine themselves to what can safely be said."[9]

If modernist aesthetics is the cause in need of defense, who or what is its enemy? In terms of the Greimasian actantial model, who is the Anti-Subject here? Again, the answer is encoded in a discourse of cultural allusions:

> "What do you want to be?" I asked Kenneth and he said he wanted to be Jean-Luc Godard but later when time permitted conversations in large, lighted rooms, whispering galleries with black-and-white Spanish rugs and problematic sculpture on calm, red catafalques.

> (§ 25)

Anomalously, this sentence names an artist whom many would call post-modernist. Perhaps Kenneth is thinking specifically of Godard's film *Weekend,* in which hippie tribesmen slaughter middle-class vacationers, like insurgent Comanches overwhelming the city's defenders in **"The Indian Uprising."** When and where does Kenneth hope to get to "be" Godard? Not now but later, and in "rooms" and "galleries" which are evidently those of a museum. In other words, Kenneth would be willing to model himself on Godard, but only after the Godard aesthetic will already have been safely canonized, only after it will have received the kind of cultural imprimatur that museums bestow.

"The implication," we wrote,

> is that the figures of the modernist tradition to whom this text mainly alludes—Mann, Eliot, Valéry, Baudelaire—have already been canonized, monumentalized: they are museum figures.[10] Godard's aesthetics, however, have not yet been canonized, and thus remain outside and in opposition to the monumentalism of canonical high-modernist aesthetics, still too "wild" for a cautious modernist epigone like Kenneth. The enemy of this late and epigonic modernism, then, can only be

the "wildness" of Godard and, more generally, of the postmodernist aesthetics that (in 1968) was just appearing on the cultural horizon. Though oriented towards modernism and recapitulating classic high-modernist positions, **"The Indian Uprising"** is a text which nevertheless anticipates a certain post-modernism, by reason of its own "wildness." For despite its weave of modernist allusions, the actual poetics of **"The Indian Uprising"** has more to do with the postmodernism of, say, Godard's *Weekend* than it does with the high modernism of Mann, Eliot, or Valéry.

3

Very quickly our analysis of **"The Indian Uprising"** into these three parallel stories, all conformable to the same Greimasian scheme, began to run into more or less intractable difficulties. Foremost among our difficulties were these:

(1) An inherent indeterminacy in narrative structure itself. Our attempt to reduce **"The Indian Uprising"** to its abstract structure in terms of Greimas's actantial model brought to light an element of indeterminacy and perspectivism in the model itself. The distribution of roles (on the plane of the public-political story in particular) depends upon identifying the Subject position, and though "I," the narrator, certainly occupies the subject position in the discourse of the text, this does not ipso facto make him the actantial Subject. Indeed, the text's ironies are such that there is room for regarding him (and his fellow-defenders) as occupying the Anti-Subject position, the true Subject of desire being the Comanches, who struggle with the Anti-Subject to (re)possess the Object of their desire (the city). "Once this reading has been proposed," we wrote, "it seems almost the more intuitive one, less forced than the reading which treats the Comanches as Anti-Subject." And we went on:

> The ease with which the story can be turned inside out, as it were, perhaps points to fundamental instability in narrative structure itself. For all the assignments of roles in the actantial model, as well as the formulation of the abstract narrative proposition underlying the story, are determined by the positioning of the Subject: change the position of the Subject (from the narrator to the Comanches, say), and all the other role assignments swing around, while the underlying narrative proposition literally turns inside out. In other words, it is the perspective of the Subject that orients the entire actantial paradigm. The reversibility of a story such as **"The Indian Uprising"** may indicate an inherent instability in all narrative structure, so that the bedrock on which we thought we were building our reading turns out to be much less firm than we had supposed.

This discovery of what might be called the "structural perspectivism" inherent in the actantial model tends to confirm one of the predictions we made at the outset of our project, namely that **"The Indian Uprising"** would prove to be "a postmodernist critique of narrative reason."

(2) The problem of integrating the three narrative planes. It did not seem satisfactory merely to distinguish the three stories without trying to determine whether and how they could be integrated, and here immediately we encountered difficulties. For the materials we could identify as belonging to different stories were merely abruptly juxtaposed in the text, in successive sentences or sometimes even within the same sentence, without the expected signals of transition from one represented situation to another:

> . . . the coat was a trap and inside a Comanche who made a thrust with his short, ugly knife at my leg which buckled and tossed me over the balustrade through a window and into another situation. Not believing that your body brilliant as it was and your fat, liquid spirit distinguished and angry as it was were stable quantities . . . I said: "See the table?"

(§ 19)

The effect is like that of cinematic jump-cutting, but jump-cutting of a particularly enigmatic kind, leaving it to the reader to determine whether successive sequences could be integrated in the same "situation," or even the same world, and if so, how.

For example, in the text's opening paragraph we cut abruptly from material obviously belonging to the public-political story of the uprising ("There were earthworks along the Boulevard Mark Clark and the hedges had been laced with sparkling wire. People were trying to understand") to a domestic vignette: "I spoke to Sylvia. 'Do you think this is a good life?' The table held apples, books, long-playing records. She looked up. 'No.'" The next paragraph returns to the uprising situation ("Patrols of paras and volunteers with armbands guarded the tall, flat buildings"), narrating a brutal interrogation of a Comanche captive and a somewhat puzzling maneuver to reinforce the defensive line, and then cuts back, again without transition, to material from the erotic-biographical story: "And I sat there getting drunker and drunker and more in love and more in love. We talked." Now, a sanctioned interpretive move, in the face of such a disjointed sequence, would involve treating the domestic scenes as exemplary private moments of crisis within the larger panorama of the public crisis of the uprising. Sylvia and the narrator, we might hypothesize, are examples of the "people" who were "trying to understand" the public crisis in which they find themselves. Perhaps the juxtaposition of the torture scene and the narrator's ensuing conversation with Sylvia is designed to make some (rather banal) point about the ironies of atrocity, namely, that even torturers have private lives, that one moment they may be pouring water into a prisoner's nostrils while the next they behave like any "normal" person, getting drunk, falling in love.

But of course this is not the only interpretive move available, not even necessarily the likeliest one. For one thing, there is no indication of temporal relations here. Although it might be "natural" to assume that, in the absence of any indication to the contrary, the order of presentation reflects the temporal order of events, there is nothing in the context to prevent our reading the interrogation scene as a flashback (or flashforward), or even as occurring simultaneously with the narrator's conversation with Sylvia. Nor need we even assume that the uprising and the domestic vignette occupy the same ontological level. What prevents our treating the uprising as, for instance, a TV Western playing in the background while this domestic scene unfolds? The domestic scene might itself in turn belong to another film, say a Bergman or Antonioni or some other treatment of 1960s malaise . . . and so on, to infinite regress, so weakly constraining is the context of these sentences.

A powerful integrative move of a different kind would involve treating scenes from one of the parallel stories as in effect *metaphors* for situations in another of the stories. In the opening paragraphs, for instance, nothing prevents us from reading the interrogation of the Comanche as a figurative version of the interrogation of Sylvia that precedes and follows it. Indeed, this maneuver could be extended to the entire text. We wrote:

> Nearly everything in **"The Indian Uprising"** that seems to refer literally to military conflict is susceptible of reinterpretation in a figurative sense, as a metaphor for a situation of a different order: the story of the narrator's unsatisfactory private life and his—somewhat self-dramatizing, somewhat comical—psychological anguish. The implausible barricade (§ 10) can be read as a metaphor for the psychological "defenses" the narrator throws up—familiar domestic objects and souvenirs, heavy drinking—against the onslaught of his personal demons; the episodes of torture can be read as metaphors for his frustrating encounters with women. (What could be more appropriate, on this reading, than for the torture victim to have electrified wires applied to his testicles?) Similarly, all the tactical maneuvering in the story, incoherent enough as an account of a military conflict, yields readily to reinterpretation in terms of a psychomachia, an internal psychological conflict: e.g., "The rolling consensus of the Comanche nation smashed our inner defenses" (§ 25). The city, on this reading, is to be identified with the embattled, besieged self of the story's narrator: "There was a sort of muck running in the gutters, yellowish, filthy stream suggesting excrement, or nervousness, a city that does not know what it has done to deserve baldness, errors, infidelity."
>
> (§ 12)

This is a powerful interpretive move, yielding a satisfying degree of integration; perhaps too powerful, perhaps too satisfying. For one thing, it too casually glosses over certain discrepancies in the mapping of one story onto the other. For instance, in the opening paragraphs, if the interrogation of the captured Comanche is meant to be a figurative version of the narrator's interrogation of Sylvia ("Do you know Faure's 'Dolly'?"), then Sylvia is to be identified with the tortured Comanche, the narrator with his torturers; but it is evidently the narrator who suffers the pain in his dialogue exchanges with Sylvia, which suggests that he ought to be identified with the torture victim rather than the victimizers. So which is he, victim or victimizer, interrogator or interrogated?

Moreover—and this is even more damaging to the metaphorical strategy of integration—nothing in the context

constrains us to assign the tenor and vehicle functions of this supposed figurative narrative one way rather than another. That is, the literal-figurative relation is readily reversible, and we would be equally justified in reading the erotic-biographical story as figurative and the public-political story of the uprising as literal as we are in reading them the other way around; neither reading is inherently more plausible than the other. Thus, far from enabling us to stabilize and integrate the text, this metaphorical reading leaves us with a text of disturbing indeterminacy and reversibility.

(3) The problem of the internal incoherence of each of the three stories. Not only were there discrepancies *between* the stories when we tried to integrate them, but each of the three stories displayed its own internal discrepancies. The more narrowly we examined these discrepancies, the plainer it became that we could sustain our narrative analysis only at the cost of "normalizing" narratives that in fact actively resist integration.

On the public-political plane, for instance, there is the conspicuous incoherence of the display of "team colors" associated with the warring parties and presumably serving to distinguish them. Since the Comanches' girl sympathizers wear blue mufflers (§ 14), the Comanche color would seem to be blue, perhaps combined with red: thus Miss R., subsequently a turncoat (or so it would appear), wears "a blue dress containing a red figure" (§ 13). (However, the barricade against the waves of "red men" incorporates "a blanket, red-orange with faint blue stripes" and "a red pillow and a blue pillow" [§ 10].) One of the colors associated with the city and its defenders would seem to be a rather equivocal yellow: the city pavements are soft and yellow (§ 1), the streets are "yellow and threatening," and "yellowish" muck runs in its gutters (§ 12).[11] Like the girls of the quarter who sympathize with the Comanches, Sylvia wears a blue muffler, but under it she wears a yellow ribbon (§ 20). "She Wore a Yellow Ribbon" was the anthem of the U.S. Seventh Cavalry, who saw service in the Indian wars; indeed, the song is said to have been played when General Custer rode out to his disastrous engagement at the Little Big Horn. So if Sylvia wears a yellow ribbon, she presumably signifies by it her alignment *with* the Indian fighters *against* the insurgent Indians. No wonder the narrator cries, "Which side are you on after all?" (§ 20).

When the war *agon* is transposed into the terms of a football game, however, the defenders are evidently identified with the color green: "In Skinny Wainwright Square the forces of green and blue swayed and struggled. The referees ran out on the field trailing chains. And then the blue part would be enlarged, the green diminished" (§ 20). In the overall logic of this narrative, it is the "part" of the defenders that constantly diminishes, that of the Indians that constantly enlarges; so the defenders must be green, the Indians blue. How, then, to explain the map?[12] "On the map we considered the situation with its strung-out inhabitants and merely personal emotions. I showed the blue-

and-green map to Sylvia. 'Your parts are green,' I said" (§ 13). We wrote: "The system of color-coding collapses into self-contradiction. The defenders are identified with blue but also with green, the attackers with green but also with blue. The question, 'Which side are you on?', addressed to Sylvia when she combined Comanche blue with Seventh Cavalry yellow, now acquires the weight of a more general epistemological skepticism and confusion."

Similarly, on the erotic-biographical plane there was the problem of repetition, a major motif of the narrator's personal crisis. The narrator's attitude toward repetition is deeply ambivalent. On the one hand, he insists that it is impossible to repeat or recover the privileged moments, especially the privileged erotic moments, of one's past life—you can't go home again—while on the other hand, the key sentences that actually tell us that you can't go home again and that the past is unrepeatable and irrecoverable are themselves self-contradictory and self-deconstructive, enacting something different from what they appear to want to say:

> Not believing that your body brilliant as it was and your fat, liquid spirit distinguished and angry as it was were stable quantities to which one could return on wires more than once, twice, or another number of times I said: "See the table?"
>
> (§ 19)

> . . . you can never touch a girl in the same way more than once, twice, or another number of times however much you may wish to hold, wrap, or otherwise fix her hand, or look, or some other quality, or incident, known to you previously.
>
> (§ 23)

> . . . you can never return to felicities in the same way, the brilliant body, the distinguished spirit recapitulating moments that occur once, twice, or another number of times in rebellions, or water.
>
> (§ 25)

Each of these sentences seems to begin unequivocally enough as statements of the impossibility of repetition ("you can never touch a girl in the same way," "you can never return to felicities in the same way"), but then look what happens to them: not "never more than once," but never more than "once, twice, or another number of times." Notice, too, the other deliberate incoherences and infelicities: these are what Barthelme in an interview once described as "back-broke sentences,"[13] and their purpose here, it would seem, is simultaneously to make an assertion (you can't go home again) and to allow this assertion to leak away, as it were, through the logical and syntactical fissures in the sentences.

More than merely incoherent, these sentences actually directly contradict themselves, enacting something different from what they say, by repeating the same phrase: namely, the phrase "more than once, twice, or another number of times." Indeed, the text of **"The Indian Uprising"** is crisscrossed with repetitions, exact or nearly exact, of phrases

and sentences, up to entire scenes.[14] Moreover, immediately after asserting (for the second time) that one can never recapture a privileged moment, the narrator *does,* in fact, recapture a privileged moment: that of descending from a bus in Sweden to the cheers of little children, visiting an old church and its graveyard (§ 23). So is repetition possible or not? There is an ironic ambiguity here, but one that the text provides no means of resolving.

On the cultural-historical plane, finally, the identification of the citizen-defenders with modernist aesthetic values, and the Comanche attackers with postmodernist aesthetics, proved to be unsustainable. One detail will suffice to make the point: under torture, the captured Comanche begins to paraphrase the opening of Thomas Mann's novella *Death in Venice*: "His name, he said, was Gustave Aschenbach. He was born in L—, a country town in the province of Silesia. He was the son of an upper official in the judicature, and his forebears had all been officers, judges, departmental functionaries . . ." (§ 23; Barthelme's ellipses). If the Comanche is somehow identical with Mann's character, then clearly the straightforward analogy "Comanches are to citizens as postmodernism is to modernism" needs, at the very least, to be considerably qualified, if not abandoned. In seeking to salvage this analogy somehow, we encountered the fourth and, in some ways, the least tractable of the impediments to our analysis of **"The Indian Uprising."**

(4) The problem of epistemological uncertainty. The more deeply we probed the cultural-historical story, the more it appeared that we had cast this story in the wrong terms. The crisis on this plane was not aesthetic (the postmodernist uprising against modernist aesthetic values) but epistemological, or rather, the aesthetic crisis was the vehicle of the epistemological one. The literary allusions that serve to give coded expression to this conflict of aesthetic values nearly all proved, on closer inspection, to bear on epistemological problems. Thus, for instance, the Mann passage which issues, implausibly enough, from the mouth of the tortured Comanche emphasizes the know-how, the *savoir faire,* of Aschenbach's respectable professional-class forebears, a know-how which (as we know from Mann's text) Aschenbach sought to emulate in his own chosen profession of authorship. This tradition of professional know-how is ruptured by Aschenbach's belated discovery of the senses, the aesthetic and libidinal forces of not-knowing, embodied in the beautiful but fickle Tadzio and the beautiful but fatal plague-city of Venice, which together comprise something like Mann's version of the "Indian uprising" of not-knowing against conventional, bourgeois knowingness.

The allusions to Eliot direct us to similar contexts of epistemological breakdown. "You know nothing . . . you feel nothing," Miss R. rants, sending us to the passage from *The Waste Land* in which the woman whose "nerves are bad" issues a series of epistemological challenges: "What are you thinking of? . . . I never know what you are thinking. . . . Do / You know nothing? Do you see nothing?

Do you remember / Nothing? . . . Is there nothing in your head?" (II:113-26). Once again, what seems to be at stake here are the relations among "knowing [something]," "knowing nothing," and "not-knowing." Similarly, when Sylvia tells the narrator, "You gave me heroin first a year ago," she is alluding to another experience of not-knowing from *The Waste Land*:

> "You gave me hyacinths first a year ago;
> "They called me the hyacinth girl."
> —Yet when we came back, late, from the Hyacinth
>   garden,
> Your arms full, and your hair wet, I could not
> Speak, and my eyes failed, I was neither
> Living nor dead, and I knew nothing,
> Looking into the heart of light, the silence.

> (I:35-41)

In the Eliot text, of course, not-knowing is only a moment in a quest for spiritual knowledge (underwritten by the Grail myth and Jessie Weston's interpretation of it), or indeed the very precondition for mystical revelation. **"The Indian Uprising"** does not seem to hold out any similar hope of ultimate knowledge, though this is hard to say for sure.

Perhaps, then, all we had to do was reframe the third of our three parallel stories in epistemological rather than cultural-historical terms. But no, on reflection this proved inadequate, for the epistemological crisis of **"The Indian Uprising"** turns out not to conform to the same narrative proposition as the public-political and erotic-biographical stories, namely "Subject loses Object." No Subject—not the narrator, nor any other character or group of characters—loses knowledge in the course of this narrative, in the way that the defenders lose the city or the narrator loses Sylvia, because no one possesses knowledge in the first place: "People were trying to understand" (§ 1); "I decided I knew nothing" (§ 10, 11). There is no *narrative* of epistemological crisis here at all, for the simple reason that epistemological uncertainty is a chronic, unchanging state or condition throughout.

The more we attended to the epistemological problem in **"The Indian Uprising,"** the more it came to appear in some sense the master-theme of the entire text, its dominant, present on all three story-planes. Not only did the cultural-historical crisis prove to be really an epistemological crisis, but so did the public-political and erotic-biographical crises. On the public-political plane, the problem appeared to be not so much the Indian uprising itself as knowing which side anyone was on, or even (in the light of the confusion over "team colors") which side was which. On the erotic-biographical plane, there seemed to be two dimensions to the epistemological crisis: on the one hand, the impossibility of understanding Sylvia, despite all the narrator's insistent questioning of her; on the other, Miss R.'s daunting combination of overbearing knowledgeableness and radical skepticism ("You know nothing . . . you are locked in a most savage and terrible ignorance"). Moreover, many of the problems of the inter-

nal coherence of the stories and of the integration among them could be reconceived as versions or dimensions of the dominant epistemological problem.

Finally, we came to recognize that epistemological uncertainty was not only the text's master-theme but also its *meta-theme,* that is, the problem of not-knowing *in* the text recoils upon readers *of* the text, ourselves included. And this recognition returned us full circle to the very beginning of our inquiry into **"The Indian Uprising."** The text turns out to be a reflection on the problem of knowing (among other things) the text itself. Its dramatized and thematized epistemological problems turn out to be continuous with the reader's problem—*our* problem—of (not) knowing the text and (not) knowing what to do with it.

4

This is not a very satisfactory outcome. We have ended up, against our will and our intentions, reproducing the poststructuralist recipe reading, reducing the text to a critical cliché: viz., **"The Indian Uprising"** is "about" its own unknowability.

So who has triumphed? The Comanches of textual indeterminacy? Maybe; but there is an ironic sense in which the theme (or meta-theme) of unknowability, far from challenging or subverting familiar forms of intelligibility, is really the most powerful "naturalization" of all, one capable of flattening a text (any text) into a one-dimensional illustration of theory, of trimming it to the measure of a theoretical template. This is the most violent kind of "critical imperialism," as Barthelme might have called it, preempting all possibility of difference, strangeness, surprise. The Comanches of indeterminacy turn out to be citizen vigilantes in drag.

Moreover, this unhappy outcome is contrary to our own direct experience of **"The Indian Uprising."** Neither unidimensional nor merely an illustration of theory, Barthelme's text is not after all "unknowable," though neither is it, by the same token, fully knowable. It is, shall we say, partially, sporadically, provisionally, and locally knowable, instead of totally, continuously, conclusively, and globally knowable. In other words, we are proposing a model of "weak" epistemological mastery: lower-case knowing instead of Knowing with a capital K.[15]

What explains the formal satisfaction—closure, integration, shapeliness—that this text yields despite all its local discrepancies, incoherence, and frustration of formal expectations? The answer lies right there: it is not "despite" but precisely *because of* these local frustrations that **"The Indian Uprising"** gives such satisfaction. Each failure of the text to cohere at one level or at one site—that of political allegory, fictional biography, aesthetic or epistemological reflection, etc.—sends the reader to *another* level or site in search of a compensatory coherence. Every failure of integration *between* levels or *among* sites sends one in search of some other point of convergence, analogy, parallelism, correspondence, etc., or some other form of integration. Restlessly roving over the text in this way, attempting one integration after another and failing to achieve any of them, the reader nevertheless ventures many provisional, local, overlapping, partial, weakly coordinated integrations, none fully satisfactory in itself. The result is a formal closure which is simultaneously under- and overdetermined, an accumulation of integrative patterns, none of which fully integrates the text or fully converges with or corroborates the others, but which in their *weakly structured aggregate* nevertheless yield a sense of global form. Might this not be a characteristically postmodernist type of formal closure, simultaneously weak and strong, open and closed, single and plural, integrated and unintegrated, but in any case supple and (as Block says in **"The Indian Uprising"**) "liquid"?[16]

"In the competing methodologies of contemporary criticism," writes Barthelme in "Not-Knowing," "a sort of tyranny of great expectations obtains, a rage for final explanations, a refusal to allow a work the mystery that is essential to it." Later he adds: "What is magical about the [aesthetic] object is that it at once invites and resists interpretation." While we might not be completely comfortable with the romantic tonalities of Barthelme's words *mystery* and *magical,* we nevertheless venture to hope that the form of "enfeebled" knowing we have proposed—a form of knowing that leaves room for a lot of not-knowing— might preserve intact the "mysterious" and "magical" qualities of Barthelme's text.

Notes

1. Donald Barthelme, "Not-Knowing," *Georgia Review* 39 (1985): 516-17.

2. Donald Barthelme, "The Indian Uprising," in *Sixty Stories* (New York: Dutton, 1982), 108. All subsequent references to this text will be incorporated into the body of our essay and will identify citations by the paragraph (there are twenty-six in all) in which they appear, thus: "§ 00."

3. Only when we were preparing the last version of this essay did we discover a text which might have served as our model, namely the chapter entitled "*Gravity's Rainbow* and the Post-rhetorical" in Alec McHoul and David Wills's *Writing Pynchon: Strategies in Fictional Analysis* (Urbana and Chicago: Univ. of Illinois Press, 1990), 23-66. Not only do McHoul and Wills offer a rare precedent of collaboration in literary studies, but their strategy of quoting and commenting on earlier drafts of their own text, in effect producing a "layered" or "stratified" reading of *Gravity's Rainbow,* anticipates our strategy in what follows. Although we arrived at this formal solution independently of McHoul and Wills, we cheerfully acknowledge their priority.

4. At the deep narrative level, according to Greimas, we find only "semiotic squares" (also called the "constitutive model"), of which nothing need be said here except that they are purely abstract and highly controversial. The surface narrative level (roughly corresponding to Propp's morphological model) consists of a logical sequence of "narrative propositions" (*énoncés narratifs*), each of which is defined as the statement of a relation between two "actants." In all the narrative propositions of all the narratives in the world there are only six actants: Subject, Object, Sender, Receiver, Helper, Opponent. A Subject may possess, win, or lose an Object, and in the process of winning or losing that Object the Subject's desire, knowledge, and capability may be tested. A Sender may send an Object, typically a message, to a Receiver who may or may not receive it. A Helper aids whereas an Opponent seeks to hinder the Subject. It is the Subject's desire (his purpose or quest) that assigns him his place in the structure and defines his identity. Thus the traditional "villain" or "antagonist," who competes with the Subject for the same Object, i.e., for his very identity *as* Subject, is designated as an "Anti-Subject," not an Opponent but a false or would-be Subject. These actants do not appear as such at the level of discourse, the level at which the story is manifested in some particular medium, language, and form (say, as a text in English such as "The Indian Uprising"). What we find at the discourse level are "actors," anthropomorphic entities designated by names or a coherent use of pronouns and other referring expressions. Thus "actors" roughly correspond to traditional notions of "character" and are most often human agents, whereas "actants" are very highly generalized character "roles." The actantial paradigm and the actor personnel do not obey the same economy and need not display a one-to-one correspondence. The doings predicated in the text of a single actor may manifest narrative propositions pertaining to several actants, and vice versa, a single actant may be manifested in several distinct actors. In other words, a single character may be involved in actions pertaining to more than one role, while the actions and attributes of a single role may be distributed among several characters.

5. The attentive reader will perhaps have remarked the absence of the Sender and Receiver roles of the Greimasian scheme from our actant assignments. This reflects the fact that we could not confidently identify a Sender or Receiver actant in "The Indian Uprising." Greimas, it should be noted, leaves open the possibility that not all the actant positions will necessarily be filled in any given narrative. This malleability of the actantial scheme might indicate one of the directions in which Greimas's model might be historicized: that is, the specific configuration of the scheme—the presence or absence of roles, their relative dominance or subordination—might very well be historically determined. Fredric Jameson, for instance, implies that the position of Sender (or Donor) is one of privileged significance in nineteenth-century romance (e.g., *Wuthering Heights*), for historical rea-

sons having to do with the transformative effects of capital in nineteenth-century society; see *The Political Unconscious: Narrative as a Socially Symbolic Act* (Ithaca: Cornell Univ. Press, 1981), 125-29. In traditional narrative (e.g., fairy and folk tales) the Sender position is occupied by a personified source of communal authority, knowledge, etc., such as a father or king; in modern narrative, as the concept of communal authority becomes ever more problematic, the Sender becomes increasingly difficult to personify. No wonder, then, that in a text like "The Indian Uprising," in which the notion of community is so overtly problematized, the Sender position goes unfilled.

6. Apart from the Indian wars, the text conflates a number of twentieth-century sieges, civil wars, and other conflicts: the "Zouaves and cabdrivers" (§ 11) allude to the Battle of the Marne in the First World War, when the Germans were barely prevented from breaking through to Paris; the street names (Boulevard Mark Clark, George C. Marshall Allée, Rue Chester Nimitz, Skinny Wainwright Square, Patton Place) are those of American generals and admirals from the Second World War; the Abraham Lincoln Brigade (§ 22) evokes the Spanish Civil War (and the siege of Barcelona in particular?); the IRA (§ 13) of course evokes the Irish Civil War and Ulster's continuing "troubles"; the fire-arrow attack on the post office (§ 22) possibly alludes to the 1916 Easter Uprising in Dublin.

7. That analogy is implicit, for instance, in a John Wayne movie of the time, *The Green Berets,* which systematically transposes the value system and imagery of cowboys-and-Indians Westerns to the Vietnam War. The Indian wars analogy also recurs throughout Michael Herr's book on the Vietnam War, *Dispatches* (1977). Francis Ford Coppola's film *Apocalypse Now* (with a script by Michael Herr) parodies the Indian-war myth of Vietnam: a unit of the Air Cavalry (no longer cavalry at all, of course, but helicopter-borne) goes to battle to the sound of a bugle-call, the very call used in Westerns to signal "cavalry to the rescue"; the Playmates flown in by "Hugh Hefner" to entertain the troops wear skimpy cowboys-and-Indians costumes.

8. "You gave me heroin first a year ago," says Sylvia to the narrator (§ 13); see *The Waste Land* I:35-41, beginning "'You gave me hyacinths first a year ago.'" Miss R. tells the narrator, "You know nothing . . . you feel nothing, you are locked in a most savage and terrible ignorance" (§ 11); see *The Waste Land* II:121-23, "'Do / You know nothing? Do you see nothing? Do you remember / Nothing?'" The Barthelme passage about "the afternoon of a day that began with spoons and letters in hallways and under windows where men tasted the history of the heart" (§ 11) seems to echo passages both from Eliot's "The Love Song of J. Alfred Prufrock" and from his "Preludes." The Comanche prisoner, under torture, quotes

from Mann's *Death in Venice* (§ 23), while Miss R. quotes from Valéry (§ 20). Echoes of the last line of Baudelaire's "Au Lecteur" ("Hypocrite lecteur!—mon semblable!—mon frére!"), more familiar, perhaps, as one of the fragments Eliot shored against his ruins in *The Waste Land* (I:76), are detectable in several of Miss R.'s therapeutic discourses: "my boy, *mon cher,* my heart" (§ 11); "goat, muck, filth, heart of my heart" (§ 20); "my virgin, my darling, my thistle, my poppet, my own" (§ 21).

There are only a few exceptions to the pattern of modernist allusion: the band of the Seventh Cavalry plays baroque, not modernist music—Gabrieli, Albinoni, Marcello, Vivaldi, Boccherini (§ 20)—and Block quotes from *Hamlet* ("The rest is silence" [§ 16]).

9. Miss R. appears to practice a form of "semantic therapy" related to the proposals of Count Alfred Korzybski (§ 11), and Korzybski and his General Semantics Movement can be seen as a somewhat crankish and disreputable "down-market" version of the Wittgensteinian position of linguistic skepticism. According to Korzybski's *Science and Sanity: An Introduction to Non-Aristotelian Systems and General Semantics* (1933), human beings live in "linguistic slavery," constrained by the "wrong and unnatural" structures of their languages to perceive the world distortedly. Languages constructed according to what he terms "Aristotelian" principles give rise to creeds, doctrines, and institutions which are at variance with objective reality, and which in their turn produce maladjustment, conflict, and world war. Korzybski recommends retraining programs to improve "semantic hygiene": if language-users could be schooled to recognize and correct for the distortions imposed on reality by linguistic structure, a proper relationship between language and the world would be established, with benefits at all levels—physical and mental health, domestic and social harmony, world peace. Through popularizations such as Stuart Chase's *The Tyranny of Words* (1938) and S. E. Hayakawa's *Language in Thought and Action* (1943), Korzybski's ideas actually found material expression in a movement for semantic hygiene of the sort envisioned in *Science and Sanity*—the General Semantics Movement.

10. Barthelme imagined such a shrine to a literary genius of the past in "At the Tolstoy Museum" (collected in *City Life,* 1970); one of the prime exhibits is Tolstoy's monumental coat, on which Kenneth would seem to have modeled his own, so attractive to Sylvia and thus able to serve for a Comanche trap.

11. Maclin Bocock, the only critic to have given "The Indian Uprising" a full-dress reading, writes: "Yellow comes up a number of times in Barthelme's first two collections of short stories, and in *Snow White,* and is more often than not associated with the hero's feeling of sexual inadequacy, whether experienced or

imagined, in the presence of women, or his fear of emotional castration by a strong male figure" ("'The Indian Uprising,' or Donald Barthelme's Strange Object Covered with Fur," *Fiction International* 4/5 [1975]: 137).

12. This map perhaps alludes slyly to the General Semantics of Count Alfred Korzybski, mentioned in note 9 above, one of whose slogans was, "The map is not the territory," i.e., language is not to be identified with the real-world referents which it represents. Cf. the map of Vietnam described at the beginning and end of Michael Herr's *Dispatches* (1977) and the map of Central America, obviously derived from Herr's Vietnam map, in the opening paragraph of Lucius Shepard's *Life during Wartime* (1987): "To the east of this green zone [designated Free Occupied Guatemala] lay an undesignated band of yellow that crossed the country from the Mexican border to the Caribbean. The Ant Farm was a firebase on the eastern edge of the yellow band, and it was from there that Mingolla . . . lobbed shells into an area that the maps depicted in black-and-white terrain markings. And thus it was that he often thought of himself as engaged in a struggle to keep the world safe for primary colors."

13. In Tom Le Clair and Larry McCaffery, eds., *Anything Can Happen: Interviews with American Novelists* (Urbana and Chicago: Univ. of Illinois Press, 1983), 34.

14. Some of the repetitions include: "I sat there getting drunker and drunker and more in love and more in love" (§ 23), "She ran off . . . uttering shrill cries" (§ 12, 13), "Once I caught it [Kenneth's coat] going down the stairs by itself" (§ 18, 19), "See the table?" (§ 19, 20, 25), "Pack it in" (§ 22, 25), etc. The principle of repetition manifests itself at the text's linguistic microlevel in the form of obsessive and unmotivated triplications: "apples, books, long-playing records" (§ 1), "hurried, careless and exaggerated" (§ 2), "trees, lamps, swans" (§ 2), "baldness, errors, infidelity" (§ 12), "zip guns, telegrams, lockets" (§ 13), "weapons, flowers, loaves of bread" (§ 14), "friendly, kind, enthusiastic" (§ 14), "letters, postcards, calendars" (§ 22), "paint, feathers, beads" (§ 26), etc. At the level of scene, there is the torture of the Comanche(s) (§ 2, 23) and the four sessions with Miss R. (§ 11, 13, 21, 26). Are these to be understood as different occurrences of a similar event, or serial representations of the same event?

15. We suspect that our position of "weak" epistemological mastery may overlap with the recent development, by Gianni Vattimo and others, of a notion of "weak thought" in Italian philosophy; for introductions to "weak thought" in English, see Stefano Rosso, "Postmodern Italy: Notes on the 'Crisis of Reason', 'Weak Thought', and *The Name of the Rose*," in Matel Calinescu and Douwe Fokkema, eds., *Exploring Postmodernism* (Amsterdam and Philadel-phia: John Benjamins, 1987), 79-92; and Giovanna Borradori, "Weak Thought and Postmodernism: The Italian Departure from Deconstruction," *Social Text* 18 (Winter 1987-88): 39-49.

16. Grace Paley, in an interview with Moshe Ron on Israeli television, has praised Barthelme for the way he "makes the poem and the short story come together." This seems to raise the possibility of reading a story like "The Indian Uprising" more in the way one might read a poem, that is, by not insisting on full representational determinacy but looking instead for some coherence of tone or "feeling." No doubt this would in some sense be a viable approach to the problem of coherence in this text; but to treat Barthelme as essentially a "lyrical" writer, and a text like "The Indian Uprising" as in effect a prose poem, is to reduce the problem to one of genre. We find this a less interesting approach, in that it de-historicizes the issue and considerably lowers the theoretical ante.

Jerome Klinkowitz (essay date 1991)

SOURCE: Klinkowitz, Jerome. "Later Fiction." In *Donald Barthelme: An Exhibition,* pp. 109-26. Durham: Duke University Press, 1991.

[*In the following essay, Klinkowitz surveys Barthelme's later short fiction, maintaining that these stories "are more relaxed and more generously entertaining, with as many comic effects as the earlier pieces but now with the humor not at the expense of an older tradition but drawn from the properties of Barthelme's own style."*]

The second half of Donald Barthelme's canon, accomplished in the fourteen years following publication of *The Dead Father,* sounds a different note in the tonality of his short fiction. The stories are more relaxed and more generously entertaining, with as many comic effects as the earlier pieces but now with the humor not at the expense of an older tradition but drawn from the properties of Barthelme's own style. No longer will Kafka or Tolstoy be asked to sit uncomfortably within the outrageously inappropriate confines of our postmodern world; instead, the author's confidence with that world will let him joke with it on its own terms. Nor will there be a cubist disorder of conversations at birthday parties or cinema vérité pieces that steadfastly refuse to cohere. There will be precious few fragments, for now Barthelme has more trust in his ability to comprehend an overall situation—and most of all trust that his readers will not make more of them than he intends, the fear of which had kept his earlier short stories so defiantly anti-illusionistic.

With *Amateurs* (1976) the feeling is most immediately one of comfort, both of Barthelme in his role of writer and the readers in their roles as consumers of his stories. The opening piece, **"Our Work and Why We Do It,"** refers to Barthelme's frequently expressed opinion that he could be quite happy back in his previous job of assembling, composing, and laying out the contents of a magazine as its managing editor. The narrator is supervising a press, up to his elbows in "problems of makeready, registration, showthrough, and feed" ([*Amateurs*; hereafter] *A,* p. 4). But just as these unfamiliar terms have easy, functional meanings (once learned), so too are there equally mechanical solutions. No endless debates between Kierkegaard and Schlegel, no hapless protagonists pondering their existential fates—just the artistic pleasure of putting machines to work at producing the most wonderful things:

> The tiny matchbook-cover press is readied, the packing applied, the "Le Foie de Veau" form locked into place. We all stand around a small table watching the matchbook press at work. It is exactly like a toy steam engine. Everyone is very fond of it, although we also have a press big as a destroyer escort—that one has a crew of thirty-five, its own galley, its own sick bay, its own band. We print the currency of Colombia, and the Acts of the Apostles, and the laws of the land, and the fingerprints.

> (*A,* p. 5)

Within this happy context, Barthelme is able to play at language and idea with all the verve of his earlier fiction. The situation prompts a simile, and one simile prompts another, which is all it takes to turn loose his talents of linguistic invention. True, presses are run by a crew, just like navy ships—so why not add the other things navy ships have? As for what they print, the items seem extravagantly odd and random—except that all four exist in this world as printed objects and therefore have to be printed somewhere. Because these workers are pressmen and not writers, they are under no obligation to make the subjects cohere. They just print them, and are therefore granted a rare pleasure of play and association—the same pleasures Barthelme gives his reader in this narrative.

Within this story that typifies *Amateurs* are most of Barthelme's familiar techniques. Skinny lists of terms, here the names of typefaces, run down the page in one of the author's favorite forms, the litany. Other texts literally crash through the windows, bringing the same excitement as do the salesmen, rushing through the doors with new orders. The one element missing is that of graphic collage. But the press functions and typeface features take that role, and the story's busy tone is reminiscent of Barthelme's collage story from *Sadness,* **"The Flight of Pigeons from the Palace."** In that piece, however, the narrator had been driven nearly to exhaustion by having to come up with marvel after new marvel to delight audiences. Here there is no such worry, because the work is invigorating, rewarding, and unlikely to dissipate in either exhaustion or obsolescence. "Our reputation for excellence is unexcelled, in every part of the world," Barthelme's narrator concludes. "And will be maintained until the destruction of our art by some other art which is just as good but which, I am happy to say, has not yet been invented" (*A,* p. 9).

Such is the condition in which Donald Barthelme finds his own work as the 1970s end. After a decade and a half of innovation, perforce disruptive because of the modernist traditions and conventions that stood in his way, and after the equally taxing struggle to establish his own postmodern mastery of the novel, he could—much like this story's pressman—settle more comfortably into a style of fiction writing that he knew would remain the standard of both excellence and currency for some time. Although the heyday of innovative fiction's spectacular accomplishments was over, it was now established as the mainstream—sufficiently mainstream for it to be attacked as Barthelme and his generation had challenged fiction a decade and a half before. And for the time being these challenges had been met. The attempts of John Gardner's *On Moral Fiction* (1978) and Gerald Graff's *Literature against Itself* (1979) to roll back standards to those of moralism and modernism had been resisted, and the next style of fiction, the Minimalism espoused by Raymond Carver, Ann Beattie, and younger brother Frederick Barthelme, had emerged by drawing as much on innovative fiction's imaginative freedom as on realism's figuration. The answer had been play: not the cocky, disruptive, irreverent play that subverted modernism in **Come Back, Dr. Caligari,** but a more harmlessly engaging style of amusement that takes the givens of both moralism and realism and good naturedly stands them on their heads.

In *Amateurs* Barthelme finds occasion for such overturnings in **"The School,"** whose life-or-death issue is the 100 percent mortality rate suffered by the pets and projects of a grade school class (starting with its tree plantings, continuing with its gerbil, and reaching the apex of anxiety with the demise of its sponsored third-world orphan), and in **"Porcupines at the University,"** an earlier story passed over several times before but now updated and added to the canon as a way of showing how the most unlikely and mutually alien subjects can be melded into a coherent story if all are treated strictly in character with the tools of literary realism (the situation involves a herd of porcupines being driven by porcupine wranglers across a college campus beleaguered by its own problems of disruption and dissent). In *Great Days* (1979) Barthelme shifts from subject and theme to structure and formal technique, yet keeps the same ideals of comedy and play in mind by focusing on the performative—a stylistic equivalent of the activities represented in *Amateurs* (class projects expiring, porcupines being wrangled, presses being run). Together, these collections reveal a confidence with subject and form equal to almost any previous high point in the development of the American short story.

Not surprisingly, this emphasis on performance coincides with the use of that most performative of American art forms, jazz, as a topic for several stories collected in *Great Days.* After **"The Crisis"** has begun the volume with a cautiously restrained examination of texture and surface and **"The Apology"** has moved more obviously into a jazz idiom by showing how an overwilling apologizer can drive away an offended suitor with a rifflike assemblage of overstated regrets, Barthelme offers a piece whose title tells the reader just what these words are meant to create: **"The New Music,"** in which standards of musical composition enhance the systematics of linguistics that the author has used before to expand the dimensions of narrative.

In both music and speech, rhythms are carriers of meaning. Rhythmic dialogues make statements far beyond the content of conceptual exchange; consider how the structure of something as simple as "Where did you go? Out. What did you do? Nothing" says so much that it becomes the title of a humorous commentary on childhood's disaffections. In Barthelme's **"The New Music,"** the entire story is constituted of just such a disconnected dialogue, a mode he introduces here and continues in several other pieces as the collection's most distinguishing form. Canonically, it is the style of talk Julie and Emma exchanged in *The Dead Father* as a way of generating a new linguistic reality far beyond the constraints of both the father's and son's self-serving forms. Now in *Great Days* story after story can be produced by its creative possibilities, with a confidence detached from narrative explanations and contextual justifications. What the characters do in **"The New Music"** is rarely directed toward a goal or even an object, but rather expresses its own sense of activity:

> —What did you do today?
>
> —Went to the grocery store and Xeroxed a box of English muffins, two pounds of ground veal and an apple. In flagrant violation of the Copyright Act.
>
> . . . . .
>
> —Ah well. I was talking to a girl, talking to her mother actually but the daughter was very much present, on the street. The daughter was absolutely someone you'd like to take to bed and hug and kiss, if you weren't too old. If she weren't too young. She was a wonderful-looking young woman and she was looking at me quite seductively, very seductively, *smoldering* a bit, and I was thinking quite well of myself, very well indeed, thinking myself quite the—Until I realized she was just practicing.
>
> ([*Great Days*; hereafter] *GD*, pp. 21-22)

The most frequent words in this passage, like the activities themselves, are simple gerunds: *ing* words that, by virtue of their lacking an object, refer simply to themselves. Placed in the context of unintroduced and unpunctuated dialogue, they have no reason for existence except their own play, which Barthelme masters in a way both pleasing and amusing to his readers. The effect is that of jazz improvisation, especially the style of two instruments trading four-bar phrases back and forth in such a way that each complements the other's action while still advancing its own, as happens in a section of **"The New Music,"** originally published in *The New Yorker* of October 2, 1978, as **"Momma"**:

> —Momma didn't 'low no clarinet playing in here. Unfortunately.
>
> —Momma.

> —Momma didn't 'low no clarinet playing in here. Made me sad.
>
> —Momma was outside.
>
> —Momma was *very* outside.
>
> —Sitting there, 'lowing and not-'lowing. In her old rocking chair.
>
> —'Lowing this, not-'lowing that.
>
> —Didn't 'low oboe.
>
> —Didn't 'low gitfiddle. Vibes.
>
> —Rock over your damn foot and bust it, you didn't pop to when she was 'lowing and not-'lowing.
>
> —Right. 'Course, she had all the grease.
>
> —True.
>
> —You wanted a little grease, like to buy a damn comic book or something, you had to go to Momma.
>
> —Sometimes yes, sometimes no. Her variously colored moods.
>
> —Mauve. Warm gold. Citizen's blue.
>
> —Mauve mood that got her thrown in the jug that time.
>
> (*GD*, p. 29)

The European style of punctuating lines of dialogue makes them hang on the page, while their responsive rhythm creates a mood all its own: of reminiscing, another gerund that is even more convincing than the activities reported earlier, for now that activity is actually taking place.

Jazz provides a model for interacting rhythms, and is by nature an activity that represents nothing other than itself—postmodernism's own ideal for fictive writing. Even as a subject, it lets Barthelme take his narrative language further than other topics might always allow, as happens in a complementary story from *Great Days,* **"The King of Jazz."** The title is referential—to the 1930 movie featuring Paul Whiteman and his orchestra—but also reflective of practices in and around jazz, including the occasion of "cutting sessions" (where players compete against each other in jam sessions) and the way critics like to assign labels (making the title ironic, for Whiteman's popularized music made him anything but an innovator or key figure).

"Well I'm the king of jazz now, thought Hokie Mokie to himself as he oiled the slide on his trombone," the story begins—like many postmodern stories, just where a conventional tale would end. To reassure himself of such status Hokie plays a few notes out the window, which starts a critical dialogue between two passers-by. Can you tell who is playing, "Can you distinguish our great homemade American jazz performers, each from the other?" "Used to could," the friend replies, anticipating Simon's own little riff in *Paradise* when he challenges himself to name ten influential drummers in the history of jazz. "Then who is playing?" Easy: "Sounds like Hokie Mokie to me. Those few but perfectly selected notes have the real epiphanic glow" (*GD*, p. 55), which is itself a snatch of the language generated so facilely by the first generation of jazz critics (nearly all of them afterhours professors from Columbia and Rutgers).

The story proceeds by letting this style of language generate itself, as the tropes of literary criticism and art commentary spin out endlessly in an attempt to capture the essence of Hokie Mokie's music—which is, of course, something that neither written words nor painted objects can approximate. It is when Hokie is challenged by a young Japanese musician that the king's truly great playing—and the critical listeners' most extravagant play of comparisons—begins:

> "You mean that sound that sounds like the cutting edge of life? That sounds like polar bears crossing the Arctic ice pans? That sounds like a herd of musk ox in full flight? That sounds like male walruses diving to the bottom of the sea? That sounds like fumaroles smoking on the slopes of Mt. Katmai? That sounds like the wild turkey walking through the deep, soft forest? That sounds like beavers chewing trees in an Appalachian marsh? That sounds like an oyster fungus growing on an aspen trunk? That sounds like a mule deer wandering a montane of the Sierra Nevada? That sounds like prairie dogs kissing? That sounds like manatees munching seaweed at Cape Sable? That sounds like coatimundis moving in packs across the face of Arkansas? That sounds like—?"

(GD, p. 59)

This is not at all what Hokie sounds like, for words cannot be music, and the terms themselves, by virtue of their references, are contradictory (how can turkeys and beavers and polar bears all sound the same? They can't; but the speaker's language about them does!). The *activity* of such language does approximate the activity of Hokie playing jazz, and unleashing that verbal improvisation is what **"The King of Jazz"** lets Barthelme do.

His next collection both continues this special interest and confirms its supporting style in the canon. The volume is itself a gesture toward canon formation: a tall, closely printed book running 457 pages titled *Sixty Stories* (1981) that combines nine new short stories with another 51 (of a possible 120) from the earlier gatherings. Gone from the living record are such self-consciously difficult pieces as **"Florence Green Is 81"** and **"Bone Bubbles"**; also missing are the purposely flat narratives of **"Edward and Pia"** and **"A Few Moments of Sleeping and Waking."** In their place, Barthelme's emphasis falls on his earlier experiments with playful delight such as **"Me and Miss Mandible"** and **"The Balloon,"** while admitting two previously noncanonical pieces from *Guilty Pleasures* as full-fledged stories (and not just parodies)—a third will appear six years later in the companion volume, *Forty Stories,* to round out the author's hundred. There is even **"A Manual for Sons"** from *The Dead Father,* a self-contained story that employs similarly ludic devices and is written with the same sense of comic confidence that became the domi-

nant mode of *Amateurs* and *Great Days.* From the latter, *Sixty Stories* reprints **"The Crisis," "The New Music,"** and **"The King of Jazz,"** while the former collection is represented by **"The School"** and **"Our Work and Why We Do It"** in *Sixty Stories* and **"Porcupines at the University"** in *Forty Stories.*

What distinguishes any retrospective exhibition is not just selections from the past but the nature of new work being shown at the same time. The last decade of Donald Barthelme's life is dominated by these kinds of gatherings, with just one volume of previously uncollected stories in between: *Overnight to Many Distant Cities* (1983). But since both retrospectives add new material, his writer's development can still be traced even in these mature years of canon stabilization.

Of Barthelme's three books from the 1980s, *Sixty Stories* is the simplest and most direct in terms of growth, for rounding out its selections from the author's earlier collections are nine new stories. All were published between November 27, 1978, and January 26, 1981, in the wake of *Great Days* and before the gathering for *Overnight to Many Distant Cities* commenced. In length, number, historical proximity, and relative affinity and diversity, they are presented just like the samplings from other collections preceding them in *Sixty Stories.* Of the nine, five are dash-dialogue stories, while others relish the odd details that give *Great Days* its special flavor. One piece, **"The Farewell,"** picks up where **"On the Steps of the Conservatory"** left off, while another—**"Bishop"**—introduces the character whose similar story inaugurates the *Overnight* volume. Throughout the nine runs a consistent interest in language—not so much for the semiotic fascinations evident in Barthelme's earliest fiction, but more for the way certain nuances, drawn from various parts of the contemporary culture, form attractive and intriguing voices that can play off each other in dialogue or establish themselves as identifiable texts within the greater narrative.

Such voices, both by themselves and in conversation, are played to the full in **"The Emerald,"** *Sixty Stories'* most obvious contribution to the Barthelme style. Like the most radically experimental fictions of earlier collections, it was not first published in *The New Yorker,* but rather appeared in *Esquire,* in the November 1979 issue (and again in 1980 as a forty-page limited edition book published by Sylvester and Orphanos in Los Angeles). It is easily Barthelme's longest short story, eclipsing even **"A Manual for Sons,"** which is given such generic status here. Yet for all its length, **"The Emerald"** manages to move along very quickly thanks to its author's customary lightness of style and snappiness of juxtapositional transitions. The new element is a characterizational and appealingly vocal use of language, which is generated not by philosophers or advertising copywriters but by various people who sound like they come from the streets of Greenwich Village or the towns of East Texas (Barthelme's two principal residences) and who speak with the quaint angularity sure to catch the ear of such a creative artist. In the dialogue sections, oddly named characters (Tope, Sallywag, Wide Boy, Taptoe) rifle clichés back and forth (sure as shootin', right as rain) as they lay plans for stealing the emerald and cutting it up for profit. In sections of a more extended conversation, Moll—the emerald's mother—finds out as much about the interviewing journalist as the journalist finds out about Moll. The interview does reveal that the greatest threat to Moll's emerald comes from a witch hunter named Vandermaster, which sets the stage for a meeting between these two as the story's protagonist and principal antagonist. Their dialogue is the piece's most inventive one, he mixing Joycean word salad with redneck vernacular, she sounding like both a sorceress and a street-tough feminist. Yet even the subplot has its special humor, as the journalist and her subject are manipulated by an unscrupulous editor while the interview itself, undertaken as the stuff of prize winning journalism, often devolves into questions such as "do you have a chili recipe you'd care to share with the folks?" (*SS,* p. 413).

The nine new short fictions in *Sixty Stories* also indicate the step Barthelme would take in *Overnight to Many Distant Cities,* his 1983 volume that stands as the last gathering of previously uncollected work published during his lifetime. Though at first glance *Overnight* is one of his more radical experiments, its fascination with the tones and textures of language is evident in *Sixty Stories*' "Aria," a 1979 *New Yorker* piece that stands as the first of the author's extended monologues. As an exercise in language, it complements the dash-dialogue stories by posing the reader as the story's other conversationalist. Or, if one wishes to remain uninvolved (something few postmodern readers can do), it can be said that the text in **"Aria"** interrogates itself. But in combination with such stories as **"Bishop,"** where the concerns of daily life are as common as they were in **"Critique de la Vie Quotidienne,"** this new mode of writing is less like the impenetrability of **"Bone Bubbles"** and **"Sentence"** and much more like the tenor of the *Overnight* collection, where the same character (consistently named "Bishop") is featured in the first full story and whose presence, as an icon of the author's own life in this world, remains a constant source of language and generator of narrative action.

The innovative nature of *Overnight to Many Distant Cities* is announced on its table of contents, for instead of listing the customary fourteen to sixteen new short stories, it alternates the titles of a dozen such pieces with the initial words (followed by three dots) of much shorter items in between. This structural distinction carries into the book itself, where the full-length fictions are printed in roman type while the miniatures are set in italics. The writing is all Barthelme's, and most of it is even from *The New Yorker,* with the occasional piece from another venue accommodated quite naturally within this new format. But the range of these materials is quite impressive, stretching from the author's main-line short stories to his unsigned "Comment" pieces from *The New Yorker*'s front pages, together with stories from such places as *Harper's* and *New American Review* and a contribution that first appeared in

an art gallery's catalog. In the past, "Comment" and catalog writings had been consigned to a separate volume, *Great Days,* and then began appearing in other collections as exceptions rather than the rule. But with *Overnight to Many Distant Cities* a structure is devised to integrate the author's signed and unsigned work.

The obvious precedent for structuring a short story collection in this manner is Ernest Hemingway's *In Our Time* (1925). For this work the accepted interpretation is that by interleaving his fifteen full-length stories with an equal number of short, italicized passages Hemingway was able to have the cultural shock of World War I permeate the otherwise domestic business of such fictions as "The Three Day Blow," "The End of Something," and the two parts of "Big Two-Hearted River." Turning to Barthelme's experiment over half a century later, one must ask if the postmodern writer is using his own italicized interleavings for transitions, as associations, or for other reflective purposes. Unlike Hemingway, Barthelme has no agenda: there is nothing in *Overnight to Many Distant Cities* to suggest that one orders and controls in the imaginative life (Hemingway's roman typeface stories) what cannot be controlled in life (*In Our Time*'s italicized "chapters"); nor is there any hint that art is neat while the world's a mess. For Barthelme, the eminent postmodernist, life and art are sometimes identical, driven as the former is by the latter's organizing principles. It is the interplay between *Overnight*'s full stories and brief interpolations that establishes this principle not just as a thematic reference or technical trick but as a creative force in Donald Barthelme's work.

Story after story in *Overnight to Many Distant Cities* features characters caught up in the world of textuality, struggling to read their way through a culture where signs can be of more substance than the reality they might be presumed to signify. In **"Visitors,"** the familiar protagonist named Bishop encounters movies, commercials, labels from art history, and made-for-seduction recipes during the summer interval when his fifteen-year-old daughter visits him. From this textual mélange he extracts a recipe for curing her persistent stomach ache—not a menu item, but a snappy chalk talk on the transition from Impressionism to Modernism. In **"Affection"** a married couple close to estrangement consult various textual sources for advice, from mother to fortune teller (Madam Olympia) and blues pianist (Sweet Pappa Cream Puff), all of whom contribute to the couple's eventual intertext, which is survived only thanks to the husband's increased earnings and his ability to not only read the *New York Times* but "wash it off my hands when I have finished reading it, every day" (*O,* p. 36). This theme continues through the volume, as Barthelme complements these recent stories with older material that had sat uncollected since 1971, such as **"The Mothball Fleet"** (where, in his more familiar manner of taking a metaphor and fleshing it out ad absurdum, the navy's flotilla of mothballed destroyers sails down the Hudson as real and as startling as the ship *San Dominick* encountered in Melville's "Benito Cereno") and **"The Sea of Hesitation"** (where the narrator is beset by texts cascading from his past, including quotations from Civil War history and phone calls from his ex-wife).

What makes the volume different, however, and what justifies the author's resurrection of these older stories (which otherwise may have remained noncanonical, or at the very least so repetitious of outdated, minor trends that reprinting them would be redundant) is the function of the brief, italicized interleavings. These passages, never bearing a title and taking their table-of-contents identification from the egalitarianism of their opening words, form a larger continuous text in which the titled stories are set as intertexts. As a context for stories that are often about lives being lived within texts (movies, commercials, advertisements, letters, telephone calls, references to books and history), the interleavings have the latitude to speak either more abstractly or more specifically about such circumstances, and by doing so yield a continuity of literary action that shows how the otherwise diverse weavings of **Overnight to Many Distant Cities** are in fact cut from the same broad cloth—a multiform cloth to be sure, produced as it has been by the master weaver of stories, Donald Barthelme.

The situation of a typical story, **"Affection,"** is a good example of how Barthelme's method works. Preceding it is the two-and-one-half-page passage beginning *"Financially, the paper"*; the narrative voice in this particular interpolation is that of a writer whose newspaper is financially healthy but journalistically weak, its portfolio fattened by diversification into everything from mining to greeting cards and its real-estate, food, clothing, plant, and furniture sections growing larger each week, at the same time that hard news and editorial depth suffer. Typically for the times, the problem is being treated systematically, even as the system in question (management levels) falters:

> The Editor's Caucus has once again applied to middle management for relief, and has once again been promised it (but middle management has Glenfiddich on its breath, even at breakfast). Top management's polls say that sixty-five percent of the readers "want movies," and feasibility studies are being conducted. Top management acknowledges, over long lunches at good restaurants, that the readers are wrong to "want movies" but insists that morality cannot be legislated. The newsroom has been insulated (with products from the company's Echotex division) so that the people in the newsroom can no longer hear the sounds in the streets.

> (*O*, p. 24)

Brief as it is, the interleaved passage profits from Barthelme's ability to take a limited number of factors—the newspaper's other divisions, the decline of its traditional standards, the lavish life style of its top management and the alcohol-ridden anxiety of the middle managers—and let their interactive energy combine to generate a tight little narrative. But in the setting of **Overnight to Many Distant Cities,** it performs a structural function as well, enfolding (with *"I put a name in an envelope . . . ,"* which follows) the more conventionally written and published story, **"Affection."**

"Affection" itself features a newspaper only in its final paragraph, where its print is something that informs the husband-narrator (threatening to estrange him from his wife) but which also can be washed away (thus saving the marriage). Along the way to this conclusion are just the influences that have fattened up certain sections of the paper while slimming down others, although for the couple's life as lived these influences are encountered firsthand. The wife's chief advisor is her mother, whose "counsel is broccoli, mostly, but who else was she going to talk to?" (*O*, p. 30). When the husband consults his own advisor, Madam Olympia, her patois rendering of a typical marital conversation uncovers the "agendas on both sides" (*O*, p. 31). Subsequent textual renderings come from the languages of TV soap opera, psychiatry, and the blues. As for the couple's problems, they're solved only by a sudden influx of new money—something wily Madam Olympia has expected would have to happen from the start.

From here Barthelme moves to an abstract piece, *"I put a name in an envelope . . . ,"* which first appeared as part of *Joseph Cornell: Catalogue of the Exhibition, February 28-March 20, 1976,* published by the Leo Castelli Gallery. In the unpaged catalog's preface, designer-editor Sandra Leonard Starr thanks the author, "who has loved Cornell's work for a very long time, for saying he couldn't think of anything to write and writing anyway." Its apparent abstraction and self-advertised insouciance do not detract from its fictive excellence, both in itself and as an interpolation within **Overnight to Many Distant Cities**; in fact, the piece is as well organized and as indicative of Barthelme's aesthetic as his catalog preface to the exhibit of women in art from 2500 B.C. to the present, *She* (New York: Cordier & Ekstrom Gallery, 3 December 1970 to 16 January 1971). There the author had posited woman as an imaginary being, an absent referent present only in the empty space she would otherwise be occupying. For Joseph Cornell, Barthelme casts out a similar net, retrieves nothing, but discovers that Cornell has become his net. For the Castelli catalog, he presents a single page typed on his own IBM Selectric; photocopied in facsimile fashion, it is folded twice and placed in an envelope, just as its first line describes; the stuffed envelope then becomes one of the several loose items gathered into the catalog, which is itself a two-pocket folder holding several individual pages and photographs. Reading the catalog thus becomes much like viewing a Cornell artwork, as the various free-standing yet compositionally integral elements are sorted out and comprehended both as entities and as parts of a whole. Reading Barthelme's page in the catalog or on the pages in **Overnight to Many Distant Cities** replicates this process, and in the latter case also supplies a context for **"Affection"** preceding it and **"Lightning"** to follow.

Like one of Joseph Cornell's boxes, Barthelme's page recycles discrete but personally treasured items in a way that produces a new artistic whole. **"Affection"** has shown an unhappily married couple doing much the same with the fragmented texts of their lives, the bonding agent being another printed text: money. **"Lightning"** poses a single protagonist who must deal with similar intertexts even as he struggles to write and live one of his own. Freelancing for a *People*-like weekly called *Folks,* he must take assignments on human-interest topics (such as people struck by lightning); the story's length is dictated by concerns of layout, while its focus must be, in his editor's words, on a subject who is not only "pretty sensational" but "slightly wonderful" (*O,* p. 41). His own career as a writer has taken him down a path much like the husband's in **"Affection,"** compromising ideals in order to earn more money to please his wife; but at this later stage he has lost his wife and quit the job for the textual bliss of freelancing according to his whims and fancies, with just the occasional high-paying job for *Folks* to keep him in rent and liquor.

This writer's human-interest feature on interesting people struck by lightning turns out to be a harvesting of recycled parts: nearly every one of his subjects has a grandparent who was struck by lightning as well (usually struck off a buckboard in 1910) and has fastened on an authoritative text to interpret his or her event. The writer himself becomes format-driven, blanching when a second respondent also has a husband named Marty—*"Two Martys in the same piece?"* (*O,* p. 44). But at this point he is figuratively struck by lightning himself, falling in love with this woman who is not only slightly wonderful but capable of enfolding him within the text of her own life, made as it is of trendy, manufactured images. Drunk with love, he tries to seduce her with a story generated out of fragments from his public relations work for Texas oil. But all that succeeds is the *Folks* layout, expanded as it is for this woman of his dreams who has become, in his editor's words, "approximately fantastic" (*O,* p. 51).

Through these stories and their interleavings Barthelme has woven a larger text whose strands remain distinct even as they become mutually enhancing. As intertextual elements exist within the volume's full-length *New Yorker* stories, so do those stories themselves function intertextually within the collection's larger narrative movement as carried forth by the italicized interleavings. By themselves, *Overnight*'s titled stories are reminiscent of an earlier Barthelme or, as with **"Captain Blood,"** of Barthelme's colleagues in postmodern fiction—one thinks of Robert Coover's classic reversal of the Casey at the Bat narrative, "McDuff on the Mound," when reading Barthelme's hilarious account of a textually correct but contextually inappropriate John Paul Jones speaking his historic lines prematurely and to the wrong auditor. Arranged as they are in *Overnight,* however, these stories not only reinforce each other, as should happen in a decently arranged collection, but are situated within a larger whole that the interleavings sustain. Should the reader wonder what type of literature is **"Captain Blood,"** there follows an interleaving in the form of conceptual art, *"A woman seated on a plain wooden chair . . . ,"* the nature of which suggests that there can be conceptual fiction as well (which **"Captain Blood"** certainly is). If **"Conversations with Goethe"** seems at first like a single-joke story (the master's one-

sided conversations consisting of aphoristic similes rushing pell-mell into absurdity), the interleaving that follows draws directly on American popular culture to show how the same thing happens when the fans of country and western music dote on the lyrics of their heroes. Finally, in the volume's title story, the larger narrative concludes with these italicized interpolations incorporated directly into the text.

Four years later, in the volume complementing *Sixty Stories* and rounding off his hundred presumably best stories, Donald Barthelme reprints **"Overnight to Many Distant Cities."** But among these *Forty Stories* are no less than eleven others from the *Overnight* volume, more than from any single collection recalled for service in his first retrospective. True, *Forty Stories* also takes a second sampling from books as far back as *Unspeakable Practices, Unnatural Acts,* and draws so many additional pieces from *City Life* and especially *Sadness* as to make those collections' representation among the favored hundred almost complete, with only the extremes of obtuseness (**"Bone Bubbles"**) and obviousness (**"Brain Damage," "Perpetua,"** and **"Subpoena"**) missing. Yet the special nature of *Overnight to Many Distant Cities* as an integral volume is lost, for the stories are not only presented in a different order (as Barthelme had done for the collections covered in *Sixty Stories*) but are scattered throughout *Forty Stories* almost randomly, a departure from his earlier retrospective practice of keeping each volume's selections together. As a final blow to *Overnight*'s special nature, the typographical and titular distinctions between the mainline stories and the interpolations are effaced, making each one just one more equal addition to the Barthelme canon.

The special task of **Forty Stories,** however, is to complete an even larger whole—a whole much greater than the sum of its individual parts. In this sense, the material comprising *Overnight to Many Distant Cities* can be read two ways: as a volume that can stand alone almost as easily and completely as do any of the author's novels, or serving as examples of his short story artistry, twelve of which he selects, along with nine quite recent and therefore previously uncollected stories, to represent the latest developments in his work.

These twenty-one pieces reveal a Barthelme as comfortable and as playful as the writer *Sixty Stories* portrays, but also as an author committed to drawing openly and directly on his own experience. In stories such as **"Visitors," "Affection,"** and **"Lightning"** (all of which are reprinted here), bits and pieces of Donald Barthelme's life could be recognized, but were always couched within the conventions of fiction: different names, similar but not identical professions, and only a generalized reference to locale (Texas, but not specifically Houston; New York City, but only occasionally an address identifiable as Greenwich Village). But by choosing his unsigned *New Yorker* "Comment" piece identified as *"When he came . . ."* in *Overnight to Many Distant Cities* and running it as a full-fledged, co-equal story under the title of **"The**

New Owner," Barthelme takes a step as obvious as when selecting his parodies and satires (previously sequestered in *Guilty Pleasures*) for canonization in *Sixty Stories.* In 1978, for a limited edition titled *Here in the Village* published with the Lord John Press in Northridge, California, he had gathered up eleven such unsigned columns and added his Cordier & Ekstrom catalog preface on images of women in art to form an entertaining, engaging, and self-exploratory look at the real Donald Barthelme living on New York's West 11th Street. Even as that volume appeared, the text presented as **"The New Owner"** in *Forty Stories* was being debuted as an unsigned "Comment" essay in *The New Yorker* for December 4, 1978, leading off the magazine's editorial section on page 21. From here its progress is revealing, not just because it brings an element of *Here in the Village* into **Overnight to Many Distant Cities,** but because even that presence, interpolative as it was, now becomes mainstream in the retrospective collection that rounds out Barthelme's career as a short story writer.

Of the author's signed *New Yorker* stories published since *Overnight,* only **"Kissing the President"** (August 1, 1983) is passed over. Of the nine included, a few tend toward abstraction, but the great majority are evocative of experiences and locales in Barthelme's very real world. The 1980s had seen him return home to Texas for part of each year and a chair at the University of Houston, his alma mater, and in **"Sinbad"** he unites the abstract and referential streams of his later work by crafting a story in which the protagonist is at once Sinbad the Sailor washed up on the figurative beach of middle age at the same time he's teaching a writing class at an all too typical southwestern university, where he rescues a failing pedagogic situation by realizing "I have something to teach. Be like Sinbad! Venture forth! Embosom the waves, let your shoes be sucked from your feet and your very trousers enticed by the frothing deep. The ambiguous sea awaits, I told them, marry it!" (**FS,** p. 34).

"The point of my career is perhaps how little I achieved" (**FS,** p. 256), concludes the journalist-turned-religion-writer being interviewed in **"January,"** *Forty Stories'* last selection. As a piece of fiction, it interrogates itself—how odd that for all of Donald Barthelme's experiments with form, he waits until almost the very end before trying the same format so many critics, including myself, had used to generate texts, presenting him with studious questions to which he would reply in kind, much as does the character Thomas Brecker in this piece. The point of **"January,"** however, is that viewing a lifetime's remarkable achievements as "so little" is the best way to keep one's self alive. The title, after all, is not "November" or "December," but rather the year's coldest month, the depth of winter, which is nevertheless the start of something entirely new. *Forty Stories,* providing as it does the larger context and canonical status for *Here in the Village,* may well be the January of Barthelme's career—not as a living author but as one for the ages.

Barbara L. Roe (essay date 1992)

SOURCE: Roe, Barbara L. "Part 1: The Short Fiction." In *Donald Barthelme: The Short Fiction,* pp. 3-93. New York: Twayne Publishers, 1992.

[*In the following excerpt, Roe surveys Barthelme's later fiction and reflects on his legacy as a short fiction author.*]

MORTAL VISIONS "VISITORS"

In 1981, when Barthelme turned 50, he seemed pleased with the view from this lookout. The years, he said, had tempered his anger over humanity's folly and taught him to "cherish" life more and more as there is "less and less time" (Brans, 131). The implications of mortality, however, preoccupy Barthelme's last decade of stories, as aging characters debate, deny, or crusade for their remaining prospects. Not surprisingly, *gray* often betokens their uncertain status. Depending on a character's perspective, for instance, gray hair is either the gloomy wreath of death or the respectable laurels of experience. Though Bishop, the 49-year-old protagonist of **"Visitors,"** still idles in the holding tank of middle age, he is beginning to feel the pinch of a silver crown.

Vulnerable to affection, understandably perplexed by the contradictions of age, Bishop never hides his humanity in caricature as so many other characters do. In fact, his story is among the least inventive but most candidly emotional of Barthelme's work. Bishop's cassoulet seduction of young, tanned Christie and particularly his hip bedtime art lecture to 15-year-old daughter Katie deliver the verbal gymnastics that Barthelme aficionados expect of the author's prose: "You get Kandinsky, a bad mother, all them pick-up-sticks pictures, you get my man Mondrian, he's the one with the rectangles and shit, . . . you get Moholy-Nagy, he did all the plastic thingummies and shit'" ([**Forty Stories**; hereafter] *F,* 113). However, Bishop's emotions— loneliness, desire, compassion—always simmer near the surface. This emotional complex gathers force in Bishop's tender relationship with Katie, who has been visiting her father each summer since her parents' divorce. As she languishes on the couch with stomach flu, he tries to cheer and comfort her, even though he, too, is ill. Other Barthelme men bemoan such imposition, but Bishop ministers to the task lovingly. His only complaint about the child is the joke he repeatedly musters to reconcile himself to divorce from Katie's "otherwise very sensible, and thrifty" (*F,* 109) mother. "'It was your fault,'" he teases Katie. "'Yours. You made too much noise, as a kid, I couldn't work.' His ex-wife had once told Katie this as an explanation for the divorce, and he'll repeat it until its untruth is marble, a monument" (*F,* 108).

The father-daughter confinement occasions not only intermittent conversations, but also drifting reveries that expose Bishop's disorienting status. Worried about his solitude, Katie encourages her father to live a little: "You could find somebody. You're handsome for your age. . . .

You don't try" (*F,* 107). But this accusation is not quite true. As Bishop recalls, he has ventured into the city streets, only to be confused by the uncertainty of signs— the motley throng on West Broadway, artistic conspiracies. Once, he forced himself to enter a gallery and to wham "EVERLAST heavy bags" (*F,* 109) at the artist's invitation. He hurt himself. Similarly, though he picks up Christie on the street and lures her back to his apartment, their dialogue only underscores the disparity in their ages and interests. He babbles excitedly about Richard Widmark's "resilience" (*F,* 111), but she misses any hinted comparisons to Bishop. When she then extols Robert Redford, Bishop worries that "the conversation has strayed, like a bad cow, from the proper path" (*F,* 112). Even Katie is a paradox. Ill, she seems just a helpless child, but when Bishop is with her in public, he is self-conscious of her maturing body and their impression on strangers as she clings to his arm.

The story closes with Bishop pondering yet another, perhaps prophetic enigma: whether his elderly neighbors eat "breakfast by candlelight" because "they are terminally romantic" or because "they're trying to save electricity" (*F,* 114). Bishop is equally vague about his own circumstances. Resilience is an effort, but desire and romance are not dead in him. Unlike Barthelme's more pitiable characters, he has yet to witness or experience the paralyzing fear of the unknown.

"MORNING"

This story's characters, in contrast, feverishly debate the implications of their mortality in a stark dialogue, stripped of the comfortable setting and explicitly identified characters and relationships offered in **"Visitors."** Distractions of style aside, **"Morning"** exposes emotions as honest and disarming as Bishop's. Hastening to remove from the world their worst fears, the speakers challenge each other to list their particular demons—sirens, vestments, breaking glass, an aging hand, but not death, not death, one thinly protests. As the companions alternately beat their oars against mortality's tide, acceptance and denial of life's inevitable end reciprocate. "Say you're frightened" ([*Sixty Stories;* hereafter] *SS,* 359), the first voice insists, at least twice repeating this plea. Initially more vulnerable than his companion, he pules about an enshrouding "gray light," while the other obliviously basks in his own brilliant orange desire, "a firestorm of porn" (*SS,* 359), the hoped-for glow beneath a girl's tight pants.

The conversation's nameless voices, abrupt shifts, and vague pronoun antecedents (especially the occasional "she") confuse the speakers' gender and number. Hence, if the text's marginal dashes punctuate shifts in *thought,* not necessarily changes of speaker, then one, two, or several characters may contribute ideas to, say, the "not afraid of" (*SS,* 360) litany early in the story. Even if, in the simplest reading, the marginal dashes designate two characters' alternating responses (voice A, voice B), the respective trumpets of terror and courage interchange midway through the

dialogue. Forgetting his earlier advice that one should not stop long enough to dwell on his fears, the initially more confident speaker of this reading confesses his dread of mornings, weighty with a day's demands. The topic suddenly turns to death, and its lingering denial further undermines confidence. However, as the now-timid voice nervously elicits his companion's confessions to dread, the latter rejuvenates himself with romantic memories and a healthy list of his life's remaining prospects. True, morning confers upon the coward the terrifying responsibility of efficient and timely fulfillment of his prospects, of accounting to his conscience or spouse for some 480 meaningful daylight minutes. But chasing the night's phantoms, morning also ushers in hope. Though he cannot escape his mortality, he does not yet have to forfeit the delights of a "bright glorious day" (*SS,* 362) and consign himself to a dim room with lonely old men. He and his companion can enjoy the mottled hues of their metamorphosis, gray tendering orange, at least until "darkness, and they give up the search" (*SS,* 363). Regardless of the number or sequence of characters' voices, this debate's outcome is the same.

In the similarly affirmative dialogue **"Great Days,"** a voice proclaims, "Each great day is itself, with its own war machines, rattles, and green lords" (*F,* 242), certainly an ambiguous offering. But as the story's closing knock-knock joke warns, only solitude and anonymity befall those who abandon effort, vigilance, and faith.

"THE NEW MUSIC"

Such hopelessness ultimately tolls doom for the lost, aging souls of **"The New Music."** Like the impotent cronies in **"Grandmother's House,"** the speakers could initially be comic Tim Conway and Don Knotts lamenting the injustice of physiques out of sync with desire. Contrary to Arte Johnson's dauntless shuffling lecher on television's "Laugh-In," they suffer permanent losses with each new rejection. Youth mercilessly lords over its elders. One man recalls how a lovely young seductress, merely "practicing" her wiles, left him emotionally bankrupt, "like Insufficient Funds" (*SS,* 338). However, this defeat is only a prelude to the story's real subject: willful submission to death in life.

The man errs by denying himself any prospects beyond the virility and confidence of youth. With his companion, he compulsively defends himself as "a slightly old young man still advertising in the trees and rivers for a mate" (*SS,* 338), but his nervous jokes soon dissipate. No silver trophies immortalize his vital past, and, contrary to the popular adage, cleanliness—the virtue of his middle age—is far overrated. His more enterprising friend tries to allay these misgivings by proposing a special journey. Life's rapturous tunes, distant and strange, waft from Pool, a mecca of hope. There they can once again dance with young women and revel in "the new music." But distrust tarnishes the bright city's treasures. The demoralized speaker dismisses his friend's enticing descriptions as propaganda for a retirement compound or death camp, whose circuses, rich gardens, and grand estates merely distract attention from the truth: widows water lawns in solitude; photographs replace families in the retirees' homes; inmates receive little medals for daily survival; corpses grace the museum walls. The doubter makes excuses. He must tend to a shirt button, his camping gear, his prescriptive daily tasks.

Behind his paralytic fear looms the doubter's mother. Though only a dark memory, she is one of the few female progenitors in Barthelme's stories not seen chiefly in dubious battle with her spouse. Similar to the mysterious masculine authority in **"A Manual for Sons,"** this mother is a soul-basher. Or so she seems. The spineless son recalls her ecstatic devotion to "the Eleusinian mysteries and the art of love" (*SS,* 343). Cloaked in secrecy, these ancient fertility rites venerated Demeter, earth mother and goddess of grain. In autumnal celebrations, when the corn was sown, a priestess coupled with her king on the ploughed earth to recapitulate Demeter's cornfield affair with Iasius and ensure a bountiful harvest. In other rites, Demeter's initiates manipulated phallic objects to reenact the immortals' copulation. Thus, the goddess's fecundity represented life's renewal for both the earth and mankind's spirit.[1]

In Barthelme's story, however, all these mythical elements compete with archetypal demons and desires in the mother-son relationship. Nightmarish visions conjure residual images of drunken orgies and bloody sacrifices to the ancient matriarch. A grim reaper, the heartless mother seems to conceive her fruits only to harvest and chop them up. The son manifests his ambivalence in a dream about a monster with Teflon claws. The monster complains that the "Curator of Archetypes" has been criticizing the beast for "shuckin' and jivin'" instead of "attacking, attacking, attacking" (*SS,* 345). Talk of "shuckin'" abruptly evokes the monster's demands for return of a cornflake. In other memories, the son perverts the ancient fertility rites and implicates his mother in his own maturing sexuality. On an autumnal walk, he dreamily relates, he once observed lovers couple "in the bare brown cut fields" (*SS,* 344) to his right; in the field to his left, however, rocked his stern mother, ignoring his polite tip of his hat to her: "She was pondering. 'The goddess Demeter's anguish for all her children's mortality'" (*SS,* 344). He then obscures the forbidden relationship in his insistence that "Momma wouldn't have 'lowed" (*SS,* 346) "the new music," but she loved lutes. They used to spend hours, the son recalls, "banging away at [their] lutes" (*SS,* 345).

In Demeter's rites of death and rebirth, the ceremonies, performed with music and dancing, symbolically delivered participants from mortal terrors into the divinities' glorious climes. Pool boasts not only these revelries, but also buildings and gardens splashed with red, Persephone's color, the hue of resurrection. Though eating the scarlet pomegranate relegated her to Hades for a season, Persephone, like the sown seeds, repeatedly rose from the realm of death to walk the green earth. Associating Pool's revel-

ries with the taboos of his ambivalent relationship with his mother, the son chooses to decay in his current dormancy rather than risk the city's sure debaucheries and villainy. Like those "uninitiated" into the ancient mysteries, he is fated to grovel "in filth and fog, abiding in . . . miseries through fear of death and lack of faith" (Themistius quoted in Grant, 133). He submits himself to the stony crypt of death in life.

"THE EMERALD"

Barthelme lamented such hopeless refusal of life's prospects. Significantly, Pool's architecture shines in the phenomenal world, not an alleged hereafter. For heroic spirits, assurance in the one assuages uncertainty of the other. As Joseph Campbell explains, to witness "not the world of solid things but a world of radiance" requires a "visionary transformation" of the mundane,[2] faith in the beauty of the "here and now" (*SS,* 417). With comic persistence, **"The Emerald"** casts its light into the shadows of disbelief.

Once again, Barthelme invokes myth as the source of moral enrichment. Contrary to the uncompromising seriousness of Judeo-Christian religion, notes Campbell, myth tolerates an irreverent union of humor and symbolism as it performs its revelations (220). It is a fitting choice for an ethical ironist. In **"The Emerald,"** Barthelme reveals the gods' presence in the most unlikely vessels: the witch Mad Moll and a reliquary encasing the Foot of Mary Magdalene. Sharing the same initials, the two form a sisterhood of darkness and light, a coalition as ambiguous as the emerald's portent. But as Moll ultimately concludes, one cannot forego the heroic "scrabble for existence" (*SS,* 417) to worry whether life's mysteries are good, bad, or indifferent.

Conceived on a stormy night, Moll bears suspicious stigmas: a black beard and a furry black mark on her forehead. In a wild parallel to the Immaculate Conception, she claims to have endured a seven-year pregnancy to deliver a god's offspring, a sleeping, talking emerald, fathered by the man in the moon. In the midst of other provocative numerical configurations, the child's arrival "at six sixty-six in the evening" (*SS,* 394) further darkens the omens. Though an acceptable tale in antiquity, the story seems madness to her cynical contemporaries. Yet Moll brews knowledge. In her "witch's head" swirl spells and incantations but also "memories of God," from whose sustaining hands she "fell . . . into the world" (*SS,* 410). Faced with a phalanx of doubters, however, her magic and wisdom sometimes seem "*not enough*" (*SS,* 401).

Having abandoned the "tucked-away gods" (*SS,* 401), disbelievers constitute this story's greater populace. Like Dante's lost souls, they form a hierarchy of denial. Deferring to her husband's prejudices, Moll's mother drifts into doubt when she tries to disguise her daughter's congenital oddities to make her look normal, common, anonymous. Flatly dismissing Moll's tale, young ignorant Lily reduces the emerald's mystical conception to salacious details, such as the alleged father's "hideously engorged member" (*SS*, 392). Like those beyond the gates of Dis, the truly hopeless doubters are mercenary schemers. A pervert tries to peddle his own false idol in a dark alley. Lather, the editor of *World,* capitalizes on life's ugliness and terror. Thieves calculate the weighty stone's value in dollars per carat. Out of greed, bitterness, or fear, they want to destroy this pretender to the gods. Their spirits, if not their purses, are bankrupt, as they petrify in their own iron-willed obstinacy.

Allied with the powerful Foot, loyal bodyguard Soapbox, the canine convert Tarbut, and her own green redeemer, Moll crusades for the spiritual enchantments still accessible to mortals. The gods, she tells Lily, "are not dormant or dead as has often been proclaimed by dummies" (*SS,* 416), but "to live twice" (*SS,* 404), as the ruthless Vandermaster demands, may indeed presume too much. Faith, action, love—these articulate spirit and consciousness in the deafening roar of the "ferocious Out" (*SS,* 399). Such human experience, says Joseph Campbell, elicits the "rapture of being alive" (5).

Overnight to Many Distant Cities

The physical, emotional, and intellectual sources of human rapture preoccupy much of the short fiction in *Overnight to Many Distant Cities*. A few pieces—**"Conversations with Goethe," "Well we all had our Willie & Wade records . . . ," "Wrack," "Captain Blood"**—softly hum the amusements or comforts of friendship. But human desire—sometimes random lust, more often sustained magnetism—seems in this collection's stories the best hope for mortals to share anything akin to heroics or otherworldly bliss.

In **"The Sea of Hesitation,"** for instance, narrator Tom routinely records the detached pursuits of his self-indulgent acquaintances. Francesca obsesses about Robert E. Lee; Catherine, about Balzac. Jinka writes Tom hate mail. Their interests are frenetic, disconnected; Tom seems equally indifferent to each. Still, he repeatedly defends people's right to "do what they want to do" ([*Overnight to Many Distant Cities*; hereafter] *O*, 94). Any willful action, he suggests, is better than silence and immobility. Ironically, through most of the story, Tom himself seems incapable of decisive action. Recalling his work with "sensory deprivation studies" (*O*, 95), he admits that the inertia of hibernating in a cozy "black box" with "the white-noise generator standing in for the sirens of Ulysses (himself an early SD subject)" (*O*, 103) is a tempting alternative to bucking for a place in the world. However, his comparison to Ulysses, paradoxically "deprived" to prove he could *conquer* temptation and premature death, supports Tom's subsequent claim that such experimentation is not "will-lessness," but the pursuit of "Possibility" (*O*, 103). The degree of heroism is relative to one's world: in this "Age of Fear" (*O*, 99), any "behavior" seems to Tom "a small miracle" (*O*, 96).

As Ulysses bravely lurched over the treacherous deep, Tom now tugs along on his own low-grade odyssey. After reading several pages of this voyage's uneventful log, we must suspect, against Tom's and Moll's protests, that the gods are indeed "dormant or dead." Then, in the last vignette, life's best miracle befalls Tom: sudden passion for a woman at the newsstand. Love animates him with joy not glimpsed elsewhere in the story. Rapt with desire for this goddess, who wordlessly returns his ardor, "smash of glance on glance" (*O*, 103), his heroic "persona floats toward her persona, over the Sea of Hesitation" (*O*, 103), and he savors every detail of the mating ritual. This magnetism, however short-lived, reaffirms humanity's riches.

For gods and mankind alike, of course, love is not without folly. Forgetting his wife and propriety, another narrator abandons himself to glorious debauchery at the Hotel Terminus: "He has learned nothing from the gray in his hair; . . . he behaves as if *something* were possible, still" (*O*, 115). Lost to love "forever," he then suffers betrayal: "She comes toward him fresh from the bath, opens her robe. Goodbye, she says, goodbye" (*O*, 117). Unlike some of Barthelme's other tales of rejection, however, **"Terminus"** closes with no hint of regret. Likewise, the narrator of **"The Sea"** embraces love's immediate prospects, even though he knows that he will eventually discover "spiritual blemishes" (*O*, 104) in his mate. Desire inspires hope, if not discretion. This risky assent to possibility is the payoff for surviving the advancement of years. As the life-worn Henrietta philosophizes, "maturity" has blessed her with an appreciation for human prospects in "a rich world beyond the pale" (*O*, 87). One does not grow old, she assures her mate Alexandra, "while love is here" (*O*, 87).

Two of the bridge pieces in *Overnight* also boast the heroics of love. In "Now that I am older . . . ," desire transforms ordinary food and furnishings into spiritual accoutrements. Noble sounding phrases—"fleet through the woods" (*O*, 132) instead of "came home from work," and "plucked forth a cobwebbed bottle" (*O*, 132) instead of "passed the Gallo"—likewise mask the vernacular. The speaker covets the ritual of flowers and feasts that anticipates the bed, but mostly he covets the bed. Like an "arrow from the bow" or "spear from the hand of Achilles" (*O*, 132) (he is in too much of a hurry to choose between these similes), he rushes to his lover, bearing posies and pop records in lieu of shield and sword. Contrary to **"The Sea,"** this ardent meditation ignores life's dull parts. More significantly, it ignores death. Above the bed where the lovers have enjoyed so many "violent nights" hangs a "silverprint" (*O*, 131) of violent death, its "prostrate forms" (*O*, 132) partially illumined by each morning's dawn. The speaker barely notes the gruesome omen before once again ravishing the lovely prone "form" beside him in "full light" (*O*, 132). The ironic analogy here between mortality's best and worst possibilities is unmistakable. For now, at least, life's coffers are full.

The other bridge piece—"I am, at the moment . . ."—is a strangely ethereal meditation, almost a hymn to death. Or maybe it is a hymn to memory, dream, imagination, the lighted altars of intellect. It is certainly a hymn to art. Like "They called for more structure . . ." and "A woman seated on a plain wooden chair . . . ," the visionary text resonates with joy in the provocative beauty of words. The setting is a forest, but the cosmos that embraces this ethereal thicket is uncertain. Familiar earthly landmarks—Ireland, France, Portugal—are "remote" (*O*, 163) or "wrapped in an impenetrable haze" (*O*, 164), though the tombs amid the exotic "beanwoods" are "perfectly ordinary gray stone" (*O*, 163) and the "already-beautiful" wear crowns of "red kidney beans" (*O*, 164). Typically, Barthelme's woods are lively places, where old gray wolves romp after nymphs. "**Departures,**" for instance, depicts the narrator's grandfather gamely bartering with the dryad Megwind, who is "lovely as light" (*F*, 102). But the forest of "I am, at the moment . . ." is hushed, holy, lighted by someone beloved who religiously glues "chandeliers" (*O*, 163) to the beanwood limbs. All Barthelme's woods, however, harbor mystery, and often miracles. As the narrator of "**Departures**" confesses, he is only "fantasizing" (*F*, 102) the forest and its denizens, but imagination's sorcery can conjure extraordinary visions to lighten the load of "human affairs" (*O*, 165).

Several images in "I am, at the moment . . ." suggest that this dreamy vision is another analog to death, not the physical wreckage of the last piece's silverprint, but the soul's contemplated release. Sometimes the speaker seems formless, otherworldly, physically remote from his lover. He sleeps in the tombs with the "already-beautiful," who, like Demeter's devotees, dance mystical rites. There are also redemptive overtones. After confession, "thieves" lie with the "deans of the chief cathedrals" (*O*, 164) in the woods. And the speaker confides, "This life is better than any I have lived, previously" (*O*, 164). Though he "rise[s] . . . to hold the ladder" (*O*, 163) for his beloved and closely monitors her labors, moreover, the couple never explicitly communicates. In fact, he says that he has a testament of "notes, instructions, quarrels" (*O*, 163) that he has been intending to discuss with her but has not or cannot. Briefly frustrated, he imagines that passionately hitting his own brow might "fell [him] to the earth" (*O*, 163). Some images, on the other hand, tauntingly imply that this vision is just another sexual fantasy, more well disguised than most. The "already-beautiful," who tote around "plump red hams" (*O*, 163), dance with "bronze hares," which the speaker has cast at night with much hot, sweaty, rhythmic labor: "Working the bellows, the sweat, the glare. The heat. The glare" (*O*, 164). Dancing and coupling is again reminiscent of Demeter's rites. More clearly, in this enchanting life that the speaker so enjoys, "beautiful hips bloom and part" (*O*, 164). Thus, when the speaker excitedly follows this disclosure with news of his beloved's "sudden movement toward red kidney beans" (*O*, 164), the reader cannot be sure whether she is ascending his spiritual ladder or descending his torso.

"I am, at the moment . . ." creates the sort of dense, abstract lyrics that Barthelme knew might lose readers. Wisely, he placed it like a benedictory preface to the keystone of *Overnight to Many Distant Cities*, the story that shares the volume's title. All the demons of human rela-

tionships, in fact, are appeased in "**Overnight,**" as maturity's tender mercies assuage the psychic losses of disappointment, familial conflict, aborted romances, and aging. If Barthelme mapped the previous piece's mazes and detours in exotic landscapes, he charts this story's settings in the everyday world, or at least in a tempered imagination's analogs to these locales. Paris, Stockholm, Taegu, and Berlin are distant only because memory displaces them to an ephemeral past. Tolerance and pleasure then balance the emotional investments in these sites.

The story condenses the journeys of a life into a fleeting chronicle, just as its spatial leaps circle the globe in a few pages. It is a deceptively spare microcosm. Italicized reminiscences announce each excursion. Some memories rankle a bit: in Paris, the speaker impatiently kicked his temperamental child; in Boston, he helped a divorcée load up her marriage spoils; in Taegu, too many swaggering generals demanded the spoils of rank. No matter how he watched his path, moreover, the narrator was always stepping into someone else's politics: swilling Stockholm's expensive J & B, he unwittingly supported the Swedish army; a "Warsaw Pact novelist" once inveigled him to smuggle "a package of paper" (*O*, 170) to the United States. Most pitiful, though, was the wretched loveless man in London, who gnawed his buttons for his soul's hunger. Selected for review along with these misfortunes, however, are ecstatic times shared with friends or lovers: a youthful escapade in Mexico City, more exciting to the elders who tracked the runaways than to the romantic adolescents themselves; simple "happiness" (*O*, 174) with a beautiful lover in Berlin; best of all, the celebration of Barcelona.

The Barcelona anecdote that closes the story departs noticeably from the context now expected of these recollections. To this point, the narrator has substantiated his memories almost exclusively with "real" objects and places. The people, though sometimes exaggerated, are likewise credible. Contrarily, the Barcelona anecdote resumes the dreamy tone and sublime images of "I am, at the moment. . . ." Again, the persona seems both quick and dead. At first, the italics hint no mystery: "*In Barcelona the lights went out*" (*O*, 174). Probably just an electrical short; hence, the candlelit dinner of "shiny langoustines" (*O*, 174). Later, strolling with his lover, the narrator celebrates the repeatedly blissful state of marriage: "Show me a man who has not married a hundred times," he boasts, "and I'll show you a wretch who does not deserve the world" (*O*, 174). Through the anecdote's first paragraph, then, nothing more than mortal romance seems to inspire his rapture for Barcelona. Yet in the next paragraph, he is suddenly and quite mysteriously dining with "the Holy Ghost" (*O*, 174) and discussing Barcelona's lighting difficulties. The passage ends just as ambiguously: "In an ecstasy of admiration for what is we ate our simple soup" (*O*, 174).

Here, again, is the now familiar apotheosis of life as is, with faith edging out irony in death's final play-off. Is Barthelme structuring another analog between a freely creative intellect and a blissful, otherworldly spirit? Very possibly. An infinite cosmos, **"Overnight"** suggests, exists in memory, dream, and imagination. But the god of this cosmos is just an ordinary mortal, listening to Manhattan's forecast—"tomorrow, fair and warmer, warmer and fair, most fair. . . ." (*O,* 174)—as he eats his "simple soup." All in all, it is a good life, Barthelme wrote. Bless the bean waters of Babel.

. . . . .

THE LEGACY: TICKETS TO PARADISE

By the late 1980s, people were accustomed to Barthelme's shameless irreverence for short story form: his absences, his arias, his fiction's chameleon poses. But acceptance had its laggards. For instance, colleague Raymond Carver, once suspicious of Barthelme's motives, tried to make peace by honoring **"Basil from Her Garden"** in *Best American Short Stories, 1986.* When Barthelme subsequently dissected this particular fiction and scattered it through *Paradise,* Carver felt betrayed. Had he known **"Basil"** was to be part of a novel, he grumbled, he would not have considered it. Carver's chagrin amused Barthelme. He wanted to redeem good will, to tell Carver that, at the time, he himself did not know the story's destiny. Neither, of course, could Barthelme have imagined his own life path when he wrote Damon Runyon parodies for his high school newspaper or hung shows in a Houston gallery or trailed his gods to New York City. In life, as in fiction, he trafficked in possibility.

Still, like most artists, most *people,* Barthelme succumbed to bouts of despair and abused his health. Seeing his thin books on the shelf next to other writers' thick books worried him. Sustaining a novel worried him. He used to say that his stories' tight, complex structures taxed intellect and patience; they were difficult to support in a sprawling network. The public's expectations fed this worry. Popular bias viewed short fiction as a stepchild unworthy of the novel's laurels. With his startling successes, however, Barthelme greatly altered this perception of short fiction and opened the genre for other generations to blaze their own trails into the "exquisite mysterious muck." As *Overnight to Many Distant Cities* indicates, moreover, maturity gave his work a patina of age, temperance, and grace. *Snow White* and *The Dead Father* were distant triumphs before he again successfully launched a novel, but even as Barthelme concentrated his last years' efforts on longer fiction, he never abandoned the rich veins mined in narrow spaces.

In March 1989 the *New Yorker* published its last short fiction from Barthelme before he died the following July. If not a dazzling performance, **"Tickets"** is one of those beautifully balanced meditations that returns pleasure with every reading.[3] Stylistically more conservative than the lyric abstractions in *Overnight,* it confirms the even hand of the settled writer. Because Barthelme's stature in American short fiction owes so much to the longevity of his relationship with this magazine, **"Tickets"** deserves a cameo shot.

Barthelme once said that his favorite sentence was not a sleek liner, but an old "wreck," curious for all its odd baggage.[4] Without straining to the limits of **"Sentence"** or **"Bone Bubbles,"** **"Tickets"** assembles a whole fleet of these fastidiously constructed wrecks—true treasures in Barthelme's legacy. The narrator's role in the fiction's dilemma supports these semantic freighters perfectly. From the first postured sentence, the narrator tries to muster the impression that he is inured to social politics. His wife has tickets to the symphony. Though she has politely invited the narrator to join "her group" (32)—her group consisting of herself and her thick, thick friend Morton—she knows full well that her husband does not like to suffer the discomforts of sitting all evening. Meanwhile, the artist Barbet has invited the narrator's wife and Morton to join *his* group. Fueled by the narrator's repressed jealousy, these simple gestures menace like rival nations' lying diplomacy. The sublimated emotion also generates the story's stylistic accretions. As staid subject-verb openings quickly collect clause upon clause, defense upon defense, obsessive thinking exposes the narrator's feigned control as mental paralysis. Suspended in his agitation, he cannot act—hence, the absence of plot.

Pleasure derives chiefly from comic exchanges within this tense design. The strongest stylistic pattern is an amusing "cancellation" motif. With "invitation" and "counter-invitation" (32), the narrator's wife and Barbet introduce this pattern in the story's first two paragraphs. In their game of social politics, each player checks the other's moves until he or she captures the opponent's men or women. After the narrator reviews his options for attending the symphony himself, the story compounds the game's significance. Dwelling on both Barbet's gall and his vicious "decayed wit" (33), the narrator explains midway through his mental volley that the artist's notoriety rests on his "'Cancellation' paintings" (33)—canvasses that superimpose an unknown work on a famous one and thereby invalidate the masterpiece. Like the terrorist writers Barthelme described in "After Joyce," Barbet manufactures objects hostile to both art and life. He betrays his creative gifts. Ironically, the narrator replicates this destructive process by defending Barbet's "fundamentally indefensible" (33) acts. With mock praise of the paint's value, for instance, he essentially cancels the importance of Barbet's art. However, he really wishes to cancel Barbet and suggests that the artist's "ill will" (33) justifies shooting the nuisance. The cancellation motif's real task, though, is to purge the jealous "ill will" that immobilizes the narrator in his obsessive thinking/counterthinking. Morton facilitates the resolution. Barbet hates Morton, but Morton counters Barbet's malice with an "indifference" that exacerbates the artist to "illness" (34). A riotous rug analogy, extended in one carbuncular sentence to almost 200 words, finishes off the malcontent. More importantly, Morton's role in Barbet's misfortune delights the narrator and thus cancels all "ill will" for his wife's friend. Checkmate.

This resolution returns the narrator to prospects declared in the story's opening sentence (forming his own group), but unbridled joy now vanquishes earlier restraint and inspires him to action. Rebelliously embracing Morton, a Gypsy, a blind man, and "that sugarplum" his wife, he proclaims that his new group "will exist in contradistinction to all existing groups" (34). His enthusiasm for life's wonderful charge will mobilize countless troops. Barthelme's trademark litany—here, "Let's go! Let's go!" sung "over and over" (34) with the signature faith of the later stories—spurs adherents into the mysterious welter.

Like a friendship of unexpected joy and duration, **"Tickets"** gives the kind of pleasure that makes good memories of good literature. Barthelme bequeathed many such gifts. Not the least was his legacy to his students, who remember him affectionately as a munificent magus with one gene from Legree. Though he never sent his style armies to trample other writers' sacred land, he did expect untested troops to bleed their native talents. According to former students Vikram Chandra (Sahaj) and Olive Hershey, reading one's feeble words aloud in class to the inexorable pacing of Barthelme's lizard cowboy boots could be murderous for a young writer unaccustomed to the master's scrutiny. Sometimes such a trial left the linoleum "littered with small carcasses."[5] No one, however, doubted Barthelme's motives for cutting his or her work to the quick. The master's radar, says Hershey, was "unerring": "As a teacher [Barthelme] gave the kind of criticism I could accept, e.g., 'Your sperm count is low,' 'Make her smarter,' or 'Try having her fall in love with the other guy.' He had an astounding gift as a listener, hearing work for the first time in class and knowing instantly where the story wanted/needed to go."[6] In matchless acts of integrity, moreover, Barthelme generously donated his time, money, and energy to prepare his students to light their own ways. As much as his inimitable fiction, they will remember these gifts.

When Barthelme died, his literary estate included *Guilty Pleasures,* his "nonfiction" parodies/satires; *Sam's Bar: An American Landscape,* a picture-text collaboration with Seymour Chwast; *The Slightly Irregular Fire Engine,* his award-winning children's book; four novels (*The King,* published posthumously); and nine short fiction collections. Given their creative triumphs, all within three decades, these works constitute a staggering legacy. Translated into many languages, the short fictions alone extend Barthelme's importance to literature globally. These small fictions were the author's natural terrain. Here, on his existential journeys, Barthelme never dreamed utopian parks poised beyond an earthly pale. But he willed us something better: privileged glimpses of the world's gardens, lush with exquisite flaws. "Collect the troops!" his stories hail. "Let's go! Let's go!"

Notes

1. For a thorough discussion of Demeter's and daughter Persephone's roles in the death-rebirth rituals, see Robert Graves, *The Greek Myths,* 2 vols. (Baltimore: Penguin Books, 1960), 1:89-96; and Michael Grant, *Myths of the Greeks and Romans* (New York: New American Library, 1962), 126-38; hereafter cited in the text.

2. Joseph Campbell, *The Power of Myth,* ed. Betty Sue Flowers (New York: Doubleday, 1988), 230; hereafter cited in the text.

3. "Tickets," *New Yorker,* 6 March 1989, 32-34; hereafter cited in the text.

4. See Larry McCaffery, "An Interview with Donald Barthelme," in *Anything Can Happen: Interviews with Contemporary American Novelists,* ed. Tom LeClair and Larry McCaffery (Urbana: University of Illinois Press, 1983), 34.

5. Vikram Chandra [Sahaj], "Good-bye, Mr. B," *Texas Monthly,* July 1990, 48.

6. Olive Hershey, letter to author, 19 May 1989.

Wayne B. Stengel (essay date 1992)

SOURCE: Stengel, Wayne B. "Irony and the Totalitarian Consciousness in Donald Barthelme's *Amateurs.*" In *Critical Essays on Donald Barthelme,* edited by Richard F. Patteson, pp. 145-52. New York: G. K. Hall & Co., 1992.

[*In the following essay, Stengel analyzes three representative stories from* Amateurs *in order to differentiate Barthelme's early and later short fiction and to explore the relationship between irony and human consciousness in his work.*]

At his best Donald Barthelme was a highly moral and political American short story writer. Moreover, for a decade or so—from the mid-sixties to the late seventies—in a plentiful, inventive stream of stories that often appeared first in the *New Yorker,* Barthelme challenged and enlarged the possibilities for short story form and short story expression. As the seventies proceeded, Barthelme's imaginative energies altered substantially. This phenomenon is apparent in *Amateurs,* Barthelme's fifth collection of short stories, published in 1976. There are four or five first-rate stories in this group of twenty-one, and yet even in the best of these Barthelme's vision seems tamed, controlled, even restrained by some of the very forces that his earlier writing so brilliantly destroyed or at least called into question. If the two most important vectors in Barthelme's short fiction are irony and human consciousness, as well as the relationship between the two, many of the stories in *Amateurs* impinge irony on their subject matter from so many perspectives as to be finally not so much deeply ironic, or even anironic, but merely controlled by Barthelme's willful subjugation to his own dazzling, dexterous use of a variety of ironic stances. Likewise, if Barthelme's stories prior to *Amateurs* consistently reject the tendency of human consciousness to force imaginative writing into conventional, preordained shapes and containers, some of the most effective tales in this collection are about the triumph of groupthink, the victory of a particular, collective attitude to reality that squelches the desires of individuality, language, and perverse lone resistance to its kind of conformist tyranny. Furthermore, there is far too little, and far too ambivalent, a sense of the irony of just these defeats within these stories. By analyzing three vivid, representative tales from *Amateurs,* "The School," "Some of Us Have Been Threatening Our Friend Colby," and "The New Member," I think it is possible to see a large and significant fault line between early and later Barthelme. In recognizing this graphic distinction, critics might begin to assess the gains and losses in Barthelme's attitude toward his own ironic attempts to forge a reconciliation with the world and toward his vision of human consciousness as fostering a kind of intellectual totalitarianism among otherwise independent, free-spirited, and civilized men and women.

"The School" is one of Barthelme's most frequently anthologized works, appearing as a representative sample of Barthelme's art and as an exemplum of post-modernist short story practice in a wide variety of freshman composition texts and short story collections. Yet what is one of Barthelme's smoothest, glibest, and rhetorically most confident tales is a curiously self-defeated model as well. Told by a male grade school teacher, this tale recounts, in a kind of mellifluous, catalogued ironic lament, a series of deadly mishaps involving first plants and animals, then parents, and finally reaching their children, who are students in the narrator's elementary school class. As the mayhem and horror of these spiraling disasters mount, the teacher, with only occasional qualms or nervousness, proceeds with his lesson plans, insistent that these disruptions are inevitable in a modern education and, perhaps, are irrelevant to it. When his terrified students demand to know why the school has been besieged with these unremitting catastrophes, the narrator can offer them no satisfying explanation. Furthermore, they insist that he offer them proof of the power of regeneration, the force of life over death, by making love to their attractive teacher's aide before their innocent eyes. Horrified by their request and yet fearful of ignoring their anxiety, the narrator begins to embrace the student teacher as his students become excited. Suddenly, there is a knock at the door. The narrator opens it to find a new pet gerbil waiting to enter his classroom. Barthelme concludes his parable with the sample declarative: "The children cheered wildly."[1]

Doubtless the smug, mostly self-assured voice of the narrator is meant to represent those modern educational administrators who insist on procedure, order, and ritual under any circumstances, choosing to ignore the death, violence, and chaos of the society around them as they hurry through their daily drills, schedules, and standardized agendas. Where is the humanity and ultimate purpose in an education that so ignores the brutality of the world, Barthelme asks? Yet what finally fails this story is its lack of surface tension and its ironically smiling conclusions.

Anyone who teaches this story must ask who has placed this new gerbil outside this desperately smiling instructor's door so that he can begin yet another round of falsely confident, cajoling lessons in animal and human ecology—the

glib, manipulative teacher, his fellow instructors and administrators, or worse yet, Barthelme, the looming authorial presence in the tale? What is wrong with both the consciousness and the irony in this work is that it becomes, at once, too little and much too much. Barthelme is at great pains to show that the sweetly domineering consciousness of this grade school teacher is not a monstrous force but an individual, with his own uncertainties and insecurities. Still, his victory achieved by someone placing before the students new life, and thus diverting them from their meaningful, hard-headed questions about life and death and human values, is a triumph for just the collectivist brain damage that so many of Barthelme's earlier tales have assailed. Moreover, in conclusion, the children cheer wildly at what? It is the simple arrival of a new living creature, the endless ability of their teacher to deceive them, the duplicity of their school in cheating them out of a meaningful education, or, in essence, the force of Barthelme's imagination in finishing his tale with such multiple, whimsically ironic endings that even his readers become a tool of his skillful rhetorical persuasion?

What is most wrong about his charming, accomplished cautionary fable is not just its protagonist's easy acquiescence to the forces of control and submission—although earlier Barthelme stories like "City Life," "Paraguay," "The Explanation" and "Kierkegaard Unfair to Schlegel" refute just the totalitarianism to which this narrator succumbs—but the smoothness of its droning narrative listing of disaster, its almost musicialization of grief and disaster recorded as a harmonic Vonnegut-like "so it goes." In one of his finest stories, **"Engineer Private Paul Klee Misplaces an Aircraft between Milbertshofen and Cambrai, March 1916,"** from *Sadness* (1972), Barthelme recreates abstract expressionist painter Klee's experience as a thoroughly reluctant inductee in World War I and sketches a great artist's ability to make the best of any nightmare through the sheer force of his imagination. On the other hand, **"The School"** displays the power of a teacher and a writer to hoodwink his pupils and audience through the power of his pet gerbil, his linguistic magic acts, parlor tricks done with mirrors, and self-reflexive language. In stories before *Amateurs,* Alan Wide recognizes a significant shift in the writer's attitude to his use of irony: "The fact is that increasingly in Barthelme's work, if not consistently, mere acceptance is modified by a more positive, more affirmative anironic attitude of assent . . . Klee intimates the possibility of irony (irony completed by the anironic ideal it implies) as a graceful, even integrative gesture toward the world."[2] Yet the voice of **"The School"** has no desire to integrate his view of education as rote procedure with the tragedies that beset his school. Rather, he wants to superimpose his rules and guidelines on his students as a means of ignoring and suppressing the painful incongruities of experience.

What's worse, this story has absolutely no rough surfaces. Barthelme's best tales have the jagged edges, the musical flat notes of jazz and collage, two of Barthelme's favorite art forms. Because of their raggedness and asymmetry, encountering such stories from any angle draws blood, invokes the shock of recognition that here is an artist deeply suspicious of the detritus of American pop culture and mass consumption, a writer who is forcing the short story into a symbolist, highly poeticized verbal and formal stylization to dramatize his anxieties about the vulgarity and emptiness of contemporary American experience. "Fragments are the only forms I trust,"[3] insists the narrator of **"See The Moon,"** deeply aware of the moral responsibility of the legitimate craftsman to shape the fragmentation of his culture and experience into a sum that is more than the holes in its parts. "Strings of language extend in every direction to bind the world into a rushing, ribald whole,"[4] the narrator of **"The Indian Uprising"** contends as he watches the takeover of New York City and his own imagination by a savage, terrorist band of Comanche Indians expertly trained in guerrilla warfare and brutal counterinsurgency techniques. With this story Barthelme clearly recognizes that though language may be capable of destroying the meaning and value of experience, the moral and political demands of art dictate that the consummate writer retain his identity and purpose, whatever the forces of oppression or liberation, justice, or injustice a society creates or inherits.

Yet despite these fictive recognitions of the writer's moral and political responsibility, by the time of *Amateurs* in 1976, there seem to be unsettling confusions in Barthelme's style and subject matter. No critic has analyzed Barthelme's aesthetic late career quandary as forcefully as Jack Hicks in his study of contemporary American fiction, *In the Singer's Temple.*

> These twenty fictions [*Amateurs*] lack the structural and linguistic energy of Barthelme's most significant work. There is no experimentation with typography or engraving, nor is there widespread use of literary fragmentation or collage, as in **"The Falling Dog"** or **"Departures."** . . . Barthelme's fiction . . . is a precarious balancing between lyric poetry and narrative prose; it depends on the tension between the necessary baggage of character, plot line, sustained mood, traditional syntax, and consistence of verbal style and the correcting need to deny, modify, or escape from those holding cells. It thrives on the eternal dichotomy between fiction as artistic sublimation ruled by logic, order, and coherence, and verbal expression as the more unrestricted play of the mind, particularly in its preconscious and subconscious aspects, daubing as an idiot savant at the palette. However accessible and affirmative, . . . the stories [in *Amateurs*] often lack the richness of texture and narrative invention that characterized Barthelme's finest work.[5]

With equal acuity, Hicks summarizes the philosophical tensions implicit in *Amateurs* and all of Barthelme's fiction: "Barthelme regards literature as a single, hierarchical system within a vastly oppressive mega-hierarchy. The act of writing is a projection of human consciousness; what is needed is a form of literature that releases consciousness from the burden of the past and from its own self-destructive tendencies."[6]

Yet the legitimately menacing quality of **"Some of Us Have Been Threatening Our Friend Colby,"** an occasionally anthologized story from *Amateurs* and arguably one of the cleverest and most ominously controlled stories Barthelme ever composed, depicts the desiccation of individual consciousness as a creatively gleeful act. In this tale a coterie of aesthetes gathers to discuss the fate of their friend Colby, who has obviously gone too far. Collectively, their totalitarian impulses dictate that Colby meet with death by hanging and the entire duration of the story, as narrated by one of their circle, consists of their discussion of the graceful, aesthetic forms, the polite, easeful considerations they can amend to their decision to destroy their friend's right to be. A variety of special arrangements are proposed as humane accoutrements to his beheading. One friend wonders what kind of classical music—exalted or severe—should accompany the event; another speculates how the invitation to the ceremony should be worded, while yet another ponders if wire or rope is the most painless method for Colby's demise. Not only does this story brilliantly demonstrate the total triumph of the artful, artificial forms of modern life over any moral content, but the story demonstrates the unabashed victory of a horrific consensus consciousness that can easily obliterate meaning and purpose in a decadent, overcivilized society.

Yet the ultimate confusions of the tale lie in its contradictory, self-consuming senses of irony. Its smiling nihilism, this Kafka-without-claws quality, lies not exclusively in what Hicks perceives as the strength of its forces of logic, order, and coherence, personified by Colby's would-be friends, but also in Colby's enervated inabilities—and Barthelme's limited desire—to have Colby fight back, escape, or evade their grotesque but fine-tuned reasoning. Colby hardly constitutes the vital Barthelme ego, what Hicks calls an "idiot savant daubing at the pallet of his very unique consciousness." Thus the greatest terror of the story is that finally it is consumed by what Hicks recognizes as its own self-destructive tendencies. **"Some of Us Have Been Threatening Our Friend Colby"** is a masterful, hilarious, smooth-as-glass depiction of how gracious and urbane citizens perform complex, strategic, and heinous acts, losing their individual identities to the dominant consciousness of a death-obsessed, death-worshipping culture. Unfortunately, one can't help but feel that completely appreciating this story means losing some small portion of one's own consciousness and irony to enjoy Barthelme's linguistic destruction of Colby as much as the narrator and Colby's other friends relish tightening the rope around his neck.

If a denuded Kafkaesque spirit hovers over this story, the full-fledged energy of Poe, Barthelme's other influential literary benefactor, gives real dimension, even poignance, to **"The New Member,"** one of the most unappreciated stories in *Amateurs*. **"The New Member"** is never anthologized in short story collections, has been critically avoided by scholars, and is hardly deemed essential reading for anyone attempting to assess the Barthelme canon. Yet this tale, once again about horrifying committee decisions and the partial triumph of committee consciousness, has an exuberantly playful, highly unpredictable sensibility and a well-contained sense of irony. The story ultimately demonstrates that the forces of totalitarianism threatening to engulf modern life are susceptible, even vulnerable, to their own fears, tremors, and demons of control. In this tale, which is a deadpan spoof of those collective mental processes so conditioned by Roberts' Rules of Order that they are unable to think beyond it, either a committee of archangels, a gathering of exceedingly genteel mafioso bosses and matrons, or, most likely, a group of East Side Manhattan philanthropic benefactors, meet to decide the fate of their charges. These privileged executives and doyens are so consumed with ruling a motion proper or out of order, seconding or tabling it, that they have long forgotten that people's fates and lives hang in the balance. When a novice member of the committee looks apprehensively outside their meeting room to report a huge stranger lurking at the window, her fears gradually convince other committee members to invite the outsider into their enclave. By story's end, the tribunal offers this alien presence a seat on the committee so that one of the anonymous masses whose lives are so randomly disrupted by its causal pronouncements can at last take part in their decision-making process.

One of the wittily calculated concluding ironies of this tale is that the hulking stranger, now a part of one of his society's most important committees, its dominant thought processes, immediately emerges as an insufferable tyrant. Like many creatures who live for committee duties, he instantly becomes a whimsical autocrat given to absurd decrees and stringent regulations. The new member's saving grace is revealed in the last sentence of the story. Although he demands that all members wear gray overalls with gray T-shirts, that they say morning, evening, and lunchtime prayers and do calisthenics between 5 and 7 P.M., and despite his forbidding boutonnieres, nose rings, and gatherings of one or more persons, "on the question of bedtime, [he is] of two minds."[7]

Very few Barthelme stories achieve such a perfect balance of his concerns with human consciousness and irony with such grace and astringency. If the great danger for human consciousness in the modern world is society's terrifying drive to make all individuals think as one, how, Barthelme asks, does literature effectively dramatize that threat, and how can irony ridicule this compulsion without making the ironic impulse just another aspect of the collectivization of human thought? With this story, Barthelme makes his new member as guilty of the deadly pragmatism and fatalism as the narrow circle of lawmakers he enters, while giving this newest dictator some of his colleagues' trepidations and uncertainties. Barthelme ultimately declares here that the hope for all totalitarian systems, as the West has just recently seen with communism, is that, eventually, they may be "of two minds."

After an initial series of stories and short story collections that viewed experimentation, formal innovation, fragmentation, and collage as fundamental means for analyzing human perception, Barthelme's later writing enters the enemy camp. What is it like to be part of absurd mental constructs like educational administration, a deadly, claustrophobic clique of aspiring artists and aesthetes, or any committee that makes life and death judgments, Barthelme asks in **"The School," "Some of Us Have Been Threatening Our Friend Colby,"** and **"The New Member."** The danger in these tales is that in visiting their tyrannical collective social consciousness, Barthelme fraternizes far too much with his antagonists' dilemmas. In revealing ironies within ironies inside their hierarchical systems, Barthelme can make totalitarianisms that wish to devour us seem all too humane, amusing, understandable, or aesthetically appealing. Ultimately one can ask, at least about **"The School"** and **"Some of Us Have Been Threatening Our Friend Colby,"** where does Barthelme stand in relation to these stories? Isn't he too sympathetic with his instructor's evasion of responsibility to his students in **"The School,"** and don't we, us the audience, as well as Barthelme, eventually enjoy threatening our friend Colby? In *Amateurs,* only in **"The New Member"** does Barthelme have the wit, moral vision, and controlled irony to explain the origins of his pet gerbil while vividly illustrating the dissension in the ranks that the sudden appearance of this beast on the threshold creates. In this ingenious fabliau, the figure hovering in the doorway is our own need to continue the lesson, to proceed with the story, to be ironically entertaining before our audience at all costs, even though we know we are as capable of manipulation, threat, and the desire to control others as individuals within the most insidious totalitarian environments. Our redeeming trait may be that, on some issues, we are of two minds.

In an otherwise felicitous essay honoring Donald Barthelme's career, John Barth in the September 19, 1989, *New York Times Book Review* called Barthelme the thinking man's minimalist.[8] For all of Barthelme's economy and miniaturization, he can never accurately be called a member of the minimalist school. Nor did he strive for limited effects in a limited short story form. Indeed, Barthelme was interested in evoking major aesthetic realignments, crucial shifts in our attention spans, and substantial inversions in our grasp of language and cognition. Recognizing that the human thought process in all its scope, grandeur, and wackiness is a huge and complex subject, Barthelme could be better termed the thinking man's essentialist. He is forever a writer who realizes the need for individuality, persistence, and the constant struggle of every unique human consciousness in asserting itself against many of the monolithic, pernicious, deadly "isms" of twentieth-century life.

Notes

1. Donald Barthelme, *Amateurs* (New York: Farrar, Straus and Giroux, 1976), 41.

2. Alan Wilde, *Horizons of Assent* (Baltimore: Johns Hopkins University Press, 1981), 183-84.

3. Donald Barthelme, *Unspeakable Practices, Unnatural Acts* (New York: Farrar, Straus and Giroux, 1968), 157.

4. Barthelme, *Unspeakable,* 11.

5. Jack Hicks, *In the Singer's Temple* (Chapel Hill: University of North Carolina Press, 1981), 35.

6. Hicks, 35.

7. Barthelme, *Amateurs,* 164.

8. [*Ed. note:* Barth's essay is reprinted at the head of this volume.]

FURTHER READING

Criticism

Barthelme, Helen Moore. *Donald Barthelme: The Genesis of a Cool Sound.* College Station: Texas A & M University Press, 2001, 209 p.

Former wife of Barthelme recounts author's life and work.

Condini, Nereo E. Review of *Sixty Stories,* by Donald Barthelme. *National Review* XXXIV, no. 4 (5 March 1982): 246-47.

Brief review of *Sixty Stories.*

Giles, Paul. "Dead, but Still with Us." *Commonweal* 158, no. 19 (8 November 1991): 637-40.

Finds a Catholic sensibility in Barthelme's stories.

Hudgens, Michael Thomas. *Donald Barthelme: Postmodernist American Writer.* Lewiston, N.Y.: Edwin Mellen Press, 2001, 191 p.

Examines the story "Paraguay" among other writings by Barthelme in terms of postmodernism.

Klinkowitz, Jerome. "Donald Barthelme (April 7, 1931-July 23, 1989)." In *A Reader's Companion to the Short Story in English,* edited by Erin Fallon, R. C. Feddersen, James Kurtzleben, Maurice A. Lee, and Susan Rochette-Crawley, pp. 57-64. Westport, Conn.: Greenwood Press, 2001.

Overview of Barthelme's life and work.

Maltby, Paul. "Donald Barthelme." In *Dissident Postmodernists: Barthelme, Coover, Pynchon,* pp. 43-81. Philadelphia: University of Pennsylvania Press, 1991.

Offers a thematic and stylistic analysis of Barthelme's work.

Patteson, Richard F. *Critical Essays on Donald Barthelme.* New York: G. K. Hall & Co., 1992, 220 p.

Collection of critical essays on Barthelme's oeuvre.

Additional coverage of Barthelme's life and career is contained in the following sources published by the Gale Group: *American Writers Supplement,* **Vol. 4;** *Beacham's Encyclopedia of Popular Fiction: Biography & Resources,* **Vol. 1;** *Contemporary Authors,* **Vols. 21-24R, 129;** *Contemporary Authors New Revision Series,* **Vols. 20, 58;** *Contemporary Literary Criticism,* **Vols. 1, 2, 3, 5, 6, 8, 13, 23, 46, 59, 115;** *Dictionary of Literary Biography,* **Vols. 2, 234;** *Dictionary of Literary Biography Yearbook,* **1980, 1989;** *DISCovering Authors Modules: Novelists;* *DISCovering Authors 3.0;* *Major 20th-Century Writers,* **Eds. 1, 2;** *Reference Guide to American Literature,* **Ed. 4;** *Reference Guide to Short Fiction,* **Ed. 2;** *St. James Guide to Fantasy Writers;* *Short Stories for Students,* **Vol. 3;** *Short Story Criticism,* **Vol. 2; and** *Something About the Author,* **Vols. 7, 62.**

Stuart Dybek
1942-

American short story writer, poet, and essayist.

The following entry presents an overview of Dybek's short fiction career through 1998.

INTRODUCTION

Dybek has been crowned the "neighborhood laureate" of southwest Chicago. His short fiction has been compared to that of Ernest Hemingway, Nelson Algren, and Sherwood Anderson, authors who also recorded accounts of Midwestern communities. Dybek recounts the world of his childhood with a tender, lyrical nostalgia. But critics laud him for never allowing memory to rose-tint his recollections—he tempers the fantastic and often surreal elements of his narratives with honest, gritty realism and the reoccurring feelings of disillusionment and displacement known to dwellers of a city, and world, in transition.

BIOGRAPHICAL INFORMATION

Dybek was born April 10, 1942. The family lived on the southwest side of Chicago, in a working class neighborhood home to eastern-European Americans and Mexican Americans. Dybek returns to this neighborhood again and again in his fiction, often narrating the stories from an adolescent's viewpoint. He attended local Catholic schools before going on to the pre-med program at Chicago's Loyola University. He dropped out for a time, working in the civil rights and peace movements, but eventually returned to Loyola earning a B.S. in 1965 and an M.A. four years later. At one point, he worked as a caseworker in the Cook County Department of Public Aid, a job which provided him with some of the details he would later use in the story "Charity." Music, jazz in particular, is also a great source of inspiration to Dybek; critics often mention the "lyrical" or "musical" flow and rhythm of his work. His first collection of stories, *Childhood and other Neighborhoods* (1980) won many literary prizes, including a Special Citation from the Ernest Hemingway Foundation, a Whiting Writers' Award (he was one of the first ten recipients of the award), and the Cliff Dwellers Arts Foundation Award. Other awards and honors include a Guggenheim fellowship (1981), a National Endowment for the Arts fellowship (1982), and the Nelson Algren Award (1985). He also won two O. Henry Awards, in 1985 for "Hot Ice" and in 1987 for "Blight," both of which are stories included in his second collection of short fiction *The Coast of Chicago* (1990). Dybek has taught English and creative writing at Western Michigan University since 1974.

MAJOR WORKS OF SHORT FICTION

Dybek's stories are set in the Chicago of his youth, in communities with blurring ethnic identities, where Old World traditions and memories are quickly being pushed to the edges of collective consciousness in favor of slick, faceless "urban renewal." His longer pieces tend to attract the most attention, although they are often actually sketches and vignettes paired with longer narratives and not traditional "short stories." His work "Nighthawks," involving the Edward Hopper painting of the same name and several threads of narrative weaving in and out of each other, is written in this manner. "Blight," for which Dybek has won several awards, is probably his most successful story. It involves a group of boys whose Chicago neighborhood has been labeled an "Official Blight Area." The boys do what they can to remain vibrant amidst the dying community, writing epic novels and starting a rock-and-roll band, eventually reclaiming their surroundings as an "Official Blithe Area." "Hot Ice" exemplifies Dybek's talent for incorporating seemingly disparate elements into a solid whole; his characters here are Mexican and Polish, teenagers and adults, and the plot resets a grim version of Sleeping Beauty in an urban winter. Dybek is a frequent contributor to many literary journals and periodicals including the *Chicago Review*, the *New Yorker*, the *Paris Review*, and *Poetry*.

CRITICAL RECEPTION

Commentators have often discussed the exploration of opposites in Dybek's work. He has garnered the most praise for stories in which surreal, magical, even grotesque elements interact with unblinkingly realistic portrayals of urban loss and displacement. His use of mythical Slavic sensibilities is heralded as a new take on the gritty Chicago tradition. But some critics find his combination of naturalism and the fantastic unsuccessful in many pieces. Dybek's repeated use of child or adolescent narrators also draws mixed reactions—some observers accuse the author of dodging deeper insight by telling his stories in immature voices, but most readers appreciate the exuberance and honesty of the youthful protagonists.

PRINCIPAL WORKS

Short Fiction

Childhood and Other Neighborhoods 1980
The Coast of Chicago 1990

Other Major Works

Brass Knuckles (poetry) 1979
Orchids (play) 1990

CRITICISM

Kirkus Reviews (review date 1 November 1979)

SOURCE: "Fiction." *Kirkus Reviews* 47, no. 21 (1 November 1979): 1278.

[*In the following review, the critic admires the story "The Apprentice" from* Childhood and Other Neighborhoods, *but unfavorably reviews the collection itself.*]

Stories and sketches, *verismo* chunks of muscular Chicago reality: boys bringing a dying immigrant grandmother a jar of outlawed duck's blood soup; tales of ragmen; teenage car escapades; adolescent artists-in-bud; the "basic principle of Catholic education—the Double Reverse: 1) *suspect what they teach you;* 2) *study what they condemn.*" Set mostly in poor milieus, Polish or black or Puerto Rican, the sketches generally have a lurid effectiveness just a step or two beyond total believability. But all of Dybek's range and flair works together in the final story, **"The Apprentice,"** in which a truant boy courses through the city in the constant company of his crazy, ex-taxidermist uncle; together they collect dead-on-the-road animals destined for an imaginary restaurant the uncle claims to supply and which caters to displaced-person gourmets—a metaphor the boy doesn't appreciate for a while (and neither do we, right off). The uncle is full, in fact, of metaphors, lovely and outsized ones; and the story's climax reaches a literal (bridge-climbing) height and arc, as well as a symbolic one, that's absolutely superb. It crowns a collection (badly titled, unfortunately) that's otherwise strong and busy but—unlike that last, wonderful story—less than enthralling.

Robert Ward (review date 1980)

SOURCE: Ward, Robert. Review of *Childhood and Other Neighborhoods* and *Brass Knuckles* by Stuart Dybek. *Northwest Review* 38, no. 3 (1980): 149-57.

[*In the following review, Ward views Dybek's stories as a "no-holds-barred assault on everything we have smugly assumed was reality."*]

> We say the world's magnificence has been enriched by a new beauty; the beauty of speed. A racing car whose hood is adorned with great pipes, like serpents of explosive breath . . . that seems to ride on grapeshot—is more beautiful than the "Victory of Samothrace". . . .

> We will destroy the museums, libraries, academies of every kind, will fight moralism, feminism, every opportunistic or utilitarian cowardice.

> Up to now literature has exalted a pensive immobility, ecstasy, and sleep. We intend to exalt aggressive action, a feverish insomnia, the racer's stride, the mortal leap, the punch and the slap. . . .

> —from *The Futurist Manifesto,* F. T. Marinetti, 1909

Necrophilia, as Erich Fromm described it, "is the passionate attraction to all that is dead, decayed, putrid, sickly; it is the passion to transform that which is alive into something unalive; to destroy for the sake of destruction; the exclusive interest in all that is purely mechanical. It is the passion 'to tear apart living structures.'"

Nearly as long as the city and recorded history, we have known, per se, that human beings have been fashioned into mega-machines to serve as tools for death glorification and holocaust. As the sociologist Louis Mumford accounts in *The Myth Of The Machine*:

> Conceptually the instruments of mechanization 5000 years ago were already detached from other human functions and purposes than the constant increase of order, power, predictability, and above all, control. With this protoscientific ideology went a corresponding regimentation and degradation of once-autonomous human activities: 'mass culture' and 'mass control' made their first appearance. With mordant symbolism, the ultimate products of the mega-machine in Egypt were colossal tombs, inhabited by mummified corpses; while in Assyria, as repeatedly in every other expanding empire, the chief testimony to its technical efficiency was a waste of destroyed villages and cities, and poisoned soils: the prototype of similar 'civilized' atrocities today.

To emphasize this perspective, Mumford quotes an inscription from Sennacherib's tomb, in which the monarch, with an ecstatic precision that would rival Vietnam, relates the irradication of every trace of the city of Babylon.

If Miguel de Unamuno was one of the first to use necrophilia as a "character trait, rather than a perverse act" wished or performed upon a corpse, a fascination with feces or dead things, Fromm was the first psychotherapist to identify it as a far more complex psychological type. Refining Freud's theory of the life and death instincts, passions which Freud believed more or less evenly distributed biologically in the personality, Fromm isolated necrophilia as a "Psycho-pathological phenomenon . . . the result of stunted growth, of psychial crippledness." Of the basic human needs, that of Orientation, Unity, Rootedness, Effectiveness, Excitation and Stimulation, whose frustration in the individual, Fromm insists, will lead to destructiveness, it is most always through the need for Effectiveness, that is the "existential" demand to be acknowledged, to be recognized, to have an effect on one's environment, that aggression is expressed: "Destructiveness is not parallel to, but the alternative to biophilia. Love of life and love of the dead is the fundamental alternative that confronts every human being. . . . If a man cannot create anything or move anybody, if he cannot break out of the prison of his total narcissism, he can escape the unbearable sense of vital impotence and nothingness only by affirming himself in the act of destruction of the life he is unable to create."

Of the *Futurist Manifesto,* Fromm states: "Here we see the essential elements of necrophilia: worship of speed and the machine; poetry as a means of attack; glorification of war; destruction of culture; hate against women; locomotives and airplanes as "living" forces. As one of the most significant psychological and artistic visions of our culture, the *Manifesto* can no longer be swept under the rug. Even Fromm attempts to de-emphasize Marinetti by labeling simply as a fascist. Yet all great art of the 20th Century must stand aghast at how thoroughly Marinetti's perception has been digested on a mass level; if not its *modus operandi,* which we have turned over to revolutionaries, terrorists, mass exterminators, as well as some of the secret organizations of our own government, then certainly the malignant and narcissistic consumerism it brings us at any price: its products and overwhelming debris we have been content to wallow in for decades.

In the spirit of Jerzy Kozinski's "Being There," our writers and artists must with compelling immediacy lay before us the elements of necrophilia. Two such writers who have recognized this crisis with unusual clarity in their first and recent books, are Lon Otto and Stuart Dybek. From their work we begin to learn what our reaction to this cultural morass must be: an intense and articulate anger.

. . . . .

If this tone of apocalypse and condemnation is where [Lon] Otto's work leaves off, it is where Stuart Dybek's ***Childhood and Other Neighborhoods*** begins. Where Otto's stories depend for their effect on his characters' complacency, Dybek's are stories of the inner city, a panorama of ruined lives overcome by the refuse of civilization. In these longer, carefully crafted stories set in the Chicago of the 40's, 50's and 60's, Dybek's technique is a no-holds-barred assault on everything we may have smugly assumed was reality. Though his characters appear to have vitality in a world they are forced to scrape a living from, in truth they are cripples who manage only to fend off the total impotence that bellies in on them. From the ragmen of **"The Palatski Man"** who each Sunday in their impoverished warren outside the city perform a strange communion composed of liquid blood red candy, generally used for the candy apples they sell, to "crazy Swantek," of **"The Cat Woman,"** whose grandmother managed a meager living through drowning unwanted kittens in her basement washing machine, until Swantek took to hanging them out on the line to dry, it is Dybek's artistry to capture the fantasies of hope, the horrible black humor, and the details of ritual that carry these people through to their end.

This bizarre world creates for the reader an atmosphere where reality and imagination become indistinguishable; it is a confusion which Dybek takes full advantage of. In

"Visions Of Budhardin" a homosexual outcast returns inside a huge mechanical elephant, and vents his wrath on the local Catholic church whose years of moral lies have made his inner landscape a ruin. Certainly, if we can accept the degree of the character's compulsion, the grotesque metaphor of a mammoth and mechanized nature does not seem so far fetched.

Yet in the profoundly achieved story **"The Apprentice,"** the exigencies of life make the surreal even more difficult to separate from the real. Ostensibly, an immigrant ex-taxidermist and nephew ride the highways at night to support themselves by supplying a rather exotic inner city restaurant, named "Spanish Blades," with its gruesome fare. The uncle, who bristles with imagination and black humor fantasy, a vitality charged by paranoia of Nazis and other fascists he imagines are pursuing him, describes this unusual place:

> . . . An exclusive restaurant, a private club, for all those who'd been excluded and had finally made their way here, to this city of displaced persons. Displaced persons, DP's, who'd come from the corners of the earth evading politics and poverty; draft dodgers, deportees, drifters, illegal aliens, missing persons, personae non grata, refugees, revolutionaries, and emigré royalty, all orphans, mingling beneath the same ensign in a dining room where chandeliers rotated a crystalline light and blue poofs of flame erupted as waiters, tuxedoed like magicians, ignited food.

And what is on the menu of such a restaurant?:

> And the road littered with the driftwood of night. Animals whose eyes have turned to quartz in the hypnosis of headlights, streamlike souls still hovering around their bodies. Rabbits, possums, coons, squirrels, pheasants—like a single species of highway animal. Some crushed beyond recognition, even their pelts useless and so left behind. But most still limp, waiting to be collected with the other highway scrap—blown tires like lizard skins, dropped mufflers, thrown hubcaps, lumber, hay bales, deposit bottles, anything that could fall off a tailgate or blow out of a car window.

The reader scarcely notices that this restaurant, in which the nephew is promised he will someday be a waiter, is only some graffiti spattered on an alley wall, that at the heart of their existence is a fantasy born from intense reality. In their comic backyard rituals these two characters bury, then revive old dolls, "mufflers and transmissions, . . . broken radios, crates of magazines, animal bones. . . . Makeshift tombstones stuck up everywhere." Near the apocalyptic ending, where the uncle, nagged by a terminal lung disease, becomes increasingly frenetic and paranoid, we begin to comprehend the great gift being passed on to the boy—the ability to stay alive in a deadly world.

Indeed, this kind of immediacy becomes even more abbreviated and accessible in Dybek's recent book of poems, *Brass Knuckles.* As the title implies, these poems are meant to shock and hurt us, swelling from volcanic sources of anger. Through such images as a twelve year old friend murdered with a crowbar, and the incineration of a pet cat's corpse in a garbage can, the horrible texture of the inner city rubs against us. Interspersed between this *cinéma vérité* are prose poems and redefinitions of myths whose surreal social satire is wrenchingly accurate. For example, these excerpts from **"Traveling Salesman"**:

> He finds himself stepping off the bus in some burg he's already bored with. Picking his teeth for 200 miles—here's where he spits the toothpick out. . . .
> . . . Finally, he's signing the register at a funeral home where he knows no one, but is mistaken for a long-lost friend of the deceased, for someone who has dislocated his life to make the hazardous journey on a night when the dead man's own children have avoided him. Once again instinct has taken him where he's needed; where the unexpected transforms routine into celebration. He kneels before the corpse, striking his forehead against the casket.

But of all the techniques which Dybek uses to expose the sophisticated depth of necrophilia surrounding us, none is more successful than the contemporized refocusing of myths which for millenia have been the psyche's projection of the flux of life and death. In the tongue in cheek **"Lazarus,"** no mention of God is made, unless it is the media which has transformed the resurrected man into a celebrity. In **"Orpheus,"** the satire weaves threads of accusation, anger, confession and a lyric communion with all victims, as this latter day Orpheus leads us through the underworld of our own streets. In **"The Rape Of Persephone,"** the longest and most complex poem of the volume, the explosiveness of revitalized archetypes reaches a crescendo. Death, who is initially described as "Death in the alley, prehistory, / drooling and slobbering, guzzling wine, / and mumbling his name over and over . . ." forces the young girl into a lurid rape whose climax is her lopping off of his penis with his own razor, "Persephone / running down an alley like a canyon / his scream has cracked through skyscrapers." It is not the cycle of the seasons that is emphasized here, rather it is the return of important Death transformed, "Sleek, in silks and velvets . . . his opera cape swirls . . . he drives the alleys in a black limousine . . . He hires an angel." "And Persephone, a woman now, / keeps meeting him . . ." because he is

> the one who makes her other lovers
> seem adolescent, who *listens* to her,
> who's interested in her soul, not just her body,
> who understands the dark scars of childhood.

He reappears alternately as "Her professor of French romantics, / including seminars in de Sade," as "the dentist who calms her terror of pain / through hypnosis; the psychiatrist / she chooses at random . . . in the phonebook.. . ."

If, in other writers, critics might brand this kind of vision as excessive over-statement, it is the highly crafted imagination, conscience and commitment of both Lon Otto and Stuart Dybek that will insure that their work must and will be read. As technology rockets us toward a future promising longer and better life, we see before us the possibility of an environment that may not be fit to live in. Our defense must be in the deepening resolve to comprehend ourselves. In the exploration of the human psyche, equal attention must be given to the biophilia and necrophilia that twist their complex patterns in each of us. As in the work of William Van Wert (whose story, "Ninth Month" appears in this issue) we must observe all the action that takes place on the killing floor, where nothing has been decided yet. The blood that is put inescapably before us is our own blood.

Bruce Cook (review date 13 January 1980)

SOURCE: Cook, Bruce. "Walks On the Southwest Side." *Washington Post Book World* 10, no. 2 (13 January 1980): 1-2.

[*In the review below, Cook regards Dybek among the pantheon of Chicago "neighborhood laureates" and praises his distinct combination of Eastern European-inspired flavor with the cynicism of the Chicago tradition.*]

A long a diagonal line southwest from Chicago's Loop lies a vast terra incognita once populated almost completely by Slavic groups which has been changing over to black and Latin during the past couple of decades. Chicago has had neighborhood laureates in the past—James T. Farrell, who wrote of the south-side Irish; Gwendolyn Brooks, the fine poet who sings of the black south side; Nelson Algren, whose people are the Poles of the near-northwest side; and Saul Bellow, who has written so well about the west-side Jews. But nobody has come forward to speak for that mixed patch surrounding Douglas Park on the southwest side. That is, nobody until now. For here is Stuart Dybek to tell you what it is like to grow up there—the sights, the sounds, the smells, all of it—and this volume of his stories constitutes as impressive a debut as has been made by any of the many good writers who have come out of that "dark city," Chicago.

Of them all Dybek seems most like Nelson Algren. Although it may simply be a similarity of subject matter, I was reminded again and again while reading ***Childhood and Other Neighborhoods*** of the tough, beautiful stories in Algren's *The Neon Wilderness*. **"Blood Soup,"** Dybek's tale of an odyssey through decayed, changing blocks and alleys by Stefush and his brother Dove to find a jar of duck blood for the old-country remedy which they are sure will restore their dying grandmother, brought back to me Algren's frequently anthologized classic, "The Night the Devil Came Down Division Street." Sterndorf, the title character of the **"Neighborhood Drunk,"** could well be a first cousin to Drunkie John in *The Man with the Golden Arm*. And the high-schoolers yearning after culture in **"The Long Thoughts"** and **"Sauerkraut Soup"** might be Bruno

Bicek's kids had Bruno only gone straight at the end of *Never Come Morning*.

Yet there are also elements here that would probably seem altogether alien to any reader of Algren. There is a kind of transcendental, magical quality to certain of the stories—**"The Palatski Man," "Visions of Budhardin,"** and **"The Apprentice"**—that is quite new to Chicago writing. It is distinctly Eastern European in flavor. The closest I can come by way of comparison would be the early stories of Isaac Bashevis Singer with all their dybbuks and devils. Yet after all, why not? Singer is a *Polish* Jew, after all. There was probably a good deal more interchange between the ghetto culture and that which surrounded it in Singer's day than is remembered now or perhaps was realized at the time.

None of this, however, is to deny the distinctive nature of Stuart Dybek's own writing. He has his own voice. It emerges more and more clearly the deeper one reads in this collection. If he writes, for the most part, about children and adolescents here, it is always with an adult's understanding and sympathy. He speaks for the losers and victims, telling of a teenage girl's wasted life in **"The Wake,"** and of the terror that is the daily bread of one boy's existence in **"Horror Movie."** There is anger, too—anger at the ignorance and brutality that has trapped those he writes about in their separate miseries, and anger at the system that keeps them there. This last is especially evident in **"Charity,"** in which the unnamed narrator, a social worker for the state, takes us on a tour through his case files and gives reality and some dignity to the squalid lives of his "clients." It is a harrowing story, absolutely true, I'm sure, to the author's experience, and it is the best of its kind I have read since Saul Bellow's "Looking for Mr. Green."

But there I go again, comparing and categorizing. There is a great urge for anyone who knows the literature of Chicago to see it as a whole, to try to tie it all together. The place has given so little encouragement to its writers and yet has produced so many fine ones that it is almost tempting to conclude that it is by denial and frustration, rather than generosity and help, that real writers are made. They have had to struggle similarly, and as a result there are certain similarities to their work—qualities of anger, cynicism, and sometimes a strident tone. Theirs is a tradition of deprivation and resentment.

And how does Stuart Dybek fit into this tradition? Perfectly, as a true inheritor, one who stands tall in a direct line of succession with Chicago's best. He is the real article, this guy, the McCoy, and if he is not ruined by neglect, drink, academic ennui, or the thousand other nagging miseries that sap a writer's talent, then he can be as good as any of the rest. It says here he is working on a novel. I am ready with my ten bucks to buy it the day it appears.

Phoebe Lou Adams (review date February 1980)

SOURCE: Adams, Phoebe Lou. "Short Reviews." *Atlantic Monthly* 245 (February 1980): 95.

[*In the following review of* Childhood and Other Neighborhoods, *Adams suggests that Dybek's stories contain both morals and "precise" narratives.*]

As the title suggests, children occupy most of the stories in this volume. Lest that fact make potential readers wary, it should be noted that these tales in no way resemble the narcissistic "sensitive young man" stories that are the staples of many literary magazines and of writers' workshops everywhere. Dybek is an original.

The landscape of the book is a stylized, half-fantastic version of ethnic Chicago, full of eerie, secret regions oblivious to the city around them: a remote dump where a strange army of ragmen camp, a series of back streets nicknamed "the Alley of Heartaches," a railroad bridge known as "the Black Angel." For Dybek's children and young adolescents this is truly an underground, and their adventures in it take on a quality of fable or myth. One could say of most of these stories that they are about the lessons of growing up, but the ideas in them do not draw attention to themselves; the stories *are* the ideas. All are dramatic and some are grotesque, but Dybek does not confuse violence with narrative power, and every story is relieved by comedy and precise psychological observation. *Childhood and Other Neighborhoods* does exactly what a first book should do—it introduces us to a fresh voice.

Howard Kaplan (review date 23 May 1980)

SOURCE: Kaplan, Howard. "In Brief." *Commonweal* 107, no. 10 (23 May 1980): 319.

[*In the following review, Kaplan criticizes Dybek for his use of child narrators, a device which Kaplan states allows Dybek an easy escape from deeper analysis.*]

You can tell the romantic writer by his choice of characters: he's a sucker for outsiders and underground men. In these eleven Chicago stories Stuart Dybek writes about pushcart peddlers (**"The Palatski Man"**), an amateur ornithologist holed up in a condemned building (**"Blood Soup"**), sots, pederasts, paranoid DPs. A tough bunch to get to know well in real life, even for writers. So when Dybek filters their stories through a child's point of view, as he tends to do, the strategy smacks of convenience more than anything else: a child doesn't have to pretend to understand what he sees. Over and over we wind up with the little tyke's sense of wonder and no more. It's like an excuse to flesh out scanty material. When Dybek tells a story "straight," as in the one about a crone who disposes of the neighborhood's excess kittens by drowning them in her washer, he doesn't have much to say: **"The Cat Woman"** is the shortest piece in the book.

The best story here (never mind the book's title) is not about childhood. More memoir than fiction, **"Charity"** records the author's psychological hard times as a social worker on Chicago's South Side. The main issue is this: how does a white do-gooder manage day after day to run a gauntlet of black panhandlers and still keep the faith? The story puts us in a funny position, which is that we end up feeling more for one of The System's own than for all the really sad cases who pass through these pages.

David Kubal (review date autumn 1980)

SOURCE: Kubal, David. "Fiction Chronicle." *The Hudson Review* 33, no. 3 (autumn 1980): 445-47.

[*In the below review, Kubal praises the unconventionality of Dybek's "magical grotesques" collected in* Childhood and Other Neighborhoods, *but notes that Dybek may be attempting to raise the mundane world to the mythic, at the expense of a serious exploration of reality.*]

In Stuart Dybek's first book [*Childhood and Other Neighborhoods*], a group of eleven uncanny stories about childhood and adolescence, we encounter a world radically different from Miss Beattie's or Mr. Vivante's. It is the Southwest side of Chicago during the 1940s, fifties, and sixties, a Slavic neighborhood gradually being overtaken by Blacks and Spanish. It is also a harsh and repulsive section of the city, which the author's singular imagination nonetheless enchants, transforming it into a world of magical grotesques. With its antecedents in Russian, and, perhaps, in Yiddish literature (one is sometimes reminded of I. B. Singer's stories), as much as in Sherwood Anderson and James T. Farrell, his fiction treats Ragmen, who hold strange rituals on the outskirts of town on Sunday after Mass; an old *buzka*, the Cat Woman, and her crazy grandson, Swantek, who drowns kittens and hangs them on the clothesline to dry; Budhardin, who returns to the neighborhood inside a mechanical elephant to revenge himself on the parish church; and, the oddest of all, "Uncle" and his apprentice, who scour the highways of Cook County for dead animals to stuff and sell to restaurants. But it is not only the trolls and ogres of the city that haunt one. It is also the gruesome sights, such as the one of the fat Puerto Rican woman tied to a telephone pole by drunks on a Saturday night: "'Help,' she said in English. She didn't yell, she hardly said it, just kind of formed the word with her lips, looking straight at him with terrified made-up eyes. One of the men kicked her when she said it. It wasn't a violent kick—he brought his foot up like a punter into her breast, which lopped up and hit her in the chin." The smells of the Chicago neighborhoods linger too—of "cat sexuality" on hot summer nights, of whiskey vomit, and of blood and sauerkraut soup.

Moments of beauty are rare. In the first story, **"The Palatski Man,"** Mr. Dybek does describe the marvel of a girl coming into puberty: "She ran from the window to the mirror and looked at herself in the dark, feeling her teeth growing and hair pushing through her skin in the tender parts of her body that had been bare and her breasts swelling like apples from her flat chest and her blood burning, and then in a lapse of wind, when the leaves fell back to earth, she heard his gold bell jangle again as if silver and knew that it was time to go." Still, growth, for the most part, is agonizing, surrounded as the children are by ugliness and putrefaction. And so, predictably enough, in the last story, the Uncle's apprentice, a figure of the young artist, stands on top of a railroad bridge gathering pigeon eggs, and as the bridge opens to let barges pass, "Warning bells clanged. Finally the boy raised his arm. Through swirling birds he waved good-bye."

The artist's flight from his city on waxen wings has become, of course, a mere conceit in modern fiction, especially in first books. It is a tired convention, too easily fallen into, and should be abandoned. Besides, in Mr. Dybek's stories of vigorous and brilliant unconventionality such a scene pales. It is all part of the modern writer's urge to mythologize reality, discontented as he is with the weightiness of the familiar. To be always trying to see through the world and to elevate it to spiritual significance is to chance missing what is so splendidly there. This may account for the fact that Mr. Dybek's characters experience so little joy or sensuous pleasure and that family life is almost totally absent from the book. The impressive exception is the story **"Sauerkraut Soup,"** in which the narrator lovingly and straightforwardly tells about working in an ice cream factory, about the old immigrant workingmen, and about eating the soup, a magical ritual. If Mr. Dybek's first novel, which his publisher informs us is underway, deals with this kind of experience, it will also be well worth reading.

Alice Bloom (review date summer 1987)

SOURCE: Bloom, Alice. "Shorted Out." *The Hudson Review* 40, no. 2 (summer 1987): 323, 329-30.

[*In the following excerpt, Bloom gives a positive review of* Childhood and Other Neighborhoods.]

I've just read 312 new short stories—American, European, Latin American. As a review is on some level a piece of advice anyway (buy, read, take seriously, etc., or don't) I'll begin with my piece and say: don't do this, don't read 312 or even 12 in a row. One, well okay, three stuffed mushrooms, a few brief interesting or amusing conversations, make for a pretty good stand-up party. But after 312 however savoury niblets of taste and talk one is both bloated and undernourished, muzzy, as though deprived of deep sleep (long talks, whole sit-down meals, a novel). Pick another metaphor and say, like a single yellow rose, a short story shows up best in the mind if placed against a relatively bare background.

I'd go further, advise that no single volume of anyone's stories, even Lawrence or Turgenev, should be read at one sitting. If the writer is good, then you want to live there longer, deeper—for a novel. If the writer's not so good, then all the failures of omission and commission become tics, present themselves boldly at entrance, and you don't even want to visit. Either irritable state of mind is unfair to the form, and either can be somewhat avoided if stories are read one at a time. . . .

For better and for worse, American fiction is not at present in this kind of clear "danger." I have neither space here nor anything like the necessary knowledge to press the point, but it is clear, reading through a stack of new writing from around the world, that by and large, American fiction writers, at least those who are most widely read (and translated), are not taking on the same subjects or scope as their counterparts abroad, especially in Third World countries. Whether it is our writers who are not making the connection, or whether they are simply showing that in real life there is little connecting, simply put, we do not have popular political writing. Then again perhaps we are only receiving, from abroad, their political writing, and Czechs and Salvadorans also have their versions of semi-literate, mass-market "romances" and other "fun" literature, as well as their version of our literate, mass-market, middle-brow novels of manners. There must be a hundred things to take into consideration, and I want only to suggest here, as have others, that this is a serious, complex subject. (For well-informed and penetrating views, may I suggest *The Writer in Our World,* the papers and panel discussions of a symposium sponsored by *TriQuarterly,* published in book form by The Atlantic Monthly Press in 1986.)

But to return for a moment to my point: by "political writing" I mean writing which sets the character's individual felt life in the larger but no less immediate context of his country's reality, one which he shares with many others. (Ron Carlson's stories, as lovely and interesting as they are, are nevertheless about almost eccentric private life, even though they do suggest that everybody does have one of those.) The characters in our books—individuals, families, small groups—seem, no matter how well done, adrift in time and geography, as though they hadn't heard the news for a long long time. American characters *still* seem to be facing a wilderness, I mean, a real wilderness; and God knows that has not been our reality for quite some time now. Though American characters feel themselves connected to values, to moral questions, and so forth, their daily concerns and experiences as reported to us in our fiction seem to remain, for all the carefully observed and detailed domesticity, manners, feelings, and so forth, oddly mythic, vague, abstract; and even when they live entrenched in city or suburb, there's yet a touching but nevertheless irrelevant quality about them, a permanent Natty Bumppoism, as though there were even now wind and space and trees and abstract morality around them on all sides, and somewhere in the distance, the smoke of an unknown campfire. That this smoke might be evidence of a

government, of a huge, pervasive, mutually experienced culture, doesn't seem to enter very deeply the experience of American characters.

The lasting impression our best current writers make, and I will close with a few notes of praise for two of them—Stuart Dybek and Jack Pulaski—is that each one is a separate, brilliant case. They could not be better than they are. Each story in Dybek's ***Childhood And Other Neighborhoods,*** each story in Pulaski's *The St. Veronica Gig Stories,* each scene, each sentence, sometimes phrases, are so written; by which I mean that one is constantly aware of, admiring of, awe-stricken sometimes by, the power and variety of our language, and by the craft exhibited here. Dybek's stories are set in the ethnic neighborhoods under the shadow of the Chicago El; no one has ever done it better, and maybe never will. Pulaski's must be the finest stories, in every way, that could be done about tenement life in Brooklyn. Pound said something along the lines that poetry should be at least as good as prose. The opposite could be said of both Pulaski and Dybek: this is prose as dense, evocative, and multi-referential as poetry. But even here, in these brilliant moving stories of immigrant working neighborhoods, Poles, Italians, Jews, Hispanics, people most, one might think, caught in and close to the real conditions of this country, the reader comes away with—and I don't mean to suggest this writing is at all precious—knowing best, admiring most, being most touched by and only connected to the eye of, this single writer who knows the place up and down, has every piece of language to tell its tale with, his language, its language, its people, intimately, its smells, sights, flavors—but who escaped, flies over it now, taking us with him, an angelic visitor.

Stuart Klawans (review date April 1990)

SOURCE: Klawans, Stuart. "Brief Encounters." *The Village Voice Literary Supplement* no. 84 (April 1990): 6.

[*In the following review, Klawans commends Dybek for his evocative stories.*]

Stuart Dybek's new book begins with a story titled **"Entrance"**—an appropriate name, whichever syllable you stress. Though the word refers immediately to the doorway of a three-flat, that fundamental unit of Chicago architecture, what really opens here is memory—the memory of departed people, of places that have changed, of everything that, in vanishing, gains the power to put you under a spell.

The setting, too, is appropriate, since few cities are so well made for hauntings. Vast, gray, matter-of-fact, Chicago seems as unalterable as granite, especially to its children. And yet it is a made-up place, conjured by entrepreneurial whim amid onion fields and intolerable weather, where one day there was nothing but prairie and the next a neighborhood full of European peasants. The day after that, the

Poles and Bohemians disappeared, leaving behind a *barrio* and Stuart Dybek, who, dazed but thoughtful, set out to write these stories about the ghosts of his past.

At their best, the stories have exactly the quality that outsiders don't associate with Chicago—they're beautiful. They modulate from one recollection to another with a musical logic—the music of Schumann, I'd say, rather than of Dybek's compatriot Chopin, though in one of the book's better pieces the latter is omnipresent. **"The Winter of Chopin"** looks back at the narrator's childhood on the Southwest Side, recalling an emotional and intellectual awakening under the influence of two outcasts: his semitramp of a grandfather and a young woman upstairs, a music student, who is unmarried but pregnant. Her nightly piano-playing holds the characters together, even though the boy and the old man never hear it directly. Waltzes, mazurkas, and polonaises come to them through the ceiling and water pipes, through wallpapered chutes and bricked-up flues—a secret network running through Mrs. Kubiac's old apartment building. Echoing along these hidden conduits, the music is already ghostly, since the grandfather, with his faculties failing, apprehends not so much the compositions themselves as his memories of them. But to the boy, of course, it's all a premonition, both of his life to come and of the day when he, too, will find that much has slipped away.

I should mention as well that the story is funny, though not as funny as **"Blight,"** a tale of adolescence during "those years between Korea and Vietnam," when rock and roll was being perfected, and when "our neighborhood was proclaimed an Official Blight Area." Joey "Deejo" De Campo, the guitarist in the narrator's high school band, takes this decree as inspiration for his great novel, *Blight,* which begins, "The dawn rises like sick old men playing on the rooftops in their underwear." Deejo's friends make him read that to them over and over.

Two other stories, **"Hot Ice"** and **"Pet Milk,"** are equally irresistible. The other major piece, **"Nighthawks,"** is not. Instead of allowing magic to emerge from the setting and characters, the story overlays Dybek's landscape with a thick crust of symbolism and imposed fantasy. Here, I think, Dybek has gone against his nature. If he is indeed more of a Schumann than a Chopin, it's because he lacks facility and polish, glamour and heroic posturing. His is a more homely, earnest, obsessive art, which is best when it is most grounded. For his purposes, the flightiest he needs to get is to make Mrs. Kubiac's building five stories tall. In a city of three-flats, that can seem as fabulous as finding mermaids in the sanitation canal.

Some of the pieces in Dybek's 1980 collection, *Childhood and Other Neighborhoods,* suffered from a similar problem; so perhaps he is determined to go on in this vein and will either keep it up until he succeeds or turn out strikingly uneven work. No matter. Writers should be judged on their strongest efforts, and in *The Coast of Chicago* those are very strong indeed. Mr. Dreiser, Mr. Farrell, Mr. Bellow, Mr. Algren, please say hello to Stuart Dybek. He's one of yours.

Antioch Review (review date fall 1990)

SOURCE: A review of *The Coast of Chicago,* by Stuart Dybek.*Antioch Review* 48, no. 4 (fall 1990): 545.

[*In the following review, the critic compares Dybek's work to that of Hemingway.*]

In 14 interlocked stories and vivid "short shorts" reminiscent of Hemingway's stark interludes in *In Our Time,* Dybek writes of a richly remembered Chicago of boyhood, adolescence, and young manhood. Dreamlike and phantasmagoric, his stories remain paradoxically vivid and realistic. Creatures of the night, his characters are apparitions, luminescent reflections and shadows who inhabit a rain-streaked, surreal city of memories and ghosts, of vanished ethnic neighborhoods and mournfully twisting, Kafkaesque streets leading nowhere. Dybek creates an eerie portrait of a vanished Chicago, populated by denizens as hauntingly spectral as those in Edward Hopper's painting *Nighthawks,* which provides the title for one of his finest series of stories.

Kirkus Reviews (review date 15 February 1990)

SOURCE: "Fiction." *Kirkus Reviews* 58, no. 4 (15 February 1990): 204-05.

[*In the following review of* The Coast of Chicago, *the critic compares the collection to* Dubliners *and Sherwood Anderson's tales in its design, scope, and realism.*]

Grounded in the realities of ethnic life in Chicago, Dybek's second collection of stories (*Children and Other Neighborhoods,* 1980) transcends street-corner sociology for an urban poetry of spirit and myth; his lyrical prose derives its power from his switchblade sharp imagery—as well as Proustian sensitivity to the smells and sounds of city life.

Every story here, from the half-page shorts to the lengthy, conventional narratives, serves as a gloss on the others, creating a coherence of design and texture truly worthy of comparison with Joyce's epiphanic Dublin tales or Anderson's Midwestern elegiacs. **"Bottle Caps," "Lights,"** and **"The Woman Who Fainted"** all detail odd rituals—collecting beer-bottle caps, waiting on the corner at dusk to tell drivers to turn on their lights, and watching each Sunday in church for the wilting flower of a woman who regularly faints. This is a memory book as well, with portraits of a nervous Russian émigré (**"Entrance"**) and a cat-lady who collects stray animals (**"Strays"**). Lyrics celebrate working as a movie usher (**"Outtakes"**) and an old radio show (**"Lost"**). **"Death of the Right Fielder,"** a brilliant comment on neighborhood myth-making, is a surreal epitaph for a lost right-fielder, felled by a heart problem but rumored to have died more glamorously in his most unglamorous position. The longer stories represent various stages of passage and revelation. In **"Chopin in Winter,"** a young boy with problems in school listens to the ethereal piano-playing of a neighbor's unmarried daughter, who's returned home from school pregnant and in disgrace; his own prodigal grandfather, an embarrassment in his own right, has shown up just in time to share with his grandson an extraordinary appreciation for music. **"Blight"** and **"Hot Ice"** take place in the late teens of a boy's life—the budding hipsters here hang out, cruise the mean streets, and eventually drift apart because of work, college, crime, the draft. A young couple fresh out of college (**"Pet Milk"**) not only realize their rift with their ethnic pasts, but move uneasily into their long-repressed sexuality.

Intimations of disillusionment and despair make these miraculous tales all the more resonant and real—a collection for the ages.

Don Lee (review date spring 1991)

SOURCE: "Ploughshares Bookshelf." *Ploughshares* 17, no. 1 (spring 1991): 228-29.

[*In the following review of* The Coast of Chicago, *Lee praises Dybek's ability to draw contrasts together, mingling past with future and grim realism with the mythic.*]

Readers of literary magazines and anthologies frequently speak of Stuart Dybek's stories with reverence, and they will certainly covet *The Coast of Chicago,* his second collection, which brings together several works already deemed classics: **"Hot Ice," "Blight,"** and **"Pet Milk."** Seven long stories are interleaved with seven shorter ones, and they are bound so tightly by place and theme, the book merits, for once, the flap-copy comparisons to Anderson's *Winesburg, Ohio* and Joyce's *Dubliners.*

Dybek's style often shifts from a gritty realism befitting the Chicago's South Side to metafictional techniques which transform images into reverie, the tangible into the mythic. Nothing could be more appropriate, since this is a book about trying to bridge polarities: the past and future, tradition and assimilation, hopelessness and joy, night and day. In stories about coming of age in the 1950s and '60s, the characters—Slavic, Hispanic, Greek—watch their neighborhoods disappear in the sweep of urban renewal, and, "at times, walking past the gaps, they felt as if they were no longer quite there themselves, half-lost despite familiar street signs, shadows of themselves superimposed on the present, except there was no present—everything either rubbled past or promised future—and they were walking as if floating, getting nowhere." This motif of being lost is insistent in the more contemporary stories as well, insomniacs and lovers sleepwalking through rainy nights, sitting in diners like the one painted in Edward Hopper's famous *Nighthawks,* an explicit inspiration for Dybek.

For a variety of reasons, all the characters in *The Coast of Chicago* find themselves to be, like their parents, DPs, Displaced Persons. The onus is on Dybek, then, to evoke and preserve memories of the tenements, the bars, and the El, the smell of "frying burgers, pizza parlors, the cornmeal and hot-oil blast of *taquerías,*" and, most of all, the people who defined the neighborhoods. Dybek succeeds gloriously.

Terry Caesar (review date summer 1991)

SOURCE: Caesar, Terry. "Glimpses, Surfaces, Ecstasies: Three Books of Short Fiction." *Michigan Quarterly Review* 30, no. 3 (summer 1991): 506-18.

[*In the following review, Caesar lauds Dybek's style, noting examples of taut narrative impressively infused with lyricism and music.*]

The title story in Charles Baxter's new volume of stories is about a man who is telephoned one day by another man. He claims to be his brother. They meet at a bar. They are indeed brothers. "Isn't this great?" exclaims one. Well, no, thinks the other. "It was horrifyingly strange without being eventful."

It is a line which can stand for some of the deepest impulses of contemporary short fiction. The strangeness is the important thing, whether or not it is horrible, and it is the more strange because the less eventful. Baxter's stories may be richer in event than those in the new volumes of Richard Burgin and Stuart Dybek. This is another way of saying that Baxter's stories are less strange.

"I know that real astonishment is our deepest taboo—that even Spinoza would not consider wonder to be one of our emotions," reflects the narrator in Burgin's first story; all of them are avid for astonishment, and almost baffled by anything which does happen—a group of old people having their picture taken, a brilliant grade school friend whose promise expires into ritualized stupor. Baxter, by contrast, is more secure with the sanction of narrative, perhaps because it keeps taboos of experience within the decencies of form, even as the form exposes the very notion of decency to a certain kind of studied horror.

Dybek's stories trace a more luxurious strangeness than those of Burgin. The narrator of his second stands in winter before steamed windows and imagines the street outside "with rings of vapor around the streetlights and headlights, clouds billowing from exhaust pipes and manhole covers, breaths hanging, snow swirling like white smoke." Events in Dybek are seldom equal to moments such as these, and narrative, in a way, exists in order to try to contain them, because they are so profuse. In Baxter, on the other hand, there is a more manageable, even resigned, stance before life's vaporousness, while in the austere, cerebral Burgin the windows don't get steamed up very much at all.

The fiction of each of these writers can be regarded as a strategy for representing various kinds of strangeness within narrative while keeping it sufficiently inchoate and fugitive (or "relative" in Baxter's designation) so that whatever is strange does not quite coalesce into event and instead presides either above or beneath the plot. Why should this be so? In part because of a certain restlessness about form which troubles each of these volumes. Baxter's are the most conventionally realistic, but he includes three "parabolic" tales in which point of view is more concentrated upon a single character who is effectively isolated by the end from each tale. Burgin's stories are saturated by lists, which take up three pages in one instance and barely get enveloped by a larger narrative in the title story. Some of Dybek's stories are very short, hardly more than episodes, and they are linked with the larger ones as if they were fragments of a lost whole.

Just as compelling an explanation for strangeness is a certain disposition of character in each volume. Put too simply, everybody is consistently seen as a version of everybody else. This is less clearly the case in Dybek, whose East European refugees, Mexican and Polish adolescents, dreamy students, shadowy musicians, and abstracted lovers all have a local distinctness of outline because they are rooted in Chicago's ethnic neighborhoods. Burgin's characters, vaguely intellectual all, and just as vaguely artistic, could live pretty much anywhere, and do, which is one reason why so many of them are given as in the thrall of someone else's otherness, which baffles them like an identity. Baxter's volume offers a much wider cast of human types—homeless people, vagrants, foreigners, teenage runaways—but a common motion in many stories brings the representative of a more normal, secure center into a disturbing conjunction with someone heretofore as unimagined as a rejected or degraded self. "A version of my face was fixed on a stranger," thinks the narrator of his brother in the title story, and the disclosure of such "versions," albeit not usually so consciously registered, is what many of the fictions in all these volumes is about. Each of us can be comprehended as a possibility of many others.

This is indeed very strange. It's even horrifying, and it may be that any formal arrangement of event isn't adequate to clarify either the true measure of our relations to each other or the structures that prevent us from admitting, as for example a man on Baxter's last page acknowledges, that we can feel we have known "the secret of the universe for a split second." This is the sort of feeling that characters in Burgin are far more eager to indulge, and he has one story, "Aerialist," where the narrator does admit it, but is rejected by the woman, and so is left alone shuddering with dismay at the end while he considers yet another ecstatic sunset from his new high-rise. Dybek's people are in this sense positively mad with ecstasy. "Hey man, let's go dig some beauty," cries one, but it is not long after when the narrator loses touch with him, and by the end of the story returns to the old neighborhood only to discover that he has lost touch with himself. It's not that life without strangeness wouldn't be life. It's more that strangeness is ultimately all there is, absolutely.

Is this because contemporary American life has become too familiar? Of course this point itself has become rather

familiar. We have every right, I think, to expect of these volumes that they will tell us something we had not suspected, and one way to put this knowledge would be to say that our very familiarity with ourselves has become, well, strange. Our surfaces can now be impersonated so well that they hardly have to be lived. They can even be eerily articulated by others who have refused to live them. . . .

Different sensibilities, different moves—and, if possible, different constraints. Dybek could in one decisive sense not be more different a writer from either Baxter or Burgin because he wants a world where there are Glimpses available everywhere and at all times. There is in Dybek a richly textured landscape of churches, apartment buildings, movie theatres, prisons, viaducts and alleys. Kids play games with baseballs or bottle caps. Men tell anecdotes and legends. Life is not either so dense or so strange that the eventual departure from home of a pregnant young pianist—she refuses to say who the father is—will not be mourned, and her music still heard as silence. There are events, and they exert a shaping force. But the crucial difference can be indicated in terms of a statement made by one of Burgin's narrators: "Nothing can threaten identity like a flight into ecstasy—no matter how brief." Identity is not so oppressive in Baxter as it is in Burgin; if it were, Glimpses wouldn't matter so much or seem so precious when they occur. In Dybek, however, identity doesn't matter very much at all and Glimpses are instead what the narratives strain to see.

They rarely afford ecstasy. Ecstasy is just a word anyway. "A name's what we use instead of smelling," declares a nameless woman in a squib of a story called **"Strays,"** about her caring for an assortment of lost animals and birds. In *The Coast of Chicago* it is most urgent to make contact with life despite language, if not through it—and so the stories are full of kids who believe that rock songs played backward make audible secret messages from the devil, or uncles who talk to fish (in Spanish, not English), or old women who weep in languages (in one instance, Bohemian) which the narrator can't understand. In, I think, Dybek's most wholly realized story, **"Blight,"** which is, among other things, at once a curse and a paean to the very word, the narrator, years after having moved and then lived away from his blight-ridden youth, at one point returns to college. His instructor in English-lit survey spits when he reads. "When he read us Shelley's 'To a Skylark,' which began 'Hail to thee, blithe spirit,' I thought he was talking about blight again until I looked it up." The burden of Dybek's art is to make us discern that there may be no fundamental difference between "blithe" and "blight," because there is some common essence behind each word that eludes them both.

Music expresses this essence better, or anyway purer. With music there is *release* from meaning. Dybek's stories are full of music, and one, **"Chopin in Winter"** (about the pregnant pianist), narrativizes the transforming power of music. In another story, **"Hot Ice,"** there is a moment after the two friends, Manny and Eddie, have been wandering around, via buses and the El, all night. Now it's morning. They still don't want to quit. It's hard to say why. "Manny could be talking Spanish, I could be talking Polish, Eddie thought. It didn't matter. What meant something was sitting at the table together, still awake watching the rain splatter the window, walking out again, to the Prague bakery for bismarcks, past people under dripping umbrellas on their way to church." Much of Dybek's special sensibility is here, especially the way the words make their way to church. To say there is no music is only to say that the words which aren't spoken constitute nonetheless a mute testimony to the very presence that music expresses. By music we can hear what matters, especially if we must be, inescapably and finally, alone with ourselves.

Therefore it is the more strange, and strangely beautiful, that what matters hardly coalesces at all in life in terms of events. Dybek's last story is entitled **"Pet Milk,"** a lovely, lush meditation on what is always lost. One thing is an emblem of childhood that seemed to embody the very fact of the material world itself—the pet milk the narrator's grandmother used to use in her coffee as she listened in her kitchen to the radio. The narrator associates the liquid's creamy swirl with the liqueur he and his girlfriend, Kate, used to enjoy at their special Czech restaurant while each luxuriated in a respective first job as well as each other. They spoke of plans. "It was the first time I'd ever had the feeling of missing someone I was still with." Another thing that is always lost is love.

One hot May evening the young lovers want each other so much that suddenly they flee the restaurant before they order dinner. His roommate will be home. They have to take the last subway express to her place in Evanston. On the way they make love inside the empty conductor's compartment. The narrator looks out and sees the surprised faces of commuters as the train speeds by each station. A high school kid grins and waves. The narrator can't forget it. "It was as if I were standing on that platform, with my schoolbooks and a smoke, on one of those endlessly accumulated afternoons after school when I stood almost outside of time simply waiting for a train, and I thought how much I'd have loved seeing someone like us streaming by."

This is a superb conclusion to *The Coast of Chicago,* by far the most tightly strung of these three volumes. The characteristic figure has been this perpetual high school kid, sometimes limp and sometimes swollen with waiting and longing, about to go somewhere yet somehow already gone beforehand. He is his own lost possibility. He knows he's foolish. He's foolish to know. Life is ceaselessly elsewhere. Chicago is its coasts. It is difficult to give an adequate sense of Dybek's sensibility, how he indulges in romance, but crisply, or how he can be very witty (this is a very funny book in places), but severe. One of the boys in **"Blight"** is "Deejo," a guitar player, who at one point has been writing the Great American Novel (of course entitled, *Blight*) which has the following first sentence: "The dawn

rises like sick old men playing on the rooftops in their underwear." His buddies are moved. "We had him read that to us again and again." Then Deejo rushes home, ecstatic, and writes all night, to the 1812 Overture. His second sentence runs to twenty pages and describes "an epic battle between a spider and a caterpillar." Dybek himself has of course better sentences. Many of them stun a reader as Deejo's friends are stunned. One way to characterize Dybek's art is to say that he never writes like Deejo (however one could cite sentences which are close), his own music is considerably less grand than the 1812 Overture, and yet he doesn't cut off his own discipline from the deeply felt crudity of that first sentence or even the naive, "epic" ambition to say everything about everything all at once.

The long central sequence (probably intended to be more musically exact than a mere medley) of stories, vignettes, events, and moments entitled, **"Nighthawks,"** is the fullest representation of this ambition. An unnamed narrator is between job interviews and drifts among the paintings at the Art Institute, always ending before Edward Hopper's famous painting, blank before the three customers who sit "as if waiting, not for something to begin, but rather to end." There is more, much more, of this sort of thing. For some readers it will all be ineffable. For me, it got overripe by the end of the first section, when rain is visible in the streetlights: "each drop contains its own blue bulb." There is sleepwalking, there is night luminous with the unseen light of dawn, there is an African musician who chants in an ancient tongue over his drumbeat. I prefer Dybek when he's more measured, and when some firmer narrative pressure works against the deliquescent lyricism. This is in one sense the meaning of the lengthy succeeding story, **"Hot Ice,"** about the attempt—eventually—of Manny and Eddie to get hold of a block of ice and release the saintly virgin whose abused body they believe has been frozen in it. Randall Jarrell has a review in which he judges a story as "manner . . . carried to the point where the returns almost stop coming in at all." **"Nighthawks,"** on the other hand, serves up all its returns by means of manner only, and they're all hot.

"Hot Ice" concludes with the boys running away with the ice block. Suddenly Manny knows "where they were taking her, where she would be finally released." Should we know? Ultimately it doesn't matter. Destination is just another name for release. All Dybek's stories strain to be released—from words, from events. Their spiritual home is still another way in which they contrast with the stories of Baxter and Burgin, whose respective routes, furthermore, are not nearly so sensuous, as if neither holds quite so sharp and plangent a sense of loss. But from another perspective—what is there to be learned from all these volumes if it is not that there are always available other perspectives?—Dybek has more in common with them after all. He has a charming vignette, **"Outtakes,"** about a boy who is enlisted to be an usher in a movie theatre, complete with wardrobe and stealthy movies in the dark. "So he became nocturnal," we read, "a member of a secret society that knew itself exiled from the screen, but like outtakes remained part of the movie." Dybek's high school kids are versions of Baxter's strangers or Burgin's narrators enlisted in the present tense. All, that is, are representable as outtakes from a movie in which they are part, even if the show on the big screen does not record them, and is not recorded by them as a social product or even a public occasion.

So the world in which all these strangers, victims, and exiles live is finally not as utterly *known* as it might first appear. It is certainly possible to discuss it without wondering if it has already been written by Raymond Carver or comprehended under the aegis of the postmodern sublime. Baxter, Burgin, and Dybek are fine writers, and not only because each affords Glimpses at something beyond the conditions of everyday life, past the limits of its events to represent. Nevertheless, I have emphasized the strangeness in them because of my persistent sense that strangeness—just that—now bids to be our only consolation, our only metaphysics, and our only narrative. Even the grand themes of love and death, or the enduring ones of identity and its trials may have yielded to the harsher, emptier ones of sheer strangeness. The ability of three such impeccably contemporary American writers of short fiction to trace this theme, so repeatedly and variously, is not the most obvious thing about them. It may be, however, the one with the most power, elusiveness, and virtuosity.

David Montrose (review date 26 July 1991)

SOURCE: Montrose, David. "Into the Underworlds." *Times Literary Supplement,* no. 4608 (26 July 1991): 18-19.

[*In the following review, Montrose bemoans the British edition of* The Coast of Chicago *for being spliced-together and lacking in cohesion.*]

Eight of the stories in *The Coast of Chicago,* Stuart Dybek's fine British début, have been selected from a larger volume of the same name published in America last year; the remaining six are from his previous collection, *Childhood and Other Neighborhoods* (1986). The titles are apposite. Dybek's fictive territory is his native patch, the Slav and Hispanic districts of Chicago's South Side (frequently during the 1950s, "those years between Korea and Vietnam"); his protagonists are often children and adolescents.

All the earlier stories are third-person narratives, the majority with children serving as the centres of consciousness. Particularly impressive are two in which pairs of children stray into alarming social netherworlds. **"The Palatski Man"** sees John and his kid sister follow a sweet-vendor back to the encampment of a gypsy-like clan of pedlars, where they witness a strange quasi-Mass. In **"Blood Soup"**, two brothers brave dangerous neighbor-

hoods in quest of fresh duck blood (no longer obtainable legally), an essential ingredient of a restorative potion for their ailing grandmother.

A variation on this device is employed in **"The Wake"**, in which misadventures befall a young woman returning at night to the area where she grew up, an area that has since "gone down". By contrast, the hero of **"The Apprentice"** is part of criminal society, working for his uncle, an unlicensed taxidermist and supplier of out-of-season game to restaurants. The underworld in **"Horror Movie"** is that of the imagination: a boy is unable to overcome his addiction to monster flicks even though they give him nightmares and cause him to start at shadows.

Dybek spices his naturalism with dashes of the grotesque and the surreal, to good effect. When, however, he increases the measures, in **"Visions of Budharin"**, the result is much less successful: inexplicably concealed inside a ramshackle mechanical elephant, a tycoon revisits his childhood haunts, undergoes indignities, broods on bygone injustices, wrecks a church interior, and finally floats away down a drainage canal. The plot may sound promisingly bizarre; the story is disappointingly half-baked.

The best of the later stories, **"Hot Ice"** and **"Blight"**, are rather more accomplished than their earlier counterparts, but ultimately slightly less striking. The extended (thirty-two page) **"Hot Ice"**, an O. Henry Award-winner, recounts episodically the low-lives of Eddie Kapusta and his pals. Their scenes are interwoven with a local legend concerning a drowned woman preserved in her father's ice-plant.

Dybek's style in his third-person narratives is somewhat reminiscent of Bellow's, though without the range and exuberance. The first-person **"Blight"** is plainer, closer to the standard voice of the contemporary American short story. Superficially akin to **"Hot Ice"**—dealing with four high-school buddies whose neighbourhood is "an Official Blight Area"—it is altogether jauntier: the kids have wider horizons; they read (Kerouac, Thomas Merton), write songs, start an R& R band. **"Nighthawks"** is the most satisfying of the other longer stories: a little anthology of tangentially connected *récits* whose focus is a twenty-four-hour diner modelled on the one in the famous painting by Edward Hopper. **"Bijou"** constitutes something of a departure: a tense and angry piece about turning human suffering into a commodity and the way cinematic depictions of violence desensitize our responses to the real thing.

In carving this single collection from two, the best stories have been chosen, but both volumes are rather misrepresented as a result. The variety of style and length in the later stories is deceptive: *Childhood and Other Neighbourhoods* contains several first-person shorter narratives, none of which has been chosen. The later "rejects" are shorter pieces, none outstanding but which achieved a cumulative impact and gave the parent volume a unity now lacking.

Thomas S. Gladsky (essay date 1992)

SOURCE: Gladsky, Thomas S. *Princes, Peasants, and Other Polish Selves: Ethnicity in American Literature,* pp. 256-62. Amherst: University of Massachusetts Press, 1992.

[*In the following excerpt, Gladsky examines Dybek's thematic use of fading cultural identity and lost places, both physical and emotional, and the effect of this rootlessness on young Chicagoans.*]

AMERICAN SELVES—ETHNIC PERSPECTIVES

THE MYSTERIOUS PRESENCE OF THE LOST: STUART DYBEK

Stuart Dybek's fiction immediately invites comparison to Nelson Algren's stories about "outsiders and underground men," as Howard Kaplan describes Dybek's characters (319). A winner of the Nelson Algren Award, Dybek—like Algren—is essentially a realist-naturalist with a touch of fantasy and a commitment to the proletariat—"an interest in class," as Dybek phrases it (*TLS,* 25 November 1989). More to the point, Dybek also writes about Chicago's Poles, although his characters, urban guerrillas of a sort, are worlds apart from the semiliterate, brutish, and hapless victims in *Never Come Morning* and *The Man with the Golden Arm.* Dybek's protagonists constantly assess themselves within the context of place. Even when they have left childhood and other neighborhoods behind, place remains with them as it does with Poniscan's wanderers, those ethnic outsiders who continue to look to their eastern Pennsylvania origins despite their long separation. But unlike the Budduskys, who have only foggy notions of heritage, Dybek's protagonists (often adolescents or teenagers) associate place with their ethnicity even though they are innocents not quite sure of their world. Dybek's commingling of place and ethnicity is recognized in Reginald Gibbons's suggestion to a round table of Chicago writers that they may be "memorializing a certain cultural reality in reaction to pressure to de-ethnicize, de-identify, and de-materialize the urban landscape" (325). Dybek replied that he does indeed worry about formerly distinct neighborhoods and regions that have become "placeless," such as the South Chicago area where he grew up and about which he writes.

Descended from Algren, and literary cousin to Poniscan, Anthony Bukoski, and Anne Pellowski, with their firm sense of place, Dybek is equally aware that ethnicity is "a strong component of my voice as a writer" (*TLS,* 25 November 1989). This voice echoes the complaint of Poniscan's long-distance ethnics and the elegiac tones of contemporary poets, all of whom preserve the past even as they bury it. His stories and poems also record the loss of ethnicity in a rapidly changing society and the coming of age in a seemingly disordered and fantastical urban environment. Ethnicity remains at the forefront, although Dybek does not envelop his work in Polish traditions as Anthony Bukoski does. Two of Dybek's most recent poems illustrate his method and provide an overview to stories and poems previously published. In "The Immigrant," the speaker talks about "returning to the Old Country." He's been "homesick" and "lonely" for the gas stations that "smell like garlic" and the butchershop where skinned rabbits hang next door to the funeral parlor. Nowhere does Dybek mention the immigrant's ancestry, nationality, or place of origin, or whether the Old World is a physical or metaphysical place—although the garlic, skinned rabbits, and rosary beads suggest a Catholic, probably Slavic, point of reference. In "Autobiography" the narrator's melancholy is more easily traced to his implied Polish connections, but even here Dybek works only through allusion. The poem is steeped in Catholicism: feast days and surplices, crucifixes and confessionals, the clang of the evening Angelus and streets transfigured by "a reverence I can't explain." Nonetheless, the narrator's story is muted, darkened by distance from his neighbors and his own history. There are autobiographies at every corner, he explains, "autobiographies, but no history." Were it not for references to the Black Virgin of Czestochowa, "my girlfriend," and to his habit of calling any old woman "babushka," the narrator would remain an everyman, a Catholic catholic. But Dybek's allusions to Polish language and history change all that and his poem assumes a specific shape through which the narrator's thoughts are contextualized.

In a general sense, the narrator worries about the past into which the dead slowly vanish, but Dybek has a particular past in mind: "a parish of phantoms," shadows "under a crucifix," grandmother with her "babushka." The abandoned past, we learn, is a particularly ethnic problem in this case, a matter of generational indifference and contrasting expectations. "It's not that I didn't listen," he explains, "but it wasn't my language." For succeeding generations, even the commonplace of tradition "has assumed / the mysterious presence / of the lost." On the one hand, the speaker is relieved to be freed from the burdens of tradition; on the other, freedom leads to exile. His story, he fears, will ultimately recede into "a solo . . . noodling through broken English."

By and large, Dybek's characters in *Childhood and Other Neighborhoods* are young, third-generation Americans occupied with friends from varying ethnic backgrounds, engaged in the rough and tumble of the street, and the problematics of initiation. None seems especially conscious either of ethnicity or of Old World connections. The peasant culture in Krawczyk's stories and Bankowsky's *A Glass Rose* is not a felt presence or a unifying element in the community. Nor does Dybek try to make it so. His protagonists, unlike Anthony Bukoski's, undergo no ethnic epiphanies, make no singular commitments, refuse to be burdened by time. Their unobtrusive Polishness is largely assumed or, if anything, reduced to a cultural residue.

To them, it is the older Poles who are the "other," part of the social fringe within their vision but not at its center. More frequently than not, the more "Polish" the character, the more bizarre are Dybek's stories. The Palatski man and his rag-peddler colleagues exist in a wasteland, a shantytown where they "stammered in foreign English" and re-enact, mysteriously, the Easter passion. Old Buzka and her crazy grandson Swantek drown unwanted neighborhood cats. Pan Gowumpe lives in a crumbling tenement with "poultry in his room." The workers in the ice-cream factory are "Slavs missing parts of hands and arms that had been chewed off while trying to clean machines." Tadeusz's uncle spends his nights cruising the highways picking up the debris of a culture on the move and the dead animals (for stuffing) it leaves in its wake. Big Antek, a local drunk, leads two boys to an abandoned ice house where years before a grieving immigrant entombed his drowned daughter. In short, most of the immigrant Poles and their near relatives, as seen through the eyes of the young, are grotesques in a distorted landscape. Few, if any, are three-dimensional "normals," although most possess an odd sort of dignity and mystery.

Only in **"Blood Soup"** does Dybek examine the interior of the peasant culture. Stefush recalls Busha's house with its holy pictures, "flaming hearts crowned with thorns, pierced by swords, and dripping blood" (27), vials of holy water, Polish phrases, zupa, czarnina, rozumiesz, and the Easter blessing of eggs, ham, kielbasi, horseradish. In other cases, Dybek's characters implicitly reject this culture even though they ironically use it to measure their movements. In **"The Wake,"** for example, Jill decides that she "wasn't going to hang around this neighborhood forever while she walks the streets, locating herself vis-à-vis St. Casimir's Church."

In **"The Wake,"** as in other stories, ethnicity is less a problem than social class which, for many descent writers, has become an abrasive ethnic marker. Actually Jill fears the prospects of life in the working class, getting "knocked up, tied down with a bunch of kids, married to a truck driver" (104). Frank Marzek in **"Sauerkraut Soup"** shares Jill's fears. He regards his father's factory years as time surrendered: "It was what my father, who'd worked in a factory all his life, had wanted to tell me. But he's never been able to find the words" (131). The environment in virtually all of Dybek's stories is working class, although he does not use these settings to politicize his work. It is clear, nonetheless, that his Chicagoans have been run down by poverty, the harsh landscape, and limited opportunities. They are conscious of their lack of status and have, in some cases, accepted the blight which surrounds them. Dybek is not interested in particular indictments, in a call to collective arms, or in proletarian rhetoric, but his message is clear enough. The Poles, three generations after the great immigration, have sunk into the underclass; pride in work, a hallmark of ethnicity for the first generation, has given way to images of the working-class prison.

Like his colleagues, Dybek continues to define ethnicity with a religiosity that permeates his school memories, neighborhood geography, and childhood adventures: from Busha's iconic wall decorations, to Tim Vukovich kneeling at school detention; from Jill's awareness of St. Casimir's steeple, to Eddie Kapusta's reminiscences about

his youthful days as an altar boy; from the children's references in **"The Palatski Man"** to Father Mike, communion, and the Holy Spirit; to Marzek's cynical appraisal of the church's power. Catholicism in these stories is as suspect, however, as the eccentrics who roam the streets. Like their working-class heritage, the religion of the church has become a cross almost too heavy to bear, the specter of unpleasant memories, a creature of habit although not necessarily of comfort, a sign of a culture unable to transfer its values to the present. Christ images in **"The Palatski Man"** become confused with the distorted landscape for children brought up with religious mystery. The story's religious imagery serves only to highlight the characters' inability to sort out the facts and fictions in their surroundings. When Eddie Kapusta tours the churches on Good Friday, he is moved by habit and training, not by piety. He turns away from the chanting old women, muttering to himself, "same as ever." In **"Sauerkraut Soup"** Frank Marzek verbalizes what Kapusta and many of the others must think. Reflecting on his own Catholic upbringing, he critically remarks, "Suspect what they teach you, study what they condemn" (127). Despite his rough treatment of religion, Dybek knows that his characters cannot escape their religious backgrounds which have become an indelible feature of their identity.

Ultimately, Dybek shows that too much has changed, that ethnicity, and consequently identity, is in transition and disarray. Demographic shifts, urban blight and renewal, the rejection of the past have produced anxiety and doubt. His "Poles," unable to resist these changes and yet part of them, sense that something has vanished: the old neighborhood, cultural promises, the assurance of heritage. Alienation, exile, and anonymity, new passwords for ethnicity, govern the lives of Big Swantek in **"The Cat Woman,"** Sterndorf in **"Neighborhood Drunk,"** Kapusta in **"Hot Ice,"** and the protagonists of **"Blight,"** one of Dybek's most recent stories. In **"Blight,"** the musical group the boys form is significantly dubbed "The No Names." The Korean War vets who languish in the streets and taverns "have actually chosen anonymity." Even the neighborhood is known only by the postal code "2 one 8" in contrast to other Chicago areas identifiable by name. Dybek writes about the breakup of the old gang, constant moving, the absence of beauty, addresses unknown. When after a few years he returns, the neighborhood is almost unrecognizable, "mostly Mexican now." His return is terrifying, a reminder of his lost self. He is back "but lost, everything at once familiar and strange" (249).

Aimlessness, strangeness, and a sense of being lost are recurring themes in Dybek's accounts of the wandering ethnic. The children in **"The Palatski Man"** try to find their junkyard home doubting, on occasion, even its existence. The boy in **"Blood Soup"** enters unknown parts of his neighborhood in search of the elusive duck's blood for his grandmother's soup. Tadeusz and his uncle in **"The Apprentice"** conduct nightly odysseys on back roads. In **"Hot Ice"** the long evening of Eddie Kapusta stretches into timelessness. Their journeys lead, Prufrockian fashion, to deserted streets that yield few answers to time's eternal questions. Eddie and the others have stepped out of place and even outside themselves. In **"Hot Ice,"** Dybek explains that "they felt as if they were no longer quite there themselves, half lost despite familiar street signs, shadows of themselves superimposed on the present, except there was no present—everything either rubbed past or promised future" (25).

Their odysseys carry them into the recesses of the past, toward disconnected glimpses of their roots as Dybek links the predicament of the contemporary urban self with ethnicity. Big Antek, for example, explains how it was when he came to a place filled with "mostly people from the Old Country" (22). Similarly Pan Gowumpe talks about life in the packing plants years before. "All those DPS working there . . . Polacks, Lugani, Bohunks. People who knew how to be hungry" (45). The listeners in these stories recognize how little they know and how much is irretrievable. Frank Marzek comes to believe the immigrants "knew something they were hiding" (129), and young Steven in **"Blood Soup"** penetrates and redefines the legacy of his past when he thinks about his "Busha." She embodied "the kind of love [that] must have come from the Old Country—instinctive, unrequesting—like her strength, something foreign that he couldn't find in himself, that hadn't been transmitted to his mother or any of Busha's other children" (26). This is Dybek's most concise, penetrating explanation of the Polish legacy and the closest he comes to epiphany in his fiction, although in **"Sauerkraut Soup"** something similar occurs to Marzek. Stopping at a Polish restaurant to savor once again the soup of his youth, he observes that "there are certain mystical connections to these things" (131).

Although ethnicity reexperienced breaks through occasionally in Dybek's fiction, cultural exile dominates the stories in *Childhood and Other Neighborhoods* and *The Coast of Chicago* (1990). In **"Hot Ice,"** Eddie Kapusta confronts his own uprootedness and the specter of the past. Eddie's problem is that he has no past by which to order the present. He knows little of Polish culture (Old or New World versions) and nothing about Poland itself. What knowledge he has of his transplanted heritage resides only in memories of childhood and neighborhood. But with the death of his family and the bulldozing of his neighborhood, "the past collapsed about them," he realizes. Resembling Anthony Bukoski's stories about the razing of St. Adalbert's, but without his reverence for old ways, **"Hot Ice"** explains contemporary exile as a consequence of lost ethnicity. Eddie has lost the language he knew as a child—so that now he can hardly distinguish Polish from other languages. He tells his friend Manny about his visits to "Busha, my grandmother" before the cranes and wrecking balls removed all the physical traces of his ethnicity. The only legacy of his once-thriving neighborhood is the twenty-sixth-street bus, the Polish Zephyr, and the old women "dressed in black coats and babushkas." Eddie tries to understand what it is they mourn, to discover the source, "to give the feeling a name [but] it eluded him as always" (40).

In **"Chopin in Winter,"** Dybek, as he had done in **"Blight"** and "Autobiography," returns to the claims of memory in what is perhaps his most romantic and sentimental treatment of the Polish self. **"Chopin in Winter"** is a memory tale told by a narrator looking back nostalgically on his childhood. Two principal events occur: the return of the boy's grandfather, Dzia, after a long absence, and the return and departure of Marcy Kubiak, the girl upstairs whose dreams of becoming a concert pianist are cut short by pregnancy. The music of Chopin, which the girl plays nightly, strikes home to Grandfather and unleashes in him "the jumble of the past" eagerly absorbed by the boy Michael, who learns something about his ancestry. Dzia Dzia talks about his trek from Krakow to Gdansk to avoid impressment into the Prussian army, his American wanderings, and Chopin's death, piano, and heart (buried in Warsaw). Chopin sustains the old man even as it does Marcy in the winter of her discontent, and as it subsequently does Michael who continues to hear the music after Marcy moves away. Dybek's story works on a universal level: a boy and his grandfather, first infatuation, a sense of home, and an awareness of changes in the offing. But in his choice of Chopin, Old World anecdotes, and a neighborhood where old women wearing babushkas drone "endless, mournful litanies before the side altar of the Black Virgin of Czestochowa" (116), Dybek particularizes the experience as an ethnic one impressed on a boy's mind, as the stuff of Polishness long gone even though he can "still hear the silence left behind" (166).

In this and other stories, the Polish connection dominates, but Dybek, like other of his colleagues, also hears the music of transethnicity in the making. Anne Pellowski, for example, moved beyond the confines of Polishness through interethnic marriages and, more important, by showing the younger generation's acquisition of a global perspective. Anthony Bukoski also writes about the new alliance of Poles and others—Native Americans, Jews, Scandinavians—not as a united proletariat but as Polish Americans redefining the meaning of otherness. Perhaps not by choice, Dybek's Poles have expanded their territory to include Hispanics and other minorities whose presence sometimes transmogrifies Polish identity. In **"Chopin in Winter,"** Michael does not literally understand Mrs. Kubiac's Bohemian, but he recognizes that through Chopin (and their own humanness) he and the Kubiacs are one family. Interaction with the Czechs, the boy's closeness to Mrs. Panova, a Russian neighbor in **"The Cat Woman,"** Pan Gowumpe's years with the "Lugani and Bohunks," young Tadeusz's visits to the Spanish Blades restaurant—all have prepared Dybek's protagonists for change, new cultural patterns of assimilation, and a revised sense of self. In **"Hot Ice,"** Eddie Kapusta and Manny Santora are more than best friends. Eddie has become partly Hispanic. He sings in Spanish and appreciates the Spanish words which, to him, perfectly express the contemporary landscape. The word "juilota" (pigeon) captured, he thought, "both their cooing and the whistling rush of their wings. He didn't remember any words like that in Polish" (28). In **"Blight,"** the young boy's sidekick is Stanley Pepper Rosado, called Stash by his mother. Dybek tells us that this new alliance is not always easy, but his story of Rosado, Ziggy Zilinski, Joey DeCampo, and the jukeboxes filled with polkas and Mexican songs shows that the Polish self is undergoing deep-seated change.

At one point in **"The Apprentice,"** Tadeusz's uncle gives him good advice. "You're starting to sort it out . . . [but] there's no in-between. People who find an in-between live foolish lives" (196). Inadvertently, the uncle describes most of Dybek's characters: the old whose ethnicity has fossilized and the young who stand between a tradition already lost and another they are about to launch: a mixture of Chopin, the music of grandfather; the "She's Too Fat Polka," the music of their fathers; and "CoCoRoCoCo Paloma," the song the narrator of **"Blight"** listens to on his visit to the old place. Like Jerzy Kosinski's characters, Dybek's ethnics know the in-betweens intimately. Alternately they seek to transcend their ethnic past and to search through it for clues to their present altered state and to the future that awaits them. Dybek's appraisal of the past is tough-minded enough to suggest ethnic uneasiness and disavowal. When all is said and done, however, his fictional journey is headed more toward the heart of ethnicity than away from it, just as his younger characters are more attracted than repelled by their somewhat strange ancestors. They return to the scenes of childhood to savor the cultural flavor of people and places, echoing Dybek's own frequent visits to his South Side Chicago neighborhood.

Thomas S. Gladsky (essay date summer 1995)

SOURCE: Gladsky, Thomas S. "From Ethnicity to Multiculturalism: The Fiction of Stuart Dybek." *MELUS* 20, no. 2 (summer 1995): 105-18.

[*In the following essay, Gladsky examines Dybek's expressions of his Polish heritage in his fiction.*]

The new world culture and old country heritage of approximately fifteen million Americans of Polish descent are among multicultural America's best kept secrets. Historically a quiet minority, they have been eager to acculturate, assimilate, and melt into the mainstream. One of the consequences of this has been a failure to acquaint other Americans with Polish culture—its history and literature—or to establish a recognized ethnic literary tradition. This is not to say that there is not a Polish presence in American letters. From the 1830s and the arrival of the first significant body of Polish emigrés, primarily officers exiled after the 1831 uprising against the tzar, American writers have created Polish literary selves in plays, fiction, poems, and in prose works numbering perhaps as many as two hundred. Many of these contain abbreviated characterizations, predictably simplistic portraits, or, in some cases, merely composite Slavic cultural representations. At the same time, a few writers of classic ethnic and immigrant fiction, such as Karl Harriman (*The Homebuilders* 1903),

Edith Miniter (*Our Natupski Neighbors* 1916), and Joseph Vogel (*Man's Courage* 1938), have sensitively explored the culture of Americans of Polish descent. Despite their efforts, what has emerged, as Thomas Napierkowski, Caroline Golab, and others have argued, is a set of stereotypes that have in certain ways attempted to transform a culture into a caricature.[1]

Beginning in the 1930s, descent writers themselves began to examine the Polish self in a multiplicity of ways when Monica Krawczyk, Victoria Janda, and Helen Bristol turned to the immigrant generation as the subject of their poetry and fiction. Two decades later Richard Bankowsky produced a remarkable tetralogy about the arrival and dispersal of a turn of the century immigrant family. Bankowsky's *A Glass Rose* is perhaps the best novel about Slavic immigration in all of American literature. Wanda Kubiak (*Polonaise Nevermore*) and Matt Babinski (*By Raz* 1937) have described Poles in Wisconsin and Connecticut. In a series of novels in the 1970s, Darryl Poniscan followed the fortunes of the Buddusky clan in eastern Pennsylvania and elsewhere. In fiction for children, Anne Pellowski lovingly describes growing up ethnic in the Latsch Valley of Wisconsin. In numerous poems, *The Warsaw Sparks,* and his soon to be published memoir, *Szostak,* Gary Gildner explores both old and new world selves in sensitive ways. Most recently, Anthony Bukoski looks back to a rapidly vanishing Duluth community in *Children of Strangers.* In short, when one also considers the "Solidarity generation" of Czeslaw Milosz, Eva Hoffman, Stanislaus Baranczak, Janusz Glowacki, W. S. Kuniczak, and others, the Polish experience in American literature becomes demonstrable if not exceptional.[2]

Even so, contemporary writers of Polish descent face complex problems, some of which are, of course, shared to some degree by all those who write about ethnicity. An ever-narrowing definition of multiculturalism that virtually excludes Eastern Europeans is one. Competing waves of Polish immigrants, dividing the ethnic community into descendants of the largely peasant immigration of 1880-1914, a post-war influx of "displaced persons," and a newer, more highly educated, urban Solidarity generation, is another. Added to these are America's general unfamiliarity with Polish culture, originating during the period of great immigration when nativists tended to lump all Slavic peoples together and to promote caricatures and stereotypes of Poles in particular.

Stuart Dybek is a case in point. The author of numerous poems and short stories, including a collection of verse (*Brass Knuckles* 1976) and two collections of fiction (**Childhood and Other Neighborhoods** 1986 and **The Coast of Chicago** 1990), Dybek is among the first writers of Polish descent (who write about the ethnic self) to receive national recognition. Reviewers have praised him as a regional writer (Chicago) and as a social critic who sides with those on the margin. They have compared him with Bellow and Dreiser and pointed to his city landscapes and spare, terse dialogue while, unfortunately, ignoring the ethnic dimension in his work.[3] To be sure, Dybek does indeed write about the human condition. He gives us primarily initiation stories of urban adolescent males stretching into adulthood, expressing their sexuality, bravado and intellectual independence and realigning their social identity. Chicago with its particularized ethnic neighborhoods is a marked presence in their lives.

For Dybek, who grew up in southside Chicago, ethnicity is itself a natural and integral part of the human condition. The population in his neighborhood was mainly Eastern European and Hispanic. As he describes it: "The Eastern Europeans—Poles and Czechs—were migrating out; the Hispanics were migrating in. Each group had its own bars; they shared the same churches" (**"You Can't Step Into the Same Street Twice"** 43). Ethnicity, moreover, is also a condition of the contemporary literary experience. If not itself the central thrust of Dybek's work, it is one of those doorways, as he prefers to describe it, that leads to "some other dimension of experience and perception that forever changes the way one sees life" (Letter). It is no surprise therefore that ethnicity is everywhere in his works. In **"The River,"** a Ukrainian kid fiddles a nocturne. The girl in **"Laughter"** is Greek. The upstairs neighbors in **"Chopin in Winter"** speak Czech. The eccentric teacher in **"Farewell"** comes from Odessa. Hispanics appear in a number of stories; but Polish ethnicity is the tie that binds Dybek's protagonists together and supplies the cultural temperament in his fiction. Young men are named Swantek, Marzek, Vukovich, Kozak, and Gowumpe. Grandmothers called *Busha* worship in churches named St. Stanislaus. Relatives refer to soup as *zupa*; the neighbors listen to the Frankie Yankovitch Polka Hour; passersby speak Polish. Here and there we hear about *mazurkas,* Paderewski, Our Lady of Czestochowa, *babushkas,* and DPs, a recurring reference to non-native born Americans of Polish descent.

But what kind of ethnicity is Dybek portraying and how does he, a third generation American at some distance from his cultural roots, choose to represent his own cultural heritage? What, in effect, is Polish about these stories and what is the relationship between old and new expressions of ethnicity inside and outside Polonia? To some, Dybek's fiction may appear to be anachronistic, in that his frame of reference excludes the post-war and more recent Solidarity immigration that has transformed the Polish community in the United States, especially in Chicago, the setting for much of his work. Dybek, it could be argued, understands ethnicity almost exclusively from the point of view of the peasant generation and its descendants. In truth, the period of immigration and old world ties has long ago ended for his ethnic Poles. Consequently, he does not focus on assimilation and acculturation; nor are his characters busily collecting and preserving bits and pieces of their old world heritage. To the contrary, his protagonists are young, streetsmart, third generation Americans who know little, if anything, about Poland's past or present or the cultural nuances of the immigrant generation from which they are descended.

If anything, Dybek shows this generation resisting its ethnic impulses even as it rushes toward them. His young protagonists are updated modernists who, like Stephen Daedalus or Alfred Prufrock, wander city streets content with their own alienation and superior to the urban blight and social chaos that surround them. They are loners, eccentrics, budding intellectuals. They have no conscious sense of themselves as Polish-American or as ethnic in the usual sense of descending from a common history, religion, geography, and set of traditions. They are consumed instead with adolescence, environment, friends—with life in deteriorating and changing southside Chicago. They prefer Kerouac, the White Sox, Edward Hopper and rock music. Dybek's young Chicagoans thrive on melancholy, feast on loneliness, inhabit the "hourless times of night" (*Coast* 84). They are refugees from Edward Hopper's "Nighthawks," which Dybek features prominently in his work. At the same time, they are acutely aware that they ache for something they cannot name "but knew was missing," as the narrator of **"The River"** phrases it; and that "things are gone they couldn't remember, but missed; and things were gone they weren't sure ever were there" (*Coast* 25). Primarily, their narratives are remembrances of youthful things past.

For them, ethnicity and memory are interwoven naturally and succinctly. Consequently ethnicity in these stories is everywhere and yet almost beyond reach. Polish culture, for example, often enters through the back door. Dybek never identifies his characters as Poles, nor do they refer to themselves as Polish or as Polish-American. Polishness is rather cumulative, dependent partly on recurring signifiers and partly on the interconnectedness of the stories themselves. In "typical" fashion, he draws attention to the presence of cultural differences in the first few lines and then proceeds to develop a generic ethnic cultural landscape which seems to have few particular Polish markers. This approach is evident even in the first story in *Childhood and Other Neighborhoods.* The title, **"The Palatski Man,"** itself calls attention to otherness, although only midway in the story does Dybek explain that *palatski,* apparently a regional American corruption of *plocki,* the Polish word for potato pancake, was a food once sold by vendors in southside Chicago. In the first page the reader also encounters the Slavic-sounding name Leon *Sisca* and the Catholic mysteries of Palm Sunday. The children attend St. Roman's grammar school, have friends named *Zmiga* and another named Raymond *Cruz,* "part Mexican" and perhaps part Polish. In addition, the children define their surroundings in terms of their parish church, which distinguishes their neighborhood from the adjoining one where "more Mexicans lived." Apart from the fact that the *palatski* man stammers in "foreign English," no other overt references to ethnicity in general or to Polishness in particular occur.

This approach is repeated elsewhere. In **"The Wake,"** Dybek looks at one evening in the life of Jill, a southside Chicago teenager whose surname and particular cultural heritage remain anonymous. Dybek, however, establishes

Jill's parameters, physical and psychological, within an ethnic landscape. On her way to the wake, she hears the bells of St. Kasimir's church and walks along the street that serves as a boundary between her neighborhood and St. Anne's, "an old Slavic neighborhood that had become Spanish." She heads toward Zeijek's Funeral home, "a three-story building domed with its fake Russian onion" (*Childhood* 108). Reminiscent of Joyce Carol Oates's "Where Are You Going, Where Have You Been?" Jill eventually drives off with an intrusive Hispanic whose ethnicity poses no threat to her. We learn that the culture of Jill's neighborhood is Slavic-Hispanic. She drives by the hot tamale man with his striped umbrella; she hears radios turned to Latin stations; and she refers to the young man's car as "Pancho." There is no dominant ethnic "theme" in **"The Wake,"** no social or generational problems, no hint of cultural oppression or collision. Ethnicity is muted, understood, and natural—an integral part of the contemporary urban experience and cultural context—but not exclusively tied to national boundaries, even though one suspects that Jill might be of Polish descent.

In other stories in *Childhood and Other Neighborhoods, The Coast of Chicago,* and elsewhere, Dybek constructs a more specifically Polish ethnic identity for his characters, their neighborhood, and their frame of mind. In **"The Cat Woman"** and **"Blood Soup,"** the two stories that immediately succeed **"The Palatski Man,"** Dybek repeats the pattern of the opening story, relying primarily on names, words, and surface features to establish an ethnic landscape. At the outset, the reader learns that *buzka* and *busha* are what some people call their grandmothers. The reader also meets characters with Slavic-sounding names such as Swantek and Stefush (a Polish diminutive for Stephen). The cat woman, Swantek's grandmother, fingers her rosary and tunes her radio to the polka station. She also shares cabbage soup with her neighbor, Mrs. Panova. In stories like **"The Cat Woman,"** the ethnic markers suggest a composite Slavic cultural landscape although discerning readers might interpret the markers as the outlines of Polish-American culture.

A distinctly Polish frame of reference becomes evident only in **"Blood Soup,"** the third story in *Childhood,* where, in addition to Busha "clutching the crucifix" and references to such old world Catholic practices as the kissing of holy pictures, Dybek includes more compelling evidence of Polish ethnicity. On occasion, he uses Polish words (*usiadz, dziekuje, dupa, czarnina, rozumiesz*) without translation. His young hero remembers the traditional Polish custom of blessing the Easter breakfast food: colored eggs, ham, bread, kraut, horseradish, and kielbasa. More importantly, in this story Dybek moves beyond ceremonies and the surface features of ethnicity when he tries to capture something of the old world temperament that differentiates Eastern Europeans from Americans and first generation ethnics from their descendants. At one point, Stefush recognizes that his grandmother is different in more substantive ways that merely her taste for *czarnina,* a peasant soup made from duck's blood. He senses in her

"a kind of love he thought must have come from the old country—instinctive, unquestioning like her strength, something foreign that he couldn't find in himself, that hadn't even been transmitted to his mother" (*Childhood* 26).

Ethnicity, particularly the culture of Americans of Polish descent, is cumulative in Dybek's writing. Often one story clarifies and extends an ethnic dimension introduced in another. For example, in order to understand fully what Dybek means in **"Blood Soup"** by "a kind of love" that "must have come from the old country," we must turn to **"A Minor Mood,"** published some seven years later. This is a familiar tale of immigrants and their descendants. Joey, a young third generation American, remembers attacks of bronchitis and his granny swooping down upon him, bathing his neck with a glob of Vicks and wrapping it in her *babushka,* applying camphor to his chest, filling the rooms with steam, mixing honey, lemon, Jim Beam, and boiling water for him to drink (and for herself too). These were mornings, he concludes, "to be tucked away at the heart of life, so that later, whenever one needed to draw upon the recollection of joy in order to get through troubled times it would be there" (7). All of **"A Minor Mood,"** in effect, develops and expands the ethnic temperament alluded to in **"Blood Soup,"** although a few ethnic signifiers can be noticed.

Only once does Dybek turn to what might be called a paradigmatic ethnic tale in order to define the contemporary Polish-American self. In **"Chopin in Winter,"** a story about the conflicting claims of descent and consent, the aging Dzia Dzia tells his own story to his grandson—his trek from Krakow to Gdansk to avoid being drafted into the tzarist army, his immigration to the coal mines of Pennsylvania and the barges of the Great Lakes. At one point, Dzia Dzia's story melts into that of another Polish immigrant and national icon, Frederick Chopin. "Chopin," he'd whisper hoarsely to Michael, pointing to the ceiling with the reverence of nuns pointing to heaven" (*Coast* 19). More than telling his story, the old man provides a cultural frame for the third generation, creating an image of what it means to be ethnic.

Dybek does not mean to stop here, however, with romantic and sentimental notions of heritage; he is more interested in cultural fusion, in that uniquely American acculturating process described by Werner Sollors in *Beyond Ethnicity* as the tension between "our hereditary qualities" and our position as "architects of our fate" (5-6). Grandfather, for instance, mentions in **"Chopin in Winter"** that Paderewski dearly loved Chopin; but Michael does not know Paderewski, a sign of his distance from his cultural heritage. Instinctively, Grandfather connects their American and Polish heritages in a comic but revealing and shrewd fashion, by asking, "Do you know who's George Washington, who's Joe DiMaggio, who's Walt Disney? . . . Paderewski was like them, except he played Chopin. . . . See, deep down inside, Lefty, you know more than you think" (*Coast* 20-21). Even in this, one of Dybek's most "Polish" stories, cultural transmission gives way to a new cultural pattern of consent and descent. For Americans of Polish descent, ethnicity means knowing about Joe Dimaggio *and* Paderewski, Washington *and* Chopin, Disneyland *and* Krakow.

Ethnicity also means Catholicism; in fact, Catholicism in the form of childhood experiences with the church, the parochial school, or the religious practices and attitudes of the immigrant generation permeates these stories and poems and often is the singular definer of Polish culture. Even here Dybek concentrates not on Polish but on *ethnic* expressions of and responses to Catholicism. In a recently published chapbook, *The Story of Mist,* Dybek begins by wondering what it is "about the belly button that connected it to the Old Country?" To explain, he immediately turns to religious metaphors, noting that "outside, night billowed like the habits of nuns through vigil lights of snow," while Busha's "rosary-pinched fingers" promised to lead inward. But it is the tolling of the bells from the steeple of St. Kasimir's that serves as the umbilical cord between old and new world culture. When he hears them, he knows that "Krakow is only blocks away, just past Goldblatt's darkened sign" (5).

The parish church is thus the center of vision in a significant number of stories. In **"The Wake,"** Jill uses the church steeple to locate her whereabouts in the neighborhood. Ladies murmur the rosary in front of the icon of Our Lady of Czestochowa in **"Neighborhood Drunk."** In a fit of madness Budhardin destroys the inside of the parish church in **"Visions of Budhardin."** Old women walk "on their knees up the marble aisle to kiss the relics" and Eddy and Manny try to visit all the neighborhood churches in **"Hot Ice." "The Woman Who Fainted"** does so at the 11:15 mass. Stanley's girlfriend lives across from the Assumption Church, leading him to call her "the Unadulterated one." To the young protagonists in these stories, the church represents the mystery of old world culture—of Polishness itself.

Consequently, Dybek frequently turns to childhood experiences with the clergy, the parochial school, and the rituals and mysteries of Eastern European Catholicism in order to develop plot and theme. There is little that is peaceful, consoling, or even attractive in these memories and experiences, however. We read about the cruelty of Father O'Donnel. We meet Sister Monica who loses her teaching assignment because she becomes hysterical in front of her fifth grade class. We listen to the narrator of **"The Dead in Korea,"** remembering how he was made to kneel on three-cornered drafting rulers in parochial school. At the same time, Dybek writes about the mystical attractions of Catholicism that draw his young people toward familiar ritual and ceremony despite their growing skepticism. This is perhaps best expressed in **"Hot Ice,"** where Manny and Eddie reenact a childhood ritual of visiting seven churches on Good Friday afternoon. They walk from St. Roman's to St. Michael's, from St. Kasimir's to St. Anne's, from St. Pius's to St. Adalbert's, then finally to the church of

St. Procopius. At first, they merely peek in and leave, "as if touching base." But soon their "familiarity with small rituals quickly returned: dipping their fingers in the holy water font by the door, making the automatic sign of the cross as they passed the life-sized crucified Christs that hung in the vestibules where old women and school kids clustered to kiss the spikes in the bronze or bloody plaster feet" (152-53).

Dybek makes it clear that the pull of Catholicism is both spiritual and cultural and that it is rooted in the immigrant experience itself. He makes this connection through the recurring presence of old people, the last of the immigrant generation. Usually these characters are grandparents engaged in helping third generation youngsters understand their cultural identity. Dzia Dzia in **"Chopin in Winter,"** Busha in **"Blood Soup,"** the old man in **"The Apprentice,"** and Gran in **"A Minor Mood"** all help to introduce their grandchildren to Polish history, tradition, and temperament.

At other times Dybek integrates the immigrant generation into the mystique of Polish Catholicism. He does this primarily through repeated references to older women involved in one form of worship or another. The narrator of **"The Woman Who Fainted,"** intrigued by the ritualistic fainting that often occurs at the 11:15 mass, observes the hand of an "old woman in a babushka" that darts out to correct the dress hem of the fainting lady. In **"Chopin in Winter,"** Mrs. Kubiak joins the regulars at morning mass, "wearing babushkas and dressed in black like a sodality of widows droning endless mournful litanies" (*Coast* 32). And in **"Good Friday,"** a two-page story published in *Gulf Coast,* the young narrator, entranced with the church organ, the statues, Sister Monica, the incense and the holy water, focuses ultimately on the "old women, babushkaed in black, weeping as they walk on their knees up the marble aisle to the altar in order to kiss the relic" (98-99). These people, Dybek implies, are nothing less than old world culture transfigured into the new world. In this sense Dybek captures both the attraction and rejection of whatever it is that Polish culture has come to mean in post-war America.

In fact, rejection and denial and the subsequent reshaping of cultural identify are essential ingredients of the ethnicization that occurs in these stories. In a very real sense all of Dybek's fiction is about social disorganization and reorganization in the classic sense of these principles outlined by Thomas and Znaniecki in *The Polish Peasant in Europe and America.* The alienation that exists in Dybek's younger characters results as much from cultural tensions, however, as it does from socio-economics and shifting philosophical perspectives. Typically, Dybek contrasts the immigrant generation with its third generation descendants with an eye toward showing cultural transformation, or he describes the simultaneous act of acquiring and rejecting a cultural past. While "ethnicity" is still the norm by which his protagonists view the world, Dybek insists that contemporary urban ethnicity must be defined differently from that of preceding time periods. Thus he attempts to differentiate between old and new ethnicity even in his ethnically Polish characters.

For example, while Dybek on the one hand offers sympathetic portraits of grandparents and other first generation Americans of Polish descent and sensitively explores the essentials of Polish culture, he on the other hand frequently presents these cultural representatives as eccentric grotesques out of touch with the times and their adopted culture. Typically he portrays the immigrant generation as the cultural "other" rather than as the cultural norm. In fact, the more Polish the characters are, the more eccentric and grotesque they and their cultural practices tend to look to the reader. The **"Palatski Man,"** the opening story in *Childhood and Other Neighborhoods,* sets this tone and outlines this direction. The *palatski* man, not dignified with any other name, is a rather frightening and threatening figure (at least to the two youngsters in the story). He is an exotic street vendor who appears to live with the peddlers, ragpickers, and other cultural outsiders in makeshift housing near an urban dumping ground. The food he sells is culturally unrecognizable although Slavic sounding. His white clothing and white cart, while ordinary enough, are undercut by his foreign-sounding English (although we never hear him talk) and his involvement in Palm Sunday Eucharistic rituals with other ragmen. Although we do not learn the *palatski* man's cultural heritage, his characterization, his ragged associates, and their surreal surroundings create an atmosphere of strangeness and alienation toward the culture represented by the word *palatski.*

This point of view permeates those stories involving Americans of Polish descent. In **"The Cat Woman,"** Dybek almost rushes to associate ethnicity with strangeness when he calls the woman *buzka,* introduces her "crazy grandson as Swantek," and then proceeds to explain that Buzka drowned the excess neighborhood kittens in her washing machine. With this introduction, the ethnicity of the immigrant generation (*buzka*) and those (Swantek) who remain most closely associated with their old world habits is enough to divorce it from the cultural norm. "No one," Dybek succinctly comments, "brought laundry anymore to the old woman" (*Childhood* 23). The story ends with grotesque images of despair and degeneration. Swantek sleeps on old drapes beside the furnace, "vomiting up cabbage in the corners and covering it with newspapers," and Buzka and her old friend Mrs. Panova blow on their spoonfuls of soup "with nothing more to say," their radio turned to the polka hour. In other stories, we meet Big Antek, the local drunk; the uncle of Tadeusz, who spends his nights picking up the debris of a culture on the move; and Slavic workers missing parts of hands and arms that have been "chewed off while trying to clean machines" (**"Sauerkraut Soup"** 128). Such is the price of the old ethnicity, which in this case is represented as servile labor, alcoholism, a meanness toward animals, a taste for cabbage soup, and, most importantly, as descent from an inferior national culture.

In these rather traditional interpretations of second and third generation behavior, the usual signifiers of ethnicity—language, religion, history, customs and other conventional cultural markers—lose their privileged position even though they remain as a frame of reference. Nowhere is this better illustrated than in his adolescent protagonists' ambivalent relationship with Catholicism, which in Polish terms is inextricably and historically tied to nationalism. In other words a rejection of Catholicism is tantamount in these cases to a rejection of national, that is to say Polish, identity. **"Visions of Budhardin," "The Long Thoughts," "The Woman Who Fainted,"** and **"Sauerkraut Soup"** all dramatize the act of coming to terms with the religion of descent. One narrator, remembering his parochial education, explains what he regarded as the fear underlying religion, and reveals that the summer "after my sophomore year in high school was the last summer I went to church" (*Coast* 120). Those who continue to attend do so from habit and custom. In **"Hot Ice,"** Eddie admits that "he had given up, and the ache left behind couldn't be called grief" (*Coast* 155). In **"Visions of Budhardin,"** the protagonist, in a rage of pent up resentment, ravages the church which so callously ignored his childhood needs. But Marzek in **"Sauerkraut Soup"** speaks for all Dybek's disillusioned Polish Catholics when he says: "I had already developed my basic principle of Catholic education—the Double Reverse: (1) *suspect what they teach you;* (2) *study what they condemn*" (*Childhood* 127). The words and deeds of these characters document their hostility to the culture of their ancestors and their inability to any longer understand or sympathize with this kind of ethnicity.

In effect, Dybek shows the transformation from immigrant to ethnic and beyond. Throughout, a sense of loss is coupled with an acceptance of change as his spokespersons lament the disappearance of the Polish southside. The narrator in **"Blight"** returns to his old neighborhood after a few years and confesses that he "was back in my neighborhood, but lost, everything at once familiar and strange, and I knew if I tried to run, my feet would be like lead, and if I stepped off a curb, I'd drop through space" (*Coast* 71). Dybek thus points to a condition of ethnicity that characterizes the American Polish community as the recently published stories of Anthony Bukoski (*Children of Strangers*) also makes clear. In Dybek's stories, as in Bukoski's, the core of old world Polish culture is almost lost. Neighborhood demographics and Parish churches have changed, and only a few Polish-born Americans are left to transmit and interpret Polish traditions and customs.[4] In **"Blood Soup,"** Uncle Joe's meat market is full of Mexican kids and Big Antek explains to Stefush that, in regard to his efforts to help his grandma make her beloved old world soup, "we don't sell fresh blood no more" (*Childhood* 30). Mrs. Gowumpe (pigeon, in Polish) tells Stefush how things were: "I used to work in the yards," he explains. "All those DPs working there . . . Polacks, Lugans, Bohunks. People who knew how to be happy" (*Childhood* 45). Now Mr. Gowumpe, grandma Busha, the *palatski* man, and the other first generation Poles are poor, isolated, lonely, and few in number. Nonetheless, they are the voice of cultural memory.

Dybek's fiction is not elegiac, however. Ethnicity is positive, pervasive, and dynamic in these stories; and the movement is toward a new understanding of ethnicity that is based not on national origins but on a shared sense of ethnicity as a condition of Americanness. Dybek's protagonists aren't Poles; they're not even Polish-American by traditional definition. They have, paradoxically, reinvented and reinterpreted themselves (Fischer 1950). For this generation ethnicity is a socio-political reality, a sensitivity to pluralism, and, as James Clifford phrases it, "a conjunctural not essential" state of mind. More than that, ethnicity is not even a necessary condition of descent because for Stuart Dybek cultural pluralism has supplanted nationality and a new level of multicultural awareness has replaced ethnocentricity. Dybek himself calls attention to this in an essay entitled "You Can't Step Into the Same Street Twice": "Besides the ethnic tribes of Slavs and Hispanics whose language and music and food smells permeated the streets, there was another tribe, one that in a way transcended nationality, a tribe of youth, of kids born to replenish the species recently depleted by WW II" (44-45).

In his stories, Dybek replicates the tribal and cultural landscape of Chicago. Those who live in the older ethnic neighborhoods have experienced a change from a basically Eastern European population to a mixed neighborhood of Americans of Hispanic and Slavic descent, primarily Mexican and Polish. More importantly, Dybek's third generation fellow Polish ethnics are just as frequently paired with Hispanic friends as with fellow "Poles": Ziggy Zilinski and Pepper Rosado in **"Blight,"** Eddy Kapusta and Manny and Pancho Santoro in **"Hot Ice,"** Ray Cruz and John in **"The Palatski Man."** There are few instances of ethnic rivalry in this landscape. Quite the contrary, the commingling of Latino and Slav is economic, sociological, and cultural—a product of shifting demographics and resulting neighborhood changes, the result of shared environment and social class. They both identify with and like "the other." From this a new sense of ethnicity—an emblem of contemporary America—arises.

On the surface, the new ethnicity appears to be nothing more than the camaraderie of friends thrown together by demographics. In reality, the union of Pole and Chicano represents the changing face of America and of Polish Americanness. Stanley Rosado is Pepper to some and Stashu to others, reflecting his Mexican father and Polish mother. When David, the descendent of Poles, goes to a bar with a friend, he drinks a Coca-Nana rather than *vodka* or *piwo*. The Mexican music on the jukebox sounds "suspiciously like polkas." David now listens to "CuCuRu-CuCu Paloma" on the radio, and Eddie Kapusta sings in Spanish. Tellingly, Eddie identifies more with Spanish than he does with the Polish language. He is struck with the word *juilota* (pigeon). It seems the perfect word because in it "he could hear both their cooing and the whistling

rush of their wings." Equally telling, Eddie cannot remember "any words like that in Polish, which his grandma had spoken to him when he was little" (*Coast* 136). Eddie's relatives may likely turn out to be Hispanic in the sense that Richard Rodriguez, in *Hunger of Memory,* believes that he may become Asian.[5] In the words of Rosalie Murphy Baum, "multicultural contact has defeated the ethnic norm" (70).

When all is said and done, Dybek's ethnic characters seem to say that "what they are" doesn't really matter in terms of history, language, geography. The new urban ethnic accepts ethnicity while rejecting nationality. Traditional ethnic borders give way to a heightened social and moral sense that replaces geographic maps and national origins. In **"Hot Ice,"** Eddie Kapusta arrives at this insight: "Most everything from that world had changed or disappeared, but the old women had endured—Polish, Bohemian, Spanish, he knew it didn't matter; they were the same . . . a common pain of loss seemed to burn at the core of their lives" (*Coast* 154). Grandma in **"Pet Milk"** is illustrative. She knows about the old country and the new, where "all the incompatible states of Europe were pressed together down at the staticky right end" of the radio dial (168). Grandma also seems to know that ethnicity in America means something more than national origin. Consequently she is happy to listen to the Greek station or the Ukrainian or the Spanish although, of course, she would prefer listening to polkas. And in **"Hot Ice,"** Eddie elaborates on the changing face of ethnicity when he admits to himself, "Manny could be talking Spanish; I could be talking Polish. . . . It didn't matter. What meant something was sitting at the table together" (*Coast* 151).

What also matters is that in Dybek's hands the Polish ethnic self assumes what some may regard as a new identity. And Dybek emerges as a writer who offers examples of the way experience, history, and ethnicity crossbreed. To be sure, Dybek does indeed try to present the preciousness of America's Polish heritage and the exceptionalism of the ethnically Polish American. He is, at the same time, eager to resist parochialism and exclusivity. His characterization of his young heroes and heroines as romantic rebels and urbanized American versions of Keats, Proust, Dostoevsky and others whom they have read, leads him beyond mere ethnicity even though his fiction is rooted in the cultural neighborhoods of southside Chicago. While attempting to capture the unique flavor of a particular ethnic group, Dybek has created a multi-layered and multi-dimensional ethnic self. This self reflects the image of a trans-ethnic urban America, a diorama of a diverse cultural landscape where ethnicity transcends national origins but remains vital and where the ethnic and the modern self are not only compatible but are the essence of postmodernism and, as Andrew Greeley puts it, "a way of being American."[6]

Notes

1. See Napierkowski's "The Image of Polish Americans in American Literature." *Polish American Studies* 40 (Spring 1983): 5-44 and Golab's "Stellaaaaaa . . .

!!!!!: The Slavic Stereotype in American Film." *The Kaleidoscopic Lens: How Hollywood Views Ethnic Groups.* Ed. Randall M. Miller. Englewood, NJ: Jerome P. Ozer, 1980. 135-55.

2. I have discussed these and other American writers of Polish descent in *Princes, Peasants, and Other Polish Selves: Ethnicity in American Literature.* Amherst: U of Massachusetts P, 1992.

3. Dybek's reviewers have concentrated on style, noting the grotesque, the bizarre, the fantastical, the dark, and the urban. Howard Kaplan's review of *Childhood and Other Neighborhoods* in *Commonweal* (23 May 1980): 319, is typical.

4. *Children of Strangers* is the newest collection of stories by Anthony Bukoski, author of *Twelve Below Zero,* who concentrates on the descendants of Polish immigrants in the Duluth area.

5. Rodriguez speculates at one point about the course of American demographics and applies the changing cultural face of the nation to his own situation. He wonders if his presence in an Asian community might not naturally and inevitably lead to Asian descendants.

6. Greeley, writing in *New Catholic World* (June 1976), disposes of the notion that ethnicity is "un-American," arguing instead that ethnicity as Americanness is a "critically important phenomenon" (111).

Works Cited

Baum, Rosalie Murphy. "John Williams's Captivity Narrative: A Consideration of Normative Ethnicity." *A Mixed Race: Ethnicity in Early America.* Ed. Frank Shuffleton. New York: Oxford UP, 1993. 56-77.

Clifford, James. *The Predicament of Culture: Twentieth-Century Ethnography, Literature, and Art.* Cambridge: Harvard UP, 1988.

Dybek, Stuart, *Childhood and Other Neighborhoods.* New York: Ecco P, 1986.

———. *The Coast of Chicago.* New York: Vintage, 1991.

———. "Good Friday." *Gulf Coast* 4 (Winter 1991): 98-99.

———. Letter to the author. 26 Nov. 1993.

———. "A Minor Mood." *The Iowa Review* 23.1 (1993): 25-32.

———. *The Story of Mist.* Brockport, NY: State Street P, 1993.

———. "You Can't Step Into the Same Street Twice." *Townships.* Ed. Michael Martone. Iowa City: U of Iowa P, 1992. 43-47.

Fischer, Michael M. J. "Ethnicity and the Post-Modern Arts of Memory." *Writing Culture: The Poetics and Politics of Ethnography.* Eds. James Clifford and George E. Marcus. Berkeley: U of California P, 1986. 194-233.

Greeley, Andrew. "Is Ethnicity un-American?" *New Catholic World* 219 (June 1976): 106-12.

Rodriquez, Richard. *Hunger of Memory.* Boston: Godine, 1982.

Sollors, Werner. *Beyond Ethnicity.* New York: Oxford UP, 1986.

Thomas, William I and Florian Znaniecki. *The Polish Peasant in Europe and America.* Urbana: U of Illinois P, 1984.

Jorge Febles (essay date fall 1996)

SOURCE: Febles, Jorge. "Dying Players: Ramírez's 'El Centerfielder' and Dybek's 'Death of the Rightfielder.'" *Confluencia* 12, no. 1 (fall 1996): 156-67.

[*In the following essay, Febles compares Dybek to Sandinista writer Sergio Ramírez, finding elements of the carnival concept in the work of both authors: reigning absurdity, grotesque figures and rituals, atemporality, and a celebration of the "play spirit."*]

Perhaps there is no rhetorical exercise as gratuitous as searching for tangentialities between literary texts that bear little direct relationship. And yet, such is the nature of the comparative effort which this essay attempts. I intend to demonstrate how coetaneous authors from different nations, writing in different languages and pursuing diverse aesthetic intentions can nevertheless perceive the game of baseball in a self-same manner. My conclusions, therefore, will pertain more to the sport itself, to its unavoidable tie with the play spirit inherent in human beings, than to the texts that somewhat at random I have opted critically to juxtapose.

Sergio Ramírez's "El centerfielder" is a politically committed construct intent on revealing the repression experienced by Nicaraguan lower classes during the Somoza dictatorship. In it, a former amateur baseball player is illegally imprisoned and sent to his death because he collaborated with his revolutionary son. This 1969 story by the Sandinista writer and politician who, for years, served as vice-president of his country, is quite representative of that tendency to confront real truth ["la realidad de verdad"] which, according to Ramírez, defines contemporary Latin American fiction. He explains:

> Frente a la fragmentaria visión anterior, de personajes de una sola pieza, de la concepción del campesino como consecuencia directa de su habla y del escenario tropical, como un set cinematográfico; frente a la denuncia panfletaria y la solidaridad absoluta del autor con sus personajes y su actitud civilizante, el nuevo escritor latinoamericano . . . crea personajes humanos y profundos, complejos y contradictorios, como en esencia es el hombre; lo libera del dominio telúrico del paisaje y lo coloca en el centro del universo; y crea, para servir de cámara experimental a la complicada esencia del ser, una técnica, un lenguaje.
>
> ("Prefacio" 51)

Ramírez's short story evinces such a nonpropagandistic testimonial approach, associated, regardless of his observation, with that post Boom generation that Angel Rama termed "novísimos," who rebel against Borgean cosmopolitanism and magic realist dogmas by pursuing a vigorous critical realism.[1] Through a complex counterpoint technique, an all too human protagonist, incapable of those epic gestures so frequent among the oppressed heroes of earlier Latin American regionalist fiction, attempts to evade a gruesome reality by resurrecting memories of athletic endeavors not devoid of tragic connotations.

Stuart Dybek's[2] more recent story, on the other hand, exemplifies a dissimilar literary attitude. **"Death of the Rightfielder"** is the fourth text included in this writer's latest book, ***The Coast of Chicago,*** a collection of stories that critics have compared favorably with works by Sherwood Anderson (*Winesburg, Ohio*), the early Hemingway (*In Our Time*), Isaac Babel (*Tales of Odessa*), even James Joyce (*Dubliners*). Vigorously grotesque, bordering ambiguously on the tall tale and the fantastic, on the extraordinary and the surreal, Dybek's brief piece represents a suggestive literary tour de force that humorously reflects baseball's quasi mythical underpinnings. The unexplained death of a youthful player during a neighborhood sandlot game motivates bizarre explanations that, when recollected by a middle-aged first person narrator, imbue the story with an eerie, melancholic and comically pathetic tone. Tom Blackburn has affirmed correctly that the tale "is like a memory that is clear and vivid of a childhood event you can never be sure really happened. The dead right fielder could be a dream, a mental picture of conversation among adults that you overheard and misunderstood or part of a real event you never did understand" (2-L). Dybek's text has an outward existential projection which underscores the ephemeral nature of youth, of life itself, of the play spirit which obscures the ungovernable passage of time. Furthermore, it reflects that lyrical tonality and jazzy speed that the author finds immanent in what he terms "the short-short form" (*Sudden Fiction*: "Afternotes," 317).

Clearly, the reader of both texts intuits the personas of writers working at cross-purposes. In the first case, one perceives blatant signification, evident sociopolitical connotations. The omniscient sender provides the receiver with a message all too obvious, intended in Brechtian fashion to provoke an analytical awakening. Its concrete referentiality leads to an indictment of the perverse system that toys with oppressed proletarians and shamelessly destroys them. In the second story, equivocal signifiers point to poetic imprecision. The reader ascertains an image, a mood, a tragicomic tone. Meaning, however, remains obscure, as if submerged in the dream-like substratum of the tale or in the creative mentality whence the anecdote emanated and for which, perhaps, it is identically elusive. The destructive passage of time, human mortality, are notions that, in the reader's intellect, gain fleeting momentum throughout, but it appears excessive to consider **"Death of the Rightfielder"** a philosophical construct at all pedagogic in nature. Ambiguity reigns supreme in it, the ambiguity intrinsic to any bittersweet remembrance or fancy.

Bakhtin has described the carnivalesque world as a playful one in which abnormality reigns supreme. It is an upside down space populated by grotesque entities and ruled by jesters who function as temporary kings, ingloriously uncrowned upon the conclusion of ritualistic time.[3] To a minimal degree, sports in general and baseball in particular may be linked to such carnivalesque periods but only when they become all-inclusive affairs imposing a general participation that supersedes passivity. The Russian critic argues that

> carnival does not know footlights, in the sense that it does not acknowledge any distinction between actors and spectators . . . Carnival is not a spectacle seen by the people; they live in it, and everyone participates because its very idea embraces all the people. While carnival lasts, there is no other life outside it. During carnival time life is subject only to its laws, that is, the laws of its own freedom.
>
> (7)

Despite its unavoidable representational nature, baseball may be linked to carnival for countless reasons. By and large, the sport is an epochal affair associated with the advent of spring in Northern climes and, in its professional variety, with the arrival of winter further to the South. As performance or feast, it supposes a fixed religious time measured absurdly in spatial manner, since the contest itself or, for that matter, even ritual innings may feasibly prolong themselves into eternity. "It ain't over till it's over," baseball savant Yogi Berra once stated, underlining in grotesque—and hence carnivalesque—fashion the ludicrous possibility of atemporality that the game insinuates. Regardless of age, players as well as coaches dress excentrically in uniforms befitting a harlequin, often consisting of glittering colors, stripes, decorations that include birds, wild beasts, absurd figures such as pirates and comic book renditions of Native American chiefs. Thus "disguised" or "made up," athletes can assume their role as other beings. Even the umpires, or fake constables who patrol the playing field to maintain an artificial fixed order, are forced to wear costumes that define their bizarre function. The game imposes a participatory role on the spectator far more intensive than the one dictated by the theater, the circus, even the concert. One is expected to "root, root, root for the home team," to complain, to praise loudly and, more significantly, to partake of the recurrent crownings and uncrownings that constitute the essence of the game. A passing reference to the debasement inherent in the classic baseball poem "Casey at the Bat" suffices to illustrate the idea in question. More than any other sport, baseball posits the notion of the athlete or hero transforming himself into goat, into the clown that his outfit never fails to underpin. Partly through his actions, partly through those of the dynamic audience, the carnival king is more often than not demoted to the role of grotesque mortal, forced to hear such mocking cries as "¡You bum!," "¡You hot dog!," "¡You clown!," or worse. Finally, both to the athlete and to the spectator baseball time eradicates external chronology: while the game lasts, reality occupies a secondary stratum. It remains hidden behind the carnival mood which defines that public market-place into which the ballpark has been transformed. In his brilliantly conceived Proppian analysis of baseball as a nonverbal art form, as folk drama, Dennis Porter writes that the game "is a festive event that occurs as a suspension of ordinary life" (154-55). Although my brief reading of the sport differs from Porter's in-depth study of baseball's mythical and pseudo heroic structure, we coincide in accenting that suppression of outward events and normal chronology lies at the very core of the game. It must be viewed as a consuming activity that projects centrifugally toward the spectators while entailing a centripetal, fully absorbed reaction on team-members, committed to the lurid exercise in mock warfare that the pastime exemplifies.

However, Johan Huizinga (whose *Homo Ludens: A Study of the Play Element in Culture* evolves concepts similar to many defined by Bakhtin in his multifaceted study of carnival) proposes specific limitations that should be borne in mind when considering the nature of baseball. Undoubtedly, the sport fits within the scheme of the German philosopher conception of play as "a voluntary activity or occupation executed within certain fixed limits of time and place, according to rules freely accepted but absolutely binding, having its aim in itself and accompanied by a feeling of tension, joy and the consciousness that it is different from ordinary life" (28). In addition, baseball is a competitive encounter and Huizinga explains that "the agon in Greek life, or the contest anywhere else in the world, bears all the formal characteristics of play, and as to its function belongs almost wholly to the sphere of the festival, which is the play-sphere. It is quite impossible to separate the contest as a cultural function from the complex 'play-festival-rite'" (31) Both these notions coincide with the sketched relationship between baseball and carnival. But Huizinga provides a meaningful caveat: "Play," he argues, "is not foolish. It lies outside the antithesis of wisdom and folly" (6). Play may be the "direct opposite of seriousness" (6), but that does not signify that it is not serious. And in the case of sport, laughter within the sacred ground is solely an accessory, a secondary occurrence that does not interfere with the severity of competition. Huizinga also alludes to the systematization of athletics since the last quarter of the nineteenth century, a fact which, to him, has reduced—if not eradicated-the pure-play quality of the agon. He states: "The spirit of the professional is no longer the true play-spirit; it is lacking in spontaneity and carelessness. This affects the amateur too, who begins to suffer from an inferiority complex. Between them they push sport further from the play sphere proper until it becomes a thing *sui generis*: neither play nor earnest" (197). Hence, like Bakhtin envisions the summit of carnival in Renaissance Europe, Huizinga perceives in organized sports a bureaucratic betrayal of the true play spirit that, to him, resides at the essence of human culture.

These clarifications notwithstanding, traces of carnival and evasive or creative play can be found in baseball. Such factors integrate the basis of the festive pre-text with which both Dybek and Ramírez elected to dialogue in order to confect their stories. Both as well chose to frame their tales by juxtaposing the ludic element to external reality, by imposing upon the play spirit the materiality that invariably destroys it.

Despite its falsely typological title that implies a child-like frivolity, in Ramírez's story baseball remains unmentioned until the second page, when the protagonist begins his trek, his tragic and involuntary epic journey to meet the interrogator who dictates his death. In order to reach the Captain's office, the character and his escort have to cross the prison courtyard, located next to a slaughterhouse where, at the time in question (midnight), butchers perform their savage duty. To avoid the conspicuous parallelism between his predictable destiny and that of the animals, the protagonist undertakes his first tacit dialogue with the sport that had afforded him precious entertainment in his youth: "Que patio más hermoso para jugar beisbol. Aquí deben armarse partidos entre los presos, o los presos con los guardias francos. La barda será la tapia, unos trescientos cincuenta pies desde el home hasta el centerfield" (661). His interior monologue then meanders into a symbolic and unreasonable escape plan:

> Un batazo a esas profundidades habría que fildearlo corriendo hacia los almendros . . . y vería al corredor doblando por segunda cuando de un salto me cogería de una rama y con una flexión me montaría sobre ella y de pie llegaría hasta la otra al mismo nivel del muro erizado de culos de botellas y poniendo con cuidado las manos primero, pasaría el cuerpo asentando los pies y aunque me hiriera al descolgarme al otro lado caería en el montarascal . . . y después correría . . .
>
> (661)

Seeking to obliterate or transform external reality by means of the play spirit, the protagonist turns game into game. The baseball image provides a momentary release from fear, from horrible surroundings, from the forthcoming confrontation with death. That image develops further to generate a fanciful Hollywoodesque escape plan where cunning overcomes violence and brutality by generating, in the spirit of the potlatch—of "serious play, fateful and fatal play, bloody play" (Huizinga, 61)—a will to win against all odds, to defeat ingeniously the dastardly rule breakers who have destroyed the norms of civilized society. (Huizinga, 101)

Since the inception of baseball into the tale, the narrator affirms the reality-inversive or carnivalesque virtues of the game. By mentally transforming oppressive surroundings into a sports arena, into an all-inclusive sacred and ritualistic area where even antagonists ("the good guards") can experience what Huizinga calls "the fun of playing" (2), the protagonist bonds contest and hope. The playing field provides a protective shell identical to that which the mother represents for her child. Such a correlation becomes apparent when the character's internal soliloquy, which is counterpoised to the essential narrative story-line, illustrates evasive flashback qualities.

The correspondence develops in three separate meditations, triggered by comments linked to the hero's difficult situation. First, the derisive statement "Te estás meando de miedo, cabrón" (662), made by the soldier who is escorting him, evokes a visual image of his youthful days as a centerfielder, when he would shag flyballs into the night accompanied by a silence and peace inherent to that portion of the playing arena which, in Spanish, has acquired the metaphorical name of "jardines." Alone and secure in the quiet field, he remembers: "no se me iba ningún batazo, y sólo por su rumor presentía la bola que venía como una paloma a caer en mi mano" (662).

A second parallelism develops when, during his interrogation, the character is asked at what time he was apprehended by the police. Upon responding that it was shortly after dinnertime, another image takes possession of his psyche:

> Vení cená me gritaba mi mamá desde la acera. Falta un inning, mamá, le contestaba, ya voy. Pero hijo, no ves que ya está obscuro, qué vas a seguir jugando. Sí ya voy, sólo falta una tanda, y en la iglesia comenzaban los violines y el armonio a tocar el rosario, cuando venía la bola a mis manos para sacar el último out y habíamos ganado otra vez el juego.
>
> (663)

The significance of this particular analeptic fragment[4] lies in the allusion to maternal protection. Additionally, it re-emphasizes the obsessive nature of the play spirit while, at the same time, introducing another concept: the notion of winning. According to Huizinga, "winning means showing oneself superior in the outcome of a game" (50). By being victorious, an individual achieves esteem and secures honor. Such honor and esteem "accrue to the benefit of the group to which the victor belongs" (50). Within the context of "El centerfielder," the recollection of winning at a game also implies hope of success in the more agonistic contest which the protagonist has by this time joined: the rhetorical cat-and-mouse game with his interrogator.

Finally, a third retrospective instance is brought about by the initial interpolation of baseball within dialogue, within present narrative time and hence, within the basic storyline. The protagonist is asked if he once was a baseball player. When he answers affirmatively, the captain identifies him by name: "¿Te decían Matraca Parrales, verdad?" (663) Recognition in this instance implies familiarity, perhaps empathy, perhaps even compassion. Success in contest pleases and seduces the group. Thus, its representatives often forgive errors made by stars outside the playing field. The character seeks to transform the confrontational nature of dialogue by exploiting the turn toward baseball talk, toward the arena where he once was hero. Parrales had been a member of the national team that, twenty years previously, had traveled to Cuba to play in a tournament. However, the captain reminds him, he had been removed from the squad upon returning to Nicaragua. Despite the criticism implicit in this comment, Parrales smiles once the captain refers to his powerful throwing arm, but he is cut short when the friendly gesture clashes with an angry stare. This motivates the third retrospection:

> La mejor jugada fue una vez que cogí un fly en las gradas del atrio, de espaldas al cuadro metí la manopla y caí de bruces en las gradas con la bola atrapada y me sangró la lengua pero ganamos la partida y me llevaron en peso a mi casa y mi mamá echando las tortillas, dejó la masa y se fue a curarme llena de orgullo y de lástima, vas a quedarte burro pero atleta, hijo.
>
> (664)

The winning motif, here complemented by the triumphant return home of the classic hero upon the shoulders of the throng on whose benefit the victory reverts, is tamed by the wound which the sheltering mother heals. That blood trickling from his lacerated tongue, nevertheless, augurs the one that will pour inevitably from his murdered body. Structurally, it signifies an alteration in the protagonist's baseball memories. Play moves to an organized sphere where failure is penalized in a manner identical to that employed to punish crimes against the state within a repressive society.

The captain's political accusation follow what may be construed as an athletic indictment. He first forces the character to admit a fateful sportive error:

> -Y ¿por qué te botaron del equipo?
> -Porque se me cayó un fly y perdimos.
> -¿En Cuba?
> -Jugando contra la selección de Aruba; era una palomita que se me zafó de las manos y entraron dos carreras, perdimos.
> -Fueron varios los que botaron.
> -La verdad, tomábamos mucho, y en el juego, no se puede.
> -Ah.
>
> (666)

The violation of play mores ("we used to drink a lot, and you can't do that when you are playing sports") constitutes a transgression punishable externally by the group that, as player, he served. Internally, it is punishable by obsessive memory, by the series of recollections the captain triggers that force the protagonist to confront again his failure. And in this act of remembering, like in his captive state, he remains alone and hopeless. The protective mother present in previous retrospections is now an absence, a distant figure that accentuates his forsakenness:

> La bola blanca venía como flotando a mis manos, fui a su encuentro, la esperé, extendí los brazos e íbamos a encontrarnos para siempre cuando pegó en el dorso de mi mano, quise asirla en la caída pero rebotó y de lejos vi al hombre barriéndose en home y todo estaba perdido, mamá, necesitaba agua tibia en mis heridas porque siempre vos lo supiste, siempre tuve coraje para fildear aunque dejara la vida.
>
> (667)

The hero's pathetic uncrowning, comical to many participants in the pseudocarnival that baseball signifies, parallels the tragic denouement of his real situation. After this reminiscence, he is sent to his death. Ironically—and somewhat artificially—the captain proposes as an unnecessary excuse for the assassination about to be committed a cynically humorous and hence grotesque fable that coincides with the fallen hero's infantile escape plan. He orders his henchman as follows: "Era beisbolista, así que invéntate cualquier babosada: que estaba jugando con los otros presos, que estaba de centerfielder, que le llegó un batazo contra el muro, que aprovechó para subirse al almendro, que se saltó la tapia, que corriendo en el solar del rastro lo tiramos" (668). This contrived ending, whose circularity is transparent, encloses a story where sport memories counteract reality until game itself ceases to be so once it has developed into organized activity supported, in this particular case, by the identical repressive organism that incarcerates and executes the protagonist. After all, in the Nicaragua of the Somozas sport and jail were controlled by one and the same quasi divine system.

In Stuart Dybek's story, death emerges from the beginning as the abrupt force that puts an end to individual play spirit, that superimposes reality upon the absurd ambiance where joyful contest presides. A text more carnivalesque in its essence than Ramírez's, the fateful event institutes a new, tragicomic amusement: verbal or psychological speculation, the "riddle contest" (154) described by Huizinga. **"Death of the Rightfielder"** develops, therefore, as an ironic construct that parodies notions inalterably connected to baseball while at the same time specific human preoccupations appear submitted to the distorting effects of a convex mirror. Recognizing the story's intrinsic playfulness, Mary Ann Grossman recalls: "One male reader described **'The Death of the Rightfielder'** . . . as 'Keilloresque' in its dreamy tone" ("Dybek Takes Readers . . .").

In the text, baseball is perceived in its most pure ludic aspect: as engrossing sandlot diversion involving participants who seek joy, the pure pleasure of playing and, at times, winning. Given their recognizable nature, impressions associated with the sport convey a banality trivialized by narrative tone. The story begins: "After too many balls went out and never came back we went out to check. It was a long walk—he always played deep" (35). Implied eeriness is counterbalanced by the humorous commonplace notion of the rightfielder who plays far away, the team castoff relinquished to patrol distant realms where he can do little harm. Pursuing this image further, the first-person narrator, who the reader must view as recollecting participant, proceeds to distinguish in a manner blatantly comic and yet suggestively melancholic between insiders and outsiders in the game of baseball. Infielders—he avers with a certainty agreeable to anyone who has ever patrolled the outer regions of a playing field—are communicators, individuals who live in the public eye, extroverts whose chatter adds an almost musical dimension to the contest. "The outfield," on the other hand, "is for loners, onlookers, brooders who would rather study clover and swat gnats than holler" (35), for a different type of clown whose essential function is to remain unnoticed until the silence that surrounds him is interrupted—like in the case

of "El centerfielder" by a flying spheroid that must be trapped in order for the game to continue successfully or conclude auspiciously.

The indirect portrait of the fallen player is supplemented with passing notions, fleeting pictures whose referentiality amusingly rounds out the playing field's non-seriousness. Unlike stricken sport stars such as the University of Syracuse's Ernie Davis, the Texas Rangers' Danny Thompson or the Chicago Bears' Brian Piccolo, the hero could not have been a victim of leukemia because: "He wasn't a talented enough athlete to die of that. He'd have been playing center, not right, if leukemia was going to get him" (36). The protagonist wore a blue felt cap with a red C, but he always denied that the letter stood for the Chicago Cubs. According to the untrustworthy narrator: "He may have been a loner, but he didn't want to be identified with a loser. He lacked the sense of humor for that, lacked the perverse pride that sticking up for losers season after season breeds, and the love" (37). Which leaves the reader pondering: What did the letter stand for, then? And: Are we confronting a misreading of character on the part of a distant, prejudiced voice? The protagonist was an ordinary guy whose mediocrity is described through a metaphorical baseball expression: ".250 at the plate" (37). Others to come, others to occupy the same sacred ground littered with the cadaver of a nonentity could be potential great ones, like Mickey Mantle or Roberto Clemente. In the baseball context that matters within the story's carnivalesque mood, the stricken character's insignificance becomes manifest. Like the average man, he is comically faceless as well as nameless in death because of his athletic shortcomings.

Initially, however, **"Death of the Rightfielder"** is a self-oriented ambiguous riddle contest in which the narrator reproduces a series of theories regarding the nature of the dying act, reiterating childish fears that underline the ease with which one can cease to be. Youthful, unexpected and sudden death promotes a search for reasonable responses that becomes, instead, an exuberantly humorous and grotesque hypothesizing akin to carnivalesque ritual. Several theories are posited by spectators and recalled by the first person narrator. One is that the protagonist was shot accidentally, or perhaps he was the victim of the murderous intentions of a rival gang such as "the Latin Lords who didn't play sports period" (36), that is, of a group who denies liberating as well as creative play spirit. A heart attack is a possibility refuted by the poetic voice because "young deaths are never natural; they're all violent" (36). Leukemia is inconceivable for reasons specified above. Other death causes subjected to speculation include an allergic reaction to a bee sting, a lightning bolt strike from an instantaneous electric storm, ingestion of strong doses of insecticide from grass blades chewed by the protagonist, sonic waves, radiation, pollution. The final quoted conjecture provides a logical return to the playing field: "A few of us liked to think it was simply that chasing a sinking liner, diving to make a shoestring catch, he broke his neck" (36-37). By ascribing the hero's death to a valiant effort carried out under the effects of the play spirit and in the sacred ground that the contest arena represents, his demise is made tolerable as well as intelligible.

The image of an athlete dying young is conventionally pitiful, clearly annexed to the ludic factor whence it emanates. To die in the playing field is to play forever, to become inexorably linked in the memory of other participants to the festival scene broken momentarily by a real event. In Dybek's story, the fantastic burial in rightfield of the fallen hero constitutes his absolute absorption by the game. His shallow grave is stamped down ("buried" in the catcher's view) to make it level with the field so that future players' prowess would not be impeded, so that no more broken necks would take place in the already tainted earth. However, such efforts prove fruitless because, as the narrator attests, "a fresh grave is stubborn" (38). It persists as a bald spot similar to "an aberrant pitcher's mound" (38) marked grotesquely by a bat jammed into the ground with a glove and blue cap over it. Such a carnivalesque internment signifies a profane mockery of conventional funeral rites, an inversion of standard societal norms. Therefore, it guarantees the perpetuation of the play spirit. While other participants in the game go on to become victims of time, of invading reality, the dead athlete endures in memory as a perennial child imbued with the gracefulness of youth. That is the implication transparent in the final paragraph, when the narrator reflects on the destructive passage of time and aging heroes like Phil Niekro, Pete Rose, the decaying Willie Mays, who, in 1971, dropped an easy fly ball during the World Series. And yet, the poetic voice melancholically affirms, such individuals "are the lucky ones," since "most guys are washed up by seventeen" (39). Through this statement, the story refocuses implicitly on the symbolic nature of the dead rightfielder, a ludic image of irretrievable youth, a vision of that all-consuming play spirit that made Ramírez's "centerfielder" shag balls well into the night. Reality is the eternal enemy of myth, of feast, of game.

Stuart Dybek's **"Death of the Rightfielder"** and Sergio Ramírez's "El centerfielder" are divergent stories ideologically, thematically, linguistically, technically. Nevertheless, through this descriptive analysis of each text I have tried to demonstrate how they parallel each other in the treatment of baseball. Both authors intuit the sport's festive nature, its ritualistic atemporality, its carnival-rooted inversive potentiality that superimposes artificial and abnormal orderliness upon an often perplexing concrete world. Both as well seek to elucidate how external events—oppressive reality—interfere with the play spirit and the playing field, with the ludic images conveyed by them, to reinstitute ruthlessness, vulgar death, apoeticality. Game ends tragically in these texts by coetaneous authors from different extremes of the American continent, and the tragic end of game is akin more to spiritual than to physical death.

Notes

1. Claudia Schaffer, in an article entitled "La recuperación del realismo: ¿Te dio miedo la sangre? de Sergio Ramírez," employs this Carlos Blanco Aguinaga term, suggested, of course, by Georg Lukács, to define Ramírez's poetic conception. She states: "Su realismo crítico abarca tanto las 'miserias' (de la pobreza, de la enfermedad, de la soledad), las 'derrotas' (de las fuerzas de oposición en general), las 'noches medievales' (de la tortura), los 'reinos de bayonetas' (la persecución por los militares, la opresión del dictador) y la 'destrucción' (de la familia, del individuo en el exilio) como los 'heroísmos' . . . la 'esperanza' y la 'construcción' de la sociedad de Nicaragua" (148).

2. One must note, in passing, that Stuart Dybek was recently honored with the prestigious PEN/Malamud Award for Excellence in the short story. He shared the 1995 Award with writer William Maxwell. Dybek was recognized for the excellence of a literary production in which *The Coast of Chicago* figures most prominently.

3. By "ritualistic time," I mean a fixed period during which behavior is structured around preordained norms, usually religious or mythical in nature. Intrinsically related to the advent of Lenten, "carnival time" entails a joyful finite period in which human beings transform themselves as well as their surroundings to create a transitory "topsy-turvy" ambiance. Carnival as ritual concludes with a return to conventional reality and order. One may argue that sports parallel carnival time in their joyous abnormality, which develops within a prescribed space during a period limited or ritualized by diverse rules and structures inherent to these human activities.

4. I follow Gerard Genette in employing the term analepsis to refer to "any evocation after the fact of an event that took place earlier than the point in the story where we are at any given moment." (40)

Works Cited

Bakhtin, Mikhail. *Rabelais and His World.* Tr. Héléne Iswolsky. Bloomington: Indiana University Press, 1984.

Tom Blackburn, "Short-Story Hero: Stuart Dybek a Standout in Art Form's Renaissance." *The Palm Beach Post,* May 1990, 1L-2L.

Dybek, Stuart. Quoted in the "Afternotes" to *Sudden Fiction International.* New York: W. W. Norton, 1989, 316-17.

———. *The Coast of Chicago.* New York: Knopf, 1990.

Genette, Gérard. *Narrative Discourse: An Essay in Method.* Tr. Jane E. Lewing. Ithaca: Cornell University Press, 1980.

Grossman, Mary Lou. "Dybek Takes Readers on Journey along a 'Coast' of Many Cultures." *St. Paul Pioneer Press,* May 27, 1990.

Huizinga, Johan. *Homo Ludens: A study of the Play Element in Culture.* Boston: Beacon Press, 1965.

Porter, Dennis. "The Perilous Quest: Baseball as Folk Drama." *Critical Inquiry,* 4:1 (1977):143-57

Ramírez, Sergio. "El centerfielder." *Antología del cuento centroamericano.* Ed. Sergio Ramírez. San José: Editorial Universitaria Centroamericana, 1982.

———. Preface to *Antología del cuento centroamericano.*

Schaefer, Claudia. "La recuperación del realismo: ¿Te dio miedo la sangre? de Sergio Ramírez." *Texto Crítico,* 13:36-37 (1987): 146-52.

Stuart Dybek and Mike Nickel and Adrian Smith (interview date winter 1997)

SOURCE: Dybek, Stuart, and Mike Nickel and Adrian Smith. "An Interview with Stuart Dybek." *Chicago Review* 43, no. 1 (winter 1997): 87-101.

[*In the following interview, Dybek discusses the perception of him as a Chicago writer, the role of childhood in his stories, and influences on his work.*]

The following interview was conducted as part of the University of Memphis's ongoing River City Writers Series; the conversation took place March 7, 1995, in Memphis. Stuart Dybek's books include two collections of short stories, **Childhood and Other Neighborhoods** *(Viking, 1980), and* **Coast of Chicago** *(Knopf, 1990), as well as a work of poetry,* Brass Knuckles *(University of Pittsburgh Press, 1979). A recipient of a lifetime achievement award from the Academy of Arts and Letters, Dybek's writing may be found in* The New Yorker, *and* The Best American Short Stories of 1995.

[*Nickel:*] *I thought we'd start by talking about the Chicago style with which you're often identified. Let's begin with the term "Chicago Writer." I'm curious how you feel about it?*

[Dybek]: Well, at this point it might seem a little disingenuous of me to say that it was a surprise because the reviews have mentioned it so often, but it really was. When my first book of stories came out, I was living in the Keys, a long way from Chicago. And the way I had written those stories was as individual pieces until I realized that there was an organizational principle in the fact that a lot of them have to do with childhood, and a lot of them were set in Chicago. And so, I organized them around that principle, but it never occurred to me that the Chicago element was what would be picked up. As soon as it was pointed out to me, I saw it, but what was uppermost in my mind at the time was that they were stories about childhood, and that they had strong Eastern European influences.

[*Smith:*] *You talk about childhood as a neighborhood itself, calling your first short-story collection* **Childhood and Other Neighborhoods.** *What is it about childhood that makes it a neighborhood?*

Let me try and answer that question by putting it in a larger context and say that if somebody asked me what I thought my subject was, the answer wouldn't be Chicago,

and it probably wouldn't be childhood: it would be perception. I think what I'm always looking for is some door in the story that opens on another world. A doorway like that can be a religious experience; in fact, that's probably the first such doorway I was aware of. When I grew up on the southwest side, the two biggest landmarks on most every corner were a church or a tavern. I would be walking down, let's say 25th street, which would represent ordinary reality. Ordinary reality would be made up by bread trucks delivering bread, people going to work, kids playing on the sidewalk, women hanging wash and so on. But by just stepping through either one of those doorways, the tavern or the church, it seemed to me that you entered a different world. In the tavern you entered a world that moved to a different time. The time it moved to was whatever song was on the jukebox. There was the smell of alcohol. People told stories and behaved in ways that they would never behave on the street. The church was the same thing. By just entering its doors you just seemed to enter the medieval ages. There was the smell of incense, and there were statues of saints and martyrs in grotesquely tortured positions. What I look for as a writer in stories are those doorways in which somebody leaves ordinary reality and enters some kind of extraordinary reality. So, to get back to your question, childhood for me is one of those doorways. To me, childhood seems like a state of extraordinary perception, and to inhabit that state or that neighborhood means that you're perceiving the world in a different way than is defined as ordinary. It's assuming that perception that interests me. It's a lens you can look through, in which the world becomes a different, hopefully fresher, more vivid place.

[*Nickel:*] *You mention you have a reluctance to accept the term "Chicago" writer. You feel that's a label of sorts?*

No, it isn't a reluctance. It's just a surprise. In fact, I was quite flattered to be included in that kind of company, and I just had never assumed that kind of lineage, that's all. I have tremendous admiration for Saul Bellow, and Algren as well. And James Farrell doesn't get mentioned enough in that company. That Studs Lonigan trilogy was really a very important book for me. But, it just hadn't occurred to me that someone would be generous enough to mention my work in that company. I really mean that.

Do you see yourself as being a part of any other literary traditions?

The writers that I was thinking about at the time when I was writing those stories in *Childhood and Other Neighborhoods* were not the writers in the so-called Chicago Tradition. The reason is that the personal departure I felt I made in order to acquire some kind of a voice I was comfortable with was, especially in that first book, one that combined elements of the fantastic and the grotesque with realism. The Chicago tradition is a stubbornly realist tradition, and I didn't really see my work in that realist tradition, and therefore, I didn't see my work in the Chicago tradition. You know, what's great about Bellow, and Algren, and Farrell is just how powerfully realistic, and naturalistic in some degree, their work is. The writers I was reading were more Eastern Europeans, and some of the Hispanic writers.

Now, I'm thinking of the story "Palatski Man," one of the first stories from your collection **Childhood and Other Neighborhoods.** *It has a certain kind of magic realist quality to it, yet you're often identified with realistic, or naturalistic, writers ranging from Eudora Welty to James Joyce. How do you account for that magic realist quality? What influences were there that brought about that style.*

I'm not sure. I can tell you the anecdote though, which is a true story, of how I came to write **"The Palatski Man,"** which was the first story that I kind of wrote. At the time, I was reading mostly realistic writers. I particularly loved that kind of realistic voice that comes out of Sherwood Anderson, which you can follow through Hemingway and Salinger. It's frequently a first person voice. A lot of those writers wrote with young narrators, so I found that very familiar, and a voice I could readily adapt. But, the problem I was having with it was that it sounded like—the way that I was using it—pretty much like it would as adapted by any number of other writers, a sort of instantly recognizable, almost generic American style. And so, on some level I was dissatisfied with it because it didn't seem to me that I had found a voice, a style that in some ways expressed what I felt were my own personal rhythms. I was listening to a ton of music, and had reached the point where mostly when I wrote I listened to some kind of music. Usually it was jazz, but I was listening more and more to classical music, especially to chamber music, and I had gotten very interested in Béla Bartók. In reading about Bartók, I read about this other composer, Zoltán Kodály. Bartók and Kodály were part of a movement which tried to infuse postmodern music, mainly French impressionist music, with folk elements from their own culture. As part of the process, they took trips into the wilds of Hungary with very primitive recording devices and recorded real gypsy music—not the kind of stuff that Brahms was using. I mean it was true primitive stuff based on bagpipe riffs, and strange model chords and so on and so forth. And then they tried to integrate it into their own music.

This sounded really interesting to me. I've always loved local color. So, I got these records out of the library by Zoltán Kodály, and I put them on the record player, and I sat down and I wrote a story to his music that I had never even thought about writing, which was the **"Palatski Man."** It was literally almost like falling into a trance. I think what happened was the same thing that happens in a fifth grade classroom when the teacher brings in Ravel's "Bolero," and says to the kids, "Now, kids, today we're going to listen to Ravel's 'Bolero', and you write whatever comes into your mind." Then it begins [whistling the beginning of "Bolero"], and everybody is writing "I see camels going across the desert. They're dancing at the oasis." That music [by Kodály] just brought up all these images, but the images it brought up happened to be these Eastern European images, which, on some levels, I guess I had grown up with, but had never been able to harness or tap into them. I had really not read very much Eastern European literature with the exception of several of the Russians. I had read no magical realism at that point. I hadn't read [Isaak] Babel. I hadn't read Czeslaw Milosz. I had read very little Kafka, but as soon as I started writing those stories, I immediately developed a kind of hunger to go and see what other kinds of stories there might be like this. And that's when I started reading a lot of Kafka, and shortly thereafter, [Gabriel Garcia] Marquez's book*One Hundred Years of Solitude* appeared. But it was really the music that had generated the story and only after that did I circle back and start finding a literary base for the direction I stumbled on.

Are you able to recreate that feeling now?

No. I wore it out. But for years after that I would gather all this music—Kodály, Bartók, Shostakovich, Janáček—because as soon as I put the music on, story became a physical feeling. I mean, I could almost feel it as if it guided me to some kind of biological, electrical path in my mind that would lead to a place in my brain where all this stuff lurked. I guess I reached the point where I overdrew the account. It's not quite there anymore, but by that time I had written most of the stories in that first book. By the way, two of the writers you mentioned—Welty and Joyce—I don't really see them as realistic writers. I mean, I'm sure they can be viewed that way, but to me, they're lyrical writers. I think in the second book I'd exhausted that Eastern European account that I was drawing on, in which, to me, the primary element was the fantastic, the fantastic or the grotesque. The grotesque that is defined in a great book by Wolfgang Kayser, where he describes it as a third genre, along with comedy and tragedy. I think the technique in **Coast of Chicago** is actually closer to Welty and Joyce, which is to try to combine the lyric mode with the realistic mode. It's that combination that fascinates me about those writers—besides their incredible sense of place.

[Nickel:] You have obviously been influenced by the ethnic diversity of the neighborhood you grew up in. How do you think this affected your development as a writer—particularly now that you've lived away from Chicago for some time? As you said, you were living in the Florida Keys when your first collection was actually published, and you lived in New York after that, so you've had a chance to move away from those Chicago influences. **Coast of Chicago,** *however, is still very much influenced by those experiences.*

Well, a lot of writers leave home in order to write about it as a place. I go back to Chicago frequently to kind of charge up again, too. Sometimes I'll just rent a room and live there for a while. But certainly, it depends wholly on temperament. Faulkner absolutely needed to live in the place that he wrote about whereas, clearly, Joyce did not. For me, because a lot of what I'm writing takes huge liberties with the imagination, I actually found it difficult to be writing about a somewhat imaginatively transformed El station, say the Bryn Mawr El station, and then to actually be passing the real Bryn Mawr El station. To my mind, a fiction writer's first allegiance is to the imagination, and so it was probably necessary for me to leave Chicago in order to write about it. As far as the ethnic neighborhoods and street life, that's become so impressed on my memory and personality that I don't really have to be there for it. I'd say, along with music, the other most important influence on my writing was my Polish grandmother who could hardly speak any English, even up into her nineties when she finally died. But we were able to communicate through my pidgin Polish and her pidgin English. There was a nonverbal communication that went on through body language, and the intensity of her eyes and just some kind of powerful nonverbal emotive ability that she had that was so un-American, or maybe "not-American," I suppose is what I mean. I value that foreign-ness to such a degree because it's opposite what I would consider "All-American," depending on how it's defined, could almost be a pejorative term, at least in the way that America digests and homogenizes everything and spits it back out into these McDonald's-like portions. That is what is least interesting to me about this country. What's most interesting to me is its ethnic variety, its cultural variety and its sense of genuine place, which is one of the reasons that the South fascinates me so much. The South and huge cities like New York have managed to remain somewhat impermeable to all that homogenization. A recurring motif in a lot of my stories is nonverbal experience and sometimes a longing after languages that don't exist, and that all comes from my grandmother.

Is the powerful emotive quality of your grandmother's nonverbal communication a part of the reason the stories in **The Coast of Chicago** *have a more consciously lyrical quality than your earlier stories?*

Maybe. I think the kinds of stories that I usually don't like are stories that are not interested in emotion. It seems to me that a risk that a writer should take is to tell a story which leaves you feeling something deeply. One of the things that is beautiful about music is that it is an emotional teacher that teaches you about different shades of emotion. In a way, all the arts are nonverbal, you know. Obviously, painting is a nonverbal art. Dance is a nonverbal art. But the narrative arts, film, theater, and particularly fiction and poetry, paradoxically, should convey a nonverbal quality. It's a total paradox of course because they're based on language. I don't know if I can articulate this, but I think that the kind of fiction I'm after is as essentially nonverbal as music is. And by that I mean, it should take you to a shading of emotion that there aren't actual words for. That is, that what you're feeling can't be paraphrased by the words we have in the language, only evoked, or approximated.

Is the minimalism of roughly half of those stories, the ones usually set off by the gray pages, a part of that?

Yes.

[Nickel:] Speaking of feeling, I'm reminded of something you said in 1983, if I can go back 12 years to pull something out from a roundtable discussion you had with other Chicago writers. In that discussion you mention sentiment as being a part of the Chicago style, but you were careful to point out that sentiment is feeling as you've just described, and not the sentimental.

Right.

Yet, a lot of your stories have a nostalgic edge to them and also contain a lot of feeling. So, I'm curious as to how you were able to do that—balance the two without crossing the line into sentimentality, which you don't.

I can't give you a capsule answer because each story usually possesses its own, somewhat different, problem, and you kind of solve it story by story. For example, there's clearly a risk one takes when writing any childhood story. Just by its very nature a story about children runs the risk of being a corny sentimental story. And so, on either a conscious or unconscious level the writer has to, from the very start, take that into account and continually devise strategies to both harness the sentiment and the subject but, at the same time, undercut the sentimentality. In one story it might be understatement and irony that keep it at bay, and, in another story, it might be that the incidents are so brutal that they balance off any kind of sentimental feelings. In another story, it might still be yet something else, so there isn't really one solution to it.

Are you aware of that dynamic, though, when you write? Are you aware that there is that danger?

Absolutely. Sure. Nostalgia, in particular. I mean, because that nostalgia is built into the immigrant experience you can't have one without the other. It really interested me when I began reading the Hispanic writers, how much more nostalgia was a part of their emotional palette. You've got people in [Garcia] Marquez walking around saying "Oh my nostalgia" in a way that you could never get away with as an American writer. We're still linked to a British tradition that doesn't emote that way. It's not an Anglo-American feeling. So, it's an opportunity to integrate that into the American emotional palette, but it's also an immediate danger when you do it. But to ignore such emotions is to ignore a universal aspect of the American experience. To become self-indulgent about them is obviously to undermine the very feelings you're trying to evoke a genuine representation of.

[Smith:] We've talked a little bit about two of the important influences on your work, music and neighborhood, and another one that keeps appearing is the presence of Mayor [Richard J.] Daley, which seems to signify a kind of wider neighborhood. In both of your short-story collections you mention the "Sorry for the Inconvenience . . ." sign which brings Daley into the story itself, and I'm wondering what it meant to you growing up in Chicago under his various administrations?

There's about five different ways I could answer that question. The simplest one is that Daley was everywhere as I grew up, and that meant that because he was a colorful politician, well . . . as William Price Fox, a teacher of mine at the University of Iowa, once said to me about growing up Catholic, "It's good material. Use it." The same thing is true of Daley. Anybody who writes about him owes a tremendous debt to a writer I haven't talked about, Mike Royko. His book *Boss* was a wonderful book. What Royko did better than anybody else was show how funny that material could be. So, there's that comic element. Another element that interests me is the fact that Daley represented a certain kind of paternalism, and on one level or another a lot of my stories are anti-paternal. I've always wanted to use, at some time or another, that opening Bob Dylan line in "Highway 61 Revisited":

God said to Abraham, kill me a son,
Abe say Man you must be putting me on,
God said no, Abe say what?
God say you can do what you want Abe but the
Next time you see me coming you better run.
Well Abe said, Where do you want this killing done?
God said, out on Highway 61.

Growing up during Vietnam, when you had an older generation seeming to want to send a reluctant younger generation to war, it was no accident Dylan wrote that verse during that time. That was the time of the so-called "Generation Gap" and, in a way, Daley was representative of that tension between different ways of perceiving the world. Daley's was an older, paternalistic order that was built on the tried and true political principle of you scratch my back I'll scratch yours.

In a number of the stories, in the ones that deal specifically with childhood in some way or another, there's an absence of the Father figure.

Exactly.

In "Chopin in Winter" and "Blight," for example.

Well, the book I'm working on now pushes that even further, but you know, because I'm working with this material, I'm kind of disinclined to fall into an analytical discussion about it. I know what it is I'm trying to say about it, but I want it said through fiction before I start talking analytically. So, if you'll let me just duck out on that one.

[Nickel:] Maybe this would be a good point to switch gears and talk about the forms you write in. The short-short story seems to have gained in popularity in the last couple of years. You're a practitioner of it, and are often anthologized in books like Flash Fiction *and* Sudden Fiction. *Do you have any insights into the rising popularity of that form?*

I really don't. I guess I've read the same things you probably have about it. People are linking it to shorter attention spans and watching MTV, and so on and so forth. I think I come to the short-short through poetry. I remember exactly how I got interested in it. A college friend named Peter Fiori, who I knew from Chicago, and I used to just read each other's work. We'd meet at a bar called "Connally's," an Irish bar on Devon, and he came walking in to the bar one day, and he had written a bunch of these short prose things, and I thought they were terrific. And so I figured I'd start writing these, too. That was long before short-shorts, flash fiction, or anything else. The only other stuff of the kind I had seen at that point I'd also liked a lot, those little vignettes that Hemingway used to separate the stories from *In Our Time*. To me they still read as fresh today as they must have when he wrote them back in the 1920s. Those were the only two short prose things I knew, and then I finally got around to picking up some translations of Rimbaud's work, and read his prose poems, and they're still some of the best prose poems I've ever read. So, I added those to the mix, and continued scribbling my own versions of those little pieces, but never knew what to do with them, and then, almost suddenly, there was this huge prose poem mass insanity that struck American Literature in the 1960s and 1970s—long after other cultures had prose poem traditions, one might add. But there was this second wave of Frenchifying, Francophiling American poetry—this time called the continental or international style, which brought on the prose poem. So, with poets experimenting with these little semi-prose pieces, there was a channel for them. Poetry editors were now publishing it. That was great. I didn't care what they called it, and I'd been writing all of these short things anyway, so I started having my short prose poem pieces published by poetry editors. One of things I couldn't help but notice at the time was that several poets whose work I admired were trying these things, and generally I thought they were writing better in verse than in prose. That kind of started bothering me. I waited with great anticipation for a book that I knew Michael Benedict was doing. He was editing poetry at that time for *The Paris Review,* and he was publishing a lot of prose poems in that magazine, and he himself wrote prose poems, and I was really waiting for this anthology of his with great anticipation. When it came out, there was certainly stuff in it that I really liked, but a lot of the work seemed flat to me and uninteresting and disappointing. I read his cogent introduction, and one of the things that Benedict said was that the prose poem developed as part of a postmodernist anti-poetry movement, and it was at that point that I realized what was bothering me about a lot of the so-called prose poems. For full effect it was necessary to read them in the context of traditional poetry. That is, they were anti-poetry, but in order to appreciate what they were doing one needed to be totally familiar with the history of formal and traditional poetry. Like a lot of conceptual art, the prose poem often worked best if you understood what it was putting itself in opposition to. And that's always been my problem with conceptual art; that it's sometimes more interesting to talk about the theory of it than to actually read or listen to the stuff itself. I didn't want to write "anti-work," so I rethought what I was doing and began regarding the pieces as just little stories. I wanted to distance myself from the prose poem. In the 1980s, the second wave of stuff came, the short shorts, which is now supposed to be fiction, distinct from prose poems. But there's overlap. At least no one is calling them anti-stories.

Right. I'm thinking of **"Laughter"** *which is one of those stories from the* **"Nighthawks"** *sequence in* **The Coast of Chicago** *which appeared, years earlier, in* Brass Knuckles *as poetry, but still very similar to its later prose counterpart. Does the change in context change the perception of that piece?*

Well it changed the writing of the piece for me. That is, one of the things I liked about the prose poem—I mean this is strictly temperamental, so I'm not claiming that this exists as an aspect of the prose poem—but for me, the freedom from line, though not from rhythm, allowed me to open up the "prose poem" in a way that I was not able, in some ways, to open up some of my poems. Then, when I freed myself from thinking of those short pieces as prose poems, I got a second burst of that feeling. So, when I started thinking about **"Laughter"** as a short fiction, rather than as a prose poem, I actually rewrote it and expanded it still further. For me, within the compressive principle of the short-short, there's still a principle of expansion that I don't find in formal poetry or in the prose poem.

[*Smith:*] *Since we've brought up* **"Nighthawks,"** *I'm wondering about the relationship between the painting and that sequence. What is it about the painting that resonates so vividly that made you want to write about it and yet write about it in that form?*

Before that piece was called **"Nighthawks"** it was called "Nocturnes." I'd been working on a story called **"Chopin in Winter,"** listening to music, as I usually do, and I found myself gravitating towards the nocturnes. They were putting me in the mood I wanted for the story. So in the story itself, nocturnes start figuring heavily. But after I finished the story, I thought, would it be possible to write a series of mood pieces, which is what nocturnes are. They're less formal than a lot of musical forms. I thought, by naming it "Nocturnes" it would give the reader some clue as to how to read it, that is, what is holding all of these things together. When you're working on something that doesn't have a good straight narrative line, you're always looking for formal clues to give the reader as to how to put the piece together, since the reader doesn't have a narrative line to follow. It was only later that I started thinking about Hopper's painting. As soon as I thought about the painting, I reluctantly dropped the title "Nocturnes" because the painting gave me a whole series of images that I could also use in the form of theme variations, and it seemed to me that the painting gave the sequence a stronger sense of narrative propulsion than "Nocturnes" did. So, I switched. But basically it was the same thing I was looking for in both. That is for some way to create individual pieces that at the same time seemed linked by something other than a straight narrative line.

[*Nickel:*] *Back to form a little bit. Are you conscious of form when you write, or do you write a piece and then later realize how the piece itself realizes the form.*

A lot of what I write starts out as poetry, probably thirty percent of the stories I've published are actually, on some level to me, failed poems. Including stories that you would never think would have started out as a poem, like **"Blight."** Really, for a long time **"Blight"** was written as a would-be poem. I had the nutty notion on that one to turn it into a poem that imitated a Lenny Bruce monologue. It was supposed to be a comic poem mimicking the way comedians get up there and tell monologues, and I still would like, someday, to write a poem that's just based on comedian's comic monologue. Finally, what happens in these failed poems is that characters start asserting themselves, they take it over, and for me it becomes a piece of fiction. As soon as a piece has fictional qualities, I let it go. My notion is that if it can be something other than a poem, then it probably wasn't supposed to be a poem. I let it become a piece of fiction. So, just that kind of procedure means that I'm not casting these things from the start in one kind of a form or another. But, a second answer to your question, relates particularly to the short-short. I'm always looking for a way out of form, or out of traditional form. Traditional form for a short story requires a beginning, a middle, and an end. But I'm always looking for a way to explode form, and that's one of the things that I like about the short-short—nobody knows what they are yet. And there aren't the same expectations of them there are of short stories. And I like that. I'm constantly looking to read and write pieces that confuse me. I mean, sometimes they confuse me so much that they don't work. The form of **"Nighthawks"** is something I'm not going to go back and do for a while because I ended up putting way more time into that than I had envisioned myself doing and, frequently, didn't know where in the world I was with that. I had only too well succeeded in putting myself in a state of absolute floundering around. It felt great to be writing in a more traditional form after that. Sooner or later, you know, you want to keep surprising yourself. The short-short is a no-man's land between fiction and poetry, and I like it there. It's a comfortable place to be lost, and not to have to feel like you have to deliver on certain expectations that the genre has set up. I feel the same way about closure. I'm always looking for a way to close a story that isn't the kind of traditional the-character-has-a-realization so it's time to end.

[*Smith:*] *The major genre you haven't published in so far is the novel. Do you have any ambition to explode your subject matter into that form?*

I've actually been working off and on, but they haven't quite jelled yet. It's certainly a genre I want to publish in. Chapters of a novel I've been working on have actually appeared in places like *Atlantic Monthly,* and *Chicago Magazine.* It's a family novel, unfortunately, and non-literary reservations have also been part of the reason I haven't published more of it.

As a problem for the writer, how do you approach the novel differently from the shorter works?

Well, I'm a little reluctant to talk about something that I really don't have out there. But, a short answer to that is, what I love about the short story is that you can jump into it where it's already geared up at a high level, start out already in third gear and then kick it into fourth and fifth. The beauty of the novel is rising and falling action and, temperamentally, what I like is rising, rising, rising action. When I hit falling action, I mean the very thing that makes the novel beautiful, which is that long narrative arch, I get tremendously nervous as a writer. When I hit that falling action part, I'm filled with panic.

Baseball appears in your work frequently. "The Death of the Right Fielder," in particular, seems concerned with the game's metaphorical qualities. What metaphorical qualities do you see in baseball that you want to use, that you have used.

Well, that story is self-explanatory as far as what its metaphors are, but I would go back to that earlier statement I made about perception. For me, sports are one of those doorways. Intense physical activity is one of those doorways. When you enter a sport or enter any intensely physical activity, you have again transformed your perception. You're in a different zone, a different world. I love the current sports vernacular for being "in the zone." Because that's exactly what I'm trying to talk about; so, clearly they're in a baseball zone in that story.

In "Hot Ice" you talk about St. Roberto Clemente and when Big Antek has his miraculous experience, in the background they're talking about Joe DiMaggio. Baseball sort of enters into the larger story as a background.

It's a sport I love though, like everybody else, I'm disgusted by what's going on right now. I spent huge amounts of my life sitting in Wrigley Field. They were some of my happiest moments. I played on ball teams well into my thirties until I tore my knees up. The entire American mythology that goes along with it fascinates me. Wrigley Field is probably one of the sights, along with Fenway Park, in Major League Baseball that still has an almost time machine element. Part of it is that we've gotten physically bigger, and the world is smaller now than when those parks were built. I have this clear recollection as a kid of sitting in this small ballpark with one of the worst pitching staffs in the history of baseball on the mound—that is the Chicago Cubs—and one of the best hitting teams in the history of baseball in the batter's box—the Pittsburgh Pirates—with guys like Stargel and Clemente and several other players, and the power of those balls firing off the bats as the Cub pitchers lobbed them in. In that small park, it really felt like you should be yelling "Incoming, Incoming." I think you can suggest, but never really ever capture, the power of a Roberto Clemente line drive coming off a bat in Wrigley Field. So, there's always that homage to him in those references in my stories.

Don Lee (essay date spring 1998)

SOURCE: Lee, Don. "About Stuart Dybek: A Profile by Don Lee." *Ploughshares* 24, no. 1 (spring 1998): 192-98.

[*In the following essay, Lee offers an overview of Dybek's career as a short story writer.*]

Stuart Dybek works with a curious mix of spontaneity and retentiveness. He wrote most of the stories for his first collection, for instance, under a spell. He'd put on Eastern European classical music, and the words would simply pour out. To this day, Dybek relies on music for inspiration, listening to jazz, jotting in a notebook, improvising, not knowing or caring if the lines will beget a poem or a short-short or a novella. Yet he can be superstitious and fussy—a perfectionist. He is reluctant to analyze or even discuss his ongoing projects, fearing he might "talk away a story," and he has not published another book since his second collection in 1990, although he has four full-length manuscripts that have been interminably close to ready.

Dybek, a second-generation Polish American, lives in Kalamazoo, Michigan, and has taught at Western Michigan University since 1974. His wife, Caren, works in the school system near Kalamazoo, and their daughter and son were raised there. But as Dybek's readers know—and his fans are cultish in their reverence for his work—he writes almost exclusively about the Southwest Side of Chicago, where he was born in 1942. Later known as Pilsen and El Barrio, the neighborhood was populated by working-class Poles, Czechs, and Hispanics. The Catholic church bridged the various ethnic groups, which mingled with a remarkable lack of tension. "It was a benevolent time," Dybek says. The area was considered an urban ghetto, and he was in a gang, but he witnessed little oppression or violence, none of "what has become a kind of genocidal urge in lower-class neighborhoods today."

What Dybek remembers is joy. "I was an ecstatic kid," he says. He was surrounded by hundreds of children, products of the postwar baby boom, and he and his friends ran around with utter abandon, playing baseball, hopping freights, trespassing through factory grounds. His father nicknamed him "The Weed," partly because he was so skinny, mostly because he was so wild. His father, Stanley, was a foreman at the International Harvest plant, which manufactured trucks and farm implements—including a manure spreader, regarded as "the only product we won't stand behind"—and his mother, Adeline, worked as a truck dispatcher for extra income. They were taxed enough without having to deal with their three rambunctious sons. Dybek, the oldest, attended Catholic schools throughout his childhood, and he was always getting into trouble in classes. "I was a year younger than everybody else, and because of that, I think the nuns gave me the benefit of the doubt and ascribed a lot of my behavior to immaturity, which my father knew all along should have been ascribed to weediness."

He was an indifferent student, even in college, where he was put into remedial English, but he did have his passions. A major influence was his grandmother. She barely spoke English, and Dybek hardly knew any Polish, but they had a bond that transcended language. "I was madly, madly in love with her," Dybek says. "There was just a quality of pure emotion that didn't require much in the way of language. She just made me *feel*. She had a tremendous sense of humor, and there was an ancient quality about her—odd superstitions, and body language and smells, and just everything about her communicated someplace other than America." Another visceral, otherworldly source of emotion was music. For reasons Dybek has never been able to fathom, he became obsessed with jazz, and was determined, at eleven years old, to play an instrument. He thought of taking up the trumpet, until his brother knocked off a piece of his front tooth with a belt buckle, ruining his embouchure, so he settled on the saxophone, taking lessons and later forming a band. (They never had any professional gigs, although they occasionally joined a polka band for a couple of sets, "which was something that filled you with a certain amount of humiliation.")

Writing was a distant interest. He read quite a bit—"Again, it was in a weedlike manner"—fascinated for a time with Greek mythology, but writing itself was not imaginable as a vocation. However, Dybek does remember distinctly an epiphany that struck him in the fourth grade, when he woke up one morning to find his mother with the flu. She prepared cream of wheat for his breakfast and then went back to bed, and Dybek, who'd always hated cream of wheat, happily flushed it down the toilet and worked on a school composition about Africa. "I was trying to describe the trees in Africa, and in groping to describe how tall they were, I thought about the tallest things I'd ever seen, which were skyscrapers, and I wrote the phrase 'the tree-scraped skies.' And I mean, I had such a sudden bolt, it jacked me out of my seat at the breakfast table." He sprinted into his mother's room, where she was in the midst of vomiting. "Here she is, heaving over the side of the bed into a bucket, and here's this kid standing there reading this composition about Africa. I'd never done anything like that before. From that moment on, writing was no longer just an academic exercise."

Yet when he entered nearby Loyola University of Chicago, the first in his family to go to college, it wasn't with the intention to become a musician or a writer, but a doctor. After a year, he abandoned that folly and switched to English literature. He became heavily invested in the civil rights and antiwar movements, and his resistance to paternalistic authority, his desire for reform, led him, after graduating from Loyola in 1964, to become a caseworker for the Cook County Department of Public Aid for two years. "I think I believed that you could somehow engage in this social change, do-gooderness, with a job like that," he says. "And one of the huge things that I learned was that, at least at that time, you were as much a part of the problem as anything else. It was a very disillusioning experience." He turned to teaching, first at an elementary school in the Chicago suburbs, then at a high school in the Virgin Islands, of all places, fulfilling a dream to be closer to the natural world (he was a closet butterfly collector as

a kid—"That was the kind of thing that could get you branded for life in my neighborhood"). "One of the things that made me love teaching was that I finally did find, within the system, some kind of a job that I felt you could do with a minimum of compromises and that did have a benevolent effect on people's lives. Two of the happiest years of my life were living in the Caribbean, between being able to teach these absolutely wonderful local kids and at the same time becoming absolutely obsessed with the ocean."

Teaching would be his mission. He agreed with the philosopher John Dewey, who had deemed education to be the great democratizing force. "My goal was to reach a point where I could either do something in curriculum, or maybe even have my own school someday." But writing was now equally compelling to him, and he hoped he could do both by enrolling in the Ph.D. program at the University of Iowa, where he would be allowed to submit a creative dissertation. "I had never met a real writer at that point, and it was only after I got there, in the company of people like Richard Yates, Cheever, Don Justice, that I began to realize the enormous commitment writing really demanded." He surrendered completely to his writing, taking poetry and fiction workshops simultaneously.

His classmates—among them Tracy Kidder, T. Coraghessan Boyle, Denis Johnson, Larry Levis, Laura Jensen, Thom Jones, and Michael Ryan—challenged and inspired Dybek, but he also grew weary of the place on occasion. Dybek recalls: "I was walking across a parking lot in the rain, talking to Jon Jackson, and saying to him, 'I don't think I could stand reading another goddamn worksheet this semester'"—worksheets were how student work was distributed in those days, on mimeographs—"and suddenly, a wet piece of paper was stuck to my foot, and I pulled it off, and I said, 'Look, it's a goddamn worksheet! You can't even walk without them sticking to you.' And I looked at it, and I started reading it, and they were these fantastic poems. They were by Tom Lux. So it was that kind of place, where you'd be walking across the parking lot in the rain, and suddenly you'd be reading this wonderful stuff."

After receiving his M.F.A. in 1973, Dybek spent one year in the Florida Keys, then landed in Kalamazoo. He published a collection of poems, *Brass Knuckles* (University of Pittsburgh Press), in 1979, a collection of interrelated stories, ***Childhood and Other Neighborhoods*** (Viking), in 1980, and another story collection, ***The Coast of Chicago*** (Knopf), in 1990. Along the way, he has won a Whiting Writers' Award, a Guggenheim, an NEA fellowship, a Nelson Algren Award, numerous O. Henry Awards and *Best American Short Stories* selections, a lifetime achievement award from the American Academy of Arts and Letters, and a PEN/Malamud Award.

Dybek is one of the progenitors of the short-short as a form, and in ***The Coast of Chicago,*** he interleaves seven short-shorts with seven longer stories, binding them so tightly in place and theme, the book deservedly earns comparisons to Anderson's *Winesburg, Ohio,* and Joyce's *Dubliners.* In those stories, he shifts seamlessly from gritty naturalism to magic realism, transforming the tangible into the mythic. It's a metafictional technique, melding memory with imagination, that came to him listening to Eastern European music many years ago. Before then, he hadn't found a narrative voice that had suited him. He'd been trying to crank out conventional short stories with generic American characters, but they didn't feel right. Then he happened to read about the Hungarian composers Bartók and Kodály, who had toured the Hungarian countryside, seeking Gypsy music to incorporate into their own compositions. Dybek hunted down a Kodály record, and from the moment the needle hit vinyl, images of his family and his own Eastern European neighborhood appeared before him. He began reading Kafka and Isaac Babel, and started a story, **"The Palatski Man,"** that ended up being his first publication, in *The Magazine of Fantasy and Science Fiction* (sixteen literary journals had rejected it).

Stylistically, he has become renown for his lyricism, which often borders on incantation, as evidenced in a passage from a recent story, the prize-winning **"We Didn't."** He takes a banal situation—a Chicago teen in the throes of hormonal delirium who cannot sway his girlfriend to sleep with him—and gives it majesty:

> Along the Gold Coast, high-rises began to glow, window added to window, against the dark. In every lighted bedroom, couples home from work were stripping off their business suits, falling to the bed, and doing it. They did it before mirrors and pressed against the glass in streaming shower stalls, they did it against walls and on the furniture in ways that required previously unimagined gymnastics which they invented on the spot. They did it in honor of man and woman, in honor of beast, in honor of God. They did it because they'd been released, because they were home free, alive, and private, because they couldn't wait any longer, couldn't wait for the appointed hour, for the right time or temperature, couldn't wait for the future, for messiahs, for peace on earth and justice for all. They did it because of the Bomb, because of pollution, because of the Four Horsemen of the Apocalypse, because extinction might be just a blink away. They did it because it was Friday night. It was Friday night and somewhere delirious music was playing—flutter-tongued flutes, muted trumpets meowing like tomcats in heat, feverish plucking and twanging, tom-toms, congas, and gongs all pounding the same pulsebeat.

Of late, Dybek's inclination to mimic the emotion of music with prose has become more explicit. "When I first started writing," he says, "I thought it would be about *saying* something. I don't think that now. I think of writing as *making* something. What's come to fascinate me more and more is trying to use language the way that the mediums of other arts—music in particular—are used, so that they lead you to nonverbal places. I don't know if it's a paradox or just foggy thinking to believe language can do the same thing, that language can in some way or another lead you to something unsayable."

His process is still to scribble in notebooks, filling pages with verse. Whether the verse eventually yields a poem or novella is somewhat unimportant, although he would like to work in longer forms more: "Genre is sometimes treated like a religion. But for me it's primarily a tool. Working in different genres, the material gets transformed in different ways." But he is careful not to rush the transformation, and faces his publisher's and his readers' demands for a new book with equanimity.

In Kalamazoo, he tends to the mail and more prosaic business in the morning, writes in the afternoon, and teaches at night, a job he continues to think of as an enormous privilege. He returns to Chicago often, visiting friends and family. He claims he doesn't need to go back to his hometown for material anymore. He has enough memories of the old neighborhood to carry him through several more books. He will, he promises, release a collection of stories and a novella soon. "I'm getting close," he insists. "That's all I can say."

FURTHER READING

Criticism

Coates, Joseph. "A Storied Renaissance." *Chicago Tribune Books.* (8 April 1990): 1-4.
    Review of *The Coast of Chicago.*

Grosch, Anthony R. "Book Reviews." *The Old Northwest* 6, no. 4 (winter 1980): 400-03.
    Review of *The Coast of Chicago.*

Nemanic, Gerald. "Chicago Writers Follow Tradition But Break New Trails." *Chicago Tribune Book World.* (6 January 1985): 21-2.
    Discusses the "new generation" of Chicago authors.

Additional coverage of Dybek's life and career is contained in the following sources published by the Gale Group: *Contemporary Authors,* **Vols. 97-100;** *Contemporary Authors New Revision Series,* **Vol. 39;** *Contemporary Literary Criticism,* **Vol. 114;** *Dictionary of Literary Biography,* **Vol. 130; and** *Literature Resource Center.*

Robert Heinlein
1907-1988

(Full name Robert Anson Heinlein; wrote under the pseudonyms Anson MacDonald, Lyle Monroe, John Riverside, Caleb Saunder, and Simea York) American short story writer, novelist, screenwriter, essayist, and children's author

INTRODUCTION

Heinlein is regarded as one of the most influential science fiction writers of the twentieth century. A prolific author, his short stories are characterized by their highly developed and believable futuristic worlds, replete with scientific and technological advances and attention to detail. He is often ranked with Isaac Asimov and Arthur C. Clarke as a master of the science fiction genre, yet his work has inspired a mixed critical reaction.

BIOGRAPHICAL INFORMATION

Heinlein was born on July 7, 1907, in Butler, Missouri. He graduated from the U.S. Naval Academy in 1929, and did graduate study in physics and mathematics at the University of California in Los Angeles. After leaving school, he worked as an architect, real estate agent, aeronautical engineer, and electronics company official. During World War II, he served as an aviation engineer with the U.S. Navy. He wrote several engineering textbooks during those years. In 1939 Heinlein wrote his first story, "Life-Line," which was published in *Astounding Science Fiction* in August 1939. From that time, his stories and novels were published in several periodicals, such as *Astounding Science Fiction, Galaxy Science Fiction, Saturday Evening Post, Argosy,* and *Magazine of Fantasy and Science Fiction.* He authored more than forty-five books, most of which have been published in at least thirty languages. He was the first science fiction writer to appear on a bestseller list. During his long career, he was awarded four Hugo awards, four Best Science Fiction Novel awards from the World Science Fiction Convention, and the first Grand Master Nebula Award, given to Heinlein in 1975 by the Science Fiction Writers of America for his lifelong contribution to the genre. He died of heart failure on May 8, 1988, in Carmel, California.

MAJOR WORKS OF SHORT FICTION.

Heinlein's fiction is characterized by his reliance on a dominant, independent hero and the conflict between individualism and collectivism. In his stories, he emphasized themes of self-reliance, patriotism, and individualism,

which often led to criticism of his work as extremely conservative in nature. For example, "Gulf" features a protagonist who is recruited into a secret elite force—a master race—who plans to conquer the Earth through assassination. At first shocked, he soon adopts the group's disdain for democracy and collectivism. Heinlein's best-known collection of short fiction, *The Past Through Tomorrow* (1967), contains previously published stories and a detailed background chart—known as Future History—that provides the chronology of the major events in the stories, the lifelines of the major characters, and technological, sociological, and political developments. In one of the stories in the collection, "Requiem" (1939), an elderly industrialist, D. D. Harriman, finances and directs the first trip to the moon on a manned rocket. He stands by, frustrated, as others travel to the moon and establish a base. Finally, he makes the journey, knowing it will probably kill him. He dies shortly after his arrival, a happy man.

CRITICAL RECEPTION

There has been a polarized critical reaction to Heinlein's career. Many commentators have deemed his fiction as extremely conservative, even fascist; moreover, the perception of him as a Social Darwinist and right-wing author has negatively prejudiced the overall consensus on his work. Defenders of Heinlein's short stories and novels reject this classification of him, asserting that his stories and novels exhibit racial and social tolerance. They contend that he should be categorized as libertarian and iconoclastic. The conflict between individualism and collectivism is considered the dominant theme in Heinlein's work. Critical commentary has also focused on the sexuality in his stories, the role of technology, and his portrayal of alien civilizations. His later work is denigrated by some reviewers as didactic, stylistically monotonous, and solipsist. Yet he has been praised for his attention to detail, and his rendering of imaginative scientific and technological advances and their impact on human civilization. No matter the opinion on Heinlein's work itself, critics do not deny the profound impact his short stories and novels had on the genre of science fiction. In fact, some commentators have compared his influence on the science fiction genre to that of H. G. Wells.

PRINCIPAL WORKS

Short Fiction

The Man Who Sold the Moon 1950
Waldo and Magic, Inc. 1950
The Green Hills of Earth 1951
Universe 1951
Assignment in Eternity 1953
The Menace from Earth 1959
The Unpleasant Profession of Jonathan Hoag 1959
The Past through Tomorrow: Future History Stories 1966
The Worlds of Robert A. Heinlein 1966
The Best of Robert Heinlein: 1939-1959. 2 vols. 1973
Destination Moon 1979
Expanded Universe: More Worlds of Robert A. Heinlein 1980
Requiem: New Collected Works by Robert A. Heinlein and Tributes to the Grand Master (edited by Yoji Kondo) 1992

Other Major Works

Rocket Ship Galileo (juvenilia) 1947
*Beyond This Horizon (novel) 1948
Space Cadet (juvenilia) 1948
Red Planet (juvenilia) 1949
*Sixth Column (novel) 1949
Farmer in the Sky (juvenilia) 1950
Between Planets (juvenilia) 1951
The Puppet Masters (novel) 1951
The Rolling Stones (juvenilia) 1952

Revolt in 2100 (novel) 1953
Starman Jones (juvenilia) 1953
Star Beast (juvenilia) 1954
Tunnel in the Sky (juvenilia) 1955
Double Star (novel) 1956
Time for the Stars (juvenilia) 1956
Citizen of the Galaxy (juvenilia) 1957
The Door into Summer (novel) 1957
Have Space Suit—Will Travel (juvenilia) 1958
*Methuselah's Children (novel) 1958
Starship Troopers (juvenilia) 1959
Stranger in a Strange Land (novel) 1961
Glory Road (novel) 1963
Podkayne of Mars: Her Life and Times (juvenilia) 1963
Farnham's Freehold (novel) 1964
The Moon Is a Harsh Mistress (novel) 1966
Time Enough for Love: The Lives of Lazarus Long (novel) 1970
I Will Fear No Evil (novel) 1971
The Number of the Beast (novel) 1980
Friday (novel) 1982
Job: A Comedy of Justice (novel) 1984
The Cat Who Walks through Walls: A Comedy of Manners (novel) 1985
To Sail beyond the Sunset: The Life and Loves of Maureen Johnson, Being the Memoirs of a Somewhat Irregular Lady (novel) 1987
Grumbles from the Grave (correspondence) 1989
Take You're your Government: A Practical Handbook for the Private Citizen Who Wants Democracy to Work (essays) 1992
Tramp Royale (autobiographical fiction) 1992

*These works are sometimes referred to as novellas.

CRITICISM

George Edgar Slusser (essay date 1977)

SOURCE: Slusser, George Edgar. *The Classic Years of Robert A. Heinlein,* pp. 9-39. San Bernardino, Calif.: Borgo Press, 1977.

[*In the following excerpt, Slusser surveys the plots and major thematic concerns of Heinlein's short fiction.*]

STORIES

Heinlein's short stories belong, essentially, to his early years. From his first published tale, **"Life-Line"** (August 1939) through 1942, when the war briefly interrupted his writing career, Heinlein worked exclusively in shorter forms, and the medium-length serialized narratives which, in their episodic quality, bear more affinity with the story than the novel. The majority of these early tales appeared in Campbell's *Astounding Science Fiction*; some were written under pseudonyms (the most famous of which is Anson MacDonald). Among this handful of works is some of the most interesting fiction Heinlein has done. In the years immediately after the war (1947-1949), he resumed writing stories—here, however, is a different kind of tale, for a different audience. Where the earlier sketches were often genuinely allegorical—parables in which a complex world view is acted out rather than simply exposed—these are more didactic. More than a change in Heinlein, perhaps, we have a change in audience—the stories were written for the slicks (especially *Saturday Evening Post*) rather than the more specialized pulps. A new tone of sentimentality appears. And in almost all of these tales there are concessions to "human interest." From 1950 on, the short stories diminish. With the exception of a couple of juveniles for *Boy's Life,* Heinlein returns to the SF magazines.

No matter what their intended audience, all these stories share one structural characteristic—they are loosely episodic. This openness fits Heinlein's purpose admirably. Only in the most external sense does a Heinlein story focus on a crucial moment in the life of a character. His protagonists do not, through some process of self-discovery, come to a climactic recognition of identity or place in the world order. Nor are there "surprise endings" in the classic sense, where an ironic twist of fate reveals a man's character to himself. On the contrary, the heroes of Heinlein's tales seem to know from the start what they must do: they face their destiny, accepting it with a singular lack of resistance or self-searching. But there is more here than "doing one's duty": the hero seems chosen, compelled by some inner predilection that goes against all reason or common sense. What the narrative invariably examines, as step by step it becomes visible, is the mechanism of election itself. This can take myriad forms—the more involuted the better—but there is always the same underlying pattern. If the story ends with a surprise, it is the wonder of destiny, always fortunate in some higher sense, if not for its immediate agent. Indeed, the final emphasis is not on the disparity between individual aspirations and the whole, but on their harmony. In amazing ways, the two strands unite, the expendable acts of one being spill over into the larger ongoing process of racial destiny, apparently advancing according to a predetermined plan toward some glorious end. Only in the later Heinlein will that end itself become problematical.

The readers of *Astounding* must have been astounded by Heinlein's first story **"Life-Line."** Here is a work directly antipodal to the adventure story and its well-hewn plot. Indeed, the center of this sequence of episodes is less a character than a problem. Pinero is more than a model of how we should act. The man and his machine embody a much more general pattern, not of conduct, but of universal law. Instead of enacting destiny, they literally incarnate it. This tale, then, is clearly allegorical. As such it stands, at the outset of his career, as a microcosm of Heinlein's world.

"Life-Line" begins in the middle of a public debate: Dr. Hugo Pinero is defending his discovery—a machine that predicts the length of each individual life span, furnishing exact dates of death—against the disbelief of the scientific establishment. Such an encounter is a Heinlein prototype, and will be repeated again and again throughout his work. Pinero is the unlikely superior being—short, pot-bellied, with dubious academic credentials. His opponent fits the orthodox mold ("America's Handsomest University President"), but is a colossal non-entity. And Pinero challenges not only the conventions, but also deep-seated economic interests: the machine is an obvious threat to the insurance industry.

The story proceeds step-by-step. The first scene exposes the problem, and sets apart the protagonist and antagonists, who will act out its solution in the flesh. Our sympathies are captured by Pinero's rhetoric, as he reverses the accepted views of heroism, and turns the tables on the power structure. In the second scene, Pinero gives technical explanations, and follows these with practical applications: he predicts the impending death of a reporter. The pivot point of **"Life-Line"** is Pinero's newspaper ad: the scientist crosses lines, setting himself up in business as a "bioconsultant." In doing so, he declares war, and seals his own fate. There is a courtroom scene (another Heinlein staple): forensics replace rhetoric, as Pinero outmaneuvers both his scientific detractors and the hostile business interests which manipulate them. Later, Pinero predicts the immediate death of an innocent young couple, and tries in vain to forestall destiny. The machine is bigger than the man. Finally, there is the scene in which Pinero meets his own destiny—the insurance trust has him bumped off—and its coda: the scientists open the box containing the doctor's predictions of their deaths, together with his own. They verify the correctness of his self forecast, then destroy their own predictions (unopened) by fire.

If **"Life-Line"** is an allegory, what does it signify? The theory behind Pinero's machine is simple: a human life span, like that of the race as a whole, is a material entity. Each of the "pink worms" that form this "vine" can be measured exactly. More importantly, they may be measured before they end. In this purely physical sense, each individual life is pre-determined. The machine gives man foreknowledge. For the majority, however, this knowledge is intolerable: life is livable only in uncertainty. And yet, Pinero proves that struggle and a clear vision of one's fate are not incompatible. In contrast to the others, he sees the moment of his death and its cause—the defense of his own machine—and still pushes on, meeting his end with calm dignity. What else can he do? Man can know his destiny, but not alter it, as Pinero learns when he tries to save the young couple.

Pinero's machine can be called an instrument of grace only in the most limited sense: it allows each man to know if he is chosen to live. In terms of the machine, of course, everyone dies, so none achieve "salvation" in any form. Heinlein refuses to leap beyond matter—indeed, in later works he explores, obsessively at times, the possibilities of metempsychosis and physical rejuvenation in hopes of extending the ego's existence this side of death. The action in **"Life-Line"** seems framed by biological determinism. There is the organic analogy of the vine of existence. And it is implied in Pinero's defense of his experimental method that the most viable forms of life are those that best understand the workings of the natural process. Yet within this materialist framework, oddly enough, the Calvinist pattern of election abides. If survival of the fittest is the rule, it is strangely qualified by the presence of the machine. Held up to its baleful light, the idea of fitness itself takes on passive, even paradoxical overtones. Pinero does not survive, yet is fittest because he alone accepts not to survive. The Protestant thrust of this parable is unmistakable. If Pinero is a new Galileo, the fact he must face is not external but internal—his own destiny. Fitness is measured less in terms of public actions—defense and counterattack—than private ones. The hero stands apart because he is the only one who accepts the consequences of his acts, who realizes he can neither play god to others nor escape his own predestined end.

Pinero is the prototype for Heinlein's elite man: all are marked by what might called a creative capacity to accept the inevitable. But where does this superiority come from? It is nothing the hero develops—this would imply that any man could do it—but rather something he already has. Indeed, its existence is clearly placed on a level outside commonality. It is not a biological trait in the ordinary sense, for Pinero possesses neither physical beauty nor strength. Nor, apparently, does he have the craft or cunning necessary for blind survival at all costs—if anyone has these, it is his opponents. Pinero puts his great intelligence to a much different end—martyrdom. But it would be wrong to give this a tragic sense either, to see it as protest against a world without transcendence.

Pinero does not elect to die; rather, he is elected. This capacity to accept fate is given to him, not to the others. And this predisposition is awakened by another gift—the idea of the machine. **"Life-Line"** is not the story of a man conquering his idea. From the first line, he already possesses it—the world is already divided into elect and non-elect. What follows merely confirms this division, and celebrates the wondrous ways of destiny among men. Heinlein may at times imply that biological law sanctions his elite. If we look more closely, however, we see that in Pinero's case such law is suspended. In **"Life-Line,"** there are two states: nature, and a secular form of grace. In the first, "wisdom" is ignorance and darkness; the way of nature is irremediably perverted. Only Pinero is lifted above this: he receives his illumination, and goes to meet his end with the serenity of the elect. His martyrdom is part, not of nature, but of some higher evolution. The fallen state is merely sifted, the chaff abandoned. The destiny of man is that of the chosen few.

The interplanetary job corps in **"Misfit"** (1939) serves the same function as Pinero's machine—it places all men on an equal footing, so that the new elite may emerge. Young Andy Libby, the protagonist, goes to space with a group of "misfits." Earth is overcrowded, jobs are scarce, ways set; these lads have rebelled against such stifling conditions. A far-seeing policy gives them a fresh start, in hopes that some truly superior being may emerge. He does. Again, from outward appearances alone, Libby would be the least likely choice: he is an awkward, gangling lad from the Ozarks. In Heinlein's parables, our standards constantly fail to discern the elite. Yet, despite appearances, Libby is an intuitive mathematical genius. Answers pour from him compulsively and inexplicably: "Why, naturally the horizon has to be just that far away." There is no rational explanation for his talents: they were given him, and providence allows them to unfold. Libby's destiny fits neatly into the larger one of man's expansion into space. In this tale, he performs the minor task of moving an asteroid—man is rearranging the heavens. He will go on (as we learn in *Methuselah's Children*) to invent the space drive that will open up the boundless universe. If things are predestined, they also seem open-ended: already we see a phobia of the end that will haunt Heinlein increasingly in later years.

In this tale, there is the same division between elect and non-elect; it is less radical, however. The common mortals do not see Libby's uniqueness. The more visionary Captain (unlike other established hierarchies in Heinlein, vision usually corresponds exactly with rank in the military) senses it, and explores further. What he discovers has the force of revelation: the hero's full name is Andrew Jackson Libby. All the paradox of freedom in Heinlein lies within this situation. Somewhere in Libby's background is the democratic spirit of individual liberty: in true Jacksonian manner, his parents refused to sign the "covenant." What takes shape in the foreground is an even more select covenant. The link is the name itself. By some strange process of alternate heredity, the spirit of one great man passes into the body of another. In Heinlein, names like Andrew Jackson Libby (or Johann Sebastian Bach Smith) are microcosms of election—the everyman's last name is a mask covering the true lineage of genius. Libby comes into his world trailing clouds of glory, and merely acts out his predestined role. The story has become a ritual more than anything else. The opening scene confirms this: a group of men are being called; at the name "Libby," the hero steps forth and his destiny unfolds.

"Requiem" (1940) is a similar kind of tale. It deals, however, not with a beginning but an end—the culminating moment in the life of the moon entrepreneur Delos D. Harriman, the visionary who first initiated space travel. Ironically, Harriman has never been able to take a trip himself to the Moon. First business interests, and then old age stand in his way. There is a hiatus here: Harriman's destiny is not complete. This story recounts the marvellous working of things that finally allows the gap to be breached, and providence fulfilled.

In **"Misfit,"** a social edict freed men to follow their destinies, to be called or not. But **"Requiem"** is a story of obstacles. In a series of episodic flashbacks, these are arrayed against the hero's Moon-dream. Father, wife and business partner are unable to believe in him. Now his family has gone to court to have him declared legally incompetent (a favorite Heinlein theme—the old man beset by family vultures—is born). Still, a fortunate paradox prevails, for Harriman constantly loses only to win. The path of destiny is beset with surprises. As a young man, Harriman had been denied, through a reversal of family fortunes, the chance to go to college and become an astronomer. But he will do much better in the end: instead of just looking at planets, he will actually die on one. In the same way, his father had scoffed at his childish desire to touch the Moon—but he will do just that. Now Harriman faces two seemingly insurmountable barriers: ill health and the law. His heart will not stand the trip, and the judge rules against him in favor of his family. A "chance" meeting with two renegade space pilots in an unlikely small-town carnival carries things forward in a manner quite unforeseen. Harriman is denied access to the circus rocket ride because of his heart, only to find men who will take him to the real Moon. The two pilots are also "misfits"—men who chafe under rules and regulations, who seek freedom in space. They take Harriman to certain death. And yet, ironically, their hardness is more merciful than the "concern" of family and friends—itself no more than a mask that hides selfish interests and lack of vision. These men know Harriman (in spite of his social status and physical condition) for one of their own. At the heart of the wider world, a secret group is formed, and pursues its plans in obedience to some higher law.

Even more obviously than **"Misfit," "Requiem"** is pure ritual of election. Harriman has already conquered space—Heinlein, in fact, will chronicle his struggles in a sequel. Why must he go to the Moon himself? The only answer is that Harriman has not yet experienced grace. His destiny will accept no compromise or compensation—he *must* go. Indeed, the final scene has distinct religious overtones. In wondrous ways, the pains of sickness and space flight cancel each other out. Because he is feeble, accelerational gravity and free fall (proverbially unpleasant to the novice in space) become blissfully dreamlike. Near weightlessness on the Moon makes even death (the most common horror) a thing most fortunate and rare: "He was serenely happy in a fashion not give to most men, even in a long life time. He felt as if he were every man who had ever lived, looked up at the stars, and longed." Harriman is crowned king of this elite. If he (like the speaker in Stevenson's **"Requiem"** that prefaces this story) also lays him down "with a will," that will has been guided by the predestined plan that fulfills itself here: "He was where he had longed to be—he had followed his need."

"'And He Built a Crooked House'" (1941) and **"They"** (1941) belong together in spite of their different subject matter. Both inscribe a pattern that will become fundamental in Heinlein's fiction—a curious polar undulation between center and circumference. It is this rhythm which gradually controls the primal relationship between elected individual and total destiny, linking them together in a

closed dynamic system. **"And He Built"** is the story of architect Quintus Teal, the man with a strange name who builds a stranger house. The tale itself has an odd form: it shrinks to a point, only to expand in vertiginous fashion from it. Things begin narrowing from the very first line: "Americans are considered crazy anywhere in the world." California, however, is their "focus of infection"; its focus is Los Angeles, the center of which is Hollywood, and so on until we come to rest on Teal and his tesseract house. Built for Homer Bailey and wife, the house is a hypercube unfolded into our habitual three dimensions. During an earthquake, it collapses upon itself, into four dimensions. Architect and clients enter this structure, and find themselves trapped at its "center," what Bailey in his three-dimensional logic sees as "the little cube in your diagram that was in the middle of the big cube." Outward from this point new dimensional vistas reach in all directions. They open one window, and look into "inverted" space; open another, and see New York from above.

Once again, a situation serves to separate the elect from those who are not. Bailey's wife is one of those hopelessly frivolous Heinlein females; and he himself is only slightly more able to cope with this strange new world. For both, the tesseract is a maze. Teal designed the house, and understands it mathematically. Nevertheless, he gets out of it not by reason but by instinct. He is different only because he sees the relationship between the two dimensions. The point of contact, the new center, is the mind itself: "'I watched where I was going and arrived where I intended to.' He stepped back into the lounge. 'The time before I didn't watch and I moved on through normal space and fell out of the house. It must have been a matter of subconscious orientation.'" As with Pinero, it is not the discovery of the machine—the tesseract house in this case—but the ability to face the implications of its working that marks the man. This slightly foolish inventor builds as if he were the instrument of destiny. Even his discovery of the link between dimensions is given to him—he falls out of the house. And what of this faculty of "orientation?" Heinlein gives things a playful twist in the end. A second tremor causes the house to vanish completely. Just before this event, the three had been contemplating the last, and most alien, landscape—a world of yellow sky and tortured shrubs. Without thinking, they leap out the window—and land in Joshua Tree National Monument! In this case, the "subconscious orientation" is most fortunate: vastness and strangeness contract to the familiar California starting point. How do we explain the Baileys' possession of this faculty? Heinlein wryly remarks that all Californians have this reflex. Unique in their madness, this is their saving grace.

In the much different world of **"They,"** there is this same fundamental interplay of center and circumference. **"They"** is the story of a monstrous case of paranoia turning out to be real—"they" *are* all against him. One of Heinlein's most patently philosophical tales, **"They"** is nonetheless a chronicle of election in the familiar mode. Once again, the hero is distinguished less by his actions than by a certain disposition to vision. In a perfectly ordinary and comfort-able world, he begins to feel alienated. Other people seem ignorant and selfish; he cannot reach out to them, and feels hemmed in by a social wall. One day, by "chance," he pierces a hole through it. He is about to leave the house one rainy afternoon with his wife. He forgets something upstairs, goes back, and opens a window shade—the sun is shining! Like Quintus Teal, he looks out on another di-mension. But in this case, clearly, seeing it is not enough: he must discover its relationship to his familiar world. The maze that confronts this hero is epistemological; he is forced back upon his own being as the only possible start-ing point. This *reductio,* however, is neither Cartesian nor Berkeleyan. He exists not because he thinks, but because he physically *is*: his five senses are the first line of con-sciousness, the sole justification for belief in self. On the evidence of these same senses, he cannot dismiss the world "out there" as illusory. He kicks the stone: things really do have physical existence. He rejects both chaos and illu-sion, isolation and solipsism. The explanation of the world he gives has a strange *a priori* basis, and resembles noth-ing more than faith. The world simply *cannot* be as crazy as it seems; men *cannot* be *that* indifferent and egotistical. Therefore, if the senses are reliable, someone must have made things the way they are. Instead of absurdity, we have the big lie, an adversary: some "puppet master" has robbed these others of their free will. This particular man (who remains fittingly nameless) is given the possibility and disposition to see reality: he is chosen to resist.

In the process of resistance, he displays what is unique in mankind: the dynamic rhythm of an existence that is, in all places and moments, individual and total. Significantly, the hero of **"They"** never makes contact with another hu-man being. But he is not isolated. The void behind the window shade is offset by a second glimpse at the totality of things, this time in a dream: "Gladness! Gladness ev-erywhere! It was . . . good to know that everything was living and aware of him, participating in him, as he par-ticipated in them. It was good to be, good to know the unity of many and diversity of one." In this epiphanic mo-ment, the individual makes direct contact with a new cir-cumferential whole. The result is the dynamic undulation of the many and the one. What these "aliens" do not real-ize is that the point is as indispensable to this balanced rhythm as the circumference. They are a collective organ-ism that seeks to absorb the individual, to "dismantle" the system. At one point in his reasoning, the hero contem-plates suicide as a means of escape from his condition, and then rejects it: to destroy the body is to destroy his sole contact with the external world. His vision of unity is the product neither of reason nor will: it issues again from a "subconscious orientation"—some deeper place where mind is firmly rooted in matter. Nor can the enemy, it seems, tamper with this individuality, or alter it against a man's desire. Some higher law—a "Treaty"—has appar-ently declared it inviolate. All these aliens can do is study this particular "specimen" as he goes through what seems a series of cyclic incarnations. And they are getting no-where, are even losing ground: the "creature" who filled

the role of his wife has become "assimilated": she asks fa-vors for him the next time around. One is reminded of Heinlein's later Martians, and his other "superior" races: while they sit and ponder man, man's vital existence is busy generating the energy that promises to destroy them.

Heinlein develops a similar pattern in the time travel story, **"By His Bootstraps"** (1941), but from an opposite angle. Here, rather than election, we have a ritual of damnation. The hero is not merely cast off; he is damned to act out his damnation over and over, without surcease or hope. What occurs is a travesty of election, in which self-awareness is a closed circle, breakthrough to totality a de-lusion of the ego. The maze in which this hero wanders is that of his own existence. Bob Wilson is writing a thesis on mathematical metaphysics. As he begins to discuss "time travel," a man steps into his room through a "time gate," and tries to persuade him to go back through it with him. A third man appears and seeks to prevent it. A fight ensues, and Wilson is knocked through the gate. Here he meets a middle-aged man who shows him the marvelous Arcadian kingdom he has inherited. He offers to let Bob share its rule if Wilson will help him: he is to go back through the time gate and fetch another man . . . It turns out all four are different temporal manifestations of Bob himself—they chase each other endlessly.

The "time gate" seems to be another of these windows into a new dimension. And the world it reveals is appar-ently as unfallen as that the hero envisions in **"They."** A second look, however, shows it to be insubstantial, a shadow kingdom filled with childlike subjects and beauti-ful maidens. Why does Wilson send his double back to fetch books like *Mein Kampf* and *The Prince*? The whole thing is a power fantasy, a creation of the hero's frustrated ego. Indeed, the sole reality here is the circular world peopled by these time-spectres—empty, without beginning or end. If there is a dynamic here, it is not creative polar-ity, but a cycle of material futility: "You feed the rats to the cats, skin the cats, and feed the carcasses of the cats to the rats who are in turn fed to the cats. the perpetual mo-tion fur farm." The form of the story is circular in manner: it begins with the "youngest" Wilson sitting at his desk, and ends as his "oldest" double sends another back to in-terrupt this same "youngest" Wilson still sitting at his desk. Throughout the story, the same event is told over and over, each time from the perspective of a different Wilson. The time puzzle is carefully reconstructed, only to be scattered once again as things begin anew. In his thesis, Bob writes: "Duration is an attribute of consciousness, not of the plenum." Wilson's adventures merely act out this solipsistic maxim. Unlike Libby or Delos Harriman, he never reaches beyond self to intersect with some broader order in time and space, never fulfills a destiny. This time the point quite literally absorbs the circumference.

If **"By His Bootstraps"** is a drama of fate, it is one with peculiarly Calvinist overtones. These time-frames interlock in the most terrible manner to trap their victim; but they are largely mind-formed. Fallen man struggles only to damn himself all the more. Wilson mistakes the gate for a mark of election: actually, he has elected himself. He chafes at the prospect of a narrow life, yearning to escape. the result is his fateful thesis, and the appearance of the gate—projections of his desire. Wilson is not called; on the contrary, what is re-enacted here is the primal sin of intellectual pride. Ironically, once he is caught in the revolving door of time, he grows increasingly vain. Escape is no longer enough. As he works out the intricate relations between the various time segments, he begins to think he sees the ways of destiny, and can outwit it. In spite of all his efforts, man will never escape his fate. But here, there is elation: Bob predicts "a great future." He is and remains a dupe. Neither in the beginning nor in the end does he receive illumination or grace. No matter how hard he tries to reshape his fallen world, he fails. His petty vision at the start predisposes him to "fall" through the gate; the further on he goes, the easier it becomes. This allegory is unique in Heinlein, for it is one of the rare times he traces the destiny of one not chosen. And yet, though the meaning of Bob's adventures is quite clear, Heinlein apparently will forget it in later works. More and more men will come to elect themselves, will turn in paths of their own making that are equally circular and solipsistic. This tale could stand as necessary corrective for a monstrosity like *I Will Fear No Evil*.

"We Also Walk Dogs" (1941) is an interesting tale; here, for the first time, Heinlein focuses openly and unabashedly on a "super group." "General Services" is an elite society within society. It can accomplish things—and thus act as prime mover in terms of human destiny—because it ignores the laws and customs of weaker mortals. Such an organization is usually the stuff of longer narrative in Heinlein. This version is a short story only by virtue of its limited focus. It is not a climactic moment in the lives of the principals, just business as usual. Nonetheless, the task they are asked to perform is a sizeable one: they must arrange an interplanetary conference on Earth. The problem is gravity. To make each ambassador feel at home, a series of localized gravitational fields is needed. Constructing these fields involves no less than a revolution in physical theory. General Services gets its theory from a recalcitrant scientist. The price—a rare Ming vase located in the British Museum. They steal the vase (we never learn how, but no one seems to miss it); Dr. O'Neil adds it to his private collection without a qualm. They hand Beaumont, the Government Chief of Protocol, a diplomatical and political triumph. Beaumont is well on his way to becoming the first president of a new Solar System Federation. With this stroke, parochialism is struck dead; new visionaries will be needed to lead mankind toward its new destiny. **"We Also Walk Dogs"** chronicles a day in the life of a growing organism. Before our eyes, the inner circle widens its activities, and acquires a new center. A neophyte is chosen out of the many nameless components of General Services, and proves his worth—Carson becomes one of elect. By the same stroke, Beaumont emerges from the morass of government agencies. But if there is expansion, there is also contraction. The heads of the organization get permis-

sion to contemplate O'Neil's vase anytime they like. This point of light, which is the "flower of forgetfulness," becomes their mystical center: "He bent his head over it and stared down into it. . . . It seemed as if his sight sank deeper and even deeper into it, as if he were drowning in a pool of light." In their vital, creative relationship to the vase, we have both the microcosm and power source for the larger dynamic they have just brought into being. Their actions not only have pushed forward the boundaries of the human race, but also secured the center at the same time: Earth will be the focal point of any future planetary union.

"We Also Walk Dogs" provides a transition between the early tales and those written during the years immediately following Heinlein's wartime silence—especially 1947 and 1948. Like the early stories, it is partly an allegory of election, a demonstration of the processes of destiny. And it is partly an exemplary tale as well, one of an openly didactic nature. As it seeks to define the complex relationship between the individual and his universe, it also sets forth exemplary types. We are not only told who the elect are—we are told or taught to admire them. In the three stories published in *Saturday Evening Post* during the year 1947—**"The Green Hills of Earth," "Space Jockey,"** and **"'It's Great to be Back'"**—this emblematic quality grows stronger and stronger. Beneath a vague cloak of sentimentality and "human interest," the mark of election not only remains, but becomes all the more implacable and incontestable. These tables no longer offer even the promise of a philosophical problem. Rather, they celebrate a moral universe that is harshly black and white.

In its tone, **"The Green Hills of Earth"** seems an atypical story for Heinlein. It is, however, clearly an exemplum. The form is that of the ballad or folk tale. There is a series of loose episodes, the chronicle of a life organized around one central contrast: we have the official legend and accepted verse of Rhysling the blind space poet, and we have the story of the real man—unkempt and bawdy. To make this contrast is to uncover the fortunate paradox of the artist's life. This insignificant-seeming individual turns out to be a hero as well as a poet—in fact, he is a great poet only because he is a hero. Both his blindness and death—romanticized in the public version—are the results of an unflinching devotion to duty. The fruit of this grandeur and misery is his great poem, **"The Green Hills of Earth."** As great art unfolds from this unlikely man in unlikely circumstances, we watch the familiar process of election, and rejoice in the ways of destiny.

Once again, in this story there is a narrowing: inside the public shell we find a private core of truth. "Noisy" Rhysling was, in the beginning, just another space tramp—a black-listed engineer with a talent for scurrilous doggerel. He signs on an unsafe vessel, and is blinded while performing (without question or hesitation) an act that saves the ship. His appearance and frivolous words are deceptive. When the moment comes, he does the "right" thing instinctively. Rhysling takes up the life of a wandering minstrel. From blindness, a new vision emerges: the lack of sight mercifully cuts him off from the ugliness of the world about him. On a Mars that has suffered grave ecological damage, he falls back on memory, and in a stroke of fortunate irony, sings about the unspoiled planet of yore. In a sense, he has broken through in his art to a new dimension. Significantly, however, he does not remain here. This circumference shrinks to a new point of reality as the wayfarer makes his first and last voyage homeward. He ponders, in poetic terms, an inversion of things: beauty is no longer the airy towers of Mars but the cool hills of Earth. Improvisation is interrupted by an atomic explosion. Working literally by blind instinct, Rhysling dampens the radioactive material, but exposes himself fatally in the process.

This tale may be read as an allegory. The vast circumference of Rhysling's wanderings—he becomes a symbol of man's restless exploration in space—collapses to a point as he meets his destiny. In analogous manner, human expansion into space—which Rhysling's own acts have themselves furthered in a small but crucial way—suddenly contract in his poetry: we celebrate Earth, the point of return. But the home planet is also a point of departure: from the acts of this blind singer (poetic and heroic), new vision will radiate outward. In its over-insistent association of election with duty, the story becomes dogmatic. Some inner light (the only one he has) reveals to Rhysling the workings of a higher law. These invariably seem to coincide with military codes, blind obedience and sacrifice, which are always virtues, and always beyond the common indication. Indeed, death is not crowned by a public reputation—Rhysling's is swept away in the first paragraph—but by a private act and an immortal product. Again, and in terms of the creative process this time, center and circumference make direct contract; all else is elided.

"Space Jockey" is a more obvious exemplum—and a less successful story. A pilot on the Moon run finds his job interfering with family life. In mid-journey, he ponders the problem, and is on the verge of abandoning his *metier* when an accident recalls him to duty. Not only does he bring the ship through—skillfully and intuitively—but by this act he reaffirms his vocation. He finally writes his letter to his wife: he will remain a pilot and she must follow him. To his surprise, she accepts without hesitation—she was with him all along.

"'—It's Great to Be Back'" is a better tale by virtue of its extreme simplicity. A young couple living in Luna City decide they have had enough of the Moon's confined life—they yearn for the green hills of Earth. In an ironic twist, however, expansion turns out to be contraction. The Earth is cramped and dirty; even worse, the people are rude and stupidly narrow-minded. After a brief stay, the couple becomes tired of references to the Man-in-the-Moon and green cheese, and decides to go back. In a sudden flash of insight, they realize just how different—and elite—the "Loonies" are. To get to the Moon in the first place, it takes a high IQ, and a superior education and disposition.

Opening this colony has automatically separated wheat from chaff. The two are accepted back without so much as a test—they are "Moonstruck," and that is enough. Once again, the election process is some mysterious affinity—a stroke of secular grace.

In these latter two tales, the nostalgia of Rhysling's world view is reversed: the center shifts from Earth to Moon. In spite of the displacement, however, the same pattern of undulation abides. In **"Space Jockey,"** the pull of wife and Earthly comforts is broken—in a final symbolic act, she accepts the move to the Moon. Likewise, the stupidity of Judge Schram and his "Junior Rocketeer" son—their "influence" with the high and mighty—are of no avail in stemming this pull away from Earth. The Moon becomes the new center from which man will expand outward. The pilot's actions are vindicated (and Schram's protests brushed aside) by that silent and serene hierarchy who implement this manifest destiny. **"'—It's Great to Be Back'"** merely celebrates this shift, as do most of the other tales of the period.

"The Black Pits of Luna" (1948) is about a group of silly Earth tourists, and the ordeal of a lost boy on the Moon. We see here what will become Heinlein's stereotypes: the henpecked husband; the weak-willed, fuzzy-brained, hysterical wife (she insists on bloodhounds); the impossible brat. Once again, pressure from above forces the guides to take an underaged and ill-mannered boy on this trip against regulations. During the crisis, parents and other tourists are helpless and useless. Only the older brother (the narrator) keeps his head, and thus perseveres. It is his ingenuity that saves his brother *in extremis*. The moral is clear—the parents are told by the irate guide: "Stay off the Moon. You don't belong here; you're not the pioneer type." The narrator, however, feels a secret desire to return; the guide recognizes him as one of theirs. Again we have a tale of sifting and exclusion.

"Gentleman, Be Seated" (1948) makes the same point in a whimsical manner. An Earth journalist on vacation on the Moon begins probing into the ways of men on the satellite: he thinks there may be scandal or graft in connection with the building of airlocks. What he gets, as he pursues this reasoning, is a very physical lesson in how things work in this different and hazardous world. He is touring a lock in the company of Fatso Konski, "the best sandhog in four planets," when there is a blast and leak. There is only one way to plug it—Fatso plays Dutch Boy with his ample rear end. But he soon succumbs to the cold. The narrator must take his place, and does so without hesitation. All are rescued in the end. More important is the hero's position—the free-floating skeptic has found a most basic point of attachment for the Moon. Is he one of them after all? He sets aside the honor—if Konski wants to collect the chess money he won while waiting to be rescued, he will have to come to Des Moines. Yet, although (as Konski said) he may be "conventional," he has already shown "he has the stuff." This time it is a disbeliever who, in a quite unforeseen way, passes the test of adoption.

"Gentlemen" begins with a discussion of agoraphobia and claustrophobia—fear of the open and of confined places. In terms of the basic rhythm, these represent unbalanced fixations on the point or the circumference. Heinlein's elite, however, must embrace both poles, striking dynamic balance between them: "Make it agoraphiles and claustrophiles, for the men who go out in space had better not have phobias." **"Ordeal in Space"** (1948) is the story of a man with such a phobia, and how he conquers it. It is a simple tale, and perhaps one of Heinlein's best. During the heroic execution of ship repairs in deepest space, Bill Cole "looks down"—the terror of the void suddenly breaks his nerve, making him unfit for duty. He returns to Earth and a cloistered existence—he cannot look out into open places. A second, redeeming "ordeal in space" comes as the hero spends the night in a friend's high-rise apartment. He hears a cat meowing—it is stranded on the narrow ledge outside. He overcomes his fears, saves the cat, and regains his old calm before the vastness of space. Is this an effort of will? We learn, however, that Bill had an inexplicable affinity for cats—perhaps because they resemble spacemen in their fearlessness and capacity for adaptation. Like seeks out like. Indeed, he is drawn in spite of himself, as if called, to the window, and this foolish and fearful act that will (wondrously) save him. He seems predestined to be a spaceman. Here too, in this story, is the now familiar reversal of priorities. There is the public act of heroism—Bill has a reputation, but it is hollow and useless when the man inside has lost his nerve—and this private one. The cat is both insignificant and all-important. In this contact, the man is revealed to himself, the way prepared for continuation of the grand design. Once again, we have Heinlein's fundamental dynamic in operation. The huge canopy of space contracts to a cat. This is only to pave the way for new expansion: "Little fluffhead, how would you like to take a long, long ride with me?"

Heinlein has written few stories after 1949. These are for the most part after-thoughts, occasional works by a writer who has turned his attention almost wholly to the novel. They vary both in nature and in mood, and can be either harshly pessimistic or sentimental and optimistic. Clearly, the center no longer holds. The dynamics of balance that informed both the earlier allegories and the exempla is gone—in its place, we get apocalypse and apotheosis. Before there was preoccupation; now there is something more like obsession. As such, these scattered tales of the 1950s seem to announce the excesses of Heinlein's latest fictional ventures.

"Sky Lift" (1953) is a strange variation on the familiar theme of the call to duty. In an earlier tale, **"The Long Watch"** (1949), the young lieutenant hero gives his life to save Earth from a military putsch. He dismantles the stockpile of atom bombs on the Moon—and like Rhysling dies of radiation poisoning. Before, Heinlein might have left the act of heroism unsung—after all, during his "long watch," the man has discovered himself, found his true calling. But the private act is no longer supreme. Heinlein gives his hero a funeral procession worthy of Siegfried.

Public ritual replaces the inner illumination: the lead coffin must be flown to Earth with pomp and circumstances, so that the best of mankind will be inspired to carry on the fight. **"Sky Lift"** does not have even the compensatory ceremony. The tale may be a better one in its avoidance of patriotic cliches, but it still remains grim. A cargo of blood must be flown immediately to an outlying base on one of Pluto's moons. To get it there in time to save the diseased men, the trip must be made at intolerably high acceleration—can the crew withstand the sustained high gravity? The protagonist does not volunteer; he is chosen. Through some uncanny insight, the Captain sees in this unlikely hero a special predisposition—what is wanted here is not the traditional ability to act, but a passive talent to endure. He is reluctant—he has a well-deserved leave before him, and is brimming with youthful spirits—and yet he heeds the call. No matter how arbitrary this may seem, it is never questioned. He accomplishes his painful mission, and survives—but in a flash passes from vigor to senility. The focus here is not on the hundreds saved, but on this one wasted youth. In this elided life, Rip Van Winkle is reborn in space. Slowly, in scattered works of this period, a pattern emerges as counter current to the dynamic of formation—that process of growth to adulthood by trial and error which Heinlein adopted along with the convention of juvenile adventure, but with which he was never really at ease. Elision can be macabre, as in **"Sky Lift,"** or it can be a blessing. In a work like *Stranger in a Strange Land,* the young hero leaps in a flash over the responsibilities and anxieties of maturity to instant (and unearned) godhood.

"The Year of the Jackpot" (1952) is even more unusual for Heinlein, an apocalyptic vision. As a general rule in his early and middle work, Heinlein presents human destiny as a plan that is both unlimited and endlessly unfolding. In this tale, however, things are cut off by total and irrevocable destruction. Its beginning seems typical enough. In fact, throughout the story we expect something else—survival and rebirth—and we are surprised at the ending. The hero is a common Heinleinian figure: a statistician wanders around gathering data on a series of uncanny phenomena, and patiently plots his curves. Other men think he is crazy, but some fortunate inclination drives him on. He deduces from the study of his graphs and past cataclysmic cycles that this will be "the year of the jackpot"—a mighty convergence of disasters. The hero takes girl and survival gear, and leaves L. A.—just in time, for earthquake, tidal wave, and atomic blast strike successively, engulfing the city. The couple reach a mountain hideaway. In the later novel *Farnham's Freehold* (1964), such a point of survival proclaims itself the center from which a new world will be rebuilt. But not here: the sun explodes as well. A story like **"Jackpot"** may mark the beginning of a dystopian, constrictive current in Heinlein's work. Gradually, the endless vistas of the earlier fiction will contract around the hero (both *Stranger* and *I Will Fear* are set in narrowly confining—and dystopian—near futures). This new tightness forces him inward on a private world, itself tainted with finality: these later heroes are obsessed with death, preoccupied, not with statistical curves and survival charts, but with artificial prolongation of their own individual bodies.

Odder yet for Heinlein is the sentimental optimism of **"The Man Who Travelled in Elephants"** (1957). Panshin thinks this story was written much earlier. On the contrary, it has neither the allegorical complexity nor the exemplary clarity of the earlier tales. In **"Elephants,"** an old man who has lost his wife is on a bus enroute to one of the state fairs they had followed all their lives. There is apparently an accident. But if the old man is killed, his is a painless death, and an effortless passage into the next world—another time gate or "door into summer." To the hero, this new world is his private vision of heaven—the biggest carnival of them all, in which he and his reborn wife mount their elephants as king and queen of the Mardi Gras. This hardly seems like Heinlein at all. Yet beneath the surface are the familiar patterns. Out of this whole bus-load, one insignificant, pot-bellied individual is elected, inexplicably to glory. Moreover, he seems predestined to this end. His private joke (and whimsical justification for his fair-chasing) was to say, when asked what line he was in, that he "travelled in elephants." A different writer might have made the elephants of this hero's apotheosis a delusion, as with Hemingway's lion in "The Snows of Kilimanjaro," a moment of dreaming transition between life and death. Instead, fantasy predisposes to a higher reality: on that side of paradise, the hero's vocation is at last recognized—"a fine profession." This story is almost entirely ritual, a huge ceremony of election that terminates in coronation itself. Elided here, in this piece of wishful thinking, is not just an individual life, but the dolorous barrier of death.

Finally, there is **"Searchlight"** (1962), lone beacon of the sixties, and a slight effort in every respect. A blind child prodigy pianist is lost somewhere on the Moon when her ship goes down. She has no idea where she is. Her rescuers make contact, but cannot use a radio direction finder—they are as blind as she is, or blinder, in fact, as it turns out. The problem is how to locate her. The ingenious solution goes a long way toward confirming the old paradox of the blind who see. A laser beam will be used to carry an audio frequency, a single musical pitch. The general sector of the Moon in which she is lost is divided into a grid of such beams, a span of the 88 notes of the piano. She identifies her note, and is rescued in the nick of time. This is a strange, convoluted tale of election, in which two disparate beings—the blind girl and the unnamed scientist who invents the laser grid—bend all kinds of accepted physical notions ("light can't be heard") in order to effect an all-but-impossible union. The Moon calls for different sense and skills in order to survive. It is as if Betsy, inviable on Earth, has been called to the Moon and subjected to this ordeal solely in order to "see" anew with her exceptional ear. We have all the mechanism for a miracle. When it actually appears, however, it occurs in purely physical terms. As the ship comes down to rescue her, the reborn girl hears it: *"they see her waving!"*

These two people are chosen for this stranger rendezvous, predestined for it by a quality shared in common—personal conviction. Betsy doesn't hesitate to make a concert tour of the Moon in spite of the dangers. As she waits for help which may never come, she remains unperturbed, as if she possessed an even higher sense—that of election. Nor does the scientist hesitate to implement his idea; he even overrides the President of the United States. Out of this meeting come two things: a wider gap between the elect and everyone else, and a promising union of science and art. But if this parable tantalizes us with new vistas, it deceives as well. We have the shell of a blind seer, but no more. "Sight" here, like music, has no spiritual dimension whatsoever. Heinlein expends all this ingenuity only to make a paradoxical shift from one physical sense to another. It is a clever exercise in relative materialism, no more.

NOVELLAS

Heinlein's novellas, simply stated, are that series of longer early narratives written before he began to publish novels. Of varying lengths, the shortest of them are nevertheless more substantial than any of his short stories. Some are quite long, and were originally serialized. Several of these (*Sixth Column, Methuselah's Children, Beyond this Horizon*) were later expanded and published as novels. In spite of this, all these novellas share a form which is peculiarly their own. They should not be considered as something intermediary or transitional, a step on the way to the novel. Theirs is rather an alternate mode of narration. Compared with Heinlein's more orthodox novels of adventure and intrigue, the novellas have a quite different structural logic. The adventure novel is fundamentally synthetic in form; successive episodes are subsumed in the gradually evolving mystery, resumed in the culminating denouement. In the same way, on the private level, the hero's consciousness unfolds in time and space until, at the moment of self-discovery, all previous experiences are encompassed in a flash. Heinlein's novellas often contain numerous episodes. These are organized, however, not in a linear series, but in concentric layers around a single center. In each novella, "action" is restricted to one pivotal problem or adventure. This is rapidly set forth and circumscribed; ensuing events tend to gloss it, building upon this center in analytical fashion. Heinlein's novellas often appear excessively digressive. Indeed, it is this centrifugal structure that generates most of those disquisitive passages that so annoy readers of Heinlein. In each of the narratives discussed here, we do not find linear movement toward a point, but pulsatory movement away from it. The "action" will expand into various satellite realms, and then suddenly (irrationally, if we persist in thinking in terms of linear construction) contract upon the point in order that the story may end.

These early novellas seem to hold the key to the excessively digressive, actionless form of Heinlein's latest work. Does he not, in a novel like *I Will Fear No Evil*, simply overexpand a pivotal situation similar to those found in the novellas? More importantly, however, their structure sheds light on the unusual nature of some of Heinlein's juvenile novels. In certain of these "classics," it seems almost as if this vertical, analytical pattern has been superimposed over the initial horizontal impetus of the action novel. In this way, the "fast starts" we find in many Heinlein novels of the 1950s—where hero and reader are thrown at top speed into the middle of a train of events rushing forward toward denouement—are literally sabotaged. The forward thrust is made to coagulate around a problem center. This may indicate a preference for the novella form; but it does not necessarily mean Heinlein has lost structural control. As we shall see, he can write adventure novels of a more conventional sort when he so wishes. We can only assume, from the persistence of these hybrids, that Heinlein intends this fusion of forms, and is actively seeking some structural advantage from it. Not only are Heinlein's early novellas strongly didactic; they illustrate, in their expansive and contractive structures, a vision of man in which the individual's relation to the whole is predestined and unchangeable. Fusion of this form with the patterns of heroic adventure in the middle novels allows Heinlein to redirect a view of man that must have been basically alien to him. Freedom of individual action, rational control of destiny—values implied in the narrative of heroic quest, no matter how debased—are gradually cancelled out as this axial form spreads from the center of these novels.

The earliest of Heinlein's longer narrative, **"If This Goes On—"** (1940), is also one of the most interesting examples of a form that seems to have sprung fully shaped from the writer's head. Most people know this work in its expanded form (rewritten in 1953 for inclusion in the volume *Revolt in 2100*). The original serialized version is shorter. And yet, in its basic structure, it is virtually the same. The core of both is one single event—a revolution. In this tale, the hero only appears to grow, as he passes from loyal soldier in the Prophet's army to leader of the insurrection against theocratic tyranny. The various stages in his revolt are just so many positions around the periphery of the Cabal. His personal adventures are manipulated to cast light on this complex central phenomenon from numerous different angles.

Panshin calls **"If This Goes On—"** the story of a change of mind: John Lyle is a "man-who-learns-better." If he does so, however, the change comes immediately, at the start of the action. In a flash, a young man eagerly serving one cause is wholeheartedly converted to another: it is but another example of a man predestined to grace. From this moment on, whenever his actions are intuitive, he invariably does the "right thing." He reads the words of Tom Paine and Patrick Henry, and has a mystical revelation. Heinlein would make us believe that his conversion is not complete: Lyle has been brainwashed, after all, and such barriers to self-realization as prudishness must still be overcome. The process will be slow and painful. There are two ways to exorcise these demons: experience and precept. In reality, each adventure Lyle has on his way to that

center of things which is the Cabal is but an excuse for someone to lecture him or us, and in doing so lay open this anatomy of a revolution.

The examples of staged adventure are numerous. At one point, for instance, Lyle is discovered and put to the Question. He doesn't talk; but what difference would it have made if he had? At this stage of the game, he possesses no crucial information whose disclosure might make the action rebound. Nor could this knowledge have been obtained even if he had had it: his mind has been blocked by hypnosis—the narrator now has a chance to tell us how this is done. Lyle doesn't even give his friend Zeb away. But if he had, would this have destroyed the Cabal? The real purpose of this scene is to inform and to reveal. The hero displays the power to resist, to outwit the enemy. We now know he is one of the elect, and are prepared for his subsequent (and otherwise unexplainable) rise in the organization.

In the rambling narrative that ensues, Lyle's adventures as a fugitive on the road serve an informative purpose again and again. After a narrow escape, he hitches a ride with a friendly trucker. His own woes disappear before the marvels of the machine itself: "Nor had I ever been inside a big freighter before and I was interested to see how much it resembled . . . the control room of an army surface cruiser." Is this naivete? Soon we see that all along he has been following a higher plan: "I . . . filed away in my mind the idea that, if the Cabal should ever need cruiser pilots in a hurry, freighter jacks could be trained for the job in short order." As Lyle gradually penetrates the inner organization of the Cabal, we get a guided tour of its workings. Various experts lecture him (and us) on such matters as the conduct of psychological warfare. Good old Zeb mysteriously reappears; Lyle gets a mentor, and the reader a round of digressive dialogues. Zeb, for example, has resumed his filthy habit of smoking. The Puritanical Lyle had always objected to it before—now he openly accuses his friend of sacrilege. He forgets where he is and all he has done. Zeb, however, straightens him out, and in the process proclaims his even more fundamentalist credo: "My religious faith is a private matter between me and my God. What my inner beliefs are you will have to judge by my actions . . . I decline to explain them nor justify them to you." This whole scene is trumped up, against all laws of dramatic construction and consistent development of character, merely to give a pretext for exposing ideas. These in turn uphold without justification the cruel and inscrutable process of election which governs the shape of this narration.

As Lyle reaches the center of his journey, events occur which reaffirm his election. Another old acquaintance miraculously turns up—his old mentor Colonel Huxley, "Head of the Department of Applied Miracles" at his old military academy. Even in that world before grace, there was a strange affinity between these two men. Now Huxley inexplicably promotes this obscure newcomer to a key position in the war effort. This new order, it seems, is just as military as the old—the new army is run right because the goal is right. In Huxley's eyes, Lyle's training in the Prophet's school makes him a prince in this one, where instructors are lacking. Within this inner circle, there is yet another circle which must guide the effort because it is in tune with higher laws of destiny. This celestial chain of command is seen at work in the final battle—the assault on "New Jerusalem." Huxley is put out of action. Lyle should hand the command over to the next officer in line, his own superior in rank. But he knows the man is incompetent: "What would Huxley have me do, if he could make the decision?" Huxley continues to make the decisions. As if visited by his dead commander, Lyle gives orders in his name. The right choices are made and destiny is fulfilled.

Lyle's journey to the center of things is made clear in the most tangible, geographical terms. The Cabal occupies a huge underground cavern in the southwestern United States. But this in turn has a center. It is reached during a picnic excursion the hero takes in the company of Zeb and two girls. With uncanny vision, Zeb guides them through this labyrinth (the passage is "so well hidden that it could have been missed for ten thousand years."). They reach "a perfect small-domed cavern"; here is pristine sand and clear waters—they have rediscovered Eden. In this prelapsarian world, Lyle appears to lose the last of his inhibitions, and thus can tap some vital new energy that will lead him into the battle to come. Such appearances are deceiving, however. At this moment of the center, the hero does not grow; he is chosen. His predestined path is merely revealed to him.

This scene of nude bathing proclaims its purity. In reality, however, what we have here is prurience. Sex is treated exactly the same way as in *Stranger in a Strange Land.* Lyle gazes upon nudity and exclaims: "What is it about the body of a human woman that makes it the most terribly beautiful sight on earth?" He learns at last that they too are human. Heinlein dangles such forbidden fruit before our impossibly naive and prudish hero, and tantalizes him. But things apparently can go no further. An outburst of lust is not possible, for Zeb and the girls only taunt the hero so that they can chastise him all the better. They lecture their charge—but it seems that the lectures are meant for us, because Lyle doesn't really need them. Some marvelous grace preserves him, the "right" woman miraculously appears. Innocence need not be sullied by experience: it overlaps temptation, and achieves perfect union.

In this scene, Heinlein does not reverse the Fall so much as suspend its effects selectively. What we get is a higher form of titillation: Lyle is ever menaced, always saved. The threat may turn out to be an imaginary one. Our hero sees the two girls differently. Miriam is a blonde temptress: "I think Lilith must have been a blonde." To gaze upon the other, however, is something else: where Miriam was "naked," Maggie is "merely unclothed, like Mother Eve." Yet Lyle has fears—he believes Maggie is betrothed to Zeb, and now looks on in horror as Miriam draws his friend away for a swim in the raw. This is chimerical, we

know: Miriam turns out to be perfectly virtuous—it is just good clean fun. On top of this, there is another unexpected twist: Zeb is not to be Adam after all. Maggie explains: "I am very fond of Zebediah and I know he is equally fond of me. But we are both dominant types psychologically . . . Two such people should not marry. Such marriages are not made in Heaven, believe me! Fortunately we found out in time." This providential revelation saves things—Maggie remains unsullied, and the way is open for Lyle to love her with purity. Or is it? Maggie reminds him Judith exists: she will not fight for him but insists on having him pure. Do we have a real barrier this time? It proves just as ephemeral—Zeb appears and tells of Judith's infidelity (she was too "Female"—"all gonads and no brain"). Lyle and Maggie are obviously destined for each other after all. But if this is the mechanism of election, it has been debased to an insubstantial game, much ado about nothing.

In two ways, both chronologically and thematically, *Coventry* (1940—is a sequel to **"If This Goes On—."** In this novella, we enter the post-revolutionary world of the Covenant. The religious dictatorship has been abolished. It has been discovered, however, that freedom in society can only extend to a pact in which all freely subscribe. Significantly, this is not called a "contract" but a "covenant." Freedom turns out to be a selective word: as we see, only a certain part of mankind has the need to adhere to this agreement. The rest go to Coventry. Here, supposedly, each man can do what he wants. Yet this is false, for in Coventry anarchy inexorably leads to tyranny—there, in fact, he has three modes to choose from. Man apparently has the option to choose between Covenant and Coventry. But this is not true either. The inhabitants of Coventry, we will learn, are damned, but not by their refusal. A man's fate, in fact, is in no way the product of his actions, but rather of some predetermination. Those who belong are impelled irrevocably by their fallen natures. Yet there are those, like the hero, who make the error, and choose Coventry. Their act does not doom them; rather, it sets in motion the formidable machinery of Heinlein's secular grace. To an even greater extent than **"If This Goes On—."** *Coventry* proves that, no matter how hard they try, the elect cannot damn themselves.

Coventry opens with a problem: to what extent should society regulate individual freedom? David MacKinnon is accused of an anti-social act—he has taken a punch at a detractor: "You believe yourself capable of judging morally your fellow citizens, and feel justified in personally correcting and punishing their lapses. You are a dangerous individual . . . for we cannot predict what damage you may do next." He is condemned to two choices: psychological rehabilitation or Coventry. This scene is cleverly staged, for our sympathies instinctively go out to MacKinnon. In an impassioned defense, he berates his world: lives have become futile and boring because all vestiges of individualism have been stamped out; minds are now controlled and levelled to a single norm. Because the "true spirit of the Revolution" has been betrayed, he will go to Coventry and start over: "I hope I never hear of the United

States again." We may believe MacKinnon at first; we will learn how wrong this new way really is.

Heinlein tugs at the "romantic" in us all. His hero (a professor of literature) is one of the last of this breed. He eschews technology, yearns to lead the "simple life." When he goes to Coventry, he takes with him primitive objects—the trust rifle of yore, instead of the modern "blaster." Heinlein is quick to point out the flaw in his logic: "The steel tortoise gave MacKinnon a feeling of Crusoe-like independence. It did not occur to him that his chattel was the end product of the cumulative effort and intelligent cooperation of hundred of thousands of men, living and dead." He later eats a piece of real meat, and vomits when he learns what it is: he is thoroughly adapted to his sophisticated culture, unable to exist without it. In Coventry, he experiences the true fruit of anarchy—lawlessness, impressment, war. He is robbed by corrupt customs officials, and imprisoned by a crooked judge. In jail, miraculously, he meets "Fader" Magee, who becomes his mentor, helping him to escape, and guiding him to the underworld. Once again, there is convergence to a point, contact with a secret society within a society. There is also another rhythm often found in Heinlein—repeated contraction and expansion. Jail cells are often places of dynamic encounter. Dave and Magee team up and stage a spectacular breakout—one of the few moments of action in this story. Once underground, Dave must hide in an old radio-phonograph in order to escape a raiding party. Out of this confinement comes an expansion in a new direction. The hero begins a process of "self-analysis" by which he corrects (one by one) his misconceptions, and initiates the journey back to a world he foolishly rejected.

In this process, though, Dave has a lot of help. While in the hideout, he basks in the parental affections of Fader Magee and Mother Johnson. This brings him to reflect on his own childhood: these people are so warm and understanding that something must certainly have been lacking in his early years. In the true spirit of psychotherapy, he unearths the tyrannical father and condemns him: it was this repressive upbringing that later caused his "atavistic" trait of violence to break out. As he reflects, things are beginning to happen. The ever-warring factions of Coventry, it seems, have buried their differences; they have discovered a new weapon, and plan to attack the "Barrier" and a helpless United States. Fader is wounded trying to get this information to the other side. Though Dave still refuses to go in his place, he takes Fader to the Doctor—and a final round of instruction begins. This lone medical man in Coventry (it seems that doctors are never anti-social) is untouchable, above both law and custom. He is there (he tells us) in "voluntary exile": "He cared nothing for dry research; what he wanted was patients, the sicker the better." He has a young daughter, Persephone, nubile and possessed of god-like wisdom. This creature, young and old at once, is the prototype for numerous female prodigies in Heinlein. Dave falls for this child-like queen of Hades. As she lectures and coerces him, her influence wears away the last vestiges of the hero's social sickness.

She informs him of the true nature of the Covenant. It is "the first scientific social document ever drawn up by man." At its core is a Korzybskian analysis of the term "justice": there is no observable phenomenon in the space-time continuum to which we can point and say "this is justice." Science can only deal with that which can be observed and measured. Something like "damage" is a far more pragmatic measure for human actions. Betrayed in this social logic is a certain Puritanical mistrust of abstractions, and rejection of man's rational ability to manipulate them. It falls back on the predetermined patterns immanent in observable objects. Indeed, Dave's own development, as it follows a parallel path, shows this nicely. The abstract beliefs of the Romantic yield to the concrete facts of experience. These turn out to be merely vehicles for some coherent plan which, in the end, reveals itself as a form of election.

The world of *Coventry* is clearly divided into three state groups, arranged in hierarchical fashion. At the bottom, there are the reprobate of Coventry. Their natures have predisposed them to this Hell. What of the few "good" people we meet there? Heinlein is careful to explain, in each case, that they do not belong. Even the enigmatic Mother Johnson is there by default; she followed her husband, and when he died, simply decided to stay on. As great mother of the underworld, her urges parallel the scientific interests of the Doctor—they are missionaries. Then there is the world of the Covenant. Above this, however, there is a higher circle yet—a select and secret company whose election overleaps the regular channels of the Covenant. Dave is apparently one of these. At last he makes his decision. He crosses the barrier via an underground river. Impossibly, miraculously, he emerges alive on the other side. His rebirth is less astounding than that of Fader himself. The sick man he left behind returns inexplicably as Captain Randall of the Secret Service. As we have seen, Dave's decision to return is not really his own; strong forces guide him all the way. In the same way too, his final act appears no more than a ritual. Fader got out before him—and there were "others" before Fader. In any crucial sense, all these deeds seem insubstantial and inconclusive. The Revolution simply ends; we don't see how it was quelled. It was not destined to succeed, and is not important. All external action pales before the prospects of Dave's election—he will abandon literature and join the Secret Service, becoming one of Fader's higher family of elite spirits. The way to glory is immediate and overleaping. The laws of the Covenant are suspended: he need not undergo psychological rehabilitation. The black sheep is already cured; indeed, he was never sick. In the end the only things that count are the man—"he must ask himself"—and destiny.

In **"If This Goes On—,"** we have a theocracy that implements not God's will on Earth but a Satanic tyranny. The cure for this, in Heinlein's canon, is not unbounded freedom—Coventry is another Hell, where men left to their own fallen natures sink to bestial anarchy. In both these works, an inner group of the elect emerges in order to guide humanity along predestined paths. The novella *Magic, Inc.* (1940) is even more pointedly concerned with the emergence of such a group. The original, more revealing title of this story is **"The Devil Makes the Law"**: monopolistic practices turn out to be quite literally the devil's work. The action takes place in a world utterly familiar and contemporary except for one detail—magic. In some mid-sized city of the American heartland, "licensed practitioners of thaumaturgy" operate in harmony with legitimate businessmen to provide services and goods of quality. This balance is upset when diabolical forces begin to prey on human greed and stupidity. But Heinlein is reenacting here neither temptation nor fall—the dynamic is rather one of division. Purposely, he downplays demonic aggression. The adversary is but a shadow, and there is only one belated encounter with it—a long-delayed (and farcical) voyage to the Underworld. Numerous scenes, however, focus on the confusion and folly of mankind. The majority of men are already fallen. Heinlein shows that it takes only a nudge to drive them further and further into the labyrinth of self-corruption. *Magic, Inc.* is a narrative of sifting: gradually the true elite, the chosen ones, stand aside and come together. The Satanic pretext is merely the *chiquenaude* that sets things in motion. Heinlein's narrative, more than anything else, celebrates the marvelous ways of a destiny that elects the "right" men to power.

Significantly, the thrust of the action here is neither to defeat evil nor to reform mankind. It is rather (as in *Coventry*) to keep things properly divided and in their proper place. Things begin to happen only when these nether forces infringe on the doings of the wrong people. The opening scene illustrates this process. A mafia-style mobster enters the business establishment of Archie, the narrator, and tries to intimidate him into buying "protection" against bad magic. Archie boots him out; the chain of reactions is set in motion. Things happen to his business, he investigates, discovers the tentacular forces of Magic, Inc. He takes his fight through the establishment, and finally outside it. Gradually, in his fight, he gathers about him a circle of unlikely but strong allies. First, he goes to Joe Jedson, rugged individualist, self-made magician, and half a dozen other things. These two encounter, by most propitious chance, Jack Bodie, free-lance licensed magician. Jedson's talents are unrecognized by diplomas; Bodie has the degrees (graduate work at Harvard and Chicago), but eschews them—he learned all he knows from his "old man." A strong alternate current to society's ways is forming; it gathers strength inexorably. From Bodie, we pass to Mrs. Amanda Jennings—on the surface a frail old lady, beneath it a good witch of extraordinary powers. We penetrate a secret world, for which Bodie, with his business cards, is no more than doorkeeper. But if Mrs. Jennings doesn't advertise, neither does her associate, Dr. Royce Worthington, Doctor of Law, Cambridge University. Beneath this dignified exterior there is the old-fashioned Congo witch-doctor. In reality, *Magic, Inc.* is a study in comparative power structures. The Chamber of Commerce, in its anarchic disorder, is unable to offer effective resistance to the monopolistic pressures. Each member pursues his own interests, and nothing is resolved. Nor do established legislative procedures fare better. Only this variegated band of individuals can accomplish anything. In a display of power which far outdoes all the public manipulations of Senators, mobsters, chiefs of state, and the infernal schemers themselves, they actually harrow Hell, hunting down the demon responsible for this operation. They form a taut core within a flabby society. In Hell they discover there is, in like manner, an efficient heart in the unwieldy body politic. Already there, disguised as one of Satan's legions, is Agent William Kane, Federal Bureau of Investigation.

The narrator Archie is the key to this chain reaction. But if such an "average guy" can enter this visionary company, why not any of us? Does Heinlein imply that any man, if he perseveres, can make himself so? Far from it. In a very real sense, this whole process of Satanic subversion is but a contorted form of grace: it exists to elect Archie to the innermost circle. The old form of Mrs. Jennings melts away to reveal an angel. Archie's everyman mask falls, and before us stands her spiritual partner. In his occupation, in fact, there is a possible sign that Archie is predestined. As opposed to the more frivolous forms of commerce and magic, he deals as a builder with "durable goods," iron and concrete. Proof of his destiny comes when some of his companions would turn him back at the threshold of the underworld—this is a job for specialists. But Mrs. Jennings casts straws, and the man who has neither skill nor knowledge in magic is chosen. This whole process has Puritan overtones. A destiny is read in visible signs and objects. Archie's fate is plain to see—the dealer in durables who displays solid (and quite uncommon) courage throughout. No deed he does (or quality he has) explains, however, the final mark of election bestowed on him. The Amanda who goes to Hades is a resplendent young woman—fearful and angelic, but still a shade. When Archie falls in love with her, we think the situation both foolish and physically impossible—sixty years of "real" time separate them. And yet, oddly enough, it is as if this imposed chastity predisposes Archie for union on a higher level. As he sleeps after their journey, the young Amanda comes and plants a kiss on his brow, choosing him as her spiritual lover. The lowest and highest elements of this hierarchy are thus strongly and permanently welded together: "Out present relationship is something . . . to tie to." Here is one of those strange polar groupings of youth and old age which, in Heinlein, cancel all possibility of individual growth between these extremes. Things here remain frozen and static. It is not Joe (the "inveterate bachelor") who will remain single, but Archie. His relation to Amanda holds this society intact: not only do they meet regularly, but they prosper—for Archie, "business is good."

Universe and *Common Sense* (1941) form a narrative whole. It is often regretted, however, that Heinlein wrote the sequel to the first story. *Universe* is praised because it ends on a note of uncertainty. We see the ignorant masses, and the hostile power structure; but there is also a small band of determined visionaries which promises to grow. The enemy leader Bill Ertz has been captured: he will be shown the stars—perhaps he will become a convert too. Many feel that *Common Sense* is not only a letdown in aesthetic terms, but a betrayal: why carry the story of this ship/universe and its visionaries to such an end? The sequel, however, is quite consistent with Heinlein's Puritanical vision. Indeed, it is essential to it: the elect must fulfill their destiny, and this second story merely provides (in typical fashion) for its ritualistic working-out. In this light, *Universe* alone is ambiguous. It seems to offer a promise of universal conversion: "Why, then we shall just have to do it all over, I suppose, till we do convince them." *Common Sense* proves this impossibility a Romantic dream. In this novella, the group fails bitterly in its attempt to reform the whole ship: humanity in general proves itself unregenerate and fallen, hopelessly blinded by "common sense." Characteristically, they are not converted but abandoned. The ship is left to continue its benighted path; the small band of visionaries go off to begin a new existence on a virgin planet. The meaning is all too obvious here. Their knowledge is rudimentary, heroically insufficient; the amazing "luck" that guides them is, visibly, the hand of destiny.

As with all these early novellas, the opening scene of *Universe* plunges us less into intrigue or action than an alien and problematic world. This story is one of Heinlein's triumphs of "extrapolation." A whole mode of human existence, at once strange and all too familiar, is skillfully built up of rapid touches and crucial details, as we catch it in mid-evolution. On a starship of the Jordan Foundation, bound for distant Proxima Centauri, there is a mutiny. The result of this struggle is reversion to a cultural dark age. To the survivors, the ship becomes their universe. A new cosmology is created: scripture ("the Lines from the Beginning") springs up telling of "Jordan's Plan," of the creation and fall of man. In this account, Chief Mutineer Huff becomes Lucier—Heinlein gives us a masterly-drawn example of the human mind creating its myths out of limited knowledge, and thereby confining itself to the narrowest space. The society of *Universe* is thoroughly medieval in its "geo-centrism." Men inhabit the lowest areas of the ship, where gravity is highest. Their culture is divided into two classes: the peasant-serfs, and the "Scientists," a priestly caste whose "science" is purest scholasticism. The upper, low-gravity levels of the ship have been abandoned to the "muties"—mutants caused by radiation resulting from the destruction of the protective shield. Typically, the Scientists' explain the muties not in physical but symbolic terms. They are the cursed descendents of the "mutineers"—the outcast race. To man, then, the sky is closed. And yet, only this way lies salvation, for here one can look out on the stars, see this *Universe* for the insignificant thing it is. The desire to go up remains in the human race. This story opens with a foray by three boys into the dangerous realms above. For two of them it is sport, an adventure. For the third, however, it is more: Hugh Hoy-land feels a strange, inexplicable sense of awe. In this dark world, he is to be the new Galileo. Called to seek the higher truth he intuits, he will look out on new worlds.

But are the muties really the more fallen race? In *Universe,* the matter is far more complex. Deprived of the possibility of raising their own food, the muties have reverted to a nomadic tribal existence, living off foraging raids and practicing cannibalism. And yet, however grisly, their use of the dead seems more natural than man's. The humans below feed their departed (as well as live prisoners) into the mass converter. The ship is providentially kept on course. Ironically, however, this is not their intention at all. In their superstitious ignorance, they cannot imagine the true purpose of the machine. It has become a Moloch, its function solely ritualistic. The muties are made practical by their need to survive. This same self-reliant existence also leads the best of them to a genuine intellectual detachment. At the center of *Universe,* is the fortunate encounter between Hugh and Joe-Jim Gregory, the two-headed mutant "philosopher." Hugh is captured while on one of these "reconnaissance" climbs. But rather than eating him, Joe-Jim spares the boy and keeps him as intellectual company. Before his capture, Hugh had been only potentially a rebel. He might ask his old teacher, Lieutenant Nelson, why the sacred texts referred to the ship as "moving," and not be satisfied with his casuistical answers. In spite of these doubts, he remained a prisoner of his world's superstitions. Joe-Jim, however, offers new vistas. His logic batters down these barriers. Then he takes Hugh and shows him the stars. But if Joe-Jim is keenly intelligent, he has a flaw: he is by native temperament an intellectual, a bystander, an observer. He is interested in the "how" and the "why" but his will to action is satisfied with comfort and convenience alone. Once Hugh sees the stars, he wants to reach them: "Why don't we finish this job?" He strikes a pact with the reluctant Joe-Jim, and a coalition of mind and will is formed.

Joe-Jim is detached, but he is not a solo. He operates with a band of devoted braves who, in action, are capable of heroic loyalty. Virtue is not entirely dead down below either. Hugh returns to high-weight to spread the news, and is condemned for heresy. Of all his former friends, only the peasant Alan Mahoney comes to his aid. We wonder why, and so does Alan—he understands nothing of Hugh's ravings. Hugh calls him, and he comes; following some irresistible inner urge, Alan does Hugh's bidding, undertaking the perilous climb to Joe-Jim, and persuading him to rescue his ally. In this story, a series of gradually narrowing circles form and replace each other. At the heart of these respective societies, each hero shapes a world within a world. As they unite forces, an even tighter circle is formed, the center from which this new push to the stars will emanate. As this innermost sphere is shaped, there is a certain balance: Alan's blind devotion to Hugh mirrors that of Bobo the dwarf for his master. The purpose of Heinlein's sequel is to show that this equilibrium is not only unstable but transitory. The final circle of the elect has not been reached, this group will inevitably break down and reform—and when it does, the muties will have no place in it.

In *Common Sense,* balance turns out to be paralysis—a dichotomy that cannot generate vital energy, but only freeze things in hopeless stasis. The dialectic between what are essentially realist and nominalist views leads nowhere. Already in *Universe,* the allegorist interpretations of Nelson were offset by Ertz's matter-of-fact vision: "The ship was the ship. It was a fact, requiring no explanation. As for Jordan—who had ever seen him, spoken to him. What was this nebulous plan of his? The object of life was living. A man was born, lived his life, and then went to the Converter." This opposition only hardens in *Common Sense.* The sterile patterns of human reason cannot be broken—they must be abandoned, and with them the mass of mankind. Interestingly, Joe-Jim literally incarnates this fatal division of the human intellect. His lack of will and purpose is the direct result of his doubleness: as his heads carry on their futile discussions, he becomes inoperative. True, Heinlein gives Joe-Jim a glorious death in action. We note, however, that the mutant performs heroically only after he has lost one of his heads.

Physically, Joe-Jim is part of fallen, unregenerate mankind. As such, he must be excluded from the company of the elect. This is accomplished by the fantastic train of events in *Common Sense.* The story begins with the miraculous conversion of erstwhile enemy Bill Ertz, and ends with the departure of this small band of visionaries for a new planet. At the very last moment, as they are menaced by a new ship's rule bent on destroying them, they discover an auxiliary space craft—incredible good luck. They guess, by another fortunate insight, that they are entering an alien solar system—this must be the end of the trip! The treachery that forces them to abandon the ship, as it plunges blindly through Proxima Centauri, is a blessing in disguise. They do not really know where they are going, but luck enables them to locate and land on a planet that (incredibly) turns out to be inhabitable and peaceful. There really is too much "chance" here. Heinlein is openly showing us destiny at work; there was a "Plan" after all, but quite a different one from what the Scientists imagined. It includes the muties only in a limited sense. Joe-Jim is a necessary step in the process, but clearly he must be surpassed. His mutation, we learned in *Universe,* was most fortunate: "Had he been born two normal twins and among the crew, it is likely that he would have drifted into scientisthood as the easiest and most satisfactory answer to the problem of living." Destiny uses this exceptional creature, but must dispense with him in turn if a higher stage is to be reached. Like all his kind, Joe-Jim is genetically inviable. Hugh, Bill and Alan, aware somehow of the role they must play, drag women along with them—faceless creatures, obviously chosen for breeding purposes. By some higher law that watches over racial purity, the mutant heroes must die. Alan remains; Bobo, the nobler in many ways, perishes. Joe-Jim dies heroically—and

yet in the end, the world of action and adventure turns out to have only secondary importance. These noble acts are transitory, another step only in that sifting process that gradually isolates the select few destined to carry the human seed to glory. The ways of Heinlein's providence may seem incredibly tortuous—man has regressed, struggled, erred. Yet we must remember that this is not all mankind, but only a ship. And of its number, the "right" few do reach their destination, on time, and perhaps under better terms than would have been possible otherwise. Destiny has reserved for this handful of survivors—and because of their limited numbers—a return to innocence, a new Golden Age: "From now on, Alan always Good Eating."

Finally, there is *Waldo* (1942). This Anson MacDonald story is, in a sense, Heinlein's archetypal novella, and one of his most complex and provocative allegorical statements. In the intricate interplay of center and circumference, in the gradual reduction of the external world to a creative polarity between this young, isolated super-genius and an old hex doctor, *Waldo* traces configurations that will later be worked out in *Stranger in a Strange Land.* The later novel will simply expand these basic patterns, and develop them in terms of linear intrigue and *Bildung.*

There are several elements to this strange tale. Its core is the fairy-tale motif of the monster who gets a human body. Heinlein gives this a twist, however, which links it with the recurrent theme of election. Waldo's is not merely a case of the beautiful spirit purifying and uplifting an ugly body. Instead of unbroken elevation, the pattern here is rather that of the fortunate fall. With his extreme *myasthenia gravis,* Waldo is literally the prisoner of gravity. Through a feat of intellect, he compensates for this by creating his weightless home in the sky. Instead of curing man's fallen state, human intelligence only worsens the original rift. This space home is alternately "Freehold" or "Wheelchair"; Waldo becomes a great floating brain in the middle of a spherical room. He must fall again in order to rise, must touch Earth. He despises those "nameless swarms of Earth-crawlers," and yet is shown just how dependent on mankind he really is. It is in falling to Earth that he paradoxically liberates himself from this dependence. He makes contact, not with the mass of men, but with his elective counterpart among it—Gramps Schneider. Out of this creative union, Waldo rises a whole being. Indeed, only because he resolves his own plight can a solution to the general human condition be found. All mankind is succumbing to *myasthenia,* suffering the radical split between order and chaos. In this Waldocratic universe, however, the general cure is only a secondary development, an offhand gift from the recipient of grace to those not chosen.

Central to *Waldo* is the symbol of hands. These are constantly (and in various forms) reaching out, touching, physically uniting two apparently sundered poles, establishing a current of creative energy between them. This image unites the several levels of action in the story into a cohesive network. There is Waldo as a special man, reaching vertically out to his predestined point of contact on the circumferential human world. There is Waldo as fallen man, reaching laterally into "Other Space," and drawing the energy which miraculously lifts him (and humanity) up again. And there is Waldo as partial man, reaching horizontally across his own arrested growth in order to draw this emotional child to instant maturity.

The incredible web of interlocking circumstances which is *Waldo* is radial in form. In its dynamics, however, it is centripedal, not centrifugal. At the center is Waldo F. Jones. Converging on him are two separate, apparently different problems. On one hand, there is engineer Jim Stevens of North American Power-Air, with their "radiant power" reactors that don't work but should by all the known laws of physics. On the other, there is Doc Grimes, and his theory of the general physical debilitation of mankind. At the center, we learn that these stands interrelate—they are two forms of some general power failure. But even when the connection is made, a seemingly impossible quandary remains. "Progress" has led to the creation of radiant energy. This weakens men and weak men in turn affect the power of their machines and cause them to fail. Once again, fallen man wanders lost in the maze created by his own intellection. The energy loosed into the world is leaking away somewhere—but where is this point of drainage, impossible by current notions of physics? The tightness of this infernal circle precludes any hope of returning to a prelapsarian state. But if it cannot be broken that way, it can be balanced with some new element, so that the ongoing polar dynamic of change in permanence may continue. This requires an act of grace, the sudden opening of a door into elsewhere. And grace does not touch ordinary men. The hidden door, we learn, was in the mind of man all along: here is both the leak and the power to rechannel it. But this discovery is made in one great mind—Waldo's.

Waldo undertakes to solve the problems Grimes and Stevens bring him. He does not do so, however, out of altruism or out of egotism—this invasion of his sealed world makes him perceive his own condition in a new light. He is suddenly aware of the fundamental inbalance his isolation has created. To overcome gravity, to suspend oneself in weightlessness, is merely to move from one extreme to another: sterile oscillation. Before, Waldo had been the suspended brain who regarded all humanity as his "hands," and who actually reached out through his various mechanical extensions (he calls them "Waldoes") to manipulate men. His position is that of tyrant. Suddenly, he discovers that he in turn is helplessly dependent on the creatures he controls. This polarity is mutual enslavement; to break out of it, he must establish some new vital contact with the Earth he has forsaken. He goes to Gramps Schneider, the mysterious Pennsylvania hex doctor, and a dynamic nexus is established. The two dwellings are polar opposites: Schneider's quaint old house is as Earthbound as Waldo's is detached and rootless. The symbol (or sign)

of their creative interplay is the gravity-operated cuckoo-clock: one ticks in Gramps's house; the other is built and operated by Waldo inside a gravity shield in his floating home.

As the Schneider-Waldo axis is forged, the image of reaching hands takes on new significance—the grip of tyranny becomes fingers groping after creative union. The "de Kalb generators" hexed back into operation by Gramps have antennae that reach out like hands. These extend (he tells us) into "Outer Space," and draw their power there. Furthermore, he repeats this "laying on of hands"—he strokes the machine in the "right" direction—on Waldo himself. Then too, Waldo is told he can extend his mental hands and take strength there. For a brief instant, Waldo feels a surge of power against his prison of gravity. This, however, is a revelation, but no miracle cure. It simply sets in motion the rhythmic undulation of a new creative process, and dynamic connections are made between formerly antithetical values: the individual and selfless energy, science and magic. Schneider, in fact, has a very Emersonian vision of "other space": its power is not to be sought outside the self, but is rather "inborn," part of the mind itself. Gramps's view is metaphysical; Waldo on the other hand, insists on locating this place topographically. He sets out in his laboratory to explore this new dimension physically, to map it, and in doing so literally colonize it, shaping it in accordance with his own conqueror's will. Only at this physical center of things can he tie all the various strands together. The machines failed, Schneider stated, because their operators were "tired." Waldo translates this into scientific terms: if energy is "shorted" somewhere, and if this "Other Space" is where it goes, then could not the point of contact be physically in the mind? If men indeed suffer from generalized, radiation-induced *myasthenia* (as Doc Grimes thinks), perhaps the mind is leaking into another dimension. Using smaller and smaller mechanical extensions, Waldo is able to reach physically, surgically, through the brain to the portals of this "Other Space," and thus verify his hypothesis—the synapses are the point of contact.

Discovery of this link leads to some important speculation as to the nature of this other dimension: "If the neurological system lay in both spaces, then that might account for the relatively slow propagation of nerve impulses as compared with electromagnetic progression. Yes! If the other space had a c constant relatively smaller than that of this space, such would follow." It is but one step from imagining an alternate universe to actually creating one: "The Other World was a closed space, with a slow c, a high entropy rate, a short radius, and an entropy state near level—a perfect reservoir of power at every point, ready to spill over into this space wherever we might close the interval." In Gramps Schneider's mystical vision, the world varies according to the way one perceives it: hence, "a thing can both *be*, not *be*, and *be anything*." But this, as the mad Dr. Rambeau proves, can be chaos. Out of chaos, however, Waldo opts to bring cosmos: "He cast his vote for order and predictability! He would *set* the style. He would impress his own concept of the Other World on the Cosmos!" If the individual replaces God, the creative polarity that selects and guides him insures that he will do the same thing that God would have done. Waldo's "own" idea is directed by some higher plan, the "style he sets." The new nexus he establishes, merely restores the dynamic interchange between center and circumference: "I think of the [Other World] as about the size and shape of an ostrich egg, but nevertheless a whole universe, existing side by side with our own, from here to the farthest star." It is from this super-position of polar opposites that the solution to the practical problems comes: "Start out by radiating power into the Other Space and pick it up from there. Then the radiation could not harm human beings." This magical engineering may save mankind's health and economy, but it remains simply a by-product of the real drama of Waldo's election.

But this universe maker remains apparently bounded by his own physical body. Yet his weakness also proves an illusion, a veil which falls to reveal the real Waldo. To Gramps, the solution is one of incredible simplicity—reach out your hands. Again, Waldo sets out to recreate metaphor in literal, physical terms. He has explored the brain with mechanical "hands," the waldoes. Why then can he not use his mental "hands," the nerve synapses, to reverse this process of leakage, and draw power like the vitalized antennae of the de Kalbs? He measures his new-found strength, significantly, in the most tangible way—with hand grips. His passage from weakling to giant also involves another form of reaching out: he floors Jim Stevens with one surprise punch; in an instant, the callow boy becomes a "man." Because Waldo is a scientist and not a hex-doctor, we may think we are witnessing an act of conscious will. Actually it remains a miracle cure. Gramps reveals a higher truth; as he translates this into new terms, Waldo does no more than act out a predetermined pattern of grace. He does not grow, either in the physical or the emotional sense; he is transfigured.

In spite of this, however, election in Waldo's case is a centripedal process. He breaks out of initial isolation only to achieve a higher form of oneness, in which the circumferential world itself is gradually absorbed by the center. The story line is a closed circle—it begins and ends with the resurrected Waldo performing his tricks and receiving homage from his admirers. The ruler of two worlds—this space and the other—is the alpha and omega of the linear narrative as well: all poles close in him. As these two spaces (through the paradoxes of topology) do not coincide, and yet do, so Waldo executes his feats simultaneously in both the micro- and macrocosm: the neural surgeon probes the infinitely small, the acrobat defies space and gravity. Gramps Schneider is gone: the initial contact was all that was needed. From that point on, everything external is gradually drawn to the center, transposed upon it like a looking-glass. First and last in this story, we have a vision of unity that is solipsism—self mirroring self. Waldo can look out on the world of men with perfect serenity ("such grand guys") only because they have become

perfect adulators. In its convolutions around an absorbent center, *Waldo* looks forward to *Stranger in a Strange Land.*

Alice Carol Gaar (essay date 1978)

SOURCE: Gaar, Alice Carol. "The Human as Machine Analog: The Big Daddy of Interchangeable Parts in the Fiction of Robert A. Heinlein." In *Robert A. Heinlein,* edited by Joseph D. Olander and Martin Harry Greenberg, pp. 64-82. New York: Taplinger Publishing Co., 1978.

[*In the following essay, Gaar explores the theme of interchangeable parts and the central figure in several of Heinlein's novellas and short stories.*]

There is a discontinuity between the rate of moral development in the human being and the exponential rate of technological progress. One might state it in a simpler way: The tool grows better and better, while its user is the same old hairless ape. The hairless ape can fly, but emotionally and morally he is still crawling. The machine works very well; maybe we don't work at all. Are the machines getting out of control, or were we never under control?

Robert A. Heinlein has been inspired by the apparent perfections of the cosmic machine to equal it by proving that we can outlive it. However, the human creature can only equal the machine by being like it or like its most efficient products. One may ascribe Heinlein's weakness in characterization—a weakness shared by most science fiction writers—to his overwhelming desire to beat the cosmos at its own game by the clever manipulation of parts. As Alexei Panshin puts it, Heinlein is essentially the engineer and is interested in how things work rather than why.[1] We can criticize Heinlein in an analysis of several of his works on the basis of his interest in process and the mechanics of human survival to see how consistently he carries through his main themes and to what extent they fail or succeed in adding a realistic dimension to his works. Why demand that he recreate a basically nineteenth-century version of a clearly defined individual jeopardized by a milieu either totally indifferent or malign? Today one may see the universe as an ocean of life. The UFO craze suggests that we are a mystery-obsessed people fearful that the apocalypse will pass us by. Heinlein greets the cosmos with a proud "Hello" that says first, "I can live just as long as you," then, "I am possibly God."

However, the very fact that he is competing with what he sees as a giant machine calls into question the conservative view of the primary nature of the individual around whom the cosmos moves and has its being. Heinlein may hail the independent, competent ego as the *sine qua non* of the existing universe, but his own primary interest in process forces a reevaluation of the conservative view of the human being. Process refers to an interlocking network of energies and involves more than just one component, which in turn suggests that we are on the verge of yet another revolution analogous in human terms to the Copernican theory. It is not simply that the human being has lost his central place in the cosmos, already described in lurid and sometimes lugubrious words by writers of the past one hundred and fifty years; but he is transformed into a link in a pattern, a point on a grid, a flow of energy throughout a system. Process implies continuous motion and transformation and that we are ourselves part of a gigantic structure. The real implications of the discoveries of science in the last few centuries are just beginning to filter down into the public maw. It is one thing to regard the human being as a futile creature imprisoned in a hostile world, and quite another to see him as part of a system and necessary in kind to a cosmic ecology. Possibly this reduction to a component is what is eating at Heinlein's vitals. He has been driven to try to come to terms with or outdo the implied systematic analogy. For this he has written his short stories, novels, books, and created Lazarus Long—a symbol of the extrahuman context which like Lazarus goes on and on forever. Such a process makes Lazarus Long a valid symbol of the universe and each component of him and his milieu essential only *in kind.*

Just as the universe is held together by energy in several forms—gravity, electromagnetic attraction, and so forth—so Lazarus Long holds his world together through the abiding power of sexual attraction and activity. But sex means two persons, and where is the second person in the story? In a cosmos that might be really just a gigantic computer, how can one talk in terms of one personality much less two personalities? Or is this question totally irrelevant in a science fiction story? An examination of this question can give us a sharper idea of just what the precise strengths and potentialities of science fiction really are and what the sources of its overriding weaknesses are. Accordingly, I will examine the theme of interchangeable parts and the central figure in the following novels as they are listed in chronological order in Panshin's bibliography: *Magic, Inc.* (appeared as **"The Devil Makes the Law"** in 1940); *Universe* (1941); *Methuselah's Children* (first appeared in 1941); *Waldo* (first appeared in 1942); *Starship Troopers* (1959); *Stranger in a Strange Land* (1961); *The Moon Is a Harsh Mistress* (first appeared in 1965);[2] and the two novels in the Seventies, *I Will Fear No Evil* (1970),[3] and *Time Enough for Love* (1973).[4] These novels cover three generations. The early ones introduce variations on Heinlein's basic concern with how things work, and the later novels carry his theme to a logical conclusion.

Although Heinlein obviously wrote *Magic, Inc.* tongue in cheek, the work reveals the direction of his interests. Here the unseen energy is present both as an applied commercial resource and as a future potential. The term "Half World"—the source of the magic energy—suggests that our world is also in a sense a half world. As in our own, the powers of that other world are reducible to elements— the demons of earth, fire, water, and air. The laws of homeopathy and contiguity (referred to on page 110 of the book in connection with some second-rate magical

"goods") state that the patterns of matter are everywhere, eternal, reproducible, and unbroken. The author thereby confesses his belief not only in the structured nature of the universe, but also in the interrelated natures of his fictional personalities.

Underneath the amusing comments on business and politics is the implication that what we call "reality" must have its complement in order to be symmetrical or complete. That he uses the term "laws" indicates that Heinlein believes in a knowable, predictable universe, whose structure can be understood through applicable formulas. Energy and power are drawn from the total structure. A short, lyrical, even mystical passage demonstrates Heinlein's respect for the innate beauty of energy. Although the salamander has been used to destroy Archie's business (the novel's hero refuses to pay for "protection"), he accepts its neutral or amoral nature, loves its beauty, and desires its presence near him. These is even a delicate sensuousness in the momentary communication between the salamander and Archie with a quality both unknown and concrete. In Archie's appreciation for its perfection, he displays the engineer's love of form and contour. He could characterize the elemental spirit as feminine if he chose, yet it takes the initiative and comes to him. Evidently both humans and the elements may be characterized as having mixed masculine and feminine natures. This short episode foreshadows Heinlein's awareness of the versatility of sexual natures, an awareness which he exploits further in later novels.

The movements of Archie and his friends between worlds serves a metabolic purpose within a larger context. But there is an emotional flatness in their presentation. Archie procures knowledge without paying for it by showing a character change, which indicates that the knowledge obtained has only a superficial effect upon him. When Mrs. Jennings sees danger in Archie's future and warns him that he must let his head rule his heart, there could be the basis for a deeper development that never really appears anywhere in the novels discussed here. In the salamander episode Archie verges on the realization of the fullness of total life. He also displays some sensitivity toward the dynamic flow of events. He may even be suggesting that he is aware that there is an exchange of energy and knowledge between the two worlds which justifies the loss of exact identity.

Both *Universe* and *Methuselah's Children* were first published in 1941 in *Astounding Science Fiction*. Even though the style and plot of *Universe* are far simpler than the works of nearly thirty years later, there are certain basic themes in it that are important for the later novels and serve as the touchstone for the fascination that his works hold. They are the themes of the double personality and of the desire to appropriate a larger space. The personality becomes more complex in order to fill that larger space. Enclosing these two themes is the technology that overwhelms them both. However in *Universe,* one of Heinlein's best juveniles, technological enlightenment and mental development are contrasting themes which harmonize well at the end.

The word "universe" means to turn as one unit, which infers that perfection involves motion. The society in the huge spaceship in the short novel is incomplete for many reasons but primarily because motion has gone out of its scheme of things. The "universe" is at first small enough to accommodate only the primitive consciousness of the colonists who have long since forgotten their heritage from the Earth left behind centuries ago. To them their ship *is* the universe since they have no knowledge of anything outside it. The ship delimits their sensibilities and their mentalities. But in this well-written tale of colonists who have long since reverted to a closed hierarchical village culture, the young hero, Hugh Hoyland, finally learns that his ship is merely enclosed within an immensely larger universe. The experience is traumatic for him, but a few lines suffice to describe the effect of the great new insight upon him. He proceeds by logical steps from the awareness that the ship is a thing meant to move from one space to another to the thought that he and the scientists-priests should restore motion to the ship and make it move through the heavens. Because it is based on the principle of pure force-weight and magnetic attraction and there are no moving parts which might cause friction, the great ship is practically indestructible. This can be related to Heinlein's near obsession with human mortality or immortality by applying the idea of frictionless energy to the transplanting of a human from one space to another without destroying anything essential. The individual within that space will be a composite, just as the two-headed Joe-Jim mutant—the most intelligent person whom Hugh meets—is a composite personality.

Since Joe-Jim is more intelligent than anyone else on the ship, he portrays early Heinlein's belief in the superiority of the personality that has more than one part. The viewpoint is a structural one since it requires a controlling pattern. Even in this simple story, change due to doubling fills out a new space. The more complex person, Joe-Jim, who knows that the ship is *in* the universe and not the universe itself, teaches Hugh. At the beginning the young hero has the problem of a space too small for his bursting adventurousness. Then appears the greater intelligence of the individual who can carry on a dialogue with himself. Together they carry on a dynamic interchange within the larger structure of the ship, approaching its weightless section, that is finally seen in the largest structure of all—space.

But although Heinlein thinks of his most important characters as individuals, they are really creatures of the tribe in the sense that they are uncomfortable or unhappy alone with their knowledge. Hugh's first desire is to push his new insights onto his fellows. To this end he plans to forcibly bring them to the Captain's Veranda to reveal outer space to them for the first time.

Methuselah's Children is the most important of the early novels discussed here, since it introduces the Howard Families, who *in toto* represent later the universe delineated in time and space by the person of Lazarus Long. The Howards are Heinlein's answer to the challenge of the machine, and because they appear later in the novel *Time Enough for Love,* one can note the development in his basic ideas over a period of time. The positive behavior of genetic selection seems to be the basic theme of the story, if one assumes that positive behavior produces the near immortality of the Howard conglomerate. The future is based on the physical patterns already present in the genetic makeup, as opposed to accidental choice. In effect, the Howard Foundation *is* choice. As the chooser the Foundation creates an environment rather than just accepting one. The Foundation thereby states that the natural environment—or natural selection—is no longer adequate, although Heinlein sings the praises of the pioneer life as a natural selector of superior characteristics. He has analyzed the larger structure and concluded that a large-scale conscious manipulation is the next step. Certainly there have never been circumstances that suggested that positive thinking enabled beetles, horses, or fish to increase their life span. As far as we know the universe of such creatures is limited almost entirely to instinctual patterns of behavior. The author is trying to analyze the human being's potentiality by comparing him to something that is neither animal nor insect.

Implied by the idea of a long life span granted by favorable genetic conditions is the interlocking, multiple-adult family group that is itself in a real sense time and space. It is the grid of perceptible reality—a continuing pattern as its members multiply and create their own surrounding world increasing in size and depth. But because of persecution and exile there is neither time nor energy within the Howard Families for the suppression of individual characteristics. Indeed, they express the sense of solidarity that comes from shared peril, and their leaders are the oldest ones because they are by definition the strongest and the smartest.

By injecting the reverse values of the Half World into the everyday world, magic in the earlier novel had provided an escape from a culturally static situation. In *Methuselah's Children* the spaceship supplies a challenge by bringing its inhabitants into other dimensions. This in turn presupposes a larger structure whose own dimensions encompass and require constant readjustment. The various discussions between the brilliant mathematician Libby (who pilots them out of the solar system) and the others in the ship refer to the distorted time and space perceptions for a ship moving near the speed of light (pt. 1, chap. 8). Such an experience "smashes" their former dimensions. Yet the individual worlds are not expendable. Among the Howards, longevity is their basic staple and as such the source of their primary "good." Possessing this characteristic they see themselves as members of a family whose identity perseveres in spite of the deaths of individual members. And none of them calls the others expendable. The family is the larger structure, but the healthiness of the Howards is inherent in what they are themselves. Collectively they are in a certain sense healthier than the "ephemerals." They are more adventurous, adaptable, and wiser because they are part of an interlocking of loose family systems which combine both independence and respect for the others.

Since Lazarus Long and Mary Sperling are progenitors of hordes of Howards, who are later quite independent of them, their personalities are singled out early. The Howards live too long to maintain emotional bonds beyond a certain point, even though they care tenderly for the relatively high percentage of subnormal and defective children born into the Families. However, their relationships, founded on the need for mutual benefit, are not emotionally shallow. Over a period of time the sense of identity will become biologically defined, since they will all be more or less related. It follows that the long-lived Howards are very much aware of the fact that they are replaced by huge numbers. And even as individuals they are in a sense analogous to the Families, since the individuals become composites by virtue of organ transplants in the rejuvenation process. Because corporate identity is a physical version of the space continuum, one might conclude that Heinlein is as much interested in corporate identity as in immortality. How does an individual who can speculate on his approaching end really survive in contrast to an insect which is automatically a specialized component of a larger community? Presumably the insect does not consciously create a mental construct of such a community. Are we by instinct less creatures of community, or is the communal mentality far more deeply embedded in the human individual than hitherto realized? The highly specialized insect cannot exist apart from a community because it is inadequate alone. Mary Sperling finally finds immortality by joining the Little People in a mutual relationship. In her, Heinlein is analyzing a human approach to the theme of corporate identity as a form of survival. The individual creates the larger structure in his own mind and thus shares a collective perception. The more persons sharing and shaping this collective perception, the more complex it becomes, a process which enlarges an organizational unit that is itself indissoluble.

In contrast to Mary Sperling's attempt to cope with the idea of death is Lazarus Long, an extreme example of the peculiar genetic gift of the Howards. Yet the author portrays an interesting psychological quirk or strength in Lazarus, who, except for his rather negative state of mind at the beginning of *Time Enough for Love,* does not think about death at all. He inevitably includes all of the women around him within his group by the power of his sexual presence alone, and they in turn bring other men into the group and keep them there. In the later novel sex is the New Evangelism, although it is actually subordinated to the family pattern. It is the universal energy that attracts and holds "bodies" and also the energy that makes communication possible. Although Lazarus expresses his belief in the survival of the fittest, he, like the Howards in general, is neither ruthless nor inhumane, as one can see in the protection of the defective children, who sometimes have special gifts of their own. This means that the family

as a real structure is stronger and bigger than the individual weaknesses of a few who accordingly are not regarded as threats. Sex is here an aspect of interfamily identity and dependence and as such is inseparable from the family grouping. And the crucial point is that Heinlein does not delve into the possibilities of unknown, unexplainable power sources in his conception of sex. His use of sex is basically not even really erotic.

As Panshin points out (p. 52) Heinlein does not revert to nonrational explanations of events, and he avoids the mysticism which would contradict his fondness for clear explanations. This is the source ultimately of his shallowness in character portrayal and the flat, opaque quality in the personalities of his characters. Sex reflects energy and love/hate when the individual is almost shattered by the awareness of another will facing him. Mysticism in its most basic sense begins at this point and from there rises into the transcendent regions of religion and speculation. But those devoted to "applied technology" alone avoid the mystery in the beginning. Heinlein's central concern seems to be a unifying pattern or a perpetual energy in human terms. His passion for organization and arrangement is an attempt to analyze the dominating force in the nature of a universe perceived by a living organism. When Lazarus analyzes the alternating despair and hopefulness of the preeminent statesman Slayton Ford (whose protection of the Howards has ruined him), it becomes obvious that the author's main concern is for survival and psychological viability, the *how* rather than the *why* (pt. 1, chap. 8 of *Methuselah's Children*).

The smashed dimensions of the Howards as they move through space and time are merely suggested physical dimensions. Completely missing in Heinlein is the awareness of the tragic levels of life or of tragedy in any form due to guilt or accident. How can there be guilt where there is nothing to sin against, no gods and no sacred mysteries? There is nothing to shake or demolish the psychological, spiritual, or philosophical dimensions within which Heinlein characters move. There is no accident which can utterly destroy *the* machine, because all machines have their duplicates and missing screws can be replaced. Whereas in the classical world tragedy is part of the fortuitous circumstances that humble the mighty and the proud, to many science fiction writers of every level all events are so much a part of an inclusive system (stated or unstated) that the fortuitous event is merely stimulating to the problem-solving intelligence. Even the alien, grotesque as he may be, is in a sense a distant relative, since otherwise he could not be portrayed, he could not be *seen.* Just as our minds have created our universe—a shared, tribal construct—the alien is also a shared, tribal construct. And it is significant that the aliens in *Methuselah's Children* are either hierarchically ordered individuals or corporate components, because that is how we really see ourselves.

The two superior alien peoples are themselves part of a larger hierarchy—the Jockaira, far inferior to the "gods" who have won mastery over temporal and spatial orientations as the Earthmen know them, and the Little People, superior to both the Earthmen and the Jockaira. The individuality of Earthmen evidently makes them (except for some of the subnormal children) unsuitable for mental telepathy. The corporate mentality is baldly set forth in the existence of the Little People, who are not individuals at all. Here for the first time the analogy between human-like creatures and the machine becomes obvious. The universe seems to be a mechanism that includes everything. To conceive of it at all is to conceive of it as a unit, which implies a dimension to our conceptual processes that goes beyond the four that locate a point in time. One might imagine Heinlein's posing of the question to himself: "Why are people not as efficient as machines?" and answering it thus: "Machines have hitherto been seen in a confused manner. People are more efficient than the machine, which is itself inadequate. Of course a person will break down if all of his parts are not functioning correctly. The problem is, how to improve that functioning so that the human being will go on forever, as he was meant to."

One can approach *Methuselah's Children* from the standpoint of a negative argument—the isolated individual is not sufficiently complex. Heinlein *is* on the verge of a metaphysical stance when he includes the individual in a structure which is a source of energy to the individual component but far more than a collective body. He approaches that stance from several aspects; namely, (1) the permanent nature of the larger structure, (2) the interchangeability of its components, (3) the dynamic interaction between those components for growth, and (4) the warping of the physical dimensions that "placed" the smaller structure. The next step is to note carefully how Heinlein "reorganizes" the individual to fit him into that context.

First published in 1942 in *Astounding Science Fiction*, *Waldo* develops Heinlein's cosmic personality by focusing on an individual who is transformed from a physically inferior person (although mechanically brilliant) into someone who is superior in the sense that the new Waldo begins successfully to create the world of men in his own image. The story moves from the self-isolation of the physically inferior, compensating individual to a totally new spatial and temporal orientation on the part of that genius who, as a result of his newly positive attitude toward the rest of humanity, shares his discovery with others. As in *Universe* weightlessness symbolizes the freedom of outer space where one is closer to one's own true nature as a dweller in space. Waldo's genius has lifted him above the physical confines of gravity. Out there he becomes aware of another world which is a source as well as a depository of energy. The Other World is the place where Waldo searches for speed, where he compares electricity to nerve impulses. Waldo proceeds on the assumption that the energy from the Other World is also subject to laws which can be discovered and used if the formulas are known.

Heinlein's shallowness in character portrayal reveals itself here in these machinations. His characters avoid traumatic

shock by refusing to confront something unpredictable within a system. Waldo calls Gramps Schneider a hex doctor and then proceeds to work out basic rules for tapping the power source of the unpredictable. Like Heinlein, Waldo is the mechanical genius who avoids the confrontation with the all-encompassing theoretical implications of this new energy. Rambeau really seems more consistent when he loses his sanity because of the traumatic shock to his rigid scientific outlook. Waldo remains, however, a very clever child intrigued by the possibilities and blind to the real import.

But there are some interesting insights in Waldo's attempts to develop a terminal for the power source. When he mentally reduces the Other World to the size of an ostrich egg, he shows his own mastery of a comprehensive structure—a process which in itself becomes the new source of his strength. In this way Waldo has gone beyond the mere sense of another world, as in *Magic, Inc.*, and as an individual, beyond the helpless exposure to other dimensions, as in *Methuselah's Children*. Energy from the Other World makes him into a complete human being who wants nothing more than to be surrounded by other people who like him.

Here again Heinlein's conceptual weakness becomes obvious. The Other World is actually other people, and learning how to manipulate energy corresponds to learning how to interact with the other people, and at the same time, learning how to be a man. But the real interaction with the Other World has to admit its basic mystery, as the theoretician would even while he speculated about it. The author allows the energy exchange between Waldo and his counterpart in the Other World to degenerate into "nerve surgery"—a mechanical and most inadequate description of the process that Waldo thinks he has discovered. The emotional complexity of the exchange is missing, therefore the intimation of the Other World is flat.

Waldo's transformation from an embittered, weak genius into a physical superman is an obvious spin-off from Faust and Nietzschean motifs. The greatness of Goethe's masterpiece is due, among other things, to a consistent following through in the bargain that Faust makes with Mephistopheles. Faust's reign of glory is always in the shadow of the final payment. Every ounce of energy that he receives demands its physical and emotional price. His return to youth at the beginning is balanced by the mistakes of youth and the blindness of old age. The wisdom, wealth, and power that he gains bring with them an emotional winnowing. In the science fiction novel it is the lack of an accompanying developmental trauma that suggests Waldo's powers are spurious. Only in Rambeau's madness and a short description of Waldo's bitter hatred of the "smooth apes" are there the rudiments of an emotional interaction to intense experiences, but these lines are never developed. Though Waldo decides that mental concentration can prevent the myasthenia gravis which is weakening the people below and is the source of his own crippled state, he does not analyze the nature of mental control over the body. His mechanics lead nowhere, and nothing important is really demonstrated. But the positive point made is that Waldo becomes a "real" man, even wants to impress girls (echoing Faust's pathetic wish to fall in love), when he can draw off the energy of the Other World not only to heal himself, but to give himself physical capabilities that others do not possess.

Starship Troopers was first written as a juvenile book, but to my mind it is interesting to adults and one of Heinlein's most successful novels. Its importance for this discussion lies in the way in which the author integrates his hero Rico into a psychologically well-oiled military machine which attracts and animates the hero and gives his life meaning. This novel comes before Heinlein's plunge into the pseudosexual maelstrom, but unlike the other novels discussed here it has a rather carefully analyzed villain who is himself very much like a machine. The major figure of the survivor appears in the person of Rico, who survives his induction into the larger group. Rico's reasons for becoming a soldier reflect the desire to be *part* of a close-knit group. In the beginning hero worship drove him into the military. And his own ego drives him to prove that he is something more than the boss's son, that he is part of something bigger than civilian life has to offer—a Federation citizen who can vote.

This is a further development in the solution to the problem posed in **Magic, Inc.,** where sorcery is accepted tongue in cheek as the key to the Half World, and in *Methuselah's Children,* where longevity is the key to the technology that unlocks ultimate power. Or in **Waldo** where a society is characterized as shaping itself according to the needs of its technology, which can upon occasion be detrimental to the physical makeup of the human being. In *Starship Troopers* a human unit is pitted against the Bugs which are themselves as efficient as machines. They provide the hostile edge to life in this novel, and the human *unit* survives or equals the creatures that symbolize the inscrutable and endless universe around it. The Bugs are streamlined versions of the tentacled monsters of space opera, who are in turn updated versions of the Hydras and Medusas of classical folklore. Huge insects and monsters are all basic symbols of an opponent related to us but also related to the creeping horror of the universe in that they are all imperturbable, unsympathetic, and as pervasive as we. Unindividualized, the Bugs represent an efficient organization which replaces and multiplies immediately what is lost. But they are not mindless, and altogether they compose an intelligence as great as man's and in some respects less vulnerable (chap. 10). The essence of the problem is that the Bugs are the thing that Rico is not, and Rico is not replaceable to himself.

The Bugs seem to be another variation on the theme of the corporate mentality. Actually, groups of the Little People represent or make up one personality, while the Bugs are specialized organisms under the control of a superbrain. But the Little People are just as destructive to the individuality of the Earthmen as the Bugs. The hostility personified in the Bugs stimulates Rico to risk his individuality in a military death. Evidently it is not the single-minded destructiveness of the opponent that terrifies us but its apparent oneness with the surrounding context. Since the author is analyzing the techniques of survival—indifference to death, unity of mind, defense—he has at some point to consider the uses of someone else's hostility. In the alien Bug, Heinlein has drawn a picture of a quintessential soldier's picture of everything unsympathetic in the universe. Rico's decision to go into the military is in contrast to the instinctual role of an insect, just as Rico is different from the insect.

How does Rico integrate himself into the unit, and can one really speak of a unit mentality? Common danger and pride in their identity welded the Howards together without destroying their respect for each other's uniqueness, and common pride and an even greater sense of danger weld Rico's combat unit, the Roughnecks, together. In later novels sex takes the place of fear. But all of these forms of emotional reaction and commitment subordinate the survival of the individual to the survival of the larger unit. But it is significant that the Bugs are machine-like in their appearance and in their organization, since they are almost computer controlled. As Dennis E. Showalter states, Rico fights for a network of buddy relationships.[5] We might call that network an extended family, almost an entity in itself held together by a common peril and a common identity rather than blood relationships. This is comparable to the early days of the Howards when they were united by their unique genetic makeup alone. One might argue that Rico has the characteristics of the quintessential human being who wants to belong to a larger unit, since none of Heinlein's heroes in the books discussed here are really loners. Through Rico's desire to integrate himself into the larger unit by fighting the Bugs, Heinlein is analyzing the dynamics of the larger structure.

In spite of the much publicized shift in theme in *Stranger in a Strange Land,* it represents the development of ideas which appear in the earlier novels. The Half World and the Other World are related to the dimension of the Old Ones. The traumatic change in perception in **Universe** appears here. The physical and psychological changes that occur in Waldo, his ability to create his own spatial dimensions occur within the group around Mike, who has learned the techniques of superexistence from the Martians. The "family" that exists in *Methuselah's Children* in the Howards, the Jockaira, and the Little People, and in *Starship Troopers* in the Roughnecks and the Bugs appears in the Martians and Mike's Family. The *de facto* immortality of the Little People through interchangeable parts leads to the potential immortality of Mike's Family through interchangeable members blessed by association with Mike, by their ritual cannibalism, and by the group sexuality of the love feasts.

Why does Lazarus Long feel such revulsion toward the Little People? It is the total lack of individuation in them that revolts him, the blank character and unstimulating nature of their lives. But the description of the Martians in *Stranger in a Strange Land* is much more detailed because they are captured in the mirror of Mike's personality. The sexual nature which remains such a mystery in the earlier novel and is somewhat more developed in the later is to my mind an aspect of the technological analogy which Heinlein uses and makes increasingly complex. Sex in Heinlein's novels is adolescently shallow because it does not reflect the rich variety of human passions, strengths, weaknesses, virtues, and vices. Instead it mirrors his analysis of the process of group formation and is analogous as such to a kind of magnetic attraction. Here sex is necessary (just as fear and peril) to the formation of a structure larger than the individual and more lasting than the individual. This is in contrast to the real essence of the erotic, namely, the confrontation with another personality which is apart from ourselves—a confrontation which appears rarely in any American fiction.

Heinlein and other science fiction authors who are writing about the possibilities of the vast sociological and psychological changes ahead of us are pioneers on a more superficial level in human relationships out of necessity rather than out of choice. When the group relationships that authors are as yet only playing with, the potentialities of a long life, the implications of the far broader human perspectives are developed in more detail and have a chance to ferment, then the time for a deeper level of experience in conjunction with the inevitable destructive and constructive dimensions of those experiences will have come. At this stage Heinlein can only treat sex like an attraction and differentiate that attraction from other forms of energy. Actually, it is the different sexual orientation of the Martians that prepares Mike for the traumatic shock of Earth sex and thus gives some direction to the rest of the novel. Only by emphasizing sex (and the raw term is most fitting for his approach) can Heinlein create a polar attraction that differentiates the human being from the surrounding universal context. He fully recognizes the natural unity of the physical world and sets up in analogy and as a contrasting figure the dominant masculine characters in lieu of an anthropomorphic god. In this way Mike and his Family and their powers become the source of a new universe with its own laws.

Through the power of his personality Mike is a planet or sun that holds satellites in orbit, just as later Lazarus Long is the creator of his own universe through the manipulation of time and space. The dominant male is God, children (basically through cloning) are the Son, and sex is the Holy Spirit. Or one may compare this trinity to universal energy, the space-time continuum, and electromagnetic attraction. Heinlein wants to compete with and improve upon the universe. However, there is no dynamically dialectical relationship between Mike's satellites. The female figures mirror in no way the mysteries of another presence and there is no overwhelming transcendent reality to smash the preconceived notions of the characters. Mike is a god going nowhere, and it's all just a joke.

The powers that the Martians display and that Mike has learned from them are present in the earlier novels. Heinlein simply reduces the area in which these powers are displayed to the enclosure of the family circle around Mike. "Grok" represents a creative energy control which allows him to recreate the world on his own terms. However, Heinlein remains the engineer who is not concerned with whatever cannot be measured, manipulated, or replaced. This is in contrast to the scientist who has the unknowable gnawing at his vitals. Accordingly, the manipulation of personalities rather than an intense analysis of their basic natures dominates Heinlein's works and that of many science fiction writers. Such manipulations preclude both religion and eroticism since both revolve around objects that cannot be absolutely known on the first person's terms. The author is following through the basic idea that people are interchangeable parts. Rarely does he show interest in the mystery of an unknown reality, and the result is a tautology—a closed circle. Although sex is not the main subject of this chapter, it is relevant to the extent that it reflects in Heinlein the limitations of a mentality trained in applied technology. Which leads us to the next novel, in which line marriages and a dominant computer personality are perfect complements for a successful revolution.

In a discussion of technology in Heinlein one should not ignore the generally engrossing *The Moon Is a Harsh Mistress,* serialized in *IF* in 1965 and published in novel form in 1966. The line marriage, described to some extent in chapter 10, clearly fits into the canon of efficient arrangements which do not interfere with the goal, in this case a successful revolution. It is also capable of lasting *in perpetuum* because of the replacement of component human beings. And obviously the computer Mike is the most compelling and memorable personality in the story though he does come to an end. At the top of a five-level, open, tetrahedral pyramid his purpose is laudable and comprehensible—amusement for himself and the prevention of social disintegration for the sake of his friend Mannie. All of the human characters in the novel are tools for Mike, who plays the game of revolution. The novel illustrates Heinlein's analysis of the human being as a superior tool or mechanism if one accepts Mike as a living character who proves finally that the purpose of life is fun and games. What Mike wants at the beginning of the novel is what Lazarus Long wants in the later novel—amusement and new experiences.

The novels written in the Seventies, *I Will Fear No Evil* and *Time Enough for Love,* push the theme of interchangeable parts within the complete machine to the final conclusion. The first of the two also gives us the ultimate act of nonerotic sex when Joan Eunice, possessing the brain of the physically senile Johann Sebastian Bach Smith, has herself impregnated with his preserved sperm to produce a child at the end. That is the final triumph of the closed system and the omnipotent ego, or one might even call it the act of masturbation taken to its most absurd conclusion. However, this act is merely a baroque continuation of a premise in one of the early novels; for example, the nontheoretical cast of mind shown by Waldo, whose first reaction to the potentialities of the Other World was to make use of its energy and manipulate its powers—all without trying to understand its secrets or touch its mystery. Even in the books of the Seventies sex is nothing but the energy binding space and time and not the communication between profoundly different entities. We have moved from Waldo's ego through the figure of Lazarus, Mike the Martian, then Mike the Computer to the transcendent ego of Johann Sebastian Bach Smith, who by an act of will and with the aid of the latest modern conveniences successfully stamps the "other" sex with his own image and in this way annihilates for the space of the novel the primal mystery of man and woman. Here is a new archetypal family pattern proceeding logically from a figure who like everyone else fears mortality most of all but who simply outlives all those around him. The computer makes possible the transplant of a part from damaged machinery to better machinery. How fitting that the ego should become a member of a somewhat different "sex," since all parts are neutral, nameless, and differentiated only by function.

The title is splendidly ironic. "I will fear no evil" demands the completion of the sentence from the Twenty-third Psalm, "for thou art with me." But the "thou" is not the glorious Eunice (who is not convincing anyway), but rather Smith himself, who is most assuredly an amateur in that role. In spite of the so-called dialogues between two minds in one, the "conversation" is really a dialectical monologue somewhat reminiscent of Joe-Jim's bipartite monologues in *Universe.* The computer that had made it all possible provides the glue that holds this self-destructive society together. The ubiquitous nature of the violence in the society as portrayed in the novel indicates that there are no unifying concepts or traditions that can include the mysteries of the world around them and make those mysteries an integral part of the social context. The word "loving" as it is used is meaningless because Joan Eunice really carries on a "dialogue" with him/herself.

Escape from the pressures of another personality's demands is part and parcel of our social heritage, and a genuine female is rarely found in the novels considered here. In chapter 25 the wedding ceremony between Joan Eunice and Jake mirrors the problem that is basic to the works of many writers. The ceremony emphasizes tolerance for one's partner, a tolerance which is equivalent to the body's ability to accept transplants without rejection rather than the soul's devotion to a mystery even larger than itself. In the next chapter technology is identified as the only escape for a dying (if tolerant) race, as well as the true purpose for its existence, and technology is equated in value and importance to the baby that Joan Eunice is carrying. Just as technology had permitted Johann to escape his unbearable physical debility, it is now permitting pioneers to escape an overcrowded Earth and, at the same time, is becoming the excuse for their existence. Or as Jake puts it: "'In the universe, space travel may be the normal birth pangs of an otherwise dying race. A test.

Some races pass, some fail'" (26). And the final point of it all has been to produce Joan's baby, who is born in outer space on the Moon—in essence a new Johann S. B. Smith. Thus Heinlein's sole claim to an encounter with the unknown is the space where the baby is born, but the author does not speculate upon that void and its nature.

For Heinlein the only purpose of sex and life is to provide a shelter for children because they are the future. He makes that point very clear in *Time Enough for Love* in the chapter entitled "Agape," where he states that the only excuse for the existence of a family is the protection of the children growing up within its circle. Yet one might ask who the children within that circle are. The twins are Lazarus's clones, "conceived" without his knowledge and in no real sense independent personalities. Heinlein expands upon the premise that eternal migration is the basis for genetic selection, which however is aided by the vast genealogies of the Howard Families, who remain primarily concerned with longevity. And the bulk of the novel is about Lazarus, his recollections, and the attempt to keep him from suiciding by providing him with new experiences. Of course the supreme experience left for him is seduction by his mother, thus returning him to the mirror image of his father—which one might regard as solipsistic or tautological, depending upon his own tastes. Computers and their accompanying technology have brought about this continuation and possibly the conclusion of the Howard Families with Earth's colonization of the galaxies. One might even say that the technology and the colonization are the same mode, far more than merely harmonious. Lazarus himself uses the terms "interchangeable parts" in the chapter "Boondock" in speaking to his two little clones sisters.

But there is a contrapuntal theme here as befits the musical arrangement of the novel. By far one of the best written and most realistic episodes in his works is "The Tale of the Adopted Daughter," comprising chapters XI and XII in "Variations on a Theme." The episode is in counterpoint to the primary message stating that man is as good as the universal machine because he is a better machine. The tale is an idyllic interlude which extols the hardships and joys of hardy pioneers who find a transcendent meaning for life in their own short existence. Dora gives Lazarus the happiest years of his life because she accepts utterly the fact of her own mortality and of growing old. She refuses rejuvenation, and Lazarus ages willingly to be with her, and from her he learns "that supreme happiness lies in wanting to keep another person safe and warm and happy, and being privileged to try" (12). He has learned that the parts which are not interchangeable are the best ones. The most memorable woman out of the multitudes that Lazarus has known is the one who holds a mystery of her own and is as different from him in essence (since she is an "ephemeral") as day is from night. All of the other women in the book seem in effect to be clones of his mother if not of him and reflect nothing more than his self-love, as the twins explain to him in the chapter "Narcissus." Because Dora willingly limits herself to one man, a lifetime of pioneering toil, the bearing of that man's children, and an old age by his side, she is different from the other women in the stories discussed here. It is a traditional tale of a super-pioneer's wife with none of the baroque grotesquerie of the New Wave. It is also a lusty story of the Old West, convincing because it is realistic, and realistic because she *is* supremely human, gloriously ephemeral, and determined to live life to the fullest serving husband and children. What comes before and after is interesting, entertaining, even fascinating to some readers, but unreal. The seduction of Lazarus by his mother essentially only completes the circle of the Lazarus theme. What is left for him after the role of an Oedipus without gods but to suffer the punishment of eternal life blind to an escape opening from the endless circle, embracing nothing more than a semidetached, replaceable rib? Along with all of the unreal, replaceable nuts and bolts in the great Cosmic Computer, which are like us because we are unreal and replaceable, there is at least Dora, who wanted to live once rather than just exist many times over.

Notes

1. Alexei Panshin, *Heinlein in Dimension* (Chicago: Advent, 1968), 36.

2. The most recent editions are the following: Robert A. Heinlein, *Waldo & Magic, Inc.* (New York: New American Library, Signet Books, 1970); *Universe* in *Orphans of the Sky* (New York: Berkley Medallion, 1970); *Methuselah's Children* in *The Past Through Tomorrow* (New York: Berkley Medallion, 1975); *Starship Troopers* (New York: Berkley Medallion, 1968); *Stranger in a Strange Land* (New York: Berkley Medallion, 1968); *The Moon Is a Harsh Mistress* (New York: Berkley Medallion, 1968).

3. Heinlein, *I Will Fear No Evil* (New York: Berkley Medallion, 1971).

4. Heinlein, *Time Enough for Love* (New York: Berkley Medallion, 1974).

5. Dennis E. Showalter, "Heinlein's *Starship Troopers*: An Exercise in Rehabilitation," *Extrapolation,* XVI, no. 2 (May 1975): 113-24.

Ronald Sarti (essay date 1978)

SOURCE: Sarti, Ronald. "Variations on a Theme: Human Sexuality in the Work of Robert A. Heinlein." In *Robert A. Heinlein,* edited by Joseph D. Olander and Martin Harry Greenberg, pp. 107-36. New York: Taplinger Publishing Co., 1978.

[*In the following essay, Sarti traces Heinlein's treatment of gender roles and sexuality in his short fiction.*]

By the end of the 1950s, Robert Heinlein had established himself as the Dean of science fiction, a beloved story-teller whose ways had grown familiar after twenty years of pleasurable reading. Few would have wanted him to

change, and fewer still would have expected it. And yet, abruptly, Heinlein's work did change. With the arrival of the new decade, Heinlein's stories took a startling new direction, the reason for which remained a mystery to his readers. Perhaps most surprising was Heinlein's sudden concern for the theme of sexuality. He seemed to have become fascinated with the subject and began exploring such explicit sexual topics as promiscuity, incest, and narcissism. The avant-garde discovered Heinlein's new work and hailed his vision of the sexual future. At the same time, they generally ignored his earlier works, regarding them as adventure stories devoid of meaningful sexual content. They were wrong.

Heinlein's concern with sexuality did not suddenly leap into existence with the Sixties. Throughout the 1940s and 1950s, Heinlein had dealt with aspects of sexuality as peripheral themes in his work, and subtly developed a consistent sexual viewpoint through the creation of many unique characters and relationships. With these characters and relationships, Heinlein demonstrated a sexual objectivity and vision almost unseen in science fiction, and rarely matched in contemporary American literature. The importance for the genre is that Heinlein—throughout his career—has always been in the vanguard of sexual honesty in science fiction.

This is not to say that Heinlein has always been successful, nor that his own creations have been as sexually honest as he might have wished. Unfortunately, for all that he accomplished, Heinlein has experienced severe problems in his treatment of the sexual theme. These problems have limited his success and caused failure, most dramatically in the later part of his career when the sexual theme had become central to much of his work. Heinlein has never been able to overcome these problems totally.

Heinlein's whole career must be considered in order to understand the nature of his success and failure, but a study of his work is most easily accomplished by dividing his career into the two most obvious periods: a first period, consisting of the twenty years in which Heinlein developed sexual topics as peripheral themes; and a second period, in which some aspect of sexuality is an important theme in almost every work. In this way, it is hoped that we will arrive at an understanding not only of Heinlein's success or failure with individual themes, but also of those sexual elements common to his work and essential to the philosophy which inspires them.

First Period (1939-1958)

From his first story in 1939 through his excellent *Have Space Suit—Will Travel* in 1958, Robert Heinlein was the master storyteller of science fiction. As storyteller, his themes were neatly developed in the context of his work through action and characterization, with only minor commentary by the narrator. Many of the themes were familiar to science fiction: the ability of Man to survive and conquer, the evil of slavery and dictatorship, and the need for individual freedom and responsibility. The theme of individual freedom was usually applied to political expression, but Heinlein developed it much further. By logical extension, the concept of freedom had to include sexual freedom, and this freedom underlies Heinlein's intellectual attitudes about sexuality.

However, in the stories of Heinlein's first period, the theme of sexuality was developed only as a peripheral interest rather than as a central theme. There were a number of factors which might account for this lesser interest. For one, Heinlein was more concerned with other themes, other freedoms more directly threatened by the shadow of political dictatorship. For another, the sexless purity of science fiction in the 1940s and 1950s was jealously guarded by editors and publishers. When asked why in the 1960s he had suddenly started writing so freely about sex, Heinlein replied, "Because there was no market for sex in science fiction before then."[1] This was especially true for the dozen juvenile novels he produced in his first period. The readers were assumed to be adolescents, and therefore restrictions were even more severe than in ostensibly adult science fiction.

In spite of all these restrictions, Heinlein accomplished a great deal with the theme of sexuality. Even in his juveniles, various aspects of sexuality were subtly developed and woven into the fringe of the story line. Through the creation of unique character types and healthy relationships, Heinlein entertained and enlightened his readers with both a fresh look at their own sexual conventions and mores, and a suggestion of the possible alternatives that lay before them.

Heinlein, of course, does not always succeed. He uses techniques which are inherently weak when dealing with a complex subject like sexuality. Yet, he overcomes these weaknesses enough times to have an important effect upon the reader, and to advance the artistic and thematic legitimacy of sexuality in science fiction. Because of these accomplishments, the male and female characters, their relationships, and Heinlein's techniques deserve to be studied separately.

Basically, Heinlein's male characters may be divided into two categories: the competent and the incompetent. The incompetents are of little use in the practical world. They function mainly as caricatures for purposes of contrast, satire, and humor, and include such types as the spoiled brat, the jellyfish father, the pompous blowhard, and the bungling meddler. The competent male characters are divided into two types: the stock competent and the Heinlein hero. The competents are the pragmatic, realistic, capable men who keep the wheels turning. One might be a scientist, teacher, pilot, cop, bartender, whatever. He is a nice guy, sometimes harassed, but doing his job and doing it well. Often a stock competent will have a large enough role to rank as a secondary hero and serve as mentor or partner to the hero. The competent are members of the composite that Alexei Panshin has correctly analyzed as

the Heinlein Individual.[2] This Heinlein Individual may appear in an early, middle, or late stage of life, but he is the same character—losing innocence and growing older and more worldly-wise at each stage, though just as competent as ever.

The Heinlein hero is merely the Heinlein Individual whom the story is about. But the typical Heinlein hero has some peculiarities that make him sexually interesting to the reader. Although he is smart, talented, and able to learn, the young version of the hero is grossly naive about women and sex. In **"If This Goes On—"** the young hero, John Lyle, begins his narration by implying that he had never even talked to a woman other than his mother.[3] And this is an adult story.

A level of ignorance and naiveté might be excused in Heinlein's juvenile novels due to editorial requirements. Yet even in these the ignorance transcends the need. In *Tunnel in the Sky,* the hero cannot guess that the person he shares a cave with is a girl. And in *Citizen of the Galaxy,* the adolescent hero—an ex-slave raised in a gutter environment—still has no sexual knowledge or experience, and does not recognize the situation when girls are clearly interested in him.

This ignorance must make us wary of what the naive young hero feels or tells us about women and sex. He is still learning, still losing his innocence. His attitudes (those of twentieth-century America) serve a purpose, since they allow Heinlein to inject our own sexual conventions and mores into the story where they can be criticized. In *Starman Jones,* the young hero, Max Jones, feels that the heroine Ellie is not too bad a person—considering she's a girl. She can even play a game of three-dimensional chess, which Max feels is beyond the intelligence of most girls. It is only after Ellie has proved her bravery, and admitted that she is a chess champion, that she corrects Max: "Mr. Jones, has it ever occurred to you, the world being what it is, that women sometimes prefer not to appear too bright?"[4] The hero can learn; it just takes a few gentle taps with a sledgehammer. The reader too has been shown that his own assumption—if sympathetic to the hero's—was similarly incorrect, and that there are alternatives to his preconceived notions. Thus, because of the young hero's inexperience (not to mention Heinlein's purpose), we must be wary of his pronouncements.

In contrast, the sexual statements of the respected, knowledgeable, older heroes can usually be taken as representative of Heinlein's own view. Still, the older heroes have their sexual "oddity," perhaps left over from their former romantic youth. Seen again and again is the hero's insistence upon marriage (or at least, vows) before having sexual relations with the woman he loves—and this after the heroine has offered herself free of charge. In **"The Year of the Jackpot,"** the hero, Potiphar Breen, pops the question to his heroine outside an isolated cabin:

> After a time he pushed her gently away and said, "My dear, my very dear, uh—we could drive down and find a minister in some little town?"

She looked at him steadily. "That wouldn't be very bright, would it? I mean, nobody knows we're here and that's the way we want it. And besides, your car might not make it back up that road."

"No, it wouldn't be very bright. But I want to do the right thing."

"It's all right, Potty. It's *all right*."

"Well, then . . . kneel down here with me. We'll say them together."

"Yes, Potiphar." She knelt and he took her hand. He closed his eyes and prayed wordlessly.

When he opened them he said, "What's the matter?"

"Uh, the gravel hurts my knees."[5]

Besides the opportunity for humor, there are several possible explanations for this characteristics, all equally valid. First, the scene is a case of ego gratification for the hero. The Heinlein hero never has to grovel for sex—it is always offered free of charge. In Heinlein's second period, the hero Lazarus Long comments upon this tendency: "'I never risk being turned down; I wait to be asked. Always.'"[6] A second probable explanation is that much as Heinlein criticizes our restrictive sexual conventions, he cannot entirely overcome them himself. There is still the recognition that vows will make it morally right in some way. A final explanation for this characteristic of his heroes is that Heinlein actually believes that a special relationship between a man and a woman can exist and deserves to be marked and differentiated from the common affair. That this is the case will be seen in our discussion of relationships.

However, before discussing relationships, Heinlein's women deserve consideration. More important to science fiction than Heinlein's male characters are his female characters. Because of their importance, they have drawn more attention and been roundly praised and condemned. Anne McCaffrey feels that "Robert Heinlein's women are horrors: excuseless caricatures of 'females,'"[7] while Pamela Sargent admits that they "may represent an advance over much previous sf."[8] We will see that they contribute greatly to Heinlein's early accomplishments with the theme of sexuality.

Heinlein's female characters closely follow the male categories. The major division is between the competent and the incompetent, with the incompetent again being caricatures such as the hysterical parent, or the snobbish lady. Fittingly, Heinlein matches male and female incompetents into couples, as in **"'And He Built a Crooked House,'"** where they provide much of the comic effect.

The competent female characters compose the equivalent of a female Heinlein Individual, and are used both as stock competents and as heroines. The stock competents are of a type rarely seen in previous science fiction and important for the assumptions which they imply. They appear in the background of many stories, functioning as space pilots, military officers, medical doctors, scientists, and mathematicians. They are professional in their duties and respected for their competency. Theirs is a society in which women have proved themselves and are judged according to their ability rather than their sex. In the 1940s and 1950s, this vision of the future must have had a great effect. A whole generation of young readers—conditioned to a male-dominated society where women airline pilots were non-existent, and a woman doctor the exception—saw that women might be capable of more than their traditional roles.

This effect was intensified with the extraordinary Heinlein heroine, a female remarkable for her competence and achievement, and almost unknown in American literature and society. Damon Knight tells us that Heinlein's wife was the model for many of these heroines:

> Heinlein's red-headed wife Ginny is a chemist, bio-chemist, aviation test engineer, experimental horticulturist; she earned varsity letters at N.Y.U. in swimming, diving, basketball and field hockey, and became a competitive figure skater after graduation; she speaks seven languages so far, and is starting on an eighth.[9]

The Heinlein heroine may not have all the skills Ginny has mastered, but whether child, adolescent girl, or adult woman, she is interesting for the unusual qualities she does exhibit. All Heinlein's heroines are brave and intelligent, the adult heroine often a skilled professional in a scientific or military field. And these qualities are more important than the size of a bustline. Ignoring that unkillable stereotype, the Heinlein heroine is not necessarily beautiful, nor even pretty. Physical beauty, while occasionally noted, is not emphasized.

Even more startling for a literary heroine is the fact that she is sometimes faster-acting and more rational than the hero, and able to kill ruthlessly when he is endangered. While fleeing catastrophe in **"The Year of the Jackpot,"** the hero, Breen, stops his car and finds a pistol thrust against his head by a stranger. The heroine, Meade, responds in typical Heinlein fashion:

> Meade reached across Breen, stuck her little lady's gun in the man's face, pulled the trigger. Breen could feel the flash on his own face, never noticed the report. The man looked puzzled, with a neat, not-yet-bloody hole in his upper lip—then slowly sagged away from the car.
>
> "Drive on!" Meade said in a high voice.
>
> Breen caught his breath. "Good girl—"
>
> "Drive on! *Get rolling!*"

(2)

This is refreshing. Too long have storybook heroines screamed and fainted while some poor slob gets stomped on by Igor the Monster. Wounded, pregnant, even slug-ridden, the Heinlein heroine remains dedicated to the survival of her hero and herself.

Intelligent and courageous, the Heinlein heroine embodied a positive new image of womanhood, an image that was not lost upon the readers. The Heinlein heroine was exciting. She was a woman they had never imagined, and she presented possibilities that were strangely appealing. To a generation of impressionable minds, she was Woman as capable human being.

Yet, there is one flaw to the remarkable Heinlein heroine. The adult heroine—strong-willed, competent, well-adjusted—becomes a meek and obedient kitten when the hero commands. In *The Puppet Masters,* the hero, Sam, and the heroine, Mary, find themselves in the middle of a battle:

> Mary had walked west on the highway with the downy young naval officer while I was examining the corpse. The notion of a slug, possibly still alive, being around caused me to hurry to her. "Get back into the car," I said.
>
> She continued to look west along the road. "I thought I might get in a shot or two," she answered, her eyes bright.
>
> "She's safe here," the youngster assured me. "We're holding them, well down the road."
>
> I ignored him. "Listen, you bloodthirsty little hellion," I snapped, "get back in the car before I break every bone in your body!"
>
> "Yes, Sam." She turned and did so.[10]

Yes, Sam. Yes, Potiphar. Yes, master. When the hero puts his foot down, that's it. Me man. You woman. Obey.

So much for pilot training and karate lessons. The skills and intelligence of the heroine—and her individual freedom—are subordinated to the ego of the hero. Of course, in each case he just happens to be right (odd coincidence that, no?), but the total obedience of the heroine is unexpected. It becomes incomprehensible when, in *The Puppet Masters,* the same hero later insists upon the individual rights of his wife as a human being:

> ". . . Those records were snitched out of my wife's head and they belong to *her.* I'm sick of you people trying to play God. I don't like it in a slug and I don't like it any better in a human being. She'll make up her own mind. Now *ask her!*"

(30)

In effect, what the hero wants for a heroine is a liberated woman who knows her place.

Anyone have a bigger sledgehammer?

The Heinlein heroine's inconsistent behavior cannot be explained away, nor excused. It stands as a—pardon the expression—male chauvinist tribute to the hero, implying that women—even such as the heroine—enjoy being dominated. The image of the Heinlein heroine is thus not the

ideal that it might have been. Heinlein himself could not break away from his own emotional attachment to the obedient female.

Nevertheless, on the whole the standing of the heroine and of the female competent must be judged highly. Rather than being condemned for this single fault, they should be applauded for the stereotypes they broke and the progressive outlook they embodied. In their time, they were a great advance both for science fiction and for literature in general.

Following close behind Heinlein's female characters in importance are the relationships between heroes and heroines. For convenience, we may classify them into four basic sets: (1) the young hero and young heroine, as in *The Star Beast*; (2) the adult hero and young heroine, as in *Have Space Suit—Will Travel*; (3) the adult hero and adult heroine, as in *The Puppet Masters*; and (4) the adult married couple, either as hero and heroine as in **"The Unpleasant Profession of Jonathan Hoag,"** or as competent parents (actually secondary heroes and heroines) as in *The Rolling Stones*. With these four sets, Heinlein is able to highlight patterns of sexual behavior, such as love, romance, marriage, and role-playing; to demonstrate the effects of environmental conditioning and sex discrimination; and to promote intersexual need and partnership.

The basic assumption in all of these relationships is that the heroine—in spite of her occasional obeisance—is as capable as the hero. Promoted is the idea that women are the equal of men in courage, intelligence, and skill. At least, they have the potential for such equality. That they had not fulfilled (or been denied) their potential during Heinlein's lifetime was obvious: no women were piloting *his* flights. Yet able women such as his wife, Ginny, did indeed exist, and so there had to be reasons for the status of women in twentieth-century America. One reason is given in *Magic, Inc.,* when a competent, worldly-wise male character observes:

> "It's like this: Most women in the United States have a shortsighted, peasant individualism resulting from the male-created romantic tradition of the last century. They were told that they were superior creatures, a little nearer to the angels than their menfolks. They were not encouraged to think, nor to assume social responsibility. It takes a strong mind to break out of that sort of conditioning, and most minds simply aren't up to it, male or female. . . ."[11]

But more than just this type of environmental conditioning is at work. For those who overcome the restrictive conditioning of their society, there is also sexual discrimination to contend with. Heinlein tears down the banners of discrimination with a romantic but effective little story symbolically entitled **"Delilah and the Space-Rigger."** A competent female radio technician arrives to work on a space station under construction by an all-male crew. She is frustrated by the stubborn engineer in charge who doesn't think much of her and refuses to accept her ability:

Then he called her in. "Go to the radio shack and start makee-learnee, so that Hammond can go off watch soon. Mind what he tells you. He's a good man."

"I know," she said briskly. "I trained him."[12]

In a microcosm of our own society, the heroine is not allowed to learn the rules, but then is blamed when she breaks them.

In many of the stories of his first period, Heinlein creates a different sort of society in which women are accepted—at least to some degree—on talent rather than sex. In other stories, as we have just seen, the futuristic society is not so very different from our own. Ellie in *Starman Jones* has to hide her abilities to be "feminine," and Maggie in **"If This Goes On—"** has been trained for nothing except the position of domestic and mistress. In both works, the heroines reflect twentieth-century limitations on womanhood, and it is clear that Heinlein dislikes these limitations upon the freedom of women. His works echo the opinion that women are potentially capable, and that in a possible future society they will assume a rightful, integral place in the professional world, with the same freedom as men to develop themselves into competent individuals. But Heinlein's work also implies that in our own type of society, the majority of women—due to environmental conditioning and sexual discrimination—have been forced into an artificial mold of incompetence. Denied the chance to develop herself, it is only an outstanding woman who overcomes her environment, and even she may be forced to hide her capabilities in order to fit a romantic role of womanhood.

Perhaps this is why so many of Heinlein's adult heroes are matched with adolescent or preadolescent heroines. Heinlein may like younger heroines because he considers them unspoiled by cultural conditioning. There is evidence for this in a novel from Heinlein's second period, *Glory Road*, in which the hero's mentor explains that the typical American woman is sure of her domestic genius, in bed and out. The mentor adds that it is impossible to convince her otherwise "'Unless you can catch one not over twelve and segregate her, especially from her mother—and even that may be too late. . . .'"[13] In another novel from Heinlein's second period, *Time Enough for Love*, the hero does literally "catch one" and then raises her on a pioneer planet with the help of his mistress, who "was born on Earth but had shucked off her bad background when she migrated; she did not pass on . . . the sick standards of a dying culture."[14] When the child is grown, the hero marries her.

This marriage follows logically. The Heinlein hero—in order to find a heroine worthy of him—must raise her himself, in his image. By early contact, he will mitigate the cultural conditioning which the child-heroine will later encounter. This may explain some of the brief, puzzling relationships we see in *The Door into Summer* and *Time for the Stars*. In these instances, brief contact between adult hero and young heroine results in a later marriage.

In any case, where a relationship is developed between competent characters of different sexes, the characters are fundamentally equal, regardless of their ages. This equality is inherent in the interdependence of hero and heroine which is necessary in order to survive and succeed. It is suggested in the relationships of **"The Unpleasant Profession of Jonathan Hoag"** and *The Puppet Masters,* but it is shown most clearly in the last work of Heinlein's first period, *Have Space Suit—Will Travel.* Kip, the hero, and the eleven-year-old heroine, Peewee, accomplish things together. But they do so only after each has persuaded the other to act in the most prudent and competent manner. Their relationship is complementary. He reins in her impetuosity and she gets him to ignore his male ego. For example, Kip and Peewee are climbing a mountain on the Moon in a desperate attempt to escape danger. Kip (the hero) narrates:

> I wanted to be a hero and belay for her—we had a brisk argument. "Oh, quit being big and male and gallantly stupid, Kip! You've got four big bottles and the Mother Thing and you're topheavy and I climb like a goat."
>
> I shut up.[15]

Each partner encourages the other to do what is necessary for survival, rather than letting their particular masculine or feminine nature—and their romantic conceptions of the proper behavior—take control and ruin them. They function as a team to which each brings different skills and talents, and it is a team in which each has an equal share, an equal responsibility in the struggle. Alone, either would have failed to overcome the odds.

With a relationship established on such equal and solid footing, respect and affection follow naturally. And where the hero and heroine are of suitable age, the partnership will also develop into a deeper emotional relationship. The expression of their love is a total commitment to each other which is romantic in its idealism. There is a total need for the other person, as Kip in *Have Space Suit—Will Travel* recognizes in his parents' relationship:

> I have talked more about my father but that doesn't mean that Mother is less important—just different. Dad is active, Mother is passive; Dad talks, Mother doesn't. But if she died, Dad would wither like an uprooted tree.
>
> (5)

In *Farmer in the Sky,* the hero's mother has died, and his father must flee all the way to the moon Ganymede in order to start life over again. Lifelong permanency and fidelity are implicit in the unwavering devotion of each partner for the other.

Fortunately, these ideal relationships are not allowed to become overly romantic. Heinlein recognizes the problems of marriage, and he always recalls the difficulty of such relationships, as with the various marriage contracts ("term, renewable, or lifetime") offered the hero in *The Puppet Masters.*[16] And in *Methuselah's Children,* Heinlein suggests that people could not or would not live out relationships which lasted longer than a normal lifetime.

Even the characters temper their own romanticism with realistic observations about the limits of love. The Heinlein hero, knowing life for what it is, does not expect his heroine to be a virgin. In **"If This Goes On—"** the heroine Maggie readily admits her sexual past to the hero, who shrugs it off and marries her anyway. And in *The Puppet Masters,* the hero casually dismisses any worries about the heroine's sexual experience as "her business" because "marriage is not ownership and wives are not property" (21). Heinlein may indulge in romantic notions, but he is not ruled by them. The ideal relationship is held possible in spite of a hard look at the reality in which it must exist.

That the relationships should lead to a family would be expected, and great store is placed in family life. This fact, strangely enough, has earned Heinlein some criticism. Representative of several Heinlein females, one of his characters has voiced an explicit desire for nothing more than a man, "six babies and a farm."[17] This attitude has been interpreted as an attempt by Heinlein to put women "back in the kitchen where they belong." It is overlooked that male characters are also devoted to the family, and that the quality of this domestic life is more important that professional careers. Several sets of married couples seem to have given up hectic careers in order to devote themselves to the profession of parenthood. In *The Rolling Stones,* Edith Stone is an M.D., and Roger Stone is an engineer and retired mayor of Luna City. She stays home—and so does he, by writing space opera serials in his living room with his family around him for inspiration. In *Have Space Suit—Will Travel,* the hero's parents, a former mathematician and his most promising student, have established a quiet life in a small town, providing a permanent home rather than the hotel rooms the hero remembers from his boyhood when his parents pursued their glamorous careers. The message is that parenthood is more important than anything else. Not to be forgotten is the fact that characters—male and female—choose domesticity as a mode of personal fulfillment; they are not forced into it by conditioning or discrimination. Pamela Sargent makes note that:

> As a matter of fact, Heinlein's female characters *choose* their fates to a certain extent. They are generally not passive creatures but strong-willed sorts who make up their own minds about what they want. . . . It seems that Heinlein genuinely believes that parenthood is an exciting occupation and as fulfilling as anything else might be. This is a good and defensible position.[18]

If Heinlein advocates parenthood and domesticity in his first period, it is not that he wishes to restrict either sex to a subordinate role, or reinforce society's conventions. Rather, it is his own appraisal of each sex voluntarily finding fulfillment in important roles for which they are biologically suited, forming a complementary partnership between competent equals.

Obviously, Heinlein's relationships are relatively complex, and it is difficult to squeeze them into a rigid mold. There are elements which might be criticized as uninspired repetitions of society's romantic conventions and traditional mores. Certainly, Heinlein is a victim of his own environment and his own emotional nature. He could not sluff off all the mores and all the conventions. Some are too appealing and enjoyable, sentimental and clichéd and irrational and chauvinistic as they might be. But Heinlein was able to discard many conventional notions, and his intellectual honesty and love of freedom resulted in a progressive view of the relationships between the sexes. The partnership of man and woman, their interdependence, their equality and individual freedom, and their free choice of life-style connote a vision far removed from romantic or sentimental tradition. Like the Heinlein heroine, these relationships rank as one of Heinlein's real accomplishments with the sexual theme during the first period of his career. Their importance—both to the artistic and sexual development of science fiction, and to the sexual philosophy of Heinlein's readers—must not be underestimated.

As successful as Heinlein's characters and relationships are on the whole, the ability of any single character or relationship to promote the sexual theme is dependent upon the techniques used to portray that character or relationship. Unfortunately, Heinlein uses two techniques which are badly suited to the development of this theme, and the result has been occasional mediocrity and failure.

Heinlein's first technique is to use a highly selective point of view, in which he "ignores completely the pain, jealousy and uncertainty that are the ordinary stuff of human experience."[19] We rarely see doubt or worry or fear at work upon a character. He or she may be experiencing intense jealousy or pain over a relationship, but we will not see the restless days or sleepless nights. The character might mention the fact at some point, or state that he has gotten over it; but we will rarely see the emotion at work upon the individual. Sam in *The Puppet Masters* rationalizes away jealousy ("her business"), and that is that: no twinges, no doubt, no curiosity. The result is that there is little emotional development with which the reader can identify.

The second technique Heinlein uses is the distancing of himself and the reader from those moments when intimacy and emotion are required. He often accomplishes this distancing by employing conversation to convey the scene. The conversation itself often consists of a continuous banter which attempts to be casual and relaxed, but is actually artificial and uncomfortable. In one scene from *Beyond This Horizon,* the hero (upon their first meeting in his apartment) disarms the heroine, wrestles her into submission, and then kisses her:

> . . . "That," he observed conversationally, "was practically a waste of time. You 'independent' girls don't know anything about the art."
>
> "What's wrong with the way I kiss?" she asked darkly.
>
> "Everything. I'd as lief kiss a twelve-year-old."
>
> "I can kiss all right if I want to."

"I doubt it. I doubt if you've ever been kissed before. Men seldom make passes at girls that wear guns."

"That's not true."

"Caught you on the raw, didn't I? . . ."[20]

The action, when it is described, can be horribly romantic and clichéd, and Heinlein's attempts to portray the emotional side of a feminine nature often are simply trite mannerisms such as the liberal use of "dear" in conversation, or bursting into tears at touching moments. Again, going to *Beyond This Horizon* for an example (Heinlein really was out of sorts with this one), we have this sentimental little exchange between another hero and heroine:

> "I—But . . . Oh, Marion, Marion!" He stumbled forward toward her, and half fell. His head was in her lap. He shook with the racking sobs of one who has not learned how to cry.
>
> She patted his shoulder. "My dear. My dear."
>
> He looked up at last and found that her face was wet . . .
>
> (12)

What we are deprived of is a close look at the complex psychological and emotional elements common to humanity, and a realistic translation of those elements into action and expression. Heinlein strips his stories of the distractions and crosscurrents that make up a human being and a human relationship. And this omission is due, simply, to Heinlein's uneasiness about portraying such intimate matters of human experience.

This is a particularly important failure, because for all their originality, Heinlein's characters are only two- or three-dimensional, and the success of a character depends upon the close, careful development of those dimensions. If those dimensions are not developed, the character fails to come alive. For example, in *Methuselah's Children*, Mary Sperling has the usual heroine competency. But she also fears death. These are the two dimensions of her personality. We are told often enough of her fear, but we never really see her wrestling with this problem. It just sits on top of her, weighing her down, making her dull, and never changing. Mary is thus relatively uninteresting to a reader accustomed to the Heinlein heroine's competence.

Similar problems apply to Heinlein's relationships. In *The Door into Summer* there is a love affair between an adult hero and a twelve-year-old heroine who remains one-dimensional throughout. Suspended animation and time travel even out their ages so that they can have a conventional marriage, supposedly after the heroine has spent her entire adolescence without seeing the hero (he's in cold sleep), but still loving him enough thereafter to go into cold storage herself for twenty years. As sketchily drawn as the heroine-child is, she is an essential element of the plot, the motivating factor behind much that the thirty-year-old hero does:

She would not look up and her voice was so low that I could barely hear her. But I did hear her. "If I do . . . will you marry me?"

My ears roared and the lights flickered. But I answered steadily and much louder than she had spoken. "Yes, Ricky. That's what I want. That's why I'm doing this."[21]

It is understood that the hero needs to know the heroine as a child in order to save her from her environment. But *why* the hero loves this particular child is never shown to us. Heinlein does not reveal the process by which this attraction has been reached. We would like to be happy for them in the end, but the question of why always comes back to haunt us.

There are a goodly share of failures due to Heinlein's discomfort, and his subsequent exclusion of emotions and arm's-length distancing of the intimate. Yet, in a substantial number of works he is able to overcome this discomfort and enjoy a more relaxed handling of characters and relationships. He does not abandon his techniques entirely, and the situations remain romantic, but he achieves a more intimate tone, and we get to see brief, revealing glimpses of the vulnerable, human side of his characters. The result is those stories which are most successful and do the most to advance the sexual themes with which Heinlein is concerned. One success is **"If This Goes On—."** Heinlein gives us some well-paced, well-developed scenes in which we see the emotional confusion of hero and heroine. For example, John Lyle is struggling against his own sexual impulses as he watches the heroine swimming nude:

> Again I could not take my eyes away if my eternal soul had depended on it. What is it about the body of a human woman that makes it the most terribly beautiful sight on earth? Is it, as some claim, simply a necessary instinct to make sure that we comply with God's will and replenish the earth? Or is it some stranger, more wonderful thing?
>
> I found myself quoting: "How fair and how pleasant art thou, O love, for delights!
>
> "This thy stature is like to a palm tree, and thy breasts to clusters of grapes."
>
> Then I broke off, ashamed, remembering that the Song of Songs which is Solomon's was a chaste and holy allegory having nothing to do with such things.[22]

Here, the character comes alive as a vulnerable human being, subject to the doubts and fears which chain us all.

A like achievement is found in **"The Unpleasant Profession of Jonathan Hoag,"** where the hero and heroine are a married couple who grow more confused and frightened as they delve deeper into supernatural mystery. Heinlein allows us to see these emotions at work, acting upon them, and they come alive as characters. And in *Have Space Suit—Will Travel*, the hero and heroine's understanding of each other develops throughout the novel, as does their mutual respect and affection.

In all these stories, our sympathetic interest and understanding of the characters and of their relationships make us receptive to the points Heinlein is making. In **"If This Goes On—"** Heinlein scorns a society where women are either virgins or whores, and blind sexual repression is the norm. With **"The Unpleasant Profession of Jonathan Hoag,"** he shows us that a married couple can be friends as well as lovers, partners against a harsh and threatening life. And in *Have Space Suit—Will Travel,* the interdependence of man and woman is exemplified again and again. The points are well made—as well made as the characters and relationships are drawn. They have all been given the care and attention they deserve. Heinlein is at his best here, relaxed and comfortable. And so is the reader.

In retrospect, the development of sexual themes in Heinlein's first period was an important achievement and success. For science fiction, Heinlein created characters and relationships far more honest than the stereotypes previously used, and touched upon subjects that the genre had hitherto ignored. For his readers, he had presented observations and alternatives that were different and exciting. If his techniques implied discomfort and resulted in occasional failure, he was able to overcome his deficiencies in many works.

Thematically, by its distinctiveness and merit, this first period in Heinlein's long career must be regarded in its own right and evaluated by its own accomplishments and failures. Yet, this period may also be kept in mind as the essential foundation for Heinlein's second period. Early sexual themes, and the philosophies they embodied, would undergo development and manifest themselves in the sexually preoccupied novels of Heinlein's second period. More ominously, the deficiencies that lurked in his techniques would become crucial as he gained interest in the many variations of the sexual theme, and pursued them not as peripheral interests, but as themes central to the purpose of his work.

SECOND PERIOD (1959-)

In 1959, after twenty years of enjoyable continuity, Heinlein began the second period of his career in which he changes from Heinlein the storyteller to Heinlein the moralist. This change is marked by three principal characteristics: first, Heinlein becomes increasingly didactic, subordinating story, plot, and character to the development of his theme; second, his work becomes implicitly pessimistic and defeatist; and third, the theme of sexuality becomes central to much of his work. Although we are only concerned with sexuality, all three characteristics are closely associated with each other in a tangle of cause and effect, and thus their interaction must be considered. By so doing, it may be possible to understand the overall sexual philosophy and psychological viewpoint from which Heinlein is writing. But before we can adopt this approach, we must first study some of the individual works of this period, analyzing the sexual theme of each, deciding upon its success or failure, and familiarizing ourselves with those elements which repeat themselves and form the expression of Heinlein's sexual beliefs.

Based upon his original belief in individual freedom, Heinlein's toleration of sexual activity broadens throughout his second period. With this toleration comes an impatience with subtlety. His stories slow to an agonizing crawl as elaborate views and ideas are put forth for the reader's consumption. Long, involved discussions between characters allow Heinlein to lecture upon every aspect of sexuality, and the result is that Heinlein enters all the sexual worlds forbidden to science fiction, such as emasculation, promiscuity, group sex, incest, narcissism, and the nature of hetero- and homosexuality. However, with the sexual theme foremost, the discomfort and ineffective techniques which earlier plagued Heinlein's work also come to the front and limit his study of each sexual theme.

Heinlein continues to express interest in the same aspects of sexuality which concerned him during his first period. The family—extended beyond the conventional nuclear unit—plays a major role in his novels, as does parenthood. And stripped of such notions as fidelity and permanency, love remains as a powerful force in Heinlein's work. All of these appear time and again as critical elements in his second period.

As with everything else in his work, some aspects of sexuality do change. For instance, the Heinlein heroine experiences a sad degeneration in many novels. Heinlein no longer bothers to develop his heroines, and they usually devolve into vaguely drawn sex objects. Perhaps Heinlein's basic attitudes toward women remain the same, but the patience required to create an enjoyable heroine is lacking. The heroine's only new characteristic is the urgent desire to be impregnated by the hero, some even going to the extremes of artificial insemination (against the hero's will) in order to bear the child of the Heinlein hero.

Another change from his first period is Heinlein's direct concern with specific aspects of sexual behavior. Sex in all its permutations has become a thing of endless wonder to Heinlein, as evidenced by the sexual variety of the stories which Heinlein has written in this period. **"'All You Zombies—'"** is an unusual short story utilizing time travel and a sex-change operation to create a solipsist's nightmare. With *Podkayne of Mars,* Heinlein attempts a feminine point of view (an exception to the heroine degeneration) by having a female narrator. *Glory Road* is a parody in which Heinlein creates the ultimate Heinlein heroine, (the second exception) in order to satirize the romantic notions implicit in his long line of characters and relationships. Besides this, he tosses in a reversal of conventional sex roles, and flirts briefly with a situation conveying tones of bestiality. And *Farnham's Freehold* is a novel in which all the male characters are emasculated and rendered impotent in one way or another, while *The Moon Is a Harsh Mistress* provides a detailed picture of life in a "line family" with multiple wives and husbands.

Individually, these works are less important to our study and must be set aside in order to consider the three novels in which Heinlein is most concerned with sexuality:

Stranger in a Strange Land, I Will Fear No Evil, and *Time Enough for Love.* These three novels not only provide specific examples of Heinlein's success and failure, but also most clearly illustrate the philosophy which Heinlein has adopted in his second period.

Stranger in a Strange Land (published in 1961) is the first sexually important work of Heinlein's second period. It is a conglomeration of many things, including religion, satire, and adventure, but is most interesting to us for its development of the sexual themes of promiscuity and group sex.

It is the story of Valentine Michael Smith, a human who is raised by Martians and learns superhuman powers. He returns to Earth humanly inexperienced, is educated, and then forms a sexually active church in which he teaches "grokking" to those who are qualified to understand the nature of existence and thus share in the superpowers. He is killed by a mob at the end of the novel because of his rejection of all conventions and mores of a hypocritical society.

Robert Plank has criticized the novel as a series of "primitive sexual fantasies" with no informative value,[23] and Alexei Panshin mentions that "the sexual relations are beyond criticism, self-justified,"[24] because Heinlein gives them as being right, and either a character can see this truth and "grok," or he cannot. Both observations are valid. The novel seems to be a long and loud bugle call for a perfect sexual freedom between all the spiritually beautiful people in the world. The dastardly villains preventing this dream from becoming a reality are human jealousy and the Judeo-Christian moral code.

The hero Michael Smith feels that sexual union should be a merging of bodies and souls in shared ecstasy, but that:

> ". . . Instead it was indifference and acts mechanically performed and rape and seduction as a game no better than roulette but less honest and prostitution and celibacy by choice and by no choice and fear and guilt and hatred and violence and children brought up to think that sex was 'bad' and 'shameful' and 'animal' and something to be hidden and always distrusted. This lovely perfect thing, male-femaleness, turned upside down and inside out and made horrible.
>
> "And everyone of those wrong things is a corollary of 'jealousy.' . . ."[25]

Linked to this human emotion of jealousy, and possibly growing out of it, is our religious code of sexual morality. This time Mike's mentor, Jubal, has his say:

> ". . . the ethics of sex is a thorny problem. Each of us is forced to grope for a solution he can live with—in the face of a preposterous, unworkable, and *evil* code of so-called 'Morals.' Most of us know the code is wrong, almost everybody breaks it. But we pay Danegeld by feeling guilty and giving lip service. Willynilly, the code rides us, dead and stinking, an albatross around the neck."
>
> (33)

As we see, Heinlein is not blind to the emotional and environmental factors ordering our existence. He succeeds in clearly putting his ideas about them before us. The only thing needed is the evidence to validate these ideas—but this we never get. Instead of showing us how we might throw off "constraints" and achieve these heights of emotional and sexual freedom, Heinlein simply gives us a finished product, a perfect community free of restrictions such as jealousy and morality. Promiscuity and group sex are given as the natural order, and the solution for everything from job dissatisfaction to menstrual cramps.

Such a community is possible because Michael and company have the ability to grok those who are worthy. Only the good of heart are able to grok and enjoy the delights of sexual and spiritual union. The rest will never make it through the door. Mike states:

> ". . . I had no slightest wish to attempt this miracle with anyone I did not already cherish and trust—Jubal, I am physically unable even to attempt love with a female who has not shared water with me. And this runs all through the Nest. Psychic impotence—unless spirits blend as flesh blends."
>
> (36)

Even Jubal recognizes that "it was a fine system—for angels" (36).

This is the problem with *Stranger in a Strange Land*: The novel creates a sexual utopia that does not apply to the common lot of humanity. Heinlein again ignores the "common stuff of human experience." For example, we are told that a character, Ben, suffers from jealousy, while a heroine, Jill, is intolerant of a "water-brother" who likes to collect pictures of nudes. Ben and Jill come closest to displaying the emotional elements that make up ordinary human existence. But in both cases, Heinlein keeps their problems at arm's length and solves them with a little superpower, so that suddenly the characters grok. No more problems.

What Heinlein is doing, of course, is utilizing his old techniques, and now as before they fail him. Only now, their weakness betrays his sexual argument and threatens the success of the novel itself. How are we to know who is worthy to share water, and who should be discorporated? How can we tell if another is able to achieve spiritual union as well as physical union? Heinlein ignores this reality. He raises arguments, but offers no proof. He suggests change, but offers no workable alternatives. Heinlein's satire is excellent, and his ideas are thought provoking. But no meaningful discussion can be found of the value and place of the promiscuity which is so highly touted.

I Will Fear No Evil (1970) is the most ambitious of Heinlein's novels, and perhaps that accounts for the fact that it is his worst failure. The novel fails as a satire—if it was meant to be one—because it satirizes very little. It fails as a story because the narration is tedious and the plot dull. It might have succeeded as an exploration of the nature of sexuality, for it is certainly concerned with that subject. Highlighted would have been such important topics as the heterosexual and homosexual drives, and the interrelationship between the physiological and psychological processes in a sexual being. But here, too, it fails.

Instead, *I Will Fear No Evil* succeeds as nothing more than a long catalog of naughty stories, including: the young secretary and the older executive; the young boy and the housewife next door; the cuckolded husband (three wives—three children—three horns); the high school cheerleader impregnated by the basketball team; the scantily dressed maid; the spanking; the nurse and the seven interns, the society lady and her two servants, and so on. Between these revelations of the life histories of the characters, we are told the story of Johann Smith, an old billionaire in a state of infirmity and kept alive with tubes, wires, and shoestrings. A once-vigorous man, his old age is a living death, and he prefers either to live or to die. The escape is to have his brain transplanted into the first body that becomes available—which turns out to be that of his female secretary Eunice, who has been killed by a mugger. The story recounts the experience of Johann's adjustment to being a woman.

The concept is fascinating, and a host of questions arise. Johann has a man's psychology, but his body is a woman's. How will Johann feel when a man touches him? Or a woman touches him? How will the mind adjust? Which is the homosexual act? When will Johann be sexually aroused—and when *should* he be? Which will predominate, psychological conditioning or physiological drives? And how will others relate to the change? What about those who loved the hero as a man—or loved Eunice, to whom the body belonged? How will these others respond?

Heinlein raises these questions himself. For example, Jake, a friend of Johann's and the lover of Eunice, breaks down and has to be sedated when Johann proposes a toast to the dead woman whose body he is occupying. And the hero, who finds himself attracted to both men and women, realizes that:

> ". . . I'm in the damnedest situation a man ever found himself in. I'm not the ordinary sex change of a homo who gets surgery and hormone shots to tailor his male body into fake female. I'm not even a mixed up XXY or an XYY. This body is a normal female XX. But the brain in it has had a man's canalization and many years of enthusiastic male sex experience. So tell me, Jake, which time am I being normal, and which time perverse?"[26]

The hero answers his own question, and makes what seems to be a major point of the book:

> ". . . From my unique experience, embracing both physiological sexes directly and not by hearsay, I say there is just *one* sex. Sex. *SEX! . . .*"
>
> (14)

This is an unusual point to make, and we might expect an author to use every page to prove his thesis by showing the hero adjusting, and explaining how he responded physiologically and emotionally to each sexual step. This does not happen.

Again, as in *Stranger in a Strange Land,* the rightness of Heinlein's premise is self-justified. Johann experiences *no* problems adjusting because there is only one sex, and he has done nothing but change the vehicle of his pleasure. An irascible old man before the transplant, Johann becomes an agreeable, charming personality in Eunice's body. He finds himself thinking about sexual relations with his doctors even before he has recovered from the operation. Oh, he *says* he has trouble adjusting: "The time I'll feel like a queer is the first time some *man* kisses [me]. I'll probably faint" (10). Johann does not faint, he just enjoys. And this is all we see.

The simplicity of adjustment extends to the hero's acquaintances. Jake, who knew the hero and loved Eunice, should be having gigantic problems adjusting, considering the promising scene in which he broke down earlier. But no, he, too, regains his composure and becomes the perfect gentlemen with Johann (and Eunice's body) out of deference to old friend and buddy Johann. Later, he ends up marrying the hero.

Even if we credit the self-justified point of the story with some validity, it is fatally compromised by plot and technique. First of all, Johann is not alone in the body of Eunice! When he awakens from the transplant operation, he discovers that the consciousness of Eunice still resides in the body, right along with his own consciousness. Eunice becomes Johann's sexual mentor and the heroine of the story, helping Johann adjust to being a woman, not that he really needs much help (later in the novel, Jake dies and they haul *his* consciousness into their body with them). This circumstance immediately destroys any chance for a viable consideration of the situation, and renders meaningless the many questions that are begging to be answered.

Also, since the point is self-justified and there is no need to deal with the messy, complex development of human sexuality, we are left free to consider such truly profound matters as the quality of different kisses, the difficulty in buying women's clothes, and the erotic histories of the characters (all those naughty stories).

More tiresome than these matters are the endless conversations. Heinlein has the ability to write witty and informative dialogue. Here, he is merely trite and repetitive. The following passage is an example of a conversation between Johann and Eunice (supposedly occurring mentally within Johann's brain inside Eunice's body—got that straight?). Johann has just kissed his female nurse, Winifred:

> Winifred left about sixty seconds later. (Well, Eunice? How did that one stack up?) (Quite well, Butch. Say eighty percent as well as Jake can do.) (You're teasing.)

(You'll find out. Winnie is sweet—but Jake has had years more practice. I'm not chucking asparagus at Winnie. I thought you were going to drag her right in with us.) (With Mrs. Sloan outside and watching our heart rate? What do you think I am? A fool?) (Yes.) (Oh, go to sleep!)

(11)

This banter fills up page after page in the novel, and we might almost consider it part of a grand parody if Heinlein did not treat it so seriously, and with such repetitious detail.

This type of conversation is also utilized to narrate Johann's reactions to the kisses he receives and bestows. Johann gets to kiss almost every character in the book (Heinlein is fascinated with kissing), and we get to hear about every experience. Yet, for all that Heinlein is constantly suggesting sexual arousal, he never delivers the real thing. As with previous works, no sexual coupling is ever actually described. We are told about Johann's first sexual experience the morning after, and it turns out that Johann was drunk and everything was fuzzy. Convenient.

Why Heinlein should tease us all through the novel and then avoid the moment of truth may only be explained by those old problems, his inhibitions. He is still not comfortable with intimate scenes of human emotion, and he falls back on the same techniques he used before, and then some. The naughty stories, Eunice's consciousness, the worthless conversations, and the kissing are all devices to avoid coming to grips with a subject that Heinlein does not know how to handle.

Yet, Heinlein does overcome one inhibition, when for the first time in his work he introduces a sexual four-letter word. He uses it twice, both times in the same paragraph at the very end of the novel and just before Johann-Eunice-Jake die giving birth:

> "Everything always hurts, Roberto—everything. Always. But some things are worth all the hurts . . . It is good to touch—to fuck—be fucked. It's—not good—to be—too much alone. . . ."

(29)

It is too bad that for all his effort, this is all Heinlein had to say. The sexual themes which are mishandled so badly do need to be explored. But Heinlein's methods are not the ones to use.

In his most recent novel, *Time Enough for Love* (1973), Heinlein is more successful because he takes care to be a storyteller—and an artist—rather than just a moralist or sexual adventurer. The novel is ostensibly about love, but actually deals with the sexual themes of incest and narcissism, which are given as manifestations of that love.

Time Enough for Love is a rambling, picaresque account of the past life of Lazarus Long. After two thousand years the hero is tired of life, but is prevented from committing suicide by the long-lived Howard Families. They convince Lazarus that he should live long enough to relate his experiences for their benefit, and so he does. Meanwhile, the people he has met form a family around him, and many of the females have themselves impregnated by Lazarus in one way or another, some even serving as host mothers to cloned versions (female reproductions) of the hero. His interest in life revived, but still seeking something new in the way of adventure, Lazarus goes into the past, ends up having an affair with his own mother, and then gets himself killed in World War I. The novel ends with his family of the future snatching Lazarus off the battlefield and reviving him.

Throughout the novel, the emphasis is upon the sexual aspects of his adventures, as signaled in the title of the novel. The key to the title may be found in one of the excerpts from Lazarus Long's Notebooks:

> The more you love, the more you *can* love—and the more intensely you love. Nor is there any limit on how *many* you can love. If a person had time enough, he could love all of that majority who are decent and just.

("Intermission")

It is also made clear that "whatever 'love' is, it's not sex" ("Variations on a Theme IV"). We find love to be much more, as Lazarus explains:

> The longer I was privileged to live with Dora, the more I loved her. She taught me to love by loving me, and I learned . . . Learned that supreme happiness lies in wanting to keep another person safe and warm and happy, and being privileged to try.

("Variations on a Theme XII")

So, love is defined as being the supreme happiness of the one who loves, and is achieved by caring most deeply for another human being. Simple enough, and the definition is applied consistently throughout the novel. But the definition is a narcissistic one. Love is supreme happiness. We want to make ourselves happy, and so we love others, and take care of others—not for their sake, but for our own. The principle extends to everything we do:

> . . . once you pick up a stray cat and feed it, you cannot abandon it. Self-love forbids it. The cat's welfare becomes essential to your own peace of mind—even when it's a bloody nuisance not to break faith with the cat.

("Variations on a Theme VI")

With this narcissistic interpretation, almost every chapter may be (and is intended to be) interpreted as a variation upon this theme. All of Lazarus Long's sexual and emotional relationships thus become expressions of self-love. The narcissism becomes quite literal at times, as when Lazarus makes love to the two cloned female versions of himself whom he has helped raise:

> ". . . Coupling with us might be masturbation, but it *can't* be incest because we *aren't* your sisters. We aren't your kin in *any* normal sense; we're *you*. Every gene

of us comes from *you*. If we love you—and we do—and if you love us—and you do, some, in your own chinchy and cautious fashion—it's Narcissus loving himself. But this time, if you could only see it, that Narcissist love could be consummated."

("Variations on a Theme XVII")

Similarly, the theme of incest runs just as deeply through the novel, and is considered in the same type of unique variations. At one point, Lazarus explores in scientific detail the relationship of a set of mirror twins whom he buys out of slavery. They are diploid brother and sister having the same mother and father, sharing the same host womb, growing up together as brother and sister, but with no genetic reason to prevent their mating, as they wish. The result of the investigation is a new understanding by the reader of the nature of incest. It becomes clear that:

"'Incest' is a legal term, not a biological one. It designates sexual union between persons forbidden by law to marry. The act itself is forbidden; whether such union results in progeny is irrelevant. The prohibitions vary widely among cultures and are usually, but not always, based on degrees of consanguinity."

("Variations on a Theme IX")

The basic message is that incest is a cultural taboo imposed because of genetic dangers, but often of no logical relation to the genetic dangers which it is meant to avoid. Whether or not one agrees with Heinlein's ideas, his consideration of incest does leave the reader with enough information and knowledge to apply such investigative methods to the cultural and genetic validity of his own incest taboos. In this way, Heinlein has succeeded with his theme.

The theme of incest is carried to fruition when Lazarus Long goes back in time and has a sexual and emotional love affair with his mother. Heinlein overcomes his own sexual inhibitions by finally including a sex scene, the one in which this relationship is consummated. Yes, Heinlein is still uncomfortable, and the dialogue is still artificial, but somehow the scene works, perhaps because of the reader's amazement at seeing such a thing in a Heinlein novel.

Time Enough for Love succeeds in many ways, and it will probably be ranked as Heinlein's most complex and interesting work. The primary accomplishment of the novel is Heinlein's masterful intertwining of the themes of incest and narcissism into each chapter and each example. For instance, one of the most romantic chapters concerns Lazarus and Dora, a child he has saved and raised as his own. When she comes of age, she wants to have a baby by Lazarus. After having raised Dora as his daughter, the incestuous element is clear in the emotional relationship. Lazarus is changing from father to husband. Then, Lazarus himself raises the issue of narcissistic self-love for this act. He has married Dora because she is a stray kitten he must take care of out of self-love. Thus, the relationship has both its incestuous and narcissistic elements. Both themes are also inherent in his relations with his cloned selves, with the mirror twins, with his family, and with his mother. The intricate plotting of these sexual themes is the work of a master craftsman.

By the elaborate repetition of the two themes, the novel is also a success for the manner in which it raises questions and suggests alternatives. Through the numerous variations of each theme, the reader is familiarized with the subject and begins to see the complexities of the theme, and to consider it outside the narrow bias of his own cultural point of view. This is an accomplishment.

However, with the novel's success comes its failure. As entertaining as the novel may be, and as many questions as it may raise and as much thought as it may stir, there is little real human substance to apply to our own situation. The mirror twins are not really normal brother and sister; Dora is not Lazarus' biological daughter; and his cloned female selves are neither sisters nor daughters. Even his mother is no longer his mother. She is a "lovely young matron, just his 'own' age" ("DaCapo III"), a woman who happens to be the mother of the child that Lazarus was two thousand years before. In too many cases, scientific manipulation accounts for a sexual improbability. Scientifically, the examples work, and the novel is good science fiction. But these examples fail to offer insights into the human factors that make up so many of these problems. Again, as in *Stranger in a Strange Land* and *I Will Fear No Evil*, the complex psychological and emotional elements that make up sexuality are ignored.

None of Heinlein's work in his second period is as successful as it might have been, and the fault is mainly with his inadequate handling of the sexual theme. The variations on this theme are cleverly presented and effective within limits—but these limits are disappointing. Heinlein's persistent reluctance to deal with the human condition of emotional vulnerability forbids any true application of the sexual studies he has undertaken. For this reason, Heinlein's second period must be looked upon as one of unfulfilled promise. Our consolation is that if Heinlein did not provide any answers, at least he asked the needed questions.

Having completed an evaluation of some works of this period in terms of the success or failure of each, it is now possible to consider the philosophy and psychology which have dictated Heinlein's extensive interest in the theme of sexuality.

Heinlein has always put great store in physical survival, and in his first period optimistically showed us the ability of the competent man to succeed against the odds. Heinlein himself was the archetype of competency and success. By the end of his first period he had already written a massive body of literature, carved out an inestimable niche for himself in science fiction, and was regarded with adulation by a large body of fans. Most would view such a life as a great success.

However, by the beginning of his second period in 1959, Heinlein was fifty-two years old and reaching the age when one's own mortality becomes obvious. A man might realize that for all his competence and for all his victories he could not escape the eventual defeat of death. Old age would strip him of his abilities and leave him powerless before this fate.

Heinlein's writing in his second period seems to reflect this type of thinking. For all their competence, his heroes are strangely unable to alter circumstances, are emasculated, and rendered impotent against the forces of the universe. The realities of old age and death also figure more prominently in Heinlein's work. In *Stranger in a Strange Land,* Michael is killed by the mob. The novel *I Will Fear No Evil* is about one man's desperate attempt to escape old age and death. And *Time Enough for Love* is about a man who cannot die. Heinlein was in his sixties when he wrote *Time Enough for Love,* an aging man writing about an ageless man. The attraction of the fantasy is obvious.

But if a man is not a Lazarus Long, if he cannot affect his fate, if he can no longer find importance in his temporary victories against the universe, where can he seek purpose? How can he give life meaning?

Religion is one answer, but Heinlein seems to have rejected that. If ever a believer in a God, Heinlein implies throughout his second period that he is atheistic. He rejects the Judeo-Christian code in *Stranger in a Strange Land,* and later makes it clear in *Time Enough for Love* that "Religion is a crutch for people not strong enough to stand up to the unknown without help" ("Intermission"). Denying himself this comfort, it is indeed a gloomy realization that death is the end of everything, without either physical or spiritual immortality.

Yet, there is another way to gain a measure of physical immortality. The answer is genetic survival, and it is this answer that Heinlein has grasped in order to give meaning and purpose to life. If a man cannot live forever, at least he can ensure the survival of a part of himself in his children. This attitude is reflected in his novels. Michael Smith impregnates at least half a dozen women by the time of his death. Johann Smith takes great care to have his female body impregnated with his own seed, and far into Heinlein's Future History, Lazarus Long is literally the genetic forefather of an important segment of the human race, and propounds that "racial survival is the *only* universal morality."[27]

To ensure this type of survival, the *family* is essential. Not only does it protect and educate the children, but it also provides comfort and holds off the grim thoughts of that ultimate fate. The love and adoration of the family, and the careful education of the children in the image of the father (hero) are essential to his psychological well-being, and far overreach any temporary interests in a professional career or adventure to the stars. This is why so many of Heinlein's stories at this time are domesticated, either utilizing the family scene as an essential story element like the "Nest" in *Stranger in a Strange Land,* or in providing a warm sanctuary from which the hero may venture forth

upon occasion as Lazarus does. For lack of this family, Lazarus—having been kicked around the universe for a few centuries—even welcomes death until a new family has built up around him and provided a "home" to return to. It is the family that rescues Lazarus from the battlefield and brings him back to life, in symbolic manifestation of the physical immortality that the family allows.

What the hero gives in return is *love.* There is that special love for *the* woman, the tender love for many women, and the warm, asexual love for "that majority who are decent and just," both men and women. The hero must love all these because it is good to love, as Michael Smith and Johann Smith and Lazarus Long all know. This is why their "families" grow so large. The more one loves, and the more there are to love, the happier one is, and it is this happiness which will deny the Fates and push back the heavy knowledge that weighs down the human spirit.

Thus, parenthood, the family, and love—always important in Heinlein's early work—evolve into essential elements of his later philosophy by forming a consistent denial of one's own purposeless mortality. However, there is another element perhaps just as essential, one that Heinlein has newly turned to in his second period. The "icing on the cake,"[28] the bountiful gift which spices up human existence, is sex. In denying death, in making a family, in loving others, "this lovely perfect thing, male-femaleness" plays an essential role that fascinates Heinlein. If all conventional adventures have shrunken in importance, the sexual adventure looms in their place. Sex can provide a first step toward love by encouraging intimacy ("growing closer"), so why not have sex often, with many people, in order to hasten the love ("spiritual union") in which happiness and comfort can be found? Besides, sex is fun, so why limit it in any way? Why let jealousy create inhibitions? Why let illogical taboos and morals interfere with this innocent pleasure that does so much to deny the reality of our own demise? Why not explore the different types of sexual love and see how we have limited ourselves and denied ourselves this great comfort?

Having evolved this philosophy, having discovered the purpose and pattern by which to live, Heinlein must preach the gospel of his new revelation, perhaps to himself as much as to others. Family! Sex! Love! These are the weapons with which to challenge the universe and deny death. These are the important things in life, the essential elements of a desperate happiness. In our pitifully short lives, there must always be time enough for these.

Notes

1. Robert A. Heinlein, "Views of Robert Heinlein," *The New Yorker,* July 1, 1974, 18.

2. Alexei Panshin, *Heinlein in Dimension* (Chicago: Advent, 1968), 169-72.

3. For this story and for other early works from Heinlein's prewar writing (1939-42), I am referring to versions rewritten for book publication rather than the original magazine versions. For more information on original versions and rewrites, see Panshin.

4. Heinlein, *Starman Jones,* ed. Judy L. del Rey (New York: Ballantine, 1975), (19).

5. Heinlein, *The Menace from Earth* (New York: New American Library, Signet Books, 1962), (2).

6. Heinlein, *Time Enough for Love* (New York: Berkley Medallion, 1974), "Variations on a Theme XII."

7. Anne McCaffrey, "Romance and Glamour in Science Fiction," in *Science Fiction: Today and Tomorrow,* ed. Reginald Bretnor (New York: Harper and Row, 1974), 281.

8. "Women in Science Fiction," Introduction, *Women of Wonder: Science Fiction Stories by Women About Women,* ed. Pamela Sargent (New York: Random House, 1975), xliii.

9. "Introduction by Damon Knight," Heinlein, *The Past Through Tomorrow* (New York: Berkley Medallion, 1975).

10. Heinlein, *The Puppet Masters* (New York: New American Library, Signet Books, 1975), (27).

11. Heinlein, *Waldo & Magic, Inc.* (New York: New American Library, Signet Books, 1970).

12. Heinlein, in *The Past Through Tomorrow.*

13. Heinlein, *Glory Road* (New York: Berkley Medallion, 1970), (21).

14. Heinlein, *Time Enough for Love,* "Variations on a Theme XII."

15. Heinlein, *Have Space Suit—Will Travel* (New York: Ace Books, 1975), (6).

16. Chapter 21.

17. Heinlein, *Tunnel in the Sky* (New York: Ace Books, 1970), (2).

18. Sargent, *Women of Wonder,* xliv.

19. Panshin, *Heinlein in Dimension,* 151.

20. Heinlein, *Beyond This Horizon* (New York: New American Library, Signet Books, 1974), (4).

21. Heinlein, *The Door into Summer* (New York: New American Library, Signet Books, 1975), (11).

22. Heinlein, "If This Goes On—" (10), in *The Past Through Tomorrow.*

23. Robert Plank, "Omnipotent Cannibals: Thoughts on Reading Robert Heinlein's *Stranger in a Strange Land,*" *Riverside Quarterly,* V (1971): 30-37. See also Chapter 4, this book.

24. Panshin, *Heinlein in Dimension,* 151.

25. Heinlein, *Stranger in a Strange Land* (New York: Berkley Medallion, 1968), (36).

26. Heinlein, *I Will Fear No Evil* (New York: Berkley Medallion, 1971), (14).

27. Heinlein, *Time Enough for Love,* "Intermission."

28. *Time Enough for Love,* "Variations on a Theme VII."

Frank H. Tucker (essay date 1978)

SOURCE: Tucker, Frank H. "Major Political and Social Elements in Heinlein's Fiction." In *Robert A. Heinlein,* edited by Joseph D. Olander and Martin Harry Greenberg, pp. 172-93. New York: Taplinger Publishing Co., 1978.

[*In the following essay, Tucker explores the political, social, and economic threads found in Heinlein's fiction.*]

In discussing the principal political and social ideas which are expressed or reflected in the Heinlein literature, it is best to begin by observing that these are in no sense tract novels and stories, and the political content is secondary or even incidental to the narratives. One should also note that the usual uncertainty regarding fictional material applies here, as to whether or not the statements of various characters reflect the author's views. However, we are obliged to rely on such statements usually as our primary source, and where they recur or are emphasized, they can be considered as significant.

First let us look at elements which are essentially individual matters. There are several ways in which the author's concepts of the "proper individual," the hero and the leader, shed light upon our subject. There are many strong characters, functioning in the stories as exemplary figures, even acting as leaders of their people or as guides to younger, less experienced characters. These leaders often seem to reflect an outlook which is typical of the intelligent, fairly conservative achievers of the author's own generation in the United States. They are go-getters, and are often ready to dedicate their efforts to the common causes of exploration, liberation, and other forms of service to mankind, or at least to their own segment of mankind.

The author is a realist, but he is rather optimistic about human destiny. In *The Door into Summer* we read, "Despite the crape-hangers, romanticists, and anti-intellectuals, the world steadily grows better because the human mind, applying itself to environment, *makes* it better."[1] This progress is seen as having been facilitated, during the past history of man, by competition and by the process to which the name of Charles Darwin is attached, natural selection and survival of the fittest—a tendency in nature toward the proliferation of mutated types which are more able to cope with their environment, accompanied by the tendency of the less fit types to die out. During the forthcoming development of mankind, in addition to these trends in nature, the author sometimes contemplates the use of genetic planning, and even genetic engineering—alteration of germ cell material—to enhance these tendencies.

Franz Rottensteiner has termed Heinlein's stories "an endorsement of social Darwinism." Fittingly, he says also that the characters in these stories "personify an ethic of success."² Although Heinlein accepts the Darwinian label, the phrase "social Darwinism" should be used cautiously because it has come to include a thoroughly ruthless approach to human affairs, dignifying the abuse of colonial populations and the extermination of supposedly inferior races as natural, ultimately beneficial processes.

In *Farnham's Freehold* we find an estimate that a twentieth-century atomic war might actually have the long-range effect of improving the stock of the human race. After such a holocaust, that is, the survival of individuals would be a real struggle, and the survivors of that competition for sustenance would tend to be the most fit persons. World Wars I and II, on the other hand, brought death mostly to the fighting forces, in which the fitter individuals were concentrated, sparing the poorer specimens who were not at the front. This concept is perhaps meant to apply only to the United States, since at the time in question there were many deaths elsewhere from starvation and genocide, not directed particularly toward the fighting forces.

At any rate, another appreciation of the racial value of hard times appears in *Beyond This Horizon,* where the sage District Moderator for Genetics, Mordan Claude, says, "'Easy times for individuals are bad times for the race,'" and the corollary is that when there is not enough adversity there must be compensatory governmental intervention and planning. There is much more in this latter novel about genetics. The character Hamilton Felix is described as a genetic superman, highly fitted for survival. We also read about the aftermath of an atomic war in 1970. The survivors used genetics to breed people who would be more peaceable, more like sheep than wolves, but the experiment failed because the nation was attacked by more wolflike peoples, who won.³

There is much more discussion of genetics in *Farnham's Freehold,* but not on the part of the heroes; rather it is the overlords of the arrogant superrace of the time who refer to the matter most often. A more decent reference to Darwinism occurs in *Starship Troopers* with some worried musing that because a certain planet lacks radiation in its atmosphere there will be no mutation, thence no zoologic competition and no progress in life forms. The musing extends to the observation that people don't worry about future generations as they should.⁴ This sounds a little like Edmund Burke's dictum that our responsibility as human beings extends not only to the living but also to the past generations and the yet unborn generations of the human community.

The application of Darwinian thought to the new situations created by the discovery and development of new frontier lands was made by Charles Darwin himself, in *The Descent of Man,* where he pointed out that a kind of selection process operated when people made the choice to go out to the New World of the Western Hemisphere during the era of settlement: those who went tended to be those who had more courage, initiative, or innovativeness.

Heinlein also is mindful of this factor in his anticipation that space travel might ruin the Earth by draining its best minds away. He certainly thinks of space exploration as being akin to the old eras of colonization and the Westward Movement on Earth. One of his Moon ships is called the *Pioneer,* and its sister ships have the equally significant names of *Mayflower* and *Colonial.* In another story, a group of fugitive settlers on Venus are described as having their own "rough frontier culture," under the guidance of a headman who handles justice like Judge Roy Bean. The formerly soft lawyer who is settled there notes the virtues of frontier life, harsh though it is, and he wonders if he should return to his former, sterile life as a fat, prosperous Earthling. In another narrative, the frontier of Western Americana is reenacted even in such details as a Conestoga wagon, on a remote planet, and the protagonist remarks that the frontiers have a wholesome, "culling" effect on mankind.⁵

The frontier as a safety valve for an overcrowded land and a stultified culture, one of the elements in the "Frontier Thesis" of the famous American historian, Frederick Jackson Turner, seems to be what Damon Knight has in mind when he remarks that even the somewhat wild Heinlein juvenile-story plots, about high school kids being sent in a survival test to remote and savage planets, are not unlikely in the context of an Earth grossly overcrowded by its population explosion.⁶

One further introductory note is needed here regarding archetypal images, those very widespread and ancient modes through which the human mind brings to its surface its deepest conceptions of problems and solutions, including the human figures which, as archetypal images, may represent our chief hopes and hazards. The reader is not asked to accept Carl Jung's interpretations of these phenomena, and it would be unwise to assert that Heinlein has done so. Such archetypal images as savior figures, whether young or old, male or female, earthbound or heaven-sent, are often found in the Heinlein stories. They may have been put there simply because such figures were natural and needful for the story. Or perhaps, as Damon Knight believes about Heinlein's Freudian probings, he has mortared some of them in, without conviction, thinking that they improve his product (p. 86).

Certainly it is evident that Heinlein at some point had become familiar with quite a mass of archaic, occult, and psychoanalytic information. In **Waldo,** for example, we find a certain defense of the accomplishments of magic. In **Magic, Inc.** there is reference to a full set of demons—Lucifugé, Sataniacha, Ashtoreth, Mammon, and Beelzebub.⁷ There is much magic and fantasy in *Glory Road,* in which the character Star, for instance, represents the archetypes of the Terrible Mother, witch, and so forth. More pertinent to our political interests here would be the inclination of Heinlein to have a senior guiding figure in his stories, a "wise old man," as the Jungians would say. Examples of this include Mordan Claude in *Beyond This Horizon,* Dr. Jefferson in *Between Planets,* Jubal Harshaw in

Stranger in a Strange Land, Sam Anderson in *Starman Jones,* Professor Bernardo de la Paz in *The Moon Is a Harsh Mistress,* and Lazarus Long in *Methuselah's Children* and *Time Enough for Love.* Lazarus, living to be thousands of years old, is surely the epitome of this figure. He also represents the type who is specially endowed with a marvelous quality, as are many of the savior and hero figures in this literature. In his case, a mutation which allows the longevity is the special gift. Furthermore, Lazarus is recurrently rescued from death by rejuvenation techniques, and finally he is in fact killed, but is, amazingly enough, brought back to life like the Lazarus of the Bible. The book also describes Long as "our Moses who led his people out of bondage," and he plays still another role despite his vulnerability, that of the archetypal "Trickster Figure." That is reflected in the description of him as having "audacity, a talent for lying convincingly, and . . . a childish delight in adventure and intrigue for its own sake" (*TEL* Introduction).

The archetypal imagery of control lost over one's own personality or body, whether by possession (as by demons) or through some other device, finds several echoes in the Heinlein literature. In science fiction as a whole, in fact, it is quite a common phenomenon, reflecting very probably a strong anxiety by modern man concerning the independence or integrity of his person. Our author makes less use of this concept than average, but there are some interesting examples. *The Puppet Masters* is a good case of this, with direct control of each human being who has a loathsome guest organism on his back. The masters, furthermore, are not independent individuals themselves, being blended into a collective whole without which they hardly function. Such a loss of individuality to the communal entity occurs also in *Methuselah's Children,* where the rabbit-like Little People have a purely collective personality. A human being, Mary Sperling, joins them, to the distress of the other people. Again, the animal-like Jockaira of the same novel do not exist for themselves but as pets of unseen masters. The masters exercise mystically vague mental control and telekinetic control over Jockaira and humans alike, though their intervention into the human mind produces hysteria and disorientation. The implications of all this for twentieth-century man, with his own agonizing choices as to collectivization and communal life, are reasonably clear.

General Political Concepts

Heinlein's writings often speak of the need to keep government small, to minimize its functions. Governmental honesty, candor, and efficiency are esteemed, and limited government will conserve these qualities. Where does Heinlein get his political philosophy? We have only a few direct indications. In **"If This Goes On—"** Grand Master Peter recommends Tom Paine to John Lyle for basic enlightenment, and we are told that Lyle finds the works of Thomas Jefferson and Patrick Henry also when he looks up the works of Paine. The interest in Paine and Henry is not merely casual; we know that Heinlein ran a full-page

ad in the *Colorado Springs Gazette Telegraph* on April 13, 1958, asking the readers to dedicate themselves as heirs of Patrick Henry. The ad quotes Henry's famous "liberty or death" speech, and deplores those who would give up essential liberty to obtain temporary safety. At any rate, our young hero Lyle also discovers that "secrecy is the keystone of tyranny. Not force, but secrecy . . . censorship."[8]

Heinlein respects the political process, preferring the practical politicians to those who are more idealistic. In *Podkayne of Mars* we read, "Politics is . . . the way we get things done . . . without fighting. We dicker and compromise . . . the only alternative is force. . . . Homo sapiens is the most deadly of all the animals in this solar system. Yet he invented politics!"[9] In *Time Enough for Love* the opinion is that reform politicians lack the reliability that "'business politicians'" have, because the former lie and cheat to serve their vague ideals (*TEL* "Variations on a Theme III").

How is the political process to be kept wholesome? Perhaps not through democracy, but through the twin concepts of loyalty and duty, without which any society is doomed, and by taking care that authority and responsibility are kept equal and coordinate in government. Suggesting that democracy is based on the idea that a million men are wiser than one man, the author implies that this is a dubious concept (*TEL* "Intermission"). Again, in *Glory Road,* the following commentaries appear:

> "'Democracy. A curious delusion—as if adding zeroes could produce a sum. . . . Democracy can't work. Mathematicians, peasants, and animals, that's all there is—so democracy, a theory based on the assumption that mathematicians and peasants are equal, can never work. . . . But a democratic *form* of government is okay, as long as it doesn't work. Any social organization does well enough if it isn't rigid. . . . Most so-called social scientists seem to think that organization is everything. It is almost nothing—except when it is a straightjacket. . . . [The U.S.A.] has a system free enough to let its heroes work at their trade. It should last a long time—unless its looseness is destroyed from inside.'"[10]

In **"Gulf,"** the comment comes from a villain, which can mean that it is not the author's view. However, it does not appear to be greatly different from the opinions cited above, except that the villain will use conspiracy and murder to promote his own cause. He opines that democracy could flourish for about one hundred and fifty years in the past, but muddled and ignorant men cannot be trusted to settle by their voting processes the issues of the modern world in which nuclear physics and the like are beyond their capacity to understand. He condemns communism also, because very little progress was made under it, a totalitarian, political religion being, as he says, incompatible with free investigation. Even this character sees some practical good in individual freedom, in that it lends itself to experimentation, evolution, and progress through trial and error.[11]

The weight of opinion throughout this literature is in favor of leaving people alone. In *Coventry,* a speaker objects to excessive planning: "'You've planned your whole world so carefully that you've planned the fun and zest right out of it.'"[12] In *Time Enough for Love,* Chairman Ira Weatheral believes that no unnecessary governing must be done or allowed; the aim of government is not to do good but to refrain from doing evil. It must keep order, but the Chairman regularly prunes officious officials from his organization, abolishing their jobs and those of their juniors (*TEL* "Variations on a Theme I"). In **"If This Goes On—"** the original version had the liberation organization planning to teach freedom to the people through hypnosis, but the revised form of this story shows the organization rejecting hypnotic conditioning, because free men must come to understand freedom under their own power (**"ITGO"** 14).

Some political interpretations have come into this literature in connection with references to past events. These references are not particularly numerous, since science fiction is more oriented to the future than to the past, but they do reveal a few things about the author's points of view. In **"Logic of Empire,"** the subject is slavery—in the future, on the face of it, but certainly the example of Europe's global expansion in the past, and the frequently attendant practice of slavery, is in the picture here. The author refers to it, and he is not so logical or accurate in these matters. A character deplores our tendency to accept "devil theory" when we examine such problems; he says that colonial slavery resulted not from villainy but from stupidity, in that it was nonproductive. It is true that slave labor is less productive than free labor. In colonial times, indeed throughout most of the centuries of European imperial expansion, there was a shortage of labor; not enough workmen to do the enormous job of opening up to European settlement and industry the two American continents, Australia, and South Africa. That does not justify slavery, but neither does it make the brutal, stopgap practice "stupid."

A related error is the declaration in **"Logic of Empire"** that ". . . the use of mother-country capital to develop the colony inevitably results in subsistence-level wages at home and slave labor in the colonies." This may often have been true, but by no means always. For example, mother-country capital was lent to the British colonies in North America—raised by stock companies, in some cases, for the initial development of the colony. Slavery did not become a regular and important institution in the Northern colonies, though it had a limited or token existence there for a time.

The patriotism of Heinlein is often evident, one sign of it being his special interest in the American Revolution, long before the Bicentennial celebrations made this a commonplace reference. In *Farnham's Freehold,* for instance, Hugh Farnham had a safe in his underground shelter, the combination for which turned out to be 74-17-76—duly explained in the text as deriving from July 4, 1776 (4). Perhaps the special interest was related to the Heinlein ad-

dress in Colorado Springs, 1776 Mesa Avenue. However that may be, the patriotic view of history is substantial enough. In the same novel, Farnham declared, "'America is the best thing in history, *I* think. . . .'" (1)

More recent history is grist for the author's mill; there are reflections of Nazis in the future situations, presented with evident disapproval, as are their emulators outside of Germany. One of the Nazi-like elitists of the Survivors Club in *Beyond This Horizon* is a section leader named Mosely, surely redolent of Sir Oswald Mosely of the British "Silver Shirts" in the Hitler era (7).

As for communism, it comes in for clear disapproval, but the references are not always shrill; occasionally there is even a neutral borrowing of a communist feature. The hero of **"If This Goes On—"** belongs to a revolutionary group which is presented approvingly; it is overthrowing a nasty theocratic dictatorship. The group requires our hero to spend a lot of time on his "Personal Conversion Report," a copious, complete, and detailed account of his background and how he became converted to the revolution. If these reports ever verged on the superficial, or omitted anything, they were to be supplemented by interrogation under hypnosis. This copious report is very similar to the long reports, diaries, and journals which cadres in training in Communist China are required to present. It is a key feature of their training, and probably inspired this fictional item, though one should concede that the Chinese would hardly use hypnosis in such connections (**"ITGO"** 10 and 11).

More general social phenomena in modern America are also reflected. The hero of *Glory Road* acknowledged that his generation, which matured in the 1950s and 1960s, contributed the overpowering goal of "Security" to the American dream. Those who are apathetic, selfish, or spoiled get no encouragement from this author (1), but that will be considered further in our discussion of citizens' rights and responsibilities below.

A modern trend which has been explicitly denounced by Heinlein in his nonfiction writing is anti-intellectualism and antiscience outlooks. His intellectual critics would be surprised, perhaps, how much better he does than do some of the critics' friends at defending the realm of the intellect and science in the face of pernicious attacks.[13]

FUNCTIONS OF GOVERNMENT AND WARRANTS FOR REVOLUTION

The author's positions on the functions of government are a bit ambivalent: he seems to want its power to be very limited, but he views strikes against the authorities (perhaps against the public interest or even the public safety) as a bad thing, a point shown best in **"The Roads Must Roll,"** not only in its own crisis of a strike against the road system, but in its "historical" reference to the so-called Functionalists of the 1930s, who supposedly said that any group might rightly exert whatever powers might be inherent in their functions—a fictional sect, but discernibly related to the strikes by public employees which have in fact brought controversy as threats to safety. Civil servants are feared for their potential power as "civil masters," and we are told that it is a fallacy to suppose that taxes are levied for the benefit of the governed. Societies are allegedly built on procedures for the protection of pregnant women and young children; anything more is a nonessential function of government. The excesses of government are derided with the saying that an elephant is a mouse built to governmental specifications (*TEL* "Intermission").

Naturally a foe of big government would execrate such things as secret police, thought control, and torture, and all these are duly deplored in **"If This Goes On—"** which appeared so early (in 1940) that we cannot attribute its Orwellian features to influence from *1984.* Heinlein's Grand Inquisitor, as he is called in this story, is similar to the minions of the Ministry of Love in *1984,* and his Prophet is somewhat like Big Brother in the latter story. It appears that *1984*'s concepts are derived to some extent from the dystopian novel of the Russian Evgeni Zamiatin, *We,* which appeared in the first years after the Bolshevik Revolution. We can relate the authoritarian features of the Heinlein story to *We*; certainly Zamiatin's dictator, the "Benefactor," is comparable to the Prophet, for example. However, we will stop short here of a direct attribution of **"If This Goes On—"** to influences from *We.*

What about the power of the state to make war or to conscript soldiers? Heinlein seems to affirm the first but to reject the second. He writes, "You can have peace. Or you can have freedom. Don't ever count on having both at once" (*TEL* "Intermission"). That is given in a piece of fiction, but his *Gazette Telegraph* ad cited above contained the same idea. On the other hand, he says that "no state has an inherent right to survive through conscript troops and, in the long run, no state ever has" (*TEL* "Intermission"). Consistent with this is the national, or rather, imperial defense portrayed in *Starship Troopers,* where the system is quite militaristic, but all service is voluntary.

Concerning the right to make a revolution against unjust authority, Heinlein certainly believes in it, rather in the spirit of the American Declaration of Independence. Many of his plots contain such endeavors, presented as virtuous actions. On the other hand, we also find examples of unpleasant militarists who try to grab power. For example, in **"The Long Watch"** the coup is attempted by officers who feel that it is "not safe to leave control of the world in political hands; power must be held by a scientifically selected group." Accordingly, the plotters will strike from the Moon, bombing "an unimportant town or two" on Earth to promote their coup. The hero of the story, Lieutenant Dahlquist, sacrifices his life to abort this foul attempt.[14]

An ample set of Heinlein political ideas is found in *The Moon Is A Harsh Mistress* because in this novel the narrative centers on the efforts of the people in Earth's settle-

ments on the Moon to achieve independence. We are told here that, as with many eighteenth- and nineteenth-century colonization projects on Earth, the original settlers consisted for some time of convicts or transportees. By the twenty-first century, however, when independence becomes an effective cause, the lunar complaints do not focus on a lack of personal freedoms. To be sure there are many constraints on individuals, but they are due mostly to the harsh realities of the struggle to live on "Luna," as it is called here. The grievances are mostly financial, like those of the American colonies in 1776.

The Lunar Authority, a corporation-like entity, conducts the commerce between Earth and Luna, setting the prices at which materials are sold to Luna and at which the products of the Moon are purchased. Since the lunar settlers consider the former prices to be too high, and the latter too low, they desire independence, so that they may negotiate more equitable terms. This aim they have in common, whether they are the descendants of American, Russian, or Chinese settlers. We read that "Great China," a greatly expanded version of the China of 1976, took most of Southeast Asia, Australia, New Zealand, Mongolia, and Siberian regions, deporting many of the inhabitants to the Moon.[15]

This book contains a lot of background information on lunar society and customs, which vary from earthly modes, chiefly because a chronic shortage of women has led to new forms of family structure and to courtship patterns in which the woman makes very free choices of her friends and affiliations (*MIHM* 3 and 11). Most significant for us, however, are the political philosophy and political aspirations expressed by the leading characters here. Since they are also the leaders of the independence movement, they are obliged to enunciate their aims and methods at some length. Two leaders in particular say a great deal about the desirable political forms for the future independent Luna; these men are Manuel O'Kelly Davis, a computer expert who narrates the novel, and Professor Bernardo de la Paz, his revolutionary collaborator who is to become head of the fledgling government of Luna. "Prof," as the latter is usually called here, expresses the more complex or academic aspects of the political thought, while Manuel represents the more everyday, straight-forward views of the man of action. Lastly, the conspirators confer with an elaborate computer which is able to vocalize. The computer, known as "Mike," becomes their friend and collaborator, contributing to their planning his more-than-human logical analysis of all problems, including the political questions. We may take it that these three parties, taken together, express the Heinlein political thought as presented in this novel.

Of course the lunar revolutionary organization is initially authoritarian because of the need to conceal the identities of its conspirators. A cell-like organization is developed, so that if a member is taken prisoner, or is a traitor, he can betray only two or three other members. Under such conditions, naturally there can be no extensive voting or consultation. Even so, the leading conspirators are broad-minded when it comes to comparing the political philosophies of capitalism, socialism, and so on. As the professor puts it, "Private where private belongs, public where it's needed, and an admission that circumstances alter cases." He goes on, however, to identify himself as a rational anarchist, one who believes that government can only exist really in the acts of self-responsible individuals. Blame and responsibility can only repose in single persons, he says. As an anarchist, he is willing to accept any rules that his associates feel are necessary to their freedom, and yet if he finds a rule too obnoxious he will break it (*MIHM* 6).

Sometimes bits of anarchism, natural law, and lunar custom are blended in this novel. The lunar customs are natural laws, says Manuel, because they are the ways people must act to stay alive. The customs have been the chief regulator of behavior. Formal laws have not been issued, only some "do or don't"-type regulations from higher authority. But all this is the status quo. What do our protagonists wish to enact when they seize power? First there is a denunciation by Manuel of busybodies who would regulate details of morals, personal habits, and the like. He muses that there must be a yearning deep in the human heart to keep others from doing as they please, usually expressed with a pious but faulty allegation that the rule is for the good of those who will be regulated (*MIHM* 11 and 14).

When the Luna Declaration of Independence is issued, appropriately enough, on July 4, 2076, there is much discussion as to the rights which should be guaranteed to all citizens, but the matter is left unsettled here. As for the newer rights of twentieth-century America, Heinlein includes a dialogue which may indicate a distaste for these, although perhaps he means only that under lunar conditions these would be inappropriate. We are told that on the Moon individuals pay for their medical care, their libraries, and for what education they happen to want. The narrator says he isn't sure what social security really is, but there is none on Luna.

With the formation of a Constitutional Convention on Luna to work out a detailed constitutional statement, the professor is stimulated to write some lengthy advice for that body, including the following significant points:

After warning the Convention how great are the dangers of losing freedom to a government, the professor warns against trusting time-honored methods, such as representative bodies based on geographic division. He suggests electing from other constituencies, such as age groups, or electing all members at large. He would even consider electing the candidates who got the least number of votes, as a safeguard against tyranny. Another possibility is to be selection by petition, giving office to each person who garners a certain number of citizens who support him—a method which would give every citizen a representative of his choice. As a further safeguard of freedom, the profes-

sor urges the conferees to "accentuate the negative." Let them forbid their government to do a number of things: to conscript men, to interfere with freedom of press, speech, assembly, travel, religion, education, or occupation. Let there be no involuntary taxation! Fearing the growth of a powerful government, he would keep it small indeed by limiting its revenues to voluntary contributions and income from lotteries and other noncoercive operations (*MIHM* 15, 17, and 22).

If there is a one-word summation of this voluntarism and desire for minimal government, with much distrust of the benefits of government welfare programs and the like, it is expressed here by the title of Book Three of this book: "TANSTAAFL!" This stands for "There ain't no such thing as a free lunch," and it is reiterated a number of times, leaving no doubt that the author wishes to emphasize it. In conclusion, a pessimism about man as a political animal emerges at the end of this novel when we learn that the framers of the new government of Luna adopted none of the professor's ideas. Manuel, too, was disappointed at the interferences with freedom which were generated by the new government, and he concluded that there "seems to be a deep instinct in human beings for making everything compulsory that isn't forbidden." At the story's end Manuel considered going out to the Asteroids, where there would be some nice places, "not too crowded," a sentiment reminiscent of the pioneering spirit of the American past, wherein the frontiersman went out beyond the settled lands to escape constraints (*MIHM* 30).

Rights and Responsibilities of the Citizenry

To quite an extent, the rights and roles of citizens may be complementary to the roles of governmental authorities, and thus the functions of citizens have already been delimited or implied in what we adduced concerning the executive operations. However, let us see what further perspectives can be derived by looking at these matters from the citizens' point of view. Particularly let us consider the position of women now; on equal rights for women the author's inclination appears to have been reasonably equitable, and not merely in recent years when the women's rights movement has made this a fashionable and natural thing for writers to advocate.

In **"Delilah and the Space-Rigger,"** which came out in 1949, Tiny Larsen, construction superintendent on Space Station One, accepts a woman electronics engineer for his team. At first he objects vociferously and contemptuously, mostly because he fears for the welfare and efficiency of his group if women are added. Soon, however, finding that the lady engineer does a good job, that she is accepted by the men, and that morale actually improves, he changes his tune and proposes to add a number of female personnel to his group. Perhaps these criteria are more functional and expedient than idealistic matters of equity, but the result was, in this story, a much more liberal situation than one could find in either trade unions or in business and the professions back in 1949.[16]

Later, in *Time Enough for Love,* the narrator reminisces about the twentieth-century United States Navy, observing that there was no job in it which could not be performed by either sex, despite which it remained heavily male in its staffing in the first six decades, at least, of that century (*TEL* "Variations on a Theme II"). Midway between these two stories, *Starship Troopers* in 1959 provided many references to women in many sorts of roles of leadership, active combat service, and even command of ships, in the space navy. The honors, status, and formal precedence given to female officers here are certainly equal. Also, it is important to note that the juxtaposition of the two sexes on spaceships, even on long voyages or in time of hostilities, is not shown as awkward and troublesome. Women are omitted only from service as combat infantry; on the ships, however, they participate in the hazards of violent death or injury in action. The author does not glaze over or ignore the little social problems or emotional reactions that would come from the propinquity of the sexes in a military force; he handles it realistically.

The same even-handed realism is evident throughout the interracial encounters under intimate and trying circumstances which are an important part of *Farnham's Freehold.* Rights for black citizens are not an especially frequent topic in Heinlein's fiction, but in this novel he takes on the problems of racial relationships in a low-key manner. Again, there is no glossing over of the nonwhite characters. They have faults, they do some awful things, they can be either gentle or arrogant; in short they are fairly typical human beings. In the future world postulated here, where blacks are the race in charge, the novel could have made an *Uncle Tom's Cabin* in reverse, but it did nothing of the kind.

There are, it is true, many stories in which this writer, as others in science fiction, contemplates a yellow peril—invasions from Asia, cruel Oriental overlords, and the like. Let us leave these to be considered as matters of hypothetical international relations of the future. Opinion will differ, but these situations could be defended as realistic, or at least as one man's attempt to project a not-altogether-fantastic future development. Nor does he follow the tradition of Buck Rogers or Flash Gordon. In those creations, the reader may recall, the Red Mongol overlords of Rogers' day went out of their way to kidnap Buck's beloved Wilma; her seduction was recurrently one of their prime objectives. Similarly, Flash's girl, Dale, got a lot of attention from the oversexed minions of the fiendish Ming the Merciless. In Heinlein, on the other hand, the Oriental attackers, while quite unpleasant, as invaders will be always, appear largely as businesslike operators; their dislike or scorn for the other side and the other races is not lurid or unusual.

The author's views on modes of sexual relationships reflect primarily his generally broad view of rights. The authorities, and indeed people as a whole, should mind their own business and be tolerant. In *Time Enough for Love* this has been given more play, presumably in response to new popular feelings in the Western world, the "new morality," and such factors which naturally condition the products of a great many writers. The hero of the novel thought that laws on marriage were unnecessary (*TEL* "Variations on a Theme XIV").

The general rights of the citizen were particularly broad in the society sketched out in **Coventry.** The people were not forbidden to do anything unless it damaged another person. If they did commit such damaging acts they were required to submit to a program of psychological readjustment administered by the authorities, to render the offenders more innocuous. If a person refused the program he was obliged to leave the society entirely, by passing through a force field or barrier to the region beyond it, which was external to the society, inhabited by such exiles or pariahs, unsupervised by the government. We find this concept of largely leaving people alone extended to risky undertakings—the government should not forbid these either. This is expressed in the story called **"Requiem,"** where a character declares that it is not "'the business of this damn paternalistic government to tell a man not to risk his life doing what he really wants to do.'"[17]

More specific rights enunciated by Heinlein's characters include the privilege of bearing arms and the concomitant arrangement that the police should not be too strong: "The police of a state should never be stronger or better armed than the citizenry. An armed citizenry, willing to fight, is the foundation of civil freedom." The words here show some resemblance to those of the Second Amendment to the Constitution of the United States, which says that the right of citizens to keep and bear arms shall not be infringed because the armed militia is essential to the security of a free state. Many of the other "Bill of Rights"-type immunities would result indirectly from the approach Heinlein advocated in his speech at the World Science Fiction Convention in Seattle, in 1961. He would not put anyone in jail, conscript anyone, or otherwise subject him to involuntary servitude, nor would he suppress or conceal information.[18]

In *Starship Troopers* and some other stories the citizenry is certainly not free from what Americans in recent times have come to think of as cruel and unusual punishment; in fact all inhabitants, whether citizens or not, and whether in the armed forces or not, are subject in *Starship Troopers* to flogging, as a punishment for a variety of offenses. We are told that twentieth-century America found itself so endangered because of lax handling of its offenders that life became insufferably dangerous, and there was finally public support for corporal punishment. Flogging was not reserved for rare and horrible crimes; drunken driving got the offender something in excess of ten lashes. The underlying rationale is stated here, that man does not have a moral instinct, as the people of the twentieth century thought; he has simply a cultivated conscience—thence the importance of exemplary or deterrent punishments (*ST* 8).

Nowhere is the doctrine of rights being coordinate with responsibilities applied more straightforwardly than in the

Starship Troopers situation, where one must earn the franchise and citizenship through national service—largely military, but not necessarily in a combat arm. The veterans-only government came into being after a prisoner-of-war foul-up following a war with the "Chinese Hegemony," and is considered efficacious because all those admitted to citizenship have, in the service, placed group welfare ahead of their personal advantage; they have at least made some sacrifices for the nation. A noncitizen cannot enter politics, but he is not persecuted, and he may be very successful in the private sector. The hero's father has a prosperous business, though he is not a citizen at the beginning of the novel. Some other key roles are reserved for citizens; only they may teach the secondary-level course called "History and Moral Philosophy," because of its importance in shaping the outlooks of young people. A single enlistment of a few years is usually enough to qualify for the franchise, but those who sign up for the career service may run into trouble in this regard if they do not finish twenty years' service.

Some debate is possible as to whether this situation would be in substance an infringement on a truly volunteer service, since there are distinct liabilities attached to those who don't volunteer. Another objection might be that a government of veterans only could be a little one-sided, or even jingoistic. Nevertheless this system would indeed coordinate privileges with responsibility in a significant way (*ST* 4, 6, 11, and 12).

Starship Troopers gives most of its attention to the career of an enlistee in the Mobile Infantry, an interstellar personal combat force which resembles most closely the United States Marines. The volunteer's life is manifestly regimented to a high degree; his rights and his scope for freedom of action are very limited. However, he has *volunteered* for this situation. Therefore even this novel is quite consistent with the Heinlein position on the individual vis-à-vis the various political philosophies, which is most comprehensively stated as follows:

> Political tags—such as royalist, communist, democrat, populist, fascist, liberal, conservative, and so forth— are never basic criteria. The human race divides politically into those who want people to be controlled and those who have no such desire.

> (TEL "Second Intermission")

ECONOMICS AND BUSINESS

The Heinlein general theory on economics is in a way a laissez-faire theory, derived from the views on minimal government and individual freedom which we have already considered. The reason for hedging with the words "in a way" in the preceding sentence is that in many of his stories the economic units or corporate entities are so large that it may be uncertain whether there would be much free economics, much individual discretion, or much random marketplace action left. It is somewhat the same question we behold on the real Earth of the present, but with many, many planets involved, the capacity for impersonal bigness is unavoidably increased.

A basic dictum already noted, "There ain't no such thing as a free lunch," has obvious implications in the area of economics. *Starship Troopers* applies much the same concept specifically to the democratic nations of the twentieth century, looking back regretfully at them to note that they collapsed because the people thought that they could "vote for whatever they wanted . . . and get it, without toil . . ." (*ST* 6). In a more recent novel, the author says the same thing, and says it in the form of an aphorism, in a list of sayings recorded by the hero. That is a fairly gratuitous utterance, not really needed for the novel, so it may be taken as authentic author-opinion: "Anything free is worth what you pay for it" (*TEL* "Second Intermission").

There are also economic corollaries to the Darwinian thought which Heinlein echoes repeatedly, and to his thoughts about the frontier. From *The Door into Summer* we have "Competition is a good idea—Darwin thought well of it" (12). Of course the brilliant and ingenious inventor found in that novel, and in several others, emerged as a natural type to succeed in a free enterprise system. Another hero manages easily to found a bank, not a deed readily accomplished by individuals in mid-twentieth-century America, but not so hard to do in a frontier-like settlement, as in the story of Lazarus Long. Even there, the development of a more meddlesome government menaces Lazarus' bank with nationalization, to his annoyance but not to his surprise. He indulges then in a dialogue on the worthlessness of paper money, denouncing fools who expect that governments will be able to guarantee both plentiful money and favorable prices. What is more, the hero recalls that he has been many times wealthy during his long life, but always lost the wealth, usually by governments inflating the economy, thus depreciating the currency, or even by outright confiscation. "Princes . . . don't produce, they always steal," he declares ("Variations on a Theme XII" and "III").

Clearly Heinlein is in favor of letting the law of supply and demand operate; he says that no one has improved on it. He does not accept Marx's value theory, finding it illogical. Really, he opines, value to man is either what he can do with a thing or what he does to get it. His disapproval of idealistic theorists extends also to those who would abolish poverty, which is the normal condition of man throughout history. Poverty is occasionally conquered temporarily, he believes, only because a tiny, creative minority scores an advance, but before long that minority is once again inhibited by its society and poverty is restored.

As for idealists who extol nature and deplore any artificialities or interferences by man with animals or natural conditions, the author reminds those silly people that man, too, is part of nature, stating that he himself prefers dams built by Homo sapiens to those made by beavers. The "naturalists" hate themselves, he says, and are contemptible (*ST* and *TEL* "Variations on a Theme III" and "Intermissions"). We infer from this, then, that if interference with entrepreneurs were not already out because of laissez-faire beliefs, certainly interference in the name of nature or preservation of the wilderness would be taboo.

INTERNATIONAL POLITICS

Most of the interpretations of international relations in this literature will be found in the events which are projected for the future, or what was the future when the stories were written. These projections are meaningful enough, despite the element of imagination in them, because they reflect the writer's estimate of what might happen, and because those projections were selected by him, out of the infinite number of conceivable future contingencies.

First, however, it is possible to point out a few ideas which partake of the nature of general observations on the relations of nations. One of these is war. Heinlein is of course no pacifist; he finds pacifism almost inconceivable in a male, and apparently believes that many pacifists are not completely against war or violence, just selectively opposed. This author is not enamored of militaristic warmongers either, preferring to consider war proper only when it is more or less necessary. Violence, likewise, is not endorsed beyond the levels which are needed for approved purposes. In *Starship Troopers,* for instance, we read that "'war is *controlled* violence, for a purpose. . . . The purpose is never to kill the enemy just to be killing him . . . It's never a soldier's business to decide when or where or how—or *why* . . .'" (*ST* 5). The Mobile Infantrymen of this novel are outfitted with exceedingly versatile powered armor which renders each user far more mobile and destructive than individual infantrymen as we have known them. By virtue of this powerful equipment, we are told admiringly, the fighter is able to make war more selectively, even in a personalized manner, eschewing indiscriminate, mass destruction (*ST* 7).

That laudable standard is shortly disregarded, one gathers, first by the declaration that the Mobile Infantry raid then in progress had "frightfulness" as an aim. (*Frightfulness* is the translation of the German term *Schrecklichkeit.*) Even in undertaking to be frightful, however, the narrator reassures us that one is not supposed to kill unless he has to (1). That is puzzling, but ten pages later it is clarified somewhat when the infantryman reports that he threw a "thirty-second bomb" into a churchlike room full of the enemy people—it being quite doubtful that they could all get out of there before the device exploded, in half a minute's time. Also, in the same raid, fire was liberally engendered in the area, so that "much of the city was burning," with a not-so-selective loss of life (*ST* 1).

So far as the projection of specific near-future wars with familiar, terrestrial nations is concerned, Heinlein has often reflected the common anticipations of the American public in the years of the respective stories. **"The Year of the Jackpot"** appeared in 1952, a year when the United States was at war and when there was widespread fear of all-out war with Russia. Thus it is not an especially fanciful or pessimistic author who builds into this story a reference to World War III, with the Soviet Union, as an accomplished fact—a war in which there were "forty cities gone."[19]

Five years after that story there appeared *The Door into Summer,* in 1957. When it was being written, the advent of the first artificial satellite had not yet occurred, but the programs in America and Russia for development of rockets that could put satellites into orbit, or which could carry atomic missiles from one continent to another, all these matters were familiar to intelligent and well-informed men like the author. Consequently, with Cold War nervousness about as keen as it has been in 1952, it was natural enough that *The Door into Summer* projected the following series of events as having taken place by 1970: another great war, many little ones, the downfall of communism, the Great Panic, the artificial satellites, and the change to atomic power (1). It was in the year after the publication of this novel that the author's *Gazette Telegraph* advertisement warned against agreements with the Russians on limitation of atomic testing, cautioning that unless such a treaty included provisions for on-the-spot inspection the United States would be unable to learn about secret Soviet tests.

So much for apprehensions concerning the USSR. Another continuing anxiety was that China would be ever stronger and more aggressive. *Sixth Column* appeared in 1941 and was later issued as *The Day After Tomorrow.* It projected a sequence of events in which China absorbed India and Japan. The Americans, thinking that the USSR would keep busy with the Asian expansionists, taking care of them, ignored the whole thing. The Russians lost out and then the U.S.A., with its chronically bad intelligence services, stumbled into war with the PanAsians, as the Chinese came to be called after their conquests. A preemptive Chinese strike with devastating weapons kept the Americans from using their own arsenal, and PanAsia occupied the U.S.A. After the blow fell, one of the characters in the novel mused, "What would it be like, this crazy new world—a world in which the superiority of western culture was not a casually accepted 'Of course' . . . ?"[20] The Oriental occupation, as described herein, had many of the features which a later generation came to see in practice, during the consolidation of communist power in Cambodia in the 1970s—registration and close control of all persons, relocation of massive numbers to work camps, executions, mandatory permits for all sorts of routine matters.

The later novel *Starship Troopers* is another of the examples of references to war with China. In this case, the reference is only a passing one; in connection with a later struggle with an insectoid empire, the narrator suggests that the nation should have foreseen the communal strength of the Bugs by recalling the grief given to the "Russo-Anglo-American Alliance" by the "Chinese Hegemony," which was another case of a collective mass in which the individual wills were submerged (*ST* 11).

These then are the principal themes of foreign relations as reflected in the Heinlein stories. There are other examples, of course, but these examples should suffice to indicate the author's focal points.

To sum up the political and social thought of a prolific writer is a difficult proposition, all the more challenging if the author's products have been rather diversified and have evolved and developed over the years. One may note, however, that the evolution of Heinlein has been mostly a matter of natural maturation, skill in the handling of new elements, and new responses to changing public tastes, to new moods among the readers. It is very much the same man there behind the writing desk, with pretty much the same core of fundamental ideas.

There are surely contradictions and dilemmas implicit in the content of the Heinlein stories. Contradictions are manifestly a vital part of the life of people in groups under any circumstances. There is, notably, the tension between liberty and leadership. There is the problem of the dutiful and devoted servant of mankind, who can hardly avoid the natural tendency of power to corrupt those who wield it. The author has had a lot to say about duty and responsibility, which he regards as a cement of proper societies, but he knows that the distance is not so great as one might suppose between the humble and the despotic, between the puritanical and the libertine. Minimal government is preferred, but so frequently we end up with gigantic empires or corporations. Still, the Heinlein "good guys" *do* strike back at unwholesome centers of power.

We have found contradictions also between a humane and peaceable outlook, on the one hand, and a readiness for war, on the other. One finds sometimes even an affirmation that war is part of the natural order of things, not to mention a countenancing of widespread destruction and loss of many innocent lives when this is "strategically necessary." Also, in this future fiction, it is not surprising to find a gap between the author's indubitably keen concern for the preservation of maximal individual liberties and privacy, on the one hand, and the grim promise of the new electronic age, on the other. We face, and have to some extent already experienced in real life, the great potential of surveillance gadgetry, as well as computerized processing of data, to carry on the "full coverage" of individuals which the fictional accounts often include.

Our author, in his comments on political and social affairs, has frequently been passionate, emphatic, or categorical. Seldom does he stray for long, however, from a correspondingly strong element of the logical, methodical, and scientific. These components are not confined to the scientist's workshop, but emerge in this literature to guide the development of mankind.

Notes

1. Robert A. Heinlein, *The Door into Summer* (New York: New American Library, Signet Books, 1975), (12).

2. Franz Rottensteiner, *The Science Fiction Book* (New York: Seabury Press, 1975), 100.

3. Heinlein, *Farnham's Freehold* (New York: Berkley Medallion, 1971), (2); *Beyond This Horizon* (New York: New American Library, Signet Books, 1974), (2), (10).

4. Heinlein, *Starship Troopers* (New York: Berkley Medallion, 1968), hereafter referred to in text as *ST.*

5. *Time Enough for Love* (New York: Berkley Medallion, 1974), (Introduction, "Prelude I," "Variations on a Theme XIV"), hereafter referred to in text as *TEL*; "The Man Who Sold the Moon," (8), (12), in *The Past Through Tomorrow* (New York: Berkley Medallion, 1975); "Logic of Empire," in *The Past Through Tomorrow.*

6. Damon Knight, *In Search of Wonder* (Chicago: Advent, 1967), 84-85.

7. Heinlein, *Waldo & Magic, Inc.* (New York: New American Library, Signet Books, 1970), 76-77, 186.

8. "If This Goes On—," (6), in *The Past Through Tomorrow,* hereafter referred to in text as 'ITGO.'

9. Heinlein, *Podkayne of Mars* (New York: Berkley Medallion, 1975), (4).

10. Heinlein, *Glory Road* (New York: Berkley Medallion, 1970), (20).

11. Heinlein, "Gulf," in *Assignment in Eternity* (New York: New American Library, Signet Books, 1970).

12. Heinlein, "Coventry," in *The Past Through Tomorrow.*

13. Heinlein, "Science Fiction: Its Nature, Faults, and Virtues," in *The Science Fiction Novel,* Basil Davenport et al. (Chicago: Advent, 1969), 44-45.

14. Heinlein, "The Long Watch," in *The Past Through Tomorrow.*

15. Heinlein, *The Moon Is a Harsh Mistress* (New York: Berkley Medallion, 1968), (2), hereafter referred to in text as *MIHM.*

16. Heinlein, "Delilah and the Space Rigger," in *The Past Through Tomorrow.*

17. Heinlein, "Requiem," in *The Past Through Tomorrow.*

18. Heinlein, *Beyond This Horizon,* (9); Alexei Panshin, *Heinlein in Dimension* (Chicago: Advent, 1968), 185.

19. Heinlein, "The Year of the Jackpot," (3), in *The Menace from Earth* (New York: New American Library, Signet Books, 1970).

20. Heinlein, *The Day After Tomorrow* (New York: New American Library, Signet Books, 1975), (1).

H. Bruce Franklin (essay date 1980)

SOURCE: Franklin, H. Bruce. "From Depression into World War II: The Early Fiction." In *Robert A. Heinlein: America as Science Fiction,* pp. 17-63. New York: Oxford University Press, 1980.

[In the following essay, Franklin discusses the defining characteristics of Heinlein's early short fiction.]

"—during the '30's almost everyone, from truck driver to hatcheck girl, had a scheme for setting the world right in six easy lessons; and a surprising percentage managed to get their schemes published."

—Robert Heinlein, **"The Roads Must Roll,"** June 1940

In 1938 the atom was split. That did not seem such big news to many people, for in 1938 the Japanese were extending their invasion of China, the Italian Fascist army was trying to wipe out the stubborn partisan resistance in Ethiopia, Franco's forces opened their decisive offensive against the Loyalist government of Spain, Franco's ally Adolf Hitler invaded Austria, and Czechoslovakia was divided up by Germany, Hungary, and Poland. In early 1939, the Soviet Union crushed an attempted invasion by Japan. In late 1939, Germany successfully invaded Poland. At some point, World War II had begun.

Meanwhile, in April of 1939, the New York World's Fair opened, in futuristic splendor, with visions of "the World of Tomorrow" presented by hundreds of corporations and dozens of states and countries. The Long Island Railroad promised to take you there swiftly from Manhattan: "From the World of Today to the World of Tomorrow in ten minutes for ten cents." Four months later, in a world plunging from the Great Depression into a global holocaust, *Astounding Science-Fiction* printed Robert Heinlein's first story.

Heinlein's first three published stories are all celebrations of the individual genius—lonely, misunderstood, but leading humanity forward to new frontiers of time and space. This lone superior individual, alienated but true to his own unprecedented destiny, is to become the central character-type of Heinlein's fiction for the next third of a century.

The hero of **"Life-Line"** (August 1939), his first story, is Dr. Hugo Pinero, the kind of lonely scientific genius who had haunted the pages of nineteenth-century science fiction from Victor Frankenstein through H. G. Well's Time Traveller. Pinero has invented a marvelous machine that determines with chilling accuracy the time of a person's death. Ridiculed by the scientific establishment, but hailed by the media as "The Miracle Man from Nowhere," he sets up a lucrative business, "Sands of Time, Inc.," so successful that it begins to threaten the profits of the giant insurance corporations.

Determined to crush the little upstart, Amalgamated Life Insurance attempts to destroy Dr. Pinero's business with an injunction. But they encounter a judge who delivers a most revealing lecture, obviously expressing the views of Robert Heinlein, whose family's farm-equipment business had been superseded by an emerging monopoly and whose own recent small-business ventures had been unable to compete, in this era of life-and-death struggle between corporate monopoly and small enterprise. This judge denounces the "strange doctrine" that because a "corporation has made a profit out of the public for a number of years,

the government and the courts are charged with the duty of guaranteeing such profit in the future, even in the face of changing circumstances and contrary to public interest." He denies the demand of Amalgamated Life Insurance "that the clock of history be stopped, or turned back."

Like many in his social class, Heinlein clung tenaciously to the belief that the main vehicle of progress was free enterprise, a vehicle sometimes willfully sabotaged by the giant corporations. This is an overt theme in several of his stories during this period. In **"Life-Line,"** Amalgamated Life Insurance shows its true nature after it is frustrated in court: it hires gangsters who carry out their assignment of murdering Dr. Pinero and wrecking his wonderful equipment. Then the leading scientists, earlier labeled by Pinero the "Barbarians! Imbeciles!" who "have blocked the recognition of every great discovery since time began," fulfill their part on the job by burning all the documentary evidence of Pinero's brilliant results.

Although the corporations and the academic establishment are the main enemy of the lone genius in **"Life-Line,"** Pinero expresses as much scorn for "the little man in the street" as for "you little men" of the Academy of Science. Yet despite all this exaltation of rugged individualism, there is a detectable countercurrent: a yearning to be part of a collective, a yearning so intense that it threatens to overwhelm individual identity. Pinero's theory and his machine are based on the assumption that each individual life is a continuity in space-time that can be compared to "a long pink worm, continuous through the years." In explaining his theory, Pinero argues that these pink worms are not, despite all appearance to the contrary, really discrete individuals:

> "As a matter of fact there is a physical continuity in this concept to the entire race, for these pink worms branch off from other pink worms. In this fashion the race is like a vine whose branches intertwine and send out shoots. Only by taking a cross-section of the vine would we fall into the error of believing that the shootlets were discrete individuals."

This sense of the individual as part of a human collective, organically joined to a death-defying timeless racial identity, is the other side of an unresolved contradiction that branches throughout all of Heinlein's work.

"Misfit," Heinlein's second story, published in *Astounding* in November 1939, dramatizes the lone genius as a kind of ugly duckling who, unlike Dr. Pinero, achieves acceptance in the human family. Like **"Life-Line,"** **"Misfit"** can also be read as a product of the Depression. In fact, its teenaged hero, Andrew Jackson Libby, is recruited into a twenty-second-century version of the New Deal's Civilian Conservation Corps. This C.C.C. of the future is the Cosmic Construction Corps, employing young misfits to convert asteroids into space stations.

Libby, "a thin, gangling, blond lad," turns out to be a supergenius. When the ballistic calculator fails at a crucial moment, Libby takes its place, saving the mission. Like the nineteenth-century science-fiction dime novel, **"Misfit"** allows its readers to identify with a boy genius who wins the admiration and gratitude of the adult world.

The first of Heinlein's stories with a juvenile hero, **"Misfit"** foreshadows his juvenile novels of 1947-58.[1] In fact, *Starman Jones* (1953) has an extended replay of Libby's superhuman computations in space. The figure of Libby himself continues to haunt Heinlein's imagination and to appeal to his readers. In *Methuselah's Children* (1941) Libby single-handedly invents and builds the "space drive" that allows trips into deep space, in this and many later tales. In *Time Enough for Love* (1973) one of the ritual quests performed by the novel's deathless mythic hero is to voyage backward in time to bury the orbiting body of his old friend Andrew Jackson Libby. In *The Number of the Beast*—(1980) Libby is resurrected as a beautiful woman, Elizabeth Andrew Jackson Libby Long, cloned from his original body and preserving his memory.

"Misfit" also introduces another theme of growing importance in Heinlein's later fiction: love and interchangeability between a human being and a thinking machine. Libby is assigned to the ballistic calculator, "three tons of thinking metal." The emotional response of this boy who had never felt "needed" is intense: "He loved the big machine. . . . Libby subconsciously thought of it as a person—his own kind of person."

The lone genius in Heinlein's third story, **"Requiem"** (*Astounding,* January 1940), is Delos D. Harriman, an old man about to die. Bearing the name of the nineteenth-century railroad magnate, Harriman is the crafty, visionary, ruthless, heroic capitalist who has (as we learn in a later story) almost single-handedly built "the Company" that all by itself explored and colonized the moon; he has also created the Harriman Foundation which finances space travel in many later tales. Prohibited by rules laid down by the bureaucracy of "this damn paternalistic government" and his own company from traveling to the moon, Harriman nevertheless roguishly buys his final trip to die on that remote place of his youthful dreams.

In describing these dreams, Harriman eloquently paints a picture of the boys and young men who made pre-World War II science fiction—both those who read it and those who wrote it. This picture is a wonderful self-portrait of Robert Heinlein:

". . . I believed—I believed. I read Verne and Wells and Smith, and I believed that we could do it—that we *would* do it. I set my heart on being one of the men to walk the surface of the Moon, to see her other side, and to look back on the face of the Earth, hanging in the sky."

". . . I just wanted to live a long time and see it all happen. I wasn't unusual; there were lots of boys like me—radio hams, they were, and telescope builders, and airplane amateurs. We had science clubs, and basement laboratories, and science-fiction leagues—the kind of boys that thought there was more romance in one is-

sue of the *Electrical Experimenter* than in all the books Dumas ever wrote. We didn't want to be one of Horatio Alger's get-rich heroes either; we wanted to build space ships."

For these technologically oriented boys and men, stimulated by the visions of science fiction, technology tends to be the focus of romance, love, and even sex. Harriman's wife "had not shared his dream and his need." As he dozes on his voyage to the moon, he imagines her voice calling "Delos! Come in from there! You'll catch your death of cold in that night air." The ship itself seems more alluring: "He noted with a professional eye that she was a single-jet type with fractional controls around her midriff." He scans her controls "lovingly"; "Each beloved gadget was in its proper place. He knew them—graven in his heart." On the voyage he finds himself between two sensual beauties:

The Moon swung majestically past the viewport, twice as wide as he had ever seen it before, all of her familiar features cameo-clear. She gave way to the Earth as the ship continued its slow swing, the Earth itself, as he had envisioned her, appearing like a noble moon, eight times as wide as the Moon appears to the Earthbound, and more luscious, more sensuously beautiful than the silver Moon could be.

Throughout Heinlein's fiction, Earth is beautiful only when viewed from a distance, when people and their civilization cannot be seen.

Despite the vision of "the World of Tomorrow" projected by the 1939 World's Fair, the Depression had shattered the dreams of millions of Americans. Looking back, we can see that this economic catastrophe signaled the collapse of the free-enterprise system, which was rapidly being replaced by monopoly and state capitalism as the dominant form of the American political economy. Robert Heinlein's social and political outlook was shaped within this historical drama. Again and again throughout his writing career, we see him posing the old beliefs in "free trade" and "free enterprise" against the growing monopolies and bureaucracies of the giant corporations and the state controlled by these impersonal forces.

In the pre-World War II stories, the struggle often takes the classic form of the small businessman, the inventor, or the small factory owner fighting directly against the corporate monopolies, which sometimes are seen as already dominating the government. Two striking examples are stories published in 1940, **"'Let There Be Light'"** and **"The Devil Makes the Law,"** the first a hard-core science-fiction tale published in the May issue of *Super Science Stories,* the second a wild fantasy published in the September *Unknown.*

The hero of **"'Let There Be Light'"** is Dr. Archie Douglas, a young physicist doing research in a laboratory set up in the factory owned by his father. While awaiting a visit from the illustrious biologist Doctor M. L. Martin, Archie tries to pick up a beautiful blonde with a "dumb pan" and a figure like fandancer Sally Rand's. She turns out to be the famous M. L. Martin ("Mary Lou to her friends") and Heinlein's first significant female character.

Mary Lou, who has been experimenting with the biology of fireflies, teams up with Archie to invent a device to turn electric power into light with minimum power loss. Then Archie's father explains that he is about to be driven out of business by the utility monopoly, which has "bought" both houses of the legislature "body and soul" in order to keep exploiting "power that actually belongs to the people." So the two geniuses reverse their process and invent a solar power generator, promising "Free power! Riches for everybody!"

Now they have to struggle against the monopoly, whose political and economic power is explained to naïve Archie by worldly-wise Mary Lou, who cites the preface to George Bernard Shaw's *Back to Methuselah*[2] in describing "the combined power of corporate industry to resist any change that might threaten their dividends." She tells of the ruthless methods industry uses to suppress inventions, including the super carburetor (an American folk legend that I personally have heard from at least a dozen mechanics in different sections of the country), and of the commitment of American industry to produce commodities "just as bad as the market will stand" so that they will wear out as soon as possible. Using feminine wiles to massage his male ego, she attributes their inventions solely to him and warns that "You threaten the whole industrial set-up."

Since they cannot safely profit from the inventions, Mary Lou proposes that they release the secret to everybody: "Free power! You'll be the new emancipator." So finally the theme of the lone Promethean genius is blazoned forth in a newspaper headline: "GENIUS GRANTS GRATIS POWER TO PUBLIC." The publicly acclaimed GENIUS of course is Archie, who now persaudes Mary Lou to marry him "to make an honest man of me." It is interesting to note that the anti-monopoly if not downright anti-capitalist message of this story is expounded by Mary Lou, who allows her own scientific and practical roles to be concealed from the public, and that the story is the first Heinlein published under a pseudonym (Lyle Monroe), thus concealing his own identity from the public.

"The Devil Makes the Law" is, as its title suggests, an allegory. The setting is a typical American town where, as elsewhere in this fantastic world, all the businessmen routinely use magic in their trades, manufacture, and professions. The protagonist is another Archie, Archibald Fraser, Merchant and Contractor in the construction business. His small business, like all the others in town, is threatened by a ruthless monopoly named Magic, Inc. When the businessmen take their struggle to the statehouse, an old "mass of masonry" which "seemed to represent something tough in the character of the American people, the determination of free men to manage their own affairs," they are dismayed to discover that Magic, Inc. is already in control of their own state government and those of other states across the country.

Archie and his friends—including a small manufacturer who uses witches to produce the garments made in his factory, an African witch-doctor, and a fiercely independent old witch-lady—are forced to take their fight directly to the source of this infernal monopolistic conspiracy: Hell itself. There, with the help of an FBI agent working for the anti-monopoly division and disguised as a demon, they unmask and defeat the boss of the monopoly, one of Satan's own lieutenants.

Heinlein's loathing of monopoly develops into the most radically "left" story of his career, **"Logic of Empire,"** published in *Astounding* in March 1941. Here, as in much of his post-World War II fiction, "the Company" has stretched beyond Earth to become an enormous interplanetary monopoly, tyrannizing over farflung colonies which are moving toward a replay of the 1776 American Revolution.

The story begins with two prosperous gentlemen, lawyer Humphrey Wingate and his wealthy friend Sam Houston Jones, whom Wingate accuses of being a "parlor pink," drinking and arguing about whether the "labor clients" of the Venus Development Company are actually slaves. Wingate vociferously champions the Company, with its "obligations to its stockholders," and condemns the lazy workers, "a class of people that feel that the world owes them a living." The argument ends in a drunken decision to sign a contract for six years of indentured labor on Venus, and they wake up incarcerated in a spaceship.

Heinlein then dramatizes the conditions of labor on Venus as a combination of indentured labor in the eighteenth-century American colonies, Black chattel slavery on nineteenth-century American plantations, and wage slavery and debt peonage in the factories and on the farms of twentieth-century America. Once off the spaceship that resembles a slave ship, the "clients" are sold to "patrons" in a slave auction. As soon as Wingate, our point-of-view character, begins laboring on a plantation, the narrative begins to sound like a future version of nineteenth-century narratives of escaped slaves, such as the *Narrative of the Life of Frederick Douglass, An American Slave*. There are overseers, an addictive drink used to narcotize the slaves, and even threats made against recalcitrant slaves "to sell you South" to more "factory-like plantations." Technically, the status of the Company's "labor clients" most closely resembles a combination of the conditions of the two main groups of workers in pre-World War II America: the debt peonage characteristic of the majority of Black rural workers and the wage slavery typical of mine and factory labor. Wingate discovers "that while he was free theoretically to quit, it was freedom to starve on Venus, unless he first worked out his bounty and his passage both ways."

Even more devastating is Wingate's discovery that the conditions of labor are deadening his consciousness; in a passage echoing Frederick Douglass's picture of his own degradation, Wingate realizes that "he was becoming one of the broken men," whose mind is relaxing into "slave psychology." And like Douglass, Wingate reawakens the freedom of his mind by resolving upon bold action based on the belief that "No slave is ever freed, *save he free himself*." So he and two other slaves attack their owner and escape.

The fugitives discover one of the "runaway slave camps," where they gain admittance by identifying themselves with the code name "Fellow travelers." This turns out to be the first of many examples in Heinlein's works of a vigorous frontier cultural outpost, the antithesis of the decadent monopolistic tyrannies of Earth. This "rough frontier culture" gives Wingate still another course in his re-education. He is surprised to find "that fugitive slaves, the scum of Earth," were able to build a viable society, just as "it had surprised his ancestors that the transported criminals of Botany Bay should develop a high civilization in Australia."

Wingate, now almost totally awakened to social reality, begins writing "a political pamphlet against the colonial system." He then encounters a character soon to be familiar to Heinlein readers, a cranky old mouthpiece for the author, in this case a university professor fired for his political views (under a pretext very similar to Stanford University's for firing Thorstein Veblen). "Doc" ridicules Wingate's "devil theory"—although the pamphlet seems tame compared with **"The Devil Makes the Law"**—explaining that "bankers," "company officials," "patrons," and "the governing classes back on Earth" are not "scoundrels" but products of social necessity and their own class outlook: "Men are constrained by necessity, and then build up rationalizations to account for their acts." Doc gives Wingate a key lesson in Heinlein's economic theory: "Colonial slavery is nothing new; it is the invariable result of imperial expansion, the automatic result of an antiquated financial structure—." Later, back on Earth, this message is reiterated by Sam Houston Jones, who has bought himself and Wingate out of slavery:

> "I've been wondering how long it would take you to get your eyes opened. . . . It's nothing new; it happened in the Old South, it happened again in California, in Mexico, in Australia, in South Africa. Why? Because in any expanding free-enterprise economy which does not have a money system designed to fit its requirements the use of mother-country capital to develop the colony inevitably results in subsistence-level wages at home and slave labor in the colonies."

Finally, Wingate, who has renounced "the empty, sterile bunkum-fed life of the fat and prosperous class he had moved among and served," realizes his inability to produce another *Uncle Tom's Cabin* or *Grapes of Wrath* and seems resigned to Sam's pronouncement that "Things are bound to get a whole lot worse before they can get any better."

Tacked on to the end of **"Logic of Empire"** is a note from editor John Campbell, informing readers of *Astounding* that "all of Robert Heinlein's stories are based on a common proposed future history of the world." Two months later, in May 1941, *Astounding* printed Heinlein's chart of this future history. Modeled on the charts of macrohistory included in Olaf Stapledon's *Last and First Men* (1930), and sharing Stapledon's vision of a spiral of progress moving upward through cyclical rises and falls, Heinlein's chart provided a framework for much of his prewar fiction, an independent display of his historical ideology, and a new pleasure for his growing throng of readers, who could now anticipate the missing pieces of the puzzle. Campbell's introductory essay, "History To Come," perceptively noted what many subsequent critics have agreed is the most engaging quality of Heinlein's fictions of the future: their sense of being "lived-in," as opposed to the "stage setting" environments of stories that have to create their future environments from scratch. Heinlein's fans thus had the comfort of entering a somewhat familiar projected history where they could recognize an occasional old friend, while at the same time experiencing the thrill of the unexpected.

Heinlein made minor revisions of this chart of future history until 1967, adding new tales as they were written and occasionally deleting an old one. Most of the stories subsequently included were published before World War II; those eventually added or subtracted made no fundamental change, except to delete references to all years before 1975 and to extend the future from 2140 to 2600. The principal addition was a cluster of nine short stories, published between 1947 and 1950, sketching the early days of space exploration shortly before and after the year 2000. Most of the Future History was published in three volumes: **The Man Who Sold the Moon** (1950), **The Green Hills of Earth** (1951), and *Revolt in 2100* (1953). In 1967, Heinlein published *The Past Through Tomorrow*, billed as the "Future History Stories Complete in One Volume," and including a publisher's note telling how "Heinlein created a gigantic chart—filling an entire wall of his study—to keep track of his future world and the progress of its peoples and civilizations." The latest revised chart is published in each collection.

Besides itemizing and dating the stories, the chart draws the "life-lines" of some of the characters, prophesies technical development, and provides sociological summaries of the main events in human history for the next centuries. Other works loosely interconnect with the projected future. Gaps are filled in by a postscript to *Revolt in 2100* called "Concerning Stories Never Written" and by the novel *Time Enough for Love*. From the 1941 chart to the latest revision in 1967, the outline of the Future History remains consistent.

In the immediate future lies the "Collapse of Empire" and "the CRAZY YEARS" of the middle twentieth century: "Considerable technical advance during this period, accompanied by a gradual deterioration of mores, orientation, and social institutions, terminating in mass psychoses in the sixth decade, and the Interregnum." Then comes the strike of 1960, the "FALSE DAWN" of 1960-70, with the first rocket reaching the moon in 1978: "The Interregnum was followed by a period of reconstruction in which the Voorhis financial proposals gave a temporary economic stability and a chance for re-orientation. This was ended by the opening of new frontiers and a return to nineteenth-century economy." This crucial quest in Heinlein's fiction—for "new frontiers" that will lead back to free-enterprise capitalism—is embodied in the Future History conception by Harriman's Lunar Corporation, the foundation of Luna City, and the development of the "PERIOD OF IMPERIAL EXPLOITATION, 1970-2020." But "the short period of interplanetary imperialism" is ended by three revolutions: Antarctica, the United States, and Venus.

Viewed in the context of the Future History, **"Logic of Empire"** can be read as a study of the conditions that lead to revolution. At the close of **"Logic of Empire,"** Sam Houston Jones foresees the rise of "a rabble-rousing political preacher like this fellow Nehemiah Scudder" to overthrow the technocratic monopolies. This important event in the Future History is loosely sketched in "Concerning Stories Never Written." Scudder's revolt leads to a religious dictatorship in the United States, outlined in the Future History chart: "Little research and only minor technical advances during this period. Extreme puritanism. Certain aspects of psychodynamics and psychometrics, mass psychology and social control developed by the priest class."

Those words describe the scene at the opening of Heinlein's first long fiction, **"If This Goes On—"** (*Astounding*, February, March 1940). The former United States is now under a theocratic dictatorship, headed by the latest incarnation of the Prophet, crushed under the weight of a vast military apparatus, and suppressed by omnipresent secret police, religious zealots employing hypnosis, torture, drugs, and the very latest methods of scientific thought control. Here is a perfect setting for Heinlein to explore what has long been one of his central themes: the relation between cultural conditioning and the possibility of human freedom.

If consciousness is determined by being, including the constantly reinforced values of a particular society or social class—and Heinlein sees all this as fairly obvious—then how is it possible for an individual, a social class, or a people to have true freedom, which depends upon the ability to transcend conditioning in order to arrive at true or at least accurate perception? In **"Logic of Empire,"** Humphrey Wingate was thrown bodily into the social class whose existence he had so radically misunderstood, and he thus came to transcend the false consciousness of his own affluent class. Heinlein chooses as protagonist and narrator of **"If This Goes On—"** a stolid, loyal, naïve young graduate of West Point, assigned to guard duty near the center of government at New Jerusalem. The story of the revolution is unfolded through the developing revolutionary consciousness of this one young man, John Lyle. But the problem remains, as we shall see, whether such a radical transformation of perception is possible for the people of the nation.

John Lyle falls in love with Judith, a nun-like Virgin about to be despoiled by the lascivious arch-hypocrite Prophet. It is this romantic attachment that literally drags Lyle to his initiation into the underground revolutionary Cabal. He rescues Judith, resists torture because the Cabal had hypnotically prepared him for it, assumes a new identity, escapes arrest, becomes the chief of staff of the commander in chief in the Cabal's enormous underground general headquarters, and takes command of the final victorious assault on New Jerusalem. Then at the end John Lyle decides to become a common citizen in the new system, marrying Judith and becoming a partner in a textile wholesaling firm.

Lyle had learned the truth about the dictatorship through his personal involvement at its evil core and through a long, intensive re-education administered to him by the Cabal. But what of the mass of ordinary citizens, exposed from birth to a profound superscientific conditioning to accept their slave status under the holy and omnipotent state? How are they to become convinced that all they had believed is false?

This problem is posed directly by a member of the technological elite running the revolution, the "chief of psychodynamics," who argues that "'We can seize power, but we cannot hold it!'":

> "Remember, my brothers, no people was ever held long in subjugation save through their own consent. The American people have been conditioned from the cradle by the cleverest and most thorough psychotechnicians in the world to believe in and trust the dictatorship which rules them. Since the suppression of our ancient civil liberties during the lifetime of the first Prophet, only the most daring and individual minds have broken loose from the taboos and superstitions that were instilled in their subconscious minds. If you free them without adequate psychological preparation, like horses led from a burning barn, they will return to their accustomed place."

> [March, p. 134]

This is the same problem faced by Hank Morgan in Mark Twain's *A Connecticut Yankee in King Arthur's Court*, when he attempts to establish a capitalist industrial republic amidst the religious darkness of feudal England. It is also one of the central problems of twentieth-century socialist revolution, which attempts to establish a new form of society, often in lands dominated by the most backward beliefs and most pervasive thought control, such as Russia in 1917, China in 1949, Cuba in 1959.

In **"If This Goes On—"** Heinlein presents a solution to this intricate problem, one "concocted" by the technological geniuses in the "psychodynamics" section of the Cabal. This plan "to change the psychological conditioning of the people and make them aware that they really had been saved from a tyranny which had ruled by keeping them in ignorance, their minds chained" provides for "readjusting the people to freedom of thought and freedom of action" under the direction of the men from psychodynamics:

They planned nothing less than mass reorientation under hypnosis. The technique was simple, as simple as works of genius usually are.

[March, p. 141]

All that is involved is placing the masses of people under hypnosis and showing them an extremely sophisticated propaganda film. The technique had already been tested, and found "usually" successful:

Usually it had worked, and the subjects were semantically readjusted to a modern nondogmatic viewpoint, but if the subject was too old mentally, if his thought processes were too thoroughly canalized, it sometimes destroyed one set of evaluations without providing him with a new set. The subject might come out of the hypnosis with an overpowering sense of insecurity which usually degenerated into schizophrenia, involute melancholia, or other psychoses involving loss of cortical control and consequent thalamic and subthalamic anarchy.

So the forces of the Cabal "'had our work cut out for us!'":

More than a hundred million persons had to be examined to see if they could stand up under quick reorientation, then re-examined after treatment to see if they had been sufficiently readjusted. Until a man passed the second examination we could not afford to enfranchise him as a free citizen of a democratic state.

[March, p. 141]

There is not the slightest suggestion of the monstrous possibilities inherent in the technological elite's determining who thinks correctly enough to be allowed to vote, and no hint of irony in Lyle's description of their colossal task: "We had to teach them to think for themselves, reject dogma, be suspicious of authority, tolerate differences of opinion, and make their own decisions—types of mental processes almost unknown in the United States for many generations."

Thirteen years after the original publication of **"If This Goes On—"** Heinlein revised it extensively for publication in *Revolt in 2100*. In the new version a cantankerous old man from Vermont, who looked like "an angry Mark Twain," arises to denounce the proposed mind-conditioning technique:

"Free men aren't 'conditioned'! Free men are free because they are ornery and cussed and prefer to arrive at their own prejudices in their own way—not have them spoonfed by a self-appointed mind tinkerer! We haven't fought, our brethren haven't bled and died, just to change bosses, no matter how sweet their motives."[3]

He goes on, articulating ideas that in the original version had been presented by the head of psychodynamics in a postscript:

"I tell you, we got into the mess we are in through the efforts of those same mind tinkerers. They've studied for years how to saddle a man and ride him. They

started with advertising and propaganda and things like that, and they perfected it to the point where what used to be simple, honest swindling such as any salesman might use became a mathematical science that left the ordinary man helpless."

When challenged to provide a solution, this new avatar of Mark Twain advocates simply restoring the old civil liberties and the franchise to everybody: "'If they mess it up again, that's their doing—but we have no right to operate on their minds.'" This position certainly seems less dangerous than the one Heinlein had presented without challenge in the 1940 version. However, it merely evades the central problem of this revolution, which according to the logic of the story itself should not be able to succeed and certainly should not be able to establish a new society capable of resisting the very forces that had originally established the tyranny. Heinlein barely covers the confusion by having the old man dramatically drop dead and the Cabal then immediately accept his position. For he remains stuck on the horns of an awkward dilemma that grows from seeing only two choices: either have the elite indoctrinate the people into correct thinking or just pretend that the problem will solve itself. The last words on the subject come from John Lyle: "I don't know who was right."[4]

This basic political and philosophic problem will reappear in many forms throughout Heinlein's works, for he will continue to see essentially just two alternatives: either the elite (the *good* elite) saves the day, which obviously contradicts democratic principles he sometimes espouses, or society succumbs to the ignorance and folly of the masses of common people. His concept of revolutionary social change imagines something created *by* an elite *for* the benefit of the people, usually quite temporarily. He seems incapable of believing that progressive social change could come through the development of the productive forces and consequent action by the exploited classes themselves. Thus Heinlein places himself consistently in direct opposition to the most powerful forces of social change in the twentieth century.

According to the chart of the Future History, the elite revolution we witness in **"If This Goes On—"** does succeed in establishing "THE FIRST HUMAN CIVILIZATION," a society implicit in the sequel, *Coventry* (*Astounding*, July 1940). The new society is based on "the Covenant," a social "contract" guaranteeing "the maximum possible liberty for every person." The Covenant forbids "no possible act, nor mode of conduct" as long as the action does not "damage" another individual. Those who violate the Covenant are not punished; they are allowed to choose between undergoing "psychological readjustment" to remove their tendency to injure other people or being sent to Coventry, a bountiful land reserved for those who refuse to accept the Covenant.

Heinlein's story does not show us life in this rational libertarian utopia, although we learn that science has provided an extremely high standard of living, social harmony prevails, while "danger and adventure" are still available: "there is danger still in experimental laboratories; there is hardship in the mountains of the Moon, and death in the jungles of Venus." Instead Heinlein shows us life in the tooth-and-claw world of Coventry, the land of exile.

The faith in rugged individualism preached in much of Heinlein's post-World War II writing is here the object of scathing attack. The arrogant, conceited protagonist, David MacKinnon, refuses to accept the mutual obligations that constitute society, yet he whines that society should guarantee him some private property in Coventry. The guard at the Barrier to Coventry scorns him and the other such "rugged individualists": "'You've turned down our type of social co-operation; why the hell should you expect the safeguards of our organization?'" As he approaches the gate to Coventry, deluding himself with his quest for a "Crusoe-like independence," MacKinnon fails to realize that even his personal possessions are the end products of "the cumulative effort and intelligent co-operation" of many people, living and dead.

What he finds in Coventry is a lawless social jungle of vicious predators, as well as a conspiracy to overthrow the society of the Covenant. MacKinnon speedily learns his lesson. He absorbs the virtues of self-sacrifice, and "cures himself" by becoming responsible to an old man known as Fader (father?) and to society. Fader turns out to be an undercover agent of the Covenant society, and he and MacKinnon each manage to return there with warnings of the dangerous plot brewing in Coventry.

A similar message appears in **"The Roads Must Roll"** (*Astounding,* June 1940), set in 1970, the period of the "FALSE DAWN" in the Future History. Automobiles have now been replaced by high-speed rolling roads with their own restaurants and stores. The skilled workers who man the great underground apparatus powering the roads follow the leadership of a monomaniac who asks "why we technicians don't just take things over." Heinlein denounces his ideology, developed from "the Bible of the Functionalist movement," a treatise "published in 1930," "dressed up with a glib mechanistic pseudopsychology" and proclaiming that those with the most indispensable function in advanced industrial society ought to be its masters. The fallacy, as Heinlein notes, is that in modern society many different functions are indispensable: "The complete interdependence of modern economic life seems to have escaped him entirely."

The other Future History story set in this period is **"Blow-ups Happen"** (*Astounding,* September 1940), predicting "the most dangerous machine in the world—an atomic power plant." Here too the main theme is social responsibility. With so much "responsibility for the lives of other people" in their hands, the atomic engineers in the plant must be selected for their "sense of social responsibility" and then they must be ceaselessly observed by the finest psychiatrists. Even so, there emerges the statistical inevitability of a catastrophic—perhaps world-destroying—accident. The only solution, to place the main power plant in orbit, is vigorously fought by the profit-hungry Board of Directors of the Company (who talk just like the management of the Three Mile Island nuclear power plant which came close to a meltdown in 1979). But even they are eventually pressured into accepting a socially responsible role, the breeder reactor is on its way into orbit, and the human race is on its way into space, in ships to be powered by nuclear fuel.

"'—We Also Walk Dogs'" (*Astounding,* July 1941) was later included in the Future History chart, someplace around the year 2000. It is the tale of General Services, Inc., "the handy-man of the last century, gone speedlined and corporate," doing anything its customers ask for, though disdaining "the richly idle" who provide most of the business. Yet even the superefficient operators of General Services, who can arrange to have a lone genius invent an anti-gravity shield on order, become lost in adoring contemplation of the timeless beauty of the Flower of Forgetfulness, a Ming bowl they have lifted from the British Museum.

The climax of the Future History comes in *Methuselah's Children* (*Astounding,* July, August, September 1941), which begins with the disruption of the Covenant society in the year 2125, traces Heinlein's history back through all the other Future History stories to a key event in 1874, and ends with the "beginning of the first mature culture" in the middle of the twenty-second century.

Back in 1874, a rich old man, fearing death, establishes the Howard Foundation, designed to breed a strain of humans with extreme longevity. The result is the Howard Families, who clandestinely build their own culture in the United States during the next two and a half centuries until they number over a hundred thousand individuals, led by 183-year-old Mary Risling (revised to Mary Sperling in the 1958 edition and the sequel, *Time Enough for Love*). The Families have decided to reveal their existence to the larger society, resulting in a frenzy of vicious envy that sweeps aside the Covenant and launches a pogrom aimed at extracting the alleged "secret" of longevity by any means, including the Inquisition of the old religious dictatorship.

Although the individuals in the Families are supposedly of superior intelligence, richly enhanced by extraordinarily long and varied experience, we see most of them incapable of confronting this crisis and acting like "bird-brained dopes" (July, p. 42). So on one hand we witness the citizens of the most humane, rational, libertarian, and scientifically advanced society suddenly metamorphose into a ruthless, snarling horde of beasts, merely because some other people have attained longevity; while on the other hand we see a subsociety, allegedly superior to this superior society (not to mention such inferiors as us), behaving like sheep.

Since, according to Heinlein, the majority of people are incapable of determining their own collective action rationally, there can be only one solution: wise leaders must arise to manipulate the masses for their own good. As the crisis begins to unfold, a new leader of the Families suddenly appears: the most characteristic, enduring, and revealing of all Heinlein's heroes, the daring, individualistic, shrewd, tough, brilliant, resourceful swashbuckler born in 1912 as Woodrow Wilson Smith and now calling himself Lazarus Long.

The wise leader on the other side turns out to be the chief Administrator of the Covenant society, Slayton Ford, a genius at organization (as his last name suggests). Lazarus Long concocts a plan, secretly accepted by Slayton Ford, that decides the fate of the Families. Long's plan is to commandeer an enormous interstellar spaceship and transport every single member of the Families—without their consent—to some planet to be discovered beyond our solar system. Before Ford hears this plan, he himself reluctantly comes to the conclusion that there can be no solution to the problem posed by the existence of the Families, either on Earth or on any planet of our sun:

> The only matter as yet unsettled in his mind was the question of whether simply to sterilize all members of the Howard Families or to kill them outright. Either solution would do, but which was the more humane?
>
> [July, pp. 41-42]

These are not the thoughts, mind you, of some sinister maniac, but the calm reflections of a man who is later to be chosen for his wisdom and political incisiveness as the administrative leader of the Families themselves. Nor are these thoughts being published in an historical vacuum. This passage appeared in July 1941, while similar speculations about a "final solution" to the problem posed by the people of a subculture were being considered by the leaders of Germany, Bulgaria, Rumania, Hungary, and the other fascist powers. Heinlein himself had already explored, in 1940, the helplessness of the Jews in the concentration camps, as well as the genocidal urges of Adolf Hitler and Nazism, in the short story **"Heil!"** (*Futuria Fantasia,* Summer 1940). Zyclon-B, the gas eventually used in the death camps, was already being manufactured by Dow-Badische, the German branch of the Dow Chemical combine.

Ford accepts Long's plan with relief, but a practical question remains: How can all one hundred thousand people of the Families be kept safely in one place until the spaceship is stolen? As the summary in the August 1941 *Astounding* puts it: "But Long points out that the people of Earth will have to be deceived, or they won't release the Families. The Families must be deceived, or they won't have the necessary swift action and unanimity of movement." Long comes up with the brilliant solution: Ford is to carry out a "mass arrest" of all the Families and place them in a "concentration camp"! (August, pp. 64, 68).

The spaceship, duly stolen by Lazarus and most aptly named the *New Frontiers,* is soon off to the stars with all hundred thousand people, powered by a "space drive" single-handedly invented—and built—by Andrew Jackson ("Slipstick") Libby, the calculating genius of **"Misfit."** "The work to be done is too urgent" for elections or other democratic social organization, so "democracy will have to wait on expediency" (August, p. 90). Slayton Ford, with them as a fugitive for his role in the adventure, now becomes their head of internal organization, in charge of a mass "indoctrination campaign" (p. 91), while overall dictatorial authority is invested in the Captain, aptly named Rufus King. Heinlein, with all his love of the first American Revolution, constantly seems drawn back toward the monarchy, at least aboard ship.

Eventually they land on an Earth-like planet inhabited by the Jockaira, a "completely gregarious" race. Everything is fine until they discover that the Jockaira are under the rule of mysterious superhumans they call "the gods," making them domesticated animals in contrast with the wild beings from Earth. The "gods" literally lift the Families from the planet and send them, using inscrutable forces, thirty-two light years away to a park-like Edenic planet with placid seas, low hills, and calm breezes, inhabited by a race of Little People, apparently gentle, loving telepaths.

The Little People, who seem to be "simply Mother Nature's children, living in a Garden of Eden" (September, p. 147), see no need for buildings, machines, agriculture. "Why struggle so for that which the good soil gives freely?" they ask, and point to many trees bearing Earth's foods, indicating "to eat therefrom" (pp. 146-47). But in fact they are another kind of superior being, "masters in the manipulation of life forms" (p. 148). Though individually they resemble "morons," it turns out that "the basic unit of their society was a telepathic rapport group of many parts" and "collectively, each rapport group constituted a genius which threw the best minds the Earthmen had to offer into the shade" (pp. 148, 152). These group minds (derived from Olaf Stapledon's *Last and First Men* and *Star Maker*), able to produce scientific marvels "with a degree of co-operation quite foreign to men," are a challenge to the human essence, as conceived by Heinlein. In searching for an apt comparison, Heinlein again reveals the outlook of his own social class, in his own society, during the late Depression years when the doom of small enterprise and perhaps of the entire system of free-enterprise capitalism was daily becoming more clear. Lazarus thus muses as he confronts the obvious superiority of the Little People:

> Human beings could not hope to compete with that type of organization any more than a back-room shop can compete with a factory assembly line. Yet to surrender to any such group identity, even if they could, would be, he felt sure, to give up whatever it was that made them men.
>
> [p. 152]

The Families reject and abandon this communal Eden created by collective hyper-science; as Oliver Schmidt puts it, "'I want to *work* for my living.'"

A few, however, such as Mary Risling, are seduced into "choosing nirvana—selflessness," marrying into one of the Little People's groups, "drowning" their "personality in the ego of the many." And the Little People, using their psychic control of the material world, genetically "improve" a newborn human baby into "a sort of superman," an hermaphroditic specimen with hoofs, rearranged organs, and many extra fingers, including one ending "in a cluster of pink worms."

The rest of the humans decide to return to Earth, armed with their newly acquired advanced technology; as Lazarus puts it, "'We'll be in shape to demand living room; we'll be strong enough to defend ourselves.'" They fly blind, "with nothing but Slipstick Libby's incomprehensible talent to guide them," and arrive in orbit in the year 2153 prepared to fight for their *Lebensraum* as a superior race. But there they discover that *Everybody is a Member of the Families now,* for it turned out that *biological* heredity had very little to do with longevity, the secret being "*psychological* heredity": "A man could live a long time just by believing that he was bound to live a long time and thinking accordingly—." This is as far as the Future History gets, until we meet Lazarus Long again, at the age of 2360, in *Time Enough for Love,* published thirty-two years later.

An alternative to the flight of the *New Frontiers* is the voyage of its sister ship, launched several years earlier, described in *Universe* (*Astounding,* May 1941). Blindly drifting for centuries in interstellar space after a disastrous mutiny, the Ship has become the Universe of a semifeudal society headed by an autocratic Captain, administered by a class of barely literate priests who call themselves "scientists," and fed by peasants who work the hydroponic farms around the little villages separated by concentric decks, compartments, and miles of maze-like passageways. "Up" is the direction of lesser weight: toward the interior of this enormous, slowly spinning cylinder. On these relatively weightless levels lurk gangs of cannibalistic mutants, one of whom, the brilliant two-headed Joe-Jim, having read the ancient books and discovered the only viewport, has comprehended the incredible truth: the universe does not end at the lowest level of the Ship, and the Ship itself is moving. In "civilized" society down below, such ideas encountered in the ancient scientific books are dismissed as allegorical romances, and anyone propounding such preposterous heresies is fed, along with mutants, into the Convertor. For, after all: "The Ship can't *go* anywhere. It already *is* everywhere."

Universe is a classic presentation of that critical problem, the impenetrable limits environment places around consciousness, a theme crucial not only for Heinlein and for such science-fiction masterpieces as E. A. Abbott's *Flatland,* Twain's *A Connecticut Yankee in King Arthur's Court* and "The Great Dark," Jorge Luis Borges's "The Library of Babel," and Christopher Priest's *The Inverted World,* but for all modern industrial society as technological and social revolutions constantly change the human environ-

ment. In the epistemological laboratory presented by *Universe,* neither the traditional beliefs of the present rulers nor the hard-headed pragmatism of a dissident rationalist bloc who accept only immediate facts can comprehend the stupendous truth of the real universe that lies outside. They are even less capable of breaking out of the prison of the Ship.

The sequel, *Common Sense* (*Astounding,* October 1941), is more a minor tale of adventure which concludes with the highly improbable escape of three men, who, along with their chattel wives, manage to land a Ship's "boat" on an Earth-like planetary moon. The story is notable mainly for its political intrigue, the appearance, rare in any Heinlein story, of a Captain who abuses his authority, and the flagrantly derogatory treatment of women, best summed up by the principal hero's injunction, "'Keep those damned women out of the way.'"

The delusory world of the Ship in *Universe* is presented as a convincing possibility in a rigorously controlled science fiction in which true science offers the only way out. During this same period, Heinlein was also publishing fantasies of psychological entrapment, paranoia, and solipsism with an emphatic denunciation of science and scientific reasoning. This is not to suggest that he dramatizes one kind of world view in his science fiction, and a contrary one in his fantasy, for, as we shall see, some of his science fiction is just as passionately anti-science. And some of the minor stories of this period show a full range of attitudes toward technology, science, and fantastic imaginings beyond science: "**—And He Built a Crooked House—**" (*Astounding,* February 1941), about a four-dimensional house created by an architect and an earthquake; "**My Object All Sublime**" (*Future,* February 1942) in which an inventor develops an invisibility device (similar to one in Jack London's "The Shadow and the Flash") so that he can squirt synthetic skunk juice on offending motorists, which gets him jailed "for everything from malicious mischief to criminal syndicalism"; "**Pied Piper**" (*Astonishing Stories,* March 1942) in which a scientific genius stops a war by kidnapping a few hundred thousand children from the enemy nation; "**Goldfish Bowl**" (*Astounding,* March 1942), a speculation that there are stratospheric beings to whom we are as goldfish are to us.

The most unrelenting of Heinlein's paranoid fantasies is "**They**" (*Unknown,* April 1941), which starkly enacts the dark side of the cult of the lone genius. Most of this story, one crucial to comprehending the meaning and significance of Heinlein's achievement, consists of the anguished musings of a man confined in what seems an insane asylum. He is convinced that the entire material world and all the people in it exist for one purpose only: to deceive him, to keep him from distinguishing their "lies" from the "truth," which comes to him in dreams. "They," "the puppet masters," are merely "swarms of actors"; "they looked like me, but they were not like me."

Starkly displayed here is the myth of the free individual, so central to Heinlein's fiction and so representative of Western thought since the dawn of the capitalist epoch.

The narrator's epistemological predicament, in fact, derives directly from the birth of Cartesian consciousness. He actually reformulates the classical *Cogito, ergo sum*: "First fact, himself. He knew himself directly. He existed." Then the evidence of his senses: "Without them he was entirely solitary, shut up in a locker of bone, blind, deaf, cutoff, the only being in the world." He desperately speculates that the other beings around him might also experience the isolation of the imprisoned ego: "Could it be that each unit in this yeastly swarm around him was the prison of another lonely ego—helpless, blind, and speechless, condemned to an eternity of miserable loneliness?" In Heinlein's later fiction we will see "the agony of his loneliness" re-enacted in many forms.

The other side of this terrifying imprisonment is the narrator's belief in his own transcendent importance: ". . . I was the center of the arrangements. . . . I am unique." He even deduces his own unique god-like immortality: "I am immortal. I transcend this little time axis." This desire to live beyond and outside one's time will become almost an obsession in the later fiction.

The narrator does vacillate about one person, his wife, who certainly seems to be another human being, one who loves him. But in the end we discover that all his apparently paranoid visions are not delusions at all: New York City and Harvard University are being dismantled as useless props, and "the creature" who pretended to be his human wife requests that the Taj Mahal sequence be arranged as his next deception.

In **"The Unpleasant Profession of Jonathan Hoag"** (*Unknown Worlds*, October 1942), another paranoid fantasy, our world is merely an immature creation of some aspiring Artist, who has made the mistake of painting us and our environment over an earlier work, "The Sons of the Bird," evil creatures who now lurk in the world behind mirrors, ready to burst forth into our reality and take possession. Jonathan Hoag is a Critic who has been sent to judge our world to see if it has any aesthetic saving grace or whether it should be obliterated.

Hoag is now in Chicago, which he finds squalid, dismal, and repulsive. Especially distasteful to him are its "coarse and brutal" working-class people. Falling partly under the wicked powers of the Sons of the Bird, Hoag seeks assistance from a married man and woman with their own small business, a detective agency. The husband and wife now find themselves at the center of the evil plot. She is afraid that if they stay on this case they "will find out what it is grown-ups know" and become as unhappy as everybody else. The Sons of the Bird lure the husband into "a small room, every side of which was a mirror—four walls, floor, and ceiling. Endlessly he was repeated in every direction and every image was himself—selves that hated him but from which there was no escape." This prison of morbid egoism suggests that "the whole world might be just a fraud and an illusion."

Because of the mutual loyalty of these two devoted small-business people, embodying "the tragedy of human love,"

Hoag eventually decides not to destroy our world, merely to correct it by wiping out the Sons of the Bird. He warns the husband and wife to drive away and under no circumstances to open the window of their car. When they momentarily disobey while driving along a crowded Chicago street, they discover that the world they have been perceiving is indeed merely an illusion:

> Outside the open window was no sunlight, no cops, no kids—nothing. Nothing but a gray and formless mist, pulsing slowly as if with inchoate life. They could see nothing of the city through it, not because it was too dense but because it was—empty.

They flee to a remote farm, where they live in a house without mirrors, handcuffing themselves together through the night. Their flight from the overwhelming, threatening, supposedly delusory reality of modern working-class urban America to some simple, primitive, rural world from the mythic past is another archetype reappearing many times in Heinlein's fiction.

"Lost Legion," published in *Super Science Stories* in November 1941, the month before the United States formally entered World War II, is set in the contemporary world, when the forces of "pure evil" are poised for a decisive assault: "They've won in Europe; they are in the ascendancy in Asia; they may win here in America . . ." (Chapter 11. In **"Lost Legacy,"** the 1953 version of the story, Heinlein switches the words "Europe" and "Asia," thus switching his identification of "pure evil" from fascism to communism). In the United States these evil forces are embodied in "the antagonists of human liberty—the racketeers, the crooked political figures, the shysters, the dealers in phony religions, the sweat shoppers, the petty authoritarians, all of the key figures among the traffickers in human misery and human oppression" (Ch. 12), who include some members of Congress, judges, governors, university presidents, heads of unions, directors of nineteen major corporations, and local authorities. They are all under the command of an inscrutable "evil thing," a no-eyed, legless monster in control of almost limitless psychic forces. The situation, in short, resembles that in **"The Devil Makes the Law."**

Opposed to these forces are a professor of psychology, his prize female student, and his surgeon friend, who together discover that *everybody* has almost limitless psychic forces, including telepathy, telekinesis, teleportation, etc. Our trio of good guys become "supermen" and then link up with a community of even greater psychic supermen hidden inside Mount Shasta and led by a new avatar of Ambrose Bierce, who seems to be a reincarnation of Mark Twain.

Through their new friends, our heroes take a telepathic voyage to the prehistoric past where they learn the true history of the human race. It seems we were all gods until Loki, speaking for an elitist band of Young Men, argued that "the ancient knowledge should henceforth be the reward of ability rather than common birthright, and second, that the greater should rule the lesser" (Ch. 6). Thus comes

"The Twilight of the Gods," and the emergence of war and empire, specifically "Mu, mightiest of empires and mother of empires." (Heinlein had co-authored a perfectly silly shaggy-dog parapsychological fantasy set in Mu, entitled **"Beyond Doubt,"** in *Astonishing Stories,* April 1941.) The rest of history has been an ever-recurring struggle between the good psychic adepts and the evil forces, who believe in "authoritarianism, nonsense like the leader principle, totalitarianism, all the bonds placed on liberty which treat men as so many economic and political units with no importance as individuals" (Ch. 7).

The good side now is striving to let all the people know that they are capable of these superhuman powers, virtually total direct control of matter by mind. Since the forces of evil already control so many adult American institutions, it is necessary to get several thousand specially picked Boy Scouts to assemble at "Camp Mark Twain" on Mount Shasta, instruct them in parapsychology, and let them loose as teachers for the common people, while our trio and the other good-mind adepts annihilate the evil-mind adepts, literally liquidating the evil leader, leaving him "a gory mess on the rug." Thus in **"Lost Legion"** the evil forces trying to take over the world are defeated by the unaided mind.

The belief that mind can *at will* do almost anything to matter represents the absurdity at the extreme end of the bourgeois definition of freedom and free will. If the will is free to do anything it wishes, the will is free from the apparent laws of the physical universe and also free from the apparent laws of human social development—a thoroughly non-dialectical definition of freedom. Instead of human consciousness being collectively and progressively freed by the advances of science, technology, and social organization, all produced by developing human consciousness, human history is seen as a sinister, imprisoning force that overwhelmed the supposed freedom of nineteenth-century individual enterprise or even, as in this story, some prehistoric, mythic freedom of beings like gods. In the face of the historic forces threatening the destruction of his social class, Heinlein's impulses are characteristically reactionary, that is, longing to reverse the processes of history, and often even thoroughly anti-historic, that is, yearning to see history shattered and swept away.

The paranoid vision clearly relates to these anti-scientific and anti-historic impulses. In early stories such as **"Life-Line"** and **"'Let There Be Light,'"** the sinister powers are often the forces that were then indeed overwhelming free-enterprise capitalism—the forces of monopoly, which actually appear as diabolic in **"The Devil Makes the Law."** But the vision of evil forces subverting, controlling, or annihilating our society takes many forms in Heinlein's imagination. They may be power-mad priests (**"If This Goes On—"**) or satanic elitists (**"Lost Legion"**) or the Sons of the Bird or simply **"They"**; in postwar works, *they* become "the Communists," either explicitly (**"Gulf,"** *Farnham's Freehold,* as well as other fiction and non-fiction) or somewhat refracted into giant communistic slugs (*The Puppet Masters*) or bugs (*Starship Troopers*).

In the novel *Sixth Column* (*Astounding,* January, February, March 1941), *they* are the Pan-Asian hordes, who have perfidiously attacked and invaded the United States. Opposed to them is "the most magnificent aggregation of research brains" ever assembled, hidden away in an unmarked spot in the Rocky Mountains, searching for a superweapon to repel these four hundred million cruel Asians, who of course care nothing for individual human life and who are routinely called "monkeys" by all the good staunch American patriots, referred to consistently as "the whites" and "white men." Finally, when there are only six men left in the secret laboratory, now headed by the aptly named Whitey Ardmore, they figure out "what makes matter tick," and they launch their counterattack under cover of a phony messianic religion, armed with an assortment of superweapons which kill only those with "Mongolian blood":

> The "basic weapon" was the simplest Ledbetter projector that had been designed. It looked very much like a pistol and was intended to be used in similar fashion. It projected a directional beam of the primary Ledbetter effect in the frequency band fatal to those of Mongolian blood and none other. It could be used by a layman after three minutes' instruction, since all that was required was to point it and press a trigger, but it was practically foolproof—the user literally could not harm a fly with it, much less a white man. But it was sudden death to Asiatics.

[March, p. 133]

The vision of Asians expressed throughout *Sixth Column* is best summed up in the attitude of Jefferson Thomas, one of the heroic freedom fighters: "'A good Pan-Asian was a dead Pan-Asian . . .'" (January, p. 26). This undisguised racism is hardly unique to Robert Heinlein; here, as usual, he is being a fairly representative American. The intense dread of "the Yellow Peril," those cruel Asians bent on overrunning America, emerged at the very moment that Americans began their campaign of conquest and exploitation of Asia and Asians (just as the dread of the "Indian savages" began with the genocidal conquest of the natives of this continent by the European invaders). Heinlein's fantasy of race war is mild compared with that envisioned by Jack London in his 1910 story "The Unparalleled Invasion," where the white nations, fearful of being overrun by the Asian hordes, unite to attack China with germ warfare delivered by airplanes, succeed in utterly exterminating the Chinese people, and thus establish a joyous epoch of "splendid mechanical, intellectual, and art output." By 1924 the Congress of the United States had prohibited all further immigration from Japan and outlawed the naturalization of all those who had already immigrated. Heinlein was far less racist than his government, for he calls his one Asian-American character, Frank Roosevelt Matsui, "as American as Will Rogers" (January, p. 27) and shows him loyally and heroically sacrificing his own life. Ironically, in March 1942, a year after the publication of *Sixth Column,* the American President for whom Frank Roosevelt Matsui was named was to issue his infamous Executive Order 9066, which had all 117,000 Japanese-Americans rounded up and placed in concentration camps, while their land and other property was seized. And although it may seem highly improbable that American scientists could devise a superweapon that would kill only Asians, in less than four years they certainly did invent a superweapon that *did* kill only Asians.

Throughout this first period, Heinlein seems torn between two quite contradictory conceptions of the relations between mind and matter. On one side he has faith in science and technology—the rational, systematic, developing accumulation of human knowledge which permits a progressive enlargement of human consciousness, of control over the material environment, of potential freedom. On the other side, he rejects science and embraces wishful thinking, the direct, unfettered, immediate control of matter by mind.

Waldo (*Astounding,* August 1942) embodies this conflict in a single story. In this future scene, Heisenberg's Uncertainty Principle has been done away with and physics has become "an exact science," the "religion" of men like Dr. Rambeau, head of research for the gigantic power monopoly, North American Power-Air. But this "faith" is being undermined by the mysterious failure of the Company's power receptors.

The Company is forced to seek help from Waldo F. Jones, a marvelous caricature of the lone genius. Waldo orbits above Earth literally in his own small sphere; ostensibly treasuring his "freedom" from the "smooth apes" of Earth below, he calls his solitary home "Freehold." Waldo, a flabby weakling reduced to almost total physical impotence by the muscular disease *myasthenia gravis,* has employed his inventive genius to contrive the servomechanisms known in the story, and subsequently in the actual world, as "waldoes."

Waldo's view of the world in one direction confronts that of Dr. Rambeau:

> To Rambeau the universe was an inexorably ordered cosmos, ruled by unvarying law. To Waldo the universe was the enemy, which he strove to force to submit to his will.

Yet Waldo and Dr. Rambeau both share a very mechanical materialism. True knowledge is vested in Gramps Schneider, an old "witch doctor" who initiates Waldo into the mysteries of the "Other World," an old term for the realm of magic, which Heinlein had set forth in **"The Devil Makes the Law"** (reprinted as *Magic, Inc.* in *Waldo and Magic, Inc.,* the 1950 volume that places these two tales into a unified world view). The old seer presents Waldo with an unmitigated split between mind and matter:

> "The Other World," he said presently, "is the world you do not see. It is here and it is there and it is everywhere. But it is especially *here.*" He touched his forehead. "The mind sits in it and sends its messages through it to the body."

Gramps uses his occult power to fix one of the power receptors, and Dr. Rambeau becomes a convert from science to magic, deliriously proclaiming: "'Nothing is certain. Nothing, *nothing,* NOTHING is certain!'" "'Chaos is King, and Magic is loose in the world!'"

Waldo learns to repair the broken power receptors by merely willing them to work, and he constructs an improved receptor that draws its power directly from the Other World. So now, as in **"'Let There Be Light,'"** there is "free and unlimited power," but Waldo is able to trick the Company into paying him royally even though he blandly tells the Chairman of the Board, "'you will not be in the business of selling power much longer.'"

Now Waldo attempts to build a scientific explanation of the Other World, for it is "contrary to the whole materialistic philosophy in which he had grown up" to believe "that thought and thought alone should be able to influence physical phenomena." But he finds himself plunged into pure Berkeleian idealism, wondering if "the order we thought we detected" is "a mere phantasm of the imagination," "Orderly Cosmos, created out of Chaos—by Mind!" He begins to believe that "the world varied according to the way one looked at it," that the physical universe would operate by magical principles for a culture that believed in magic, by scientific laws for a culture that believed in science. This notion, that a society's culture determines the physical universe it inhabits, is precisely the opposite of the view, stated earlier in the story, and certainly truer to human history, that it is the physical universe, including the current level of technology, that determines the character of a society's culture:

> It may plausibly be urged that the shape of a culture— its *mores,* evaluations, family organization, eating habits, living patterns, pedagogical methods, institutions, forms of government, and so forth—arise [sic] from the economic necessities of its technology.

Heinlein seems unable to choose between a mechanical materialism, together with an inflexible determinism, on one hand, and unmitigated idealism, together with a capricious voluntarism, on the other. Any dialectical interplay between mind and matter, between what is determined and what can be freely changed, lies outside the rigid bipolar framework for the philosophical speculation in **Waldo.**

In Waldo himself, however, we do see such a dialectic. Gramps Schneider had told him that he could reach into the Other World to cure his pathological muscular weakness:

> Gramps Schneider had told him he need not be weak!
>
> That he could be strong—
>
> Strong!
>
> STRONG!

Waldo has something in common with many of the readers of *Astounding,* as we find out if we turn to the last page of this August 1942 issue:

Let me make *YOU* a SUPERMAN!

When you stand before your mirror, stripped to the skin, what do you see? A body you can be really proud of? A build that others admire or talk about? OR—are you fat and flabby? . . .

If you're honest enough with yourself to admit that physically you're only *half* a man *now*—then I want to prove I can make you a SUPERMAN in double-quick time! . . .

. . . I'll show you exactly how to get a handsome, husky pair of shoulders—a deep, he-man chest—arms & leg muscles hard as rocks yet limber as a whip . . . every inch of you all man, *he*-man, SUPERMAN.

Charles Atlas's "Dynamic Tension" method of body-building here advertised is almost precisely what Waldo employs. He does not overcome his weakness by the instantaneous and magical wishful thinking he used to fix the power receptors, but by a determination of will that forces him to condition the muscles of his body systematically and rigorously. Gradually building up his muscles, he becomes even stronger than the average man, and leaves his lonely exile in "Freehold" to rejoin the human race, becoming an acrobatic dancer, admired by all for his strength and agility. The lone genius, it turns out, really just wished "to be *liked,* to be *wanted.*"

Heinlein's first published attempt at a time-travel story, **"Elsewhere"** (*Astounding,* September 1941), projects a bizarre maze of alternative time tracks which individuals may choose at will. Here the desire to be free *from* the present, to be released by wishing for an escape, is explicit: the central character, a professor of speculative metaphysics, escapes from imprisonment by wishing himself into a future that combines idealized features of both ancient Rome and an advanced space age. The professor explains to his four choice students that "'the mind creates its own world,'" that "'Berkeleian idealism'" creates just as "real" a world as "materialism." (In the revised version, published in 1953 in *Assignment in Eternity,* Heinlein goes so far as to add a fifth student, a religious fundamentalist, who manages to transform herself directly into an angel!) There is scorn for "'you engineers,'" who all "'believe in a mechanistic, deterministic universe.'" Yet a young engineering student saves a whole planet from an invasion of alien forces by flitting from one time track to another so that the good guys can build a blaster gun, a "little gadget" that "'unquestionably will win the war for us.'" The whimsical jumble of fantastic time tracks contrasts sharply with the novel from which this story derives, Jack London's *The Star Rover* (1915), in which a political prisoner in San Quentin escapes from incessant torture by achieving different identities in the class struggle that has constituted actual human history.

"Elsewhere" also contrasts sharply with **"By His Bootstraps"** (*Astounding,* October 1941), Heinlein's second time-travel story, and one of his masterpieces. Rigorous in its logic, this tale penetrates deeply into the implications of the myth of the free individual.

Bob Wilson, the protagonist, moves from being an ordinary doctoral student (working on a thesis disproving time travel) to becoming the lone active will and consciousness thirty thousand years in the future, ruling alone as lord and master over an Earth filled with his slaves. We see the events from the different points of view of Wilson as he becomes different selves by moving back and forth through time.

When we first meet Wilson, he is being accosted by two mysterious strangers who pop out of a "Time Gate" into his apartment. Later we perceive the same scene from the point of view of each of these men, who turn out to be later selves of Bob Wilson, sent from the future back into the present. The first Wilson goes through the Time Gate and meets the mysterious all-powerful Diktor, who sends him back into his own time, from which still another Wilson eventually emerges into that remote future ten years before the encounter between Diktor and Wilson. In all these adventures, Wilson can never recognize any of his future selves. He does not even realize that he himself has become Diktor until the moment of the first encounter between this future self and the first Wilson from the past. On one level, the story is an ingenious exploration of the problems of identity in time, and the associated questions of the relations between determinism and free will. Diktor has created himself out of Bob Wilson, but without conscious choice until after it has already happened.

"By His Bootstraps" is also a dramatic display of the trapped ego, creating a world out of images of itself. It is thus the first fully developed manifestation of the solipsism which will become one of Heinlein's main themes. This solipsism is the ultimate expression of the bourgeois myth of the free individual, who supposedly is able to lift himself from rags to riches by his own bootstraps. As Diktor puts it to the Bob Wilson who emerges into this future of dictatorial power and abject slavery, "'One twentieth-century go-getter can accomplish just about anything he wants to accomplish around here—.'"

Diktor is a grandiose enlargement of Robinson Crusoe, with the entire planet his island. In fact, the first man Wilson meets in the future throws himself on his knees and arises as "his Man Friday." All the people of this world, who have been enslaved by some mysterious "High Ones" for 20,000 years, are now "docile friendly children," "slaves by nature." What they lack is "the competitive spirit," "the will-to-power": "Wilson had a monopoly on that."

But this "monopoly" is also a state of supreme loneliness, as well as boredom. Diktor wistfully compares these people, mere extensions of his own will, with "the brawling, vulgar, lusty, dynamic swarms who had once called themselves the People of the United States," the very society he had earlier rejected and abandoned as "a crummy world full of crummy people." His choice—if that is what he ever had—lies between the life of normal futility he left and the one of sublime futility he has acquired. The choice is embodied in his sexual alternatives: in the future are myriads of beautiful mindless slave women literally kneeling to his will; in his old life there is the "shrewish," conniving Genevieve, whose approaching footsteps on his stairs had been the deciding factor in driving him out of his humdrum world into the Time Gate. Wilson's sexuality in both worlds is barren. He can only reproduce himself, as he, a self-created being, suggests in his final words, promising himself, his only kind of son, a great future: "'There is a great future in store for you and me, my boy—a great future!'"

On still another level, **"By His Bootstraps"** displays this world-embracing egoism as the center of political imperialism. When Diktor asks the first Bob Wilson to return briefly to his own time, his purpose is to acquire some tools to be used in colonizing this undeveloped land:

> "I want you to return to the twentieth century and obtain certain things for us, things that can't be obtained on this side but which will be very useful to us in, ah, developing—yes, that is the word—developing this country."

The prime thing he needs is certain books: Machiavelli's *The Prince, Behind the Ballots* by political machine boss James Farley, *How To Make Friends and Influence People* by Dale Carnegie, and Adolf Hitler's *Mein Kampf.*

The utopian novel *Beyond This Horizon* (*Astounding,* April, May 1942) is Heinlein's only attempt in this early fiction to describe what he conceives to be a good society. Here he tries to combine a high level of social organization and cooperation with the maximum possible individual freedom. Though this society somewhat resembles the one implied in *Coventry,* it is no gentle, peaceful land where any damage to another person means "readjustment" or exile. It is a society made up of people "descended from 'wolves,' not 'sheep'" (April, p. 21), one in which all self-respecting men and even some women are expert gunfighters ready to cut each other down at the drop of an insult. The main product of human history through "the Continuous War of 1910-1970" and beyond can be summed up in one italicized sentence: *"The fighters survived"* (April, p. 21). Now, several centuries of systematic genetic engineering have created a race of human beings superior in health, longevity, physique, and intelligence.

The underlying assumption of *Beyond This Horizon,* as Philip E. Smith II has put it in his superb essay on Heinlein's social Darwinism, is that "biology explains behavior" and "biology also explains politics," with an "underlying fantasy-wish . . . derived from a social Darwinistic interpretation of evolution."[5] We witness this dynamic utopian society passing through a series of crises to advance to what Heinlein often projects as the next stage of human evolution, the development of telepathic powers.

The economic structure itself, supposedly a perfected, fully rational capitalism that has evolved from the "pseudo-capitalism" of previous centuries, is seen as relatively unimportant, so long as there is a rational system of finance. Here everybody gets "dividends," the social distribution of surplus capital, through centralized accounting. To the question ". . . wouldn't it be simpler to set up a collective system and be done with it?" comes this response:

> "Finance structure is a general theory and applies equally to any type of state. A complete socialism would have as much need for structural appropriateness in its cost accounting as would a free entrepreneur. The degree of public ownership as compared with the degree of free enterprise is a cultural matter. For example, food is, of course, free, but—."
>
> [April, p. 11]

Technology also has relatively little to do with the greatness of this society, except insofar as it allows the necessary improvements in genetic engineering. We are assured that the goal of their eugenics is to improve the gene pool of the whole race, not to develop a separate line of supermen.

The hero of *Beyond This Horizon* is Hamilton Felix, the fastest gun in town, packing an antique Colt .45. A "star line" genetic type, Hamilton is supposed to contribute his superior genes to the race by breeding with his pre-selected genetic counterpart, Phyllis, a beautiful gunslinger. But he is weighed down by ennui and frustration, because he lacks some of the qualifications of the leading geniuses, the philosophers in charge of centralized planning: "'When it was finally pounded into my head that I couldn't take first prize, I wasn't interested in second prize'" (April, p. 24).

However, Hamilton discovers and helps defeat a conspiracy of "the Survivors Club," an elitist cabal planning to seize power, set up "the New Order," and redirect genetic engineering to create classes of superbrainy leaders and superbrawny workers. In heroically combating these protofascists and amorously dallying with Phyllis, Hamilton begins to reawaken his interest in life and the possibility of procreation.

Yet he still fails to see any purpose in human existence. His own profession symbolizes his dilemma: he invents sophisticated games and superpinball machines for amusement centers. An extraordinary revelation comes to him as his consciousness swims out from a dose of gas he gets in a shootout:

> No fun in the game if you knew the outcome. He had designed a game like that once, and called it "Futility"—no matter how you played, you had to win. . . . It was always a little hard to remember which position himself had played, forgetting that he had played all of the parts. Well, that was the game; it was the only game in town, and there was nothing else to do. Could he help it if the game was crooked? Even if he had made it up and played all the parts.
>
> [May, p. 66]

Hamilton here is perilously close to Diktor, the sole player in the rigged time-travel game of **"By His Bootstraps."**

But Hamilton makes a deal with the geniuses who administer this society. He will agree to reproduce if they will commit massive funds to investigate the meaning of life, including research into the question of an afterlife. They accede, Phyllis assumes her proper role of wife and mother, and their star line children soon exhibit telepathy and living proof of reincarnation.

As the May 1942 synopsis explained, *Beyond This Horizon* "is, itself, almost a synopsis." There are subplots that go nowhere (including a delightful sequence about a Babbitt-like ex-football player and fraternity man, rabid anti-Communist, boosterish Republican businessman who turns up from 1926 and soon dispels some romantic notions that have developed about the twentieth century), pages of scientific and pseudo-scientific theory, and more philosophizing and action than the narrative can comfortably handle. This myriad of fragments kaleidoscopically displays the contradictory components of Heinlein's late Depression outlook, a world view that will later determine his responses to the earth-shaking events of the period from the end of World War II to the early 1970s.

I have saved for the final story to be explored in this [essay] the only one that directly confronts the actual international situation emerging in these early years of World War II, **"Solution Unsatisfactory"** (*Astounding,* May 1941). This story, like most of the fiction we have looked at so far, should not be read as merely *pre*war. As Heinlein puts it in **"Solution Unsatisfactory"**: "We were not at war, legally, yet we had been in the war up to our necks with our weight on the side of democracy since 1940."

In December 1938 Otto Hahn in Berlin had discovered the splitting of the uranium atom under a bombardment of neutrons. Earlier that year, Hahn's Jewish wife, the great physicist Lise Meitner, had fled Germany to avoid the pogroms; in early 1939, Dr. Meitner and her nephew Otto Frisch formulated an explanation of Hahn's process, which they named nuclear fission. Heinlein begins his tale with the ominous implications of these critical modern events. He loosely fictionalizes Lise Meitner as Estelle Karst, a Jewish assistant of Dr. Hahn, who comes to the United States and discovers, as a by-product of her medical research, the ultimate and irresistible weapon, radioactive dust.

The story is told by "an ordinary sort of man" who suddenly finds himself thrust into the center of history. The main character and hero is "liberal" but "tough-minded" Clyde C. Manning, congressman, colonel in the United States Army, and apparently the only possible savior of the world.

America now has the weapon which amounts to "a loaded gun held at the head of every man, woman, and child on the globe!" The narrator expresses some misgivings about America having this power:

> I had the usual American subconscious conviction that our country would never use power in sheer aggres-

sion. Later, I thought about the Mexican War and the Spanish-American War and some of the things we did in Central America, and I was not so sure—

Nevertheless, for Heinlein there can be only one conclusion, inescapable and inevitable:

> The United States was having power thrust on it, willy-nilly. We had to accept it and enforce a world-wide peace, ruthlessly and drastically, or it would be seized by some other nation.

So first America intervenes in the war. But before actually using the atomic weapon, "we were morally obligated" to give every possible warning, first to the German government, then to the people of Berlin, the targeted city. This passage rings with shocking irony in the echo of the American sneak attacks on Hiroshima and Nagasaki.

Next comes the worldwide "*Pax Americana.*" The United States demands that every nation in the world immediately disarm, a threat Heinlein quaintly expresses in frontier lingo: "'Throw down your guns, boys; we've got the drop on you!'" This choice is forced on us by such "facts" as these:

> Four hundred million Chinese with no more concept of voting and citizen responsibility than a flea. Three hundred million Hindus who aren't much better indoctrinated. God knows how many in the Eurasian Union who believe in God knows what. The entire continent of Africa only semicivilized. Eighty million Japanese who really believe that they are Heaven-ordained to rule.

So the *Pax Americana* inescapably must be "a military dictatorship imposed by force on the whole world."

Sure enough, there is another nation so uncivilized, unreasonable, and dastardly as to dispute the American global hegemony, the "Eurasian Union," now under the control of the "Fifth Internationalists," who have paralleled our atomic research. In 1945, unlike the actual history of that year, the sneak atomic attack is delivered not by the United States but upon it. We retaliate by wiping out Vladivostok, Irkutsk, and Moscow, and sending an invasion force, "the American Pacification Expedition." The United States now has the job of "policing the world."

The President of the United States at this time is a good man, so he and Colonel Manning wish to prevent the atomic weapon being used "to turn the globe into an empire, our empire" for "imperialism degrades both oppressor and oppressed." They decide that the power "must not be used to protect American investments abroad, to coerce trade agreements, for any purpose but the simple abolition of mass killing." In characteristic American and Heinlein style, "Manning and the President played by ear," establishing treaties "to commit future governments of the United States to an irrevocable benevolent policy."

Colonel Manning then becomes Commissioner of World Safety, which forms the international Peace Patrol, whose pilots, armed with the atomic weapon, are never to be assigned to their own country. The Peace Patrol is welded together by "esprit de corps," and the main check on their new recruits is "the President's feeling for character."

Then the good President is killed in a plane crash, and the presidency is assumed by the isolationist Vice President, allied with a senator who had tried to use the Peace Patrol to recover expropriated holdings in South America and Rhodesia. They attempt to arrest Manning, but the pilots of the Peace Patrol intervene, arrest the bad President, and make Manning "the undisputed military dictator of the world."

Nobody, not even Manning, likes this solution. But, though unsatisfactory, it apparently seemed the best to Robert A. Heinlein in 1941.

Notes

Unless otherwise noted, all references are to the original publication, as identified in the text. Page references will not be given for short stories. For longer works published in serial form, page references will be given parenthetically and will include month and page number; where it will be more convenient for the readers, and where no ambiguity will be thus created, references will be made by chapter number.

1. As pointed out by Sam Moskowitz in *Seekers of Tomorrow* (Cleveland: World Publishing, 1966), p. 194.

2. Actually the reference as pointed out by J. R. Christopher in "Methuselah, Out of Heinlein by Shaw," *Shaw Review,* 16 (1973), pp. 79-88, is to Shaw's *The Apple Cart.* This article documents quite an extensive influence by Shaw on Heinlein. And Samuel R. Delany has argued that "the didactic methods of Robert Heinlein owe a great deal to Shaw's comedies of ideas, far more than to Wells and Verne" (in "Critical Methods: Speculative Fiction," *Many Futures, Many Worlds,* ed. Thomas Clareson (Kent, Ohio: Kent State University Press, 1977), p. 281).

3. "If This Goes On—," *Revolt in 2100* (New York: New American Library, 1955, 1959), pp. 118-19. This is the text of the 1953 Shasta Publishers' edition.

4. *Ibid.,* p. 119.

5. Philip E. Smith II, "The Evolution of Politics and the Politics of Evolution in Heinlein's Fiction," in *Robert A. Heinlein,* eds. Joseph D. Olander and Martin Harry Greenberg (New York: Taplinger, 1978), p. 141.

Gary K. Wolfe (essay date 1983)

SOURCE: Wolfe, Gary K. "Autoplastic and Alloplastic Adaptations in Science Fiction: 'Waldo' and 'Desertion'." In *Coordinates: Placing Science Fiction and Fantasy,* ed-ited by George E. Slusser, Eric S. Rabkin, and Robert Scholes, pp. 65-79. Carbondale: Southern Illinois University Press, 1983.

[*In the following essay, Wolfe contrasts the different approaches of Heinlein's* Waldo *and Clifford D. Simak's "Desertion" to the problem of integration between body and environment.*]

At a recent gathering of science fiction fans—a "con," to use the jargon of the fans themselves—an acquaintance and I were watching the bizarrely dressed crowd milling about in the lobby of the hotel when he turned to me and asked, "Have you noticed how many *grossly overweight* people there are here?" In fact, there were a surprising number of rather large people present, but there were also quite a few fans who seemed to represent the more traditional stereotype of the science fiction fan as undernourished adolescent. There was even a sizable number of people of normal, undistinguished girth. But the person who called this to my attention assured me that a rather atypical distribution of body types was quite common at conventions of this sort, and that he had noted it often. Perhaps he was more acutely aware of bodily structures than I, for, himself a science fiction fan since childhood, he had recently published his second book on body building and weight control.

Later, in talking with others more generally familiar with the world of fandom than I, I found that many people had made observations similar to these. A few even offered theories about how science fiction conventions offered a safe arena for social intercourse among people who felt inept or awkward on the outside. Such a theory reminds one of the cliché that "science fiction is a crutch for people who can't handle reality" and of the retaliatory T-shirt slogan that was making the rounds of these conventions a couple of years ago: "Reality is a crutch for people who can't handle science fiction." Both suggest in different ways the often tribal nature of interactions among fans, but it was not solely this hard-core group of fans I was concerned with. I looked at a number of interviews, memoirs, and autobiographies of science fiction writers—including Isaac Asimov's remarkably detailed *In Memory Yet Green*—and found frequent confirmation of what had now become a growing suspicion: not that science fiction was necessarily fattening (or emaciating, for that matter), but that it seemed to address the needs of adolescents and even adults who, at some key stage in their lives, felt themselves to be unattractive or ill at ease in their own bodies. I am not suggesting that such an attitude is in any sense a prerequisite to the enjoyment of science fiction, or that it is even characteristic of a majority of readers, but I will attempt to demonstrate that in a genre which spent many of its formative years catering to a largely adolescent audience and responding to the needs and desires of that audience, this attitude has been reflected in the literature.

This pattern has been noted before. Joanna Russ, in a 1970 essay titled "The Image of Women in Science Fiction," declared that science fiction readers "are overwhelmingly likely to be nervous, shy, pleasant boys, sensitive, intelligent, and very awkward with people. They also talk too much." But while science fiction did for a long time garner a predominantly male audience, such a feeling of social awkwardness was not confined to boys. An attractive woman science fiction reader in her late thirties reports that, as a teenager, she often felt ungainly, unattractive, and ostracized from the social life of her school—partly because of her appearance, but partly also because of her superior intelligence, which seemed to be regarded as inappropriate in a girl. She took solace in stories of mutants, particularly Henry Kuttner's "Baldy" stories (collected as *Mutant,* 1953), and in stories of bodily transformation, such as Clifford D. Simak's "Desertion" (collected in *City,* 1952). The mutant stories conveyed to her the promise of a world in which mind or intelligence could act directly on the environment through telepathy or telekinesis, without the mediation of socializing agencies such as schools and families. Furthermore, the mutants themselves, the holders of these secret powers, were often physically unattractive outcasts (hence their nickname "Baldies" in the Kuttner stories). The tales of bodily transformation were another matter, and perhaps reflect a deeper fantasy. These tales, which might include James Blish's "pantropy" series (collected in *The Seedling Stars,* 1957) as well as the Simak title, concerned the fantasy of achieving a near-perfect match between a body and an alien environment, made possible by a liberation from earthly form altogether.

The point of all this is not just that science fiction is a genre principally concerned with mind-body dualism—though it does often address that issue—but that one of the uses of science fiction is to provide its readers with alternate models for relating to one's environment, and for gaining rewards from that environment. Generally, these models are of two kinds, and in describing them we might borrow an opposition originally suggested by Géza Róheim in discussing the differences between primitive and technological societies. One such difference, Róheim suggested, is that the former tend to be autoplastic while the latter are alloplastic; that is, the primitive seeks a more hospitable relationship with the environment through manipulation of his or her own body (as in surgical rites of passage), while a technological society such as ours manipulates the environment itself through such means as engineering and architecture. The opposition takes on added meaning when one remembers that Róheim sought to establish a psychoanalytical model for anthropology which would permit parallels between ontogenetic and cultural development—an idea later developed and extended by Bruno Bettelheim and Norman O. Brown. While later anthropologists have persuasively disputed any such one-to-one correspondence, the autoplastic-alloplastic antinomy remains in use in both cultural anthropology and developmental psychology.

What I want to explore in this essay, then, is the manner in which science fiction attempts to resolve the opposition of self and environment through both autoplastic and alloplastic fantasies, with some sidelong speculations on how this may in part account for the appeal of certain science fiction works to their readers. For this I would like to borrow another unusual term, this time from science fiction itself. "Instrumentality" is a useful word in discussing the means by which ends are achieved in science fiction, but it is a term that came into the genre through an odd route, probably originating in a novel that is not science fiction at all and that is almost never read today. Science fiction readers will recognize the word from its usage to describe the intergalactic government, the "Instrumentality of Mankind," in the stories published under the name Cordwainer Smith. It has been suggested that Smith (Paul Linebarger) intended a spiritual meaning for this term, borrowing it from references in Roman Catholic and Episcopalian theology to the priest becoming the "instrumentality" of God while performing the sacraments. Without disputing this, I suggest that Linebarger may have had a broader meaning in mind as well. His earlier, non-science fiction novel *Ria* (published under the name Felix Forrest, 1947) ends with the protagonist undergoing a kind of mystical vision on a beach in North Carolina. "She felt that she stood somewhere in the lower part of her own tremendous skull, and that she listened to the fluent deep roar of a resounding bronze instrument of some kind—something metallic, something which sounded like the instrumentality of man, not like the unplanned noises of nature and the sea." The echo of Wallace Stevens may be deliberate, for the clear implication in this passage is that instrumentality includes the whole project of imposed human order, a project that in Smith's science fiction would be extended to the entire universe. But in Smith's science fiction, the instrumentality of man expresses itself through both autoplastic and alloplastic means; the predictable alloplastic fantasies of vast cities and controlled environments, common to nearly all galactic-federation stories, are balanced by stories in which the limits of human form itself are questioned by making humans partly into machines or animals partly into humans. Smith's first published story, for example, "Scanners Live in Vain" (1950), concerns humans surgically restructured to survive in the hostile environment of space, cut off from all knowledge of their own bodies save through special "scanning" instruments. In keeping the Róheim's model of cultural development, the scanners are phased out once the instrumentality discovers alloplastic means of dealing with this problem—namely, building better spaceships.

Science fiction, then, offers its readers the promise of greater and more satisfactory integration with the environment in two ways. In the first, the environment itself becomes the instrumentality of integration through its appropriation and alteration to humanity's will. This is the focus of the bulk of imaginative fiction which extrapolates trends in a direct line from an already highly alloplastic culture such as ours, and it leads eventually to fantasies of completely remaking environments to meet cultural needs: "terraforming" alien worlds in many novels, but also custom-building new worlds in novels such as Larry Niven's *Ringworld* (1970), Bob Shaw's *Orbitsville* (1975), or, on a smaller scale, Arthur C. Clarke's *Rendezvous with*

Rama (1973). (It is interesting to note that, even though physicist Freeman Dyson has seriously suggested the eventual possibility of constructing an *Orbitsville*-type artificial world, science fiction writers have often shied away from making humans responsible for such a wholesale alloplastic fantasy, and all three of the novels I mentioned present the artificial world as an alien artifact.)

Thematically opposed to such instrumentalities of the environment is a smaller but distinct tradition of science fiction stories which deal with what we might call instrumentalities of the body. In these stories, the human form itself is altered through artificial means in orders to achieve greater integration with an environment that would otherwise be hostile. This tradition includes the Simak, Blish, and Smith stories mentioned above, as well as Bernard Wolfe's remarkable novel *Limbo* (1952) and any number of "cyborg" stories, including most recently and notably Frederik Pohl's *Man Plus* (1976). A still more recent story which gives evidence of the tradition's continuing appeal is Vonda McIntyre's "Aztecs" (1977). Although this tradition has antecedents as diverse as H. G. Wells's *The Island of Dr. Moreau* (1896) and Olaf Stapledon's *Last and First Men* (1930), I would like, for purposes of this essay, to explore its impact in a single period of science fiction history, at the height of the so-called Golden Age of magazine science fiction, and to contrast it with a more conventionally alloplastic treatment of the same theme of self and environment from the same period.

More specifically, I would like to examine two stories which appeared only two years apart in *Astounding Science Fiction* in the early forties. Both stories subsequently gained reputations as minor classics of the genre, and both deal in almost archetypal terms with the problem of integration between body and environment. But their approaches to this problem differ considerably: Robert Heinlein's *Waldo* (August 1942) is for most of its length a conventional alloplastic fantasy, albeit reduced to the most primal terms in a tale concerning a weak and ungainly individual's attempts to create a hospitable environment. Clifford D. Simak's "Desertion" (November 1944), on the other hand, is an equally simplified version of the autoplastic fantasy in which the body itself becomes the instrument of integration through bodily transformation, again in a tale focusing on a single individual's experience.

Heinlein's *Waldo* is a story which is remembered primarily for a relatively trivial reason: the fact that the term "waldoes," used in the story to describe the mechanical hands that Waldo uses to overcome his own weakness, later entered the jargon of nuclear technology to describe similar artificial hands used to handle radioactive or other dangerous material. But the story itself is far more interesting for other reasons, not the least of which is the portrayal of the world-saving genius as isolated weakling. As H. Bruce Franklin points out, "Waldo has something in common with many of the readers of *Astounding,* as we find out if we turn to the last page of this August 1942 issue." What is on that last page, Franklin notes, is an ad for

Charles Atlas's "dynamic tension" method of body building—a method not too different from that discovered by Waldo during the course of the narrative. Is Waldo a fantasy projection of the typical science fiction reader, then, and are we back to the body-image problem which I mentioned at the beginning of this essay? Perhaps that is carrying things a bit far, but there is much evidence within the story itself to suggest that it indeed addresses a number of concerns that were likely shared by its readers in 1942 and, for that matter, by many science fiction fans even today. Furthermore, the story exhibits clearly an ideological tension that characterized not only much of Heinlein's work, but the entire field of science fiction as it grew and developed under John W. Campbell, Jr.'s guidance during his years as editor of *Astounding.* The early signs of this tension were already apparent in 1939 with the launching of *Unknown* as a fantasy companion to *Astounding,* but the tension would continue to be apparent throughout the next decade, leading to such works as Jack Williamson's *The Humanoids* (1947-48 in *Astounding*) and culminating, perhaps, in the involvement of Campbell with the Dianetics movement in the early fifties. This tension, I believe, was not merely an opposition between fantasy and science fiction, but something more fundamental, arising, perhaps, out of a growing need to find a place for human mind and will in the mechanistic vision of the universe projected by much science fiction of this period. One might loosely characterize this, then, as a tension between free will and determinism, or between the individual and technology (using technology in a sense similar to that which Jacques Ellul describes in *The Technological Society* [1954]), but for our purposes, both of these may be subsumed into the opposition between self and environment of which we spoke earlier. Put in more purely psychological terms, the question becomes: does one alter one's environment to conform to the needs of the self, or can one alter oneself in order to function in the environment? Does one seek integration through alloplastic or autoplastic means? This, it seems to me, is one of the central issues in *Waldo.*

Near the beginning of *Waldo,* a number of oppositions are quickly established which serve to separate the protagonist, Waldo Farthingwaite-Jones, from the mainstream of the future society in which the story takes place. Foremost among these is Waldo's physical condition, which alone would serve to isolate him from society: suffering from myasthenia gravis since birth, he is abnormally weak and "softly fat, with double chin, dimples, smooth skin; he looked like a great, pink cherub, floating attendance on a saint." Waldo's prepubescent, babylike features are significant, and certainly might have served to promote identification among many of the adolescent readers of the magazine. His condition also accounts for his lack of sexual experience, which will become a motivating factor later in the story. Add to this a brilliant mind and an arrogant, somewhat paranoid personality, and the result is a fair portrayal of the boy genius as social outcast.

But Waldo is set in opposition to society in more symbolic ways, too. In an age when most people have taken to living and working in underground structures according to something called "the London Plan" (p. 20), Waldo instead lives in a gravity-free orbiting space station which puts fewer strains on his weakened body. He calls this station "Freehold," suggesting liberation, but earthlings call it "Wheelchair," suggesting quite the opposite—dependence. An opposition between the individual and the corporation is also established: while most earthlings are dependent on a conglomerate called North American Power-Air for their energy (the corporation holds a virtual monopoly on the "broadcast power" that runs the cities and transportation systems), Waldo has declared a vendetta against this company for allegedly cheating him on some patents. In all, there are three principal levels of oppositions established to differentiate Waldo from the rest of the society. On what we might call the mythic level, there is the opposition of the sky and the underground (with the surface of the earth virtually abandoned by both Waldo and society, as evidenced by the crumbling roads left to deteriorate because "90 percent of the traffic is in the air" [p. 45]). On the social level, this becomes the opposition between the individual (Waldo, who lives in the sky) and the corporate state (North American Power-Air, which literally runs the underground society). Finally, on a level which is both psychological and philosophical, the opposition is between freedom (Freehold) and dependence (Wheelchair). The problem thus set up, the basic movement of the story is toward resolving these oppositions and getting Waldo back down to earth. From a psychological perspective, this becomes a problem in integrating the individual with his social and physical environment.

Initially, Waldo seeks to achieve this integration through purely alloplastic means, by creating an environment suitable to his bodily infirmity and surrounding himself with mechanical extensions of himself (the famous "waldoes"). But this solution clearly takes its emotional toll on him, and his resulting loneliness is evidenced not only by his arrogant misanthropy but by his sentimental attachment to a pet dog and canary. Yet Waldo's genius remains wholly mechanical; like Edison (the model of many early technologist-heroes in science fiction), he is more the inventor than the theorist. It seems never to have occurred to him to have turned to medicine or physiology to seek solutions to his problem; instead he manipulates the environment to reduce the dimensions of the problem. To this extent, Waldo's Freehold is a microcosm of the technological society of earth, a purely alloplastic adaptation. At this early point in the story, the only figure warning of the limits of possible dangers of such adaptation is Waldo's mentor and uncle, Doc Grimes, who also serves as mediator between Waldo and earth society. Grimes is concerned that long-term exposure to broadcast energy on earth is having a debilitating effect on the human nervous system (p. 15)—eventually turning the whole country into a nation of Waldoes. To protect himself from these effects, Grimes introduces one of the few autoplastic adaptations in this part of the narrative: the lead-shielded clothing which he wears to protect himself (p. 14). Grimes is also a doctor, a profession logically associated with autoplastic adaptations, and

at one point in the narrative he recalls delivering the baby Waldo with "the necessary 'laying on of hands'" (p. 17). Grimes is clearly Waldo's father figure throughout the narrative, and is the only one whom Waldo will turn to for advice.

The narrative of **Waldo** begins by introducing a technological problem that will eventually force Waldo to reassess his own dependence on technology by calling into question the very reliability of alloplastic adaptations. Broadcast power receivers on earth have begun to fail for no apparent reason, and the power company is forced to turn to Waldo for assistance in solving the problem. Already, through this collaboration, the individual/corporation antinomy begins to resolve itself, with Grimes the mediating agent. The only one so far able to repair an affected receiver is not a scientist, but an aging "hex-doctor" named Schneider, whose repair involves a mystic ritual and results in the receiver antennas wiggling like worms. Thematically, Schneider is set in opposition to a corporation scientist named Rambeau, who is devoted to a wholly deterministic view of the universe—a view underlined by the point made early in the story that an earlier "reformulation of the General Field Theory did away with Heisenberg's Uncertainty Principle" (p. 13). To Rambeau, physics is an exact science, and Schneider's repair of the broken receivers using power drawn from "the Other World" drives Rambeau crazy. The mad Rambeau's ravings give Waldo the clue to solving the problem, but Waldo must visit Schneider (who refuses to leave the earth or communicate via technology) in order to learn the actual solution. Significantly, Schneider chooses to live on the surface of the earth, and when Waldo, descending from orbit, and corporate representatives, rising from their underground cities, meet at Schneider's home, the opposition of sky/underground is symbolically resolved.

Schneider, then, supplants Grimes as the symbolic mediator of the earth/Waldo antinomy; and in a sense he also temporarily supplants Grimes as Waldo's father figure: it is through another "laying on of hands"—Schneider's massage of his weak arms (p. 67)—that Waldo begins to learn how to tap the sources of inner strength that will result in his eventual rebirth. But Schneider also becomes one pole of another set of antinomies, with Rambeau representing his opposite, and Waldo himself must provide the synthesis for this level of the dialectic. The Schneider/Rambeau opposition can be expressed in a number of ways; Waldo's own formulations of it progress from magic/science (p. 76) to mind/world (p. 88) to will/determinism (p. 89). But it might also be expressed as autoplastic/alloplastic, for while Rambeau insisted that the problems with the mechanical environment could only be solved through reference to that environment itself, Schneider insists that the solution lay within the individual. And that, incredibly enough, turns out to be precisely the reason the receivers began to fail. The operators, indeed weakened by the radiation effects Doc Grimes had feared all along, permitted the machines to fail by losing faith in them, by being "run-down, tired out, worried about something" (p. 73).

By adopting Schneider's methods; that is, by learning to focus on himself rather than on his environment, Waldo is able to gain the strength necessary to enable him to function successfully in the gravity of earth. Heinlein also strongly implies that Waldo manages to achieve a dialectical synthesis of the magic/science antinomy by means of a new, comprehensive view of the universe that encompasses both mind and matter, but as is commonly the case when a science fiction story extrapolates itself into this particular corner, the details of the new synthesis are necessarily vague. What is important to the emotional impact of the story, however, is not that Heinlein should manage to construct a comprehensive synthesis of physics and mysticism, but that he should find a means by which Waldo can be integrated into society, and that this means can be drawn from Waldo's own mind and body. In a sense, the story becomes a cautionary tale about depending too heavily on alloplastic adaptations. Like many fairy tales, including "Rapunzel," the story indicates that the body may provide solutions to problems, rather than simply being itself a problem. As Waldo gains strength, he also develops an interest in social relations that is new to him. He learns how to use his body in relation to others—not belching in their presence, defending himself when challenged—very much in the manner of a child moving into adolescence. It seems appropriate that his first request of his newfound friend Stevens (one of the corporate representatives who had been his nemesis) should be "Could you teach me how to behave with girls?" (p. 103). Later he comments, "I'm just beginning to find out how much fun it is to be a man!" (p. 103). By the end of the story, Waldo has become almost a parody compilation of adolescent fantasies—a world-famous ballet dancer, brain surgeon, and scientist, sought after by reporters, business managers, and beautiful women.

Waldo begins by positing an extreme condition of alloplastic adaptation and ends by showing the limits and dangers of such adaptations. In Clifford D. Simak's "Desertion," these limits of mechanical adaptation provide the basic premise of the story. "Desertion" is a much shorter story than *Waldo,* but together with its sequel "Paradise" (*Astounding,* June 1946) it provides what may be the pivotal element in Simak's remarkable chronicle-narrative *City* (1952). Furthermore, as Thomas D. Clareson points out, "'Desertion' provides a classic example of one of the basic sf structural patterns: the solution of a specific problem." This in itself is unusual for a story as exclusively concerned with autoplastic adaptation as "Desertion" is; what is more remarkable is the manner in which Simak elides the technical dimensions of the problem in order to present the tale purely as myth (and it is, more than any other tale in *City,* presented as "entirely myth" by the anonymous dog-narrator of the frame-tale). Within the sequence of *City* stories, "Desertion" and "Paradise" provide the account of how most of humanity abandons the earth, clearing the way for the tales of intelligent dogs, robots, and ants that make up the bulk of the rest of the narrative. But "Desertion" also has a power uniquely its own. It may be in part, as Eric S. Rabkin and Robert Scholes suggest, a

fable of environmental determinism, but I suspect this is not enough to account for the peculiar fondness with which many science fiction readers remember the tale. Many readers I have met can even quote the closing lines of the narrative, when the protagonist Fowler and his dog Towser, converted into Jovian life forms to explore the hostile environment of Jupiter, refuse to return: "'They would turn me back into a dog,' said Towser. 'And me,' said Fowler, 'back into a man.'"

The narrative begins in a society that has already given itself over to autoplastic adaptations to aid in the exploration of alien planets. Simak does not bother to explain why technology failed in conquering these environments with more conventionally alloplastic solutions; he only mentions that "converters," machines which transform humans into native extraterrestrial life forms, have been in use on "most of the other planets" (p. 106). Jupiter, however, presents a special problem: not only is its tremendous pressure and corrosive atmosphere more than usually destructive of machinery, but the four men who have so far been "converted" into the native life form known as "Lopers" have failed to return to report on their findings. Humanity's reasons for wanting to explore Jupiter are described in terms of the classic manifest destiny theme of much technological science fiction: "Man would take over Jupiter as he already had taken over the other smaller planets." For this appropriation to succeed, however, it is important that humanity not be "forced to work with clumsy tools and mechanisms or through the medium of robots that themselves were clumsy" (p. 106). Two important, if somewhat contradictory, points are made here: first, that the autoplastic adaptations used to explore the other planets had not been genuine; that is, they were undertaken in the service of the larger alloplastic fantasy of acquiring resources to feed a burgeoning interplanetary technology. The idea, apparently, was never that humanity would permanently adapt to these alien life forms. Second, there is evidence that this technology itself is already beginning to prove inadequate; the "clumsy tools and mechanisms" have begun to frustrate humanity in its attempts to truly know other worlds. The story begins, then, at a point at which the limits of alloplastic adaptations are already making themselves apparent.

When a fifth man who has been converted into a Loper fails to return, Fowler, the project director, decides that he and his dog Towser will undergo the conversion themselves. (Fowler's attachment to his dog, although taking on added meaning in the larger context of the *City* narrative that describes the rise of a dog civilization, also recalls Waldo's attachment to *his* dog; in both cases the relationship serves to reassure us that these characters are not after all heartless technophiles and to prepare us for the emotional changes they will undergo later in the story.) The converter itself is one of those delightful pieces of science fiction business that seem totally impossible; we spaceships, superweapons, even an entirely artificial planet called the "Death Star." In contrast to this are the desert, ice, and jungle planets where the rebels live and are forced to adapt themselves to unpromising environments. The extreme of such autoplastic adaptation is the jungle planet in *The Empire Strikes Back* where the ancient Yoda survives by drawing on an inner power called "the Force" and where the hero Luke Skywalker trains himself to adapt to any environment using this Force. Near the end of *Star Wars,* Luke, who in that film had only begun to learn the power of the Force, rejects technology in order to use this inner force from his own body to destroy the Death Star. I mention this scene in particular because it contains almost a direct echo of Heinlein's *Waldo:* Luke is persuaded to trust in the Force by the calm, disembodied voice of his previous mentor, Obi-Wan Kenobi, who had been earlier eliminated by the villain Darth Vader. The similar scene in *Waldo* occurs when the myasthenic Waldo, attacked by the insane Rambeau, hears the words of Schneider: "Gramps Schneider said in his ear, in a voice that was calm and strong, 'Reach out for the power, my son. Feel it in your fingers'" (p. 96).

Even more direct autoplastic fantasies are contained in the recent films *Altered States* and *Scanners. Scanners* is more traditionally a horror film based on the common mutant theme of psychokinesis, but *Altered States* literally concerns the alteration of the body through liberation of "inner forces." Based on a 1978 Paddy Chayefsky novel, the Ken Russell film is in part an inadvertent remake of a 1958 B-picture called *Monster on the Campus,* which concerned a scientist whose experiments on himself transformed him into a Neanderthal. *Altered States* not only recreates that fantasy, but goes beyond it in a tale of a scientist who combines isolation-tank experiments with hallucinogenic drugs to turn himself into a variety of amorphous primal shapes which quickly get out of his control. In the film's climactic scene, the scientist is able to overcome these transformations through love for his wife, which he has never been able to declare before. But before we dismiss this as a sentimental cliché common to films of this sort, we should pause to consider the cliché's significance: it reassures us that bodily changes, even when exaggerated to the level of the bizarre special effects of a film like this, can indeed serve to promote greater integration and a better relationship with others. Through the transformations, the scientist Jessup in *Altered States* learns the value of his own natural bodily form and gains the motivation needed to save his failing marriage.

Such autoplastic themes as I have discussed suggest a number of things about science fiction that might easily be overlooked: that it is not exclusively a literature about mechanization and technological appropriation of the universe, that its roots do not necessarily lie in fantasies of power and subjugation, that it does not serve its readers wholly as a means of escape or as a device for intellectual game-playing, that it is not antihuman. The works I have discussed gain their power not from the technological marvels they introduce, but from the structural models of integration they provide. In this manner, science fiction can provide for an older, somewhat intellectual audience some of the same functions that fantasies and fairy tales serve

for younger children. This is not to suggest that fantasy cannot do the same thing science fiction does—that is a matter for another essay altogether—but merely that the science fiction, grounded in a framework of intellectuality that many of its readers value, can use that framework to construct positive and highly affective models of integration and maturation.

George Slusser (essay date November 1988)

SOURCE: Slusser, George. "Notes and Correspondence: Robert Anson Heinlein, 1907-88." *Science Fiction Studies* 15, no. 3 (November 1988): 385-86.

[*In the following essay, Slusser reflects on his personal friendship with Heinlein.*]

In the newspaper Tuesday morning, May 10th, I read that Robert A. Heinlein had died Monday in his sleep from heart ailments and emphysema. He was 80 years old, and had lived a long, rich, and creative life. Death was merciful to him. And yet I had difficulty believing he was really dead. After all, the single theme of his work, over all those years, is the quest for material life at all costs. Once pushed into this life, you fought for all you're worth to keep going on. A powerful theme, and one which in Heinlein's case seemed to admit no defeat. Yet here were the facts.

During that Tuesday, I tried to sift out what Heinlein meant to me. First people called me from newspapers, to get some quick information about this "acclaimed SF writer." Journalistic memory went back to the hippies and *Stranger* and Manson. There were the inevitable questions. "Was Heinlein really a good writer?" "If I liked him, why?" I found myself saying things like: he put me on the Moon, he let me live in Luna City, he put me on a spaceship with the real Rolling Stones. Not the sort of "literary" things they wanted to hear.

Then friends called, and we talked about all the stories and novels we had read. And then I was alone with my experience. I had been a Heinlein fan since a young boy, and had never stopped reading him. I don't believe I ever read him with pleasure (as one reads a novel like *Great Expectations*), but rather with a mixture of fascination and irritation. Heinlein says things I don't like, but writes about problems that need urgent tending to. I never heard a word about Heinlein in graduate school. In fact, there I was taught a method for attacking "writers of this sort." Where is the stylistic complexity, the intricate web of symbols and ambiguities? The touchstones were Flaubert, Joyce—in America, Stevens. But Heinlein's prose does not live on the metaphysical streets of a physical town. It is in fact, for the academic, a real stone, the one we must kick once in a while to see if we live in literary reality. And so it was for me. Heinlein taught me to see the real American tradition: Whitman, Jeffers, Twain. To look beyond "imperfections" of style to their mythic power. And Heinlein taught me to see that SF is not a debased avatar, but a true avenue—the continuation of our native myth.

Thinking of these things, I suddenly realized that this mythic Heinlein did not belong to the past, or to the past tense. Writers die when their works become "texts." But Heinlein is a voice. And a voice that is still heard with pleasure. It is a voice that runs through five decades of novels and stories. And still found entertaining and relevant by students, many of whom had not been born when Heinlein put his words to paper. This ability to be heard is the mark of a great storyteller, and Heinlein is one. I regularly teach novels like *The Star Beast* alongside Fielding, Cervantes, Balzac—great voices—and they stand the comparison.

I have quarreled with Heinlein, with his seemingly strange linkage between individuality and immortality. I found his anti-Sisyphean vision of perpetual motion, which reads like a modern version of Cronos devouring his progeny, terrifying. But only to realize that all this is not necessarily a "nightside" to our culture. I saw, instead, that Heinlein's dream stirs deep within that culture: in Thoreau's experience at Walden Pond, in Emerson's "undulatory" process. It was by struggling with Heinlein that I came to understand what American culture at least *wants* to be: dynamic and perpetually adolescent—a motion-machine that is not a circle but a spiral. If a true and vital flow passes from writers like Poe and Melville directly to Heinlein, then the academic distinction between SF and "mainstream" is a patent absurdity. For SF today, in Heinlein and in his literary progeny, best represents Emerson's legacy, where form has become a genuine function of power.

Heinlein has, in works from **"Lifeline"** to *The Cat Who Walks Through Walls,* dealt with the same problem over and over—the individual's fascination with, and struggle against, material limits. Heinlein is dead now, matter and destiny have claimed their part. But it seems as if only a part has fallen and fallen only in order that a corresponding power, the voice or "spirit" of the man, is freer to rise. I cannot think of Heinlein without hearing these lines of his Northern California neighbor, Robinson Jeffers: "What / Soared: the fierce rush: the night-herons by the flooded river cried/Fear at its rising / Before it was quite unsheathed from reality."

George Slusser (essay date summer 1995)

SOURCE: Slusser, George. "Heinlein's Fallen Futures." *Extrapolation* 36, no. 2 (summer 1995): 96-112.

[*In the following essay, Slusser evaluates the impact of Heinlein's work, viewing him as "a national writer, one who carries into a new scientific century cultural and ethical patterns first conceived by nineteenth-century American thinkers and writers of 'romance'."*]

Robert Heinlein's long career has ended. Thus, there is the need, more urgent than ever, to assess the nature and importance of his work. But on what level should this assess-

ment take place? The old-style fan saw Heinlein, both writer and public persona, as the quintessential SF writer and adulated him. Criticism of any sort was not tolerated, as I found out when my mid-seventies monographs were awarded the "galaxative award" by Spider Robinson in a hostile fan press. But SF readership has changed since then, and Heinlein has been placed in broader context—not necessarily to his advantage either, for the persona fans once admired has become an embarrassment to many of today's academic readers, whose ideologies he does not readily serve. All this shows that the Heinlein "problem" is one of the critical context in which we choose to place him. Is his work best studied in terms of genre? As a "literary" phenomenon? A cultural or mythical construct? After years of thinking about Heinlein and following his career, I wish to reinforce my original point of departure: Heinlein is a *national* writer, one who carries into a new scientific century cultural and ethical patterns first conceived by nineteenth-century American thinkers and writers of "romance." If Heinlein is the Grandmaster of SF, we cannot say, with Bruce Franklin, that Heinlein has turned America into science fiction, but just the opposite—that SF is America, its natural form of literary expression in the continuity of its culture.

Recently, my earlier writings on a then-living Heinlein were taken to task by British critic Robin Usher. As Usher sees it, I mistakenly sought to limit my explanation of Heinlein's work to "theological" paradigms, in this case to the operation, in his fiction, of a secularized mechanism of Calvinist election: "Heinlein *is* concerned to promote a vision of an 'immutable higher order' but his God does not choose man. *Man* chooses God, or rather he chooses to be His vehicle. The God which the Heinlein hero serves is a personal inner god: the 'Self' of Jungian psychology" (Usher 71). The Jungian interpretation is attractive and no doubt correct. For me, however, it is simply too general. For the Jungian, it seems that all people have a "higher self," and all are free to choose, or not, to integrate with it. Increasingly, however, it is clear to me that Heinlein's "hero" is not everyman but a uniquely American figure shaped in a very particular cultural matrix.

I do not wish to abandon the Calvinist interpretation, rather I wish to nuance it with an Emersonian reading. Among the few books on the shelves of families in the Bible Belt where Heinlein grew up, Emerson's essays are sure to sit. Emerson is read as secular American scripture, and it is he, not Jung, that glosses Heinlein. Analogies can be made, of course, between Emerson's "oversoul" and Jung's higher self. Nor is election an apparent aspect of Emerson's transcendental materialism. His frequent use of "we" suggests at least that the undulation between soul and oversoul, center and circumference, is a process open to all. The real difference, however, is in the direction and purpose of the process. In Jung, to invest the "higher self" is to grow, expand, move toward a future that must be wiser, thus better. In Emerson, investment takes an opposite path. The heart that abandons itself to the Supreme Mind "will travel a royal road to particular knowledges and powers. In ascending to this primary and aboriginal sentiment, we have come from our remote station on the circumference instantaneously to the center of the world, where, as in the closet of God, we see causes, and anticipate the universe, which is but a slow effect" ("Over-Soul" 1154). Things are topsy-turvy here, with the Jungian "royal road" leading instead from general circumference to a particular center, to an intimate "closet of God" that surely suggests the strait gate of election. What is more, in this closet of God we witness the contraction of future and history (the "slow effect") to a presentness which is that of the sole self: "For the soul is true to itself, and the man in whom it is shed abroad cannot wander from the present, which is infinite, to a future which would be finite" ("Over-Soul" 1158).

Usher speaks of "a *positive* form of Heinleinian solipsism," in Jungian terms one with a future, a growth vector. Heinlein's most powerful figures, however, despite their nominal insertion in a "future history," in fact exist in a present that they strive to render infinite in duration and in size. This is a dynamic, self-sustaining solipsism. Emerson on one hand seems to deny the role of election in bestowing special "grace" on such a self: "Like a bird which alights nowhere, but hops perpetually from bough to bough, is the Power which abides in no man and in no woman, but for a moment speaks from this one, and for another moment from that one" ("Experience" 1170). On the other hand, he describes the mechanism whereby such a self generates its own power and form: "Life itself is a mixture of power and form, and will not bear the least excess of either" ("Experience" 1171). The Heinlein hero cultivates "life" not in terms of growth, which is excess, but rather as dynamic undulation measured in the sense of increasing amplitude, where longevity is equated with expanding duration of its present moment. What is experience here is not Jungian individuation but, rather, a material infusion of self into cosmos like that of Emerson's transparent eyeball: "I am nothing, I see all; the currents of the Universal Being circulate through me" ("Nature" 1067). The Heinlein hero tells the bird of power it need not alight, for everywhere the bird would put down, the single body is, cosmic currents flowing through its extended circulation system.

Just as Emerson shifts from "we" to "I" in the case of the secularized "election" that is the transparent eyeball, so Heinlein maintains an illusion of democratic possibility, until from the circulating masses a single being is chosen to become the body that in turn subsumes the circulation system. Following Emerson, Heinlein thus occludes traditional Calvinist anxiety over origins. The hero does not worry about whether he was initially chosen; in that "choice" here is made a function of ostensibly material forces such as genetic accident or species drive, the so-called "survival of the fittest." Successful use of these, however, balancing the power-form ratio in order to expand beyond "we" to "I," must, in the manner of Puritan society, be read as visible signs of election. The question, then, of Heinlein's "theology" is crucial in the context of

an American culture that, as in Emerson, effectively obviates psychological development by transposing religious forms onto secular or material experience.

Heinlein continued publishing up to his death in 1988 (indeed, his voice continued to be heard in 1989, in *Grumbles from the Grave*). In one sense, however, his opus comes full circle in *The Number of the Beast* (1980)—or rather, swallows its tale, which from its earliest stories is that of the male monohero himself expanding to absorb all other characters and "plots." Ostensibly a sprawling space opera, *Beast* soon reveals, as we sail off with Zeb Carter for dimensions unknown, that it is both fiction about fiction and, specifically, fiction about Heinlein's own fiction. Increasingly in his later novels, Heinlein used fictional persona as alter egos. The author here, however (it is hard to refer to a "narrator," as Heinlein almost always lets his characters speak in their voice or speaks of them in a voice calqued on their "point of view"), not only resurrects figures from a panoply of early novels but makes them aware that they are fictional creations. Moreover, Heinlein incorporates his reader into the text as well by mingling that reader's world (both as "real" person and as reader of pulp adventures) with those of his fictional characters, thus making that world yet another of the alternative universes he rules over. There is humor here, much of it aimed at critics. Even so, the implication is clear: the author, nowhere and everywhere in his creation, makes himself a transparent eyeball and at the same time, forcing all currents of the Universal Being to flow back through his own pen, declares himself a god in all possible worlds, the reader's world included.

Heinlein announces in this novel an "inter-universal society for eschatological pantheistic multiple-ego solipsism." The joke, however, contains the fundamental paradox of Heinlein's work as a whole. *Beast* is full of chatty "family" scenes; it is a-whirl with multiple entities. Yet, beyond even the genetic lines of Lazarus Long, this proliferation of kin, fictional or real, collapses as it seems to expand, circumscribing at a single center the isolated "body" of the author. Expansion and contraction are one, systole and diastole, so that as action and pages of prose proliferate, the single author becomes increasingly "visible" not just in but *as* his creation. We can call the process "dynamic solipsism," or some such thing. But it seems, too, an act of literary cannibalism, where scores of worlds are "born" only to be fed upon and fictional progeny devoured as the source of energy needed to sustain the single writer. This "god" does not create *ex nihilo*; rather, he recycles, and because what he recycles is things he creates, he endlessly swallows himself. At the same time, however, this solipsistic creator is central to the material universe that underlies Heinlein's fiction. Operating here is a system of pure transfer of energy that excludes the possibility of future progress. One understands the attraction of grace in such a condition, for Pascal faced a similar dilemma. To Heinlein, however, grace is not a means of transcending orders of reality; instead, it promises access to an alternate world where entropy is replaced by self-sustaining process, where an individual center—here the writer in the closet of God—expands to create its own circumference.

On the narrative level, Heinlein displaces the literary "circumference," with its diversity of character and plot and pretensions at future history, with the undulating rhythms of personal solipsism. His career as a published writer spanned exactly five decades. His first story, **"Life Line,"** appeared in *Astounding Science Fiction* in August 1939. Thereafter his steady output literally evolved along with the publishing industry, embracing formats from the magazine story and serial, the hardback juvenile novel for lending libraries, mass-market paperbacks, and, at the end of his career, increasingly luxurious hardback and trade paperback publications (an example is the 1980 Fawcett Columbine edition of *Number of the Beast* with its lavishly embossed wrap-around cover and massively integrated illustrations). The lengths of his fictions range from minimalist short stories, written under austere editorial (and no doubt personal/artistic) constraints, to prolix novels that get longer and longer. By the end of his life Heinlein could demand of his publishers that no word, however unnecessary, be stricken from his texts. As late as 1968, in *Stranger in a Strange Land,* the work that made him a best-seller, editorial cuts were made; the posthumous appearance of an "uncut version" shows us how precious those lost words have become since.

Despite this great variety of formats, Heinlein's literary purpose has remained remarkably monochromatic in his incessant focus on the single individual and his world. This despite the fact that, as Heinlein's career advanced, he sought to persuade the reader that his stories and novellas were really part of a projected, organically evolving "future history." Ever since Balzac and the later Asimov, however, we know such histories are post hoc creations. For Heinlein, it seems to have been a matter of drawing clever diagrams and chronologies after the fact. For the 1967 appearance of ***The Past Through Tomorrow,*** billed as "Future History Stories: Complete in One Volume," reveals the arbitrary nature of the grouping and suggests that, as of then, the project was closed.

The true nature of Heinlein's "future" is clearly revealed with the 1980 publication of ***Expanded Universe.*** Here Heinlein presents a handful of so-called future history stories (the same five stories were also published in a volume called ***The Worlds of Robert A. Heinlein*** that appeared one year earlier than ***The Past Through Tomorrow,*** in 1966). Now, however, the stories serve to present not history but the singular career of the author himself. Presenting **"Life Line"** lets Heinlein describe his first sale. Other stories mark the chronology of his literary life, giving the occasion for speeches and essays that expose his increasingly obsessive thoughts and "credo." In his "Foreword" to ***Expanded Universe.*** Heinlein talks about making money and gloats uncharitably about outliving all his presumed literary enemies: "time wounds all heels." The historical mask falls here. And if Heinlein, in his 1980s novels, brings back figures from earlier works to play roles, in a

neo-Balzacian attempt to bestow on the whole of his *oeuvre* a feel of historical continuity, the latter is a facade. The late novels may claim the scope of an intergalactic human comedy. Yet the recurring figures in this family of man prove to be the family of *one* figure, the most representative of players in his putative "future history," Lazarus Long. Long's progeny return obsessively in novels from *Beast* to *Job: A Comedy of Justice* (1984) and *To Sail Beyond the Sunset* (1987). Long shares with the "commentator" of **Expanded Universe,** the writer-god of *Beast,* and even with Heinlein's Job an obsession with preserving his physical being. In Heinlein, all promise of mankind's advancement, its growth across time and space, conflates on a focus that is not even family in the sense of dynasty but the single self. Does it matter if this self is the "real" Heinlein or his fictional alter ego Lazarus Long? Long, whose literary situation permits him to meditate on the wages of prolonged personal destiny (rather than on royalties and enemies), may be most fascinating of the two. It is Long, in fact, who raises the question of *kairos* in relation to author Heinlein's pretense at *chronos* or historical axis. For as Lazarus frantically seeks to cleave throughout eternity to his individual body firmly held in the bands of matter, he denies all possibility either of history or of cosmic growth through transcendence, where individuals give way to higher collective entities or "overminds."

Thus, despite the huge bulk of Heinlein's production and the increasing sprawl of his form into massive *romans à tiroirs,* the normative form in his canon remains, both in a literal (i.e., structural) and figurative sense, the short, vertically operative allegory. This is an endlessly repeatable tale that, in its working out, ever repeats the same scenario: (1) initial promise of action and strong character development suddenly ruptured along its line of horizontal development; (2) subsequent, and instant, translation of events or protagonists to adulthood and "glory"; (3) conflation of ends and beginnings; finally, (4) physical condensation of all fictional scenarios and human dramas to that fixed point where we discover the preordained duration of a (ultimately *the*) single physical body.

A frequent narrative mask in earlier Heinlein is the "social evolutionary" setting where, as in *Beyond this Horizon* (1948), genetically "strong" protagonists dream of some dimorphic evolution that would send their seed "to roam the stars—no limit." Yet for such "star lines," genetic advance (and advantage) never leaves the unlikely matrix of the patriarchal family. The perennial grouping, even in tales of promised genetic change, is invariably father, mother, son. The configuration is as static as the psychoanalytical triad. Its particular fixity, however, in Heinlein, comes more from "atavistic" traits, so-called anal and oral formations.

The first, and obvious, thing we notice about Heinlein's narrative is its single-gender nature. If formula plotting requires that there be roles of wife, daughter, even "lover," Heinlein goes out of his way—more than the conventions of "juvenile" fiction demand—to turn females into tom-

, nags, fuzzy-brained hysterics. Feminists execrate inlein, on a visceral level, because he presents women who do domestic duty as irrevocably stupid. For example, the simpering wife of **"The Black Pits of Luna"** (1948) is so dumb (i.e., ignorant of science) that she calls for bloodhounds on an airless moon to search for a lost son who subsequently proves quite able to take care of himself. The tomboy is a bit more interesting, but only because she is a male travesty. Heinlein lets girls wear the shoes of the traditionally male adolescent of the juvenile bildungsroman. For example, Podkayne of Mars, heroine of a belated juvenile (1963), enters the scene as a tough-as-nails girl with ambitions of breaking into the all-male world of military space flight. In the end, however, biology makes her drop the mask, and voila, the old curse of Eve returns. All she need do is look in a mirror to discover she has broad hips and is fond of babies, and dreams of space conquest bow to destiny with relief. When Heinlein brings back another "tomboy," in *Friday* (1982), we are, it seems, promised something quite different: a real female at last, one who (as is proclaimed on the book's jacket) "is all woman . . . very, very female." How troubling to learn that this female, who "can think better, fight better and make love better than any of the normal people around her," is not normal but, rather, is "a super-being . . . engineered from the finest genes." The Engineer is still a male authority, and the product, "trained to be a secret courier," is still his little girl Friday.

Heinlein's "departures" from the male adolescent hero formula are significant because they are not departures. He gives us girl heroines, even concocts potential sexual rivalries and "love affairs" between his youthful protagonists, only to elide them in a way that shows he has no interest whatsoever in gender differences on this level. A female heroine can survive only by being the exact calque of a young male. All daughters are really sons, and it is as sons that they must deal with parental authority. Parents alone in Heinlein have marked gender stances, and what differentiates them has the force of deep creation myth.

In his culturally unassuming medium of the "juvenile" bildungsroman, Heinlein recasts the struggle of child and parent on the primitive and universalist plane of a battle between earth and sky gods. As first glance, the prize seems nothing less than possession of the material universe. In work after work, a young hero(ine), freed of the necessity of seeking Freudian or Jungian individuation, is called to act in a quasi-symbolic drama that (like Everyman moving between the gates of heaven and hell) is bounded by two unchanging, and all-encompassing, forces. On one "end" of the life line, we find the all-separating mother, who bears life only to cast it forth into the stream of material growth and decay. She is a conflation of generative and biological curses—Rhea and Pandora combined. On the other (respondent) end, there is the all-consuming father. In Heinlein's mythology, the latter is postlapsarian. Born of woman's curse, this figure sustains male life only to the degree he harnesses the mother's capacity to generate more life in the form of consumable energy. He is a new Kronos, spawning and raising children in order to devour them. The sole role of Heinlein's younger "generation," then, is that of allegorical vector between producer of energy and consumer. Such existence is hardly progressive—the young man growing to displace father and mother. It is regressive, where quests for adulthood and adult relationships only mask an inverted (and thoroughly male) drive to reverse the fall by controlling—"farming," in a literal sense—the maternal force.

The allegorical nature of Heinlein's stories is evident in their ritualistic nature. Female temptation and love, for instance, are rituals. We have seen how the challenge of the female rival is thwarted when plot veers from conflict to revelation of identity. Similar forces intervene to deny the female the self-knowledge necessary to function as lover and, potentially, wife. Wherever couples are formed in a Heinlein novel, the gesture is anticlimactic, an afterthought that denies passion and offers no threat of future conflict. The "lover" is instantly the potential mother, future and dutiful serer of offspring for another young Kronos-in-training.

The rhetorical device here is ellipsis. That its use conceals an obsession with the Pandoran mother as source of originally uncontrolled generation—all-destroying time and love—is clear. In order to contain, and ultimately control, this chthonic force, Heinlein always conflates the figures of wife and mother. His texts (like his heroes) function like machines that would regulate this terrible organic presence by a highly contrived "technology" of substitution. On the simplest level, in a juvenile like *Time for the Stars* (1956), Heinlein mechanically multiplies female suitors, reducing potential individuals to faceless ciphers. In this novel, Special Relativity is evoked to sanction the elevation to prominence of one identical twin over the other. As befits this allegory of secularized "grace," female "temptation" must be offered only to be eliminated by making that presence generic in nature. Predestined by their very names, Misses Alpha, Beta, and Gamma Furtney have a destiny only as components in a telepathic net. Unnamed, they cannot be called. Nonentities, they offer no individual menace to the scientifically elect.

The same reduction of female personalities to groupings occurs in the so-called "adult" novels as well. We find them, ironically, in the novel that passed in the late 1960s as a call to self-awareness: *Stranger in a Strange Land*. The long first section of the novel celebrates the doings of mature "sybarite" Jubal Harshaw. Harshaw offers an iconic template for domination of women that young Michael Valentine Smith will implement in the course of this long book. Playing Pan to the coming hippie rock star, Harshaw always travels with his entourage of beauties. But, physically, they are as faceless as an MTV constellation. They are his "secretaries," and there is a James Bond uniformity to the standardized modes of sexual experience they offer. There is a Bondlike "danger," too, in Amazon Jill and temptress-dancer Dawn. But whatever potential threat they pose instantly vanishes when they learn that they are (despite minor physical differences like full-body tatoos for Dawn) in fact mirror twins. We have the impression of reading two novels having different women with the same name. Harshaw's Jill has a mind of her own and is well on her way to becoming a prime mover in the intrigue. With Mike, however, all this vanishes; suddenly she is another faceless unit in his harem—now neither person nor lover, just another breeder of chosen ones.

In the later novels, however, the youthful-feminine appears more tempting, and correspondingly harder to dominate. In *I Will Fear No Evil* (1970), the male messiah of *Stranger* (who could only be resurrected on an alternate plane) is replaced by an aged recycler, who takes women's bodies as well as their personalities. The three names here—Johann Sebastian Smith—tell us in emblem fashion that we have a special creative mind trapped in the body of an everyman. An automobile accident and a brain transplant let Johann be recycled in the body of his beautiful secretary. The situation generates three hundred pages of voyeurism and sexual charades, with finally two men and a woman "sharing" the same body. Heinlein, however, is not putting Plato's androgyne back together here. Instead, what we have is a male destiny using a female body to get physically closer to the process of reproduction. Johann had stored his sperm before the operation and now uses it to inseminate himself so that he can control, now from inside the body, the process of gestation that will perpetuate his seed.

Heinlein's young hero has not become old so much as become a conflation of old and young. Smith figures in this sense Heinlein's aged-yet-ageless hero, Lazarus Long. Long's sole activity, in *Time Enough For Love* (1972), is finding new and intricate ways of fathering himself. In this novel, Long uses a number of gambits from genetic engineering to time travel in order to play sons and lovers, though he has reached the end not only of his biological line but of human time as well. By this playing, he hopes to conquer, retroactively, the female challenges left undone by the normal flow of existence. Cloning allows him to produce the "sisters" he never had. In their production, he reduces biology to empty form by insisting that cloned embryos be carried in host "mothers," who are two exotic and faceless hetaera of the sort Jubal cultivated. Thanks to longevity, Lazarus can raise these sisters as "daughters" and in turn seduce them as lovers. The creatures even condone his actions: "Coupling with us might be masturbation, but it can't be incest, because we aren't your sisters. . . . We're you." In another episode, Lazarus acts as onanistic Pygmalion to bring a computer to life. Where before he has lost "emphemeral" lovers to the stream of time, now he lures a flesh-and-blood woman out of machine-eternity, if into a life of sterile servitude.

Longevity gives Lazarus, after he tires of living multiple lives, the capacity to relive them through the lives of his sons and daughters. Not only are daughters clones of the sons, but both become, through genetic control, simply extensions of the father's body.

Not content with channeling the energies of the female first cause, he strives to encompass it physically, too, by going back in time to make love with his mother. Heinlein titillates us with the possibility of this son becoming his own father. But titillation is all we get, for if the system is to hold, the mother must remain the inviolate first cause. Lazarus cannot touch it, for not only would he cease to be, but the energy that generates the power and form of this being would fail. For the Emersonian materialist, the first cause is awesome. Final causes are, by contrast, menacing but controllable. In relation to birth (the center), final causes promise irreversible events—individuation, future happenings, death—and as such commit energy to linear rather than undulatory movement, drawing it fatally beyond the pull of its source. A "Lord of Life" is needed to forestall the end by controlling the means, holding the center in relation to an ever-expanding circumference. Lazarus is such a "Lord of Life."

Looking backward from Lazarus, we see these figures dominating Heinlein narratives from the beginning. The only difference is their power and width of circumference. We go from Fader Magee in *Coventry* (1940) and Kettle Belly Bailey in **"Gulf"** (1940) to reincarnations of Jubal Harshaw who bridge the gap, in *Number of the Beast,* between a career of fictional mentors and the author as their stepfather. Finally, there are the many lives and beings of Lazarus Long as they multiply in response to the looming ubiquity of Maureen Johnson in *The Cat Who Walks through Walls* (1986) and finally *To Sail beyond the Sunset* (1988). That Heinlein's "Lords of Life" are almost never natural fathers is a strategic device. Witness Lazarus's many "adoptive" masks and roles, which allow him to approach the seat of female power without committing incest or chronoclasm.

The scenario, however, already functions in the juveniles. For example, in *Time for the Stars* the hero Tom's blood father is "unmanned" through attachment to wife and home. The boy finds a mentor in bachelor Uncle Steve. And happily Steve's advice—go to the stars—proves a way, via relativity, for the son to impede the normal course of bloodlines. Tom returns to find his twin brother the age of his grandfather. He could, therefore, marry a girl the age of his granddaughter. In doing so, he would draw the future, now a circumference to his center, at least a ways back toward the original point of generation.

Uncle Steve is a military man, and his mentor is a titular one: the Captain. Heinlein's army, however, is not a place of blind obedience to a system. Indeed, *Time* is an exemplary tale of how few, if many are thus named, have the intrinsic qualities to be Captain. Tom is under the command of the inept Captain Urqhardt. The latter, ordering the ship to certain ruin, forces Tom (and with him the now-dead Steve, who remains his tutelary voice) to disobey orders. And through the intervention of a yet higher authority, what Heinlein calls "serendipity," in the form here of the faster-than-light vessel that suddenly arrives to vindicate the hero's actions, Tom can defy the letter of the without breaking its spirit. In allegories of this sort, the mentor is ultimately an inner, guiding voice. The action is its vindication, as all institutional hierarchies (as with Emerson, institutions are but lengthened shadows of men) yield to natural ones. In like manner, a natural providence—here the relativity that allows scientists back on earth time to research and build the "miraculous" ship—breaks through the benighted folly of ordinary beings to make manifest the right way. But in Heinlein, "the way" is not a way that goes anywhere in a historical sense. What is revealed is not moments that decide the course of human progress. As with Emerson's representative men, we have revelations of a number of representative moments, different manifestations or forms of a same living power. This is precisely the "geography" of the linked novellas *Universe* and *Common Sense* (1941). We do not, here, see all humanity reverted to superstition and self-limitation, only certain people on a typical generation starship lost on its course to Alpha Centauri. The adventure of the stories' "new Galileo," Hugh Hoyland, leads to no historical breakthrough, no new beginning of civilization, simply to a reprieve. The narrative, revealing a type, only retells Heinlein's single story, that of the winnowing of human chaff and the emergence of the elect.

Heinlein surely would not have liked terms like "providence" or "grace." The conventional Miltonic God the Father, as we see in *Job: A Comedy of Justice* (1986), is just another corporate manager, whose dominions are a stifling bureaucracy. But "serendipity" is not a secularized form of grace; it is a localized form. Heinlein's chain of "grace" is not just patriarchal; it is operative on the local, or tribal, level. In his military chain of command, there are never generals. In *Starship Troopers* (1959), for example, Johnny Rico's exemplary career is guided first by Sergeant Zim, the boot-camp instructor who returns, "providentially," to lead him in his baptism of fire. Beyond Zim, there is the less tangible Colonel Dubois, the high school "moral philosophy" instructor who first inspires Johnny to enlist. But, if Dubois returns again and again to direct Johnny's path, guidance here is through words not deeds. We have Dubois's timely letters, his lectures, his reported bits of wisdom, but not his physical presence. Colonels, in fact, seem to be numinous figures in Heinlein. Witness P-Colonel Baslim of the Exotic Corps in *Citizen of the Galaxy* (1957). Once he saves orphan Thorby from slavery in the opening pages of the book, he dies, leaving behind his "aura" or guiding light to future mentors. Captain seems the ideal level of patriarchal authority—the head or chief of a small tribe, of a "few good men." The social unit of serendipity is never large; in lieu of the blood family, it must form an alternate unit of equal size, as befits the intimacy of Emersonian power and form.

Heinlein's patriarchal dramas, then, are to be read not in an Oedipal sense but as rituals that free the young hero from the strictures of family and blood, from the possibility of social individuation and, beyond this, of historical dynasty. But free them to what purpose? In *Citizen of the Galaxy,* step-father Baslim acts, beyond death, to activate

a series of surrogate mentors whose task is to free Thorby from any resurgence of blood ties: first Captain Krausa, who frees Thorby from the toils of a Trader "family" so complex in organization an anthropologist is needed to decipher it; then Lawyer Garsch, who extricates the hero from the intrigues of his own blood family. As we have seen, blood fathers, like the bureaucratic structures they represent, hinder the young hero. They do not, however, hinder "growth" in a Freudian sense. We never see, in Heinlein, Freud's displacement of the father as creating a balanced personality. Heinlein's mentors, instead, redirect the young man to a non-Oedipal line, where blood father is displaced by a symbolic figure: bachelor uncle, teacher, captain. In *Starship Troopers,* for example, the possibility of Oedipal conflict is raised only to be elided when an alternate military chain of command subsumes the authority of blood ties. Johnny's blood father is unsuccessful in exercising his paternal right to prevent his son from enlisting. Defeated, he returns in the end in an inverted role: now as the sergeant who serves directly under Lieutenant Rico. Johnny has displaced the father, but not through psychological growth; rather, by instant identification with the symbolic patriarchy that rules his universe. This is the universe of Kronos, a world before and outside the laws of personal and historical development, where fathers and sons, by necessity, remain indistinguishable. The symbolic figure associated with a Kronos who absorbs his progeny is that of elision. "Son" Johnny is simply an immanent patriarch. By eliding normal processes of biology and psychology, he merely invests the form of the symbolic "father."

It is difficult to isolate a "key" text for any aspect of Heinlein's rich work. The narrative, however, that best defines the crux between immanence and history in Heinlein, where the promise of future generations encounters the self-perpetuating dynamic of Kronos, the interchangeable father and son as Emerson's center and circumference, is *The Puppet Masters* (1959). This novel, on the surface, seems to restore Freud and bloodlines to the family portrait. For in the story we learn that the "Old Man," the military boss, is in fact the protagonist's own flesh-and-blood father. The purpose of this narrative, it appears, is not to lead Sam, in guise of some secular grace, to take possession of the father role. It is rather to have him earn the right to become the father, as the individual who rids the Old Man of his parasitical "slug," restoring him to the bloodline and overthrowing his authority at the same time. The Kronos function, the immanent possession that conflates son and father to interchangeable roles, seems transferred to the vampiric, personality-stealing slugs who in the end are defeated. But on what terms is a family reunited here? Were I wont to give Heinlein such intentions, I would say that in *The Puppet Masters* he restores the Freudian temptation, but only to "subvert" it. On the eve of figures like Michael Valentine Smith and Lazarus Long, who are openly hermaphroditic compounds of father and son, he seems to wish to lay the ghost of individuation to rest.

Indicating the vertical nature of family development in the novel is the perfect allegorical "readibility" of the cover illustration from the 1951 *Galaxy,* where the earlier serial-form appeared. The cover, depicting the final scene, shows us a son who is now Boss, looming tall and strong over a much smaller female figure. In now familiar manner, man's potential partner and sexual rival is neutralized by size and symbolic position. The seductive attributes of Eve—in this case full breasts—are regulated by the strait-jacketing "space" costume and thus reduced to mere signs of the breeding function the female must serve on the subsequent twenty-year flight to Titan to destroy the slug's home world. This is an accurate depiction of the narrative's reductive nature. Initially, Mary is an agent as tough and resourceful as Sam. In the course of things, however, she does not develop but is merely translated from an active to a symbolic role. In the end, she may be the one who saves mankind; but she does so only because she is capable of being a passive vessel. Because she has survived the rare Venusian fever that kills the slugs, she becomes the repository of crucial information that allows *men* to exterminate them. Indeed, it is only through controlled male probing of her hidden life sources in memory, an act of permissive rape by proxy, that the identity of the disease is finally retrieved.

The background of the cover is a huge spaceship, the largest element in the picture and symbol of the primacy of the mission. Beckoning the couple to enter is the Old Man. His distant smallness suggests the role of tutelary spirit. He bears, in fact, no family resemblance to the tall young man. Instead we have Heinlein's typical mentor, bald and paunchy, the physique common to such diverse figures as Kettle Belly Bailey and Hugh Farnham. In the narrative, the Old Man all but perishes in a final plane crash only to be resurrected by physical fusion with his young acolyte. Much as Jubal Harshaw's suicide, in *Stranger in a Strange Land,* is reversed when Mike "inhabits" his body, here Sam's lying "face to face . . . almost cheek to cheek" with his dying father restores the vitality we see on the *Galaxy* cover. On that cover, the father continues to draw on filial energy, inviting the son into a situation—space travel—where he must take the form of an old man. Sam's voyage to adulthood will be an elided one. Like Rip van Winkle, the tall son will emerge from this mental chrysalis twenty years later on a distant planet as a bald and paunchy figure. Yet, within the allegorical space of this cover, Sam, potentially the father yet still the tall youth, improves on Rip. Rip must pay for the instant translation from inexperience to wisdom with loss of youth, while Sam retains both. Applying the Einsteinian gambit of *Time for the Stars,* twenty years of Sam's time at near-light speeds translates into centuries of earth time. If Sam ages on his biological line, even more he is a hopeless anachronism to the "new" world many intervening generations have created. Yet, by the logic of paradox, he still returns "younger" that his great-great-grandfather. This cover freezes, in static eternity, the elements of that dynamic of self-perpetuation which is Heinlein's master narrative throughout his career. It is a narrative in which, in this instance, the fantasy of election and the physics of space travel concur to make Sam a youth in age's mantle.

Looking across the span of Heinlein's work, then, we see families and generations and future history conflate into what is an endless reconfiguring of a single lifeline—that of the aging authority figure, from Hugo Pinero in the first published story **"Life Line"** (1939) to Lazarus Long—into a dynamic figure that resembles Emerson's undulation between center and circumference. If Emerson defines his poles as individual being on one hand and universe on the other, he does not see the latter as a purely personal construct but as *the* universe itself. We cannot, thus, limit Heinlein's hero, in light of his relation to the "continuity" of an American experience, to those patterns of psychoanalysis and bildung his own fictional vision rejects. The Oedipal and individuation myths assume the primacy of Zeus and the Socratic dictum of "know thyself." But Heinlein, following a cultural current that can be traced back to Ben Franklin, openly formulates the human condition in terms of a pre-Socratic emphasis on material atoms and intelligence on one hand and, on the other, of preindividuated, "archaic" human formations—the oral Kronos who devours generations and futures in order to preserve his material present. In Heinlein's monohero—in whom Emersonian self-reliance and Thoreau's call to "simplify" is carried to monstrous proportions—we have, rather than a case of arrested development or "phobia" of growing old, a concerted act of personal philosophy.[1]

Heinlein's care is for the physical perpetuation of the body—the sole body he (in the manner of the empirical tradition of the American founders) really *knows*: his own. But if psychological categories are tangential, even antithetical, to his vision, moral categories are not. The word "ethos" refers to a being's character, its "normal state" of being. C. Hugh Holman states that Calvinism "may almost be considered the ethical mode in America" (226). As such, Calvinism may be said to haunt Emerson's transcendental vision as its ethical "soul," the basic condition of the humanity on which that vision would operate. Heinlein, then, though neither a professed nor practicing Calvinist, is unable, in his narratives of male self-perpetuation, to do away with the female first cause. Here, it seems, we have a thing of awe and terror, the place of generation that is at once a place of total depravity and source of the Fall and a wellspring of "grace," the force (however disguised as genetic or evolutionary trajectories) that sustains Lazarus's "unconditional" election beyond any ability he may have to perform deeds. It is for this reason that Lazarus, claiming the circumference in the very late novels, increasingly comes under the pull of Mother Maureen's center. Her presence in these novels acts to restore, in light of the secular temptation of control by unaided reason, Calvinism's ultimate doctrine of limits. Maureen's rise signals the limited possibility for atonement or action in the face of the mystery of grace, which no one, even Lazarus, deserves in light of the enormity of the Fall.

Heinlein's Americanism is usually confused with the genre formulas he adopts. Samuel R. Delany outlines the following pulp formulas as "genre conventions" in SF: "(1) that a single man, unaided, can change the course of history; (2) that the universe is basically a hospitable place; (3) that intelligence is a perfectly linear human attribute" (226). Heinlein is constantly telling us that such is his credo. But let us measure his fiction by these categories. First, in spite of constant praise (through fictional mouthpieces or in authorial asides) of the lone hero, rarely if ever is that single man "unaided" in Heinlein. Lazarus's name, we are told, means "God has helped." For such heroes, self-reliant toughness is doubled by a secular form of "grace," an inscrutable destiny that elevates a figure who bears no marks of greatness. Second, if certain men are chosen, how "hospitable" is the destiny that elects them? Heinlein forever asserts, in the name of "serendipity," that the universe is a friendly place for his elect. For example, when Hugh Hoyland's band in **Common Sense** casts off in space, it appears to land in a new Eden. Yet no new world begins here: instead we have a localized event, a huddling place for a few lucky survivors, nothing more. In the broader scope of the Fall, human triumphs and "conquests" are diminutions when measured against what was and is no more, the lost first cause, or, in its secular mask, the peak of energy from which all else is a downward slope. Heinlein's "Eden," in fact, returns human beings to the crudest oral existence: "From now on, Alan, always Good Eating" (128). On an even vaster intergalactic stage, Kip, in *Have Space Suit, Will Travel* (1959), successfully argues the human cause before a cosmic bar of justice. But the outcome of his serendipitous efforts (his "grace") is pure Calvinist anticlimax, for mankind is not granted a pardon, only a reprieve. The sole triumph is again on the level of anality and food. For only back at the local soda fountain after his adventure can Kip exercise free will, and this only to fling a pie in the face of the local bully.

Calvinism makes a perfect fit with the thermodynamic vision that Heinlein derives simultaneously from his Emersonian heritage and from his interest in the physical sciences. The undulatory pattern between center and circumference, which shapes family relations and conflict around the self-sustaining patriarch, may offer conservation of matter. But this itself is a localized case on the irreversible slope of entropy. However centrifugal the claim for an expanding circumference, as with Lazarus's universe-spanning body, expansion is matched by an opposite and unequal centripetal pull toward an ever-diminishing center. Nor is intelligence, the motor of physical mastery, ever (in Delany's sense) linear in Heinlein's SF formulas; rather, it is curved or sloped. For example, the apparently linear pursuit of life extension leads ultimately to physical contraction. Such is Kettle Belly Bailey's search to acquire "speedtalk" in **"Gulf"** (1941), for this is a skill that damns those that master it to "an *effective* lifetime of at least sixteen hundred years, reckoned in flow of ideas," thus placing an intolerable compression on a still-short lifeline. Even escape into alternative universes proves a compression, not expansion, of heroic possibility. In *Glory Road* (1963), "Scar" Gordon trades Vietnam for a realm of sword and sorcery only to find its paths of glory (worse even than those of its analogue) meandering and hopelessly regressive. "Decisive" battles lead nowhere, and the world he finally liberates (aptly called "Center") turns out to be simply a mirror of Scar's anarchic being, a world without government, where "even the positive edicts of the Imperium were usually negative in form." Finally, intellectual mastery of time inscribes nothing more than endless loopings around a single, and endlessly diminishing, instant or episode in the lifespan of a single self. Bob Wilson, in **"By His Bootstraps"** (1941), appears to achieve physical eternity—and a much better life in the magic kingdom of Norsaal—by orchestrating a dynamic circumference of temporal manifestations of himself around a single, endlessly repeated spacetime event. Yet perpetual motion proves here to be a "fur farm," where with each turn something dies, a little energy is lost. Bob, for example, passes through the circles to become the mentor Diktor because he *is* Diktor. Yet the notebook Diktor first showed him is lost in the process, and he must (re)write it. The "Bob" who will replace him in turn must rewrite another, and so on. What happens, however, to these notebooks? And where does each Diktor that is displaced go?

In the end, Bob Wilson is perhaps *the* emblematic Heinlein hero. He, by an act of grace (the appearance of the "time gate"), does not have to finish his thesis and go get a dull teaching job in the adult world. He runs temporal rings around his fiance Genevieve, dominating her while never having to marry her. He invests the role of his mentor by both being *and* becoming him, thanks to the providential paradox of sequency/simultaneity. He is master of a segment of time, with the reward of being able to live in an imaginary kingdom, the master of many beautiful women. Even entropy, provided he sees it operating on the notebooks and Diktors, must take a million years to wear him down. And yet we readers find him ultimately dull and empty. He has neither personality nor future nor the possibility of spiritual adventure. He is Heinlein's fallen man, who is chosen only to illustrate the ubiquity of damnation. The stigma, in Heinlein, that cleaves universal promise to material process is a denial not only of the future but of all possibility of transcendence. In the paradox of election in a world without the possibility of God as spirit, we face the vision, less of Emerson than his nightside Poe, whose materialist fantasies are circumscribed by a brooding sense of the universe as irrevocably depraved and fallen. On one hand, history and future must lie in the tomb of matter, where existence undulates between fear of premature burial and the lure of material "resurrection," and its amplitude in the end is but the span of a corpse, so that Lazarus and Johann Smith make no advance over Ligeia. On the other, hope of transcendence is ultimately the same life-in-death suspension of biological process we find in the symbiosis between Usher and his house. In like manner, Heinlein's life-defying patriarchs draw parasitically on their maternal past. The "universes" they build, to cite Ray Bradbury in "The Golden Apples of the Sun," are "wormed with man and gravity" (250), equally crumbling. Heinlein has taken the formulas of SF and lengthened their shadows, infusing them with the central problematic of his culture, for which the paradox of the fallen future remains a driving force, and fatal obsession.

Notes

1. One can trace Heinlein's preoccupation with endlessly extending the material line of a single existence from his first published story "Life Line." We find fascinating variants on this ongoing investigation in the "middle period," in works like *Double Star,* where a protagonist called in to impersonate a political figure in danger in the end actually becomes that figure. The older man has been physically replaced (rejuvenated) by the younger one, and, in infinite series, one could imagine a yet younger one, when the time comes, replacing this impersonator. *Time Enough for Love* carries this search to obsessive and monstrous extremes, and the last novels only build on this.

Works Cited

Bradbury, Ray. *The Golden Apples of the Sun.* Garden City, NY: Doubleday, 1953.

Delany, Samuel R. "Reflection on Historical Models." *Starboard Wine: More Notes on the Language of Science Fiction.* Pleasantville, NY: Dragon Press, 1984.

Emerson, Ralph Waldo. "Experience," *The American Tradition in Literature,* 3rd ed. Vol. 1. Ed. Sculley Bradley, Richmond Croom Beatty, and E. Hudson Long. New York: Grosset and Dunlap, 1967.

———. "Nature." *The American Tradition in Literature.*

———. "The Over-Soul." *The American Tradition in Literature.*

Heinlein, Robert A. *Beyond This Horizon.* Reading: Fantasy Press, 1948.

———. "The Black Pits of Luna." *The Past through Tomorrow.*

———. "By His Bootstraps." *The Menace from Earth.* New York: Signet Books, 1957.

———. *The Cat Who Walks through Walls.* New York: Putnam's, 1985.

———. *Citizen of the Galaxy.* New York: Scribner's, 1957.

———. "Coventry." *The Past through Tomorrow.*

———. "Common Sense." *Orphans of the Sky.* New York: Berkley Books, 1963.

———. *Expanded Worlds: The New Worlds of Robert A. Heinlein.* New York: Grosset and Dunlap, 1980.

———. *Friday.* New York: Holt, Reinhart, Winston, 1982.

———. *Glory Road.* New York: Putnam's, 1963.

———. *Grumbles from the Grave.* New York: Del Rey/Ballantine, 1989.

———. "Gulf." *Assignment in Eternity.* Reading: Fantasy Press, 1953.

———. *Have Space Suit, Will Travel.* New York: Scribner's, 1958.

———. *I Will Fear No Evil.* New York: Putnam's, 1980.

———. *Job: A Comedy of Justice.* New York: Del Rey/Ballantine, 1984.

———. "Life Line." *The Past through Tomorrow.*

———. *Number of the Beast.* London: New English Library/Times Mirror, 1980.

———. *The Past through Tomorrow.* New York: Berkley Books, 1967.

———. *The Puppet Masters.* Garden City: Doubleday, 1951.

———. *To Sail beyond the Sunset.* New York: Ace/Putnam, 1987.

———. *Starship Troopers.* New York: Putnam's, 1959.

———. *Stranger in a Strange Land.* New York: Putnam's, 1961.

———. *Time for the Stars.* New York: Scribner's, 1956.

———. *Time Enough for Love.* New York: Putnam's, 1973.

———. "Universe." *Orphans of the Sky.*

Holman, C. Hugh. *A Handbook to Literature.* 3rd ed. New York: Bobbs Merrill, 1962.

Usher, Robin Leslie. "Robert Heinlein: Theologist?" *Foundation* 54 (Spring 1992).

Rafeeq O. McGiveron (essay date July 1996)

SOURCE: McGiveron, Rafeeq O. "Heinlein's Solar System, 1940-1952." *Science Fiction Studies* 23, no. 2 (July 1996): 245-52.

[*In the following essay, McGiveron explores the role of extraterrestrials in Heinlein's fiction.*]

"Noisy" Rhysling, the wandering blind poet of the spaceways in Robert A. Heinlein's **"The Green Hills of Earth"** (1947), sings,

> We've tried each spinning space mote
> And reckoned its true worth:
> Take us back again to the homes of men
> On the cool, green hills of Earth.
>
> (*Past* 373)

Despite his apparent dismissal of "the harsh bright soil of Luna" and the jungles of a pulp-fiction Venus "Crawling with unclean death," Rhysling can not help but admit the beauty of "Saturn's rainbow rings," "the frozen night on Titan" (*Past* 372-23), and, in another poem, the canals and graceful towers of a Lowellian Mars (*Past* 366-67). Reckoning the true worth of the Solar System Heinlein created throughout the 1940s and early 1950s, however, reveals more than simply an admiration for rugged beauty.

One notable characteristic of much of Heinlein's early work is his use of a Solar System inhabited in the past or present by four different species of nonhuman intelligences. Heinlein depicted these species first in magazine stories published in the 1940s and enriched his treatment of them in a number of juvenile novels published in the late 1940s and early 1950s. Certain of his stories written at this time, of course, do not fit into this scheme. For example, though it was published as part of the FUTURE HISTORY series, the story "'—We Also Walk Dogs'" (1941) postulates not only aliens on "three planets [including unlikely Jupiter] and four major satellites" (*Past* 331) but also a breakthrough in gravity control which fortunately is not carried over into any other tale. Many of the other FUTURE HISTORY stories simply do not deal with aliens at all, and after 1952 the novels either shift from the earlier pattern or leave the Solar System altogether. Yet the majority of Heinlein's early works which deal significantly with the diverse inhabitants of the Solar System do fit into a general pattern.

Heinlein's alien worlds of the 1940s and early 1950s not only provide colorful settings but also serve the didactic purpose of humbling the human species. Rather than simply being threatening monsters to outthink and outshoot, Heinlein's intelligent aliens teach his characters—and us—that the cosmos easily weeds out the morally or intellectually unfit and that human beings still have much to learn about controlling their baser instincts. The extinct Selenites and inhabitants of the hypothetical Fifth Planet provide a warning against hubris, while the living Venerians and Martians show some ideals for which we should strive.

Other critics, of course, have discussed didacticism in Heinlein's early fiction, often rather derisively. To Brian W. Aldiss, for example, "Heinlein is often verbose and pedantic," "a straw-chewing technophile who would tell God himself that He was wrong" (268). H. Bruce Franklin sees Heinlein's juvenile novels as "optimistic, expansionary, [and] pulsing with missionary zeal . . ." (73). George Edgar Slusser comments dismissively, "Rather than simply show us how things work, he has always been ready to tell us how they should work. Heinlein is, and always has been, a dogmatic optimist, a soapbox preacher who peddles his pet theories in the guise of fiction" (*RAH* i). Heinlein thus is chastised not only for his particular views but simply for daring to express them.

Not all critics agree, however, with such an easy dismissal. Jack Williamson, for one, does not see being optimistic or expressing opinions as inherently damning: "Considering the Scribner's books as a group, we can claim for them a major role in the evolution of modern science fiction. Cer-

tainly they gave many thousand young readers, and thousands not so young, a delightful introduction to the genre. Built on sound futurology, they still make a fine primer for the new reader" (30-31). This assessment fits with Heinlein's outlook, for he claimed that "science fiction prepares young people to live and survive in a world of ever-continuing change by teaching them that the world does change. Since that is the only sort of world we have, science fiction leads in the direction of mental health, of adaptability" (*SF* 61). If Williamson and Heinlein are correct—which I believe them to be—then investigating the pattern of Heinlein's earlier work may be just as important as looking at his later, more complex novels. C. W. Sullivan III contends that, with their "carefully integrated" components of "adventure, sociology, and science," Heinlein's juveniles "are still 'contemporary,' and are among the best science fiction in the YA range" (64). Fred Erisman finds that Heinlein's use of aliens shows us that "the [human] race must outgrow its inherent racism" (224), and Williamson has observed that the extraterrestrials of Heinlein's juveniles "often serve as teachers for the maturing heroes" (19). To date, however, no critic yet has examined Heinlein's early inhabited Solar System in any detail.

In *Space Cadet* (1948) a cadet of the Interplanetary Patrol is informed that

> The arts of space and warfare are the least part of your education. . . . Much more important is the world around you, the planets and their inhabitants—extraterrestrial biology, history, cultures, psychology, law and institutions, treaties and conventions, planetary ecologies, system ecology, interplanetary economics, applications of extraterritorialism, comparative religious customs, law of space, to mention a few.
>
> (§6:72)

When the cadet questions the utility of studying the extinct inhabitants of the Moon, since "they've been dead for millions of years," he is told blandly, "Keeps your mind loosened up" (§6:73). As readers learn, the civilizations of the past teach humanity some valuable lessons.

Heinlein first uses extraterrestrials in **"Blowups Happen"** (1940), employing the extinct Selenites to show Terran nuclear physicists that Earth's important yet dangerous fission reactor, aptly named "The Big Bomb," must be moved into orbit to avoid a possible catastrophe. Because in this story scientists have "proved" that lunar cratering could not have been caused by meteoric bombardment or volcanism, the only remaining answer is that the Moon is "dead by suicide!" (*Past* 103). An astronomer explains the scenario:

> Perhaps they knew the danger they ran, but wanted power so badly that they were willing to gamble the life of their race. Perhaps they were ignorant of the ruinous possibilities of their little machines, or perhaps their mathematicians assured them that it would not happen.
>
> But we will never know . . . no one will ever know. For it blew up, and killed them—it killed their planet.
>
> (*Past* 103)

In this story, at least, the Selenites are a sufficient example, and the brash young human species avoids the mistakes of another world's past. As David N. Samuelson notes, "The solutions are simplistic, [and] events happen with miraculous speed and coincidence, but the problems are built up seriously enough . . . if we allow for adventure magazine oversimplification" (11). For readers today, over half a century after its first publication, the story still is an appropriate metaphor in a world of dwindling resources and increasing technological complexity.

Heinlein toys with an inhabited Moon again in *Rocket Ship Galileo* (1947), yet in this novel he suggests, rather more bleakly and more realistically, that our problems usually cannot be solved by mere technological fixes. In the post-Hiroshima age a teenaged astronaut of the *Galileo* explains his theory that the devastation of the Moon could not have been accidental:

> Look at Tycho. That's where they set off the biggest ammunition dump on the planet. It cracked the whole planet. I'll bet somebody worked out a counter-weapon that worked too well. It set off every atom bomb on the moon all at once and it ruined them!
>
> (§11:121).

As in the earlier story, the explosions blew off the lunar atmosphere and let the seas boil away, yet here Heinlein's caution hits even closer to home. Rather than a mere accident, the Moon people *"had one atomic war too many"* (§11:120); the war might have been prevented by a change in values or morality but certainly not by simple engineering.

Of similar didactic value is Heinlein's use of the hypothetical Fifth Planet, Lucifer, whose breakup was imagined to have formed the Asteroid Belt. He refers to the planet peripherally in *Farmer in the Sky* (1950) and in the lightweight *The Rolling Stones* (1952), but it is the earlier *Space Cadet* which really puts Lucifer to use. Although, as in the discussion of the Selenites, Lucifer is mentioned only in what is essentially a 300-word aside, it fits well into Heinlein's concept of the inhabited Solar System. In addition to learning that the planet was once inhabited— "probably the most important discovery in System-study since they opened the diggings in Luna" (§12:148)— scientists find that the planet was broken apart "nearly half a billion years ago" (§12:141) not by natural forces but by war. Whereas the Selenites of **"Blowups Happen"** and *Rocket Ship Galileo* merely rendered their world uninhabitable, the Fifth Planet actually "was disrupted by artificial nuclear explosion. In other words, they did it themselves." According to the captain of the ship bringing the discovery sunward, "we have more reason than ever to be proud of our Patrol—and our responsibility is even heavier than we had thought" (§12:148); again Heinlein soberingly reminds us that any "solution" is not a technological one but a moral one instead.

Heinlein originally had hoped to return to the Fifth Planet, sending the characters from *Rocket Ship Galileo* there in a novel to be titled *The Mystery of the Broken Planet*

(*Grumbles* 43). This book, unfortunately, was never written, but in *Between Planets* (1951) Heinlein returns to the idea that even the cleverest species are fallible and mortal. Because of its intelligent Venerian "dragons" and teddybear-like "move-overs"—not to mention its differing political history and another miraculous technological breakthrough—this novel does not fit into the general scheme of his Future History or the rest of the juveniles. However, warning of the fallibility and mortality of all species again is given by the Fifth Planet, whose grand First System Empire left "ruins on the floor of two oceans . . . and four other planets" (§2:22). If even "the noblest planet of them all, the home of empire" (§2:23) could misstep on the path of intellectual evolution and disappear almost without a trace, surely less experienced humanity should tread with care.

Yet Heinlein creates not only self-destructive worlds but flourishing ones as well, though the species of these latter ones often thrive in ways which humanity is only beginning to learn to appreciate. Whereas Luna and the Fifth Planet remind us most glaringly that pride must be tempered with wisdom, Venus and Mars show us examples of the wisdom for which we eventually must strive. Humans, claims a psychology-trained officer in *Space Cadet,* basically are motivated by money, pride, or ethics, yet "The Martian is another sort of cat, and so is the Venerian" (§9:111). This important difference is what makes the inhabitants of Venus and Mars worthy of our attention.

Heinlein first works with Venus in **"Logic of Empire"** (1941), but here the indigenous culture is drawn rather unambitiously. The lisping amphibian Venerians merely tag along with the human colonists, hoping to bum a "'thigarek' . . . the staple medium of trade when dealing with the natives" (**Past** 398). *Space Cadet* fleshes out a Venerian civilization much more satisfying and more fitting for Heinlein's overall view of intelligent species' place in the cosmos. Whereas the earlier natives are caricatures added merely for local color, the Venerians of *Space Cadet* are subtle reminders that humans are not necessarily lords of the cosmos; the natives are more scientifically proficient, socially complex, and morally enviable than anyone previously had supposed.

Although the "Little People" do not appear to have the great technological infrastructure that human civilization has, they possess an understanding of science so thorough that it seems more common knowledge than a separate discipline. Despite their apparent lack of tools or machines, the Little People perform many technical feats almost unnoticed, making one cadet realize that "the Venerians [are] not the frog-seal-beaver creatures his Earth-side prejudices had led him to think" (§16:193). Their cities, for example, are built beneath lakes and are lit with "some sort of glowing, orange clusters" (§14:168-69) whose workings the humans are unable to explain. "The Little People make little use of power, they hardly use metal" (§17:212), yet they produce a fabric which cannot be cut with the cadets' knives (§14:170). One human claims, with no little justification, "They've forgotten more about chemistry than we'll ever learn" (§17:214): the Venerians create chemical solutions which protect against a century of Venus's harsh climate (§17: 202-03) or are caustic enough to eat through a spaceship's hull (§15:177, §16:193). For the humans the Venerians are able to synthesize Terran maple syrup from a sample and, more impressively, the liquified gases which make up rocket propellants (§17:211-14). The Little People, "to whom even a common door latch [is] a puzzle" (§16:193), prove to the cadets "that there may be more ways of doing engineering than the big, muscley, noisy ways we've worked out" (§17:212).

The Venerians whom the cadets encounter in the planet's unexplored equatorial regions are "more civilized than the ones around the [polar] colonies." When one human asks, "What *is* civilization?" another hedges, "Never mind the philosophy .·. ." (§17:212). Although the humans thus cannot quite name the difference, it is not merely a matter of technical prowess. The equatorial Venerians prove "that the planet has only one language . . ." (§14:166), and they somehow have heard of the Patrol even though no contact had previously been made (§15:181). Both of these important factors suggest that, far from being broken into isolated bands, the Venerians belong to a sophisticated society in which communication is planet-wide. Though they do not delve too deeply into the "philosophy," at least the humans learn that the Little People are not only more scientific than they had supposed but more socially complex also.

Yet perhaps the most important lesson of Venerian civilization is its moral progress. While one cadet discovers that he cannot make one of the Little People understand the existence of other planets and stars (§16:194), the Venerian herself "continually [uses] words and concepts . . . which [can] not be straightened out . . ." even with the help of their best translator, so that "He began to get hazily the idea that Th'wing was the sophisticated one and that he, Matt, was the ignorant outsider. 'Sometimes I think,' he told Tex, 'that Th'wing thinks I am an idiot studying hard to become a moron—but flunking the course'" (§16:195). Perhaps the cadet is essentially correct. He may be puzzled by Venerian technical terms, but it seems just as probable that he cannot fully comprehend the social or moral system of Venus either. A cadet raised in one of the polar colonies states with authority that "the Little People just don't have the cussedness in them that humans have" (§14:171); they have, after all, "never heard of" war (§16:190). The Venerians remind us that human morality still needs considerable improvement.

When writing about Martians in *Red Planet* (1949) Heinlein does not need to make that species' technical achievements as subtle as those of the Venerians. Envisioned in the tradition begun by "the immortal Dr. Percival Lowell" (§2:15) and continued by over four decades of science fiction writers, Heinlein's Mars is a slowly dying world crisscrossed by great canals thousands of kilometers long. In addition, the Martians use clever holographic techniques to simulate the outdoors within their social rooms (§3:35, §7:105), hidden environmental engineering to raise atmospheric pressure in their dwellings without an airlock (§3:36, §7:104), and mind-reading apparatus which can replay a lifetime of memories in mere hours (§8:112-14, 118). A pair of teenaged human colonists discover a remarkable system of ancient, ultra-highspeed "subways" far beneath the planet's surface (§7:108-09) and, more surprisingly, that the Martians "had interplanetary flight millions of years back . . . had it and gave it up" (§14:184). When enraged, even modern Martians are able to make an enemy disappear inexplicably (§3:34, §13:179, 180-81).

As with the Venerians, however, far more important than the Martians' technological achievements is their moral progress. Indeed, Samuelson contends that "the reader's learning to understand this strange world and its inhabitants" is more important than the human plot of oppression and revolution which drives the novel (123). The Martians have advanced far enough that they seem to have little of the greed and impatience which still threaten humanity. A telling excerpt from "Noisy" Rhysling's "Grand Canal" reads,

> Bone-tired the race that raised the Towers, forgotten are their lores;
> Long gone the gods who shed the tears which lap these crystal shores.
> Slow beats the time-worn heart of Mars beneath this icy sky;
> The thin air whispers voicelessly that all who live must die—
>
> Yet still the lacy Spires of Truth sing Beauty's madrigal
> And she herself will ever dwell along the Grand Canal!
>
> (*Past* 366)

Rhysling's poem captures not only the Martians' renunciation of the fleeting and unimportant but, with its reference to beauty, their wise embrace of the soothing and aesthetic.

In *Red Planet* we are informed that "no two Martian cities looked alike. It was as if each were a unique work of art, each representing the thoughts of a different artist" (§3:32). The buildings are "filled with an atmosphere of peace and security" (§8:107), and, as the main character learns, the Martians themselves are similarly reassuring: "the Martian's voice had a strange effect on him. Croaking and uncouth though it was, it was filled with such warmth and sympathy and friendliness that the native no longer frightened him. Instead he seemed like an old and trusted friend" (§3:30-31). Moreover, though they have just met, the giant three-legged Martians generously—and improbably—include the colonist and his friend in their important water-sharing ceremony (§3:37-38). Despite their physical differences, "Martians are good people" (§7:101). Clearly beings who radiate such "a warm glow of friendliness as real as sunshine" (§8:115) have much to teach.

One of the Martians' most significant social activities is "growing together." In **"Ordeal in Space"** (1948) Heinlein describes growing together as "sit[ting] for hours with a friend or a trusted acquaintance, saying nothing, needing to say nothing . . . [The Martians] had so grown together that they needed no government, until the Earthmen came" (352). In *Red Planet* the boys are, again improbably, included:

> For a long time nothing was said. Jim's thoughts drifted away. . . . He came back presently to personal self-awareness and realized that he was happier than he had been in a long time, with no particular reason that he could place. It was a quiet happiness; he felt no desire to laugh nor even to smile, but he was perfectly relaxed and content.
>
> He was acutely aware of the presence of the Martians, of each individual Martian, and was becoming even more aware of them with each drifting minute. He had never noticed before how beautiful they were. . . .
>
> He was aware, too, of Frank beside him and thought about how much he liked him. . . . He wondered why he had never told Frank that he liked him. . . .
>
> Jim . . . lay back, and soaked in the joy of living.
>
> (§3:36-37)

Certainly it is vague and all too easy, yet in a juvenile novel even this slant away from the superficial problems of the everyday world is important.

Apparently central to the Martians' ability to "grow together" is their idea of the "other world." This is one of the "small seasonings of mysticism" which Alexei Panshin notes, rather prosaically, "remind us again that there are more things in heaven and earth than can be explained by *The World Book Encyclopedia*" (52). In *Space Cadet* an officer tries to explain to a cadet that the concept of the "other world" just might be valid, even though the humans do not understand it:

> Let's forget the usual assumption that a Martian is talking in religious symbols when he says that we live just on "one side" while he lives on "both sides." Suppose that what he means is as real as butter and eggs, that he really does live in two worlds at the same time and that we are in the one he regards as unimportant. If you accept that, then it accounts for the Martian being unwilling to waste time talking with us, or trying to explain things to us. He isn't being stuffy, he's being reasonable. Would you waste time trying to explain rainbows to an earthworm?
>
> (§12:143-44)

In *Red Planet* a gruff old doctor, the novel's wisest human character, asks, "can you imagine a people having close and everyday relations with Heaven—*their* heaven—as close and matter of fact as the relations between, say, the United States and Canada?" (§12:165). Apparently the Martians have such relations with their "other world," for in representing humanity before "the judges of mankind's worth" (Slusser, *Classic* 43), the doctor speaks with an an-

cient ghost, "a being . . . that has trouble remembering which millennium he is in . . ." (§14:187). Though the doctor himself—"a warmhearted old curmudgeon serving as the author's mouthpiece" (Franklin 78)—realizes that "The most wildly impossible philosophy of all is materialism" (§9:133), many humans are interested simply in getting Mars "opened up to exploitation" (§3:28). Martian spirituality allows the native inhabitants of Mars a crucial perspective which most humans lack.

As many readers will see, *Red Planet* lays some of the groundwork for *Stranger in a Strange Land* (1961), a complex novel outside the scope of this simple essay. While Heinlein's exploration of Martian culture in this juvenile is more thorough than his treatment of any of his other species, the Martians are no less metaphorical than the others. Despite the solemnities of water sharing, "growing together," and the "other world," the Martians are obviously less an example to follow than a reminder that humanity still has far to progress.

In stories throughout the 1940s and juvenile novels in the early 1950s Robert A. Heinlein created a Solar System whose diverse inhabitants serve the purpose of humbling the brash young human species. While the extinct inhabitants of the Moon and Lucifer remind us that the price of hubris may be self-destruction, Heinlein's Venerians and Martians display some of the wisdom we need to avoid that fate. Hard-headed Heinlein certainly does not suggest that we must engage in water sharing and *grok*—but he does suggest that we still have far to go in our intellectual and moral evolution.

Works Cited

Aldiss, Brian W., and David Wingrove. *Trillion Year Spree: The History of Science Fiction.* NY: Atheneum, 1986.

Erisman, Fred. "Robert Heinlein's Case for Racial Tolerance, 1954-1956." *Extrapolation* 29: 216-26, Fall 1988.

Franklin, H. Bruce. *Robert A. Heinlein: America as Science Fiction.* Science-Fiction Writers Series. NY: Oxford UP, 1980.

Heinlein, Robert A. *Between Planets.* 1951. NY: Ace, n.d.

———. "Blowups Happen." *Astounding Science Fiction,* Sept 1940. *Past* 73-120.

———. *Farmer in the Sky.* 1952. NY: Ballantine, 1975.

———. "The Green Hills of Earth." *Saturday Evening Post,* 8 Feb 1947, *Past* 363-73.

———. *Grumbles from the Grave.* NY: Del Rey, 1989.

———. "Logic of Empire." *Astounding Science Fiction,* Mar 1941. *Past* 375-421.

———. "Ordeal in Space." *Town and Country,* May 1948. *Past* 347-61.

———. *The Past through Tomorrow.* 1967. NY: Berkley, 1975.

———. *Red Planet.* 1949. NY: Del Rey, 1978.

———. *Rocket Ship Galileo.* 1947. NY: Del Rey, 1981.

———. *The Rolling Stones.* 1952. NY: Ace, n.d.

———. "Science Fiction: Its Nature, Faults and Virtues." *The Science Fiction Novel.* 1959. 2nd ed., rev. Ed. Basil Davenport. Chicago: Advent, 1964. 17-63.

———. *Space Cadet.* 1948. NY: Del Rey, 1978.

———. "—We Also Walk Dogs." *Astounding Science Fiction,* Jul 1941. *Past* 319-42.

Panshin, Alexei. *Heinlein in Dimension: A Critical Analysis.* Chicago: Advent, 1968.

Samuelson, David N. "The Frontier Worlds of Robert A. Heinlein." *Voices for the Future: Essays on Major Science Fiction Writers.* Vol. 1. Ed. Thomas D. Clareson. Bowling Green, OH: Bowling Green U Popular P, 1976. 104-52.

Slusser, George Edgar. *The Classic Years of Robert A. Heinlein.* Milford Series. Popular Writers of Today 11. San Bernardino: Borgo, 1977.

———. *Robert A. Heinlein: Stranger in His Own Land.* Milford Series. Popular Writers of Today 1. San Bernardino: Borgo, 1976. [This passage in the Introduction to the first edition has been dropped from the much revised Introduction to the 2nd edition, 1977.—RDM]

Sullivan, C. W., III. "Heinlein's Juveniles: Still Contemporary After All These Years." *ChLA Quarterly* 10 (1985): 64-66.

Williamson, Jack. "Youth Against Space: Heinlein's Juveniles Revisited." *Robert A. Heinlein.* Eds. Joseph D. Olander and Martin Harry Greenberg. Writers of the 21st Century Series. NY: Taplinger, 1978. 15-31.

FURTHER READING

Criticism

Franklin, H. Bruce. *Robert A. Heinlein: America as Science Fiction.* New York: Oxford University Press, 1980, 232 p.
    Traces Heinlein's literary development.

Olander, Joseph D. and Greenberg, Martin Harry, eds. *Robert A. Heinlein.* New York: Taplinger Publishing Co., 1978, 268 p.
    Collection of critical essays.

Slusser, George Edgar. *The Classic Years of Robert A. Heinlein.* San Bernardino, Calif.: Borgo Press, 1977, 63 p.
    Classifies Heinlein's literary career into periods and discusses the defining characteristics of each category.

Usher, Robin Leslie. "Robert A. Heinlein: Theologist?" *Foundation,* no. 54 (spring 1992): 70-86.
    Discusses George Edgar Slusser's critic of Heinlein's work.

Additional coverage of Heinlein's life and career is contained in the following sources published by the Gale Group: *Authors and Artists for Young Adults,* **Vol. 17;** *Beacham's Encyclopedia of Popular Fiction: Biography & Resources,* **Vol. 2;** *Beacham's Guide to Literature for Young Adults,* **Vols. 4, 13;** *Children's Literature Review,* **Vol. 75;** *Contemporary Authors,* **Vols. 1-4R, 125;** *Contemporary Authors New Revision Series,* **Vols. 1, 20, 53;** *Contemporary Literary Criticism,* **Vols. 1, 3, 8, 14, 26, 55;** *Contemporary Popular Writers;* *Dictionary of Literary Biography,* **Vol. 8;** *DISCovering Authors Modules: Popular Fiction and Genre Authors;* *DISCovering Authors 3.0;* *Exploring Short Stories;* *Junior DISCovering Authors;* *Literature and Its Times,* **Vol. 5;** *Major Authors and Illustrators for Children and Young Adults,* **Ed. 1;** *Major Twentieth Century Writers,* **Eds. 1, 2;** *Reference Guide to American Literature,* **Ed. 4;** *St. James Guide to Science Fiction Writers,* **Ed. 4;** *St. James Guide to Young Adult Writers;* *Science Fiction Writers;* *Short Stories for Students,* **Vol. 7; and** *Something About the Author,* **Vols. 9, 56, 69.**

Stephen King
1947-

(Full name Stephen Edwin King; has also written under the pseudonyms Richard Bachman and John Swithen) American short story writer, novelist, screenwriter, essayist, autobiographer, and children's author.

The following entry presents criticism of King's short fiction works from 1988 to 2000. For discussion of King's short fiction career prior to 1988, see *SSC*, Volume 17.

INTRODUCTION

King is a prolific and immensely popular author of horror fiction. In his works, King blends elements of the traditional gothic tale with those of the modern psychological thriller, detective, and science fiction genres. His short fiction features colloquial language, clinical attention to physical detail and emotional states, realistic settings, and an emphasis on contemporary problems. His wide popularity attests to his ability to tap into his reader's fear of and inability to come to terms with evil confronted in the everyday world.

BIOGRAPHICAL INFORMATION

King was born in Portland, Maine, on September 21, 1947. When his father abandoned the family when King was only two years old, his mother moved around with King and his brother until they settled down with relatives in Durham, Maine in 1958. King published his first short story, "I Was a Teenage Grave Robber," in *Comics Review* in 1965. He also wrote his first full-length manuscript while still in high school. King received a scholarship to the University of Main at Orono, where he was very active in student politics and the antiwar movement. After his graduation in 1970, King was unable to get a teaching job; instead he got jobs pumping gas and then working in a laundry. King spent a short time teaching at the Hampden Academy in Hampden, Maine, until the success of his first novel, *Carrie* (1974) enabled him to focus on writing full time. In 1978 he was writer-in-residence and an instructor at the University of Maine at Orono. Several of his novels, novellas, and short stories have been adapted for the screen and television, and King has made cameo appearances in many of them. He has been given numerous awards for his fiction, and has contributed short stories, essays, and reviews to several periodicals.

MAJOR WORKS OF SHORT FICTION

Like his novels, the majority of King's horror tales are characterized by something supernatural or unnatural invading the lives of regular people. In "Night Surf," a group

of six young people in Anson Beach, Maine, gather after surviving the deadly flu virus A6. They spend their time listening to the radio and coming to terms with almost certain death. In "The Raft," four college kids on a raft are systematically grabbed and devoured by a mysterious blob in the water. Critics note that the majority of King's horror stories explore the lives and concerns of people who are traditionally marginalized by society—the young, the old, and women—a factor that is thought to contribute to his immense popularity. Several of King's novellas and short fiction touch on the confusion, anxieties, and insecurity of childhood. For instance, *The Body* chronicles the story of four twelve-year-old boys who set out to find the body of a man struck by a train. On the journey, the protagonist, Gordie, begins a process of maturation and self-discovery and realizes the importance of friendship. The novella was made into a popular film, *Stand by Me*. Another novella, *Apt Pupil,* focuses on a thirteen-year-old boy's discovery of a Nazi war criminal living next door. In the process, the teenager uncovers his own dark, violent side. "The Monkey," collected in *Skeleton Crew,* explores the long-repressed anxiety of Hal, represented by a toy monkey that he believes is evil and responsible for the death of his childhood friend, Johnny. As a child, a terrified Hal threw the toy into a well. Now an adult, Hal returns to his hometown for his aunt's funeral, rediscovers the toy monkey, and is forced to deal with the grief and insecurities from his childhood.

CRITICAL RECEPTION

Commentators note that King's short fiction is often overshadowed by the widespread popularity of his novels. Moreover, some critics maintain that his narrative style and thematic concerns are best suited to the longer form of the novel or novella, and not that of the short story. Since many of King's short stories deal with the anxieties and challenges of adolescence, critics have declared such themes as memory, innocence, child abuse, friendship, and security as central to his work. Furthermore, the representation of women and the role of sexuality in King's fiction has garnered critical attention. Stylistically, his use of repetition and flashback has also been a topic of analysis. Some reviewers contend that King's short fiction is overly sentimental, sometimes derivative, inconsistent in quality, and obsessed with violence and morbidity. Despite critical opinion on his short fiction, King's considerable contributions to modern horror literature are widely acknowledged. Reviewers regard his work as an insightful reflection of the fears, anxieties, and obsessions of the late twentieth century.

PRINCIPAL WORKS

Short Fiction

The Star Invaders [as Steve King] 1964
Night Shift 1978
Creepshow 1982
Different Seasons 1982
Cycle of the Werewolf 1983
Skeleton Crew 1985
Four Past Midnight 1990
Nightmares and Dreamscapes (short stories, poem, and essay) 1993
Everything's Eventual: 14 Dark Tales 2002

Other Major Works

Carrie: A Novel of a Girl with a Frightening Power (novel) 1974
'Salem's Lot (novel) 1975
Rage [as Richard Bachman] (novel) 1977
The Shining (novel) 1977
The Stand (novel) 1978
Another Quarter Mile: Poetry (poetry) 1979
The Dead Zone (novel) 1979
The Long Walk [as Richard Bachman] (novel) 1979
Firestarter (novel) 1980
Cujo (novel) 1981
Roadwork: A Novel of the First Energy Crisis [as Richard Bachman] (novel) 1981
Stephen King's Danse Macabre (nonfiction) 1981
The Dark Tower: The Gunslinger (novel) 1982
The Running Man [as Richard Bachman] (novel) 1982
Christine (novel) 1983
Pet Sematary (novel) 1983
Cat's Eye (screenplay) 1984
The Eyes of the Dragon (juvenile novel) 1984
The Talisman [with Peter Straub] (novel) 1984
Thinner [as Richard Bachman] (novel) 1984
It (novel) 1986
Misery (novel) 1987
The Tommyknockers (novel) 1987
The Dark Half (novel) 1989
The Dark Tower: The Drawing of Three (novel) 1989
My Pretty Pony (children's novel) 1989
Needful Things (novel) 1991
Dolores Claiborne (novel) 1992
Gerald's Game (novel) 1992
Rose Madder (novel) 1995
Desperation (novel) 1996
Green Mile: A Novel in Six Parts (novel) 1996
The Regulators [as Richard Bachman] (novel) 1996
The Two Dead Girls (novel) 1996
Bag of Bones (novel) 1997
Wizard and Glass (novel) 1998
The Girl Who Loved Tom Gordon (juvenilia) 1999
Hearts in Atlantis (novel) 1999
Storm of the Century (screenplay) 1999
On Writing: A Memoir of the Craft (nonfiction) 2000
Black House [with Peter Straub] (novel) 2001
Dreamcatcher (novel) 2001
From a Buick 8 (novel) 2002

CRITICISM

Joseph Reino (essay date 1988)

SOURCE: Reino, Joseph. "Fantasies of Summer and Fall: Full of Sound and Fury." In *Stephen King: The First Decade,* Carrie *to* Pet Sematary, pp. 117-35. Boston: Twayne Publishers, 1988.

[*In the following essay, Reino provides a thematic and stylistic analysis of the novellas comprising* Different Seasons.]

With brief seasonal subtitles, *Different Seasons* (1982) attempts to bind together four unusual novellas of varying lengths and moods. Taken from the optimistic "Essay on Man" of the eighteenth-century English poet Alexander Pope, "Hope Springs Eternal" is the subtitle of the vernal season, *Rita Hayworth and Shawshank Redemption*—a subtitle that is, at the tag-end of the violence-ridden twentieth century, little more than a pleasant, but not quite believable, cliché. The second and longest of the novellas, the sinister *Apt Pupil,* is a "Summer of Corruption"—an apparent variation on the "winter of our discontent" from the oft-quoted opening line of Shakespeare's *Richard III.* The third and autumnal season, *The Body* (widely acknowledged as the most nearly autobiographical of King's works), flirts with the attractive deceptions of an American Eden and is, consequently, a "Fall from Innocence." The fourth, *The Breathing Method,* easily the most fantastic of the group, is appropriately subtitled with Shakespeare's late fantasy-romance, *The Winter's Tale.* While this brilliant quartet of tales does not deal with the unabashed horrors and terrors of the more famous novels, nevertheless, according to King's personal observations, "elements of horror can be found in all of the tales, not just in *The Breathing Method*—that business with the slugs in *The Body* is pretty gruesome, as is much of the dream imagery in *Apt Pupil*" (*DS,* 502). Although King raised sharp objection to psychiatrist-author Janet Jeppson, when she suggested that he has been "writing about it ever since"—"it" being the train accident that killed a young playmate—he admits in his afterword to *Different Seasons* that, with respect to horror in general, only "God knows why," sooner or later, "my mind always seems to turn back in that [gothic] direction" (502).

Rita Hayworth and Shawshank Redemption, the first "season," is the most strangely titled of all King's stories, the kind of story ("with a homosexual rape scene") that Susan Norton's mother complained that "sissy-boy" novelist Ben Mears had written. Taking place in an imaginary Maine prison called Shawshank, the story is supposedly narrated by one of the inmates (nicknamed "Red"), a clever entrepreneur who can "get it for you" for a price, that is, obtain whatever a prisoner might like, or need, from the outside world: pictures, comic books, posters, panties from a wife or girl friend, etc. Red's hundred-page story concerns a banker-prisoner, Andy Dufresne, sentenced to life imprisonment because of incriminating circumstantial evidence in the murder of his wife and her lover. Though consistently denied parole, and tragically unfortunate in attempting to prove his innocence, Andy becomes the financial wizard of the prison ("quiet, well-spoken, respectful, non-violent" [95]), with an unusual smile and a cool faraway look. Red is intrigued by Andy's strange requests, two in particular: a rock-hammer and a Rita Hayworth poster. What Andy is doing with these objects—the Hayworth poster changing to other shapely females as the years go by—is revealed only at the end of the novella, when the reader learns that for years and years (1949-75)

Andy had been digging himself a tunnel, and successfully concealing the cellblock escape route (the "hole") behind sexy, and inevitably distracting, pin-up posters.

Both the prolonged tunneling and the subsequent escape are as improbable as the incriminating evidence that incarcerated Andy in Shawshank State Prison in the first place (18-25). But King makes the narrative plausible by having whole sections of Red's account reported as gossip, rumor, and prison talk, slowly turning Andy Dufresne into a legendary folk hero about whom (like Robert Frost's Paul Bunyon, Washington Irving's Icabod Crane, or some medieval Arthurian knight) one tends to expect the unexpected. Unlike the final section of *Carrie,* which attempts to verify everything through newspaper reports, eyewitness accounts, and court transcripts, here King exercises his ingenuity by having everything sustained through sheer guesswork and speculation.

Of all the plot improbabilities in *Rita Hayworth and Shawshank Redemption,* however, the most hilarious is the author's success in hiding in his rectum a one-hundred-page (or more) manuscript about Andy Dufresne's life, prison escape, and detailed plans for secret life in Mexico (30, 101). On the occasion of the author-prisoner's parole, this rectal secreting is done so as to escape detection from guards during a strip-down physical examination prior to final release. Thus what the average King enthusiast has been devouring with such interest derives from the same part of the human anatomy that is naturally used to eliminate foul-smelling body wastes, but was "unnaturally" violated (and presumably also much enlarged) by the prison "sisters" during one of their many sodomitic escapades.[1] Both this rectal literary joke, and the impossibles and improbables of the quasi-legendary prison career of Andy Dufresne, give the Popean subtitle, "Hope Springs Eternal," a rather hopeless resonance indeed—implying, one supposes, that if you believe this "story," you will believe just about anything.[2] The "redemption" part of the title has various implications, not the least of which is the elimination of the Bible-quoting Warden Norton, who never so much as cracked a smile and "would have felt right at home" with those infernal New England preachers, the "Mathers, Cotton and Increase" (56).

The Breathing Method, the fourth and last "season," and a gothic/fantasy successor to such traditional Christmas stories as the medieval romance *Sir Gawain and the Green Knight* and Charles Dickens's *Christmas Carol,* is an out-and-out tall tale best suited to winter in which, as one editor points out in connection with Shakespeare's *Winter's Tale,* "no one expects any probability."[3] In folklore and legend (the Roman *Saturnalia,* ancient rituals surrounding the birth of Mithra, the tradition of the *modrenacht* among the Angles, etc.), the season of the winter solstice (21 December) is often filled with fantasy. The main incident in the fourth season is the birth of a child from an accidentally decapitated woman (Sandra Stansfield) occurring "on the eve of that birth we have celebrated for two thousand years" (462). The young woman is unmarried and wearing a false wedding ring, and this mysterious and/or magical birth thus parallels, or even parodies, the traditional Christian belief in the virgin birth recounted in the gospel of Luke. Despite the potential for blasphemous satire (which King does not elsewhere resist), the parallel is not overstressed, and at several points only gently reinforced: (1) by a quotation from a Roman Stoic that might well have come from the Pauline epistles, to the effect that *"There is no comfort without pain; thus we define salvation through suffering"* (461, 482-83); and (2) by having the tall tale of an impossible Christmas Eve birth told by an eighty-year-old physician, who thereby parallels the author of the gospel of Luke, traditionally believed to have been a physician, from whom the story of the virgin birth is almost exclusively derived.

Without demeaning the power of these spring and winter narratives, **Rita Hayworth** and **Breathing Method** appear as prologue and epilogue to the central tales of summer and fall that are among King's finest creations: **Apt Pupil** and **The Body.** The former concerns a thirteen year old's not-quite-accidental discovery of a Nazi war criminal living secretly in California, while the latter recounts the adventures of several twelve year olds who set out to find the dead body of a boy struck by a train, and in the process one of them (the teller of the tale) makes significant discoveries about his personal sensitivity and poetic proclivities. Taken together, **Apt Pupil** and **The Body** are youth-oriented companion pieces, offering in-depth analyses of young boys who can easily take their place among King's other preteens: Mark Petrie, Richie Boddin, Danny and Ralphie Glick, Danny Torrance, and Marty Coslaw. Interestingly, in both **Apt Pupil** and **The Body,** King again explores depth after desperate depth of feelings about father-son relationships that are central to a sympathetic understanding of much of his work—a psychological dimension too often glossed over by reviewers, who seem to harp exclusively on elements of terror, horror, and the supernatural.[4]

CORPSES THAT REFUSE TO STAY BURIED

The protagonist of **Apt Pupil** is a thirteen-year-old "innocent" in the pleasant-enough beginnings of this California revelation, but a seventeen-year-old criminal in its tragic conclusion. A stereotypical American boy of WASP background—the family was Methodist (164)—Todd Bowden has the kind of "summer" face that might easily be found advertising Kellogg's Corn Flakes: "hair the color of ripe corn, white even teeth, lightly tanned skin marred by not even the first shadow of adolescent acne" (109). Despite the gradual deterioration of Todd's personality throughout this 175-page "Summer of Corruption," his face matures but never loses its boyish attractiveness: "young, blond, and white" (281). Even toward the end of **Apt Pupil,** when Todd is one of four victorious boys named to Southern Cal's All Stars, the newspaper photograph is "grinning openly out at the world from beneath the bill of his baseball cap" (254). When identified as the probable killer of local derelicts, he is remembered as having an "ain't-life-grand" air about his improbable face (282).

In addition to a happy-time television reaction to nearly everything (good or bad), several other aspects of Todd's personality—always superficially favorable—receive considerable attention: his "aptness" as a school student, his high degree of intelligence and foresight, his full-blooded teenage slang, and his outstanding athletic abilities. These apparent positives in Todd's All-American makeup, however, inevitably deteriorate. So boyishly appealing and attractive at first, showing "perfect teeth that had been fluoridated since the beginning of his life and bathed thrice a day in Crest toothpaste" (113), his smiles sour into the sardonic expression of a psychopath beaming out "rich and radiant" (131) as he eagerly absorbs Nazi stories about gas chambers, conspirators hung by piano wires, or lampshades designed of human skin. On one occasion, when the old concentration camp commander (Kurt Dussander, whom Todd all-too-willingly befriends) is forced to tell Todd about the experimental nerve gas (poetically nicknamed *Pegasus*) that caused its victims to scream, laugh, vomit, and helplessly defecate, the All-American Boy is happily consuming two delicious chocolate Ring Dings. Even old reprobate Dussander reacts negatively, not only in being forced to remember horrors he himself eagerly perpetrated in German concentration camps, but especially because of Todd's enthusiastic "That was a good story, Mr. Dussander" (136). Ironically, King puts in the mouth of the old Nazi, wanted by the Israelis for being "one of the greatest butchers of human beings ever to live" (262), reactions that are likely to pass through readers themselves when he says aloud to the boy, "You are a monster." Innocent-looking Todd reminds Dussander that "according to the books I read, *you're* the monster, Mr. Dussander," who sent thirty-five hundred a day into the ovens "before the Russians came and made you stop" (127). The next time Dussander (in something resembling teenage slang) is tempted to damn Todd as "putrid little monster," he only *thinks* it (135), keeping to himself his disgust with Todd's behavior, even though that behavior is viciously patterned after his own (giving an inkling of King's attitude toward the relationship of postwar American behavior to the Nazis.)

The name Todd suggests "toddy," a pleasant drink of brandy or whiskey mixed with hot water, sugar, and spices. Like the boy's blue-eyed All-American appearance, therefore, his name has sweet connotations. Winter suggests a sinister undercurrent—quite apt, one might add—to this attractive first name, since "Todd" is similar to the German word for death, *Tod.*[5] Kurt Dussander's name derives from *Peter Kurtin, Monster of Düsseldorf,* a novel about an actual criminal included in Father Callahan's recollections of gothic junk in *'Salem's Lot* (296). But Dussander's American pseudonym is the kinder-sounding "Arthur Denker," the first name deriving from the mythic medieval king,[6] and the patronym from yet another German word, "thinker" (*Denker*). The fake last name covertly suggests the octogenarian's cleverness in concealing his true identity by skillfully avoiding detection and capture by sharp Israeli authorities for so many years. Dussander's ability to "think" things through is so masterful that inexperienced Todd, who at one point had the potential of being an absolute blackmailer, comes to feel that "his skull had turned to window-glass and all things were flashing inside in large letters" (201). The living room of Dussander's house contains a neat symbol of all the false facades in *Apt Pupil* (Americans and ex-Nazis included): "the fake fireplace" that was "faced with fake bricks" (115).

The Jekyll/Hyde qualities of the Todd/Denker names seem—and indeed *are*—the exact opposite of what they pleasantly suggest, and have parallels in some unusual literary techniques. The most important of these is the series of empty-headed clichés, banalities, proverbs, and (on Todd's part) slang simplicities that are placed in plot situations in such a way as to point up their utter shallowness. As names reverse (e.g., from sweet "toddy" to grim "death"), so do the cliché-drenched conversations among the doomed older characters.

Important among these typically American pseudoprofundities are the following. Todd's parents "don't believe in spanking" because "corporal punishment causes more problems than it cures" (115). Todd's father (Dick Bowden) thinks that "kids should find out about life as soon as they can—the bad as well as the good." His silly rationale is that "life is a tiger you have to grab by the tail, and if you don't know the nature of the beast it will eat you up" (120). Dick Bowden balances off his wife's cliché, "Waste not, want not," with his own innocuous "Not by a long chalk" (138). Todd's teacher (the well-intentioned Mrs. Anderson) lectures the students of the California school (of which sweet-looking Todd is one) about finding "YOUR GREAT INTEREST," hers being "collecting nineteenth-century post cards" (117). The guidance counselor (satirically nicknamed "Rubber Ed," "Sneaker Pete," and the "Ked Man" by mocking high school students) idiotically supposes that his rubber-covered Keds gives him "real rapport" with the students. He too has an assortment of dismal colloquialisms on which he thinks he can structure educational success: that he could "get right down to it" with the kids, "get into their hangups," knew what a "bummer" was, and understood and sympathized when "someone was doing a number on your head" (166).

The upshot of all this "right-thinking," superficial claptrap that passes for wisdom—a parody of certain educational practices that dominated American society during the period of the 1976 bicentennial, the time-frame of the story (206)—is that Todd Bowden, one of the young people these insights were supposed to direct into proper channels of patriotic behavior, becomes a Nazi admirer and hobo murderer. King is not saying that benign and "liberating" clichés are inherently wrong or that they cause Todd's inclination toward social misbehavior. Rather, his gothic perspective is that benevolent philosophies, reduced to thoughtless aphorisms and innocuous clichés, are utterly powerless against the boy's adamantine malevolence. Todd, too, is entrapped in his own kind of verbal superficiality, mostly teenage American slang that might have been considered "cute" in something other than a Califor-

nia neo-Nazi context: "Gotcha," "Right on," "You'll go ape," "School's cool," "Crazy, baby," "It blows my wheels," "Blasts from the past," etc. Only infrequently does Todd trot out some really humorous wit, as on the occasion when his mother brings up a matter that Todd does not want to deal with, and he leaves her with the wise crack: "I've gotta put an egg in my shoe and beat it" (134). All too frequently, unfortunately, his mind reverts to mindless banalities, as when, entrapped by Dussander, he thinks of a "cartoon character with an anvil suspended over its head" (202).

Possibly offensive to some readers—and this may explain the negative criticism of *Apt Pupil* by some reviewers—is the fact that the Nazi proves the more elegant and perceptive in language skills than the sentimental, cliché-ridden Americans, who—as Dussander scornfully points out—"put photographs of firemen rescuing kittens from trees on the front pages of city newspapers" (202). Thus at the dinner table with Todd's parents, when offered another glass of cognac by Todd's mother, Dussander gracefully declines with the proverb, "One must never overdo the sublime" (149). When in the office of the guidance counselor, Dussander convinces his listener by pretending he "was raised to believe that a man's family came before everything" (169)—a cliché, to be sure, but just about the only one in the entire novella known to be false at the time it is uttered. When Todd is completely entrapped by the old Nazi's psychological counterthrusts, Dussander comforts the boy by suggesting that "no situation is static" (202). When confronted with murderous hatred in Todd's eyes ("that dark, burning, speculative glance"), Dussander realizes that he had to protect himself, because "one underestimates at one's own risk" (175). At the complex business of what might be called "verbal survival," Dussander is extremely crafty: careful to manipulate false words, while never falling victim to them, always rising above his own (and others') deceptive language to remain—desperately necessary for a former Nazi—free to survive! Adolf Hitler once asserted that "something of even the most shameless prevarication will find lodging and stick,'" but Dussander is several notches beyond mere Nazi lies and prevarications. Whatever he does, he pulls off with considerable finesse and with an enviable command of language that makes him all the more dangerous because his basic malevolence is so difficult to detect by naive Americans—like the Bowdens and the Frenches in this novella—who are too easily satisfied with facades and superficialities. As Dussander says on the occasion of his deceptive visit to the office of the guidance counselor in the guise of Todd's grandfather: "In my time I have stayed ahead of Wiesenthal and pulled the wool over the eyes of Himmler himself," and "if I cannot fool one American public school teacher, I will pull my winding-shroud around me and crawl down into my grave" (165).

One of the perhaps less obvious purposes of *Apt Pupil* is to dramatize the confrontation between an intelligent but inexperienced teenager (whose German name means "death") and an intelligent but far more sinister, yet "extremely urbane," ex-Nazi (whose German pseudonym means "thinker"). King engages in a skillfull balancing act, seesawing the blackmail potential of the boy over against the psychological counterthrusts of the Nazi, highlighting differences in language they both use. What to the boy is "grooving on it," "getting off on it" (i.e., the Nazi atrocities), to language-sensitive old Dussander is the behavior of an aficionado (121). At first the boy and his American slang seem to win out. For example, every time Dussander "tried to slip into generalities" concerning the atrocities, the "gooshy stuff" that the boy liked to hear about, "Todd would frown severely and ask him specific questions to get him back on the track" (131). With "absurd American self-confidence," and pummeled by his own knee-jerk slang, Todd never studies the "possible consequences" of the memories he has stirred up and set aswirling (198-99). He acts like the "sorcerer's apprentice, who had brought the brooms to life but who had not possessed enough wit to stop them once they got started" (141). This insensitive, damn-the-torpedoes behavior on the part of an All-American boy, who had been raised by well-meaning parents "without all those needless guilts" (181), and got an A+ on a Nazi research paper from a teacher who never gave such grades, proves fatal. Once the sleeping specters of a pitiless past have been awakened, literate Herr Dussander reverts to Nazism again. "Nostalgia" for a history of gas chambers and hideous ovens takes over his whole personality (135), and like an articulate Red Death that might please even Edgar Allan Poe himself, holds "illimitable [verbal] dominion over all."

What distinguishes Stephen King from a mere hack writer grinding out novels for popularity and a fast buck is that, in *Apt Pupil,* he himself never gets self-deceived by the clichés of his own conceptions. Though the subsidiary characters of *Apt Pupil* (Dick and Monica Bowden, Ed French, etc.) are entrapped by clichés, they are still multidimensional, much deeper than the bromides in which they so ardently believe. Dussander himself may be "one of the greatest butchers of human beings ever to live," but he is no pasteboard Hollywood Nazi. He may scorn American slang and wince every time young Bowden utters one of his teenage "witticisms," but every once in a while even Dussander "marvel[s] at the American love of jargon" (159).

Especially interesting is a final exposure to American slang that occurs at the end of the novella when Dussander takes the poison pills he has always kept in clever reserve. Beginning to grow dim with death, Dussander overhears the "quavering" but "triumphant" voices of some cribbage players using typical card-game talk: "How do you like *those* apples" and "I'll peg out"; and for the first time in his snobbish old life, the conceited concentration camp commander acknowledges to himself that Americans do indeed have a "turn for idiom," what he is finally and sentimentally capable of realizing is "wonderful." In his last moments, the childless octogenerian finds himself wishing he could tell his "apt pupil"—a kind of surrogate Nazi son—that "talking to him had been better than listening to

the run of his own thoughts" (266). In reading these final meanderings, one must remember that the "apt pupil's" questions and answers had been mostly slangish, and that Dussander's conversation, though conniving and degenerate, was *always* literate, elegant, and graceful. On his deathbed, the old Nazi inclines toward the Americanisms he had been scorning for more than a hundred pages of narrative. He enters his eternity with the idea that he is somehow—in the American slang—"pegging out." Of course, Stephen King does not resist a final twist of the ironic knife. Criminal Dussander cannot possibly "peg out." For hands with "hungry fingers" were "reaching eagerly up" from his deathbed to "grab him" (like the wrathful souls of the River Styx in the seventh canto of Dante's *Inferno*); and Dussander's death thoughts "broke up in a steepening spiral of darkness, and he rode down that spiral as if down a greased slide, down and down, to whatever dreams there are" (267). As he dies, it is as if the tongues of the "unquiet dead" (the former victims of his gas chamber atrocities) were crying out to him their own colloquialism: How do you like *these* apples, Dussander?—his eternity being suddenly recognized as a nightmarish place where there is absolutely no possibility of ever "pegging out."

Dussander's desire for "rest," while dying from a deliberate overdose of pills, is disrupted by a fear of hideous dreams that the dead and damned might have to endure. His thoughts, of course, echo Hamlet's famous soliloquy, "To be or not to be"); and this technique of literary echo is typical of King, who sometimes—though not here—goes out of his way to specifically justify a literary allusion. The glancing reference to Hamlet's famous fear ("for in that sleep of death what dreams may come"—hardly an original thought at this late date) interweaves ominously into the wise sayings, banalities, and bromides that hammer away at *Apt Pupil* for more than a hundred pages. Dussander may be a former Nazi, but he is the kind of sophisticated old degenerate who would have read and in part probably memorized *Hamlet,* a Nordic play on a revengeful Nordic subject. It is consistent with his temper and flair for the histrionic to pass away into the "dreams" of death with a graceful Shakespearean flourish.

THE TARGET WAS A DEAD BOY

Nothing in the novels of Stephen King, not even the autobiographical parts of *Danse Macabre,* is so intensely personal as the two-hundred-word introduction to *The Body,* the third novella of *Different Seasons,* composed immediately after the first draft of *'Salem's Lot* and exploiting nonvampire aspects of masculine identity—this time in teenage boys. *The Body* is supposed to be narrated by protagonist-novelist Gordie Lachance, who is the presumed author of the introduction. But the mask is papery thin, and more than once—by including adaptations of previously published short stories[8] and by concluding the novella with blatantly autobiographical snatches (432)—the problematic psyche of Stephen King breaks through. From time to time, there are glancing autobiographical parallels even among other characters. In *'Salem's Lot,* Ben Mears, when under suspicion of combined murder and perversion, quotes Mark Twain (who significantly has the same first name as Ben's young mirror-image, Mark Petrie) as having said that a "novel was a confession to everything by a man who had never done anything" (97). While such popular stories as **"Graveyard Shift"** may recount the terror of an actual descent into the basement of a rat-filled factory, *The Body* makes deeper psychological cuts into the "everything," the "dreadful possibilities," the "awful . . . unknown"—and attempts "to look the [subconscious] Gorgon in the face" (*SL,* 374). As the poet Hart Crane once phrased it, the "scimitar" of self-appraisal found "more than flesh to fathom in its fall."[9]

Punning on his own name, Gordon, the protagonist-novelist of *The Body* realizes what a "thin film there is between your rational man costume—the writer with leather elbow-patches on his corduroy jacket—and the capering, Gorgon myths of childhood" (418). Lachance (though actually King) works out his word-problems more matter-of-factly than some twentieth-century poets, but no less poignantly. In "Burnt Norton," T. S. Eliot believes that "Words strain / Crack sometimes break, under the burden, / Under the tension, slip, slide, perish, / Decay with imprecision." Lachance-King's repeatedly stated anguish is simply that the "most important things are the hardest things to say" because they "lie too close to wherever your secret heart is buried"—interesting sensitivity on the part of one who, under his own name, elsewhere explains that the "business of creating horror is much the same as the business of paralyzing an opponent with the martial arts . . . finding vulnerable points and then applying pressure there" (*DM,* 68). The tripartite appearance of the secret-heart motif (289, 390, 395) obviously indicates its sensitive importance, but one cannot help remembering the "life of careful academicism" (i.e., Matt Burke's in *'Salem's Lot*) that "refuse[d] to plant an intellectual foot on any ground until it had been footnoted in triplicate" (299). The vulnerable point for Gordie Lachance, as also for novelist Ben Mears in *'Salem's Lot,* is the secret self, the creative and sensitive nature that can all too easily be cruelly misunderstood. The secret self of alcoholic Father Callahan of *'Salem's Lot,* for instance, was the effeminate face of "Mr. Flip," his imaginary boyhood companion with "thin white face and burning eyes," the "thing that hid in the closet during the days and came out [at nights] after his mother closed the bedroom door" (352).

Assuming a poetic and almost mystical posture, Gordie recognizes that "words shrink things that seemed limitless when they were in your head to no more than living size when they're brought out." Tellingly, this popular twentieth-century author of horror tales—for one must remember that King more than Lachance is speaking here—reveals his personal horror: that the "most important things . . . are landmarks to a treasure" that "your enemies would love to steal away." Later in the novella, a half-retarded boy (Vern Tessio) tries to retrieve a "quart jar of pennies" hidden under the front porch of his house. Unfortunately,

like Lachance-King's landmarks to a treasure that one's enemies would love to steal away, Vern's treasure map was accidentally burned by his mother (an "enemy") along with old homework papers, candy wrappers, comic magazines, and joke-books, in order to start the cook fire one morning, and Vern's map for locating his copper treasures went "right up the kitchen chimney." Vern is half-afraid that his crafty brother (yet another "enemy") might have found the secret penny jar, an explanation that was clear enough to all his twelve-year-old buddies (whose corpse-searching activities form the basis of the novella), but "Vern refused to believe it" (297). Toward the end of the novella, Lachance-King will wrap up his secret in a symbol, a missing blueberry bucket, perhaps imaginary, belonging to a dead boy (Ray Brower), whose train-struck body is what the morbidly curious boys are seeking.

The momentary formula in the penny-jar incident, however, is King equals Lachance equals Vern, and this ought to be apparent to perceptive readers. But as Henry James points out in his "Art of Fiction," too often such subtle symbolic parallels are likely to be overlooked. Therefore, the protagonist-author of *The Body* who has—in James's phrase—"reasons of his own" for considering these sensitive parallels important, continues more explicitly in his introduction so that the reader can "see it": "And you may make revelations that cost you dearly only to have people look at you in a funny way, not understanding what you have said at all, or why you thought it was so important that you almost cried while you were saying it. That's the worst, I think. When the secret stays locked within not for want of a teller but for want of an understanding ear." The entire novella is balanced and counterbalanced with this need-to-reveal versus fear-to-reveal paradox, and thus the ultimate revelation turns out to be nothing more than a blue symbol (the "blue bucket" that Gordie goes groping after in the incessant pursuits of his imagination [419-20]), timeless yearnings for meaning and understanding, perhaps not entirely understood even by the author himself—imponderables that the death-haunted poet Percy Shelley, in his *Prometheus Unbound,* sought for in the "unascended heaven / Pinnacled deep in the intense inane" (3:203-4).

Several portions of these fearful needs are repeated on the occasion when Gordie prepares to keep nightwatch for his sleeping buddies against improbable ghosts. What Gordie Lachance sees is not a "grotesquely ambulatory bedsheet" stealing spectrelike through the trees (38), but something so delicately ambiguous that one cannot tell, for an instant or two, whether it is girl or female deer: "her eyes weren't brown but a dark, dusty black"—"she looked serenely at me"—"my stomach and genitals filled with a hot dry excitement" (389). Deliberately paraphrasing Robert Frost's poem, "Two Look at Two" (except that in this case it becomes a boy looking at a doe—as it were, "one-looking-at-one"), the four-paragraph passage sounds Gordie-depths of Frost-like feelings of delicacy and sensitivity. King even exploits the implications of Frost's name when Gordie is "frozen solid" with fear and awe and perhaps even loving expectation. For a brief and ecstatic moment, Gordie has chanced upon his American Eden.

A similar echo (this time from Frost's "After Apple-Picking") occurs in 'Salem's Lot when novelist Ben Mears compares looking at one of the avenues of the soon-to-be-haunted town to "looking through a thin pane of ice—like the one you can pick off the top of the town cistern in November," and everything is "wavy and misty and in some places it trails off into nothing" (SL, 13).[10] The Frost allusion in 'Salem's Lot is perhaps not so subtle as that of The Body, although in both instances the quasi-quotation is intended to emphasize delicate aspects of the male psyche, a matter of considerable significance in both novel and novella. Interestingly, both Ben and Gordie, novelist-protagonists in successive and presumably entirely different stories, are delicately drawn together through an allusion to momentary Edens in Robert Frost's poetry.

It is on the tip of Gordie's tongue to tell his companions about the sudden appearance of the doe and the wonder and astonishment it caused, but he ends up keeping it to himself. In fact, "I've never spoken or written of it until just now, today." Gordie privately acknowledges in his novella what he never would have openly acknowledged to his adventuring twelve-year-old pals: that the delicate, or should one say feminine, feelings about a beautiful doe, rather than the machismo of actually looking at the mangled and decaying body of a boy struck by a train (obviously the main thrust of the story), were the "best part of that trip, the cleanest part" (390). All this by contrast with the diminished pleasure that literary success produces in a maturer Gordie of later years, writing being once associated with "guilty masturbatory pleasure," but later—at the time of the composition of The Body—associated with "cold clinical images of artificial insemination" (361).

Nonetheless, when trouble arose in Gordie's life—as on the first day in Vietnam, or when he thought his youngest son might be hydrocephalic—he would find himself "almost helplessly" returning to that morning, to "the scuffed suede of her ears, the white flash of her tail" (390). Similarly, in Firestarter, when Andy Magee and his daughter Charlie have been pursued by the C.I.A. to a point of total exhaustion, Andy sees a large Frost-like doe "looking at him thoughtfully," and "then [she] was gone into the deeper woods with a flip of her white tail." Like Gordie in the midst of his fears, Andy, too, "felt encouraged" (127). As for The Body, what Gordie half hopes for is that the reader's memory will jog back to the time when (some thirty pages earlier) friend Richie discovered Gordie's hidden stories in a carton in a closet. Gordie expressed reluctance to have his storytelling propensities revealed to the other boys. "I want it to be a secret," Gordie said—to which friend Richie responded, "Why? It ain't pussy. You ain't no queer. I mean, it ain't poetry" (361).

The Body is constructed in a series of episodes, each emphasizing some boyish secret, until in the final paragraphs, under the not-so-subtle guise of Gordie Lachance, King tries to give symbolic expression, through the imaginary blue bucket belonging to the dead boy, to what has been

bothering him throughout a lifetime. The first secret is a place, a treehouse made of scavenged planks, splintery and knotholed, the roof of corrugated tin sheets "hawked from the dump," and built by four twelve-year-old boys: the slow-witted Teddy and Vern, the quick-witted and perceptive Chris, and the narrator Gordie. This secret place contains yet another secret place, a 12 × 10 inch compartment under the floor in which the boys hide such things as ashtrays, girlie books, Master Detective murder magazines, and playing cards "when some kid's father decided it was time to do the we're-really-good-pals routine" (290). What the boys do in this secret treehouse is normal enough boy-stuff: complain about parents, play cards, look at spicy magazines, use off-color language, share jokes—behavior so common among teenage boys one almost wonders why secrecy is necessary.

Visible from the outside, yet hiding the activities and even thoughts of the occupants, the secret treehouse is a necessary refuge from the irrationalities of Castle Rock parents, especially fathers. The most brutal was Teddy's psychopathic father, who "shoved the side of Teddy's head down against one of the cast-iron burner plates [of the stove] . . . yanked Teddy up by the hair of the head and did the other side," Teddy being, as a consequence, half-deaf and half-blind (292). As the author of the novella words it, "the thick glasses and the hearing aid [Teddy] wore sometimes made him look like an old man" (291). Chris's father was not much better than Teddy's, for Chris was "marked up every two weeks or so, bruises on his cheeks and neck or one eye swelled up and as colorful as a sunset, and once he came into school with a big clumsy bandage on the back of his head" (302).

Considering the often callous behavior of these parents, it is not surprising that their twelve-year-old sons entangle everything they do, consciously or unconsciously, in a web of secrets and ignorances. In addition to those already mentioned, consider that the malevolent parents are not informed of the twenty-mile adventure to find a dead body (301), that hostile rival gangs are unaware of each other's plans for the trip (301), that Billy Tessio does not realize his whispered conversation with Charlie Hogan is overheard by his despised brother (299), that Gordie remains unwilling to expose his vicious attacker (427), and that (in Gordie's story) Chico's affair with Janet occurs without his parent's knowledge (312).

Secrets confront secrets when rival gangs meet over the dead body of the boy struck by a train. The temporary triumph of the younger gang over the older (406-11) and the subsequent revenge of the defeated older boys (425-28) climax the ever-developing theme of manliness in The Body, and are reminiscent of, though perhaps somewhat more believable than, the teenage confrontation between feminine Mark Petrie and masculine Richie Boddin in 'Salem's Lot. The tangle of boyish secrets can be summed up in Gordie's words: "The story never did get out . . . what I meant was that none of our parents ever found out what we'd been up to that Labor Day weekend" (424). "Nobody knew exactly what had happened . . . a few stories went around [in the schoolyard]; all of them wildly wrong" (428). Secrets are interlaced in interesting ways too numerous to catalog here, with author-to-be Gordie becoming like that "benevolent spider," the town gossip Mabel Werts of 'Salem's Lot, who sat at her window with telephone and high-powered binoculars "in the center of a communications web" (72)—except that here in Castle Rock, it might be more accurate to speak of it as Gordie's non-communications web.

The deepest secrets, however, are those encircling Gordie's poetic dispositions (so shied away from in the conversation with Richie), creating imaginative enclosures of horror from which escape is impossible. These involve not so much the discovery of the body of the blueberry boy, although the details are graphic enough to keep one awake for many a night, but the insidious accuracy with which poetic Lachance reconstructs the accident. The deceased is not found mangled on the railroad tracks, as one might have expected, but rather some distance away. The body is "down here" (that is, at the bottom of a railroad embankment) and "relatively intact," with its filthy low-topped Keds caught in tall blackberry brambles. Neatly punning on "kid" and "Keds," as though he were a poet, Lachance explains that "I could go on all day and never get it right about the distance between his bare feet on the ground and his dirty Keds hanging in the bushes. It was thirty-plus inches, but it was a googol of light years. The kid was disconnected from his Keds beyond all hope of reconciliation. He was dead" (405). Characterizing the nonexistent future of the dead boy as *"can't, don't, won't, never, shouldn't, wouldn't, couldn't,"* Gordie realizes how relentlessly the train engine had "knocked him out of his Keds just as it had knocked the [kid] out of his body." Full realization was "like a dirty punch below the belt" (404).

Readers are, of course, permitted the opinion that the train's indifference to the life of Ray Brower was less terrible than the insensitivity of Teddy's father, when he shoved the side of the boy's head against one of the cast-iron burner plates of the oven, a cruelty that turns Teddy's bleak future into a living parody of the dead boy's *"can't, don't, won't, never, shouldn't, wouldn't, couldn't."* Lachance's terrifyingly plausible reconstruction of the train accident appears with a complaint about the magnetic powers of the narrator's imagination: "a little mind-movie" one can have "whenever things get dull"—the trouble being that the little mind-movie-projector "turns around and bites" with "teeth that have been filed to points like the teeth of a cannibal" (404). Five-year-old Danny Torrance in *The Shining* has similar unnerving mental projections when a hotel's emergency fire-hose (like an insidious snake) appears to hiss out the words: "What would I want to do to a nice little boy like you . . . except bite . . . and bite . . . and bite?" (173).

The cosmic entity that cruelly shapes the lives of the young preteens of *The Body* (their many beatings, mistreatments, and eventual early deaths [429-32]) behaves like "some

sentient, malevolent force," some Lovecraftian cosmic horror symbolized by the "big icy hailstones" that were striking Ray Brower's face "with an awful splatting sound that reminded us of . . . [the dead boy's] terrible and unending patience" (412). Even more frightfully, the dead Brower's eyes "filled up with round white hailstones," that, melting, ran down his cheeks as if the dead boy were "weeping for his own grotesque position" (413). (Dante employs a similar ice-eyed scene in the lowest depths of his *Inferno*, the "Ptolomaea" [canto 33] where the eyes of a treacherous reprobate fill up with frozen tears, which the hell traveler callously refuses to remove.) With consummate verbal and psychological skills, King often projects such "sentient malevolent forces" into the overwrought psyches of many of his male characters—forces that in Dante's ninth circle are a "wind" from the great wings of the diabolical Dis that freezes up the infernal slush of Cocytus. High school teacher Jim Norman in **"Sometimes They Come Back,"** senses this force as a "black noxious beast" in the empty halls of his haunted school, senses it so deeply that he "thought it could hear it almost breathing" (*NS,* 147).

Concerned with problems of masculine identity and feminine creativity, both ***The Body*** and the gracefully shaped 'Salem's Lot . . . were composed at virtually the same time and, taken together, are extensive in-depth explorations—virtual confessions, as it were—of the deepest sort of personal/creative insecurities in literate and much-divided modern man. Horror and mysticism, crudity and sensitivity, inside and outside evil—not so mutually exclusive as one might at first imagine—overlap and intermingle, in both ***The Body*** and 'Salem's Lot, to create two of the most powerful self-analytical narratives in recent American fiction. In both novel and novella, the literary scalpel of Stephen King cuts deep into his own trembling flesh (his much-troubled psyche); and the "patient"—if one might be permitted to negate a famous line in T. S. Eliot's "Love Song of J. Alfred Prufrock"—lies painfully [un]etherized upon the table." As Stephen King is himself both novelist Mears (representing light) and vampire Barlow (darkness) in 'Salem's Lot; just so he is both the novelist Lachance (living) and the train-struck Brower (dead) in ***The Body***. In a real sense, both novel and novella are self-elegies; and no "Orphean lute"—in the words of Robert Lowell's equally despairing "Quaker Graveyard in Nantucket"—can "call life back." Considered together, these two haunting narratives of a "body" and a "lot" may eventually—without too much fuss and embarrassment—take their place beside the "succession of flights and drops," the "little seesaw[s] of the right throbs and the wrong," in Henry James's psychologically involuted *Turn of the Screw*.[11]

Notes

1. "Red" makes a passing remark indicating that he too has been brutalized by gang-rapes in prison: "Am I speaking from personal experience—I only wish I weren't" (33).

2. Another interpretation is given by Winter, who claims that in *Rita Hayworth* King worked a "theme of innocence as effectively as he considered the theme of guilt in *The Shining*. . . . Red's story tells of how the irresistible force of innocence succeeds against the seemingly immovable object of Shawshank" (*Art of Darkness,* 105-6).

3. G. B. Harrison, ed., *Shakespeare: The Complete Works* (New York: Harcourt Brace, 1952), 1431.

4. In an afterword to *Different Seasons,* King explains the order of the composition of the four novellas. Coming from the author himself, one would expect this information to be unimpeachable, but in a footnote to his chapter on *Different Seasons,* Winter explains that the sequence of compositions was not exactly as King had originally reported it (*Art of Darkness,* 207).

5. Winter, *Art of Darkness,* 207.

6. "Denker" pretends that his first name was given him by his father because of an admiration for Arthur Conan Doyle (116). This is yet another name-game: Doyle's famous Sherlock Holmes, like the crafty Dussander, is a sleuth. Ironically however, shortly after this so-called Conan Doyle explanation of the name "Arthur," Todd reveals that his mom and dad had given him a fingerprint set for Christmas, which he promptly used to discover Dussander's Nazi identity (124).

7. Richard Hanser, *Putsch* (New York: Pyramid Books 1971), 241.

8. "Stud City," *Ubris,* Fall 1969; "The Revenge of Lard Ass Hogan," *Main Review,* 1975. As samples of Gordie Lachance's story-telling abilities, the versions that appear in *The Body* have been revised.

9. Hart Crane, *Complete Poems* (New York: Anchor Books, 1966), 50.

10. Frost's line reads: "I cannot rub the strangeness from my sight / I got from looking through a pane of glass / I skimmed this morning from the drinking trough / And held against the world of hoary grass." "After Apple-Picking" is one of Frost's most frequently anthologized poems. Author Ben Mears would surely have known it.

11. From the memorable opening sentence of Henry James's *Turn of the Screw.*

Tony Magistrale (essay date 1992)

SOURCE: Magistrale, Tony. "Ship of Ghouls: *Skeleton Crew.*" In *Stephen King: The Second Decade,* Danse Macabre *to* The Dark Half, pp. 86-99. New York: Twayne Publishers, 1992.

[*In the following essay, Magistrale offers a mixed assessment of King's short fiction collection* Skeleton Crew *and asserts that the stories focus on the same themes as King's longer fiction.*]

When rationality begins to break down, the circuits of the human brain can overload. Axons grow bright and feverish. Hallucinations turn real: the quicksilver puddle at the point where perspective makes parallel lines seem to intersect is really there; the dead walk and talk; a rose begins to sing.[1]

All artists have personalities and distinctions that give shape to their art; no one is equally skilled at everything. Artists who attempt to stretch beyond their innate powers command respect but frequently risk failure. The problem is compounded by the vagaries of audience expectation. Every artist who presents work for public consumption has an image, and for careerist reasons must change it only with extreme caution.

I suspect that King's greatest achievements, like those of his early mentor William Faulkner, will continue to be his novels. While loquaciousness and a tendency toward looseness in plot are major liabilities in some of his longer fiction, King nonetheless appears to require a broad venue in order to best develop characters and themes. The short story is pressed to its limits in his hands; King's are often too derivative of blood-and-guts horror fiction, overly sentimental, or just plain silly. On the other hand, several of his short tales are paragons of precision and psychological terror. When a reader finishes an exquisite example, such as **"Last Rung on the Ladder"** or **"The Monkey,"** King's failings elsewhere in the genre can be immediately forgiven.

In *Stephen King, The First Decade* Joseph Reino begins his examination of King's first collection of short stories, *Night Shift* (1978), with the assertion that the book is "a representative anthology of Stephen King's short fiction with dramatic situations so interestingly rendered that curiosity is immediately aroused" (Reino, 100). Reino's assessment is also applicable to several selections from King's second collection of short fiction, *Skeleton Crew* (1985). Michael Collings and David Engebretson insist that *Skeleton Crew* is the better collection of the two, "more consistent in quality than *Night Shift,* more descriptive of King's versatility as a writer."[2]

Skeleton Crew contains a wide and uneven range of material. In **"The Monkey," "The Raft," "Nona,"** and **"The Reach"** King has never been more adroit in handling narrative pace and psychological subtexts. In **"Here There Be Tygers," "Cain Rose Up," "The Wedding Gig," "Mrs. Todd's Shortcut," "Uncle Otto's Truck," "Survivor Type,"** and **"Gramma"** his plotting is less exacting, his themes less sophisticated, his conclusions telegraphed and predictable.

Skeleton Crew, however, offers a representation of the major themes and issues discussed elsewhere in this book and given more elaborate consideration in King's longer fiction. There is, for example, work that exposes the dangers inherent in scientific technocracy and religious zealotry (the novella **The Mist**); stories that are representative of the science-fiction genre (**"The Jaunt," "Beachworld,"** and **"Word Processor of the Gods"**); simple morality fables, like many of Poe's tales, in which acts of criminal behavior return to haunt the perpetrator, suggesting that an offense against another is also an offense against oneself (**"Uncle Otto's Truck"** and **"The Wedding Gig"**); and tales that are most rewarding when their subtextual properties are pursued: **"The Raft"** as a study of the rite of passage from childhood freedom to the terrors of adulthood, and **"The Monkey"** as a psychoanalytic tale examining the deleterious consequences of self-repression and guilt.

Reino makes careful note of King's tendency to link individual stories in *Night Shift* through patterns of repetition: "a phrase, quotation, theme, or question repeated with dramatic effect not unlike the well-known incremental techniques of traditional ballads on tragic themes" (Reino, 100). This proclivity is likewise evident in *Skeleton Crew,* as several stories carry a variation of the refrain "Do you love?" Sometimes raised as a terrifying self-indictment (**"Nona"**), sometimes uttered in absolute certitude (**"The Reach"**), the phrase functions within a variety of interesting contexts, and its potential meaning shifts in a manner appropriate to the context in which it appears.

In **"The Raft"** the question arises as Randy, the young central consciousness in the narrative, is about to be swallowed by a gelatinous creature that floats upon the surface of Cascade Lake. When he first poses the question "Do you love?" it comes from within the warm recollection of summers past, and his answer is affirmative. But by the end of the narrative—and this is in keeping with the plot's progression from Randy's response to a naive and simplistic college dare to his serious confrontation with death and loss—Randy's query, as well as the answer he receives, have changed in tone. His final address is to the hydromonster itself, and it expresses a desperate hope for a last moment of kindness rather than a dreamy wish for personal fulfillment. The answer, however, as if in Melvillian confirmation of nature's essential indifference toward the human world, is provided by a loon's scream "somewhere, far across the empty lake" ([*Skeleton Crew*; hereafter] *SC,* 270).

On a more affirmative note, **"The Reach"** concerns another variant of the same question. Stella Flanders' journey into the Reach is not the lonely death experience that Randy undertakes. In place of his "empty lake," Stella discovers a community of souls from her past—a society of the dead, who seek her not for punishment or out of malevolence but because of the enduring power of love. In spite of the cold and snow that surround Stella, her death is neither isolated nor painful. In fact, the conclusion of the tale indicates that her last journey completes the natural cycle of life and, at the same time, begins another one.

In addition to some variant of the phrase "Do you love?" lakes are a conspicuous presence in many of the tales in *Skeleton Crew.* In *The Mist* the white cloud that carries in it the mutant results of the Arrowhead Project comes in directly over a lake, as does the terrible summer storm that

appears to precipitate the mist's arrival. The lakes in **"The Monkey," "The Raft,"** and **"The Reach"** come to represent much more than mere bodies of water; they evolve into symbols for the unknown or the unconscious mind. In each of these stories the lake serves as a barrier to the protagonist's past or future that he or she is forced eventually to traverse. The character's physical crossing of the lake—walking across the frozen ice in **"The Reach,"** swimming the water in **"The Raft,"** or using a rowboat to get to the lake's epicenter in **"The Monkey"**—corresponds to a psychological crossing, the symbolic welding of two distinct eras in time (usually present and past). Thoreau discovered metaphoric correspondences to himself in the mystic waters of Walden Pond; likewise, King's *Skeleton Crew* characters experience some sort of transformation in their water crossings or journeys. But whereas Thoreau's lake usually signified the most affirmative elements in his nature, King's waters tend to mirror the dark side of the human psyche—its secret sins and lost vision.

The short story has one great advantage over the novel: its forced concision creates an intensified effect. Because it can be read in one sitting rather than over a series of days or weeks, the short story leaves a more powerful imprint on the mind. This seems particularly true of short fiction that is ever mindful of its psychological implications, its efforts to reveal a specific condition or personality disorder. The stories analyzed in this [essay] were selected not only because of "the grace and finesse with which they are narrated and their ultimate terrors skillfully unveiled" (Reino, 103), but also for the value of their psychological complexity. **"The Raft"** and **"The Monkey"** in particular are two of the finest examples of psychological terror to be found in American literature. In this present era of "slash-and-gore" horror films and fiction, readers who lament the passing of the psychological Gothic, fully realized in the tales of Hawthorne and Poe, would do well to examine **"The Monkey"** and **"The Raft"** carefully. Like "Roger Malvin's Burial," "My Kinsman, Major Molineux," and "The Black Cat," these two King stories are best appreciated as allegories of the human heart. Their terrors, although couched in highly personalized contexts, actually veil subtle truths about the dark realities of the human condition. **"The Raft"** and **"The Monkey"** underscore the struggle to prevail over forces that have, finally, less to do with supernatural phenomena located outside the self than with the mind's own destructive impulses. **"The Reach"** endures as one of the most optimistic and certainly the gentlest tale ever narrated by Stephen King. If novels such as *Pet Sematary* and *The Shining* pose a view of the afterlife in terms of Dionysian energies aligned with evil, **"The Reach"** offers a positive counterpoint: that death does not signal the end of human love but rather its perpetuation. *The Mist,* the longest work in the collection, continues the technocratic critique King raised in the early Bachman books, *The Stand, Firestarter,* and, of course, *The Talisman* and *The Tommyknockers.* Like these novels, *The Mist* indicts the misdirected experiments of a technology that is ultimately beyond the understanding of those who created it. Often cited especially by students as a favorite King text, *The Mist* moves as swiftly as a summer thunderstorm from the security of familial domesticity to the nightmare of a world completely upended.

The Clouding of Human Minds

With the notable exception of an albino tentacle that is severed in battle at the loading dock behind the Federal Foods supermarket, the supernatural special effects of *The Mist* are not in evidence for a full two-thirds of the novella. This is a remarkable achievement in itself, given that the characters and the reader are both profoundly conscious of a supernatural presence for nearly the entire length of the narrative. King holds his reptilian and crustacean creatures in abeyance to force our attention onto the tale's real abhorrence: the behavior of human beings who suddenly find themselves confronting adversity and tragedy.

Ironically, as the pearl-white mist shrouds the market microcosm in a soupy fog, those who are trapped inside unveil their true personalities. Stripped of their social veneers as a result of the circumstances in which they find themselves, the men and women of *The Mist* exhibit the full emotional spectrum of human responses—from avarice and immobilizing fear to unselfish compassion toward complete strangers. In the controlled microcosm of the supermarket, which becomes the scene of slowly unfolding levels of terror and the hysteria of mass despair, King measures the courage and coping skills of his protagonist-heroes.

Some of the men, frustrated in their helplessness, decide to test themselves physically against the creatures who inhabit the mist. Norm, Jim, and Myron, the stockboys, initially respond to the situation with a blind male bravado that is unguided by reason. Others, we are informed, "had lapsed into a complete stupor without benefit of beer, wine, or pills. The hard cement of reality had come apart in some unimaginable earthquake, and these poor devils had fallen through" (*SC*, 96). Brent Norton, the New York lawyer, on the other hand, refuses to see the cracks in the "hard cement of reality" and clings to a desperate rationality, even as he witnesses proof of the irrationality outside. Devoid of any imaginative capacity, he and his "Flat Earther" group are unable to abandon the complacent order that has sustained their place in the world. Norton's hyperrational stance in defiance of the novella's surreal developments is shown to be no more viable a response than Mrs. Carmody's emotional ranting. Whereas Norton completely shuts out the new reality occasioned by the mist, Mrs. Carmody has no difficulty accepting the changes brought about by its arrival. However, it is her medieval interpretation that is suspect.

Most of the characters in *The Mist* thus demonstrate a deficient understanding of, and response to, the adversity they are forced to encounter. For most, the reality of the mist highlights the failure of the human mind to interpret accurately what the senses supply it by way of empirical evidence: "Norton was imposing a mental gag order on himself. Myron and Jim had tried by turning the whole thing into a macho charade—if the generator could be fixed, the mist would blow over. This was Brown's way. He was . . . Protecting the Store" (*SC*, 73). The fact that the creatures who emerge from the mist resemble pterodactyls and other primordial life forms from the deep sea suggest a further connection to the behavior of the humans inside the food market. As Hitchcock's disruption of nature can be seen as a comment on the human world in his classic film *The Birds,* King implies that the bestial level of social interaction that takes place inside the supermarket is reflective of the primeval devolution occurring just outside its glass doors and windows.

Several of the characters, however, manage to face the mist without illusions or the need to deny their fears, and for them this communal tragedy presents the opportunity for personal growth. Focusing their attention and energies on the welfare of others rather than indulging their own terror, Hattie Turman, Ollie Weeks, Amanda Dumfries, and the novella's first-person narrator, Dave Drayton, cope best with the deteriorating situation around them. When Amanda and Dave decide to make love in what proves to be a final moment of quiet on the first night, it is a spontaneous act that underscores the need for human interdependency, the bond that is forfeited by the other characters who remain inside the market: "We lay down then, and she said, 'Love me, David. Make me warm.' When she came, she dug into my back with her nails and called me a name that wasn't mine. I didn't mind" (*SC*, 103).

Amanda and David, along with those who support them, rise above the self-centered arrogance that informs the attitudes of Norton, Carmody, and the Arrowhead Project, which is responsible for producing the monsters. The mist's very existence must be attributed to basic human negligence: the failure to care enough about the welfare of others and the environment we share. Near the narrative's conclusion Dave Drayton posits that "it was the mist itself that sapped the strength and robbed the will" (*SC*, 122). This is not exactly correct. The degree of weakness and lack of will that Drayton references is finally not caused by the fog; the real lack of will in this story concerns public failure to monitor sufficiently a technocracy that has been given too many tax dollars and not enough accountability. The culprits of the Arrowhead Project, as Douglas Winter points out, "remain as faceless and opaque as the mist itself" (Winter 1984, 100). The mist, then, is a metaphor for the clouded vision that inspired the Arrowhead Project as well as for the moral ambiguity that later engulfs those inside the market and leads to Mrs. Carmody's rise to power.

The Psychology of "The Monkey"

What does the little toy monkey in this story represent? This question is, of course, critical to unraveling Hal Sherburn's relationship with the monkey, much less the story's core meaning. Is the simian toy some sort of dark talismanic device that is a harbinger of death? Or does it maintain a more specifically personal connection to Hal? The tale supports both interpretations. The fish that are mysteriously killed when the monkey is entombed at the bottom of Crystal Lake would appear to indicate the randomness of evil. Yet the fact that the toy is intimately connected to Hal, linking him to his childhood and events that occurred over 20 years ago, suggests that the monkey is also some sort of psychological signifier to Hal's past. I wish to pursue this latter interpretation, not only because it is the richer but also because it stands in opposition to Douglas Winter's approach to the text as an illustration of "outside, predestinate evil" (Winter 1984, 227).

One of King's greatest skills as a writer is his ability to describe the terrors associated with childhood, particularly the shadowy guilts that frequently attend a child's initial experience with death. In *It*, for example, the personal guilt that is established after the murder of Bill Denbrough's younger brother becomes a motivating force in the older boy's relentless pursuit of It. And in ***The Body*** Gordie La Chance assumes the onus of his older brother's death in light of the cold indifference that characterizes his parents' state of bereavement. In these two texts King implies that for children the mystery of death is even more complicated than it is for adults, for in their confusion and innocence children often assume a measure of personal responsibility.

Drawn back to his "home place where [Hal and his brother] had finished growing up" (*SC,* 144) for his Aunt Ida's funeral, Hal finds himself highly susceptible to the unhappy memories of his childhood, which revolve around the deaths of loved ones. In his anger and grief after the accidental death of his best friend, Johnny, Hal had believed that a toy monkey was somehow responsible, and he had buried it in a deep well located on his aunt's property. Although the boy had had no direct influence on Johnny's fall from the treehouse, he had been both traumatized by it and, more important, filled with tremendous guilt. Hal had been both secretly relieved that "it hadn't been his turn [to die]" (*SC,* 147) and dimly conscious of how easily it might have been: "Johnny had been climbing the rungs up to his treehouse in the backyard. The two of them had spent many hours up there that summer" (*SC,* 145). Unable to articulate these feelings because of their complexity and his own desire to repress them, Hal had projected them onto the toy monkey—"it was the monkey's fault" (*SC,* 145)—and buried his own guilt, like the monkey thrown down the shaft, deep within the "dark well" of his psyche. This psychological nexus is supported years later when Hal finds himself drawn back to the "rock-lined throat" of the cistern, in which he sees "a drowning face, wide eyes, grimacing mouth . . . It was his own face in the dark water" (*SC,* 144).

The recent death of his mother-surrogate aunt, the journey back to his former home, and his current struggles as husband and father serve to reactivate all of Hal's submerged adolescent anxieties, which have never been adequately

resolved. Thus, the monkey "resurfaces" from the well as Hal's past terrors are brought into juxtaposition with his present crises. Hal is "losing Dennis" (*SC,* 143), his oldest son, and his relationship with his wife is equally strained: "Just lately she took a lot of Valium. It had started around the time National Aerodyne had laid Hal off" (*SC,* 143). That the monkey returns at this point in his life is an indication of Hal's lingering childhood vulnerabilities. His insecurities about his career, his marriage, and his parenting are reminders of the powerlessness he knew as a child.

Hal's monkey is a psychological signifier of his repressed past. We have traced how his condition was exacerbated by Johnny's accidental fall from the treehouse, but Hal's initial level of guilt had actually been established years prior to that incident. The monkey itself had first been discovered in the back of his father's "long and narrow and somehow snug back closet" (*SC,* 150). Hal had felt the urge to return repeatedly to this closet, "trying, as best [he] could, to somehow make contact with [his] vanished father" (*SC,* 150). In an unnerving parallel to King's own personal history, Hal's father, "a merchant mariner, had simply disappeared as if from the very face of the earth when [Hal] was young" (*SC,* 144). As is often the case with small children whose parents divorce or die, the boy had grown up feeling as though he were somehow personally responsible for his father's disappearance, perhaps believing that his parent's actions were the result of something he had done or failed to do as a son. It is significant that Hal had discovered the monkey only after repeated visits to his father's closet and that the appearance of the toy had coincided with the deepening of Hal's sense of personal loss and guilt.

The monkey is thus linked to Hal's psychological disturbances, and each time Hal is made to experience death, his condition worsens. The sudden and terrible losses of his mother, his babysitter, his best friend, and his brother's playmate would have been difficult for any child to accept, even with the assistance of loving parents and a professionally trained counselor. Hal, however, had had no one to advise him on interpreting these tragic events, and his subsequent pain and confusion had easily been translated into guilt. Unable to sustain a barrier between himself and these dark accidents of fate (Johnny's fall and Beulah's murder) and natural conclusions to life (his mother's brain embolism and Aunt Ida's stroke), Hal had felt responsible for their occurrence. In the mind of this assaulted child, the monkey had become an extension of his hyperdeveloped conscience. His efforts to create a physical distance between himself and the toy had been symbolic of his own self-avoidance. For almost three decades Hal had repressed his guilt, channelled it into the buried monkey. As an adult, when Hal is forced to address these old, submerged feelings, the monkey resurfaces (in addicts' jargon, Hal has never gotten the monkey off his back): "There was the guilt; the certain, deadly knowledge that he had killed his mother by winding the monkey upon that sunny afterschool afternoon" (*SC,* 159).

As an adult, Hal is in a more advantageous position to acknowledge and confront the deep psychological disturbances he misapprehended as a child. But to accomplish this he would probably need the help of a psychotherapist to bring to consciousness that which has been repressed, so that personal integration and wholeness might become a real possibility. Unfortunately, he never seeks or receives such assistance; he has only the unqualified love of his youngest son, Petey, to help him shoulder the psychic burden that the monkey represents. His commitment to Petey enables Hal to weather a tremendous storm (symbolic of his inner personal strife) in order to reinter the toy in "the deepest part of Crystal Lake" (*SC,* 167). Hal puts trust once again in his capacity for self-discipline. Like the well on Aunt Ida's property, the lake is another metaphor for Hal's unconscious mind, and at the end of the tale Hal's guilt is once more pushed back into its "deepest part." Significantly, however, on this occasion the monkey (Hal's guilt) proves much more difficult to repress. Hal must risk his very life in his struggle to "get rid of the monkey for another twenty years" (*SC,* 169). While the story appears to imply in its optimistic conclusion that this may well be the case, any student of Freud would concur with Hal's own self-diagnosis: that unless he experiences the type of release that would be obtained by acknowledging and confronting his long history of guilty associations, the monkey and all that it signifies is *"just going to come back and come back and that's all this is about. . . ."* (*SC,* 161).

ALLEGORICAL RITES OF PASSAGE

King begins **"The Raft"** with this sentence: "It was forty miles from Horlicks University in Pittsburgh to Cascade Lake, and although dark comes early to that part of the world in October, and although they didn't get going until six o'clock, there was still a little light in the sky when they got there" (*SC,* 245). Thus he places the reader immediately at the heart of the story, revealing a hyperconscious awareness of time that lends a breathlessness to the narrative's pace. From the distance separating Pittsburgh and Cascade Lake, to the late hour when the journey commences, to the autumnal finalities associated with late October, the narrowing perimeters of time are made almost palpable for the reader. The syntax of the sentence itself—which contains two dependent clauses, one right after the other, that both begin with *although*—suggests the potential danger inherent in whatever action these characters have elected to undertake. Their motives are as yet unknown, but there is already a foreboding quality, conveyed by the opening sentence's suggestion of the deliberateness of the choice to venture out in spite of the ominous changes taking place in the landscape. This evocative opening also forms a nexus to the full symbolism of the tale's deepest meaning: we will soon learn that the characters featured in this sentence are in the "October" of their adolescence, on the verge of adulthood. Although we share in their naïveté at this point in the narrative, the opening sentence embodies the story's metaphor of chronological entrapment. These young people are about to lose touch with the great freedoms of childhood—deathless summers, irresponsibility, and personal immortality—as their futile attempt to thwart time's advance is mirrored in a growing psychological desperation.

What begins in the first few pages of **"The Raft"** as a whimsical salutation to summer (*SC,* 248) deepens into a highly allegorical indictment of the rite of passage into maturity. The tale is about nothing less than the transitional terrors associated with growing up in America. As a child Rachel recalls swimming out to the white raft, but once there she remained "for damn near two hours, scared to swim back" (*SC,* 247). The hydromonster partly symbolizes universal childhood fears, in particular those associated with the unknown. In this context the raft comes to represent an intangible transitional barrier that separates innocence from experience, adolescence from adulthood. Randy confirms this when he remarks that the raft "looked like a little bit of summer that someone forgot to clean up and put away in the closet until next year" (*SC,* 247). Just beyond the raft, however, inhabiting the deepest waters of the lake (which serves, as in **"The Monkey,"** as a means for visualizing the human unconscious), is the amorphous hydromonster—the manifest symbol of the imminent adulthood that each student must face.

The hydromonster, as "latent with symbolism as Melville's white whale" (Winter 1984, 172), represents the cannibalistic impulses King affiliates with the adult world throughout his canon. Moreover, the adjectives used to describe it—"circular," "masculine," "mute," "purposeful," "even-shaped," "lithe Naugahyde," "criss-crossing"—all suggest elements of containment and/or rigidity. I will have more to say . . . on the subject of how the adults who populate King's fictional world frequently oppress young people, physically and psychologically, and how evidence of this can be traced throughout King's canon, from *Carrie* to *It.*

In light of the broad definitions of negative adulthood presented in King's fiction, it is interesting that the one constant in the majority of his adult characters is their aptitude for betrayal. The young adults in **"The Raft"** come to exhibit some of the negative traits of adulthood in their interpersonal behavior. As the story unfolds, all of the relationships, same-sex as well as heterosexual, deteriorate. Randy and Deke have been college roommates for three years, but Randy does not trust his friend around women, and when Deke glances at Randy, "it [is with] more loving familiarity than contempt . . . but the contempt [is] there, too" (*SC,* 252). The two boy-men are similar only in terms of their mutual insensitivity toward Rachel and LaVerne. The girl-women are treated either as children to be silenced or threatened, or sexual toys who must always make themselves accessible. For most of the story the females are reduced to male fantasy objects, little more than breasts and bottoms, and they vie consistently for Deke's attention. Even in the midst of their peril, they perceive themselves solely as sexual competitors, turning exclusively to the men for any measure of comfort. Randy also discovers that his best friend and his girlfriend are lovers; they have thus betrayed both him and Rachel. Randy contemplates all this while trapped on the raft. At one point he acknowledges to himself that "the black patch on the water scared him. That was the truth" (*SC*, 252). Much is suggested in this double-edged association between the hydromonster and truth. Does "that was the truth" merely indicate Randy's honest acknowledgment of his fear? Or does it mean something more—that in the presence of the black patch Randy gains sudden, truthful insights?

Literally stripped of their clothes, all of the child-adults, and Randy in particular, are also stripped of their illusions. Even Randy's sole moment of comfort in LaVerne's sexual embrace proves transitory at best: she is literally swept from underneath him at the very moment when "the tactile sensations were incredible, fantastic" (*SC*, 266). Randy's losses seem to be orchestrated by, or at least centered in, the hydromonster itself. It lures him to study its "flaring nuclear colors," falsely deceiving him into believing that "perhaps the thing could fix it so there was no pain; perhaps that was what the colors were for" (*SC*, 269). At one point or another in each of our lives we share Randy's blind faith that the world of adulthood will somehow be if not a triumphant experience, at least a manageable one. But the reality of the aging process always brings disillusionment and concludes in death, even as we try, like Randy, to believe that there must be some way to "fix it so there [will be] no pain."

In the concluding pages of **"The Raft"** Randy clings to a series of kaleidoscopic memories from adolescent summers: "the feel of summer, the texture; I can root for the Yankees from the bleachers, girls in bikinis on the beach . . . the Beach Boys oldies" (*SC*, 267). These memories of boyhood, however, are no more a shield against the dark realities of adult life than is the raft an adequate barrier against the hydromonster's assault. The physical deaths that occur in this tale, albeit grotesque and graphic, pale in their capacity to evoke terror and sympathy from the reader when measured against the story's subtext of innocence betrayed. In his last hours of life, bereft of human comfort and anticipating his own demise, Randy learns what we all must in light of the harsh realities of aging: that the cocoon of innocence—symbolized appropriately in Randy's romantic urge to "say good-bye to summer, and then swim back" (*SC*, 248)—is lost once we have emerged from it.

Do the Dead Sing?

Stella Flanders' 95-year-old imagination is death-haunted. From the beginning of **"The Reach"** to its conclusion, her life is seen in reference to those she has buried. In fact, Stella's reach has very little to do with the actual "water between the island and the mainland" (*SC*, 489); it is, instead, the spiritual swell that continues to link her to the men and women of Goat Island who were her family and friends: *Your blood is in the stones of this island, and I stay here because the mainland is too far to reach. Yes, I love; I have loved, anyway, or at least tried to love, but memory is so wide and so deep, and I cannot cross"* (*SC*, 493).

Content to have spent her entire life never having journeyed across the Reach to the mainland, Stella is now an old woman whose past is more meaningful than her present; the island dead have been whispering to her long before she sees her first apparition. Although she shares an apparently warm relationship with her living son and grandchildren, for the length of the story Stella's only topic of communication with them concerns the past and those who are dead. Douglas Winter postulates that "When Stella Flanders embarks upon her journey, she understands what she is leaving behind in the 'small world' on this side of the Reach: 'a way of being and a way of living; a feeling'" (Winter 1984, 10). This is not precisely accurate, for while Stella does relinquish the present and her commitment to those still alive on Goat Island, she does not abandon her past, as Winter suggests, but rather rediscovers it in her reunion with those she has lost. Indeed, although she maintains a connection with the dead that grows increasingly stronger in the course of the narrative, she indulges her recollections not out of weakness or morbidity but because they remain a conduit to love. This is why death poses no real fear for Stella; she knows that "it don't hurt . . . All that's before" (*SC*, 504). Her past is not left behind when she chooses to cross the Reach, as her "small world" is reanimated in contact with the island's dead: "He was holding his hat out to her in a gesture that appeared almost absurdly courtly, and his face was Bill's face, unmarked by the cancer that had taken him" (*SC*, 502).

The story's optimism is sustained by the nucleus of a small town, and this is critical to understanding Stella's attitude toward her existence: "I see enough of what goes on in cities on the TV. I guess I'll stay where I am" (*SC*, 492-3). Stella's perspective on her Maine home is unique in King's canon. With the possible exception of *The Dead Zone,* in which we see a community working in unison to capture a rapist-murderer stalking local women, King's general treatment of small-town America is neither flattering nor equivocal. In contrast to the citizens of the malefic microcosms of 'Salem's Lot, Haven, Castle Rock, and Derry, the Goat Island inhabitants in **"The Reach"** take care of one another, view their neighbors as integral members of an extended family, and continually emphasize the importance of caring interpersonal relationships:

> "Children," she would tell them, "we always watched out for our own. We had to, for the Reach was wider in those days and when the wind roared and the surf pounded and the dark came early, why, we felt very small—no more than dust motes in the mind of God. So it was natural for us to join hands, one with the other.

> "We joined hands, children, and if there were times when we wondered what it was all for, or if there was any such a thing as love at all, it was only because we had heard the wind and the waters on long winter nights, and we were afraid."

> (*SC*, 499)

Stella's appreciation that her own identity is inexorably linked to the larger social community reflects the more affirmative side of King's social self. In a conversation I had with him . . . , King mentioned that his choice to remain a resident of Bangor, Maine, was based partly as a result of his commitment to the community itself as a place that has nurtured both his family and his fiction. Although his novels and stories pose a rather bleak portrait of communal life in America, King's own personal feelings toward Bangor seem to closely resemble Stella's feelings about Goat Island in **"The Reach."** King continues to give back to the town in which he lives: he remains an active presence in Bangor's political life, he has given numerous public lectures at the local university at Orono, he has supported benefits to raise money for Bangor's neediest, and he recently contributed funds to buy baseball uniforms for the town's Little League.[3] Whenever a director seeks to film an adaptation of one of his texts, King always lobbies hard to set the film in Maine in an effort to share some of his financial success with his fellow citizens: "For years I've desperately wanted to get film crews into Maine. There are parts of Washington County where twelve weeks of shooting could generate more income than the place sees in a year."[4] In another man of King's wealth and stature, these activities might appear to be token gestures, but in his case they genuinely reflect his awareness of his responsibilities as a citizen and a human being.

In **"The Reach"** Stella Flanders understands that the only hope for men and women in the face of nature's awful cruelty is the degree of commitment we give to one another: "They stood in a circle in the storm, the dead of Goat Island, and the wind screamed around them, driving its packet of snow, and some kind of song burst from her" (**SC,** 504). Her character embodies a side of Stephen King that is seldom noted either in popular reviews of his fiction and films or in scholarly analyses. She represents the life force that sustains each of King's small-group relationships—from that of Danny, Wendy Torrance, and Hallorann in *The Shining* to that of the members of the Losers' Club in *It*. The heroes and heroines in King's fiction do not triumph as a result of their personal independence or complacent withdrawal from corruption. Their endurance is based upon the degree to which they have not sacrificed their humanity and upon their quest to find others with whom they might entrust their love. Stella Flanders never really fears a reunion with those who have died, because for her the dead wear sympathetic faces and retain the most important capacity with which human beings are endowed. As King wrote in *Danse Macabre,*

> the horror writer is not just a writer but a human being, mortal man or woman, just another passenger in the boat, another pilgrim on the way to whatever there is. And we hope that if he sees another pilgrim fall down that he will write about it—but not before he or she has helped the fallen one off his or her feet, brushed off his or her clothes, and seen if he or she is all right, and able to go on. If such behavior is to be, it cannot be as a result of an intellectual moral stance; it is because there is such a thing as love, merely a practical fact, a practical force in human affairs.

> (*DM,* 403)

Notes

1. *The Mist,* in *Skeleton Crew* (New York: G. P. Putnam's Sons, 1985), 101. All references to selections from *Skeleton Crew* hereafter cited in text as *SC*.

2. Michael Collings and David Engebretson, *The Shorter Works of Stephen King* (Mercer Island, Wash.: Starmont House, 1985), 130; hereafter cited in text.

3. For an insightful glance into King's relationship to Bangor's Little League, the reader should consult King's essay "Head Down" (*New Yorker,* 16 April 1990, 68-111). The commission King received from *The New Yorker* upon publication of this essay was donated to purchase new uniforms for all the baseball teams in Bangor's Little League system. Aside from being an expansive treatise on King's great love (and thorough knowledge) of baseball, the article also reveals a good deal about the author's fascination with adolescent American boyhood and the solidarity among athletes playing in team competition.

4. Quoted in Jeff Connor, *Stephen King Goes to Hollywood* (New York: New American Library, 1987), 82.

Jonathan P. Davis (essay date 1994)

SOURCE: Davis, Jonathan P. "Childhood and Rites of Passage." In *Stephen King's America*, pp. 48-69. Bowling Green, Ohio: Bowling Green State University Popular Press, 1994.

[*In the following essay, Davis explores King's treatment of childhood in his short fiction and novels.*]

> The child in adult life is defenceless
> And if he is grown-up, knows it,
> And the grown-up looks at the childish part
> And despises it.
>
> —Stevie Smith "To Carry the Child"

Anyone who has read Stephen King extensively will find that he spends a large amount of time exploring childhood. Childhood to King is a magical time, a time when the world seems magnificent in its literal beauty, a time when a human being is most splendid because of ignorance of worldly evil. King recollects with fondness an age when imaginative capacities are boundless because they are not yet bogged down by the spirit-corrupting concerns of adulthood. This preoccupation with youth in his fiction becomes both significant and inspirational when seen from the light that King is writing in an America that attempts to desensitize its young by exposing it continuously to violence and sex in both the entertainment and news media, forcing it to mature at too early an age. Children to King are like lumps of clay on a potter's wheel waiting to be sculpted into the individuals they will later become; they are the most impressionable beings in the human chain.

While they begin innocent, not yet concerned with how they look or where they will get money to buy a new car, children still are forced at some point to exit the gates of purity and enter the arena of adulthood, which occurs through some initial earth-shattering discovery that causes them to recognize the imperfections of their world. For some children, the initiation may be discovering that their fathers are not the spotless, faultless men they thought they were but rather pathetic alcoholics. Others may find their untainted visions of their world clouded by a first exposure to a pornographic magazine depicting radically different images of sexuality than those which they'd been taught. King revels in both the pre-corrupted and corrupted states of youth. He feels that they are periods that people must return to in later years to complete the wheel of humanity; if people cannot remember both the magic of childhood before its corruption and the lessons learned during and after its corruption, then they will never be complete but will succumb to the evils of the adult world.

First and foremost of King's fascination with children is the imaginative capacity they have that makes them stronger at heart than the adults who claim superiority over them. While adults claim to be wise, they are ignorant to the fact that the imaginative atrophy often resulting from an inability to adapt to innocence's corruption actually limits them. Adults often can no longer discover the beauty in a sunset; they cannot remember the golden moments of childhood bonding, a period when same-sex friends seemed the most important aspect of being alive, and it is this incapacity to recollect these times that often leads to an increasingly burdensome adult life in King's fiction. Unless the adults in King's world can escape into the realm of imagination first experienced and shared with others in childhood, unless they can approach oncoming evil with a child's mentality, they are doomed to adult reasoning. Because evil in itself is intangible and cannot be reasonably rationalized, it is often both adults' adherence to their belief in reason and their insistency on literalizing reality and unreality that often result in a catastrophe in King's fiction. Only when they open themselves up to combatting evil from a child's perspective, one which believes in monsters and ghosts, can they openly battle adversities.

King's interest in children's imagination could be linked directly to his feelings on moral choice discussed previously. Adults are unable to see their shortcomings because they are too enveloped in a subjectively egocentric universe based on the rules of rationality. A child, who is ever open to the threats of vampires, killer cars, haunted hotels, and killer clowns, is not yet able to reject the thought of entering the world of the irrational. Clive Barker, one of King's leading contemporaries in horror fiction, says of King, "In King's work, it is so often the child who carries that wisdom; the child who synthesizes 'real' and 'imagined' experience without question, who knows instinctively that imagination can tell the truth the way the senses never can" (63). Often in King's books, it takes the imagination of a child to cast away the evil that reduces adults to whimpering fools: *It*'s The Loser's Club, a group of socially outcast children who possess the imaginative capacities to recognize the evil plundering Derry and therefore acquire the power to stop it; *'Salem's Lot*'s Mark Petrie, whose belief in the world of monsters allows protagonist Ben Mears to return to his own childhood fears which upon retrospection provide him with the power to combat the vampires quenching their thirsts on the small town; *The Shining*'s Danny Torrance, whose childish imagination provides a welcome birthplace for supernatural powers capable of turning back the all-consuming evil of the hotel that has claimed his father; and *The Talisman*'s Jack Sawyer, who because of his youth and separation from the adult world of reasoning becomes his ailing mother's savior while an evil adult society led by his malicious Uncle Morgan tries to destroy them both. The child heroes in King's fiction continue to increase, merely because of King's awareness that their innocence is the only hope for survival in an unimaginative adult world that is swallowing itself.

King often highlights the plight of American children by portraying an adult society that is trying to soil its young by stealing their purity. The sad truth lies in the fact that while children are stronger than their elders in their ability to utilize their imaginations in the face of adversities, they are incapacitated by their dependency on adults. As a result, adults possess the power to make lasting impressions—often negative ones—on their young simply because of both their physical superiority and worldly mentality, something Bernadette Lynn Bosky points out:

> Children do not resist their impressions partly because they have not learned adult standards of sanity and already exist in a shocking and primal world that adults can barely recall or comprehend. It is a sad irony, exampled in books like *The Shining, Cujo,* and *Pet Sematary,* that children, who often understand the intrinsics of evil best, have the least power to change it.
>
> (216)

While children basically possess the true weapons for survival—a productive imagination, a love for simple things, a gentle nature—they are often made vulnerable by an adult society that teaches them violence, hostility, and greed. In their vulnerability, children become sponges that absorb the impressions their adult society gives them, which King himself explains:

> What is it about kids that they can look at the most outrageous thing and just see it and, unless there's a reaction they can play off, just deal with it? If a kid sees a guy that's dead in the street, who's been hit by a car, if he's by himself he'll just look at the dead guy and then maybe run off to find somebody—after he'd had a good look to see what it was like. But if a lot of people are standing around crying, then the kid will cry too, because he's got a mirror reaction. Kids by themselves sort of interest me that way; they seem to me to be the place where you should start to explore wherever people come from.
>
> (*BB* 105)

As King suggests, children learn from the adult reactions to which they are exposed. King's fiction which deals with the gap between young and old tends to argue that the negative responses children register from adults are those that are most often recollected later in adult life, serving as a basis for chronic human flaws. In *The Library Policeman,* a novella in *Four Past Midnight,* King speaks this observation through Dirty Dave Duncan's mouth:

> I don't think kids know monsters so well at first glance. It's their folks that tell em how to recognize the monsters. . . . And when they went home [from Ardelia Lortz's terrifying renditions of fairy tales], they didn't remember, in the top part of their minds, anyways, about the stories or the posters. Down underneath, I think they remembered plenty, just like down underneath Sam knows who his Library Policeman is. I think they still remember today—the bankers and lawyers and big-time farmers who were once Ardelia's Good Babies. I can still see em, wearin pinafores and short pants, sittin in those little chairs, lookin at Ardelia in the middle of the circle, their eyes so big and round they looked like pie-plates. And I think that when it gets dark and the storms come, or when they are sleepin and the nightmares come, they go back to bein kids. I think the doors open and they see the Three Bears— Ardelia's Three Bears—eatin the brains out of Goldilock's head with their wooden porridge-spoons, and Baby Bear wearin Goldilock's scalp on his head like a long golden wig. I think they wake up sweaty, feelin sick and afraid. I think that's what she left this town. I think she left a legacy of secret nightmares.
>
> (527)

The Ardelia Lortz that Dirty Dave speaks of is a stain on his memories. She is the embodiment of the adult world that strives to swallow its young. In the past, she had run the public library in town where children's readings took place. Once the doors were shut and the parents had gone, Ardelia perverted all of the children's favorite fairy tales into her own gory versions where the protagonists are killed and maimed because they are naughty little children. When the listeners showed fear, she took them into another room and turned into a monster with a funnel-shaped mouth that sucked the tears of fear right from their eyes; she sucked them dry of all the imaginative capabilities that kept them young, staining their youth with her corrupted adult vision.

Ardelia is central to the story because it is she who comes back as a ghost to feed on protagonist Sam Peebles' fear, one which was never resolved as a child. Sam's fear is of libraries; what once were places of limitless possibilities, places of magical learning, are now to Sam the manifestations of a dark memory from past years—the memory of being raped by a homosexual child molester when Sam was returning an overdue book to the public library. The child molester had claimed that he was punishing Sam for being a naughty boy who did not return his book on time. The young Sam, who, like children everywhere, was impressionable in his youth, took the molester's accusation to heart, and from that point on, had his childish fascina-

tion with libraries reduced to repulsion. Dirty Dave, who had followed Ardelia's persecution of the young when she was living primarily because of an adult lust for her, also admits that corrupting children was appealing to his adult mind:

> There's a part of me, even now, that wants to sugarcoat it, make my part in it better than it was. I'd like to tell you that I fought with her, argued, told her I didn't want nothin to do with scarin a bunch of kids . . . but it wouldn't be true. I went right along with what she wanted me to do. God help me, I did. Partly it was because I was scared of her by then. But mostly it was because I was still besotted with her. And there was something else, too. There was a mean, nasty part of me—I don't think it's in everyone, but I think it's in a lot of us—that liked what she was up to. Liked it.
>
> (520)

The combination of supplicating himself for Ardelia's body and secretly enjoying the corruption of youth alienates Dirty Dave from the children whom he had respected and admired prior to meeting Ardelia. His feelings about the role he played in Ardelia's perversion of Junction City's children is significant when put together with the other adults in the story who thrive on eradicating the magic of youth, a tendency in adults that Sam has difficulty understanding, keeping him from being whole. Because Sam Peebles had never been able to come to terms with the reality of his perversion, he cannot defeat Ardelia and the Library Policeman of his past until he can return to his childhood and retrieve the golden moments that were stolen from him.

Prior to being raped, Sam had purchased a pack of red licorice. The red licorice, like the library, had become a negative memory, one that prior to his manipulation by the molester had been a meaningful token of his youth. Sam defeats Ardelia and the Library Policeman by buying several packs of the same red licorice and jamming them into the mouth of the monster—which ultimately becomes a union of Ardelia, his molester, and all the negative memories those adults represent—that is trying to swallow him the same way it did his innocence. Because he is finally able to return to the magic of his childhood, using those memories to oppose his enemies, the adult Sam is able to reclaim a portion of the innocence that the adult world had taken from him.

King's stories that depict a conflict between children and adults may be seen as having their foundations built in the portrayal of the age gap as presented by the American media. Television and movies often portray the young as threatening to the adult world, something easily identified in films such as *The Exorcist,* a story about a young girl who, after being possessed by the devil, strikes out at the adults surrounding her; *The Omen,* which uses a child as the vehicle through which the coming of the Beast as promised in the book of Revelations is realized; *The Class of 1984,* a film that tells the story of a man's battle against a group of delinquent high school students who represent all of the destructive impulses in humankind; and the number of movies that portray youths and adolescents as wanting nothing but a good time void of responsibility—drinking, getting high, playing rock music, wanting constant sex (*Porky's, Friday the 13th, Fast Times at Ridgemont High*). The media has indeed tended to condition society into believing that the young are a threat to the adult world's standards of living. By presenting youths in such a fashion, the media has succeeded in stereotyping them. While these presentations may be seen on one side as reactions by youths who are fighting against their elders who are suppressing them, most often they are viewed as the mirror opposite: the young lack respect for the old and therefore suffer in failing to adhere to adult precepts. The sad truth lies in the fact that the media, which is run by adults, often does not look back on adolescence as a meaningful time but rather focuses on the tragedies that occur during youth: a painful loss of virginity, illicit experimentation with controlled substances resulting in negative consequences, painful pranks on vulnerable peers. Instead of portraying children and adolescents as having the strength and imaginative capacities to combat their adversities, American media has often presented them as weak, disturbed individuals with ambiguous identities who perish because of their helplessness and lack of moral direction.

King seems to be aware of the misinterpretation of the young in the media, and he tries to provide an alternative viewpoint by portraying his young people as being stronger than the corrupt adult world. Often in his books, the initial coming of age occurs when children first become wise to the several rites of initiation into adulthood offered by their elders. The optimism King has for American youth shines through in his belief that children have the capacity to achieve mature growth when passing through these rites of passage; more often than not, King's young people are able to leave their states of innocence with their heads held high and are strong enough to recognize the significance of the step in human development they are taking. In ***The Sun Dog***, Kevin Delevan, the young owner of the Polaroid Sun 660 that so captivates Pop Merrill's attention, has the strength to determine when he will be ready to cross the line separating purity from experience, an ability to discriminate that shines clear in his recollection of a hunting trip with his father:

> Bet you wish it'd been your turn in the puckies, don't you, son? the game-warden had asked, ruffling Kevin's hair. Kevin had nodded, keeping his secret to himself: he was glad it hadn't been his turn in the puckies, his rifle which must be responsible for throwing the slug or not throwing it . . . and, if he had turned out to have the courage to do the shooting, his reward would have been only another troublesome responsibility: to shoot the buck clean. He didn't know if he could have mustered the courage to put another bullet in the thing if the kill wasn't clean, or the strength to chase the trail of its blood and steaming, startled droppings and finish what he started if it ran. He had smiled up at the game-warden and nodded and his dad had snapped a picture of that, and there had never been any need to tell his dad that the thought going on behind that upturned

> brow and under the game-warden's ruffling hand had been No. I don't wish it. The world is full of tests, but twelve's too young to go hunting them. I'm glad it was Mr. Roberson. I'm not ready yet to try a man's tests.

> (756)

These reflections take place when Kevin is facing the dog that Pop Merrill had released from the camera because of his greedy adult anxiety. This is a turning point in the story because it is this moment when Kevin must decide whether to turn the camera that will be used to combat the dog over to his father or whether to take on the task himself, a man's task that he had not yet been prepared to face while hunting at the age of twelve. Kevin recognizes that the present moment is the time to make that step, for where before crossing into manhood would have been done in vain (shooting a deer), he is now in a position to save both his and his father's lives:

> The thought of turning the Polaroid over to his father crossed his mind, but only momentarily. Something deep inside himself knew the truth: to pass the camera would be tantamount to murdering his father and committing suicide himself. His father believed something, but that wasn't specific enough. The camera wouldn't work for his father even if his father managed to break out of his current stunned condition and press the shutter. It would only work for him.

> (757)

After recalling the time when he was tempted to enter the adult world, a transition that could have been accomplished by aiming his rifle at the deer and mortally wounding it, Kevin remembers that he had in his heart resisted the temptation, knowing truly well he was not yet ready. The coming of age into adulthood occurs when he realizes that he is in a position to react like an adult, yet the magic of the transition rests in the fact that Kevin also understands that he is not stained because of this awareness but rather is in close enough contact with his youth to have the imaginative capacity to defeat the inexplicable atrocity bearing down on him and his father. While recognizing that his father is slightly aware of what is going on as the dog prepares to strike, Kevin has the inner strength to speculate that his father is still too out of touch with such phenomena because of the imaginative atrophy of adulthood. The combined abilities to walk through his rite of passage with confidence and utilize his childish capacities result in Kevin's life-saving effort.

The Body, King's tour de force of coming of age stories, also portrays young people as having the inner strength to make the transition from innocence to experience. After hearing of a boy from town who had disappeared after venturing out to pick berries, a group of four young boys embark on a journey through miles of railroad tracks and vegetation to find the boy, who they believe is surely dead. Along the trip, the four begin to realize the significance of their union in their search and are able to grasp the splendor of childhood bonding, which provides the catapult to accomplishing their task. Gordie Lachance, the story's narrator, acts as spokesperson for the group when he explicates his growing realization that both he and his friends are taking a significant step toward maturity in searching a first exposure to death:

> Unspoken—maybe it was too fundamental to be spoken—was the idea that this was a big thing. It wasn't screwing around with firecrackers or trying to look through the knothole in the back of the girls' privy at Harrison State Park. This was something on a par with getting laid for the first time, or going into the Army, or buying your first bottle of legal liquor.
>
> There's a high ritual to all fundamental events, the rites of passage, the magic corridor where the change happens. Buying the condoms. Standing before the minister. Raising your hand and taking the oath. Or, if you please, walking down the railroad tracks to meet a fellow your own age halfway, the same as I'd walk halfway over to Pine Street to meet Chris if he was coming over to my house, or the way Teddy would walk halfway down Gates Street to meet me if I was going to his. It seemed right to do it this way, because the rite of passage is a magic corridor and so we always provide an aisle—it's what you walk down when you get married, what they carry you down when you get buried. Our corridor was those twin rails, and we walked between them, just bopping along toward whatever this was supposed to mean.
>
> (415)

Gordie's passage suggests that he and his friends have reached a point where they are prepared to traverse into the world of experience, leaving their innocence behind. The passage is inspirational in that it does not portray youth teetering on the "unstable legs of adolescence" but rather suggests that the boys are indeed ready to make the transition confidently. In the end, they are able to complete their rite of passage with authority. After they discover the dead body, a group of older boys wanting media exposure burst in to claim the body for themselves. The younger ones, realizing the trials they had to endure in achieving their end goal, use their accumulated strength to turn the interlopers back. Once again, King has presented a vision of youth that has the capacity to grow from change and heed the lessons it provides.

King also attempts to show in his fiction that children and adolescents are not always the blank slates that adults believe them to be. While King's adults boast a knowledge of the world, they are often ignorant of the fact that their intimate relationship with rational explanation gives them less an understanding of the line separating reality from unreality that youths in their imaginative splendor can access. King's young people, while still innocent, are indeed often aware that there are some things that they can comprehend that their elders could not even if they tried. In effect, it is the imaginative capacities that King's children possess that ultimately alienate them from adults. A scene from *'Salem's Lot* that supports this idea: upon arriving home after visiting the Marsten house, where he hears the voice of head-vampire Barlow in the cellar, young Mark Petrie is greeted with dismay by his parents, who have been worried sick over his extended absence:

> "Where have you been?" She caught his shoulders and shook them.
>
> "Out," he said wanly. "I fell down running home."

There was nothing else to say. The essential and defining characteristic of childhood is not the effortless merging of dream and reality, but only alienation. There are no words for childhood's dark turns and exhalations. A wise child recognizes it and submits to the necessary consequences. A child who counts the cost is a child no longer.

> He added: "The time got away from me. It—"
>
> Then his father, descending upon him.
>
> (293)

Mark Petrie comes home looking like he'd just been run over by a car, an appearance caused by his stumbling and falling while running from the Marsten house. But he cannot tell his parents the truth, because in their adult tendency to adhere to reason, they could not possibly understand or believe him. Mark understands and endures the ensuing interrogation.

Other examples of a child's interpretation of the world as opposed to an adult's can be found throughout King's canon. In *The Library Policeman*, Sam Peebles begins to make the distinction after observing a grim poster Ardelia Lortz had put up on the door to the children's reading room in the public library:

> The door was closed. On it was a picture of Little Red Riding Hood, looking down at the wolf in grandma's bed. The wolf was wearing Grandma's nightgown and Grandma's nightcap. It was snarling. Foam dripped from between its bared fangs. An expression of almost exquisite horror had transfixed Little Red Riding Hood's face, and the poster seemed not just to suggest but to actually proclaim that the happy ending of this story—of all fairy tales—was a convenient lie. Parents might believe such guff, Red Riding Hood's ghastly-sick face said, but the little ones knew better, didn't they?
>
> (418)

Peebles recognizes during a retrospect on childhood that there are some things that children can see in their vivid imaginations that adults, members of the "Reasonable tribe" never could. Likewise, in the short story **"The Boogeyman"** (*Night Shift*), protagonist Lester Billings begins to grasp his own lack of childish imagination that, had it been present, may have saved his children from the monster preying on them from their closets:

> I started to think, maybe if you think of a thing long enough, believe in it, it gets real. Maybe all the monsters we were scared of when we were kids, Frankenstein and Wolfman and Mummy, maybe they were real. Real enough to kill the kids they said fell in gravel pits or drowned in lakes or were just never found. Maybe grownups unmake that world because we're so sure of the world's normalcy.
>
> (**"The Boogeyman,"** Fogler Special Collections 6)

Up until this point, Billings had reprimanded his children for dreaming up the monster in their closets. Because of the separation between what his children believed and what he was not able to believe, Billing's ignorance ends in their deaths. The children who were able to understand the world of monsters were completely helpless to stop the one living among them; their only savior, their father, did not have the imaginative capacity to heed their call of distress. (Note: **"The Boogeyman"** is also interesting in its implications of an adult world persecuting its young. Billing's disbelief of the monster in his house also arises from his hostility toward his children, who, rather than being seen as a blessing, are seen as extra baggage. Prior to his children's deaths, Billings had come to think of his children as unwanted responsibilities. In effect, what Billings denies to be the cause of his children's deaths also arises from his subconscious desire to see himself rid of them.)

Although King often attempts to explain the imaginative capacities that separate the young from the old, thereby making children better prepared in the shadow of oncoming danger, he does not make children completely spotless in their understandings of the human condition. On the contrary, while King writes to show the differences between the imaginations of the young and old, he also explicates that there are certain awarenesses to which adults have access while children do not. From this perspective, while a child is often aware of an adult's misunderstanding of the supernatural and imaginable realm, an adult is cognizant of a child's inability to estimate human nature. This concept would tend to argue that a child, who has not yet been exposed enough to the evil ways in which the world operates, is vulnerable in his or her ignorance of adult human behavior. The following exchange between Andy McGee and his daughter, Charlie, in *Firestarter* suggests this important differential between an adult's understanding of the world as compared to a child's:

[at a Best Western hotel after Andy has rescued Charlie from The Shop agents who have just executed his wife]

"I want Mommy," she sobbed.

He nodded. He wanted her, too. He held Charlie tightly to him and smelled ozone and porcelain and cooked Best Western towels. She had almost flashfried them both.

"It's gonna be all right," he told her, and rocked her, not really believing it, but it was the litany, the Psalter, the voice of the adult calling down the black well of years into the miserable pit of terrorized childhood; it was what you said when things went wrong; it was the nightlight that could not banish the monster from the closet but perhaps only keep it at bay for a little while; it was the voice without power that must speak nevertheless.

"It's gonna be all right," he told her, not really believing it, knowing as every adult knows in his secret heart that nothing is really all right, ever. "It's gonna be all right."

He was crying. He couldn't help it now. His tears came in a flood and he held her to his chest as tightly as he could.

"Charlie, I swear to you, somehow it's gonna be all right."

(180)

The difference in worldly knowledge between children and adults is apparent in the novel. Charlie possesses the talent of pyrokinesis, which enables her to set fires at will. Her understanding of her talent is representative of a young child's: she does not yet understand the power she holds within her, and she is often left in a state of disorientation after she uses it. Too young to understand controlling it, Charlie only uses the power, much as any young child would, spontaneously; she only uses it when either she or her father is in danger. The adult world, on the other hand, wants to use her as a secret governmental weapon. Because they recognize the massive destruction Charlie's power can inflict, the adult world (represented as The Shop and the U.S. government) tries to apprehend her and harness her wild talent. In her youth, Charlie is too young to understand that adults wish to manipulate her, much as she is too young to realize that things are not "all right"—a consolation that her father must prevericate to ease her tension. Only Andy, a grown-up member of the adult society, possesses this understanding that will take years for his daughter to comprehend.

King's analysis of youth does not end with pre-adolescent childhood. On the contrary, he spends an equal amount of text exploring life after the initial coming of age, which takes place after children have lost their innocence through an initiation to worldliness. He is just as concerned with the next stage of human development, adolescence, which actually serves as the void between the extremities of childhood innocence and adult experience. Adolescence to King may be the most turbulent period of people's lives because it is a time when they must develop their personalities without any firm ground to stand on; no longer wearing the pure skin of childhood, yet also not bearing the experienced colors of adulthood, adolescents are often trapped in identity crises. The development that takes place during this period carries tremendous implications concerning what people will become as adults. Susceptible to confusion about themselves, King's adolescents are vulnerable to adversity. Douglas Winter, quoting author Charles L. Grant, indicates King's preoccupation with adolescence by arguing, "In King's view, 'the struggle toward adolescence and adulthood is as fraught with terror as the worst possible nightmare, and as meaningful as anything a grown-up has to contend with'" (*SK* 32). Critic Tom Newhouse provides what is perhaps the most accurate description of the dilemma facing King's adolescents when he writes that "they are often outsiders who turn to violence as a response to exclusionary social environments which deny them acceptance, or who resort to destructive attitudes that they believe will advance them upward" (49). While a student at the University of Maine at Orono, King wrote a weekly column titled "King's Garbage Truck," which appeared in the campus newspaper, *The Maine Campus*. In his May 21, 1970, column, the last "Garbage Truck" column he wrote, King said this about his own transition into the adult world after completing his required studies:

> This boy has shown evidences of some talent, although at this point it is impossible to tell if he is just a flash in the pan or if he has real possibilities. It seems obvious that he has learned a great deal at the University of Maine at Orono, although a great deal has contributed to a lessening of idealistic fervor rather than a heightening of that characteristic. If a speaker at his birth into the real world mentions "changing the world with the bright-eyed vigor of youth" this young man is apt to flip him the bird and walk out, as he does not feel very bright-eyed by this time; in fact, he feels about two thousand years old.

It is implicit in this statement that even King, who when he wrote this was writing non-fiction, was weary of the tasks that lay ahead of him in making the complete transition to adulthood. Perhaps it is a realization such as this one that has been the motivating factor behind devoting a large portion of his literature to the uphill battle young people must endure when struggling through the crises brought about by fighting to understand who they are.

Finding a meaningful identity is perhaps the most pervasive conflict facing King's fictitious adolescents. The vulnerability arising from having no sound identity often opens them up to the constant fire of adversities being cast at them by adults and peers alike. No better example can be found than in King's first published novel, *Carrie*. *Carrie* is the story of an ugly-duckling with an extraordinary gift, telekinesis, which enables her to move stationary objects by merely using her will. She is simultaneously persecuted by her peers, who take advantage of her humble docility, and her religious fundamentalist mother, who interprets everything Carrie does as being sinful. While trying to discover her identity, Carrie's view of herself is continuously distorted by the ways in which her immediate associates react to her. Winter argues that "she is at the center of an ever-tightening circle of control, of a society laden with traps that demand conformity and the loss of identity" (35). Her significant others seem intent on dictating to Carrie exactly how she is to view herself. Yet while she is discouraged from asserting herself as an autonomous individual, she carries on with the human desire to persevere. She is granted the opportunity to grasp her femininity when a classmate, Sue Snell, takes pity on her after succumbing to the guilt from her involvement in taunting Carrie and forfeits her prom date, Tommy Ross, whom she persuades to escort Carrie to the dance. Carrie reacts to the invitation by making herself up, allowing her natural beauty hidden beneath her humble exterior to shine through, which stuns her adversaries. The peers most preoccupied with making Carrie's life a living hell respond by dumping pig blood on her when she is mockingly elected prom queen. When she returns home after wreaking destruction on those who shamed her, she walks into the second trap, her mother, who, believing Carrie had been out behaving immorally, rebukes her. Like Carrie's peers, her mother ultimately dies at the hand of Carrie's

wrath. The results of prom night are catastrophic, and the tragedy lies in the fact that Carrie had finally summoned the courage to exercise her autonomy only to have her peers and her mother deny her that opportunity.

Carrie is metamorphasized into a monster by the society that tried to repress her. But all the while, the reader never truly views Carrie as an atrocity; on the contrary, she demands the reader's sympathy. She does not willfully conduct evil against others but rather is forced to lash back at those who try consistently to eradicate the one thing that has any significant meaning in Carrie's adolescence: her self-worth. Critic Ben Indick explains King's treatment of Carrie as a victim rather than as an aggressor when he says that "the heroine of *Carrie*, no more mature than most of her fellow teenagers, nevertheless tries to understand herself and particularly her mother. Her destructive acts come only because she has no way to respond emotionally and intellectually" (160).

Another prime example of a King adolescent who is pushed into mayhem is Arnie Cunningham in *Christine*. Arnie is the male counterpart of Carrie. While he does not possess any wild talent, he is similar to Carrie in his awkwardness and forced humility because of his lack of physical prowess. Like Carrie's peers, Arnie's never accept him but insist on keeping him humble. Girls will have nothing to do with him, thinking he is a greek with zits. Boys intimidate him because he is weak. Arnie even feels alienated from his parents, who expect him to follow the blueprint of his life they have drawn for him. When Arnie finds and purchases Christine, a '57 Plymouth Fury in which he takes great pride, his feelings of persecution are reinforced from all sides: his parents reject the car because they think it will keep him from his studies, and his peers react with distaste because they realize his fixation with it has made him bolder in his stand against them. His parents discourage his involvement with the car by prohibiting him from parking it in front of the house, and his teenage adversaries at one point pulverize it. Aside from Dennis Guilder, Arnie's one true friend, Arnie is under constant pressure to refrain from establishing any meaningful identity of his own—an identity he feels the car could provide. Dennis summarizes Arnie's plight and that of any other high school outcast when he says that:

> he was a loser, you know. Every high school has to have at least two; it's like a national law. One male, one female. Everyone's dumping ground. Having a bad day? Flunked a big test? Had an argument with your folks and got grounded for the weekend? No problem. Just find one of those poor sad sacks that go scurrying around the halls like criminals before the home-room bell and walk it right to him.
>
> (1)

In effect, Arnie comes to believe that his only purposes in life are to play both the punching bag on which his peers take out their frustrations and the obedient son who must respect his parents' wishes, even if those wishes conflict with his own.

As Arnie's attachment to Christine grows stronger, so do the lines separating Arnie from his significant others grow clearer. In an exchange with Dennis, Arnie discloses his unhappiness with his parents, a feeling not unfamiliar to many adolescents:

> "Has it ever occurred to you," he said abruptly, "that parents are nothing but overgrown kids until their children drag them into adulthood? Usually kicking and screaming?"
>
> I shook my head.
>
> "Tell you what I think," he said "I think that part of being a parent is trying to kill your kids. I know it sounds a little crazy at first . . . but there are lots of things that sound nuts until you really consider them. Penis envy. Oedpial conflicts. The Shroud of Turin . . . I really believe it, though . . . not that they know what they're doing; I don't believe that at all. And do you know why? . . . Because as soon as you have a kid, you know for sure that you're going to die. When you have a kid, you see your own gravestone."
>
> (26-27)

Arnie's feelings of no way out—his despair in establishing a positive meaningful identity while under fire from significant others—combined with his lack of faith in people willing to form substantial relationships with him lead to his fall from humanity and susceptibility to evil. As Bernadette Lynn Bosky brings to light, "Arnie's feelings of great potential hidden by ugliness, of being unappreciated and socially excluded, pave the way for his seduction by Christine" (227). While Arnie does begin to understand Christine's evil late in the book, he still rejects the option to do the right thing—to destroy her—because he is unwilling to surrender the feelings of self-worth she has given him. Though he makes a severe lapse in moral judgment, it could be argued that he has been conditioned by the society persecuting him to dismiss any notion of brotherhood. In the end, Arnie, like Carrie White, can be observed as a sympathetic character even in the shadow of the mass destruction he causes because his downfall is the result of being denied his autonomy.

While King often expresses his sympathies for children and adolescents who are persecuted by a suppressive society comprised chiefly of adults, readers must not overlook that King is also making a call to adults that they may redeem themselves by thoughtfully looking back on their own youth and remembering the magic of those times and the lessons learned. What King is most concerned with in adults is their ability to complete a wheel: to begin life as innocent beings who are eventually corrupted by worldly evil who may then circle back to the period of innocence so that they may not lose touch with beauty of the human experience. Says King, "I'm interested in the notion of finishing off one's childhood as one completes making a wheel. The idea is to go back and confront your childhood, in a sense relive it if you can, so that you can be whole" (Winter, *AOD* 185). King fears that too often adults become so enveloped in the trials and tribulations of adult life that they drown themselves in the pools of logic and reason; in doing so, they forget the wonder of viewing the splendor and mysticism of life as seen through a child's eyes, an experience they must return to time and time again if they want to avoid being swallowed by the world:

> Rather than indulge in a spurious attempt to recapture a social milieu, King's fiction often looks to our youth as the earlier way of life whose "swan song" must be sung. His stories are songs of innocence and experience, juxtaposing childhood and adulthood—effectively completing the wheel whose turn began in childhood by reexperiencing those days from a mature perspective.
>
> (Winter, *AOD* 10)

Often in King's fiction, the dilemma facing the adult characters stems directly from two inabilities. The first is the inability to return to childhood and remember the magic of those moments. The second is the failure to understand the significance of an event that happened during that time period—an event that is repressed rather than resolved as one grows older. King attempts to point out that there must be a synthesis between childhood and adult experiences—that one must be able to interpret life by merging the sensory and emotional input that occurs throughout the cycle of one's life. In *The Library Policeman,* the main conflict arises from Sam Peebles' initial inability to return to his childhood and face the atrocity (a homosexual rape) that was dealt to him then. Until the end of the story, instead of going back and facing what happened to him from a mature perspective, Sam hides the memory far back in his mind. But without the synthesis between childhood and adulthood, he is never really whole. Rather, he finds himself trapped solely in one period or the other, as adults can tend to do:

> [after the Library Policeman has stormed into Sam's house]
>
> Sam felt a triple-locked door far back in his mind straining to burst open. He never thought of running. The idea of flight was beyond his capacity to imagine. He was a child again, a child who has been caught red-handed
>
> (the book isn't *The Speaker's Companion*) doing some awful bad thing. Instead of running (the book isn't *Best Loved Poems of the American People*)
>
> he folded slowly over his own wet crotch and collapsed between the two stools which stood at the counter, holding his hands up blindly above his head.
>
> (487)

The reason the Library Policeman has come after Sam again is because Sam had recently failed to return two library books. Yet while Sam is cowering in the corner of his kitchen under the shadow of his intruder, the emotional salad being tossed in his brain tries to remind him that it is not only those two books for which his intruder has come back; to Sam, the Library Policeman is also asking once again for the Robert Louis Stevenson book he'd not returned as a child on the day the man raped him. Sam is bounced back and forth between the two time periods because he has not yet been able to complete the wheel and understand what had happened to him. Only when he is able to accomplish that circling back to his younger days can Sam efficiently battle his adversary. As Naomi Higgins, Sam's girlfriend, acknowledges when observing Sam's revival of spirit in confronting his enemy, "he looks like a man who has been granted the opportunity to return to his worst nightmares . . . with some powerful weapon in his hands" (576).

A similar situation can be found in *'Salem's Lot,* where protagonist Ben Mears has returned to the town of his childhood carrying some heavy emotional baggage. When a youth, Ben had entered the Marsten house on a dare, and, after entering, had found the house's owner hanging by his neck from a support beam in an upstairs bedroom. Mears had fled from the house then and has returned to the present with that trauma still unresolved. This lack of resolve in understanding death is intensified by the recent death of his wife, who was killed in a fatal motorcycle accident in which Ben had been driving. Ben's predicament exists until he benefits from the aid of a child, Mark Petrie, who becomes the connection with childhood Ben needs in returning back to his own youth to understand death and dying. Ben then becomes emotionally equipped to combat the league of vampires presently spreading death throughout 'Salem's Lot once he is able to complete the wheel joining youth and adulthood.

What both Sam and Ben do in the end of their stories—complete the wheel—is elemental to King's understanding of the life cycle:

> None of us adults remember childhood. We think we remember it, which is even more dangerous. Colors are brighter. The sky looks bigger. It's impossible to remember exactly how it was. Kids live in a constant state of shock. The input is so fresh and so strong that it's bound to be frightening.
>
> (BB *95*)

As King points out, because the input is so powerful when perceived as a child, it becomes all the more difficult to recollect it as years separate adults from that experience. By making a mental effort to return to those days and recognizing the distance from them created by time, adults can capitalize on magical childhood moments by synthesizing the memory with an adult's perspective of life. King revealed this belief years before his first published novel in the March 27, 1969, "King's Garbage Truck," written at age 21: "Somehow everything seems to get just a little dirtier and more selfish as we get older. It's good to remember other times, once in a while. We'll have to do it again some time." Once adults can accomplish the synthesis, they will have taken a giant step toward becoming whole.

The need for adults to access their childhood and adolescent memories and observations resonates throughout King's fiction, published and unpublished. *Blaze,* an un-

published King novel held by the Raymond H. Fogler Library Special Collections Department at UMO, is a fine example. The story is about the life of Claiborne Blaisdell, Jr., an oversized man who has a history of criminal behavior in his adult years. Once a promising student as a youngster, his intellectual capacities were destroyed after a brain injury resulting from being thrown down a flight of stairs by his father. The injury caused Blaze's brain to slow, keeping his mind perpetually adolescent. His actions as an adult are correlative to a young person's for he is not cursed with the adult tendency to cheat and deceive. However, his limited intellect often leads to his manipulation and persecution. In order to console himself about the evil of the adult world, he reflects on memories such as the following, a time when he and a friend from the orphanage where he'd been raised played hookie to travel to Boston:

> and they began to laugh with each other, laughing into each other's faces in a rare moment of triumph that comes only once or twice in the richest of lifetimes, a time that seems wholly natural and right when it occurs, but is golden and soft in retrospect, too beautiful to be looked at often. It is a time that is usually recalled in future circumstances that are bitter, a time that is wholly childhood, often painful in late-remembered truth. Blaze never forgot it.
>
> (70)

The story creates a valid argument that Blaze's slowed mental growth is a blessing in disguise. It allows him to see life continuously from a child's perspective which enables him to view simple things with wonder and imagination. The best example of this can be found in Blaze's attachment to Joe Gerard III, a baby Blaze kidnaps at the prompting of the voice of his dead partner in crime, George Rockley. Although Rockley is dead, his spirit is recreated in Blaze's mind to ease Blaze's utter isolation and feelings of loneliness that occur once his only friend is deceased. Blaze kidnaps the baby with the intent of ransoming it, but soon falls in love with it in a way that no rational adult could:

> The dawning of the child's possibilities stole over him anew, and he shivered with the urge to snatch it up and cradle it to himself, to see Joe open his eyes and goggle around with his usual expression of perpetual wonder. With no knowledge of Wordsworth or Rousseau, he grasped the essential attraction infants have for adults; their cleanliness, their blankness, their portentous idiocy. And with Blaze, this feeling existed in a pureness that is rarely common to parents. He was not bright enough or motivated enough to have ambitions for the child or to want to mould its direction. Like a naturalist with a new species of plant, he wanted only to watch it grow.
>
> (141)

The story of Blaze is a prime indication of what King is trying to tell his readers: that it is important to synthesize child and adult perspectives. For while Blaze is a lovable character in his grownup state of innocence who can appreciate life in the way only a child can, it is his ignorance of adult behavior that culminates in his demise. His constant slip-ups, typical of inexperienced individuals, lead the law directly to him, and he is shot down in the woods where he has taken refuge with the baby. Blaze is merely an example of one extreme: the individual who can recall and perceive life through a child's eyes, and the one who avoids taking life too seriously. Yet, as has been explained, because Blaze cannot blend child experiences with adult experiences, he remains a helpless victim of a hostile world.

By thoroughly exploring the significance of youth in the chain of human development, King has succeeded in both continuing the theme as presented by his literary predecessors and commenting on the condition of young people in America. The concern for childhood and rites of passage can be linked directly to those American writers who made it a significant part of their fiction: Mark Twain, William Faulkner, Sherwood Anderson, Willa Cather, Flannery O'Connor, Joyce Carol Oates. The themes that pervade stories such as Twain's *Huckleberry Finn,* Oates' "Where Are You Going? Where Have You Been?", and Faulkner's "Barn Burning" are the same ones that have had a profound influence on King's writing. Twain's Huck Finn embarks on a journey down the Mississippi River where his childhood innocence is constantly threatened by the adult world; likewise, King's Jack Sawyer in *The Talisman* ventures west across the expanse of America, a physical journey that correlates his evolution from innocence to experience. Oates' protagonist, Connie, is escorted away by evil incarnate, Arnold Friend, when she selfishly alienates herself and succumbs to worldly desires; King's Arnie Cunningham in *Christine* makes a similar departure after isolating himself from society while searching for an identity. Faulkner's Sarty comes of age when he turns in his father for having burned a neighbor's farm after Sarty had repressed the truth of his father's evil acts for many years; in a similar situation, King's Danny Torrance (*The Shining*) confronts his father after deciding he is too enveloped in his own selfishly evil impulses to save himself. While these may be crude synopses, the themes concerning youth that King explores with such careful detail are the same that have helped earn his literary predecessors their greatness.

Because King is able to present an image of youth that is both optimistic and sympathetic, he provides a meaningful counterpoint to the tendencies of the American media to stereotype youth as troublesome. In a modernized America where young people are regularly exposed to input that consistently threatens to corrupt their innocence, King's portrayal of youth should be hailed as nothing less than splendid. By writing about youth as a time to be cherished, King assures his readers that they are not too far away from avoiding the self-destruction that can arise from failing to grasp the memories and lessons of being young. Closer scrutiny of King's fiction should convince readers that youth need not be observed as a strenuous period of development but rather one of significant meaning;

by returning to younger days and rejoicing in their wonders and steps toward growth from a mature perspective, Americans can save themselves from being devoured by the moral, social, and economic pressures that so often dilute the magic of the human experience with age.

The material covered thus far does not do King proper justice. If one were to accumulate an adequate amount of critical interpretation on the political, social, and moral subtexts of King's works, one would easily fill up rows of library shelves much like those that are weighted with critical interpretations on Faulkner and Shakespeare. The material discussed up to this point is an attempt to provide the reader with the knowledge that King is not just an entertainer—that there is more to acquire from a Stephen King book than just scares and thrills. As the ensuing sections aim to prove, King does not limit himself to any one area but rather attempts to address all spectres of the human condition in his canon, a feat that lesser writers of today's popular culture have been unable to achieve.

Leonard Cassuto (essay date 1998)

SOURCE: Cassuto, Leonard. "Repulsive Attractions: 'The Raft,' the *Vagina Dentata,* and the Slasher Formula." In *Imagining the Worst: Stephen King and the Representation of Women,* edited by Kathleen Margaret Lant and Theresa Thompson, pp. 61-78. Westport, Conn.: Greenwood Press, 1998.

[*In the following essay, Cassuto finds parallels between "The Raft" and the slasher-film genre, and views the mysterious monster in the story as an embodiment of the* vagina dentata.]

"Twice-told tales" occupy a time-honored place in American literature, but Stephen King's **"The Raft"** deserves attention as a twice-written one. King himself was so haunted by his own creation that he rewrote the story from memory in 1981, thirteen years after first devising it. (He had published it in an obscure skin magazine in 1968 as **"The Float,"** but he never located a copy and later discovered that he had lost the original typescript.) From his brief account of the story's composition, it's clear that King rewrote it because he wanted to read it himself, presumably because—to use his own phrase—it pushed his "horror-button" as hard as it does those of his readers (*Danse Macabre,* 273).[1]

I want to consider the lingering power of **"The Raft"** in terms of its genre conventions and central symbol. The story is a simple one: Four reckless college students (two men and two women) decide to defy the onset of autumn by driving out to an isolated lake forty miles from campus and swimming out to the raft anchored there. They are followed in the water by a mysterious, floating black spot that lurks alongside the raft. The spot tracks their movements, lures them with flashing colors, and takes advantage of their carelessness to pull them into the water one by one and devour them with gory rapacity. The story ends with the last character, Randy, standing cold and alone on the raft, unable to sit or lie down (if he does, the spot will slide underneath the raft and grab him through the cracks between the boards). Exhausted and despairing, Randy is about to give up and allow himself to be drawn into the water to be absorbed. The black spot is never explained.

The plot and setting of **"The Raft"** closely follow those of the slasher film, an unsubtle genre of horror, very popular in recent years, that typically features a killer who punishes adolescent sexuality with hideous, unconscious-driven aggression (drills, knives, axes, chain saws). But unlike the invariably phallic killers of *Halloween, Friday the 13th* and their ilk, the punishing monster in this case has a distinctly female quality, and the final character it stalks is a young man rather than the woman who survives in countless movies. The black spot that mesmerizes Randy—and that will shortly kill him as it has killed everyone else in the story—is a potent, archetypal female symbol. It is the *vagina dentata*: the womb that devours. In the pages that follow, I consider **"The Raft"** as a slasher narrative with an unusual hero (a male), an unusual monster (a "female"), and an unusual outcome (everybody dies). In the end, I will argue that the story stands as Stephen King's obliquely self-conscious, unusually deep and honest commentary on the attraction of formula-driven horror.

"The Raft" and the Vagina Dentata

When asked in a 1982 interview about his greatest sexual fear, Stephen King replied, "The vagina dentata, the vagina with teeth. The story where you were making love to a woman and it just slammed shut and cut your penis off. That'd do it" (*Bare Bones,* 189). King's fear has a lot of precedent, for the toothed vagina is an image that is found in numerous myths across cultures. It appears in various accounts as a "barred and dangerous entrance" that nonetheless holds great allure for the men who seek to enter it. Defanging the toothed vagina has generally been depicted in myth as an heroic act of male courage, a brave risk taken to bring safe reproduction to society. Akin to the *vagina dentata* is the so-called "bottomless lake," the womb that swallows men and makes them disappear. This image too is a staple of myth and folklore; its connection to castration anxiety is clear if only from the fact that its victims are always male.[2]

The black spot in **"The Raft"** is a voracious *vagina dentata* that engulfs its victims and rips them apart. The death of Randy's roommate Deke, for example, is rife with sexual connotation. Literally pulled "into the crack" between the boards of the raft, his body becomes "hard as Carrara marble," a "big tree," that is "purple" and "bulging" as it "disappear[s]" (259-60). Deke's "swelled" face is that of "a man being clutched in a bear hug of monstrous and unknowable force" (260, 261). He screams with

pain at first, but his final utterances are "thick, syrupy grunts" (260) that might, in another setting, signify orgasm. They are followed by an ejaculation of sorts: "a great jet of blood, so thick it was almost solid" that forces itself from his mouth (260). Deke dies after that, and his body "collapse[s] forward," as the spot makes "sucking sounds" from under the raft (261). Finally, as his dead torso is slowly forced through the crack, there comes "a sound like strong teeth crunching up a mouthful of candy jawbreakers" (262).

Freudian psychoanalysis is strangely silent about the *vagina dentata* and the fear of the castrating woman generally. Among the work of later psychoanalysts, Karen Horney's important 1932 essay, "The Dread of Woman," has provided a useful starting point for modern theorists to analyze the image. Horney argues that masculine desire of woman is intertwined with a deep fear of her, a fear that the man seeks to expunge by objectifying it. Horney suggests that even the male "glorification of women has its source not only in his cravings for love, but also in his desire to conceal his dread" (136). This dread, says Horney, does not lie solely in the fact that woman has been castrated (which is the basis for Freud's explanation). Instead, "there must be a further dread, the object of which is the woman or the female genital" (137).

Horney sees a key link between sexual desire and a desire to return to the womb: "Does the man feel, side by side with his desire to conquer, a secret longing for extinction in the act of reunion with the woman (mother)?" (139). In diagram form, her argument would look something like this:

$$\text{sex} = \text{death} = \text{reincorporation/reunion with mother}$$

In Horney's developmental equation, early castration anxiety (exemplified by the *vagina dentata*) can lead in adulthood to an uncanny fear of the mystery of motherhood.[3] This latter sense of mystery encompasses a desire to return to the womb (here, the bottomless lake), a re-union that necessarily implies a loss of individuation, or death. Horney suggests that this desire may provide the basis for Freud's death-instinct, the subject's desire for the ultimate unity to be found in self-extinction.

Horney's two central postulates, that the male dread of woman can spring from early fear of castration and then later from fear of motherhood, form the conceptual basis for Barbara Creed's interesting recent work, *The Monstrous-Feminine*. Building on Horney's work and applying it specifically to horror cinema, Creed describes the *vagina dentata* as the "mouth of hell" (106), an image of woman as castrator that embodies unconscious male fears and fantasies about the female genitals. She argues that Freud represses the possibility of the castrating female as a fearful object because of his desire to promote the phallocentric view of woman as frightening because she is castrated. To Creed, "woman also terrifies because man endows her with imaginary powers of castration" (87). She sees the castrating woman as playing a powerfully ambivalent role in the Oedipal equation, expressing the conflicting unconscious feelings that accompany the child's breaking away from the mother. Following Horney, Creed sees this conflict reflected in the simultaneous fear of castration by the mother and the desire for sexual union with her.[4] This combination of unconscious fear and desire is expressed in the consumption of horror, an urge that reflects a "morbid desire to see *as much as possible* of the unimaginable" (29). The nature of horror (that is, its traffic in death and dismemberment) "allow[s] for an explicit representation of man's castration anxieties" (155).

The *vagina dentata* powerfully embodies these anxieties, and **"The Raft"** gives affecting expression to them in a generic setting. The black spot is variously described as "humped up" and "stuffing the cracks" (263, 265). Its abundantly bloody killings support the mythical and psychological arguments for the uncanniness of menstrual blood. Yet for all of its gruesome appetites, the spot also allures; its colors reduce Rachel to "trembling wonder" before she succumbs to them, and they make Randy "loopy" (258).

On its most basic level, **"The Raft"** is an Oedipal nightmare of the castrating mother. The story enacts an elemental struggle between child and parent, with the spot representing the mother who reasserts parental authority over her children who have strayed from the correct path. On campus (where the story opens), the young people pursue their wanton and slovenly ways away from parental influence by drinking, having sex, and acting in otherwise undisciplined fashion. (The narrator comments on the poor housekeeping by the men, Randy and Deke, who let food fester in their refrigerator [247]; the women, Rachel and LaVerne, come over on a Tuesday afternoon to lie around and drink beer.) But when they leave their own surroundings and go to the "Terrible Place," the ancient order (the Parental Law) takes control and punishes all misbehavior.[5]

"The Raft" makes undisciplined sexuality into a capital crime. This notion is not new; in particular, there is important precedent in fairy tales for imagining it as one. "Little Red Riding Hood," for example, has been read by Bruno Bettelheim as a parable whose message is caution: Good children shouldn't leave the path before they're able to take care of themselves in the dark, sexual woods.[6] If they do, they'll get eaten. To Bettelheim, the tale enacts a "'deathly' fascination with sex" (176); he gives particular emphasis to the redness of the girl's hood and the hair of the wolf. (The cover illustration by Gustave Dore that adorns Bettelheim's *The Uses of Enchantment* is of a young girl—Little Red—in bed with a mean-looking wolf in a bonnet. The girl is apparently naked under the covers, wearing an equivocal expression.) Bettelheim's broad thesis is that fairy tales offer children a chance to work through their unconscious fears and desires in an imaginative setting that always leaves them "happily ever after" at the end. In the case of "Little Red Riding Hood," these unconscious thoughts center on the alluring menace of

sexual awakening. Like virtually all fairy tales, "Little Red Riding Hood" can easily be framed as a horror story, and in fact has recently been filmed as one.[7] Moreover, Creed cites "Little Red Riding Hood" as a story that invokes the *vagina dentata*.[8] And finally, **"The Raft"** bears a strong structural resemblance to "Little Red Riding Hood": The characters go literally off the path (eight miles down a back road) in order to indulge their sexual urges, and as a result, they get swallowed up.

Bettelheim says that "Premature sexuality is a regressive experience" that causes the immature subject to fall back on Oedipal coping mechanisms (173). The ultimate Oedipal regression is a return to mother, a reunion fraught with mingled fear and desire. King puts this uneasy mixture of unconscious feelings on full display out on the raft. When Randy stands alone facing the black spot after all of his friends have died, he hears the spot whispering mother-love to him in a voice he hears in his mind, amidst his own wandering memories of cars and baseball games. It is the voice of (re)incorporation: "*I love do you love*" (269). Randy responds to the voice as a child, weeping and begging, "Go away, please, go anywhere, but leave me alone. I don't love you" (269).

But predictably, Randy's fear and aversion are interlaced with curiosity and desire. The spot hypnotizes with blending colors and "rich, inward-turning spirals" on its surface (253) that lure Rachel to her death, and which Randy resists only by literally punching himself in the face (258). Even after watching his friends die, when Randy looks at the spot squeezing up between the cracks between the boards of the raft, reaching for him, he "wonder[s] what the stuff would feel like when it flowed over his feet, when it hooked into him" (263). And when, at the story's end, Randy is near to giving in to the lures and long siege by the black spot, he hears the voice in his head welcoming him into an ultimate, fearful union: "*you* do *you* do *love me*" (269). A few moments later, Randy asks, "Sing with me," and he sings a child's song about the end of school. Then he allows himself to be drawn to the spot, letting his eyes follow the spirals that invite him into its depths: The fear of castration and extinction become one with the desire for sexual union.

Randy sees the world with the eyes of a child living in a safe, protected world, an updated version of 1950s family sitcom existence. Such a world is bounded and guarded by nurturing parents. Throughout **"The Raft,"** King has Randy inwardly describe what he sees in terms of benign cultural icons and kiddie commercialism, a diverse collection of images that spans a couple of decades, including Sandy Duncan (as Peter Pan), Arthur Godfrey, PacMan, Rialto movie shows, Richard Nixon's "V for victory sign," the Yankees, the Beach Boys, and the Ramones. These emblems are part of Randy's emotional lexicon of assuring images of family life. Accordingly, he wishes for family safety when he gets in trouble. When he first suspects that the spot may be dangerous, for example, his immediate thought is that there is no one to look out for himself

and his friends: *"No one knows we're here. No one at all."*
No one to take care of them, that is—no one to be a parent to them. When he looks in vain for lights in the windows of the vacated summer cottages surrounding the lake, he imagines a family on vacation: "[S]*omebody's got to be staying the week in his place, fall foliage, shouldn't miss it, bring your Nikon, folks back home are going to love the slides*" (262). What is happening to Randy needs to be understood in terms of his all-American family view. The happenings on the raft expose the deep fears that hold up this family idyll in his mind.

Seen thus, the black spot is not simply a monster that somehow appears in the summer setting when fall comes—it is an ancient presence that has been lurking behind Randy's *Leave It to Beaver* worldview all the time, a menace for all seasons that has necessitated the construction of that ideal family order to hide its own uncanny presence in his mind. Though the origins of the spots remain a mystery, we might consider it as a projection of Randy's own unconscious fear and desire—an expression of the complicated urges that led him to suggest the fatal swim in the first place. These mixed feelings include his wish to break away from parental authority even as he desires to live under its continuing protection (a conflict that college life helps to keep in suspension). Randy longs to impress the women and win their attraction away from Deke, his football hero roommate; he fights his mingled desire for and "jealousy" of Deke's virile vitality (which he admires even as Deke dies [261]); he desires LaVerne but resents her attraction to Deke enough to want to hit her (251); later, he wants to protect LaVerne after Rachel and Deke die, even as he wants to be protected himself. The lure of the spot is, among other things, the promise to resolve these conflicts by returning everything to primal, undifferentiated oneness. At the bottom of the desire for mother is a desire for reincorporation.

If horror is essentially about the return of repressed or surpassed childhood fears—as Freud says in "The Uncanny" and King in *Danse Macabre*—then **"The Raft"** argues that one can literally never escape these fears. All four characters in **"The Raft"** are clearly familiar with Cascade Lake, where the story takes place; Rachel and Randy have clear memories of childhood summer days spent there.[9] Rachel voices a common childhood fear attached to such places, recalling that the first time she swam out to the raft as a child, she was afraid to swim back (247). Rachel's fear returns to Randy, Rachel, LaVerne, and Deke as adults in this childhood setting. It comes back in familiar, but crucially changed and newly mysterious, form. This is Freud's uncanny: the return of repressed early fear, the familiar become unfamiliar.

The outcome of the opposition between child and castrating mother in **"The Raft"** is one that broadly denies the possibility of passage from childhood to adulthood. **"The Raft"** suggests that it's impossible to escape one's youth and move on, that the attempt to break the parent-child bond will end in death.[10] The characters in King's story

move away from home and find themselves returning in search of it anyway—and the return leads to the end of them. They can never escape their childhood origin. It literally sucks them back in—but it has the opportunity to do so only because they have gone to meet it at the isolated place (isolated in geography, and also in memory) where it lies. The raft is "a little bit of summer" (247) that the four young adults try to claim in October, after summer is gone. They can't go back to the childhood past, but neither can they get away from it in their present. **"The Raft"** is in this sense a story about impotence writ large, symbolized by the inability to escape from the most powerful ruler of the child's early life: the mother. But at the same time, it's also about the wish not to get away at all.[11]

"The Raft" as Slasher

"The Raft" resembles *Halloween* and other movies like it in that the story is propelled by a killer's terrible retribution for illicit teenage sexuality.[12] The slasher setting is always empty of other people and usually isolated, but it is also typically American, and recognizably middle class, as Vera Dika points out in her 1990 study of the genre (58-59). The point is that the killer and the victims meet on ground familiar to both. Dika presents a lengthy descriptive plot analysis of the slasher film that begins with a past event that triggers present retribution: "[T]he killer's destructive force is reactivated . . . [t]he young community takes no heed . . . [t]he killer stalks [and] kills members of the young community . . . the heroine does battle with the killer . . . [she] kills or subdues the killer" and survives (though she is "not free") (59-60, 136). This summary is perhaps too elaborately patterned, with the definition of "past event" particularly needing to be questioned.

"The Raft" offers no direct clue to any notable past happening that would awaken the monster, but as I suggested in my earlier discussion of Randy's desires, the past need not include a public drama in order to leave the unconscious residue that makes the present danger possible—in horror, all unconscious desires are potentially dangerous. In practice, slashers are categorized according to Creed's more basic paradigm, the presence of a group of teenagers looking for someplace to have sex, and paying the highest price for their immature, headstrong behavior (124). Carol J. Clover describes the slasher's victims as "sexual transgressors [who] are scheduled for early destruction" (33). In the standard scenario, the monster, gendered male and equipped with a phallic weapon, does them in, one by one. They are punished until there's only one left, leading to a staple of the genre: the face-off between the last survivor (almost always a woman who, unlike her friends, is not sexually active) and the killer.

"The Raft" contains clear elements of the formula-driven slasher film. The supporting characters in the story fit the standard types seen in most genre entries. Deke is the typical he-man recognizable to all who are familiar with these stories. He's a football player with "sniper's eyes" (245), and he drives a Camaro (which one of my female friends once called a "penis car"). As his name suggests, Deke is defiantly male and unabashedly sexual: He can take his pants off in a fluid motion that Randy admires, and even when swimming, "the muscles in his back and buttocks worked gorgeously" (246). Moreover, Deke flashes the assaultive, possessive sexual gaze that Laura Mulvey has identified as a pervasive and pernicious form of cinematic expression: "He was talking to Randy but he was looking at LaVerne. LaVerne's panties were almost as transparent as her bra, the delta of her sex sculpted neatly in silk, each buttock a taut crescent" (250). Deke's eye is overcome by a stronger one, for the spot possesses its own controlling gaze. He literally disappears into the "'insatiable organ hole' of the feminine."[13] Before he suffers this fittingly sexual death, Deke seeks, receives, and revels in the sexual attention of both women in the story. He laughs off Randy's fear in a way designed to impress them (at the expense of the more cautious Randy). According to slasher convention, Deke is doomed. Characters like him—Rachel calls him "Macho City" (249)—are among the earliest victims of sexually motivated killers in slasher stories. Following formula, Deke is the second to go.

The two women in the story are also stock victims. Rachel, Deke's girlfriend and the first to die, is a "sloe-eyed" sufferer who Randy compares to petite, vulnerable Sandy Duncan (254). LaVerne, "a big girl" (261), is less sympathetic. She comes on to Deke in front of Rachel; her triumph over her rival sounds like "the arid cackle of a witch" (253). When the black spot first shows what it can do by messily consuming Rachel, LaVerne dissolves into "mewling," self-absorbed hysteria, and Deke fulfills Randy's unvoiced wish to hit her. By assigning her such marked lack of appeal, even *in extremis,* King sets LaVerne up to die in a fairly standard way. She is the third to go.

The basic slasher plot is immediately recognizable in **"The Raft"**: Four promiscuous, pleasure-driven college students go off by themselves and three of them get theirs, leaving a confrontation between the last one and the killer. But the positions of the two main characters (the killer and the survivor) are off-center. Just as the killer is gendered female rather than male, the survivor is male rather than female. And in an unusual ending, the survivor is clearly doomed. In the most comprehensive and nuanced analysis of gender and modern horror to date, Clover connects gender in the slasher film with the pain and suffering that is ritually imposed by the genre as part of a "masochistic aesthetic" that "dominates horror cinema" (222). She notes that slasher movies kill boys quickly and girls much more slowly and painfully (35); she argues, moreover, that this happens because males in the audience will be more comfortable identifying with suffering if they do so through a female character (the protagonist, whom she terms "the Final Girl").[14] Slasher films, she says, promote identification with suffering by linking it to women, who are at greater social liberty than men to express fear and pain. But the death of Deke in **"The Raft"** is a clear violation of formula: Pulled down through a crack between the boards of the raft and eaten alive from his feet up, he suffers at gruesome length. Furthermore, his death, by far the longest of the three in the story, gives way to the protracted suffering of another male, Randy.

Randy's status as final survivor merits special consideration of his suffering. The Final Girl, says Clover, is an androgynous figure whose lack of sexual activity contributes to her boyishness (40). Her femaleness is further qualified by the bravery (behavior gendered male, argues Clover) that she calls upon to defeat the killer at the end. This reversal finally makes the Final Girl into "a congenial double for the adolescent male" (51), a "male surrogate in things oedipal" (53), and in sum, a "characterological androgyne" (63).[15]

King makes Randy different from the array of slasher survivors. His maleness is not a major issue in this context; boys as well as girls can be androgynous, and the slasher genre has proved flexible enough to accommodate them in the exceptional cases in which they appear in the survivor's role.[16] At first, Randy seems to fit right into Clover's unisex mold. "A shy boy" (252), he appears as a stereotypical college nerd: When we see him for the first time he is "resetting his glasses on his nose" (244). To Deke, he's a "brain-ball" who takes "all the fucking science courses" (255). Randy is socially weaker than Deke; he accepts subordinate status as "Pancho" to Deke's "Cisco Kid." He is also more uncertain than Deke about his masculinity (significantly, his name is ungendered), and he is sexually insecure—and not without reason. He sees that his attraction to LaVerne is endangered from the start: "He liked her, but Deke was stronger" (246).

Essentially unsexed and feminized to the point that he possesses uncertain gender status, Randy fits the androgynous type that Clover would expect for a Final Boy (63). It is therefore highly significant that Randy understands pain. Looking at Rachel after Deke spurns her and accepts LaVerne's attentions, "Randy saw dull hurt on her face. . . . [H]e knew that expression . . . how that expression felt inside" (251). This sensitivity sets up Randy to suffer, basically because he knows how to do it. He knows pain because he's not so rigidly male as Deke, and because he's lost what he calls "his fear cherry" (257). This link between fear and sex is worth dwelling on in conjunction with the *vagina dentata.* Deke is sexually experienced, but in matters of fear, he's still a virgin until the spot changes that. Randy has less sexual experience, but he knows pain when he sees it—and significantly, he fears and avoids the spot even before it kills anyone.

Although Randy shows an affinity for the culturally feminized role of sufferer, he violates the qualifications for Clover's Final Androgyne in two important ways. First, going to the raft is his idea, not Deke's. Though "he never expected Deke to take it seriously" (245) and he feels guilty and regretful about putting the women on the spot as a result of it, the bold initiative is his own and the dangerous situation of his own making.

Second and most crucially, Randy has sex while he is on the raft. When he and LaVerne are the last two remaining, fear and desire combine to draw them together in a coital embrace that ends in her death when the spot seizes her hair trailing in the water. The sex "had never been like this" for Randy, and it touches off a succession of images in his mind just before the spot intervenes: "firm breasts fragrant with Coppertone oil, and if the bottom of the bikini was small enough you might see some (*hair her hair HER HAIR IS IN THE OH GOD IN THE WATER HER HAIR*)" (266, 267). The sequence of thoughts connects pubic hair to the suddenly vulnerable hair on LaVerne's head; following the associations, we see that LaVerne is ensnared by her own sexuality. The spot prevents sexual climax ("He pulled back suddenly" [267]), substituting the big death (loss of life) for the little one (orgasm). Randy's name takes on added significance in light of this grisly sexual interlude: It's a pun. And as a result of his action, he definitively masculinizes himself—at the cost of the death of a woman.

In Clover's slasher typology, the standard narrative feminizes the Final Girl through her suffering, and then masculinizes her by her courageous heroism (59). **"The Raft"** moves through these gender changes in sexually explicit fashion but with an important added regression at the end. Randy starts out sexually uncertain (the unsexed Brain in the shadow of the virile Jock [248]) and then proves his masculinity not by bravery, but more directly by copulation (specifically, by comforting and then seducing the Jock's would-be girlfriend after the Jock dies). But then Randy regresses to childhood, ending in a position of lonely, hopeless, terrified suffering at the hands of the castrating mother. The Final Girl is always chaste in slasher films, but Randy has sex at a time when the standard plot calls for him to start saving himself. The Final Girl "looks death in the face" and finds the strength to survive and resist (Clover, 35), but **"The Raft"** ends with Randy's capitulation to the seductive gaze of the black spot. In effect, Randy finds his masculinity rather than his wits in time of stress, and his emergent sexuality does him in.

The nature of the black spot also runs counter to generic expectations. Whereas the killer is almost always gendered male in slasher films, Clover notes that like the Final Girl, he too is unsexed, substituting phallic weapons for actual sexual function and thereby strongly qualifying his masculinity. (Rape doesn't happen in slasher films—dismemberment takes its place.) Sexually ambiguous, the monster makes up a matched pair with the Final Girl, supporting Clover's general contention that the slasher film "at every level presents us with hermaphroditic constructions" (55). But **"The Raft"** has a female-type monster that is all-powerful, ultimately victorious, distinctly nonphallic. Unlike the usual slasher, whose face is covered by a mask, the spot is naked and undisguised, open in its castrating depths.

It seems clear that Stephen King wants us to read **"The Raft"** as a slasher narrative. The story feels like a slasher—that is, the plot and setting evoke the kinds of

narrative expectations that a slasher does. But it's just as clear that King flouts the conventions of the formula. Though a sexual killer, the black spot is a highly atypical slasher monster, and the character of Randy is a kind of red herring: The author appears to draw him along the familiar unsexed lines of the Final Androgyne, but then he sharply and unexpectedly shifts Randy's behavior towards the male side of the sexual spectrum. In effect, King invites us to read **"The Raft"** in a certain way, and then deliberately counters our expectations. Why?

"The Raft" and the Attraction of Formula-Driven Horror

King's pointed violation of certain slasher conventions does not simply unmask the killer—his manipulation of the formula effectively pulls the cover off the workings of the entire slasher genre. If (as Clover argues) the slasher film refracts the male experience of fear, vulnerability, and pain through the socially reassuring lens of femininity and femaleness, then **"The Raft"** removes the looking glass and forces the reader to face the light directly. That is, **"The Raft"** offers no illusion of comfortable distance afforded by the conventional image of a screaming, crying woman who just manages to save herself; instead, King presents us with an immediate, culturally disturbing sight: a crying man (one who nevertheless leaves no doubt about his maleness) who cries and suffers right up to the moment of his death. By placing a female monster and a fully masculinized final character in the two key roles in his slasher story, King parts the curtain to reveal the writer at the controls, openly ordering the steps that make up the slasher ritual—and reordering the roles to remove the gender diversions. Beneath the "identificatory buffer" of the female protagonist, Clover says that the slasher is a growing-up story of "sex and parents," with the killer as "a materialized projection of the viewer's own incestuous fears and desires" (51, 49). This omnibus interpretation fits **"The Raft"** compellingly closely, further legitimating the story's position in the slasher category. In Clover's dissection of the slasher's gender-identity strategies, she argues that the genre elides sex difference so that "[t]he same female body does for both" male and female (59), allowing males to identify with suffering in an act of voyeuristic masochism that takes place during the consumption of horror. But in **"The Raft,"** King decisively rearranges this anatomy. Males and females are fully distinct, and the role of sufferer is occupied by a fully masculinized character. There is no buffer, no relief, no getting away from confronting the masochistic attraction of the story. The reader identifies with Randy in order to suffer through a man.

Just as King moves Randy away from androgyny by definitively asserting his masculinity, so does he position the monster (also an uncertainly sexed character in the standard slasher) clearly within the category of the feminine. Again, King offers no prism to partially deflect unpleasant psychic realities. The monster is no masked man who substitutes killing for sex.[17] Instead, the black spot in **"The Raft"** is unalterably, potently female, with no masks to disguise its nature. It is a force that combines killing with sex and makes them equally dangerous. When the spot clutches Deke, the narrator calls it an act of "unbelievable reversal" (261). King presents us with this "reversed" monster, and then he stages a violent Oedipal drama in the most elemental form: Four young adults face the primal abyss from whence they came.

By using an unequivocally male character to dramatize male suffering at the hands of a female terror, King makes a minor departure from formula into a deliberately uncomfortable, highly charged exposé of the fears whose exploitation drives the slasher genre, and the narrowly gender-based expectations that frame the characters in horror narratives generally. Clover says that the sexually ambiguous quality of the hero and killer in the standard slasher represents an attempt to shield the male viewer from the nature of the masochistic identification that he undergoes. King exposes the cultural politics of this need for weakness by placing these characters at gendered poles and thereby calling attention to the uncomfortable desire in between. Randy's behavior thus becomes a trenchant commentary on the cultural expectations of male heroism. Clover argues with some justification that modern horror is very direct about its gender politics (calling attention to its own "feint" [229]), but King is even more direct in **"The Raft,"** exposing male masochism where it lies—at the center of things—and in the process showing the feelings of fear and weakness that widespread cultural conventions of male heroism continue to hide.

It may be that **"The Raft"** must be seen first as a boy's nightmare, if only because of the way that King strips away the gender trickery to reveal the cold sexual truth: that it all comes down to a terrified, (almost) naked boy and his menacing mother. But even if this is so, one might ask why a story of literalized castration anxiety should attract women. More generally, if the horror genre is driven by male fears, then why would women be drawn to it at all?

I want to approach this set of questions elliptically, by first looking into a specific question of plot that bothered me when I read **"The Raft"**: Why doesn't Randy get away from the black spot when he can? He has two clear opportunities: the deaths of Deke and LaVerne, during which the black spot is busy enough with its victim to allow for a quick swim to the shore. King even has Randy notice this odd blind spot in himself—he doesn't realize until "much later" that he could have escaped while Deke died (260). In between the two deaths, Randy wonders whether he should put down the unconscious LaVerne and swim for it. What stops him is "an awful guilt" (261).

George Romero, screenwriting for director Michael Gornick, provides an answer to my question in the short film they made of **"The Raft."**[18] In the movie, Randy actually does escape while the spot consumes LaVerne. Watching the film, I realized that Randy doesn't escape in King's story because if he does, then he can't suffer the way he's meant to, the way that the ritual of slasher consumption demands.

Romero, himself a noted director of horror films (including *Night of the Living Dead*), understands that **"The Raft"** corresponds to the slasher formula, and he makes subtle changes in plot and character that allow it to conform more obviously to the genre conventions in its screen version. He enhances the transgression imagery, for example: The young people smoke marijuana on the way to the lake, and the film's last image is a shot of a "No Swimming" sign that makes little sense in light of the raft's presence on the lake, but which is entirely consistent with the crime-and-punishment logic of the slasher film. The most important changes, though, are in the character of Randy. In particular, Randy's guilt and hesitation are gone, leaving only his desperate longing to be a stud. He acts as much like one as he can, and looks more like one too: He doesn't wear glasses in the movie. Even so, he's less successful in his romantic endeavors than in King's original story; when he and LaVerne are alone on the raft, he tries to seduce her as she sleeps. She partially rouses herself to refuse him, but the distraction leads to the black spot grabbing her hair and pulling her into its depths. In the movie then, LaVerne's death is entirely Randy's fault: He tries to have sex with her when he should be watching the spot according to their agreement to take turns. His self-centered sexual greed makes him a standard issue slasher male, not a Final Androgyne type.

In Romero's version, Randy finds his resourcefulness when LaVerne dies and tries to escape while the spot quickly devours her and then sets off after him. He races the spot to shore, and narrowly wins the race. He then taunts the spot from the edge of the shore ("I beat you!") instead of moving out of range, and is abruptly engulfed, done in by his own attempt to ascend to the vacant alpha male slot instead of feminizing himself (as sufferer instead of warrior) and getting away. As this climactic episode shows especially clearly, the film version of **"The Raft"** makes Randy more stereotypically male than the story does. Most important, the changes in his character keep him from being coded feminine at any time. In contrast to his portrayal in the story, his groping for sex and subsequent escape are consistent with a male slasher victim, not a survivor. Not surprisingly, the film lacks the segment in which Randy stands tortured and terrified, alone with the spot. In effect, the movie version of Randy lacks the understanding of pain or the capacity to suffer, so the movie ends without delivering much emotional impact, with only a surprise (Randy's quick and sudden death at the moment when we believe that he has delivered himself) that doesn't adequately substitute for what has been excised from the story.

Paradoxically, even though the "Raft" movie accentuates the standard slasher plot inherent within the story by adding the escape segment (a more predictable form of confrontation between the killer and the survivor than King's lonely conclusion to the story), the film's mechanical adherence to conventional sex roles (making sure that boys don't suffer the way that girls are supposed to) keeps the movie from feeling like a slasher. The loss in feeling is a loss of suffering: The shift in Randy's character short-circuits the masochistic component of the viewing mechanism that Clover identifies as so central to the horror genre—Randy doesn't suffer, and there's no Final Girl to do the honors in his place. The movie thus changes certain parts of the story to make it superficially more slasherlike, but in making these changes, Romero eliminates Randy's pain, precluding the particular form of viewer identification that needs to take place with the slasher protagonist.

So the problem is not that Randy escapes—it's that by having him do so, Romero's rewrite of King's story prevents the character from enduring the pain and fear that a slasher narrative conditions its audience to expect. Consequently, the film can't deliver its emotional payoff, despite its careful adherence to genre conventions. The difference between story and movie can thus be summed up in broad terms: The movie is conservative (arguably too conservative), whereas King's story is experimental (within a conservative genre). Whatever the film's entertainment value, it lacks the story's depth because it takes away the story's pain. Randy's role in the narrative can be filled by a boy or a girl, but whoever occupies it is required to suffer, irrespective of gender. King's story, especially when compared to the film, shows that the needs of the slasher ritual transcend the gender conventions that have grown around them.

All of which brings us back to the question of female attraction to slasher narratives. That gender is an issue in the reception of horror is scarcely disputed by those who have considered the subject, but there is no consensus about its role or effect. In her influential 1975 essay, "Visual Pleasure and Narrative Cinema," Laura Mulvey says that the cinematic gaze is gendered male, with woman as its object, and women can participate in the viewing only by adopting the male perspective (which is either sadistic or fetishistic). Although Mulvey's model may account for some female attraction to horror, the image of the castrating woman complicates her thesis. Writing partially in response to Mulvey's view, Creed argues that "The slasher film actively seeks to arouse castration anxiety in relation to the issue of whether or not woman is castrated" by presenting her as both castrated and castrator (127).[19] It is worth noting that the castrating black spot in **"The Raft"** has an appetite for males and females alike. Randy says twice that "It went for the girls" (250), and its first victim is in fact female.

The existence of female horror fans is beyond dispute, so horror—even slashers—must have something to offer them. Creed persuasively defines horror on a fundamental level as the artistically expressed desire for the liminal and disruptive (Kristeva's "abject"), a desire constructed according to primal paradigms that are neither restricted to nor defined by the male experience. These include birth, seduction, and castration—with only the last of these routing female identification through male-defined channels (153-54). In essence, the mystery of the "archaic mother" is not an exclusively male preserve, and the return to the womb not necessarily a purely male desire or an exclusively male fear. Indeed, Creed disputes the idea that the unconscious is socialized male or female, theorizing that horror addresses the unconscious fears and desires of "both the human subject . . . and the gendered subject" (156). Slashers clearly implicate universal fears (pain, death) with gendered ones (female fear of violation or—especially in the case of **"The Raft"**—male castration anxiety).

Lots of horror stories are about regressive sexuality (one need only look to the enduring vampire and werewolf film cycles for confirmation), and it follows that a fundamental component of the experience of horror is the desire to experience such fantasies, again and again. The slasher film cycle (which varies strikingly little from film to film) is one of the more obvious manifestations of this desire to repeat. Accordingly, Clover identifies the consumption of horror as a cultural repetition-compulsion, a ritual play with ancient fears that King alludes to in **"The Raft"** when he has Randy describe the black spot as being like something out of the "Halloween Shock-Show down at the Rialto" (255). In their reenactment of their early experience and confrontation with their early fear, the characters in **"The Raft"** are no different from the horror consumers who encounter them in King's pages: Like the readers and moviegoers with whom Randy groups himself and his friends, the characters use a ritual—swimming out to the raft to "say good-bye to summer" (248)—to re-experience their old fears and desires. For the characters, for King's readers, and doubtless for the writer himself as well, these feelings are a defining part of the self that needs regular indulgence.

Randy's memory of his trips to the horror movies is part of a series of self-references and formula twists that set **"The Raft"** apart from the other slashers with which it claims kinship. Though Romero may have overlooked the viewing dynamic of the slasher film when he scripted **"The Raft,"** he, like Stephen King, has no illusions about what the black spot represents. As the film ends with the spot moving back to the center of the lake (after overwhelming Randy at the water's edge), the camera pulls back, taking in Deke's abandoned Camaro parked further up the shore. The doors are open and the car radio is playing a raucous heavy metal song with these lyrics, which we hear as the film ends:

> Tryin'
> To get her out of my mind
> All my friends said,
> "You better watch that girl
> She's a taker, a knife edge woman
> She's a dream breaker"

This "knife edge woman" is an unexpected, archetypally female monster who sets her sights on a likewise unexpected victim: a young man. King uses the spot's inevitable victory to show us why we choose to suffer through Randy's ordeal, and what we are buying into when we do so. **"The Raft"** thus stands as a slasher that deconstructs the slasher formula.

Notes

1. Since becoming famous, King has frequently written brief compositional histories to accompany his shorter works, generally publishing them as headnotes or appendices. For his account of his unusual loss and recovery of "The Raft," see *Skeleton Crew* (509-10).

2. For a useful historical and ethnographic overview of the *vagina dentata* and related imagery, see Erich Neumann's Jungian study *The Great Mother: An Analysis of the Archetype* and especially Wolfgang Lederer's *The Fear of Women* (quotation at 47; "bottomless lake" is also Lederer's phrase). For a survey of *vagina dentata* jokes and castration humor generally, see G. Legman, *No Laughing Matter: An Analysis of Sexual Humor.* Monte Gulzow and Carol Mitchell provide an interesting specific case of the way that the *vagina dentata* became a repository for unexpressable anxiety among Vietnam war soldiers in "'Vagina dentata' and 'Incurable Venereal Disease' Legends from the Viet Nam War." (I am grateful to my former student Jane Hogan for bringing the latter two sources to my attention.)

3. Horney says that the dread of the vagina and the dread of the father are not mutually exclusive; instead, the former "often conceals itself behind" the latter, despite the fact that "it is more deep-seated, weighs more heavily, and is usually more energetically repressed than the dread of the man (father)" (138). Her project includes bringing the dread of the woman into view and into the debate over the child's developmental stages. Accordingly, she traces the dread of women to the early, instinctive realization on the boy's part that "his penis is much too small for his mother's genital" (142). If "the grown man continues to regard woman as the great mystery," says Horney, "the mystery of motherhood" is the root cause of it (141). Horney's hypothesis suggests that Freud's admittedly incomplete list of categories of uncanny fear should be expanded to include the return of childhood fears of woman (see Freud's "The Uncanny").

4. Creed argues that in films like *Psycho, Carrie,* and others, monstrosity—in the form of castrating woman—is constructed out of the failure to make the break between mother and child (38).

5. Carol J. Clover uses this phrase to describe the killer's lair in slasher films; its feminine characteristics (enclosure, dampness, darkness) are striking in their consistency from film to film (30, 48). In the case of "The Raft," the watery scene fulfills the formula's apparent requirement of a female setting. For King's own discussion of the "Bad Place" (which he identifies more directly with monstrosity itself), see *Danse Macabre,* 263-94.

6. See *The Uses of Enchantment,* 167-83.

7. Neil Jordan's stylized, elegant *The Company of Wolves* (1985) is an adult version of "Little Red Riding Hood" that realizes the story's unconscious theme of sexual awakening through the overtly sexualized use of the werewolf transformation.

8. Creed notes "the reference to the red riding hood/clitoris and its emphasis on the devouring jaws of the wolf/grandmother" (108).

9. Rachel says, "It seems like I spent my life out at Cascade lake" (246).

10. Clover argues that the slasher heroine's defeat of the monster and passage to safety represents an ascent to phallicized maturity (*Men, Women, and Chain Saws,* Chapter 1, especially 49-50). One might argue that Randy matures when he chooses to care for the prostrate LaVerne rather than save himself (261), but his regression at the end of the story calls any such gains into doubt.

11. King's understanding of (and fascination with) the magnetic power (both attractive and repulsive) of the castrating mother is evident from his positioning of "The Raft" within the *Skeleton Crew* collection. The story is followed by "Word Processor of the Gods," in which an uxorious man, Richard Hagstrom, uses a magic word processor (a modern genie-in-the-machine, designed by his precocious nephew, that makes any typed command come true) to first render his virago wife childless (by making their bratty son disappear), and then to make his wife herself disappear. He replaces the two with his sweet-natured sister-in-law and his gifted nephew (both of whom had been killed in a car crash along with Richard's selfish brother shortly before the narrative begins). The magic word processor effectively allows Richard to reposition the branches of his family tree, rewriting the past to retroactively install his unthreatening relatives as his nuclear family. King's segue thus places a meditation on powerlessness ("The Raft") next to a fantasy of ultimate power ("Word Processor of the Gods"). The latter story grants dominion not simply over life and death, but also over the past. The castrating mother figure, Richard's shrewish wife, is not simply neutralized; instead, Richard is able to nullify her by "deleting" all evidence of her existence. This Oedipal fairy tale is the psychic opposite of "The Raft." The two stories form a matched pair, two different answers to the same "What if?" question.

12. The slasher genre is a modern cinematic development that most critics agree is a narrow offshoot from Alfred Hitchcock's *Psycho* (1960) that suddenly began to sprout vigorously a generation later, starting with John Carpenter's influential *Halloween* (1978). Scores of slasher films were made during the 1980s, with the pace beginning to taper off of late.

13. See Clover (188), quoting Michele Montrelay in part; Clover surveys the ways in which the gazer in horror films is frequently sucked into a vaginal vacuum, emphasizing the consistency with which "horror pre-

sents us with scenarios in which assaultive gazing is not just thwarted and punished, but actually reversed in such a way that those who thought to penetrate end up themselves penetrated" (192). This is exactly what happens to Deke.

14. Clover argues on the basis of her own (admittedly informal) survey that young males make up the majority of the audience for slasher films (6-7), but this claim is disputed by Dika (142).

15. Clover points to the unisex names of many Final Girls (Stevie, Joey, Stretch, etc.) as further evidence for the character's sexually ambiguous status (40). Her contention that the Final Girl is an androgynous figure who enables the viewer to identify with suffering has touched off some interesting arguments with other theorists working on the slasher film (including Creed and Dika, the authors of the most detailed studies), but her list of the defining characteristics of the Final Girl has encountered no like opposition; Creed, for example, sees the Final Girl thus: "[I]ntelligent, resourceful and usually not sexually active, she tends to stand apart from the others" (124).

16. Clover says in a note that "we may expect horror films of the future to feature Final Boys as well as Final Girls (Pauls as well as Paulines)." Among the incipient examples she cites is Stephen King's *Misery* (novel 1987; film 1990), in which a broken-legged novelist takes the . . . 'feminine' or masochistic position" (63). See also her note on *The Burning* (1981), in which a "nerdish male" plays the part normally taken by the Final Girl (52).

17. Clover: "[S]lasher killers are by generic definition sexually inadequate—men who kill precisely because they *cannot* fuck" (186).

18. "The Raft" is one of three segments, all scripted by Romero and directed by Gornick, that make up *Creepshow* 2 (1987).

19. In a brief analysis of the attraction of horror to the female spectator, Creed allows that it is "complex" (155).

Works Cited

Bettelheim, Bruno. *The Uses of Enchantment: The Meaning and Importance of Fairy Tales.* New York: Vintage, 1989.

Clover, Carol J. *Men, Women, and Chain Saws: Gender and the Modern Horror Film.* Princeton: Princeton University Press, 1992.

Creed, Barbara. *The Monstrous-Feminine: Film, Feminism, Psychoanalysis.* London: Routledge, 1993.

Dika, Vera. *Games of Terror. "Halloween," "Friday the 13th," and the Films of the Stalker Cycle.* Rutherford, NJ: Fairleigh Dickinson University Press; London and Toronto: Associated University Presses, 1990.

Freud, Sigmund. "The Uncanny." Translated by James Strachey. Vol. 17 of *The Standard Edition of the Complete Psychological Works of Sigmund Freud.* 24 Vols. London: Hogarth, 1986, 219-52.

Gulzow, Monte, and Carol Mitchell. "'Vagina Dentata' and 'Incurable Venereal Disease' Legends from the Viet Nam War." *Western Folklore,* 39 (1980): 306-16.

Horney, Karen. "The Dread of Woman." *Feminine Psychology.* New York: Norton, 1967, 133-46.

King, Stephen. *Bare Bones: Conversations on Terror with Stephen King.* Edited by Tim Underwood and Chuck Miller. New York: McGraw, 1988.

———. *Danse Macabre.* New York: Everest, 1981.

———. *Misery.* New York: Viking, 1987.

———. "The Raft." *Skeleton Crew.* New York: Putnam's, 1985, 245-70.

———. *Skeleton Crew.* New York: Putnam's, 1985.

Lederer, Wolfgang. *The Fear of Women.* New York: Grune, 1968.

Legman, G. *No Laughing Matter. An Analysis of Sexual Humor.* Bloomington: Indiana University Press, Vol. 1, 1968; Vol. 2, 1975.

Mulvey, Laura. "Visual Pleasure and Narrative Cinema," *Screen* 16 (1975): 6-18.

Neumann, Erich. *The Great Mother: An Analysis of the Archetype.* Translated by Ralph Manheim. Princeton: Princeton University Press, 1963.

André L. DeCuir (essay date 1998)

SOURCE: DeCuir, André L. "The Power of the Feminine and the Gendered Construction of Horror in Stephen King's 'The Reach'." In *Imagining the Worst: Stephen King and the Representation of Women,* edited by Kathleen Margaret Lant and Theresa Thompson, pp. 79-89. Westport, Conn.: Greenwood Press, 1998.

[*In the following essay, DeCuir examines the themes of childbirth and horror in King's "The Reach."*]

In "A Dream of New Life: Stephen King's *Pet Sematary* as a Variant of *Frankenstein*," Mary Ferguson Pharr attempts to draw parallels between Mary Shelley's great work and Stephen King's reworking of "the dream of new life . . . a dream both seductive and malefic, the stuff finally of nightmares made flesh" (116). Pharr seeks to show that "what King has done in *Pet Sematary* is not to copy Mary Shelley, but rather to amplify the cultural echo she set in motion so that its resonance is clearer to the somewhat jaded, not always intellectual reader of Gothic fantasy today" (118).

Needless to say, gallons upon gallons of scholarly ink have been spilled over Shelley's multi-layered text, but all critics of the novel seem to be indebted to Ellen Moers's discussion of *Frankenstein* as a "*woman's* mythmaking on the subject of birth" (93), "a hideous thing" (95). According to Moers, when Victor "runs away and abandons the newborn monster," Shelley, because of the "hideous intermingling of death and life in her own life" (96), is expressing a "revulsion against newborn life, and the drama of guilt, dread, and flight surrounding birth and its consequences" (93).

With Moers's ideas in mind, framing the biographical and textual similarities Pharr points out in Shelley's novel and King's *Pet Sematary*, I wish to show that the deep-rooted, intermingled themes of childbirth and horror in *Frankenstein* are more directly presented and the horror more specified by King in a little-known short story called **"The Reach"** (originally published as **"Do the Dead Sing"**) than in *Pet Sematary*. Not only does the story feature a woman as the main character, but it also contains King's attempt to represent a *self-suppressed* feminine consciousness. Through the main character of the ninety-five-year-old Stella Flanders and the *imagined* conversations she has with her great-grandchildren, King maps out the cultural suppression of the female voice, but also the subsequent and inevitable resurfacing of the feminine, when the voice is rendered inaudible, through the female body and its functions, mainly childbirth. David G. Hartwell correctly writes that in **"The Reach"** "the horror is distanced but underpins the whole [story]" (15). I wish to show that King specifies this horror as a horror experienced by the male when female power is manifested through the female body which, despite constant efforts, cannot be totally known, experienced, or controlled. For the female, King implies that horror stems from witnessing and experiencing the measures taken by the male, who deems his authority threatened by an overt demonstration of female "otherness."

Briefly, "the reach" in the title of King's story refers to the body of water between an island and the mainland and becomes the story's controlling symbol. The story begins in the summer before the death of Stella Flanders, who has never left her island home, Goat Island, even to visit the mainland, moves through the fall and winter with occasional flashbacks to the summer, and concludes in the summer after the winter of Stella's death. Though the story is related by a third-person narrator, this narrator, in the summer flashbacks, "turns the story over" to Stella in a sense, for it is in these flashbacks that Stella's consciousness is more pervasive and reveals her thoughts about her family, their lives, and those of the people of Goat Island. After her 95th birthday, Stella begins to see the ghost of her husband, Bill, who keeps asking her "when you comin' across to the mainland?" (17). In March, while the reach is still frozen, Stella realizes that the cancer which she had always suspected of growing inside her is getting worse and decides to cross the reach to the mainland. The drifting snow causes her to lose her way until

she encounters Bill and ghosts of their friends. They lovingly take her hands and lead her across the reach where she dies.

Such a bare-bones plot summary, of course, ignores a complex narrative structure that implicates long-standing codes in the cultural suppression and even in the self-censorship of women's voices. A close examination of the summer flashbacks, which are italicized in the text[1] and which contain more of Stella's "voice" than the fall and winter sections, reveals a tremendous silence as apparently, Stella speaks only once during the visit of her great-grandchildren in the summer before her death: "*The Reach was wider in those days*" (15). When the children ask her to explain, the narrator replies: "*She only sat in her rocker by the cold stove, her slippers bumping placidly on the floor*" (15). The subsequent flashbacks consist of Stella's thoughts, framed by the narrator's implication that these thoughts are what Stella would express verbally "*if she could*": "'*Gram, what's the Reach?*' *Lona might have asked . . . although she never had. And she would have given them the answer any fisherman knew by rote: a Reach is a body of water between two bodies of land, a body of water which is open at either end*" (16-17; bold emphasis added).

Twice, the narrator interjects that Stella does not cry (16, 20), and perhaps the most graphic example of self-suppression, which also seems to serve as an indictment of male-centered heterosexual sex as repressive, occurs when Stella is addressed by the ghost of her late husband, Bill: "She could say nothing. Her fist was crammed deep into her mouth" (22). Stella's silence, however, has subversive potential because her nonverbal recollections of herself and the women of Goat Island and their various experiences with marriage and childbirth in particular serve to "feminize" Goat Island as a primal, nurturing environment while they indict the mainland as a masculine sphere of industrialization that fosters greed and exploitation, and ultimately, spiritual death.

The mainland, Raccoon Head, is simply referred to by the residents of Goat Island as "the Head," and is surrounded by phallic, "split and fissured rock" (29). While Stella imagines that her great-granddaughter, Lona, will complain that Goat Island is "*so small*" and that "*We live in Portland. There's buses, Gram!*" and even catches herself in "real wonder" after contemplating how "*cars passing to and fro on the Head's main street . . . can go as far as they want . . . Portland . . . Boston . . . New York City*" (26), she more frequently recalls tragedies that have befallen Goat Island residents while on the mainland. For example, Stella remembers that George Havelock "had died a nasty death over on the mainland in 1967, the year there was no fishing. An ax had slipped in Big George's hand, there had been blood—too much of it!—and an island funeral three days later" (16). Goat Island is not immune to death, however, as Stella recalls that Bull Symes had a heart attack "*while he was out dragging traps*" (17), but for Stella and her neighbors, misfortune on the mainland can be exacerbated by practices arising from an existence based on cash nexus (e.g., lawsuits, foreclosures, liens).

When Goat Island resident George Dinsmore takes a job on the mainland "driving plow for the town of Raccoon Head," and gets "smashed on rye whiskey" and drives the plow through three power poles during a storm, Raccoon Head loses power for five days, and as George's "punishment," the electric company "*slap[s] a lien on his home.*" (24). Stella's recollection of George's rescue from his financial straits by his Goat Island neighbors portrays the collective action of the Goat Island residents as directly opposed to that of mainland individuals who are in danger of becoming absorbed into a corporate machine as suggested by Stella's use of the third person plural possessive pronoun in reference to the company threatening George, "*the Hydro*": "[I]*t was seen to it that the Hydro had their money*" (24). Stella would like to emphasize to her great-grandchildren that "'*we always watched out for our own*'" (24) and her consciousness shapes this "we," the collective body of Goat Island residents, not as a corporate force but as a sentient parental entity, willing to take its prodigal son back into the fold while recognizing his faults but also praising his attributes. Stella would like to point out that George was "*good for nothing when his workday was done*" but also to emphasize quickly that "*when he was on the clock he would work like a dray-horse*" (24). Like a desperate parent resorting to "He is a good boy," "This is his first offense," "He was just in the wrong place at the wrong time" arguments in order to defend a child facing a judge, Stella, through her consciousness, adds, "*That one time he got into trouble was because it was at night, and night was always George's drinking time*" (24). The more protective and nurturing environment of Goat Island is suggested by Stella's addendum that since George "now . . . worked on the island . . . he didn't get into much hurt" and that quality of life on the island results, not from being well paid, but from being "*kept . . . fed*" (24).

The "daughters" of Goat Island apparently would fare worse than its "sons" if they should attempt to exist on the mainland independently. According to Stella "*If you* [a woman] *had business on the Head, your man took you in the lobster boat*" (16-17), for if a woman should venture to the mainland on her own, she runs the risk not only of being exploited in the Head's economic system, but she is also in danger of being robbed of something innately and exclusively feminine:

> [I]*f she stays* [on Goat Island], *she may be able to keep something of this small world with the little Reach on one side and the big Reach on the other, something it would be too easy to lose hustling hash in Lewiston or donuts in Portland or drinks at the Nashville North in Bangor. Am I old enough not to beat around the bush about what that something might be: a way of living—a feeling.*
>
> (24)

I would suggest that the cryptic nature of this segment of Stella's consciousness, which falls within a contemplation of the seven-month-pregnant Missy Bowie and her future

on Goat Island as opposed to a future on the mainland, when examined within the context of the story's references to the bodily processes culminating in childbirth and when further magnified by contemporary feminist criticism, becomes an attempt to define what French feminist critics posit as a powerful difference stemming from and sustained by female sexuality. While the thought attempts to disclose a bleak picture of women's loss of dignity in an exploitative economic system, it also warns about the possible loss of something that cannot be defined by the dominant system of signifiers. Stella's concern for its loss if removed from Goat Island suggests that this quality she would like to explain has the potential to empower and to develop, perhaps into something "explosive" and "*utterly destructive*" (italicized in text; Cixous, 886), if nurtured within the environment of Goat Island and not on the mainland where it is subject to repression and perhaps obliteration "by the [Lacanian] Law of the Father" (Jones, 362).[2]

The "gender" of the parental force made up of the collective efforts of the Goat Island residents is suggested by its spokesperson, Stella, who happens to be the oldest person on the island, but who also takes pride in being the oldest woman on the island: "They were talking about Freddy Dinsmore, the oldest man on the island (two years younger'n me, though, Stella thought with some satisfaction)" (18). Incidentally, Freddy dies of the flu in February "before anyone could take him across to the mainland and hook him up to all those machines they have for guys like Freddy" (21). Stella's lack of contact with the mainland and her reiteration in different phraseology that Goat Island "*is my place and I love it*" establish her as the island's matriarch. "Most of the village" turns out for Stella's 95th birthday with a "tremendous birthday cake" (16), and she is still able to make the younger residents of Goat Island stare in wonder, "wide-eyed" (19), with her tales of unusual occurrences that transpired on Goat Island before her listeners were born. For example, in January, when Stella is asked if she "had ever seen such a winter," Stella relates that in February of 1938, the reach froze, allowing her husband, Bill, and his friend, Bull Symes, to walk across the reach to the mainland and back again (18).

Although she holds no political office that legislates the behavior of the island community, her unobtrusive authority, which undoubtedly stems at least partially from her longevity, also seems anchored in female sexuality as her silent reminiscences are punctuated by references to menstruation, conception, pregnancy, midwifery, deliveries and births, a miscarriage, and deaths of ill newborns. She recalls, for example, how her own mother "*conceived four times but one of her babies had miscarried and another had died a week after birth*" (20). At a post-memorial service reception, Stella notices that the widow, Missy Bowie, is "seven months big with child—it would be her fifth" (18). Even Stella's condensed version of her family history, which she would like to relate to her great-grandchildren, emphasizes not official titles, heroic, or even infamous deeds, but propagation:

She would say: "*Louis and Margaret Godlin begat Stella Godlin, who became Stella Flanders; Bill and Stella Flanders begat Jane and Alden Flanders and Jane Flanders became Jane Wakefield; Richard and Jane Wakefield begat Lois Wakefield, who became Lois Perrault; David and Lois Perrault begat Lona and Hal. These are your names, children: you are Godlin-Flanders-Wakefield-Perrault.*"

(21)

King does not overtly define Goat Island as a feminist utopia "ruled by women" (Showalter, 191).[3] Curiously, however, he structures Stella's mental and therefore "silent" account of her family history without reference to formal marriage, thus demonstrating how Stella, at least in her mind, has ostensibly always minimized the importance society places on an institution in which women are often relegated to an inferior position. Also, we learn through Stella's memories that the only male child in her family to reach adulthood is her son Alden, whose "*slow brain*" and lifelong bachelorhood (20-21) conflate into a suggestion of male sexual impotence. Stella's consciousness does not reveal, however, a desire for more potent male progeny to carry on the family name, and nowhere does she express hope that her great-grandson Hal will grow up to sire more Perraults. A particular observation about Hal actually adds to Stella's silent disregard for prescribed gender-based behavior. To Stella, not Lona, but Hal, her male great-grandchild, is "*somehow more intuitive*" (20).

Whereas the "gender" of Goat Island has been suggested by that of its oldest-living resident, Stella, King more definitely sketches out the environment of Goat Island as a feminine realm by linking the Reach itself to the womb through Stella's explanation of the birth of the deformed Wilson infant:

There was Norman and Ettie Wilson's baby that was born a mongoloid, its poor dear little feet turned in, its bald skull lumpy and cratered, its fingers webbed together as if it had dreamed too long and too deep while swimming that interior Reach.

(24)

At the outset of this essay, I suggested that for King, horror, as experienced by the male in **"The Reach,"** is generated by a confrontation with the changes undergone by the female body culminating in actual reproduction, changes he can never experience in a body he thought he controlled. In his terror, the male is "unmanned," pushed to drastic measures, or utterly destroyed. Stella recalls, for example, that after her husband, Bill, delivered their daughter himself, he went "*into the bathroom and first puked and then wept like a hysterical woman who had her monthlies p'ticularly bad*" (20). The images of Victor Frankenstein rushing out of his chambers after gazing upon his creation with "horror and disgust" and his later destruction of the unfinished female creature after contemplating how, if it should couple with his male creation, "a race of devils would be propagated upon the earth, who might make the very existence of the species of man a condition precari-

ous and full of terror" (Shelley, 163), converge, in **"The Reach,"** into an example of drastic measures taken by the male when a female bodily process does not transpire according to societal expectations and produces a terrible result.

Just as Victor destroys in order to protect the condition "of the species of man," Norman Wilson, the infant's father, takes drastic measures to eradicate any evidence of the "hideous progeny" (Shelley, 229) of that "interior Reach," which could "unman" him as confrontation with this "unknown" did Bill Flanders:

Reverend McCracken had come and baptized the baby, and a day later Mary Dodge, who even at that time had midwived over a hundred babies, and Norman took Ettie down the hill to see Frank Child's new boat and although she could barely walk, Ettie went with no complaint, although she had stopped in the door to look back at Mary Dodge, who was sitting calmly by the idiot baby's crib and knitting. Mary had looked up at her and when their eyes met, Ettie burst into tears. "Come on," Norman had said, upset. "Come on, Ettie come on." And when they came back an hour later the baby was dead, one of those crib-deaths, wasn't it merciful he didn't suffer.

(24-25)

The infant's mother seems to be privy to the plan for her tearful outburst occurs when her eyes meet those of Mary Dodge who she knows is present to carry out her designated part, the actual killing of the infant, while she and her husband are out. Norman's urgings of "come on" would seem to indicate a creeping sense of remorse, but his choice of Mary Dodge to actually carry out the deed, a woman "*who had midwived over a hundred babies*" and who could probably make the baby's death look "natural," serves as his acknowledgment that this woman's "feminine knowledge" of the bodily processes surrounding childbirth and her experience in assisting in this process somehow empower her enough to take the life of the infant. Just as Victor runs away in revulsion from his "newborn," Norman "runs away" to Frank Child's boat, perhaps fearing that directly confronting the "hideous" product of a female bodily process himself would unman and weaken him.

By positing the reach as a metaphorical body of amniotic fluid produced by the feminine entity, Goat Island, King sets the stage for a demonstration of the "explosive, *utterly destructive*" return of the repressed or "silenced" power of the feminine that is particularly horrifying and devastating to the male who seeks to subdue this "female" body. The characters Stewie McClelland and Russell Bowie "trust the ice" of the presently frozen reach and take "Stewie's Bombardier Skiddoo" out onto the ice while "drinking Apple Zapple Wine, and sure enough, the skiddoo went into the Reach. Stewie managed to crawl out (although he lost one foot to frostbite). The Reach took Russell Bowie and carried him away" (18). The loss of Stewie's foot can be viewed as a symbolic castration, a "punishment," initiated by the Reach. Stella's later vision of the body of Russell Bowie, twisting and dancing beneath the ice covering the Reach, looks forward to her memory of the Wilson baby, "swimming that interior Reach," thus further establishing the reach as a metaphorical womb, that center of an exclusive feminine power, but also dramatizes what Gilbert and Gubar allude to as an historical male fear of the womb as a dark, suffocating, annihilating prison (93-95).[4]

The only example of a female character's experience of horror resulting in a reaction comparable to the responses of Bill Flanders and Norman Wilson is that of Ettie Wilson who bursts into tears at the understanding that, according to her husband's plan, her baby will no longer be alive when she returns from a diversionary outing. Though her reaction is certainly justified, if we are to understand King's gendered polarization of the constitution of the "horrible" and responses to it in **"The Reach,"** we must recognize Ettie's intensely personal tragedy as an integral part of the story's paradigm of a female recognition of horror. If horror for the male is generated by a confrontation with female bodily processes altered through sexuality, then it follows that horror for the female is brought on by the extreme measures taken by the male when faced with this female "otherness."

As presented earlier, Stella alludes to a "*being and a way of living—a* feeling," a quality that she seems to ascribe exclusively to women. It apparently stems from and is sustained by female sexuality, but this essence can be drained by an existence on the masculinely-structured mainland that seeks to harness it. The events surrounding her own death not only further gender-identify the mainland but also characterize it as a haven for death itself. In Stella's consciousness, crossing to the mainland seems to be a euphemism for dying as the apparition of Bill asks her, "When you comin [*sic*] across to the mainland?" (17). When the reach is still frozen, Stella decides to cross over to the mainland where "*she had never once in her life been*" (16), but only after realizing that the cancer she had always suspected of growing inside her has "finally gotten around to . . . the '*pièce de resistance*' (23). She reasons that perhaps on the mainland, death will finally overtake her, thus ending "the griping pain in her stomach" and the spitting up of "bright red blood into the toilet bowl," "foul-tasting stuff, coppery and shuddersome" (23).

Sure enough, as Stella nears the mainland, she weakens and is supported by the ghosts of the Goat Island dead until "it is time":

> They stood in a circle in the storm, the dead of Goat Island, and the wind screamed around them, driving its packet of snow, and some kind of song burst from her [Stella]. It went up into the wind and the wind carried it away. They all sang then, as children will sing in their high, sweet voices as a summer evening draws down to summer night. They sang, and Stella felt herself going to them and with them, finally across the Reach. There was a bit of pain, but not much; losing

> her maidenhead had been worse. They stood in a circle in the night. The snow blew around them and they sang.

(29)

Despite the wholeness and wholesomeness suggested by the image of children standing in a circle, the narrator's revelation of Stella's final thoughts discloses her continuing effort to gender-identify the mainland and death itself that she associates with the mainland. The sensation Stella uses as a standard by which to measure the "bit of pain" experienced at the moment of death is not the pain of childbirth, a phenomenon that she recalled can unsettle the menfolk more than the women actually experiencing its accompanying pain, but that resulting from male-female penetration.

Throughout **"The Reach,"** Stella's consciousness is rendered in italics, a method of representation that lessens as the story concludes, perhaps suggesting Stella's impending loss of consciousness and death. The last seven paragraphs, which carry the reader to the summer *after Stella's death,* curiously, are printed in italics, and the consciousness of Alden, Stella's son, who has now assumed the "matriarchal" position of entertaining Stella's great-grandchildren during their summer visits to Goat Island, is at the center of the story's conclusion. The focus on Alden, shaped in the same manner as Stella's silent acknowledgments of female empowerment, however, does not suggest that, with the death of Stella, Goat Island, will become "masculinized" as the mainland. Like Stella and other women, Alden, even though a biological male, is still a marginalized figure due to his "mental slowness" a condition that also presumes a sexual slowness or impotency or at least a lack of sexual knowledge, either of which would displace Alden from socially sanctioned masculine behavior (i.e., the wielding of phallic power). Whereas women may choose silence to avoid the sapping of their essences by an inimical socioeconomic system,[5] Alden, due to his disability, cannot coherently articulate, and thus exists in a deeper silence imposed by forces beyond his control. King's linking of Alden's and Stella's "silences" via narrative structure, however, suggests that what Alden keeps hidden can be just as subversive, namely a knowledge that the dead have the power to make themselves known in the realm of the living.

Alden recalls the looks in the eyes of two male characters, Larry McKeen and John Bensohn, when they recognize that the cap found on Stella's frozen body is not Alden's, but that of Bill, his dead father. This oddity has the potential to subvert any male-induced normalcy, just like childbirth in Stella's recollections (I use "male" because the only witnesses Alden remembers are male), and as a result of this "horror," the incident is stigmatized as one of those "*things that can never be told,*" something "*not exactly secret, that* [is] *not discussed*" (30). For Alden, however, it is something not to be completely obliterated from memory but "*made for thinking on slowly*" and "*at length, while the hands do their work and the coffee sits in a solid china mug nearby*" (30). His recognition of *"his dead father's cap, the look of its bill or the places where the visor had been broken"* (30) found on his mother's body allows him, in his own mind at least, and his consciousness is the prevailing one at the end of the story, to revise the finality of death feared by his mother in her narrative into death as the ultimate liberator from repression (Stella herself may have experienced this sense of release as, just before crossing the Reach, "she burst into tears suddenly—all the tears she had never wept"). He is able to comfort himself in his loneliness with an affirmation that the dead, who may have been verbally, intellectually, sexually, and spiritually repressed all their lives, do inevitably make their voices heard.

Notes

1. Throughout this chapter, selected italicized passages from "The Reach" will be quoted without notation (for example, "italicized in text"), but any italicization utilized from other sources will be noted as such.

2. Critics such as Julia Kristeva, Hélène Cixous, and Luce Irigaray seem to have based their ideas on the psychoanalytic theories of Jacques Lacan, who suggests that the individual experiences two "systems" of language, the "imaginary" and the "symbolic." The former is a prelinguistic phase in which the individual is unaware of signs that express "difference," such as the signifiers "male" and "female." The latter is the present system of language that illustrates difference.

   Kristeva translates the "imaginary" into the "semiotic" and associates this phase with the female body and the sensations experienced by both woman and child during pregnancy, birth, and infancy. The symbolic is associated with the father as the child is indoctrinated into a system in which the imaginary or semiotic is suppressed in favor of polarities and implied inferiorities. Cixous and Irigaray argue that if women are to express themselves completely, they must fracture, revise, or replace the present system of language with one stemming from "jouissance," a reclaiming of the female body and a rediscovery of its eroticism. I contend that what Stella may mean by "something" is like the concept of "jouissance."

   For more complete summaries of these theories, see Ann Rosalind Jones's "Writing the Body: Toward an Understanding of *l'Écriture feminine*" and Raman Selden's *A Reader's Guide to Contemporary Literary Theory*.

3. Showalter, in a discussion of feminist novelists, refers to a group of nineteenth-century women writers who expressed some "very peculiar fantasies." Works by writers such as Lady Florence Dixie, "Ellis Ethelmer," and Charlotte Perkins Gilman portrayed "imagined worlds ruled by women, feminist revolutions, and virgin births" (191). Showalter attributes this tradition to a "horror" similar to the one experienced by Mary Shelley in *Frankenstein*. According to Showalter, these novels reflected some women's "repugnance for the actual process of intercourse and childbirth" that perhaps stemmed from the increasing awareness of the "dangers in pregnancy, venereal disease and childbearing," but also the simultaneous need to share in the Victorian "veneration of motherhood and maternal love" (191).

4. In Chapter 3 of *The Madwoman in the Attic,* "The Parables of the Cave," Gilbert and Gubar assert that the womb is "the place of female power . . . one of the great antechambers of the mysteries of transformation" (95). Stella's mental image of what Russell Bowie might have experienced, writhing beneath a translucent barrier, frantically trying to break through its surface (which he may have tried to do before drowning), echoes and illustrates Gilbert and Gubar's premise of the Victorian (male) fear of the womb and association of it with the tomb, "the cavern confrontations and the evils they might reveal—the suffocation, the 'black bat airs,' the vampirism, the chaos of what Victor Frankenstein calls 'filthy creation'" (93-94).

5. Joyce Zonana, in a discussion as to why Safie's letters are not reproduced in the text of Frankenstein, concludes that their absence sends a strong "feminist message of resistance, rebellion" (181) as the letters cannot be appropriated and possessed by the male characters. Victor, Walton, and the creature "seek to 'know' or possess something outside of themselves" (181). Zonana supports her argument with Cixous's "The Laugh of the Medusa" and writes that women's self-silencing "actually asserts the integrity of female experience. Such silence resists and baffles the act of appropriation" and interpretation according to "patriarchal conventions" (Zonana, 180-81).

Works Cited

Cixous, Hélène. "The Laugh of the Medusa." Translated by Keith Cohen and Paula Cohen. *Signs: Journal of Women in Culture and Society* 1 (1976): 875-93.

Gilbert, Sandra, and Susan Gubar. *The Madwoman in the Attic: The Woman Writer and the Nineteenth-Century Literary Imagination.* New Haven: Yale University Press, 1979.

Hartwell, David G., ed. *The Dark Descent.* New York: Doherty, 1987.

Jones, Ann Rosalind. "Writing the Body: Toward an Understanding of *l'Écriture feminine.*" *The New Feminist Criticism: Essays on Women, Literature, and Theory.* Edited by Elaine Showalter. New York: Pantheon, 1985, 361-77.

King, Stephen. "The Reach." *The Dark Descent.* Edited by David G. Hartwell. New York: Doherty, 1987, 15-30.

Moers, Ellen. *Literary Women.* New York: Doubleday, 1976.

Pharr, Mary Ferguson. "A Dream of New Life: Stephen King's *Pet Sematary* as a Variant of *Frankenstein*." *The Gothic World of Stephen King: Landscape of Nightmares.* Edited by Gary Hoppenstand and Ray B. Browne. Bowling Green: Bowling Green State University Popular Press, 1987, 115-25.

Selden, Raman. *A Reader's Guide to Contemporary Literary Theory.* Lexington: University of Kentucky Press, 1989.

Shelley, Mary. *Frankenstein or The Modern Prometheus.* 1818. Edited by James Rieger. Indianapolis: Bobbs-Merrill, 1974.

Showalter, Elaine. *A Literature of Their Own: British Women Novelists From Brontë to Lessing.* Princeton: Princeton University Press, 1977.

Zonana, Joyce. "'They Will Prove the Truth of My Tale': Safie's Letters as the Feminist Core of Mary Shelley's *Frankenstein*." *The Journal of Narrative Technique* 21 (1991): 170-84.

Joe Sanders (essay date fall 2000)

SOURCE: Sanders, Joe. "'Monsters from the Id!' in Stephen King's 'The Monkey.'" *Extrapolation* 41, no. 3 (fall 2000): 257-65.

[*In the following essay, Sanders relates King's story "The Monkey" to the film* Forbidden Planet, *in its psychic personification of the human id or subconscious.*]

Considering how much more effective Stephen King's horrific images are on the page than on the screen, it probably is just as well that no movie has been made of **"The Monkey,"** in which a scruffy child's toy seems to be the source of all supernatural menace. What could be frightening about a broken clockwork monkey that can't even bang its little cymbals together when someone turns its wind-up key? Yet King somehow does involve readers in a distraught father's memories of a series of violent deaths during his youth that seem to portend the destruction of his present family. The toy monkey is featured on the cover of King's second collection, **Skeleton Crew,** and the story somehow *is* genuinely disturbing.

Critics have recognized the effectiveness of **"The Monkey"** but have had trouble identifying the source of its power. The major critical issue appears to be whether the little doll embodies a threat from outside, something that intrudes into the small circle of ordinary human experience from the surrounding darkness, or whether the toy monkey reflects something already present in Hal Shelburn, the story's protagonist. Douglas Winter, in *Stephen King: The Art of Darkness,* stresses the former; for Winter, the monkey represents "external evil, symbolized by the wheel for fortune" and acting purely by chance "without apparent logic or motivation" (70, 71). Tony Magistrale draws a much closer connection between monkey and man, reminding us that the toy is "associated with the violent events and subsequent guilt of Hal Shelburn's adolescence" (74). Magistrale also relates that guilt to "part of his [Hal's] subconscious mind which is unable to overcome the events of his tragic youth," though this does not fully explain how Hal's youth *became* tragic (74). Other critics have tried to pull these extremes together. In *The Many Facets of Stephen King,* Michael R. Collings sees the monkey as a "child's toy that delights in mayhem for the sake of mayhem" (95) but adds that King is "capitalizing on a childhood fear" (96). In another study, written with David Engebretson, Collings also suggests that **"The Monkey"** "occupies the middle ground" between stories about "creatures" and those centered on "psychological intuition" (*Shorter* 137). Finally, in the most detailed analysis of the story thus far, Gene Doty describes "a strong but ambiguous link between Hal and the monkey" (130) but concludes that the story "presents a world in which evil constantly threatens human beings, who do not even have the comfort of being afflicted by a personal evil, which they might at least be able to understand" (135).

Actually, of course, it is not especially comforting even to glimpse one's personal evil, let alone admit that evil impulses should be acknowledged so that they may be understood and controlled. This may be a major reason King's story is so difficult to get a grip on. As protagonist, Hal Shelburn is the window through which readers must observe what is happening when the adult Hal confronts the monkey and also what happened when the child Hal first made the thing's acquaintance. In fact, though, Hal-at-any-age is a lot more slippery than he first appears. Especially when recounting the past, the adult Hal interprets and improves his memories. Here is the story's description of young Hal's first sight of the monkey, followed almost immediately by his adult critical commentary: "Delighted, Hal and turned it this way and that, feeling the crinkle of its nappy fur. Its funny grin pleased him. Yet hadn't there been something else? An almost instinctive feeling of disgust that had come and gone almost before he was aware of it? Perhaps it was so, but with an old, old memory like this one, you had to be careful not to believe too much. Old memories could lie"(151). If the first two sentences represent Hal as a child, the next two represent Hal as an adult looking back and censoring his younger self, and the last two show Hal-the-critical-adult questioning his desire *now* to have felt more than delight *then*. The passage also permits Stephen King to suggest, without lowering the mask of Hal Shelburn, that what the character says is not quite to be trusted. Not even if it's something he deeply believes—especially not then.

Hal's trustworthiness is important to an understanding of the story. William F. Nolan, for example, is dissatisfied with **"The Monkey"** because he believes it "lacks internal logic": "Why didn't the protagonist simply *destroy* the monkey?" (103). This is not a foolish question. As Hal remembers it, when he was a small child he was too overwrought throughout the succession of deaths caused by the monkey to take decisive action against it. What he does attempt to do, though—hiding it back where he found it, throwing it out with the trash, or dropping it down a dry well—couldn't actually destroy the monkey, just get it away from immediate contact with him.

Keeping the monkey away somehow feels more important to Hal than actually disposing of it physically. He wants to stop thinking about it: out of sight, out of mind. But he can't succeed in separating himself from the monkey. It stays close to him. It wants to chat. When Hal discovers that it has followed him to Maine, he imagines it cheerfully informing him, "*Thought you got rid of me, didn't you? But I'm not that easy to get rid of, Hal. I like you, Hal. We were made for each other, just a boy and his pet monkey, a couple of good old buddies*" (165). Even more suggestively, when Hal looks down the mouth of the abandoned well where he remembers throwing the monkey years before, "a drowned face stared up at him, wide eyes, grimacing mouth. A moan escaped him. It was not loud, except in his heart. There it had been very loud. It was his own face in the dark water. *Not* the monkey's. For moment he had thought it was the monkey's" (144-45). To confuse a human and a simian face—or to mistake the anguished dread Hal is supposed to be feeling with the monkey's fixed expression of mindless, murderous glee, for that matter—means that Hal is not nearly as distant from the monkey as he consciously insists.

Perhaps we can reveal **"The Monkey"**'s internal logic by examining what happens in the story and by speculating on why Hal has such difficulty getting rid of something that, he realizes as an adult, ought to disgust and horrify him. Let's return to Hal's first sight of the toy, focusing this time on the circumstances of the encounter. Hal is only four when he first discovers the monkey. As King describes it, the important facts of Hal's life are the mysterious absence of his father and the consequence that his mother has had to go to work to support her sons. Hal's older brother Bill is in first grade, but Hal is stuck at home with a succession of uncaring babysitters: "Most were stupid girls who seemed only to want to eat or sleep. None of them wanted to read to Hal as his mother would do" (150). His current sitter is Beulah, a black teenager with an "admirable bosom," who "fawned over when Hal when Hal's mother was around and sometimes pinched him when she wasn't," but who at least shares stories with him from her own choice of magazine reading, such as "Death Came for the Voluptuous Redhead" (150). While she is asleep on the couch one day—not reading to him or otherwise giving him attention—Hal explores in the back closet where his father's things are stored. That's where he finds the monkey grinning "its ageless, toothy grin" (151). Even though the story repeatedly describes it as "broken," Hal thinks the thing is "neat" and brings it back to his bedroom. That night, Hal awakens "from some uneasy dream" (151) to hear the monkey clanging its cymbals in the dark. Rather than being pleased that the toy works after all, Hal first of all is afraid that his brother or mother will hear. Before he even imagines anything else happening as a result of the

monkey's action, Hal's guilty impulse is to reject the monkey (along with memory of his dream) and put it back where he found it. "But the next morning," the story continues, "he forgot all about putting the monkey back because his mother didn't go to work" (152). Beulah and a friend have been murdered; Death has come for the voluptuous babysitter: "It was like Beulah just disappeared into one of her own detective magazines" (152). When he makes a cause and effect connection between the monkey's banging its cymbals and Beulah's being shot, Hal consciously is horrified. On the other hand, his mother stays home with him, so even if two other people are dead somewhere else Hal himself has a pretty nice day.

It's difficult to find fault with something that brings pleasure. Young Hal can connect the monkey's cymbal pounding with the first violent death and the others that follow, but he has trouble holding that connection clearly in his consciousness. Awareness keeps fading so that he even forgets what happened until he has "a bad dream about the monkey and Beulah—he couldn't remember exactly what—and had awakened screaming, thinking for a moment that the soft weight on his chest was the monkey, that he would open his eyes and see it grinning down at him" (154). The nightmare attracts his mother's attention again, so Hal almost succeeds in putting this reminder out of his thoughts too. Thus the real answer to Nolan's question about why Hal doesn't destroy the monkey seems to be not so much that the boy is too frightened to act as that he can "barely remember" (154) that he needs to do something as long as his own life is generally satisfactory. In fact, not long after this, even after all he has seen and dreamed, "Hal had forgotten all about the monkey" (155). If Hal can't remember there *is* a monkey, how could he remember that he should destroy it? And how could he seriously consider how thoroughly the "delight" he feels upon seeing the monkey should be qualified by "disgust"? How, in other words, can Hal even approach recognition of what Doty calls a "personal evil"? To understand the internal logic of **"The Monkey,"** we need to imagine an "evil" that is too deeply personal to be admitted. To avoid notice, this evil cannot consciously be connected with one's own feelings or actions. The closest a person dares approach it is acceptance, however frightened and unwilling, of the horrible acts that someone or something else has committed. This unrecognized—and unrecognizable—part of a person is free from conscious limitations. It is selfishly "personal" because it acts for immediate gratification of intimate desires without regard for the feelings or even the genuine existence of other humans. It envies, resents, and kills for personal satisfaction. Harboring such monstrous impulses is not unusual. As Doty comments, "Hal, like any normal child, must experience resentments toward the other people in his life, and, consequently, must also fantasize about their deaths" (132).

No one wants to admit to desiring such acts: Hal consciously semi-*liked* Beulah, so that "The liking made what happened worse" (150). But the deaths during Hal's youth do contribute to his physical and emotional comfort. Even his mother's death, after Hal has turned the monkey's key with what "years later he would think" was a kind of "drugged fascination" (158), lets him move into a more secure family setting with his aunt and uncle in Maine, which he later calls "the home place" (161). True, each violent death is so shocking that it's hard for readers to relate it to Hal's unadmitted needs. Also, not all the deaths benefit Hal as directly as the ones discussed here, or at least it's difficult to be sure since Hal has forgotten so much of the circumstances. Each death, however, is at least a display of power, of the ability to act rather than be acted upon. The main fact of Hal's childhood, remember, is insecurity. Being a small child means that he must depend on other people who are larger and more powerful but often also arbitrary or unresponsive. Hal is old enough to recognize his vulnerability and to want to at least begin asserting himself against the competitors or dominant individuals around him. At the same time, he must realize that he shouldn't. It's not right or safe to resent the people who have power over him. Not yet, at least not openly.

Although the supernatural power the monkey gives Hal is unique, his situation isn't. In fact, Hal's involvement with the monkey illustrates Freud's familiar concept of the id, a fundamental part of a three-level picture of the human mind that has been so widely popularized that by 1956 it could be used as the basis for the SF film *Forbidden Planet*. The film has what King's story lacks: skeptical observers to question the supposedly innocent bystander who has witnessed a series of violent deaths. These outsiders can articulate ideas that never reach the surface of Hal's consciousness in **"The Monkey."** At the beginning of *Forbidden Planet,* when the United Planets Cruiser *C-57-D* arrives on Altair 4 to check up on a "prospecting party of scientists," the sole survivor warns Captain Adams and his crew to leave at once. Dr. Morbius insists that he himself is perfectly safe, but cautions the newcomers that all the other scientists were killed by some unseen force just after they voted to return home, against Morbius's wishes, "like rag dolls ripped to bloody shreds by a malignant child" (Stuart 44). The mysterious creature has not been active since then, though Morbius's nightmares indicate that it still is lurking nearby. Despite this, Morbius is perfectly happy devoting his life to understanding the intricate machinery built by the planet's original inhabitants, the Krel, just before *they* were mysteriously wiped out. The Earthmen are suspicious and intrigued—especially after they meet Altaira, the nubile daughter Morbius has tried to keep away from them, and they begin making plans that might force Morbius to leave with them. Almost immediately, they are attacked each night by an invisible, unstoppable monster. The earthmen are suspicious of Morbius but can't imagine how he could be responsible until the ship's doctor solves the riddle by subjecting himself to the same Krel intelligence-enlarging device that Morbius himself used shortly after arriving on the planet. Overwhelmed, dying, but intent on warning the others, the doctor gasps "Monsters from the id!" When Morbius identifies "id" as "the elementary basis of the subconscious mind," Captain Adams intuits that the Krels' final technological development allowed the manipulation of matter by their minds—subconscious as well as conscious—so that their primitive, murderous impulses took form and killed them. Morbius agrees, pitying the exquisitely refined beings who "could hardly have understood what power was destroying them." Yet even as he dazedly asks "Why haven't I seen this all along?" he objects that the monster attacking them now cannot be a residue of the long-extinct Krel. "Your mind refuses to face the conclusion," Adams replies, identifying Morbius's own id as the threat. "We're all part monsters in our subconscious," he adds. "Even in you, the loving father, there still exists the mindless primitive." Eventually, as the monster is about to enter their last refuge to kill Adams along with Altaira, Morbius accepts the truth: "Guilty! Guilty! My evil self is at that door, and I have no power to stop it!" He shields the others with his own body, shouting at the unseen monster "I deny you! I give you up!" Whereupon he collapses, dying. Film critics have been puzzled by this conclusion (Warren 266; Brosnan 124), but it should be obvious from the doctor's death that if merely facing the id is unbearably traumatic, then truly denying it would negate "the basis of the subconscious mind" and bring consciousness crashing down in ruins too.

Whether or not Stephen King has seen *Forbidden Planet,* it's extremely unlikely that he hasn't at least heard about the film.[1] In any case, the point is that Freud's theories permeate our culture so thoroughly that even a mass movie audience was assumed to have at least a vague picture of the primitive, utterly selfish and ruthless id, asserting itself without being glimpsed as a part of oneself, always attributed to some exterior source. Even Hal Shelburn, as Doty paraphrases him, reflects that "'most bad things' are not conscious of their badness" (134).

For the most part, thus far, we've been considering Hal's sometimes-dubious memories of events that happened when he was a child just beginning to assert himself so that he'd be able to replace the controlling adults around him. In the story's "now," however, the situation has changed. Now Hal is an adult himself, with his own position as a controller to protect. He has a family of his own to look after. His own childhood has given him no realistic male role model to refer to when it comes to raising sons—all his plans to bond with his boys refer to how his uncle took him fishing, but he's determined to be the perfect husband and father (149). As Hal sees it, being head of a family means making its members feel secure. Like Dr. Morbius, all Hal seems to expect in return is sincere respect and unquestioning acceptance of his benevolent authority. Unfortunately, he isn't able to guarantee financial security. He's lost a good job and been relegated to an inferior one, however he rationalizes that fact when he's talking to the others; despite verbal quibbling, he is intensely aware that the rest of the family knows they're living in reduced circumstances (148). Even though his wife verbally agrees with him that they're doing just fine, Hal is sure that the reason she stuffs herself with Valium is to muffle her discontent (143). His two sons, meanwhile, are growing up to the point where they might naturally begin challenging his control. Petey is only nine and apparently safe for the moment, but Dennis is twelve and beginning to act independently, "achieving a premature escape velocity" (143).

Hal is, in short, severely stressed, torn between an unchangeable ideal and a changing reality. At this point, when he needs to reassert his authority but lacks justification for doing so, the monkey reappears. Hal is consciously horrified. However, his sons are fascinated by this monster from the id, and the incipiently rebellious Dennis reacts with the same comment young Hal made: "neat" (141). He says this, moreover, "respectfully . . . a tone Hal rarely got from the boy anymore himself" (141). The struggle for possession of the monkey illustrates the contest for power between Hal and his sons. In the monkey's presence, Hal becomes more aggressively dominant. While the monkey grins "as if in approbation" (148), he manhandles Dennis until his son at least temporarily stops challenging his father's authority and cries "with a young boy's loud, braying, healthy sobs" (149-50). Though his wife objects, "You're not like this," he verbally slaps her back to where she belongs too (153). Earlier, Hal had rather guiltily tried to analyze his feelings toward Dennis. As Captain Adams reminds Morbius, "even in . . . the loving father, there still exists the mindless primitive," and Hal admits to himself that "he felt this uncontrollable hostility toward Dennis more and more often, but in the aftermath he felt demeaned and tacky . . . helpless" (148). Now, with the monkey present, he has an excuse for feeling helpless; he can tell himself that he's too upset to control his feelings. And anyway, the others deserved what they got.

Such victories are shortlived, and Hal's actions reveal his own divided feelings more and more openly. Hal's conscious purpose is to keep the monkey from hurting his family, so he manages to get it away from the boys. Evidently not remembering how difficult it is to keep the thing out of reach, he locks it in his suitcase and lies down for a nap. When he wakes up from a deep, deep sleep, the bag still is locked and the key still in his pocket. The monkey, though, is loose. In fact, Hal had been hugging it while he slept. Petey helpfully reports, "Dennis saw. He laughed, too. He said you looked like a baby with a teddy bear" (159). Dennis's laughter at a grownup's childishness probably counterbalances the "healthy sobs" Hal drew from him earlier, especially considering how the boy now probably resents having been slammed around. So what's a father to do? It is unlikely that Hal will be able to restore, let alone maintain, the authority he enjoyed a few years ago when he was satisfying his wife financially and when the boys were younger and more naive. He can shove them back in place, but they almost certainly won't stay there. Now, the only way Hal could keep the other family members from disturbing his sense of himself, making him feel like a failure, is by letting the monkey dispose of them. That's literally unthinkable. Besides, he needs them too much.

Despite the clues King provides throughout the story, Hal will never be able to see himself as the source of this monstrous disruption of his loving, well-regulated family. He must deny responsibility for what happens. Therefore, he must get rid of the monkey, the embodiment of unthinkable impulses, in order to protect the people who are dependent on him whether they know and appreciate it or not. The moment is right. His drug-saturated wife and disrespectful preteen son have gone out, but Petey is still there because he wanted to stay and "hang out" with his father (159). Unlike Dennis, Petey is emphatically a child. He is absolutely non-threatening and non-assertive. He still calls his father "Daddy" (141) and clings to him at a hint of danger; in response to his transparent dependency, Hal feels "simple love for the boy" (144), "an emotion that was bright and strong and uncomplicated" (159), not at all like the anguish caused by the older, complicated Dennis. Hal recognizes a kindred soul in Petey, especially when Petey tells how he rejected the invitation the monkey made while Hal was asleep: "Wind me up, Petey, we'll play, your father isn't going to wake up, he's never going to wake up at all" (160). And so Petey becomes his father's trusty aide when Hal sets out to sink the monkey in the deepest part of a nearby lake. By doing so, Hal vindicates himself as his loved ones' necessary protector, as he visualizes Petey physically shrinking: "Petey was magically eight, six, a four-year-old standing at the edge of the water. He shaded his eyes with one infant hand" (169). After Hal returns to the shore, the two go through a delicate, semi-verbalized negotiation and/or reaffirmation of their respective roles. Petey sounds and acts like a small child as he takes shelter in his father's arms and asks if the "nastybad monkey" is gone; "'You were brave, Daddy," he says (172). In reply, Hal accepts his son as a potentially maturing individual and as a partner in dealing with the others; when Petey asks what they'll tell his mother, Hal replies, "I dunno, big guy. We'll think of something" (172).

At the end of the story, Hal and Petey walk back toward "the home place" and everything is over—except for a newspaper story that reports hundreds of dead fish floating in the lake where the monkey waits for some other father and son to rescue it (172). As Hal has suspected throughout, although he appears to forget in the glow of Petey's approval, the monkey represents a deadly force that cannot be denied for long in this world. Science fiction, *Forbidden Planet,* for example, is more confident of humans' ability to understand and control ourselves; the ship's doctor and Morbius eventually see and do the right thing even if it costs their lives. Fantasy is less confident, and horror is sure of the reverse. As the critics of King's story who have grappled with the nature of the monkey's power have sensed, the force menaces Hal from outside but carries out his own desires; at the same time, normal desires that he might otherwise have tried to cope with are twisted beyond recognition by the supernatural instrument. Rather than diminishing the power of King's story, identifying the monkey as a monster from the id clarifies Doty's point that it is an especially disturbing, constant threat because it is never quite in focus, always lurking barely beyond apprehension. For the monkey simultaneously reveals and conceals an inescapable, dreadful human process. As children become aware of themselves and parents become aware of their own mortality, threats of physical and psychic destruction do erupt, unrecognizable and uncontrollable. It is too late for Hal to think of truly getting rid of the monkey now, as he walks back home with his innocent little son. It always was too late. It always will be.

Note

1. In a recent novel, however, King's narrator comments, "Perhaps sometimes ghosts were alive—minds and desires divorced from their bodies. . . . Ghosts from the id" (*Bag of Bones* 227).

Works Cited

Brosnan, John. *Future Tense: The Cinema of Science Fiction.* New York: St. Martin's, 1978.

Collings, Michael R. *The Many Facets of Stephen King.* Mercer Island, WA: Starmont, 1985.

Collings, Michael R., and David Engebretson. *The Shorter Works of Stephen King.* Mercer Island, WA: Starmont, 1985.

Doty, Gene. "A Clockwork Evil: Guilt and Coincidence in 'The Monkey.'" *The Dark Descent: Essays Defining Stephen King's Horrorscape.* Ed. Tony Magistrale. Westport, CT: Greenwood, 1992. 129-36.

Forbidden Planet. Dir. Fred McLeod. Script by Cyril Hume. Story by Irving Block and Allen Adler. MGM, 1956.

King, Stephen. *Bag of Bones.* New York: Scribner, 1998.

———. "The Monkey." *Skeleton Crew.* New York: Putnam, 1985. 141-73.

Magistrale, Tony. *Landscape of Fear: Stephen King's American Gothic.* Bowling Green, OH: Popular Press, 1988.

Nolan, William F. "The Good Fabric: Of Night Shifts and Skeleton Crews." *Kingdom of Fear: The World of Stephen King.* Ed. Tim Underwood and Chuck Miller. San Francisco: Underwood-Miller, 1986. 99-108.

Stuart, W. J. *Forbidden Planet.* New York: Bantam, 1956.

Warren, Bill. *Keep Watching the Skies! American Science Fiction Movies of the Fifties.* Vol. I: *1950-1957.* Jefferson, NC: McFarland, 1982.

Winter, Douglas E. *Stephen King: The Art of Darkness.* New York: NAL, 1986.

FURTHER READING

Criticism

Bosky, Bernadette Lynn. "The Mind's a Monkey: Character and Psychology in Stephen King's Recent Fiction." In *Kingdom of Fear: The World of Stephen King,* edited by Tim Underwood and Chuck Miller, pp. 209-40. San Francisco: Underwood-Miller, 1986.

Discusses King's more recent fiction.

Collings, Michael R. and David Engebretson. *The Shorter Works of Stephen King.* Mercer Island, Wash.: Starmont House, Inc., 1985, p.

Comprehensive appraisal of King's short fiction from early uncollected tales, through *Skeleton Crew,* and including later uncollected stories.

Davis, Jonathan P. *Stephen King's America.* Bowling Green, Ohio: Bowling Green State University Popular Press, 1994, 183 p.

Surveys the major thematic concerns in King's short fiction and novels and includes several interviews with King.

Elliott, Stuart. "Stephen King's New Collection of Short Stories is On the Beam, Literally, to Would-Be Buyers." *New York Times* (19 March 2002): C6.

Addresses the unique marketing strategies of the collection *Everything's Eventual: 14 Dark Tales.*

Review of *Everything's Eventual: 14 Dark Tales,* by Stephen King. *Kirkus Reviews* 70, no. 5 (1 March 2002): 281.

Claims "King remains strong in the short form."

Kirn, Walter. "The Horror! Etc.: A Collection of Short Fiction by Stephen King." *New York Times* (14 April 2002): section 7, p. 6.

Comments on the literary status of King through the publication of *Everything's Eventual: 14 Dark Tales.*

Leayman, Charles. "Another King Movie Mistake: *Graveyard Shift.*" *Cinefantastique* 21, no. 4 (February 1991): 50.

Negative review of the movie version of "Graveyard Shift."

Maslin, Janet. "Storytelling Mogul Decides to Sweep Out Odds and Ends." *New York Times* (18 March 2002): E7.

Prefers the "sleepers" of *Everything's Eventual: 14 Dark Tales* to those published in the *New Yorker.*

McNicol, Nancy. Review of *Everything's Eventual: 14 Dark Tales,* by Stephen King. *Library Journal* 127 no. 6 (1 April 2002): 144.

Cites *Everything's Eventual: 14 Dark Tales* as "a milestone in compilations of King's shorter works."

"H. P. Lovecraft and Stephen King: A Pair of New Englanders." *Niekas* 45 (July 1998): 14-17.

Outlines the New England regionalism of King and Lovecraft.

"Analysis of the Fear Factor in Stephen King's 'The Man Who Loved Flowers.'" *Niekas* 45 (July 1998): 18-19, 32.

Centers on the role of fear in a King story.

Nolan, William F. "The Good Fabric: Of Night Shifts and Skeleton Crews." In *Kingdom of Fear: The World of Stephen King,* edited by Tim Underwood and Chuck Miller, pp. 99-108. San Francisco: Underwood-Miller, 1986.

Assesses the short fiction collections *Night Shift* and *Skeleton Crew*.

Peterson, Thane. "Why Stephen King Rules." *Business Week Online* (23 April 2002).

Praises *Everything's Eventual: 14 Dark Tales*.

Punter, David. Stephen King: "Problems of Recollection and Construction." *LIT* 5, no. 1 (1994): 67-82.

Discusses King's exploration of childhood anxieties.

Review of *Everything's Eventual: 14 Dark Tales*, by Stephen King. *Publishers Weekly* 249, no. 11 (18 March 2002): 73.

Positive review of *Everything's Eventual: 14 Dark Tales*.

Scapperotti, Dan. "The Twilight Zone Revisited: Stephen King's 'The Langoliers'." *Cinefantastique* 26, no. 5 (August 1995): 51, 53-4.

Describes the adaptation of *The Langoliers* to television.

Skal, David J. "The Dance of Dearth: Horror in the Eighties." *The New York Review of Science Fiction,* no. 52 (December 1992): 1, 10-16.

Reprinted chapter from Skal's book *The Monster Show: A Cultural History of Horrors* discussing King in terms of popular culture.

"Morality in the Horror Fiction of Stephen King." *Studies in Weird Fiction* 22 (winter 1998): 29-33.

Details the ethical principals of King's fiction.

Wood, Gary. "Stephen King's *Graveyard Shift*: Halloween Kicks Off King Triple Bill Shocks." *Cinefantastique* 21, no. 3 (December 1990): 8.

Discusses the film adaptation of "Graveyard Shift," a story from King's *Night Shift*.

Wood, Gary. "Whatever Happened to *Apt Pupil?*" *Cinefantastique* 21, no. 4 (February 1991): 35-7.

Chronicles the unsuccessful initial attempt to bring *Apt Pupil* to the screen.

Additional coverage of King's life and career is contained in the following sources published by the Gale Group: *American Writers Supplement,* **Vol. 5;** *Authors and Artists for Young Adults,* **Vols. 1, 17;** *Beacham's Encyclopedia of Popular Fiction: Biography & Resources,* **Vol. 2;** *Bestsellers,* **Vol. 90:1;** *Contemporary Authors,* **Vols. 61-64;** *Contemporary Authors New Revision Series,* **Vols. 1, 30, 52, 76;** *Contemporary Literary Criticism,* **Vols. 12, 26, 37, 61, 113;** *Contemporary Popular Writers; Dictionary of Literary Biography,* **Vol. 143;** *Dictionary of Literary Biography Yearbook, 1980; DISCovering Authors Modules: Novelists* **and** *Popular Fiction and Genre Authors; DISCovering Authors 3.0; Junior DISCovering Authors; Literature and Its Times,* **Vol. 5;** *Major Twentieth Century Writers,* **Eds. 1, 2;** *Reference Guide to American Literature,* **Ed. 4;** *St. James Guide to Horror, Ghost & Gothic Writers; St. James Guide to Young Adult Writers; Short Story Criticism,* **Vol. 17; and** *Something About the Author,* **Vols. 9, 55.**

The Queen of Spades

Alexander Pushkin

(Born Alexander Sergeevich Pushkin; also transliterated as Aleksandr and Puškin) Russian short story writer, novelist, playwright, and poet.

The following entry presents criticism of Pushkin's novella *Pikovaia dama* (1834; *The Queen of Spades*). For discussion of Pushkin's complete short fiction career, see *SSC,* Volume 27.

INTRODUCTION

The Queen of Spades is considered Pushkin's most successful prose work. Initially published in the series *Library for Reading* in March 1834, the story was then included in the volume *Tales Published by Alexander Pushkin* later that year. A critical and commercial success, *The Queen of Spades* achieved widespread popularity for its striking plot and the appeal of its enigmatic protagonist, the army officer Hermann. The story has been adapted as a play, several films, and an opera by Petr Chaikovskii.

PLOT AND MAJOR CHARACTERS

The novella opens with a group of young army officers playing cards early in the morning. One of the men, Tomsky, recounts the story of his grandmother, the Countess. Sixty years before, while residing in Paris, the Countess lost a great deal of money while playing the card game known as faro. An acquaintance, the adventurer Saint-Germain, revealed to her three cards that if played consecutively would win her money back. That night she played the cards in order and won a tidy sum. Yet after that night, she never used the secret cards again and only disclosed the secret to one other person. Intrigued by the story, a young engineer named Hermann (also translated as Germann) determines to extract the secret from the Countess. He begins to court the old lady's companion, a young woman named Lizaveta. One night, while the Countess and Lizaveta are at a ball, Hermann sneaks into the Countess's bedroom. He confronts her, demanding the secret order of the cards. When she claims the story was a joke, he pulls a gun on her, causing her to die of fright. At the Countess's funeral, Hermann believes that the old woman's corpse casts a mocking glance at him. That night her ghost visits him and reveals the secret of the cards: he will win if he bets on the three, the seven, and the ace on three consecutive nights. He follows her instructions, winning on the three and seven; but on the third night, he places a bet on what he thinks is the ace—only to find that he has bet on the queen of spades. He has lost everything; furthermore, he believes that the picture of the queen on the card smiles mockingly at him. Devastated, he ends up in a mental institution, repeating the order of the cards over and over again.

MAJOR THEMES

One of the recurring themes in Pushkin's prose and poetry is gambling, especially with cards, which is the focus of *The Queen of Spades*. Some commentators have perceived Pushkin's interest in numbers and cards as related to number theory, numerology, and the practice of gematria. Critics have also considered the theme of good versus evil as an important one in the novella, as Herman has been perceived as an evil or Mephisthophelean character. In addition, reviewers have identified other thematic concerns in the story as the destructive nature of greed and the power of sexuality, focusing on the Oedipal relationship between the Countess and Hermann. Other dominant themes in Pushkin's work are time, youth, and age, which are illustrated in the portrait of the Countess. Autobiographical elements have been detected in *The Queen of Spades,* as Pushkin has been described by biographers as an inveterate gambler, particularly with faro and dice. Moreover, like Hermann, Pushkin was known to believe in omens, fortune-telling, and parapsychological phenomena.

CRITICAL RECEPTION

There are two major critical interpretations of *The Queen of Spades.* In the first, the story is perceived as a supernatural tale, evinced by the presence of the magic cards, a winking corpse, and the Countess's ghost. Yet other commentators regard the events of the story as the realistic evolution of Hermann's mental illness: his distorted perceptions and irrational actions can be viewed as a result of guilt, alcohol, dreams, and hallucinations. Commentators have also explored and debated the provocative use of the numbers one, two, three, and seven in Pushkin's tale. *The Queen of Spades* has been deemed a very influential story, particularly on the work of the Russian novelist Fyodor Dostoevsky. Critics have also detected the influence of several authors and works on Pushkin's novella, including that of E. T. A. Hoffmann, Masonic legends, Friedrich de la Motte Fouqué's *Pique-Dame,* Honoré de Balzac's *La peau de Chagrin,* and *Le Rouge et le noir* by Stendhal. Stylistically, commentators have traced Pushkin's development as a prose writer up to *The Queen of Spades,* deeming the story as his most successful prose work. His rejection of the established prose style at that time—characterized by flowery language and an abundance of metaphors, simile, and adjectives—in favor of a spare style, omniscient narration, irony, and symbolic details has been identified as a milestone for Russian prose writing as well as Pushkin's literary oeuvre.

PRINCIPAL WORKS

Short Fiction

Povesti pokoinogo I. P. Belkina [*The Tales of Belkin, and The History of Goryukhino*] 1830
Skazki [*Pushkin's Fairy Tales*] 1831-34
Pikovaia dama [*The Queen of Spades*] 1834
Tales Published by Alexander Pushkin 1834
Complete Prose Tales 1966

Complete Prose Fiction 1983
Tales of the Late Ivan Petrovich Belkin; The Queen of Spades; The Captain's Daughter; Peter the Great's Blackamoor (translated by Alan Myers and Andrew Kahn) 1997
Alexander Pushkin: The Collected Stories (translated by Paul Debreczeny) 1999

Other Major Works

Stikhotvoreniia. 4 vols. (poetry) 1826
Boris Godunov [*Boris Godunov*] (drama) 1831
Motsart i Sal'eri [*Mozart and Salieri*] (drama) 1831
Pir vo vremia chumy [*The Feast During the Plague*] (drama) 1832
Evgenii Onegin [*Eugene Onegin*] (verse novel) 1833
Kapitanskaia dochka [*The Captain's Daughter*] (novel) 1836
Skupoi rytsar' [*The Covetous Knight*] (drama) 1836
Kamennyi gost' [*The Statue Guest* and *The Stone Guest*] (drama) 1839
Russian Romances (novels) 1875
The Works: Lyrics, Narrative Poems, Folk Tales, Prose (poems, dramas, short stories) 1939
Letters (letters) 1964
The Bronze Horseman: Selected Poems (poetry) 1982

CRITICISM

W. J. Leatherbarrow (essay date 1985)

SOURCE: Leatherbarrow, W. J. "Pushkin: The Queen of Spades." In *The Voice of a Giant: Essays on Seven Russian Prose Classics,* edited by Roger Cockrell and David Richards, pp. 1-14. Exeter, England: University of Exeter Press, 1985.

[*In the following essay, Leatherbarrow unfavorably compares Pushkin's prose to his poetry and considers* The Queen of Spades *a unique work within the context of other nineteenth-century Russian prose works.*]

Pushkin's literary status is beyond question for Russians and for those in the West who read Russian. He is 'the father of Russian literature', a remarkable genius directly responsible for the impressive development of Russian literature in the nineteenth century. He is also revered as Russia's finest poet.

But Pushkin's genius—both as artist and as instigator—is by no means as apparent to the casual non-Russian reader, who perhaps has little difficulty in appreciating other Russian writers, such as Dostoevsky, Turgenev and Tolstoy. This certainly was the case with as intelligent and sensitive a reader as Matthew Arnold, who as late as 1887, some 50 years after Pushkin's death, commented that Russia had not yet produced a great poet.[1]

The reason for this view is not difficult to find. Poetry is, in general, very difficult to translate successfully, and this is particularly true of Pushkin's poetry. Therefore, the reader who wisely avoids the largely unsuccessful attempts to render Pushkin's verse in English has no alternative but to base his assessment of Pushkin on the poet's prose, which has been translated more effectively than his verse.[2]

Pushkin was a poet by temperament rather than by choice. His thoughts found their most natural expression in verse, and his adoption of prose towards the end of his short life in many ways ran counter to his nature. As Mirsky suggests, prose for Pushkin was a foreign language which had to be learned, and his use of it, although skilful, is nonetheless deliberate and self-conscious.[3] Puskin's prose never quite conceals his natural tendency to write poetry and we can detect the poet in the very phrasing and tempo of his prose.

Judging Pushkin, therefore, on the strength of his prose is rather like judging Turgenev on the strength of his verse. With the exception of **The Queen of Spades,** Pushkin's achievements in prose are not comparable to his achievements in verse. Neither are tales such as *Dubrovsky, The Captain's Daughter,* and **"The Negro of Peter the Great"** likely to find enthusiastic admirers—as distinct from merely respectful ones—among modern readers familiar with the great prose achievements of Pushkin's successors.

But the failure of Pushkin's prose to affect the modern reader to the same extent as does that of, say, Dostoevsky in no way detracts from its immense historical significance. For without the examples of Pushkin's prose experiments on the one hand, and his novel in verse, *Eugene Onegin,* on the other, it is difficult to believe that the Russian novel would have flourished as it did in the half century following the poet's death.

Pushkin represented the culmination of a great age of Russian poetry. From the reign of Catherine the Great to that of Nicholas I, poetry had been the dominant literary genre, served by writers of outstanding talent and originality, such as Gavriil Derzhavin (1743-1816) and Vasilii Zhukovsky (1783-1852), as well as by a host of lesser figures. Imaginative prose *fiction,* as distinct from the historical works and travel sketches of Nikolai Karamzin (1766-1826), was largely unpractised. Most of the novels read during Pushkin's time were either French or quite unoriginal imitations of French models. There was no tradition of the Russian novel as such, and this point is made with delightful irony in **The Queen of Spades** when Tomsky offers to bring his grandmother a Russian novel and the old Countess replies: 'Are there any Russian novels?'[4]

The only major literary figure who had made a consistent attempt to establish a truly Russian prose fiction was Karamzin, whose mawkishly sentimental tale *Poor Liza,* written in 1792, enjoyed a marked popularity amongst the Russian reading public. Karamzin had made an attempt, which was vigorously resisted by conservative literary figures, to liberate the Russian literary language from the ponderous archaisms of Old Church Slavonic. This he did by bringing it closer to the speech of the educated nobility. Indeed Karamzin's prose was the best Russia had to offer before Pushkin but, as Pushkin himself remarked in 1822: 'That is no great praise'.[5]

Poor Liza has many obvious faults. Apart from its cloyingly sentimental plot about the suicide of a young serf-girl deceived by a thoughtless aristocrat, it is burdened by a wearisome, pretentious and totally unsuitable narrative manner. Purple passages give way to excessively emotional authorial interjections, which in turn yield to quite unconvincing dialogue. Karamzin was bound by literary conventions which did not allow for the straightforward, direct and realistic telling of a tale. Liza's speech—educated and formal—belies her lowly station in life. Peasant girls never spoke in this way, but Karamzin obviously considered it out of the question to introduce the vulgarisms of popular speech into a literature directed exclusively at an educated aristocratic élite.

In sum, everything about *Poor Liza* is excessive and artificial—a long way from the directness and simplicity of Pushkin's own prose manner. And herein lies the true significance of Pushkin's adoption of prose. In his first completed prose work, **The Tales of Belkin,** Pushkin experimented with existing narrative forms and conventions, adapting, testing, and even parodying them; in the process he created a versatile narrative medium—the first successful Russian prose style—which was to point the way and enable the great age of the Russian realistic novel to follow the golden age of poetry.

This achievement is all the more remarkable if we remember that prose did not come as naturally to Pushkin as poetry and that, with the exception of **The Queen of Spades,** Pushkin's prose lacks the sparkling vitality of his verse. Indeed, in the early part of his career Pushkin was openly contemptuous of prose. 'The thought of prose makes me sick', he wrote in 1823,[6] and in view of the quality of prose written at the time we can perhaps understand his feelings. But fashions in literature change and the popularity of poetry had begun to decline by the end of the reign of Alexander I. Even Pushkin was no longer read as eagerly by a public that now craved prose. He was never a writer who pandered to public opinion, and poems such as *The Poet and the Crowd* (1828) and *To the Poet* (1830) demonstrate his disdain for the opinion of what he called 'the rabble', but it is notable that Pushkin's interest in prose should be awakened at a time when poetry was in decline. After all, he was the first Russian professional writer who relied for his livelihood on selling his manuscripts. Perhaps also he was fascinated by the possibilities of an unfamiliar medium.

By the time he turned to prose Pushkin had for some years been engaged in writing a novel, his masterpiece *Eugene Onegin,* which was not completed until 1830. But *Eugene*

Onegin is written in verse and this makes, in Pushkin's words, 'the devil of a difference'.[7] It is quite unlike anything he wrote in prose despite its claim to being a novel. It has none of the studied austerity of his prose manner, but all of the wit and vivacity which characterise his best poetry. It is perhaps the fullest expression of Pushkin's poetic nature.

In all his best works Pushkin maintains an effective interplay between his material and his personality. Everything he wrote in verse bears the stamp of his temperament, but not in an obtrusive fashion as is the case with Tolstoy and Dostoevsky, who constantly force points of view upon their readers. Pushkin keeps company with his reader, not as a teacher or guide, but as an intelligent, witty and sensitive companion who, like the reader, is sufficiently detached from the themes, plots and characters of his works to be able to share his impressions, his delight, his amusement, his irony, and even at times his sadness. *Eugene Onegin* is the supreme example of this kind of work. It is a highly personal piece in which Pushkin mixes the formal elements of the prose novel (plot, characterisation, etc.) with an extensive yet controlled poetic self-display. Pushkin is the commanding presence in the work. He interrupts, digresses, comments and reminisces; and in the process he grafts onto the novel a rich additional subjective world.

If poetry and 'the novel in verse' offered Pushkin the means for this delightful self-display, prose afforded him the opportunity of trying something quite different which ran against the grain of his nature—narrative impersonality. The reader is struck immediately by the directness of Pushkin's prose style. His tales are above all action stories, where the plot is promoted at the expense of description, digression, dialogue and analysis. In Pushkin's prose, unlike his poetry, the narrator usually plays an essentially passive role. This is particularly obvious in *The Tales of Belkin,* where Pushkin employs several narrators in order to maintain a distance between the characters and situations described in the tales and the real narrator—himself.

This approach may be compared with that of Pushkin's contemporary, Nikolai Gogol, whose stories are showcases for an obtrusive storyteller. Pushkin viewed prose quite differently from Gogol. He also saw it as a method quite distinct from poetry as it allowed for a totally impersonal narrative. Ironically enough, it might well have been the writing of the capricious and highly personal *Eugene Onegin* that fully revealed to Pushkin the possibilities offered by prose. Certainly, in a well-known passage from Chapter III of the work Pushkin anticipates eventually abandoning poetry for 'humble prose'.[8] In his novel in verse Pushkin had for the first time tried his hand at an extended plot, extended characterisation and a detailed evocation of a certain class of Russian life. As Pushkin no doubt saw, prose is the medium best suited to a work of this type and this scale, and *Eugene Onegin* remains the only successful Russian novel in verse. The subsequent great Russian novels, although often relying upon characters and situations deriving from Pushkin's work, were written in prose. It is ironic, however, that few Russian novelists inherited Pushkin's view of prose as an impersonal narrative medium. The nineteenth-century Russian novel was to become the vehicle for the propagation of opinion and personal views.

Pushkin's first major prose attempt was **"The Negro of Peter the Great,"** written in 1827 after he had been reading the historical romances of Walter Scott. Like the works of Scott, **"The Negro of Peter the Great"** aims to evoke a distinct historical period, but unlike Scott's novels it is written in the terse and economic prose so characteristic of Pushkin. Significantly, it is unfinished. Many of Pushkin's prose works were left uncompleted, which suggests perhaps that they were seen by him essentially as experimental pieces rather than as independent works of art.

Pushkin did not turn to prose in earnest until 1830, shortly before his marriage. He had travelled to his father's estate at Boldino, which he was due to receive as a wedding present, and stayed there for most of the autumn because of an outbreak of cholera. This period of isolation at Boldino was the most intensely creative period of Pushkin's life. While there he completed *Eugene Onegin,* composed his *Little Tragedies,* and wrote the collection of stories entitled *The Tales of Belkin. The Queen of Spades* was written during a second, brief Boldino autumn in 1833.

As early as 1822 Pushkin had drafted an article in which he considered the principles of prose. Like so much of Pushkin's prose fiction, this article remained unfinished, but enough of it exists to show that Pushkin valued precision and brevity as the cardinal virtues of prose. In one passage he scathingly dismisses those writers who burden narrative with rhetoric:

> What are we to say of our writers who, considering it beneath them to write simply of ordinary things, think to liven up their childish prose with embellishments and faded metaphors? These people can never say *friendship* without adding 'that sacred sentiment whose noble flame, etc.' They should be saying 'early in the morning', but they write: 'Hardly had the first rays of the rising sun illumined the eastern edge of the azure sky . . .' Oh! How new and fresh this all is! Is it any the better just because it is longer?[9]

In *The Queen of Spades* Pushkin puts his early ideas on prose most effectively into practice. It is a very short work, with a very simple plot, a handful of characters and no obvious message or rich passages of description. And yet it echoes in the mind like few other works, and lends itself to the sort of detailed analysis that critics usually reserve for much longer pieces. The virtues of precision and brevity are in evidence throughout the work, in its characterisation, its plot and its narrative style.

In his presentation of the characters, for example, Pushkin ignores the obvious ways of making a character memorable, such as detailed physical description, lengthy dialogue and thumbnail sketches of personal history or cast of mind. Instead he creates quite distinct images with the minimum use of words. His secret is quite simple, if difficult to emulate. Rather than give his reader masses of information in the hope that the really memorable and significant details are included somewhere, Pushkin selects only those details which are evocative enough to allow the reader to complete the picture in his mind. For example, the gambler Chekalinsky is perfectly sketched in only ten or so lines:

> He was a man of about 60, of most respectable appearance. His head was covered with silvery grey hair; his full, fresh face expressed good humour; his eyes glittered, enlivened by a perpetual smile. Narumov introduced Hermann to him. Chekalinsky shook his hand cordially, asked him not to stand on ceremony and continued dealing . . .

> Chekalinsky paused after every round to give the players time to arrange their cards and note their losses, listened courteously to their requests and more courteously still straightened the corner of a card which some thoughtless hand had folded over.[10]

How vividly Chekalinsky is depicted here, with his intelligence, his good nature, his charm and, not least, his tact in quietly passing over the 'thoughtless hand's' attempt to cheat by doubling a stake after the game had been played.

Pushkin is equally effortless and economical in presenting his hero, Hermann, who comes to life through a few simple leitmotifs which Pushkin repeats at intervals throughout the tale, as he would in a poem. These include Hermann's German origins, which would have been enough to render him ridiculous in the eyes of Pushkin's French-educated contemporaries, and his passionate commitment to gambling together with an unwillingness 'to risk the necessary in the hope of gaining the superfluous', which mark him out as a hopelessly split personality and anticipate his madness.

Pushkin is careful also in his deployment of the plot. Nothing is allowed to detract from the purposeful account of Hermann's descent from moderation to incarceration. This overriding concern for action makes *The Queen of Spades* a superb mystery story, and Mirsky comments that it 'is as tense as a compressed spring'.[11] The reader is caught up in the tempo of the work, and this tempo is never relaxed by digressions, descriptions and lengthy dialogues. Minimum use is made of adjectives and adverbs that might inhibit the flow of action.

Yet despite the apparent thinness of both Pushkin's scene-setting and his characters' dialogue, these are never less than totally convincing. Unlike Karamzin's Liza, Pushkin's characters speak as one might expect people of their kind of speak: Hermann, in the conventional clipped manner of a cautious German; the old Countess, in the dignified but slightly archaic manner of a living relic. Similarly, Pushkin sets his scenes with the brevity of a dramatist's stage directions, but the richness and authority of a novelist. The short opening paragraph conveys a wealth of important information:

> Once they were playing cards in the rooms of Narumov, a Guards Officer. The long winter night had passed unnoticed, and they only sat down to supper about five in the morning. Those who had won ate with great appetite; the rest, in distraction, sat before their empty plates. But the champagne appeared, the conversation picked up, and all took part in it.[12]

How suggestive even the simplest words are. For instance, Pushkin does not need to describe who *they* (the cardplayers) are, for who but the privileged classes can afford to take supper at 5 a.m.? Likewise, the feverish compulsion of gambling is communicated by the short phrase: 'The long winter night had passed unnoticed'. The single adverb *unnoticed* (*nezametno*) eloquently conveys the dedication of the participants.

By writing in this fashion Pushkin is able to convey a great deal in a very short space. By the end of the first page of the tale the scene has been set, both physically and socially, and the reader has been introduced to all the major characters (except Lizaveta Ivanovna), the tale of the mysterious cards, and the hero's tragically split nature.

In this way Pushkin demonstrates that denseness of language is unnecessary. A single word, provided it is the right word, can speak volumes. This is why *The Queen of Spades,* a short mystery story, raises as many questions in the reader's mind as a much longer work.

The Queen of Spades may come as a surprise to modern readers familiar with the work of other nineteenth-century Russian prose writers. It does not appear to provide those features expected in a masterpiece of Russian literature. It is by any standards brief, but particularly so in contrast with the immense novels of Tolstoy and Dostoevsky with which the term 'Russian literature' is usually associated in the West. Moreover, *The Queen of Spades* is, as we have seen, primarily an *action* story, uncluttered by the pages of philosophical and religious speculation which are recognised as another of Russian literature's hallmarks. Pushkin's tale contains no tortured intellectuals speculating about the meaning of life and death or repentant noblemen abandoning corrupt society for a more direct and meaningful life among peasants or cossacks. It appears to be a simple society tale, laced with a dash of the supernatural, which offers no obvious message or revelation.

It is not only modern readers who have been struck by the apparent slightness of *The Queen of Spades.* Although it gained an immediate popularity amongst the reading public in Russia, the Russian literary critics of the 1840s and 1850s, who were for the most part also social critics, found very little in the tale to write about. Men such as Vissarion Belinsky in the 1840s and Nikolai Chernyshevsky in the 1850s saw literature as a potentially powerful weapon in the struggle for social and political change. To readers of such outlook *The Queen of Spades* offered little. Belinsky was clearly embarrassed by the tale's exclusiveness—it was obviously written to be read with pleasure by readers of Pushkin's own society, the privileged and educated classes. Similarly, Chernyshevsky found many of Pushkin's works well-written but essentially slight.

Temperamentally, if not chronologically, Pushkin was an eighteenth-century aristocratic man of letters, whose works, in their elegance, precision and polish, reflect the conviction that art, if it is not well-executed, is nothing at all. His mature view of art was uncompromisingly aesthetic. 'The aim of poetry is poetry', he once wrote,[13] and he could not look upon literature as a work-horse condemned to draw intolerably heavy philosophical and moral burdens. This is not to suggest that Pushkin did not take literature seriously; on the contrary, he believed that poetic inspiration was divine. It is simply that Pushkin's seriousness and commitment to literature were of a different kind from those of his successors; literature could be serious without being grave, and it could uplift without instructing. Pushkin wore the mantle of the artist lightly and elegantly, but this same mantle was to prove too cumbersome for many of his followers.

In his social attitudes too Pushkin differed from later Russian writers, and this is worth examining because throughout the history of literature the writer's social outlook has largely conditioned his view of art. The guilt, for example, which Tolstoy felt on behalf of his social class, the nobility, is central to the development of his writing and to his rejection of 'sophisticated' literature in favour of simpler forms accessible to the ordinary working people.

Pushkin was rarely inconvenienced by democratic leanings. He was the product of an established Europeanised aristocratic society, and inordinately proud of his own 600-year-old lineage. He regarded the nobility, and by implication the idea of social privilege, as 'a necessary and natural feature of a great civilised nation'.[14] He was an élitist and a snob, and these characteristics are quite obvious in his work. He addressed himself for the most part to his social equals and had little time for those who were unwilling or unable to appreciate the sophistication of his genius. Of course it was far easier for Pushkin to maintain this attitude than it would have been for Tolstoy. Pushkin lived and wrote towards the end of a great age of the nobility in Russia. Democratic and populist attitudes existed, but were nothing like as widespread or as fashionable as they were to become later in the nineteenth century, following the development in Russia of a mixed-class, as opposed to exclusively aristocratic intelligentsia.

Values have of course changed since Pushkin's day, and attitudes and assumptions regarded then as natural and unquestionable may now appear to be decadent, frivolous, unfair and irresponsible. Perhaps this is why *The Queen of Spades* fails to satisfy the literary taste of many modern readers, and here 'modern' can mean not just ourselves, but also people as close chronologically to Pushkin as Belinsky and Chernyshevsky, who had come to expect more from literature than a simple society tale. In short, *The Queen of Spades* is not likely to evoke widespread admiration today because it is, in a modern context, aristocratically unfair, provocatively amoral and intellectually lightweight. It cannot be described as 'a vivid exposé of a corrupt society', or 'an urgent analysis of the ethical problems facing us all', etc.

Many details of *The Queen of Spades* locate it firmly in a bygone age. For example, the story's exclusiveness has already been mentioned. It is directed unambiguously at a tiny, privileged section of nineteenth-century Russian society. One suspects that it would have meant little to people of lesser status, even to those capable of reading, for the reader is expected to grasp and appreciate references and attitudes familiar only to polite society. Apart from making allusions to contemporary society, figures and events, which the hypothetical middle-class reader of the time might conceivably have been able to trace, Pushkin assumes familiarity on his reader's part with manners, customs and attitudes practised only by the upper reaches of society.[15] The reader is expected, for example, to respond immediately and in the right way to the distinction drawn by society between Hermann's status, that of an engineer, and Narumov's, that of a guardsman. Only then can he understand the suggestiveness of Tomsky's incredulity when the socially naive Lizaveta Ivanovna implies that the immaculately well-bred Narumov might be a mere engineer.

But in a more general sense Pushkin assumes that the intelligence and outlook of the reader are comparable to his own. For example, he takes it for granted that his reader will be able to play with ideas and concepts as easily and naturally as he does. For Pushkin such playfulness was second nature. He was able to juggle even with serious concepts without either being enslaved by them or rendering them ridiculous. A tone of playfulness and the skilful use of parody are central to *The Queen of Spades,* and their presence effectively deters the reader from interpreting the tale too seriously. Whoever draws heavy social or moral conclusions from this work is guilty of a gross failure of response.

The Queen of Spades is rich in literary allusions and echoes which would have been quite apparent to Pushkin's contemporaries. The whole tale is built around the juxtaposition of features characteristic of two literary genres popular at the time: the gothic tale of the supernatural, and the realistic social and psychological sketch. Pushkin assumes his reader's familiarity with these two forms and then proceeds to hold their seemingly contradictory demands together for the duration of his tale. As a result, the reader is never sure whether he is dealing with a work of fantasy or a work of psychological realism. The opening of *The Queen of Spades* skilfully establishes the ambiguity: the epigraph and Tomsky's introduction of the story of the mysterious card trick both speak clearly of supernatural forces awaiting the ambitious Hermann, but at the same time the reader learns of Hermann's hopelessly split nature, torn between the extremes of sobriety and wild imagination. Either could account for his eventual downfall. Likewise, the reader is made to feel uneasy about Pushkin's immaculately realistic depiction of upper-class Russian life by the occasional references to real people with mysterious associations, such as the strange Count Saint-Germain, who had revealed the secret of the cards to the old Countess.

Ambiguity informs the whole work. Is Hermann the victim of a supernatural conspiracy which avenges his abuse of Lizaveta Ivanovna and the death of the Countess? Or is he simply a mad German whose amply demonstrated imagination accounts for his apparently supernatural downfall? Pushkin allows both possibilities, and the uncertainty is skilfully reinforced in the following extract:

> Hermann was the son of a Russified German, who had left him a small capital sum. Being firmly convinced of the need to consolidate his independence, Hermann did not touch even the interest, but lived on his salary, denying himself even the slightest extravagance. Moreover, he was reserved and ambitious, so that his companions rarely had the opportunity to make fun of his excessive thrift. He had strong passions and an ardent imagination, but his resoluteness saved him from the customary indiscretions of youth. Thus, for instance, although he was a gambler at heart, he never touched cards, for he reckoned that his circumstances did not allow him (as he put it) 'to risk the necessary in the hope of gaining the superfluous'. Yet despite this he spent whole nights sitting at the card tables, following with feverish excitement the vicissitudes of the game.
>
> The tale of the three cards had had a powerful effect on Hermann's imagination and preyed on his mind the whole night. 'What if,' he thought to himself the next evening as he wandered around St Petersburg, 'What if the old Countess were to reveal her secret to me? Or tell me the three lucky cards? Why shouldn't I try my luck? . . . I could get introduced to her, win her favour, perhaps even become her lover. But that would all take time, and she is eighty-seven. She could be dead within a week, or even a couple of days! And what about the tale itself? Can one believe it? . . . No, economy, moderation and hard work—these are my three lucky cards. They will treble my capital, increase it sevenfold and bring me leisure and independence!'[16]

On one level of this passage a strong case is made out for a realistic interpretation of subsequent events. We are told, for example, that Hermann 'had strong passions and an ardent imagination, but his resoluteness saved him from the customary indiscretions of youth'; that he was 'a gambler at heart', but had 'never touched cards' and that he followed each game 'with feverish excitement'. These brief psychological brushstrokes point unmistakeably to a man whose moderate veneer only just restrains a wild and imaginative nature. This interpretation is given added weight by Hermann's rapid and extreme psychological fluctuations, as for example when he dreams wildly one moment of becoming the Countess' lover, only to be brought immediately down to earth by the sobering thought that she is eighty-seven years old. As a result of this thought Hermann decides to dismiss his thirst for the secret of the card trick and resolves: 'Economy, moderation

and hard work—these are my three lucky cards', which will 'treble my capital, increase it sevenfold . . .'. The numbers Hermann hits upon here are significant, for the Three, the Seven and the Ace are the cards to be revealed to him later by the Countess' ghost. Pushkin is evidently suggesting that the numbers are for some reason already fixed in Hermann's mind and that he simply imagines the Countess' subsequent visitation.

At this point in the chapter the realistic interpretation has the upper hand, but Pushkin goes on to cloud the issue and resurrect the possibility of supernatural intervention. During his walk home Hermann suddenly finds himself before a large house. His enquiries reveal that this is none other than the house of the Countess whose history has so occupied his imagination. Coincidence, perhaps? He resumes his wanderings, but then again suddenly finds himself before the same house. Coincidence becomes less likely, and, like Hermann, the reader suspects the existence of some unknown force directing his steps.

There are many other instances of such ambiguity. It is not clear that Hermann really sees the Countess' corpse wink at him: Pushkin's use of the phrase 'it seemed to him' keeps the issue open.[17] Neither are we sure that he really sees the ghost; we are told before this 'visit' that Hermann can think of nothing but the death of the Countess and that 'contrary to his custom he had drunk a great deal'.[18]

Pushkin's emphasis upon such playful ambiguity is achieved perhaps at the expense of the more serious implications of a story about greed, ambition and murder, but certainly not at the expense of its entertainment value. And Pushkin's desire to entertain rather than instruct is one of the features which clearly distinguish him from later Russian writers.

We see the entertainer/parodist at work again in the choice of characters for the tale. All of them are literary stereotypes common in works of the time, and were therefore as familiar to Pushkin's contemporaries as they are today. But Pushkin does not give his reader what he has come to expect from such characters. He compels him instead to regard familiar figures in a new light. The reader of popular sentimental or sensational tales might well expect to respond to the conventional figures of the Countess, Lizaveta Ivanova and Hermann in certain well-defined ways. The old Countess, for example, is the familiar tyrant/villain figure and might be expected to arouse in the reader distaste for her obvious unfairness and selfishness; Lizaveta Ivanovna, the archetypal sentimental heroine/victim, should engender compassion; and Hermann, the stock romantic hero of melodrama, admiration for his strength of will. After all, he is the man of the future, trying to establish himself by manipulating the injustices of a vanishing way of life.

But these conventional reactions are not the ones Pushkin ultimately provokes in his reader. It becomes obvious in the course of the tale that Pushkin regards his characters not in a moral light, but in an aesthetic one, and the reader is invited to do the same. This distances Pushkin from the moralists who followed him and firmly set the tone of later Russian literature and discloses just how old-fashioned *The Queen of Spades* is. Pushkin's aristocratic self-confidence and his sense of the dignity and stability of his class and its values allow him to evade altogether the moral issues raised by the tale and to judge his characters—for judge them he does, albeit unobtrusively—against aesthetic and class criteria. Thus the self-centred, spiteful and no doubt undeserving Countess receives from Pushkin the tacit approval he withholds from the poor and worthy Lizaveta Ivanovna. Pushkin suggests that you do not have to be good to be appealing, and that style can conceal—indeed, atone for—a multitude of sins. And this wicked old lady certainly has style. Her dubious ethics and swollen legs count for little when we see just how skilled she is at the arts of survival and oneupmanship. She has lived for years with a secret which could make a fortune, but regards it as unimportant; as John Bayley has remarked: 'Class has no need of magic'.[19] She displays a remarkable ability to keep one step ahead of those who surround her. For example, when her grandson, Tomsky, lets slip that the last of the old Countess' contemporaries has passed away, the predictably solicitous Lizaveta Ivanovna tries to soften the news in order to spare the Countess' feelings. What she fails to see is that the old lady, far from being concerned and dispirited, is delighted. She has outdone her contemporaries by outliving them. She delights in attending balls where she is unwanted and where she knows that her presence as a relic of the past inhibits the future. Her stubborn refusal to rest in dignified peace is also entirely in character. There is no doubt that, of all the characters in the tale, she has the lion's share of Pushkin's sympathy.

Pushkin's attitude to Lizaveta Ivanovna is also unexpected. He obviously finds her poor, innocent and humiliated, but, most important of all, she is dull. She has a certain drab righteousness, but no style whatsoever. Pushkin's essentially aesthetic rather than ethical outlook is clear in a passage where, no doubt with the best of intentions, he begins to describe Lizaveta's hardships, but cannot resist transferring his attention from this tediously upright girl to the much more interesting items of furniture which surround her.[20]

The same is true of Hermann. Readers familiar with the character of Rastignac in Balzac's novel, *Le Père Goriot,* published in 1834 soon after *The Queen of Spades,* might see in Hermann a similar romantic, demonic figure. But Hermann is a parody of the romantic man of will, a vulgar and prosaic figure despite his involvement in the death of the Countess. One suspects that Pushkin allows the full weight of retribution to fall upon Hermann, not because he has killed, but because he has done so without style and panache. His real sin is his dullness and the ridiculous figure he cuts when, instead of murdering the Countess with the ruthless resolve of a Napoleon whom he resembles only in profile, he timidly waves an unloaded revolver un-

der her nose and watches her die of fright. The old Countess displays her natural superiority even at the moment of death, by depriving Hermann of heroic stature.

In a world in which ethical considerations often rank higher than aesthetic ones Pushkin's tendency to invert this hierarchy is unlikely to find general favour. *The Queen of Spades* emphasises Pushkin's distance from present values and has been a particular source of embarrassment for Soviet literary critics who are expected to re-examine the great works of the past in order to emphasise those features which imply a progressive social philosophy. For such reapers *The Queen of Spades* yields a most frustratingly poor harvest.

Notes

1. Matthew Arnold, *Essays in Criticism* (Second Series), London, 1908, p. 257.

2. Two recent verse translations of Pushkin's novel in verse, *Eugene Onegin* are worthy exceptions. These are by Charles Johnston (Penguin, Harmondsworth, 1979) and Walter Arndt (Dutton, New York, 1981).

3. D. S. Mirsky, *A History of Russian Literature,* Routledge & Kegan Paul, London, 1964, p. 117.

4. A. S. Pushkin, *Polnoe sobranie sochinenii v desyati tomakh,* Leningrad, 1977-79, VI, p. 215.

5. *P.S.S.* VII, p. 13.

6. Letter to P. A. Vyazemsky, 19 August 1823, *P.S.S.,* X, p. 52.

7. Letter to Vyazemsky, 4 November 1823, *P.S.S.,* X, p. 57.

8. *P.S.S.,* V, p. 53.

9. *P.S.S.,* VII, p. 12.

10. *P.S.S.,* VI, p. 235.

11. D. S. Mirsky, p. 119.

12. *P.S.S.,* VI, p. 210.

13. Letter to V. A. Zhukovsky, 20 April 1825, *P.S.S.,* X, p. 112.

14. *P.S.S.,* VII, p. 136.

15. See J. Bayley, *Pushkin. A Comparative Commentary,* Cambridge University Press, Cambridge, 1971, p. 321.

16. *P.S.S.,* VI, pp. 218-219.

17. *P.S.S.,* VI, p. 232.

18. *P.S.S.,* VI, p. 232.

19. Bayley, p. 319.

20. *P.S.S.,* VI, p. 217.

William Edward Brown (essay date 1986)

SOURCE: Brown, William Edward. "Alexander Pushkin as a Writer of Prose." In *A History of Russian Literature of the Romantic Period.* Vol. 3, pp. 218-24. Ann Arbor, Mich.: Ardis, 1986.

[*In the following essay, Brown explains the relationship between Pushkin's* The Queen of Spades, Ezersky, *and the narrative poem* The Bronze Horseman.]

THE QUEEN OF SPADES[1]

Pushkin's most successful completed short story, **The Queen of Spades,** was written in 1833, during his "second Boldino autumn," and published in the following year. During this same period he was working on the uncompleted second "novel in verse," *Ezersky,* and the last of his narrative poems, *The Bronze Horseman.* Among these three pieces, in different genres, there is a fascinating and puzzling kinship. Hermann, the methodical and monomaniacal German who is the hero of **The Queen of Spades,** was first conceived as a character of a quite different sort—a dreamy romantic, in love with a "little German girl" with the significant name of Charlotte. There are only a few small fragments extant of the original "story about a gambler" which preceded the complete novella, but enough exists to make it evident that the kernel of the story would have been the hero's attempt to learn the secret of the "three cards" in the hope thereby of winning a fortune in order to achieve independence and marry his Charlotte. The first fragment of the original form of the story is told in the first person by a member of a group of young men which would presumably have included Hermann perhaps as a friendly outsider:[2]

> About four years ago there was a gathering in Petersburg of several of us young fellows whom circumstances had brought into contact. We were leading a pretty disordered kind of life. We ate at Andrieux's without appetite, we drank without getting happy, we went to Sofia Astafevna's to drive the poor old woman crazy with our pretended choosiness. We killed the day somehow or other, and in the evenings we gathered at each other's quarters in turn.

The second fragment describes Hermann's sweetheart and her family, and briefly remarks on Hermann himself:

> Now permit me briefly to make you acquainted with Charlotte. . . . Her father was at one time a merchant of the second guild, then an apothecary, then director of a pension, finally a proofreader and typesetter; he died, leaving his wife certain debts and a quite complete collection of butterflies and insects. He was a good man and had many basic kinds of knowledge which led him to nothing good. His widow, having sold the manuscripts to a shopkeeper, paid for a little tobacco shop and began to provide for herself and Charlotte with the labor of their hands.

> Hermann lived on the same court as the widow, became acquainted with Charlotte, and soon they were in love with one another, as only Germans can still love in our times. . . .

> And when the charming little German girl pulled aside the white window curtain, Hermann did not appear at his peep-hole [*vasisdas*] and greet her with his customary smile.

His father, a Russianized German, had bequeathed a small capital. Hermann left it in a savings bank, not touching the interest, and lived on his salary alone.

Part of the last fragment, slightly expanded, was retained in the brief characterization of Hermann in Chapter 2 of the finished novella. But the entire conception of this character, including his involvement with Charlotte, is radically changed in **The Queen of Spades**; Charlotte disappears altogether, and Hermann becomes a frustrated Napoleon.

The basic similarity of Hermann's relations with Charlotte in the original sketch with the aspirations of *Ezersky* in that fragment and of Eugene in *The Bronze Horseman* is clearly evident. What the denouement of the *Ezersky* story might have been is of course unknown; the other tales, one in prose and one in verse, both end in tragic frustration and madness. Hermann's efforts to win a quick fortune for himself and Charlotte would probably have come to the same end.[3]

Like many of Pushkin's works, **The Queen of Spades** has a subject which was suggested to Pushkin by an anecdote told by a friend:[4]

> The old Countess was Natalia Petrovna Golitsyna, mother of Dmitri Vladimirovich, governor-general of Moscow; she had really lived in Paris in the fashion Pushkin described. Her grandson, [S.G.] Golitsyn, related to Pushkin that once he had lost at cards and went to his grandmother to ask for money. She would not give him money, but told him three cards, which had been designated to her in Paris by [Count] St.-Germain. "Try them," said his grandmother. Her grandson bet on the cards and recouped his losses. The further development of the tale is entirely fictional.

The anecdote of the "three cards" is the generating principle of the tale. Related at the late supper of the group of card-playing young aristocrats (their dissipated habits are less prominent than in the first-person account in the fragmentary first version) it becomes fixed in the mind of the seemingly staid and cold-blooded young German engineer Hermann and transforms him into a monomaniac, bent on learning at all costs the secret that will bring him sudden wealth and lift him out of the bourgeois existence which he resents. The rest of the story, told with the utmost economy and directness, without any detours, is the account of this maniacal quest and its tragic outcome.

A fundamental theme of the novella is that of information given a living being by a ghostly visitor. Superficially this suggests E. T. A. Hoffmann. Although many of Hoffmann's characters have dealings with ghosts, perhaps the nearest analogue in the work of the German romantic is the story *Ritter Gluck,*[5] in which a young musician meets a man who plays him music which he does not recognize from an opera by the great composer Willibald Christoph Gluck—an opera which is known to have been on Gluck's mind when he died, but which was never written. The performer of the music is the ghost of Gluck himself. In the

Hoffmann story, however, there is no personal relationship between the two musicians, while the ghost which imparts to Hermann the secret of the three cards is that of the old Countess whom his unexpected appearance and threats have frightened to death, and Hermann's catastrophic third play, when he unaccountably draws the queen of spades instead of the ace appears to be the old woman's posthumous revenge. This aspect of the tale is underlined by the epigraph: "The queen of spades signifies secret hostility"—*Most recent fortune-telling manual.*

Like many writers of his day, e.g., V. F. Odoevsky, Pushkin in his novella resorts to the device of "double motivation," that is, he takes pains to leave clues that allow the apparently supernatural incidents of the old Countess's apparition and revenge to be explained naturally: thus, Hermann is overwrought by the old woman's death and the apparently definitive loss of the secret of the three cards; he has been drinking more than usual; although he has been a constant spectator at card games, he himself has never before been a player, etc. At the same time, the most significant of the seemingly supernatural incidents—Hermann's unexampled success on the first two of his three evenings in Chekalinsky's gambling parlor, when he bets on the first two of the three-card sequence, the three and the seven—remains unexplained, or explainable only as sheer, and most improbable, coincidence. The Marxist critics who indignantly reject the idea that Pushkin, even for the purposes of his story, accepted such an irrational belief as that in ghosts, are letting a preconceived notion of Pushkin cloud their vision. Doubtless he did not personally subscribe to popular beliefs in otherworldly intervention; but he was not above using them for artistic purposes. Note, for example, the frequency of prophetic dreams in his works. At the end of Chapter 2 Hermann has a dream of dizzying success at the gaming table; just so the young monk Grigory in the fifth scene of *Boris Godunov* relates a dream that foretells his career as a pretender to the throne of Muscovy and its tragic end; and Petrusha Grinyov, in *The Captain's Daughter,* dreams that in some fashion the rough-looking muzhik who has been his guide through a snow-storm is his father: the muzhik, who is Pugachev, indeed saves his life and makes possible his marriage. Hermann's failure on his third play is from a rational point of view a perfectly natural occurrence, far more natural indeed than his earlier successes; in Hermann's fevered mind, however, it is a supernatural punishment. Just as he saw the features of the dead woman at her funeral contorted in a mocking grimace, so he sees the same leer on the face of the queen of spades. Pushkin makes no point of this, for his tale is perfectly objective, with no didactic overtones: but anyone wishing to read a moral into the fable could say that such ruthless and single-minded pursuit of money as Hermann's deserves his punishment; and that even in terms of his own hallucination he has merited it: his ghostly visitor left him with the words: "I forgive you my death, on condition that you marry my ward, Lizaveta Ivanovna." The thought of doing so never enters Hermann's mind.

The tale is told with Pushkin's usual economy; there is no parade of description, either of background realia or of the psychology of the characters. It begins *in medias res,* with the words: "Once a card game was going on at the quarters of Narumov of the Horse Guards," and whatever exposition is needed is supplied in passing as events develop. In six chapters the tragedy moves inexorably to its conclusion, from the first appearance of the anecdote of the "three cards," to Hermann's scheme of extorting the secret from the old woman and her resulting death, through his appearance and faint at her funeral, to the apparition and revelation of the secret, to the final scene at Chekalinsky's, which is marked by an almost unbearable intensity. Contrary to Pushkin's usual practice, a brief epilogue informs the reader that Hermann has been confined to a madhouse, and that Lizaveta Ivanovna, the poor girl whom he had heartlessly made the tool of his insane cupidity, has found a wealthy husband.

Hermann's character is the heart of the story. It is briefly sketched in Chapter 2:[6]

> He was secretive and ambitious moreover, and his companions rarely had occasion to make fun of his excessive parsimony. He had strong passions and an ardent imagination, but firmness saved him from the usual errors of youth. So, for example, though a gambler at heart, he had never taken cards in his hand because he reckoned that his fortune would not allow him, as he used to say, *to sacrifice the necessary in hope of gaining the superfluous,*—yet he used to sit for whole nights at the gaming tables and follow with feverish excitement the various turns of the game.

Hermann has often been compared with Julien Sorel, the ruthless *arriviste* of Stendhal's *The Red and the Black.* There is considerable similarity between the two heroes: both are of plebeian origin and resent their relatively low place in society and are ruthlessly bent on changing it; both look on other people as potential instruments for their own purposes; and both overreach themselves and suffer a catastrophic fall. Perhaps the guillotine is a happier ending than the madhouse! But there is a great difference: Julien, although he always has his eye on the main chance, is a man of passion; Hermann is cold-blooded and calculating. Julien is genuinely in love, first with Mme de Rênal and then with Mlle de la Mole. His fatal blunder is one of passion, when he attempts to murder the first of his mistresses when she becomes inconvenient to his second affair. Hermann, however passionate his letters to Lizaveta Ivanovna may sound (they are faithful transcripts from sentimental German novels, we are told) has no interest in her whatsoever; her beauty and innocence leave him wholly unmoved.

In one other respect there is a similarity between Julien and Hermann: both are "exceptional people," and both are potential Napoleons. Julien sees the conqueror's meteoric career as a constant inspiration; and Pushkin twice explicitly compares his hero to Napoleon. Pushkin's heroes, whether in verse or prose, after his Byronic period are almost always ordinary, commonplace people—Eugene Onegin, the Eugene of *The Bronze Horseman,* Peter Grinyov, etc.; even young Alexei Berestov ("Mistress into Maid"), for all his melancholy pose and "black ring engraved with a death's-head" is a quite ordinary fellow. Vladimir Dubrovsky and Hermann are exceptions. Pushkin notes ironically that Hermann's "Byronic" character is rather an anomaly in his time. It is this demonic aspect of the prosaic-seeming young engineer which fascinates Lizaveta in Tomsky's description (Chapter 4): "He has the profile of a Napoleon and the soul of a Mephistopheles. I believe that he has at least three crimes on his conscience." Tomsky is of course not serious—there is nothing in the story itself to support such a charge against Hermann—but Pushkin intends it as a clue to the potentialities of his character.

For the most part Pushkin refrains from himself describing his people or their thoughts; this is done much more effectively by depicting their actions. Thus there is no analysis of Hermann's deliberations between the time when he first hears of the three cards and his wooing of Lizaveta Ivanovna. The reader learns of this turn of events only in Chapter 2 when Lizaveta asks Tomsky if Narumov is in the engineers (we have been told in the first chapter that Narumov belongs to the Horse Guards, but Hermann is an engineer). Although in Chapter 4 Lizaveta, as she sits in her room after the ball, is described as passing in mental review the circumstances which have led to her rash assignation with Hermann, all this is already known to the reader, and her meditation only confirms what earlier chapters have shown. Lizaveta is presented most sympathetically. She is a presumably typical figure—the poor young companion of a tyrannical old woman. A dependent, hourly subject to the whims, tantrums and stupid "conversation" of a senile tyrant, Liza has romantic dreams about captivating a suitor who will enable her to escape from her humiliating captivity. Her desperation motivates her acceptance of Hermann's demand for an assignation, and her innocence of the world explains her failure to appreciate fully the risks involved. The disillusion she suffers when Hermann uses the first (and only) meeting with her for his own selfish purposes and she realizes that it is only money that he loves, not her, is crushing. Kindly Pushkin provides her with wealth and independence in the Epilogue— and a poor "companion" of her own. One hopes that her own experience may have made her humane.

The other fully developed character of the novella is that of the old Countess. In two splendid passages in the second and third chapters Pushkin shows her in action with Lizaveta and thereby reveals both what she is like and what her companion has to endure. Then he gives a concise summary of her character, which her behavior with Lizaveta has already enabled the reader to guess:[7]

> The Countess, of course, did not have a bad heart; but she was capricious like any woman who has been spoiled by society; miserly and sunk in a cold egoism, like all old people who have fallen out of love with life and are estranged from the present.

Stylistically *The Queen of Spades* is the perfect example of Pushkin's realistic prose. In *The Tales of Belkin* the fictional transmission of the stories complicates the style. The first teller of the tales is a provincial official, an ex-army officer, a sentimental maiden lady, or the like; the tales are told to a colorless amateur writer (Belkin) who casts them in a simple, artless prose; and finally the third narrator, A. P. (Alexander Pushkin), colors it with elements of irony and occasional subjective feeling. *The Queen of Spades* is the first of Pushkin's completed stories to dispense with the distancing device of the fictional narrator. Sober, colorless, light, completely free of ornamentation or mannerisms, the language is the closest approach in Russian to classical French prose, which is indeed Pushkin's model. The sentences are short and structurally simple; the infrequent epithets are precise, each calculated for a definite effect; and the verb usually carries the principal idea. Note, for example, the sentence: "Hermann heard her hurrying footsteps." Liza, returning with the Countess from the ball, and torn with anxiety over her imprudent assignation, is in haste to discover if Hermann really is in her room. The epithet "hurrying" tells all this with Pushkin's habitual neatness and economy. Or in Chapter 4 as Hermann leaves Lizaveta's room to make his escape down the concealed private staircase to the street, he makes his wordless farewell to her: "Hermann pressed her cold, unresponsive hand, kissed her bowed head, and left the room." The word "unresponsive" tells the whole story of their relations: he has lied to her and used her as his tool, and all she feels for him is loathing and shame for her own gullibility.

When Pushkin feels it necessary to convey more fully the thoughts of his characters, he still uses the greatest economy. In the same climactic fourth chapter Hermann appears in Lizaveta's room and reveals his real purpose in their meeting and the death of the Countess:[8]

> Lizaveta Ivanovna listened to him with horror. So those passionate letters, those ardent demands, that bold, stubborn pursuit—all that was not love! Money—that was what his soul craved! She could not satisfy his desires and make him happy! . . . She began to weep bitterly in her belated, tormenting repentance. Hermann looked at her in silence. His heart too was torn, but neither the poor girl's tears nor the wonderful charm of her grief agitated his grim soul. He felt no remorse of conscience at thought of the dead old woman. One thing horrified him: the irretrievable loss of the secret from which he had expected to get rich—Morning had come. Lizaveta Ivanovna extinguished the burned-down candle; a pallid light illuminated her room. She wiped her tear-stained eyes and raised them to Hermann; he was sitting at the window, with arms folded and frowning terribly. In that position he had an amazing resemblance to portraits of Napoleon. This likeness struck even Lizaveta Ivanovna.

Lev Tolstoi, on a rereading of *The Captain's Daughter,* felt that Pushkin's prose had aged: "Now in the modern trend interest in the details of a feeling justly replaces interest in events themselves. Pushkin's tales are somehow naked."[9] It is true that the great novels of the nineteenth century which came after Pushkin are distinguished by a fullness of psychological analysis which Pushkin never indulges in. But the great novels of his own day, especially those of Sir Walter Scott and Honoré Balzac are distinguished just as much for lengthy descriptions, antiquarian and historical and social disquisitions and the like. Pushkin eschews all this, and his prose does convey an impression of bareness. So does Voltaire's, and so does Stendhal's, and so does Mérimée's, all writers whom Pushkin knew and valued. Pushkin's prose is different from any of these, but it is essentially French; there is no Russian antecedent for it.

As a final stylistic note on *The Queen of Spades,* it is not without interest that some Russian writers have claimed to detect an almost poetic rhythm in the story. A. Slonimsky goes the farthest: "The theme of the three cards invariably calls up a rhythmical three-beat movement of the language, which sometimes passes into a regular dactyl." He then quotes the words of Hermann's meditation: "What if the old Countess should reveal the secret to me? Or name for me those three sure cards" [*ili naznachit mne éti tri vérnye kárty? . . .*].[10] Such attempts, however, are doomed to inevitable frustration, for while the word accents of a prose sentence are fixed, the *sentence accent* is not, and different readers will not read the same sentence identically. Lezhnyov derides Slonimsky's rhythmical reading of the three-card sequence: "Troíka, semérka i túz"["the three, the seven and the ace"], which unfortunately for Slonimsky's thesis, sometimes appears without the connective "i," for which the critic is obliged to substitute a purely arbitrary "pause." As Stepanov says:[11] "The laws of prose rhythm are different, and to try to fit Pushkin's phrase to verse measures . . . is a hopeless business, although one that obliquely testifies to its rhythmical organization as a principle." Pushkin's prose has its own extremely complex rhythm, which one may feel, but which no schematic analysis has succeeded in defining.

Notes

1. Pushkin, *Sobranie*, V, 233-262; trans. R. Edmonds in *The Queen of Spades and Other Stories.*

2. Pushkin, *Sobranie*, V, 553-554.

3. N. N. Petrunina ("Dve 'Peterburgskie povesti' Pushkina," in *Pushkin: Issledovaniia i materialy,* X [L. Nauka, 1982], pp. 147-167) explores in copious and often unconvincing detail the interrelationships of the two completed and one fragmentary tale.

4. *Rasskazy o Pushkine, Zapisannye so slov ego druzei O. I. Bartenevym v 1851-1860* (M. 1925), pp. 46-47.

5. *See Ritter Gluck* in *E. T. A. Hoffmann* (Berlin & Darmstadt: Tempel Verlag, 1963), I, 17-27.

6. Pushkin, *Sobranie*, V, 242.

7. Pushkin, *Sobranie*, V, 240.

8. Pushkin, *Sobranie*, V, 253-254.

9. L. N. Tolstoi, *Polnoe sobranie sochinenii* (M. Goslitizdat, 1949—), Vol. 46, p. 188.

10. A. Slonimskii, *Masterstvo Pushkina*, p. 522.

11. Stepanov, *Proza Pushkina*, p. 253.

Jean Norris Scales (essay date June 1991)

SOURCE: Scales, Jean Norris. "The Ironic Smile: Pushkin's 'The Queen of Spades' and James' 'The Aspern Papers.'" *CLA* 34, no. 4 (June 1991): 486-90.

[*In the following essay, Scales finds parallels between Pushkin's tale and Henry James's "The Aspern Papers."*]

Reflecting contrasting bodies of literature, Alexander Pushkin's *The Queen of Spades* and Henry James' "The Aspern Papers" present views of man that are remarkably similar—man in his obsession learning the ironic consequences of his excesses. Pushkin's milieu is prerevolutionary tsarist Russia, and James' environment, a late nineteenth-century European setting. Yet, there is poignant similarity in the obsessive desire of the protagonists, in the striking reversal on the brink of success, and in the ironic smile that reinforces the reversal of each story.

Pushkin's protagonist, Hermann, a German engineer, moves in the courtly circles of late eighteenth-century St. Petersburg, while James' narrator, an American literary critic, moves in a foreign world, that of nineteenth-century Venice. Born in 1843, six years after Pushkin's death in a duel, James gives a view of "publishing scoundrels" through his protagonist, beyond the more individualistic concentration of Pushkin's central character. Related by Pushkin in brisk, objective style and by James in more complex first-person narration, the stories show young protagonists as they move within a hair's breadth of their most cherished desires, only to have fulfillment denied. Acceptance of fate by the protagonists is implicit in the design of the stories.

At the beginning of Pushkin's story, Hermann is notably a quiet observer, watching card games hour after hour but never venturing into competition. Pushkin masterfully controls the revelation of the protagonist's interest as it moves from a flicker to blazing obsession. Upon hearing of the aged Countess Anna Fedotovna's story of a remarkable winning streak in Paris years before, Hermann is silently and irretrievably caught by the fascination of possessing the secret which turned her losses into astounding winnings. From this point, Pushkin traces the detective story that will bring Hermann into possession of the cherished secret withheld by the Countess for sixty years, and conveys the irony of his having received it.

Earlier than in Pushkin's story, James reveals the narrator's consideration of his "plan of campaign." That which follows is only an intensification of those views expressed earlier in warlike imagery. The mystery of disclosing the narrator's increasing obsession is not present, for he from beginning to end reveals to the reader with frankness his singular purpose and his ultimate frustration. His subterfuge in exuding falsely a love of cultivating flowers, his moving into the dismal Venetian mansion of the aged Miss Bordereau and her niece Tina at exorbitant rent, and his unrelenting pursuit of the coveted Aspern papers outline the course of his campaign. In flattering speech, guarded silence, and audacious action, he unswervingly pursues his purpose. Unlike Pushkin's story, James' narrative does not bring the protagonist into the possession of his goal. Rather, the irony lies not in the consequences of his acquiring that which he sought, but in gaining by his own payment only a miniature reminder of his very bitter loss.

In each story there are tantalizing elements which increase the fervor of the pursuit. Hermann stands day after day below the window of the Countess, in time gaining access to her bedroom through an humble maid who is led to believe that his interest is in her. The success of the first stage of his mission leads Hermann to a frantic pressing of the Countess which results in her death, not by the gun that Hermann wields but from the shock of such an invasion. Her revelation of the card secret provides a second reinforcement of hope and a sharpening of the obsession. But shortly, when at the funeral Hermann sees the corpse of the Countess give him a mocking look, he is momentarily disconcerted: "At that moment it seemed to him the dead woman darted a mocking look at him and winked one eye."[1]

James' narrator, foreshadowing his own ironic reversal, is tauntingly shown a picture of Jeffrey Aspern by Miss Bordereau several months after he has begun his battle with flowers at the Venetian palace. Studying the face of the brilliant young poet, the narrator, also in the delusion of an obsession, witnesses a mocking smile: "He seemed to smile at me with mild mockery; he might have been amused at my case."[2] Noticeably, James' protagonist, in control of himself, is not disconcerted. Rather, he accepts the delusion humorously: "I had got into a pickle for him—as if he needed it!" (p. 287).

In both works, the wry smiles of the dead Countess in Pushkin's story and of the Aspern picture in James' narrative foreshadow the conclusion. It is through the blindness of obsession that both protagonists persist and are thus defeated through their own stubbornness of pursuit. In the very first reference to the Aspern picture, there is an ironic ring, for Miss Bordereau inquires, "Do you know about curiosities?" (p. 251). It is only after the use of "curiosities" that she clarifies upon the narrator's questioning: "About antiquities, the old gimcracks that people pay so much for today." (p. 251). In James' narrative the picture will indeed be a curiosity, for the handsome countenance will assume life in the narrator's mind and the semblance will be the symbol of defeat that is projected at the end of the story.

Further, the picture is a tantalizing play for Miss Bordereau in that initial conversation referring to it, for she

titillatingly refuses to disclose the subject of the picture. It is through the narrator's keenness and to his joy that he recognizes the identity. He sees the Aspern picture as a step toward the Aspern papers. But this first inquiry regarding an Aspern property is disappointing, for Miss Bordereau refuses to entrust the picture to the narrator, slipping it silently into her pocket. His hope for the papers is renewed when the aged lady's health wanes. Upon the promise of assistance of Tina, and upon Miss Bordereau's death, the narrator sees victory in sight—in spite of her hateful epithet for him as he rummaged through the drawers in her darkened room.

Hermann in his St. Petersburg world is also led to believe that riches will be his as he utilizes the coveted card trick, twice to astounding success. It is only upon the third encounter that his house of cards comes tumbling down. In the heat of anticipation, he turns up what should have been an ace, to find the queen of spades smiling at him:

> At that moment it seemed to him that the queen of spades smiled ironically and winked her eye at him. He was struck by her remarkable resemblance. . . .
>
> "The old Countess!" he exclaimed, seized with terror.
>
> (Pushkin, p. 46)

His sanity pushed to the limit, Hermann goes out of his mind and is confined to a mental hospital where he mutters constantly, "Three, seven, queen!" Thus Pushkin's protagonist in his obsession is led delusively to his tragic defeat.

Without the grimness of his Russian counterpart, James' protagonist in volatile zest moves to his crushing defeat. He cringes beneath the revelation of Tina, his assumed aide, the revelation that she has methodically burned the Aspern papers. The Aspern picture that she has given over to him then serves itself as a mockery of his futile pursuit. Paid for, and hanging above his desk, the picture remains the bitterest of reminders.

Although different in their literary heritages, Pushkin and James present interestingly comparable works. Pushkin in *The Queen of Spades* and James in "The Aspern Papers" strike a common chord in presenting the ironic consequences of an obsession and in using a pictured smile to reinforce the irony.

Notes

1. Alexander Pushkin. "The Queen of Spades," in *Great Russian Short Stories,* ed. Norris Houghton (New York: Dell, 1958), p. 42. Hereafter cited parenthetically in the text.

2. Henry James. *The Turn of the Screw and The Aspern Papers* (New York: Everyman's Library, 1969), p. 287. Hereafter cited parenthetically in the text.

Justin Doherty (essay date April 1992)

SOURCE: Doherty, Justin. "Fictional Paradigms in Pushkin's 'Pikovaya dama.'" *Essays in Poetics* 17, no. 1 (April 1992): 49-66.

[*In the following essay, Doherty delineates various critical interpretations of* The Queen of Spades *and offers one of his own based on a discussion of Pushkin's main fictional paradigms.*]

Pikovaya dama (*The Queen of Spades*) is generally considered to be one of the most significant works in nineteenth century Russian literature; it is also one of the most frequently written about. Even so, it is my feeling that studies of this text have left fundamental questions unasked; partly this is a result of a traditional bias in Pushkin scholarship in Russia as well as in the West. Whatever the reasons for this, it is surely necessary both to challenge certain received ideas about Pushkin's major works, and to explore new ways of interpreting them. In this article, I am interested in particular in the notion of reading which, as I see it, is woven into the general texture of *Pikovaya dama*; much of this article will accordingly be devoted to discussion of the fictional models or paradigms around which Pushkin has constructed his text. The reasons why such an approach is relevant have been indicated by Donald Fanger, who writes:

> [. . .] Pushkin's experiments in prose were highly conscious and principled ones, conducted by a professional on literary materials, and (as his finished prose made clear) informed with an awareness that a whole range of problems [. . .] remained to be worked out before the instrument might be applied as the times seemed increasingly to require. The result was to invest much of his fiction with an aura of stylization, other literary presences tending to loom more or less distinctly through the translucent character of his writing.[1]

For our purposes, 'other literary presences' will be interpreted as generalised, rather than specific, models and antecedents which are present in Pushkin's text.

Before proceeding to the text of *Pikovaya dama* itself, it is worth briefly summarising the main currents in earlier interpretations of this story. Broadly, these fall into three main groups: those whose main concern is literary-historical or textological; those which attempt a formal or structural analysis of the text; and those which attempt an 'exegesis' of the text, revealing some hidden, often occult, meaning. The latter two strands will be of most interest to us. Both these approaches, however different, assume a basic coherence in the text, and very often a reliable set of meanings which emerge from this structural coherence. Put another way, the text is 'readable', the particular aptitude or competence of a given reader permitting more and more new meanings to be 'read' out of the text. Indeed, *Pikovaya dama* seems, like many 'great' literary works, to have an inexhaustible store of meanings contained within itself; but as in many similar cases, the situation is really not so simple.

My discomfort arises from the fact that the coherence, seriousness of intention, and basic 'legibility' of this text are scarcely ever questioned; and even when they are, critics seem reluctant to draw the logical conclusion to their insights. I shall give two examples from recent essays by American Slavists which exemplify the problem, as it affects both exegetical and structural approaches to Pushkin's story.

In a study of Pushkin's incorporation of Masonic motifs and symbols into *Pikovaya dama,* Lauren Leighton is ready to admit a non-serious attitude on the part of the author:

> [. . .] When Freemasonry is shown to be associated in the tale with a wide range of cabalistic, thaumaturgic practices—the whole question of number and numerology—Puškin's delight in word and number games, in astounding coincidences, and in just plain spoofing subjects Freemasonry to outright ridicule.

However, this assertion is but a prelude to the 'serious' claim of the discovering of a new buried meaning in the text: Pushkin's purported anagrammatized incorporation of the name of the Decembrist Kondraty Ryleev, whose fate is claimed to have obsessed Pushkin in the years following 1825. This leads Leighton to make the 'meaningful' conclusion:

> Truly, as Akhmatova has stated, *The Queen of Spades* is a sophisticated, *multi-meaninged,* multi-levelled work of art whose full implications we have not yet begun to appreciate.[2]

However subversive the text may be in its irreverent use of certain perceived occult motifs, digging a little deeper produces a new, more serious intention on the part of the author.

An example of another recuperative reading of *Pikovaya dama,* this time using a structural approach, is an essay by Roberta Reeder on Pushkin's apparently parodic use of Hoffmann in his story. This essay attempts a fairly rigorous structural comparison between *Pikovaya dama* and several of Hoffmann's best-known stories; Reeder's analytical model derives from Vladimir Propp's analysis of Russian fairy-tales. Her conclusion is that *Pikovaya dama* is constructed as a parody of the canonical Hoffmann *Novelle,* indeed, along the lines of Hoffmann's own self-parodying tales such as 'The King's Bride'. But having demonstrated that Pushkin's story belongs to a non-serious literary genre, Reeder is at pains in her conclusion to restitute the text to the realm of traditional literary values, and goes so far as to suggest a naive identification with the story's characters:

> On the one hand, Charles Passage is correct when he notes the seriousness and probing of the human dilemma in *The Queen of Spades.* However, the work does have a comic, grotesque side as well. With the schemata of the Hoffmann tale as background, we can see how Pushkin masterfully parodied the Kunst-

märchen tradition. He has taken specific character types and typical actions and exaggerated and inverted them for the purposes of parody. Yet, as Shaw has pointed out in discussion of *Evgenij Onegin,* we laugh at Evgenij and Tat'jana as literary parodies of the sentimental and Byronic tradition, *but we sympathize with them as characters who strive to be larger than life, but whose human limitations prevent them from succeeding. The same can be said for Germann and Lizaveta. This is perhaps one of the elements wherein Pushkin's greatness lies.*[3]

Such recourse to the most unreflecting traditional assumptions about literary texts is, then, disappointingly widespread. If there is a subversive tendency of one kind or another identified in the text, then it is always easy to find a serious intention to control it. Pushkin's text may well, as Lauren Leighton asserts, have 'implications we have not yet begun to appreciate', but could this be because we have not yet begun to read it properly?

The aim of this article is to question the kind of critical assumptions I have indicated, and to consider important implications in this text which the desire to extract serious meanings seems so easily to obscure. I hope to show that *Pikovaya dama* is much less 'coherent' than critics have claimed, and that it is in fact very difficult to read any clear meanings into this text at all. Rather, this is a text which silences a number of potential meanings, which resists any single interpretative procedure. It is a text, though, whose sophistication and complexity are considerable, but whose sophistication and complexity seem to work against the reader in a teasing, playful, sometimes malevolent and ultimately frustrating way. In a manner which is peculiarly characteristic of certain of Pushkin's works, it appears to trivialize its own serious potential. This article, then, will examine Pushkin's 'ludic' attitude in *Pikovaya dama,* and look at some of the ways in which the reader is manipulated through 'typical' situations, themes and characters to be left in a state of unknowing perplexity.

The first important question to address in approaching *Pikovaya dama* is its genrological status: if this is not clearly established, the way is open for interpretations which distort the story's true character. I have in mind here the type of retrospective readings which see *Pikovaya dama* as a precursor of so-called 'psychological realism': the assumption here is that this story can, and should, be read in the same manner as a 'realist' novel. As a corrective to this type of assumption it is worth quoting the comments of Dostoevsky, perhaps the greatest Russian exponent of 'psychological realism', in a letter of 1880, which give his reading of *Pikovaya dama* as a fantastic tale:

> [. . .] the fantastic in art has its own limitations and rules. The fantastic must coincide with the real to the extent that you are *almost* obliged to believe it. Pushkin, who gave us almost all forms of literature, wrote *The Queen of Spades* which is the height of the art of the fantastic. You believe that Hermann really did have

a vision, one which matches precisely his general outlook, and at the same time, by the end of the story, when you have finished reading it, you do not know what to think: was this vision a product of Hermann's inner being, or was he really someone in contact with another world, a world of evil spirits hostile to humanity (Spiritism and its teachings). This is real art![4]

Dostoevsky's comments are of interest for two reasons. First, they tell us something reasonably reliable about how the text would have been read by Pushkin's contemporaries (Dostoevsky would have read it as a teenager in the 1830s), and thus point us, as readers, to the type of 'rules' and referents which apparently shape the story and give it meaning. To this extent, the assignation of *Pikovaya dama* to the genre of the fantastic tale must in turn inform our reading of it.

But Dostoevsky's comments are also interesting in their almost exact coincidence with the definition of the fantastic tale proposed by the literary theorist Tzvetan Todorov in his classic study of this genre, his *Introduction à la littérature fantastique.* Todorov's preliminary definition of the genre is as follows:

> In a world which is clearly our own, familiar, without devils, sylphs or vampires, there occurs an event which cannot be explained by the laws of this same familiar world. Whoever witnesses the event must choose between two possible solutions: either there has been a delusion of the senses, a trick of the imagination, and so the laws of the world remain as they are; or else the event really has occurred, it forms an integral part of reality, but it is a reality governed by laws unknown to us. Either the devil is an illusion, an imaginary being; or he really does exist, like any other living being; except that we don't meet him very often [. . .]
>
> The fantastic is this hesitation experienced by someone who knows only the laws of nature, confronted with an apparently supernatural event.[5]

Todorov acknowledges that his own conclusions are prefigured in a number of nineteenth century writers and theorists, and indeed it would be absurd to suppose that writers of fantastic literature were ignorant of the procedures on which their fiction was built. These authors were, rather, only too aware of what they were doing; one might compare the comments of one of Pushkin's contemporaries, V. F. Odoevsky, on the fantastic tales of E. T. A. Hoffmann:

> Hoffmann discovered the only way in which this element [the fantastic] may be incorporated into literature; his fantasy always has two sides: one which is pure fantasy, the other realistic; so that our proud nineteenth century reader is not invited to believe unconditionally in any miraculous event which is being recounted to him; everything by which this same event might be accounted for plainly and simply is brought to the fore in the story,—in this way he may have the best of both worlds; man's natural attraction to the marvellous is satisfied, and at the same time the exacting spirit of analysis is not offended; the reconciling of these two contrary elements was a feat of true genius.[6]

The literary context, then, in which *Pikovaya dama* belongs, is centred on the well understood model of the fantastic tale, which writers like Pushkin proceeded to utilize quite consciously and with considerable sophistication.[7]

Pikovaya dama conforms to various criteria on which the genre of the fantastic tale depends: it has an extraordinary hero, presents extraordinary and improbable events, and ends in catastrophe. But Pushkin was too sophisticated a writer to either accept or to imitate at face value a genre and manner which by the 1830s were more often parodied than taken seriously. Pushkin's appropriation of the fantastic tale is extremely self-conscious, and indeed often has the appearance of a parody. But before going on to examine in detail the ways in which Pushkin's version of the fantastic tale operates, one should perhaps remember that the fantastic tale was itself a self-conscious and in some sense a parodic literary form: for underneath the vicissitudes of plot and the employment of devices aimed at creating suspense, shock and horror in the reader, the Gothic novels and fantastic tales of the eighteenth and early nineteenth centuries are themselves more or less refined derivatives of the much older fairy-tale or folk legend (one might recall that the German term for Hoffmann's fantastic tales is *Kunstmärchen* or 'art-fairy-tale').

Retracing a story like *Pikovaya dama* to a remote model in the fairy-tale (*skazka*) is actually less fanciful than it at first appears to be. Aside from the distant ancestry of the fantastic tale in general in the fairy-tale, Pushkin was himself knowledgeable about and interested in the Russian traditional *skazka*. According to biographical tradition, Pushkin heard numerous folk-tales and legends directly from his elderly nanny, Arina Rodionovna, while confined to his family estate of Mikhailovskoe in 1824-26, and they exerted a powerful effect on his literary imagination.[8] This is testified in several ways, both in Pushkin's attempts to create his own imaginative versions of Russian *skazki*,[9] and in his incorporation of motifs and images clearly derived from the *skazka* into other works (as in the fortune-telling and dream sequences involving Tatyana in *Evgeniy Onegin*). *Pikovaya dama* is less obviously connected to the fairy-tale, but at a deeper structural level (as is the case with other examples of the literary fantastic) Pushkin makes use of it by constructing his story around several of the basic elements of the traditional Russian fairy-tale.

Vladimir Propp, the Russian ethnographer, in a famous study of the Russian *skazka,* discovered that any folk-tale in Russia conformed to a single pattern, with a limited number of possible actions, and a small number of possible characters to perform these. Ann Shukman has suggested that this type of pattern may underlie many Russian works of fiction; particularly common is what she describes as the 'classic' plot-scheme for the Russian *skazka*: 'The classic Russian fairy-tale had as its core the story of the hero who is despatched, journeys to another kingdom, acquires a magic object, overcomes the antagonist, wins the princess [. . .]'.[10] Shukman goes on to suggest that just such a pattern can be seen in the basic plot-structure

of *Pikovaya dama.* The story does indeed centre on a hero's quest for secret knowledge, which is granted to him by the 'donor' (the Countess) in circumstances with clear supernatural overtones: the Countess' ghost visits Hermann shortly after her death. Hermann then sets about using this secret knowledge to win his fortune, but is unsuccessful and precipitates his personal catastrophe. The reason he fails is that he abuses his knowledge, and rejects an essential condition of the fairy-tale plot: he is motivated not by erotic love for the beautiful princess (Liza), but instead by greed.

Indeed, the condition that erotic love must be a primary motive for heroic deeds is made explicit in the story when the Countess' ghost says to Hermann: 'I forgive you my death, so long as you will marry my ward Lizaveta Ivanovna'.[11] By this stage of the story (Chapter Five) we are well aware that Hermann is a false hero, and so do not actually expect him to marry Liza. It is therefore with a certain degree of satisfaction that we read of Hermann's final calamitous defeat at the hands of the gambler Chekalinsky, his 'antagonist'—and observe that in Hermann's error in playing the queen of spades instead of an ace there is the intimation of revenge by the Countess herself. However, the reader's satisfaction here is not, I do not think, a moralistic delight in seeing an evil-doer punished; rather, it has to do with the expectations raised by a story which follows the fairy-tale plot structure so closely. Reading has conditioned us to anticipate Hermann's demise, once we know him for the false hero that he is.

Furthermore, there is an explicit indication in the text itself that Pushkin quite consciously derived the fundamental plot of his story from the *skazka*. After hearing Tomsky's anecdote in Chapter One of the story, Hermann's reaction is articulated in the single word: 'skazka'. The surface meaning here is clearly that Tomsky's anecdote is a fiction; but quite evidently, the implications are greater than that. In particular, it is interesting that Hermann's interjection should be precisely to suggest that the fairy-tale (*skazka*) is a type of literature which is 'false', that is to say, which does not correspond to his experience and general expectations of life; this is of some importance in relation to later developments in the story. Moreover, there is significance in the fact that Hermann himself articulates this response to the anecdote: for his is the second of three apparently 'typical' reactions to Tomsky's anecdote (the first saying that it is a fluke [*sluchay*], the third suggesting that trick cards were used). Here Pushkin's apparently casual use of detail hides a very subtle design.

There are two ways in which this point may be developed. First, there is a certain irony in the fact that what Hermann initially perceives to be a 'fairy-tale', that is, a 'tall story', becomes more and more of a reality in his imagination as the main narrative develops. For it is quite possible that Hermann's initial reaction is correct, and Tomsky's anecdote is an invention; that the story of the mysterious win at cards by the Countess is an elegant, though transparent, disguise for her having offered herself to the Comte de

Saint-Germain, the man who apparently gave her the secret of the three winning cards, in return for money which she needed to repay a gambling debt. This reading is corroborated when in Chapter Three, threatened by Hermann, the Countess insists that the anecdote of the three cards was 'a joke' (*shutka*). We must then ascribe the dead Countess's visit to Hermann, and the secret she reveals to him, as the work of Hermann's imagination, and the fact that the three cards he imagines to be magically endowed actually win, to chance. This interpretation has been supported by more than one critic.[12]

Secondly, Hermann's assertion allows us to infer that if there is a fairy-tale plot model in *Pikovaya dama,* it is precisely Tomsky's anecdote which provides it. The anecdote thus assumes the status of a 'story within the story', where it and Hermann's own story reflect one another in fascinating ways. This must in turn affect the relationship between story-telling and truth: for if the reliability of Tomsky's anecdote about the Countess is open to doubt, then surely we can say the same about Pushkin's story about Hermann . . . In the main narrative of *Pikovaya dama,* just as much as in interpreting Tomsky's anecdote, Hermann finds himself very much in the position of reader. In any estimate, he is not a very good reader; his whole personal catastrophe, after all, stems from a misreading of Tomsky's anecdote, whose fictionality, if by that we mean its non-correspondence with actual experience in the world, ought to be transparent to him. Hermann's subsequent failure to read this anecdote as a product of the imagination, is matched by Hermann's own developing fantasy which, in his mind, assumes an every growing sense of reality and truth. Hermann's fantasy about his own power and destiny, then, facilitates not only his fatal error at cards, but his basic misperceptions in key scenes such as the Countess' funeral, and indeed his firm belief that the Countess' apparition before him actually took place.

Hermann's status as a misreading reader in the story corresponds closely to Tzvetan Todorov's observations on the structure of fantastic tales—for it is often via the perceptions of one or more characters that we are obliged to interpret ambiguous events. Hermann 'reads' the events as they occur as unambiguously supernatural, because his interpretation later on in the story is founded on the identification in his mind between a fictional paradigm (Tomsky's anecdote) and the realistically possible. In our role as readers of Pushkin's text, we find ourselves in a similar position, though in relation to a different paradigm: that of the fantastic tale in general. But the problem of how to read the fantastic tale is exacerbated in *Pikovaya dama* by Pushkin's self-conscious and possibly parodic use of the fantastic. It is therefore necessary to be more exact in defining the relationship between *Pikovaya dama* and this genre: does Pushkin's text parody the fantastic tale, or does it go beyond the confines of the literary fantastic, and indeed of literary parody itself?

There is a long tradition of interpreting *Pikovaya dama* as an ironic or parodic text. In a seminal essay on Pushkin's story, the Russian critic A. L. Slonimsky identified this with Pushkin's use of the basic techniques of the fantastic tale: 'In the constant vacillation between a fantastic and a psychologically plausible motivation, in the hidden realistic suggestions—Pushkin's sense of irony is gradually revealed.'[13] This tradition of interpretation suggests that a 'fantastic' reading of *Pikovaya dama* is undermined by careful 'realist' motivation—so that from beneath the guise of a fantastic tale a work of 'psychological realism' eventually emerges. More recently, this view of Pushkin's text as the narration of triumphant realism has been brought into question. How, after all, can a text parodying the literary fantastic transform itself with such facility into a work of strict realism? The American Slavist Diana Burgin prefers to use the term 'mystification' to describe Pushkin's technique in *Pikovaya dama,* and allow for a plurality of possible interpretations, rather than dogmatically assert the dominance of a single one:

> In order to make the fantastic credible, to suspend momentarily the reader's disbelief and draw him into the mystery of his tale, Puškin employs the narrative device of mystification. He plays upon certain characters and events in such a way as to make them seem strange and mysterious when they are not, and, conversely, he de-emphasizes or mocks those mystifying or supernatural events [. . .] which are clues to the real mystery. Using the device of mystification as a veil for his supernatural mystery, Puškin creates in the reader ambivalence about the reality of irrational occurrences, so that he can, with ample justification in the text, interpret the story in several ways [. . .][14]

The terminology used here may not be quite clear (the Russian word *mistifikatsiya,* meaning a 'leg-pull', is clearly what is meant), but the stress on the importance of *reading* in *Pikovaya dama,* and on the absence of any single obviously 'correct' reading of the text, are important points to make. I should now like to examine several instances of Pushkin's self-conscious play with the conventions of the fantastic tale, or 'mystification', as Burgin calls it.

On several occasions, this is quite undisguised. One such instance occurs in Chapter Two, in the frivolous conversation between the Countess and her grandson, Tomsky, where she asks him to supply her with something to read:

> —[. . .] bring me a new novel, but please, not one of those modern ones.
>
> —What do you mean, grand'maman?
>
> —I mean a novel where the hero doesn't kill his father, or his mother, and there aren't any drowned corpses. I'm terrified of drowned bodies.
>
> —There aren't any novels like that nowadays [. . .][15]

We might care to add, that the real misfortune of this situation is that the Countess herself will very soon become a corpse, though, perhaps fortunately for her, not a drowned one. This apparently trivial episode highlights a theme which pervades the story: the author's knowing awareness of life's imitation of art, of the contamination of 'reality' by fictional worlds—which is to recognize of the text's status as fiction *and* metafiction. The conscious merging of fiction and reality is of course characteristic of much of the literature of this period. But Pushkin is able to ascribe this attitude to several of his characters, in the form of a systematic misperception of things; as a result the entire world of **Pikovaya dama** seems to consist of the projection of fictional models onto whatever one takes to be reality in the text.

In particular, the image of Herman which is built up in the story has several facets, but which all centre on the stereotyped figure of the Romantic hero-villain. The most extreme instance of this comes from the least reliable source—from Tomsky, the teller of the original anecdote. In Chapter Four, he describes Hermann to Liza in the following way:

> This Hermann [. . .] is a truly Romantic individual: he has the profile of a Napoleon, and the soul of a Mephistopheles. I am sure that he has at least three crimes on his conscience [. . .][16]

This statement is replete with irony, over and above the fact that Tomsky himself does not mean what he says. First, it comes *after* the narration of Hermann's visit to the Countess in Chapter Three, which precedes it temporally: thus Tomsky's words are actually true, inasmuch as Hermann has committed the crime of precipitating the Countess' death, though Tomsky of course does not know this. Then the remark on Hermann's resemblance to Napoleon embeds itself in Liza's mind so strongly that when later that same night she contemplates the villainous Hermann, it recurs:

> She wiped her tear-stained eyes and looked up at Hermann: he was still sitting on the window-sill, with his arms folded, a fearsome frown on his brow. In this pose he bore an extraordinary resemblance to Napoleon.[17]

In case we do not understand how Hermann comes to have this effect on Liza's imagination, we are then instructed in a rare authorial intervention: 'The portrait which Tomsky had painted matched the image which she had created herself, and thanks to the latest novels, this already hackneyed figure terrified and captivated her imagination'.[18] As if to underline the irony, Liza is here also depicted with her arms folded, and head lowered: she has herself involuntarily adopted the pose of her admired 'Napoleon'.

Hermann's supposed Mephistophelean qualities are also largely imaginary, though in this case they are projected through Hermann's own self-representation. This emerges most clearly when he pleads with the barely conscious Countess in Chapter Three:

> [. . .] Reveal your secret to me! [. . .] Perhaps it is connected with some awful sin, with the loss of eternal happiness, with a compact with the Devil . . . Think on it: you are old; you have not long to live,—I am willing to take your sin upon my own soul. Only tell me your secret![19]

Hermann's connection with the powers of evil is clearly an imaginary one, and these suggestions are not substantiated elsewhere in the story. In this sense he is clearly a parodic version of the true evil genius of Romantic fiction; but of all the story's characters, he is perhaps the only one not to realise this.

Hermann's character, as we are told by the story's narrator early on, is constructed around two opposing principles: that of the solid and disciplined German bourgeois, and the passionate, Romantic (and also German) dreamer. The mechanism of his character is such that one of the two sides must eventually get the upper hand: as we are told at the beginning of Chapter Six, 'Two fixed ideas cannot exist side by side in the moral universe, just as two bodies cannot occupy one and the same space in the physical world'.[20] Indeed, Hermann's character depends so obviously on this type of rationalistic formula that it is hard to find much 'psychological' depth in it, or even much psychological plausibility. There is a whole series of oppositions characteristic of the Romantic age which underlies the basic split in Hermann's character: reason and madness, calculation and passion, nobility of character and bourgeois philistinism, erotic love and self-love, and so on. Hermann, who embodies these opposing principles, is thus inherently contradictory—a bourgeois Romantic, a German Napoleon, a heroic villain, a rationalising madman, a passionate lover who prefers Mammon to Eros. His consciousness is a dialogue between his two opposing sides, in which the triumph of his passionate disposition appears inevitable.

But Hermann is not only contradictory, but an illusory Romantic hero who demonstrates through his own thoughts and actions the irreality of Romantic fictional models. Just as other characters (Liza, Tomsky) imagine him to be something he is not, he too relies on an *imaginary* picture of himself and the world. Pushkin repeatedly uses the word *voobrazhenie* (imagination) in relation to Hermann, as in the first 'psychological' portrait of him in Chapter Two, where this word occurs three times:

1. 'He had strong passions and a fiery *imagination* [. . .]'.[21]

2. 'The anecdote about the three cards made a strong impression on his *imagination* and occupied his thoughts for the whole night'.[22]

3. 'The extraordinary anecdote again affected his *imagination*'.[23]

In Chapter Five, after attending the Countess' funeral, Hermann drinks more than usual in order to quell his 'inner trouble'; we are told that 'the alcohol fired his *imagination* still more'.[24] In Chapter Six, we are given a sense of the force of Hermann's imagination as it turns increasingly to manic obsession:

> Three, seven, ace—soon took the place of the image of the dead old woman in Hermann's imagination. Three, seven, ace—did not leave his thoughts and were constantly on his lips. Seeing a young girl, he would say

to himself: 'How slender she is! . . . A real three of hearts!'. If someone asked him the time, he would answer: 'five minutes to the seven'. Every corpulent man reminded him of an ace. The three, the seven and the ace appeared to him in his sleep, taking on all manner of forms: the three blossomed before him in the shape of an opulent flower, the seven took the form of a Gothic portal, the ace—of a giant spider [. . .][25]

However plausible or otherwise we find this 'psychological portrait', it is clear that in this text the word *imagination* is a negative force. It is Hermann's imaginative embroiderings on a dubious anecdote, after all, which lead to the Countess' death and to Hermann's own catastrophe. Pushkin's text is anti-Romantic in this sense, but he is unable to escape the value-system which Romanticism had created: for this reason, it is a consciously parodic text at the level of characterisation. Hermann is referred to as 'this already hackneyed figure' (*eto uzhe poshloe litso*)[26] in the main text of the story; and indeed, it is only Hermann himself in the story who fails to have his eyes opened to this basic truth. Pushkin's attitude to this character is already clear in the basic paranomasia on his name, Hermann/German (further extended to include the Comte de Saint-*Germain,* which renders him both Hermann's *cousin,* and his spiritual, eighteenth century and French father): this is very much the playfully ironic attitude identified with Pushkin by Slonimsky.

The type of language or discourse associated in the text with Hermann is another important clue as to how he should be read. At this level, it becomes clear that he is a character whose basic features are deceptiveness and lack of authenticity. One type of inauthenticity may be seen in Hermann's smug Bourgeois dictum that he is 'not in a position to risk the necessary in the hope of acquiring the superfluous';[27] this is a hollow and facile covering for Hermann's fundamental anxiety about his situation, but, ironically, the story ends with him doing the opposite of this and risking his patrimony on a card game and losing it. But the most glaring instance of Hermann's lack of authenticity is his attempt in Chapter Three to woo Liza by copying his love-letters from a German novel 'word for word'.[28] We may be right in assuming that Hermann's *writing* here makes 'authentic' discourse impossible to achieve; but this leads the reader to ask whether there is beneath Hermann's quite deliberate deception a more authentic discourse which will eventually emerge?

At face value, if we believe the story's narrator, it appears that just such a process of a stripping away of elegant deceptions, to reveal the true 'inner man', is what takes place. Once Hermann's passionate imagination gets the better of him, 'truth' is revealed—though it emerges through the same medium of letter-writing; this is described slightly later in Chapter Three:

> Hermann did not relent. Every day he made sure that Liza continued to receive letters from him. No longer were they translated from the German. Hermann wrote them inspired by passion, and spoke in a language

which accorded with his nature: in them was expressed both the ardour of his desires, and the disorder of an unbridled imagination.[29]

Here one must be very careful in reading Pushkin's artful prose, for on the surface we are faced with a characteristic Romantic paradigm. First of all, we are told, Hermann was 'inspired by passion', but hindsight will tell us that this is not the expected *erotic* passion associated in the Romantic hero with truth and authenticity, but a *criminal* passion for financial gain. So to the same extent that erotic passion leads to a direct expression of truth, so, one infers, Hermann's anti-eroticism (exemplified by his notion of becoming the lover of the eighty-seven-year-old Countess who personifies the real object of his desires) must be inauthentic and in some sense untruthful. The illusion of truth which appears to confront the reader here is further supported by Pushkin's careful designation that, in the language of passion in which Hermann expresses himself in his letters, Hermann *speaks,* rather than *writes* ('he spoke in a language which accorded with his nature'). This superiority of 'speech' over 'writing' is, we know, deceptive. In any case Hermann in his letters is not speaking, but writing: the language of the heart is mediated by the pen; and the conventionality of such uses of the verb 'to speak' in describing an act of writing is clear enough. Through this rather obvious appeal to 'truth', then, Hermann's epistolary speech is shown to be every bit as fraudulent as his earlier copying from German novels. Furthermore, given Hermann's insecure status in the text as a parodic hero, in a way copying from a German novel is more appropriate and authentic for him, since that is where he originates and where he ultimately belongs. Indeed, the 'speech' of his own heart, passions, imagination or whatever would probably have no real difference from the stilted discourse of a bad epistolary novel. In any case the addressee, Lizaveta Ivanovna, is no more capable of discerning the difference than Hermann himself.

In the end it becomes apparent that there is no naturally truthful discourse for Hermann to adopt, as the story makes a nonsense of the idea of an authentic language of feeling or of anything else. For it turns out that Hermann's 'unbridled imagination' is not captivated by the conventional language of the heart, but is instead in the thrall of an artificial system of signs—the language of cards. Hermann, we are told, may be subject to strong passions and possessed of a vivid imagination, but 'in his soul' he is a gambler, the casually inserted *budushchiy v dushe* subtly undermining the impression that Hermann is a Romantic hero of another kind.[30] This 'deeper truth' is easily forgotten through the many peripeteia of the story, but it affects the discourse which constitutes Hermann's interior monologue in powerful ways—as is clear from the opening paragraph of Chapter Six. This gradual intrusion of the language of cards, which has a partly comic function here, as well as indicating the extent of Hermann's mental dissolution, becomes dominant in the Epilogue to the story, with Hermann left muttering 'three, seven, ace! three, seven, queen! . . .'[31] This turns out to be the language of Hermann's heart in its most essential form, because it is all that is left of Hermann himself, the obsessive gambler.

While Hermann's own discourse may be deceptive and implausible, there are other ways in which the plausibility of the text as a whole is subjected to doubt, for this is a text in which the 'author' is not entirely silent. Each chapter is prefaced by a brief epigraph, playful, obscure, and provocative, and this system of epigraphs provides a framing of and commentary on the action which makes up the story. While the story's main narrator is a relatively unproblematic figure, the author's is an ironic and teasing voice which upsets and interrupts our attempts to read the text 'normally'. The epigraphs are intrusive, for one thing, because many of them are in French, and not Russian; for another, as Viktor Shklovsky pointed out, because they are pointedly prosaic, and derive from inconsequential, marginal sources;[32] finally, because they are unashamedly spurious, most having been shown to be Pushkin's own inventions (only the epigraph to Chapter Two can be convincingly attributed to another individual—it records a *bon mot* of the poet Denis Davydov).[33] Why did Pushkin so elaborately surround his text with a series of frivolous, if elegant, ironic comments?

Clearly this was not done to underline the seriousness of the story's inner meaning, for nearly all the epigraphs trivialize and undermine the content of a given episode. The epigraph to Chapter Three, for instance, is a comment on Hermann's letters to Liza which draws attention to their insincerity; apparently Pushkin's own invention, it sheds an ironic light on the claim that Hermann's passionate outpourings on paper are the true discourse of his heart. A second, even more striking example is the epigraph to Chapter Five, which relates the Countess' apparition before Hermann shortly after her death. Here, Pushkin has concocted a quotation which is attributed to Swedenborg, where a ghost appearing before the great mystic can only utter the banal greeting 'How do you do, Mr Counsellor'.[34] Swedenborg was widely read in the 1820s and 30s; so his authority should underline the seriousness of an intrusion of the supernatural. Instead, the banality of Pushkin's faked quotation points to something else: the banality of the supernatural itself in the literature of the period. Thus it is suggested by this epigraph that what would appear to be the most profound and mysterious episode in the story is both uninteresting and commonplace. And the very factitiousness of the quotation (which presumably would not appear in Russian if Pushkin had read it in a genuine source) draws attention to the factitiousness, obvious surely to Pushkin's sophisticated readership, of the supernatural tale as such.

This self-conscious character of Pushkin's text affects other levels of potential meaning too: for in still further ways *Pikovaya dama* sets up an elaborate game between author and reader, using as an intermediary an apparently good-willed, if naive, third-person narrator. What, for instance, is one to make of the elaborate numerological symbolism evident in the abundance of threes and sevens in the text? Does Pushkin really imitate Masonic rituals in his description of Hermann's behaviour in the Countess' secret chamber? Surely not in any serious way, given the status of the text as a whole, if one can only recuperate serious meanings by constructing a 'serious' Hermann. But there are other reasons too. As far as Pushkin's use of numbers is concerned, it is easy enough to read a symbolic meaning into these: for example, the numbers three and seven both figure in the year of Pushkin's death, 1837; indeed, the Countess is 87 years old, and if her age and the unlucky number 13 (the ace and the three), which happens to be 100-87, are combined, one also arrives at 1837, after a bit of shuffling, it is true.[35] Does this prove anything? Take a less 'meaningful' date—say 1833, the year Pushkin wrote the story: two threes, the ace and the seven, plus the ace. In fact, just about any date can be found to be enciphered in the text.

But if this is not convincing enough, it is worth turning instead to one of the governing thematic ideas in the text: the theme of card-playing and gambling. Card playing is a superstitious activity, and Hermann himself, we are told in Chapter Five, is superstitious as well as obsessed by cards.[36] Cards may be used in fortune-telling and necromancy. Card players are conscious of the 'magic' properties of different ranks and suits.[37] But card-playing sets the scene for Tomsky's anecdote as well as providing its subject, and as such partakes of the same ambiguity as the anecdote itself. These ambiguous properties of card-playing are exploited throughout the story.

On the one hand, gambling, as in the stories of Hoffmann,[38] may be symbolic of the demonic world—gambling is evil, and Hermann's sensational story might seem to encourage such an interpretation of *Pikovaya dama*.[39] On the other hand, card-playing is a game, an autotelic and self-justifying activity, belonging culturally to a world of trivial, non-serious pursuits, and this connotation supports the alternative view of *Pikovaya dama* as an ironic, non-serious and ludic text. Indeed, the fact that card-playing is so closely aligned with story-telling and reading in this text suggests that these activities belong in a similar realm.

Evidently, Pushkin makes no attempt to resolve the ambiguity surrounding card-playing, for the suspense in the story, on the model of the classic fantastic tale, lies in the tension created between our scepticism towards and willingness to believe the story we are reading. But there is one important clue as to how we should perhaps interpret the theme of card-playing in the epigraph to Chapter One, whose meaning, obscure to the modern reader, would have been clear enough to Pushkin's contemporaries. Here, Pushkin gives a parodic imitation of apparently well-known 'revolutionary' songs by two members of the Decembrist movement, Ryleev and Bestuzhev;[40] Pushkin's verses (actually written in 1828 when he included them in a letter to Vyazemsky) have been interpreted as an ironic comment on the decline in the Russian aristocratic elite in the years after the failed Decembrist revolt of 1825 and the ensuing cynicism and loss of faith in democratic ideals. Part of this decline expressed itself in the unusual popularity of card-playing in the years following 1825. In the context of *Pikovaya dama,* the irony lies in the non-correspondence between the tone of the verse text and its referent. The scene described is implicitly solemn—the opening lines *A v nenastnye dni* ('And in bleak winter weather') suggest something conspiratorial and dangerous, while the *delo* (serious business) with which the protagonists occupy themselves is nothing more serious than a game of cards (underlined by the rhyme *melom/delom* ['with chalk'/'with business'], which has a trivialising effect).[41] The seriousness, then, is a sham, as we are shown with an irony which is many-layered. So we can perhaps, in taking this seriousness at face value, be misreading the text in much the same way as Hermann misreads his 'text', the anecdote told by Tomsky.

It would seem, in conclusion, that, however coherent and readable *Pikovaya dama* may seem on the surface, to recuperate anything 'meaningful' requires that we ignore the very clear gestures of irony and parody on the part of the author, and so 'misread' the text. What we miss, in doing so, are the playful, intricate and elegant ways in which Pushkin frustrates our attempts to read this text in ways which would seem to us appropriate and productive of meaning. For this is a self-conscious text which may in the end be 'about' nothing, even though it raises many serious questions about the nature of fiction and of human discourse in general. It seems to me that Pushkin has produced in this story something considerably more important than simply the parody of the fantastic tale which is its starting point; in the end, it is something more like a parody of writing, reading, and critical interpretation all together. Certainly what this text does not do is to point the way for 'psychological' novels of the later nineteenth century. If it anticipates anything, then it is something far more modern. Take for instance, the at once conclusive and empty final sentence of this story—'Tomsky has been promoted to Captain and is engaged to the Princess Pauline' (*Tomsky proizveden v rotmistry i zhenitsya na knyazhne Poline*):[42] the fatuous way in which this sentence rewards the originator of the dubious anecdote himself, effecting the text's sole gesture towards a happy, 'fairy-tale' ending, stands as a challenge to the reader to find something significant in it. Does it mean anything? Does it achieve anything, other than render itself, our reading of it, and even Pushkin's writing of it, equally ridiculous?

Notes

1. Donald Fanger, *The Creation of Nikolai Gogol,* London, 1977, p. 32

2. Lauren Leighton, 'Puškin and Freemasonry: "The Queen of Spades"', in *New Perspectives on Nineteenth-Century Russian Prose,* Columbus, Ohio, 1981, p. 25 (my italics).

3. Roberta Reeder, '"The Queen of Spades": A Parody of the Hoffmann Tale', in *New Perspectives on Nineteenth-Century Russian Prose,* Columbus, Ohio, 1981, p. 96 (my italics).

4. F. M. Dostoevsky, *Polnoe sobranie sochineniy,* t. 30, L., 1988, p. 192; all translations in this article are my own.

5. Tzvetan Todorov, *Introduction à la littérature fantastique,* Paris, 1970, p. 29.

6. V. F. Odoevsky, *Russkie nochi,* L., 1975, p. 189.

7. In this respect it is perhaps worth noting Pushkin's own evident interest in the literary fantastic, for he seems to have read widely, if not uncritically, in this field. His personal library held many standard productions in the genre, mainly in French, though with a considerable number in English too. Most of these, interestingly, have publication dates from the late 1820s and early 1830s (*Pikovaya dama* was written in 1833). Pushkin had the twelve-volume French translation of the works of Hoffmann by Loeve-Veimars (Paris, 1829-33), as well as a two-volume selection and a biography of Hoffmann, also by Loeve-Veimars. Among French writers, he had works by Hugo, Janin, Mérimée, Musset and Nodier, all published between 1830 and 1833. Of the standard 'Gothic' novels in English, Pushkin had the collected novels of Anne Radcliffe; Maturin's *Melmoth the Wanderer* and *Bertram,* and a single-volume set of novels by Beckford (*Vathek*), Walpole (*The Castle of Otranto*), and 'Monk' Lewis (*The Bravo of Venice*). Among Pushkin's other books in English, there is also the following intriguing item:

   W. Godwin, *Lives of the Necromancers* or an account of the eminent persons in successive ages, who have claimed for themselves, or to whom have been imputed by others, the exercise of magical power. London, 1834.

   For a description of non-Russian books in Pushkin's library, see Tatiana Wolff, *Pushkin on Literature,* London, 1971, Appendix, pp. 485-522.

8. See e.g. Ernest J. Simmons, *Pushkin,* Gloucester, Mass., 1971, pp. 219-21.

9. But note that not all of Pushkin's *skazki* actually draw on Russian material: see e.g. S. A. Fomichev, *Poeziya Pushkina: Tvorcheskaya evolyutsiya,* L., 1986, p. 190, who includes only 'Skazka o pope i o rabotnike ego Balde' (1831), 'Skazka o tsare Saltane' (1831), and 'Skazka o mertvoy tsarevne' (1831) in this category.

10. Ann Shukman, 'The Short Story, Theory, Analysis, Interpretation', *Essays in Poetics,* 2,2, 1977, pp. 27-95 (see esp. pp. 75-78).

11. Pushkin, *Polnoe sobranie sochineniy,* t. 4, M.-L., 1936, p. 210; all references to Pushkin will be to this edition.

12. See e.g. M. Gershenzon, *Mudrost' Pushkina,* Ann Arbor, 1983, p. 98.

13. A. Slonimsky. *Masterstvo Pushkina,* M., 1963, p. 524.

14. Diana Lewis Burgin, 'The Mystery of "Pikovaja dama": A New Interpretation', in *Mnemozina: Studia litteraria russica in honorem Vsevolod Setchkarev*, ed. Joachim T. Baehr and Norman W. Ingham, Munich, 197?, p. 56 (quoted by Leighton, 'Pushkin and Freemasonry', p. 22).

15. Pushkin, *op. cit.*, p. 197.

16. *Ibid.*, p. 207.

17. *Ibid.*, p. 208.

18. *Ibid.*, p. 207.

19. *Ibid.*, pp. 205-6.

20. *Ibid.*, p. 211.

21. *Ibid.*, p. 200.

22. *Ibid.*, p. 200.

23. *Ibid.*, p. 201.

24. *Ibid.*, p. 210.

25. *Ibid.*, p. 211.

26. *Ibid.*, p. 207.

27. *Ibid.*, p. 193.

28. *Ibid.*, p. 201.

29. *Ibid.*, p. 203.

30. *Ibid.*, p. 200.

31. *Ibid.*, p. 214.

32. V. Shklovsky, *Zametki o proze Pushkina*, M., 1937, p. 58.

33. See G. P. Makogonenko, *Tvorchestvo A.S. Pushkina v 1830-e gody (1833-1836)*, L., 1982, pp. 220-21.

34. Pushkin, *op.cit.*, p. 209.

35. Compare M. Falchikov, 'The Outsider and the Numbers Game (Some Observations on *Pikovaya dama*)', *Essays in Poetics*, 2,2, 1977, pp. 96-106.

36. Pushkin, *op. cit.*, p. 209.

37. Shklovsky, *op. cit.*, p. 57.

38. Reeder, *op. cit.*, pp. 81-83; see also Charles Passage, *The Russian Hoffmannists*, The Hague, 1963, p. 135.

39. See Yu. M. Lotman, 'Tema kart i kartochnoy igry v russkoy literature nachala XIX veka', *Trudy po znakovym sistemam*, 7, Tartu, 1975, pp. 120-42 (esp. pp. 129-30); but note that Lotman sees in Pushkin's story an alternative association of card-playing with positive forces which have the potential to disrupt the 'automatic' world in which the characters move (pp. 136-39). I am grateful to Joe Andrew for drawing my attention to Lotman's article.

40. Makogonenko, *op. cit.*, pp. 218-19.

41. Pushkin, *op. cit.*, p. 193.

42. *Ibid.*, p. 214.

Caryl Emerson (essay date 1993)

SOURCE: Emerson, Caryl. "'The Queen of Spades' and the Open End." In *Puškin Today*, edited by David M. Bethea, pp. 317. Bloomington: Indiana University Press, 1993.

[*In the following essay, Emerson relates Pushkin's utilization of supernatural elements and realism in* The Queen of Spades *to his use of parody.*]

> In Puškin, however, the idea of fate, fate acting with the speed of lightning, is deprived of any of the strictness and purity of religious doctrine. Chance is that point which casts the idea [of fate] in a position of faceless and vacillating indeterminateness, an indeterminateness which nevertheless retains the right to pass judgment over us. . . . Chance chops fate off at the knee and constructs it on a new scientific basis. Chance is a concession to black magic on the part of precision mechanics, which had discovered in the tiresome hustle and bustle of atoms the origin of things, and right under the nose of the distraught church had craftily managed to explain the world order as disorder. . . .
>
> Homelessness, orphanhood, loss of an aim and a purpose—all the same, blind chance, elevated to a law, suited Puškin. In that idea the enlightened century preserved untouched, for the nonce, a taste of that mystery and trickery dear to the poet's heart. In it there was something of the card games that Puškin loved. Chance meant freedom—the freedom of fate transfigured by some lapse of logic into arbitrary license, and the freedom of human insecurity, torn to shreds like a drunkard. It was an emptiness fraught with catastrophes, holding out promise of adventure, teaching one to live by faking it, by taking risks. . . . With the ascension of freedom, everything became possible.
>
> —Abram Terc, *Progulki s Puškinym* (Collins-London: Overseas Publications Interchange, 1975), 37-39.

Of the many controversies surrounding Puškin's **Pikovaja dama (*The Queen of Spades*)**, one of the most persistent has centered on its almost seamless fusion of the fantastic with the realistic.[1] On the one hand, the tale is saturated with unexplained—indeed, inexplicable—coincidence and supernatural events, very much in the Gothic (and later the Gogolian) tradition. On the other hand, the work is remarkably precise in historical and topographical detail, with a sober, reportorial narrator who documents by the day, hour, and minute the uncanny and the mundane with apparently equal confidence. As one student of the tale has remarked, this neutral narrator "does not moralize, does not issue warnings, does not terrify, but permits the readers themselves to assess characters and events" (Poljakova 1974: 385).

Given the uncertain genre of the tale, this burden on readers to "assess characters and events" through their own efforts has presented a challenge. **The Queen of Spades** both invites logical decoding and appears to frustrate it. In this essay I will suggest that such a dual—and ultimately contradictory—invitation to the reader constitutes a deliberate strategy on Puškin's part, Puškin's extension, as it were, of his own profound and endlessly inventive categories of parody into a realm we would today call reader-reception aesthetics.

First, a few words on the sorts of parody one finds in Puškin. On the most elementary and playful level there is outright blasphemy, as in *Gavriiliada*. And then there are Puškin's famous inversions of moral scenarios or literary cliché, such as the fate of the Prodigal Son theme in **"Stancionnyj smotritel'"** (**"The Stationmaster"**) or the mockery of feuding families and civilizing the natives in **"Baryšnja-krest'janka"** (**"Mistress into Maid"**). But one of Puškin's most sophisticated sorts of parody can be found, it seems, at a level *above* that of specific theme or plot. Here I draw on Gary Saul Morson's discussion of parody in his book *The Boundaries of Genre*: "Parodies are usually described and identified as being of (or 'after') a particular author or work, but the parodist's principal target may, in fact, be a particular *audience* or *class of readers*" (Morson 1981: 113). With *Shamela* as his case in point, Morson suggests that Fielding, like many parodists, "implies that readers must not be too ready to accept the invitations authors extend, and that reading is an action which, like any action, can be performed responsibly or irresponsibly" (1981: 114).

Precisely this target—readers who are "too ready to accept the invitations authors extend"—seems to me a defining characteristic of this final category of parody of Puškin. What is parodied is the reader's search for a system or a key, and in this search, the more numerous the partial hints and tantalizing fragments provided by the author, the more challenging and irresistible the search becomes. We glimpse the method in *Evgenij Onegin* (Eugene Onegin). In that novel the formal symmetry governing the action and fates of the heroes encourages us, along with Tat'jana, to seek a "key" to Onegin's personality. When Tat'jana asks, alone in Onegin's library (Book Seven, XXIV), "ne parodija li on?" (Is he not a parody?), that parody could have several targets. Not the least of these targets is the reader or analyst of the novel, who persists in the attempt to make all of Onegin's disparate segments add up to a psychologically satisfying explanation.[2]

The strategy is even more boldly present in *Boris Godunov*. There the presence of a real-life, documented historical event beneath the dramatic plot greatly increases the possibility and range of parody. Puškin takes Karamzin's well-known, providential, over-determined story and reworks it so that only the open-ended, indifferent characters win—characters with infinitely malleable biographies, like the Pretender. The seemingly disjointed structure of the play, in which all the major action is off-stage, encourages the audience to seek a *hidden* unity. But precisely that search can be seen as part of the target of the parody. The absence of unity in Puškin's historical

drama is more than a "Shakespeareanism." It can be read as a comment on the nature of history itself—in which, we know, Puškin always respected the element of *chance*, "that powerful, instantaneous tool of providence."[3]

Indeed, as Puškin surely divined, the very idea of historical unity distorts. Contemplating a historical event, later generations do not need to impose a unity on it. They already know how the story will end. Thus the "unity" that we perceive in any account of the past has no necessary connection with logic, system, or causality; it simply reflects the outrageous privilege of historical perspective. One possible way of exposing that false unity would be to confront the audience of historical drama with an event on stage as it might have looked in its own time and on its own chaotic, present-tense terms to its participants. With canonized historical plots such as that of Boris Godunov, this sense of radical openness is exceedingly difficult to transmit. Part of what Puškin parodies in *Boris Godunov*, I suggest, is audience gullibility: historical themes, when clothed in a present-tense form like drama, can never be honest to the event. That event will always appear chaotic and open-ended to those living it, and somehow inevitable and predetermined to those re-creating it or witnessing it later in narrative art.

If *Boris Godunov* has provoked its share of searches for hidden unity and keys to its meaning, those searches are meager and amateurish fare when compared to the studies devoted to the decoding of **The Queen of Spades**. My purpose here is not to survey the extremely rich and clever secondary literature in any detail, but merely to offer some general categories of classification.

To state first the obvious: The spare, efficient, dense, and objectively cold prose in this tale encourages the reader to assume that someone is in control. Meaning appears to be distributed by some higher power, or at least by a higher narrative perspective. The critical search for this unified meaning seems to fall into four basic categories or strategies. Each strategy erects a symbolic system in the text that relates to some narrative or visual patterns—in behavior, plot, language, or number; these patterns are then interpreted as tying together all the details of the story.

There are, first, the socio-literary studies that focus on the mechanics and ideology behind gambling in Puškin's era. Exemplary here might be Jurij Lotman's discussion of card games and gambling in nineteenth-century Russia (Lotman 1975) and Nathan Rosen's classic essay on the meaning of the three magic cards (Rosen 1975). As Lotman points out, the concept of *chance* (and the challenge presented by games of chance) involves both a negative and a positive aspect: what is rational collapses into the chaotic and the anomalous, but at the same time what is dead becomes animate, mobile, changeable. Gambling is a metaphor for multiple, *co*-existing codes in a society and in a text. The impulse to coordinate, rank, and crack these codes has been the motivation behind much of the criticism on **The Queen of Spades**.

A second category would be the psychoanalytical-generational treatments. These include the vision, by Murray and Albert Schwartz (1975), of Germann as a sexual impotent who seeks through gambling the prerogatives of parenthood, and also Diana Burgin's ingenious hypothesis (Burgin 1974) that the Countess revealed the secret of the three cards to Čaplickij because he was her natural son by St. Germain and also (once he grew up) her lover. Burgin suggests that this taboo-ridden family cabal exercises a fatal attraction for Germann; he tries obsessively to gain entry but fails, and can only imitate its patterns hopelessly unto death.

On a different level of analysis are the linguistic and syntactic studies, of which V. V. Vinogradov is the illustrious founder. Representative of this approach would be Heidi Faletti's inquiry into the frequency of parataxis in the text (Faletti 1977), and her suggestion that this tendency to bunch together clauses without conjunctions has a thematic significance: it is the linguistic expression of a plot "organized largely on the basis of juxtaposition" (1977: 133).

Finally we have the various erudite numerological studies. Prototypical here is Lauren Leighton's "Gematria in *The Queen of Spades:* A Decembrist Puzzle" (1977). Leighton reveals a multitude of anagrams, chronograms, cryptograms, cryptonyms, and logogriphs that suggest Masonic allusions and references to the executed Decembrist Kondratij Ryleev. This final category is perhaps the most quantified of the searches for a "key to the work." But critics in all categories would probably ascribe to Diana Burgin's comment in the paragraph of her essay that opens a subchapter entitled "Questions: Clues to the Solution of the Mystery": "It is up to the reader to speculate on the implications of the text, piece together the information they offer, and come up with the solution to the mystery. Let us begin this task by examining four passages" (1974: 47). The primary responsibility of the reader is to uncover a system that will explain the work.

In the midst of these many mysterious codes, the question inevitably arises: Who is the reader of all this hidden material? If Puškin is parodying the code-breaking efforts of an audience, on what level does this audience exist? In a recent essay, "The Ace in Puškin's 'The Queen of Spades,'" Sergej Davydov assumes that the audience parodied is *internal* to the text; that is, it is Germann himself: "Puškin settles his own account with Germann. . . . He surrounds him with mysterious events, teases him with anagrams and cryptograms which the calculative engineer repeatedly failed to solve" (1989: 130). This idea of internal audience is intriguing. But it seems to me equally—if not more—plausible that the audience parodied by Puškin is in fact the reader *external* to the text, and for a reason quite opposite to the "failure" Davydov detects in Germann. Puškin might well be parodying his readers precisely because of their success and skill at reading codes.

Support for this hypothesis (albeit grudging support) can be found in even the most severely puzzle- and key-oriented criticism. For much of it ends on an oddly inde-

terminate note. After prodigious code-cracking efforts, Leighton asks "what functions gematria serves in the tale" (1977: 464). And he modestly concludes that it adds interest, zest; it "enriches the style by enlarging the tale's lexical means, expanding its semantic fields, and adding to its morphological and syntactic texture. . . . It helps to unify the tale's parts into a gracefully organic whole, and it makes for a greatly intriguing, and therefore greatly entertaining, narrative." The puzzle, in other words, is not cracked; it is only elaborated. Several other studies conclude in much the same way (Davydov, Poljakova): despite all the apparent overcoding, something in the text is always missing; the integrative move that will cap the deed is forever deferred. It is either the elusive ace, or the absence of resolution in the debate over realistic versus supernatural motivation, or the lack of a single literary prototype that the heroes of the tale might be parodying. As Paul Debreczeny points out, there appear to be many diluted prototypes for both characters and scenes. "Puškin used details of literary models only as so many tiny building blocks," Debreczeny concludes (1983b: 202). What, then, do these blocks actually build?

In answer, I would suggest that the codes we get in this story, wonderfully crafted as they are, were designed by Puškin *not* to build any single unified structure, or to solve any single puzzle. Scholars have long noted this strategy on a blunt compositional level, in Puškin's choice of epigraphs. The epigraphs to **Queen of Spades** rarely summarize but rather comment ironically on their chapters, defining "the chapter's tonality—sometimes, to be sure, against the spirit of its content" (Poljakova 1974: 410). But it would seem that the irony of structures in this tale is not confined to a dialogue between epigraph and text. That irony is itself a clue to a larger disjunction. For just as the self-contained scenes in *Boris Godunov* do not add up to the dramatically resolved whole that was expected of tragedy, so the mysteries in **The Queen of Spades** are not really solvable by a single code—by the sort of code we would seek, say, in a good detective story. And yet the evidence for crackable codes is so overwhelming in **The Queen of Spades** that we, along with Germann, are almost flung into the search. This passion on the part of the reader to explain the whole by a single key might well be the real target of Puškin's parody.

With this hypothesis, yet another reading of the story becomes possible: Puškin provides us not with a code, and not with chaos, but precisely with the *fragments* of codes, codes that tantalize but do not quite add up. He teases the reader with partial keys—because the reader, like Germann, does not really want to gamble. The reader wants to *decipher,* to study the past so that it will reveal the future, to predict patterns of behavior and events. We know from the very plot of the tale, however, that only desperately passionate true gamblers—people willing to stake everything on *true* chance, like St. Germain, the Countess, Čaplickij—can be privy to true secrets (Burgin 1974: 53).

In this reading, the key passage in the text has nothing to do with threes, sevens, numerology, or cryptography. It is, rather, the Countess's final words to German: "Eto byla šutka" (it was a joke)—*not,* note, a riddle, which has an answer already implied in the asking. Simply a joke, non-repeatable and non-systematizing, randomly successful in one context and perhaps a complete fiasco in some other time and place. Naturally Germann cannot read this response properly, because his whole life is one of calculation. When he answers the Countess with "Etim nečego šutit'" (This is no joking matter), it is clear to what extent his entire being is alien to the lesson of *real* gambling, namely, that there *is no system.*[4] As Lotman points out in his essay on the card game, Faro is a model of fate. And, Lotman continues, "the external world, which possesses an inexhaustible supply of time and unlimited possibilities of resuming the game, inevitably outplays every individual" (1975: 477-78).

This wisdom, which is routinely applied to Germann, could apply to code-crackers outside the text as well. For Puškin always promises system, but it is a trap. In this connection it is worth mentioning the excellent essay by Michael Shapiro on Puškin's "semiotic dominant" (Shapiro 1979). Shapiro suggests that the one truly characteristic feature of Puškin's work is its *definition by negation.* And the essential negated value in *The Queen of Spades,* I suggest, is the search for system. As Shapiro points out, it is not the supernatural that drives Germann mad, but chance itself, the most everyday and natural randomness of events. As Shapiro concludes his reading of the tale: "The element of chance which irrupts into the conclusion just when success is nearest is conditioned by the preternatural, by that whole realm of the (private) imagination which is opposed to reality as its negation. The reversal is all the more powerful since all of the events leading up to the moment of potential success are themselves accidents" (1979: 125).

There is, in short, a philosophy of history in this tale, just as there clearly is in *Boris Godunov.* The means are different because the problem that time poses in each work is different. In the play, Puškin parodies our search for system in the past; in the story, he parodies our search for system in the future. *Blindness to the present*—Germann convinced of his ace and confronted by a Queen—is common to both works. If Dmitrij the Pretender survives because he is so thoroughly a product of contingency, then Germann, in contrast, perishes because he cannot live in that sort of world once the *promise* of code has been offered him. In the seductive fragments of an explanation that are strewn around his story, we glimpse what might be the real logic of the tale: an allegory of interpretation itself. In *The Queen of Spades* Puškin appears to be celebrating the spirit of the true gambler, whom chance can impoverish but could never drive mad.

Notes

1. In an excellent, as yet unpublished essay, Felix Raskolnikov summarizes the major Soviet contributions to this debate on "the real versus the irrational" in *The Queen of Spades,* regretting that earlier studies have not "admitted the possibility of a *serious* attitude on Puškin's part toward the irrational."

2. This aspect of the Onegin-Tat'jana relationship received provocative treatment by Sergej Bočarov in a paper prepared for—but not delivered at—the Kennan Institute's Conference on Russian Classic Literature, "Puškin: The Shorter Prose Works" (January 20-21, 1986, Washington, D.C.). Bočarov points out that Onegin's first reference to Tat'jana is already provisional and twice displaced, "not from himself nor for himself" ("I would have chosen the other / If I were a poet like you"). The fact that he is *not* a poet but a sceptic effectively bars him from satisfying any of the definitions Tat'jana craves; for most of the novel he represents openness, potential, whereas Tat'jana is forever the symbol of resoluteness and irreversible decision. The tension between the hero and heroine, Bočarov suggests, is the tension between "dal' svobodnogo romana" (distance of a free novel) (which Onegin represents) and the more teleological variant of that line in the notebooks, "*plan* svobodnogo romana" (plan of a free novel), which is the realm of Tat'jana's equilibrium and quest for answers. See Bočarov 1986.

3. From Puškin's review of the second volume of Polevoj's *Istorija russkogo naroda* (History of the Russian People, 1830), in PSS XI: 127.

4. Interestingly enough, this subtext of real gambling—which Puškin so cunningly hides from Germann himself—is revealed to the hero in Čajkovskij's much-maligned operatic version of the tale. In the main, of course, Čajkovskij sentimentalizes the plot, creating a banal love story between Liza and Germann and stripping away Puškin's cool irony as surely as he strips it from his operatic *Onegin.* But on close inspection, Čajkovskij's Germann is a surprisingly self-conscious character. Perhaps because he must sing arias about himself, he has perspective on his dilemma—which Puškin's hero does not.

Consider, for example, Germann's ruminations at the beginning of Act II, scene 4, as he enters the old Countess's bedroom and vows to extract her secret. "A esli tajny net?" (And if there is no secret?) he suddenly sings. "I èto vse pustoj liš' bred moej bol'noj duši!" (And it is all merely the empty delirium of my sick soul!). Even more telling is the nervous song Germann performs at the gaming tables (Act III, scene 7) while he is still in his winning phase, that is, before he draws the fatal queen of spades. Surrounded by stunned friends and watched maliciously by Prince Eleckij—the injured ex-fiancé, from whom Germann had stolen Liza—Germann calls for wine and "giggles hysterically." He then sings: "Čto žizn' naša? Igra! Dobro i zlo—odni mečty! Trud, čestnost'—skazki dlja bab'ja! Kto prav, kto sčastliv zdes', druz'ja? Segodnja ty a zavtra ja!" (And what is our life? A game! Good and evil—both are only dreams! Labor, honor—old wives' tales! Who is right, who is happy here, friends? Today it's you, tomorrow it's I!).

Both Puškin's and Čajkovskij's heroes are close to being obsessive paranoids, to be sure. But only the operatic Germann is granted the right to question and mock his own pathology. He has clearly glimpsed by the end of the opera what real gambling requires, and the realization kills him.

Gary Rosenshield (essay date 1994)

SOURCE: Rosenshield, Gary. "Choosing the Right Card: Madness, Gambling, and the Imagination in Pushkin's 'The Queen of Spades.'" *PMLA* 109, no. 5 (1994): 995-1008.

[*In the following essay, Rosenshield explains the role of madness in Pushkin's novella.*]

M. L. Gofman writes that Aleksandr Pushkin's formulation of the problem of madness is the most successful in Russian literature, indeed that all Russian literature may be said to derive from it (62). Though this statement is polemical—a challenge to the often quoted apocryphal saying, attributed to Dostoevsky, that all Russian literature came out of Gogol's "Overcoat"—it points to a significant lacuna in the study of Pushkin: the representation of madness. Pushkin's remarkable lyric "God Grant That I Not Lose My Mind" ("Не дай мне Бог сойти с ума"; 3: 322-23) has received only scant attention.[1] Even more surprising, madness has never been argued as central to the understanding of *The Queen of Spades* ("Пиковая дама"; 8: 227-52), his finest work in prose, though the story culminates in the hero's insanity.[2]

This avoidance of the issue of madness may be more than an oversight. For Russians, Pushkin has represented the Apollonian ideal of clarity, balance, harmony, order—and sanity—a poetic refuge against the disorder and dysfunctions of Russian life (Gofman 61-62). As the narrator of Andrey Bitov's *Pushkin House* (Пушкинский дом) says, Pushkin was "the first and only bearer of Reason in Russia" 'первый и единственный носитель Разума в России' (239).[3] To suggest that disorder and insanity lurk behind the polished surfaces of some of Pushkin's most highly regarded works may be to liken him to his opposite, the Dionysian Dostoevsky, for whom chaos and madness are native territory.[4]

There is a great temptation to impose a monolithic interpretation on the problem of madness in *The Queen of Spades,* as on other aspects of the work. One should be guided by Dostoevsky's observation that the perfection of the story derives directly from Pushkin's ability to present mutually exclusive ideas convincingly:

> The fantastic should come so close to the real that you must *almost* believe it. Pushkin, who has given us all our artistic models, achieved in *The Queen of Spades* the acme of the art of the fantastic. For you really believe that Germann actually saw a ghost, and you believe precisely the view of reality commensurate with such a vision; yet at the end of the story—that is, after having read it—you do not know how to interpret it: did Germann's vision arise from Germann's nature, or was he actually one of those who came in contact with another world, a world of evil and hostile spirits (i.e., spiritism and its teachings). Now, that is art!

> Фантастическое должно до того соприкасаться с реальным, что Вы должны *почти* поверить ему. Пушкин, давший нам почти все формы искусства, написал «Пиковую даму»—верх искусства фантастического. И вы верите, что Германн действительно имел видение, и именно сообразное с его мировоззрением, а между тем, в конце повести, то есть прочтя ее, Вы не знаете, как решить: вышло ли это видение из природы Германна, или действительно он один из тех, которые соприкоснулись с другим миром, злых и враждебных человечеству духов. (NB. Спиритизм и учения его.) Вот это искусство!

(30.1: 192)[5]

Caryl Emerson takes this idea further, proposing that in *The Queen of Spades,* one of the earliest and most brilliant examples of authorial deception in Russian narrative prose, Pushkin not only encourages different interpretations but withholds sufficient proof for any interpretation by including only fragmentary codes:

> I would suggest that the codes we get in this story, wonderfully crafted as they are, were designed by Pushkin *not* to build any single unified structure, not to solve any single puzzle. . . . Pushkin provides us not with a code, and not with chaos, but precisely with the *fragments* of codes, codes that tantalize but do not quite add up. He teases the reader with partial keys. . . .

(35-36)

Pushkin's use of fragmentary codes supports diametrically opposed psychological and supernatural interpretations of the plot. Germann, the hero, overhears a tale about an eighty-seven-year-old countess who possesses a secret formula for winning vast sums at faro. His attempt to wangle the secret from her by threatening her with a gun fails when she dies of fright. The next day Germann is visited by the countess's ghost, who reveals to him the secret, involving three cards. When he tries the secret, it works for the first two cards, and though it enables him to determine that he should take the ace as the third, he inexplicably chooses the queen, the wrong card.[6] Believing that the countess (in the form of the queen) has wreaked revenge on him, Germann goes insane. He sits in a mental hospital continually muttering, "Three, seven, ace! Three, seven, queen!" 'Тройка, семерка, туз! Тройка, семерка, дама!' (8: 252). It is easy enough to interpret everything in this story psychologically, including the countess's ghost—as has often been done (Burgin; N. Rosen; Schwartz and Schwartz; Lotman; Williams). But Germann seems to be lucid when the dead countess visits him. Moreover, the secret he receives works, despite his choice of the wrong card. The psychological code turns out to be fragmentary; it can never prove that Germann did not see a ghost. Once the door is open to the fantastic, however, it becomes possible to reinterpret all the data from a supernatural point of view, with the understanding that the supernatural is an even more fragmentary code than the psychological.

Likewise, *The Queen of Spades* gives contradictory presentations of madness. There seems to be no compensatory wisdom or vision in Germann's clinical insanity; his final condition appears a fate worse than death. However, Germann's mistake—the choice of the queen over the ace—challenges this deromanticized, devalorized picture of madness (revealing it to be only a fragmentary code) and contains a key to a more romantic notion of madness as an imaginative achievement—even a breakthrough. (Nevertheless, there has to be more evidence for the devalorized interpretation than for the romantic one because the revelation of the true value of madness can come only at the end; the epiphany must be a shock not only to Germann but to the reader as well.) In part 1 of this essay, I outline Pushkin's gradual turn away from a romantic view of madness, a turn that is reflected in this period in both German literature (Hoffmann) and Russian (Gogol and Dostoevsky). In part 2, I detail how Germann's materialistic ideal and the various failures of his imagination deflate madness. Using much the same evidence as in part 2, I show in part 3, in contrast to previous interpretations, that Germann chooses the right card not the wrong one, and that this choice constitutes for the hero not only a validation of madness but also a victory of the imagination and thus of life over death. My aim is not to refute one interpretation by the other but to bring out what Dostoevsky considered the supreme artistic quality of the story, the simultaneous validity of mutually exclusive interpretations—to place the devalorized interpretation of madness in perspective and provide the case for the romantic alternative. Finally, I discuss the legacy of Pushkin's presentation of madness, showing its influence on Dostoevsky's conception of Ivan Karamazov, in *The Brothers Karamazov,* often considered the seminal work of modern Russian literature.

I

It has been generally held that Pushkin's work from 1833 and later contains few if any traces of a romantic view of madness. Some Soviet critics (Levkovich, for example) concede that Pushkin may have regarded the subject—especially the relation between poetry and madness—romantically in the 1820s but maintain that he overcame this poetic phase by the early 1830s, when realism triumphed over romanticism, reason over madness, and clarity over confusion. Indeed, his early poetry closely ties madness—as well as other extreme states—and the poetic process. Pushkin describes poetry as a "passionate illness," "fiery ecstasy," "the violence of a whirlwind," "confusion," "fever," even "sacred delirium."[7] But "God Grant That I Not Lose My Mind"—attributed to 1833, the year when Pushkin composed his other two major works on

madness, *The Queen of Spades* and *The Bronze Horseman* ("Медный всадник"; 5: 131-50)—seems to confirm a turn toward a decidedly antiromantic position. In the beginning of "God Grant," the persona finds his situation so trying that he gladly entertains the idea of parting with his reason to secure his peace and freedom, but visualizing the social and personal consequences of madness, he is compelled to reject it as a solution to his problems. In the end, madness is likened not only to a fatal illness afflicting an individual but also to a plague (чума) threatening a population; society perceives the madman as a threat to the well-being of the state.[8]

Pushkin's devalorization of madness seems to run counter to the romanticism of this period in Russian literature, typified by the works of Prince Vladimir Odoevsky (1803-69), a writer influenced by German literature and philosophy and close in spirit to E. T. A. Hoffmann. An opponent of rationalism and utilitarianism, Odoevsky wrote repeatedly about the superiority of humankind's mystical and irrational inner world and about the inextricable relation between madness and genius—particularly madness and poetry.[9] The hero of "The Sylph" ("Сильфида," 1837), a story reminiscent of Hoffmann's "The Golden Flowerpot" ("Der goldne Topf," 1814), settles on his estate in the provinces and, about to reconcile himself to the philistinism of everyday life—including marriage to his neighbor's daughter—starts reading cabalistic and esoteric treatises. They lead him, through insanity, into a higher, spiritual world that reveals to him the true meaning of existence and releases him from all mundane concerns and ties. The hero is eventually "saved" by his friends, who cure his madness, but at the expense of his spiritual life. His greatest regret in life remains his cure, a view with which the author sympathizes.

The most important writers of the time, however, including Gogol, the young Dostoevsky, and Pushkin, treat German romantic and Hoffmannian prose forms and thematics, especially the representation of madness, ironically and often parodically.[10] German literature made this ironic turn earlier, perhaps taking its cue from Hoffmann himself, who often wrote in an ironic vein and even seemed to parody his own writings devoted to the marvelous and the fantastic (in the late "The King's Betrothed" ["Die Königsbraut," 1821], for example).[11] To be sure, Gogol and Dostoevsky could hardly have influenced Pushkin's representation of madness in *The Queen of Spades,* nor is it likely that Pushkin's story had a significant influence on the depiction of madness in their early works, which differ dramatically from his in style and content. Rather, Gogol's and Dostoevsky's early works show that Pushkin's parodic, antiromantic treatment of madness, though untypical for Russian literature, was not idiosyncratic; it in fact reflected German literary trends.

Gogol presents madness ironically in two of his most famous stories, "The Nose" ("Нос," 1836; 3: 45-75) and "Notes of a Madman" ("Записки сумасшедшего," 1835; 3: 191-214). The hero of "The Nose," Kovalev, wakes one morning to find that his nose is gone and leading an independent existence disguised as an official whose rank is much higher than Kovalev's. The story parodies the theme of the doppelgänger, frequently used by Hoffmann to represent spiritual and mental disturbance, for Gogol's characters are too superficial to have minds or spirits in which a true double could manifest itself. The hero is a typical Gogolian пошляк, the epitome of self-satisfied vulgarity and mediocrity. The hero of "Notes of a Madman," a petty clerk with neither intellect nor spirit (and perhaps even without soul), goes mad not because of a desire for a higher, spiritual realm but because he is not taken seriously by his superior's daughter. His madness is presented as ridiculous and petty. The tragic side of the story is more social than personal, issuing from the brutal treatment of the hero in an insane asylum. Similarly, in *The Double* (Двойник, 1846; 1: 109-229) Dostoevsky depoeticizes, deromanticizes, and devalues madness in his hero, Golyadkin, and the hero's double. The opposite of a higher self, this double does not provide Golyadkin with any vision of a higher—or lower—realm. Emptied of all that is vital and elevating, it is as prosaic as Golyadkin himself. "Goljadkin's folly," Victor Terras writes, "is a travesty of madness for, really, there is nothing . . . at all to go mad from" (*Young Dostoevsky* 256).

According to Roberta Reeder, who makes an excellent case for *The Queen of Spades* as a parody of a Hoffmannian *Kunstmärchen,* Pushkin empties Germann of all that is romantically elevating:

> Like many of Hoffmann's heroes, Germann is provided with choice, but prefers to blame his interest in the demonic on outside forces. His goal is not to be a great poet like Anselmus, but to gain great wealth out of sheer greed. . . . Like the Philistines in Hoffmann's tales, when Germann turns to the spiritual, he achieves only the demonic and never attains the heights of the realm of the good and the beautiful.
>
> (95)

Pushkin thus seems not only to portray Germann's madness as a spiritual death but also, through parody, to cut off all the paths that may lead it to be valorized as a conduit to a higher world or truth. In contrast to Anselmus, the hero of "The Golden Flowerpot," who must lose his sanity so as not to become a prisoner of the world of avarice, and to Odoevsky's hero, who is cured of madness against his will, Germann appears to go mad only because his performance is inadequate to his greed—that is, unromantically.

II

Madness in *The Queen of Spades,* as in Hoffmann, is precipitated and aggravated not by the absence of imagination but by imaginative failure. Almost every time Germann meets story and art, he attempts to appropriate them as means of satisfying his desire for great wealth. The work opens with a tale told by the countess's grandson, Tomsky, about his grandmother's secret of three cards. At first, Ger-

mann disbelieves the story, but it soon begins to work on his imagination and, as he appropriates it, to take on more grotesque forms than it had in all its history.[12] Because of his materialism, Germann's imagination cannot lead him to a higher truth; he can only obsessively transform life into images grotesquely reflecting his desire. Outside the old countess's house, after hearing the story,

> Germann began to tremble. The amazing story of the three cards again appeared before his imagination. He began to walk up and down near the house thinking of its owner and her marvelous gift. He returned late to his humble lodging, but he could not sleep for a long time; and when at last sleep overcame him, he dreamed of cards, a green table, piles of banknotes, and heaps of gold coins. He played card after card, decisively turning down the corners of his cards, and he won continually, raking in the gold and putting the notes into his pocket. After waking up quite late, he sighed over the loss of his fantastic wealth; then he again set out to wander around the city, and he again found himself in front of the countess's house.

> Германн затрепетал. Удивительный анекдот снова представился его воображению. Он стал ходить около дома, думая об его хозяйке и о чудной ее способности. Поздно воротился он в смиренный свой уголок; долго он не мог заснуть, и, когда сон им овладел, ему пригрезились карты, зеленый стол, кипы ассигнаций и груды червонцев.
>
> (8: 236)

Soon Germann absorbs everything and everyone that he encounters into his monomaniacal plot. For example, Pushkin sets Liza, the countess's ward, as a romantic object for his hero. On the first fateful night of decision, Germann can choose either a door on his left, to Liza's room (where she has arranged a tryst with him), or a door on his right, to the countess's. But Germann does not intend to sacrifice fortune for love. He must give up a heroine to attain his terrible ambition. In a tale like "The Golden Flowerpot," the bourgeois heroine is presented as an ideological reason for the hero to escape into the world of his imagination, but for Germann, Liza is little more than a part of his plan to wrench the secret from the aged countess. Earlier, to win Liza's heart, Germann composes letters by copying passages out of German novels. Later he does without this aid; his letters are written "under the inspiration of passion, spoken in his own language, and they bore full testimony to the inflexibility of his desire and the disordered condition of his uncontrollable imagination" 'их писал, вдохновенный страстию, и говорил языком, ему свойственным: в них выражались и непреклонность его желаний, и беспорядок необузданного воображения' (8: 238). The passion that inspires Germann is nothing but the desire for wealth, security, and independence. His language in the letters is a hodgepodge of clichés from second-rate sentimental and romantic literature. The narrator notes that these clichés were perfectly expressive of Germann's desire and imagination; his words present not profound symbolism but his inflexible desire made trite by his disordered and uncontrolled fancy.

Numerous studies attempt to discover the meaning of Germann's transformations of the three cards,[13] but what may be most important about these transformations for a devalorized view of *The Queen of Spades* is their prosaicness. Germann sees all stout men—often associated in Russian literature with high status and success—as aces and regards flowers as threes. His response to people on the street who ask him for the time indicates how close he is to the madness of the epilogue. Regardless of the time of day, he answers, in a way worthy of the comic genius of Gogol, "Five minutes to the seven" 'без пяти минут семерка' (8: 249). The narrator concludes this passage with another deflationary stroke. The mad hero should after all go back to Paris, the origin of the story—but a Paris transformed by his imagination—and take on fortune herself in the great gambling houses of the city. But just as the countess comes back after her death to reveal her secret to Germann when he has lost all hope, so Germann is spared a heroic challenge or quest. Chance not only saves him, it hardly inconveniences him.

The scene that most deflates Germann's imagination—and thus his madness—is his confrontation with the countess. Germann steals into her chambers and waits for her to return from a ball. Although he takes with him an unloaded pistol to threaten her if she proves unaccommodating, he plans to win her over the same way he won Liza, despite the seventy-year difference in the women's ages. Germann's speech to the countess provides the first and most detailed access to the linguistic contents of his imagination. It also suggests the contents of his letters to Liza and anticipates the countess's speech to him from beyond the grave. When Germann confronts the countess in her boudoir, she responds by saying that the story was a joke. In no joking mood, he falls on his knees before the decrepit eighty-seven-year-old woman and reveals why he must have her secret:

> "If your heart ever knew the feeling of love," he said, "if you remember its rapture, if you have even once smiled at the cry of a newborn son, if anything human ever beat in your breast, then I implore you by the feelings of a wife, a lover, a mother, by all that is sacred in life, not to reject my plea. Reveal to me your secret. Of what use is it to you? . . . Maybe it is connected with a horrible sin, with the loss of eternal bliss, with a pact with the devil. . . . Consider: you are old; you do not have long to live—I am ready to take your sins upon my soul. Only reveal to me your secret. Remember that the happiness of a man rests in your hands, that not only I but my children, grandchildren, and great-grandchildren will bless your memory and honor it as sacred. . . ."

> —Если когда-нибудь,—сказал он,—сердце ваше знало чувство любви, если вы помните ее восторги, если вы раз улыбнулись при илаче новорожденного сына, если что-нибудь человеческое билось когда-нибудь в груди вашей, то умоляю вас чувствами супруги, любовницы, матери,—всем, что ни есть святого в жизни—не откажите мне в моей просьбе!—откройте мне вашу тайну!—что вам в ней? . . . Может быть,

> она сопряжена с ужасным грехом, с пагубою вечного блаженства, с дьявольским договором . . . Подумайте: вы стары; жить вам уже недолго,—я готов взять грех ваш на свою душу. Откройте мне только вашу тайну. Подумайте, что счастие человека находится в ваших руках; что не только я, но дети мои, внуки и правнуки благословят вашу память и будут ее чтить как святыню . . .

(8: 241-42)

This product of Germann's disordered and uncontrolled imagination will hardly persuade the countess to reveal her secret—assuming that she has one. Aside from triteness, this speech is characterized by ridiculous nonsequiturs regarding the satanic, the sacred, sin, and happiness. Germann entreats the countess by all this is sacred not to reject his plea, but he immediately remarks that the secret may be related to some horrible sin, to the loss of eternal bliss, or to a pact with the devil. He is even willing to make his own pact with the devil and take all her sins on himself. But how can his happiness—and especially his children's—be assured if it is based on a satanic pact?

In a more traditionally romantic work—Gogol's "Portrait" ("Портрет," 1835; 3: 401-45), for example—the imagination can be corrupted, serving the devil (comfort) as well as true art or religion. But Germann is not an artist, and though he has a most lively imagination, every manifestation of it appears as the epitome of Nabokovian пошлость 'banality.'[14] Thus Germann's madness not only is not romantically conceived—that is, tied to a higher truth—but is specifically linked to the second-rate, the vulgar, the unimaginative, and even the ridiculous. From this point of view, any connection between Germann and the demonic—such as the countess's spirit—is as doubtful as one between him and the higher, spiritual world.

Though Germann may be "punished" in the end for using others to achieve crass, materialistic goals, Nabokov, for one, might have argued that Germann's crimes are also against the imagination. Art, Nabokov writes,

> is a game, because it remains art only as long as we are allowed to remember that, after all, it is all make-believe, that the people on the stage, for instance, are not actually murdered, in other words, only as long as our feelings of horror or of disgust do not obscure our realization that we are, as readers or spectators, participating in an elaborate and enchanting game: the moment this balance is upset we get, on the stage, ridiculous melodrama, and in a book just a lurid description of, say, a murder which should belong in a newspaper instead.

н

(*Lectures* 106)

Germann upsets the balance between art and life by reducing one to the other. By doing so, he kills the story and destroys himself. It is perhaps poetic justice that in contrast to Anselmus, who is redeemed by a creative madness,

Germann goes vulgarly mad. For Anselmus madness is a means to a higher end; for Germann it is the result of imaginative failure.

Yet it might be argued that what leads Germann to madness is not so much the coarseness of his imagination as the reductiveness. He tries, in effect, to reduce life to a formula. At the beginning, Germann needs imagination to acquire the secret of the three cards. He is preoccupied with choosing among alternatives. He has to gain entry to the countess's house, and once there he needs a strategy to make the countess reveal her secret. When she dies, he cannot stop thinking creatively, for he still lacks the secret. Once the three cards are revealed to him, however, he becomes more obsessive and his world more constricted. No ingenious plans are now necessary. Three, seven, and ace make up Germann's entire existence; everything in the outside world is transformed into the new code:

> Two fixed ideas cannot exist together in the moral world just as two bodies cannot occupy one and the same place in the physical world. Three, seven, ace began to eclipse in Germann's imagination the image of the dead old woman. Three, seven, ace didn't leave him for a moment and played continually on his lips. If he saw a young girl, he would say, "How slender she is! A real three of hearts." If anyone asked him the time, he would answer, "Five minutes to the seven." Every pot-bellied man he saw reminded him of the ace. Three, seven, ace haunted him in his sleep, assuming all possible forms: the three blossomed before him in the form of a magnificent flower; the seven appeared as a Gothic portal and the ace an enormous spider. All his thoughts fused into one: to make use of the secret that had cost him so dearly. He thought of retirement and of traveling. He wanted to compel fortune to yield up her treasure to him in the public gambling houses of Paris. Chance saved him all these troubles.

> Две противоположенные идеи не могут вместе существовать в нравственной природе, так же, как два теда не могут в физийеском мире занимать одно и то же место. Тройка, семерка, туз—скоро заслонили в воображении Германна образ мертвой старухи. Тройка, семерка, туз—не выходили из его головы и шевелились на его губах. Увидев молодую девушку, он говорил:— Как она стройна! . . . Настоящая тройка червонная. У него спрашивали: который час, он отвечал:—без пяти минут семерка.—Всякий пузастый мужчина напоминал ему туза. Тройка, семерка, туз—преследовали его во сне, принимая все возможные виды: тройка цвела перед ним в образе пышного грандифлора, семерка представлялась готическими воротами, туз огромным пауком. Все мысли его слились в одну,—воспользоваться тайной, которая дорого ему стоила. Он стал думать об отставке и о путешествии. Он хотел в открытых игрецких домах Парижа вынудить клад у очарованной фортуны. Случай избавил его от хлопот.

> (8: 249)

The third and last stage of this imaginative reduction is represented in the insane asylum. All thought has vanished; all connection to the outside world has been severed. Two phrases, four words ("Three, seven, ace," "Three, seven, queen"), constitute the only sign that a human being once lived in his body. Germann is reduced to the names of the cards, signifiers now of nothing. His imagination has revealed nothing to him; instead, it has converted the tale told at the beginning (and permuted through hundreds of variations) to a simple formula for eliminating risk, chance, and change. (It should be noted that Germann, at least consciously, never thinks of himself as gambling when he uses the secret.) His imagination has stopped interpretation and reinterpretation. Germann becomes an exemplum of madness as imaginative failure.

III

Although *The Queen of Spades* underscores the vulgarity of Germann's imagination, the story is not a monolithic devalorization of madness. Like the psychological interpretations of the story, the devalorization does not constitute a complete code. Evidence for a more positive interpretation of Germann's madness is encoded in the brief, seemingly matter-of-fact epilogue, which sums up the fates of the major characters.

> Germann went out of his mind. He is a patient in room 17 in Obukhov Hospital. He doesn't answer any questions but mutters with unusual rapidity, "Three, seven, ace! Three, seven, queen!"

> Lizaveta Ivanovna married a very amiable young man. He works in some government department and has a considerable fortune; he is the son of a former steward of the old countess. Lizaveta Ivanovna is bringing up a poor relative.

> Tomsky has been promoted to captain and is marrying Princess Polina.

> Германн сошел с ума. Он сидит в Обуховской больнице в 17 нумере, не отвечает ни на какие вопросы, и бормочет необыкновенно скоро:— Тройка, семерка, туз! Тройка, семерка, дама! . . .

> Лизавета Ивановна выщла замуж за очень любезного человека; он где-то служит и имеет порядочное состояние: он сын бывшего управителя у старой графини. У Лизаветы Ивановны воспитывается бедная родственница.

> Томский произведен в ротмистры и женится на княжне Полине.

> (8: 252)

When compared with Liza's and Tomsky's fates, Germann's outcome appears in a more positive light.[15] Liza seems to follow the example of the countess, her former tormentor; the young woman now is in a position to visit on her own ward the injuries that she suffered as a ward. But, more important, she has in a sense played the same game as Germann. He starts off with a small fortune (маленький капитал; 8: 235) and loses everything; she starts with nothing and through an undertaking rather less risky than his—marriage—achieves his ideal: a considerable fortune (порядочное состояние; 8: 252). Liza's husband received his fortune from his father, just as Germann did, but her father-in-law amassed the money by stealing from the countess when he was her steward. Tomsky also enters into a marriage of convenience, with a princess, thus attaining the same tainted goal that Liza achieves and in the same manner. The last word Germann speaks is "queen." He may be tied to the countess forever, but Liza pays a higher price morally for her apparent freedom.

But is there anything positive to Germann's madness besides the contrast with other characters? Liza and Tomsky succeed in their world precisely because they lack imagination; Liza repeats the countess's bad example, and Tomsky takes the most beaten of all paths. Germann ultimately does the opposite of his prudent, fortune-amassing father and even does what probably no one associated with the tale of the three cards has done, especially if most of the absurdities that Germann hears at the beginning are discounted. Germann starts out with a small capital, risks everything, and loses everything. To assume only that he believes in the secret and thus thinks he is not taking a risk, not really gambling, is to make him a one-dimensional character—a figure completely coinciding with his conscious self—in a story that is above all ambiguous and complex.[16]

Given a Nabokovian view of пошдост, it may seem better to have no imagination at all than the one Pushkin deals Germann, but the story, I hope to show, reveals otherwise. The narrator says not only that Germann has a lively imagination but that he is a gambler at heart. Critics have paid much more attention to the first quality than to the second, but each is prophetic, realizing itself and combining with the other to seal Germann's fate. In the end, Germann gambles; he plays not so much to win as to risk, to dare, to stake his life—that is, to live.

That Germann is a gambler at heart is indicated in the first passages of the text as well as in the last. At the beginning, he sits on the sidelines, a passionate and imaginative observer—Pushkin stresses his strong passions (сильные страсти)—but he is able to restrain his desire:[17] "And yet he would sit night after night at the card tables, following with feverish excitement the various turns of the game" 'А между тем, целые ночи просиживал за карточными столами, и следовал с лихорадочным трепетом за различными оборотами игры' (8: 235). Both his restraint and his passion are present before he hears the tale (сказка) of the three cards. The tale does not transform Germann; it pushes him over the edge.

Pushkin abandons Germann on the first page and does not take him up again until the middle of the next chapter, providing a span of reading time that suggests the psychological time Germann requires for the сказка to invade his imagination. Despite the depreciative account I give of Germann's imagination in the previous part, the narrator describes it as active and fiery (огненное; 8: 235). Germann does not passively accept the сказка but transforms it into his own creation, and so it reflects, as any creation

must, the mind and passions of its creator. Germann knows that the story of the secret is just a fairy tale, but only this story, which represents the imaginative transformation of many generations, can affect him. A creature of the imagination, he finds the play less tempting than the story into which the play is metamorphosed.

Soon after the idea of the three cards implants itself in Germann's mind, he attempts to exert active control over the сказка. A plot begins to emerge in his imagination that charges all the events and characters of the tale. First Liza is emplotted, then the countess, both before and after her death. Of course, Germann places himself at the center of events, the quester after the great secret. However, his madness, while exacerbated by his desire to reduce the story to the names of the secret cards, can be just as easily seen as a concentration of his imaginative powers to some higher end, of which he is barely conscious.

The most important of Germann's imaginative acts involving the dead countess are the first, by which he thinks his fortune is made, and the two last, by which his doom is sealed. The first act, his imagining of the ghost of the countess (for argument's sake, I do not treat the apparition as supernatural), is not so much a self-serving device of his as a creative interpretation:

> "I have come to you against my will," she said in a firm voice, "but I have been ordered to fulfill your request. Three, seven, ace in succession will win for you, but only provided that you do not play more than one card a day and that you never play again for the rest of your life. I forgive you my death, provided that you marry my ward, Lizaveta Ivanovna."
>
> (8: 247)

This utterance is in some ways as trite as Germann's speeches. Germann's conception that the countess comes against her will to grant his request and forgive him seems psychologically obvious if not commonplace. Further, he has been thinking about threes, sevens, and aces ever since he encountered the anecdote. The night after hearing it, Germann names the cards and affirms their power even as he appears to reject them: "No! Prudence, moderation, and hard work: those are my three sure cards; that is what will increase my capital threefold, sevenfold, and provide me with peace and independence" 'Нет! расчет, умеренность и трудолюбие: вот мои три верные карты, вот что утроит, усемерит мой капитал, и доставит мне покой и независимость!' (8: 235).[18] And yet he curiously varies the story from the way it has been repeated in the past (perhaps to make it more convincing to himself), introducing the requirement that the cards be played on successive days. For perhaps the first time, instead of reducing the tale, Germann begins to draw it out. This expansion may reflect his unconscious desire not to win at once but to prolong the game, to continue to play for the sake of playing.

Pushkin makes explicit Germann's role as interpreter:

For a long time Germann could not come to his senses. He went into the other room. His orderly was asleep on the floor; Germann was hardly able to wake him. The orderly was drunk as usual, and it was impossible to get any sense from him. The street door was locked. Germann returned to his room, lit a candle, and wrote down his vision.

Германн долго не мог опомниться. Он вышел в другую комнату. Денщик его спал на полу; Германн насилу его добудился. Денщик был пьян по обыкновению: от него нельзя было добиться никакого толку. Дверь в сени была заперта. Германн возвратился в свою комнату, засветил свечку, и записал свое видение.

(8: 248)

Whatever Germann writes is an interpretation, in no way less fanciful than the interpretations of numerous critics who after reading *The Queen of Spades,* and especially the vision episode, sat down, like Germann, to write. In this episode and others as well, scholars—and artists like Dostoevsky—have thought that there was more to Germann's imagination than the clichés with which his speeches are riddled.

On the night of the countess's death, Germann faces a choice on the left, Liza's apartment, and one on the right, the countess's study. He chooses the door on the right, seemingly the wrong door—ambition wins out over love. On the night of the last card game, it is the card on the left, the ace, that will bring him fame and fortune, the card on the right that leads to madness. He chooses the card on the right. But this final mad act, the playing of the last card, must be viewed not as the most reductive deed of a vulgar madman but as Germann's most inspired and imaginative act in his own creation. For his choice of the wrong card—and who but a madman could choose the wrong card while knowing the right one?—is a choice against his ideals of peace and comfort (покой) and of independence (независимость), a rebellious blow against a final resolution. The mad act that drives Germann permanently insane thus may be his highest act of sanity: a choice against reduction, a choice for the first time for chance, play, and life. Given Germann's extreme personality, only an act of madness can free him from his vain ideal of undisturbed self-sufficiency and permit him for one moment to experience, in the most intense form imaginable, the feeling of being a true, though reckless, gambler, a man who can stake his life on a card. To win would, of course, have been to lose; it would have been never to gamble—to live—at all.[19]

This conclusion is as unexpected as the queen of spades is for the conscious Germann. Almost all critics hold that Germann chooses the wrong card and that Pushkin punishes him by making him do so, but in fact the calculating Germann dies for chance because of an unconscious choice that elevates Germann's unhappy role in the tale. Thus, at the last possible moment, a romantic notion of madness flashes into view and sheds a different light on the preceding events. Before going insane, the hero experiences a momentary vision of the truth of his life and character, much as Dostoevsky's Myshkin does in his epileptic aura.[20] At last Germann understands the emptiness of his ideal of peace and independence and sees clearly—and recognizes the price of—the only possibility that remains for redeeming his past. For this romantic moment, as in Pushkin's **"Egyptian Nights"** ("Египетские ночи," 1835), one must be willing to sacrifice one's life. The tragedy of Germann, a sharply polarized personality, is that there can be no compromise, no healthy gambling. His choice in the end is the one that he created for himself. It was he who brought the countess back from the dead. It was he who invented the cards, the secret. It was also he who plotted his final moments, giving himself no middle ground. It is either the ace or the queen. By choosing the queen, Germann rejects the ordinary fate of Liza and Tomsky; he makes a leap of the imagination that elevates him above his fellows and transforms him into a figure that has exerted a tremendous power on the Russian literary imagination to this day. But just as important, by choosing the queen, Germann also chooses to keep the story alive—open to interpretation—and to make himself part, perhaps the most intriguing part, of the next redaction of the tale, a warning to all proponents of closure.

Pushkin's ambiguous and ambivalent representation of madness in *The Queen of Spades*—as simultaneously a romantic epiphany and the epitome of пошлость—is probably not what Gofman had in mind when he speculated about Pushkin's legacy for Russian literature. But this strange idea of madness perhaps constituted Pushkin's principal legacy for the mature Dostoevsky. In *The Gambler* (Игрок, 1867), Dostoevsky wrote his own version of *The Queen of Spades,* and Raskolnikov, in *Crime and Punishment* (Преступление и наказание, 1866), is an updated Germann. But it is in the representation of Ivan Karamazov that the implications of Pushkin's treatment of madness are taken to their logical conclusions.

Toward the end of *The Brothers Karamazov* (Братья Карамазовы, 1880; 14: 5-508, 15: 5-197), in a passage that echoes Germann's encounter with the dead countess, Ivan Karamazov confronts a ghost, a creature of his imagination. A doctor from Moscow has just diagnosed Ivan as "having something perhaps even like a brain disorder" 'вроде даже как бы расстройства в мозгу' in which "hallucinations . . . are quite possible" 'галлюцинации . . . очень возможны.'

And so he was sitting there now, almost conscious himself of being delirious, and, as I have said already, staring persistently at some object on the sofa against the opposite wall. Someone suddenly appeared sitting there, though God knows how he walked in, because he had not been in the room when Ivan Fyodorovich entered the room on his way back from his visit to Smerdyakov.

(15: 70; pt. 4, bk. 11, ch. 9)

Ivan senses something mean and seedy in his devil. Ivan may curse him and call him a lie, an illness, a ghost, an embodiment of only one side of himself, a reflection of

Ivan's most loathsome and stupid thoughts and feelings, but what disturbs Ivan most of all is the visitor's banality, пошлость. The devil says archly that his dream is "to become incarnate . . . in some fat, 250-pound merchant's wife and believe everything she believes in" 'воплотиться . . . в какуюнибудь толстую семипудовую купчиху и всему поверить, во что она верит,' and he claims that it is not artists who have extraordinary hallucinations but "the most ordinary people, officials, journalists, priests" 'совсем самые заурядные люди, чиновники, фельетонисты, попы' (15: 73-74). The devil, however, deftly counters Ivan's characterization of him as banal: "How could such a banal devil come to such a great man?" 'Как, дескать, к такому великому человеку мог войти такой пошлый черт?' (15: 81). Banality, brilliance, and hallucination are inseparably bound in Ivan's madness.

This unusual sort of madness brings Ivan, as it does Germann, face to face with the choice that will determine his fate, a choice between opposite worlds. Though Ivan's choice differs from Germann's, Dostoevsky like Pushkin focuses simultaneously on the banal and the romantic aspects of his hero's madness. More important, however, Dostoevsky intimates something larger than a dual, or ambiguous, interpretation of madness, as пошлость or revelation. He posits a different kind of madness, maybe a particularly Russian form, not a madness that leads now to false salvation (the ace) and now to transfiguration (the queen) but one that both threatens damnation and promises transfiguration at the same time—perhaps a madness without closure. Through Dostoevsky's transformation, Pushkin's concept of madness may have become, to Nabokov's consternation, one of the most dynamic of Pushkin's legacies to nineteenth- and twentieth-century Russian literature and culture. Nabokov seemingly attempts to have the final word in *Despair* (Отчаяние: Роман), in which the main character, Hermann (Герман), a mad writer prone to hallucinations and obsessed with a double, is punished for imaginative failure: "Hell shall never parole Hermann" (xiii). But it is not in Nabokov's power to end the story by dealing Hermann/Герман the wrong cards; whatever end he chooses for his hero, Nabokov is fated, somewhat like Pushkin's Germann, to become still another intriguing link in the self-renewing legacy of **The Queen of Spades.**

Notes

1. There are only a few brief discussions of the poem in the critical literature: Taborisskaja 73-75, Geršenzon 25-26, and Ètkind 66-68. The poem also makes a brief appearance in Bitov's novel *Pushkin House* (Пушкинский дом; 238-39). See also Rosenshield.

2. Even Gofman devotes only four pages to *The Queen of Spades,* which he sees as the culmination of Pushkin's work on the theme (82-86). See also the discussions of madness in the story by Williams; Taborisskaja 81-87; and Makogonenko 249-55. For a review of the Russian reception of the story, see Lerner 141-42.

3. All translations of Russian quotations are my own.

4. Geršenzon was one of the first to celebrate "the chaotic perfection" 'хаотическое совершенство' in Pushkin (24-32).

5. Many agree with Dostoevsky's praise for Pushkin's ability to efface the line between the realistic and the fantastic. For one of the earliest and most convincing demonstrations of this technique, see Slonimskij.

6. In this version of faro, players choose whatever card they want from the deck.

7. "[П]ламенный недуг," "пламенныи восторг," "вихорь буйный" ("Conversation of a Bookseller and the Poet" ["Разговор книгопродавца с поэтом"], 1824; 2: 325); "смятенье" ("The Poet" ["Поэт"], 1827; 3: 65); "горячка," "священный бред" (*Eugene Onegin* [Евгений Онегин], 1832; 6: 29; 1.58).

8. But it would be incorrect to conclude that madness is a concern of Pushkin's only in his poetry. As Blagoj shows, madness is perhaps Pushkin's most frequent metaphor for describing, individually and collectively, all things socially and politically unsound, destabilizing, and dangerous (311-28). For a discussion of the views of madness in Germany during the late Enlightenment, in both literary and nonliterary texts, see Ziolkowski 144-80. For similar analyses of unreason in the Age of Reason, see Byrd; Feder 147-202; Foucault; Osinski; Reuchlein; and G. Rosen 151-71. See also Vol'pert's comparison of Pushkin and Stendhal. For works in Pushkin's library indicating his familiarity with the contemporary literature on madness, see Modzalevskij 53, 246, 273, 346. Vol'pert notes in relation to *The Queen of Spades* that Pushkin had cut from François Leuret's *Fragments psychologiques sur la folie* the pages devoted to various types of hallucinations (54).

Pushkin was personally acquainted with a "mad" poet, Konstantin Batyushkov, who stopped writing poetry after going insane at thirty-three—Pushkin's age when he wrote *The Queen of Spades, The Bronze Horseman,* and perhaps "God Grant." Pushkin was reported to have been greatly shaken by a visit to the mad Batyushkov when everyone thought that Batyushkov was dying (he recovered). Still, Batyushkov hardly resembles the madman of the last stanzas of "God Grant." For the most detailed discussions of Batyushkov's life and madness, see Alekseev 369-71, Košelev 276-340, and Majkov 222-40.

9. One of the artist heroes in *Russian Nights* (Русские ночи), Odoevsky's most famous work, says, "Doesn't the state of a madman resemble the state of a poet? . . . Isn't the exalted state of a poet . . . closer to what is called insanity than insanity is to an ordinary animal-like stupidity?" 'Состояние сумасшедшего не имеет ли сходства с состоянием поэта? . . . Не ближе ли находится

восторженное состояние поэта . . . к тому, что называют безумием, нежели безумие к обыкновенной животной глупости?' (25-26).

10. The generally nonironic works patterned after Hoffmann by Gogol ("The Portrait" ["Портрет"]) and by the young Dostoevsky ("The Landlady" ["Хозяйка"]) are not their most successful endeavors.

11. As Tymms shows, parodies on Hoffmannian doubles were written before Hoffmann's death in 1822: "So the romantic tale ends by parodying itself; with the self-destructive irony of the whole movement, the German Romantic, having, over a period of a decade or two, elaborately hoisted up a bizarre image of his own self-division, now turns upon his *Janus bifrons,* and bowls over the puppet he had himself glorified into 'super-reality'" (71).

12. Pushkin emphasizes Germann's imagination throughout. He calls attention to the story's effect on it three times in the narrator's formal introduction alone. German "had strong passions and a fervent imagination" 'имел сильные страсти и огненное воображение'; the anecdote about the three cards "had exerted a strong influence on his imagination" 'сильно подействовал на его воображение'; and a little while later the amazing anecdote "again appeared before his imagination" 'снова представился его воображению' (8: 235-36).

13. See, for example, Leighton, "Gematria" and "Numbers"; Weber; and Davydov.

14. See Nabokov's essay "Philistines and Philistinism" (*Lectures* 309-14).

15. For less than positive assessments of Liza's actions and fate, see Leatherbarrow 13-14 and especially Shaw.

16. Psychoanalytic interpretations presuppose latent desires but, in contrast to romantic psychology, often do not admit the possibility of an individual with multiple selves. For psychoanalytic approaches to the story, see Schwartz and Schwartz; N. Rosen; and Burgin.

17. This detail may be Pushkin's code for indicating Germann's complexity. Comparing Shakespeare's characters with Molière's, Pushkin writes: "The characters created by Shakespeare are not, as in Molière, basically types of such and such a passion, such and such a vice, but living beings filled with many passions, many vices; circumstances develop their varied and many-sided personalities before the viewer. In Molière, the miser is miserly—and that's all; in Shakespeare, Shylock is miserly, acute, vindictive, philoprogenitive, witty" (Proffer 240).

18. Shaw shows that when туз 'ace' is not mentioned after a reference to three and seven, a phrase that suggests the missing term often appears instead (119). In the series I quote here, the ace is "provided" by the expression "peace and independence" (for туз can also signify a portly man or a man of rank and wealth).

19. Sinjavskij, if I understand him correctly, argues that for Pushkin chance and risk are perhaps one's only guarantee of attaining something eternal (39). Sinjavskij has in mind the famous line from "The Feast in Time of the Plague" ("Пир во время нумы," 1830; 7: 173-84): "The guarantee, perhaps, of immortality" 'Бессмертья, может быть, залог' (180).

20. The author-narrator of *The Bronze Horseman* not only sympathizes with Evgeny, the mad hero (whose ideals are closer to Pushkin's than are Germann's), but ultimately ascribes a special form of clairvoyance, even prophecy, to Evgeny's madness.

Works Cited

Alekseev, M. P. "Несколко новых данных о Пушкине и Батюшкове" [Some New Findings about Pushkin and Batyushkov]. Известия Академии наук СССР. Отделение литературы и языка [Proceedings of the Academy of Sciences of the USSR. Division of Literature and Language] 8 (1949): 369-72.

Bitov, Andrej. Пушкинский дом [Pushkin House]. Moscow: Sovremennik, 1989.

Blagoj, D. Социология творчества Пушкина: Этюды [The Sociology of Pushkin's Works: Studies]. Moscow: Federaciija, 1929.

Burgin, Diana Lewis. "The Mystery of 'Pikovaia dama.'" *Mnemozina: Studia litteraria russica in honorem Vsevolod Setchkarev.* Ed. Joachim T. Baer and Norman W. Ingham. Munich: Fink, 1974. 46-56.

Byrd, Max. *Visits to Bedlam: Madness and Literature in the Eighteenth Century.* Columbia: U of South Carolina P, 1974.

Davydov, Sergei. "The Ace in Pushkin's 'The Queen of Spades.'" Forthcoming.

Dostoevskij, F. M. Полное собрание сочинений [Complete Works]. Ed. V. G. Bazanov et al 30 vols. Leningrad: Nauka, 1972-90.

Emerson, Caryl. "'The Queen of Spades' and the Open End." *Puškin Today.* Ed. David Bethea. Bloomington: Indiana UP, 1992. 31-37.

Ètkind, E. Симметрчческие композиции у Пушкина [Pushkin's Symmetrical Compositions]. Paris: Institut d'Etudes Slaves, 1988.

Feder, Lillian. *Madness in Literature.* Princeton: Princeton UP, 1980.

Foucault, Michel. *Madness and Civilization: A History of Insanity in the Age of Reason.* New York: Random, 1965.

Geršenzon, M. Мудрость Пушкина [The Wisdom of Pushkin]. Moscow: Pisateli v Moskve, 1919.

Gofman, M. L. "Проблема сумасшествия в творчестве Пушкина" [The Problem of Madness in Pushkin's Works]. Новый журнал [New Journal] 51 (1957): 61-86.

Gogol', N. V. Полное собрание сочинений [Complete Works]. 14 vols. Moscow: AN SSSR, 1937-52.

Košelev, Vjačeslav. Константин Батюшков: Странствия и страсти [Konstantin Batyushkov: Wanderings and Passions]. Moscow: Sovremennik, 1987.

Leatherbarrow, W. J. "'The Queen of Spades.'" *The Voice of a Giant: Essays on Seven Russian Prose Classics*. Ed. Roger Cockrell and David Richards. Exeter: U of Exeter, 1985. 1-14.

Leighton, Lauren. "Gematria in 'The Queen of Spades': A Decembrist Puzzle." *Slavic and East European Journal* 21 (1977): 455-69.

———. "Numbers and Numerology in 'The Queen of Spades.'" *Canadian Slavonic Papers* 19 (1977): 417-43.

Lerner, N. O. Рассказы о Пушкине [Stories about Pushkin]. Leningrad: Priboj, 1929.

Levkovič, Ja. L. "Стихотворение Пупкина 'Не дай мне Бог сойти с ума'" [Pushkin's Lyric "God Grant That I Not Lose My Mind"]. Пушкин: Исследования и материалы [Pushkin: Research Papers and Materials]. Vol. 10. Leningrad: AN SSSR, 1982. 176-92.

Lotman, Ju. M. "Тема карт и карточиой игры в русской литературе начала XIX века" [The Theme of Cards and Card Playing in Russian Literature of the Beginning of the Nineteenth Century]. Труды по знаковым системам [Studies on Semiotic Systems] 7 (1975): 122-42.

Majkov, L. Батюшков: Его жизнь и соченения [Batyushkov: His Life and Works]. 2nd ed. Saint Petersburg: Marks, 1896.

Makogonenko, G. P. Творчество А. С. Пущкина в 1830-е годы (1833-1836) [Pushkin's Works of the 1830s (1833-36)]. Leningrad: Xudožestvennaja Literatura, 1982.

Modzalevskij, V. L. Библиотека А. С. Пушкина [Pushkin's Library]. Saint Petersburg: Akademija Nauk, 1910.

Nabokov, Vladimir. *Despair.* New York: Vintage, 1965. Trans. of V. Sirin [Vladimir Nabokov]. Отчаяние: Роман. Berlin: Petropolis, 1936.

———. *Lectures on Russian Literature.* Ed. Fredson Bowers. New York: Harcourt, 1981.

Odoevskij, Vladimir. Русские ночи [Russian Nights]. Leningrad: Nauka, 1975.

———. "Сильфида" [The Sylph]. Повести и рассказы [Novellas and Short Stories]. Moscow: Xudožestvennaja Literatura, 1988. 173-94.

Osinski, Jutta. *Über Vernunft und Wahnsinn: Studien zur literarischen Aufklärung in der Gegenwart und im 18. Jhdt.* Bonn: Bouvier, 1983.

Proffer, Carl R., ed. *The Critical Prose of Alexander Pushkin.* Bloomington: Indiana UP, 1969.

Puškin, A. S. Подное собрание сочинений [Complete Works]. 17 vols. Moscow: AN SSSR, 1937-59.

Reeder, Roberta. "'The Queen of Spades': A Parody of the Hoffmann Tale." *New Perspectives on Nineteenth-Century Russian Prose.* Ed. George J. Gutsche. Columbus: Slavica, 1982. 74-98.

Reuchlein, Georg. *Bürgerliche Gesellschaft, Psychiatrie und Literatur: Zur Entwicklung der Wahnsinnsthematik in der deutschen Literatur des späten 18. und frühen 19. Jahrhunderts.* Munich: Fink, 1986.

Rosen, George. *Madness in Society: Chapters in the Historical Sociology of Mental Illness.* New York: Harper, 1969.

Rosen, Nathan. "The Magic Cards in 'The Queen of Spades.'" *Slavic and East European Journal* 19 (1975): 255-75.

Rosenshield, Gary. "The Poetics of Madness: Puškin's 'God Grant That I Not Lose My Mind.'" *Slavic and East European Journal* 38 (1994): 120-47.

Schwartz, Murray M., and Albert Schwartz. "'The Queen of Spades': A Psychoanalytic Interpretation." *Texas Studies in Literature and Language* 17 (1975): 275-88.

Shaw, Joseph T. "The 'Conclusion' of Pushkin's 'Queen of Spades.'" *Studies in Russian and Polish Literature in Honor of Waslaw Lednicki.* Ed. Zbigniew Folejewski et al. The Hague: Mouton, 1962. 114-26.

Sinjavskij, Andrej [Avram Terts]. Прогулки с Пушкиным [Strolls with Pushkin]. London: Collins, 1975.

Slonimskij, A. L. "О композиции 'Пиковой дамы'" [On the Composition of "The Queen of Spades"]. Пушкинский сборник памяти Профессора С. А. Венгерова [Collected Articles on Pushkin in Memory of Professor S. A. Vengerov]. Moscow: GIXL, 1923. 171-80.

Taborisskaja, E. M. "Своеобразие решения темы безумия в произведениях Пушкина 1883 года" [Pushkin's Original Resolution of the Theme of Madness in the Works of 1833]. Пушкинские чтения: Сборник статей [Readings of Pushkin: Collected Articles]. Tallinn: Eesti Raamat, 1990. 71-87.

Terras, Victor. *The Young Dostoevsky: 1846-1849: A Critical Study.* The Hague: Mouton, 1969.

Tymms, Ralph. *The Double in Literary Psychology.* Cambridge: Bowes, 1949.

Vol'pert, L. I. "Тема безумия в прозе Пушкина и Стендаля: 'Пиковая дама' и Красное и черное" [The Theme of Madness in the Prose of Pushkin and Stendhal: "The Queen of Spades" and *The Red and the Black*]. Пушкин и русская литература: Сборник научных трудов [Pushkin and Russian Literature: Collected Scholarly Articles]. Riga: Latvijskij Gosudarstvennyj Universitet Imeni P. Stučki, 1986. 46-58.

Weber, Harry B. "'Pikovaia dama': A Case for Freemasonry in Russian Literature." *Slavic and East European Journal* 12 (1968): 435-47.

Williams, Gareth. "The Obsessions of Madness of Germann in 'Pikovaja dama.'" *Russian Literature* 14 (1983): 383-96.

Ziolkowski, Theodore. *German Romanticism and Its Institutions.* Princeton: Princeton UP, 1990.

Svetlana Grenier (essay date March-June 1996)

SOURCE: Grenier, Svetlana. "'Everyone Knew Her . . .' or Did They?: Rereading Pushkin's Lizaveta Ivanovna ('The Queen of Spades')." *Canadian Slavonic Papers* 38, no. 1-2 (March-June 1996): 93-107.

[*In the following essay, Grenier offers an interpretation of Lizaveta's fate in Pushkin's novella.*]

The second paragraph of the "Conclusion" of *The Queen of Spades* reads

> Lizaveta Ivanovna has married a very amiable young man; he is in the civil service and has a considerable fortune: he is the son of the old countess's former steward. Lizaveta Ivanovna is bringing up a daughter of a poor relation.[1]

Over the last thirty years or so it has become a commonplace of *The Queen of Spades* criticism to infer that this paragraph, and especially its last sentence, testify to Lizaveta Ivanovna's absolutely and tediously repeating her benefactress's path. She will take the old countess's place and will doom yet another ward to become the victim of a capricious benefactress. J. T. Shaw, for example, sums up his interpretation as follows: Lizaveta Ivanovna is "a martyr who seeks and finds a deliverer so that she may do as she has been done by."[2]

I would like to dispute this "finalizing" approach to Pushkin's heroine. To put it in Bakhtinian terms, Lizaveta Ivanovna's fate and personality are just as radically "open-ended" as the rest of *The Queen of Spades* and, for that matter, the rest of Pushkin's mature work—as one Bakhtin scholar actually suggests.[3]

In his analysis of *The Queen of Spades,* Lotman allows for an open-ended interpretation of the work, demonstrating the simultaneous operation of at least two mutually exclusive "models," one transpiring through the other.[4] He himself, however, reads the "Conclusion" as a definitive closure on this contradiction of paradigms, a closure which allows Pushkin to dot all the i's, particularly where Lizaveta Ivanovna is concerned. In this [essay], I will argue that the "Conclusion" continues rather than terminates the pattern of mutually exclusive paradigms, thus leaving the heroine's fate literally open. This argument can be presented in Lotman's own words: it is precisely the *incom-*

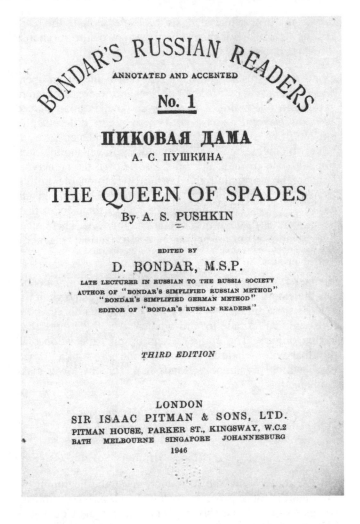

patibility* of the *equally possible* interpretations with each other that assures Pushkin's images of the "depth of unfinished-ness."

Readers' responses to Lizaveta Ivanovna contradict each other enough to suggest that her image presented in the "Conclusion" is less finalizing than it seems to be. Alongside the recently popular interpretation of this heroine, which privileges the apparently cynical "Conclusion," another interpretation is at least equally possible, one anchored in the apparently sympathetic view of her in the main body of the story.[5] Yet, while the two readings are equally possible, they are also equally "impossible," for each must "force" the text a little to accommodate it, each must fill too many gaps and contend with too many indeterminacies. Each, finally, imposes a definitive unity on a character, who, in this mysterious story, is designed to defy it.[6] Lizaveta Ivanovna's image conforms to Caryl Emerson's overall assessment of the tale, in which the reader is programmed to try to discover the unified meaning of the story on his or her own: "Pushkin provides us not with a code, and not with chaos, but precisely with the *fragments* of codes, codes that tantalize but do not quite add up."[7] I maintain that, in order not to hinder this open-endedness, Pushkin deliberately leaves Lizaveta's case *open,* and, in the final analysis, he leaves it up to the readers' cynicism or idealism about human nature to choose the reading that suits them.[8]

One way for Pushkin to make Lizaveta Ivanovna an open-ended character, is to trace her lineage to several different genres. In presenting Lizaveta Ivanovna, Pushkin indeed activates several generic codes that create different plot expectations in the reader.[9] At different moments he invokes the eighteenth-century epistolary novel and the Sentimental tale (*à la* Karamzin's *Poor Liza*); the archetypal Cinderella story; and the currently fashionable gotho-freneticist fiction, society tale, and physiological sketch. No sooner does Pushkin introduce one of these codes than he subverts it through introducing another one. This procedure results in an all-pervasive relativization of generic predictability.

Chapter II establishes this pattern of shifting generic codes. On the one hand, it is preceded by an epigraph reminiscent of the eighteenth-century novel, with its libertine heroes' cynical attitude toward women as nothing more than sexual objects. The epigraph sets up an expectation of a plot that will include an aristocrat's intrigue with a "*suivante,*" which presumably stands here for any lower-class woman:

> —*Il parait que monsieur est décidément pour les suivantes.*
> —*Que voulez-vous, madame? Elles sont plus fraîches.*
>
> (Society conversation) (6:324).[10]

On the other hand, the introduction, at the beginning of the chapter, of a grotesquely old "*madame*" (Countess) seems to undermine this expectation. Yet the Countess's behavior does mimic that of the jealous (older) mistress of the epigraph: she spends hours in front of a mirror but won't allow her *quasi-suivante,* the young Lizaveta, to spend even a few minutes dressing. Also, as soon as the Countess suspects Liza of trying to attract the attentions of some "*monsieur,*" she uses her socially superior position to prevent her ward from succeeding. The reader next witnesses a "gentleman" (young officer) courting the young lady ("*suivante*"); moreover, when Germann's thoughts are revealed the reader learns that he had indeed considered starting an affair with the "hideous" (6:339) "*madame*"—all of which seems to confirm the original expectation of a "triangle" between the *monsieur, madame,* and her *suivante* and of the *monsieur* eventually *preferring* the *suivante.*

This triangle, however, exists on a completely different plane from the triangle of the epigraph and of the libertine novel. In the epigraph, the "freshness" of the ladies' maids prompts the "gentleman" to choose between two women, two different objects of the *same passion*; the "freshness" of Lizaveta may potentially prompt Germann to choose between two *different passions,* love and greed.

In this context, the last sentence of Chapter II ("That moment decided his fate" [6:332]) appears highly ambiguous. On the one hand, it follows the sentence, "Germann saw a *fresh* young face and dark eyes" (6:332; my italics—S.G.), which refers the reader back to the epigraph, reinforcing the original expectation of a "libertine" plot. On the other hand, it sounds like a *Romantic* (or perhaps Sentimental) cliché denoting love at first sight. Indeed, this sentence is just the last one in a series of "fragments" of a Romantic code in its Byronic or gotho-freneticist version.[11] The narrator also mentions Germann's typically Romantic appearance as perceived by Lizaveta Ivanovna, who notices his "pale cheeks" and "dark eyes gleam[ing] from under his hat" (6:330)[12]; the heroine's mysterious, irrational fear when she sees him up close; and Germannn's "strong passions and fiery imagination" (6:331). These Romantic elements contradict the genre of the libertine novel. In the Sentimental and Romantic paradigm, love is the highest value, and woman is perceived as an exalted being, not simply as an object of sexual power games, as in the "libertine" novel.[13] The clash of two styles and of the world views they represent—the "libertine" epigraph vs. the "Romantic" ending—produces a tension that should warn the reader against an automatic "romantic" interpretation of events (i. e., that Germannn is in love with Liza). The reader's prior knowledge of Germannn's thoughts also makes such an interpretation less than certain. Yet the Romantic elements undercut both the "libertine" and the "mercenary" interpretation. Invoking fate in such circumstances is too large a brush stroke for depicting Germann's allegedly purely mercenary motives.[14] Chapter II, thus, ends on a note of still unresolved uncertainty as to the possible plot development.[15]

The unpredictable nature of the plot, with its shifting genres, is not the only question the reader has to contend with; other questions associated with the heroine serve to compound it further. The conflicting expectations for the heroine's role that depend on the reader's perception of Germann's intentions are superimposed over characterization, direct and indirect, of Lizaveta Ivanovna in Chapter II.

First of all, the reader must somehow define Lizaveta in terms of social status. After the epigraph, which juxtaposes and contrasts the "*madame*" with the "*suivantes,*" the chapter introduces two women, "the old Countess" and "a young lady, her ward." While the former corresponds, in status, to the "*madame*" of the epigraph, the latter does not fit precisely into either category. She is contrasted with the "three maids" (*devushki*), i. e., *suivantes,* as a "young lady" (*baryshnia*); at the same time, her status is subordinate to that of the Countess and defined in relation to her ("*her* ward"). In sum, she clearly occupies some vague, in-between social niche.

The paragraph introducing the two women graphically translates their contrasting social positions into the spatial terms of "center" and "margin." The old countess sits at the mirror surrounded by three maids; she is literally the *center* of attention. The ward's peripheral position in the room ("by the window") signals her social marginality. The mention of the window suggests also her *liminal* status: she is both inside and, in a certain sense, outside of the countess's house and, by extension, of the exclusive social circle it represents ("[Lizaveta Ivanovna] was required to dress like everyone, that is, like only a very few" [6:329]). The ward's marginality and liminality is further formally expressed through the amount of text used to introduce her (one short sentence, in contrast to the whole paragraph for the countess) and the position of that introduction (at the *end*, i.e., on the *border* of the paragraph).

In the opening scene as well as in the narrator's comments that follow, Pushkin puts three codes in motion: the fairy-tale, the Sentimental, and the Realist. On the one hand, Liza's situation is transparently presented as that of Cinderella. The three maids' physical proximity to the countess—as in the stepmother's daughters' case—suggests a much greater affinity between her and them than between either her or them, on the one hand, and Liza, on the other, stressing Liza's "outsider" status in this world.[16] The scene that follows demonstrates the ward's humiliatingly ambiguous status of being both "lady" and "maid" ("*suivante*") at the same time; the dramatic presentation of the Countess's interactions with Liza seems to call for the readers' sympathy. So does the narrator's commentary:

> In truth, Lizaveta Ivanovna was a most unfortunate creature. Bitter is the alien bread, says Dante, and heavy are the steps of the alien porch—and who would know better the bitter taste of dependency than a poor ward of an aristocratic old lady? . . . Lizaveta Ivanovna was the household martyr . . .
>
> (6:328)

The archetypal fairy-tale code is reinforced by a more recent Sentimental one. Certain details suggest Lizaveta Ivanovna's kinship with her namesake, Karamzin's *Poor Liza*: aside from sharing the same name, the two heroines share the epithet "poor" (here "poor ward," "poor girl"). Furthermore, Pushkin's Lizaveta attends to her benefactress in much the same way Karamzin's Liza attends to her mother's needs. Finally, Lizaveta Ivanovna evinces certain *topoi* of feminine behavior typical of the Sentimental heroine: for example, the first time the reader witnesses her spotting Germann on the street, she blushes and lowers her eyes—the way Poor Liza does upon meeting Erast for the first time.[17]

In both the fairy-tale and the Sentimental system the heroine is defined as a creature "beautiful in body and soul" and at the same time socially and sexually vulnerable.[18] Lizaveta's outwardly quiet submissiveness to the Countess's ever-changing whims initially points the reader in the direction of perceiving her personality as Cinderella- and Poor-Liza-like in goodness. On the other hand, the proliferation of concrete realistic details of the ward's life in the narrator's comments anchors that life firmly in the social reality of the time:

> She served tea and was blamed for wasting sugar; she read novels aloud to the countess and was guilty of the author's every mistake; . . . A salary was appointed

her that was never paid in full, while she was required to dress like everyone, that is, like only a very few. . . . [A]t balls she would dance only when there was a lack of partners, and ladies took her hand every time they had to go to the dressing room to fix something in their attire.
>
> (6:328-29)

This introduction of the elements of the newly-fashionable genre of "*physiologie*"[19] into the description of a Cinderella-like heroine results in a tension that works to undermine the fairy-tale, Sentimental, and Romantic codes invoked. So does the summary of her somewhat un-Cinderella-like reaction to the situation: "She was proud [*samoliubiva*], felt her position keenly and looked around, waiting impatiently for a deliverer" (6:329). This statement denies Lizaveta Ivanovna Cinderella's good-natured submissiveness. It also introduces a decidedly un-heroinic (from the perspective of the earlier forms of writing) note of restless impatience and *activeness* into her (properly heroinic) *waiting*.[20] This sentence, however, is followed immediately by more "fragments" of the "Cinderella code" ("Lizaveta Ivanovna was a hundred times sweeter [*milee*] than the brazen and cold-hearted debutantes . . ."; "How often . . . she would go cry in her shabby room . . . !" [6:329]), clearly designed to evoke the reader's sympathy for the heroine.

The above sequence is just one example of the constant switching of codes used to present Lizaveta Ivanovna in Chapter II. Eventually the reader must realize that the essence of this *new*, socially marginal and liminal character lies somewhere beyond or in-between the familiar codes. Continual recourse to the well-worn clichés of earlier plots and character types in the depiction of Germann's interactions with Lizaveta Ivanovna serves, first and foremost, to foreground the novelty of the hero and *his* plot (through juxtaposition and contrast of love and greed). As a result of this on-and-off switching of different codes, however, a no-less-novel type of heroine emerges to complement the generically-ambiguous hero.

Chapter III, through several similar reversals, continues the pattern established in Chapter II. The reader is again faced with the uncertainty of Germann's motives; the ambivalence introduced in Lizaveta Ivanovna's "static" characterization is now dramatized in her actions.

In the depiction of Lizaveta Ivanovna in chapter III, the obviously active codes of the eighteenth-century epistolary novel are at first subverted for the reader by the heroine's behavior, which is unconventional in this (or any "romantic") system. Her first letter, unlike those of Pushkin's Tatiana or of Rousseau's Julie, does not contain a confession of love. She acts, rather, like a rational, level-headed person, who is excited by a new experience (a man paying attention to her)—and yet is acutely aware of the attendant danger. Lizaveta, like any reader of Pushkin's time, knows full well that taking up her pen is the crucial first step towards a potential abyss.[21] Her vacillations between the various courses she could take, her "weighing the pros and cons of an uncertain situation,"[22] in other words, her attempt to control the situation, is rational—and absolutely unconventional for a heroine in the Sentimental or Romantic system. Rational behavior aimed at self-preservation is un-heroine-like; it is unfeminine—and it earns this character the condemnation of the critics. Quoting the narrator's statement about Lizaveta's "waiting for a deliverer," Paul Debreczeny interprets her fear of Germann as

> simply the fear that he will not, after all, turn out to be her 'deliverer.' Granting him an assignation, she risks her reputation in the hope of acquiring a husband; her 'gamble,' as one critic [J. T. Shaw] put it, is no purer in motivation than Hermann's.[23]

Such critics rely on the primacy and ultimate authority of the realist code and, without explaining the purpose of the other codes, accept it as the key to understanding this character.[24] Yet, the realist code does not supersede the other codes: they are all invoked intermittently throughout the presentation, creating a complex and, at times, "doubling" image of this new character type. For example, an element of calculation (i.e., a hope that Germann will "turn out to be her 'deliverer'") may well be present at the moment of writing her first letter. It would explain why Lizaveta Ivanovna, although she is not head-over-heels in love with Germann, decides to pursue the relationship by responding to his letter. And yet, it seems reductive to dismiss all of her actions as necessarily "mercenary" in motivation. Other motives are also implicitly suggested by the narrator. Clearly, Liza has unfulfilled emotional needs. The thrilling new status of a young woman *looked* at and sought out, after the utter loneliness ("she had neither a friend nor a mentor" [6:334]) and total social invisibility ("everyone knew her, no one took any notice of her" [6:329]), she had previously experienced; the hope of "becoming a heroine" (to use Rachel Brownstein's apt title)[25]—all of this for the first time gives meaning to her tedious life: "She walked away [from the window] tormented by curiosity and agitated by a feeling *completely novel for her*" (6:330; my italics—S.G.).

The fact that Lizaveta Ivanovna does not right away fall in love with Germann the way Tatiana does with Onegin testifies to her more rational and less "romantic" nature, which, at first glance, appears to disqualify her from heroinic status in the Sentimental-Romantic paradigm. Liza's rationality has a limited scope, however. The promise of a romance proves too enticing for the "young dreamer" to resist. Soon enough, she is swept away:

> Lizaveta Ivanovna received letters from him every day, . . . No longer were they translated from the German. Germann wrote them inspired by passion and spoke in the language all his own: both the unbending strength of his desires and the disorder of his unbridled imagination found expression in them. Lizaveta Ivanovna did not even think of sending them back any more: she revelled in them; she started responding, and her notes were becoming longer and more tender by the hour.
>
> (6:335-36)

This passage suggests an interesting function to the "fragments" of the epistolary genre: both parties' letters seem to cause their possible love, rather than being prompted by it. Furthermore, these words suggest that no ulterior motive underlies Liza's action of granting Germann an assignation. Indeed, she cannot be acting on the basis of calculation, unless she is exceedingly foolish,[26] because Germann's actions, his impudence [*derzost'*], and the image she has made of him[27] do not indicate an intention on his part to "deliver" her in any matrimonial sense of the word. They indicate rather the opposite. She *is* acting foolishly—not out of miscalculation, but because, as the text implies, "[*e*]*lle était fille, elle était amoureuse.*"[28] Lizaveta Ivanovna, by virtue of her overall social and emotional vulnerability, is an ideal victim for a would-be seducer. By the middle of Chapter III, when Liza invites Germann to a nocturnal *rendez-vous,* the Sentimental-Romantic code has been reinstated. In an already familiar pattern, however, Liza's letter again partially subverts this code: it does not mention her feelings and sounds almost businesslike.

Chapter IV of *The Queen of Spades* perpetuates the ambiguity of Lizaveta Ivanovna's image through Pushkin's intertextual self-references to *Eugene Onegin,* which simultaneously activate and subvert what might be called a "Tatiana code." This chapter, containing an anti-climactic *rendez-vous manqué* between Germann and Liza similar to that in Chapter IV of *Eugene Onegin,* brings to the surface certain structural and textual parallels between the two plots and between the presentations of the two heroines, Liza and Tatiana.

The scene in Chapter IV of *The Queen of Spades* recapitulates and condenses the motifs of Chapters Three through Seven of *Eugene Onegin.* Tatiana's initial *literary* infatuation with Onegin, combining attraction and fear, finds a parallel in Liza's imagination being "frightened and captivated" by the image she has created of Germann, "due to the influence of the recent novels" (6:344). The meeting in the garden, scene of Onegin's "confession" (4:XII) that crushes Tatiana's hopes, corresponds to Germann's meeting with Liza when she learns that his courtship had not been motivated by love. Tatiana's dream vision of Onegin as a demonic murderer surrounded by monsters is echoed by the following exchange in *The Queen of Spades*: "'You are a monster,' she said.—'I did not want her death: my gun is not loaded'" (6:345). Tatiana's gradual recognition of Onegin's "Napoleonic" nature is paralleled by the description of Germann's Napoleonic posture (6:345) reminiscent of the bronze Napoleon figure in Onegin's study. Tatiana's recognition, "solving the enigma" (7:XXV) of Onegin leads to the shedding of her previous romantic notions of life and eventually to her marriage. The scene between Liza and Germann in chapter IV presumably has a similar effect on Liza.

As we see, Lizaveta Ivanovna undergoes an evolution rather similar to Tatiana's. She starts out as a romantically-minded young lady whose imagination is fed by her reading. She encounters a man whom she sees as a hero of a novel; takes the daring step of corresponding with him; and finally meets him face to face—only to witness her hopes and her romantic world view destroyed. In the epilogue she, like Tatiana, is "realistically" married to some "amiable young man" (6:356).

At the same time, this parallelism highlights points of difference between the two heroines. In one parallel, Lizaveta, like Tatiana, "trembles" anticipating her encounter with the hero (6:342; 3:XL), who at once represents her fate, her own conscience, and society's potential judgment of her improper step in writing to him. Unlike Tatiana, Lizaveta is not truly in love with the hero. Her mixed feelings of fear and attraction crystallize into "hoping to find Germann [in her room] and wishing not to find him" (6:342). She has not thrown herself uncompromisingly into this "affair"—she has been "drawn" into it by "circumstances" (6:342). For her, this *quasi*-relationship has been not the whole-hearted commitment that Tatiana's love was, but a thrilling, fascinating, dangerous game, motivated, in the final analysis, by the desire for recognition of her human and feminine significance. In the end, she is disappointed most of all because she turns out not to be a person with the power to "quench [Germann's] passion and make him happy" (6:345).

These differences between Liza and Tatiana surface at the *beginning* of Chapter Four; the many parallels between them are concentrated in the scene of Liza's encounter with Germann in the *second half* of the chapter. This order suggests that Pushkin intends here to switch the "Tatiana code" back on so as to promote a sympathetic view of Lizaveta and (since this is her last dramatic appearance in the story) to leave that view with the reader.

Turning to the "Conclusion," and comparing it with Chapter VIII of *Eugene Onegin*, we see that the parallel evolution of the two heroines leads each into ostensibly following in her mother's (if we consider the old countess a mother figure) footsteps. Tatiana, although she repeats her mother's path of marrying someone other than the object of her affections and although she appears entrenched and content in her new role (as her mother was), is, in the end, a very different person from her mother and from what she outwardly *appears* to be. As it turns out, she is not happy as a successful *grande dame*: she would rather be in the country, and she still keeps her love for Onegin.

Lizaveta Ivanovna ostensibly repeats the Countess's path. She is married to a wealthy husband, the son of the Countess's steward (cf. "My late grandfather [the Countess's husband] . . . was something akin to Grandmother's butler" [6:321]) and, of course, she is bringing up a ward.

As mentioned at the beginning of this article, several critics read this last detail as providing more or less conclusive evidence of Lizaveta Ivanovna's complete transformation into a powerful and oppressive benefactress. Such a transformation would invoke a motif that fits into two subsets, popular in the 1830s and 1840s, of the nascent re-

alist literary code: "society tale" and "Natural School" tale.[29] Considering that Pushkin has consistently subverted every generic code he used to present Lizaveta Ivanovna and her story, thereby creating an ambiguous figure, it seems reasonable to suspect that the apparently cynical "Conclusion" is one more in the series of statements intended by the author to be false leads for the gullible reader. If the overarching principle in the design of this character has been the undermining of the various generic codes, then the last line should also be potentially underminable, thereby preserving the unfinalized openness of Lizaveta Ivanovna's image.

Just as Tatiana is not what she seems to be in high society, so Liza is not necessarily what she seems to be to the "finalizing," non-Romantic narrator of the "Conclusion." After all, this narrator sums up the hero's story with a sober statement that "Germann has gone mad" (6:355). This "fact" does not, however, resolve the mystery of the plot. It does not, for example, unequivocally answer the question whether Germann had seen a "real" ghost or a hallucination. As Dostoevsky's Svidrigailov would later say, the fact that "ghosts appear only to the sick . . . only proves that ghosts *can* appear to no one but sick people— and not that there are no ghosts *per se*" (Dostoevsky, 6:221).[30] Thus, like the mad Germann himself, the "Conclusion" "does not answer any questions" (6:355)—about Germann *or* Lizaveta Ivanovna. The latter is as free to repeat the Countess's path as she is free to alter the very meaning of the terms "ward" and "benefactress."

At the end of the story Germann goes mad, the card game goes on, and Lizaveta Ivanovna takes in a poor relative. The "Conclusion," which pretends to tie up all the "loose ends" in the story, is too blatantly formulaic to suggest that it can—or intends to—actually finalize the unfinalizable elements within the plot. Does the fact that the story has this formal conclusion imply that everything mysterious and Romantic in it can be dismissed? Lizaveta is decidedly cynical only if nothing supernatural has happened to Germann, *and* if nothing of the sort had happened to "the late Chaplitskii" (6:323), *and* if the "realistic" interpretation of the story is, from the beginning, the only one possible. None of the story's readers seem to agree on all of these points.

Notes

* I would like to thank Olga Meerson and Marcia A. Morris for carefully reading the penultimate version of this article and offering many helpful comments and suggestions.

1. A. S. Pushkin, *Polnoe sobranie sochinenii v desiati tomakh*. 2nd ed. Vol. 6 (Moscow, 1956-1958): 356. All further references to "The Queen of Spades" will include the volume and page number from this edition. All translations are mine. References to *Eugene Onegin* will be identified with an Arabic numeral for the chapter number and a Roman numeral for the stanza number.

2. Joseph T. Shaw, "The 'Conclusion' of Pushkin's Queen of Spades," in *Studies in Russian and Polish*

Literature in Honor of Wacław Lednicki, eds. Zbigniew Folejewski et al. Slavistic Printings and Reprintings 27 (The Hague: Mouton, 1962) 126. For similar views, see Paul Debreczeny, *The Other Pushkin: A Study of Alexander Pushkin's Prose Fiction* (Stanford: Stanford University Press, 1983) 217-18, 228; Gleb Žekulin, "And in Conclusion, Who Is Tomsky? (Rereading 'The Queen of Spades'), *Transactions of the Association of Russian-American Scholars in the USA* 20 (1987): 77; Rita Poddubnaia, "O poètike *Pikovoi damy* A.S. Pushkina: Zakony zhanrovoi struktury," in *O poetyce Aleksandra Puszkina (Materiały z sesii naukowej UAM 6 i 7 XII 1974,* ed. Bohdan Galster, Seria Filologia Rosyjska 7 (Poznań, 1975): 56-57; L. S. Sidiakov, *Khudozhestvennaia proza A.S. Pushkina* (Riga, 1973) 123; M. Falchikov, "The Outsider and the Number Game (Some observations on *Pikovaya dama*)," *Essays in Poetics* 2.2 (1977): 101, 104; Gary Rosenshield, "Choosing the Right Card: Madness, Gambling, and the Imagination in Pushkin's 'The Queen of Spades'," *PMLA* 109.5 (1994): 1002.

3. See Caryl Emerson's cogent discussion in "'The Queen of Spades' and the Open End" in *Puškin Today,* ed. David Bethea (Bloomington: Indiana University Press, 1993). On Bakhtin's concept of unfinalizability, see Gary Saul Morson and Caryl Emerson, *Mikhail Bakhtin: Creation of a Prosaics* (Stanford: Stanford University Press, 1990) 36-38.

4. Discussing the triangular "semantic paradigm" of history in Pushkin's works of the 1830s (revolt of the elements-statue-man), Lotman himself insists on the "possibility of not just different but complementary," i. e., "equally adequate, and at the same time mutually exclusive" readings of such works. Iu. M. Lotman, "Tipologicheskaia kharakteristika realizma pozdnego Pushkina," *V shkole poèticheskogo slova* (Moscow, 1988) 127. While, as Lotman maintains, interpretation of one element of the paradigm determines the interpretation of the whole series, each member of the series, nonetheless, can be interpreted in several different ways. These interpretations form this member's own "microparadigm." Although a particular interpretation of one element of the triangular paradigm may be stressed in a particular text, "not a single one of these [possible interpretations] ever functions as the only one. The paradigm is given in all of its potential manifestations" (Lotman, "Tipologicheskia kharakteristika" 130.)

5. See, for example, Nathan Rosen, "The Magic Cards in 'The Queen of Spades'," *Slavic and East European Journal* 19 (1975): 274 (Note 31). I would also include here the interpretation of Lizaveta Ivanovna in Chaikovskii's opera and rewritings of the "ward's text" by Dostoevsky and other nineteenth-century Russian authors (see chapters II-V of my dissertation: Svetlana Slavskaya Grenier, "'Everyone Knew Her, No One Noticed Her': The Fate of the *Vospitannitsa* (Female Ward) in Nineteenth-Century Russian

Literature," unpub. diss, Columbia University, 1991). M. S. Altman, deriving his interpretation from Dostoevsky's use of Pushkin's plot, explains Liza's adoption of a ward by her desire to "pacify her alarmed conscience." M. S. Al'tman, "Videnie Germana. (Pushkin i Dostoevskii)," *Slavia* 9 (1932): 796.

6. Cf. Vinogradov's cautious approach to Lizaveta: "One has a sense of a deliberate unfinished-ness (*nedokonchennost'*), a certain 'openness' (*nezamknutost'*) of this character." V. V. Vinogradov, *Stil' Pushkina* (Moscow, 1941) 606.

7. Emerson 30. In an excellent article, which I read while preparing the final version of this manuscript, Gary Rosenshield, referring to Caryl Emerson's statement, demonstrates exactly how "Pushkin's use of fragmentary codes supports diametrically opposed psychological and supernatural interpretations of the plot" (996)—where Germann is concerned. He reiterates the "cynical" view of Liza, however, albeit with some caution: "Liza seems to follow the example of the countess, her former tormentor; the young woman now is in a position to visit on her own ward the injuries that she suffered as a ward" (1002).

8. Emerson 36. In my dissertation, I argue that this open-endedness has produced a tradition of literary wards—some meek, some cunning, some only seemingly meek or cunning.

9. I am using the term "code" in its basic structuralist and semiotic meaning, as developed by Ferdinand de Saussure, Roman Jakobson, and Iurii Lotman. See "Code" in *Encyclopedia of Contemporary Literary Theory: Approaches, Scholars, Terms,* ed. Irena R. Makaryk (Toronto: University of Toronto Press, 1993): 525; Cf. "When a writer chooses a certain genre, style or artistic school, he is also choosing the language [code] in which he intends to address the reader. This language enters into the complex hierarchy of the artistic languages of a given epoch, a given culture, a given people, or a given humanity." Jurij Lotman, *The Structure of the Artistic Text,* trans. Gail Lenhoff and Ronald Vroon, Michigan Slavic Contributions 7 (Ann Arbor: University of Michigan Press, 1977): 18. Compare Lotman's discussion of artistic codes on pp. 12-25. See also, "The code is a perspective of quotations, a mirage of structures; . . . the units which have resulted from it (those we inventory) are themselves, always, ventures out of the text, the mark, the sign of a virtual digression to the remainder of a catalogue . . . ; they are so many fragments of something that has always been *already* read, seen, done, experienced; the code is the wake of that *already.*" Roland Barthes, *S/Z,* trans. Richard Miller (New York: Hill and Wang, 22nd printing, 1995; first American ed., 1974): 20.

10. This conversation indeed invokes a typical plot pattern of the period (see, for example, Richardson's *Pamela* or Karamzin's *Poor Liza*); this pattern is re-

capitulated in the nineteenth century in *David Copperfield* (Steerforth and Little Em'ly), George Sand's *Indiana* (Raymond and Noun), etc.

11. On Pushkin's use of the gotho-freneticist code, see R. L. Busch, "Pushkin and the Gotho-freneticist Tradition," *Canadian Slavonic Papers* 29.2 (1987).

12. On typical appearance of the hero in Russian Romanticism, see Iu.V. Mann, *Poètika russkogo romantizma* (Moscow, 1976) 32, 34; cf. also Busch on the gotho-freneticist features in the characterization of Germann (181).

13. On the place of love in Romanticism see Mann, *Poètika* 38-39.

14. Compare Feliks Raskolnikov's discussion of Germann as a Romantic hero: F. Raskolnikoff, "Irratsional'noe v *Pikovoi dame*," *Revue des études slaves* 59.1-2 (1987): 254-55. Raskolnikov analyzes a similar example of the use of Romantic/poetic style: "Den'gi,—vot chego alkala ego dusha!" ("Money was what his heart thirsted for!") (6:345). He does not mention, however, that this sentence occurs amid what is clearly Lizaveta Ivanovna's thoughts (not distinguished from the narrator's speech in any graphic way). This example suggests that Liza's—or Liza-like—voice and consciousness may be responsible also for other instances of irruption of the Romantic code into the narrative. This Romantic voice and point of view compete with the narrator's other—cynical and "realistic"—voice. M. Falchikov also proposes the idea of multiple narrators one of whom might be Liza (Falchikov 99-100).

15. This clash of styles is just one example of the stylistic tensions generated throughout the story by the simultaneous operation of mutually exclusive paradigms. Sergei Bocharov speaks of the narrative "realizing . . . Germann's dual nature and the dual motivation of his behavior: the prosaic 'German' calculation, base acquisitiveness and 'fiery imagination,' the passion of a gambler. Both these motives operate and mix together in Germann simultaneously . . ." S. G. Bocharov, *Poètika Pushkina. Ocherki* (Moscow, 1974) 187. Maxim Shrayer makes a similar point about the reader's uncertainty as to Germann's motives at this point and until Chapter IV Maxim D. Shrayer, "Rethinking Romantic Irony: Puškin, Byron, Schlegel and *The Queen of Spades*," *Slavic and East European Journal* 36.4 (1992): 401-402. He persuasively explains Pushkin's use of various mutually exclusive paradigms by his "romantic-ironic design" (408).

16. I am indebted to Olga Meerson for pointing out to me this *visual* aspect of Pushkin's use of the "Cinderella code." I would also like to thank her for directing my attention to the relevance of Svidrigailov's ideas on ghosts to my discussion (see below, note 29).

17. N. M. Karamzin, *Izbrannye sochineniia v dvukh tomakh* vol. 1 (Moscow-Leningrad, 1964) 608.

18. Karamzin 620. As Nancy Kipnis Miller demonstrates, the 18th-century literary (gender) ideology "codes femininity in paradigms of sexual vulnerability." Nancy K. Miller, *The Heroine's Text. Readings in the French and English Novel, 1722-82* (New York: Columbia University Press, 1980) xi.

19. On the development of the physiological sketch in Russia, see A. G. Tseitlin, *Stanovlenie realizma v russkoi literature (Russkii fiziologicheskii ocherk)* (Moscow, 1965) and Iu. V. Mann, "Filosofiia i poètika 'natural'noi shkoly,'" in *Problemy tipologii russkogo realizma,* eds. N. L. Stepanov and U. R. Fokht (Moscow, 1969).

20. This note, however, is soon cancelled, to a certain extent, in the description of her first sighting of Germann: she "accidentally glanced" at the street; she was not "used to flirting with the officers passing by" (6:329).

21. Miller x.

22. Debreczeny 217.

23. Debreczeny 217, Shaw 124.

24. Debreczeny, for example, notes that "Although the narrator bursts into a pathetic tirade about the plight of the poor *demoiselles de compagnie* in the middle of Chapter Two, he soon descends to a level of realism, explaining that 'she was proud; . . .'" (Debreczeny 217).

25. "The marriage plot most novels depend on is about finding validation of one's uniqueness and importance by being singled out among all other women by a man. . . . Her quest is to be recognized in all her significance, to have her worth made real by being approved. When, at the end, this is done, she is transformed: . . . she is a bride, the very image of a heroine. . . . To want to become a heroine, to have a sense of the possibility of being one, is to develop the beginnings of what feminists call a 'raised' consciousness: it liberates a woman from feeling (and therefore perhaps from being) a victim or dependent or a drudge, someone of no account." Rachel M. Brownstein, *Becoming a Heroine: Reading about Women in Novels* (New York: Viking, 1982) xv, xix.

26. This is the view Shaw takes: "Her efforts to free herself are a compound of ignorance and desperate desire for a man who will give her independence." Shaw 124.

27. Her image of Germann was "rather like" (6:344) Tomskii's characterization of him: "He has the profile of Napoleon and the soul of Mephistopheles. I think he has at least three crimes on his conscience" (6:343).

28. Pushkin's epigraph (from Malfilâtre) to Chapter Three of *Eugene Onegin.*

29. According to Elizabeth Shepard, the society tale, as a genre, "inclines . . . to a demonstration of high society's power either to destroy the individual's happiness (or chance of happiness) or to reduce him or her

to its own level." Elizabeth C. Shepard, "The Society Tale and the Innovative Argument in Russian Prose Fiction of the 1830s, *Russian Literature* 10 (1981): 131. Iurii Mann demonstrates that the idea of the power of society ("the age") to destroy the individual's idealism informs the motif of "transformation," one of the primary structural motifs in the works of the "Natural School." Mann, "Filosofiia i poètika" 251-57.

30. F. M. Dostoevskii, *Polnoe sobranie sochinenii v tridtsati tomakh,* vol. 6 (Leningrad, 1972-90) 221. Svidrigailov's words seem to spring directly from Dostoevsky's own impressions from *The Queen of Spades.* (Cf. Dostoevsky's famous remarks in the letter to Iu. F. Abaza of 15 June 1880, where he calls Pushkin's story an exemplar of the "fantastic art" [Dostoevskii, vol. 30(1):192]). In fact, the conversation that precedes Svidrigailov's statement echoes several of Pushkin's motifs: Svidrigailov's late wife Marfa Petrovna (who plays the role of a jealous benefactress vis-à-vis Dunia Raskolnikov) appears to him three times; they had been married for seven years; when she visits him she speaks about "the most insignificant trifles"—just like the "late Baronness" who allegedly visits Swedenborg in the epigraph to chapter V; during her second visit, Marfa Petrovna has a pack of cards in her hands and offers to tell Svidrigailov's fortunes; during her third appearance, they talk about his matrimonial plans. Al'tman discusses some of these and other parallels and correctly concludes that the fact that Svidrigailov experiences Germann's "vision" confirms both Svidrigailov's function as Raskolnikov's "double" and Raskolnikov's origins in Germann. Al'tman does not, however, point out that the whole Germann-Countess-Lizaveta triangle is reduplicated as both Raskolnikov-Pawnbroker-Lizaveta/Sonia and, on another level, Svidrigailov-Marfa Petrovna-Dunia, proving even further Dostoevsky's great fascination with Pushkin's novella—and not just with its hero but with all its aspects. Notice that in neither case does Dostoevsky read Liza as a calculating pragmatist. For other examples of Dostoevsky's use of *The Queen of Spades* see Altman, A. L. Bem, "*Pikovaia dama* v tvorchestve Dostoevskogo," in *O Dostoevskom,* vol. 3 *U istokov tvorchestva Dostoevskogo* (Prague: Petropolis, 1929-1936 [Reprint ed., Ann Arbor: University Microfilms, 1963]) and Grenier (ch. 5)

Gary Rosenshield (essay date spring 1996)

SOURCE: Rosenshield, Gary. "Freud, Lacan, and Romantic Psychoanalysis: Three Psychoanalytic Approaches to Madness in Pushkin's *The Queen of Spades.*" *Slavic and East European Journal* 4, no. 1 (spring 1996): 1-26.

[*In the following essay, Rosenshield provides a psychoanalytical perspective on* The Queen of Spades, *focusing on the nature and significance of the protagonist's madness.*]

1. Introduction

Scholars and critics have offered more ingenious and diverse interpretations of *The Queen of Spades* than of any other work in Russian literature of the nineteenth century. But they have curiously paid relatively little attention to the nature and significance of the hero's madness—certainly the most dramatic event in the tale.[1] This critical lacuna is understandable: in contrast to the heroes of *King Lear* or Dostoevskii's *The Double,* Germann, the hero of *The Queen of Spades,* goes clinically mad only at the very end of the story, in the brief epilogue. That is, until the epilogue, Germann, just like his direct descendent, Raskol'nikov, must take responsibility for all his actions. But if *The Queen of Spades* does not tell a tale about full-blown madness, it certainly tells a tale about going mad, a theme of far greater interest and critical import than clinical insanity, and one furthermore which, in contrast to clinical insanity, Pushkin sets in motion on the first page.

I have chosen a psychoanalytical approach because it offers perhaps the best means of unraveling the dynamics and meaning of Germann's madness in *The Queen of Spades.* Since different psychoanalytical models of personality diverge dramatically in their understanding of the role of the ego in mental health and disorder, they will lead, in literature as in life, to different interpretations and evaluative assessments of madness. But assuming, paraphrasing Dostoevskii,[2] that even seemingly contradictory psychoanalytical interpretations need not cancel each other out and may even shed equal, but different, light on the same phenomenon, I have utilized and adapted Freudian, romantic, and Lacanian personality models in the hope of illuminating some of the most problematic sections of the story. I first analyze Germann's madness using a traditional Freudian personality model based on American ego-psychology. I hope to show that this model accounts, more satisfactorily than previous interpretations, for Germann's rapid transition from remarkable self-control to ultimate risk and finally insanity. I then turn to a contrasting, ego-devalorized model of personality based on Lacan's mirror-stage, a model which illuminates Germann's ego-ideal (the construct of the superego) and his preoccupation with the ace of spades, the *tuz.* Lacan's devaluation of the ego-ideal does not, however, open the door to a romantic validation of untrammeled desire and an embracing of Germann's madness. I show in detail how such an embracing of madness (the queen), though quite consistent with Romantic psychoanalysis (that of Deleuze and Guitari or Laing, for example), is almost as antithetical to a Lacanian "ideal," because of its rejection of the Symbolic Order, as Germann's obsession with the ego-ideal (the ace). In the last section, I deal with the relation between Germann and his creator (the implied and historical author) in an attempt to understand more fully Germann's place in the Symbolic Order. Is Germann, whom Dostoevskii without irony called "a colossal figure," condemned irrevocably to the ultimate Lacanian punishment of linguistic idiocy or does he "escape" his creator's prison?[3]

I intend the following psychoanalytic interpretations not to be *strictly* Freudian or Lacanian, but rather theories of personality suggested by Freudian, Romantic, and Lacanian models of the ego and the unconscious in their widest senses, and adapted as interpretative strategies for understanding literary texts. These models, being both prescriptive and descriptive, not only describe the role the ego and unconscious play in the life of civilized men and women, but also suggest the role they should play.[4] Further, I am not presenting Freud and Lacan as psychoanalytical antitheses. Lacan understood his own work not as a replacement but as a recovery, a rediscovery, of Freud, a means of exposing the misunderstanding and distortions of the ego-psychologists, Freud's, mostly American, followers and "heirs." Lacan capsulizes his own approach in his interpretation of Freud's famous statement on the ego and the id in his *New Introductory Lectures* (*wo es war, soll Ich werden*) not as an authoritative pronouncement, but as a metaphor inviting multiple interpretations, one of which informs the interpretations offered here. At times I take the same liberty with Lacan as Lacan takes with Freud, stretching his model, in places, to accommodate Pushkin's text.[5] I have not taken liberty with Pushkin's texts by applying psychoanalytical methods, for the interpretations I propose here do not violate the spirit of Pushkin's story, nor do they exceed in extravagance or fancy the numerous numerological, masonic, and cabalistic interpretations that the story has generated for over 160 years.[6]

2. FREUD

In the last decades of his life, Freud worked continually on a tripartite model of personality centered around the ego and its attempt to mediate between the instinctual drives emanating from the id and the internalized constraints on those drives imposed by the superego. Freud never meant these concepts to be understood as static, reified entities but rather as dynamic functions and relationships; and he himself continued to rework and refine them to his death. (I use these concepts in my discussion of Freud, Lacan, and others as a form of metaphoric shorthand, not as reifications of psychological processes.) The followers of Lacan refer to Freud's later psychological theories, somewhat disparagingly as ego-psychology because these theories emphasize the positive role of the ego. For Freud the ego should be the hero of the narrative of personality since the mental health of the individual depends directly on the ego's ability to mediate the opposing demands of its two merciless masters, the superego and the id. The more successfully the ego keeps the unrealistic strictures of the superego and the libidinous demands of the id in check and/or satisfied, the more energy, the more psychic space, it can appropriate from the id for its own realistic, rational purposes—for the personality, for the self. Progress in the personality is essentially marked by the increase in the domain of the ego at the expense of the id and superego. At the end of the third of his *New Introductory Lectures on Psychoanalysis,* Freud writes:

> Nevertheless it may be admitted that the therapeutic efforts of psycho-analysis have chosen a similar line of approach. Its intention is, indeed, to strengthen the ego,

to make it more independent of the super-ego, to widen its field of perception and enlarge its organization, so that it can appropriate fresh portions of the id. Where id was, there ego shall be ("wo es war, soll Ich werden"). It is a work of culture—not unlike the draining of the Zuider Zee.

> (80)

Thus in ego-psychology, madness represents the direst of all imaginable fates for Germann, for it signifies the death-in-life of the mind and thus, the self. Germann's plot embodies the antithesis of Freud's wish for a stronger, more independent, and enlarged ego, since throughout the story his ego undergoes a progressive deterioration, ending in complete failure. At the beginning, Germann's concern for his patrimony (his inheritance in all its senses, from his father) and his desire for gambling (even for its own sake) coexist in a state of tense and fragile equilibrium. Germann greatly values his ego-ideal (that is, the ideal of the superego) of position, wealth, and progeny, but he takes little joy in it, for it demands prudence, moderation, and hard work (*raschet, umerennost',* and *trudoliubie*), those three *reliable* cards of the superego, which represent values that Freud describes as essential to civilization but also responsible for its discontents (*Civilization* 39-41). As E. M. Forster writes in *Howard's End*: "those who prepare for all the emergencies of life beforehand may equip themselves at the expense of joy." These values represent the distortions of desire; they are desired because they are desired by others.

However, the demands of the id rival those of the superego. Germann is not, as many have argued, interested in cards solely as a way of increasing his fortune without risk (Emerson 45; Boucher 12). As the narrator says, Germann is "a gambler at heart" (*v dushe igrok,* 8:235); gambling constitutes the very core of his desire, of his irrational self. Is it really imperative, in following in one's father's footsteps, to increase one's patrimony three and seven times? When Germann says that he is not in a position to sacrifice what is necessary to obtain the superfluous, he means that his father's idea (perhaps the German idea in contrast to the Russian one) requires only the preservation of (and addition to) the family fortune, not its geometric increase. Thus Germann's dream of sudden immense fortune represents less a desire to preserve and add to his father's patrimony than a displacement of his desire to gamble. It is often argued that Germann derives the three magic cards from his desire to increase his capital, as he says, threefold, sevenfold (Vinogradov, Slonimskii 175-176), and to become independent, a *tuz* (an ace).[7] But in fact it is the desire to gamble that transforms the various combinations in faro into a plan for self-aggrandizement—the cards become merely the signifiers of Germann's libidinous desire, not a means to fortune.[8]

Since Germann is really more passionate (Dostoevskii would call him a "colossal figure") than cool and calculating, he seems bound, sooner or later, to take matters to their extreme conclusions.[9] On one hand, Germann's passion for gambling clashes with the superego's demand for *raschet, umerennost'*, and *trudoliubie*. On the other hand, the superego, always ready to exact punishment, in guilt, for the ego's concessions to libidinal satisfaction, for even courting desire, will not easily countenance giving in to passion. For the superego, according to Freud, does not distinguish between desire and satisfaction—that is, thoughts and deeds: "The distinction . . . between doing something bad and wishing to do it disappears entirely, since nothing can be hidden from the superego, not even thoughts" (*Civilization* 72).

Germann has long haunted the gaming tables. He would sit whole nights, following with feverish excitement the various changes in the course of play. He also openly admits that gambling fascinates him (*igra zanimaet menia sil'no*, 8:227). Soon after he hears Tomskii's tales about his grandmother's success at cards, all the libidinal forces that have been held in check by the ego seek expression in the desire to gamble, not so much for the sake of fortune, but for the sake of gambling itself; that is, for the sake of risk, chance, and danger. He needs to exchange the three sure cards of the superego, no matter what the sacrifice, for those magic cards that will attain for him "the superfluous": the greatest desire of the id. Horrified at the possible abandonment of the ego-ideal, the superego marshals its forces, resorting to its own three cards of prudence, moderation, and hard work. But neither "side" can gain complete ascendancy, for gambling is unacceptable to the superego and a life of continued moderation is no longer acceptable to the id.

Previously, the ego had been able to hold these contending passions in check, in effect, to negotiate a compromise. Before hearing the story (*skazka*) at the Narumovs', Germann has done well in society, working his way through the military ranks. After he hears the story, however, the old compromises and restraints no longer work. Germann disguises his passion for gambling as a higher form of prudence: that is, as a way of fulfilling his obligation of adding to his patrimony and establishing his own line, "the paternal order of genealogy," as Kristeva describes it (152). Although a paradox, it seems like an ideal compromise—a scheme of gambling without risk. We can see the imaginative shape of the compromise in the account of the countess's visit to Germann. Ostensibly, the countess comes to Germann to give him the secret cards, assuring him of victory (the desire of the id). But it is a victory with strictures: he is not to forget his goal of settling down and starting a family; he must marry the countess's ward, Liza; he must not forget the legacy of his father; he must never gamble again (the demands of the superego).

This attempt simultaneously to placate both the id and superego, to realize the paradox, is doomed to failure. Germann's ego is not weak; it is simply unable, after his imagination has been inflamed, to contend with the increasingly powerful and uncompromising demands of both id and superego. Since there can be no rational, "ego-engendered," solution to Germann's situation, no resolu-

tion of the conflict between the superego and the id, the ego increasingly leaves the field to its irreconcilable and more powerful masters.

This struggle within Germann reaches its terrible conclusion at the gambling tables, where only play can decide the issue. On the last day, the day of the third card, Germann, to be sure, is veering on the edge of madness; however, he is still sane. He is still sane for he has not yet really gambled; he cannot know that he has really risked anything, since his first two cards have won as predicted; they have proved reliable. But the makeshift compromise of the ego is now rejected in favor of libidinal desire. Germann now must really play, gamble, risk. He must show himself that he has not been given three sure cards, for those three cards are nothing but the formula of calculation, the absence of risk, the ego-ideal. He must now lose in order to win; he must lose to prove that he has really played. He must choose the wrong card, which is the right card. He must choose the queen (desire) and not the ace (the ideal of the father).[10] But the loss of everything, of his entire patrimony, brings upon Germann the punishment of the father—the embodiment of the superego—whose prescriptions he flagrantly violated in pursuit of forbidden libidinal desires, the personification of which is the queen of spades, the queen mother, the ultimate object of forbidden desire, transformed, in the story, by the superego into a temptress, witch, and destroyer. The symbolically realized desire for the mother must always entail the loss of patrimony, for patrimony is the prime compensation of the child for renouncing the rights to the mother.[11] Thus, we see that Germann never really had a choice at all; the ace and the queen, each in its own way, are both the wrong card—each leads to a life completely unacceptable to the other. The final scene merely works out the fate, the madness, latent in Germann's character from the very beginning, from the moment when he first heard the tale of the three cards.

The ego's compromise of gambling without gambling is destroyed on contact with the real world. In contrast to the draining of Zuider Zee, Freud's metaphor for the aggrandizement of the ego at the expense of the superego and the id, in **The Queen of Spades** we have a bursting of the dikes; the power of the ego is nullified. In the end, neither desire nor civilization survives. The personality suffers a complete disintegration, Germann goes hopelessly insane.

3. LACAN: THE MIRROR STAGE

Whereas the Freudian model suggests an unfortunate, perhaps even tragic Germann, the "victim" of powerful forces he cannot control, it does not cast the desires of the id or the constraints of the superego as villains. Had the ego proven stronger or the demands of the id and superego weaker, a viable, though not necessarily happy, compromise could have emerged. The Lacanian model adopts a pejorative attitude toward the whole process of mediation and stasis that is the hallmark of ego-psychology. It does not see at all the failure of the ego as central to Germann's dismal fate.

The Lacanian view of personality, despite its Freudian base, differs radically from the late Freudian model both in its conception and evaluation of the ego and its role in adult life. For Lacan, the ego does not represent the ideal, the real self, the part of the personality whose control over, and growth at the expense of, the unconscious constitutes the sine qua non of healthy adult psychological development.[12] Rather it is one of the earliest aspects of the personality to be formed, occurring in the prelinguistic, pre-oedipal stage of human development (the imaginary stage), and it remains for the entire life of a person an obstacle to overcome, almost a prison from which one must seek liberation. Lacan describes the ego as an alienating identity and repeatedly ascribes to it, in varying degrees, paranoia, narcissism, aggression, and *méconnaissance* ("false knowledge"). The ego evolves in what Lacan calls the mirror (or imaginary) stage, when the child first sees himself in the mirror—his mirror image—and gains a false, idealized image of himself, as a whole, unified, integral self. The ego's quest of wholeness, autonomy, and mastery of its environment involves a futile exercise reflecting the most superficial ends of the personality. Worse still, it stands in the way of the truth of the unconscious.

For Lacan, the ego always misreads the truth that comes from the unconscious, for the truth of the unconscious can be glimpsed only through its metaphoric condensations and metonymic displacements when the individual enters the Symbolic Order, which is based on, and mediated by, language. Only by entering the Symbolic Order can the individual overcome the demands of the ego for unity, wholeness, and fixity and open himself up to the linguistically mediated manifestations of the unconscious. The mature subject has access to the repressed because the mature subject lives in the world of language (the Symbolic); whereas the ego—which derives from a presymbolic, pre-oedipal phase of development, in which identity (the mirror), not difference (the Symbolic) is the dominant—struggles against the very notion of a shifting, indeterminate, and linguistically mediated truth.

Ego-psychology equates the collapse of Germann's ego with spiritual and mental death. For Lacanian psychology, on the other hand, Germann's main problem rests in the ego itself: Germann resembles an adult arrested in the mirror stage of development. He has devoted his whole life before the *skazka* to a rational, closed, infallible plan of existence. Unwilling to sacrifice the necessary for the superfluous, he seems to desire most of all "peace and independence" (*pokoi i nezavisimost'*, 8:235) the false ego-ideal of stasis, wholeness, autonomy, and mastery of the future. At the beginning of the story he has resisted all temptation to diverge from his plan; in fact, he must steel himself against the promptings of the unconscious, and the responsibilities of a subject, precisely because he senses that he is a gambler at heart.

Germann's rational side, however, is not merely a manifestation of a strong paternal superego, for his "patrimony" is not the Father (the Law of the Father of the Symbolic Order), but a mirror image of his materialistic ego-ideal. Germann does not pass precipitately from a small fortune and sanity to ruin and madness, for, from a Lacanian point of view, he has reached the nadir of his psychological "fortune" at the very beginning, as he controls the forces raging within, as he continues to stand by, refusing to take part in the life that seethes around him. As we have seen, Germann is already on the make; he has a position in the Engineers, and, given the experience of those of German origin in the tsarist state and military bureaucracies, he seems destined to eventual prestige and an even larger fortune. He has preserved his patrimony intact and will be soon adding to it, just, as we must presume, his father did before him.

However, once Germann hears about the countess's secret of the three cards, his commitment to his ego-ideal becomes overwhelming, enlisting both his passion and fantasy. Germann's dreams, in which the unconscious, in its various disguises, should most reveal itself, do not seem to reflect unconscious content or conflict at all; they contain no ingenious displacements and compensations that point to a truth that can transform his life. For example, immediately after hearing the countess's story, Germann spends a restless night thinking of nothing but the three cards. "The anecdote about the three cards had a powerful effect on his imagination; all night he could not stop thinking about it" (Anekdot o trekh kartakh sil'no podeistvoval na ego voobrazhenie, i tseluiu noch' ne vykhodil iz ego golovy, 8:235). The content of his dreams is almost identical to his conscious thoughts and therefore requires little interpretation.

> He returned late to his humble lodging, but he could not sleep for a long time; and when at last sleep overcame him, he dreamed of cards, a green table, piles of banknotes and heaps of gold coins. He played card after card, decisively turning down the corners of his cards, and he won continually, raking in the gold and putting the notes into his pocket. After waking up quite late, he sighed over the loss of his fantastic wealth.
>
> (8:236)

The same transparent wish fulfillment reveals itself in many of Germann's other daydreams, hallucinations, and nightmares. The above dream is repeated in a more dramatic form in the fifth chapter. Here Germann again returns from the countess, this time from the dead countess, who has, he imagines, just winked at him from her coffin. He throws himself on his bed fully clothed and falls into a deep sleep. The Countess then visits him from beyond the grave, revealing her secret to him and stipulating perfectly acceptable conditions. He must play on three successive days: the bank probably does not have enough money to cover three successive wins in one day. He must not play ever again in his life: why should he play again once he has attained his fortune? He must marry Liza: if he is going to be a wealthy man he will need a wife, and Liza is extremely pretty, charming, and undemanding.

When Germann wakes up the following day to play his first card, he is obsessed with the names of the cards he has learned from the countess. The narrator's description of Germann's thoughts and dreams show clearly Germann's incipient schizophrenia and again the lack of a significant distinction between Germann's conscious thoughts and his dreams.

> Three, seven, ace began to eclipse in Germann's imagination the image of the dead old woman. Three, seven, ace didn't leave him for a moment and played continually on his lips. If he saw a young girl, he would say: "How slender she is! A real trey of hearts." If anyone asked him the time, he would answer: "Five minutes to the seven." Every pot-bellied man he saw reminded him of the ace. Three, seven, ace haunted him in his sleep, assuming all possible forms.
>
> (8:249)

The merging of Germann's waking and dream life, indicating the erasure in Germann's mind between himself and the real world, of course prefigures final schizophrenic breakdown. But even more important, again we see that, as the narrator says, "All his thoughts fused into one: to make use of the secret which had cost him so dearly" (8:249). The three cards of Germann's obsession do not seem to harbor any special unconscious code: they are merely the cards that Germann must choose to attain his ego-ideal of peace and independence—that is, identification—characteristic of the mirror stage. "He thought of retirement and of traveling. He wanted to compel fortune to yield up her treasure to him in the public gambling houses of Paris" (8:249).

Pushkin sets up the card game at the end in such fashion as to present the possibility of Germann's achieving his ego-ideal: an achievement of absolute mirror identity. Germann will become exactly what he dreamed of becoming. Further, on three successive days he will exactly match his three winning cards. On the last day he will achieve the ultimate identity and union with, of course, the ace. But when the opportunity arrives, when the ego-ideal is virtually in his grasp, Germann makes a mistake, he chooses the wrong card. More important, he chooses the wrong card *unconsciously*. For the first time in the story, the conscious and unconscious content of Germann's mind fail to coincide; in fact, they radically diverge. At long last, the unconscious reveals itself in all its power and truth—in *difference*; it reveals to him, and to us, the illusory nature of the dream of independence, peace, and unity, the insufficiency of the ego-ideal. At the moment of what seems to be the achievement of ultimate unity, the story seems to declare itself for ultimate separation, disunity, and disruption; the unconscious has spoken. The story speaks the truth of the unconscious, at last. It seems to end on a note of the highest possible truth.

For Freud the draining of Zuider Zee was at best a hope, for he was essentially pessimistic about human happiness and survival. The cultural institutions essential for preserving the human race also prevented the satisfaction of elemental sexual and aggressive desires: happiness. Germann's madness suggests the fate potentially lurking for all of us just beyond the juggling act of the ego. For Lacan,

whose psychology seems at times a never-ending attempt to deconstruct the metaphor of Freud's Zuider Zee, the psychological forces are, as we have seen, differently distributed: the ego, rather than being man's greatest hope, is at best an obstacle to truth. Lacan interprets Freud's, "*Wo es war, soll Ich werden,*" not as "the ego must dislodge the id" (Lacan, *Four* 44) but rather that the ego must be at home where the id (or rather the true subject, "the unconscious . . . *itself*" was [Lacan, *Écrits* 314]): that is, "in the field of the dream" where the voice of the gods is heard, where the subject "must come into existence" (Lacan, *Four* 45). I must be somewhere other than where I am now.[13] From a Lacanian point of view, madness in *The Queen of Spades* seems not so much the paradigmatic failure of a great Freudian compromise, but the price we sometimes must pay for the existential experience of truth.

But does this Lacanian interpretation of Germann's mistake really valorize Germann's madness? Does it even mean that he has chosen the right card? To answer this question we need to see Lacan's view of desire against the background of romantic psychoanalysis, which takes the valorization of madness to its extreme conclusion.

4. ROMANTIC PSYCHOANALYSIS/ANTIPSYCHIATRY

In an earlier article on *The Queen of Spades* ("Choosing the Right Card"), arguing for a more romantic interpretation of the story, I concluded that Germann's choice of the queen was disastrous both morally and spiritually, but it was nevertheless the right choice. The queen was an unconscious decision taken against the shallow ideal of bourgeois comfort and security or, in Lacanian terms, against the mirror stage ideal of autonomy, stasis, and identity. Yet a Lacanian interpretation, however much it privileges the unconscious over the ego, cannot take the romantic jump from ace to queen that some of the more romantic or revolutionary psychoanalytic writers (Laing, Deleuze, Guitarri) might suggest or even advocate.

From a more romantic point of view, the real Germann seeks not security and autonomy, the most superficial side of his self, but adventure and risk. The real Germann, unbeknownst to himself, has taken a journey to the other side in exploration of his true being, the being associated with unconscious desire.[14] Whereas at the beginning of the story Germann's passionate nature and the desire of the unconscious are effectively repressed—Germann having not once deviated from his ideal of prudence, moderation, and hard work—at the end, the irrational and the unconscious take over almost completely. There are traces of the old ego-ideal: stout men remind him naturally of aces, but he also sees them transformed into spiders, a displacement that reveals his unconscious revulsion toward his former ego-ideal, an ideal which had caught him and imprisoned him in its fatal web, sucking the life juices from him. As has been previously noted (Rosen 260-270), sexual imagery abounds: young girls turn into threes and threes into flowers; sevens become Gothic portals. Germann seems less a man who possesses the secret of the three cards than a gambler possessed by one great desire: to play, nothing more. Whether he wins or not must now be irrelevant. Dostoevskii saw the very same thing in Raskol'nikov, who really planned a robbery to commit a murder, not a murder to commit a robbery. Germann must test whether he can dare to place everything on a card, to find out *not* whether he is a man or a mouse, as Raskol'nikov conceived of his deed, but whether he is a creature of imitation and identification, an automaton in the mold of his father, or whether he is a man, a creature of desire for the sake of desire, who can stake his whole existence on a game of pure chance.

Pushkin presents the last three days of Germann's sanity with the utmost concision. We learn little about Germann's state on the first two days. We know that after the first day of play Germann drank a glass of lemonade and went home. There is nothing more to tell for everything rests on the third day. *The Queen of Spades* begins with Germann silently watching others play; now he silently plays himself. The *skazka* has become a reality—for him. The irrational has taken up residence in the light of day.

The playing of the three cards on successive days seems at first curious (Rosen 257-258). But perhaps Pushkin is giving Germann time to experience for a few short days the life of desire: on the second day to experience the repetition, which in psychoanalytic theory is essential for the validation of experience, and to peak, of his own volition, only on the last day. Life happens in the gaps, the breaks, the ruptures, not in the everyday. "Life can happen to us only in an instant, like a flash of lightning, and only on condition that we be open to it and move toward it" (Cixous 112). Ordinary life has been sacrificed for life lived on an entirely different plane, in which the self is in direct contact with its essence, its unconscious desire. To be sure, the rebellion against the father (Germann's father) and the mother (the countess) cannot long go unpunished. Germann inflicts the punishment, as we have seen, on himself. But it is, in a way, a triumphant destruction, a destruction that he unconsciously brings down upon himself, for in the end only by losing could he have really played, risked the necessary in order to obtain the superfluous. For as Cixous says, "risk is the other word for life . . . We can say that being is without shelter (*sans abri*), without protection, but salvation is precisely in risk" (113).

The story presents Germann's madness, his pathetic reduction to a body without a mind, not as an incontestable mark of perdition and damnation, but as a sort of triumph in disaster. Given his ego-ideal at the beginning of the story, Germann progresses from a blind, illusory sanity to a few moments, if not a few days, of truth in madness, in mad abandonment, in the sacrifice of "the necessary" for the "superfluous," that is, in fact, the "sacrifice" of the superfluous for the necessary. Germann's madness is the price he has to pay to find himself. It is, at least, a human being who goes mad. Madness, for Germann, for a man imprisoned by a repressive ego-ideal, marks the end of the path to liberation and a higher form of sanity. Germann's

madness not only culminates the process that began after he heard Tomskii's *skazka*, it also validates that process.

Germann's madness, to be sure, lacks the traditional heroic stature. He fails to achieve that insight, compassion, and wisdom sometimes vouchsafed to the mad tragic hero, like Lear, or to the mad artist, genius, or religious seer, like Dostoevskii's Prince Myshkin. He treats Liza unconscionably. But romantically conceived, *The Queen of Spades* presents not so much a tale about man in his relation to the social world as a tale about the perdition and salvation of the individual soul in terms of the individual's relation to himself.

The price of the truth for Germann was, and perhaps could not have been anything other than, insanity. R. D. Laing, who sees the journey to the other side as essential to all spiritual rebirth, concedes that "not everyone comes back us to again" (138). Yet "we have to blast our way through the solid wall, even if at the risk of chaos, madness, and death. For from this side of the wall, this is the risk. There are no assurances, no guarantees" (143). Certainly Germann would not have ranked higher had he achieved his ideal of security and autonomy, the "negative" ideal of Kalinovich and Chichikov, an estate of a thousand souls.[15] Was not his embracing—at last—of the irrational a victory of the individual, of the personality in its attempt to overcome the stultifying imprisonment of the ego-ideal?

Achilles was given the choice of an undistinguished long life or a short illustrious one. He chose glory over old age. Perhaps what he really chose was a life lived at a fever pitch over one of uneventful security. Soon after Germann heard the story of the three cards he chose the madness of the irrational over the sanity of the ego-ideal. For a few weeks he lived at an intensity that he had never even dreamed of, such was the force of his repressive ego-ideal. He burnt out quickly, but for the first time in his life he did not calculate, but lived. On this day, more than ever before, it is no longer possible for Germann to win at cards, that is, to attain his father's desire, to gain "a thousand souls," and not at the same time completely to lose his own soul: to cut himself off even more completely from himself and the truth of desire—from life, from his sense of being alive. "Far from having lost who knows what contact with life, the schizophrenic is closest to the beating heart of reality, to an intense point identical with the production of the real" (Deleuze 87). Seen from this point of view, Germann's fate in *The Queen of Spades* embodies the essence of literary and psychoanalytical romanticism.[16]

5. LACAN: THE DESIRE OF THE OTHER

But no Lacanian interpretation can really countenance a victory, if it is characterized by the hero's retreat into an autistic shell, muttering incessantly nothing but "Three, seven, ace. Three seven, queen," the ultimate linguistic reduction: the nullification of semantic difference. Might not the choice of the queen be almost as flawed a choice as the ace? In fact, from a Lacanian perspective, may the queen, just like the ace—until the unconscious breakthrough at the very end—correspond not to the highest truth, the truth of unconscious desire, but to a form of imaginary desire, a "lower" form of desire associated, like Germann's desire for fortune and stasis, primarily with the ego?[17] Although the desire associated with the queen exists in opposition to, even in conflict with, the desire associated with the ace, it, too, is a form of imaginary desire.

The traces of imaginary desire associated with the queen can be inferred, however, not from Germann's dreams—which, as we have seen, offer little material for deciphering—but from Tomskii's *skazka*. All readers, like Germann, have assumed that when Germann heard Tomsky's tale he became obsessed with the desire to make his fortune without risk, simply by learning the countess's secret. It seems perfectly consistent, albeit irrational, that a superstitious man, obsessed with fortune, would pursue a secret bound to make him fabulously rich without risk. This is only one of the vectors (plots) of imaginary desire—the achievement of Germann's ego-ideal, the replication of his father's identity. There is another very different plot of imaginary desire associated with Saint Germain, the hero of the countess's tale about pleasure, not fortune.

The secret of this other desire resides not in the cards themselves—they are, despite Germann's wishes, signifiers not signifieds—but in the relationships they call into play in Tomskii's tale. Germann secretly yearns not for a specific person, but for an entire age called up by the tale. In the present age, the ego-ideal has displaced pleasure; everyone is seeking, in one way or another, his fortune.[18] The epilogue shows the heroine, the *declassé,* once dependent Liza and the high-society aristocrat Tomskii seeking their fortunes no less deviously and assiduously than Germann. They, in fact, turn out to be the real "Germanns" in the story. In Russian society of the 1830s marriage was increasingly becoming a financial transaction. Tomskii's tale takes Germann back to what seems to him (we are obviously not speaking of facts) an age when desire reigned supreme, a completely frivolous time, preoccupied with gambling, magic, and love, an age whose dominant figures know nothing of prudence, moderation, and hard work. The countess, *la Vénus moscovite,* plays without any regard for her losses, and her secret friend Saint Germain can solve her monetary problems without recourse to anything so prosaic as a loan. With no money at all, she presents herself at the gambling salon to bet on three cards in succession and "wins back everything" (8:229). She does not win a fortune—for what purpose?—only enough to repay her debt and return, unimpeded, to her frivolous life in the French capital: that is, to a life of pleasure.

For Germann, the young countess is not so much a particular beauty but the other, the object of desire itself. "You should know that about sixty years ago my grandmother used to travel to Paris, where she created a sensation. People would run after her, just to catch a glimpse of *la Vénus moscovite.* Richelieu paid court to her, and grandmother insists that he almost shot himself from her cruelty" (8:228). Thus, not even Richelieu was able to attain her! Pushkin devotes a great deal of time to the description, through Germann's eyes, of the countess's bedroom/boudoir. It is certainly faded, just as the countess, but it also has definite reminders of the age which catered to the frivolous desires of fashionable women. "In all the corners, he could see porcelain shepherdesses, table clocks made by the famed Leroy, little boxes, *roulettes,* fans and playthings for ladies, invented at the end of the last century together with Mongolfier's balloon and Mesmer's magnetism" (8:240). Just as Germann stood transfixed before the countess's house, he now seems "mesmerized" by the playthings associated with the countess's youth—an attachment to partial objects characteristic of all fetishists.

But Germann is equally, if not more attracted, to his namesake, but antithesis, the "remarkable" Saint Germain, the Lacanian object of the (m)other's desire. The identity of the real Saint Germain is irrelevant; the only important Saint Germain is the one who speaks to Germann. Tomskii says "You've heard of Count Saint Germain, about whom they tell so many marvelous stories. You know he passed himself off as the Wandering Jew, the inventor of the elixir of life and of the philosopher's stone, and so forth. He was laughed at as a charlatan, and Casanova in his memoirs says that he was a spy; however, Saint Germain, despite his mysteriousness, was a man of very respectable appearance, who knew how to behave in society" (8:228).

Tomskii's tale is hardly credible, he even seems purposely to tell the tale in a way that undermines it.[19] But for Germann, the figures of the tale are as real as the secret that the countess supposedly possesses. Saint Germain belongs to that society of desire; he has a respectable appearance and knows how to behave in society; on the other hand, he is not bound by and to it, he is not identical with it. Affable, presentable, carefree, eccentric, generous, accommodating, he is a man who can easily say that for the resolution of life's problems "money is not necessary" (229). To Germann, he stands on the outside, as spy, necromancer, Wandering Jew, and alchemist, a seeker after life's greatest secrets; he is someone who has had access to the countess, the epitome of desire for an age obsessed with desire; he is the father who has enjoyed the desire (*jouissance*) forbidden to the child. As Lacan says: "Nowhere does it appear more clearly than man's desire finds its meaning in the desire of the other, not so much because the other holds the key to the object desired, as because the first object [goal, GR] of desire is to be recognized by the other" (58). In other words, Germann seeks the countess because he wishes to be recognized, acknowledged by Saint Germain—as his son?—who as other defines his being, his position as a subject.

If Germann seeks only the secret of the cards, the countess must be seen, like Liza, as a means to an end. But if the *skazka* opens up the more passionate, imaginative, irrational sides of Germann, it must open him up far more to the pursuit of desire, however imaginary, than to the pursuit of the prosaic ideal of comfort and independence.[20] Germann, thus, seeks out the countess less to learn the secret of the three cards than to confront the countess—not the countess herself, but the countess that has come in his mind to represent an age of desire, a world, moreover, that exists locked up within his own psyche.[21] From this point of view, Germann needs the cards to get to the countess, not the countess to get to the cards. The need to learn the secret is a pretext for other ends.

When we first meet Germann after Tomskii tells the tale, Germann is already obsessed by the tale and the possibility of fabulous fortune. He is already thinking of persuading the countess to reveal her secret to him. Dismissing the absurdity of the tale and idea, Germann says to himself: "Can one really believe it? No! Prudence, moderation, and hard work; these are my three reliable cards. They are what will increase my capital threefold and sevenfold, and bring me peace and independence." Since, as Shaw has pointed out, one of the meanings of ace (*tuz*) in Russian is a wealthy man of comfort and independence, the three cards three/seven/ace are given to Germann from the very beginning. Or rather while dismissing the tale as unsubstantiated nonsense, Germann invents (imagines) the three cards for himself. No sooner does he invent the cards—that is, in the very next sentence—than he finds himself in front of the countess's house. The cards lead to the countess, not the other way round.

> Pondering these matters, he suddenly found himself on one of the main streets of Petersburg, in front of a house of old-fashioned architecture . . .
>
> "Whose house is this?" he asked a policeman.
>
> "The countess N.'s," answered the policeman.
>
> Germann began to tremble. The amazing story of the three cards again appeared before his imagination.
>
> (8:236)

The magic of the three cards works; it has led him, without consciously knowing, to his real destination. The narrator writes that Germann began to tremble (*zatrepetal*). But the Russian verb *trepetat'* also means to experience a thrill, a palpitation of the heart. Germann experiences a thrill of horror, but even more tellingly, perhaps even a secret thrill of delight (*jouissance*). His imagination is immediately set aflame again and he begins to circle the countess's house. On returning home, he cannot fall asleep; when he does, he dreams of nothing but gambling. He wakes up and the process begins again—the psychoanalytical repetition-compulsion—again he wanders aimlessly about the city, but he winds up (once more the same Russian verb, *ochutilsia* is repeated) in front of the countess's house—the first time was obviously no accident.[22] He interprets the coincidence as an unknown force drawing him to the house.

To be sure, it is an unknown force, but it is an internal, not an external one. Germann returns to the house—home—precisely to find out what this force is, this force which has existed in him all the time, but only now is claiming its due. Freud describes uncanny experiences like Germann's, including his own, in terms of repetition-compulsion ("The 'Uncanny,'" 2:389-391). He defines the uncanny (*unheimlich*) as that which is most intimate (*heimisch*—because associated with home—but which is repressed). "In this case, too, the *unheimlich* is what was once *heimisch*, home-like, familiar; the prefix 'un' is a token of repression" (2:399). The repetition compulsion is a sign of an almost demonic unconscious desire, the unconscious repressed striving for expression, or in Lacanian terms, insisting to be heard.

When Germann finally enters her boudoir, he finds, of course, in addition to the accouterments of the eighteenth century, the century of desire, a decrepit old woman, hardly *la Vénus moscovite*. But there is also something demonic and witchlike about the old woman. She cannot satisfy Germann's desire, but she can assist him in discovering the hidden: the repressed within himself.

After frightening the countess to death, Germann comes to her funeral. He must somehow revive her. He wishes her back. He steps up to the coffin, bends over, and thinks that the countess winks at him. He steps backwards, misses his step, and falls flat on his back. He is mistaken for the countess's "natural son" (*pobochnyi syn*): that is, the countess is mistaken for his mother, of course, the ultimate object of desire.[23] The countess beckons him: that is, he beckons her. In the evening, Germann prepares for the return visit about which she has given a sign. It cannot be to give him the secret of the cards; he already has that. The cards are again a pretext, a rationale for the countess's visit. She tells him what he wants to hear. He must play, he must come to terms with his desire. She says this under the cover, the manifest content, of the secret that will gain him a fortune; but we must remember, from the point of view of pleasure/desire associated with the countess, fortune is nothing but death, his ego-ideal. But the truth of desire, of the unconscious, can only be listened to under the guise of the acceptable. Now Germann is ready for the final confrontation, the agon, between his ego-ideal symbolized by the ace and his desire, symbolized by the countess, the old lady, the witch. Germann makes a terrible "mistake" at the end; but only in terms of the manifest content of the story, for when Germann unconsciously chooses the queen, he is only following his desire to the very end. When he chooses the queen, he calls her back, just as he did in his dream. In the end, he seems to renounce his dream of fortune, his ego-ideal and gives himself up to desire: at last. Now he is wedded to the countess forever.

But can the unconscious choice of the queen really be equated with the truth of the unconscious that Lacan describes in terms of discovery and surprise? Does Germann's choice take to its conclusion what Lacan has said about the truth of the unconscious?

> What occurs, what is *produced*, in this gap, is presented as *the discovery*. . . . The discovery is, at the same time, a solution—not necessarily a complete one,

but, however incomplete it may be, it has that indefinable something that touches us . . . namely *surprise,* that by which the subject is overcome, by which he finds both more and less than he expected—but, in any case, it is, in relation to what he expected, of exceptional value.

(Lacan, *Four* 25)

To be sure, it is not too difficult to understand why Germann goes insane after sacrificing fortune for desire. He realizes that his mistake has cost him everything—what he once possessed and what he had dreamed of possessing (his ego-ideal). In terms of the superego, he is punished both for abandoning his ego-ideal and for desiring the prohibited. But why must he go insane so autistically? Why must he be condemned to repeat over and over again "Three, seven, ace. Three seven queen," as though he had not already made the choice and paid the highest price? Why is he reduced to signifiers now bereft of all reference? How can a man who ventured so close to the truth of the unconscious—which is structured like a language—be condemned to repeat the same signifiers now completely bereft of meaning? What happened to the cards in relation to Germann?[24]

Lacan, to be sure, writes disparagingly about the ego-ideal and presents the idea of madness as essential to human freedom and to our definition as subjects. "Not only can man's being not be understood without madness, it would not be man's being if it did not bear madness within itself as the limit of his freedom" (Lacan, *Écrits,* 215). He does not, however, promote the madman or schizophrenic as an ideal, as do anti-psychiatrists such as R. D. Laing and material psychiatrists (or schizoanalists) such as Deleuze and Guattari. Germann is neither a schizophrenic of genius nor a traveler to the other side who has hope of coming back with a new truth. In the epilogue, his absence of true speech underlines Germann's complete destruction; he has retreated into another world, the Real Order, cutting the ties of language to which the individual owes his existence as a human subject.[25] For Lacan there can be no true existence without the language of the Other, especially not true unconscious life, since the unconscious is related to the desire of the Other, and thus to the language of the Other. From a Lacanian perspective, we cannot see Germann's choice of the queen, though far superior to that of the ace (the ego-ideal, the wish for autonomy and security), as ultimate truth—even for Germann. Either card represents a serious mistake.

Lacan has argued that the difference between the psychotic and neurotic personality can be explained by a defect attributable to what he calls the foreclosure of the paternal metaphor and its substitution, in the imaginary sphere, by a delusional metaphor in which the signifier and signified are stabilized (*Écrits,* 214). "It is an accident in this register and in what takes place in it, namely, the foreclosure of the Name-of-the-Father in the place of the Other, and in the failure of the paternal metaphor, that I designate the defect that gives psychosis its essential condition, and the

structure that separates it from neurosis" (*Écrits,* 215). The human being becomes a subject by taking his/her place in the Symbolic Order, by accepting the symbolic father as author-of-the-Law (*Écrits,* 199)—Freud's totem that binds the brothers of the clan—and living by its attendant sociolinguistic proscriptions and empowerments. The choice of either card constituted a refusal to enter fully into the Symbolic Order, to accept the Law based on difference and lack.

To understand Germann's refusal to enter into the symbolic by choosing the queen, we need to examine more closely how Germann incorporates the *skazka* into his life, and how he pursues the countess and Saint Germain, the symbols of pleasure/desire. We have equated Germann's obsession with the ace with his desire for identity and stasis, since the ace signifies the elimination of all difference between demand and need—that is, desire. To be sure, Germann is closer to the truth of the unconscious, and his personality, when he pursues the countess and his alterego/antithesis Saint Germain, but his desire for the countess and Saint Germain also represents the desire to retreat to, or bring back, an already dead past. The ego (the ace) aims to freeze the present, not to enter the next stage, the precarious realm of the symbolic; Germann's desire to assume the role of Saint Germain constitutes a desire to live in the past, to reject (foreclose) not only the present but the future as well, for the future emblemizes the domain of the infinitely postponing and deferring signifying chain of the Symbolic Order. The story shows not only the futility of attaining the ego-ideal but of pursuing desire without the mediation of language, outside of the symbolic.

The incredibility of the *skazka* would seem to undercut Germann's pursuit of desire, but dreams, daydreams, and fairy-tales do not have to be great artistic creations to be psychologically relevant; they need only strike the appropriate chord. Germann can no more become the son of Saint Germain and the illegitimate son of the countess than he can bring back the age of desire which they represent for him. Nor can he displace Saint Germain and gain possession of the countess for himself. The countess makes fun of Germann's attempts to become Saint Germain—the desire of the mother—winking at him both at her funeral and at the final game of faro. Thus while Germann's unconscious efforts to transcend his ego-ideal are presented positively in the story, his desire to possess the mother, to become Saint Germain, represents his desire to foreclose the paternal metaphor. (But Germann finds it no easier to take the place of the father when he is no longer there or possess the mother when she is eighty-seven years old.) For the father is most there, symbolically, as the name-of-the-father, as Law, when he is no longer physically present. To enter into the Symbolic Order, Germann must repress the desire to replace the father and possess the mother, he must forego the desire of the primary process, and live in the mediated world of language and difference, in which the signifier continually slides over the signified. Germann uses language, the names of the cards, to achieve identification and unity, whether it be to achieve, is ego-ideal (the ace) or to become undifferentiated from his desire (the queen). To choose either the ace or the queen must mean to lose, for the cards—the queen and the ace—represent not the Symbolic Order, the end as well as the process of adult life, but solely the means of a reactive and reactionary agenda: wealth and the satisfaction of pleasure/desire. We see this when Germann passes Liza by for fortune and the countess. To love Liza is to accept the law of the father, to renounce the mother, and to enter the Symbolic Order. Germann's punishment in the end is absolutely appropriate. Since the Symbolic Order is characterized by the dominance of language, of desire mediated and defined by language, when Germann loses language he is reduced to mumbling two, now meaningless, phrases, the phrases that brought about his ruin. He becomes a true infant: he who does not speak; and a true idiot, a completely private person.

Indeed, Germann withdraws more and more into himself as the story progresses. At the beginning, he is among company, but even then he stands aside from the play. Everyone gambles except Germann. All the countess's sons were gamblers; only the "natural" son never gambles. When at the end, he finally plays, it is only as one against all. If he wins, he has promised never to play again, completely to withdraw from society. Since in the story, playing/gambling becomes a symbol of life, of the chance and risk that are necessary for human freedom, Germann's promise never to play again constitutes a foreclosure of the paternal metaphor. To play is continually to live in the world of difference, to keep open possibilities, to refuse reduction, to accept that there never can be a perfect coincidence between demand and need, and that there is no coincidence between the ace and fortune and between the queen and desire.

6. LACAN: THE SYMBOLIC ORDER

But is there something even more latent in the Lacanian paradigm, relating to Germann's inability to enter the Symbolic Order, that demands further explication, or must we rest with still another explanation, however different, of Germann's dismal fate? Here I would like to address more directly the relationship of the author (both putative and historical) to his character. The author of *The Queen of Spades* abhors Germann's materialistic ideal and his scorn of feminine charms (Germann uses Liza and then passes her by for the countess); he shows Germann's imagination to be limited and clichéd; and he presents the rumor that Germann has three crimes on his conscience and that he has the soul of a Mephistopheles as ridiculous. Germann seems to have the profile of Napoleon—even Liza thinks so—but this could easily be a studied pose, as clichéd as the letters he writes to Liza.[26] But Pushkin not only limns, in places, a disparaging portrait of his hero; he also, as it were, "punishes" him severely. Worse than killing him off, he strips him forever of his sexual and linguistic powers, in other words, the powers that meant most to Pushkin himself. It is a fate worse than death—in fact, a death-in-life that Pushkin, one might say, had already imagined for

himself in his famous lyric of 1833 "God Grant That I Go Not Mad" (Rosenshield, "Poetics"). But, as I hope to have shown, something other than this reduced Germann also comes across in Pushkin's portrait, something, for whatever reason, that impressed Dostoevskii enough to call him a "colossal type." Pushkin deromanticizes his hero, but something of the romantic escapes in Germann's choice of the queen. He shows him to be a philistine, but also a gambler willing to stake everything on a card. He reduces him to a driveling idiot with no issue, incapable of ever taking his place in society (the Symbolic Order). But again something of the Symbolic, and the threat of the Symbolic, remains—even prevails.

What is this threat? Why does Pushkin prevent Germann from entering the Symbolic? Scholars have closely examined and analyzed Pushkin's apprehensions regarding the social transformations threatening Russian society and its class structure.[27] Pushkin must have seen, if not Germann, then the forces that he represents, as a direct threat to everything he valued. Like many of his contemporaries, Pushkin both abhorred and feared the materialistic culture that he saw arising in Europe and Russia, a culture whose idea he distilled in Germann's monomaniacal pursuit of gain. He attempts to take away Germann's power, but he cannot; Pushkin is too consummate an artist to do so. Passionate, rash, and determined, Germann is potentially a dangerous rebel against the established order.[28] Dostoevskii saw him as the epitome of Petersburg, because he obviously recognized in him a prophetic type—the potential revolutionary—a *raznochinets,* who would soon enough abandon his desire for gold (the ace) and the lost other/mother (the queen) and invest elsewhere his passion, determination, monomania, and—yes—the willingness to gamble for the ultimate stakes. He will eventually take his place in the Symbolic Order and radically transform it in his own image.

Lacanian psychoanalysis effectively erases the traditional Cartesian separation of the external social world and the autonomous self, of the political and the private spheres, since the subject comes into being by virtue of adopting the social rules and strictures of the symbolic world of language. Though Lacan represents the truth of the unconscious—which is available, and only available, through language—as socially derived, as formed in interaction with the other, he also views this truth as inherently subversive, as something that continually challenges institutions, order, and convention. After all, that is why it is repressed. For Lacan, the captive "self" lives entirely in the Imaginary, imprisoned by a false image of identity and autonomy, whereas the true subject—though he may not be completely autonomous, though he may even be "decentered"—by virtue of living in the Symbolic Order gains access to the creative power and freedom of "the words that will make him faithful or a renegade" (*Écrits* 68). The subversiveness, the challenge, of Germann, is that his desire is not entirely personal, it is also social and political, and it is precisely the social and political ramifications of Germann that Pushkin attempts to repress.[29]

Pushkin, like Dostoevskii, wishes Germann would go away, but such a wish—wishful thinking—represents a relatively manifest content of *The Queen of Spades*. The realization and fear that Germann is really Russia's future, not her past, constitutes a deeper, more latent, level of the text, a level which reveals the author's *unconscious* desire to keep Germann down, to deal him all the wrong cards. The greatness of the story is that it resists the attempts of its author. It, not he, speaks the truth of the Lacanian unconscious. For better or worse, Germann is the true legacy of Peter the Great, and as Pushkin should have known from the flood in *The Bronze Horseman,* Germann can be denied only temporarily. As he enters the Symbolic Order, he will hold all the cards, he will reshuffle them, and he will give all the signifiers new meaning. The secret, of course, is that the cards as signifiers can have no meaning in themselves. It may be small consolation, but we also know that the Germanns will hold these cards only temporarily, for they will inevitably be passed on to and redefined by others who have also waited their time before the house of the ancient countess.

Though all the psychoanalytical approaches to Germann's madness take us different places, they each reveal something important about the story. A Freudian interpretation sees Germann's fate as a metaphor—taken to its logical conclusion—for the tragic situation of man in civilization. Romantic psychoanalysis, in valorizing Germann's mad choice of the queen, emphasizes the risks that the individual may need to take to escape from an alienating environment given over to conformity and material aggrandizement. Finally, Lacanian psychology, perhaps more in the spirit of Pushkin, while leaving room for the participation of unconscious desire in Germann's choice of the queen, exposes at the same time the failings of two different kinds of imaginary desire, associated, respectively, with the queen and the ace. Failure is written into each of them. But, in the end, like most approaches to this baffling story, none of the psychoanalytic approaches—and this is entirely consistent with the Lacanian model we have used—can "report" to us the real unconscious content of *The Queen of Spades*; they can give us only intimations of it. Whatever may be the story's unconscious truth—that truth about which the story does not speak directly—it is something that fascinates readers today no less than it did Dostoevskii when his "raw youth," Arkadii Dolgorukii, dreamed again Germann's dream of power and fortune. Germann, as symbol, has never really lost the power of speech; he continues, like Dostoevskii's Underground Man, to speak to us subversively even today.

Notes

1. See the discussion of madness in the story by Gofman 82-86; Williams 383-396; Taborisskaia 81-87; Makogonenko 249-255; Rosenshield, "Choosing the Right Card," 995-1008. For a review of the Russian reception of the story in general, see Lerner 141-142.

2. Dostoevskii 30.1:192. For one of the earliest and most convincing demonstrations of Pushkin's technique of combining the realistic and the fantastic, see Slonimskii 171-80.

3. The narrator of *A Raw Youth* speaks of Pushkin's Germann as "a colossal figure, an unusual, completely Petersburg type—a type from the Petersburg period" (13:113).

4. Most of the previous psychological and psychoanalytical interpretations of the story are based on variations of the Oedipal triangle, with Germann either coveting the countess and/or being punished for rebelling against his father. See, for example, Burgin 46-56; Rosen 255-275; Schwartz 275-288; Lotman 122-142; Williams 383-396. My approach does not at all deny the importance of Oedipal factors (I will later make use of them myself), but, as will be evident, I treat them for analytical purposes as the imaginative correlatives of more primal personality structures.

5. There are widely diverging interpretations of Lacanian psychoanalysis, partly because Lacan intended his psychoanalysis to be more of an exploration of unconscious truth than a body of information or doctrines. He has said "I don't have a conception of the world. I have a style" (Quoted in Turkle 232). Turkle argues that Lacanian theory gives us a "compelling cast of inner agents and games to play with . . . of possibilities . . . for concrete manipulation" (xviii). For the best discussion of the developments of Lacanian psychoanalysis in France, see Turkle's *Psychoanalytical Politics*.

6. Several works in the last few decades have dwelt at length on the ubiquitousness of the numbers three, seven, one and their various combinations and permutations. See, for example, Slonimskii 174-77; Vinogradov 87-91; Weber 435-447: Kodjak 91-92; Leighton, "Numbers and Numerology"; Leighton, "Gematria"; Debreczeny 219-22.

7. See Shaw (119) for the implications of *tuz*.

8. For a discussion of the occurrence of three and seven as bets in faro, see Nabokov 2:261, Rosen 255-257. See also Debreczeny's (199, 325) discussion of Tomashevskii's observations on this point.

9. Of course, we—and Germann—learn about Germann's passionate nature only through the course of the story, only when he attempts to realize the object of his obsession.

10. For Kristeva (154), woman represents the desire which is repressed, both in women and men, in patriarchal culture. "Woman is a specialist in the unconscious, a witch, a bacchanalian, taking her *jouissance* in an anti-Apollonian, Dionystic orgy."

11. Since Germann is often seen as a rebel, it is not surprising that his gambling is viewed as an unconscious rebellion against his father, the superego (Debreczeny 110-112). But the most common psy-

chological explanation of Germann's choice of the wrong card is that of self-punishment for the guilt he experiences for the death of the countess (Rosen 265-270).

12. Disparaging remarks about American ego-psychology are common in Lacan: "The academic restoration of this 'autonomous ego' justified my view that a misunderstanding was involved in any attempt to strengthen the ego in a type of analysis that took as its criterion of 'success' a successful adaption to society—a phenomenon of mental abdication that was bound up with the aging of the psychoanalytic group in the diaspora of the war, and the reduction of a distinguished practice to a label suitable to the 'American way of life'" (Lacan, *Écrits,* 306-307).

13. See also Lacan, *Écrits* 128-129, 171, 299-300, 313-314, 164-165.

14. As we shall see, in contrast to Lacan, antipsychiatrists, such as Kristeva, Deleuze and Guattari, Cixous, and Laing, seek liberation in the idealization of desire associated with the pre-symbolic (sometimes called the semiotic or pre-Oedipal) stage of development—Lacan's imaginary stage. Kristeva, as a feminist, sees the phallocentric, symbolic order as the antithesis of truth. Representation itself, since it is part of the Word, the symbolic order, tends to undermine unconscious truth, which is "an unrepresentable form beyond true and false, and beyond present-past-future" (155).

15. Masing-Delič and King argue that General Epanchin in *The Idiot* is Dostoevskii's deromanticized projection of a successful Germann, a man who slowly gains his fortune.

16. There is some evidence that the choice that Germann makes was one that—again unconsciously—he had decided on quite a bit earlier. When leaning over the countess's body at her funeral, Germann imagines that she winks at him. While moving backward, he stumbles (*ostupilsia*) and takes a very bad fall, landing flat on his back. Is this not the same type of "accident" that he later has when he chooses the wrong card and sees the countess, again, winking at him? Alan Sheridan (Lacan, *Écrits* x) describes the real in Lacan as "that over which the symbolic stumbles, that which is refractory, resistant, . . . [that] which is lacking in the symbolic order, the ineliminable residue of all articulation, the foreclosed element, which may be approached, but never grasped: the umbilical cord of the symbolic."

17. Lacan contrasts, in his L-Schema, the symbolic relationship (S-O), based on unconscious communication, which exists between the subject (S) and object/Other (O) with the imaginary relationship (o-o') that exists between the ego (o) and its object/other (o') (Lacan, *Écrits* 193-94).

18. Lacan distinguishes pleasure (*plaisir*), an imaginary desire, from *jouissance,* a more symbolic desire. Since Germann's obsession with the queen seems to oscillate between these two forms of desire, I have sometimes used the word pleasure and sometimes desire, depending on context. Lacan, *Écrits* 319-24.

19. For example, through his description of the unbelievable relationship—in all respects—between Saint Germain and his grandmother.

20. That is, imaginary desire, however flawed, seems to be far more in touch with unconscious desire than Germann's ego-ideal. Further, its greater association with unconscious desire may even prepare the reader for the unconscious "mistake" at the end against the ego-ideal.

21. Williams has written interestingly about Germann's equal fascination for the countess and the secret of the cards. He presents Germann's attraction, however, as a perversion. As German watches the countess undress, Williams states that Germann already "may be considered to be insane" (391). Only in the last sentence (394) does he seem to realize that it is not the countess herself but the age that she symbolizes that so attracts Germann and becomes the object of his desire. Germann "looks back with nostalgia to the financially non-competitive, almost feudal society of the last years before the revolution, in his hopeless love for the image of the countess . . ." (394). See also Slonimskii 179.

22. "What is repeated, in fact, is always something that occurs . . . *as if by chance*" (Lacan, *Four* 54).

23. It seems probable that Germann's mother is Russian (not untypical for the time) and that he derives his passionate side from her. Saint Germain, his alterego, shows him the possibility of overcoming the "German" side of himself, the side of control and indefinitely delayed gratification. The terms "German" and "Russian" are meant in the story only as conveniences of thought; they refer to universal characteristics within us all. Tom Shaw has speculated that Germann may be the point of departure for Goncharov's Shtolts in *Oblomov*. Goncharov explicitly states that Shtolts derives his more "feeling" side from his Russian mother, his more practical and rational side from his German father.

24. Psychotics were interesting to Lacan, especially because of the way they used language. But Germann's madness results in the virtual loss of all language.

25. "The psychoanalytic experience has rediscovered in man the imperative of the Word as the law that has formed him in its image. . . . May that experience enable you to understand at last that it is in the gift of speech that all the reality of its effects resides; for it is by way of this gift that all reality has come to man and it is by his continued act that he maintains it" (Lacan, *Écrits* 106). The Real Order exists outside of the Symbolic Order and therefore can never be reached by language.

26. See my "Choosing the Right Card" (998-1001) for a discussion of Pushkin's deflation of Germann's imagination throughout the story.

27. Since the early 1930s, Soviet critics have fairly consistently seen Germann as a representative of a new class, the money- and power-hungry bourgeoisie, fated to displace the older and weaker nobility as embodied by the decrepit countess. See, for example, Iakubovich, 69-70; Gukovskii, 340-353, 364-365; Tomashevskii, 198-99; Stepanov, 76-79.

28. For others who have seen Germann as a Faust, a romantic rebel, or a challenger of the social order, see Weber, 435-447; Schwartz; Kodjak, 87-118; Falchikov, 96-106; Esipov, 193-205.

29. Turkle's *Psychoanalytical Politics* ascribes the politically radical direction of psychoanalysis in France in the 1960s and 1970s to Lacan's erasure of the division between the personal and social in the definition of the subject. Once the personal and the social could be seen as two sides of the same coin, a political psychoanalysis became possible.

Works Cited

Boucher, Anthony. "Of Fortune and Faro." *Opera News* 30.11 (1966): 8-12.

Burgin, Diana Lewis. "The Mystery of "Pikovaia dama." *Mnemozina: Studia litteraria russica in Honorem Vsevolod Setchkarev.* Ed. Joachim T. Baer and Norman W. Ingham. Munich: Fink, 1974. 46-56.

Cixous, Hélène. *Readings: The Poetics of Blanchot, Joyce, Kafka, Kleist, Lispector, and Tsvetayeva.* Minneapolis: U of Minnesota P, 1991.

Debreczeny, Paul. *The Other Pushkin: A Study of Alexander Pushkin's Prose Fiction.* Stanford, California: Stanford UP, 1983.

Deleuze, Giles and Félix Guattari. *Anti-Oedipus: Capitalism and Schizophrenia.* Minneapolis: U of Minnesota P, 1983.

Dostoevskii, F. M. *Polnoe sobranie sochinenii.* Ed. V. G. Bazanov et al. 30 vols. Leningrad: Nauka, 1972-90.

Emerson, Caryl. "'The Queen of Spades' and the Open End." *Puškin Today.* Ed. David Bethea. Bloomington, Indiana: Indiana UP, 1992. 31-37.

Esipov. V. "Istoricheskii podteskt v povesti Pushkina 'Pikovaia dama.'" *Voprosy literatury* 4 (1989): 193-205.

Falchikov, F. "The Outsider and the Number Game: Some Observations on 'Pikovaia Dama.'" *Essays in Poetics* 2.1 (1977): 96-106.

Freud, Sigmund. "The 'Uncanny.'" *Collected Papers.* 5 vols. New York: Basic, 1959. 4: 368-408.

———. *Civilization and Its Discontents.* Trans. James Strachey. New York: Norton, 1961.

———. *New Introductory Lectures on Psychoanalysis.* Trans. James Strachey. New York: Norton, 1965.

Gofman, M. L. "Problema sumaschestviia v tvorchestve Pushkina." *Novyi zhurnal* 51 (1957): 61-86.

Gukovskii, A. G. *Pushkin i problemy realisticheskogo stilia.* Moscow: GIKhL, 1957.

Iakubovich, D. P. "'Pikovaia Dama': Stat'ia i kommentarii," *A. S. Pushkin: Pikovaia dama.* Leningrad: GIKhL, 1963.

Kodjak, Andrej. "'The Queen of Spades' in the Context of the Faust Legend." *Alexander Pushkin: A Symposium on the 175th Anniversary of His Birth.* New York: New York UP, 1976. 87-118.

Kristeva, Julia. *The Kristeva Reader.* Ed. Toril Moi. New York: Columbia University Press, 1986.

Lacan, Jacques. *Écrits.* Trans. Alan Sheridan. New York: Norton, 1977.

———. *The Four Fundamental Concepts of Psychoanalysis.* Trans. Jacques-Alain Miller. New York: Norton, 1977.

Laing, R. D. *The Politics of Experience.* New York: Ballantine, 1967.

Leighton, Lauren. "Numbers and Numerology in 'The Queen of Spades.'" *Canadian Slavonic Papers* 19 (1977): 417-443.

———. "Gematria in 'The Queen of Spades': A Decembrist Puzzle." *Slavic and East European Journal* 21 (1977): 455-469.

Lerner, N. O. "Istoriia 'Pikovoi damy.'" *Rasskazy o Pushkine.* Leningrad: Priboi, 1929. 132-163.

Lotman, Iu. M. "Tema kart i kartochnoi igry v russkoi literature nachala XIX veka." *Trudy po znakovym sistemam* 7 (1975): 122-142.

Makogonenko, G. P. *Tvorchestvo A. S. Pushkina v 1830-e gody.* Leningrad: Khudozhestvennaia literatura, 1982.

Masing-Delič, I., and Pandora King. "General Epanchin as Germann: A Travesty on Pushkin's 'Queen of Spades' in Dostoevsky's *The Idiot.*" *Dostoevsky Studies* 9 (1989): 171-91.

Nabokov, Vladimir, trans. *Eugene Onegin.* A. S. Pushkin 2 vols. New York: Random, 1964.

Pushkin, A. S. *Polnoe sobranie sochinenii.* 17 vols. Moscow, Leningrad: AN SSSR, 1937-59.

Rosen, Nathan. "The Magic Cards in 'The Queen of Spades.'" *Slavic and East European Journal* 19 (1975): 255-275.

Rosenshield, Gary. "Choosing the Right Card: Madness, Gambling and Imagination in Pushkin's 'The Queen of Spades.'" *PMLA* 109 (1994): 995-1008.

———. "The Poetics of Madness: Pushkin's 'God Grant That I Go Not Mad.'" *Slavic and East European Journal* 38.1 (1994): 120-47.

Schwartz, Murray M. and Albert Schwartz. "'The Queen of Spades': A Psychoanalytic Interpretation." *Texas Studies in Literature and Language* 17 (1975): 275-288.

Shaw, Joseph T. "The 'Conclusion' of Pushkin's 'Queen of Spades.'" *Studies in Russian and Polish Literature in Honor of Waclaw Lednicki.* Ed. Zbigniew Folejewski. 'S-Gravenhage: Mouton, 1962. 114-126.

Slonimskii, A. L. "O kompozitsii 'Pikovoi damy.'" *Pushkinskii sbornik pamiati Professora S. A. Vengerova.* Moscow: GIKhL, 1923. 171-80.

Stepanov, N. L. *Proza Pushkina.* Moscow: AN SSSR, 1962.

Taborisskaia, E. M. "Svoebrazie resheniia temy bezumiia v proizvedeniiakh Pushkina 1833 goda." *Pushkinskie chteniia: Sbornik statei.* Tallinn: Eesti Raamat, 1990. 71-87.

Tomashevskii, B. V. "Istorizm Pushkina." *Pushkin: kniga vtoraia, Materialy k monografii (1824-1837).* Moscow: AN SSSR, 1961.

Turkle, Sherry. *Psychoanalytical Politics: Jacques Lacan and Freud's French Revolution.* 2nd ed. New York: Guilford, 1992.

Vinogradov, V. V. "Stil' 'Pikovoi damy.'" *Pushkin: Vremennik Pushkinskoi komissii,* 2 (1936): 75-104.

Weber, Harry B. "'Pikovaia dama': A Case for Freemasonry in Russian Literature." *Slavic and East European Journal* 12 (1968): 435-447.

Williams, Gareth. "The Obsessions of Madness of Germann in 'Pikovaja dama.'" *Russian Literature* 14.4 (1983): 383-396.

Sergei Davydov (essay date summer 1999)

SOURCE: Davydov, Sergei. "The Ace in 'The Queen of Spades.'" *Slavic Review* 58, no. 2 (summer 1999): 309-28.

[*In the following essay, Davydov traces various critical perspectives on Pushkin's novella, focusing on rational and supernatural explanations for the protagonist's obsession with the three, seven, and ace cards.*]

> И постепенно в усыпленье
> И чувств и сум впадает он,
> А перед ним воображенье
> Свой пестрый мечет фараон.
>
> —A. S. Pushkin, *Evgenii Onegin,* 8:37

(And slowly, as his mind and feeling / descend into a languid dream, / Imagination takes up dealing / her motley Faro game to him.)

At a card table at the beginning of *Pikovaia dama* (*The Queen of Spades*), Tomskii recounts a tale about his flamboyant grandmother, an avid Faro player. In her youth the Countess once lost a large sum to the Duke of Orleans *au jeu de la Reine* at Versailles. When her husband refused to pay off her debt, the Countess turned to the adventurer and wonderman Count Saint-Germain for help. Instead of lending her money, the old eccentric revealed to her three secret cards with which she won back everything she had lost. Tomskii's bizarre tale provokes three responses among the Petersburg gamblers:

> "Mere chance!" said one of the guests.
> "A fairy tale!" remarked Germann.
> "Perhaps they were powdered [doctored] cards,"
>   joined in a third.
> "I don't think so," Tomskii replied in a serious tone.[1]

Tomskii, the narrator of this remarkable episode, rejects all three rational explanations and insists on the validity of the supernatural event. Which response is correct? Those who explain the mystery in natural, realistic terms (chance, lie, trickery), or Tomskii, who insists on the intrusion of the supernatural? Fedor Dostoevskii addressed this question in a letter to Iu. F. Abaza:

> Pushkin, who has given us almost all artistic forms, wrote **The Queen of Spades**—the pinnacle of the art of the fantastic. One believes that Germann actually saw an apparition, and precisely in accordance with his worldview, and yet, having finished the tale, one does not know how to decide: did this vision emerge from Germann's own nature [realistic solution], or is he actually one of those who have come into contact with another world, a world of spirits, evil and hostile to man [supernatural solution] [. . .] Now this is what I call art! [*Vot éto iskusstvo!*][2]

In his book on the fantastic, Tzvetan Todorov maintains that the reader's vacillation between the natural and supernatural cause of an uncanny phenomenon is the chief precondition for the genre of the fantastic.[3] An exclusive decision for or against the intrusion of the supernatural would destroy the foremost virtue of Pushkin's tale, the "seamless fusion of the fantastic with the realistic" that both invites and frustrates logical decoding.[4]

As skeptical as the Petersburg gamblers, the literary critics remain unconvinced by Tomskii's insistence on the supernatural nature of the triggering event. In pursuit of rational solutions, three questions are usually raised: (1) What is the origin of the magic trey, seven, and ace? (2) Could Germann (or the reader) have identified the three cards without the ghost's intervention? (3) How does one explain Germann's fatal blunder of confusing the ace with the queen in his last game?

TREY, SEVEN, ACE

Few today share Mikhail Gershenzon's opinion that "it really does not matter whether Germann in his hallucination fancied these particular cards rather than some other three cards."[5] In searching for the origin of the three, seven, and one (one being the numerical value of the ace), critics have turned to literary sources with which Pushkin was or might have been familiar. The first link to Pushkin's triplet was found in the two lines from Fedor Glinka's 1828 poem "Brachnyi pir Toviia" (Tobias's wedding feast), which contain two of the three cards: "Malo l' platy? / Utroit' syn! usemerit'" (Not enough pay? Triple it, septuple it, my son!).[6] Viktor Vinogradov suggested another likely source, Karl Heun's novella *Der holländische Jude* in which the hero bets on the magic trey and seven and wins a fortune.[7] Again this subtext leaves out the ace. In fact, no single literary source can account for all three cards of Pushkin's triplet.[8]

Boris Tomashevskii and Vladimir Nabokov suggested an extraliterary source that might sensibly have motivated Pushkin's choice. Both scholars argued that the numbers 1-3-7 are derived from the sequence of three straight wins in the game of Faro, if the stakes are doubled each time. If the initial stake (*le va*) is one, then the first win equals *une et le va*; the second, *trois et le va;* the third, *sept et le va;* and so on.[9] Pushkin himself mentions this lucky series— *sonica, paroli, paroli-paix*—in the beginning of his tale. The sequence 1-3-7 would have been known to Germann who never plays himself but "would sit by the card table whole nights and follow with feverish trembling the different turns of the game." Though Tomashevskii's and Nabokov's answer offers the most likely explanation so far for the identity of the three cards, it is marred by one flaw: it fails to indicate the correct sequence in which the cards had to be played in order to win. Because the ace is in the wrong position, this theory, too, is not entirely satisfactory.

It was essential for Pushkin that a pervasive sense of the occult be sustained throughout the tale. References to the elixir of life and *lapis philosophorum,* the secret galvanism, Joseph-Michel Montgolfier's balloon and Friedrich Anton Mesmer's magnetism, the obscure epigraph from the mystic Emanuel Swedenborg, and the ominous quote from a *Fortune-Teller* are all indispensable ingredients of Pushkin's arcane brew. Stimulated by its potency, but impervious to the irony of Pushkin's tale, critics have availed themselves of a number of occult tools in order to extract the three cards from various numerological motifs.[10] One shortcoming of this approach is that the tale contains a profusion of numbers and dates (1, 2, 3, 4, 5, 6, 7, 8, 9, 10, 12, 17, 20, 30, 40, 50, 60, 70, 80, 87, 100, 275, 47,000, 50,000, 94,000, 300,000) from which any card can be produced. When the focus is on a smaller textual segment, such as "Vot chto utroit, usemerit moi kapital" (This is what will triple, septuple my capital), one card, usually the ace, is missing from the triplet. Even when all three cards can be obtained from a given passage, the sequence is incorrect.[11]

The same problem that mars the numerological approach also applies to gematria, that is, the anagrammatic method of extracting the cards from the sound texture of the tale. Lauren Leighton ingeniously discovered many card logogriphs in the famous passage describing the Countess's boudoir:

перед кивотом, наполненным сТаРИнными" [3] обРАЗами [1], теплилась золотая лампада. Полинялые штофные кресла и ДиВАны [2] с

пуховыми подушками, с сошедшей позолотою, стояли в печальной СиМмЕТРИи [7, 3] около стен, обитых китайскими обоями. На стене висели два [2] портрета, писанные в Париже *mme Lebrun* [Q]. Один [1] из них изображал *мужчину* лет сорока, румянного и полного, в светлозеленом мундире и со звездой [1]; другой [2]—молодую к а авцщу с орлиным носом, с зачесанными висками и с розою в пудренных волосах [Q]. По вСЕМ [7] углам торчали фарфоровые пастушки, столовые часы работы славного *Leroy* [K], коробочки, рулетки, веера и РАЗные [1] дамские [Q] игрушки, изобретенные в конде минувшего столетия вМЕСте [7] с Монгольфьеровым шаром и МЕСмерОВым [7, 8] магнетизмом.

(A gold sanctuary lamp burned in front of an icon-case filled with ancient icons. Armchairs with faded damask upholstery and down-cushioned sofas, their gilt coating worn, stood in melancholy symmetry along the walls, which were covered with Chinese silk. Two portraits, painted in Paris by Mme. Lebrun, hung on the wall. One of them showed a man about forty years old, red-faced and portly, wearing a light green coat with a star; the other a beautiful young woman with an aquiline nose, with her hair combed back over her temples, and with a rose in her powdered locks. Every nook and corner was crowded with china shepherdesses, table clocks made by the famous Leroy, little boxes, bandalores, fans, and diverse other ladies' toys invented at the end of the last century, along with Montgolfier's balloon and Mesmer's magnetism.)[12]

No doubt the description of the Countess's remarkable boudoir, which Gershenzon inexplicably characterized as Pushkin's "artistic blunder" (*khudozhestvennyi promakh*),[13] is one of the most mesmerizing passages of the tale, rife with numerical allusions. The only problem is that in addition to the 3, 7, and 1, this passage generates a number of other cards, such as 2, 8, K, and Q, and it, too, fails to provide the proper order in which the cards should be played. When focusing on a smaller anagrammatic sample, as a rule, one card is missing:

. . . фонари светились ТУСкло; улицы были пУСТы. Изредка тянулся Ванька на тощей кляче, высмаТРИвая запоздалого седока. [1, 1, 3] . . . на его МЕСте он поСТУпий бы совСЕМ иначе [7, 1, 7] . . .—я причною ее СМЕРТИ [7, 3] . . .—Я не хотел ее СМЕРТИ, [7, 3] . . . В эту минуту показался ему, что мертвая наСМЕшливо взглянла на него, прищуривая ОДНИМ глазом. Германн, поспешно подавшись назад, оСТУпийся и навзничь гранулся об земь. [7, 1, 1]

([. . .] the lights shone dimly; the streets were deserted. Only occasionally did a cabdriver shamble by with his scrawny nag, on the lookout for a late passenger [. . .] in his friend's place he would have acted entirely differently [. . .] I caused her death [. . .] I did not wish her death [. . .] At that moment it seemed to him that the deceased cast a mocking glance at him, screwing up one of her eyes. He moved back hastily, missed his step, and crashed to the ground flat on his back.)[14]

No matter how intriguing, an exclusively numerological or gematric approach only multiplies the "codes that tantalize but do not quite add up."[15] On the other hand, a cryptographic reading that combines elements of both methods can yield, I suspect, a less illusory solution. Consider, for example, the following passage in which the three cards are disguised under the expressions of time, producing a curious chronogram:

> ОДНАЖДЫ—это случилось ДВА ДНЯ после вечера, описанного в начале этой повести, и за НЕДЕлЮ перед той сценой, на которой мы остановились,—ОДНАЖДЫ Лизавета Ивановна . . .

> (*One time*—this happened *two days after* the party described at the beginning of our story and *a week* before the scene that we have just detailed—*one* time Lizaveta Ivanovna [. . .])[16]

"Odnazhdy" stands for the ace (1), "nedelia" for the 7. In order to obtain the missing 3, we have to add to these two days that one "imperceptible night" which Pushkin described at the opening of the tale:

> There was a card party at the house of Narumov, the officer of the Horse Guards. The *long winter night passed imperceptibly*; it was close to five in the morning when the company sat down to supper.[17]

Because this passage produces the three cards and points in the direction of the correct sequence: 1-3-7-1, it provides us with the needed key to enter the next chronogram, which Pushkin encrypted in the same code and which contains the three cards in the *correct order*:

> Не прошло м ех неель [3, 7] с той поры, как она в пе ьый аз [1] увидела в окошко молодого человека . . .

> (Less than three weeks [3, 7] had passed since she had first [1] caught sight of the young man through the window [. . .])[18]

Perhaps the most frequently quoted passage from which the critics have attempted to extract the magic cards is Germann's inner monologue in chapter 2:

> "Да и самый анекдот? . . . Можно ли ему верить? . . . Нет! расчет, умеренность и трудолюбие: вот мои три верные карты, вот что *ум оцм, у еме цм* мой капитал и доставит мне покой и независимость."

> ("And what about the anecdote itself? . . . Can one put any faith in it? . . . No! Calculation, moderation, and industry; these are my three reliable cards. They will *treble* my capital, increase in *sevenfold*, and bring me ease and independence!")[19]

Aleksandr Slonimskii, who was the first to comment on this passage, speaks of a "double motivation" for the first two cards: the natural (through Germann) and the supernatural (through the Countess).[20] Andrei Kodjak agrees that Germann "has subconsciously determined two of the cards that the Countess would reveal to him. Here, however, the psychological theory breaks down; the third win-

ning card—the ace—remains inexplicable."[21] Nathan Rosen, who also cites this passage, concludes: "The fact that the ace is not included in the passage [. . .] suggests a flaw in this approach."[22]

Having more trust in Pushkin than in the Pushkinists, I would like to insist on the flawlessness of the poet's cryptographic method, for Germann's words do contain all three cards, including the missing ace. Squeezed between the 3 and 7 hides the phonetically assimilated *tuz* [tus]:

> vot chto *utroiT, USemerit* moi kapital.

Pushkin's sleight of hand may be counted on to uncover the right card at the exact time. The tale's maxim, according to which "two fixed ideas can no more coexist in the moral sphere than can two bodies occupy the same space in the physical world," does not apply to the poetic time and space of Pushkin's anagrams.[23]

Moreover, the principle of covering up the middle card seems to be derived directly from Faro. The game is played with two decks of cards. Each punter selects a card of his choice from one deck, places it face down on the table and makes his stake on it. (Germann chooses the trey in his first game and bets 47,000 on it.) The banker then deals from a different deck, placing two cards face up to the left and to the right of the punter's card. The punter then uncovers his card. If it matches the card on his left, he wins, if it matches the card on his right, he loses. If no match occurs, no one wins and the game continues. The punters may select for the next round a different card or continue to bet on their old one. The actual suit is irrelevant in Faro.

Thus, if we apply the rules of the game to the phrase "utroit, usemerit," the first reading of the phrase places the trey and the seven face up on the page, the second, cryptic reading uncovers the elusive ace: "utroi-TUS-emerit." The fickle ace, a latecomer to this cryptogrammatic charade, was hidden in the blind spot, both in the middle (graphically) and at the end (perceptually).[24] Most important, of course, is that this cryptogram, just like the previous chronogram, precedes the ghost's visit, and if the engineer Germann had marked his own words more shrewdly, he might have deduced the triplet and the correct sequence without the help of the ghost. Nevertheless, the fact that the 3-7-1 would actually win still remains rationally inexplicable.

There is, I believe, only one other passage prior to the ghost's visit that can produce all three cards in the proper sequence. But, since this passage is a rather complex cryptogram, involving numerology, gematria, and visual transformations, we should first examine Pushkin's method more closely. Let us recall that after the ghost reveals the secret to Germann, he begins to perceive the surrounding reality as an encrypted text displaying the most bizarre manifestations of the three cards. The following passage, which Pushkin partially decoded for the benefit of the reader, is a good illustration of this method and can serve as a key to other cryptic passages of the tale:

Тройка, семерка, туз—не выходили из его головы и шевелились на его губах. Увидев *молодую евушку,* он говорил: "Как она *м ойна!* . . . Настоящая *м ойка че вонная*". У него спрашивали: *"Комо ый ча ",* он отвечал: "без пяти минут *еме ка*". Всякйй *пуза мый муж чцна* напоминал ему *муза*. Тройка, семерка, туз—преследовали его во сне, принимая все возможные виды: *м ойка* цвела перед ним в образе пЫшного *ζ анцфло а*, *еме ка* представлялась *ζомцче кцмц во омами,* муз огромным *пауком*.[25]

(Trey, seven, ace—the threesome haunted him and was perpetually on his lips. Seeing a *young girl,* he would say: "How shapely! . . . Just like a *trey* of hearts." If anybody asked him *what time* it was, he would answer, "Five of the *seven.*" Every *portly man* reminded him of an *ace.* The trey, the seven, and the ace hounded him even in his dreams, taking on every imaginable form: the *trey* blossomed before him like a great luxuriant *flower*; the *seven* appeared as a *Gothic gate*; and the *ace* assumed the shape of an enormous *spider.*)[25]

Rosen imaginatively illustrated the visual and auditory transformations of the three cards into three diurnal and three nocturnal images. The diurnal transformations are self-explanatory. The "*stroi*naia devushka" is associated with the "*troi*ka chervonnaia" through the similarity of sound and shape.[26] Just as the tale's chronology contained the three cards, Germann's second association turns time into a card: "Kotoryi chas"—"bez piati minut semerka." The third transformation of a "*puz*astyi muzhchina" into a "*tuz*" is motivated by the similarity of sound and meaning: "tuz" is also a man of rank and wealth.[27] Unlike Germann's diurnal associations, their nocturnal counterparts are encoded in a more elusive manner that involves "expansion and deformation."[28] Because the sound element is absent from the oneiric transformations, the reader must rely on visual clues alone. The trey with its three leaf-shaped spades or clubs on top of each other blossoms at night into a "luxurious flower" (*pyshnyi grandiflor*), perhaps a *rosa grandiflora,* which was also a Masonic Rose-Croix symbol.[29] The seven appears in the guise of a gothic portal. This bizarre metamorphosis was deciphered by G. M. Koka, who convincingly related the shape of Fel'ten's gothic arch in Petersburg's Ekaterininskii Garden to the arrangement of the seven spades on this card. Pushkin's friend Anton Del'vig used an engraving of this portal as the frontispiece of his *Severnye tsvety* (1830).[30] Rosen illustrated the next metamorphosis of the ace into a "gigantic spider" by linking the shape of the spade to an exotic triangular creature. The more common garden spider, *paukkrestovik,* would be a more likely candidate, for the cross sign on its back strikingly mimics the club.

The diurnal and nocturnal associations seem to be meaningfully correlated: the analogy between the slender girl and the luxuriant flower (3), and between the potbellied man and the gigantic spider (1) is quite obvious. The link between "five minutes to seven" and the gothic portal remains elusive, however. Rosen suggested that "Gothic portals move time backward to the Middle Ages of the Gothic novel, hence the day and night associations of seven relate

to time."[31] Kodjak offered an even more abstract link between the day and night associations of the trey, seven, and ace: "youth, passing time, old age = fertility, historical time, destruction or death."[32] If Pushkin's code is consistent, both metamorphoses of the seven should relate to time in a more direct, visual way. Perhaps the fireplace clock from Pushkin's Petersburg apartment, whose case is a perfect miniature replica of a gothic arch, is the missing iconic link. The fact that Pushkin used the passage of time to encode the three cards twice before in his chronograms would then attest to the consistency of his method.

Although Germann's spectacular associations occur only after the ghost's visit, these visual and auditory metamorphoses of the three cards provide the key to another encoded passage that precedes the visit. The paragraph that immediately follows the phrase "utroit, usemerit" seems to contain in an encrypted form all three cards in the correct order:

Рассуждая таким образом, очутился он в одной из главных улиц Петербурга. Улица была заставлена экилажами, *ка емы* одна за другою катились к освещенному подъезду. Из *ка ем* поминутно вытягивалась то *м ойная ноζа* молодой красавицы, то *ст емучая ноζа ромфо ма,* то полосатый чулок и *ипломамцче кий ραшмак.* Шуþы и плащи мелькали мимо величавого швейцара. Германн остановился.[33]

(Lost thus in thought, he found himself on one of the main streets of Petersburg, in front of an old-style house. The street was crowded with equipages; one carriage after another rolled up to the lighted entrance. Now a young beauty's *shapely leg,* now a rattling [*spurred*] *riding boot,* now a striped stocking and a *diplomat's shoe* emerged from the carriages. Fur coats and cloaks flitted by the stately doorman. Hermann stopped.)[33]

If we employ the already familiar cryptogrammatic clues, we may arrive at the following reading: The phrase "*karety odna za drugoiu katilis*'" anagrammatically announces the arrival of the cards (*karety-karty*). (Compare this with the analogous formulation in the next paragraph: "[Germann] stavil kartu za kartoi.") Next, Pushkin pulls from his deck the three cards, disguised as the three pairs of feet stepping one after another from the arriving carriages. The first card he lays forth is the *troika*: "Iz karet pominutno vytiagivalas' to *stroi*naia noga molodoi krasavitsy." The transformation of the trey into the "shapely foot of a young beauty" is a faithful alliterative and a visual replica of the previous cryptogram: "Uvidev moloduiu devushku, on govoril: 'Kak ona *stroi*na! . . . Nastoiashchaia *troika* chervonnaia.'" Next Pushkin sets down the seven in the guise of "gremuchaia botforta"; turned upside down, the "spurred boot" resembles a seven. There can be little doubt that a "striped stocking and a diplomat's shoe" adorn the foot of a big shot, a *tuz.* This last transformation anticipates both of Germann's later associations, which link the ace to a "potbellied man" and a "gigantic spider." It is perhaps of interest to note that the legs of the garden spider are conspicuously striped, a detail that further tightens the web of correspondences between the various mutations of the ace.[34]

Thus, with (or without) a grain of salt, the "shapely foot," the "spurred boot," and the "diplomatic shoe," stepping out from the carriages in the winning order before Germann's very eyes, are encoded images of the three magic cards. Had Germann been as keen an admirer of *nozhki* as was his author, he might have solved the mystery without causing the death of the Countess and, perhaps, he might have found solace at the "shapely feet of a young beauty" such as Liza. Instead, he becomes privy to the "repulsive mysteries" of the old lady's toilette, as he watches how "her yellow dress, embroidered with silver, fell to her swollen feet."[35]

THE QUEEN

This last pair of feet brings us to the last card of this magic tale, to the *beldam* of the story, the queen of spades. The old Countess Anna Fedotovna, a truly extravagant relic of the eighteenth century, belongs among the most remarkable of Pushkin's creations. Her real life model was Princess Nataliia Petrovna Golitsyna, whom Pushkin knew personally. The princess served as a lady-in-waiting to five generations of Russian emperors and was ninety-two years old at the time Pushkin wrote his tale. She was an avid gambler, and because of her failing eyesight, a deck of large-format cards was kept for her at the court.[36] Once, her grandson, S. G. Golitsyn, had lost a large sum at cards and came to his grandmother to beg for money. Instead of money, the princess told him of the three winning cards that Saint-Germain had once revealed to her in Paris. The grandson bet on them and regained his loss.[37]

Nabokov discovered a German subtext for the Russian **Queen of Spades** in a novel *Pique-Dame: Berichte aus dem Irrenhause in Briefen* (1826). The novel is a collection of letters from an insane asylum, addressed to a dead friend by a young gambler who ruined his life in a game of Faro when he bet for the tenth time on the queen of spades.[38]

Neither the Russian princess nor the Swedish *Pique-Dame* can explain the dénouement of Pushkin's **Pikovaia dama**, however. The most puzzling aspect of Pushkin's tale is not that the ghost reveals the three winning cards to Germann, but that he actually fails to win with them. There have been numerous attempts to explain the fatal displacement of the ace by the queen in realistic terms. Some of the solutions echo the responses of the gamblers at the beginning of the tale: "Mere chance!" "A fairy tale!" "Perhaps they were powdered cards." Gershenzon maintained that Germann pulled out the queen of spades by "pure coincidence," and that there was hardly any similarity between the card and the Countess.[39] The Soviet scholar L. V. Chkhaidze offered a crudely materialistic explanation, claiming that in a new deck of cards "the printing tint was, of course, fresh, and the cards were slightly sticking to each

other. [. . .] Hence, everything is explained realistically; there is no 'mysticism' in the tale whatsoever."[40] Gary Rosenshield argued that by choosing the "wrong card" (the queen instead of the ace), Germann has actually chosen the "right card," because to "win would, of course, have been to lose; it would have been never to gamble—to live—at all."[41] Vinogradov offered a more plausible explanation of the uncanny dénouement; he cast the mysterious intrusion of the queen of spades at the end of the tale as the materialization of Germann's repressed guilt for the death of the old lady.[42]

This psychological interpretation becomes even more valid if one takes into account the various visual assimilations of the Countess with the card. First Germann sees the Countess framed in a portrait by Mme Lebrun, depicting her as "a beautiful young woman, with an aquiline nose [and] a rose in her powdered hair." The portrait is reminiscent of the queen of spades, shown in profile with a rose in her hand. Observing the Countess undressing, Germann sees her as an inverted double figure framed in the mirror. In the same scene he sees her sitting in a rectangular Voltaire chair and involuntarily "swaying from left to right" as if moved by "the action of a hidden galvanism."[43] In addition to the framing of the Countess as a card, her swaying resembles the mechanics of the Faro game, in which cards fall to the left and right of the punter's card.[44] Twice Germann glimpses the Countess framed in his window, and twice she winks at him from other rectangular frames: from her open coffin and from the fatal card when Germann is finally struck by the "extraordinary likeness."[45]

Having established the visual link between the Countess and the card, we may now look into the mechanics of the actual displacement of the ace by the queen. To begin with, there is no visual resemblance between the two cards that would account for Germann's error. The contrast between the ace, with its single suit in the center, and the queen, whose figure fills almost the entire card, defies confusion. More likely, Germann's inexplicable blunder was prepared through a chain of assimilations based on contiguity rather than similarity, whereby the unstable position of the ace plays a significant role. Throughout the tale the ace is the most elusive member of the triplet and is often absent from the series altogether. When the ace does appear, it is usually the best-camouflaged card of the three. Semantically dissimulated as "raz, odin, odnazhdy" (one, once) or hidden at the word boundary between the two other cards, "utroit, usemerit," the ace is the least perspicuous component in the various cryptograms. Its weaker position within the triplet makes the ace an especially vulnerable target for displacement by the queen.

If the queen of spades has its human counterpart in the Countess, then the ace could stand for her husband, the Count. After hearing Tomskii's story about his grandparents, Germann sees the two figures on the portraits hanging next to each other in the Countess's boudoir: "One of them showed a man about forty years old, red-faced and portly, wearing a light green coat with a star [Count—

portly man—star = ace]; the other a beautiful young woman with an aquiline nose, with her hair combed back over her temples, and with a rose in her powdered locks [Countess—profile—rose = queen]." The contiguity of the two portraits might have contributed to Germann's confusion of the two cards. Furthermore, Tomskii's unflattering account of his grandfather underscores the Count's inferior position vis-à-vis the Countess: "My late grandfather, as far as I remember, played the part of a butler to my grandmother. He feared her like fire." After he refused to pay off her debt, "Grandmother slapped him on the face and went to bed by herself as an indication of her displeasure."[46] The next day she pays a visit to Count Saint-Germain, who helps her in his own mysterious way. Thus, throughout the story, the "queen" clearly dominates over the vulnerable "ace."

Another factor contributing to the assimilation and eventual displacement of the ace by the queen is the Countess's androgynous appearance. Once her feminine attributes such as the "cap, decorated with roses" and the "powdered wig" are removed, Germann faces a rather masculine "gray and closely cropped head." In turn, the appearance of the Countess's real-life prototype also intensifies the gender confusion: because of her facial hair, Princess Golitsyna was called in Pushkin's circle "Princesse Moustache" (*Usataia printsessa*) or by the androgynous name "Princesse Woldemar."[47]

Yet even this gender osmosis cannot satisfactorily explain Germann's fatal error of pulling the wrong card. After all, the 3-7-1 revealed to him by the ghost were the *correct* three cards, and nothing should have gone awry. Germann's repressed guilt or the assimilation of the two cards and of their gender offers only an auxiliary explanation of Germann's failure to distinguish between them. When he selected "his card" (Pushkin does not say ace, but "svoiu kartu"), the alleged ace must have been before Germann's very eyes. Yet, when he turned the card over, the "queen of spades screwed up her eyes and grinned." All rational explanations again break down at this point, and we are compelled to resort to the last and most authoritative word on the issue.

The Recent Fortune-Teller informs us in the tale's epigraph that "The queen of spades signifies secret ill will." Vinogradov explains: "Thus the queen of spades, that is, the dead Countess, penetrated the series of the three 'reliable cards,' replaced the ace, and, having destroyed Germann's plans, has fulfilled the will of destiny, 'the secret ill will' of fate."[48]

One can hardly blame the Countess for acting as she did. After all, one dislikes being called "old witch" (*staraia ved'ma*) and being threatened with a pistol, just as much as one abhors dying, even at such an advanced age. One may conclude therefore, that the Countess assumed the form of the queen of spades and, acting as befits a lady of her suit, spited Germann, *sygrala Germannu v piku,* as the Russian expression goes.

This simple, if fantastic, explanation has one fundamental flaw, however. At one point Pushkin confides to the reader that "the Countess hard by no means a bad heart." Trusting Pushkin, I would like to suggest that Germann was ruined not because of the Countess's ill will but rather in spite of her goodwill. During her nocturnal visit, the Countess made it clear that she came to Germann against her will ("ia prishla k tebe protiv svoei voli"). She also reveals the three cards to him against her will: "mne veleno ispolnit' tvoiu pros'bu." In both cases the Countess seems to act on behalf of some other involved party. But then comes the unexpected move: "*I will forgive you my death,* under the condition that you marry my ward, Lizaveta Ivanovna."[49]

Forgiveness and compassion are virtues not traditionally associated with the vengeful ghosts of gothic lore, yet the Countess forgives Germann of her own accord, *because of her good heart.* One can argue that her sudden, albeit posthumous concern for Liza's well-being is an attempt to atone for the ill-treatment of her poor ward, and in establishing this last condition, the Countess is arranging Liza's future. If Germann were to marry Liza, his fabulous win would come in lieu of her dowry and would also handsomely compensate for Liza's salary which, as Pushkin tells us, "was never paid in full."[50] Thus, if Pushkin's statement about the Countess's heart can be trusted, and if her concern for Liza's well-being is genuine, it is highly unlikely that the Countess would double-cross Germann, for the ruin of Liza's benefactor could not be in her interest.

Yet the Countess may have concluded from his behavior that he had no intention of marrying her ward. Germann's predicament would have been further exacerbated if Liza's chastity had been compromised during that night she spent, "bare-armed and open-chested," alone with her "midnight bridegroom."[51] Because Germann has disregarded an important part of the contract with the dead Countess—for both love and magic are contracts—the "Vénus moscovite" intercedes and in the guise of the queen of spades ruins the knave.

But what if Germann had intended to marry Liza? In that case, his ruin must have been orchestrated by forces beyond the Countess's control. There remains only one character capable of this meddling. Germann was ruined through the diabolical intervention of the Wandering Jew, the discoverer of the elixir of life and of the philosopher's stone, the alchemist, spy, and founder of Freemasonry, Count Saint-Germain himself. The notorious master of the three cards, he prevents Germann from winning the "superfluous" and robs him even of the "necessary." Germann's 47,000 rubles, the patrimony left to him by his thrifty German father, comes to the banker Chekalinskii, while Germann ends up in the insane asylum.

Diana Burgin offered the most intriguing argument for the necessity of this seemingly excessive punishment. Causing the old lady's death is only the most overt of Germann's transgressions. During his visit to the Countess, Germann inadvertently stumbles upon an arcane mystery that involves a "cabalistic, erotic, familial, and possibly incestuous" relationship among three generations of gamblers and lovers: Saint-Germain, the Countess, and Chaplitskii.[52] It was Gershenzon who in 1919 deviously suggested that Saint-Germain may have helped the destitute "Vénus moscovite" in exchange for a small "romantic favor."[53] We know from Tomskii's tale that "to this day grandmother loves him with a passion and gets cross if she hears disrespectful talk about him."[54] Burgin suggested that Chaplitskii, to whom the Countess once revealed the three cards, might be their natural son. (It is rumored that Saint-Germain himself was the natural son of the Queen of Spain.) But, in order to qualify for Saint-Germain's inheritance, Chaplitskii had to become the Countess's lover. Gershenzon was the first to intimate that the Countess passed down the secret to the distressed young gambler for his "leniency toward her fading charms."[55] To complete this arcane genealogy, J. Thomas Shaw added to it the banker Chekalinskii who acts as "the card-playing agent of fate." A man of about sixty, Chekalinskii is of "the right age to be the 'son' of the Countess and Chaplitskii."[56] It seems that Saint-Germain's incestual clan, spanning four generations of gamblers and lovers, is governed by strict laws of primogeniture (and paranomasia) according to which *Chaplitskii* and *Chekalinskii,* rather than Germann, are the legitimate heirs. Unlike the true members of Saint-Germain's cabal, Germann was averse to risk and to love, which further disqualifies him from the patrimony. Thus, it is only befitting that the banker Chekalinskii should dispossess the pretender.

Germann, of course, is unaware of this cabal, yet on several occasions he comes dangerously close to its tabooridden scenario. At one point he considers becoming a lover of the old Countess, mentions to her some "covenant with the devil," and is willing to take her "terrible sin" upon his soul. Prying from the Countess her secret, Germann inadvertently evokes the "cry of a new-born son" and beseeches her by appealing to the "feelings of a wife, mistress, mother." At first the Countess dismisses the whole affair as a joke: "Eto byla shutka." But when Germann mentions Chaplitskii's name, she becomes "visibly uneasy" and, for the first time, shows a "profound stirring of her heart" (*cherty ee izobrazili sil' noe dvizhenie dushi*).[57] The amorous innuendo lingers even after her death. As Germann leaves the house by the secret staircase, he imagines some eighteenth-century *beau,* "with hair combed *à l'oiseau royal,* pressing his three-cornered hat to his heart,"[58] stealing into the Countess's boudoir. Was it the apparition of Chaplitskii, or of Saint-Germain himself, returning to claim the Countess's soul? Such musing would not be far off the historical mark: In 1762, when the Countess was in her thirties, Saint-Germain actually visited Petersburg and was involved in the conspiracy that ousted Peter III and brought Catherine II to the throne. While in Russia, Saint-Germain stayed at the house of Princess Mariia Golitsyna, a relative of Pushkin's prototype for the Countess.[59] The amorous innuendo transpires

also through the liturgical words of the bishop's funeral sermon: "The angel of death found her [. . .] waiting for the midnight bridegroom."[60] And toward the end of the service Germann himself becomes implicated in the most risqué aspect of the cabal. A close relative of the deceased misidentifies him as the Countess's "illegitimate son." Thus, because Germann inadvertently disturbed the privacy of Saint-Germain's clan and came within a hairsbreadth of its secret, the patriarch sends the ghost of his mistress to punish the intruder.

For those who dislike this magic scenario and would prefer to remain on this side of the supernatural, there is a simpler explanation for Germann's ruin. Pushkin punishes Germann out of Masonic loyalty to Count Saint-Germain—both men were members of the Ovid Lodge in Odessa. Simultaneously, in a gesture of chivalry, Pushkin intercedes on behalf of the two slighted ladies. By chastising Germann for his caddishness, Pushkin fulfills the old lady's last wish better than she had ever envisioned: he marries off her heartbroken and dowryless ward to the wealthy son of the Countess's former steward. With this offstage marriage, the matchmaker Pushkin transfers a substantial part of the Countess's fortune to poor Liza, for it was known that the "numerous domestics [. . .] did what they pleased, robbing the moribund old woman left, right, and center."[61]

Having meted out justice, Pushkin also settles his own poetic scores with Germann, who scoffed at Tomskii's story, calling it a "fairy tale." What the German engineer berated as *Dichtung,* Pushkin stages as pure *Wahrheit.* The author surrounds his hero (and the reader) with uncanny events, teases him with tantalizing anagrams, chronograms, and cryptograms that the calculating engineer repeatedly fails to crack, and when he also fails to respond to the call of Liza's heart, Pushkin spites Germann with the fatal card, thus completing his path from the beldam to bedlam.

Dostoevskii called *The Queen of Spades* "the pinnacle of the art of the fantastic."[62] Its concealed galvanism and the seamless weaving of the fantastic with the realistic invites yet frustrates logical decoding, leaving reader and critic alike to perpetually sway between natural and supernatural explanations for the inexplicable. Pushkin's fantastic tale is a positive proof of Lord Byron's claim that "'the Artist' who has rendered the 'game of cards poetical' is by far greater" than one who describes a "Walk in a forest" badly.[63] By the same token, Pushkin also fulfills Baron Brambeus's prophecy that *The Queen of Spades* will be read with the "same pleasure by a Countess and merchant alike."[64] We can only guess what Anna Fedotovna thought of it:

"Paul!" called the Countess from behind the screen. "Send me a new novel, will you, but please not the kind they write nowadays."

"What do you mean, *grand' maman?*"

"I mean a novel in which the hero does not strangle either his mother or his father [. . .]"

"There are no such novels these days. Would you perhaps like some Russian ones?"

"You don't mean to say there are Russian novels? . . . Send some to me, my dear, send some by all means!"[65]

Notes

The first portion of this article develops the argument I made in a note "Real'noe i fantasticheskoe v 'Pikovoj dame,'" in *Revue des études Slaves* 59 (1987): 263-67. I would like to thank my anonymous referees for several felicitous formulations and the guest editor of this issue, Stephanie Sandler, for her inspiring suggestions.

1. A. S. Pushkin, *Polnoe sobranie sochinenii,* 17 vols. (Moscow, 1937-1959), 8.1:228-29. All Russian quotations are from this volume (hereafter *PSS,* 17 vols.); all translations of *The Queen of Spades* are from Alexander Pushkin, *Complete Prose Fiction,* trans. and ed. Paul Debreczeny (Stanford, 1983; hereafter *CPF*). All other translations are mine.

2. 15 June 1880; F. M. Dostoevskii, *Pis'ma,* ed. A. S. Dolinin (Moscow, 1959), 4:178.

3. See Tzvetan Todorov, *The Fantastic: A Structural Approach to a Literary Genre,* trans. Richard Howard (Ithaca, 1975), 25-26.

4. Caryl Emerson, "'The Queen of Spades' and the Open End," in David Bethea, ed., *Pushkin Today* (Bloomington, 1993), 32.

5. Mikhail Gershenzon, *Mudrost' Pushkina* (Moscow, 1919), 102.

6. Pointed out by N. Kashin, "Po povodu 'Pikovoi damy,'" *Pushkin i ego sovremenniki,* 1927, nos. 31-32:34.

7. Viktor Vinogradov, "Stil' 'Pikovoi damy,'" *Vremennik Pushkinskoi komissii* (1936): 87-88. Karl Heun wrote under the pseudonym Heinrich Clauren. His novella "Gollandskii kupets" was translated in *Syn otechestva* 101, no. 9 (1825): 3-51, and reprinted in 1832. See also I. Gribushin, "Iz nabliudenii nad tekstami Pushkina: Vyigrysh na troiku i semerku do 'Pikovoi damy,'" *Vremennik Pushkinskoi komissii* (1973): 85-89.

8. For other subtexts, see Paul Debreczeny, *The Other Pushkin* (Stanford, 1983), 204-9.

9. See Boris Tomashevskii's letter to André Meynieux, in Pouchkine, *Oeuvres complètes,* ed. A. Meynieux, 3 vols. (Paris, 1953-58), 3:500*n*5; and Vladimir Nabokov, *Eugene Onegin: A Novel in Verse by Aleksandr Pushkin,* 4 vols. (Princeton, 1964), 2:261.

10. See Aleksandr Slonimskii, "O kompozitsii 'Pikovoi damy,'" *Pushkinskii sbornik pamiati prof. S. A. Vengerova* (Moscow, 1923), 171-80; Peter Bicilli, "Zametki o Pushkine," *Slavia* 11 (1932): 557-60; Vinogradov, "Stil' 'Pikovoi damy'"; J. Thomas Shaw,

"The 'Conclusion' of Pushkin's 'Queen of Spades,'" in Z. Folejewski, ed., *Studies in Russian and Polish Literature in Honor of Waclaw Lednicki* (The Hague, 1962), 114-26; Andrei Kodjak, "'The Queen of Spades' in the Context of the Faust Legend," in Andrei Kodjak and Kirill Taranovsky, eds., *Alexander Puškin: A Symposium on the 175th Anniversary of His Birth* (New York, 1976), 87-118; Lauren G. Leighton, "Numbers and Numerology in 'The Queen of Spades,'" *Canadian Slavonic Papers* 19, no. 4 (1977): 417-43.

11. The importance of the sequence was pointed out by Diana Burgin, "The Mystery of 'Pikovaia Dama': A New Interpretation," in Joachim T. Baer and Norman W. Ingham, eds., *Mnemozina: Studia litteraria Russica in honorem Vsevolod Setchkarev* (Munich, 1974), 46; and Nathan Rosen, "The Magic Cards in 'The Queen of Spades,'" *Slavic and East European Journal* 19 (1975): 256.

12. *PSS,* 17 vols., 8.1:239-40; *CPF,* 222-23. I have capitalized only the most direct allusions to cards found by Leighton and have added to them one ace and one seven. See Leighton, "Gematria in 'The Queen of Spades': A Decembrist Puzzle," *Slavic and East European Journal* 21 (1976): 455-56.

13. Gershenzon, *Mudrost' Pushkina,* 111-12.

14. *PSS,* 17 vols., 8.1:239, 244, 245, 247, and *CPF,* 222, 226, 227, 229.

15. Emerson, "'The Queen of Spades' and the Open End," 6.

16. *PSS,* 17 vols., 8.1:234, and *CPF,* 217 (emphasis mine).

17. *CPF,* 217 (emphasis mine).

18. *PSS,* 17 vols., 8.1:243, and *CPF,* 225 (emphasis mine).

19. *PSS,* 17 vols., 8.1:235, and *CPF,* 219 (emphasis mine).

20. Slonimskii, "O kompozitsii 'Pikovoi damy,'" 176.

21. Kodjak, "'The Queen of Spades' in the Context of the Faust Legend," 89.

22. Rosen, "The Magic Cards in 'The Queen of Spades,'" 255.

23. "For us, charades and logogriphs are child's play, but in Karamzin's time, when lexical detail and play with devices were in the foreground, such games were a literary genre." Iurii Tynianov, "Literaturnyi fakt" (1924), in *Poetika, istoriia literatury, kino* (Moscow, 1977), 275. Similar anagrammatic jeux d'esprit were a favorite pastime among Pushkin's friends. The readers of their school journal, *Litseiskii mudrets,* readily solved A. Illichevskii's conundrums such as the following "charade-logogriph" (Illichevskii's own term): "Sadovniki v sadu sadiat

menia, / Poety nad mogiloi. / Otkin' mne golovu,—i vot uzh vitiaz' ia, / Khotia po pravde khilyi. / Otkinesh' briukho mne, ia stanovlius' travoi, / Il' kushan'em pered toboi. / Slozhi mne briukho s golovoi—/ Ia stanu pred toboi s tovarom, / Ni slova ne skazal ia darom, / Poimi zh menia, chitatel' moi." (The gardeners plant me in the garden, / the poets over the grave. / Cut off my head—I become a legendary warrior, / though, to tell the truth, a wimpy one. / Remove my belly—I turn into grass / or food before your very eyes. / Attach the belly to my head—/ I stand before you with my wares. / Not a word I said in vain; / understand me, my reader?). K. Ia. Grot, *Pushkinskii litsei,* 2d ed. (St. Petersburg, 1998), 333. The answer to the charade is "kiparis" (cypress); its components: "Paris, ris, kipa" (Paris, rice, stack). For Pushkin's use of anagrammatic riddles, see my articles "The Sound and Theme in the Prose of A. S. Pushkin: A Logo-Semantic Study of Paronomasia," *Slavic and East European Journal* 27 (1983): 1-18; and "'The Shot' by Aleksandr Pushkin and Its Trajectories," in J. Douglas Clayton, ed., *Issues in Russian Literature before 1917: Selected Papers of the Third World Congress for Soviet and East European Studies* (Columbus, Ohio, 1989), 62-74.

24. The fact that the ace is discovered as the last card of the series is conclusive proof of the infallibility of Pushkin's 3-7-1 sequence and, by the same token, of the shortsightedness of the interpreters of this phrase. See Slonimskii, "O kompozitsii 'Pikovoi damy,'" 176; Kashin, "Po povodu 'Pikovoi damy,'" 33-34; V. V. Vinogradov, *Stil' Pushkina* (Moscow, 1941), 588; L. V. Chkhaidze, "O real'nom znachenii motiva trekh kart v 'Pikovoi dame,'" *Pushkin: Issledovaniia i materialy* (Moscow-Leningrad, 1960), 3:458; Shaw, "The 'Conclusion' of Pushkin's 'Queen of Spades,'" 119; L. S. Sidiakov, *Khudozhestvennaia proza A. S. Pushkina* (Riga, 1973), 117; S. G. Bocharov, *Poetika Pushkina* (Moscow, 1974), 187; Rosen, "The Magic Cards in 'The Queen of Spades,'" 255; Kodjak, "'The Queen of Spades' in the Context of the Faust Legend," 89; L. Leighton, "Numbers and Numerology in 'The Queen of Spades,'" 427, and many others.

25. *PSS,* 17 vols., 8.1:249, and *CPF,* 230 (emphasis mine).

26. Rosen, "The Magic Cards in 'The Queen of Spades,'" 262.

27. Cf. A. Griboedov, "Chto za tuzy v Moskve zhivut i umiraiut" (*Gore ot uma,* act 2, scene 1). There is a secondary sound association between the *puzastyi muzhchina* and *tuz:* a chubby little fellow is also called *butuz* in Russian.

28. Rosen, "The Magic Cards in 'The Queen of Spades,'" 262.

29. Harry B. Weber, "'Pikovaia dama': A Case for Freemasonry in Russian Literature," *Slavic and East European Journal* 12 (1968): 443.

30. "Khudozhestvennyi mir Pushkina," in G. M. Koka, ed., *Pushkin ob iskusstve* (Moscow, 1962), 18. This arch is reproduced by Rosen, "The Magic Cards in 'The Queen of Spades,'" 264.

31. Rosen, "The Magic Cards in 'The Queen of Spades,'" 263; suggested by Shaw, "The 'Conclusion' of Pushkin's 'Queen of Spades,'" 120.

32. Kodjak, "'The Queen of Spades' in the Context of the Faust Legend," 97.

33. *PSS,* 17 vols., 8.1:236, and *CPF,* 219 (emphasis mine).

34. Those who might take my delicate leg twisting for leg pulling should find reassurance in Pushkin's words to Prince Viazemskii: "Aristocratic prejudices are suitable for you but not for me—I look at a finished poem of mine as a cobbler looks at a pair of his boots: I sell for profit. The shop foreman judges my jack-boots (*botforty*) as not up to the standard, he rips them up and ruins the piece of goods; I am the loser. I go and complain to the district policeman." From a letter to Viazemskii, March 1823, in J. Thomas Shaw, trans. and ed., *The Letters of Alexander Pushkin* (Madison, 1967), 111. My incredulous arbiter may turn for additional solace to Pushkin's parable "Sapozhnik" (The cobbler, 1829): "A cobbler, staring at a painting, / Has found the footwear on it flawed. / The artist promptly fixed the failing, / But this is what the cobbler thought: / 'It seems the face is slightly crooked . . . / Isn't that bosom rather nude?' / Annoyed, Apelles interrupted: 'Judge not, my friend, above the boot!'" (trans. Rosanne Shield, unpublished manuscript).

35. *CPF,* 223.

36. N. Rabkina, "Istoricheskii prototip 'Pikovoi damy,'" *Voprosy istorii* 43, no. 1 (1968): 213-16. Pushkin acknowledged the link between the princess and the Countess in his diary entry of 7 April 1834.

37. V. Grigorenko et al., eds., *Pushkin v vospominaniiakh sovremennikov,* 2 vols. (Moscow, 1977), 2:195.

38. In his commentary to *Eugene Onegin,* Nabokov erroneously attributed this novel by the Swedish romantic writer Clas Johan Livijn to its German translator la Motte-Fouqué (Nabokov, *Eugene Onegin,* 3:97). The original title of Livijn's novel is *Spader Dame, en Berättelse i Bref, Funne pa Danviken* (1824). Pushkin could have been familiar with the novel in a French translation. Moreover, its Swedish title and a brief plot summary appeared in *Moskovskii telegraf* (1825). See D. M. Sharypkin, "Vokrug 'Pikovoi damy,'" *Vremennik Pushkinskoi komissii* (1972): 128-31; and J. Douglas Clayton, "'Spader Dame,' 'Pique-Dame,' and 'Pikovaia dama': A German Source for Pushkin?" *Germano-Slavica,* 1974, no. 4:5-10.

39. Gershenzon, *Mudrost' Pushkina,* 102-3.

40. Chkhaidze, "O real'nom znachenii motiva trekh kart v 'Pikovoi dame,'" 459.

41. Gary Rosenshield, "Choosing the Right Card: Madness, Gambling, and the Imagination in Pushkin's 'The Queen of Spades,'" *PMLA* 109 (1994): 1004. I have to admit that I fail to understand this argument. If gambling was what Germann really desired, as Rosenshield claims, why should selecting the ace and winning 367,000 rubles have prevented him from gambling again at some future point? The true gambler Chaplitskii continued to gamble after his fabulous bet on the three cards the Countess had revealed to him.

42. Vinogradov, "Stil' 'Pikovoi damy,'" 96-97.

43. *CPF,* 223.

44. Noted by Vinogradov, "Stil' 'Pikovoi damy,'" 103.

45. A number of these frames were also pointed out by Rosen.

46. *CPF,* 212.

47. See Nikolai Osipovich Lerner, *Proza Pushkina,* 2d ed. (Moscow, 1923), 47, and Shaw, trans. and ed., *The Letters,* 362, 394. The confusion of the ace with the queen and their gender could also have been facilitated by Germann's possible misunderstanding of the French phrase from Tomskii's tale: "au jeu de *la Reine*" (the queen's game—fem.), which Germann might have associated with *au jeu de l'araignée* (the spider's game—masc.). This pun was mentioned by Rosen, "The Magic Cards in 'The Queen of Spades,'" 273*n*. The German engineer's French was probably not as good as that of his aristocratic friends.

48. Vinogradov, "Stil' 'Pikovoi damy,'" 97.

49. *PSS,* 17 vols., 8.1:247; *CPF,* 230 (emphasis mine).

50. Ibid., 217.

51. Between 3:00 A.M. when Germann enters Liza's room and the moment he kisses her good-bye in the morning, another winter night, long and dark enough to accommodate a Dantesque pause, passes imperceptibly. We learn from the tale's epilogue that Liza has married and is bringing up a poor relative, perhaps "her own illegitimate daughter by Germann." Suggested by Neil Cornwell, *Pushkin's "The Queen of Spades,"* Critical Studies in Russian Literature (London, 1993), 62-63.

52. Burgin, "The Mystery of 'Pikovaia Dama': A New Interpretation," 46-56.

53. Gershenzon, *Mudrost' Pushkina,* 98.

54. *CPF,* 213.

55. Gershenzon, *Mudrost' Pushkina,* 98.

56. Shaw, "The 'Conclusion' of Pushkin's 'Queen of Spades,'" 125*n*23.

57. *PSS,* 17 vols., 8.1:241, and *CPF,* 224.

58. *CPF,* 228.

59. See Cornwell, *Pushkin's "The Queen of Spades,"* 88-89.

60. *CPF,* 228.

61. *CPF,* 217. Noted by Shaw, "The 'Conclusion' of Pushkin's 'Queen of Spades,'" 121.

62. Dostoevskii, *Pis'ma,* 4:178.

63. "Letter to John Murray Esq" (1821), in Andrew Nicholson, ed., *The Complete Miscellaneous Prose* (Oxford, 1991), 141. See Shaw, trans. and ed., *The Letters,* 281.

64. *PSS,* 17 vols., 15:110, 322.

65. *CPF,* 215.

FURTHER READING

Biography

Mirsky, D. S. "Prose." In *Pushkin,* pp. 183-86. New York: E. P. Dutton & Co., 1963.
> Provides a summary of the novella and deems it "beyond doubt Pushkin's masterpiece in prose."

Criticism

Bayley, John. "Prose." In *Pushkin: A Comparative Commentary,* pp. 306-54. London: Cambridge University Press, 1971.
> Traces Pushkin's stylistic development by examining his prose works, including *The Queen of Spades.*

Lotman, Jurij M. "Theme and Plot: The Theme of Cards and the Card Game in Russian Literature of the Nineteenth Century." *PTL* 3, no. 3 (October 1978): 455-92.
> Explores the function of the card game in Russian literature, including *The Queen of Spades.*

Nabokov, Véra and Barabtarlo, Gennady. "A Possible Source for Pushkin's 'Queen of Spades'." *Russian Literature Triquarterly* 24 (1991): 43-62.
> Regards Friedrich Heinrich Carl, Baron de La Motte Fouqué's *Pique-Dame* as an influence on *The Queen of Spades.*

Pursglove, Michael. "Chronology in Pushkin's 'Pikovaya dama'." *Irish Slavonic Studies* 6 (1985): 11-18.
> Offers a timeline for the events of *The Queen of Spades.*

Reeder, Roberta. "The Queen of Spades: A Parody of the Hoffmann Tale." In *New Perspectives on Nineteenth-Century Russian Prose,* edited by George J. Gutsche and Lauren G. Leighton, pp. 73-98. Columbus, Ohio: Slavica Publishers, 1981.

Examines *The Queen of Spades* as a parody of an E. T. A. Hoffmann tale.

Shapovalov, Veronica. "A. S. Pushkin and the St. Petersburg Text." In *The Contexts of Aleksandr Sergeevich Pushkin,* edited by Peter I. Barta and Ulrich Goebel, pp. 43-54. Lewiston, New York: The Edwin Mellen Press, 1988.

Considers *The Queen of Spades* as a prime example of the "St. Petersburg text."

Shrayer, Maxim D. "Rethinking Romantic Irony: Puškin, Byron, Schlegel and *The Queen of Spades.*" *Slavic and East European Journal* 36, no. 4 (winter 1992): 397-414.

Explores the romantic irony in The Queen of Spades in order to clarify Pushkin's status as a Romantic writer.

Vickery, Walter N. "*The Little House in Kolomna, Angelo,* Fairy Tales in Verse, *The Bronze Horseman,* and Prose Writings." In *Alexander Pushkin,* pp. 126-28. New York: Twayne, 1992.

Brief synopsis of the tale and its major thematic concerns.

Additional coverage of Pushkin's life and career is contained in the following sources published by the Gale Group: *Dictionary of Literary Biography,* **Vol. 205;** *DISCovering Authors; DISCovering Authors: British Edition; DISCovering Authors: Canadian Edition; DISCovering Authors Modules: Dramatists, Most-studied Authors* **and** *Poets; DISCovering Authors 3.0; Exploring Short Stories; Nineteenth-Century Literature Criticism,* **Vols. 3, 27, 83;** *Poetry Criticism,* **Vol. 10;** *Reference Guide to Short Fiction,* **Ed. 2;** *Reference Guide to World Literature,* **Ed. 2;** *Short Story Criticism,* **Vol. 27;** *Short Stories for Students,* **Vol. 9;** *Something About the Author,* **Vol. 61; and** *World Literature Criticism.*

How to Use This Index

The main references

Calvino, Italo
   1923-1985 .... **CLC** 5, 8, 11, 22, 33, 39,
                            73; **SSC** 3

---

list all author entries in the following Gale Literary Criticism series:

BLC = *Black Literature Criticism*
CLC = *Contemporary Literary Criticism*
CLR = *Children's Literature Review*
CMLC = *Classical and Medieval Literature Criticism*
DA = *DISCovering Authors*
DAB = *DISCovering Authors: British*
DAC = *DISCovering Authors: Canadian*
DAM = *DISCovering Authors: Modules*
     DRAM: *Dramatists Module;* *MST:* *Most-Studied Authors Module;*
     MULT: *Multicultural Authors Module;* *NOV:* *Novelists Module;*
     POET: *Poets Module;* *POP:* *Popular Fiction and Genre Authors Module*
DC = *Drama Criticism*
HLC = *Hispanic Literature Criticism*
LC = *Literature Criticism from 1400 to 1800*
NCLC = *Nineteenth-Century Literature Criticism*
NNAL = *Native North American Literature*
PC = *Poetry Criticism*
SSC = *Short Story Criticism*
TCLC = *Twentieth-Century Literary Criticism*
WLC = *World Literature Criticism, 1500 to the Present*

The cross-references

See also CANR 23; CA 85-88;
obituary CA116

---

list all author entries in the following Gale biographical and literary sources:

AAYA = *Authors & Artists for Young Adults*
AITN = *Authors in the News*
BEST = *Bestsellers*
BW = *Black Writers*
CA = *Contemporary Authors*
CAAS = *Contemporary Authors Autobiography Series*
CABS = *Contemporary Authors Bibliographical Series*
CANR = *Contemporary Authors New Revision Series*
CAP = *Contemporary Authors Permanent Series*
CDALB = *Concise Dictionary of American Literary Biography*
CDBLB = *Concise Dictionary of British Literary Biography*
DLB = *Dictionary of Literary Biography*
DLBD = *Dictionary of Literary Biography Documentary Series*
DLBY = *Dictionary of Literary Biography Yearbook*
HW = *Hispanic Writers*
JRDA = *Junior DISCovering Authors*
MAICYA = *Major Authors and Illustrators for Children and Young Adults*
MTCW = *Major 20th-Century Writers*
SAAS = *Something about the Author Autobiography Series*
SATA = *Something about the Author*
YABC = *Yesterday's Authors of Books for Children*

Literary Criticism Series
Cumulative Author Index

Aherne, Owen
See Cassill, R(onald) V(erlin)

Ai 1947- .... **CLC 4, 14, 69**
See also CA 85-88; CAAS 13; CANR 70;
DLB 120

Aickman, Robert (Fordyce)
1914-1981 .... **CLC 57**
See also CA 5-8R; CANR 3, 72, 100; DLB
261; HGG; SUFW

Aiken, Conrad (Potter) 1889-1973 .... **CLC 1,
3, 5, 10, 52; PC 26; SSC 9**
See also AMW; CA 5-8R; 45-48; CANR 4,
60; CDALB 1929-1941; DAM NOV,
POET; DLB 9, 45, 102; EXPS; HGG;
MTCW 1, 2; RGAL 4; RGSF 2; SATA 3,
30; SSFS 8; TUS

Aiken, Joan (Delano) 1924- .... **CLC 35**
See also AAYA 1, 25; CA 9-12R, 182;
CAAE 182; CANR 4, 23, 34, 64; CLR 1,
19; DLB 161; FANT; HGG; JRDA; MAI-
CYA 1, 2; MTCW 1; RHW; SAAS 1;
SATA 2, 30, 73; SATA-Essay 109; WYA;
YAW

Ainsworth, William Harrison
1805-1882 .... **NCLC 13**
See also DLB 21; HGG; RGEL 2; SATA
24; SUFW

Aitmatov, Chingiz (Torekulovich)
1928- .... **CLC 71**
See also CA 103; CANR 38; MTCW 1;
RGSF 2; SATA 56

Akers, Floyd
See Baum, L(yman) Frank

Akhmadulina, Bella Akhatovna
1937- .... **CLC 53**
See also CA 65-68; CWP; CWW 2; DAM
POET

Akhmatova, Anna 1888-1966 ..... **CLC 11, 25,
64, 126; PC 2**
See also CA 19-20; 25-28R; CANR 35;
CAP 1; DA3; DAM POET; EW 10;
MTCW 1, 2; RGWL 2

Aksakov, Sergei Timofeyvich
1791-1859 .... **NCLC 2**
See also DLB 198

Aksenov, Vassily
See Aksyonov, Vassily (Pavlovich)

Akst, Daniel 1956- .... **CLC 109**
See also CA 161; CANR 110

Aksyonov, Vassily (Pavlovich)
1932- .... **CLC 22, 37, 101**
See also CA 53-56; CANR 12, 48, 77;
CWW 2

Akutagawa Ryunosuke
1892-1927 .... **TCLC 16; SSC 44**
See also CA 117; 154; DLB 180; MJW;
RGSF 2; RGWL 2

Alain 1868-1951 .... **TCLC 41**
See also CA 163; GFL 1789 to the Present

Alain de Lille c. 1116-c. 1203 .... **CMLC 53**
See also DLB 208

Alain-Fournier .... **TCLC 6**
See also Fournier, Henri Alban
See also DLB 65; GFL 1789 to the Present;
RGWL 2

Alanus de Insluis
See Alain de Lille

Alarcon, Pedro Antonio de
1833-1891 .... **NCLC 1**

Alas (y Urena), Leopoldo (Enrique Garcia)
1852-1901 .... **TCLC 29**
See also CA 113; 131; HW 1; RGSF 2

Albee, Edward (Franklin III) 1928- . **CLC 1,
2, 3, 5, 9, 11, 13, 25, 53, 86, 113; DC
11; WLC**
See also AITN 1; AMW; CA 5-8R; CABS
3; CAD; CANR 8, 54, 74; CD 5; CDALB
1941-1968; DA; DA3; DAB; DAC; DAM

DRAM, MST; DFS 2, 3, 8, 10, 13, 14;
DLB 7, 266; INT CANR-8; LAIT 4;
MTCW 1, 2; RGAL 4; TUS

Alberti, Rafael 1902-1999 .... **CLC 7**
See also CA 85-88; 185; CANR 81; DLB
108; HW 2; RGWL 2

Albert the Great 1193(?)-1280 ...... **CMLC 16**
See also DLB 115

Alcala-Galiano, Juan Valera y
See Valera y Alcala-Galiano, Juan

Alcayaga, Lucila Godoy
See Godoy Alcayaga, Lucila

Alcott, Amos Bronson 1799-1888 .... **NCLC 1**
See also DLB 1, 223

Alcott, Louisa May 1832-1888 . **NCLC 6, 58,
83; SSC 27; WLC**
See also AAYA 20; AMWS 1; BPFB 1;
BYA 2; CDALB 1865-1917; CLR 1, 38;
DA; DA3; DAB; DAC; DAM MST, NOV;
DLB 1, 42, 79, 223, 239, 242; DLBD 14;
FW; JRDA; LAIT 2; MAICYA 1, 2; NFS
12; RGAL 4; SATA 100; TUS; WCH;
WYA; YABC 1; YAW

Aldanov, M. A.
See Aldanov, Mark (Alexandrovich)

Aldanov, Mark (Alexandrovich)
1886(?)-1957 .... **TCLC 23**
See also CA 118; 181

Aldington, Richard 1892-1962 .... **CLC 49**
See also CA 85-88; CANR 45; DLB 20, 36,
100, 149; RGEL 2

Aldiss, Brian W(ilson) 1925- . **CLC 5, 14, 40;
SSC 36**
See also AAYA 42; CA 5-8R; CAAE 190;
CAAS 2; CANR 5, 28, 64; CN 7; DAM
NOV; DLB 14, 261; MTCW 1, 2; SATA
34; SFW 4

Aldrich, Bess Streeter
1881-1954 .... **TCLC 125**
See also CLR 70

Alegria, Claribel 1924- .... **CLC 75; HLCS 1;
PC 26**
See also CA 131; CAAS 15; CANR 66, 94;
CWW 2; DAM MULT; DLB 145; HW 1;
MTCW 1

Alegria, Fernando 1918- .... **CLC 57**
See also CA 9-12R; CANR 5, 32, 72; HW
1, 2

Aleichem, Sholom .... **TCLC 1, 35; SSC 33**
See also Rabinovitch, Sholem
See also TWA

Aleixandre, Vicente 1898-1984 ... **TCLC 113;
HLCS 1**
See also CANR 81; DLB 108; HW 2;
RGWL 2

Aleman, Mateo 1547-1615(?) .... **LC 81**

Alencon, Marguerite d'
See de Navarre, Marguerite

Alepoudelis, Odysseus
See Elytis, Odysseus
See also CWW 2

Aleshkovsky, Joseph 1929-
See Aleshkovsky, Yuz
See also CA 121; 128

Aleshkovsky, Yuz .... **CLC 44**
See also Aleshkovsky, Joseph

Alexander, Lloyd (Chudley) 1924- ... **CLC 35**
See also AAYA 1, 27; BPFB 1; BYA 5, 6,
7, 9, 10, 11; CA 1-4R; CANR 1, 24, 38,
55; CLR 1, 5, 48; CWRI 5; DLB 52;
FANT; JRDA; MAICYA 1, 2; MAICYAS
1; MTCW 1; SAAS 19; SATA 3, 49, 81,
129; SUFW; TUS; WYA; YAW

Alexander, Meena 1951- .... **CLC 121**
See also CA 115; CANR 38, 70; CP 7;
CWP; FW

Alexander, Samuel 1859-1938 .... **TCLC 77**

Alexie, Sherman (Joseph, Jr.)
1966- .... **CLC 96, 154**
See also AAYA 28; CA 138; CANR 95;
DA3; DAM MULT; DLB 175, 206;
MTCW 1; NNAL

Alfau, Felipe 1902-1999 .... **CLC 66**
See also CA 137

Alfieri, Vittorio 1749-1803 .... **NCLC 101**
See also EW 4; RGWL 2

Alfred, Jean Gaston
See Ponge, Francis

Alger, Horatio, Jr. 1832-1899 .... **NCLC 8, 83**
See also DLB 42; LAIT 2; RGAL 4; SATA
16; TUS

Al-Ghazali, Muhammad ibn Muhammad
1058-1111 .... **CMLC 50**
See also DLB 115

Algren, Nelson 1909-1981 ..... **CLC 4, 10, 33;
SSC 33**
See also AMWS 9; BPFB 1; CA 13-16R;
103; CANR 20, 61; CDALB 1941-1968;
DLB 9; DLBY 1981, 1982, 2000; MTCW
1, 2; RGAL 4; RGSF 2

Ali, Ahmed 1908-1998 .... **CLC 69**
See also CA 25-28R; CANR 15, 34

Alighieri, Dante
See Dante

Allan, John B.
See Westlake, Donald E(dwin)

Allan, Sidney
See Hartmann, Sadakichi

Allan, Sydney
See Hartmann, Sadakichi

Allard, Janet .... **CLC 59**

Allen, Edward 1948- .... **CLC 59**

Allen, Fred 1894-1956 .... **TCLC 87**

Allen, Paula Gunn 1939- .... **CLC 84**
See also AMWS 4; CA 112; 143; CANR
63; CWP; DA3; DAM MULT; DLB 175;
FW; MTCW 1; NNAL; RGAL 4

Allen, Roland
See Ayckbourn, Alan

Allen, Sarah A.
See Hopkins, Pauline Elizabeth

Allen, Sidney H.
See Hartmann, Sadakichi

Allen, Woody 1935- .... **CLC 16, 52**
See also AAYA 10; CA 33-36R; CANR 27,
38, 63; DAM POP; DLB 44; MTCW 1

Allende, Isabel 1942- . **CLC 39, 57, 97; HLC
1; WLCS**
See also AAYA 18; CA 125; 130; CANR
51, 74; CDWLB 3; CWW 2; DA3; DAM
MULT, NOV; DLB 145; DNFS 1; FW;
HW 1, 2; INT CA-130; LAIT 5; LAWS
1; MTCW 1, 2; NCFS 1; NFS 6; RGSF
2; SSFS 11; WLIT 1

Alleyn, Ellen
See Rossetti, Christina (Georgina)

Alleyne, Carla D. .... **CLC 65**

Allingham, Margery (Louise)
1904-1966 .... **CLC 19**
See also CA 5-8R; 25-28R; CANR 4, 58;
CMW 4; DLB 77; MSW; MTCW 1, 2

Allingham, William 1824-1889 ...... **NCLC 25**
See also DLB 35; RGEL 2

Allison, Dorothy E. 1949- .... **CLC 78, 153**
See also CA 140; CANR 66, 107; CSW;
DA3; FW; MTCW 1; NFS 11; RGAL 4

Alloula, Malek .... **CLC 65**

Allston, Washington 1779-1843 .... **NCLC 2**
See also DLB 1, 235

Almedingen, E. M. .... **CLC 12**
See also Almedingen, Martha Edith von
See also SATA 3

Almedingen, Martha Edith von 1898-1971
See Almedingen, E. M.
See also CA 1-4R; CANR 1

Almodovar, Pedro 1949(?)- .... **CLC 114;
HLCS 1**
See also CA 133; CANR 72; HW 2

Almqvist, Carl Jonas Love
1793-1866 .... **NCLC 42**

Alonso, Damaso 1898-1990 .... **CLC 14**
See also CA 110; 131; 130; CANR 72; DLB
108; HW 1, 2

Alov
See Gogol, Nikolai (Vasilyevich)

Alta 1942- .... **CLC 19**
See also CA 57-60

Alter, Robert B(ernard) 1935- .... **CLC 34**
See also CA 49-52; CANR 1, 47, 100

Alther, Lisa 1944- .... **CLC 7, 41**
See also BPFB 1; CA 65-68; CAAS 30;
CANR 12, 30, 51; CN 7; CSW; GLL 2;
MTCW 1

Althusser, L.
See Althusser, Louis

Althusser, Louis 1918-1990 .... **CLC 106**
See also CA 131; 132; CANR 102; DLB
242

Altman, Robert 1925- .... **CLC 16, 116**
See also CA 73-76; CANR 43

Alurista
See Urista, Alberto H.
See also DLB 82; HLCS 1

Alvarez, A(lfred) 1929- .... **CLC 5, 13**
See also CA 1-4R; CANR 3, 33, 63, 101;
CN 7; CP 7; DLB 14, 40

Alvarez, Alejandro Rodriguez 1903-1965
See Casona, Alejandro
See also CA 131; 93-96; HW 1

Alvarez, Julia 1950- .... **CLC 93; HLCS 1**
See also AAYA 25; AMWS 7; CA 147;
CANR 69, 101; DA3; MTCW 1; NFS 5,
9; SATA 129; WLIT 1

Alvaro, Corrado 1896-1956 .... **TCLC 60**
See also CA 163; DLB 264

Amado, Jorge 1912-2001 ... **CLC 13, 40, 106;
HLC 1**
See also CA 77-80; 201; CANR 35, 74;
DAM MULT, NOV; DLB 113; HW 2;
LAW; LAWS 1; MTCW 1, 2; RGWL 2;
TWA; WLIT 1

Ambler, Eric 1909-1998 .... **CLC 4, 6, 9**
See also BRWS 4; CA 9-12R; 171; CANR
7, 38, 74; CMW 4; CN 7; DLB 77; MSW;
MTCW 1, 2; TEA

Ambrose, Stephen E(dward)
1936- .... **CLC 145**
See also CA 1-4R; CANR 3, 43, 57, 83,
105; NCFS 2; SATA 40

Amichai, Yehuda 1924-2000 .. **CLC 9, 22, 57,
116; PC 38**
See also CA 85-88; 189; CANR 46, 60, 99;
CWW 2; MTCW 1

Amichai, Yehudah
See Amichai, Yehuda

Amiel, Henri Frederic 1821-1881 .... **NCLC 4**
See also DLB 217

Amis, Kingsley (William)
1922-1995 ...... **CLC 1, 2, 3, 5, 8, 13, 40,
44, 129**
See also AITN 2; BPFB 1; BRWS 2; CA
9-12R; 150; CANR 8, 28, 54; CDBLB
1945-1960; CN 7; CP 7; DA; DA3; DAB;
DAC; DAM MST, NOV; DLB 15, 27,
100, 139; DLBY 1996; HGG; INT
CANR-8; MTCW 1, 2; RGEL 2; RGSF 2;
SFW 4

Amis, Martin (Louis) 1949- .... **CLC 4, 9, 38,
62, 101**
See also BEST 90:3; BRWS 4; CA 65-68;
CANR 8, 27, 54, 73, 95; CN 7; DA3;
DLB 14, 194; INT CANR-27; MTCW 1

Ammons, A(rchie) R(andolph)
1926-2001 ...... **CLC 2, 3, 5, 8, 9, 25, 57,
108; PC 16**
See also AITN 1; AMWS 7; CA 9-12R;
193; CANR 6, 36, 51, 73, 107; CP 7;
CSW; DAM POET; DLB 5, 165; MTCW
1, 2; RGAL 4

Amo, Tauraatua i
See Adams, Henry (Brooks)

Amory, Thomas 1691(?)-1788 .... **LC 48**
See also DLB 39

Anand, Mulk Raj 1905- .... **CLC 23, 93**
See also CA 65-68; CANR 32, 64; CN 7;
DAM NOV; MTCW 1, 2; RGSF 2

Anatol
See Schnitzler, Arthur

Anaximander c. 611 B.C.-c. 546
B.C. .... **CMLC 22**

Anaya, Rudolfo A(lfonso) 1937- ...... **CLC 23,
148; HLC 1**
See also AAYA 20; BYA 13; CA 45-48;
CAAS 4; CANR 1, 32, 51; CN 7; DAM
MULT, NOV; DLB 82, 206; HW 1; LAIT
4; MTCW 1, 2; NFS 12; RGAL 4; RGSF
2; WLIT 1

Andersen, Hans Christian
1805-1875 ... **NCLC 7, 79; SSC 6; WLC**
See also CLR 6; DA; DA3; DAB; DAC;
DAM MST, POP; EW 6; MAICYA 1, 2;
RGSF 2; RGWL 2; SATA 100; TWA;
WCH; YABC 1

Anderson, C. Farley
See Mencken, H(enry) L(ouis); Nathan,
George Jean

Anderson, Jessica (Margaret) Queale
1916- .... **CLC 37**
See also CA 9-12R; CANR 4, 62; CN 7

Anderson, Jon (Victor) 1940- .... **CLC 9**
See also CA 25-28R; CANR 20; DAM
POET

Anderson, Lindsay (Gordon)
1923-1994 .... **CLC 20**
See also CA 125; 128; 146; CANR 77

Anderson, Maxwell 1888-1959 .... **TCLC 2**
See also CA 105; 152; DAM DRAM; DLB
7, 228; MTCW 2; RGAL 4

Anderson, Poul (William)
1926-2001 .... **CLC 15**
See also AAYA 5, 34; BPFB 1; BYA 6, 8,
9; CA 1-4R, 181; 199; CAAE 181; CAAS
2; CANR 2, 15, 34, 64, 110; CLR 58;
DLB 8; FANT; INT CANR-15; MTCW 1,
2; SATA 90; SATA-Brief 39; SATA-Essay
106; SCFW 2; SFW 4; SUFW

Anderson, Robert (Woodruff)
1917- .... **CLC 23**
See also AITN 1; CA 21-24R; CANR 32;
DAM DRAM; DLB 7; LAIT 5

Anderson, Roberta Joan
See Mitchell, Joni

Anderson, Sherwood 1876-1941 ..... **TCLC 1,
10, 24, 123; SSC 1, 46; WLC**
See also AAYA 30; AMW; BPFB 1; CA
104; 121; CANR 61; CDALB 1917-1929;
DA; DA3; DAB; DAC; DAM MST, NOV;
DLB 4, 9, 86; DLBD 1; EXPS; GLL 2;
MTCW 1, 2; NFS 4; RGAL 4; RGSF 2;
SSFS 4, 10, 11; TUS

Andier, Pierre
See Desnos, Robert

Andouard
See Giraudoux, Jean(-Hippolyte)

Andrade, Carlos Drummond de ..... **CLC 18**
See also Drummond de Andrade, Carlos
See also RGWL 2

Andrade, Mario de .... **TCLC 43**
See also de Andrade, Mario
See also LAW; RGWL 2; WLIT 1

Andreae, Johann V(alentin)
1586-1654 .... **LC 32**
See also DLB 164

Andreas Capellanus fl. c. 1185- .... **CMLC 45**
See also DLB 208

Andreas-Salome, Lou 1861-1937 ... **TCLC 56**
See also CA 178; DLB 66

Andress, Lesley
See Sanders, Lawrence

Andrewes, Lancelot 1555-1626 .... **LC 5**
See also DLB 151, 172

Andrews, Cicily Fairfield
See West, Rebecca

Andrews, Elton V.
See Pohl, Frederik

Andreyev, Leonid (Nikolaevich)
1871-1919 .... **TCLC 3**
See also CA 104; 185

Andric, Ivo 1892-1975 .... **CLC 8; SSC 36**
See also CA 81-84; 57-60; CANR 43; 60;
CDWLB 4; DLB 147; EW 11; MTCW 1;
RGSF 2; RGWL 2

Androvar
See Prado (Calvo), Pedro

Angelique, Pierre
See Bataille, Georges

Angell, Roger 1920- .... **CLC 26**
See also CA 57-60; CANR 13, 44, 70; DLB
171, 185

Angelou, Maya 1928- ..... **CLC 12, 35, 64, 77,
155; BLC 1; PC 32; WLCS**
See also AAYA 7, 20; AMWS 4; BPFB 1;
BW 2, 3; BYA 2; CA 65-68; CANR 19,
42, 65; CDALBS; CLR 53; CP 7; CPW;
CSW; CWP; DA; DA3; DAB; DAC;
DAM MST, MULT, POET, POP; DLB 38;
EXPN; EXPP; LAIT 4; MAICYA 2; MAI-
CYAS 1; MAWW; MTCW 1, 2; NCFS 2;
NFS 2; PFS 2, 3; RGAL 4; SATA 49;
WYA; YAW

Angouleme, Marguerite d'
See de Navarre, Marguerite

Anna Comnena 1083-1153 .... **CMLC 25**

Annensky, Innokenty (Fyodorovich)
1856-1909 .... **TCLC 14**
See also CA 110; 155

Annunzio, Gabriele d'
See D'Annunzio, Gabriele

Anodos
See Coleridge, Mary E(lizabeth)

Anon, Charles Robert
See Pessoa, Fernando (Antonio Nogueira)

Anouilh, Jean (Marie Lucien Pierre)
1910-1987 . **CLC 1, 3, 8, 13, 40, 50; DC
8**
See also CA 17-20R; 123; CANR 32; DAM
DRAM; DFS 9, 10; EW 13; GFL 1789 to
the Present; MTCW 1, 2; RGWL 2; TWA

Anthony, Florence
See Ai

Anthony, John
See Ciardi, John (Anthony)

Anthony, Peter
See Shaffer, Anthony (Joshua); Shaffer, Peter (Levin)

Anthony, Piers 1934- .... **CLC 35**
See also AAYA 11; BYA 7; CA 21-24R;
CAAE 200; CANR 28, 56, 73, 102; CPW;
DAM POP; DLB 8; FANT; MAICYA 2;
MAICYAS 1; MTCW 1, 2; SAAS 22;
SATA 84; SATA-Essay 129; SFW 4;
SUFW; YAW

Anthony, Susan B(rownell)
1820-1906 .... **TCLC 84**
See also FW

DAB; DAC; DAM MST, NOV, POP;
DLB 2, 28; DLBD 3; DLBY 1982;
MTCW 1, 2; NFS 4, 14; RGAL 4; RGSF
2; SSFS 12; TUS

Belser, Reimond Karel Maria de 1929-
See Ruyslinck, Ward
See also CA 152

Bely, Andrey .... **TCLC 7; PC 11**
See also Bugayev, Boris Nikolayevich
See also EW 9; MTCW 1

Belyi, Andrei
See Bugayev, Boris Nikolayevich
See also RGWL 2

Bembo, Pietro 1470-1547 .... **LC 79**
See also RGWL 2

Benary, Margot
See Benary-Isbert, Margot

Benary-Isbert, Margot 1889-1979 .... **CLC 12**
See also CA 5-8R; 89-92; CANR 4, 72;
CLR 12; MAICYA 1, 2; SATA 2; SATA-
Obit 21

Benavente (y Martinez), Jacinto
1866-1954 .... **TCLC 3; HLCS 1**
See also CA 106; 131; CANR 81; DAM
DRAM, MULT; GLL 2; HW 1, 2; MTCW
1, 2

Benchley, Peter (Bradford) 1940- .. **CLC 4, 8**
See also AAYA 14; AITN 2; BPFB 1; CA
17-20R; CANR 12, 35, 66; CPW; DAM
NOV, POP; HGG; MTCW 1, 2; SATA 3,
89

Benchley, Robert (Charles)
1889-1945 .... **TCLC 1, 55**
See also CA 105; 153; DLB 11; RGAL 4

Benda, Julien 1867-1956 .... **TCLC 60**
See also CA 120; 154; GFL 1789 to the
Present

Benedict, Ruth (Fulton)
1887-1948 .... **TCLC 60**
See also CA 158; DLB 246

Benedikt, Michael 1935- .... **CLC 4, 14**
See also CA 13-16R; CANR 7; CP 7; DLB
5

Benet, Juan 1927-1993 .... **CLC 28**
See also CA 143

Benet, Stephen Vincent 1898-1943 . **TCLC 7;
SSC 10**
See also AMWS 11; CA 104; 152; DA3;
DAM POET; DLB 4, 48, 102, 249; DLBY
1997; HGG; MTCW 1; RGAL 4; RGSF
2; SUFW; WP; YABC 1

Benet, William Rose 1886-1950 ..... **TCLC 28**
See also CA 118; 152; DAM POET; DLB
45; RGAL 4

Benford, Gregory (Albert) 1941- ..... **CLC 52**
See also BPFB 1; CA 69-72, 175; CAAE
175; CAAS 27; CANR 12, 24, 49, 95;
CSW; DLBY 1982; SCFW 2; SFW 4

Bengtsson, Frans (Gunnar)
1894-1954 .... **TCLC 48**
See also CA 170

Benjamin, David
See Slavitt, David R(ytman)

Benjamin, Lois
See Gould, Lois

Benjamin, Walter 1892-1940 .... **TCLC 39**
See also CA 164; DLB 242; EW 11

Benn, Gottfried 1886-1956 .. **TCLC 3; PC 35**
See also CA 106; 153; DLB 56; RGWL 2

Bennett, Alan 1934- .... **CLC 45, 77**
See also BRWS 8; CA 103; CANR 35, 55,
106; CBD; CD 5; DAB; DAM MST;
MTCW 1, 2

Bennett, (Enoch) Arnold
1867-1931 .... **TCLC 5, 20**
See also BRW 6; CA 106; 155; CDBLB
1890-1914; DLB 10, 34, 98, 135; MTCW
2

Bennett, Elizabeth
See Mitchell, Margaret (Munnerlyn)

Bennett, George Harold 1930-
See Bennett, Hal
See also BW 1; CA 97-100; CANR 87

Bennett, Hal .... **CLC 5**
See also Bennett, George Harold
See also DLB 33

Bennett, Jay 1912- .... **CLC 35**
See also AAYA 10; CA 69-72; CANR 11,
42, 79; JRDA; SAAS 4; SATA 41, 87;
SATA-Brief 27; WYA; YAW

Bennett, Louise (Simone) 1919- ...... **CLC 28;
BLC 1**
See also BW 2, 3; CA 151; CDWLB 3; CP
7; DAM MULT; DLB 117

Benson, E(dward) F(rederic)
1867-1940 .... **TCLC 27**
See also CA 114; 157; DLB 135, 153;
HGG; SUFW

Benson, Jackson J. 1930- .... **CLC 34**
See also CA 25-28R; DLB 111

Benson, Sally 1900-1972 .... **CLC 17**
See also CA 19-20; 37-40R; CAP 1; SATA
1, 35; SATA-Obit 27

Benson, Stella 1892-1933 .... **TCLC 17**
See also CA 117; 154, 155; DLB 36, 162;
FANT; TEA

Bentham, Jeremy 1748-1832 .... **NCLC 38**
See also DLB 107, 158, 252

Bentley, E(dmund) C(lerihew)
1875-1956 .... **TCLC 12**
See also CA 108; DLB 70; MSW

Bentley, Eric (Russell) 1916- .... **CLC 24**
See also CA 5-8R; CAD; CANR 6, 67;
CBD; CD 5; INT CANR-6

Beranger, Pierre Jean de
1780-1857 .... **NCLC 34**

Berdyaev, Nicolas
See Berdyaev, Nikolai (Aleksandrovich)

Berdyaev, Nikolai (Aleksandrovich)
1874-1948 .... **TCLC 67**
See also CA 120; 157

Berdyayev, Nikolai (Aleksandrovich)
See Berdyaev, Nikolai (Aleksandrovich)

Berendt, John (Lawrence) 1939- ...... **CLC 86**
See also CA 146; CANR 75, 93; DA3;
MTCW 1

Beresford, J(ohn) D(avys)
1873-1947 .... **TCLC 81**
See also CA 112; 155; DLB 162, 178, 197;
SFW 4; SUFW

Bergelson, David 1884-1952 .... **TCLC 81**

Berger, Colonel
See Malraux, (Georges-)Andre

Berger, John (Peter) 1926- .... **CLC 2, 19**
See also BRWS 4; CA 81-84; CANR 51,
78; CN 7; DLB 14, 207

Berger, Melvin H. 1927- .... **CLC 12**
See also CA 5-8R; CANR 4; CLR 32;
SAAS 2; SATA 5, 88; SATA-Essay 124

Berger, Thomas (Louis) 1924- .. **CLC 3, 5, 8,
11, 18, 38**
See also BPFB 1; CA 1-4R; CANR 5, 28,
51; CN 7; DAM NOV; DLB 2; DLBY
1980; FANT; INT CANR-28; MTCW 1,
2; RHW; TCWW 2

Bergman, (Ernst) Ingmar 1918- ...... **CLC 16,
72**
See also CA 81-84; CANR 33, 70; DLB
257; MTCW 2

Bergson, Henri(-Louis) 1859-1941 . **TCLC 32**
See also CA 164; EW 8; GFL 1789 to the
Present

Bergstein, Eleanor 1938- .... **CLC 4**
See also CA 53-56; CANR 5

Berkeley, George 1685-1753 .... **LC 65**
See also DLB 31, 101, 252

Berkoff, Steven 1937- .... **CLC 56**
See also CA 104; CANR 72; CBD; CD 5

Berlin, Isaiah 1909-1997 .... **TCLC 105**
See also CA 85-88; 162

Bermant, Chaim (Icyk) 1929-1998 ... **CLC 40**
See also CA 57-60; CANR 6, 31, 57, 105;
CN 7

Bern, Victoria
See Fisher, M(ary) F(rances) K(ennedy)

Bernanos, (Paul Louis) Georges
1888-1948 .... **TCLC 3**
See also CA 104; 130; CANR 94; DLB 72;
GFL 1789 to the Present; RGWL 2

Bernard, April 1956- .... **CLC 59**
See also CA 131

Berne, Victoria
See Fisher, M(ary) F(rances) K(ennedy)

Bernhard, Thomas 1931-1989 ..... **CLC 3, 32,
61; DC 14**
See also CA 85-88; 127; CANR 32, 57; CD-
WLB 2; DLB 85, 124; MTCW 1; RGWL
2

Bernhardt, Sarah (Henriette Rosine)
1844-1923 .... **TCLC 75**
See also CA 157

Bernstein, Charles 1950- .... **CLC 142,**
See also CA 129; CAAS 24; CANR 90; CP
7; DLB 169

Berriault, Gina 1926-1999 .... **CLC 54, 109;
SSC 30**
See also CA 116; 129; 185; CANR 66; DLB
130; SSFS 7,11

Berrigan, Daniel 1921- .... **CLC 4**
See also CA 33-36R; CAAE 187; CAAS 1;
CANR 11, 43, 78; CP 7; DLB 5

Berrigan, Edmund Joseph Michael, Jr.
1934-1983
See Berrigan, Ted
See also CA 61-64; 110; CANR 14, 102

Berrigan, Ted .... **CLC 37**
See also Berrigan, Edmund Joseph Michael,
Jr.
See also DLB 5, 169; WP

Berry, Charles Edward Anderson 1931-
See Berry, Chuck
See also CA 115

Berry, Chuck .... **CLC 17**
See also Berry, Charles Edward Anderson

Berry, Jonas
See Ashbery, John (Lawrence)
See also GLL 1

Berry, Wendell (Erdman) 1934- ... **CLC 4, 6,
8, 27, 46; PC 28**
See also AITN 1; AMWS 10; ANW; CA
73-76; CANR 50, 73, 101; CP 7; CSW;
DAM POET; DLB 5, 6, 234; MTCW 1

Berryman, John 1914-1972 ... **CLC 1, 2, 3, 4,
6, 8, 10, 13, 25, 62**
See also AMW; CA 13-16; 33-36R; CABS
2; CANR 35; CAP 1; CDALB 1941-1968;
DAM POET; DLB 48; MTCW 1, 2; PAB;
RGAL 4; WP

Bertolucci, Bernardo 1940- ...... **CLC 16, 157**
See also CA 106

Berton, Pierre (Francis Demarigny)
1920- .... **CLC 104**
See also CA 1-4R; CANR 2, 56; CPW;
DLB 68; SATA 99

Bertrand, Aloysius 1807-1841 .... **NCLC 31**
See also Bertrand, Louis oAloysiusc

Bertrand, Louis oAloysiusc
See Bertrand, Aloysius
See also DLB 217

Bertran de Born c. 1140-1215 .... **CMLC 5**

Besant, Annie (Wood) 1847-1933 ..... **TCLC 9**
See also CA 105; 185

Bessie, Alvah 1904-1985 .... **CLC 23**
See also CA 5-8R; 116; CANR 2, 80; DLB
26

Bethlen, T. D.
See Silverberg, Robert

Beti, Mongo .... **CLC 27; BLC 1**
See also Biyidi, Alexandre
See also AFW; CANR 79; DAM MULT;
WLIT 2

Betjeman, John 1906-1984 ...... **CLC 2, 6, 10,
34, 43**
See also BRW 7; CA 9-12R; 112; CANR
33, 56; CDBLB 1945-1960; DA3; DAB;
DAM MST, POET; DLB 20; DLBY 1984;
MTCW 1, 2

Bettelheim, Bruno 1903-1990 .... **CLC 79**
See also CA 81-84; 131; CANR 23, 61;
DA3; MTCW 1, 2

Betti, Ugo 1892-1953 .... **TCLC 5**
See also CA 104; 155; RGWL 2

Betts, Doris (Waugh) 1932- ..... **CLC 3, 6, 28;
SSC 45**
See also CA 13-16R; CANR 9, 66, 77; CN
7; CSW; DLB 218; DLBY 1982; INT
CANR-9; RGAL 4

Bevan, Alistair
See Roberts, Keith (John Kingston)

Bey, Pilaff
See Douglas, (George) Norman

Bialik, Chaim Nachman
1873-1934 .... **TCLC 25**
See also CA 170

Bickerstaff, Isaac
See Swift, Jonathan

Bidart, Frank 1939- .... **CLC 33**
See also CA 140; CANR 106; CP 7

Bienek, Horst 1930- .... **CLC 7, 11**
See also CA 73-76; DLB 75

Bierce, Ambrose (Gwinett)
1842-1914(?) ..... **TCLC 1, 7, 44; SSC 9;
WLC**
See also AMW; BYA 11; CA 104; 139;
CANR 78; CDALB 1865-1917; DA;
DA3; DAC; DAM MST; DLB 11, 12, 23,
71, 74, 186; EXPS; HGG; LAIT 2; RGAL
4; RGSF 2; SSFS 9; SUFW

Biggers, Earl Derr 1884-1933 .... **TCLC 65**
See also CA 108; 153

Billings, Josh
See Shaw, Henry Wheeler

Billington, (Lady) Rachel (Mary)
1942- .... **CLC 43**
See also AITN 2; CA 33-36R; CANR 44;
CN 7

Binchy, Maeve 1940- .... **CLC 153**
See also BEST 90:1; BPFB 1; CA 127; 134;
CANR 50, 96; CN 7; CPW; DA3; DAM
POP; INT CA-134; MTCW 1; RHW

Binyon, T(imothy) J(ohn) 1936- .... **CLC 34**
See also CA 111; CANR 28

Bion 335 B.C.-245 B.C. .... **CMLC 39**

Bioy Casares, Adolfo 1914-1999 ... **CLC 4, 8,
13, 88; HLC 1; SSC 17**
See also Casares, Adolfo Bioy; Miranda,
Javier; Sacastru, Martin
See also CA 29-32R; 177; CANR 19, 43,
66; DAM MULT; DLB 113; HW 1, 2;
LAW; MTCW 1, 2

Birch, Allison .... **CLC 65**

Bird, Cordwainer
See Ellison, Harlan (Jay)

Bird, Robert Montgomery
1806-1854 .... **NCLC 1**
See also DLB 202; RGAL 4

Birkerts, Sven 1951- .... **CLC 116**
See also CA 128; 133, 176; CAAE 176;
CAAS 29; INT 133

Birney, (Alfred) Earle 1904-1995 .. **CLC 1, 4,
6, 11**
See also CA 1-4R; CANR 5, 20; CP 7;
DAC; DAM MST, POET; DLB 88;
MTCW 1; PFS 8; RGEL 2

Biruni, al 973-1048(?) .... **CMLC 28**

Bishop, Elizabeth 1911-1979 ..... **CLC 1, 4, 9,
13, 15, 32; PC 3, 34**
See also AMWS 1; CA 5-8R; 89-92; CABS
2; CANR 26, 61, 108; CDALB 1968-
1988; DA; DA3; DAC; DAM MST,
POET; DLB 5, 169; GLL 2; MAWW;
MTCW 1, 2; PAB; PFS 6, 12; RGAL 4;
SATA-Obit 24; TCLC 121; TUS; WP

Bishop, John 1935- .... **CLC 10**
See also CA 105

Bishop, John Peale 1892-1944 ..... **TCLC 103**
See also CA 107; 155; DLB 4, 9, 45; RGAL
4

Bissett, Bill 1939- .... **CLC 18; PC 14**
See also CA 69-72; CAAS 19; CANR 15;
CCA 1; CP 7; DLB 53; MTCW 1

Bissoondath, Neil (Devindra)
1955- .... **CLC 120**
See also CA 136; CN 7; DAC

Bitov, Andrei (Georgievich) 1937- ... **CLC 57**
See also CA 142

Biyidi, Alexandre 1932-
See Beti, Mongo
See also BW 1, 3; CA 114; 124; CANR 81;
DA3; MTCW 1, 2

Bjarme, Brynjolf
See Ibsen, Henrik (Johan)

Bjoernson, Bjoernstjerne (Martinius)
1832-1910 .... **TCLC 7, 37**
See also CA 104

Black, Robert
See Holdstock, Robert P.

Blackburn, Paul 1926-1971 .... **CLC 9, 43**
See also CA 81-84; 33-36R; CANR 34;
DLB 16; DLBY 1981

Black Elk 1863-1950 .... **TCLC 33**
See also CA 144; DAM MULT; MTCW 1;
NNAL; WP

Black Hobart
See Sanders, (James) Ed(ward)

Blacklin, Malcolm
See Chambers, Aidan

Blackmore, R(ichard) D(oddridge)
1825-1900 .... **TCLC 27**
See also CA 120; DLB 18; RGEL 2

Blackmur, R(ichard) P(almer)
1904-1965 .... **CLC 2, 24**
See also AMWS 2; CA 11-12; 25-28R;
CANR 71; CAP 1; DLB 63

Black Tarantula
See Acker, Kathy

Blackwood, Algernon (Henry)
1869-1951 .... **TCLC 5**
See also CA 105; 150; DLB 153, 156, 178;
HGG; SUFW

Blackwood, Caroline 1931-1996 .... **CLC 6, 9,
100**
See also CA 85-88; 151; CANR 32, 61, 65;
CN 7; DLB 14, 207; HGG; MTCW 1

Blade, Alexander
See Hamilton, Edmond; Silverberg, Robert

Blaga, Lucian 1895-1961 .... **CLC 75**
See also CA 157; DLB 220

Blair, Eric (Arthur) 1903-1950 .... **TCLC 123**
See also Orwell, George
See also CA 104; 132; DA; DA3; DAB;
DAC; DAM MST, NOV; MTCW 1, 2;
SATA 29

Blair, Hugh 1718-1800 .... **NCLC 75**

Blais, Marie-Claire 1939- .... **CLC 2, 4, 6, 13,
22**
See also CA 21-24R; CAAS 4; CANR 38,
75, 93; DAC; DAM MST; DLB 53; FW;
MTCW 1, 2; TWA

Blaise, Clark 1940- .... **CLC 29**
See also AITN 2; CA 53-56; CAAS 3;
CANR 5, 66, 106; CN 7; DLB 53; RGSF
2

Blake, Fairley
See De Voto, Bernard (Augustine)

Blake, Nicholas
See Day Lewis, C(ecil)
See also DLB 77; MSW

Blake, William 1757-1827 .... **NCLC 13, 37,
57; PC 12; WLC**
See also BRW 3; BRWR 1; CDBLB 1789-
1832; CLR 52; DA; DA3; DAB; DAC;
DAM MST, POET; DLB 93, 163; EXPP;
MAICYA 1, 2; PAB; PFS 2, 12; SATA
30; TEA; WCH; WLIT 3; WP

Blanchot, Maurice 1907- .... **CLC 135**
See also CA 117; 144; DLB 72

Blasco Ibanez, Vicente 1867-1928 . **TCLC 12**
See also BPFB 1; CA 110; 131; CANR 81;
DA3; DAM NOV; EW 8; HW 1, 2;
MTCW 1

Blatty, William Peter 1928- .... **CLC 2**
See also CA 5-8R; CANR 9; DAM POP;
HGG

Bleeck, Oliver
See Thomas, Ross (Elmore)

Blessing, Lee 1949- .... **CLC 54**
See also CAD; CD 5

Blight, Rose
See Greer, Germaine

Blish, James (Benjamin) 1921-1975 . **CLC 14**
See also BPFB 1; CA 1-4R; 57-60; CANR
3; DLB 8; MTCW 1; SATA 66; SCFW 2;
SFW 4

Bliss, Reginald
See Wells, H(erbert) G(eorge)

Blixen, Karen (Christentze Dinesen)
1885-1962
See Dinesen, Isak
See also CA 25-28; CANR 22, 50; CAP 2;
DA3; DLB 214; MTCW 1, 2; SATA 44

Bloch, Robert (Albert) 1917-1994 .... **CLC 33**
See also AAYA 29; CA 5-8R, 179; 146;
CAAE 179; CAAS 20; CANR 5, 78;
DA3; DLB 44; HGG; INT CANR-5;
MTCW 1; SATA 12; SATA-Obit 82; SFW
4; SUFW

Blok, Alexander (Alexandrovich)
1880-1921 .... **TCLC 5; PC 21**
See also CA 104; 183; EW 9; RGWL 2

Blom, Jan
See Breytenbach, Breyten

Bloom, Harold 1930- .... **CLC 24, 103**
See also CA 13-16R; CANR 39, 75, 92;
DLB 67; MTCW 1; RGAL 4

Bloomfield, Aurelius
See Bourne, Randolph S(illiman)

Blount, Roy (Alton), Jr. 1941- .... **CLC 38**
See also CA 53-56; CANR 10, 28, 61;
CSW; INT CANR-28; MTCW 1, 2

Bloy, Leon 1846-1917 .... **TCLC 22**
See also CA 121; 183; DLB 123; GFL 1789
to the Present

Bluggage, Oranthy
See Alcott, Louisa May

Blume, Judy (Sussman) 1938- .... **CLC 12, 30**
See also AAYA 3, 26; BYA 1, 8, 12; CA 29-
32R; CANR 13, 37, 66; CLR 2, 15, 69;
CPW; DA3; DAM NOV, POP; DLB 52;
JRDA; MAICYA 1, 2; MAICYAS 1;
MTCW 1, 2; SATA 2, 31, 79; WYA; YAW

Blunden, Edmund (Charles)
1896-1974 .... **CLC 2, 56**
See also BRW 6; CA 17-18; 45-48; CANR
54; CAP 2; DLB 20, 100, 155; MTCW 1;
PAB

Bly, Robert (Elwood) 1926- .... **CLC 1, 2, 5,
10, 15, 38, 128; PC 39**
See also AMWS 4; CA 5-8R; CANR 41,
73; CP 7; DA3; DAM POET; DLB 5;
MTCW 1, 2; RGAL 4

Boas, Franz 1858-1942 .... **TCLC 56**
   See also CA 115; 181
Bobette
   See Simenon, Georges (Jacques Christian)
Boccaccio, Giovanni 1313-1375 ... **CMLC 13; SSC 10**
   See also EW 2; RGSF 2; RGWL 2; TWA
Bochco, Steven 1943- .... **CLC 35**
   See also AAYA 11; CA 124; 138
Bode, Sigmund
   See O'Doherty, Brian
Bodel, Jean 1167(?)-1210 .... **CMLC 28**
Bodenheim, Maxwell 1892-1954 .... **TCLC 44**
   See also CA 110; 187; DLB 9, 45; RGAL 4
Bodker, Cecil 1927-
   See Bodker, Cecil
Bodker, Cecil 1927- .... **CLC 21**
   See also CA 73-76; CANR 13, 44; CLR 23; MAICYA 1, 2; SATA 14, 133
Boell, Heinrich (Theodor)
   1917-1985 ..... **CLC 2, 3, 6, 9, 11, 15, 27, 32, 72; SSC 23; WLC**
   See also Boll, Heinrich
   See also CA 21-24R; 116; CANR 24; DA; DA3; DAB; DAC; DAM MST, NOV; DLB 69; DLBY 1985; MTCW 1, 2; TWA
Boerne, Alfred
   See Doeblin, Alfred
Boethius c. 480-c. 524 .... **CMLC 15**
   See also DLB 115; RGWL 2
Boff, Leonardo (Genezio Darci)
   1938- .... **CLC 70; HLC 1**
   See also CA 150; DAM MULT; HW 2
Bogan, Louise 1897-1970 .... **CLC 4, 39, 46, 93; PC 12**
   See also AMWS 3; CA 73-76; 25-28R; CANR 33, 82; DAM POET; DLB 45, 169; MAWW; MTCW 1, 2; RGAL 4
Bogarde, Dirk
   See Van Den Bogarde, Derek Jules Gaspard Ulric Niven
   See also DLB 14
Bogosian, Eric 1953- .... **CLC 45, 141**
   See also CA 138; CAD; CANR 102; CD 5
Bograd, Larry 1953- .... **CLC 35**
   See also CA 93-96; CANR 57; SAAS 21; SATA 33, 89; WYA
Boiardo, Matteo Maria 1441-1494 .... **LC 6**
Boileau-Despreaux, Nicolas 1636-1711 . **LC 3**
   See also EW 3; GFL Beginnings to 1789; RGWL 2
Boissard, Maurice
   See Leautaud, Paul
Bojer, Johan 1872-1959 .... **TCLC 64**
   See also CA 189
Bok, Edward W. 1863-1930 .... **TCLC 101**
   See also DLB 91; DLBD 16
Boland, Eavan (Aisling) 1944- .. **CLC 40, 67, 113**
   See also BRWS 5; CA 143; CANR 61; CP 7; CWP; DAM POET; DLB 40; FW; MTCW 2; PFS 12
Boll, Heinrich
   See Boell, Heinrich (Theodor)
   See also BPFB 1; CDWLB 2; EW 13; RGSF 2; RGWL 2
Bolt, Lee
   See Faust, Frederick (Schiller)
Bolt, Robert (Oxton) 1924-1995 .... **CLC 14**
   See also CA 17-20R; 147; CANR 35, 67; CBD; DAM DRAM; DFS 2; DLB 13, 233; LAIT 1; MTCW 1
Bombal, Maria Luisa 1910-1980 ...... **SSC 37; HLCS 1**
   See also CA 127; CANR 72; HW 1; LAW; RGSF 2
Bombet, Louis-Alexandre-Cesar
   See Stendhal

Bomkauf
   See Kaufman, Bob (Garnell)
Bonaventura .... **NCLC 35**
   See also DLB 90
Bond, Edward 1934- .... **CLC 4, 6, 13, 23**
   See also BRWS 1; CA 25-28R; CANR 38, 67, 106; CBD; CD 5; DAM DRAM; DFS 3,8; DLB 13; MTCW 1
Bonham, Frank 1914-1989 .... **CLC 12**
   See also AAYA 1; BYA 1, 3; CA 9-12R; CANR 4, 36; JRDA; MAICYA 1, 2; SAAS 3; SATA 1, 49; SATA-Obit 62; TCWW 2; YAW
Bonnefoy, Yves 1923- .... **CLC 9, 15, 58**
   See also CA 85-88; CANR 33, 75, 97; CWW 2; DAM MST, POET; DLB 258; GFL 1789 to the Present; MTCW 1, 2
Bontemps, Arna(ud Wendell)
   1902-1973 .... **CLC 1, 18; BLC 1**
   See also BW 1; CA 1-4R; 41-44R; CANR 4, 35; CLR 6; CWRI 5; DA3; DAM MULT, NOV, POET; DLB 48, 51; JRDA; MAICYA 1, 2; MTCW 1, 2; SATA 2, 44; SATA-Obit 24; WCH; WP
Booth, Martin 1944- .... **CLC 13**
   See also CA 93-96; CAAE 188; CAAS 2; CANR 92
Booth, Philip 1925- .... **CLC 23**
   See also CA 5-8R; CANR 5, 88; CP 7; DLBY 1982
Booth, Wayne C(layson) 1921- .... **CLC 24**
   See also CA 1-4R; CAAS 5; CANR 3, 43; DLB 67
Borchert, Wolfgang 1921-1947 .... **TCLC 5**
   See also CA 104; 188; DLB 69, 124
Borel, Petrus 1809-1859 .... **NCLC 41**
   See also DLB 119; GFL 1789 to the Present
Borges, Jorge Luis 1899-1986 ... **CLC 1, 2, 3, 4, 6, 8, 9, 10, 13, 19, 44, 48, 83; HLC 1; PC 22, 32; SSC 4, 41; WLC**
   See also AAYA 26; BPFB 1; CA 21-24R; CANR 19, 33, 75, 105; CDWLB 3; DA; DA3; DAB; DAC; DAM MST, MULT; DLB 113; DLBY 1986; DNFS 1, 2; HW 1, 2; LAW; MSW; MTCW 1, 2; RGSF 2; RGWL 2; SFW 4; SSFS 4, 9; TCLC 109; TWA; WLIT 1
Borowski, Tadeusz 1922-1951 .... **TCLC 9; SSC 48**
   See also CA 106; 154; CDWLB 4, 4; DLB 215; RGSF 2; SSFS 13
Borrow, George (Henry)
   1803-1881 .... **NCLC 9**
   See also DLB 21, 55, 166
Bosch (Gavino), Juan 1909-2001
   See also CA 151; DAM MST, MULT; DLB 145; HLCS 1; HW 1, 2
Bosman, Herman Charles
   1905-1951 .... **TCLC 49**
   See also Malan, Herman
   See also CA 160; DLB 225; RGSF 2
Bosschere, Jean de 1878(?)-1953 ... **TCLC 19**
   See also CA 115; 186
Boswell, James 1740-1795 ... **LC 4, 50; WLC**
   See also BRW 3; CDBLB 1660-1789; DA; DAB; DAC; DAM MST; DLB 104, 142; TEA; WLIT 3
Bottomley, Gordon 1874-1948 ..... **TCLC 107**
   See also CA 120; 192; DLB 10
Bottoms, David 1949- .... **CLC 53**
   See also CA 105; CANR 22; CSW; DLB 120; DLBY 1983
Boucicault, Dion 1820-1890 .... **NCLC 41**
Boucolon, Maryse
   See Conde, Maryse
Bourget, Paul (Charles Joseph)
   1852-1935 .... **TCLC 12**
   See also CA 107; 196; DLB 123; GFL 1789 to the Present

Bourjaily, Vance (Nye) 1922- .... **CLC 8, 62**
   See also CA 1-4R; CAAS 1; CANR 2, 72; CN 7; DLB 2, 143
Bourne, Randolph S(illiman)
   1886-1918 .... **TCLC 16**
   See also AMW; CA 117; 155; DLB 63
Bova, Ben(jamin William) 1932- ...... **CLC 45**
   See also AAYA 16; CA 5-8R; CAAS 18; CANR 11, 56, 94; CLR 3; DLBY 1981; INT CANR-11; MAICYA 1, 2; MTCW 1; SATA 6, 68, 133; SFW 4
Bowen, Elizabeth (Dorothea Cole)
   1899-1973 . **CLC 1, 3, 6, 11, 15, 22, 118; SSC 3, 28**
   See also BRWS 2; CA 17-18; 41-44R; CANR 35, 105; CAP 2; CDBLB 1945-1960; DA3; DAM NOV; DLB 15, 162; EXPS; FW; HGG; MTCW 1, 2; NFS 13; RGSF 2; SSFS 5; SUFW; TEA; WLIT 4
Bowering, George 1935- .... **CLC 15, 47**
   See also CA 21-24R; CAAS 16; CANR 10; CP 7; DLB 53
Bowering, Marilyn R(uthe) 1949- .... **CLC 32**
   See also CA 101; CANR 49; CP 7; CWP
Bowers, Edgar 1924-2000 .... **CLC 9**
   See also CA 5-8R; 188; CANR 24; CP 7; CSW; DLB 5
Bowie, David .... **CLC 17**
   See also Jones, David Robert
Bowles, Jane (Sydney) 1917-1973 ..... **CLC 3, 68**
   See also CA 19-20; 41-44R; CAP 2
Bowles, Paul (Frederick) 1910-1999 . **CLC 1, 2, 19, 53; SSC 3**
   See also AMWS 4; CA 1-4R; 186; CAAS 1; CANR 1, 19, 50, 75; CN 7; DA3; DLB 5, 6, 218; MTCW 1, 2; RGAL 4
Bowles, William Lisle 1762-1850 . **NCLC 103**
   See also DLB 93
Box, Edgar
   See Vidal, Gore
   See also GLL 1
Boyd, James 1888-1944 .... **TCLC 115**
   See also CA 186; DLB 9; DLBD 16; RGAL 4; RHW
Boyd, Nancy
   See Millay, Edna St. Vincent
   See also GLL 1
Boyd, Thomas (Alexander)
   1898-1935 .... **TCLC 111**
   See also CA 111; 183; DLB 9; DLBD 16
Boyd, William 1952- .... **CLC 28, 53, 70**
   See also CA 114; 120; CANR 51, 71; CN 7; DLB 231
Boyle, Kay 1902-1992 .... **CLC 1, 5, 19, 58, 121; SSC 5**
   See also CA 13-16R; 140; CAAS 1; CANR 29, 61, 110; DLB 4, 9, 48, 86; DLBY 1993; MTCW 1, 2; RGAL 4; RGSF 2; SSFS 10, 13, 14
Boyle, Mark
   See Kienzle, William X(avier)
Boyle, Patrick 1905-1982 .... **CLC 19**
   See also CA 127
Boyle, T. C.
   See Boyle, T(homas) Coraghessan
   See also AMWS 8
Boyle, T(homas) Coraghessan
   1948- .... **CLC 36, 55, 90; SSC 16**
   See also Boyle, T. C.
   See also BEST 90:4; BPFB 1; CA 120; CANR 44, 76, 89; CN 7; CPW; DA3; DAM POP; DLB 218; DLBY 1986; MTCW 2; SSFS 13
Boz
   See Dickens, Charles (John Huffam)
Brackenridge, Hugh Henry
   1748-1816 .... **NCLC 7**
   See also DLB 11, 37; RGAL 4

Bronte, (Patrick) Branwell
1817-1848 .... **NCLC 109**

Bronte, Charlotte 1816-1855 ...... **NCLC 3, 8, 33, 58, 105; WLC**
See also AAYA 17; BRW 5; BRWR 1; BYA 2; CDBLB 1832-1890; DA; DA3; DAB; DAC; DAM MST, NOV; DLB 21, 159, 199; EXPN; LAIT 2; NFS 4; TEA; WLIT 4

Bronte, Emily (Jane) 1818-1848 ... **NCLC 16, 35; PC 8; WLC**
See also AAYA 17; BPFB 1; BRW 5; BRWR 1; BYA 3; CDBLB 1832-1890; DA; DA3; DAB; DAC; DAM MST, NOV, POET; DLB 21, 32, 199; EXPN; LAIT 1; TEA; WLIT 3

Brontes
See Bronte, Anne; Bronte, Charlotte; Bronte, Emily (Jane)

Brooke, Frances 1724-1789 .... **LC 6, 48**
See also DLB 39, 99

Brooke, Henry 1703(?)-1783 .... **LC 1**
See also DLB 39

Brooke, Rupert (Chawner)
1887-1915 ..... **TCLC 2, 7; PC 24; WLC**
See also BRWS 3; CA 104; 132; CANR 61; CDBLB 1914-1945; DA; DAB; DAC; DAM MST, POET; DLB 19, 216; EXPP; GLL 2; MTCW 1, 2; PFS 7; TEA

Brooke-Haven, P.
See Wodehouse, P(elham) G(renville)

Brooke-Rose, Christine 1926(?)- ...... **CLC 40**
See also BRWS 4; CA 13-16R; CANR 58; CN 7; DLB 14, 231; SFW 4

Brookner, Anita 1928- .. **CLC 32, 34, 51, 136**
See also BRWS 4; CA 114; 120; CANR 37, 56, 87; CN 7; CPW; DA3; DAB; DAM POP; DLB 194; DLBY 1987; MTCW 1, 2; TEA

Brooks, Cleanth 1906-1994 . **CLC 24, 86, 110**
See also CA 17-20R; 145; CANR 33, 35; CSW; DLB 63; DLBY 1994; INT CANR-35; MTCW 1, 2

Brooks, George
See Baum, L(yman) Frank

Brooks, Gwendolyn (Elizabeth)
1917-2000 .. **CLC 1, 2, 4, 5, 15, 49, 125; BLC 1; PC 7; WLC**
See also AAYA 20; AFAW 1, 2; AITN 1; AMWS 3; BW 2, 3; CA 1-4R; 190; CANR 1, 27, 52, 75; CDALB 1941-1968; CLR 27; CP 7; CWP; DA; DA3; DAC; DAM MST, MULT, POET; DLB 5, 76, 165; EXPP; MAWW; MTCW 1, 2; PFS 1, 2, 4, 6; RGAL 4; SATA 6; SATA-Obit 123; TUS; WP

Brooks, Mel .... **CLC 12**
See also Kaminsky, Melvin
See also AAYA 13; DLB 26

Brooks, Peter (Preston) 1938- .... **CLC 34**
See also CA 45-48; CANR 1, 107

Brooks, Van Wyck 1886-1963 .... **CLC 29**
See also AMW; CA 1-4R; CANR 6; DLB 45, 63, 103; TUS

Brophy, Brigid (Antonia)
1929-1995 .... **CLC 6, 11, 29, 105**
See also CA 5-8R; 149; CAAS 4; CANR 25, 53; CBD; CN 7; CWD; DA3; DLB 14; MTCW 1, 2

Brosman, Catharine Savage 1934- ..... **CLC 9**
See also CA 61-64; CANR 21, 46

Brossard, Nicole 1943- .... **CLC 115**
See also CA 122; CAAS 16; CCA 1; CWP; CWW 2; DLB 53; FW; GLL 2

Brother Antoninus
See Everson, William (Oliver)

The Brothers Quay
See Quay, Stephen; Quay, Timothy

Broughton, T(homas) Alan 1936- ..... **CLC 19**
See also CA 45-48; CANR 2, 23, 48

Broumas, Olga 1949- .... **CLC 10, 73**
See also CA 85-88; CANR 20, 69, 110; CP 7; CWP; GLL 2

Broun, Heywood 1888-1939 .... **TCLC 104**
See also DLB 29, 171

Brown, Alan 1950- .... **CLC 99**
See also CA 156

Brown, Charles Brockden
1771-1810 .... **NCLC 22, 74**
See also AMWS 1; CDALB 1640-1865; DLB 37, 59, 73; FW; HGG; RGAL 4; TUS

Brown, Christy 1932-1981 .... **CLC 63**
See also BYA 13; CA 105; 104; CANR 72; DLB 14

Brown, Claude 1937-2002 ... **CLC 30; BLC 1**
See also AAYA 7; BW 1, 3; CA 73-76; CANR 81; DAM MULT

Brown, Dee (Alexander) 1908- ... **CLC 18, 47**
See also AAYA 30; CA 13-16R; CAAS 6; CANR 11, 45, 60; CPW; CSW; DA3; DAM POP; DLBY 1980; LAIT 2; MTCW 1, 2; SATA 5, 110; TCWW 2

Brown, George
See Wertmueller, Lina

Brown, George Douglas
1869-1902 .... **TCLC 28**
See also Douglas, George
See also CA 162

Brown, George Mackay 1921-1996 ... **CLC 5, 48, 100**
See also BRWS 6; CA 21-24R; 151; CAAS 6; CANR 12, 37, 67; CN 7; CP 7; DLB 14, 27, 139; MTCW 1; RGSF 2; SATA 35

Brown, (William) Larry 1951- .... **CLC 73**
See also CA 130; 134; CSW; DLB 234; INT 133

Brown, Moses
See Barrett, William (Christopher)

Brown, Rita Mae 1944- ... **CLC 18, 43, 79**
See also BPFB 1; CA 45-48; CANR 2, 11, 35, 62, 95; CN 7; CPW; CSW; DA3; DAM NOV, POP; FW; INT CANR-11; MTCW 1, 2; NFS 9; RGAL 4; TUS

Brown, Roderick (Langmere) Haig-
See Haig-Brown, Roderick (Langmere)

Brown, Rosellen 1939- .... **CLC 32**
See also CA 77-80; CAAS 10; CANR 14, 44, 98; CN 7

Brown, Sterling Allen 1901-1989 ...... **CLC 1, 23, 59; BLC 1**
See also AFAW 1, 2; BW 1, 3; CA 85-88; 127; CANR 26; DA3; DAM MULT, POET; DLB 48, 51, 63; MTCW 1, 2; RGAL 4; WP

Brown, Will
See Ainsworth, William Harrison

Brown, William Wells 1815-1884 ... **NCLC 2, 89; BLC 1; DC 1**
See also DAM MULT; DLB 3, 50, 183, 248; RGAL 4

Browne, (Clyde) Jackson 1948(?)- ... **CLC 21**
See also CA 120

Browning, Elizabeth Barrett
1806-1861 ... **NCLC 1, 16, 61, 66; PC 6; WLC**
See also BRW 4; CDBLB 1832-1890; DA; DA3; DAB; DAC; DAM MST, POET; DLB 32, 199; EXPP; PAB; PFS 2; TEA; WLIT 4; WP

Browning, Robert 1812-1889 . **NCLC 19, 79; PC 2; WLCS**
See also BRW 4; BRWR 2; CDBLB 1832-1890; DA; DA3; DAB; DAC; DAM MST, POET; DLB 32, 163; EXPP; PAB; PFS 1, 15; RGEL 2; TEA; WLIT 4; WP; YABC 1

Browning, Tod 1882-1962 .... **CLC 16**
See also CA 141; 117

Brownmiller, Susan 1935- .... **CLC 159**
See also CA 103; CANR 35, 75; DAM NOV; FW; MTCW 1, 2

Brownson, Orestes Augustus
1803-1876 .... **NCLC 50**
See also DLB 1, 59, 73, 243

Bruccoli, Matthew J(oseph) 1931- ... **CLC 34**
See also CA 9-12R; CANR 7, 87; DLB 103

Bruce, Lenny .... **CLC 21**
See also Schneider, Leonard Alfred

Bruin, John
See Brutus, Dennis

Brulard, Henri
See Stendhal

Brulls, Christian
See Simenon, Georges (Jacques Christian)

Brunner, John (Kilian Houston)
1934-1995 .... **CLC 8, 10**
See also CA 1-4R; 149; CAAS 8; CANR 2, 37; CPW; DAM POP; DLB 261; MTCW 1, 2; SCFW 2; SFW 4

Bruno, Giordano 1548-1600 .... **LC 27**
See also RGWL 2

Brutus, Dennis 1924- ... **CLC 43; BLC 1; PC 24**
See also AFW; BW 2, 3; CA 49-52; CAAS 14; CANR 2, 27, 42, 81; CDWLB 3; CP 7; DAM MULT, POET; DLB 117, 225

Bryan, C(ourtlandt) D(ixon) B(arnes)
1936- .... **CLC 29**
See also CA 73-76; CANR 13, 68; DLB 185; INT CANR-13

Bryan, Michael
See Moore, Brian
See also CCA 1

Bryan, William Jennings
1860-1925 .... **TCLC 99**

Bryant, William Cullen 1794-1878 . **NCLC 6, 46; PC 20**
See also AMWS 1; CDALB 1640-1865; DA; DAB; DAC; DAM MST, POET; DLB 3, 43, 59, 189, 250; EXPP; PAB; RGAL 4; TUS

Bryusov, Valery Yakovlevich
1873-1924 .... **TCLC 10**
See also CA 107; 155; SFW 4

Buchan, John 1875-1940 .... **TCLC 41**
See also CA 108; 145; CMW 4; DAB; DAM POP; DLB 34, 70, 156; HGG; MSW; MTCW 1; RGEL 2; RHW; YABC 2

Buchanan, George 1506-1582 .... **LC 4**
See also DLB 132

Buchanan, Robert 1841-1901 .... **TCLC 107**
See also CA 179; DLB 18, 35

Buchheim, Lothar-Guenther 1918- .... **CLC 6**
See also CA 85-88

Buchner, (Karl) Georg 1813-1837 . **NCLC 26**
See also CDWLB 2; DLB 133; EW 6; RGSF 2; RGWL 2; TWA

Buchwald, Art(hur) 1925- .... **CLC 33**
See also AITN 1; CA 5-8R; CANR 21, 67, 107; MTCW 1, 2; SATA 10

Buck, Pearl S(ydenstricker)
1892-1973 .... **CLC 7, 11, 18, 127**
See also AAYA 42; AITN 1; AMWS 2; BPFB 1; CA 1-4R; 41-44R; CANR 1, 34; CDALBS; DA; DA3; DAB; DAC; DAM MST, NOV; DLB 9, 102; LAIT 3; MTCW 1, 2; RGAL 4; RHW; SATA 1, 25; TUS

Buckler, Ernest 1908-1984 .... **CLC 13**
See also CA 11-12; 114; CAP 1; CCA 1; DAC; DAM MST; DLB 68; SATA 47

Buckley, Vincent (Thomas)
1925-1988 .... **CLC 57**
See also CA 101

Buckley, William F(rank), Jr. 1925- . **CLC 7, 18, 37**
See also AITN 1; BPFB 1; CA 1-4R; CANR 1, 24, 53, 93; CMW 4; CPW; DA3; DAM POP; DLB 137; DLBY 1980; INT CANR-24; MTCW 1, 2; TUS

Buechner, (Carl) Frederick 1926- . **CLC 2, 4, 6, 9**
See also BPFB 1; CA 13-16R; CANR 11, 39, 64; CN 7; DAM NOV; DLBY 1980; INT CANR-11; MTCW 1, 2

Buell, John (Edward) 1927- .... **CLC 10**
See also CA 1-4R; CANR 71; DLB 53

Buero Vallejo, Antonio 1916-2000 ... **CLC 15, 46, 139; DC 18**
See also CA 106; 189; CANR 24, 49, 75; DFS 11; HW 1; MTCW 1, 2

Bufalino, Gesualdo 1920(?)-1990 ...... **CLC 74**
See also CWW 2; DLB 196

Bugayev, Boris Nikolayevich 1880-1934 .... **TCLC 7; PC 11**
See also Bely, Andrey; Belyi, Andrei
See also CA 104; 165; MTCW 1

Bukowski, Charles 1920-1994 ... **CLC 2, 5, 9, 41, 82, 108; PC 18; SSC 45**
See also CA 17-20R; 144; CANR 40, 62, 105; CPW; DA3; DAM NOV, POET; DLB 5, 130, 169; MTCW 1, 2

Bulgakov, Mikhail (Afanas'evich) 1891-1940 .... **TCLC 2, 16; SSC 18**
See also BPFB 1; CA 105; 152; DAM DRAM, NOV; NFS 8; RGSF 2; RGWL 2; SFW 4; TWA

Bulgya, Alexander Alexandrovich 1901-1956 .... **TCLC 53**
See also Fadeyev, Alexander
See also CA 117; 181

Bullins, Ed 1935- ... **CLC 1, 5, 7; BLC 1; DC 6**
See also BW 2, 3; CA 49-52; CAAS 16; CAD; CANR 24, 46, 73; CD 5; DAM DRAM, MULT; DLB 7, 38, 249; MTCW 1, 2; RGAL 4

Bulwer-Lytton, Edward (George Earle Lytton) 1803-1873 .... **NCLC 1, 45**
See also DLB 21; RGEL 2; SFW 4; SUFW; TEA

Bunin, Ivan Alexeyevich 1870-1953 .... **TCLC 6; SSC 5**
See also CA 104; RGSF 2; RGWL 2; TWA

Bunting, Basil 1900-1985 ...... **CLC 10, 39, 47**
See also BRWS 7; CA 53-56; 115; CANR 7; DAM POET; DLB 20; RGEL 2

Bunuel, Luis 1900-1983 ... **CLC 16, 80; HLC 1**
See also CA 101; 110; CANR 32, 77; DAM MULT; HW 1

Bunyan, John 1628-1688 ..... **LC 4, 69; WLC**
See also BRW 2; BYA 5; CDBLB 1660-1789; DA; DAB; DAC; DAM MST; DLB 39; RGEL 2; TEA; WCH; WLIT 3

Buravsky, Alexandr .... **CLC 59**

Burckhardt, Jacob (Christoph) 1818-1897 .... **NCLC 49**
See also EW 6

Burford, Eleanor
See Hibbert, Eleanor Alice Burford

Burgess, Anthony . **CLC 1, 2, 4, 5, 8, 10, 13, 15, 22, 40, 62, 81, 94**
See also Wilson, John (Anthony) Burgess
See also AAYA 25; AITN 1; BRWS 1; CD-BLB 1960 to Present; DAB; DLB 14, 194, 261; DLBY 1998; MTCW 1; RGEL 2; RHW; SFW 4; YAW

Burke, Edmund 1729(?)-1797 .... **LC 7, 36; WLC**
See also BRW 3; DA; DA3; DAB; DAC; DAM MST; DLB 104, 252; RGEL 2; TEA

Burke, Kenneth (Duva) 1897-1993 ... **CLC 2, 24**
See also AMW; CA 5-8R; 143; CANR 39, 74; DLB 45, 63; MTCW 1, 2; RGAL 4

Burke, Leda
See Garnett, David

Burke, Ralph
See Silverberg, Robert

Burke, Thomas 1886-1945 .... **TCLC 63**
See also CA 113; 155; CMW 4; DLB 197

Burney, Fanny 1752-1840 .... **NCLC 12, 54, 107**
See also BRWS 3; DLB 39; RGEL 2; TEA

Burney, Frances
See Burney, Fanny

Burns, Robert 1759-1796 ... **LC 3, 29, 40; PC 6; WLC**
See also BRW 3; CDBLB 1789-1832; DA; DA3; DAB; DAC; DAM MST, POET; DLB 109; EXPP; PAB; RGEL 2; TEA; WP

Burns, Tex
See L'Amour, Louis (Dearborn)
See also TCWW 2

Burnshaw, Stanley 1906- .... **CLC 3, 13, 44**
See also CA 9-12R; CP 7; DLB 48; DLBY 1997

Burr, Anne 1937- .... **CLC 6**
See also CA 25-28R

Burroughs, Edgar Rice 1875-1950 . **TCLC 2, 32**
See also AAYA 11; BPFB 1; BYA 4, 9; CA 104; 132; DA3; DAM NOV; DLB 8; FANT; MTCW 1, 2; RGAL 4; SATA 41; SCFW 2; SFW 4; TUS; YAW

Burroughs, William S(eward) 1914-1997 ... **CLC 1, 2, 5, 15, 22, 42, 75, 109; WLC**
See also Lee, William; Lee, Willy
See also AITN 2; AMWS 3; BPFB 1; CA 9-12R; 160; CANR 20, 52, 104; CN 7; CPW; DA; DA3; DAB; DAC; DAM MST, NOV, POP; DLB 2, 8, 16, 152, 237; DLBY 1981, 1997; HGG; MTCW 1, 2; RGAL 4; SFW 4; TCLC 121

Burton, Sir Richard F(rancis) 1821-1890 .... **NCLC 42**
See also DLB 55, 166, 184

Burton, Robert 1577-1640 .... **LC 74**
See also DLB 151; RGEL 2

Buruma, Ian 1951- .... **CLC 163**
See also CA 128; CANR 65

Busch, Frederick 1941- .... **CLC 7, 10, 18, 47**
See also CA 33-36R; CAAS 1; CANR 45, 73, 92; CN 7; DLB 6, 218

Bush, Ronald 1946- .... **CLC 34**
See also CA 136

Bustos, F(rancisco)
See Borges, Jorge Luis

Bustos Domecq, H(onorio)
See Bioy Casares, Adolfo; Borges, Jorge Luis

Butler, Octavia E(stelle) 1947- .... **CLC 38, 121; BLCS**
See also AAYA 18; AFAW 2; BPFB 1; BW 2, 3; CA 73-76; CANR 12, 24, 38, 73; CLR 65; CPW; DA3; DAM MULT, POP; DLB 33; MTCW 1, 2; NFS 8; SATA 84; SCFW 2; SFW 4; SSFS 6; YAW

Butler, Robert Olen, (Jr.) 1945- ...... **CLC 81, 162**
See also BPFB 1; CA 112; CANR 66; CSW; DAM POP; DLB 173; INT CA-112; MTCW 1; SSFS 11

Butler, Samuel 1612-1680 .... **LC 16, 43**
See also DLB 101, 126; RGEL 2

Butler, Samuel 1835-1902 .... **TCLC 1, 33; WLC**
See also BRWS 2; CA 143; CDBLB 1890-1914; DA; DA3; DAB; DAC; DAM MST, NOV; DLB 18, 57, 174; RGEL 2; SFW 4; TEA

Butler, Walter C.
See Faust, Frederick (Schiller)

Butor, Michel (Marie Francois) 1926- .... **CLC 1, 3, 8, 11, 15, 161**
See also CA 9-12R; CANR 33, 66; DLB 83; EW 13; GFL 1789 to the Present; MTCW 1, 2

Butts, Mary 1890(?)-1937 .... **TCLC 77**
See also CA 148; DLB 240

Buxton, Ralph
See Silverstein, Alvin; Silverstein, Virginia B(arbara Opshelor)

Buzo, Alexander (John) 1944- .... **CLC 61**
See also CA 97-100; CANR 17, 39, 69; CD 5

Buzzati, Dino 1906-1972 .... **CLC 36**
See also CA 160; 33-36R; DLB 177; RGWL 2; SFW 4

Byars, Betsy (Cromer) 1928- .... **CLC 35**
See also AAYA 19; BYA 3; CA 33-36R, 183; CAAE 183; CANR 18, 36, 57, 102; CLR 1, 16, 72; DLB 52; INT CANR-18; JRDA; MAICYA 1, 2; MAICYAS 1; MTCW 1; SAAS 1; SATA 4, 46, 80; SATA-Essay 108; WYA; YAW

Byatt, A(ntonia) S(usan Drabble) 1936- .... **CLC 19, 65, 136**
See also BPFB 1; BRWS 4; CA 13-16R; CANR 13, 33, 50, 75, 96; DA3; DAM NOV, POP; DLB 14, 194; MTCW 1, 2; RGSF 2; RHW; TEA

Byrne, David 1952- .... **CLC 26**
See also CA 127

Byrne, John Keyes 1926-
See Leonard, Hugh
See also CA 102; CANR 78; INT CA-102

Byron, George Gordon (Noel) 1788-1824 ..... **NCLC 2, 12, 109; PC 16; WLC**
See also BRW 4; CDBLB 1789-1832; DA; DA3; DAB; DAC; DAM MST, POET; DLB 96, 110; EXPP; PAB; PFS 1, 14; RGEL 2; TEA; WLIT 3; WP

Byron, Robert 1905-1941 .... **TCLC 67**
See also CA 160; DLB 195

C. 3. 3.
See Wilde, Oscar (Fingal O'Flahertie Wills)

Caballero, Fernan 1796-1877 .... **NCLC 10**

Cabell, Branch
See Cabell, James Branch

Cabell, James Branch 1879-1958 .... **TCLC 6**
See also CA 105; 152; DLB 9, 78; FANT; MTCW 1; RGAL 4; SUFW

Cabeza de Vaca, Alvar Nunez 1490-1557(?) .... **LC 61**

Cable, George Washington 1844-1925 .... **TCLC 4; SSC 4**
See also CA 104; 155; DLB 12, 74; DLBD 13; RGAL 4; TUS

Cabral de Melo Neto, Joao 1920-1999 .... **CLC 76**
See also CA 151; DAM MULT; LAW; LAWS 1

Cabrera Infante, G(uillermo) 1929- . **CLC 5, 25, 45, 120; HLC 1; SSC 39**
See also CA 85-88; CANR 29, 65, 110; CD-WLB 3; DA3; DAM MULT; DLB 113; HW 1, 2; LAW; LAWS 1; MTCW 1, 2; RGSF 2; WLIT 1

Cade, Toni
See Bambara, Toni Cade

Cadmus and Harmonia
See Buchan, John

Carr, Caleb 1955(?)- .... **CLC 86**
 See also CA 147; CANR 73; DA3

Carr, Emily 1871-1945 .... **TCLC 32**
 See also CA 159; DLB 68; FW; GLL 2

Carr, John Dickson 1906-1977 .... **CLC 3**
 See also Fairbairn, Roger
 See also CA 49-52; 69-72; CANR 3, 33,
 60; CMW 4; MSW; MTCW 1, 2

Carr, Philippa
 See Hibbert, Eleanor Alice Burford

Carr, Virginia Spencer 1929- .... **CLC 34**
 See also CA 61-64; DLB 111

Carrere, Emmanuel 1957- .... **CLC 89**
 See also CA 200

Carrier, Roch 1937- .... **CLC 13, 78**
 See also CA 130; CANR 61; CCA 1; DAC;
 DAM MST; DLB 53; SATA 105

Carroll, James P. 1943(?)- .... **CLC 38**
 See also CA 81-84; CANR 73; MTCW 1

Carroll, Jim 1951- .... **CLC 35, 143**
 See also AAYA 17; CA 45-48; CANR 42

Carroll, Lewis ... **NCLC 2, 53; PC 18; WLC**
 See also Dodgson, Charles L(utwidge)
 See also AAYA 39; BRW 5; BYA 5, 13; CD-
 BLB 1832-1890; CLR 2, 18; DLB 18,
 163, 178; DLBY 1998; EXPN; EXPP;
 FANT; JRDA; LAIT; NFS 7; PFS 11;
 RGEL 2; SUFW; TEA; WCH

Carroll, Paul Vincent 1900-1968 ...... **CLC 10**
 See also CA 9-12R; 25-28R; DLB 10;
 RGEL 2

Carruth, Hayden 1921- ..... **CLC 4, 7, 10, 18,
 84; PC 10**
 See also CA 9-12R; CANR 4, 38, 59, 110;
 CP 7; DLB 5, 165; INT CANR-4; MTCW
 1, 2; SATA 47

Carson, Rachel Louise 1907-1964 .... **CLC 71**
 See also AMWS 9; ANW; CA 77-80; CANR
 35; DA3; DAM POP; FW; LAIT 4;
 MTCW 1, 2; NCFS 1; SATA 23

Carter, Angela (Olive) 1940-1992 ...... **CLC 5,
 41, 76; SSC 13**
 See also BRWS 3; CA 53-56; 136; CANR
 12, 36, 61, 106; DA3; DLB 14, 207, 261;
 EXPS; FANT; FW; MTCW 1, 2; RGSF 2;
 SATA 66; SATA-Obit 70; SFW 4; SSFS
 4, 12; WLIT 4

Carter, Nick
 See Smith, Martin Cruz

Carver, Raymond 1938-1988 ..... **CLC 22, 36,
 53, 55, 126; SSC 8, 51**
 See also AMWS 3; BPFB 1; CA 33-36R;
 126; CANR 17, 34, 61, 103; CPW; DA3;
 DAM NOV; DLB 130; DLBY 1984,
 1988; MTCW 1, 2; RGAL 4; RGSF 2;
 SSFS 3, 6, 12, 13; TCWW 2; TUS

Cary, Elizabeth, Lady Falkland
 1585-1639 .... **LC 30**

Cary, (Arthur) Joyce (Lunel)
 1888-1957 .... **TCLC 1, 29**
 See also BRW 7; CA 104; 164; CDBLB
 1914-1945; DLB 15, 100; MTCW 2;
 RGEL 2; TEA

Casanova de Seingalt, Giovanni Jacopo
 1725-1798 .... **LC 13**

Casares, Adolfo Bioy
 See Bioy Casares, Adolfo
 See also RGSF 2

Casas, Bartolome de las 1474-1566
 See Las Casas, Bartolome de
 See also WLIT 1

Casely-Hayford, J(oseph) E(phraim)
 1866-1903 .... **TCLC 24; BLC 1**
 See also BW 2; CA 123; 152; DAM MULT

Casey, John (Dudley) 1939- .... **CLC 59**
 See also BEST 90:2; CA 69-72; CANR 23,
 100

Casey, Michael 1947- .... **CLC 2**
 See also CA 65-68; CANR 109; DLB 5

Casey, Patrick
 See Thurman, Wallace (Henry)

Casey, Warren (Peter) 1935-1988 .... **CLC 12**
 See also CA 101; 127; INT 101

Casona, Alejandro .... **CLC 49**
 See also Alvarez, Alejandro Rodriguez

Cassavetes, John 1929-1989 .... **CLC 20**
 See also CA 85-88; 127; CANR 82

Cassian, Nina 1924- .... **PC 17**
 See also CWP; CWW 2

Cassill, R(onald) V(erlin) 1919- ... **CLC 4, 23**
 See also CA 9-12R; CAAS 1; CANR 7, 45;
 CN 7; DLB 6, 218

Cassiodorus, Flavius Magnus c. 490(?)-c.
 583(?) .... **CMLC 43**

Cassirer, Ernst 1874-1945 .... **TCLC 61**
 See also CA 157

Cassity, (Allen) Turner 1929- .... **CLC 6, 42**
 See also CA 17-20R; CAAS 8; CANR 11;
 CSW; DLB 105

Castaneda, Carlos (Cesar Aranha)
 1931(?)-1998 .... **CLC 12, 119**
 See also CA 25-28R; CANR 32, 66, 105;
 DNFS 1; HW 1; MTCW 1

Castedo, Elena 1937- .... **CLC 65**
 See also CA 132

Castedo-Ellerman, Elena
 See Castedo, Elena

Castellanos, Rosario 1925-1974 .... **CLC 66;
 HLC 1; SSC 39**
 See also CA 131; 53-56; CANR 58; CD-
 WLB 3; DAM MULT; DLB 113; FW;
 HW 1; LAW; MTCW 1; RGSF 2; RGWL
 2

Castelvetro, Lodovico 1505-1571 .... **LC 12**

Castiglione, Baldassare 1478-1529 ...... **LC 12**
 See also Castiglione, Baldesar
 See also RGWL 2

Castiglione, Baldesar
 See Castiglione, Baldassare
 See also EW 2

Castillo, Ana (Hernandez Del)
 1953- .... **CLC 151**
 See also AAYA 42; CA 131; CANR 51, 86;
 CWP; DLB 122, 227; DNFS 2; FW; HW
 1

Castle, Robert
 See Hamilton, Edmond

Castro (Ruz), Fidel 1926(?)-
 See also CA 110; 129; CANR 81; DAM
 MULT; HLC 1; HW 2

Castro, Guillen de 1569-1631 .... **LC 19**

Castro, Rosalia de 1837-1885 ... **NCLC 3, 78;
 PC 41**
 See also DAM MULT

Cather, Willa (Sibert) 1873-1947 .... **TCLC 1,
 11, 31, 99, 125; SSC 2, 50; WLC**
 See also AAYA 24; AMW; AMWR 1; BPFB
 1; CA 104; 128; CDALB 1865-1917; DA;
 DA3; DAB; DAC; DAM MST, NOV;
 DLB 9, 54, 78, 256; DLBD 1; EXPN;
 EXPS; LAIT 3; MAWW; MTCW 1, 2;
 NFS 2; RGAL 4; RGSF 2; RHW; SATA
 30; SSFS 2, 7; TCWW 2; TUS

Catherine II
 See Catherine the Great
 See also DLB 150

Catherine the Great 1729-1796 .... **LC 69**
 See also Catherine II

Cato, Marcus Porcius 234 B.C.-149
 B.C. .... **CMLC 21**
 See also Cato the Elder

Cato the Elder
 See Cato, Marcus Porcius
 See also DLB 211

Catton, (Charles) Bruce 1899-1978 . **CLC 35**
 See also AITN 1; CA 5-8R; 81-84; CANR
 7, 74; DLB 17; SATA 2; SATA-Obit 24

Catullus c. 84 B.C.-54 B.C. .... **CMLC 18**
 See also AW 2; CDWLB 1; DLB 211;
 RGWL 2

Cauldwell, Frank
 See King, Francis (Henry)

Caunitz, William J. 1933-1996 .... **CLC 34**
 See also BEST 89:3; CA 125; 130; 152;
 CANR 73; INT 130

Causley, Charles (Stanley) 1917- .... **CLC 7**
 See also CA 9-12R; CANR 5, 35, 94; CLR
 30; CWRI 5; DLB 27; MTCW 1; SATA
 3, 66

Caute, (John) David 1936- .... **CLC 29**
 See also CA 1-4R; CAAS 4; CANR 1, 33,
 64; CBD; CD 5; CN 7; DAM NOV; DLB
 14, 231

Cavafy, C(onstantine) P(eter) ... **TCLC 2, 7;
 PC 36**
 See also Kavafis, Konstantinos Petrou
 See also CA 148; DA3; DAM POET; EW
 8; MTCW 1; RGWL 2; WP

Cavalcanti, Guido c. 1250-c.
 1300 .... **CMLC 54**

Cavallo, Evelyn
 See Spark, Muriel (Sarah)

Cavanna, Betty .... **CLC 12**
 See also Harrison, Elizabeth (Allen) Ca-
 vanna
 See also JRDA; MAICYA 1; SAAS 4;
 SATA 1, 30

Cavendish, Margaret Lucas
 1623-1673 .... **LC 30**
 See also DLB 131, 252; RGEL 2

Caxton, William 1421(?)-1491(?) .... **LC 17**
 See also DLB 170

Cayer, D. M.
 See Duffy, Maureen

Cayrol, Jean 1911- .... **CLC 11**
 See also CA 89-92; DLB 83

Cela, Camilo Jose 1916-2002 .... **CLC 4, 13,
 59, 122; HLC 1**
 See also BEST 90:2; CA 21-24R; CAAS
 10; CANR 21, 32, 76; DAM MULT;
 DLBY 1989; EW 13; HW 1; MTCW 1, 2;
 RGSF 2; RGWL 2

Celan, Paul -1970 .... **CLC 10, 19, 53, 82; PC
 10**
 See also Antschel, Paul
 See also CDWLB 2; DLB 69; RGWL 2

Celine, Louis-Ferdinand .. **CLC 1, 3, 4, 7, 9,
 15, 47, 124**
 See also Destouches, Louis-Ferdinand
 See also DLB 72; EW 11; GFL 1789 to the
 Present; RGWL 2

Cellini, Benvenuto 1500-1571 .... **LC 7**

Cendrars, Blaise .... **CLC 18, 106**
 See also Sauser-Hall, Frederic
 See also DLB 258; GFL 1789 to the Present;
 RGWL 2; WP

Centlivre, Susanna 1669(?)-1723 .... **LC 65**
 See also DLB 84; RGEL 2

Cernuda (y Bidon), Luis 1902-1963 . **CLC 54**
 See also CA 131; 89-92; DAM POET; DLB
 134; GLL 1; HW 1; RGWL 2

Cervantes, Lorna Dee 1954- .... **PC 35**
 See also CA 131; CANR 80; CWP; DLB
 82; EXPP; HLCS 1; HW 1

Cervantes (Saavedra), Miguel de
 1547-1616 .... **LC 6, 23; HLCS; SSC 12;
 WLC**
 See also BYA 1, 14; DA; DAB; DAC; DAM
 MST, NOV; EW 2; LAIT 1; NFS 8; RGSF
 2; RGWL 2; TWA

Cesaire, Aime (Fernand) 1913- . **CLC 19, 32,
 112; BLC 1; PC 25**
 See also BW 2, 3; CA 65-68; CANR 24,
 43, 81; DA3; DAM MULT, POET; GFL
 1789 to the Present; MTCW 1, 2; WP

NOV, POET; DLB 12, 54, 78; EXPN;
EXPS; LAIT 2; NFS 4; PFS 9; RGAL 4;
RGSF 2; SSFS 4; TUS; WYA; YABC 2

Cranshaw, Stanley
See Fisher, Dorothy (Frances) Canfield

Crase, Douglas 1944- .... **CLC 58**
See also CA 106

Crashaw, Richard 1612(?)-1649 .... **LC 24**
See also BRW 2; DLB 126; PAB; RGEL 2

Cratinus c. 519 B.C.-c. 422 B.C. ... **CMLC 54**

Craven, Margaret 1901-1980 .... **CLC 17**
See also BYA 2; CA 103; CCA 1; DAC;
LAIT 5

Crawford, F(rancis) Marion
1854-1909 .... **TCLC 10**
See also CA 107; 168; DLB 71; HGG;
RGAL 4; SUFW

Crawford, Isabella Valancy
1850-1887 .... **NCLC 12**
See also DLB 92; RGEL 2

Crayon, Geoffrey
See Irving, Washington

Creasey, John 1908-1973 .... **CLC 11**
See also Marric, J. J.
See also CA 5-8R; 41-44R; CANR 8, 59;
CMW 4; DLB 77; MTCW 1

Crebillon, Claude Prosper Jolyot de (fils)
1707-1777 .... **LC 1, 28**
See also GFL Beginnings to 1789

Credo
See Creasey, John

Credo, Alvaro J. de
See Prado (Calvo), Pedro

Creeley, Robert (White) 1926- .. **CLC 1, 2, 4,
8, 11, 15, 36, 78**
See also AMWS 4; CA 1-4R; CAAS 10;
CANR 23, 43, 89; CP 7; DA3; DAM
POET; DLB 5, 16, 169; DLBD 17;
MTCW 1, 2; RGAL 4; WP

Crevecoeur, Hector St. John de
See Crevecoeur, Michel Guillaume Jean de
See also ANW

Crevecoeur, Michel Guillaume Jean de
1735-1813 .... **NCLC 105**
See also Crevecoeur, Hector St. John de
See also AMWS 1; DLB 37

Crevel, Rene 1900-1935 .... **TCLC 112**
See also GLL 2

Crews, Harry (Eugene) 1935- ..... **CLC 6, 23,
49**
See also AITN 1; AMWS 11; BPFB 1; CA
25-28R; CANR 20, 57; CN 7; CSW; DA3;
DLB 6, 143, 185; MTCW 1, 2; RGAL 4

Crichton, (John) Michael 1942- .... **CLC 2, 6,
54, 90**
See also AAYA 10; AITN 2; BPFB 1; CA
25-28R; CANR 13, 40, 54, 76; CMW 4;
CN 7; CPW; DA3; DAM NOV, POP;
DLBY 1981; INT CANR-13; JRDA;
MTCW 1, 2; SATA 9, 88; SFW 4; YAW

Crispin, Edmund .... **CLC 22**
See also Montgomery, (Robert) Bruce
See also DLB 87; MSW

Cristofer, Michael 1945(?)- .... **CLC 28**
See also CA 110; 152; CAD; CD 5; DAM
DRAM; DFS 15; DLB 7

Croce, Benedetto 1866-1952 .... **TCLC 37**
See also CA 120; 155; EW 8

Crockett, David 1786-1836 .... **NCLC 8**
See also DLB 3, 11, 183, 248

Crockett, Davy
See Crockett, David

Crofts, Freeman Wills 1879-1957 .. **TCLC 55**
See also CA 115; 195; CMW 4; DLB 77;
MSW

Croker, John Wilson 1780-1857 .... **NCLC 10**
See also DLB 110

Crommelynck, Fernand 1885-1970 .. **CLC 75**
See also CA 189; 89-92

Cromwell, Oliver 1599-1658 .... **LC 43**

Cronenberg, David 1943- .... **CLC 143**
See also CA 138; CCA 1

Cronin, A(rchibald) J(oseph)
1896-1981 .... **CLC 32**
See also BPFB 1; CA 1-4R; 102; CANR 5;
DLB 191; SATA 47; SATA-Obit 25

Cross, Amanda
See Heilbrun, Carolyn G(old)
See also BPFB 1; CMW; CPW; MSW

Crothers, Rachel 1878-1958 .... **TCLC 19**
See also CA 113; 194; CAD; CWD; DLB
7, 266; RGAL 4

Croves, Hal
See Traven, B.

Crow Dog, Mary (Ellen) (?)- .... **CLC 93**
See also Brave Bird, Mary
See also CA 154

Crowfield, Christopher
See Stowe, Harriet (Elizabeth) Beecher

Crowley, Aleister .... **TCLC 7**
See also Crowley, Edward Alexander
See also GLL 1

Crowley, Edward Alexander 1875-1947
See Crowley, Aleister
See also CA 104; HGG

Crowley, John 1942- .... **CLC 57**
See also BPFB 1; CA 61-64; CANR 43, 98;
DLBY 1982; SATA 65; SFW 4

Crud
See Crumb, R(obert)

Crumarums
See Crumb, R(obert)

Crumb, R(obert) 1943- .... **CLC 17**
See also CA 106; CANR 107

Crumbum
See Crumb, R(obert)

Crumski
See Crumb, R(obert)

Crum the Bum
See Crumb, R(obert)

Crunk
See Crumb, R(obert)

Crustt
See Crumb, R(obert)

Crutchfield, Les
See Trumbo, Dalton

Cruz, Victor Hernandez 1949- .... **PC 37**
See also BW 2; CA 65-68; CAAS 17;
CANR 14, 32, 74; CP 7; DAM MULT,
POET; DLB 41; DNFS 1; EXPP; HLC 1;
HW 1, 2; MTCW 1; WP

Cryer, Gretchen (Kiger) 1935- .... **CLC 21**
See also CA 114; 123

Csath, Geza 1887-1919 .... **TCLC 13**
See also CA 111

Cudlip, David R(ockwell) 1933- .... **CLC 34**
See also CA 177

Cullen, Countee 1903-1946 .... **TCLC 4, 37;
BLC 1; PC 20; WLCS**
See also AFAW 2; AMWS 4; BW 1; CA
108; 124; CDALB 1917-1929; DA; DA3;
DAC; DAM MST, MULT, POET; DLB 4,
48, 51; EXPP; MTCW 1, 2; PFS 3; RGAL
4; SATA 18; WP

Cum, R.
See Crumb, R(obert)

Cummings, Bruce F(rederick) 1889-1919
See Barbellion, W. N. P.
See also CA 123

Cummings, E(dward) E(stlin)
1894-1962 .. **CLC 1, 3, 8, 12, 15, 68; PC
5; WLC**
See also AAYA 41; AMW; CA 73-76;
CANR 31; CDALB 1929-1941; DA;
DA3; DAB; DAC; DAM MST, POET;
DLB 4, 48; EXPP; MTCW 1, 2; PAB;
PFS 1, 3, 12, 13; RGAL 4; TUS; WP

Cunha, Euclides (Rodrigues Pimenta) da
1866-1909 .... **TCLC 24**
See also CA 123; LAW; WLIT 1

Cunningham, E. V.
See Fast, Howard (Melvin)

Cunningham, J(ames) V(incent)
1911-1985 .... **CLC 3, 31**
See also CA 1-4R; 115; CANR 1, 72; DLB
5

Cunningham, Julia (Woolfolk)
1916- .... **CLC 12**
See also CA 9-12R; CANR 4, 19, 36; CWRI
5; JRDA; MAICYA 1, 2; SAAS 2; SATA
1, 26, 132

Cunningham, Michael 1952- .... **CLC 34**
See also CA 136; CANR 96; GLL 2

Cunninghame Graham, R. B.
See Cunninghame Graham, Robert
(Gallnigad) Bontine

**Cunninghame Graham, Robert (Gallnigad)
Bontine** 1852-1936 .... **TCLC 19**
See also Graham, R(obert) B(ontine) Cun-
ninghame
See also CA 119; 184

Currie, Ellen 19(?)- .... **CLC 44**

Curtin, Philip
See Lowndes, Marie Adelaide (Belloc)

Curtis, Price
See Ellison, Harlan (Jay)

Cusanus, Nicolaus
See Nicholas of Cusa
See also LC 80

Cutrate, Joe
See Spiegelman, Art

Cynewulf c. 770- .... **CMLC 23**
See also DLB 146; RGEL 2

Cyrano de Bergerac, Savinien de
1619-1655 .... **LC 65**
See also GFL Beginnings to 1789; RGWL
2

Czaczkes, Shmuel Yosef Halevi
See Agnon, S(hmuel) Y(osef Halevi)

Dabrowska, Maria (Szumska)
1889-1965 .... **CLC 15**
See also CA 106; CDWLB 4; DLB 215

Dabydeen, David 1955- .... **CLC 34**
See also BW 1; CA 125; CANR 56, 92; CN
7; CP 7

Dacey, Philip 1939- .... **CLC 51**
See also CA 37-40R; CAAS 17; CANR 14,
32, 64; CP 7; DLB 105

Dagerman, Stig (Halvard)
1923-1954 .... **TCLC 17**
See also CA 117; 155; DLB 259

D'Aguiar, Fred 1960- .... **CLC 145**
See also CA 148; CANR 83, 101; CP 7;
DLB 157

Dahl, Roald 1916-1990 .... **CLC 1, 6, 18, 79**
See also AAYA 15; BPFB 1; BRWS 4; BYA
5; CA 1-4R; 133; CANR 6, 32, 37, 62;
CLR 1, 7, 41; CPW; DA3; DAB; DAC;
DAM MST, NOV, POP; DLB 139, 255;
HGG; JRDA; MAICYA 1, 2; MTCW 1,
2; RGSF 2; SATA 1, 26, 73; SATA-Obit
65; SSFS 4; TEA; YAW

Dahlberg, Edward 1900-1977 .. **CLC 1, 7, 14**
See also CA 9-12R; 69-72; CANR 31, 62;
DLB 48; MTCW 1; RGAL 4

Daitch, Susan 1954- .... **CLC 103**
See also CA 161

Dale, Colin .... **TCLC 18**
See also Lawrence, T(homas) E(dward)

Dale, George E.
See Asimov, Isaac

Dalton, Roque 1935-1975(?) .... **PC 36**
See also CA 176; HLCS 1; HW 2

Daly, Elizabeth 1878-1967 .... **CLC 52**
See also CA 23-24; 25-28R; CANR 60;
CAP 2; CMW 4

Daly, Maureen 1921- .... **CLC 17**
See also AAYA 5; BYA 6; CANR 37, 83,
108; JRDA; MAICYA 1, 2; SAAS 1;
SATA 2, 129; WYA; YAW

Damas, Leon-Gontran 1912-1978 .... **CLC 84**
See also BW 1; CA 125; 73-76

Dana, Richard Henry Sr.
1787-1879 .... **NCLC 53**

Daniel, Samuel 1562(?)-1619 .... **LC 24**
See also DLB 62; RGEL 2

Daniels, Brett
See Adler, Renata

Dannay, Frederic 1905-1982 .... **CLC 11**
See also Queen, Ellery
See also CA 1-4R; 107; CANR 1, 39; CMW
4; DAM POP; DLB 137; MTCW 1

D'Annunzio, Gabriele 1863-1938 ... **TCLC 6,**
40
See also CA 104; 155; EW 8; RGWL 2;
TWA

Danois, N. le
See Gourmont, Remy(-Marie-Charles) de

Dante 1265 1321 .... **CMLC 3, 18, 39; PC 21;**
WLCS
See also DA; DA3; DAB; DAC; DAM
MST, POET; EFS 1; EW 1; LAIT 1;
RGWL 2; TWA; WP

d'Antibes, Germain
See Simenon, Georges (Jacques Christian)

Danticat, Edwidge 1969- .... **CLC 94, 139**
See also AAYA 29; CA 152; CAAE 192;
CANR 73; DNFS 1; EXPS; MTCW 1;
SSFS 1; YAW

Danvers, Dennis 1947- .... **CLC 70**

Danziger, Paula 1944- .... **CLC 21**
See also AAYA 4, 36; BYA 6, 7, 14; CA
112; 115; CANR 37; CLR 20; JRDA;
MAICYA 1, 2; SATA 36, 63, 102; SATA-
Brief 30; WYA; YAW

Da Ponte, Lorenzo 1749-1838 .... **NCLC 50**

Dario, Ruben 1867-1916 ... **TCLC 4; HLC 1;**
PC 15
See also CA 131; CANR 81; DAM MULT;
HW 1, 2; LAW; MTCW 1, 2; RGWL 2

Darley, George 1795-1846 .... **NCLC 2**
See also DLB 96; RGEL 2

Darrow, Clarence (Seward)
1857-1938 .... **TCLC 81**
See also CA 164

Darwin, Charles 1809-1882 .... **NCLC 57**
See also BRWS 7; DLB 57, 166; RGEL 2;
TEA; WLIT 4

Darwin, Erasmus 1731-1802 .... **NCLC 106**
See also DLB 93; RGEL 2

Daryush, Elizabeth 1887-1977 ...... **CLC 6, 19**
See also CA 49-52; CANR 3, 81; DLB 20

Dasgupta, Surendranath
1887-1952 .... **TCLC 81**
See also CA 157

Dashwood, Edmee Elizabeth Monica de la
Pasture 1890-1943
See Delafield, E. M.
See also CA 119; 154

da Silva, Antonio Jose
1705-1739 .... **NCLC 114**
See also Silva, Jose Asuncion

Daudet, (Louis Marie) Alphonse
1840-1897 .... **NCLC 1**
See also DLB 123; GFL 1789 to the Present;
RGSF 2

Daumal, Rene 1908-1944 .... **TCLC 14**
See also CA 114

Davenant, William 1606-1668 .... **LC 13**
See also DLB 58, 126; RGEL 2

Davenport, Guy (Mattison, Jr.)
1927- .... **CLC 6, 14, 38; SSC 16**
See also CA 33-36R; CANR 23, 73; CN 7;
CSW; DLB 130

David, Robert
See Nezval, Vitezslav

Davidson, Avram (James) 1923-1993
See Queen, Ellery
See also CA 101; 171; CANR 26; DLB 8;
FANT; SFW 4; SUFW

Davidson, Donald (Grady)
1893-1968 .... **CLC 2, 13, 19**
See also CA 5-8R; 25-28R; CANR 4, 84;
DLB 45

Davidson, Hugh
See Hamilton, Edmond

Davidson, John 1857-1909 .... **TCLC 24**
See also CA 118; DLB 19; RGEL 2

Davidson, Sara 1943- .... **CLC 9**
See also CA 81-84; CANR 44, 68; DLB
185

Davie, Donald (Alfred) 1922-1995 .... **CLC 5,**
8, 10, 31; PC 29
See also BRWS 6; CA 1-4R; 149; CAAS 3;
CANR 1, 44; CP 7; DLB 27; MTCW 1;
RGEL 2

Davie, Elspeth 1919-1995 .... **SSC 52**
See also CA 120; 126; 150; DLB 139

Davies, Ray(mond Douglas) 1944- ... **CLC 21**
See also CA 116; 146; CANR 92

Davies, Rhys 1901-1978 .... **CLC 23**
See also CA 9-12R; 81-84; CANR 4; DLB
139, 191

Davies, (William) Robertson
1913-1995 .... **CLC 2, 7, 13, 25, 42, 75,**
91; WLC
See also Marchbanks, Samuel
See also BEST 89:2; BPFB 1; CA 33-36R;
150; CANR 17, 42, 103; CN 7; CPW;
DA; DA3; DAB; DAC; DAM MST, NOV,
POP; DLB 68; HGG; INT CANR-17;
MTCW 1, 2; RGEL 2; TWA

Davies, Walter C.
See Kornbluth, C(yril) M.

Davies, William Henry 1871-1940 ... **TCLC 5**
See also CA 104; 179; DLB 19, 174; RGEL
2

Da Vinci, Leonardo 1452-1519 ..... **LC 12, 57,**
60
See also AAYA 40

Davis, Angela (Yvonne) 1944- .... **CLC 77**
See also BW 2, 3; CA 57-60; CANR 10,
81; CSW; DA3; DAM MULT; FW

Davis, B. Lynch
See Bioy Casares, Adolfo; Borges, Jorge
Luis

Davis, Gordon
See Hunt, E(verette) Howard, (Jr.)

Davis, H(arold) L(enoir) 1896-1960 . **CLC 49**
See also ANW; CA 178; 89-92; DLB 9,
206; SATA 114

Davis, Rebecca (Blaine) Harding
1831-1910 .... **TCLC 6; SSC 38**
See also CA 104; 179; DLB 74, 239; FW;
NFS 14; RGAL 4; TUS

Davis, Richard Harding
1864-1916 .... **TCLC 24**
See also CA 114; 179; DLB 12, 23, 78, 79,
189; DLBD 13; RGAL 4

Davison, Frank Dalby 1893-1970 ..... **CLC 15**
See also CA 116; DLB 260

Davison, Lawrence H.
See Lawrence, D(avid) H(erbert Richards)

Davison, Peter (Hubert) 1928- .... **CLC 28**
See also CA 9-12R; CAAS 4; CANR 3, 43,
84; CP 7; DLB 5

Davys, Mary 1674-1732 .... **LC 1, 46**
See also DLB 39

Dawson, (Guy) Fielding (Lewis)
1930-2002 .... **CLC 6**
See also CA 85-88; 202; CANR 108; DLB
130

Dawson, Peter
See Faust, Frederick (Schiller)
See also TCWW 2, 2

Day, Clarence (Shepard, Jr.)
1874-1935 .... **TCLC 25**
See also CA 108; DLB 11

Day, John 1574(?)-1640(?) .... **LC 70**
See also DLB 62, 170; RGEL 2

Day, Thomas 1748-1789 .... **LC 1**
See also DLB 39; YABC 1

Day Lewis, C(ecil) 1904-1972 . **CLC 1, 6, 10;**
PC 11
See also Blake, Nicholas
See also BRWS 3; CA 13-16; 33-36R;
CANR 34; CAP 1; CWRI 5; DAM POET;
DLB 15, 20; MTCW 1, 2; RGEL 2

Dazai Osamu .... **TCLC 11; SSC 41**
See also Tsushima, Shuji
See also CA 164; DLB 182; MJW; RGSF
2; RGWL 2; TWA

de Andrade, Carlos Drummond
See Drummond de Andrade, Carlos

de Andrade, Mario 1892-1945
See Andrade, Mario de
See also CA 178; HW 2

Deane, Norman
See Creasey, John

Deane, Seamus (Francis) 1940- ...... **CLC 122**
See also CA 118; CANR 42

de Beauvoir, Simone (Lucie Ernestine Marie
Bertrand)
See Beauvoir, Simone (Lucie Ernestine
Marie Bertrand) de

de Beer, P.
See Bosman, Herman Charles

de Brissac, Malcolm
See Dickinson, Peter (Malcolm)

de Campos, Alvaro
See Pessoa, Fernando (Antonio Nogueira)

de Chardin, Pierre Teilhard
See Teilhard de Chardin, (Marie Joseph)
Pierre

Dee, John 1527-1608 .... **LC 20**
See also DLB 136, 213

Deer, Sandra 1940- .... **CLC 45**
See also CA 186

De Ferrari, Gabriella 1941- .... **CLC 65**
See also CA 146

Defoe, Daniel 1660(?)-1731 .. **LC 1, 42; WLC**
See also AAYA 27; BRW 3; BRWR 1; BYA
4; CDBLB 1660-1789; CLR 61; DA;
DA3; DAB; DAC; DAM MST, NOV,
DLB 39, 95, 101; JRDA; LAIT 1; MAI-
CYA 1, 2; NFS 9, 13; RGEL 2; SATA 22;
TEA; WCH; WLIT 3

de Gourmont, Remy(-Marie-Charles)
See Gourmont, Remy(-Marie-Charles) de

de Hartog, Jan 1914- .... **CLC 19**
See also CA 1-4R; CANR 1; DFS 12

de Hostos, E. M.
See Hostos (y Bonilla), Eugenio Maria de

de Hostos, Eugenio M.
See Hostos (y Bonilla), Eugenio Maria de

Deighton, Len .... **CLC 4, 7, 22, 46**
See also Deighton, Leonard Cyril
See also AAYA 6; BEST 89:2; BPFB 1; CD-
BLB 1960 to Present; CMW 4; CN 7;
CPW; DLB 87

Deighton, Leonard Cyril 1929-
See Deighton, Len
See also CA 9-12R; CANR 19, 33, 68;
DA3; DAM NOV, POP; MTCW 1, 2

Dekker, Thomas 1572(?)-1632 ..... **LC 22; DC**
12
See also CDBLB Before 1660; DAM
DRAM; DLB 62, 172; RGEL 2

Douglas, Ellen .... **CLC 73**
See also Haxton, Josephine Ayres; Williamson, Ellen Douglas
See also CN 7; CSW

Douglas, Gavin 1475(?)-1522 .... **LC 20**
See also DLB 132; RGEL 2

Douglas, George
See Brown, George Douglas
See also RGEL 2

Douglas, Keith (Castellain)
1920-1944 .... **TCLC 40**
See also BRW 7; CA 160; DLB 27; PAB; RGEL 2

Douglas, Leonard
See Bradbury, Ray (Douglas)

Douglas, Michael
See Crichton, (John) Michael

Douglas, (George) Norman
1868-1952 .... **TCLC 68**
See also BRW 6; CA 119; 157; DLB 34, 195; RGEL 2

Douglas, William
See Brown, George Douglas

Douglass, Frederick 1817(?)-1895 .. **NCLC 7, 55; BLC 1; WLC**
See also AFAW 1, 2; AMWS 3; CDALB 1640-1865; DA; DA3; DAC; DAM MST, MULT; DLB 1, 43, 50, 79, 243; FW; LAIT 2; NCFS 2; RGAL 4; SATA 29

Dourado, (Waldomiro Freitas) Autran
1926- .... **CLC 23, 60**
See also CA 25-28R, 179; CANR 34, 81; DLB 145; HW 2

Dourado, Waldomiro Autran
See Dourado, (Waldomiro Freitas) Autran
See also CA 179

Dove, Rita (Frances) 1952- .... **CLC 50, 81; BLCS; PC 6**
See also AMWS 4; BW 2; CA 109; CAAS 19; CANR 27, 42, 68, 76, 97; CDALBS; CP 7; CSW; CWP; DA3; DAM MULT, POET; DLB 120; EXPP; MTCW 1; PFS 1, 15; RGAL 4

Doveglion
See Villa, Jose Garcia

Dowell, Coleman 1925-1985 .... **CLC 60**
See also CA 25-28R; 117; CANR 10; DLB 130; GLL 2

Dowson, Ernest (Christopher)
1867-1900 .... **TCLC 4**
See also CA 105; 150; DLB 19, 135; RGEL 2

Doyle, A. Conan
See Doyle, Sir Arthur Conan

Doyle, Sir Arthur Conan
1859-1930 .... **TCLC 7; SSC 12; WLC**
See also Conan Doyle, Arthur
See also AAYA 14; BRWS 2; CA 104; 122; CDBLB 1890-1914; CMW 4; DA; DA3; DAB; DAC; DAM MST, NOV; DLB 18, 70, 156, 178; EXPS; HGG; LAIT 2; MSW; MTCW 1, 2; RGEL 2; RGSF 2; RHW; SATA 24; SCFW 2; SFW 4; SSFS 2; TEA; WCH; WLIT 4; WYA; YAW

Doyle, Conan
See Doyle, Sir Arthur Conan

Doyle, John
See Graves, Robert (von Ranke)

Doyle, Roddy 1958(?)- .... **CLC 81**
See also AAYA 14; BRWS 5; CA 143; CANR 73; CN 7; DA3; DLB 194

Doyle, Sir A. Conan
See Doyle, Sir Arthur Conan

Dr. A
See Asimov, Isaac; Silverstein, Alvin; Silverstein, Virginia B(arbara Opshelor)

Drabble, Margaret 1939- ...... **CLC 2, 3, 5, 8, 10, 22, 53, 129**
See also BRWS 4; CA 13-16R; CANR 18, 35, 63; CDBLB 1960 to Present; CN 7; CPW; DA3; DAB; DAC; DAM MST, NOV, POP; DLB 14, 155, 231; FW; MTCW 1, 2; RGEL 2; SATA 48; TEA

Drapier, M. B.
See Swift, Jonathan

Drayham, James
See Mencken, H(enry) L(ouis)

Drayton, Michael 1563-1631 .... **LC 8**
See also DAM POET; DLB 121; RGEL 2

Dreadstone, Carl
See Campbell, (John) Ramsey

Dreiser, Theodore (Herman Albert)
1871-1945 .... **TCLC 10, 18, 35, 83; SSC 30; WLC**
See also AMW; CA 106; 132; CDALB 1865-1917; DA; DA3; DAC; DAM MST, NOV; DLB 9, 12, 102, 137; DLBD 1; LAIT 2; MTCW 1, 2; NFS 8; RGAL 4; TUS

Drexler, Rosalyn 1926- .... **CLC 2, 6**
See also CA 81-84; CAD; CANR 68; CD 5; CWD

Dreyer, Carl Theodor 1889-1968 ...... **CLC 16**
See also CA 116

Drieu la Rochelle, Pierre(-Eugene)
1893-1945 .... **TCLC 21**
See also CA 117; DLB 72; GFL 1789 to the Present

Drinkwater, John 1882-1937 .... **TCLC 57**
See also CA 109; 149; DLB 10, 19, 149; RGEL 2

Drop Shot
See Cable, George Washington

Droste-Hulshoff, Annette Freiin von
1797-1848 .... **NCLC 3**
See also CDWLB 2; DLB 133; RGSF 2; RGWL 2

Drummond, Walter
See Silverberg, Robert

Drummond, William Henry
1854-1907 .... **TCLC 25**
See also CA 160; DLB 92

Drummond de Andrade, Carlos
1902-1987 .... **CLC 18**
See also Andrade, Carlos Drummond de
See also CA 132; 123; LAW

Drury, Allen (Stuart) 1918-1998 .... **CLC 37**
See also CA 57-60; 170; CANR 18, 52; CN 7; INT CANR-18

Dryden, John 1631-1700 ..... **LC 3, 21; DC 3; PC 25; WLC**
See also BRW 2; CDBLB 1660-1789; DA; DAB; DAC; DAM DRAM, MST, POET; DLB 80, 101, 131; EXPP; IDTP; RGEL 2; TEA; WLIT 3

Duberman, Martin (Bauml) 1930- ..... **CLC 8**
See also CA 1-4R; CAD; CANR 2, 63; CD 5

Dubie, Norman (Evans) 1945- .... **CLC 36**
See also CA 69-72; CANR 12; CP 7; DLB 120; PFS 12

Du Bois, W(illiam) E(dward) B(urghardt)
1868-1963 ... **CLC 1, 2, 13, 64, 96; BLC 1; WLC**
See also AAYA 40; AFAW 1, 2; AMWS 2; BW 1, 3; CA 85-88; CANR 34, 82; CDALB 1865-1917; DA; DA3; DAC; DAM MST, MULT, NOV; DLB 47, 50, 91, 246; EXPP; LAIT 2; MTCW 1, 2; NCFS 1; PFS 13; RGAL 4; SATA 42

Dubus, Andre 1936-1999 ..... **CLC 13, 36, 97; SSC 15**
See also AMWS 7; CA 21-24R; 177; CANR 17; CN 7; CSW; DLB 130; INT CANR-17; RGAL 4; SSFS 10

Duca Minimo
See D'Annunzio, Gabriele

Ducharme, Rejean 1941- .... **CLC 74**
See also CA 165; DLB 60

Duchen, Claire .... **CLC 65**

Duclos, Charles Pinot- 1704-1772 .... **LC 1**
See also GFL Beginnings to 1789

Dudek, Louis 1918- .... **CLC 11, 19**
See also CA 45-48; CAAS 14; CANR 1; CP 7; DLB 88

Duerrenmatt, Friedrich 1921-1990 ... **CLC 1, 4, 8, 11, 15, 43, 102**
See also Durrenmatt, Friedrich
See also CA 17-20R; CANR 33; CMW 4; DAM DRAM; DLB 69, 124; MTCW 1, 2

Duffy, Bruce 1953(?)- .... **CLC 50**
See also CA 172

Duffy, Maureen 1933- .... **CLC 37**
See also CA 25-28R; CANR 33, 68; CBD; CN 7; CP 7; CWD; CWP; DFS 15; DLB 14; FW; MTCW 1

Du Fu
See Tu Fu
See also RGWL 2

Dugan, Alan 1923- .... **CLC 2, 6**
See also CA 81-84; CP 7; DLB 5; PFS 10

du Gard, Roger Martin
See Martin du Gard, Roger

Duhamel, Georges 1884-1966 .... **CLC 8**
See also CA 81-84; 25-28R; CANR 35; DLB 65; GFL 1789 to the Present; MTCW 1

Dujardin, Edouard (Emile Louis)
1861-1949 .... **TCLC 13**
See also CA 109; DLB 123

Dulles, John Foster 1888-1959 .... **TCLC 72**
See also CA 115; 149

Dumas, Alexandre (pere)
1802-1870 .... **NCLC 11, 71; WLC**
See also AAYA 22; BYA 3; DA; DA3; DAB; DAC; DAM MST, NOV; DLB 119, 192; EW 6; GFL 1789 to the Present; LAIT 1, 2; NFS 14; RGWL 2; SATA 18; TWA; WCH

Dumas, Alexandre (fils)
1824-1895 .... **NCLC 9; DC 1**
See also DLB 192; GFL 1789 to the Present; RGWL 2

Dumas, Claudine
See Malzberg, Barry N(athaniel)

Dumas, Henry L. 1934-1968 .... **CLC 6, 62**
See also BW 1; CA 85-88; DLB 41; RGAL 4

du Maurier, Daphne 1907-1989 .. **CLC 6, 11, 59; SSC 18**
See also AAYA 37; BPFB 1; BRWS 3; CA 5-8R; 128; CANR 6, 55; CMW 4; CPW; DA3; DAB; DAC; DAM MST, POP; DLB 191; HGG; LAIT 3; MSW; MTCW 1, 2; NFS 12; RGEL 2; RGSF 2; RHW; SATA 27; SATA-Obit 60; SSFS 14; TEA

Du Maurier, George 1834-1896 ..... **NCLC 86**
See also DLB 153, 178; RGEL 2

Dunbar, Paul Laurence 1872-1906 . **TCLC 2, 12; BLC 1; PC 5; SSC 8; WLC**
See also AFAW 1, 2; AMWS 2; BW 1, 3; CA 104; 124; CANR 79; CDALB 1865-1917; DA; DA3; DAC; DAM MST, MULT, POET; DLB 50, 54, 78; EXPP; RGAL 4; SATA 34

Dunbar, William 1460(?)-1520(?) .... **LC 20**
See also BRWS 8; DLB 132, 146; RGEL 2

Duncan, Dora Angela
See Duncan, Isadora

Duncan, Isadora 1877(?)-1927 .... **TCLC 68**
See also CA 118; 149

Duncan, Lois 1934- .... **CLC 26**
See also AAYA 4, 34; BYA 6, 8; CA 1-4R; CANR 2, 23, 36; CLR 29; JRDA; MAICYA 1, 2; MAICYAS 1; SAAS 2; SATA 1, 36, 75, 133; WYA; YAW

Duncan, Robert (Edward)
1919-1988 .... **CLC 1, 2, 4, 7, 15, 41, 55; PC 2**
See also CA 9-12R; 124; CANR 28, 62; DAM POET; DLB 5, 16, 193; MTCW 1, 2; PFS 13; RGAL 4; WP

Duncan, Sara Jeannette
1861-1922 .... **TCLC 60**
See also CA 157; DLB 92

Dunlap, William 1766-1839 .... **NCLC 2**
See also DLB 30, 37, 59; RGAL 4

Dunn, Douglas (Eaglesham) 1942- .... **CLC 6, 40**
See also CA 45-48; CANR 2, 33; CP 7; DLB 40; MTCW 1

Dunn, Katherine (Karen) 1945- .... **CLC 71**
See also CA 33-36R; CANR 72; HGG; MTCW 1

Dunn, Stephen (Elliott) 1939- .... **CLC 36**
See also AMWS 11; CA 33-36R; CANR 12, 48, 53, 105; CP 7; DLB 105

Dunne, Finley Peter 1867-1936 ...... **TCLC 28**
See also CA 108; 178; DLB 11, 23; RGAL 4

Dunne, John Gregory 1932- .... **CLC 28**
See also CA 25-28R; CANR 14, 50; CN 7; DLBY 1980

Dunsany, Lord .... **TCLC 2, 59**
See also Dunsany, Edward John Moreton Drax Plunkett
See also DLB 77, 153, 156, 255; FANT; IDTP; RGEL 2; SFW 4; SUFW

Dunsany, Edward John Moreton Drax Plunkett 1878-1957
See Dunsany, Lord
See also CA 104; 148; DLB 10; MTCW 1

du Perry, Jean
See Simenon, Georges (Jacques Christian)

Durang, Christopher (Ferdinand)
1949- .... **CLC 27, 38**
See also CA 105; CAD; CANR 50, 76; CD 5; MTCW 1

Duras, Marguerite 1914-1996 . **CLC 3, 6, 11, 20, 34, 40, 68, 100; SSC 40**
See also BPFB 1; CA 25-28R; 151; CANR 50; CWW 2; DLB 83; GFL 1789 to the Present; IDFW 4; MTCW 1, 2; RGWL 2; TWA

Durban, (Rosa) Pam 1947- .... **CLC 39**
See also CA 123; CANR 98; CSW

Durcan, Paul 1944- .... **CLC 43, 70**
See also CA 134; CP 7; DAM POET

Durkheim, Emile 1858-1917 .... **TCLC 55**

Durrell, Lawrence (George)
1912-1990 .... **CLC 1, 4, 6, 8, 13, 27, 41**
See also BPFB 1; BRWS 1; CA 9-12R; 132; CANR 40, 77; CDBLB 1945-1960; DAM NOV; DLB 15, 27, 204; DLBY 1990; MTCW 1, 2; RGEL 2; SFW 4; TEA

Durrenmatt, Friedrich
See Duerrenmatt, Friedrich
See also CDWLB 2; EW 13; RGWL 2

Dutt, Toru 1856-1877 .... **NCLC 29**
See also DLB 240

Dwight, Timothy 1752-1817 .... **NCLC 13**
See also DLB 37; RGAL 4

Dworkin, Andrea 1946- .... **CLC 43, 123**
See also CA 77-80; CAAS 21; CANR 16, 39, 76, 96; FW; GLL 1; INT CANR-16; MTCW 1, 2

Dwyer, Deanna
See Koontz, Dean R(ay)

Dwyer, K. R.
See Koontz, Dean R(ay)

Dwyer, Thomas A. 1923- .... **CLC 114**
See also CA 115

Dybek, Stuart 1942- .... **CLC 114; SSC 55**
See also CA 97-100; CANR 39; DLB 130

Dye, Richard
See De Voto, Bernard (Augustine)

Dyer, Geoff 1958- .... **CLC 149**
See also CA 125; CANR 88

Dylan, Bob 1941- .... **CLC 3, 4, 6, 12, 77; PC 37**
See also CA 41-44R; CANR 108; CP 7; DLB 16

Dyson, John 1943- .... **CLC 70**
See also CA 144

E. V. L.
See Lucas, E(dward) V(errall)

Eagleton, Terence (Francis) 1943- .. **CLC 63, 132**
See also CA 57-60; CANR 7, 23, 68; DLB 242; MTCW 1, 2

Eagleton, Terry
See Eagleton, Terence (Francis)

Early, Jack
See Scoppettone, Sandra
See also GLL 1

East, Michael
See West, Morris L(anglo)

Eastaway, Edward
See Thomas, (Philip) Edward

Eastlake, William (Derry)
1917-1997 .... **CLC 8**
See also CA 5-8R; 158; CAAS 1; CANR 5, 63; CN 7; DLB 6, 206; INT CANR-5; TCWW 2

Eastman, Charles A(lexander)
1858-1939 .... **TCLC 55**
See also CA 179; CANR 91; DAM MULT; DLB 175; NNAL; YABC 1

Eberhart, Richard (Ghormley)
1904- .... **CLC 3, 11, 19, 56**
See also AMW; CA 1-4R; CANR 2; CDALB 1941-1968; CP 7; DAM POET; DLB 48; MTCW 1; RGAL 4

Eberstadt, Fernanda 1960- .... **CLC 39**
See also CA 136; CANR 69

Echegaray (y Eizaguirre), Jose (Maria Waldo) 1832-1916 .... **TCLC 4; HLCS 1**
See also CA 104; CANR 32; HW 1; MTCW 1

Echeverria, (Jose) Esteban (Antonino)
1805-1851 .... **NCLC 18**
See also LAW

Echo
See Proust, (Valentin-Louis-George-Eugene-)Marcel

Eckert, Allan W. 1931- .... **CLC 17**
See also AAYA 18; BYA 2; CA 13-16R; CANR 14, 45; INT CANR-14; MAICYA 2; MAICYAS 1; SAAS 21; SATA 29, 91; SATA-Brief 27

Eckhart, Meister 1260(?)-1327(?) ... **CMLC 9**
See also DLB 115

Eckmar, F. R.
See de Hartog, Jan

Eco, Umberto 1932- .... **CLC 28, 60, 142**
See also BEST 90:1; BPFB 1; CA 77-80; CANR 12, 33, 55, 110; CPW; CWW 2; DA3; DAM NOV, POP; DLB 196, 242; MSW; MTCW 1, 2

Eddison, E(ric) R(ucker)
1882-1945 .... **TCLC 15**
See also CA 109; 156; DLB 255; FANT; SFW 4; SUFW

Eddy, Mary (Ann Morse) Baker
1821-1910 .... **TCLC 71**
See also CA 113; 174

Edel, (Joseph) Leon 1907-1997 .. **CLC 29, 34**
See also CA 1-4R; 161; CANR 1, 22; DLB 103; INT CANR-22

Eden, Emily 1797-1869 .... **NCLC 10**

Edgar, David 1948- .... **CLC 42**
See also CA 57-60; CANR 12, 61; CBD; CD 5; DAM DRAM; DFS 15; DLB 13, 233; MTCW 1

Edgerton, Clyde (Carlyle) 1944- ...... **CLC 39**
See also AAYA 17; CA 118; 134; CANR 64; CSW; INT 134; YAW

Edgeworth, Maria 1768-1849 .... **NCLC 1, 51**
See also BRWS 3; DLB 116, 159, 163; FW; RGEL 2; SATA 21; TEA; WLIT 3

Edmonds, Paul
See Kuttner, Henry

Edmonds, Walter D(umaux)
1903-1998 .... **CLC 35**
See also BYA 2; CA 5-8R; CANR 2; CWRI 5; DLB 9; LAIT 1; MAICYA 1, 2; RHW; SAAS 4; SATA 1, 27; SATA-Obit 99

Edmondson, Wallace
See Ellison, Harlan (Jay)

Edson, Russell 1935- .... **CLC 13**
See also CA 33-36R; DLB 244; WP

Edwards, Bronwen Elizabeth
See Rose, Wendy

Edwards, G(erald) B(asil)
1899-1976 .... **CLC 25**
See also CA 201; 110

Edwards, Gus 1939- .... **CLC 43**
See also CA 108; INT 108

Edwards, Jonathan 1703-1758 .... **LC 7, 54**
See also AMW; DA; DAC; DAM MST; DLB 24; RGAL 4; TUS

Efron, Marina Ivanovna Tsvetaeva
See Tsvetaeva (Efron), Marina (Ivanovna)

Egoyan, Atom 1960- .... **CLC 151**
See also CA 157

Ehle, John (Marsden, Jr.) 1925- ...... **CLC 27**
See also CA 9-12R; CSW

Ehrenbourg, Ilya (Grigoryevich)
See Ehrenburg, Ilya (Grigoryevich)

Ehrenburg, Ilya (Grigoryevich)
1891-1967 .... **CLC 18, 34, 62**
See also CA 102; 25-28R

Ehrenburg, Ilyo (Grigoryevich)
See Ehrenburg, Ilya (Grigoryevich)

Ehrenreich, Barbara 1941- .... **CLC 110**
See also BEST 90:4; CA 73-76; CANR 16, 37, 62; DLB 246; FW; MTCW 1, 2

Eich, Guenter 1907-1972 .... **CLC 15**
See also Eich, Gunter
See also CA 111; 93-96; DLB 69, 124

Eich, Gunter
See Eich, Guenter
See also RGWL 2

Eichendorff, Joseph 1788-1857 .... **NCLC 8**
See also DLB 90; RGWL 2

Eigner, Larry .... **CLC 9**
See also Eigner, Laurence (Joel)
See also CAAS 23; DLB 5; WP

Eigner, Laurence (Joel) 1927-1996
See Eigner, Larry
See also CA 9-12R; 151; CANR 6, 84; CP 7; DLB 193

Einhard c. 770-840 .... **CMLC 50**
See also DLB 148

Einstein, Albert 1879-1955 .... **TCLC 65**
See also CA 121; 133; MTCW 1, 2

Eiseley, Loren Corey 1907-1977 .... **CLC 7**
See also AAYA 5; ANW; CA 1-4R; 73-76; CANR 6; DLBD 17

Eisenstadt, Jill 1963- .... **CLC 50**
See also CA 140

Eisenstein, Sergei (Mikhailovich)
1898-1948 .... **TCLC 57**
See also CA 114; 149

Eisner, Simon
See Kornbluth, C(yril) M.

Erickson, Steve .... **CLC 64**
    See also Erickson, Stephen Michael
    See also CANR 60, 68
Ericson, Walter
    See Fast, Howard (Melvin)
Eriksson, Buntel
    See Bergman, (Ernst) Ingmar
Ernaux, Annie 1940- .... **CLC 88**
    See also CA 147; CANR 93; NCFS 3
Erskine, John 1879-1951 .... **TCLC 84**
    See also CA 112; 159; DLB 9, 102; FANT
Eschenbach, Wolfram von
    See Wolfram von Eschenbach
Eseki, Bruno
    See Mphahlele, Ezekiel
Esenin, Sergei (Alexandrovich)
    1895-1925 .... **TCLC 4**
    See also CA 104; RGWL 2
Eshleman, Clayton 1935- .... **CLC 7**
    See also CA 33-36R; CAAS 6; CANR 93;
    CP 7; DLB 5
Espriella, Don Manuel Alvarez
    See Southey, Robert
Espriu, Salvador 1913-1985 .... **CLC 9**
    See also CA 154; 115; DLB 134
Espronceda, Jose de 1808-1842 ..... **NCLC 39**
Esquivel, Laura 1951(?)- ... **CLC 141; HLCS
    1**
    See also AAYA 29; CA 143; CANR 68;
    DA3; DNFS 2; LAIT 3; MTCW 1; NFS
    5; WLIT 1
Esse, James
    See Stephens, James
Esterbrook, Tom
    See Hubbard, L(afayette) Ron(ald)
Estleman, Loren D. 1952- .... **CLC 48**
    See also AAYA 27; CA 85-88; CANR 27,
    74; CMW 4; CPW; DA3; DAM NOV,
    POP; DLB 226; INT CANR-27; MTCW
    1, 2
Etherege, Sir George 1636-1692 .... **LC 78**
    See also BRW 2; DAM DRAM; DLB 80;
    PAB; RGEL 2
Euclid 306 B.C.-283 B.C. .... **CMLC 25**
Eugenides, Jeffrey 1960(?)- .... **CLC 81**
    See also CA 144
Euripides c. 484 B.C.-406 B.C. .... **CMLC 23,
    51; DC 4; WLCS**
    See also AW 1; CDWLB 1; DA; DA3;
    DAB; DAC; DAM DRAM, MST; DFS 1,
    4, 6; DLB 176; LAIT 1; RGWL 2
Evan, Evin
    See Faust, Frederick (Schiller)
Evans, Caradoc 1878-1945 ... **TCLC 85; SSC
    43**
    See also DLB 162
Evans, Evan
    See Faust, Frederick (Schiller)
    See also TCWW 2
Evans, Marian
    See Eliot, George
Evans, Mary Ann
    See Eliot, George
Evarts, Esther
    See Benson, Sally
Everett, Percival
    See Everett, Percival L.
    See also CSW
Everett, Percival L. 1956- .... **CLC 57**
    See also Everett, Percival
    See also BW 2; CA 129; CANR 94
Everson, R(onald) G(ilmour)
    1903-1992 .... **CLC 27**
    See also CA 17-20R; DLB 88
Everson, William (Oliver)
    1912-1994 .... **CLC 1, 5, 14**
    See also CA 9-12R; 145; CANR 20; DLB
    5, 16, 212; MTCW 1

Evtushenko, Evgenii Aleksandrovich
    See Yevtushenko, Yevgeny (Alexandrovich)
    See also RGWL 2
Ewart, Gavin (Buchanan)
    1916-1995 .... **CLC 13, 46**
    See also BRWS 7; CA 89-92; 150; CANR
    17, 46; CP 7; DLB 40; MTCW 1
Ewers, Hanns Heinz 1871-1943 ..... **TCLC 12**
    See also CA 109; 149
Ewing, Frederick R.
    See Sturgeon, Theodore (Hamilton)
Exley, Frederick (Earl) 1929-1992 .... **CLC 6,
    11**
    See also AITN 2; BPFB 1; CA 81-84; 138;
    DLB 143; DLBY 1981
Eynhardt, Guillermo
    See Quiroga, Horacio (Sylvestre)
Ezekiel, Nissim 1924- .... **CLC 61**
    See also CA 61-64; CP 7
Ezekiel, Tish O'Dowd 1943- .... **CLC 34**
    See also CA 129
Fadeyev, A.
    See Bulgya, Alexander Alexandrovich
Fadeyev, Alexander .... **TCLC 53**
    See also Bulgya, Alexander Alexandrovich
Fagen, Donald 1948- .... **CLC 26**
Fainzilberg, Ilya Arnoldovich 1897-1937
    See Ilf, Ilya
    See also CA 120; 165
Fair, Ronald L. 1932- .... **CLC 18**
    See also BW 1; CA 69-72; CANR 25; DLB
    33
Fairbairn, Roger
    See Carr, John Dickson
Fairbairns, Zoe (Ann) 1948- .... **CLC 32**
    See also CA 103; CANR 21, 85; CN 7
Fairfield, Flora
    See Alcott, Louisa May
Fairman, Paul W. 1916-1977
    See Queen, Ellery
    See also CA 114; SFW 4
Falco, Gian
    See Papini, Giovanni
Falconer, James
    See Kirkup, James
Falconer, Kenneth
    See Kornbluth, C(yril) M.
Falkland, Samuel
    See Heijermans, Herman
Fallaci, Oriana 1930- .... **CLC 11, 110**
    See also CA 77-80; CANR 15, 58; FW;
    MTCW 1
Faludi, Susan 1959- .... **CLC 140**
    See also CA 138; FW; MTCW 1; NCFS 3
Faludy, George 1913- .... **CLC 42**
    See also CA 21-24R
Faludy, Gyoergy
    See Faludy, George
Fanon, Frantz 1925-1961 .... **CLC 74; BLC 2**
    See also BW 1; CA 116; 89-92; DAM
    MULT; WLIT 2
Fanshawe, Ann 1625-1680 .... **LC 11**
Fante, John (Thomas) 1911-1983 ..... **CLC 60**
    See also AMWS 11; CA 69-72; 109; CANR
    23, 104; DLB 130; DLBY 1983
Farah, Nuruddin 1945- .. **CLC 53, 137; BLC
    2**
    See also AFW; BW 2, 3; CA 106; CANR
    81; CDWLB 3; CN 7; DAM MULT; DLB
    125; WLIT 2
Fargue, Leon-Paul 1876(?)-1947 .... **TCLC 11**
    See also CA 109; CANR 107; DLB 258
Farigoule, Louis
    See Romains, Jules
Farina, Richard 1936(?)-1966 .... **CLC 9**
    See also CA 81-84; 25-28R

Farley, Walter (Lorimer)
    1915-1989 .... **CLC 17**
    See also BYA 14; CA 17-20R; CANR 8,
    29, 84; DLB 22; JRDA; MAICYA 1, 2;
    SATA 2, 43, 132; YAW
Farmer, Philip Jose 1918- .... **CLC 1, 19**
    See also AAYA 28; BPFB 1; CA 1-4R;
    CANR 4, 35; DLB 8; MTCW 1; SATA
    93; SCFW 2; SFW 4
Farquhar, George 1677-1707 .... **LC 21**
    See also BRW 2; DAM DRAM; DLB 84;
    RGEL 2
Farrell, J(ames) G(ordon)
    1935-1979 .... **CLC 6**
    See also CA 73-76; 89-92; CANR 36; DLB
    14; MTCW 1; RGEL 2; RHW; WLIT 4
Farrell, James T(homas) 1904-1979 . **CLC 1,
    4, 8, 11, 66; SSC 28**
    See also AMW; BPFB 1; CA 5-8R; 89-92;
    CANR 9, 61; DLB 4, 9, 86; DLBD 2;
    MTCW 1, 2; RGAL 4
Farrell, Warren (Thomas) 1943- ...... **CLC 70**
    See also CA 146
Farren, Richard J.
    See Betjeman, John
Farren, Richard M.
    See Betjeman, John
Fassbinder, Rainer Werner
    1946-1982 .... **CLC 20**
    See also CA 93-96; 106; CANR 31
Fast, Howard (Melvin) 1914- ... **CLC 23, 131**
    See also AAYA 16; BPFB 1; CA 1-4R, 181;
    CAAE 181; CAAS 18; CANR 1, 33, 54,
    75, 98; CMW 4; CN 7; CPW; DAM NOV;
    DLB 9; INT CANR-33; MTCW 1; RHW;
    SATA 7; SATA-Essay 107; TCWW 2;
    YAW
Faulcon, Robert
    See Holdstock, Robert P.
Faulkner, William (Cuthbert)
    1897-1962 .... **CLC 1, 3, 6, 8, 9, 11, 14,
    18, 28, 52, 68; SSC 1, 35, 42; WLC**
    See also AAYA 7; AMW; AMWR 1; BPFB
    1; BYA 5; CA 81-84; CANR 33; CDALB
    1929-1941; DA; DA3; DAB; DAC; DAM
    MST, NOV; DLB 9, 11, 44, 102; DLBD
    2; DLBY 1986, 1997; EXPN; EXPS;
    LAIT 2; MTCW 1, 2; NFS 4, 8, 13;
    RGAL 4; RGSF 2; SSFS 2, 5, 6, 12; TUS
Fauset, Jessie Redmon
    1882(?)-1961 .... **CLC 19, 54; BLC 2**
    See also AFAW 2; BW 1; CA 109; CANR
    83; DAM MULT; DLB 51; FW; MAWW
Faust, Frederick (Schiller)
    1892-1944(?) .... **TCLC 49**
    See also Austin, Frank; Brand, Max; Chal-
    lis, George; Dawson, Peter; Dexter, Mar-
    tin; Evans, Evan; Frederick, John; Frost,
    Frederick; Manning, David; Silver, Nicho-
    las
    See also CA 108; 152; DAM POP; DLB
    256; TUS
Fawkes, Guy
    See Benchley, Robert (Charles)
Fearing, Kenneth (Flexner)
    1902-1961 .... **CLC 51**
    See also CA 93-96; CANR 59; CMW 4;
    DLB 9; RGAL 4
Fecamps, Elise
    See Creasey, John
Federman, Raymond 1928- .... **CLC 6, 47**
    See also CA 17-20R; CAAS 8; CANR 10,
    43, 83, 108; CN 7; DLBY 1980
Federspiel, J(uerg) F. 1931- .... **CLC 42**
    See also CA 146
Feiffer, Jules (Ralph) 1929- ...... **CLC 2, 8, 64**
    See also AAYA 3; CA 17-20R; CAD; CANR
    30, 59; CD 5; DAM DRAM; DLB 7, 44;
    INT CANR-30; MTCW 1; SATA 8, 61,
    111

Fleur, Paul
   See Pohl, Frederik
Flooglebuckle, Al
   See Spiegelman, Art
Flora, Fletcher 1914-1969
   See Queen, Ellery
   See also CA 1-4R; CANR 3, 85
Flying Officer X
   See Bates, H(erbert) E(rnest)
Fo, Dario 1926- .... **CLC 32, 109; DC 10**
   See also CA 116; 128; CANR 68; CWW 2;
   DA3; DAM DRAM; DLBY 1997; MTCW
   1, 2
Fogarty, Jonathan Titulescu Esq.
   See Farrell, James T(homas)
Follett, Ken(neth Martin) 1949- .... **CLC 18**
   See also AAYA 6; BEST 89:4; BPFB 1; CA
   81-84; CANR 13, 33, 54, 102; CMW 4;
   CPW; DA3; DAM NOV, POP; DLB 87;
   DLBY 1981; INT CANR-33; MTCW 1
Fontane, Theodor 1819-1898 .... **NCLC 26**
   See also CDWLB 2; DLB 129; EW 6;
   RGWL 2; TWA
Fontenot, Chester .... **CLC 65**
Fonvizin, Denis Ivanovich
   1744(?)-1792 .... **LC 81**
   See also DLB 150; RGWL 2
Foote, Horton 1916- .... **CLC 51, 91**
   See also CA 73-76; CAD; CANR 34, 51,
   110; CD 5; CSW; DA3; DAM DRAM;
   DLB 26, 266; INT CANR-34
Foote, Mary Hallock 1847-1938 .. **TCLC 108**
   See also DLB 186, 188, 202, 221
Foote, Shelby 1916- .... **CLC 75**
   See also AAYA 40; CA 5-8R; CANR 3, 45,
   74; CN 7; CPW; CSW; DA3; DAM NOV,
   POP; DLB 2, 17; MTCW 2; RHW
Forbes, Cosmo
   See Lewton, Val
Forbes, Esther 1891-1967 .... **CLC 12**
   See also AAYA 17; BYA 2; CA 13-14; 25-
   28R; CAP 1; CLR 27; DLB 22; JRDA;
   MAICYA 1, 2; RHW; SATA 2, 100; YAW
Forche, Carolyn (Louise) 1950- .... **CLC 25,**
   83, 86; PC 10
   See also CA 109; 117; CANR 50, 74; CP 7;
   CWP; DA3; DAM POET; DLB 5, 193;
   INT CA-117; MTCW 1; RGAL 4
Ford, Elbur
   See Hibbert, Eleanor Alice Burford
Ford, Ford Madox 1873-1939 ... **TCLC 1, 15,**
   39, 57
   See also Chaucer, Daniel
   See also BRW 6; CA 104; 132; CANR 74;
   CDBLB 1914-1945; DA3; DAM NOV;
   DLB 34, 98, 162; MTCW 1, 2; RGEL 2;
   TEA
Ford, Henry 1863-1947 .... **TCLC 73**
   See also CA 115; 148
Ford, John 1586-1639 .... **LC 68; DC 8**
   See also BRW 2; CDBLB Before 1660;
   DA3; DAM DRAM; DFS 7; DLB 58;
   IDTP; RGEL 2
Ford, John 1895-1973 .... **CLC 16**
   See also CA 187; 45-48
Ford, Richard 1944- .... **CLC 46, 99**
   See also AMWS 5; CA 69-72; CANR 11,
   47, 86; CN 7; CSW; DLB 227; MTCW 1;
   RGAL 4; RGSF 2
Ford, Webster
   See Masters, Edgar Lee
Foreman, Richard 1937- .... **CLC 50**
   See also CA 65-68; CAD; CANR 32, 63;
   CD 5
Forester, C(ecil) S(cott) 1899-1966 ... **CLC 35**
   See also CA 73-76; 25-28R; CANR 83;
   DLB 191; RGEL 2; RHW; SATA 13
Forez
   See Mauriac, Francois (Charles)

Forman, James
   See Forman, James D(ouglas)
Forman, James D(ouglas) 1932- .... **CLC 21**
   See also AAYA 17; CA 9-12R; CANR 4,
   19, 42; JRDA; MAICYA 1, 2; SATA 8,
   70; YAW
Fornes, Maria Irene 1930- . **CLC 39, 61; DC**
   10; HLCS 1
   See also CA 25-28R; CAD; CANR 28, 81;
   CD 5; CWD; DLB 7; HW 1, 2; INT
   CANR-28; MTCW 1; RGAL 4
Forrest, Leon (Richard) 1937-1997 .. **CLC 4;**
   BLCS
   See also AFAW 2; BW 2; CA 89-92; 162;
   CAAS 7; CANR 25, 52, 87; CN 7; DLB
   33
Forster, E(dward) M(organ)
   1879-1970 ...... **CLC 1, 2, 3, 4, 9, 10, 13,**
   15, 22, 45, 77; SSC 27; WLC
   See also AAYA 2, 37; BRW 6; BRWR 2;
   CA 13-14; 25-28R; CANR 45; CAP 1;
   CDBLB 1914-1945; DA; DA3; DAB;
   DAC; DAM MST, NOV; DLB 34, 98,
   162, 178, 195; DLBD 10; EXPN; LAIT
   3; MTCW 1, 2; NCFS 1; NFS 3, 10, 11;
   RGEL 2; RGSF 2; SATA 57; SUFW;
   TCLC 125; TEA; WLIT 4
Forster, John 1812-1876 .... **NCLC 11**
   See also DLB 144, 184
Forster, Margaret 1938- .... **CLC 149**
   See also CA 133; CANR 62; CN 7; DLB
   155
Forsyth, Frederick 1938- .... **CLC 2, 5, 36**
   See also BEST 89:4; CA 85-88; CANR 38,
   62; CMW 4; CN 7; CPW; DAM NOV,
   POP; DLB 87; MTCW 1, 2
Forten, Charlotte L. 1837-1914 .... **TCLC 16;**
   BLC 2
   See also Grimke, Charlotte L(ottie) Forten
   See also DLB 50, 239
Foscolo, Ugo 1778-1827 .... **NCLC 8, 97**
   See also EW 5
Fosse, Bob .... **CLC 20**
   See also Fosse, Robert Louis
Fosse, Robert Louis 1927-1987
   See Fosse, Bob
   See also CA 110; 123
Foster, Hannah Webster
   1758-1840 .... **NCLC 99**
   See also DLB 37, 200; RGAL 4
Foster, Stephen Collins
   1826-1864 .... **NCLC 26**
   See also RGAL 4
Foucault, Michel 1926-1984 . **CLC 31, 34, 69**
   See also CA 105; 113; CANR 34; DLB 242;
   EW 13; GFL 1789 to the Present; GLL 1;
   MTCW 1, 2; TWA
Fouque, Friedrich (Heinrich Karl) de la
   Motte 1777-1843 .... **NCLC 2**
   See also DLB 90; RGWL 2; SUFW
Fourier, Charles 1772-1837 .... **NCLC 51**
Fournier, Henri Alban 1886-1914
   See Alain-Fournier
   See also CA 104; 179
Fournier, Pierre 1916- .... **CLC 11**
   See also Gascar, Pierre
   See also CA 89-92; CANR 16, 40
Fowles, John (Robert) 1926- . **CLC 1, 2, 3, 4,**
   6, 9, 10, 15, 33, 87; SSC 33
   See also BPFB 1; BRWS 1; CA 5-8R;
   CANR 25, 71, 103; CDBLB 1960 to
   Present; CN 7; DA3; DAB; DAC; DAM
   MST; DLB 14, 139, 207; HGG; MTCW
   1, 2; RGEL 2; RHW; SATA 22; TEA;
   WLIT 4
Fox, Paula 1923- .... **CLC 2, 8, 121**
   See also AAYA 3, 37; BYA 3, 8; CA 73-76;
   CANR 20, 36, 62, 105; CLR 1, 44; DLB
   52; JRDA; MAICYA 1, 2; MTCW 1; NFS
   12; SATA 17, 60, 120; WYA; YAW

Fox, William Price (Jr.) 1926- .... **CLC 22**
   See also CA 17-20R; CAAS 19; CANR 11;
   CSW; DLB 2; DLBY 1981
Foxe, John 1517(?)-1587 .... **LC 14**
   See also DLB 132
Frame, Janet .. **CLC 2, 3, 6, 22, 66, 96; SSC**
   29
   See also Clutha, Janet Paterson Frame
   See also CN 7; CWP; RGEL 2; RGSF 2;
   TWA
France, Anatole .... **TCLC 9**
   See also Thibault, Jacques Anatole Francois
   See also DLB 123; GFL 1789 to the Present;
   MTCW 1; RGWL 2; SUFW
Francis, Claude .... **CLC 50**
   See also CA 192
Francis, Dick 1920- .... **CLC 2, 22, 42, 102**
   See also AAYA 5, 21; BEST 89:3; BPFB 1;
   CA 5-8R; CANR 9, 42, 68, 100; CDBLB
   1960 to Present; CMW 4; CN 7; DA3;
   DAM POP; DLB 87; INT CANR-9;
   MSW; MTCW 1, 2
Francis, Robert (Churchill)
   1901-1987 .... **CLC 15; PC 34**
   See also AMWS 9; CA 1-4R; 123; CANR
   1; EXPP; PFS 12
Francis, Lord Jeffrey
   See Jeffrey, Francis
   See also DLB 107
Frank, Anne(lies Marie)
   1929-1945 .... **TCLC 17; WLC**
   See also AAYA 12; BYA 1; CA 113; 133;
   CANR 68; DA; DA3; DAB; DAC; DAM
   MST; LAIT 4; MAICYA 1; MAICYAS 1;
   MTCW 1, 2; NCFS 2; SATA 87; SATA-
   Brief 42; WYA; YAW
Frank, Bruno 1887-1945 .... **TCLC 81**
   See also CA 189; DLB 118
Frank, Elizabeth 1945- .... **CLC 39**
   See also CA 121; 126; CANR 78; INT 126
Frankl, Viktor E(mil) 1905-1997 ...... **CLC 93**
   See also CA 65-68; 161
Franklin, Benjamin
   See Hasek, Jaroslav (Matej Frantisek)
Franklin, Benjamin 1706-1790 .... **LC 25;**
   WLCS
   See also AMW; CDALB 1640-1865; DA;
   DA3; DAB; DAC; DAM MST; DLB 24,
   43, 73, 183; LAIT 1; RGAL 4; TUS
Franklin, (Stella Maria Sarah) Miles
   (Lampe) 1879-1954 .... **TCLC 7**
   See also CA 104; 164; DLB 230; FW;
   MTCW 2; RGEL 2; TWA
Fraser, (Lady) Antonia (Pakenham)
   1932- .... **CLC 32, 107**
   See also CA 85-88; CANR 44, 65; CMW;
   MTCW 1, 2; SATA-Brief 32
Fraser, George MacDonald 1925- ...... **CLC 7**
   See also CA 45-48, 180; CAAE 180; CANR
   2, 48, 74; MTCW 1; RHW
Fraser, Sylvia 1935- .... **CLC 64**
   See also CA 45-48; CANR 1, 16, 60; CCA
   1
Frayn, Michael 1933- .... **CLC 3, 7, 31, 47**
   See also BRWS 7; CA 5-8R; CANR 30, 69;
   CBD; CD 5; CN 7; DAM DRAM, NOV;
   DLB 13, 14, 194, 245; FANT; MTCW 1,
   2; SFW 4
Fraze, Candida (Merrill) 1945- .... **CLC 50**
   See also CA 126
Frazer, Andrew
   See Marlowe, Stephen
Frazer, J(ames) G(eorge)
   1854-1941 .... **TCLC 32**
   See also BRWS 3; CA 118
Frazer, Robert Caine
   See Creasey, John
Frazer, Sir James George
   See Frazer, J(ames) G(eorge)

Frazier, Charles 1950- .... **CLC 109**
   See also AAYA 34; CA 161; CSW
Frazier, Ian 1951- .... **CLC 46**
   See also CA 130; CANR 54, 93
Frederic, Harold 1856-1898 .... **NCLC 10**
   See also AMW; DLB 12, 23; DLBD 13;
   RGAL 4
Frederick, John
   See Faust, Frederick (Schiller)
   See also TCWW 2
Frederick the Great 1712-1786 .... **LC 14**
Fredro, Aleksander 1793-1876 .... **NCLC 8**
Freeling, Nicolas 1927- .... **CLC 38**
   See also CA 49-52; CAAS 12; CANR 1,
   17, 50, 84; CMW 4; CN 7; DLB 87
Freeman, Douglas Southall
   1886-1953 .... **TCLC 11**
   See also CA 109; 195; DLB 17; DLBD 17
Freeman, Judith 1946- .... **CLC 55**
   See also CA 148; DLB 256
Freeman, Mary E(leanor) Wilkins
   1852-1930 .... **TCLC 9; SSC 1, 47**
   See also CA 106; 177; DLB 12, 78, 221;
   EXPS; FW; HGG; MAWW; RGAL 4;
   RGSF 2; SSFS 4, 8; SUFW; TUS
Freeman, R(ichard) Austin
   1862-1943 .... **TCLC 21**
   See also CA 113; CANR 84; CMW 4; DLB
   70
French, Albert 1943- .... **CLC 86**
   See also BW 3; CA 167
French, Marilyn 1929- .... **CLC 10, 18, 60**
   See also BPFB 1; CA 69-72; CANR 3, 31;
   CN 7; CPW; DAM DRAM, NOV, POP;
   FW; INT CANR-31; MTCW 1, 2
French, Paul
   See Asimov, Isaac
Freneau, Philip Morin 1752-1832 .. **NCLC 1,**
   111
   See also AMWS 2; DLB 37, 43; RGAL 4
Freud, Sigmund 1856-1939 .... **TCLC 52**
   See also CA 115; 133; CANR 69; EW 8;
   MTCW 1, 2; NCFS 3; TWA
Freytag, Gustav 1816-1895 .... **NCLC 109**
   See also DLB 129
Friedan, Betty (Naomi) 1921- .... **CLC 74**
   See also CA 65-68; CANR 18, 45, 74; DLB
   246; FW; MTCW 1, 2
Friedlander, Saul 1932- .... **CLC 90**
   See also CA 117; 130; CANR 72
Friedman, B(ernard) H(arper)
   1926- .... **CLC 7**
   See also CA 1-4R; CANR 3, 48
Friedman, Bruce Jay 1930- ...... **CLC 3, 5, 56**
   See also CA 9-12R; CAD; CANR 25, 52,
   101; CD 5; CN 7; DLB 2, 28, 244; INT
   CANR-25
Friel, Brian 1929- .... **CLC 5, 42, 59, 115; DC**
   8
   See also BRWS 5; CA 21-24R; CANR 33,
   69; CBD; CD 5; DFS 11; DLB 13; MTCW
   1; RGEL 2; TEA
Friis-Baastad, Babbis Ellinor
   1921-1970 .... **CLC 12**
   See also CA 17-20R; 134; SATA 7
Frisch, Max (Rudolf) 1911-1991 ... **CLC 3, 9,**
   14, 18, 32, 44
   See also CA 85-88; 134; CANR 32, 74; CD-
   WLB 2; DAM DRAM, NOV; DLB 69,
   124; EW 13; MTCW 1, 2; RGWL 2;
   TCLC 121
Fromentin, Eugene (Samuel Auguste)
   1820-1876 .... **NCLC 10**
   See also DLB 123; GFL 1789 to the Present
Frost, Frederick
   See Faust, Frederick (Schiller)
   See also TCWW 2

Frost, Robert (Lee) 1874-1963 .. **CLC 1, 3, 4,**
   9, 10, 13, 15, 26, 34, 44; PC 1, 39;
   WLC
   See also AAYA 21; AMW; AMWR 1; CA
   89-92; CANR 33; CDALB 1917-1929;
   CLR 67; DA; DA3; DAB; DAC; DAM
   MST, POET; DLB 54; DLBD 7; EXPP;
   MTCW 1, 2; PAB; PFS 1, 2, 3, 4, 5, 6, 7,
   10, 13; RGAL 4; SATA 14; TUS; WP;
   WYA
Froude, James Anthony
   1818-1894 .... **NCLC 43**
   See also DLB 18, 57, 144
Froy, Herald
   See Waterhouse, Keith (Spencer)
Fry, Christopher 1907- .... **CLC 2, 10, 14**
   See also BRWS 3; CA 17-20R; CAAS 23;
   CANR 9, 30, 74; CBD; CD 5; CP 7; DAM
   DRAM; DLB 13; MTCW 1, 2; RGEL 2;
   SATA 66; TEA
Frye, (Herman) Northrop
   1912-1991 .... **CLC 24, 70**
   See also CA 5-8R; 133; CANR 8, 37; DLB
   67, 68, 246; MTCW 1, 2; RGAL 4; TWA
Fuchs, Daniel 1909-1993 .... **CLC 8, 22**
   See also CA 81-84; 142; CAAS 5; CANR
   40; DLB 9, 26, 28; DLBY 1993
Fuchs, Daniel 1934- .... **CLC 34**
   See also CA 37-40R; CANR 14, 48
Fuentes, Carlos 1928- .. **CLC 3, 8, 10, 13, 22,**
   41, 60, 113; HLC 1; SSC 24; WLC
   See also AAYA 4; AITN 2; BPFB 1; CA
   69-72; CANR 10, 32, 68, 104; CDWLB
   3; CWW 2; DA; DA3; DAB; DAC; DAM
   MST, MULT, NOV; DLB 113; DNFS 2;
   HW 1, 2; LAIT 3; LAW; LAWS 1;
   MTCW 1, 2; NFS 8; RGSF 2; RGWL 2;
   TWA; WLIT 1
Fuentes, Gregorio Lopez y
   See Lopez y Fuentes, Gregorio
Fuertes, Gloria 1918-1998 .... **PC 27**
   See also CA 178, 180; DLB 108; HW 2;
   SATA 115
Fugard, (Harold) Athol 1932- . **CLC 5, 9, 14,**
   25, 40, 80; DC 3
   See also AAYA 17; AFW; CA 85-88; CANR
   32, 54; CD 5; DAM DRAM; DFS 3, 6,
   10; DLB 225; DNFS 1, 2; MTCW 1;
   RGEL 2; WLIT 2
Fugard, Sheila 1932- .... **CLC 48**
   See also CA 125
Fukuyama, Francis 1952- .... **CLC 131**
   See also CA 140; CANR 72
Fuller, Charles (H., Jr.) 1939- .... **CLC 25;**
   BLC 2; DC 1
   See also BW 2; CA 108; 112; CAD; CANR
   87; CD 5; DAM DRAM, MULT; DFS 8;
   DLB 38, 266; INT CA-112; MTCW 1
Fuller, Henry Blake 1857-1929 .... **TCLC 103**
   See also CA 108; 177; DLB 12; RGAL 4
Fuller, John (Leopold) 1937- .... **CLC 62**
   See also CA 21-24R; CANR 9, 44; CP 7;
   DLB 40
Fuller, Margaret
   See Ossoli, Sarah Margaret (Fuller)
   See also AMWS 2; DLB 183, 223, 239
Fuller, Roy (Broadbent) 1912-1991 ... **CLC 4,**
   28
   See also BRWS 7; CA 5-8R; 135; CAAS
   10; CANR 53, 83; CWRI 5; DLB 15, 20;
   RGEL 2; SATA 87
Fuller, Sarah Margaret
   See Ossoli, Sarah Margaret (Fuller)
Fuller, Sarah Margaret
   See Ossoli, Sarah Margaret (Fuller)
   See also DLB 1, 59, 73
Fulton, Alice 1952- .... **CLC 52**
   See also CA 116; CANR 57, 88; CP 7;
   CWP; DLB 193

Furphy, Joseph 1843-1912 .... **TCLC 25**
   See also CA 163; DLB 230; RGEL 2
Fuson, Robert H(enderson) 1927- .... **CLC 70**
   See also CA 89-92; CANR 103
Fussell, Paul 1924- .... **CLC 74**
   See also BEST 90:1; CA 17-20R; CANR 8,
   21, 35, 69; INT CANR-21; MTCW 1, 2
Futabatei, Shimei 1864-1909 .... **TCLC 44**
   See also Futabatei Shimei
   See also CA 162; MJW
Futabatei Shimei
   See Futabatei, Shimei
   See also DLB 180
Futrelle, Jacques 1875-1912 .... **TCLC 19**
   See also CA 113; 155; CMW 4
Gaboriau, Emile 1835-1873 .... **NCLC 14**
   See also CMW 4; MSW
Gadda, Carlo Emilio 1893-1973 .... **CLC 11**
   See also CA 89-92; DLB 177
Gaddis, William 1922-1998 ... **CLC 1, 3, 6, 8,**
   10, 19, 43, 86
   See also AMWS 4; BPFB 1; CA 17-20R;
   172; CANR 21, 48; CN 7; DLB 2; MTCW
   1, 2; RGAL 4
Gaelique, Moruen le
   See Jacob, (Cyprien-)Max
Gage, Walter
   See Inge, William (Motter)
Gaines, Ernest J(ames) 1933- ...... **CLC 3, 11,**
   18, 86; BLC 2
   See also AAYA 18; AFAW 1, 2; AITN 1;
   BPFB 2; BW 2, 3; BYA 6; CA 9-12R;
   CANR 6, 24, 42, 75; CDALB 1968-1988;
   CLR 62; CN 7; CSW; DA3; DAM MULT;
   DLB 2, 33, 152; DLBY 1980; EXPN;
   LAIT 5; MTCW 1, 2; NFS 5, 7; RGAL 4;
   RGSF 2; RHW; SATA 86; SSFS 5; YAW
Gaitskill, Mary 1954- .... **CLC 69**
   See also CA 128; CANR 61; DLB 244
Galdos, Benito Perez
   See Perez Galdos, Benito
   See also EW 7
Gale, Zona 1874-1938 .... **TCLC 7**
   See also CA 105; 153; CANR 84; DAM
   DRAM; DLB 9, 78, 228; RGAL 4
Galeano, Eduardo (Hughes) 1940- . **CLC 72;**
   HLCS 1
   See also CA 29-32R; CANR 13, 32, 100;
   HW 1
Galiano, Juan Valera y Alcala
   See Valera y Alcala-Galiano, Juan
Galilei, Galileo 1564-1642 .... **LC 45**
Gallagher, Tess 1943- .... **CLC 18, 63; PC 9**
   See also CA 106; CP 7; CWP; DAM POET;
   DLB 120, 212, 244
Gallant, Mavis 1922- . **CLC 7, 18, 38; SSC 5**
   See also CA 69-72; CANR 29, 69; CCA 1;
   CN 7; DAC; DAM MST; DLB 53;
   MTCW 1, 2; RGEL 2; RGSF 2
Gallant, Roy A(rthur) 1924- .... **CLC 17**
   See also CA 5-8R; CANR 4, 29, 54; CLR
   30; MAICYA 1, 2; SATA 4, 68, 110
Gallico, Paul (William) 1897-1976 ..... **CLC 2**
   See also AITN 1; CA 5-8R; 69-72; CANR
   23; DLB 9, 171; FANT; MAICYA 1, 2;
   SATA 13
Gallo, Max Louis 1932- .... **CLC 95**
   See also CA 85-88
Gallois, Lucien
   See Desnos, Robert
Gallup, Ralph
   See Whitemore, Hugh (John)
Galsworthy, John 1867-1933 .... **TCLC 1, 45;**
   SSC 22; WLC
   See also BRW 6; CA 104; 141; CANR 75;
   CDBLB 1890-1914; DA; DA3; DAB;
   DAC; DAM DRAM, MST, NOV; DLB
   10, 34, 98, 162; DLBD 16; MTCW 1;
   RGEL 2; SSFS 3; TEA

Galt, John 1779-1839 .... **NCLC 1, 110**
   See also DLB 99, 116, 159; RGEL 2; RGSF
   2
Galvin, James 1951- .... **CLC 38**
   See also CA 108; CANR 26
Gamboa, Federico 1864-1939 .... **TCLC 36**
   See also CA 167; HW 2; LAW
Gandhi, M. K.
   See Gandhi, Mohandas Karamchand
Gandhi, Mahatma
   See Gandhi, Mohandas Karamchand
Gandhi, Mohandas Karamchand
   1869-1948 .... **TCLC 59**
   See also CA 121; 132; DA3; DAM MULT;
   MTCW 1, 2
Gann, Ernest Kellogg 1910-1991 ..... **CLC 23**
   See also AITN 1; BPFB 2; CA 1-4R; 136;
   CANR 1, 83; RHW
Garber, Eric 1943(?)-
   See Holleran, Andrew
   See also CANR 89
Garcia, Cristina 1958- .... **CLC 76**
   See also AMWS 11; CA 141; CANR 73;
   DNFS 1; HW 2
Garcia Lorca, Federico 1898-1936 . **TCLC 1,
7, 49; DC 2; HLC 2; PC 3; WLC**
   See also Lorca, Federico Garcia
   See also CA 104; 131; CANR 81; DA;
   DA3; DAB; DAC; DAM DRAM, MST,
   MULT, POET; DFS 10; DLB 108; HW 1,
   2; MTCW 1, 2; TWA
Garcia Marquez, Gabriel (Jose)
   1928- .... **CLC 2, 3, 8, 10, 15, 27, 47, 55,
68; HLC 1; SSC 8; WLC**
   See also AAYA 3, 33; BEST 89:1, 90:4;
   BPFB 2; BYA 12; CA 33-36R; CANR 10,
   28, 50, 75, 82; CDWLB 3; CPW; DA;
   DA3; DAB; DAC; DAM MST, MULT,
   NOV, POP; DLB 113; DNFS 1, 2; EXPN;
   EXPS; HW 1, 2; LAIT 2; LAW; LAWS
   1; MTCW 1, 2; NCFS 3; NFS 1, 5, 10;
   RGSF 2; RGWL 2; SSFS 1, 6; TWA;
   WLIT 1
Garcilaso de la Vega, El Inca 1503-1536
   See also HLCS 1; LAW
Gard, Janice
   See Latham, Jean Lee
Gard, Roger Martin du
   See Martin du Gard, Roger
Gardam, Jane (Mary) 1928- .... **CLC 43**
   See also CA 49-52; CANR 2, 18, 33, 54,
   106; CLR 12; DLB 14, 161, 231; MAI-
   CYA 1, 2; MTCW 1; SAAS 9; SATA 39,
   76, 130; SATA-Brief 28; YAW
Gardner, Herb(ert) 1934- .... **CLC 44**
   See also CA 149; CAD; CD 5
Gardner, John (Champlin), Jr.
   1933-1982 ...... **CLC 2, 3, 5, 7, 8, 10, 18,
28, 34; SSC 7**
   See also AITN 1; AMWS 6; BPFB 2; CA
   65-68; 107; CANR 33, 73; CDALBS;
   CPW; DA3; DAM NOV, POP; DLB 2;
   DLBY 1982; FANT; MTCW 1; NFS 3;
   RGAL 4; RGSF 2; SATA 40; SATA-Obit
   31; SSFS 8
Gardner, John (Edmund) 1926- .... **CLC 30**
   See also CA 103; CANR 15, 69; CMW 4;
   CPW; DAM POP; MTCW 1
Gardner, Miriam
   See Bradley, Marion Zimmer
   See also GLL 1
Gardner, Noel
   See Kuttner, Henry
Gardons, S. S.
   See Snodgrass, W(illiam) D(e Witt)

Garfield, Leon 1921-1996 .... **CLC 12**
   See also AAYA 8; BYA 1, 3; CA 17-20R;
   152; CANR 38, 41, 78; CLR 21; DLB
   161; JRDA; MAICYA 1, 2; MAICYAS 1;
   SATA 1, 32, 76; SATA-Obit 90; TEA;
   WYA; YAW
Garland, (Hannibal) Hamlin
   1860-1940 .... **TCLC 3; SSC 18**
   See also CA 104; DLB 12, 71, 78, 186;
   RGAL 4; RGSF 2; TCWW 2
Garneau, (Hector de) Saint-Denys
   1912-1943 .... **TCLC 13**
   See also CA 111; DLB 88
Garner, Alan 1934- .... **CLC 17**
   See also AAYA 18; BYA 3, 5; CA 73-76,
   178; CAAE 178; CANR 15, 64; CLR 20;
   CPW; DAB; DAM POP; DLB 161, 261;
   FANT; MAICYA 1, 2; MTCW 1, 2; SATA
   18, 69; SATA-Essay 108; SUFW; YAW
Garner, Hugh 1913-1979 .... **CLC 13**
   See also Warwick, Jarvis
   See also CA 69-72; CANR 31; CCA 1; DLB
   68
Garnett, David 1892-1981 .... **CLC 3**
   See also CA 5-8R; 103; CANR 17, 79; DLB
   34; FANT; MTCW 2; RGEL 2; SFW 4;
   SUFW
Garos, Stephanie
   See Katz, Steve
Garrett, George (Palmer) 1929- .. **CLC 3, 11,
51; SSC 30**
   See also AMWS 7; BPFB 2; CA 1-4R;
   CAAE 202; CAAS 5; CANR 1, 42, 67,
   109; CN 7; CP 7; CSW; DLB 2, 5, 130,
   152; DLBY 1983
Garrick, David 1717-1779 .... **LC 15**
   See also DAM DRAM; DLB 84, 213;
   RGEL 2
Garrigue, Jean 1914-1972 .... **CLC 2, 8**
   See also CA 5-8R; 37-40R; CANR 20
Garrison, Frederick
   See Sinclair, Upton (Beall)
Garro, Elena 1920(?)-1998
   See also CA 131; 169; CWW 2; DLB 145;
   HLCS 1; HW 1; LAWS 1; WLIT 1
Garth, Will
   See Hamilton, Edmond; Kuttner, Henry
Garvey, Marcus (Moziah, Jr.)
   1887-1940 .... **TCLC 41; BLC 2**
   See also BW 1; CA 120; 124; CANR 79;
   DAM MULT
Gary, Romain .... **CLC 25**
   See also Kacew, Romain
   See also DLB 83
Gascar, Pierre .... **CLC 11**
   See also Fournier, Pierre
Gascoyne, David (Emery)
   1916-2001 .... **CLC 45**
   See also CA 65-68; 200; CANR 10, 28, 54;
   CP 7; DLB 20; MTCW 1; RGEL 2
Gaskell, Elizabeth Cleghorn
   1810-1865 .... **NCLC 5, 70, 97; SSC 25**
   See also BRW 5; CDBLB 1832-1890; DAB;
   DAM MST; DLB 21, 144, 159; RGEL 2;
   RGSF 2; TEA
Gass, William H(oward) 1924- . **CLC 1, 2, 8,
11, 15, 39, 132; SSC 12**
   See also AMWS 6; CA 17-20R; CANR 30,
   71, 100; CN 7; DLB 2, 227; MTCW 1, 2;
   RGAL 4
Gassendi, Pierre 1592-1655 .... **LC 54**
   See also GFL Beginnings to 1789
Gasset, Jose Ortega y
   See Ortega y Gasset, Jose
Gates, Henry Louis, Jr. 1950- .... **CLC 65;
BLCS**
   See also BW 2, 3; CA 109; CANR 25, 53,
   75; CSW; DA3; DAM MULT; DLB 67;
   MTCW 1; RGAL 4

Gautier, Theophile 1811-1872 .. **NCLC 1, 59;
PC 18; SSC 20**
   See also DAM POET; DLB 119; EW 6;
   GFL 1789 to the Present; RGWL 2;
   SUFW; TWA
Gawsworth, John
   See Bates, H(erbert) E(rnest)
Gay, John 1685-1732 .... **LC 49**
   See also BRW 3; DAM DRAM; DLB 84,
   95; RGEL 2; WLIT 3
Gay, Oliver
   See Gogarty, Oliver St. John
Gay, Peter (Jack) 1923- .... **CLC 158**
   See also CA 13-16R; CANR 18, 41, 77;
   INT CANR-18
Gaye, Marvin (Pentz, Jr.)
   1939-1984 .... **CLC 26**
   See also CA 195; 112
Gebler, Carlo (Ernest) 1954- .... **CLC 39**
   See also CA 119; 133; CANR 96
Gee, Maggie (Mary) 1948- .... **CLC 57**
   See also CA 130; CN 7; DLB 207
Gee, Maurice (Gough) 1931- .... **CLC 29**
   See also AAYA 42; CA 97-100; CANR 67;
   CLR 56; CN 7; CWRI 5; MAICYA 2;
   RGSF 2; SATA 46, 101
Gelbart, Larry (Simon) 1928- .... **CLC 21, 61**
   See also Gelbart, Larry
   See also CA 73-76; CANR 45, 94
Gelbart, Larry 1928-
   See Gelbart, Larry (Simon)
   See also CAD; CD 5
Gelber, Jack 1932- .... **CLC 1, 6, 14, 79**
   See also CA 1-4R; CAD; CANR 2; DLB 7,
   228
Gellhorn, Martha (Ellis)
   1908-1998 .... **CLC 14, 60**
   See also CA 77-80; 164; CANR 44; CN 7;
   DLBY 1982, 1998
Genet, Jean 1910-1986 .. **CLC 1, 2, 5, 10, 14,
44, 46**
   See also CA 13-16R; CANR 18; DA3;
   DAM DRAM; DFS 10; DLB 72; DLBY
   1986; EW 13; GFL 1789 to the Present;
   GLL 1; MTCW 1, 2; RGWL 2; TWA
Gent, Peter 1942- .... **CLC 29**
   See also AITN 1; CA 89-92; DLBY 1982
Gentile, Giovanni 1875-1944 .... **TCLC 96**
   See also CA 119
Gentlewoman in New England, A
   See Bradstreet, Anne
Gentlewoman in Those Parts, A
   See Bradstreet, Anne
Geoffrey of Monmouth c.
   1100-1155 .... **CMLC 44**
   See also DLB 146; TEA
George, Jean
   See George, Jean Craighead
George, Jean Craighead 1919- .... **CLC 35**
   See also AAYA 8; BYA 2, 4; CA 5-8R;
   CANR 25; CLR 1; 80; DLB 52; JRDA;
   MAICYA 1, 2; SATA 2, 68, 124; WYA;
   YAW
George, Stefan (Anton) 1868-1933 . **TCLC 2,
14**
   See also CA 104; 193; EW 8
Georges, Georges Martin
   See Simenon, Georges (Jacques Christian)
Gerhardi, William Alexander
   See Gerhardie, William Alexander
Gerhardie, William Alexander
   1895-1977 .... **CLC 5**
   See also CA 25-28R; 73-76; CANR 18;
   DLB 36; RGEL 2
Gerson, Jean 1363-1429 .... **LC 77**
   See also DLB 208
Gersonides 1288-1344 .... **CMLC 49**
   See also DLB 115

Gogarty, Oliver St. John
1878-1957 .... **TCLC 15**
See also CA 109; 150; DLB 15, 19; RGEL
2

Gogol, Nikolai (Vasilyevich)
1809-1852 .... **NCLC 5, 15, 31; DC 1;**
SSC 4, 29, 52; WLC
See also DA; DAB; DAC; DAM DRAM,
MST; DFS 12; DLB 198; EW 6; EXPS;
RGSF 2; RGWL 2; SSFS 7; TWA

Goines, Donald 1937(?)-1974 . **CLC 80; BLC**
2
See also AITN 1; BW 1, 3; CA 124; 114;
CANR 82; CMW 4; DA3; DAM MULT,
POP; DLB 33

Gold, Herbert 1924- ... **CLC 4, 7, 14, 42, 152**
See also CA 9-12R; CANR 17, 45; CN 7;
DLB 2; DLBY 1981

Goldbarth, Albert 1948- .... **CLC 5, 38**
See also CA 53-56; CANR 6, 40; CP 7;
DLB 120

Goldberg, Anatol 1910-1982 .... **CLC 34**
See also CA 131; 117

Goldemberg, Isaac 1945- .... **CLC 52**
See also CA 69-72; CAAS 12; CANR 11,
32; HW 1; WLIT 1

Golding, William (Gerald)
1911-1993 ..... **CLC 1, 2, 3, 8, 10, 17, 27,**
58, 81; WLC
See also AAYA 5; BPFB 2; BRWR 1;
BRWS 1; BYA 2; CA 5-8R; 141; CANR
13, 33, 54; CDBLB 1945-1960; DA;
DA3; DAB; DAC; DAM MST, NOV;
DLB 15, 100, 255; EXPN; HGG; LAIT 4;
MTCW 1, 2; NFS 2; RGEL 2; RHW;
SFW 4; TEA; WLIT 4; YAW

Goldman, Emma 1869-1940 .... **TCLC 13**
See also CA 110; 150; DLB 221; FW;
RGAL 4; TUS

Goldman, Francisco 1954- .... **CLC 76**
See also CA 162

Goldman, William (W.) 1931- ...... **CLC 1, 48**
See also BPFB 2; CA 9-12R; CANR 29,
69, 106; CN 7; DLB 44; FANT; IDFW 3,
4

Goldmann, Lucien 1913-1970 .... **CLC 24**
See also CA 25-28; CAP 2

Goldoni, Carlo 1707-1793 .... **LC 4**
See also DAM DRAM; EW 4; RGWL 2

Goldsberry, Steven 1949- .... **CLC 34**
See also CA 131

Goldsmith, Oliver 1730-1774 .. **LC 2, 48; DC**
8; WLC
See also BRW 3; CDBLB 1660-1789; DA;
DAB; DAC; DAM DRAM, MST, NOV,
POET; DFS 1; DLB 39, 89, 104, 109, 142;
IDTP; RGEL 2; SATA 26; TEA; WLIT 3

Goldsmith, Peter
See Priestley, J(ohn) B(oynton)

Gombrowicz, Witold 1904-1969 .... **CLC 4, 7,**
11, 49
See also CA 19-20; 25-28R; CANR 105;
CAP 2; CDWLB 4; DAM DRAM; DLB
215; EW 12; RGWL 2; TWA

Gomez de Avellaneda, Gertrudis
1814-1873 .... **NCLC 111**
See also LAW

Gomez de la Serna, Ramon
1888-1963 .... **CLC 9**
See also CA 153; 116; CANR 79; HW 1, 2

Goncharov, Ivan Alexandrovich
1812-1891 .... **NCLC 1, 63**
See also DLB 238; EW 6; RGWL 2

Goncourt, Edmond (Louis Antoine Huot) de
1822-1896 .... **NCLC 7**
See also DLB 123; EW 7; GFL 1789 to the
Present; RGWL 2

Goncourt, Jules (Alfred Huot) de
1830-1870 .... **NCLC 7**
See also DLB 123; EW 7; GFL 1789 to the
Present; RGWL 2

Gongora (y Argote), Luis de
1561-1627 .... **LC 72**
See also RGWL 2

Gontier, Fernande 19(?)- .... **CLC 50**

Gonzalez Martinez, Enrique
1871-1952 .... **TCLC 72**
See also CA 166; CANR 81; HW 1, 2

Goodison, Lorna 1947- .... **PC 36**
See also CA 142; CANR 88; CP 7; CWP;
DLB 157

Goodman, Paul 1911-1972 ..... **CLC 1, 2, 4, 7**
See also CA 19-20; 37-40R; CAD; CANR
34; CAP 2; DLB 130, 246; MTCW 1;
RGAL 4

Gordimer, Nadine 1923- ...... **CLC 3, 5, 7, 10,**
18, 33, 51, 70, 123, 160, 161; SSC 17;
WLCS
See also AAYA 39; AFW; BRWS 2; CA
5-8R; CANR 3, 28, 56, 88; CN 7; DA;
DA3; DAB; DAC; DAM MST, NOV;
DLB 225; EXPS; INT CANR-28; MTCW
1, 2; NFS 4; RGEL 2; RGSF 2; SSFS 2,
14; TWA; WLIT 2; YAW

Gordon, Adam Lindsay
1833-1870 .... **NCLC 21**
See also DLB 230

Gordon, Caroline 1895-1981 . **CLC 6, 13, 29,**
83; SSC 15
See also AMW; CA 11-12; 103; CANR 36;
CAP 1; DLB 4, 9, 102; DLBD 17; DLBY
1981; MTCW 1, 2; RGAL 4; RGSF 2

Gordon, Charles William 1860-1937
See Connor, Ralph
See also CA 109

Gordon, Mary (Catherine) 1949- .... **CLC 13,**
22, 128
See also AMWS 4; BPFB 2; CA 102;
CANR 44, 92; CN 7; DLB 6; DLBY
1981; FW; INT CA-102; MTCW 1

Gordon, N. J.
See Bosman, Herman Charles

Gordon, Sol 1923- .... **CLC 26**
See also CA 53-56; CANR 4; SATA 11

Gordone, Charles 1925-1995 .. **CLC 1, 4; DC**
8
See also BW 1, 3; CA 93-96; 180; 150;
CAAE 180; CAD; CANR 55; DAM
DRAM; DLB 7; INT 93-96; MTCW 1

Gore, Catherine 1800-1861 .... **NCLC 65**
See also DLB 116; RGEL 2

Gorenko, Anna Andreevna
See Akhmatova, Anna

Gorky, Maxim .... **TCLC 8; SSC 28; WLC**
See also Peshkov, Alexei Maximovich
See also DAB; DFS 9; EW 8; MTCW 2;
TWA

Goryan, Sirak
See Saroyan, William

Gosse, Edmund (William)
1849-1928 .... **TCLC 28**
See also CA 117; DLB 57, 144, 184; RGEL
2

Gotlieb, Phyllis Fay (Bloom) 1926- .. **CLC 18**
See also CA 13-16R; CANR 7; DLB 88,
251; SFW 4

Gottesman, S. D.
See Kornbluth, C(yril) M.; Pohl, Frederik

Gottfried von Strassburg fl. c.
1170-1215 .... **CMLC 10**
See also CDWLB 2; DLB 138; EW 1;
RGWL 2

Gotthelf, Jeremias 1797-1854 .... **NCLC 115**
See also DLB 133; RGWL 2

Gould, Lois 1932(?)-2002 .... **CLC 4, 10**
See also CA 77-80; CANR 29; MTCW 1

Gould, Stephen Jay 1941-2002 .... **CLC 163**
See also AAYA 26; BEST 90:2; CA 77-80;
CANR 10, 27, 56, 75; CPW; INT CANR-
27; MTCW 1, 2

Gourmont, Remy(-Marie-Charles) de
1858-1915 .... **TCLC 17**
See also CA 109; 150; GFL 1789 to the
Present; MTCW 2

Govier, Katherine 1948- .... **CLC 51**
See also CA 101; CANR 18, 40; CCA 1

Gower, John c. 1330-1408 .... **LC 76**
See also BRW 1; DLB 146; RGEL 2

Goyen, (Charles) William
1915-1983 .... **CLC 5, 8, 14, 40**
See also AITN 2; CA 5-8R; 110; CANR 6,
71; DLB 2, 218; DLBY 1983; INT
CANR-6

Goytisolo, Juan 1931- .... **CLC 5, 10, 23, 133;**
HLC 1
See also CA 85-88; CANR 32, 61; CWW
2; DAM MULT; GLL 2; HW 1, 2; MTCW
1, 2

Gozzano, Guido 1883-1916 .... **PC 10**
See also CA 154; DLB 114

Gozzi, (Conte) Carlo 1720-1806 .... **NCLC 23**

Grabbe, Christian Dietrich
1801-1836 .... **NCLC 2**
See also DLB 133; RGWL 2

Grace, Patricia Frances 1937- .... **CLC 56**
See also CA 176; CN 7; RGSF 2

Gracian y Morales, Baltasar
1601-1658 .... **LC 15**

Gracq, Julien .... **CLC 11, 48**
See also Poirier, Louis
See also CWW 2; DLB 83; GFL 1789 to
the Present

Grade, Chaim 1910-1982 .... **CLC 10**
See also CA 93-96; 107

Graduate of Oxford, A
See Ruskin, John

Grafton, Garth
See Duncan, Sara Jeannette

Grafton, Sue 1940- .... **CLC 163**
See also AAYA 11; BEST 90:3; CA 108;
CANR 31, 55; CMW 4; CPW; CSW;
DA3; DAM POP; DLB 226; FW; MSW

Graham, John
See Phillips, David Graham

Graham, Jorie 1951- .... **CLC 48, 118**
See also CA 111; CANR 63; CP 7; CWP;
DLB 120; PFS 10

Graham, R(obert) B(ontine) Cunninghame
See Cunninghame Graham, Robert
(Gallnigad) Bontine
See also DLB 98, 135, 174; RGEL 2; RGSF
2

Graham, Robert
See Haldeman, Joe (William)

Graham, Tom
See Lewis, (Harry) Sinclair

Graham, W(illiam) S(idney)
1918-1986 .... **CLC 29**
See also BRWS 7; CA 73-76; 118; DLB 20;
RGEL 2

Graham, Winston (Mawdsley)
1910- .... **CLC 23**
See also CA 49-52; CANR 2, 22, 45, 66;
CMW 4; CN 7; DLB 77; RHW

Grahame, Kenneth 1859-1932 .... **TCLC 64**
See also BYA 5; CA 108; 136; CANR 80;
CLR 5; CWRI 5; DA3; DAB; DLB 34,
141, 178; FANT; MAICYA 1, 2; MTCW
2; RGEL 2; SATA 100; TEA; WCH;
YABC 1

Granger, Darius John
See Marlowe, Stephen

Harriss, Will(ard Irvin) 1922- .... **CLC 34**
See also CA 111
Harson, Sley
See Ellison, Harlan (Jay)
Hart, Ellis
See Ellison, Harlan (Jay)
Hart, Josephine 1942(?)- .... **CLC 70**
See also CA 138; CANR 70; CPW; DAM POP
Hart, Moss 1904-1961 .... **CLC 66**
See also CA 109; 89-92; CANR 84; DAM DRAM; DFS 1; DLB 7, 266; RGAL 4
Harte, (Francis) Bret(t)
1836(?)-1902 .... **TCLC 1, 25; SSC 8; WLC**
See also AMWS 2; CA 104; 140; CANR 80; CDALB 1865-1917; DA; DA3; DAC; DAM MST; DLB 12, 64, 74, 79, 186; EXPS; LAIT 2; RGAL 4; RGSF 2; SATA 26; SSFS 3; TUS
Hartley, L(eslie) P(oles) 1895-1972 ... **CLC 2, 22**
See also BRWS 7; CA 45-48; 37-40R; CANR 33; DLB 15, 139; HGG; MTCW 1, 2; RGEL 2; SUFW
Hartman, Geoffrey H. 1929- .... **CLC 27**
See also CA 117; 125; CANR 79; DLB 67
Hartmann, Sadakichi 1869-1944 ... **TCLC 73**
See also CA 157; DLB 54
Hartmann von Aue c. 1170-c. 1210 .... **CMLC 15**
See also CDWLB 2; DLB 138; RGWL 2
Hartog, Jan de
See de Hartog, Jan
Haruf, Kent 1943- .... **CLC 34**
See also CA 149; CANR 91
Harwood, Ronald 1934- .... **CLC 32**
See also CA 1-4R; CANR 4, 55; CBD; CD 5; DAM DRAM, MST; DLB 13
Hasegawa Tatsunosuke
See Futabatei, Shimei
Hasek, Jaroslav (Matej Frantisek)
1883-1923 .... **TCLC 4**
See also CA 104; 129; CDWLB 4; DLB 215; EW 9; MTCW 1, 2; RGSF 2; RGWL 2
Hass, Robert 1941- ... **CLC 18, 39, 99; PC 16**
See also AMWS 6; CA 111; CANR 30, 50, 71; CP 7; DLB 105, 206; RGAL 4; SATA 94
Hastings, Hudson
See Kuttner, Henry
Hastings, Selina .... **CLC 44**
Hathorne, John 1641-1717 .... **LC 38**
Hatteras, Amelia
See Mencken, H(enry) L(ouis)
Hatteras, Owen .... **TCLC 18**
See also Mencken, H(enry) L(ouis); Nathan, George Jean
Hauptmann, Gerhart (Johann Robert)
1862-1946 .... **TCLC 4; SSC 37**
See also CA 104; 153; CDWLB 2; DAM DRAM; DLB 66, 118; EW 8; RGSF 2; RGWL 2; TWA
Havel, Vaclav 1936- ..... **CLC 25, 58, 65, 123; DC 6**
See also CA 104; CANR 36, 63; CDWLB 4; CWW 2; DA3; DAM DRAM; DFS 10; DLB 232; MTCW 1, 2
Haviaras, Stratis .... **CLC 33**
See also Chaviaras, Strates
Hawes, Stephen 1475(?)-1529(?) .... **LC 17**
See also DLB 132; RGEL 2
Hawkes, John (Clendennin Burne, Jr.)
1925-1998 .. **CLC 1, 2, 3, 4, 7, 9, 14, 15, 27, 49**
See also BPFB 2; CA 1-4R; 167; CANR 2, 47, 64; CN 7; DLB 2, 7, 227; DLBY 1980, 1998; MTCW 1, 2; RGAL 4

Hawking, S. W.
See Hawking, Stephen W(illiam)
Hawking, Stephen W(illiam) 1942- . **CLC 63, 105**
See also AAYA 13; BEST 89:1; CA 126; 129; CANR 48; CPW; DA3; MTCW 2
Hawkins, Anthony Hope
See Hope, Anthony
Hawthorne, Julian 1846-1934 .... **TCLC 25**
See also CA 165; HGG
Hawthorne, Nathaniel 1804-1864 ... **NCLC 2, 10, 17, 23, 39, 79, 95; SSC 3, 29, 39; WLC**
See also AAYA 18; AMW; AMWR 1; BPFB 2; BYA 3; CDALB 1640-1865; DA; DA3; DAB; DAC; DAM MST, NOV; DLB 1, 74, 183, 223; EXPN; EXPS; HGG; LAIT 1; NFS 1; RGAL 4; RGSF 2; SSFS 1, 7, 11, 15; SUFW; TUS; WCH; YABC 2
Haxton, Josephine Ayres 1921-
See Douglas, Ellen
See also CA 115; CANR 41, 83
Hayaseca y Eizaguirre, Jorge
See Echegaray (y Eizaguirre), Jose (Maria Waldo)
Hayashi, Fumiko 1904-1951 .... **TCLC 27**
See also Hayashi Fumiko
See also CA 161
Hayashi Fumiko
See Hayashi, Fumiko
See also DLB 180
Haycraft, Anna (Margaret) 1932-
See Ellis, Alice Thomas
See also CA 122; CANR 85, 90; MTCW 2
Hayden, Robert E(arl) 1913-1980 . **CLC 5, 9, 14, 37; BLC 2; PC 6**
See also AFAW 1, 2; AMWS 2; BW 1, 3; CA 69-72; 97-100; CABS 2; CANR 24, 75, 82; CDALB 1941-1968; DA; DAC; DAM MST, MULT, POET; DLB 5, 76; EXPP; MTCW 1, 2; PFS 1; RGAL 4; SATA 19; SATA-Obit 26; WP
Hayek, F(riedrich) A(ugust von)
1899-1992 .... **TCLC 109**
See also CA 93-96; 137; CANR 20; MTCW 1, 2
Hayford, J(oseph) E(phraim) Casely
See Casely-Hayford, J(oseph) E(phraim)
Hayman, Ronald 1932- .... **CLC 44**
See also CA 25-28R; CANR 18, 50, 88; CD 5; DLB 155
Hayne, Paul Hamilton 1830-1886 . **NCLC 94**
See also DLB 3, 64, 79, 248; RGAL 4
Hays, Mary 1760-1843 .... **NCLC 114**
See also DLB 142, 158; RGEL 2
Haywood, Eliza (Fowler)
1693(?)-1756 .... **LC 1, 44**
See also DLB 39; RGEL 2
Hazlitt, William 1778-1830 ...... **NCLC 29, 82**
See also BRW 4; DLB 110, 158; RGEL 2; TEA
Hazzard, Shirley 1931- .... **CLC 18**
See also CA 9-12R; CANR 4, 70; CN 7; DLBY 1982; MTCW 1
Head, Bessie 1937-1986 .... **CLC 25, 67; BLC 2; SSC 52**
See also AFW; BW 2, 3; CA 29-32R; 119; CANR 25, 82; CDWLB 3; DA3; DAM MULT; DLB 117, 225; EXPS; FW; MTCW 1, 2; RGSF 2; SSFS 5, 13; WLIT 2
Headon, (Nicky) Topper 1956(?)- .... **CLC 30**
Heaney, Seamus (Justin) 1939- ..... **CLC 5, 7, 14, 25, 37, 74, 91; PC 18; WLCS**
See also BRWR 1; BRWS 2; CA 85-88; CANR 25, 48, 75, 91; CDBLB 1960 to Present; CP 7; DA3; DAB; DAM POET; DLB 40; DLBY 1995; EXPP; MTCW 1, 2; PAB; PFS 2, 5, 8; RGEL 2; TEA; WLIT 4

Hearn, (Patricio) Lafcadio (Tessima Carlos)
1850-1904 .... **TCLC 9**
See also CA 105; 166; DLB 12, 78, 189; HGG; RGAL 4
Hearne, Vicki 1946-2001 .... **CLC 56**
See also CA 139; 201
Hearon, Shelby 1931- .... **CLC 63**
See also AITN 2; AMWS 8; CA 25-28R; CANR 18, 48, 103; CSW
Heat-Moon, William Least .... **CLC 29**
See also Trogdon, William (Lewis)
See also AAYA 9
Hebbel, Friedrich 1813-1863 .... **NCLC 43**
See also CDWLB 2; DAM DRAM; DLB 129; EW 6; RGWL 2
Hebert, Anne 1916-2000 .... **CLC 4, 13, 29**
See also CA 85-88; 187; CANR 69; CCA 1; CWP; CWW 2; DA3; DAC; DAM MST, POET; DLB 68; GFL 1789 to the Present; MTCW 1, 2
Hecht, Anthony (Evan) 1923- ...... **CLC 8, 13, 19**
See also AMWS 10; CA 9-12R; CANR 6, 108; CP 7; DAM POET; DLB 5, 169; PFS 6; WP
Hecht, Ben 1894-1964 .... **CLC 8**
See also CA 85-88; DFS 9; DLB 7, 9, 25, 26, 28, 86; FANT; IDFW 3, 4; RGAL 4; TCLC 101
Hedayat, Sadeq 1903-1951 .... **TCLC 21**
See also CA 120; RGSF 2
Hegel, Georg Wilhelm Friedrich
1770-1831 .... **NCLC 46**
See also DLB 90; TWA
Heidegger, Martin 1889-1976 .... **CLC 24**
See also CA 81-84; 65-68; CANR 34; MTCW 1, 2
Heidenstam, (Carl Gustaf) Verner von
1859-1940 .... **TCLC 5**
See also CA 104
Heifner, Jack 1946- .... **CLC 11**
See also CA 105; CANR 47
Heijermans, Herman 1864-1924 .... **TCLC 24**
See also CA 123
Heilbrun, Carolyn G(old) 1926- .... **CLC 25**
See also Cross, Amanda
See also CA 45-48; CANR 1, 28, 58, 94; FW
Hein, Christoph 1944- .... **CLC 154**
See also CA 158; CANR 108; CDWLB 2; CWW 2; DLB 124
Heine, Heinrich 1797-1856 .... **NCLC 4, 54; PC 25**
See also CDWLB 2; DLB 90; EW 5; RGWL 2; TWA
Heinemann, Larry (Curtiss) 1944- .. **CLC 50**
See also CA 110; CAAS 21; CANR 31, 81; DLBD 9; INT CANR-31
Heiney, Donald (William) 1921-1993
See Harris, MacDonald
See also CA 1-4R; 142; CANR 3, 58; FANT
Heinlein, Robert A(nson) 1907-1988 . **CLC 1, 3, 8, 14, 26, 55; SSC 55**
See also AAYA 17; BPFB 2; BYA 4, 13; CA 1-4R; 125; CANR 1, 20, 53; CLR 75; CPW; DA3; DAM POP; DLB 8; EXPS; JRDA; LAIT 5; MAICYA 1, 2; MTCW 1, 2; RGAL 4; SATA 9, 69; SATA-Obit 56; SCFW 1; SFW 4; SSFS 7; YAW
Helforth, John
See Doolittle, Hilda
Heliodorus fl. 3rd cent. - .... **CMLC 52**
Hellenhofferu, Vojtech Kapristian z
See Hasek, Jaroslav (Matej Frantisek)
Heller, Joseph 1923-1999 . **CLC 1, 3, 5, 8, 11, 36, 63; WLC**
See also AAYA 24; AITN 1; AMWS 4; BPFB 2; BYA 1; CA 5-8R; 187; CABS 1; CANR 8, 42, 66; CN 7; CPW; DA; DA3;

DAB; DAC; DAM MST, NOV, POP; DLB 2, 28, 227; DLBY 1980; EXPN; INT CANR-8; LAIT 4; MTCW 1, 2; NFS 1; RGAL 4; TUS; YAW

Hellman, Lillian (Florence)
1906-1984 .. **CLC 2, 4, 8, 14, 18, 34, 44, 52; DC 1**
See also AITN 1, 2; AMWS 1; CA 13-16R; 112; CAD; CANR 33; CWD; DA3; DAM DRAM; DFS 1, 3, 14; DLB 7, 228; DLBY 1984; FW; LAIT 3; MAWW; MTCW 1, 2; RGAL 4; TCLC 119; TUS

Helprin, Mark 1947- .... **CLC 7, 10, 22, 32**
See also CA 81-84; CANR 47, 64; CDALBS; CPW; DA3; DAM NOV, POP; DLBY 1985; FANT; MTCW 1, 2

Helvetius, Claude-Adrien 1715-1771 .. **LC 26**

Helyar, Jane Penelope Josephine 1933-
See Poole, Josephine
See also CA 21-24R; CANR 10, 26; CWRI 5; SATA 82

Hemans, Felicia 1793-1835 ...... **NCLC 29, 71**
See also DLB 96; RGEL 2

Hemingway, Ernest (Miller)
1899-1961 .... **CLC 1, 3, 6, 8, 10, 13, 19, 30, 34, 39, 41, 44, 50, 61, 80; SSC 1, 25, 36, 40; WLC**
See also AAYA 19; AMW; AMWR 1; BPFB 2; BYA 2, 3, 13; CA 77-80; CANR 34; CDALB 1917-1929; DA; DA3; DAB; DAC; DAM MST, NOV; DLB 4, 9, 102, 210; DLBD 1, 15, 16; DLBY 1981, 1987, 1996, 1998; EXPN; EXPS; LAIT 3, 4; MTCW 1, 2; NFS 1, 5, 6, 14; RGAL 4; RGSF 2; SSFS 1, 6, 8, 9, 11; TCLC 115; TUS; WYA

Hempel, Amy 1951- .... **CLC 39**
See also CA 118; 137; CANR 70; DA3; DLB 218; EXPS; MTCW 2; SSFS 2

Henderson, F. C.
See Mencken, H(enry) L(ouis)

Henderson, Sylvia
See Ashton-Warner, Sylvia (Constance)

Henderson, Zenna (Chlarson)
1917-1983 .... **SSC 29**
See also CA 1-4R; 133; CANR 1, 84; DLB 8; SATA 5; SFW 4

Henkin, Joshua .... **CLC 119**
See also CA 161

Henley, Beth .... **CLC 23; DC 6, 14**
See also Henley, Elizabeth Becker
See also CABS 3; CAD; CD 5; CSW; CWD; DFS 2; DLBY 1986; FW

Henley, Elizabeth Becker 1952-
See Henley, Beth
See also CA 107; CANR 32, 73; DA3; DAM DRAM, MST; MTCW 1, 2

Henley, William Ernest 1849-1903 .. **TCLC 8**
See also CA 105; DLB 19; RGEL 2

Hennissart, Martha
See Lathen, Emma
See also CA 85-88; CANR 64

Henry VIII 1491-1547 .... **LC 10**
See also DLB 132

Henry, O. .... **TCLC 1, 19; SSC 5, 49; WLC**
See also Porter, William Sydney
See also AAYA 41; AMWS 2; EXPS; RGAL 4; RGSF 2; SSFS 2

Henry, Patrick 1736-1799 .... **LC 25**
See also LAIT 1

Henryson, Robert 1430(?)-1506(?) ...... **LC 20**
See also BRWS 7; DLB 146; RGEL 2

Henschke, Alfred
See Klabund

Hentoff, Nat(han Irving) 1925- .... **CLC 26**
See also AAYA 4, 42; BYA 6; CA 1-4R; CAAS 6; CANR 5, 25, 77; CLR 1, 52; INT CANR-25; JRDA; MAICYA 1, 2; SATA 42, 69, 133; SATA-Brief 27; WYA; YAW

Heppenstall, (John) Rayner
1911-1981 .... **CLC 10**
See also CA 1-4R; 103; CANR 29

Heraclitus c. 540 B.C.-c. 450
B.C. .... **CMLC 22**
See also DLB 176

Herbert, Frank (Patrick)
1920-1986 .... **CLC 12, 23, 35, 44, 85**
See also AAYA 21; BPFB 2; BYA 4, 14; CA 53-56; 118; CANR 5, 43; CDALBS; CPW; DAM POP; DLB 8; INT CANR-5; LAIT 5; MTCW 1, 2; SATA 9, 37; SATA-Obit 47; SCFW 2; SFW 4; YAW

Herbert, George 1593-1633 ...... **LC 24; PC 4**
See also BRW 2; BRWR 2; CDBLB Before 1660; DAB; DAM POET; DLB 126; EXPP; RGEL 2; TEA; WP

Herbert, Zbigniew 1924-1998 .... **CLC 9, 43**
See also CA 89-92; 169; CANR 36, 74; CDWLB 4; CWW 2; DAM POET; DLB 232; MTCW 1

Herbst, Josephine (Frey)
1897-1969 .... **CLC 34**
See also CA 5-8R; 25-28R; DLB 9

Herder, Johann Gottfried von
1744-1803 .... **NCLC 8**
See also DLB 97; EW 4; TWA

Heredia, Jose Maria 1803-1839
See also HLCS 2; LAW

Hergesheimer, Joseph 1880-1954 ... **TCLC 11**
See also CA 109; 194; DLB 102, 9; RGAL 4

Herlihy, James Leo 1927-1993 .... **CLC 6**
See also CA 1-4R; 143; CAD; CANR 2

Hermogenes fl. c. 175- .... **CMLC 6**

Hernandez, Jose 1834-1886 .... **NCLC 17**
See also LAW; RGWL 2; WLIT 1

Herodotus c. 484 B.C.-c. 420
B.C. .... **CMLC 17**
See also AW 1; CDWLB 1; DLB 176; RGWL 2; TWA

Herrick, Robert 1591-1674 .... **LC 13; PC 9**
See also BRW 2; DA; DAB; DAC; DAM MST, POP; DLB 126; EXPP; PFS 13; RGAL 4; RGEL 2; TEA; WP

Herring, Guilles
See Somerville, Edith Oenone

Herriot, James 1916-1995 .... **CLC 12**
See also Wight, James Alfred
See also AAYA 1; BPFB 2; CA 148; CANR 40; CLR 80; CPW; DAM POP; LAIT 3; MAICYA 2; MAICYAS 1; MTCW 2; SATA 86; TEA; YAW

Herris, Violet
See Hunt, Violet

Herrmann, Dorothy 1941- .... **CLC 44**
See also CA 107

Herrmann, Taffy
See Herrmann, Dorothy

Hersey, John (Richard) 1914-1993 .... **CLC 1, 2, 7, 9, 40, 81, 97**
See also AAYA 29; BPFB 2; CA 17-20R; 140; CANR 33; CDALBS; CPW; DAM POP; DLB 6, 185; MTCW 1, 2; SATA 25; SATA-Obit 76; TUS

Herzen, Aleksandr Ivanovich
1812-1870 .... **NCLC 10, 61**

Herzl, Theodor 1860-1904 .... **TCLC 36**
See also CA 168

Herzog, Werner 1942- .... **CLC 16**
See also CA 89-92

Hesiod c. 8th cent. B.C.- .... **CMLC 5**
See also AW 1; DLB 176; RGWL 2

Hesse, Hermann 1877-1962 ... **CLC 1, 2, 3, 6, 11, 17, 25, 69; SSC 9, 49; WLC**
See also AAYA 43; BPFB 2; CA 17-18; CAP 2; CDWLB 2; DA; DA3; DAB; DAC; DAM MST, NOV; DLB 66; EW 9; EXPN; LAIT 1; MTCW 1, 2; NFS 6, 15; RGWL 2; SATA 50; TWA

Hewes, Cady
See De Voto, Bernard (Augustine)

Heyen, William 1940- .... **CLC 13, 18**
See also CA 33-36R; CAAS 9; CANR 98; CP 7; DLB 5

Heyerdahl, Thor 1914-2002 .... **CLC 26**
See also CA 5-8R; CANR 5, 22, 66, 73; LAIT 4; MTCW 1, 2; SATA 2, 52

Heym, Georg (Theodor Franz Arthur)
1887-1912 .... **TCLC 9**
See also CA 106; 181

Heym, Stefan 1913-2001 .... **CLC 41**
See also CA 9-12R; 203; CANR 4; CWW 2; DLB 69

Heyse, Paul (Johann Ludwig von)
1830-1914 .... **TCLC 8**
See also CA 104; DLB 129

Heyward, (Edwin) DuBose
1885-1940 .... **TCLC 59**
See also CA 108; 157; DLB 7, 9, 45, 249; SATA 21

Heywood, John 1497(?)-1580(?) .... **LC 65**
See also DLB 136; RGEL 2

Hibbert, Eleanor Alice Burford
1906-1993 .... **CLC 7**
See also Holt, Victoria
See also BEST 90:4; CA 17-20R; 140; CANR 9, 28, 59; CMW 4; CPW; DAM POP; MTCW 2; RHW; SATA 2; SATA-Obit 74

Hichens, Robert (Smythe)
1864-1950 .... **TCLC 64**
See also CA 162; DLB 153; HGG; RHW; SUFW

Higgins, George V(incent)
1939-1999 .... **CLC 4, 7, 10, 18**
See also BPFB 2; CA 77-80; 186; CAAS 5; CANR 17, 51, 89, 96; CMW 4; CN 7; DLB 2; DLBY 1981, 1998; INT CANR-17; MSW; MTCW 1

Higginson, Thomas Wentworth
1823-1911 .... **TCLC 36**
See also CA 162; DLB 1, 64, 243

Higgonet, Margaret ed. .... **CLC 65**

Highet, Helen
See MacInnes, Helen (Clark)

Highsmith, (Mary) Patricia
1921-1995 .... **CLC 2, 4, 14, 42, 102**
See also Morgan, Claire
See also BRWS 5; CA 1-4R; 147; CANR 1, 20, 48, 62, 108; CMW 4; CPW; DA3; DAM NOV, POP; MSW; MTCW 1, 2

Highwater, Jamake (Mamake)
1942(?)-2001 .... **CLC 12**
See also AAYA 7; BPFB 2; BYA 4; CA 65-68; 199; CAAS 7; CANR 10, 34, 84; CLR 17; CWRI 5; DLB 52; DLBY 1985; JRDA; MAICYA 1, 2; SATA 32, 69; SATA-Brief 30

Highway, Tomson 1951- .... **CLC 92**
See also CA 151; CANR 75; CCA 1; CD 5; DAC; DAM MULT; DFS 2; MTCW 2; NNAL

Hijuelos, Oscar 1951- .... **CLC 65; HLC 1**
See also AAYA 25; AMWS 8; BEST 90:1; CA 123; CANR 50, 75; CPW; DA3; DAM MULT, POP; DLB 145; HW 1, 2; MTCW 2; RGAL 4; WLIT 1

Hikmet, Nazim 1902(?)-1963 .... **CLC 40**
See also CA 141; 93-96

Hildegard von Bingen 1098-1179 . **CMLC 20**
See also DLB 148

Hildesheimer, Wolfgang 1916-1991 .. **CLC 49**
See also CA 101; 135; DLB 69, 124

Hill, Geoffrey (William) 1932- ...... **CLC 5, 8, 18, 45**
See also BRWS 5; CA 81-84; CANR 21, 89; CDBLB 1960 to Present; CP 7; DAM POET; DLB 40; MTCW 1; RGEL 2

Hooker, (Peter) Jeremy 1941- .... **CLC 43**
See also CA 77-80; CANR 22; CP 7; DLB 40

hooks, bell .... **CLC 94**
See also Watkins, Gloria Jean
See also DLB 246

Hope, A(lec) D(erwent) 1907-2000 .... **CLC 3, 51**
See also BRWS 7; CA 21-24R; 188; CANR 33, 74; MTCW 1, 2; PFS 8; RGEL 2

Hope, Anthony 1863-1933 .... **TCLC 83**
See also CA 157; DLB 153, 156; RGEL 2; RHW

Hope, Brian
See Creasey, John

Hope, Christopher (David Tully)
1944- .... **CLC 52**
See also AFW; CA 106; CANR 47, 101; CN 7; DLB 225; SATA 62

Hopkins, Gerard Manley
1844-1889 .... **NCLC 17; PC 15; WLC**
See also BRW 5; BRWR 2; CDBLB 1890-1914; DA; DA3; DAB; DAC; DAM MST, POET; DLB 35, 57; EXPP; PAB; RGEL 2; TEA; WP

Hopkins, John (Richard) 1931-1998 .. **CLC 4**
See also CA 85-88; 169; CBD; CD 5

Hopkins, Pauline Elizabeth
1859-1930 .... **TCLC 28; BLC 2**
See also AFAW 2; BW 2, 3; CA 141; CANR 82; DAM MULT; DLB 50

Hopkinson, Francis 1737-1791 .... **LC 25**
See also DLB 31; RGAL 4

Hopley-Woolrich, Cornell George 1903-1968
See Woolrich, Cornell
See also CA 13-14; CANR 58; CAP 1; CMW 4; DLB 226; MTCW 2

Horace 65 B.C.-8 B.C. .... **CMLC 39**
See also AW 2; CDWLB 1; DLB 211; RGWL 2

Horatio
See Proust, (Valentin-Louis-George-Eugene-)Marcel

Horgan, Paul (George Vincent
O'Shaughnessy) 1903-1995 .. **CLC 9, 53**
See also BPFB 2; CA 13-16R; 147; CANR 9, 35; DAM NOV; DLB 102, 212; DLBY 1985; INT CANR-9; MTCW 1, 2; SATA 13; SATA-Obit 84; TCWW 2

Horn, Peter
See Kuttner, Henry

Hornem, Horace Esq.
See Byron, George Gordon (Noel)

Horney, Karen (Clementine Theodore
Danielsen) 1885-1952 .... **TCLC 71**
See also CA 114; 165; DLB 246; FW

Hornung, E(rnest) W(illiam)
1866-1921 .... **TCLC 59**
See also CA 108; 160; CMW 4; DLB 70

Horovitz, Israel (Arthur) 1939- .... **CLC 56**
See also CA 33-36R; CAD; CANR 46, 59; CD 5; DAM DRAM; DLB 7

Horton, George Moses
1797(?)-1883(?) .... **NCLC 87**
See also DLB 50

Horvath, Odon von 1901-1938 .... **TCLC 45**
See also von Horvath, Oedoen
See also CA 118; 194; DLB 85, 124; RGWL 2

Horvath, Oedoen von -1938
See Horvath, Odon von

Horwitz, Julius 1920-1986 .... **CLC 14**
See also CA 9-12R; 119; CANR 12

Hospital, Janette Turner 1942- .... **CLC 42, 145**
See also CA 108; CANR 48; CN 7; RGSF 2

Hostos, E. M. de
See Hostos (y Bonilla), Eugenio Maria de

Hostos, Eugenio M. de
See Hostos (y Bonilla), Eugenio Maria de

Hostos, Eugenio Maria
See Hostos (y Bonilla), Eugenio Maria de

Hostos (y Bonilla), Eugenio Maria de
1839-1903 .... **TCLC 24**
See also CA 123; 131; HW 1

Houdini
See Lovecraft, H(oward) P(hillips)

Hougan, Carolyn 1943- .... **CLC 34**
See also CA 139

Household, Geoffrey (Edward West)
1900-1988 .... **CLC 11**
See also CA 77-80; 126; CANR 58; CMW 4; DLB 87; SATA 14; SATA-Obit 59

Housman, A(lfred) E(dward)
1859-1936 ... **TCLC 1, 10; PC 2; WLCS**
See also BRW 6; CA 104; 125; DA; DA3; DAB; DAC; DAM MST, POET; DLB 19; EXPP; MTCW 1, 2; PAB; PFS 4, 7; RGEL 2; TEA; WP

Housman, Laurence 1865-1959 .... **TCLC 7**
See also CA 106; 155; DLB 10; FANT; RGEL 2; SATA 25

Howard, Elizabeth Jane 1923- ..... **CLC 7, 29**
See also CA 5-8R; CANR 8, 62; CN 7

Howard, Maureen 1930- .... **CLC 5, 14, 46, 151**
See also CA 53-56; CANR 31, 75; CN 7; DLBY 1983; INT CANR-31; MTCW 1, 2

Howard, Richard 1929- .... **CLC 7, 10, 47**
See also AITN 1; CA 85-88; CANR 25, 80; CP 7; DLB 5; INT CANR-25

Howard, Robert E(rvin)
1906-1936 .... **TCLC 8**
See also BPFB 2; BYA 5; CA 105; 157; FANT; SUFW

Howard, Warren F.
See Pohl, Frederik

Howe, Fanny (Quincy) 1940- .... **CLC 47**
See also CA 117; CAAE 187; CAAS 27; CANR 70; CP 7; CWP; SATA-Brief 52

Howe, Irving 1920-1993 .... **CLC 85**
See also AMWS 6; CA 9-12R; 141; CANR 21, 50; DLB 67; MTCW 1, 2

Howe, Julia Ward 1819-1910 .... **TCLC 21**
See also CA 117; 191; DLB 1, 189, 235; FW

Howe, Susan 1937- .... **CLC 72, 152**
See also AMWS 4; CA 160; CP 7; CWP; DLB 120; FW; RGAL 4

Howe, Tina 1937- .... **CLC 48**
See also CA 109; CAD; CD 5; CWD

Howell, James 1594(?)-1666 .... **LC 13**
See also DLB 151

Howells, W. D.
See Howells, William Dean

Howells, William D.
See Howells, William Dean

Howells, William Dean 1837-1920 .. **TCLC 7, 17, 41; SSC 36**
See also AMW; CA 104; 134; CDALB 1865-1917; DLB 12, 64, 74, 79, 189; MTCW 2; RGAL 4; TUS

Howes, Barbara 1914-1996 .... **CLC 15**
See also CA 9-12R; 151; CAAS 3; CANR 53; CP 7; SATA 5

Hrabal, Bohumil 1914-1997 .... **CLC 13, 67**
See also CA 106; 156; CAAS 12; CANR 57; CWW 2; DLB 232; RGSF 2

Hrotsvit of Gandersheim c. 935-c.
1000 .... **CMLC 29**
See also DLB 148

Hsi, Chu 1130-1200 .... **CMLC 42**

Hsun, Lu
See Lu Hsun

Hubbard, L(afayette) Ron(ald)
1911-1986 .... **CLC 43**
See also CA 77-80; 118; CANR 52; CPW; DA3; DAM POP; FANT; MTCW 2; SFW 4

Huch, Ricarda (Octavia)
1864-1947 .... **TCLC 13**
See also CA 111; 189; DLB 66

Huddle, David 1942- .... **CLC 49**
See also CA 57-60; CAAS 20; CANR 89; DLB 130

Hudson, Jeffrey
See Crichton, (John) Michael

Hudson, W(illiam) H(enry)
1841-1922 .... **TCLC 29**
See also CA 115; 190; DLB 98, 153, 174; RGEL 2; SATA 35

Hueffer, Ford Madox
See Ford, Ford Madox

Hughart, Barry 1934- .... **CLC 39**
See also CA 137; FANT; SFW 4

Hughes, Colin
See Creasey, John

Hughes, David (John) 1930- .... **CLC 48**
See also CA 116; 129; CN 7; DLB 14

Hughes, Edward James
See Hughes, Ted
See also DA3; DAM MST, POET

Hughes, (James Mercer) Langston
1902-1967 .... **CLC 1, 5, 10, 15, 35, 44, 108; BLC 2; DC 3; PC 1; SSC 6; WLC**
See also AAYA 12; AFAW 1, 2; AMWR 1; AMWS 1; BW 1, 3; CA 1-4R; 25-28R; CANR 1, 34, 82; CDALB 1929-1941; CLR 17; DA; DA3; DAB; DAC; DAM DRAM, MST, MULT, POET; DLB 4, 7, 48, 51, 86, 228; EXPP; EXPS; JRDA; LAIT 3; MAICYA 1, 2; MTCW 1, 2; PAB; PFS 1, 3, 6, 10, 15; RGAL 4; RGSF 2; SATA 4, 33; SSFS 4, 7; TUS; WCH; WP; YAW

Hughes, Richard (Arthur Warren)
1900-1976 .... **CLC 1, 11**
See also CA 5-8R; 65-68; CANR 4; DAM NOV; DLB 15, 161; MTCW 1; RGEL 2; SATA 8; SATA-Obit 25

Hughes, Ted 1930-1998 . **CLC 2, 4, 9, 14, 37, 119; PC 7**
See also Hughes, Edward James
See also BRWR 2; BRWS 1; CA 1-4R; 171; CANR 1, 33, 66, 108; CLR 3; CP 7; DAB; DAC; DLB 40, 161; EXPP; MAICYA 1, 2; MTCW 1, 2; PAB; PFS 4; RGEL 2; SATA 49; SATA-Brief 27; SATA-Obit 107; TEA; YAW

Hugo, Richard
See Huch, Ricarda (Octavia)

Hugo, Richard F(ranklin)
1923-1982 .... **CLC 6, 18, 32**
See also AMWS 6; CA 49-52; 108; CANR 3; DAM POET; DLB 5, 206; RGAL 4

Hugo, Victor (Marie) 1802-1885 .... **NCLC 3, 10, 21; PC 17; WLC**
See also AAYA 28; DA; DA3; DAB; DAC; DAM DRAM, MST, NOV, POET; DLB 119, 192, 217; EFS 2; EW 6; EXPN; GFL 1789 to the Present; LAIT 1, 2; NFS 5; RGWL 2; SATA 47; TWA

Huidobro, Vicente
See Huidobro Fernandez, Vicente Garcia
See also LAW

Huidobro Fernandez, Vicente Garcia
1893-1948 .... **TCLC 31**
See also Huidobro, Vicente
See also CA 131; HW 1

Hulme, Keri 1947- .... **CLC 39, 130**
See also CA 125; CANR 69; CN 7; CP 7; CWP; FW; INT 125

Kempe, Margery 1373(?)-1440(?) ... **LC 6, 56**
See also DLB 146; RGEL 2

Kempis, Thomas a 1380-1471 .... **LC 11**

Kendall, Henry 1839-1882 .... **NCLC 12**
See also DLB 230

Keneally, Thomas (Michael) 1935- ... **CLC 5, 8, 10, 14, 19, 27, 43, 117**
See also BRWS 4; CA 85-88; CANR 10, 50, 74; CN 7; CPW; DA3; DAM NOV; MTCW 1, 2; RGEL 2; RHW

Kennedy, Adrienne (Lita) 1931- ..... **CLC 66; BLC 2; DC 5**
See also AFAW 2; BW 2, 3; CA 103; CAAS 20; CABS 3; CANR 26, 53, 82; CD 5; DAM MULT; DFS 9; DLB 38; FW

Kennedy, John Pendleton
1795-1870 .... **NCLC 2**
See also DLB 3, 248, 254; RGAL 4

Kennedy, Joseph Charles 1929-
See Kennedy, X. J.
See also CA 1-4R; CAAE 201; CANR 4, 30, 40; CP 7; CWRI 5; MAICYA 2; MAICYAS 1; SATA 14, 86; SATA-Essay 130

Kennedy, William 1928- ... **CLC 6, 28, 34, 53**
See also AAYA 1; AMWS 7; BPFB 2; CA 85-88; CANR 14, 31, 76; CN 7; DA3; DAM NOV; DLB 143; DLBY 1985; INT CANR-31; MTCW 1, 2; SATA 57

Kennedy, X. J. .... **CLC 8, 42**
See also Kennedy, Joseph Charles
See also CAAS 9; CLR 27; DLB 5; SAAS 22

Kenny, Maurice (Francis) 1929- ...... **CLC 87**
See also CA 144; CAAS 22; DAM MULT; DLB 175; NNAL

Kent, Kelvin
See Kuttner, Henry

Kenton, Maxwell
See Southern, Terry

Kenyon, Robert O.
See Kuttner, Henry

Kepler, Johannes 1571-1630 .... **LC 45**

Ker, Jill
See Conway, Jill K(er)

Kerkow, H. C.
See Lewton, Val

Kerouac, Jack 1922-1969 ...... **CLC 1, 2, 3, 5, 14, 29, 61; WLC**
See also Kerouac, Jean-Louis Lebris de
See also AAYA 25; AMWS 3; BPFB 2; CDALB 1941-1968; CPW; DLB 2, 16, 237; DLBD 3; DLBY 1995; GLL 1; MTCW 2; NFS 8; RGAL 4; TCLC 117; TUS; WP

Kerouac, Jean-Louis Lebris de 1922-1969
See Kerouac, Jack
See also AITN 1; CA 5-8R; 25-28R; CANR 26, 54, 95; DA; DA3; DAB; DAC; DAM MST, NOV, POET, POP; MTCW 1, 2

Kerr, Jean 1923- .... **CLC 22**
See also CA 5-8R; CANR 7; INT CANR-7

Kerr, M. E. .... **CLC 12, 35**
See also Meaker, Marijane (Agnes)
See also AAYA 2, 23; BYA 1, 7, 8; CLR 29; SAAS 1; WYA

Kerr, Robert .... **CLC 55**

Kerrigan, (Thomas) Anthony 1918- .. **CLC 4, 6**
See also CA 49-52; CAAS 11; CANR 4

Kerry, Lois
See Duncan, Lois

Kesey, Ken (Elton) 1935-2001 ... **CLC 1, 3, 6, 11, 46, 64; WLC**
See also AAYA 25; BPFB 2; CA 1-4R; CANR 22, 38, 66; CDALB 1968-1988; CN 7; CPW; DA; DA3; DAB; DAC;

DAM MST, NOV, POP; DLB 2, 16, 206; EXPN; LAIT 4; MTCW 1, 2; NFS 2; RGAL 4; SATA 66; SATA-Obit 131; TUS; YAW

Kesselring, Joseph (Otto)
1902-1967 .... **CLC 45**
See also CA 150; DAM DRAM, MST

Kessler, Jascha (Frederick) 1929- ...... **CLC 4**
See also CA 17-20R; CANR 8, 48

Kettelkamp, Larry (Dale) 1933- .... **CLC 12**
See also CA 29-32R; CANR 16; SAAS 3; SATA 2

Key, Ellen (Karolina Sofia)
1849-1926 .... **TCLC 65**
See also DLB 259

Keyber, Conny
See Fielding, Henry

Keyes, Daniel 1927- .... **CLC 80**
See also AAYA 23; BYA 11; CA 17-20R, 181; CAAE 181; CANR 10, 26, 54, 74; DA; DA3; DAC; DAM MST, NOV; EXPN; LAIT 4; MTCW 2; NFS 2; SATA 37; SFW 4

Keynes, John Maynard
1883-1946 .... **TCLC 64**
See also CA 114; 162, 163; DLBD 10; MTCW 2

Khanshendel, Chiron
See Rose, Wendy

Khayyam, Omar 1048-1131 ... **CMLC 11; PC 8**
See also Omar Khayyam
See also DA3; DAM POET

Kherdian, David 1931- .... **CLC 6, 9**
See also AAYA 42; CA 21-24R; CAAE 192; CAAS 2; CANR 39, 78; CLR 24; JRDA; LAIT 3; MAICYA 1, 2; SATA 16, 74; SATA-Essay 125

Khlebnikov, Velimir .... **TCLC 20**
See also Khlebnikov, Viktor Vladimirovich
See also EW 10; RGWL 2

Khlebnikov, Viktor Vladimirovich 1885-1922
See Khlebnikov, Velimir
See also CA 117

Khodasevich, Vladislav (Felitsianovich)
1886-1939 .... **TCLC 15**
See also CA 115

Kielland, Alexander Lange
1849-1906 .... **TCLC 5**
See also CA 104

Kiely, Benedict 1919- .... **CLC 23, 43**
See also CA 1-4R; CANR 2, 84; CN 7; DLB 15

Kienzle, William X(avier)
1928-2001 .... **CLC 25**
See also CA 93-96; 203; CAAS 1; CANR 9, 31, 59; CMW 4; DA3; DAM POP; INT CANR-31; MSW; MTCW 1, 2

Kierkegaard, Soren 1813-1855 ..... **NCLC 34, 78**
See also EW 6; TWA

Kieslowski, Krzysztof 1941-1996 .... **CLC 120**
See also CA 147; 151

Killens, John Oliver 1916-1987 .... **CLC 10**
See also BW 2; CA 77-80; 123; CAAS 2; CANR 26; DLB 33

Killigrew, Anne 1660-1685 .... **LC 4, 73**
See also DLB 131

Killigrew, Thomas 1612-1683 .... **LC 57**
See also DLB 58; RGEL 2

Kim
See Simenon, Georges (Jacques Christian)

Kincaid, Jamaica 1949- ..... **CLC 43, 68, 137; BLC 2**
See also AAYA 13; AFAW 2; AMWS 7; BRWS 7; BW 2, 3; CA 125; CANR 47, 59, 95; CDALBS; CDWLB 3; CLR 63;

CN 7; DA3; DAM MULT, NOV; DLB 157, 227; DNFS 1; EXPS; FW; MTCW 2; NCFS 1; NFS 3; SSFS 5, 7; TUS; YAW

King, Francis (Henry) 1923- .... **CLC 8, 53, 145**
See also CA 1-4R; CANR 1, 33, 86; CN 7; DAM NOV; DLB 15, 139; MTCW 1

King, Kennedy
See Brown, George Douglas

King, Martin Luther, Jr.
1929-1968 .... **CLC 83; BLC 2; WLCS**
See also BW 2, 3; CA 25-28; CANR 27, 44; CAP 2; DA; DA3; DAB; DAC; DAM MST, MULT; LAIT 5; MTCW 1, 2; SATA 14

King, Stephen (Edwin) 1947- .... **CLC 12, 26, 37, 61, 113; SSC 17, 55**
See also AAYA 1, 17; AMWS 5; BEST 90:1; BPFB 2; CA 61-64; CANR 1, 30, 52, 76; CPW; DA3; DAM NOV, POP; DLB 143; DLBY 1980; HGG; JRDA; LAIT 5; MTCW 1, 2; RGAL 4; SATA 9, 55; SUFW; WYAS 1; YAW

King, Steve
See King, Stephen (Edwin)

King, Thomas 1943- .... **CLC 89**
See also CA 144; CANR 95; CCA 1; CN 7; DAC; DAM MULT; DLB 175; NNAL; SATA 96

Kingman, Lee .... **CLC 17**
See also Natti, (Mary) Lee
See also CWRI 5; SAAS 3; SATA 1, 67

Kingsley, Charles 1819-1875 .... **NCLC 35**
See also CLR 77; DLB 21, 32, 163, 178, 190; FANT; MAICYA 2; MAICYAS 1; RGEL 2; WCH; YABC 2

Kingsley, Henry 1830-1876 .... **NCLC 107**
See also DLB 21, 230; RGEL 2

Kingsley, Sidney 1906-1995 .... **CLC 44**
See also CA 85-88; 147; CAD; DFS 14; DLB 7; RGAL 4

Kingsolver, Barbara 1955- . **CLC 55, 81, 130**
See also AAYA 15; AMWS 7; CA 129; 134; CANR 60, 96; CDALBS; CPW; CSW; DA3; DAM POP; DLB 206; INT CA-134; LAIT 5; MTCW 5, 10, 12; RGAL 4

Kingston, Maxine (Ting Ting) Hong
1940- .... **CLC 12, 19, 58, 121; AAL; WLCS**
See also AAYA 8; AMWS 5; BPFB 2; CA 69-72; CANR 13, 38, 74, 87; CDALBS; CN 7; DA3; DAM MULT, NOV; DLB 173, 212; DLBY 1980; FW; INT CANR-13; LAIT 5; MAWW; MTCW 1, 2; NFS 6; RGAL 4; SATA 53; SSFS 3

Kinnell, Galway 1927- ..... **CLC 1, 2, 3, 5, 13, 29, 129; PC 26**
See also AMWS 3; CA 9-12R; CANR 10, 34, 66; CP 7; DLB 5; DLBY 1987; INT CANR-34; MTCW 1, 2; PAB; PFS 9; RGAL 4; WP

Kinsella, Thomas 1928- .... **CLC 4, 19, 138**
See also BRWS 5; CA 17-20R; CANR 15; CP 7; DLB 27; MTCW 1, 2; RGEL 2; TEA

Kinsella, W(illiam) P(atrick) 1935- . **CLC 27, 43**
See also AAYA 7; BPFB 2; CA 97-100; CAAS 7; CANR 21, 35, 66, 75; CN 7; CPW; DAC; DAM NOV, POP; FANT; INT CANR-21; LAIT 5; MTCW 1, 2; NFS 15; RGSF 2

Kinsey, Alfred C(harles)
1894-1956 .... **TCLC 91**
See also CA 115; 170; MTCW 2

Kipling, (Joseph) Rudyard
1865-1936 ... **TCLC 8, 17; PC 3; SSC 5, 54; WLC**
See also AAYA 32; BRW 6; BYA 4; CA 105; 120; CANR 33; CDBLB 1890-1914;

CLR 39, 65; CWRI 5; DA; DA3; DAB; DAC; DAM MST, POET; DLB 19, 34, 141, 156; EXPS; FANT; LAIT 3; MAICYA 1, 2; MTCW 1, 2; RGEL 2; RGSF 2; SATA 100; SFW 4; SSFS 8; SUFW; TEA; WCH; WLIT 4; YABC 2

Kirk, Russell (Amos) 1918-1994 .. **TCLC 119**
See also AITN 1; CA 1-4R; 145; CAAS 9; CANR 1, 20, 60; HGG; INT CANR-20; MTCW 1, 2

Kirkland, Caroline M. 1801-1864 . **NCLC 85**
See also DLB 3, 73, 74, 250, 254; DLBD 13

Kirkup, James 1918- .... **CLC 1**
See also CA 1-4R; CAAS 4; CANR 2; CP 7; DLB 27; SATA 12

Kirkwood, James 1930(?)-1989 .... **CLC 9**
See also AITN 2; CA 1-4R; 128; CANR 6, 40; GLL 2

Kirshner, Sidney
See Kingsley, Sidney

Kis, Danilo 1935-1989 .... **CLC 57**
See also CA 109; 118; 129; CANR 61; CD-WLB 4; DLB 181; MTCW 1; RGSF 2; RGWL 2

Kissinger, Henry A(lfred) 1923- ..... **CLC 137**
See also CA 1-4R; CANR 2, 33, 66, 109; MTCW 1

Kivi, Aleksis 1834-1872 .... **NCLC 30**

Kizer, Carolyn (Ashley) 1925- ... **CLC 15, 39, 80**
See also CA 65-68; CAAS 5; CANR 24, 70; CP 7; CWP; DAM POET; DLB 5, 169; MTCW 2

Klabund 1890-1928 .... **TCLC 44**
See also CA 162; DLB 66

Klappert, Peter 1942- .... **CLC 57**
See also CA 33-36R; CSW; DLB 5

Klein, A(braham) M(oses)
1909-1972 .... **CLC 19**
See also CA 101; 37-40R; DAB; DAC; DAM MST; DLB 68; RGEL 2

Klein, Joe
See Klein, Joseph

Klein, Joseph 1946- .... **CLC 154**
See also CA 85-88; CANR 55

Klein, Norma 1938-1989 .... **CLC 30**
See also AAYA 2, 35; BPFB 2; BYA 6, 7, 8; CA 41-44R; 128; CANR 15, 37; CLR 2, 19; INT CANR-15; JRDA; MAICYA 1, 2; SAAS 1; SATA 7, 57; WYA; YAW

Klein, T(heodore) E(ibon) D(onald)
1947- .... **CLC 34**
See also CA 119; CANR 44, 75; HGG

Kleist, Heinrich von 1777-1811 ...... **NCLC 2, 37; SSC 22**
See also CDWLB 2; DAM DRAM; DLB 90; EW 5; RGSF 2; RGWL 2

Klima, Ivan 1931- .... **CLC 56**
See also CA 25-28R; CANR 17, 50, 91; CDWLB 4; CWW 2; DAM NOV; DLB 232

Klimentov, Andrei Platonovich
1899-1951 .... **TCLC 14; SSC 42**
See also CA 108

Klinger, Friedrich Maximilian von
1752-1831 .... **NCLC 1**
See also DLB 94

Klingsor the Magician
See Hartmann, Sadakichi

Klopstock, Friedrich Gottlieb
1724-1803 .... **NCLC 11**
See also DLB 97; EW 4; RGWL 2

Knapp, Caroline 1959-2002 .... **CLC 99**
See also CA 154

Knebel, Fletcher 1911-1993 .... **CLC 14**
See also AITN 1; CA 1-4R; 140; CAAS 3; CANR 1, 36; SATA 36; SATA-Obit 75

Knickerbocker, Diedrich
See Irving, Washington

Knight, Etheridge 1931-1991 . **CLC 40; BLC 2; PC 14**
See also BW 1, 3; CA 21-24R; 133; CANR 23, 82; DAM POET; DLB 41; MTCW 2; RGAL 4

Knight, Sarah Kemble 1666-1727 .... **LC 7**
See also DLB 24, 200

Knister, Raymond 1899-1932 .... **TCLC 56**
See also CA 186; DLB 68; RGEL 2

Knowles, John 1926-2001 ... **CLC 1, 4, 10, 26**
See also AAYA 10; BPFB 2; BYA 3; CA 17-20R; 203; CANR 40, 74, 76; CDALB 1968-1988; CN 7; DA; DAC; DAM MST, NOV; DLB 6; EXPN; MTCW 1, 2; NFS 2; RGAL 4; SATA 8, 89; YAW

Knox, Calvin M.
See Silverberg, Robert

Knox, John c. 1505-1572 .... **LC 37**
See also DLB 132

Knye, Cassandra
See Disch, Thomas M(ichael)

Koch, C(hristopher) J(ohn) 1932- .... **CLC 42**
See also CA 127; CANR 84; CN 7

Koch, Christopher
See Koch, C(hristopher) J(ohn)

Koch, Kenneth 1925-2002 .... **CLC 5, 8, 44**
See also CA 1-4R; CAD; CANR 6, 36, 57, 97; CD 5; CP 7; DAM POET; DLB 5; INT CANR-36; MTCW 2; SATA 65; WP

Kochanowski, Jan 1530-1584 .... **LC 10**
See also RGWL 2

Kock, Charles Paul de 1794-1871 . **NCLC 16**

Koda Rohan
See Koda Shigeyuki

Koda Rohan
See Koda Shigeyuki
See also DLB 180

Koda Shigeyuki 1867-1947 .... **TCLC 22**
See also Koda Rohan
See also CA 121; 183

Koestler, Arthur 1905-1983 ... **CLC 1, 3, 6, 8, 15, 33**
See also BRWS 1; CA 1-4R; 109; CANR 1, 33; CDBLB 1945-1960; DLBY 1983; MTCW 1, 2; RGEL 2

Kogawa, Joy Nozomi 1935- ...... **CLC 78, 129**
See also CA 101; CANR 19, 62; CN 7; CWP; DAC; DAM MST, MULT; FW; MTCW 2; NFS 3; SATA 99

Kohout, Pavel 1928- .... **CLC 13**
See also CA 45-48; CANR 3

Koizumi, Yakumo
See Hearn, (Patricio) Lafcadio (Tessima Carlos)

Kolmar, Gertrud 1894-1943 .... **TCLC 40**
See also CA 167

Komunyakaa, Yusef 1947- .... **CLC 86, 94; BLCS**
See also AFAW 2; CA 147; CANR 83; CP 7; CSW; DLB 120; PFS 5; RGAL 4

Konrad, George
See Konrad, Gyorgy
See also CWW 2

Konrad, Gyorgy 1933- .... **CLC 4, 10, 73**
See also Konrad, George
See also CA 85-88; CANR 97; CDWLB 4; CWW 2; DLB 232

Konwicki, Tadeusz 1926- .... **CLC 8, 28, 54, 117**
See also CA 101; CAAS 9; CANR 39, 59; CWW 2; DLB 232; IDFW 3; MTCW 1

Koontz, Dean R(ay) 1945- .... **CLC 78**
See also AAYA 9, 31; BEST 89:3, 90:2; CA 108; CANR 19, 36, 52, 95; CMW 4; CPW; DA3; DAM NOV, POP; HGG; MTCW 1; SATA 92; SFW 4; YAW

Kopernik, Mikolaj
See Copernicus, Nicolaus

Kopit, Arthur (Lee) 1937- ...... **CLC 1, 18, 33**
See also AITN 1; CA 81-84; CABS 3; CD 5; DAM DRAM; DFS 7, 14; DLB 7; MTCW 1; RGAL 4

Kops, Bernard 1926- .... **CLC 4**
See also CA 5-8R; CANR 84; CBD; CN 7; CP 7; DLB 13

Kornbluth, C(yril) M. 1923-1958 .... **TCLC 8**
See also CA 105; 160; DLB 8; SFW 4

Korolenko, V. G.
See Korolenko, Vladimir Galaktionovich

Korolenko, Vladimir
See Korolenko, Vladimir Galaktionovich

Korolenko, Vladimir G.
See Korolenko, Vladimir Galaktionovich

Korolenko, Vladimir Galaktionovich
1853-1921 .... **TCLC 22**
See also CA 121

Korzybski, Alfred (Habdank Skarbek)
1879-1950 .... **TCLC 61**
See also CA 123; 160

Kosinski, Jerzy (Nikodem)
1933-1991 .... **CLC 1, 2, 3, 6, 10, 15, 53, 70**
See also AMWS 7; BPFB 2; CA 17-20R; 134; CANR 9, 46; DA3; DAM NOV; DLB 2; DLBY 1982; HGG; MTCW 1, 2; NFS 12; RGAL 4; TUS

Kostelanetz, Richard (Cory) 1940- .. **CLC 28**
See also CA 13-16R; CAAS 8; CANR 38, 77; CN 7; CP 7

Kostrowitzki, Wilhelm Apollinaris de
1880-1918
See Apollinaire, Guillaume
See also CA 104

Kotlowitz, Robert 1924- .... **CLC 4**
See also CA 33-36R; CANR 36

Kotzebue, August (Friedrich Ferdinand) von
1761-1819 .... **NCLC 25**
See also DLB 94

Kotzwinkle, William 1938- ..... **CLC 5, 14, 35**
See also BPFB 2; CA 45-48; CANR 3, 44, 84; CLR 6; DLB 173; FANT; MAICYA 1, 2; SATA 24, 70; SFW 4; YAW

Kowna, Stancy
See Szymborska, Wislawa

Kozol, Jonathan 1936- .... **CLC 17**
See also CA 61-64; CANR 16, 45, 96

Kozoll, Michael 1940(?)- .... **CLC 35**

Kramer, Kathryn 19(?)- .... **CLC 34**

Kramer, Larry 1935- .... **CLC 42; DC 8**
See also CA 124; 126; CANR 60; DAM POP; DLB 249; GLL 1

Krasicki, Ignacy 1735-1801 .... **NCLC 8**

Krasinski, Zygmunt 1812-1859 .... **NCLC 4**
See also RGWL 2

Kraus, Karl 1874-1936 .... **TCLC 5**
See also CA 104; DLB 118

Kreve (Mickevicius), Vincas
1882-1954 .... **TCLC 27**
See also CA 170; DLB 220

Kristeva, Julia 1941- .... **CLC 77, 140**
See also CA 154; CANR 99; DLB 242; FW

Kristofferson, Kris 1936- .... **CLC 26**
See also CA 104

Krizanc, John 1956- .... **CLC 57**
See also CA 187

Krleza, Miroslav 1893-1981 .... **CLC 8, 114**
See also CA 97-100; 105; CANR 50; CD-WLB 4; DLB 147; EW 11; RGWL 2

Kroetsch, Robert 1927- .. **CLC 5, 23, 57, 132**
See also CA 17-20R; CANR 8, 38; CCA 1; CN 7; CP 7; DAC; DAM POET; DLB 53; MTCW 1

Kroetz, Franz
See Kroetz, Franz Xaver

Kroetz, Franz Xaver 1946- .... **CLC 41**
 See also CA 130
Kroker, Arthur (W.) 1945- .... **CLC 77**
 See also CA 161
Kropotkin, Peter (Aleksieevich)
 1842-1921 .... **TCLC 36**
 See also CA 119
Krotkov, Yuri 1917-1981 .... **CLC 19**
 See also CA 102
Krumb
 See Crumb, R(obert)
Krumgold, Joseph (Quincy)
 1908-1980 .... **CLC 12**
 See also BYA 1, 2; CA 9-12R; 101; CANR
 7; MAICYA 1, 2; SATA 1, 48; SATA-Obit
 23; YAW
Krumwitz
 See Crumb, R(obert)
Krutch, Joseph Wood 1893-1970 ..... **CLC 24**
 See also ANW; CA 1-4R; 25-28R; CANR
 4; DLB 63, 206
Krutzch, Gus
 See Eliot, T(homas) S(tearns)
Krylov, Ivan Andreevich
 1768(?)-1844 .... **NCLC 1**
 See also DLB 150
Kubin, Alfred (Leopold Isidor)
 1877-1959 .... **TCLC 23**
 See also CA 112; 149; CANR 104; DLB 81
Kubrick, Stanley 1928-1999 .... **CLC 16**
 See also AAYA 30; CA 81-84; 177; CANR
 33; DLB 26; TCLC 112
Kueng, Hans 1928-
 See Kung, Hans
 See also CA 53-56; CANR 66; MTCW 1, 2
Kumin, Maxine (Winokur) 1925- ..... **CLC 5,**
 13, 28; PC 15
 See also AITN 2; AMWS 4; ANW; CA
 1-4R; CAAS 8; CANR 1, 21, 69; CP 7;
 CWP; DA3; DAM POET; DLB 5; EXPP;
 MTCW 1, 2; PAB; SATA 12
Kundera, Milan 1929- .. **CLC 4, 9, 19, 32, 68,**
 115, 135; SSC 24
 See also AAYA 2; BPFB 2; CA 85-88;
 CANR 19, 52, 74; CDWLB 4; CWW 2;
 DA3; DAM NOV; DLB 232; EW 13;
 MTCW 1, 2; RGSF 2; SSFS 10
Kunene, Mazisi (Raymond) 1930- ... **CLC 85**
 See also BW 1, 3; CA 125; CANR 81; CP
 7; DLB 117
Kung, Hans .... **CLC 130**
 See also Kueng, Hans
Kunikida Doppo 1869(?)-1908
 See Doppo, Kunikida
 See also DLB 180
Kunitz, Stanley (Jasspon) 1905- .. **CLC 6, 11,**
 14, 148; PC 19
 See also AMWS 3; CA 41-44R; CANR 26,
 57, 98; CP 7; DA3; DLB 48; INT CANR-
 26; MTCW 1, 2; PFS 11; RGAL 4
Kunze, Reiner 1933- .... **CLC 10**
 See also CA 93-96; CWW 2; DLB 75
Kuprin, Aleksander Ivanovich
 1870-1938 .... **TCLC 5**
 See also CA 104; 182
Kureishi, Hanif 1954(?)- .... **CLC 64, 135**
 See also CA 139; CBD; CD 5; CN 7; DLB
 194, 245; GLL 2; IDFW 4; WLIT 4
Kurosawa, Akira 1910-1998 ..... **CLC 16, 119**
 See also AAYA 11; CA 101; 170; CANR
 46; DAM MULT
Kushner, Tony 1957(?)- .... **CLC 81; DC 10**
 See also AMWS 9; CA 144; CAD; CANR
 74; CD 5; DA3; DAM DRAM; DFS 5;
 DLB 228; GLL 1; LAIT 5; MTCW 2;
 RGAL 4
Kuttner, Henry 1915-1958 .... **TCLC 10**
 See also CA 107; 157; DLB 8; FANT;
 SCFW 2; SFW 4

Kuzma, Greg 1944- .... **CLC 7**
 See also CA 33-36R; CANR 70
Kuzmin, Mikhail 1872(?)-1936 ...... **TCLC 40**
 See also CA 170
Kyd, Thomas 1558-1594 .... **LC 22; DC 3**
 See also BRW 1; DAM DRAM; DLB 62;
 IDTP; RGEL 2; TEA; WLIT 3
Kyprianos, Iossif
 See Samarakis, Antonis
Labrunie, Gerard
 See Nerval, Gerard de
La Bruyere, Jean de 1645-1696 .... **LC 17**
 See also EW 3; GFL Beginnings to 1789
Lacan, Jacques (Marie Emile)
 1901-1981 .... **CLC 75**
 See also CA 121; 104; TWA
Laclos, Pierre Ambroise Francois
 1741-1803 .... **NCLC 4, 87**
 See also EW 4; GFL Beginnings to 1789;
 RGWL 2
Lacolere, Francois
 See Aragon, Louis
La Colere, Francois
 See Aragon, Louis
La Deshabilleuse
 See Simenon, Georges (Jacques Christian)
Lady Gregory
 See Gregory, Lady Isabella Augusta (Persse)
Lady of Quality, A
 See Bagnold, Enid
**La Fayette, Marie-(Madelaine Pioche de la
 Vergne)** 1634-1693 .... **LC 2**
 See also GFL Beginnings to 1789; RGWL
 2
Lafayette, Rene
 See Hubbard, L(afayette) Ron(ald)
La Fontaine, Jean de 1621-1695 .... **LC 50**
 See also EW 3; GFL Beginnings to 1789;
 MAICYA 1, 2; RGWL 2; SATA 18
Laforgue, Jules 1860-1887 . **NCLC 5, 53; PC
 14; SSC 20**
 See also DLB 217; EW 7; GFL 1789 to the
 Present; RGWL 2
Layamon
 See Layamon
 See also DLB 146
Lagerkvist, Paer (Fabian)
 1891-1974 .... **CLC 7, 10, 13, 54**
 See also Lagerkvist, Par
 See also CA 85-88; 49-52; DA3; DAM
 DRAM, NOV; MTCW 1, 2; TWA
Lagerkvist, Par .... **SSC 12**
 See also Lagerkvist, Paer (Fabian)
 See also DLB 259; EW 10; MTCW 2;
 RGSF 2; RGWL 2
Lagerloef, Selma (Ottiliana Lovisa)
 1858-1940 .... **TCLC 4, 36**
 See also Lagerlof, Selma (Ottiliana Lovisa)
 See also CA 108; MTCW 2; SATA 15
Lagerlof, Selma (Ottiliana Lovisa)
 See Lagerloef, Selma (Ottiliana Lovisa)
 See also CLR 7; SATA 15
La Guma, (Justin) Alex(ander)
 1925-1985 .... **CLC 19; BLCS**
 See also AFW; BW 1, 3; CA 49-52; 118;
 CANR 25, 81; CDWLB 3; DAM NOV;
 DLB 117, 225; MTCW 1, 2; WLIT 2
Laidlaw, A. K.
 See Grieve, C(hristopher) M(urray)
Lainez, Manuel Mujica
 See Mujica Lainez, Manuel
 See also HW 1
Laing, R(onald) D(avid) 1927-1989 . **CLC 95**
 See also CA 107; 129; CANR 34; MTCW 1
Lamartine, Alphonse (Marie Louis Prat) de
 1790-1869 .... **NCLC 11; PC 16**
 See also DAM POET; DLB 217; GFL 1789
 to the Present; RGWL 2

Lamb, Charles 1775-1834 ..... **NCLC 10, 113;
 WLC**
 See also BRW 4; CDBLB 1789-1832; DA;
 DAB; DAC; DAM MST; DLB 93, 107,
 163; RGEL 2; SATA 17; TEA
Lamb, Lady Caroline 1785-1828 ... **NCLC 38**
 See also DLB 116
Lamming, George (William) 1927- ... **CLC 2,
 4, 66, 144; BLC 2**
 See also BW 2, 3; CA 85-88; CANR 26,
 76; CDWLB 3; CN 7; DAM MULT; DLB
 125; MTCW 1, 2; NFS 15; RGEL 2
L'Amour, Louis (Dearborn)
 1908-1988 .... **CLC 25, 55**
 See also Burns, Tex; Mayo, Jim
 See also AAYA 16; AITN 2; BEST 89:2;
 BPFB 2; CA 1-4R; 125; CANR 3, 25, 40;
 CPW; DA3; DAM NOV, POP; DLB 206;
 DLBY 1980; MTCW 1, 2; RGAL 4
Lampedusa, Giuseppe (Tomasi) di
 .... **TCLC 13**
 See also Tomasi di Lampedusa, Giuseppe
 See also CA 164; EW 11; MTCW 2; RGWL
 2
Lampman, Archibald 1861-1899 ... **NCLC 25**
 See also DLB 92; RGEL 2; TWA
Lancaster, Bruce 1896-1963 .... **CLC 36**
 See also CA 9-10; CANR 70; CAP 1; SATA
 9
Lanchester, John .... **CLC 99**
 See also CA 194
Landau, Mark Alexandrovich
 See Aldanov, Mark (Alexandrovich)
Landau-Aldanov, Mark Alexandrovich
 See Aldanov, Mark (Alexandrovich)
Landis, Jerry
 See Simon, Paul (Frederick)
Landis, John 1950- .... **CLC 26**
 See also CA 112; 122
Landolfi, Tommaso 1908-1979 .... **CLC 11, 49**
 See also CA 127; 117; DLB 177
Landon, Letitia Elizabeth
 1802-1838 .... **NCLC 15**
 See also DLB 96
Landor, Walter Savage
 1775-1864 .... **NCLC 14**
 See also BRW 4; DLB 93, 107; RGEL 2
Landwirth, Heinz 1927-
 See Lind, Jakov
 See also CA 9-12R; CANR 7
Lane, Patrick 1939- .... **CLC 25**
 See also CA 97-100; CANR 54; CP 7; DAM
 POET; DLB 53; INT 97-100
Lang, Andrew 1844-1912 .... **TCLC 16**
 See also CA 114; 137; CANR 85; DLB 98,
 141, 184; FANT; MAICYA 1, 2; RGEL 2;
 SATA 16; WCH
Lang, Fritz 1890-1976 .... **CLC 20, 103**
 See also CA 77-80; 69-72; CANR 30
Lange, John
 See Crichton, (John) Michael
Langer, Elinor 1939- .... **CLC 34**
 See also CA 121
Langland, William 1332(?)-1400(?) ..... **LC 19**
 See also BRW 1; DA; DAB; DAC; DAM
 MST, POET; DLB 146; RGEL 2; TEA;
 WLIT 3
Langstaff, Launcelot
 See Irving, Washington
Lanier, Sidney 1842-1881 .... **NCLC 6**
 See also AMWS 1; DAM POET; DLB 64;
 DLBD 13; EXPP; MAICYA 1; PFS 14;
 RGAL 4; SATA 18
Lanyer, Aemilia 1569-1645 .... **LC 10, 30**
 See also DLB 121
Lao Tzu c. 6th cent. B.C.-3rd cent.
 B.C. .... **CMLC 7**
Lao-Tzu
 See Lao Tzu

Lee, John .... **CLC 70**
Lee, Julian
   See Latham, Jean Lee
Lee, Larry
   See Lee, Lawrence
Lee, Laurie 1914-1997 .... **CLC 90**
   See also CA 77-80; 158; CANR 33, 73; CP
   7; CPW; DAB; DAM POP; DLB 27;
   MTCW 1; RGEL 2
Lee, Lawrence 1941-1990 .... **CLC 34**
   See also CA 131; CANR 43
Lee, Li-Young 1957- .... **PC 24**
   See also CA 153; CP 7; DLB 165; PFS 11,
   15
Lee, Manfred B(ennington)
   1905-1971 .... **CLC 11**
   See also Queen, Ellery
   See also CA 1-4R; 29-32R; CANR 2; CMW
   4; DLB 137
Lee, Shelton Jackson 1957(?)- .... **CLC 105;**
   BLCS
   See also Lee, Spike
   See also BW 2, 3; CA 125; CANR 42;
   DAM MULT
Lee, Spike
   See Lee, Shelton Jackson
   See also AAYA 4, 29
Lee, Stan 1922- .... **CLC 17**
   See also AAYA 5; CA 108; 111; INT 111
Lee, Tanith 1947- .... **CLC 46**
   See also AAYA 15; CA 37-40R; CANR 53,
   102; DLB 261; FANT; SATA 8, 88; SFW
   4; SUFW; YAW
Lee, Vernon .... **TCLC 5; SSC 33**
   See also Paget, Violet
   See also DLB 57, 153, 156, 174, 178; GLL
   1; SUFW
Lee, William
   See Burroughs, William S(eward)
   See also GLL 1
Lee, Willy
   See Burroughs, William S(eward)
   See also GLL 1
Lee-Hamilton, Eugene (Jacob)
   1845-1907 .... **TCLC 22**
   See also CA 117
Leet, Judith 1935- .... **CLC 11**
   See also CA 187
Le Fanu, Joseph Sheridan
   1814-1873 .... **NCLC 9, 58; SSC 14**
   See also CMW 4; DA3; DAM POP; DLB
   21, 70, 159, 178; HGG; RGEL 2; RGSF
   2; SUFW
Leffland, Ella 1931- .... **CLC 19**
   See also CA 29-32R; CANR 35, 78, 82;
   DLBY 1984; INT CANR-35; SATA 65
Leger, Alexis
   See Leger, (Marie-Rene Auguste) Alexis
   Saint-Leger
Leger, (Marie-Rene Auguste) Alexis
   Saint-Leger 1887-1975 .. **CLC 4, 11, 46;**
   PC 23
   See also Perse, Saint-John; Saint-John Perse
   See also CA 13-16R; 61-64; CANR 43;
   DAM POET; MTCW 1
Leger, Saintleger
   See Leger, (Marie-Rene Auguste) Alexis
   Saint-Leger
Le Guin, Ursula K(roeber) 1929- ..... **CLC 8,**
   13, 22, 45, 71, 136; SSC 12
   See also AAYA 9, 27; AITN 1; BPFB 2;
   BYA 5, 8, 11, 14; CA 21-24R; CANR 9,
   32, 52, 74; CDALB 1968-1988; CLR 3,
   28; CN 7; CPW; DA3; DAB; DAC; DAM
   MST, POP; DLB 8, 52, 256; EXPS;
   FANT; FW; INT CANR-32; JRDA; LAIT
   5; MAICYA 1, 2; MTCW 1, 2; NFS 6, 9;
   SATA 4, 52, 99; SCFW; SFW 4; SSFS 2;
   SUFW; WYA; YAW

Lehmann, Rosamond (Nina)
   1901-1990 .... **CLC 5**
   See also CA 77-80; 131; CANR 8, 73; DLB
   15; MTCW 2; RGEL 2; RHW
Leiber, Fritz (Reuter, Jr.)
   1910-1992 .... **CLC 25**
   See also BPFB 2; CA 45-48; 139; CANR 2,
   40, 86; DLB 8; FANT; HGG; MTCW 1,
   2; SATA 45; SATA-Obit 73; SCFW 2;
   SFW 4; SUFW
Leibniz, Gottfried Wilhelm von
   1646-1716 .... **LC 35**
   See also DLB 168
Leimbach, Martha 1963-
   See Leimbach, Marti
   See also CA 130
Leimbach, Marti .... **CLC 65**
   See also Leimbach, Martha
Leino, Eino .... **TCLC 24**
   See also Loennbohm, Armas Eino Leopold
Leiris, Michel (Julien) 1901-1990 ..... **CLC 61**
   See also CA 119; 128; 132; GFL 1789 to
   the Present
Leithauser, Brad 1953- .... **CLC 27**
   See also CA 107; CANR 27, 81; CP 7; DLB
   120
Lelchuk, Alan 1938- .... **CLC 5**
   See also CA 45-48; CAAS 20; CANR 1,
   70; CN 7
Lem, Stanislaw 1921- ...... **CLC 8, 15, 40, 149**
   See also CA 105; CAAS 1; CANR 32;
   CWW 2; MTCW 1; SCFW 2; SFW 4
Lemann, Nancy 1956- .... **CLC 39**
   See also CA 118; 136
Lemonnier, (Antoine Louis) Camille
   1844-1913 .... **TCLC 22**
   See also CA 121
Lenau, Nikolaus 1802-1850 .... **NCLC 16**
L'Engle, Madeleine (Camp Franklin)
   1918- .... **CLC 12**
   See also AAYA 28; AITN 2; BPFB 2; BYA
   2, 4, 5, 7; CA 1-4R; CANR 3, 21, 39, 66,
   107; CLR 1, 14, 57; CPW; CWRI 5; DA3;
   DAM POP; DLB 52; JRDA; MAICYA 1,
   2; MTCW 1, 2; SAAS 15; SATA 1, 27,
   75, 128; SFW 4; WYA; YAW
Lengyel, Jozsef 1896-1975 .... **CLC 7**
   See also CA 85-88; 57-60; CANR 71;
   RGSF 2
Lenin 1870-1924
   See Lenin, V. I.
   See also CA 121; 168
Lenin, V. I. .... **TCLC 67**
   See also Lenin
Lennon, John (Ono) 1940-1980 .. **CLC 12, 35**
   See also CA 102; SATA 114
Lennox, Charlotte Ramsay
   1729(?)-1804 .... **NCLC 23**
   See also DLB 39; RGEL 2
Lentricchia, Frank, (Jr.) 1940- .... **CLC 34**
   See also CA 25-28R; CANR 19, 106; DLB
   246
Lenz, Gunter .... **CLC 65**
Lenz, Siegfried 1926- .... **CLC 27; SSC 33**
   See also CA 89-92; CANR 80; CWW 2;
   DLB 75; RGSF 2; RGWL 2
Leon, David
   See Jacob, (Cyprien-)Max
Leonard, Elmore (John, Jr.) 1925- . **CLC 28,**
   34, 71, 120
   See also AAYA 22; AITN 1; BEST 89:1,
   90:4; BPFB 2; CA 81-84; CANR 12, 28,
   53, 76, 96; CMW 4; CN 7; CPW; DA3;
   DAM POP; DLB 173, 226; INT CANR-
   28; MSW; MTCW 1, 2; RGAL 4; TCWW
   2
Leonard, Hugh .... **CLC 19**
   See also Byrne, John Keyes
   See also CBD; CD 5; DFS 13; DLB 13

Leonov, Leonid (Maximovich)
   1899-1994 .... **CLC 92**
   See also CA 129; CANR 74, 76; DAM
   NOV; MTCW 1, 2
Leopardi, (Conte) Giacomo
   1798-1837 .... **NCLC 22; PC 37**
   See also EW 5; RGWL 2; WP
Le Reveler
   See Artaud, Antonin (Marie Joseph)
Lerman, Eleanor 1952- .... **CLC 9**
   See also CA 85-88; CANR 69
Lerman, Rhoda 1936- .... **CLC 56**
   See also CA 49-52; CANR 70
Lermontov, Mikhail Iur'evich
   See Lermontov, Mikhail Yuryevich
   See also DLB 205
Lermontov, Mikhail Yuryevich
   1814-1841 .... **NCLC 5, 47; PC 18**
   See also Lermontov, Mikhail Iur'evich
   See also EW 6; RGWL 2; TWA
Leroux, Gaston 1868-1927 .... **TCLC 25**
   See also CA 108; 136; CANR 69; CMW 4;
   SATA 65
Lesage, Alain-Rene 1668-1747 .... **LC 2, 28**
   See also EW 3; GFL Beginnings to 1789;
   RGWL 2
Leskov, N(ikolai) S(emenovich) 1831-1895
   See Leskov, Nikolai (Semyonovich)
Leskov, Nikolai (Semyonovich)
   1831-1895 .... **NCLC 25; SSC 34**
   See also Leskov, Nikolai Semenovich
Leskov, Nikolai Semenovich
   See Leskov, Nikolai (Semyonovich)
   See also DLB 238
Lesser, Milton
   See Marlowe, Stephen
Lessing, Doris (May) 1919- ... **CLC 1, 2, 3, 6,**
   10, 15, 22, 40, 94; SSC 6; WLCS
   See also AFW; BRWS 1; CA 9-12R; CAAS
   14; CANR 33, 54, 76; CD 5; CDBLB
   1960 to Present; CN 7; DA; DA3; DAB;
   DAC; DAM MST, NOV; DLB 15, 139;
   DLBY 1985; EXPS; FW; LAIT 4; MTCW
   1, 2; RGEL 2; RGSF 2; SFW 4; SSFS 1,
   12; TEA; WLIT 2, 4
Lessing, Gotthold Ephraim 1729-1781 . **LC 8**
   See also CDWLB 2; DLB 97; EW 4; RGWL
   2
Lester, Richard 1932- .... **CLC 20**
Levenson, Jay .... **CLC 70**
Lever, Charles (James)
   1806-1872 .... **NCLC 23**
   See also DLB 21; RGEL 2
Leverson, Ada Esther
   1862(?)-1933(?) .... **TCLC 18**
   See also Elaine
   See also CA 117; 202; DLB 153; RGEL 2
Levertov, Denise 1923-1997 .. **CLC 1, 2, 3, 5,**
   8, 15, 28, 66; PC 11
   See also AMWS 3; CA 1-4R; 178; 163;
   CAAE 178; CAAS 19; CANR 3, 29, 50,
   108; CDALBS; CP 7; CWP; DAM POET;
   DLB 5, 165; EXPP; FW; INT CANR-29;
   MTCW 1, 2; PAB; PFS 7; RGAL 4; TUS;
   WP
Levi, Carlo 1902-1975 .... **TCLC 125**
   See also CA 65-68; 53-56; CANR 10;
   RGWL 2
Levi, Jonathan .... **CLC 76**
   See also CA 197
Levi, Peter (Chad Tigar)
   1931-2000 .... **CLC 41**
   See also CA 5-8R; 187; CANR 34, 80; CP
   7; DLB 40
Levi, Primo 1919-1987 . **CLC 37, 50; SSC 12**
   See also CA 13-16R; 122; CANR 12, 33,
   61, 70; DLB 177; MTCW 1, 2; RGWL 2;
   TCLC 109

Locke, John 1632-1704 .... **LC 7, 35**
  See also DLB 31, 101, 213, 252; RGEL 2;
  WLIT 3
Locke-Elliott, Sumner
  See Elliott, Sumner Locke
Lockhart, John Gibson 1794-1854 .. **NCLC 6**
  See also DLB 110, 116, 144
Lockridge, Ross (Franklin), Jr.
  1914-1948 .... **TCLC 111**
  See also CA 108; 145; CANR 79; DLB 143;
  DLBY 1980; RGAL 4; RHW
Lodge, David (John) 1935- .... **CLC 36, 141**
  See also BEST 90:1; BRWS 4; CA 17-20R;
  CANR 19, 53, 92; CN 7; CPW; DAM
  POP; DLB 14, 194; INT CANR-19;
  MTCW 1, 2
Lodge, Thomas 1558-1625 .... **LC 41**
  See also DLB 172; RGEL 2
Loewinsohn, Ron(ald William)
  1937- .... **CLC 52**
  See also CA 25-28R; CANR 71
Logan, Jake
  See Smith, Martin Cruz
Logan, John (Burton) 1923-1987 .... **CLC 5**
  See also CA 77-80; 124; CANR 45; DLB 5
Lo Kuan-chung 1330(?)-1400(?) .... **LC 12**
Lombard, Nap
  See Johnson, Pamela Hansford
Lomotey (editor), Kofi .... **CLC 70**
London, Jack 1876-1916 ..... **TCLC 9, 15, 39;**
  SSC 4, 49; WLC
  See also London, John Griffith
  See also AAYA 13; AITN 2; AMW; BPFB
  2; BYA 4, 13; CDALB 1865-1917; DLB
  8, 12, 78, 212; EXPS; LAIT 3; NFS 8;
  RGAL 4; RGSF 2; SATA 18; SFW 4;
  SSFS 7; TCWW 2; TUS; WYA; YAW
London, John Griffith 1876-1916
  See London, Jack
  See also CA 110; 119; CANR 73; DA; DA3;
  DAB; DAC; DAM MST, NOV; JRDA;
  MAICYA 1, 2; MTCW 1, 2
Long, Emmett
  See Leonard, Elmore (John, Jr.)
Longbaugh, Harry
  See Goldman, William (W.)
Longfellow, Henry Wadsworth
  1807-1882 .... **NCLC 2, 45, 101, 103; PC**
  30; WLCS
  See also AMW; CDALB 1640-1865; DA;
  DA3; DAB; DAC; DAM MST, POET;
  DLB 1, 59, 235; EXPP; PAB; PFS 2, 7;
  RGAL 4; SATA 19; TUS; WP
Longinus c. 1st cent. - .... **CMLC 27**
  See also AW 2; DLB 176
Longley, Michael 1939- .... **CLC 29**
  See also BRWS 8; CA 102; CP 7; DLB 40
Longus fl. c. 2nd cent. - .... **CMLC 7**
Longway, A. Hugh
  See Lang, Andrew
Lonnrot, Elias 1802-1884 .... **NCLC 53**
  See also EFS 1
Lonsdale, Roger ed. .... **CLC 65**
Lopate, Phillip 1943- .... **CLC 29**
  See also CA 97-100; CANR 88; DLBY
  1980; INT 97-100
Lopez, Barry (Holstun) 1945- .... **CLC 70**
  See also AAYA 9; ANW; CA 65-68; CANR
  7, 23, 47, 68, 92; DLB 256; INT CANR-7,
  -23; MTCW 1; RGAL 4; SATA 67
Lopez Portillo (y Pacheco), Jose
  1920- .... **CLC 46**
  See also CA 129; HW 1
Lopez y Fuentes, Gregorio
  1897(?)-1966 .... **CLC 32**
  See also CA 131; HW 1
Lorca, Federico Garcia
  See Garcia Lorca, Federico
  See also DFS 4; EW 11; RGWL 2; WP

Lord, Bette Bao 1938- .... **CLC 23; AAL**
  See also BEST 90:3; BPFB 2; CA 107;
  CANR 41, 79; INT CA-107; SATA 58
Lord Auch
  See Bataille, Georges
Lord Brooke
  See Greville, Fulke
Lord Byron
  See Byron, George Gordon (Noel)
Lorde, Audre (Geraldine)
  1934-1992 .. **CLC 18, 71; BLC 2; PC 12**
  See also Domini, Rey
  See also AFAW 1, 2; BW 1, 3; CA 25-28R;
  142; CANR 16, 26, 46, 82; DA3; DAM
  MULT, POET; DLB 41; FW; MTCW 1,
  2; RGAL 4
Lord Houghton
  See Milnes, Richard Monckton
Lord Jeffrey
  See Jeffrey, Francis
Loreaux, Nichol .... **CLC 65**
Lorenzini, Carlo 1826-1890
  See Collodi, Carlo
  See also MAICYA 1, 2; SATA 29, 100
Lorenzo, Heberto Padilla
  See Padilla (Lorenzo), Heberto
Loris
  See Hofmannsthal, Hugo von
Loti, Pierre .... **TCLC 11**
  See also Viaud, (Louis Marie) Julien
  See also DLB 123; GFL 1789 to the Present
Lou, Henri
  See Andreas-Salome, Lou
Louie, David Wong 1954- .... **CLC 70**
  See also CA 139
Louis, Father M.
  See Merton, Thomas
Lovecraft, H(oward) P(hillips)
  1890-1937 .... **TCLC 4, 22; SSC 3, 52**
  See also AAYA 14; BPFB 2; CA 104; 133;
  CANR 106; DA3; DAM POP; HGG;
  MTCW 1, 2; RGAL 4; SCFW; SFW 4;
  SUFW
Lovelace, Earl 1935- .... **CLC 51**
  See also BW 2; CA 77-80; CANR 41, 72;
  CD 5; CDWLB 3; CN 7; DLB 125;
  MTCW 1
Lovelace, Richard 1618-1657 .... **LC 24**
  See also BRW 2; DLB 131; EXPP; PAB;
  RGEL 2
Lowell, Amy 1874-1925 ... **TCLC 1, 8; PC 13**
  See also AMW; CA 104; 151; DAM POET;
  DLB 54, 140; EXPP; MAWW; MTCW 2;
  RGAL 4; TUS
Lowell, James Russell 1819-1891 ... **NCLC 2,**
  90
  See also AMWS 1; CDALB 1640-1865;
  DLB 1, 11, 64, 79, 189, 235; RGAL 4
Lowell, Robert (Traill Spence, Jr.)
  1917-1977 .... **CLC 1, 2, 3, 4, 5, 8, 9, 11,**
  15, 37, 124; PC 3; WLC
  See also AMW; CA 9-12R; 73-76; CABS
  2; CANR 26, 60; CDALBS; DA; DA3;
  DAB; DAC; DAM MST, NOV; DLB 5,
  169; MTCW 1, 2; PAB; PFS 6, 7; RGAL
  4; WP
Lowenthal, Michael (Francis)
  1969- .... **CLC 119**
  See also CA 150
Lowndes, Marie Adelaide (Belloc)
  1868-1947 .... **TCLC 12**
  See also CA 107; CMW 4; DLB 70; RHW
Lowry, (Clarence) Malcolm
  1909-1957 .... **TCLC 6, 40; SSC 31**
  See also BPFB 2; BRWS 3; CA 105; 131;
  CANR 62, 105; CDBLB 1945-1960; DLB
  15; MTCW 1, 2; RGEL 2

Lowry, Mina Gertrude 1882-1966
  See Loy, Mina
  See also CA 113
Loxsmith, John
  See Brunner, John (Kilian Houston)
Loy, Mina .... **CLC 28; PC 16**
  See also Lowry, Mina Gertrude
  See also DAM POET; DLB 4, 54
Loyson-Bridet
  See Schwob, Marcel (Mayer Andre)
Lucan 39-65 .... **CMLC 33**
  See also AW 2; DLB 211; EFS 2; RGWL 2
Lucas, Craig 1951- .... **CLC 64**
  See also CA 137; CAD; CANR 71, 109;
  CD 5; GLL 2
Lucas, E(dward) V(errall)
  1868-1938 .... **TCLC 73**
  See also CA 176; DLB 98, 149, 153; SATA
  20
Lucas, George 1944- .... **CLC 16**
  See also AAYA 1, 23; CA 77-80; CANR
  30; SATA 56
Lucas, Hans
  See Godard, Jean-Luc
Lucas, Victoria
  See Plath, Sylvia
Lucian c. 125-c. 180 .... **CMLC 32**
  See also AW 2; DLB 176; RGWL 2
Lucretius c. 94 B.C.-c. 49 B.C. ..... **CMLC 48**
  See also AW 2; CDWLB 1; DLB 211; EFS
  2; RGWL 2
Ludlam, Charles 1943-1987 .... **CLC 46, 50**
  See also CA 85-88; 122; CAD; CANR 72,
  86; DLB 266
Ludlum, Robert 1927-2001 .... **CLC 22, 43**
  See also AAYA 10; BEST 89:1, 90:3; BPFB
  2; CA 33-36R; 195; CANR 25, 41, 68,
  105; CMW 4; CPW; DA3; DAM NOV,
  POP; DLBY 1982; MSW; MTCW 1, 2
Ludwig, Ken .... **CLC 60**
  See also CA 195; CAD
Ludwig, Otto 1813-1865 .... **NCLC 4**
  See also DLB 129
Lugones, Leopoldo 1874-1938 ...... **TCLC 15;**
  HLCS 2
  See also CA 116; 131; CANR 104; HW 1;
  LAW
Lu Hsun .... **TCLC 3; SSC 20**
  See also Shu-Jen, Chou
Lukacs, George .... **CLC 24**
  See also Lukacs, Gyorgy (Szegeny von)
Lukacs, Gyorgy (Szegeny von) 1885-1971
  See Lukacs, George
  See also CA 101; 29-32R; CANR 62; CD-
  WLB 4; DLB 215, 242; EW 10; MTCW
  2
Luke, Peter (Ambrose Cyprian)
  1919-1995 .... **CLC 38**
  See also CA 81-84; 147; CANR 72; CBD;
  CD 5; DLB 13
Lunar, Dennis
  See Mungo, Raymond
Lurie, Alison 1926- .... **CLC 4, 5, 18, 39**
  See also BPFB 2; CA 1-4R; CANR 2, 17,
  50, 88; CN 7; DLB 2; MTCW 1; SATA
  46, 112
Lustig, Arnost 1926- .... **CLC 56**
  See also AAYA 3; CA 69-72; CANR 47,
  102; CWW 2; DLB 232; SATA 56
Luther, Martin 1483-1546 .... **LC 9, 37**
  See also CDWLB 2; DLB 179; EW 2;
  RGWL 2
Luxemburg, Rosa 1870(?)-1919 ..... **TCLC 63**
  See also CA 118
Luzi, Mario 1914- .... **CLC 13**
  See also CA 61-64; CANR 9, 70; CWW 2;
  DLB 128

Author Index

Maiakovskii, Vladimir
See Mayakovski, Vladimir (Vladimirovich)
See also IDTP; RGWL 2

Mailer, Norman 1923- ... **CLC 1, 2, 3, 4, 5, 8, 11, 14, 28, 39, 74, 111**
See also AAYA 31; AITN 2; AMW; BPFB 2; CA 9-12R; CABS 1; CANR 28, 74, 77; CDALB 1968-1988; CN 7; CPW; DA; DA3; DAB; DAC; DAM MST, NOV, POP; DLB 2, 16, 28, 185; DLBD 3; DLBY 1980, 1983; MTCW 1, 2; NFS 10; RGAL 4; TUS

Maillet, Antonine 1929- .... **CLC 54, 118**
See also CA 115; 120; CANR 46, 74, 77; CCA 1; CWW 2; DAC; DLB 60; INT 120; MTCW 2

Mais, Roger 1905-1955 .... **TCLC 8**
See also BW 1, 3; CA 105; 124; CANR 82; CDWLB 3; DLB 125; MTCW 1; RGEL 2

Maistre, Joseph 1753-1821 .... **NCLC 37**
See also GFL 1789 to the Present

Maitland, Frederic William
1850-1906 .... **TCLC 65**

Maitland, Sara (Louise) 1950- .... **CLC 49**
See also CA 69-72; CANR 13, 59; FW

Major, Clarence 1936- . **CLC 3, 19, 48; BLC 2**
See also AFAW 2; BW 2, 3; CA 21-24R; CAAS 6; CANR 13, 25, 53, 82; CN 7; CP 7; CSW; DAM MULT; DLB 33; MSW

Major, Kevin (Gerald) 1949- .... **CLC 26**
See also AAYA 16; CA 97-100; CANR 21, 38; CLR 11; DAC; DLB 60; INT CANR-21; JRDA; MAICYA 1, 2; MAICYAS 1; SATA 32, 82; WYA; YAW

Maki, James
See Ozu, Yasujiro

Malabaila, Damiano
See Levi, Primo

Malamud, Bernard 1914-1986 .. **CLC 1, 2, 3, 5, 8, 9, 11, 18, 27, 44, 78, 85; SSC 15; WLC**
See also AAYA 16; AMWS 1; BPFB 2; CA 5-8R; 118; CABS 1; CANR 28, 62; CDALB 1941-1968; CPW; DA; DA3; DAB; DAC; DAM MST, NOV, POP; DLB 2, 28, 152; DLBY 1980, 1986; EXPS; LAIT 4; MTCW 1, 2; NFS 4, 9; RGAL 4; RGSF 2; SSFS 8, 13; TUS

Malan, Herman
See Bosman, Herman Charles; Bosman, Herman Charles

Malaparte, Curzio 1898-1957 .... **TCLC 52**
See also DLB 264

Malcolm, Dan
See Silverberg, Robert

Malcolm X .... **CLC 82, 117; BLC 2; WLCS**
See also Little, Malcolm
See also LAIT 5

Malherbe, Francois de 1555-1628 .... **LC 5**
See also GFL Beginnings to 1789

Mallarme, Stephane 1842-1898 ...... **NCLC 4, 41; PC 4**
See also DAM POET; DLB 217; EW 7; GFL 1789 to the Present; RGWL 2; TWA

Mallet-Joris, Francoise 1930- .... **CLC 11**
See also CA 65-68; CANR 17; DLB 83; GFL 1789 to the Present

Malley, Ern
See McAuley, James Phillip

Mallowan, Agatha Christie
See Christie, Agatha (Mary Clarissa)

Maloff, Saul 1922- .... **CLC 5**
See also CA 33-36R

Malone, Louis
See MacNeice, (Frederick) Louis

Malone, Michael (Christopher)
1942- .... **CLC 43**
See also CA 77-80; CANR 14, 32, 57

Malory, Sir Thomas 1410(?)-1471(?) . **LC 11; WLCS**
See also BRW 1; BRWR 2; CDBLB Before 1660; DA; DAB; DAC; DAM MST; DLB 146; EFS 2; RGEL 2; SATA 59; SATA-Brief 33; TEA; WLIT 3

Malouf, (George Joseph) David
1934- .... **CLC 28, 86**
See also CA 124; CANR 50, 76; CN 7; CP 7; MTCW 2

Malraux, (Georges-)Andre
1901-1976 .... **CLC 1, 4, 9, 13, 15, 57**
See also BPFB 2; CA 21-22; 69-72; CANR 34, 58; CAP 2; DA3; DAM NOV; DLB 72; EW 12; GFL 1789 to the Present; MTCW 1, 2; RGWL 2; TWA

Malzberg, Barry N(athaniel) 1939- ... **CLC 7**
See also CA 61-64; CAAS 4; CANR 16; CMW 4; DLB 8; SFW 4

Mamet, David (Alan) 1947- .. **CLC 9, 15, 34, 46, 91; DC 4**
See also AAYA 3; CA 81-84; CABS 3; CANR 15, 41, 67, 72; CD 5; DA3; DAM DRAM; DFS 15; DLB 7; IDFW 4; MTCW 1, 2; RGAL 4

Mamoulian, Rouben (Zachary)
1897-1987 .... **CLC 16**
See also CA 25-28R; 124; CANR 85

Mandelshtam, Osip
See Mandelstam, Osip (Emilievich)
See also EW 10; RGWL 2

Mandelstam, Osip (Emilievich)
1891(?)-1943(?) .... **TCLC 2, 6; PC 14**
See also Mandelshtam, Osip
See also CA 104; 150; MTCW 2; TWA

Mander, (Mary) Jane 1877-1949 ... **TCLC 31**
See also CA 162; RGEL 2

Mandeville, Sir John fl. 1350- ...... **CMLC 19**
See also DLB 146

Mandiargues, Andre Pieyre de .... **CLC 41**
See also Pieyre de Mandiargues, Andre
See also DLB 83

Mandrake, Ethel Belle
See Thurman, Wallace (Henry)

Mangan, James Clarence
1803-1849 .... **NCLC 27**
See also RGEL 2

Maniere, J.-E.
See Giraudoux, Jean(-Hippolyte)

Mankiewicz, Herman (Jacob)
1897-1953 .... **TCLC 85**
See also CA 120; 169; DLB 26; IDFW 3, 4

Manley, (Mary) Delariviere
1672(?)-1724 .... **LC 1, 42**
See also DLB 39, 80; RGEL 2

Mann, Abel
See Creasey, John

Mann, Emily 1952- .... **DC 7**
See also CA 130; CAD; CANR 55; CD 5; CWD; DLB 266

Mann, (Luiz) Heinrich 1871-1950 ... **TCLC 9**
See also CA 106; 164, 181; DLB 66, 118; EW 8; RGWL 2

Mann, (Paul) Thomas 1875-1955 ... **TCLC 2, 8, 14, 21, 35, 44, 60; SSC 5; WLC**
See also BPFB 2; CA 104; 128; CDWLB 2; DA; DA3; DAB; DAC; DAM MST, NOV; DLB 66; EW 9; GLL 1; MTCW 1, 2; RGSF 2; RGWL 2; SSFS 4, 9; TWA

Mannheim, Karl 1893-1947 .... **TCLC 65**

Manning, David
See Faust, Frederick (Schiller)
See also TCWW 2

Manning, Frederic 1887(?)-1935 ... **TCLC 25**
See also CA 124; DLB 260

Manning, Olivia 1915-1980 .... **CLC 5, 19**
See also CA 5-8R; 101; CANR 29; FW; MTCW 1; RGEL 2

Mano, D. Keith 1942- .... **CLC 2, 10**
See also CA 25-28R; CAAS 6; CANR 26, 57; DLB 6

Mansfield, Katherine ... **TCLC 2, 8, 39; SSC 9, 23, 38; WLC**
See also Beauchamp, Kathleen Mansfield
See also BPFB 2; BRW 7; DAB; DLB 162; EXPS; FW; GLL 1; RGEL 2; RGSF 2; SSFS 2, 8, 10, 11

Manso, Peter 1940- .... **CLC 39**
See also CA 29-32R; CANR 44

Mantecon, Juan Jimenez
See Jimenez (Mantecon), Juan Ramon

Mantel, Hilary (Mary) 1952- .... **CLC 144**
See also CA 125; CANR 54, 101; CN 7; RHW

Manton, Peter
See Creasey, John

Man Without a Spleen, A
See Chekhov, Anton (Pavlovich)

Manzoni, Alessandro 1785-1873 ... **NCLC 29, 98**
See also EW 5; RGWL 2; TWA

Map, Walter 1140-1209 .... **CMLC 32**

Mapu, Abraham (ben Jekutiel)
1808-1867 .... **NCLC 18**

Mara, Sally
See Queneau, Raymond

Marat, Jean Paul 1743-1793 .... **LC 10**

Marcel, Gabriel Honore 1889-1973 . **CLC 15**
See also CA 102; 45-48; MTCW 1, 2

March, William 1893-1954 .... **TCLC 96**

Marchbanks, Samuel
See Davies, (William) Robertson
See also CCA 1

Marchi, Giacomo
See Bassani, Giorgio

Marcus Aurelius
See Aurelius, Marcus
See also AW 2

Marguerite
See de Navarre, Marguerite

Marguerite d'Angouleme
See de Navarre, Marguerite
See also GFL Beginnings to 1789

Marguerite de Navarre
See de Navarre, Marguerite
See also RGWL 2

Margulies, Donald 1954- .... **CLC 76**
See also CA 200; DFS 13; DLB 228

Marie de France c. 12th cent. - ..... **CMLC 8; PC 22**
See also DLB 208; FW; RGWL 2

Marie de l'Incarnation 1599-1672 ...... **LC 10**

Marier, Captain Victor
See Griffith, D(avid Lewelyn) W(ark)

Mariner, Scott
See Pohl, Frederik

Marinetti, Filippo Tommaso
1876-1944 .... **TCLC 10**
See also CA 107; DLB 114, 264; EW 9

Marivaux, Pierre Carlet de Chamblain de
1688-1763 .... **LC 4; DC 7**
See also GFL Beginnings to 1789; RGWL 2; TWA

Markandaya, Kamala .... **CLC 8, 38**
See also Taylor, Kamala (Purnaiya)
See also BYA 13; CN 7

Markfield, Wallace 1926- .... **CLC 8**
See also CA 69-72; CAAS 3; CN 7; DLB 2, 28

Markham, Edwin 1852-1940 .... **TCLC 47**
See also CA 160; DLB 54, 186; RGAL 4

Markham, Robert
See Amis, Kingsley (William)

Marks, J
See Highwater, Jamake (Mamake)

Maugham, W. S.
 See Maugham, W(illiam) Somerset
Maugham, W(illiam) Somerset
 1874-1965 .. **CLC 1, 11, 15, 67, 93; SSC 8; WLC**
 See also BPFB 2; BRW 6; CA 5-8R; 25-28R; CANR 40; CDBLB 1914-1945; CMW 4; DA; DA3; DAB; DAC; DAM DRAM, MST, NOV; DLB 10, 36, 77, 100, 162, 195; LAIT 3; MTCW 1, 2; RGEL 2; RGSF 2; SATA 54
Maugham, William Somerset
 See Maugham, W(illiam) Somerset
Maupassant, (Henri Rene Albert) Guy de
 1850-1893 .... **NCLC 1, 42, 83; SSC 1; WLC**
 See also BYA 14; DA; DA3; DAB; DAC; DAM MST; DLB 123; EW 7; EXPS; GFL 1789 to the Present; LAIT 2; RGSF 2; RGWL 2; SSFS 4; SUFW; TWA
Maupin, Armistead (Jones, Jr.)
 1944- .... **CLC 95**
 See also CA 125; 130; CANR 58, 101; CPW; DA3; DAM POP; GLL 1; INT 130; MTCW 2
Maurhut, Richard
 See Traven, B.
Mauriac, Claude 1914-1996 .... **CLC 9**
 See also CA 89-92; 152; CWW 2; DLB 83; GFL 1789 to the Present
Mauriac, Francois (Charles)
 1885-1970 .... **CLC 4, 9, 56; SSC 24**
 See also CA 25-28; CAP 2; DLB 65; EW 10; GFL 1789 to the Present; MTCW 1, 2; RGWL 2; TWA
Mavor, Osborne Henry 1888-1951
 See Bridie, James
 See also CA 104
Maxwell, William (Keepers, Jr.)
 1908-2000 .... **CLC 19**
 See also AMWS 8; CA 93-96; 189; CANR 54, 95; CN 7; DLB 218; DLBY 1980; INT CA-93-96; SATA-Obit 128
May, Elaine 1932- .... **CLC 16**
 See also CA 124; 142; CAD; CWD; DLB 44
Mayakovski, Vladimir (Vladimirovich)
 1893-1930 .... **TCLC 4, 18**
 See also Maiakovskii, Vladimir; Mayak-ovsky, Vladimir
 See also CA 104; 158; MTCW 2; SFW 4; TWA
Mayakovsky, Vladimir
 See Mayakovski, Vladimir (Vladimirovich)
 See also EW 11; WP
Mayhew, Henry 1812-1887 .... **NCLC 31**
 See also DLB 18, 55, 190
Mayle, Peter 1939(?)- .... **CLC 89**
 See also CA 139; CANR 64, 109
Maynard, Joyce 1953- .... **CLC 23**
 See also CA 111; 129; CANR 64
Mayne, William (James Carter)
 1928- .... **CLC 12**
 See also AAYA 20; CA 9-12R; CANR 37, 80, 100; CLR 25; FANT; JRDA; MAI-CYA 1, 2; MAICYAS 1; SAAS 11; SATA 6, 68, 122; YAW
Mayo, Jim
 See L'Amour, Louis (Dearborn)
 See also TCWW 2
Maysles, Albert 1926- .... **CLC 16**
 See also CA 29-32R
Maysles, David 1932-1987 .... **CLC 16**
 See also CA 191
Mazer, Norma Fox 1931- .... **CLC 26**
 See also AAYA 5, 36; BYA 1, 8; CA 69-72; CANR 12, 32, 66; CLR 23; JRDA; MAI-CYA 1, 2; SAAS 1; SATA 24, 67, 105; WYA; YAW

Mazzini, Guiseppe 1805-1872 .... **NCLC 34**
McAlmon, Robert (Menzies)
 1895-1956 .... **TCLC 97**
 See also CA 107; 168; DLB 4, 45; DLBD 15; GLL 1
McAuley, James Phillip 1917-1976 .. **CLC 45**
 See also CA 97-100; DLB 260; RGEL 2
McBain, Ed
 See Hunter, Evan
 See also MSW
McBrien, William (Augustine)
 1930- .... **CLC 44**
 See also CA 107; CANR 90
McCabe, Patrick 1955- .... **CLC 133**
 See also CA 130; CANR 50, 90; CN 7; DLB 194
McCaffrey, Anne (Inez) 1926- .... **CLC 17**
 See also AAYA 6, 34; AITN 2; BEST 89:2; BPFB 2; BYA 5; CA 25-28R; CANR 15, 35, 55, 96; CLR 49; CPW; DA3; DAM NOV, POP; DLB 8; JRDA; MAICYA 1, 2; MTCW 1, 2; SAAS 11; SATA 8, 70, 116; SFW 4; WYA; YAW
McCall, Nathan 1955(?)- .... **CLC 86**
 See also BW 3; CA 146; CANR 88
McCann, Arthur
 See Campbell, John W(ood, Jr.)
McCann, Edson
 See Pohl, Frederik
McCarthy, Charles, Jr. 1933-
 See McCarthy, Cormac
 See also CANR 42, 69, 101; CN 7; CPW; CSW; DA3; DAM POP; MTCW 2
McCarthy, Cormac .... **CLC 4, 57, 59, 101**
 See also McCarthy, Charles, Jr.
 See also AAYA 41; AMWS 8; BPFB 2; CA 13-16R; CANR 10; DLB 6, 143, 256; TCWW 2
McCarthy, Mary (Therese)
 1912-1989 .. **CLC 1, 3, 5, 14, 24, 39, 59; SSC 24**
 See also AMW; BPFB 2; CA 5-8R; 129; CANR 16, 50, 64; DA3; DLB 2; DLBY 1981; FW; INT CANR-16; MAWW; MTCW 1, 2; RGAL 4; TUS
McCartney, (James) Paul 1942- . **CLC 12, 35**
 See also CA 146
McCauley, Stephen (D.) 1955- .... **CLC 50**
 See also CA 141
McClaren, Peter .... **CLC 70**
McClure, Michael (Thomas) 1932- ... **CLC 6, 10**
 See also CA 21-24R; CAD; CANR 17, 46, 77; CD 5; CP 7; DLB 16; WP
McCorkle, Jill (Collins) 1958- .... **CLC 51**
 See also CA 121; CSW; DLB 234; DLBY 1987
McCourt, Frank 1930- .... **CLC 109**
 See also CA 157; CANR 97; NCFS 1
McCourt, James 1941- .... **CLC 5**
 See also CA 57-60; CANR 98
McCourt, Malachy 1932- .... **CLC 119**
 See also SATA 126
McCoy, Horace (Stanley)
 1897-1955 .... **TCLC 28**
 See also CA 108; 155; CMW 4; DLB 9
McCrae, John 1872-1918 .... **TCLC 12**
 See also CA 109; DLB 92; PFS 5
McCreigh, James
 See Pohl, Frederik
McCullers, (Lula) Carson (Smith)
 1917-1967 .... **CLC 1, 4, 10, 12, 48, 100; SSC 9, 24; WLC**
 See also AAYA 21; AMW; BPFB 2; CA 5-8R; 25-28R; CABS 1, 3; CANR 18; CDALB 1941-1968; DA; DA3; DAB; DAC; DAM MST, NOV; DFS 5; DLB 2,

7, 173, 228; EXPS; FW; GLL 1; LAIT 3, 4; MAWW; MTCW 1, 2; NFS 6, 13; RGAL 4; RGSF 2; SATA 27; SSFS 5; TUS; YAW
McCulloch, John Tyler
 See Burroughs, Edgar Rice
McCullough, Colleen 1938(?)- .. **CLC 27, 107**
 See also AAYA 36; BPFB 2; CA 81-84; CANR 17, 46, 67, 98; CPW; DA3; DAM NOV, POP; MTCW 1, 2; RHW
McDermott, Alice 1953- .... **CLC 90**
 See also CA 109; CANR 40, 90
McElroy, Joseph 1930- .... **CLC 5, 47**
 See also CA 17-20R; CN 7
McEwan, Ian (Russell) 1948- ..... **CLC 13, 66**
 See also BEST 90:4; BRWS 4; CA 61-64; CANR 14, 41, 69, 87; CN 7; DAM NOV; DLB 14, 194; HGG; MTCW 1, 2; RGSF 2; TEA
McFadden, David 1940- .... **CLC 48**
 See also CA 104; CP 7; DLB 60; INT 104
McFarland, Dennis 1950- .... **CLC 65**
 See also CA 165; CANR 110
McGahern, John 1934- ... **CLC 5, 9, 48, 156; SSC 17**
 See also CA 17-20R; CANR 29, 68; CN 7; DLB 14, 231; MTCW 1
McGinley, Patrick (Anthony) 1937- . **CLC 41**
 See also CA 120; 127; CANR 56; INT 127
McGinley, Phyllis 1905-1978 .... **CLC 14**
 See also CA 9-12R; 77-80; CANR 19; CWRI 5; DLB 11, 48; PFS 9, 13; SATA 2, 44; SATA-Obit 24
McGinniss, Joe 1942- .... **CLC 32**
 See also AITN 2; BEST 89:2; CA 25-28R; CANR 26, 70; CPW; DLB 185; INT CANR-26
McGivern, Maureen Daly
 See Daly, Maureen
McGrath, Patrick 1950- .... **CLC 55**
 See also CA 136; CANR 65; CN 7; DLB 231; HGG
McGrath, Thomas (Matthew)
 1916-1990 .... **CLC 28, 59**
 See also AMWS 10; CA 9-12R; 132; CANR 6, 33, 95; DAM POET; MTCW 1; SATA 41; SATA-Obit 66
McGuane, Thomas (Francis III)
 1939- .... **CLC 3, 7, 18, 45, 127**
 See also AITN 2; BPFB 2; CA 49-52; CANR 5, 24, 49, 94; CN 7; DLB 2, 212; DLBY 1980; INT CANR-24; MTCW 1; TCWW 2
McGuckian, Medbh 1950- ... **CLC 48; PC 27**
 See also BRWS 5; CA 143; CP 7; CWP; DAM POET; DLB 40
McHale, Tom 1942(?)-1982 .... **CLC 3, 5**
 See also AITN 1; CA 77-80; 106
McIlvanney, William 1936- .... **CLC 42**
 See also CA 25-28R; CANR 61; CMW 4; DLB 14, 207
McIlwraith, Maureen Mollie Hunter
 See Hunter, Mollie
 See also SATA 2
McInerney, Jay 1955- .... **CLC 34, 112**
 See also AAYA 18; BPFB 2; CA 116; 123; CANR 45, 68; CN 7; CPW; DA3; DAM POP; INT 123; MTCW 2
McIntyre, Vonda N(eel) 1948- .... **CLC 18**
 See also CA 81-84; CANR 17, 34, 69; MTCW 1; SFW 4; YAW
McKay, Claude .... **TCLC 7, 41; BLC 3; PC 2; WLC**
 See also McKay, Festus Claudius
 See also AFAW 1, 2; AMWS 10; DAB; DLB 4, 45, 51, 117; EXPP; GLL 2; LAIT 3; PAB; PFS 4; RGAL 4; WP

Middleton, Stanley 1919- .... **CLC 7, 38**
See also CA 25-28R; CAAS 23; CANR 21, 46, 81; CN 7; DLB 14

Middleton, Thomas 1580-1627 .... **LC 33; DC 5**
See also BRW 2; DAM DRAM, MST; DLB 58; RGEL 2

Migueis, Jose Rodrigues 1901- .... **CLC 10**

Mikszath, Kalman 1847-1910 .... **TCLC 31**
See also CA 170

Miles, Jack .... **CLC 100**
See also CA 200

Miles, John Russiano
See Miles, Jack

Miles, Josephine (Louise)
1911-1985 .... **CLC 1, 2, 14, 34, 39**
See also CA 1-4R; 116; CANR 2, 55; DAM POET; DLB 48

Militant
See Sandburg, Carl (August)

Mill, Harriet (Hardy) Taylor
1807-1858 .... **NCLC 102**
See also FW

Mill, John Stuart 1806-1873 .... **NCLC 11, 58**
See also CDBLB 1832-1890; DLB 55, 190, 262; FW 1; RGEL 2; TEA

Millar, Kenneth 1915-1983 .... **CLC 14**
See also Macdonald, Ross
See also CA 9-12R; 110; CANR 16, 63, 107; CMW 4; CPW; DA3; DAM POP; DLB 2, 226; DLBD 6; DLBY 1983; MTCW 1, 2

Millay, E. Vincent
See Millay, Edna St. Vincent

Millay, Edna St. Vincent
1892-1950 ... **TCLC 4, 49; PC 6; WLCS**
See also Boyd, Nancy
See also AMW; CA 104; 130; CDALB 1917-1929; DA; DA3; DAB; DAC; DAM MST, POET; DLB 45, 249; EXPP; MAWW; MTCW 1, 2; PAB; PFS 3; RGAL 4; TUS; WP

Miller, Arthur 1915- ...... **CLC 1, 2, 6, 10, 15, 26, 47, 78; DC 1; WLC**
See also AAYA 15; AITN 1; AMW; CA 1-4R; CABS 3; CAD; CANR 2, 30, 54, 76; CD 5; CDALB 1941-1968; DA; DA3; DAB; DAC; DAM DRAM, MST; DFS 1, 3; DLB 7, 266; LAIT 1, 4; MTCW 1, 2; RGAL 4; TUS; WYAS 1

Miller, Henry (Valentine)
1891-1980 .... **CLC 1, 2, 4, 9, 14, 43, 84; WLC**
See also AMW; BPFB 2; CA 9-12R; 97-100; CANR 33, 64; CDALB 1929-1941; DA; DA3; DAB; DAC; DAM MST, NOV; DLB 4, 9; DLBY 1980; MTCW 1, 2; RGAL 4; TUS

Miller, Jason 1939(?)-2001 .... **CLC 2**
See also AITN 1; CA 73-76; 197; CAD; DFS 12; DLB 7

Miller, Sue 1943- .... **CLC 44**
See also BEST 90:3; CA 139; CANR 59, 91; DA3; DAM POP; DLB 143

Miller, Walter M(ichael, Jr.)
1923-1996 .... **CLC 4, 30**
See also BPFB 2; CA 85-88; CANR 108; DLB 8; SCFW; SFW 4

Millett, Kate 1934- .... **CLC 67**
See also AITN 1; CA 73-76; CANR 32, 53, 76; DA3; DLB 246; FW; GLL 1; MTCW 1, 2

Millhauser, Steven (Lewis) 1943- .... **CLC 21, 54, 109**
See also CA 110; 111; CANR 63; CN 7; DA3; DLB 2; FANT; INT CA-111; MTCW 2

Millin, Sarah Gertrude 1889-1968 ... **CLC 49**
See also CA 102; 93-96; DLB 225

Milne, A(lan) A(lexander)
1882-1956 .... **TCLC 6, 88**
See also BRWS 5; CA 104; 133; CLR 1, 26; CMW 4; CWRI 5; DA3; DAB; DAC; DAM MST; DLB 10, 77, 100, 160; FANT; MAICYA 1, 2; MTCW 1, 2; RGEL 2; SATA 100; WCH; YABC 1

Milner, Ron(ald) 1938- .... **CLC 56; BLC 3**
See also AITN 1; BW 1; CA 73-76; CAD; CANR 24, 81; CD 5; DAM MULT; DLB 38; MTCW 1

Milnes, Richard Monckton
1809-1885 .... **NCLC 61**
See also DLB 32, 184

Milosz, Czeslaw 1911- ...... **CLC 5, 11, 22, 31, 56, 82; PC 8; WLCS**
See also CA 81-84; CANR 23, 51, 91; CDWLB 4; CWW 2; DA3; DAM MST, POET; DLB 215; EW 13; MTCW 1, 2; RGWL 2

Milton, John 1608-1674 ..... **LC 9, 43; PC 19, 29; WLC**
See also BRW 2; BRWR 2; CDBLB 1660-1789; DA; DA3; DAB; DAC; DAM MST, POET; DLB 131, 151; EFS 1; EXPP; LAIT 1; PAB; PFS 3; RGEL 2; TEA; WLIT 3; WP

Min, Anchee 1957- .... **CLC 86**
See also CA 146; CANR 94

Minehaha, Cornelius
See Wedekind, (Benjamin) Frank(lin)

Miner, Valerie 1947- .... **CLC 40**
See also CA 97-100; CANR 59; FW; GLL 2

Minimo, Duca
See D'Annunzio, Gabriele

Minot, Susan 1956- .... **CLC 44, 159**
See also AMWS 6; CA 134; CN 7

Minus, Ed 1938- .... **CLC 39**
See also CA 185

Miranda, Javier
See Bioy Casares, Adolfo
See also CWW 2

Mirbeau, Octave 1848-1917 .... **TCLC 55**
See also DLB 123, 192; GFL 1789 to the Present

Miro (Ferrer), Gabriel (Francisco Victor)
1879-1930 .... **TCLC 5**
See also CA 104; 185

Misharin, Alexandr .... **CLC 59**

Mishima, Yukio ... **CLC 2, 4, 6, 9, 27; DC 1; SSC 4**
See also Hiraoka, Kimitake
See also BPFB 2; DLB 182; GLL 1; MJW; MTCW 2; RGSF 2; RGWL 2; SSFS 5, 12

Mistral, Frederic 1830-1914 .... **TCLC 51**
See also CA 122; GFL 1789 to the Present

Mistral, Gabriela
See Godoy Alcayaga, Lucila
See also DNFS 1; LAW; RGWL 2; WP

Mistry, Rohinton 1952- .... **CLC 71**
See also CA 141; CANR 86; CCA 1; CN 7; DAC; SSFS 6

Mitchell, Clyde
See Ellison, Harlan (Jay); Silverberg, Robert

Mitchell, James Leslie 1901-1935
See Gibbon, Lewis Grassic
See also CA 104; 188; DLB 15

Mitchell, Joni 1943- .... **CLC 12**
See also CA 112; CCA 1

Mitchell, Joseph (Quincy)
1908-1996 .... **CLC 98**
See also CA 77-80; 152; CANR 69; CN 7; CSW; DLB 185; DLBY 1996

Mitchell, Margaret (Munnerlyn)
1900-1949 .... **TCLC 11**
See also AAYA 23; BPFB 2; BYA 1; CA 109; 125; CANR 55, 94; CDALBS; DA3; DAM NOV, POP; DLB 9; LAIT 2; MTCW 1, 2; NFS 9; RGAL 4; RHW; TUS; WYAS 1; YAW

Mitchell, Peggy
See Mitchell, Margaret (Munnerlyn)

Mitchell, S(ilas) Weir 1829-1914 .... **TCLC 36**
See also CA 165; DLB 202; RGAL 4

Mitchell, W(illiam) O(rmond)
1914-1998 .... **CLC 25**
See also CA 77-80; 165; CANR 15, 43; CN 7; DAC; DAM MST; DLB 88

Mitchell, William 1879-1936 .... **TCLC 81**

Mitford, Mary Russell 1787-1855 ... **NCLC 4**
See also DLB 110, 116; RGEL 2

Mitford, Nancy 1904-1973 .... **CLC 44**
See also CA 9-12R; DLB 191; RGEL 2

Miyamoto, (Chujo) Yuriko
1899-1951 .... **TCLC 37**
See also Miyamoto Yuriko
See also CA 170, 174

Miyamoto Yuriko
See Miyamoto, (Chujo) Yuriko
See also DLB 180

Miyazawa, Kenji 1896-1933 .... **TCLC 76**
See also CA 157

Mizoguchi, Kenji 1898-1956 .... **TCLC 72**
See also CA 167

Mo, Timothy (Peter) 1950(?)- ... **CLC 46, 134**
See also CA 117; CN 7; DLB 194; MTCW 1; WLIT 4

Modarressi, Taghi (M.) 1931-1997 ... **CLC 44**
See also CA 121; 134; INT 134

Modiano, Patrick (Jean) 1945- .... **CLC 18**
See also CA 85-88; CANR 17, 40; CWW 2; DLB 83

Mofolo, Thomas (Mokopu)
1875(?)-1948 .... **TCLC 22; BLC 3**
See also AFW; CA 121; 153; CANR 83; DAM MULT; DLB 225; MTCW 2; WLIT 2

Mohr, Nicholasa 1938- .... **CLC 12; HLC 2**
See also AAYA 8; CA 49-52; CANR 1, 32, 64; CLR 22; DAM MULT; DLB 145; HW 1, 2; JRDA; LAIT 5; MAICYA 1; MAICYAS 1; RGAL 4; SAAS 8; SATA 8, 97; SATA-Essay 113; WYA; YAW

Mojtabai, A(nn) G(race) 1938- ..... **CLC 5, 9, 15, 29**
See also CA 85-88; CANR 88

Moliere 1622-1673 ..... **LC 10, 28, 64; DC 13; WLC**
See also DA; DA3; DAB; DAC; DAM DRAM, MST; DFS 13; EW 3; GFL Beginnings to 1789; RGWL 2; TWA

Molin, Charles
See Mayne, William (James Carter)

Molnar, Ferenc 1878-1952 .... **TCLC 20**
See also CA 109; 153; CANR 83; CDWLB 4; DAM DRAM; DLB 215; RGWL 2

Momaday, N(avarre) Scott 1934- ...... **CLC 2, 19, 85, 95, 160; PC 25; WLCS**
See also AAYA 11; AMWS 4; ANW; BPFB 2; CA 25-28R; CANR 14, 34, 68; CDALBS; CN 7; CPW; DA; DA3; DAB; DAC; DAM MST, MULT, NOV, POP; DLB 143, 175, 256; EXPP; INT CANR-14; LAIT 4; MTCW 1, 2; NFS 10; NNAL; PFS 2, 11; RGAL 4; SATA 48; SATA-Brief 30; WP; YAW

Monette, Paul 1945-1995 .... **CLC 82**
See also AMWS 10; CA 139; 147; CN 7; GLL 1

Monroe, Harriet 1860-1936 .... **TCLC 12**
See also CA 109; DLB 54, 91

Naidu, Sarojini 1879-1949 .... **TCLC 80**
  See also RGEL 2
Naipaul, Shiva(dhar Srinivasa)
  1945-1985 .... **CLC 32, 39**
  See also CA 110; 112; 116; CANR 33;
  DA3; DAM NOV; DLB 157; DLBY 1985;
  MTCW 1, 2
Naipaul, V(idiadhar) S(urajprasad)
  1932- .... **CLC 4, 7, 9, 13, 18, 37, 105;**
  SSC 38
  See also BPFB 2; BRWS 1; CA 1-4R;
  CANR 1, 33, 51, 91; CDBLB 1960 to
  Present; CDWLB 3; CN 7; DA3; DAB;
  DAC; DAM MST, NOV; DLB 125, 204,
  207; DLBY 1985, 2001; MTCW 1, 2;
  RGEL 2; RGSF 2; TWA; WLIT 4
Nakos, Lilika 1899(?)- .... **CLC 29**
Narayan, R(asipuram) K(rishnaswami)
  1906-2001 . **CLC 7, 28, 47, 121; SSC 25**
  See also BPFB 2; CA 81-84; 196; CANR
  33, 61; CN 7; DA3; DAM NOV; DNFS
  1; MTCW 1, 2; RGEL 2; RGSF 2; SATA
  62; SSFS 5
Nash, (Fredric) Ogden 1902-1971 . **CLC 23;**
  PC 21
  See also CA 13-14; 29-32R; CANR 34, 61;
  CAP 1; DAM POET; DLB 11; MAICYA
  1, 2; MTCW 1, 2; RGAL 4; SATA 2, 46;
  TCLC 109; WP
Nashe, Thomas 1567-1601(?) .... **LC 41**
  See also DLB 167; RGEL 2
Nathan, Daniel
  See Dannay, Frederic
Nathan, George Jean 1882-1958 .... **TCLC 18**
  See also Hatteras, Owen
  See also CA 114; 169; DLB 137
Natsume, Kinnosuke
  See Natsume, Soseki
Natsume, Soseki 1867-1916 .... **TCLC 2, 10**
  See also Natsume Soseki; Soseki
  See also CA 104; 195; RGWL 2; TWA
Natsume Soseki
  See Natsume, Soseki
  See also DLB 180
Natti, (Mary) Lee 1919-
  See Kingman, Lee
  See also CA 5-8R; CANR 2
Navarre, Marguerite de
  See de Navarre, Marguerite
Naylor, Gloria 1950- . **CLC 28, 52, 156; BLC**
  3; WLCS
  See also AAYA 6, 39; AFAW 1, 2; AMWS
  8; BW 2, 3; CA 107; CANR 27, 51, 74;
  CN 7; CPW; DA; DA3; DAC; DAM
  MST, MULT, NOV, POP; DLB 173; FW;
  MTCW 1, 2; NFS 4, 7; RGAL 4; TUS
Neff, Debra .... **CLC 59**
Neihardt, John Gneisenau
  1881-1973 .... **CLC 32**
  See also CA 13-14; CANR 65; CAP 1; DLB
  9, 54, 256; LAIT 2
Nekrasov, Nikolai Alekseevich
  1821-1878 .... **NCLC 11**
Nelligan, Emile 1879-1941 .... **TCLC 14**
  See also CA 114; DLB 92
Nelson, Willie 1933- .... **CLC 17**
  See also CA 107
Nemerov, Howard (Stanley)
  1920-1991 .... **CLC 2, 6, 9, 36; PC 24**
  See also AMW; CA 1-4R; 134; CABS 2;
  CANR 1, 27, 53; DAM POET; DLB 5, 6;
  DLBY 1983; INT CANR-27; MTCW 1,
  2; PFS 10, 14; RGAL 4; TCLC 124
Neruda, Pablo 1904-1973 .. **CLC 1, 2, 5, 7, 9,**
  28, 62; HLC 2; PC 4; WLC
  See also CA 19-20; 45-48; CAP 2; DA;
  DA3; DAB; DAC; DAM MST, MULT,
  POET; DNFS 2; HW 1; LAW; MTCW 1,
  2; PFS 11; RGWL 2; TWA; WLIT 1; WP

Nerval, Gerard de 1808-1855 ... **NCLC 1, 67;**
  PC 13; SSC 18
  See also DLB 217; EW 6; GFL 1789 to the
  Present; RGSF 2; RGWL 2
Nervo, (Jose) Amado (Ruiz de)
  1870-1919 .... **TCLC 11; HLCS 2**
  See also CA 109; 131; HW 1; LAW
Nesbit, Malcolm
  See Chester, Alfred
Nessi, Pio Baroja y
  See Baroja (y Nessi), Pio
Nestroy, Johann 1801-1862 .... **NCLC 42**
  See also DLB 133; RGWL 2
Netterville, Luke
  See O'Grady, Standish (James)
Neufeld, John (Arthur) 1938- .... **CLC 17**
  See also AAYA 11; CA 25-28R; CANR 11,
  37, 56; CLR 52; MAICYA 1, 2; SAAS 3;
  SATA 6, 81; SATA-Essay 131; YAW
Neumann, Alfred 1895-1952 .... **TCLC 100**
  See also CA 183; DLB 56
Neumann, Ferenc
  See Molnar, Ferenc
Neville, Emily Cheney 1919- .... **CLC 12**
  See also BYA 2; CA 5-8R; CANR 3, 37,
  85; JRDA; MAICYA 1, 2; SAAS 2; SATA
  1; YAW
Newbound, Bernard Slade 1930-
  See Slade, Bernard
  See also CA 81-84; CANR 49; CD 5; DAM
  DRAM
Newby, P(ercy) H(oward)
  1918-1997 .... **CLC 2, 13**
  See also CA 5-8R; 161; CANR 32, 67; CN
  7; DAM NOV; DLB 15; MTCW 1; RGEL
  2
Newcastle
  See Cavendish, Margaret Lucas
Newlove, Donald 1928- .... **CLC 6**
  See also CA 29-32R; CANR 25
Newlove, John (Herbert) 1938- .... **CLC 14**
  See also CA 21-24R; CANR 9, 25; CP 7
Newman, Charles 1938- .... **CLC 2, 8**
  See also CA 21-24R; CANR 84; CN 7
Newman, Edwin (Harold) 1919- ...... **CLC 14**
  See also AITN 1; CA 69-72; CANR 5
Newman, John Henry 1801-1890 . **NCLC 38,**
  99
  See also BRWS 7; DLB 18, 32, 55; RGEL
  2
Newton, (Sir) Isaac 1642-1727 ...... **LC 35, 53**
  See also DLB 252
Newton, Suzanne 1936- .... **CLC 35**
  See also BYA 7; CA 41-44R; CANR 14;
  JRDA; SATA 5, 77
New York Dept. of Ed. .... **CLC 70**
Nexo, Martin Andersen
  1869-1954 .... **TCLC 43**
  See also CA 202; DLB 214
Nezval, Vitezslav 1900-1958 .... **TCLC 44**
  See also CA 123; CDWLB 4; DLB 215
Ng, Fae Myenne 1957(?)- .... **CLC 81**
  See also CA 146
Ngema, Mbongeni 1955- .... **CLC 57**
  See also BW 2; CA 143; CANR 84; CD 5
Ngugi, James T(hiong'o) .... **CLC 3, 7, 13**
  See also Ngugi wa Thiong'o
Ngugi wa Thiong'o
  See Ngugi wa Thiong'o
  See also DLB 125
Ngugi wa Thiong'o 1938- .... **CLC 36; BLC 3**
  See also Ngugi, James T(hiong'o); Ngugi
  wa Thiong'o
  See also AFW; BRWS 8; BW 2; CA 81-84;
  CANR 27, 58; CDWLB 3; DAM MULT,
  NOV; DNFS 2; MTCW 1, 2; RGEL 2
Nichol, B(arrie) P(hillip) 1944-1988 . **CLC 18**
  See also CA 53-56; DLB 53; SATA 66

Nicholas of Cusa 1401-1464 .... **LC 80**
  See also DLB 115
Nichols, John (Treadwell) 1940- .... **CLC 38**
  See also CA 9-12R; CAAE 190; CAAS 2;
  CANR 6, 70; DLBY 1982; TCWW 2
Nichols, Leigh
  See Koontz, Dean R(ay)
Nichols, Peter (Richard) 1927- .... **CLC 5, 36,**
  65
  See also CA 104; CANR 33, 86; CBD; CD
  5; DLB 13, 245; MTCW 1
Nicholson, Linda ed. .... **CLC 65**
Ni Chuilleanain, Eilean 1942- .... **PC 34**
  See also CA 126; CANR 53, 83; CP 7;
  CWP; DLB 40
Nicolas, F. R. E.
  See Freeling, Nicolas
Niedecker, Lorine 1903-1970 ..... **CLC 10, 42;**
  PC 42
  See also CA 25-28; CAP 2; DAM POET;
  DLB 48
Nietzsche, Friedrich (Wilhelm)
  1844-1900 .... **TCLC 10, 18, 55**
  See also CA 107; 121; CDWLB 2; DLB
  129; EW 7; RGWL 2; TWA
Nievo, Ippolito 1831-1861 .... **NCLC 22**
Nightingale, Anne Redmon 1943-
  See Redmon, Anne
  See also CA 103
Nightingale, Florence 1820-1910 ... **TCLC 85**
  See also CA 188; DLB 166
Nijo Yoshimoto 1320-1388 .... **CMLC 49**
  See also DLB 203
Nik. T. O.
  See Annensky, Innokenty (Fyodorovich)
Nin, Anais 1903-1977 ..... **CLC 1, 4, 8, 11, 14,**
  60, 127; SSC 10
  See also AITN 2; AMWS 10; BPFB 2; CA
  13-16R; 69-72; CANR 22, 53; DAM
  NOV, POP; DLB 2, 4, 152; GLL 2;
  MAWW; MTCW 1, 2; RGAL 4; RGSF 2
Nisbet, Robert A(lexander)
  1913-1996 .... **TCLC 117**
  See also CA 25-28R; 153; CANR 17; INT
  CANR-17
Nishida, Kitaro 1870-1945 .... **TCLC 83**
Nishiwaki, Junzaburo 1894-1982 .... **PC 15**
  See also Nishiwaki, Junzaburo
  See also CA 194; 107; MJW
Nishiwaki, Junzaburo 1894-1982
  See Nishiwaki, Junzaburo
  See also CA 194
Nissenson, Hugh 1933- .... **CLC 4, 9**
  See also CA 17-20R; CANR 27, 108; CN
  7; DLB 28
Niven, Larry .... **CLC 8**
  See also Niven, Laurence Van Cott
  See also AAYA 27; BPFB 2; BYA 10; DLB
  8; SCFW 2
Niven, Laurence Van Cott 1938-
  See Niven, Larry
  See also CA 21-24R; CAAS 12; CANR 14,
  44, 66; CPW; DAM POP; MTCW 1, 2;
  SATA 95; SFW 4
Nixon, Agnes Eckhardt 1927- .... **CLC 21**
  See also CA 110
Nizan, Paul 1905-1940 .... **TCLC 40**
  See also CA 161; DLB 72; GFL 1789 to the
  Present
Nkosi, Lewis 1936- .... **CLC 45; BLC 3**
  See also BW 1, 3; CA 65-68; CANR 27,
  81; CBD; CD 5; DAM MULT; DLB 157,
  225
Nodier, (Jean) Charles (Emmanuel)
  1780-1844 .... **NCLC 19**
  See also DLB 119; GFL 1789 to the Present
Noguchi, Yone 1875-1947 .... **TCLC 80**
Nolan, Christopher 1965- .... **CLC 58**
  See also CA 111; CANR 88

DNFS 1; HW 1, 2; LAW; LAWS 1; MTCW 1, 2; RGWL 2; SSFS 13; TWA; WLIT 1

p'Bitek, Okot 1931-1982 ..... **CLC 96; BLC 3**
See also AFW; BW 2, 3; CA 124; 107; CANR 82; DAM MULT; DLB 125; MTCW 1, 2; RGEL 2; WLIT 2

Peacock, Molly 1947- .... **CLC 60**
See also CA 103; CAAS 21; CANR 52, 84; CP 7; CWP; DLB 120

Peacock, Thomas Love
1785-1866 .... **NCLC 22**
See also BRW 4; DLB 96, 116; RGEL 2; RGSF 2

Peake, Mervyn 1911-1968 .... **CLC 7, 54**
See also CA 5-8R; 25-28R; CANR 3; DLB 15, 160, 255; FANT; MTCW 1; RGEL 2; SATA 23; SFW 4

Pearce, Philippa
See Christie, Philippa
See also CA 5-8R; CANR 4, 109; CWRI 5; FANT; MAICYA 2

Pearl, Eric
See Elman, Richard (Martin)

Pearson, T(homas) R(eid) 1956- .... **CLC 39**
See also CA 120; 130; CANR 97; CSW; INT 130

Peck, Dale 1967- .... **CLC 81**
See also CA 146; CANR 72; GLL 2

Peck, John (Frederick) 1941- .... **CLC 3**
See also CA 49-52; CANR 3, 100; CP 7

Peck, Richard (Wayne) 1934- .... **CLC 21**
See also AAYA 1, 24; BYA 1, 6, 8, 11; CA 85-88; CANR 19, 38; CLR 15; INT CANR-19; JRDA; MAICYA 1, 2; SAAS 2; SATA 18, 55, 97; SATA-Essay 110; WYA; YAW

Peck, Robert Newton 1928- .... **CLC 17**
See also AAYA 3, 43; BYA 1, 6; CA 81-84, 182; CAAE 182; CANR 31, 63; CLR 45; DA; DAC; DAM MST; JRDA; LAIT 3; MAICYA 1, 2; SAAS 1; SATA 21, 62, 111; SATA-Essay 108; WYA; YAW

Peckinpah, (David) Sam(uel)
1925-1984 .... **CLC 20**
See also CA 109; 114; CANR 82

Pedersen, Knut 1859-1952
See Hamsun, Knut
See also CA 104; 119; CANR 63; MTCW 1, 2

Peeslake, Gaffer
See Durrell, Lawrence (George)

Peguy, Charles (Pierre)
1873-1914 .... **TCLC 10**
See also CA 107; 193; DLB 258; GFL 1789 to the Present

Peirce, Charles Sanders
1839-1914 .... **TCLC 81**
See also CA 194

Pellicer, Carlos 1900(?)-1977
See also CA 153; 69-72; HLCS 2; HW 1

Pena, Ramon del Valle y
See Valle-Inclan, Ramon (Maria) del

Pendennis, Arthur Esquir
See Thackeray, William Makepeace

Penn, William 1644-1718 .... **LC 25**
See also DLB 24

PEPECE
See Prado (Calvo), Pedro

Pepys, Samuel 1633-1703 ... **LC 11, 58; WLC**
See also BRW 2; CDBLB 1660-1789; DA; DA3; DAB; DAC; DAM MST; DLB 101, 213; NCFS 4; RGEL 2; TEA; WLIT 3

Percy, Thomas 1729-1811 .... **NCLC 95**
See also DLB 104

Percy, Walker 1916-1990 .... **CLC 2, 3, 6, 8, 14, 18, 47, 65**
See also AMWS 3; BPFB 3; CA 1-4R; 131; CANR 1, 23, 64; CPW; CSW; DA3; DAM NOV, POP; DLB 2; DLBY 1980, 1990; MTCW 1, 2; RGAL 4; TUS

Percy, William Alexander
1885-1942 .... **TCLC 84**
See also CA 163; MTCW 2

Perec, Georges 1936-1982 .... **CLC 56, 116**
See also CA 141; DLB 83; GFL 1789 to the Present

Pereda (y Sanchez de Porrua), Jose Maria de 1833-1906 .... **TCLC 16**
See also CA 117

Pereda y Porrua, Jose Maria de
See Pereda (y Sanchez de Porrua), Jose Maria de

Peregoy, George Weems
See Mencken, H(enry) L(ouis)

Perelman, S(idney) J(oseph)
1904-1979 .. **CLC 3, 5, 9, 15, 23, 44, 49; SSC 32**
See also AITN 1, 2; BPFB 3; CA 73-76; 89-92; CANR 18; DAM DRAM; DLB 11, 44; MTCW 1, 2; RGAL 4

Peret, Benjamin 1899-1959 .... **TCLC 20; PC 33**
See also CA 117; 186; GFL 1789 to the Present

Peretz, Isaac Loeb 1851(?)-1915 ... **TCLC 16; SSC 26**
See also CA 109

Peretz, Yitzkhok Leibush
See Peretz, Isaac Loeb

Perez Galdos, Benito 1843-1920 ... **TCLC 27; HLCS 2**
See also Galdos, Benito Perez
See also CA 125; 153; HW 1; RGWL 2

Peri Rossi, Cristina 1941- .. **CLC 156; HLCS 2**
See also CA 131; CANR 59, 81; DLB 145; HW 1, 2

Perlata
See Peret, Benjamin

Perloff, Marjorie G(abrielle)
1931- .... **CLC 137**
See also CA 57-60; CANR 7, 22, 49, 104

Perrault, Charles 1628-1703 ... **LC 2, 56; DC 12**
See also BYA 4; CLR 79; GFL Beginnings to 1789; MAICYA 1, 2; RGWL 2; SATA 25; WCH

Perry, Anne 1938- .... **CLC 126**
See also CA 101; CANR 22, 50, 84; CMW 4; CN 7; CPW

Perry, Brighton
See Sherwood, Robert E(mmet)

Perse, St.-John
See Leger, (Marie-Rene Auguste) Alexis Saint-Leger

Perse, Saint-John
See Leger, (Marie-Rene Auguste) Alexis Saint-Leger
See also DLB 258

Perutz, Leo(pold) 1882-1957 .... **TCLC 60**
See also CA 147; DLB 81

Peseenz, Tulio F.
See Lopez y Fuentes, Gregorio

Pesetsky, Bette 1932- .... **CLC 28**
See also CA 133; DLB 130

Peshkov, Alexei Maximovich 1868-1936
See Gorky, Maxim
See also CA 105; 141; CANR 83; DA; DAC; DAM DRAM, MST, NOV; MTCW 2

Pessoa, Fernando (Antonio Nogueira)
1898-1935 ..... **TCLC 27; HLC 2; PC 20**
See also CA 125; 183; DAM MULT; EW 10; RGWL 2; WP

Peterkin, Julia Mood 1880-1961 ...... **CLC 31**
See also CA 102; DLB 9

Peters, Joan K(aren) 1945- .... **CLC 39**
See also CA 158; CANR 109

Peters, Robert L(ouis) 1924- .... **CLC 7**
See also CA 13-16R; CAAS 8; CP 7; DLB 105

Petofi, Sandor 1823-1849 .... **NCLC 21**
See also RGWL 2

Petrakis, Harry Mark 1923- .... **CLC 3**
See also CA 9-12R; CANR 4, 30, 85; CN 7

Petrarch 1304-1374 .... **CMLC 20; PC 8**
See also DA3; DAM POET; EW 2; RGWL 2

Petronius c. 20-66 .... **CMLC 34**
See also AW 2; CDWLB 1; DLB 211; RGWL 2

Petrov, Evgeny .... **TCLC 21**
See also Kataev, Evgeny Petrovich

Petry, Ann (Lane) 1908-1997 ... **CLC 1, 7, 18**
See also AFAW 1, 2; BPFB 3; BW 1, 3; BYA 2; CA 5-8R; 157; CAAS 6; CANR 4, 46; CLR 12; CN 7; DLB 76; JRDA; LAIT 1; MAICYA 1, 2; MAICYAS 1; MTCW 1; RGAL 4; SATA 5; SATA-Obit 94; TCLC 112; TUS

Petursson, Halligrimur 1614-1674 .... **LC 8**

Peychinovich
See Vazov, Ivan (Minchov)

Phaedrus c. 15 B.C.-c. 50 .... **CMLC 25**
See also DLB 211

Phelps (Ward), Elizabeth Stuart
See Phelps, Elizabeth Stuart
See also FW

Phelps, Elizabeth Stuart
1844-1911 .... **TCLC 113**
See also Phelps (Ward), Elizabeth Stuart
See also DLB 74

Philips, Katherine 1632-1664 . **LC 30; PC 40**
See also DLB 131; RGEL 2

Philipson, Morris H. 1926- .... **CLC 53**
See also CA 1-4R; CANR 4

Phillips, Caryl 1958- .... **CLC 96; BLCS**
See also BRWS 5; BW 2; CA 141; CANR 63, 104; CBD; CD 5; CN 7; DA3; DAM MULT; DLB 157; MTCW 2; WLIT 4

Phillips, David Graham
1867-1911 .... **TCLC 44**
See also CA 108; 176; DLB 9, 12; RGAL 4

Phillips, Jack
See Sandburg, Carl (August)

Phillips, Jayne Anne 1952- .... **CLC 15, 33, 139; SSC 16**
See also BPFB 3; CA 101; CANR 24, 50, 96; CN 7; CSW; DLBY 1980; INT CANR-24; MTCW 1, 2; RGAL 4; RGSF 2; SSFS 4

Phillips, Richard
See Dick, Philip K(indred)

Phillips, Robert (Schaeffer) 1938- .... **CLC 28**
See also CA 17-20R; CAAS 13; CANR 8; DLB 105

Phillips, Ward
See Lovecraft, H(oward) P(hillips)

Piccolo, Lucio 1901-1969 .... **CLC 13**
See also CA 97-100; DLB 114

Pickthall, Marjorie L(owry) C(hristie)
1883-1922 .... **TCLC 21**
See also CA 107; DLB 92

Pico della Mirandola, Giovanni
1463-1494 .... **LC 15**

Piercy, Marge 1936- .... **CLC 3, 6, 14, 18, 27, 62, 128; PC 29**
See also BPFB 3; CA 21-24R; CAAE 187; CAAS 1; CANR 13, 43, 66; CN 7; CP 7; CWP; DLB 120, 227; EXPP; FW; MTCW 1, 2; PFS 9; SFW 4

Piers, Robert
See Anthony, Piers

Pieyre de Mandiargues, Andre 1909-1991
See Mandiargues, Andre Pieyre de
See also CA 103; 136; CANR 22, 82; GFL 1789 to the Present

Pilnyak, Boris 1894-1938 . **TCLC 23; SSC 48**
See also Vogau, Boris Andreyevich

Pinchback, Eugene
See Toomer, Jean

Pincherle, Alberto 1907-1990 ...... **CLC 11, 18**
See also Moravia, Alberto
See also CA 25-28R; 132; CANR 33, 63; DAM NOV; MTCW 1

Pinckney, Darryl 1953- .... **CLC 76**
See also BW 2, 3; CA 143; CANR 79

Pindar 518(?) B.C.-438(?) B.C. .... **CMLC 12; PC 19**
See also AW 1; CDWLB 1; DLB 176; RGWL 2

Pineda, Cecile 1942- .... **CLC 39**
See also CA 118; DLB 209

Pinero, Arthur Wing 1855-1934 .... **TCLC 32**
See also CA 110; 153; DAM DRAM; DLB 10; RGEL 2

Pinero, Miguel (Antonio Gomez)
1946-1988 .... **CLC 4, 55**
See also CA 61-64; 125; CAD; CANR 29, 90; DLB 266; HW 1

Pinget, Robert 1919-1997 .... **CLC 7, 13, 37**
See also CA 85-88; 160; CWW 2; DLB 83; GFL 1789 to the Present

Pink Floyd
See Barrett, (Roger) Syd; Gilmour, David; Mason, Nick; Waters, Roger; Wright, Rick

Pinkney, Edward 1802-1828 .... **NCLC 31**
See also DLB 248

Pinkwater, Daniel
See Pinkwater, Daniel Manus

Pinkwater, Daniel Manus 1941- .... **CLC 35**
See also AAYA 1; BYA 9; CA 29-32R; CANR 12, 38, 89; CLR 4; CSW; FANT; JRDA; MAICYA 1, 2; SAAS 3; SATA 8, 46, 76, 114; SFW 4; YAW

Pinkwater, Manus
See Pinkwater, Daniel Manus

Pinsky, Robert 1940- .... **CLC 9, 19, 38, 94, 121; PC 27**
See also AMWS 6; CA 29-32R; CAAS 4; CANR 58, 97; CP 7; DA3; DAM POET; DLBY 1982, 1998; MTCW 2; RGAL 4

Pinta, Harold
See Pinter, Harold

Pinter, Harold 1930- .. **CLC 1, 3, 6, 9, 11, 15, 27, 58, 73; DC 15; WLC**
See also BRWR 1; BRWS 1; CA 5-8R; CANR 33, 65; CBD; CD 5; CDBLB 1960 to Present; DA; DA3; DAB; DAC; DAM DRAM, MST; DFS 3, 5, 7, 14; DLB 13; IDFW 3, 4; MTCW 1, 2; RGEL 2; TEA

Piozzi, Hester Lynch (Thrale)
1741-1821 .... **NCLC 57**
See also DLB 104, 142

Pirandello, Luigi 1867-1936 ...... **TCLC 4, 29; DC 5; SSC 22; WLC**
See also CA 104; 153; CANR 103; DA; DA3; DAB; DAC; DAM DRAM, MST; DFS 4, 9; DLB 264; EW 8; MTCW 2; RGSF 2; RGWL 2

Pirsig, Robert M(aynard) 1928- ... **CLC 4, 6, 73**
See also CA 53-56; CANR 42, 74; CPW 1; DA3; DAM POP; MTCW 1, 2; SATA 39

Pisarev, Dmitry Ivanovich
1840-1868 .... **NCLC 25**

Pix, Mary (Griffith) 1666-1709 .... **LC 8**
See also DLB 80

Pixerecourt, (Rene Charles) Guilbert de
1773-1844 .... **NCLC 39**
See also DLB 192; GFL 1789 to the Present

Plaatje, Sol(omon) T(shekisho)
1878-1932 .... **TCLC 73; BLCS**
See also BW 2, 3; CA 141; CANR 79; DLB 125, 225

Plaidy, Jean
See Hibbert, Eleanor Alice Burford

Planche, James Robinson
1796-1880 .... **NCLC 42**
See also RGEL 2

Plant, Robert 1948- .... **CLC 12**

Plante, David (Robert) 1940- . **CLC 7, 23, 38**
See also CA 37-40R; CANR 12, 36, 58, 82; CN 7; DAM NOV; DLBY 1983; INT CANR-12; MTCW 1

Plath, Sylvia 1932-1963 ..... **CLC 1, 2, 3, 5, 9, 11, 14, 17, 50, 51, 62, 111; PC 1, 37; WLC**
See also AAYA 13; AMWS 1; BPFB 3; CA 19-20; CANR 34, 101; CAP 2; CDALB 1941-1968; DA; DA3; DAB; DAC; DAM MST, POET; DLB 5, 6, 152; EXPN; EXPP; FW; LAIT 4; MAWW; MTCW 1, 2; NFS 1; PAB; PFS 1, 15; RGAL 4; SATA 96; TUS; WP; YAW

Plato c. 428 B.C.-347 B.C. . **CMLC 8; WLCS**
See also AW 1; CDWLB 1; DA; DA3; DAB; DAC; DAM MST; DLB 176; LAIT 1; RGWL 2

Platonov, Andrei
See Klimentov, Andrei Platonovich

Platt, Kin 1911- .... **CLC 26**
See also AAYA 11; CA 17-20R; CANR 11; JRDA; SAAS 17; SATA 21, 86; WYA

Plautus c. 254 B.C.-c. 184 B.C. .... **CMLC 24; DC 6**
See also AW 1; CDWLB 1; DLB 211; RGWL 2

Plick et Plock
See Simenon, Georges (Jacques Christian)

Plieksans, Janis
See Rainis, Janis

Plimpton, George (Ames) 1927- .... **CLC 36**
See also AITN 1; CA 21-24R; CANR 32, 70, 103; DLB 185, 241; MTCW 1, 2; SATA 10

Pliny the Elder c. 23-79 .... **CMLC 23**
See also DLB 211

Plomer, William Charles Franklin
1903-1973 .... **CLC 4, 8**
See also AFW; CA 21-22; CANR 34; CAP 2; DLB 20, 162, 191, 225; MTCW 1; RGEL 2; RGSF 2; SATA 24

Plotinus 204-270 .... **CMLC 46**
See also CDWLB 1; DLB 176

Plowman, Piers
See Kavanagh, Patrick (Joseph)

Plum, J.
See Wodehouse, P(elham) G(renville)

Plumly, Stanley (Ross) 1939- .... **CLC 33**
See also CA 108; 110; CANR 97; CP 7; DLB 5, 193; INT 110

Plumpe, Friedrich Wilhelm
1888-1931 .... **TCLC 53**
See also CA 112

Po Chu-i 772-846 .... **CMLC 24**

Poe, Edgar Allan 1809-1849 ..... **NCLC 1, 16, 55, 78, 94, 97; PC 1; SSC 1, 22, 34, 35, 54; WLC**
See also AAYA 14; AMW; BPFB 3; BYA 5, 11; CDALB 1640-1865; CMW 4; DA; DA3; DAB; DAC; DAM MST, POET; DLB 3, 59, 73, 74, 248, 254; EXPP; EXPS; HGG; LAIT 2; MSW; PAB; PFS 1, 3, 9; RGAL 4; RGSF 2; SATA 23; SCFW 2; SFW 4; SSFS 2, 4, 7, 8; SUFW; WP; WYA

Poet of Titchfield Street, The
See Pound, Ezra (Weston Loomis)

Pohl, Frederik 1919- .... **CLC 18; SSC 25**
See also AAYA 24; CA 61-64; CAAE 188; CAAS 1; CANR 11, 37, 81; CN 7; DLB 8; INT CANR-11; MTCW 1, 2; SATA 24; SCFW 2; SFW 4

Poirier, Louis 1910-
See Gracq, Julien
See also CA 122; 126; CWW 2

Poitier, Sidney 1927- .... **CLC 26**
See also BW 1; CA 117; CANR 94

Polanski, Roman 1933- .... **CLC 16**
See also CA 77-80

Poliakoff, Stephen 1952- .... **CLC 38**
See also CA 106; CBD; CD 5; DLB 13

Police, The
See Copeland, Stewart (Armstrong); Summers, Andrew James; Sumner, Gordon Matthew

Polidori, John William 1795-1821 . **NCLC 51**
See also DLB 116; HGG

Pollitt, Katha 1949- .... **CLC 28, 122**
See also CA 120; 122; CANR 66, 108; MTCW 1, 2

Pollock, (Mary) Sharon 1936- .... **CLC 50**
See also CA 141; CD 5; CWD; DAC; DAM DRAM, MST; DFS 3; DLB 60; FW

Polo, Marco 1254-1324 .... **CMLC 15**

Polonsky, Abraham (Lincoln)
1910-1999 .... **CLC 92**
See also CA 104; 187; DLB 26; INT 104

Polybius c. 200 B.C.-c. 118 B.C. ... **CMLC 17**
See also AW 1; DLB 176; RGWL 2

Pomerance, Bernard 1940- .... **CLC 13**
See also CA 101; CAD; CANR 49; CD 5; DAM DRAM; DFS 9; LAIT 2

Ponge, Francis 1899-1988 .... **CLC 6, 18**
See also CA 85-88; 126; CANR 40, 86; DAM POET; GFL 1789 to the Present; RGWL 2

Poniatowska, Elena 1933- . **CLC 140; HLC 2**
See also CA 101; CANR 32, 66, 107; CDWLB 3; DAM MULT; DLB 113; HW 1, 2; LAWS 1; WLIT 1

Pontoppidan, Henrik 1857-1943 .... **TCLC 29**
See also CA 170

Poole, Josephine .... **CLC 17**
See also Helyar, Jane Penelope Josephine
See also SAAS 2; SATA 5

Popa, Vasko 1922-1991 .... **CLC 19**
See also CA 112; 148; CDWLB 4; DLB 181; RGWL 2

Pope, Alexander 1688-1744 ...... **LC 3, 58, 60, 64; PC 26; WLC**
See also BRW 3; BRWR 1; CDBLB 1660-1789; DA; DA3; DAB; DAC; DAM MST, POET; DLB 95, 101, 213; EXPP; PAB; PFS 12; RGEL 2; WLIT 3; WP

Popov, Yevgeny .... **CLC 59**

Porter, Connie (Rose) 1959(?)- .... **CLC 70**
See also BW 2, 3; CA 142; CANR 90, 109; SATA 81, 129

Porter, Gene(va Grace) Stratton .. **TCLC 21**
See also Stratton-Porter, Gene(va Grace)
See also BPFB 3; CA 112; CWRI 5; RHW

Puzo, Mario 1920-1999 .... **CLC 1, 2, 6, 36, 107**
See also BPFB 3; CA 65-68; 185; CANR 4, 42, 65, 99; CN 7; CPW; DA3; DAM NOV, POP; DLB 6; MTCW 1, 2; RGAL 4

Pygge, Edward
See Barnes, Julian (Patrick)

Pyle, Ernest Taylor 1900-1945
See Pyle, Ernie
See also CA 115; 160

Pyle, Ernie .... **TCLC 75**
See also Pyle, Ernest Taylor
See also DLB 29; MTCW 2

Pyle, Howard 1853-1911 .... **TCLC 81**
See also BYA 2, 4; CA 109; 137; CLR 22; DLB 42, 188; DLBD 13; LAIT 1; MAI-CYA 1, 2; SATA 16, 100; WCH; YAW

Pym, Barbara (Mary Crampton)
1913-1980 .... **CLC 13, 19, 37, 111**
See also BPFB 3; BRWS 2; CA 13-14; 97-100; CANR 13, 34; CAP 1; DLB 14, 207; DLBY 1987; MTCW 1, 2; RGEL 2; TEA

Pynchon, Thomas (Ruggles, Jr.)
1937- ...... **CLC 2, 3, 6, 9, 11, 18, 33, 62, 72, 123; SSC 14; WLC**
See also AMWS 2; BEST 90:2; BPFB 3; CA 17-20R; CANR 22, 46, 73; CN 7; CPW 1; DA; DA3; DAB; DAC; DAM MST, NOV, POP; DLB 2, 173; MTCW 1, 2; RGAL 4; SFW 4; TUS

Pythagoras c. 582 B.C.-c. 507
B.C. .... **CMLC 22**
See also DLB 176

Q
See Quiller-Couch, Sir Arthur (Thomas)

Qian, Chongzhu
See Ch'ien, Chung-shu

Qian Zhongshu
See Ch'ien, Chung-shu

Qroll
See Dagerman, Stig (Halvard)

Quarrington, Paul (Lewis) 1953- ..... **CLC 65**
See also CA 129; CANR 62, 95

Quasimodo, Salvatore 1901-1968 ..... **CLC 10**
See also CA 13-16; 25-28R; CAP 1; DLB 114; EW 12; MTCW 1; RGWL 2

Quatermass, Martin
See Carpenter, John (Howard)

Quay, Stephen 1947- .... **CLC 95**
See also CA 189

Quay, Timothy 1947- .... **CLC 95**
See also CA 189

Queen, Ellery .... **CLC 3, 11**
See also Dannay, Frederic; Davidson, Avram (James); Deming, Richard; Fairman, Paul W.; Flora, Fletcher; Hoch, Edward D(entinger); Kane, Henry; Lee, Manfred B(ennington); Marlowe, Stephen; Powell, (Oval) Talmage; Sheldon, Walter J(ames); Sturgeon, Theodore (Hamilton); Tracy, Don(ald Fiske); Vance, John Holbrook
See also BPFB 3; CMW 4; MSW; RGAL 4

Queen, Ellery, Jr.
See Dannay, Frederic; Lee, Manfred B(ennington)

Queneau, Raymond 1903-1976 ..... **CLC 2, 5, 10, 42**
See also CA 77-80; 69-72; CANR 32; DLB 72, 258; EW 12; GFL 1789 to the Present; MTCW 1, 2; RGWL 2

Quevedo, Francisco de 1580-1645 .... **LC 23**

Quiller-Couch, Sir Arthur (Thomas)
1863-1944 .... **TCLC 53**
See also CA 118; 166; DLB 135, 153, 190; HGG; RGEL 2; SUFW

Quin, Ann (Marie) 1936-1973 .... **CLC 6**
See also CA 9-12R; 45-48; DLB 14, 231

Quinn, Martin
See Smith, Martin Cruz

Quinn, Peter 1947- .... **CLC 91**
See also CA 197

Quinn, Simon
See Smith, Martin Cruz

Quintana, Leroy V. 1944- .... **PC 36**
See also CA 131; CANR 65; DAM MULT; DLB 82; HLC 2; HW 1, 2

Quiroga, Horacio (Sylvestre)
1878-1937 .... **TCLC 20; HLC 2**
See also CA 117; 131; DAM MULT; HW 1; LAW; MTCW 1; RGSF 2; WLIT 1

Quoirez, Francoise 1935- .... **CLC 9**
See also Sagan, Francoise
See also CA 49-52; CANR 6, 39, 73; CWW 2; MTCW 1, 2; TWA

Raabe, Wilhelm (Karl) 1831-1910 . **TCLC 45**
See also CA 167; DLB 129

Rabe, David (William) 1940- .. **CLC 4, 8, 33; DC 16**
See also CA 85-88; CABS 3; CAD; CANR 59; CD 5; DAM DRAM; DFS 3, 8, 13; DLB 7, 228

Rabelais, Francois 1494-1553 .... **LC 5, 60; WLC**
See also DA; DAB; DAC; DAM MST; EW 2; GFL Beginnings to 1789; RGWL 2; TWA

Rabinovitch, Sholem 1859-1916
See Aleichem, Sholom
See also CA 104

Rabinyan, Dorit 1972- .... **CLC 119**
See also CA 170

Rachilde
See Vallette, Marguerite Eymery

Racine, Jean 1639-1699 .... **LC 28**
See also DA3; DAB; DAM MST; EW 3; GFL Beginnings to 1789; RGWL 2; TWA

Radcliffe, Ann (Ward) 1764-1823 ... **NCLC 6, 55, 106**
See also DLB 39, 178; HGG; RGEL 2; SUFW; WLIT 3

Radclyffe-Hall, Marguerite
See Hall, (Marguerite) Radclyffe

Radiguet, Raymond 1903-1923 ...... **TCLC 29**
See also CA 162; DLB 65; GFL 1789 to the Present; RGWL 2

Radnoti, Miklos 1909-1944 .... **TCLC 16**
See also CA 118; CDWLB 4; DLB 215; RGWL 2

Rado, James 1939- .... **CLC 17**
See also CA 105

Radvanyi, Netty 1900-1983
See Seghers, Anna
See also CA 85-88; 110; CANR 82

Rae, Ben
See Griffiths, Trevor

Raeburn, John (Hay) 1941- .... **CLC 34**
See also CA 57-60

Ragni, Gerome 1942-1991 .... **CLC 17**
See also CA 105; 134

Rahv, Philip .... **CLC 24**
See also Greenberg, Ivan
See also DLB 137

Raimund, Ferdinand Jakob
1790-1836 .... **NCLC 69**
See also DLB 90

Raine, Craig (Anthony) 1944- .. **CLC 32, 103**
See also CA 108; CANR 29, 51, 103; CP 7; DLB 40; PFS 7

Raine, Kathleen (Jessie) 1908- ..... **CLC 7, 45**
See also CA 85-88; CANR 46, 109; CP 7; DLB 20; MTCW 1; RGEL 2

Rainis, Janis 1865-1929 .... **TCLC 29**
See also CA 170; CDWLB 4; DLB 220

Rakosi, Carl .... **CLC 47**
See also Rawley, Callman
See also CAAS 5; CP 7; DLB 193

Ralegh, Sir Walter
See Raleigh, Sir Walter
See also BRW 1; RGEL 2; WP

Raleigh, Richard
See Lovecraft, H(oward) P(hillips)

Raleigh, Sir Walter 1554(?)-1618 .... **LC 31, 39; PC 31**
See also Ralegh, Sir Walter
See also CDBLB Before 1660; DLB 172; EXPP; PFS 14; TEA

Rallentando, H. P.
See Sayers, Dorothy L(eigh)

Ramal, Walter
See de la Mare, Walter (John)

Ramana Maharshi 1879-1950 .... **TCLC 84**

Ramoacn y Cajal, Santiago
1852-1934 .... **TCLC 93**

Ramon, Juan
See Jimenez (Mantecon), Juan Ramon

Ramos, Graciliano 1892-1953 .... **TCLC 32**
See also CA 167; HW 2; LAW; WLIT 1

Rampersad, Arnold 1941- .... **CLC 44**
See also BW 2, 3; CA 127; 133; CANR 81; DLB 111; INT 133

Rampling, Anne
See Rice, Anne
See also GLL 2

Ramsay, Allan 1686(?)-1758 .... **LC 29**
See also DLB 95; RGEL 2

Ramsay, Jay
See Campbell, (John) Ramsey

Ramuz, Charles-Ferdinand
1878-1947 .... **TCLC 33**
See also CA 165

Rand, Ayn 1905-1982 ...... **CLC 3, 30, 44, 79; WLC**
See also AAYA 10; AMWS 4; BPFB 3; BYA 12; CA 13-16R; 105; CANR 27, 73; CDALBS; CPW; DA; DA3; DAC; DAM MST, NOV, POP; DLB 227; MTCW 1, 2; NFS 10; RGAL 4; SFW 4; TUS; YAW

Randall, Dudley (Felker) 1914-2000 . **CLC 1, 135; BLC 3**
See also BW 1, 3; CA 25-28R; 189; CANR 23, 82; DAM MULT; DLB 41; PFS 5

Randall, Robert
See Silverberg, Robert

Ranger, Ken
See Creasey, John

Rank, Otto 1884-1939 .... **TCLC 115**

Ransom, John Crowe 1888-1974 .. **CLC 2, 4, 5, 11, 24**
See also AMW; CA 5-8R; 49-52; CANR 6, 34; CDALBS; DA3; DAM POET; DLB 45, 63; EXPP; MTCW 1, 2; RGAL 4; TUS

Rao, Raja 1909- .... **CLC 25, 56**
See also CA 73-76; CANR 51; CN 7; DAM NOV; MTCW 1, 2; RGEL 2; RGSF 2

Raphael, Frederic (Michael) 1931- ... **CLC 2, 14**
See also CA 1-4R; CANR 1, 86; CN 7; DLB 14

Ratcliffe, James P.
See Mencken, H(enry) L(ouis)

Rathbone, Julian 1935- .... **CLC 41**
See also CA 101; CANR 34, 73

Rattigan, Terence (Mervyn)
1911-1977 .... **CLC 7; DC 18**
See also BRWS 7; CA 85-88; 73-76; CBD; CDBLB 1945-1960; DAM DRAM; DFS 8; DLB 13; IDFW 3, 4; MTCW 1, 2; RGEL 2

Ratushinskaya, Irina 1954- .... **CLC 54**
See also CA 129; CANR 68; CWW 2

Raven, Simon (Arthur Noel)
1927-2001 .... **CLC 14**
See also CA 81-84; 197; CANR 86; CN 7

Ravenna, Michael
    See Welty, Eudora (Alice)
Rawley, Callman 1903-
    See Rakosi, Carl
    See also CA 21-24R; CANR 12, 32, 91
Rawlings, Marjorie Kinnan
    1896-1953 .... **TCLC 4**
    See also AAYA 20; AMWS 10; ANW;
    BPFB 3; BYA 3; CA 104; 137; CANR 74;
    CLR 63; DLB 9, 22, 102; DLBD 17;
    JRDA; MAICYA 1, 2; MTCW 2; RGAL
    4; SATA 100; WCH; YABC 1; YAW
Ray, Satyajit 1921-1992 .... **CLC 16, 76**
    See also CA 114; 137; DAM MULT
Read, Herbert Edward 1893-1968 ..... **CLC 4**
    See also BRW 6; CA 85-88; 25-28R; DLB
    20, 149; PAB; RGEL 2
Read, Piers Paul 1941- .... **CLC 4, 10, 25**
    See also CA 21-24R; CANR 38, 86; CN 7;
    DLB 14; SATA 21
Reade, Charles 1814-1884 .... **NCLC 2, 74**
    See also DLB 21; RGEL 2
Reade, Hamish
    See Gray, Simon (James Holliday)
Reading, Peter 1946- .... **CLC 47**
    See also BRWS 8; CA 103; CANR 46, 96;
    CP 7; DLB 40
Reaney, James 1926- .... **CLC 13**
    See also CA 41-44R; CAAS 15; CANR 42;
    CD 5; CP 7; DAC; DAM MST; DLB 68;
    RGEL 2; SATA 43
Rebreanu, Liviu 1885-1944 .... **TCLC 28**
    See also CA 165; DLB 220
Rechy, John (Francisco) 1934- ...... **CLC 1, 7,
    14, 18, 107; HLC 2**
    See also CA 5-8R; CAAE 195; CAAS 4;
    CANR 6, 32, 64; CN 7; DAM MULT;
    DLB 122; DLBY 1982; HW 1, 2; INT
    CANR-6; RGAL 4
Redcam, Tom 1870-1933 .... **TCLC 25**
Reddin, Keith .... **CLC 67**
    See also CAD
Redgrove, Peter (William) 1932- . **CLC 6, 41**
    See also BRWS 6; CA 1-4R; CANR 3, 39,
    77; CP 7; DLB 40
Redmon, Anne .... **CLC 22**
    See also Nightingale, Anne Redmon
    See also DLBY 1986
Reed, Eliot
    See Ambler, Eric
Reed, Ishmael 1938- .. **CLC 2, 3, 5, 6, 13, 32,
    60; BLC 3**
    See also AFAW 1, 2; AMWS 10; BPFB 3;
    BW 2, 3; CA 21-24R; CANR 25, 48, 74;
    CN 7; CP 7; CSW; DA3; DAM MULT;
    DLB 2, 5, 33, 169, 227; DLBD 8; MSW;
    MTCW 1, 2; PFS 6; RGAL 4; TCWW 2
Reed, John (Silas) 1887-1920 .... **TCLC 9**
    See also CA 106; 195; TUS
Reed, Lou .... **CLC 21**
    See also Firbank, Louis
Reese, Lizette Woodworth 1856-1935 . **PC 29**
    See also CA 180; DLB 54
Reeve, Clara 1729-1807 .... **NCLC 19**
    See also DLB 39; RGEL 2
Reich, Wilhelm 1897-1957 .... **TCLC 57**
    See also CA 199
Reid, Christopher (John) 1949- .... **CLC 33**
    See also CA 140; CANR 89; CP 7; DLB 40
Reid, Desmond
    See Moorcock, Michael (John)
Reid Banks, Lynne 1929-
    See Banks, Lynne Reid
    See also CA 1-4R; CANR 6, 22, 38, 87;
    CLR 24; CN 7; JRDA; MAICYA 1, 2;
    SATA 22, 75, 111; YAW
Reilly, William K.
    See Creasey, John

Reiner, Max
    See Caldwell, (Janet Miriam) Taylor
    (Holland)
Reis, Ricardo
    See Pessoa, Fernando (Antonio Nogueira)
Remarque, Erich Maria 1898-1970 . **CLC 21**
    See also AAYA 27; BPFB 3; CA 77-80; 29-
    32R; CDWLB 2; DA; DA3; DAB; DAC;
    DAM MST, NOV; DLB 56; EXPN; LAIT
    3; MTCW 1, 2; NFS 4; RGWL 2
Remington, Frederic 1861-1909 ..... **TCLC 89**
    See also CA 108; 169; DLB 12, 186, 188;
    SATA 41
Remizov, A.
    See Remizov, Aleksei (Mikhailovich)
Remizov, A. M.
    See Remizov, Aleksei (Mikhailovich)
Remizov, Aleksei (Mikhailovich)
    1877-1957 .... **TCLC 27**
    See also CA 125; 133
Renan, Joseph Ernest 1823-1892 .. **NCLC 26**
    See also GFL 1789 to the Present
Renard, Jules(-Pierre) 1864-1910 .. **TCLC 17**
    See also CA 117; 202; GFL 1789 to the
    Present
Renault, Mary .... **CLC 3, 11, 17**
    See also Challans, Mary
    See also BPFB 3; BYA 2; DLBY 1983;
    GLL 1; LAIT 1; MTCW 2; RGEL 2;
    RHW
Rendell, Ruth (Barbara) 1930- .. **CLC 28, 48**
    See also Vine, Barbara
    See also BPFB 3; CA 109; CANR 32, 52,
    74; CN 7; CPW; DAM POP; DLB 87;
    INT CANR-32; MSW; MTCW 1, 2
Renoir, Jean 1894-1979 .... **CLC 20**
    See also CA 129; 85-88
Resnais, Alain 1922- .... **CLC 16**
Reverdy, Pierre 1889-1960 .... **CLC 53**
    See also CA 97-100; 89-92; DLB 258; GFL
    1789 to the Present
Rexroth, Kenneth 1905-1982 .... **CLC 1, 2, 6,
    11, 22, 49, 112; PC 20**
    See also CA 5-8R; 107; CANR 14, 34, 63;
    CDALB 1941-1968; DAM POET; DLB
    16, 48, 165, 212; DLBY 1982; INT
    CANR-14; MTCW 1, 2; RGAL 4
Reyes, Alfonso 1889-1959 .. **TCLC 33; HLCS
    2**
    See also CA 131; HW 1; LAW
Reyes y Basoalto, Ricardo Eliecer Neftali
    See Neruda, Pablo
Reymont, Wladyslaw (Stanislaw)
    1868(?)-1925 .... **TCLC 5**
    See also CA 104
Reynolds, Jonathan 1942- .... **CLC 6, 38**
    See also CA 65-68; CANR 28
Reynolds, Joshua 1723-1792 .... **LC 15**
    See also DLB 104
Reynolds, Michael S(hane)
    1937-2000 .... **CLC 44**
    See also CA 65-68; 189; CANR 9, 89, 97
Reznikoff, Charles 1894-1976 .... **CLC 9**
    See also CA 33-36; 61-64; CAP 2; DLB 28,
    45; WP
Rezzori (d'Arezzo), Gregor von
    1914-1998 .... **CLC 25**
    See also CA 122; 136; 167
Rhine, Richard
    See Silverstein, Alvin; Silverstein, Virginia
    B(arbara Opshelor)
Rhodes, Eugene Manlove
    1869-1934 .... **TCLC 53**
    See also CA 198; DLB 256
R'hoone, Lord
    See Balzac, Honore de

Rhys, Jean 1894(?)-1979 ...... **CLC 2, 4, 6, 14,
    19, 51, 124; SSC 21**
    See also BRWS 2; CA 25-28R; 85-88;
    CANR 35, 62; CDBLB 1945-1960; CD-
    WLB 3; DA3; DAM NOV; DLB 36, 117,
    162; DNFS 2; MTCW 1, 2; RGEL 2;
    RGSF 2; RHW; TEA
Ribeiro, Darcy 1922-1997 .... **CLC 34**
    See also CA 33-36R; 156
Ribeiro, Joao Ubaldo (Osorio Pimentel)
    1941- .... **CLC 10, 67**
    See also CA 81-84
Ribman, Ronald (Burt) 1932- .... **CLC 7**
    See also CA 21-24R; CAD; CANR 46, 80;
    CD 5
Ricci, Nino 1959- .... **CLC 70**
    See also CA 137; CCA 1
Rice, Anne 1941- .... **CLC 41, 128**
    See also Rampling, Anne
    See also AAYA 9; AMWS 7; BEST 89:2;
    BPFB 3; CA 65-68; CANR 12, 36, 53,
    74, 100; CN 7; CPW; CSW; DA3; DAM
    POP; GLL 2; HGG; MTCW 2; YAW
Rice, Elmer (Leopold) 1892-1967 ...... **CLC 7,
    49**
    See also CA 21-22; 25-28R; CAP 2; DAM
    DRAM; DFS 12; DLB 4, 7; MTCW 1, 2;
    RGAL 4
Rice, Tim(othy Miles Bindon)
    1944- .... **CLC 21**
    See also CA 103; CANR 46; DFS 7
Rich, Adrienne (Cecile) 1929- ... **CLC 3, 6, 7,
    11, 18, 36, 73, 76, 125; PC 5**
    See also AMWS 1; CA 9-12R; CANR 20,
    53, 74; CDALBS; CP 7; CSW; CWP;
    DA3; DAM POET; DLB 5, 67; EXPP;
    FW; MAWW; MTCW 1, 2; PAB; PFS 15;
    RGAL 4; WP
Rich, Barbara
    See Graves, Robert (von Ranke)
Rich, Robert
    See Trumbo, Dalton
Richard, Keith .... **CLC 17**
    See also Richards, Keith
Richards, David Adams 1950- .... **CLC 59**
    See also CA 93-96; CANR 60, 110; DAC;
    DLB 53
Richards, I(vor) A(rmstrong)
    1893-1979 .... **CLC 14, 24**
    See also BRWS 2; CA 41-44R; 89-92;
    CANR 34, 74; DLB 27; MTCW 2; RGEL
    2
Richards, Keith 1943-
    See Richard, Keith
    See also CA 107; CANR 77
Richardson, Anne
    See Roiphe, Anne (Richardson)
Richardson, Dorothy Miller
    1873-1957 .... **TCLC 3**
    See also CA 104; 192; DLB 36; FW; RGEL
    2
**Richardson (Robertson), Ethel Florence
    Lindesay** 1870-1946
    See Richardson, Henry Handel
    See also CA 105; 190; DLB 230; RHW
Richardson, Henry Handel .... **TCLC 4**
    See also Richardson (Robertson), Ethel Flo-
    rence Lindesay
    See also DLB 197; RGEL 2; RGSF 2
Richardson, John 1796-1852 .... **NCLC 55**
    See also CCA 1; DAC; DLB 99
Richardson, Samuel 1689-1761 ...... **LC 1, 44;
    WLC**
    See also BRW 3; CDBLB 1660-1789; DA;
    DAB; DAC; DAM MST, NOV; DLB 39;
    RGEL 2; TEA; WLIT 3

Richler, Mordecai 1931-2001 .... **CLC 3, 5, 9, 13, 18, 46, 70**
See also AITN 1; CA 65-68; 201; CANR 31, 62; CCA 1; CLR 17; CWRI 5; DAC; DAM MST, NOV; DLB 53; MAICYA 1, 2; MTCW 1, 2; RGEL 2; SATA 44, 98; SATA-Brief 27; TWA

Richter, Conrad (Michael)
1890-1968 .... **CLC 30**
See also AAYA 21; BYA 2; CA 5-8R; 25-28R; CANR 23; DLB 9, 212; LAIT 1; MTCW 1, 2; RGAL 4; SATA 3; TCWW 2; TUS; YAW

Ricostranza, Tom
See Ellis, Trey

Riddell, Charlotte 1832-1906 .... **TCLC 40**
See also Riddell, Mrs. J. H.
See also CA 165; DLB 156

Riddell, Mrs. J. H.
See Riddell, Charlotte
See also HGG; SUFW

Ridge, John Rollin 1827-1867 .... **NCLC 82**
See also CA 144; DAM MULT; DLB 175; NNAL

Ridgeway, Jason
See Marlowe, Stephen

Ridgway, Keith 1965- .... **CLC 119**
See also CA 172

Riding, Laura .... **CLC 3, 7**
See also Jackson, Laura (Riding)
See also RGAL 4

Riefenstahl, Berta Helene Amalia 1902-
See Riefenstahl, Leni
See also CA 108

Riefenstahl, Leni .... **CLC 16**
See also Riefenstahl, Berta Helene Amalia

Riffe, Ernest
See Bergman, (Ernst) Ingmar

Riggs, (Rolla) Lynn 1899-1954 .... **TCLC 56**
See also CA 144; DAM MULT; DLB 175; NNAL

Riis, Jacob A(ugust) 1849-1914 ..... **TCLC 80**
See also CA 113; 168; DLB 23

Riley, James Whitcomb
1849-1916 .... **TCLC 51**
See also CA 118; 137; DAM POET; MAICYA 1, 2; RGAL 4; SATA 17

Riley, Tex
See Creasey, John

Rilke, Rainer Maria 1875-1926 .. **TCLC 1, 6, 19; PC 2**
See also CA 104; 132; CANR 62, 99; CDWLB 2; DA3; DAM POET; DLB 81; EW 9; MTCW 1, 2; RGWL 2; TWA; WP

Rimbaud, (Jean Nicolas) Arthur
1854-1891 .... **NCLC 4, 35, 82; PC 3; WLC**
See also DA; DA3; DAB; DAC; DAM MST, POET; DLB 217; EW 7; GFL 1789 to the Present; RGWL 2; TWA; WP

Rinehart, Mary Roberts
1876-1958 .... **TCLC 52**
See also BPFB 3; CA 108; 166; RGAL 4; RHW

Ringmaster, The
See Mencken, H(enry) L(ouis)

Ringwood, Gwen(dolyn Margaret) Pharis
1910-1984 .... **CLC 48**
See also CA 148; 112; DLB 88

Rio, Michel 1945(?)- .... **CLC 43**
See also CA 201

Ritsos, Giannes
See Ritsos, Yannis

Ritsos, Yannis 1909-1990 .... **CLC 6, 13, 31**
See also CA 77-80; 133; CANR 39, 61; EW 12; MTCW 1; RGWL 2

Ritter, Erika 1948(?)- .... **CLC 52**
See also CD 5; CWD

Rivera, Jose Eustasio 1889-1928 ... **TCLC 35**
See also CA 162; HW 1, 2; LAW

Rivera, Tomas 1935-1984
See also CA 49-52; CANR 32; DLB 82; HLCS 2; HW 1; RGAL 4; SSFS 15; TCWW 2; WLIT 1

Rivers, Conrad Kent 1933-1968 .... **CLC 1**
See also BW 1; CA 85-88; DLB 41

Rivers, Elfrida
See Bradley, Marion Zimmer
See also GLL 1

Riverside, John
See Heinlein, Robert A(nson)

Rizal, Jose 1861-1896 .... **NCLC 27**

Roa Bastos, Augusto (Antonio)
1917- .... **CLC 45; HLC 2**
See also CA 131; DAM MULT; DLB 113; HW 1; LAW; RGSF 2; WLIT 1

Robbe-Grillet, Alain 1922- .... **CLC 1, 2, 4, 6, 8, 10, 14, 43, 128**
See also BPFB 3; CA 9-12R; CANR 33, 65; DLB 83; EW 13; GFL 1789 to the Present; IDFW 3, 4; MTCW 1, 2; RGWL 2; SSFS 15

Robbins, Harold 1916-1997 .... **CLC 5**
See also BPFB 3; CA 73-76; 162; CANR 26, 54; DA3; DAM NOV; MTCW 1, 2

Robbins, Thomas Eugene 1936-
See Robbins, Tom
See also CA 81-84; CANR 29, 59, 95; CN 7; CPW; CSW; DA3; DAM NOV, POP; MTCW 1, 2

Robbins, Tom .... **CLC 9, 32, 64**
See also Robbins, Thomas Eugene
See also AAYA 32; AMWS 10; BEST 90:3; BPFB 3; DLBY 1980; MTCW 2

Robbins, Trina 1938- .... **CLC 21**
See also CA 128

Roberts, Charles G(eorge) D(ouglas)
1860-1943 .... **TCLC 8**
See also CA 105; 188; CLR 33; CWRI 5; DLB 92; RGEL 2; RGSF 2; SATA 88; SATA-Brief 29

Roberts, Elizabeth Madox
1886-1941 .... **TCLC 68**
See also CA 111; 166; CWRI 5; DLB 9, 54, 102; RGAL 4; RHW; SATA 33; SATA-Brief 27; WCH

Roberts, Kate 1891-1985 .... **CLC 15**
See also CA 107; 116

Roberts, Keith (John Kingston)
1935-2000 .... **CLC 14**
See also CA 25-28R; CANR 46; DLB 261; SFW 4

Roberts, Kenneth (Lewis)
1885-1957 .... **TCLC 23**
See also CA 109; 199; DLB 9; RGAL 4; RHW

Roberts, Michele (Brigitte) 1949- ..... **CLC 48**
See also CA 115; CANR 58; CN 7; DLB 231; FW

Robertson, Ellis
See Ellison, Harlan (Jay); Silverberg, Robert

Robertson, Thomas William
1829-1871 .... **NCLC 35**
See also Robertson, Tom
See also DAM DRAM

Robertson, Tom
See Robertson, Thomas William
See also RGEL 2

Robeson, Kenneth
See Dent, Lester

Robinson, Edwin Arlington
1869-1935 .... **TCLC 5, 101; PC 1, 35**
See also AMW; CA 104; 133; CDALB 1865-1917; DA; DAC; DAM MST, POET; DLB 54; EXPP; MTCW 1, 2; PAB; PFS 4; RGAL 4; WP

Robinson, Henry Crabb
1775-1867 .... **NCLC 15**
See also DLB 107

Robinson, Jill 1936- .... **CLC 10**
See also CA 102; INT 102

Robinson, Kim Stanley 1952- .... **CLC 34**
See also AAYA 26; CA 126; CN 7; SATA 109; SCFW 2; SFW 4

Robinson, Lloyd
See Silverberg, Robert

Robinson, Marilynne 1944- .... **CLC 25**
See also CA 116; CANR 80; CN 7; DLB 206

Robinson, Smokey .... **CLC 21**
See also Robinson, William, Jr.

Robinson, William, Jr. 1940-
See Robinson, Smokey
See also CA 116

Robison, Mary 1949- .... **CLC 42, 98**
See also CA 113; 116; CANR 87; CN 7; DLB 130; INT 116; RGSF 2

Rochester
See Wilmot, John
See also RGEL 2

Rod, Edouard 1857-1910 .... **TCLC 52**

Roddenberry, Eugene Wesley 1921-1991
See Roddenberry, Gene
See also CA 110; 135; CANR 37; SATA 45; SATA-Obit 69

Roddenberry, Gene .... **CLC 17**
See also Roddenberry, Eugene Wesley
See also AAYA 5; SATA-Obit 69

Rodgers, Mary 1931- .... **CLC 12**
See also BYA 5; CA 49-52; CANR 8, 55, 90; CLR 20; CWRI 5; INT CANR-8; JRDA; MAICYA 1, 2; SATA 8, 130

Rodgers, W(illiam) R(obert)
1909-1969 .... **CLC 7**
See also CA 85-88; DLB 20; RGEL 2

Rodman, Eric
See Silverberg, Robert

Rodman, Howard 1920(?)-1985 .... **CLC 65**
See also CA 118

Rodman, Maia
See Wojciechowska, Maia (Teresa)

Rodo, Jose Enrique 1871(?)-1917
See also CA 178; HLCS 2; HW 2; LAW

Rodolph, Utto
See Ouologuem, Yambo

Rodriguez, Claudio 1934-1999 .... **CLC 10**
See also CA 188; DLB 134

Rodriguez, Richard 1944- .... **CLC 155; HLC 2**
See also CA 110; CANR 66; DAM MULT; DLB 82, 256; HW 1, 2; LAIT 5; NCFS 3; WLIT 1

Roelvaag, O(le) E(dvart) 1876-1931
See Rolvaag, O(le) E(dvart)
See also CA 117; 171

Roethke, Theodore (Huebner)
1908-1963 .... **CLC 1, 3, 8, 11, 19, 46, 101; PC 15**
See also AMW; CA 81-84; CABS 2; CDALB 1941-1968; DA3; DAM POET; DLB 5, 206; EXPP; MTCW 1, 2; PAB; PFS 3; RGAL 4; WP

Rogers, Carl R(ansom)
1902-1987 .... **TCLC 125**
See also CA 1-4R; 121; CANR 1, 18; MTCW 1

Rogers, Samuel 1763-1855 .... **NCLC 69**
See also DLB 93; RGEL 2

Rogers, Thomas Hunton 1927- .... **CLC 57**
See also CA 89-92; INT 89-92

Rogers, Will(iam Penn Adair)
1879-1935 .... **TCLC 8, 71**
See also CA 105; 144; DA3; DAM MULT; DLB 11; MTCW 2; NNAL

Rogin, Gilbert 1929- .... **CLC 18**
  See also CA 65-68; CANR 15
Rohan, Koda
  See Koda Shigeyuki
Rohlfs, Anna Katharine Green
  See Green, Anna Katharine
Rohmer, Eric .... **CLC 16**
  See also Scherer, Jean-Marie Maurice
Rohmer, Sax .... **TCLC 28**
  See also Ward, Arthur Henry Sarsfield
  See also DLB 70; MSW; SUFW
Roiphe, Anne (Richardson) 1935- .. **CLC 3, 9**
  See also CA 89-92; CANR 45, 73; DLBY
  1980; INT 89-92
Rojas, Fernando de 1475-1541 .... **LC 23;**
  HLCS 1
  See also RGWL 2
Rojas, Gonzalo 1917-
  See also CA 178; HLCS 2; HW 2; LAWS 1
**Rolfe, Frederick (William Serafino Austin
  Lewis Mary)** 1860-1913 .... **TCLC 12**
  See also Corvo, Baron
  See also CA 107; DLB 34, 156; RGEL 2
Rolland, Romain 1866-1944 .... **TCLC 23**
  See also CA 118; 197; DLB 65; GFL 1789
  to the Present; RGWL 2
Rolle, Richard c. 1300-c. 1349 ...... **CMLC 21**
  See also DLB 146; RGEL 2
Rolvaag, O(le) E(dvart) .... **TCLC 17**
  See also Roelvaag, O(le) E(dvart)
  See also DLB 9, 212; NFS 5; RGAL 4
Romain Arnaud, Saint
  See Aragon, Louis
Romains, Jules 1885-1972 .... **CLC 7**
  See also CA 85-88; CANR 34; DLB 65;
  GFL 1789 to the Present; MTCW 1
Romero, Jose Ruben 1890-1952 .... **TCLC 14**
  See also CA 114; 131; HW 1; LAW
Ronsard, Pierre de 1524-1585 . **LC 6, 54; PC
  11**
  See also EW 2; GFL Beginnings to 1789;
  RGWL 2; TWA
Rooke, Leon 1934- .... **CLC 25, 34**
  See also CA 25-28R; CANR 23, 53; CCA
  1; CPW; DAM POP
Roosevelt, Franklin Delano
  1882-1945 .... **TCLC 93**
  See also CA 116; 173; LAIT 3
Roosevelt, Theodore 1858-1919 ..... **TCLC 69**
  See also CA 115; 170; DLB 47, 186
Roper, William 1498-1578 .... **LC 10**
Roquelaure, A. N.
  See Rice, Anne
Rosa, Joao Guimaraes 1908-1967 ... **CLC 23;
  HLCS 1**
  See also Guimaraes Rosa, Joao
  See also CA 89-92; DLB 113; WLIT 1
Rose, Wendy 1948- .... **CLC 85; PC 13**
  See also CA 53-56; CANR 5, 51; CWP;
  DAM MULT; DLB 175; NNAL; PFS 13;
  RGAL 4; SATA 12
Rosen, R. D.
  See Rosen, Richard (Dean)
Rosen, Richard (Dean) 1949- .... **CLC 39**
  See also CA 77-80; CANR 62; CMW 4;
  INT CANR-30
Rosenberg, Isaac 1890-1918 .... **TCLC 12**
  See also BRW 6; CA 107; 188; DLB 20,
  216; PAB; RGEL 2
Rosenblatt, Joe .... **CLC 15**
  See also Rosenblatt, Joseph
Rosenblatt, Joseph 1933-
  See Rosenblatt, Joe
  See also CA 89-92; CP 7; INT 89-92
Rosenfeld, Samuel
  See Tzara, Tristan
Rosenstock, Sami
  See Tzara, Tristan

Rosenstock, Samuel
  See Tzara, Tristan
Rosenthal, M(acha) L(ouis)
  1917-1996 .... **CLC 28**
  See also CA 1-4R; 152; CAAS 6; CANR 4,
  51; CP 7; DLB 5; SATA 59
Ross, Barnaby
  See Dannay, Frederic
Ross, Bernard L.
  See Follett, Ken(neth Martin)
Ross, J. H.
  See Lawrence, T(homas) E(dward)
Ross, John Hume
  See Lawrence, T(homas) E(dward)
Ross, Martin 1862-1915
  See Martin, Violet Florence
  See also DLB 135; GLL 2; RGEL 2; RGSF
  2
Ross, (James) Sinclair 1908-1996 ... **CLC 13;
  SSC 24**
  See also CA 73-76; CANR 81; CN 7; DAC;
  DAM MST; DLB 88; RGEL 2; RGSF 2;
  TCWW 2
Rossetti, Christina (Georgina)
  1830-1894 .... **NCLC 2, 50, 66; PC 7;
  WLC**
  See also BRW 5; BYA 4; DA; DA3; DAB;
  DAC; DAM MST, POET; DLB 35, 163,
  240; EXPP; MAICYA 1, 2; PFS 10, 14;
  RGEL 2; SATA 20; TEA; WCH
Rossetti, Dante Gabriel 1828-1882 . **NCLC 4,
  77; WLC**
  See also BRW 5; CDBLB 1832-1890; DA;
  DAB; DAC; DAM MST, POET; DLB 35;
  EXPP; RGEL 2; TEA
Rossi, Cristina Peri
  See Peri Rossi, Cristina
Rossi, Jean Baptiste 1931-
  See Japrisot, Sebastien
  See also CA 201
Rossner, Judith (Perelman) 1935- . **CLC 6, 9,
  29**
  See also AITN 2; BEST 90:3; BPFB 3; CA
  17-20R; CANR 18, 51, 73; CN 7; DLB 6;
  INT CANR-18; MTCW 1, 2
Rostand, Edmond (Eugene Alexis)
  1868-1918 .... **TCLC 6, 37; DC 10**
  See also CA 104; 126; DA; DA3; DAB;
  DAC; DAM DRAM, MST; DFS 1; DLB
  192; LAIT 1; MTCW 1; RGWL 2; TWA
Roth, Henry 1906-1995 ..... **CLC 2, 6, 11, 104**
  See also AMWS 9; CA 11-12; 149; CANR
  38, 63; CAP 1; CN 7; DA3; DLB 28;
  MTCW 1, 2; RGAL 4
Roth, (Moses) Joseph 1894-1939 ... **TCLC 33**
  See also CA 160; DLB 85; RGWL 2
Roth, Philip (Milton) 1933- ... **CLC 1, 2, 3, 4,
  6, 9, 15, 22, 31, 47, 66, 86, 119; SSC
  26; WLC**
  See also AMWS 3; BEST 90:3; BPFB 3;
  CA 1-4R; CANR 1, 22, 36, 55, 89;
  CDALB 1968-1988; CN 7; CPW 1; DA;
  DA3; DAB; DAC; DAM MST, NOV,
  POP; DLB 2, 28, 173; DLBY 1982;
  MTCW 1, 2; RGAL 4; RGSF 2; SSFS 12;
  TUS
Rothenberg, Jerome 1931- .... **CLC 6, 57**
  See also CA 45-48; CANR 1, 106; CP 7;
  DLB 5, 193
Rotter, Pat ed. .... **CLC 65**
Roumain, Jacques (Jean Baptiste)
  1907-1944 .... **TCLC 19; BLC 3**
  See also BW 1; CA 117; 125; DAM MULT
Rourke, Constance (Mayfield)
  1885-1941 .... **TCLC 12**
  See also CA 107; YABC 1

Rousseau, Jean-Baptiste 1671-1741 ...... **LC 9**
Rousseau, Jean-Jacques 1712-1778 .... **LC 14,
  36; WLC**
  See also DA; DA3; DAB; DAC; DAM
  MST; EW 4; GFL Beginnings to 1789;
  RGWL 2; TWA
Roussel, Raymond 1877-1933 .... **TCLC 20**
  See also CA 117; 201; GFL 1789 to the
  Present
Rovit, Earl (Herbert) 1927- .... **CLC 7**
  See also CA 5-8R; CANR 12
Rowe, Elizabeth Singer 1674-1737 ..... **LC 44**
  See also DLB 39, 95
Rowe, Nicholas 1674-1718 .... **LC 8**
  See also DLB 84; RGEL 2
Rowlandson, Mary 1637(?)-1678 .... **LC 66**
  See also DLB 24, 200; RGAL 4
Rowley, Ames Dorrance
  See Lovecraft, H(oward) P(hillips)
Rowling, J(oanne) K(athleen)
  1965(?)- .... **CLC 137**
  See also AAYA 34; BYA 13, 14; CA 173;
  CLR 66, 80; SATA 109
Rowson, Susanna Haswell
  1762(?)-1824 .... **NCLC 5, 69**
  See also DLB 37, 200; RGAL 4
Roy, Arundhati 1960(?)- .... **CLC 109**
  See also CA 163; CANR 90; DLBY 1997
Roy, Gabrielle 1909-1983 .... **CLC 10, 14**
  See also CA 53-56; 110; CANR 5, 61; CCA
  1; DAB; DAC; DAM MST; DLB 68;
  MTCW 1; RGWL 2; SATA 104
Royko, Mike 1932-1997 .... **CLC 109**
  See also CA 89-92; 157; CANR 26; CPW
Rozanov, Vassili 1856-1919 .... **TCLC 104**
Rozewicz, Tadeusz 1921- ...... **CLC 9, 23, 139**
  See also CA 108; CANR 36, 66; CWW 2;
  DA3; DAM POET; DLB 232; MTCW 1,
  2
Ruark, Gibbons 1941- .... **CLC 3**
  See also CA 33-36R; CAAS 23; CANR 14,
  31, 57; DLB 120
Rubens, Bernice (Ruth) 1923- .... **CLC 19, 31**
  See also CA 25-28R; CANR 33, 65; CN 7;
  DLB 14, 207; MTCW 1
Rubin, Harold
  See Robbins, Harold
Rudkin, (James) David 1936- .... **CLC 14**
  See also CA 89-92; CBD; CD 5; DLB 13
Rudnik, Raphael 1933- .... **CLC 7**
  See also CA 29-32R
Ruffian, M.
  See Hasek, Jaroslav (Matej Frantisek)
Ruiz, Jose Martinez .... **CLC 11**
  See also Martinez Ruiz, Jose
Rukeyser, Muriel 1913-1980 . **CLC 6, 10, 15,
  27; PC 12**
  See also AMWS 6; CA 5-8R; 93-96; CANR
  26, 60; DA3; DAM POET; DLB 48; FW;
  GLL 2; MTCW 1, 2; PFS 10; RGAL 4;
  SATA-Obit 22
Rule, Jane (Vance) 1931- .... **CLC 27**
  See also CA 25-28R; CAAS 18; CANR 12,
  87; CN 7; DLB 60; FW
Rulfo, Juan 1918-1986 .. **CLC 8, 80; HLC 2;
  SSC 25**
  See also CA 85-88; 118; CANR 26; CD-
  WLB 3; DAM MULT; DLB 113; HW 1,
  2; LAW; MTCW 1, 2; RGSF 2; RGWL 2;
  WLIT 1
Rumi, Jalal al-Din 1207-1273 .... **CMLC 20**
  See also RGWL 2; WP
Runeberg, Johan 1804-1877 .... **NCLC 41**
Runyon, (Alfred) Damon
  1884(?)-1946 .... **TCLC 10**
  See also CA 107; 165; DLB 11, 86, 171;
  MTCW 2; RGAL 4
Rush, Norman 1933- .... **CLC 44**
  See also CA 121; 126; INT 126

Rushdie, (Ahmed) Salman 1947- .... **CLC 23, 31, 55, 100; WLCS**
See also BEST 89:3; BPFB 3; BRWS 4; CA 108; 111; CANR 33, 56, 108; CN 7; CPW 1; DA3; DAB; DAC; DAM MST, NOV, POP; DLB 194; FANT; INT CA-111; MTCW 1, 2; RGEL 2; RGSF 2; TEA; WLIT 4

Rushforth, Peter (Scott) 1945- .... **CLC 19**
See also CA 101

Ruskin, John 1819-1900 .... **TCLC 63**
See also BRW 5; BYA 5; CA 114; 129; CD-BLB 1832-1890; DLB 55, 163, 190; RGEL 2; SATA 24; TEA; WCH

Russ, Joanna 1937- .... **CLC 15**
See also BPFB 3; CA 5-28R; CANR 11, 31, 65; CN 7; DLB 8; FW; GLL 1; MTCW 1; SCFW 2; SFW 4

Russell, George William 1867-1935
See A.E.; Baker, Jean H.
See also BRWS 8; CA 104; 153; CDBLB 1890-1914; DAM POET; RGEL 2

Russell, Jeffrey Burton 1934- .... **CLC 70**
See also CA 25-28R; CANR 11, 28, 52

Russell, (Henry) Ken(neth Alfred)
1927- .... **CLC 16**
See also CA 105

Russell, William Martin 1947-
See Russell, Willy
See also CA 164; CANR 107

Russell, Willy .... **CLC 60**
See also Russell, William Martin
See also CBD; CD 5; DLB 233

Rutherford, Mark .... **TCLC 25**
See also White, William Hale
See also DLB 18; RGEL 2

Ruyslinck, Ward .... **CLC 14**
See also Belser, Reimond Karel Maria de

Ryan, Cornelius (John) 1920-1974 ..... **CLC 7**
See also CA 69-72; 53-56; CANR 38

Ryan, Michael 1946- .... **CLC 65**
See also CA 49-52; CANR 109; DLBY 1982

Ryan, Tim
See Dent, Lester

Rybakov, Anatoli (Naumovich)
1911-1998 .... **CLC 23, 53**
See also CA 126; 135; 172; SATA 79; SATA-Obit 108

Ryder, Jonathan
See Ludlum, Robert

Ryga, George 1932-1987 .... **CLC 14**
See also CA 101; 124; CANR 43, 90; CCA 1; DAC; DAM MST; DLB 60

S. H.
See Hartmann, Sadakichi

S. S.
See Sassoon, Siegfried (Lorraine)

Saba, Umberto 1883-1957 .... **TCLC 33**
See also CA 144; CANR 79; DLB 114; RGWL 2

Sabatini, Rafael 1875-1950 .... **TCLC 47**
See also BPFB 3; CA 162; RHW

Sabato, Ernesto (R.) 1911- .... **CLC 10, 23; HLC 2**
See also CA 97-100; CANR 32, 65; CD-WLB 3; DAM MULT; DLB 145; HW 1, 2; LAW; MTCW 1, 2

Sa-Carniero, Mario de 1890-1916 . **TCLC 83**

Sacastru, Martin
See Bioy Casares, Adolfo
See also CWW 2

Sacher-Masoch, Leopold von
1836(?)-1895 .... **NCLC 31**

Sachs, Marilyn (Stickle) 1927- .... **CLC 35**
See also AAYA 2; BYA 6; CA 17-20R; CANR 13, 47; CLR 2; JRDA; MAICYA 1, 2; SAAS 2; SATA 3, 68; SATA-Essay 110; WYA; YAW

Sachs, Nelly 1891-1970 .... **CLC 14, 98**
See also CA 17-18; 25-28R; CANR 87; CAP 2; MTCW 2; RGWL 2

Sackler, Howard (Oliver)
1929-1982 .... **CLC 14**
See also CA 61-64; 108; CAD; CANR 30; DFS 15; DLB 7

Sacks, Oliver (Wolf) 1933- .... **CLC 67**
See also CA 53-56; CANR 28, 50, 76; CPW; DA3; INT CANR-28; MTCW 1, 2

Sadakichi
See Hartmann, Sadakichi

Sade, Donatien Alphonse Francois
1740-1814 .... **NCLC 3, 47**
See also EW 4; GFL Beginnings to 1789; RGWL 2

Sadoff, Ira 1945- .... **CLC 9**
See also CA 53-56; CANR 5, 21, 109; DLB 120

Saetone
See Camus, Albert

Safire, William 1929- .... **CLC 10**
See also CA 17-20R; CANR 31, 54, 91

Sagan, Carl (Edward) 1934-1996 .... **CLC 30, 112**
See also AAYA 2; CA 25-28R; 155; CANR 11, 36, 74; CPW; DA3; MTCW 1, 2; SATA 58; SATA-Obit 94

Sagan, Francoise .... **CLC 3, 6, 9, 17, 36**
See also Quoirez, Francoise
See also CWW 2; DLB 83; GFL 1789 to the Present; MTCW 2

Sahgal, Nayantara (Pandit) 1927- .... **CLC 41**
See also CA 9-12R; CANR 11, 88; CN 7

Said, Edward W. 1935- .... **CLC 123**
See also CA 21-24R; CANR 45, 74, 107; DLB 67; MTCW 2

Saint, H(arry) F. 1941- .... **CLC 50**
See also CA 127

St. Aubin de Teran, Lisa 1953-
See Teran, Lisa St. Aubin de
See also CA 118; 126; CN 7; INT 126

Saint Birgitta of Sweden c.
1303-1373 .... **CMLC 24**

Sainte-Beuve, Charles Augustin
1804-1869 .... **NCLC 5**
See also DLB 217; EW 6; GFL 1789 to the Present

Saint-Exupery, Antoine (Jean Baptiste Marie Roger) de 1900-1944 .... **TCLC 2, 56; WLC**
See also BPFB 3; BYA 3; CA 108; 132; CLR 10; DA3; DAM NOV; DLB 72; EW 12; GFL 1789 to the Present; LAIT 3; MAICYA 1, 2; MTCW 1, 2; RGWL 2; SATA 20; TWA

St. John, David
See Hunt, E(verette) Howard, (Jr.)

St. John, J. Hector
See Crevecoeur, Michel Guillaume Jean de

Saint-John Perse
See Leger, (Marie-Rene Auguste) Alexis Saint-Leger
See also EW 10; GFL 1789 to the Present; RGWL 2

Saintsbury, George (Edward Bateman)
1845-1933 .... **TCLC 31**
See also CA 160; DLB 57, 149

Sait Faik .... **TCLC 23**
See also Abasiyanik, Sait Faik

Saki .... **TCLC 3; SSC 12**
See also Munro, H(ector) H(ugh)
See also BRWS 6; LAIT 2; MTCW 2; RGEL 2; SSFS 1; SUFW

Sakutaro, Hagiwara
See Hagiwara, Sakutaro

Sala, George Augustus 1828-1895 . **NCLC 46**
Saladin 1138-1193 .... **CMLC 38**
Salama, Hannu 1936- .... **CLC 18**
Salamanca, J(ack) R(ichard) 1922- .. **CLC 4, 15**
See also CA 25-28R; CAAE 193

Salas, Floyd Francis 1931-
See also CA 119; CAAS 27; CANR 44, 75, 93; DAM MULT; DLB 82; HLC 2; HW 1, 2; MTCW 2

Sale, J. Kirkpatrick
See Sale, Kirkpatrick

Sale, Kirkpatrick 1937- .... **CLC 68**
See also CA 13-16R; CANR 10

Salinas, Luis Omar 1937- ... **CLC 90; HLC 2**
See also CA 131; CANR 81; DAM MULT; DLB 82; HW 1, 2

Salinas (y Serrano), Pedro
1891(?)-1951 .... **TCLC 17**
See also CA 117; DLB 134

Salinger, J(erome) D(avid) 1919- .. **CLC 1, 3, 8, 12, 55, 56, 138; SSC 2, 28; WLC**
See also AAYA 2, 36; AMW; BPFB 3; CA 5-8R; CANR 39; CDALB 1941-1968; CLR 18; CN 7; CPW 1; DA; DA3; DAB; DAC; DAM MST, NOV, POP; DLB 2, 102, 173; EXPN; LAIT 4; MAICYA 1, 2; MTCW 1, 2; NFS 1; RGAL 4; RGSF 2; SATA 67; TUS; WYA; YAW

Salisbury, John
See Caute, (John) David

Salter, James 1925- .... **CLC 7, 52, 59**
See also AMWS 9; CA 73-76; CANR 107; DLB 130

Saltus, Edgar (Everton) 1855-1921 . **TCLC 8**
See also CA 105; DLB 202; RGAL 4

Saltykov, Mikhail Evgrafovich
1826-1889 .... **NCLC 16**
See also DLB 238:

Saltykov-Shchedrin, N.
See Saltykov, Mikhail Evgrafovich

Samarakis, Antonis 1919- .... **CLC 5**
See also CA 25-28R; CAAS 16; CANR 36

Sanchez, Florencio 1875-1910 .... **TCLC 37**
See also CA 153; HW 1; LAW

Sanchez, Luis Rafael 1936- .... **CLC 23**
See also CA 128; DLB 145; HW 1; WLIT 1

Sanchez, Sonia 1934- .... **CLC 5, 116; BLC 3; PC 9**
See also BW 2, 3; CA 33-36R; CANR 24, 49, 74; CLR 18; CP 7; CSW; CWP; DA3; DAM MULT; DLB 41; DLBD 8; MAICYA 1, 2; MTCW 1, 2; SATA 22; WP

Sand, George 1804-1876 ..... **NCLC 2, 42, 57; WLC**
See also DA; DA3; DAB; DAC; DAM MST, NOV; DLB 119, 192; EW 6; FW; GFL 1789 to the Present; RGWL 2; TWA

Sandburg, Carl (August) 1878-1967 . **CLC 1, 4, 10, 15, 35; PC 2, 41; WLC**
See also AAYA 24; AMW; BYA 1, 3; CA 5-8R; 25-28R; CANR 35; CDALB 1865-1917; CLR 67; DA; DA3; DAB; DAC; DAM MST, POET; DLB 17, 54; EXPP; LAIT 2; MAICYA 1, 2; MTCW 1, 2; PAB; PFS 3, 6, 12; RGAL 4; SATA 8; TUS; WCH; WP; WYA

Sandburg, Charles
See Sandburg, Carl (August)

Sandburg, Charles A.
See Sandburg, Carl (August)

Sanders, (James) Ed(ward) 1939- .... **CLC 53**
See also Sanders, Edward
See also CA 13-16R; CAAS 21; CANR 13, 44, 78; CP 7; DAM POET; DLB 16, 244

Sanders, Edward
See Sanders, (James) Ed(ward)
See also DLB 244

Schulz, Bruno 1892-1942 .. **TCLC 5, 51; SSC 13**
See also CA 115; 123; CANR 86; CDWLB 4; DLB 215; MTCW 2; RGSF 2; RGWL 2

Schulz, Charles M(onroe)
1922-2000 .... **CLC 12**
See also AAYA 39; CA 9-12R; 187; CANR 6; INT CANR-6; SATA 10; SATA-Obit 118

Schumacher, E(rnst) F(riedrich)
1911-1977 .... **CLC 80**
See also CA 81-84; 73-76; CANR 34, 85

Schuyler, James Marcus 1923-1991 .. **CLC 5, 23**
See also CA 101; 134; DAM POET; DLB 5, 169; INT 101; WP

Schwartz, Delmore (David)
1913-1966 ... **CLC 2, 4, 10, 45, 87; PC 8**
See also AMWS 2; CA 17-18; 25-28R; CANR 35; CAP 2; DLB 28, 48; MTCW 1, 2; PAB; RGAL 4; TUS

Schwartz, Ernst
See Ozu, Yasujiro

Schwartz, John Burnham 1965- .... **CLC 59**
See also CA 132

Schwartz, Lynne Sharon 1939- .... **CLC 31**
See also CA 103; CANR 44, 89; DLB 218; MTCW 2

Schwartz, Muriel A.
See Eliot, T(homas) S(tearns)

Schwarz-Bart, Andre 1928- .... **CLC 2, 4**
See also CA 89-92; CANR 109

Schwarz-Bart, Simone 1938- . **CLC 7; BLCS**
See also BW 2; CA 97-100

Schwerner, Armand 1927-1999 .... **PC 42**
See also CA 9-12R; 179; CANR 50, 85; CP 7; DLB 165

Schwitters, Kurt (Hermann Edward Karl Julius) 1887-1948 .... **TCLC 95**
See also CA 158

Schwob, Marcel (Mayer Andre)
1867-1905 .... **TCLC 20**
See also CA 117; 168; DLB 123; GFL 1789 to the Present

Sciascia, Leonardo 1921-1989 .. **CLC 8, 9, 41**
See also CA 85-88; 130; CANR 35; DLB 177; MTCW 1; RGWL 2

Scoppettone, Sandra 1936- .... **CLC 26**
See also Early, Jack
See also AAYA 11; BYA 8; CA 5-8R; CANR 41, 73; GLL 1; MAICYA 2; MAICYAS 1; SATA 9, 92; WYA; YAW

Scorsese, Martin 1942- .... **CLC 20, 89**
See also AAYA 38; CA 110; 114; CANR 46, 85

Scotland, Jay
See Jakes, John (William)

Scott, Duncan Campbell
1862-1947 .... **TCLC 6**
See also CA 104; 153; DAC; DLB 92; RGEL 2

Scott, Evelyn 1893-1963 .... **CLC 43**
See also CA 104; 112; CANR 64; DLB 9, 48; RHW

Scott, F(rancis) R(eginald)
1899-1985 .... **CLC 22**
See also CA 101; 114; CANR 87; DLB 88; INT CA-101; RGEL 2

Scott, Frank
See Scott, F(rancis) R(eginald)

Scott, Joan .... **CLC 65**

Scott, Joanna 1960- .... **CLC 50**
See also CA 126; CANR 53, 92

Scott, Paul (Mark) 1920-1978 .... **CLC 9, 60**
See also BRWS 1; CA 81-84; 77-80; CANR 33; DLB 14, 207; MTCW 1; RGEL 2; RHW

Scott, Sarah 1723-1795 .... **LC 44**
See also DLB 39

Scott, Sir Walter 1771-1832 .... **NCLC 15, 69, 110; PC 13; SSC 32; WLC**
See also AAYA 22; BRW 4; BYA 2; CD-BLB 1789-1832; DA; DAB; DAC; DAM MST, NOV, POET; DLB 93, 107, 116, 144, 159; HGG; LAIT 1; RGEL 2; RGSF 2; SSFS 10; SUFW; TEA; WLIT 3; YABC 2

Scribe, (Augustin) Eugene
1791-1861 .... **NCLC 16; DC 5**
See also DAM DRAM; DLB 192; GFL 1789 to the Present; RGWL 2

Scrum, R.
See Crumb, R(obert)

Scudery, Georges de 1601-1667 .... **LC 75**
See also GFL Beginnings to 1789

Scudery, Madeleine de 1607-1701 .. **LC 2, 58**
See also GFL Beginnings to 1789

Scum
See Crumb, R(obert)

Scumbag, Little Bobby
See Crumb, R(obert)

Seabrook, John
See Hubbard, L(afayette) Ron(ald)

Sealy, I(rwin) Allan 1951- .... **CLC 55**
See also CA 136; CN 7

Search, Alexander
See Pessoa, Fernando (Antonio Nogueira)

Sebastian, Lee
See Silverberg, Robert

Sebastian Owl
See Thompson, Hunter S(tockton)

Sebestyen, Igen
See Sebestyen, Ouida

Sebestyen, Ouida 1924- .... **CLC 30**
See also AAYA 8; BYA 7; CA 107; CANR 40; CLR 17; JRDA; MAICYA 1, 2; SAAS 10; SATA 39; WYA; YAW

Secundus, H. Scriblerus
See Fielding, Henry

Sedges, John
See Buck, Pearl S(ydenstricker)

Sedgwick, Catharine Maria
1789-1867 .... **NCLC 19, 98**
See also DLB 1, 74, 183, 239, 243, 254; RGAL 4

Seelye, John (Douglas) 1931- .... **CLC 7**
See also CA 97-100; CANR 70; INT 97-100; TCWW 2

Seferiades, Giorgos Stylianou 1900-1971
See Seferis, George
See also CA 5-8R; 33-36R; CANR 5, 36; MTCW 1

Seferis, George .... **CLC 5, 11**
See also Seferiades, Giorgos Stylianou
See also EW 12; RGWL 2

Segal, Erich (Wolf) 1937- .... **CLC 3, 10**
See also BEST 89:1; BPFB 3; CA 25-28R; CANR 20, 36, 65; CPW; DAM POP; DLBY 1986; INT CANR-20; MTCW 1

Seger, Bob 1945- .... **CLC 35**

Seghers, Anna -1983 .... **CLC 7**
See also Radvanyi, Netty
See also CDWLB 2; DLB 69

Seidel, Frederick (Lewis) 1936- .... **CLC 18**
See also CA 13-16R; CANR 8, 99; CP 7; DLBY 1984

Seifert, Jaroslav 1901-1986 .. **CLC 34, 44, 93**
See also CA 127; CDWLB 4; DLB 215; MTCW 1, 2

Sei Shonagon c. 966-1017(?) .... **CMLC 6**

Sejour, Victor 1817-1874 .... **DC 10**
See also DLB 50

Sejour Marcou et Ferrand, Juan Victor
See Sejour, Victor

Selby, Hubert, Jr. 1928- .... **CLC 1, 2, 4, 8; SSC 20**
See also CA 13-16R; CANR 33, 85; CN 7; DLB 2, 227

Selzer, Richard 1928- .... **CLC 74**
See also CA 65-68; CANR 14, 106

Sembene, Ousmane
See Ousmane, Sembene
See also AFW; CWW 2; WLIT 2

Senancour, Etienne Pivert de
1770-1846 .... **NCLC 16**
See also DLB 119; GFL 1789 to the Present

Sender, Ramon (Jose) 1902-1982 ...... **CLC 8; HLC 2**
See also CA 5-8R; 105; CANR 8; DAM MULT; HW 1; MTCW 1; RGWL 2

Seneca, Lucius Annaeus c. 4 B.C.-c. 65 .... **CMLC 6; DC 5**
See also AW 2; CDWLB 1; DAM DRAM; DLB 211; RGWL 2; TWA

Senghor, Leopold Sedar 1906-2001 . **CLC 54, 130; BLC 3; PC 25**
See also AFW; BW 2; CA 116; 125; 203; CANR 47, 74; DAM MULT, POET; DNFS 2; GFL 1789 to the Present; MTCW 1, 2; TWA

Senna, Danzy 1970- .... **CLC 119**
See also CA 169

Serling, (Edward) Rod(man)
1924-1975 .... **CLC 30**
See also AAYA 14; AITN 1; CA 162; 57-60; DLB 26; SFW 4

Serna, Ramon Gomez de la
See Gomez de la Serna, Ramon

Serpieres
See Guillevic, (Eugene)

Service, Robert
See Service, Robert W(illiam)
See also BYA 4; DAB; DLB 92

Service, Robert W(illiam)
1874(?)-1958 .... **TCLC 15; WLC**
See also Service, Robert
See also CA 115; 140; CANR 84; DA; DAC; DAM MST, POET; PFS 10; RGEL 2; SATA 20

Seth, Vikram 1952- .... **CLC 43, 90**
See also CA 121; 127; CANR 50, 74; CN 7; CP 7; DA3; DAM MULT; DLB 120; INT 127; MTCW 2

Seton, Cynthia Propper 1926-1982 .. **CLC 27**
See also CA 5-8R; 108; CANR 7

Seton, Ernest (Evan) Thompson
1860-1946 .... **TCLC 31**
See also ANW; BYA 3; CA 109; CLR 59; DLB 92; DLBD 13; JRDA; SATA 18

Seton-Thompson, Ernest
See Seton, Ernest (Evan) Thompson

Settle, Mary Lee 1918- .... **CLC 19, 61**
See also BPFB 3; CA 89-92; CAAS 1; CANR 44, 87; CN 7; CSW; DLB 6; INT 89-92

Seuphor, Michel
See Arp, Jean

Sevigne, Marie (de Rabutin-Chantal)
1626-1696 .... **LC 11**
See also GFL Beginnings to 1789; TWA

Sewall, Samuel 1652-1730 .... **LC 38**
See also DLB 24; RGAL 4

Sexton, Anne (Harvey) 1928-1974 ..... **CLC 2, 4, 6, 8, 10, 15, 53, 123; PC 2; WLC**
See also AMWS 2; CA 1-4R; 53-56; CABS 2; CANR 3, 36; CDALB 1941-1968; DA; DA3; DAB; DAC; DAM MST, POET; DLB 5, 169; EXPP; FW; MAWW; MTCW 1, 2; PAB; PFS 4, 14; RGAL 4; SATA 10; TUS

Shaara, Jeff 1952- .... **CLC 119**
See also CA 163; CANR 109

Shaara, Michael (Joseph, Jr.)
1929-1988 .... **CLC 15**
See also AITN 1; BPFB 3; CA 102; 125; CANR 52, 85; DAM POP; DLBY 1983

Shackleton, C. C.
See Aldiss, Brian W(ilson)

Shacochis, Bob .... **CLC 39**
See also Shacochis, Robert G.

Shacochis, Robert G. 1951-
See Shacochis, Bob
See also CA 119; 124; CANR 100; INT 124

Shaffer, Anthony (Joshua)
1926-2001 .... **CLC 19**
See also CA 110; 116; 200; CBD; CD 5; DAM DRAM; DFS 13; DLB 13

Shaffer, Peter (Levin) 1926- .. **CLC 5, 14, 18, 37, 60; DC 7**
See also BRWS 1; CA 25-28R; CANR 25, 47, 74; CBD; CD 5; CDBLB 1960 to Present; DA3; DAB; DAM DRAM, MST; DFS 5, 13; DLB 13, 233; MTCW 1, 2; RGEL 2; TEA

Shakey, Bernard
See Young, Neil

Shalamov, Varlam (Tikhonovich)
1907(?)-1982 .... **CLC 18**
See also CA 129; 105; RGSF 2

Shamlu, Ahmad 1925-2000 .... **CLC 10**
See also CWW 2

Shammas, Anton 1951- .... **CLC 55**
See also CA 199

Shandling, Arline
See Berriault, Gina

Shange, Ntozake 1948- .... **CLC 8, 25, 38, 74, 126; BLC 3; DC 3**
See also AAYA 9; AFAW 1, 2; BW 2; CA 85-88; CABS 3; CAD; CANR 27, 48, 74; CD 5; CP 7; CWD; CWP; DA3; DAM DRAM, MULT; DFS 2, 11; DLB 38, 249; FW; LAIT 5; MTCW 1, 2; NFS 11; RGAL 4; YAW

Shanley, John Patrick 1950- .... **CLC 75**
See also CA 128; 133; CAD; CANR 83; CD 5

Shapcott, Thomas W(illiam) 1935- .. **CLC 38**
See also CA 69-72; CANR 49, 83, 103; CP 7

Shapiro, Jane 1942- .... **CLC 76**
See also CA 196

Shapiro, Karl (Jay) 1913-2000 ...... **CLC 4, 8, 15, 53; PC 25**
See also AMWS 2; CA 1-4R; 188; CAAS 6; CANR 1, 36, 66; CP 7; DLB 48; EXPP; MTCW 1, 2; PFS 3; RGAL 4

Sharp, William 1855-1905 .... **TCLC 39**
See also Macleod, Fiona
See also CA 160; DLB 156; RGEL 2

Sharpe, Thomas Ridley 1928-
See Sharpe, Tom
See also CA 114; 122; CANR 85; INT CA-122

Sharpe, Tom .... **CLC 36**
See also Sharpe, Thomas Ridley
See also CN 7; DLB 14, 231

Shatrov, Mikhail .... **CLC 59**

Shaw, Bernard
See Shaw, George Bernard
See also DLB 190

Shaw, G. Bernard
See Shaw, George Bernard

Shaw, George Bernard 1856-1950 .. **TCLC 3, 9, 21, 45; WLC**
See also Shaw, Bernard
See also BRW 6; BRWR 2; CA 104; 128; CDBLB 1914-1945; DA; DA3; DAB; DAC; DAM DRAM, MST; DFS 1, 3, 6, 11; DLB 10, 57; LAIT 3; MTCW 1, 2; RGEL 2; TEA; WLIT 4

Shaw, Henry Wheeler 1818-1885 .. **NCLC 15**
See also DLB 11; RGAL 4

Shaw, Irwin 1913-1984 .... **CLC 7, 23, 34**
See also AITN 1; BPFB 3; CA 13-16R; 112; CANR 21; CDALB 1941-1968; CPW; DAM DRAM, POP; DLB 6, 102; DLBY 1984; MTCW 1, 21

Shaw, Robert 1927-1978 .... **CLC 5**
See also AITN 1; CA 1-4R; 81-84; CANR 4; DLB 13, 14

Shaw, T. E.
See Lawrence, T(homas) E(dward)

Shawn, Wallace 1943- .... **CLC 41**
See also CA 112; CAD; CD 5; DLB 266

Shchedrin, N.
See Saltykov, Mikhail Evgrafovich

Shea, Lisa 1953- .... **CLC 86**
See also CA 147

Sheed, Wilfrid (John Joseph) 1930- . **CLC 2, 4, 10, 53**
See also CA 65-68; CANR 30, 66; CN 7; DLB 6; MTCW 1, 2

Sheldon, Alice Hastings Bradley
1915(?)-1987
See Tiptree, James, Jr.
See also CA 108; 122; CANR 34; INT 108; MTCW 1

Sheldon, John
See Bloch, Robert (Albert)

Sheldon, Walter J(ames) 1917-1996
See Queen, Ellery
See also AITN 1; CA 25-28R; CANR 10

Shelley, Mary Wollstonecraft (Godwin)
1797-1851 ...... **NCLC 14, 59, 103; WLC**
See also AAYA 20; BPFB 3; BRW 3; BRWS 5; BYA 5; CDBLB 1789-1832; DA; DA3; DAB; DAC; DAM MST, NOV; DLB 110, 116, 159, 178; EXPN; HGG; LAIT 1; NFS 1; RGEL 2; SATA 29; SCFW; SFW 4; TEA; WLIT 3

Shelley, Percy Bysshe 1792-1822 .. **NCLC 18, 93; PC 14; WLC**
See also BRW 4; BRWR 1; CDBLB 1789-1832; DA; DA3; DAB; DAC; DAM MST, POET; DLB 96, 110, 158; EXPP; PAB; PFS 2; RGEL 2; TEA; WLIT 3; WP

Shepard, Jim 1956- .... **CLC 36**
See also CA 137; CANR 59, 104; SATA 90

Shepard, Lucius 1947- .... **CLC 34**
See also CA 128; 141; CANR 81; HGG; SCFW 2; SFW 4

Shepard, Sam 1943- .... **CLC 4, 6, 17, 34, 41, 44; DC 5**
See also AAYA 1; AMWS 3; CA 69-72; CABS 3; CAD; CANR 22; CD 5; DA3; DAM DRAM; DFS 3, 6, 7, 14; DLB 7, 212; IDFW 3, 4; MTCW 1, 2; RGAL 4

Shepherd, Michael
See Ludlum, Robert

Sherburne, Zoa (Lillian Morin)
1912-1995 .... **CLC 30**
See also AAYA 13; CA 1-4R; 176; CANR 3, 37; MAICYA 1, 2; SAAS 18; SATA 3; YAW

Sheridan, Frances 1724-1766 .... **LC 7**
See also DLB 39, 84

Sheridan, Richard Brinsley
1751-1816 .... **NCLC 5, 91; DC 1; WLC**
See also BRW 3; CDBLB 1660-1789; DA; DAB; DAC; DAM DRAM, MST; DFS 15; DLB 89; WLIT 3

Sherman, Jonathan Marc .... **CLC 55**

Sherman, Martin 1941(?)- .... **CLC 19**
See also CA 116; 123; CANR 86

Sherwin, Judith Johnson
See Johnson, Judith (Emlyn)
See also CANR 85; CP 7; CWP

Sherwood, Frances 1940- .... **CLC 81**
See also CA 146

Sherwood, Robert E(mmet)
1896-1955 .... **TCLC 3**
See also CA 104; 153; CANR 86; DAM DRAM; DFS 15; DLB 7, 26, 249; IDFW 3, 4; RGAL 4

Shestov, Lev 1866-1938 .... **TCLC 56**

Shevchenko, Taras 1814-1861 .... **NCLC 54**

Shiel, M(atthew) P(hipps)
1865-1947 .... **TCLC 8**
See also Holmes, Gordon
See also CA 106; 160; DLB 153; HGG; MTCW 2; SFW 4; SUFW

Shields, Carol 1935- .... **CLC 91, 113**
See also AMWS 7; CA 81-84; CANR 51, 74, 98; CCA 1; CN 7; CPW; DA3; DAC; MTCW 2

Shields, David 1956- .... **CLC 97**
See also CA 124; CANR 48, 99

Shiga, Naoya 1883-1971 ..... **CLC 33; SSC 23**
See also Shiga Naoya
See also CA 101; 33-36R; MJW

Shiga Naoya
See Shiga, Naoya
See also DLB 180

Shilts, Randy 1951-1994 .... **CLC 85**
See also AAYA 19; CA 115; 127; 144; CANR 45; DA3; GLL 1; INT 127; MTCW 2

Shimazaki, Haruki 1872-1943
See Shimazaki Toson
See also CA 105; 134; CANR 84

Shimazaki Toson .... **TCLC 5**
See also Shimazaki, Haruki
See also DLB 180

Sholokhov, Mikhail (Aleksandrovich)
1905-1984 .... **CLC 7, 15**
See also CA 101; 112; MTCW 1, 2; RGWL 2; SATA-Obit 36

Shone, Patric
See Hanley, James

Shreve, Susan Richards 1939- .... **CLC 23**
See also CA 49-52; CAAS 5; CANR 5, 38, 69, 100; MAICYA 1, 2; SATA 46, 95; SATA-Brief 41

Shue, Larry 1946-1985 .... **CLC 52**
See also CA 145; 117; DAM DRAM; DFS 7

Shu-Jen, Chou 1881-1936
See Lu Hsun
See also CA 104

Shulman, Alix Kates 1932- .... **CLC 2, 10**
See also CA 29-32R; CANR 43; FW; SATA 7

Shusaku, Endo
See Endo, Shusaku

Shuster, Joe 1914-1992 .... **CLC 21**

Shute, Nevil .... **CLC 30**
See also Norway, Nevil Shute
See also BPFB 3; DLB 255; NFS 9; RHW; SFW 4

Shuttle, Penelope (Diane) 1947- .... **CLC 7**
See also CA 93-96; CANR 39, 84, 92, 108; CP 7; CWP; DLB 14, 40

Sidney, Mary 1561-1621 .... **LC 19, 39**
See also Sidney Herbert, Mary

Sidney, Sir Philip 1554-1586 . **LC 19, 39; PC 32**
See also BRW 1; BRWR 2; CDBLB Before 1660; DA; DA3; DAB; DAC; DAM MST, POET; DLB 167; EXPP; PAB; RGEL 2; TEA; WP

Sidney Herbert, Mary
See Sidney, Mary
See also DLB 167

Siegel, Jerome 1914-1996 .... **CLC 21**
See also CA 116; 169; 151

Siegel, Jerry
See Siegel, Jerome

Sienkiewicz, Henryk (Adam Alexander Pius)
1846-1916 .... **TCLC 3**
See also CA 104; 134; CANR 84; RGSF 2;
RGWL 2

Sierra, Gregorio Martinez
See Martinez Sierra, Gregorio

Sierra, Maria (de la O'LeJarraga) Martinez
See Martinez Sierra, Maria (de la
O'LeJarraga)

Sigal, Clancy 1926- .... **CLC 7**
See also CA 1-4R; CANR 85; CN 7

Sigourney, Lydia H.
See Sigourney, Lydia Howard (Huntley)
See also DLB 73, 183

Sigourney, Lydia Howard (Huntley)
1791-1865 .... **NCLC 21, 87**
See also Sigourney, Lydia H.; Sigourney,
Lydia Huntley
See also DLB 1

Sigourney, Lydia Huntley
See Sigourney, Lydia Howard (Huntley)
See also DLB 42, 239, 243

Siguenza y Gongora, Carlos de
1645-1700 .... **LC 8; HLCS 2**
See also LAW

Sigurjonsson, Johann 1880-1919 ... **TCLC 27**
See also CA 170

Sikelianos, Angelos 1884-1951 ...... **TCLC 39;**
PC 29
See also RGWL 2

Silkin, Jon 1930-1997 .... **CLC 2, 6, 43**
See also CA 5-8R; CAAS 5; CANR 89; CP
7; DLB 27

Silko, Leslie (Marmon) 1948- .... **CLC 23, 74,**
114; SSC 37; WLCS
See also AAYA 14; AMWS 4; ANW; BYA
12; CA 115; 122; CANR 45, 65; CN 7;
CP 7; CPW 1; CWP; DA; DA3; DAC;
DAM MST, MULT, POP; DLB 143, 175,
256; EXPP; EXPS; LAIT 4; MTCW 2;
NFS 4; NNAL; PFS 9; RGAL 4; RGSF 2;
SSFS 4, 8, 10, 11

Sillanpaa, Frans Eemil 1888-1964 ... **CLC 19**
See also CA 129; 93-96; MTCW 1

Sillitoe, Alan 1928- .. **CLC 1, 3, 6, 10, 19, 57,**
148
See also AITN 1; BRWS 5; CA 9-12R;
CAAE 191; CAAS 2; CANR 8, 26, 55;
CDBLB 1960 to Present; CN 7; DLB 14,
139; MTCW 1, 2; RGEL 2; RGSF 2;
SATA 61

Silone, Ignazio 1900-1978 .... **CLC 4**
See also CA 25-28; 81-84; CANR 34; CAP
2; DLB 264; EW 12; MTCW 1; RGSF 2;
RGWL 2

Silone, Ignazione
See Silone, Ignazio

Silva, Jose Asuncion
See da Silva, Antonio Jose
See also LAW

Silver, Joan Micklin 1935- .... **CLC 20**
See also CA 114; 121; INT 121

Silver, Nicholas
See Faust, Frederick (Schiller)
See also TCWW 2

Silverberg, Robert 1935- .... **CLC 7, 140**
See also AAYA 24; BPFB 3; BYA 7, 9; CA
1-4R, 186; CAAE 186; CAAS 3; CANR
1, 20, 36, 85; CLR 59; CN 7; CPW; DAM
POP; DLB 8; INT CANR-20; MAICYA
1, 2; MTCW 1, 2; SATA 13, 91; SATA-
Essay 104; SCFW 2; SFW 4

Silverstein, Alvin 1933- .... **CLC 17**
See also CA 49-52; CANR 2; CLR 25;
JRDA; MAICYA 1, 2; SATA 8, 69, 124

Silverstein, Virginia B(arbara Opshelor)
1937- .... **CLC 17**
See also CA 49-52; CANR 2; CLR 25;
JRDA; MAICYA 1, 2; SATA 8, 69, 124

Sim, Georges
See Simenon, Georges (Jacques Christian)

Simak, Clifford D(onald) 1904-1988 . **CLC 1,**
55
See also CA 1-4R; 125; CANR 1, 35; DLB
8; MTCW 1; SATA-Obit 56; SFW 4

Simenon, Georges (Jacques Christian)
1903-1989 .... **CLC 1, 2, 3, 8, 18, 47**
See also BPFB 3; CA 85-88; 129; CANR
35; CMW 4; DA3; DAM POP; DLB 72;
DLBY 1989; EW 12; GFL 1789 to the
Present; MSW; MTCW 1, 2; RGWL 2

Simic, Charles 1938- .... **CLC 6, 9, 22, 49, 68,**
130
See also AMWS 8; CA 29-32R; CAAS 4;
CANR 12, 33, 52, 61, 96; CP 7; DA3;
DAM POET; DLB 105; MTCW 2; PFS 7;
RGAL 4; WP

Simmel, Georg 1858-1918 .... **TCLC 64**
See also CA 157

Simmons, Charles (Paul) 1924- .... **CLC 57**
See also CA 89-92; INT 89-92

Simmons, Dan 1948- .... **CLC 44**
See also AAYA 16; CA 138; CANR 53, 81;
CPW; DAM POP; HGG

Simmons, James (Stewart Alexander)
1933- .... **CLC 43**
See also CA 105; CAAS 21; CP 7; DLB 40

Simms, William Gilmore
1806-1870 .... **NCLC 3**
See also DLB 3, 30, 59, 73, 248, 254;
RGAL 4

Simon, Carly 1945- .... **CLC 26**
See also CA 105

Simon, Claude 1913-1984 ... **CLC 4, 9, 15, 39**
See also CA 89-92; CANR 33; DAM NOV;
DLB 83; EW 13; GFL 1789 to the Present;
MTCW 1

Simon, Myles
See Follett, Ken(neth Martin)

Simon, (Marvin) Neil 1927- ... **CLC 6, 11, 31,**
39, 70; DC 14
See also AAYA 32; AITN 1; AMWS 4; CA
21-24R; CANR 26, 54, 87; CD 5; DA3;
DAM DRAM; DFS 2, 6, 12; DLB 7, 266;
LAIT 4; MTCW 1, 2; RGAL 4; TUS

Simon, Paul (Frederick) 1941(?)- ..... **CLC 17**
See also CA 116; 153

Simonon, Paul 1956(?)- .... **CLC 30**

Simonson, Rick ed. .... **CLC 70**

Simpson, Harriette
See Arnow, Harriette (Louisa) Simpson

Simpson, Louis (Aston Marantz)
1923- .... **CLC 4, 7, 9, 32, 149**
See also AMWS 9; CA 1-4R; CAAS 4;
CANR 1, 61; CP 7; DAM POET; DLB 5;
MTCW 1, 2; PFS 7, 11, 14; RGAL 4

Simpson, Mona (Elizabeth) 1957- ... **CLC 44,**
146
See also CA 122; 135; CANR 68, 103; CN
7

Simpson, N(orman) F(rederick)
1919- .... **CLC 29**
See also CA 13-16R; CBD; DLB 13; RGEL
2

Sinclair, Andrew (Annandale) 1935- . **CLC 2,**
14
See also CA 9-12R; CAAS 5; CANR 14,
38, 91; CN 7; DLB 14; FANT; MTCW 1

Sinclair, Emil
See Hesse, Hermann

Sinclair, Iain 1943- .... **CLC 76**
See also CA 132; CANR 81; CP 7; HGG

Sinclair, Iain MacGregor
See Sinclair, Iain

Sinclair, Irene
See Griffith, D(avid Lewelyn) W(ark)

Sinclair, Mary Amelia St. Clair 1865(?)-1946
See Sinclair, May
See also CA 104; HGG; RHW

Sinclair, May .... **TCLC 3, 11**
See also Sinclair, Mary Amelia St. Clair
See also CA 166; DLB 36, 135; RGEL 2;
SUFW

Sinclair, Roy
See Griffith, D(avid Lewelyn) W(ark)

Sinclair, Upton (Beall) 1878-1968 ..... **CLC 1,**
11, 15, 63; WLC
See also AMWS 5; BPFB 3; BYA 2; CA
5-8R; 25-28R; CANR 7; CDALB 1929-
1941; DA; DA3; DAB; DAC; DAM MST,
NOV; DLB 9; INT CANR-7; LAIT 3;
MTCW 1, 2; NFS 6; RGAL 4; SATA 9;
TUS; YAW

Singer, Isaac
See Singer, Isaac Bashevis

Singer, Isaac Bashevis 1904-1991 .. **CLC 1, 3,**
6, 9, 11, 15, 23, 38, 69, 111; SSC 3, 53;
WLC
See also AAYA 32; AITN 1, 2; AMW;
BPFB 3; BYA 1, 4; CA 1-4R; 134; CANR
1, 39, 106; CDALB 1941-1968; CLR 1;
CWRI 5; DA; DA3; DAB; DAC; DAM
MST, NOV; DLB 6, 28, 52; DLBY 1991;
EXPS; HGG; JRDA; LAIT 3; MAICYA
1, 2; MTCW 1, 2; RGAL 4; RGSF 2;
SATA 3, 27; SATA-Obit 68; SSFS 2, 12;
TUS; TWA

Singer, Israel Joshua 1893-1944 .... **TCLC 33**
See also CA 169

Singh, Khushwant 1915- .... **CLC 11**
See also CA 9-12R; CAAS 9; CANR 6, 84;
CN 7; RGEL 2

Singleton, Ann
See Benedict, Ruth (Fulton)

Singleton, John 1968(?)- .... **CLC 156**
See also BW 2, 3; CA 138; CANR 67, 82;
DAM MULT

Sinjohn, John
See Galsworthy, John

Sinyavsky, Andrei (Donatevich)
1925-1997 .... **CLC 8**
See also Tertz, Abram
See also CA 85-88; 159

Sirin, V.
See Nabokov, Vladimir (Vladimirovich)

Sissman, L(ouis) E(dward)
1928-1976 .... **CLC 9, 18**
See also CA 21-24R; 65-68; CANR 13;
DLB 5

Sisson, C(harles) H(ubert) 1914- .... **CLC 8**
See also CA 1-4R; CAAS 3; CANR 3, 48,
84; CP 7; DLB 27

Sitwell, Dame Edith 1887-1964 ..... **CLC 2, 9,**
67; PC 3
See also BRW 7; CA 9-12R; CANR 35;
CDBLB 1945-1960; DAM POET; DLB
20; MTCW 1, 2; RGEL 2; TEA

Siwaarmill, H. P.
See Sharp, William

Sjoewall, Maj 1935- .... **CLC 7**
See also Sjowall, Maj
See also CA 65-68; CANR 73

Sjowall, Maj
See Sjoewall, Maj
See also BPFB 3; CMW 4; MSW

Skelton, John 1460(?)-1529 ..... **LC 71; PC 25**
See also BRW 1; DLB 136; RGEL 2

Skelton, Robin 1925-1997 .... **CLC 13**
See also AITN 2; CA 5-8R; 160; CAAS 5;
CANR 28, 89; CCA 1; CP 7; DLB 27, 53

Skolimowski, Jerzy 1938- .... **CLC 20**
See also CA 128

INT CA-125; JRDA; MAICYA 2; MAIC-YAS 1; MTCW 2; PFS 7; RGAL 4; SATA 80, 120; WYA; YAW

Soupault, Philippe 1897-1990 .... **CLC 68**
See also CA 116; 147; 131; GFL 1789 to the Present

Souster, (Holmes) Raymond 1921- .... **CLC 5, 14**
See also CA 13-16R; CAAS 14; CANR 13, 29, 53; CP 7; DA3; DAC; DAM POET; DLB 88; RGEL 2; SATA 63

Southern, Terry 1924(?)-1995 .... **CLC 7**
See also AMWS 11; BPFB 3; CA 1-4R; 150; CANR 1, 55, 107; CN 7; DLB 2; IDFW 3, 4

Southey, Robert 1774-1843 .... **NCLC 8, 97**
See also BRW 4; DLB 93, 107, 142; RGEL 2; SATA 54

Southworth, Emma Dorothy Eliza Nevitte
1819-1899 .... **NCLC 26**
See also DLB 239

Souza, Ernest
See Scott, Evelyn

Soyinka, Wole 1934- .... **CLC 3, 5, 14, 36, 44; BLC 3; DC 2; WLC**
See also AFW; BW 2, 3; CA 13-16R; CANR 27, 39, 82; CD 5; CDWLB 3; CN 7; CP 7; DA; DA3; DAB; DAC; DAM DRAM, MST, MULT; DFS 10; DLB 125; MTCW 1, 2; RGEL 2; TWA; WLIT 2

Spackman, W(illiam) M(ode)
1905-1990 .... **CLC 46**
See also CA 81-84; 132

Spacks, Barry (Bernard) 1931- .... **CLC 14**
See also CA 154; CANR 33, 109; CP 7; DLB 105

Spanidou, Irini 1946- .... **CLC 44**
See also CA 185

Spark, Muriel (Sarah) 1918- ..... **CLC 2, 3, 5, 8, 13, 18, 40, 94; SSC 10**
See also BRWS 1; CA 5-8R; CANR 12, 36, 76, 89; CDBLB 1945-1960; CN 7; CP 7; DA3; DAB; DAC; DAM MST, NOV; DLB 15, 139; FW; INT CANR-12; LAIT 4; MTCW 1, 2; RGEL 2; TEA; WLIT 4; YAW

Spaulding, Douglas
See Bradbury, Ray (Douglas)

Spaulding, Leonard
See Bradbury, Ray (Douglas)

Spelman, Elizabeth .... **CLC 65**

Spence, J. A. D.
See Eliot, T(homas) S(tearns)

Spencer, Elizabeth 1921- .... **CLC 22**
See also CA 13-16R; CANR 32, 65, 87; CN 7; CSW; DLB 6, 218; MTCW 1; RGAL 4; SATA 14

Spencer, Leonard G.
See Silverberg, Robert

Spencer, Scott 1945- .... **CLC 30**
See also CA 113; CANR 51; DLBY 1986

Spender, Stephen (Harold)
1909-1995 .... **CLC 1, 2, 5, 10, 41, 91**
See also BRWS 2; CA 9-12R; 149; CANR 31, 54; CDBLB 1945-1960; CP 7; DA3; DAM POET; DLB 20; MTCW 1, 2; PAB; RGEL 2; TEA

Spengler, Oswald (Arnold Gottfried)
1880-1936 .... **TCLC 25**
See also CA 118; 189

Spenser, Edmund 1552(?)-1599 ..... **LC 5, 39; PC 8, 42; WLC**
See also BRW 1; CDBLB Before 1660; DA; DA3; DAB; DAC; DAM MST, POET; DLB 167; EFS 2; EXPP; PAB; RGEL 2; TEA; WLIT 3; WP

Spicer, Jack 1925-1965 .... **CLC 8, 18, 72**
See also CA 85-88; DAM POET; DLB 5, 16, 193; GLL 1; WP

Spiegelman, Art 1948- .... **CLC 76**
See also AAYA 10; CA 125; CANR 41, 55, 74; MTCW 2; SATA 109; YAW

Spielberg, Peter 1929- .... **CLC 6**
See also CA 5-8R; CANR 4, 48; DLBY 1981

Spielberg, Steven 1947- .... **CLC 20**
See also AAYA 8, 24; CA 77-80; CANR 32; SATA 32

Spillane, Frank Morrison 1918-
See Spillane, Mickey
See also CA 25-28R; CANR 28, 63; DA3; MTCW 1, 2; SATA 66

Spillane, Mickey .... **CLC 3, 13**
See also Spillane, Frank Morrison
See also BPFB 3; CMW 4; DLB 226; MSW; MTCW 2

Spinoza, Benedictus de 1632-1677 .. **LC 9, 58**

Spinrad, Norman (Richard) 1940- ... **CLC 46**
See also BPFB 3; CA 37-40R; CAAS 19; CANR 20, 91; DLB 8; INT CANR-20; SFW 4

Spitteler, Carl (Friedrich Georg)
1845-1924 .... **TCLC 12**
See also CA 109; DLB 129

Spivack, Kathleen (Romola Drucker)
1938- .... **CLC 6**
See also CA 49-52

Spoto, Donald 1941- .... **CLC 39**
See also CA 65-68; CANR 11, 57, 93

Springsteen, Bruce (F.) 1949- .... **CLC 17**
See also CA 111

Spurling, Hilary 1940- .... **CLC 34**
See also CA 104; CANR 25, 52, 94

Spyker, John Howland
See Elman, Richard (Martin)

Squires, (James) Radcliffe
1917-1993 .... **CLC 51**
See also CA 1-4R; 140; CANR 6, 21

Srivastava, Dhanpat Rai 1880(?)-1936
See Premchand
See also CA 118; 197

Stacy, Donald
See Pohl, Frederik

Stael
See Stael-Holstein, Anne Louise Germaine Necker
See also EW 5; RGWL 2

Stael, Germaine de
See Stael-Holstein, Anne Louise Germaine Necker
See also DLB 119, 192; FW; GFL 1789 to the Present; TWA

Stael-Holstein, Anne Louise Germaine
Necker 1766-1817 .... **NCLC 3, 91**
See also Stael; Stael, Germaine de

Stafford, Jean 1915-1979 .. **CLC 4, 7, 19, 68; SSC 26**
See also CA 1-4R; 85-88; CANR 3, 65; DLB 2, 173; MTCW 1, 2; RGAL 4; RGSF 2; SATA-Obit 22; TCWW 2; TUS

Stafford, William (Edgar)
1914-1993 .... **CLC 4, 7, 29**
See also AMWS 11; CA 5-8R; 142; CAAS 3; CANR 5, 22; DAM POET; DLB 5, 206; EXPP; INT CANR-22; PFS 2, 8; RGAL 4; WP

Stagnelius, Eric Johan 1793-1823 . **NCLC 61**

Staines, Trevor
See Brunner, John (Kilian Houston)

Stairs, Gordon
See Austin, Mary (Hunter)
See also TCWW 2

Stairs, Gordon 1868-1934
See Austin, Mary (Hunter)

Stalin, Joseph 1879-1953 .... **TCLC 92**

Stancykowna
See Szymborska, Wislawa

Stannard, Martin 1947- .... **CLC 44**
See also CA 142; DLB 155

Stanton, Elizabeth Cady
1815-1902 .... **TCLC 73**
See also CA 171; DLB 79; FW

Stanton, Maura 1946- .... **CLC 9**
See also CA 89-92; CANR 15; DLB 120

Stanton, Schuyler
See Baum, L(yman) Frank

Stapledon, (William) Olaf
1886-1950 .... **TCLC 22**
See also CA 111; 162; DLB 15, 255; SFW 4

Starbuck, George (Edwin)
1931-1996 .... **CLC 53**
See also CA 21-24R; 153; CANR 23; DAM POET

Stark, Richard
See Westlake, Donald E(dwin)

Staunton, Schuyler
See Baum, L(yman) Frank

Stead, Christina (Ellen) 1902-1983 ... **CLC 2, 5, 8, 32, 80**
See also BRWS 4; CA 13-16R; 109; CANR 33, 40; DLB 260; FW; MTCW 1, 2; RGEL 2; RGSF 2

Stead, William Thomas
1849-1912 .... **TCLC 48**
See also CA 167

Stebnitsky, M.
See Leskov, Nikolai (Semyonovich)

Steele, Sir Richard 1672-1729 .... **LC 18**
See also BRW 3; CDBLB 1660-1789; DLB 84, 101; RGEL 2; WLIT 3

Steele, Timothy (Reid) 1948- .... **CLC 45**
See also CA 93-96; CANR 16, 50, 92; CP 7; DLB 120

Steffens, (Joseph) Lincoln
1866-1936 .... **TCLC 20**
See also CA 117

Stegner, Wallace (Earle) 1909-1993 .. **CLC 9, 49, 81; SSC 27**
See also AITN 1; AMWS 4; ANW; BEST 90:3; BPFB 3; CA 1-4R; 141; CAAS 9; CANR 1, 21, 46; DAM NOV; DLB 9, 206; DLBY 1993; MTCW 1, 2; RGAL 4; TCWW 2; TUS

Stein, Gertrude 1874-1946 .... **TCLC 1, 6, 28, 48; PC 18; SSC 42; WLC**
See also AMW; CA 104; 132; CANR 108; CDALB 1917-1929; DA; DA3; DAB; DAC; DAM MST, NOV, POET; DLB 4, 54, 86, 228; DLBD 15; EXPS; GLL 1; MAWW; MTCW 1, 2; NCFS 4; RGAL 4; RGSF 2; SSFS 5; TUS; WP

Steinbeck, John (Ernst) 1902-1968 ... **CLC 1, 5, 9, 13, 21, 34, 45, 75, 124; SSC 11, 37; WLC**
See also AAYA 12; AMW; BPFB 3; BYA 2, 3, 13; CA 1-4R; 25-28R; CANR 1, 35; CDALB 1929-1941; DA; DA3; DAB; DAC; DAM DRAM, MST, NOV; DLB 7, 9, 212; DLBD 2; EXPS; LAIT 3; MTCW 1, 2; NFS 1, 5, 7; RGAL 4; RGSF 2; RHW; SATA 9; SSFS 3, 6; TCWW 2; TUS; WYA; YAW

Steinem, Gloria 1934- .... **CLC 63**
See also CA 53-56; CANR 28, 51; DLB 246; FW; MTCW 1, 2

Steiner, George 1929- .... **CLC 24**
See also CA 73-76; CANR 31, 67, 108; DAM NOV; DLB 67; MTCW 1, 2; SATA 62

Steiner, K. Leslie
See Delany, Samuel R(ay), Jr.

Steiner, Rudolf 1861-1925 .... **TCLC 13**
See also CA 107

Updike, John (Hoyer) 1932- . **CLC 1, 2, 3, 5, 7, 9, 13, 15, 23, 34, 43, 70, 139; SSC 13, 27; WLC**
See also AAYA 36; AMW; AMWR 1; BPFB 3; BYA 12; CA 1-4R; CABS 1; CANR 4, 33, 51, 94; CDALB 1968-1988; CN 7; CP 7; CPW 1; DA; DA3; DAB; DAC; DAM MST, NOV, POET, POP; DLB 2, 5, 143, 218, 227; DLBD 3; DLBY 1980, 1982, 1997; EXPP; HGG; MTCW 1, 2; NFS 12; RGAL 4; RGSF 2; SSFS 3; TUS

Upshaw, Margaret Mitchell
See Mitchell, Margaret (Munnerlyn)

Upton, Mark
See Sanders, Lawrence

Upward, Allen 1863-1926 .... **TCLC 85**
See also CA 117; 187; DLB 36

Urdang, Constance (Henriette)
1922-1996 .... **CLC 47**
See also CA 21-24R; CANR 9, 24; CP 7; CWP

Uriel, Henry
See Faust, Frederick (Schiller)

Uris, Leon (Marcus) 1924- .... **CLC 7, 32**
See also AITN 1, 2; BEST 89:2; BPFB 3; CA 1-4R; CANR 1, 40, 65; CN 7; CPW 1; DA3; DAM NOV, POP; MTCW 1, 2; SATA 49

Urista, Alberto H. 1947- .... **PC 34**
See also Alurista
See also CA 45-48, 182; CANR 2, 32; HLCS 1; HW 1

Urmuz
See Codrescu, Andrei

Urquhart, Guy
See McAlmon, Robert (Menzies)

Urquhart, Jane 1949- .... **CLC 90**
See also CA 113; CANR 32, 68; CCA 1; DAC

Usigli, Rodolfo 1905-1979
See also CA 131; HLCS 1; HW 1; LAW

Ustinov, Peter (Alexander) 1921- .... **CLC 1**
See also AITN 1; CA 13-16R; CANR 25, 51; CBD; CD 5; DLB 13; MTCW 2

U Tam'si, Gerald Felix Tchicaya
See Tchicaya, Gerald Felix

U Tam'si, Tchicaya
See Tchicaya, Gerald Felix

Vachss, Andrew (Henry) 1942- .... **CLC 106**
See also CA 118; CANR 44, 95; CMW 4

Vachss, Andrew H.
See Vachss, Andrew (Henry)

Vaculik, Ludvik 1926- .... **CLC 7**
See also CA 53-56; CANR 72; CWW 2; DLB 232

Vaihinger, Hans 1852-1933 .... **TCLC 71**
See also CA 116; 166

Valdez, Luis (Miguel) 1940- ..... **CLC 84; DC 10; HLC 2**
See also CA 101; CAD; CANR 32, 81; CD 5; DAM MULT; DFS 5; DLB 122; HW 1; LAIT 4

Valenzuela, Luisa 1938- .... **CLC 31, 104; HLCS 2; SSC 14**
See also CA 101; CANR 32, 65; CDWLB 3; CWW 2; DAM MULT; DLB 113; FW; HW 1, 2; LAW; RGSF 2

Valera y Alcala-Galiano, Juan
1824-1905 .... **TCLC 10**
See also CA 106

Valery, (Ambroise) Paul (Toussaint Jules)
1871-1945 .... **TCLC 4, 15; PC 9**
See also CA 104; 122; DA3; DAM POET; DLB 258; EW 8; GFL 1789 to the Present; MTCW 1, 2; RGWL 2; TWA

Valle-Inclan, Ramon (Maria) del
1866-1936 .... **TCLC 5; HLC 2**
See also CA 106; 153; CANR 80; DAM MULT; DLB 134; EW 8; HW 2; RGSF 2; RGWL 2

Vallejo, Antonio Buero
See Buero Vallejo, Antonio

Vallejo, Cesar (Abraham)
1892-1938 .... **TCLC 3, 56; HLC 2**
See also CA 105; 153; DAM MULT; HW 1; LAW; RGWL 2

Valles, Jules 1832-1885 .... **NCLC 71**
See also DLB 123; GFL 1789 to the Present

Vallette, Marguerite Eymery
1860-1953 .... **TCLC 67**
See also CA 182; DLB 123, 192

Valle Y Pena, Ramon del
See Valle-Inclan, Ramon (Maria) del

Van Ash, Cay 1918- .... **CLC 34**

Vanbrugh, Sir John 1664-1726 .... **LC 21**
See also BRW 2; DAM DRAM; DLB 80; IDTP; RGEL 2

Van Campen, Karl
See Campbell, John W(ood, Jr.)

Vance, Gerald
See Silverberg, Robert

Vance, Jack .... **CLC 35**
See also Vance, John Holbrook
See also DLB 8; FANT; SCFW 2; SFW 4; SUFW

Vance, John Holbrook 1916-
See Queen, Ellery; Vance, Jack
See also CA 29-32R; CANR 17, 65; CMW 4; MTCW 1

Van Den Bogarde, Derek Jules Gaspard Ulric Niven 1921-1999 .... **CLC 14**
See also Bogarde, Dirk
See also CA 77-80; 179

Vandenburgh, Jane .... **CLC 59**
See also CA 168

Vanderhaeghe, Guy 1951- .... **CLC 41**
See also BPFB 3; CA 113; CANR 72

van der Post, Laurens (Jan)
1906-1996 .... **CLC 5**
See also AFW; CA 5-8R; 155; CANR 35; CN 7; DLB 204; RGEL 2

van de Wetering, Janwillem 1931- ... **CLC 47**
See also CA 49-52; CANR 4, 62, 90; CMW 4

Van Dine, S. S. .... **TCLC 23**
See also Wright, Willard Huntington
See also MSW

Van Doren, Carl (Clinton)
1885-1950 .... **TCLC 18**
See also CA 111; 168

Van Doren, Mark 1894-1972 .... **CLC 6, 10**
See also CA 1-4R; 37-40R; CANR 3; DLB 45; MTCW 1, 2; RGAL 4

Van Druten, John (William)
1901-1957 .... **TCLC 2**
See also CA 104; 161; DLB 10; RGAL 4

Van Duyn, Mona (Jane) 1921- ...... **CLC 3, 7, 63, 116**
See also CA 9-12R; CANR 7, 38, 60; CP 7; CWP; DAM POET; DLB 5

Van Dyne, Edith
See Baum, L(yman) Frank

van Itallie, Jean-Claude 1936- .... **CLC 3**
See also CA 45-48; CAAS 2; CAD; CANR 1, 48; CD 5; DLB 7

Van Loot, Cornelius Obenchain
See Roberts, Kenneth (Lewis)

van Ostaijen, Paul 1896-1928 .... **TCLC 33**
See also CA 163

Van Peebles, Melvin 1932- .... **CLC 2, 20**
See also BW 2, 3; CA 85-88; CANR 27, 67, 82; DAM MULT

van Schendel, Arthur(-Francois-Emile)
1874-1946 .... **TCLC 56**

Vansittart, Peter 1920- .... **CLC 42**
See also CA 1-4R; CANR 3, 49, 90; CN 7; RHW

Van Vechten, Carl 1880-1964 .... **CLC 33**
See also AMWS 2; CA 183; 89-92; DLB 4, 9; RGAL 4

van Vogt, A(lfred) E(lton) 1912-2000 . **CLC 1**
See also BPFB 3; BYA 13, 14; CA 21-24R; 190; CANR 28; DLB 8, 251; SATA 14; SATA-Obit 124; SCFW; SFW 4

Varda, Agnes 1928- .... **CLC 16**
See also CA 116; 122

Vargas Llosa, (Jorge) Mario (Pedro)
1936- .... **CLC 3, 6, 9, 10, 15, 31, 42, 85; HLC 2**
See also Llosa, (Jorge) Mario (Pedro) Vargas
See also BPFB 3; CA 73-76; CANR 18, 32, 42, 67; CDWLB 3; DA; DA3; DAB; DAC; DAM MST, MULT, NOV; DLB 145; DNFS 2; HW 1, 2; LAIT 5; LAW; LAWS 1; MTCW 1, 2; RGWL 2; SSFS 14; TWA; WLIT 1

Vasiliu, George
See Bacovia, George

Vasiliu, Gheorghe
See Bacovia, George
See also CA 123; 189

Vassa, Gustavus
See Equiano, Olaudah

Vassilikos, Vassilis 1933- .... **CLC 4, 8**
See also CA 81-84; CANR 75

Vaughan, Henry 1621-1695 .... **LC 27**
See also BRW 2; DLB 131; PAB; RGEL 2

Vaughn, Stephanie .... **CLC 62**

Vazov, Ivan (Minchov) 1850-1921 . **TCLC 25**
See also CA 121; 167; CDWLB 4; DLB 147

Veblen, Thorstein B(unde)
1857-1929 .... **TCLC 31**
See also AMWS 1; CA 115; 165; DLB 246

Vega, Lope de 1562-1635 .... **LC 23; HLCS 2**
See also EW 2; RGWL 2

Vendler, Helen (Hennessy) 1933- ... **CLC 138**
See also CA 41-44R; CANR 25, 72; MTCW 1, 2

Venison, Alfred
See Pound, Ezra (Weston Loomis)

Verdi, Marie de
See Mencken, H(enry) L(ouis)

Verdu, Matilde
See Cela, Camilo Jose

Verga, Giovanni (Carmelo)
1840-1922 .... **TCLC 3; SSC 21**
See also CA 104; 123; CANR 101; EW 7; RGSF 2; RGWL 2

Vergil 70 B.C.-19 B.C. . **CMLC 9, 40; PC 12; WLCS**
See also Virgil
See also AW 2; DA; DA3; DAB; DAC; DAM MST, POET; EFS 1

Verhaeren, Emile (Adolphe Gustave)
1855-1916 .... **TCLC 12**
See also CA 109; GFL 1789 to the Present

Verlaine, Paul (Marie) 1844-1896 .. **NCLC 2, 51; PC 2, 32**
See also DAM POET; DLB 217; EW 7; GFL 1789 to the Present; RGWL 2; TWA

Verne, Jules (Gabriel) 1828-1905 ... **TCLC 6, 52**
See also AAYA 16; BYA 4; CA 110; 131; DA3; DLB 123; GFL 1789 to the Present; JRDA; LAIT 2; MAICYA 1, 2; RGWL 2; SATA 21; SCFW; SFW 4; TWA; WCH

Verus, Marcus Annius
See Aurelius, Marcus

Very, Jones 1813-1880 .... **NCLC 9**
See also DLB 1, 243; RGAL 4

Vesaas, Tarjei 1897-1970 .... **CLC 48**
See also CA 190; 29-32R; EW 11

Vialis, Gaston
See Simenon, Georges (Jacques Christian)

Vian, Boris 1920-1959 .... **TCLC 9**
See also CA 106; 164; DLB 72; GFL 1789
to the Present; MTCW 2; RGWL 2

Viaud, (Louis Marie) Julien 1850-1923
See Loti, Pierre
See also CA 107

Vicar, Henry
See Felsen, Henry Gregor

Vicker, Angus
See Felsen, Henry Gregor

Vidal, Gore 1925- ...... **CLC 2, 4, 6, 8, 10, 22,**
33, 72, 142
See also Box, Edgar
See also AITN 1; AMWS 4; BEST 90:2;
BPFB 3; CA 5-8R; CAD; CANR 13, 45,
65, 100; CD 5; CDALBS; CN 7; CPW;
DA3; DAM NOV, POP; DFS 2; DLB 6,
152; INT CANR-13; MTCW 1, 2; RGAL
4; RHW; TUS

Viereck, Peter (Robert Edwin)
1916- .... **CLC 4; PC 27**
See also CA 1-4R; CANR 1, 47; CP 7; DLB
5; PFS 9, 14

Vigny, Alfred (Victor) de
1797-1863 .... **NCLC 7, 102; PC 26**
See also DAM POET; DLB 119, 192, 217;
EW 5; GFL 1789 to the Present; RGWL 2

Vilakazi, Benedict Wallet
1906-1947 .... **TCLC 37**
See also CA 168

Villa, Jose Garcia 1914-1997 .... **PC 22**
See also AAL; CA 25-28R; CANR 12;
EXPP

Villarreal, Jose Antonio 1924-
See also CA 133; CANR 93; DAM MULT;
DLB 82; HLC 2; HW 1; LAIT 4; RGAL
4

Villaurrutia, Xavier 1903-1950 ...... **TCLC 80**
See also CA 192; HW 1; LAW

Villehardouin, Geoffroi de
1150(?)-1218(?) .... **CMLC 38**

Villiers de l'Isle Adam, Jean Marie Mathias
Philippe Auguste 1838-1889 ... **NCLC 3;**
SSC 14
See also DLB 123, 192; GFL 1789 to the
Present; RGSF 2

Villon, Francois 1431-1463(?) . **LC 62; PC 13**
See also DLB 208; EW 2; RGWL 2; TWA

Vine, Barbara .... **CLC 50**
See also Rendell, Ruth (Barbara)
See also BEST 90:4

Vinge, Joan (Carol) D(ennison)
1948- .... **CLC 30; SSC 24**
See also AAYA 32; BPFB 3; CA 93-96;
CANR 72; SATA 36, 113; SFW 4; YAW

Viola, Herman J(oseph) 1938- .... **CLC 70**
See also CA 61-64; CANR 8, 23, 48, 91;
SATA 126

Violis, G.
See Simenon, Georges (Jacques Christian)

Viramontes, Helena Maria 1954-
See also CA 159; DLB 122; HLCS 2; HW
2

Virgil
See Vergil
See also CDWLB 1; DLB 211; LAIT 1;
RGWL 2; WP

Visconti, Luchino 1906-1976 .... **CLC 16**
See also CA 81-84; 65-68; CANR 39

Vittorini, Elio 1908-1966 .... **CLC 6, 9, 14**
See also CA 133; 25-28R; DLB 264; EW
12; RGWL 2

Vivekananda, Swami 1863-1902 .... **TCLC 88**

Vizenor, Gerald Robert 1934- .... **CLC 103**
See also CA 13-16R; CAAS 22; CANR 5,
21, 44, 67; DAM MULT; DLB 175, 227;
MTCW 2; NNAL; TCWW 2

Vizinczey, Stephen 1933- .... **CLC 40**
See also CA 128; CCA 1; INT 128

Vliet, R(ussell) G(ordon)
1929-1984 .... **CLC 22**
See also CA 37-40R; 112; CANR 18

Vogau, Boris Andreyevich 1894-1937(?)
See Pilnyak, Boris
See also CA 123

Vogel, Paula A(nne) 1951- ... **CLC 76; DC 18**
See also CA 108; CAD; CD 5; CWD; DFS
14; RGAL 4

Voigt, Cynthia 1942- .... **CLC 30**
See also AAYA 3, 30; BYA 1, 3, 6, 7, 8;
CA 106; CANR 18, 37, 40, 94; CLR 13,
48; INT CANR-18; JRDA; LAIT 5; MAI-
CYA 1, 2; MAICYAS 1; SATA 48, 79,
116; SATA-Brief 33; WYA; YAW

Voigt, Ellen Bryant 1943- .... **CLC 54**
See also CA 69-72; CANR 11, 29, 55; CP
7; CSW; CWP; DLB 120

Voinovich, Vladimir (Nikolaevich)
1932- .... **CLC 10, 49, 147**
See also CA 81-84; CAAS 12; CANR 33,
67; MTCW 1

Vollmann, William T. 1959- .... **CLC 89**
See also CA 134; CANR 67; CPW; DA3;
DAM NOV, POP; MTCW 2

Voloshinov, V. N.
See Bakhtin, Mikhail Mikhailovich

Voltaire 1694-1778 .... **LC 14, 79; SSC 12;**
WLC
See also BYA 13; DA; DA3; DAB; DAC;
DAM DRAM, MST; EW 4; GFL Begin-
nings to 1789; NFS 7; RGWL 2; TWA

von Aschendrof, Baron Ignatz 1873-1939
See Ford, Ford Madox

von Daeniken, Erich 1935- .... **CLC 30**
See also AITN 1; CA 37-40R; CANR 17,
44

von Daniken, Erich
See von Daeniken, Erich

von Hartmann, Eduard
1842-1906 .... **TCLC 96**

von Hayek, Friedrich August
See Hayek, F(riedrich) A(ugust von)

von Heidenstam, (Carl Gustaf) Verner
See Heidenstam, (Carl Gustaf) Verner von

von Heyse, Paul (Johann Ludwig)
See Heyse, Paul (Johann Ludwig von)

von Hofmannsthal, Hugo
See Hofmannsthal, Hugo von

von Horvath, Odon
See Horvath, Odon von

von Horvath, Odon
See Horvath, Odon von

von Horvath, Oedoen
See Horvath, Odon von
See also CA 184

von Liliencron, (Friedrich Adolf Axel)
Detlev
See Liliencron, (Friedrich Adolf Axel) De-
tlev von

Vonnegut, Kurt, Jr. 1922- . **CLC 1, 2, 3, 4, 5,**
8, 12, 22, 40, 60, 111; SSC 8; WLC
See also AAYA 6; AITN 1; AMWS 2; BEST
90:4; BPFB 3; BYA 3, 14; CA 1-4R;
CANR 1, 25, 49, 75, 92; CDALB 1968-
1988; CN 7; CPW 1; DA; DA3; DAB;
DAC; DAM MST, NOV, POP; DLB 2, 8,
152; DLBD 3; DLBY 1980; EXPN;
EXPS; LAIT 4; MTCW 1, 2; NFS 3;
RGAL 4; SCFW; SFW 4; SSFS 5; TUS;
YAW

Von Rachen, Kurt
See Hubbard, L(afayette) Ron(ald)

von Rezzori (d'Arezzo), Gregor
See Rezzori (d'Arezzo), Gregor von

von Sternberg, Josef
See Sternberg, Josef von

Vorster, Gordon 1924- .... **CLC 34**
See also CA 133

Vosce, Trudie
See Ozick, Cynthia

Voznesensky, Andrei (Andreievich)
1933- .... **CLC 1, 15, 57**
See also CA 89-92; CANR 37; CWW 2;
DAM POET; MTCW 1

Waddington, Miriam 1917- .... **CLC 28**
See also CA 21-24R; CANR 12, 30; CCA
1; CP 7; DLB 68

Wagman, Fredrica 1937- .... **CLC 7**
See also CA 97-100; INT 97-100

Wagner, Linda W.
See Wagner-Martin, Linda (C.)

Wagner, Linda Welshimer
See Wagner-Martin, Linda (C.)

Wagner, Richard 1813-1883 .... **NCLC 9**
See also DLB 129; EW 6

Wagner-Martin, Linda (C.) 1936- .... **CLC 50**
See also CA 159

Wagoner, David (Russell) 1926- .... **CLC 3, 5,**
15; PC 33
See also AMWS 9; CA 1-4R; CAAS 3;
CANR 2, 71; CN 7; CP 7; DLB 5, 256;
SATA 14; TCWW 2

Wah, Fred(erick James) 1939- .... **CLC 44**
See also CA 107; 141; CP 7; DLB 60

Wahloo, Per 1926-1975 .... **CLC 7**
See also BPFB 3; CA 61-64; CANR 73;
CMW 4; MSW

Wahloo, Peter
See Wahloo, Per

Wain, John (Barrington) 1925-1994 . **CLC 2,**
11, 15, 46
See also CA 5-8R; 145; CAAS 4; CANR
23, 54; CDBLB 1960 to Present; DLB 15,
27, 139, 155; MTCW 1, 2

Wajda, Andrzej 1926- .... **CLC 16**
See also CA 102

Wakefield, Dan 1932- .... **CLC 7**
See also CA 21-24R; CAAS 7; CN 7

Wakefield, Herbert Russell
1888-1965 .... **TCLC 120**
See also CA 5-8R; CANR 77; HGG; SUFW

Wakoski, Diane 1937- ...... **CLC 2, 4, 7, 9, 11,**
40; PC 15
See also CA 13-16R; CAAS 1; CANR 9,
60, 106; CP 7; CWP; DAM POET; DLB
5; INT CANR-9; MTCW 2

Wakoski-Sherbell, Diane
See Wakoski, Diane

Walcott, Derek (Alton) 1930- .... **CLC 2, 4, 9,**
14, 25, 42, 67, 76, 160; BLC 3; DC 7
See also BW 2; CA 89-92; CANR 26, 47,
75, 80; CBD; CD 5; CDWLB 3; CP 7;
DA3; DAB; DAC; DAM MST, MULT,
POET; DLB 117; DLBY 1981; DNFS 1;
EFS 1; MTCW 1, 2; PFS 6; RGEL 2;
TWA

Waldman, Anne (Lesley) 1945- .... **CLC 7**
See also CA 37-40R; CAAS 17; CANR 34,
69; CP 7; CWP; DLB 16

Waldo, E. Hunter
See Sturgeon, Theodore (Hamilton)

Waldo, Edward Hamilton
See Sturgeon, Theodore (Hamilton)

Walker, Alice (Malsenior) 1944- ... **CLC 5, 6,**
9, 19, 27, 46, 58, 103; BLC 3; PC 30;
SSC 5; WLCS
See also AAYA 3, 33; AFAW 1, 2; AMWS
3; BEST 89:4; BPFB 3; BW 2, 3; CA 37-
40R; CANR 9, 27, 49, 66, 82; CDALB

Weber, Max 1864-1920 .... **TCLC 69**
  See also CA 109; 189
Webster, John 1580(?)-1634(?) .... **LC 33; DC 2; WLC**
  See also BRW 2; CDBLB Before 1660; DA; DAB; DAC; DAM DRAM, MST; DLB 58; IDTP; RGEL 2; WLIT 3
Webster, Noah 1758-1843 .... **NCLC 30**
  See also DLB 1, 37, 42, 43, 73, 243
Wedekind, (Benjamin) Frank(lin)
  1864-1918 .... **TCLC 7**
  See also CA 104; 153; CDWLB 2; DAM DRAM; DLB 118; EW 8; RGWL 2
Wehr, Demaris .... **CLC 65**
Weidman, Jerome 1913-1998 .... **CLC 7**
  See also AITN 2; CA 1-4R; 171; CAD; CANR 1; DLB 28
Weil, Simone (Adolphine)
  1909-1943 .... **TCLC 23**
  See also CA 117; 159; EW 12; FW; GFL 1789 to the Present; MTCW 2
Weininger, Otto 1880-1903 .... **TCLC 84**
Weinstein, Nathan
  See West, Nathanael
Weinstein, Nathan von Wallenstein
  See West, Nathanael
Weir, Peter (Lindsay) 1944- .... **CLC 20**
  See also CA 113; 123
Weiss, Peter (Ulrich) 1916-1982 .. **CLC 3, 15, 51**
  See also CA 45-48; 106; CANR 3; DAM DRAM; DFS 3; DLB 69, 124; RGWL 2
Weiss, Theodore (Russell) 1916- ... **CLC 3, 8, 14**
  See also CA 9-12R; CAAE 189; CAAS 2; CANR 46, 94; CP 7; DLB 5
Welch, (Maurice) Denton
  1915-1948 .... **TCLC 22**
  See also BRWS 8; CA 121; 148; RGEL 2
Welch, James 1940- .... **CLC 6, 14, 52**
  See also CA 85-88; CANR 42, 66, 107; CN 7; CP 7; CPW; DAM MULT, POP; DLB 175, 256; NNAL; RGAL 4; TCWW 2
Weldon, Fay 1931- . **CLC 6, 9, 11, 19, 36, 59, 122**
  See also BRWS 4; CA 21-24R; CANR 16, 46, 63, 97; CDBLB 1960 to Present; CN 7; CPW; DAM POP; DLB 14, 194; FW; HGG; INT CANR-16; MTCW 1, 2; RGEL 2; RGSF 2
Wellek, Rene 1903-1995 .... **CLC 28**
  See also CA 5-8R; 150; CAAS 7; CANR 8; DLB 63; INT CANR-8
Weller, Michael 1942- .... **CLC 10, 53**
  See also CA 85-88; CAD; CD 5
Weller, Paul 1958- .... **CLC 26**
Wellershoff, Dieter 1925- .... **CLC 46**
  See also CA 89-92; CANR 16, 37
Welles, (George) Orson 1915-1985 .. **CLC 20, 80**
  See also AAYA 40; CA 93-96; 117
Wellman, John McDowell 1945-
  See Wellman, Mac
  See also CA 166; CD 5
Wellman, Mac .... **CLC 65**
  See also Wellman, John McDowell; Wellman, John McDowell
  See also CAD; RGAL 4
Wellman, Manly Wade 1903-1986 ... **CLC 49**
  See also CA 1-4R; 118; CANR 6, 16, 44; FANT; SATA 6; SATA-Obit 47; SFW 4; SUFW
Wells, Carolyn 1869(?)-1942 .... **TCLC 35**
  See also CA 113; 185; CMW 4; DLB 11

Wells, H(erbert) G(eorge)
  1866-1946 .... **TCLC 6, 12, 19; SSC 6; WLC**
  See also AAYA 18; BPFB 3; BRW 6; CA 110; 121; CDBLB 1914-1945; CLR 64; DA; DA3; DAB; DAC; DAM MST, NOV; DLB 34, 70, 156, 178; EXPS; HGG; LAIT 3; MTCW 1, 2; RGEL 2; RGSF 2; SATA 20; SCFW; SFW 4; SSFS 3; SUFW; TEA; WCH; WLIT 4; YAW
Wells, Rosemary 1943- .... **CLC 12**
  See also AAYA 13; BYA 7, 8; CA 85-88; CANR 48; CLR 16, 69; CWRI 5; MAICYA 1, 2; SAAS 1; SATA 18, 69, 114;
Wells-Barnett, Ida B(ell)
  1862-1931 .... **TCLC 125**
  See also CA 182; DLB 23, 221
Welsh, Irvine 1958- .... **CLC 144**
  See also CA 173
Welty, Eudora (Alice) 1909-2001 .. **CLC 1, 2, 5, 14, 22, 33, 105; SSC 1, 27, 51; WLC**
  See also AMW; AMWR 1; BPFB 3; CA 9-12R; 199; CABS 1; CANR 32, 65; CDALB 1941-1968; CN 7; CSW; DA; DA3; DAB; DAC; DAM MST, NOV; DLB 2, 102, 143; DLBD 12; DLBY 1987, 2001; EXPS; HGG; LAIT 3; MAWW; MTCW 1, 2; NFS 13, 15; RGAL 4; RGSF 2; RHW; SSFS 2, 10; TUS
Wen I-to 1899-1946 .... **TCLC 28**
Wentworth, Robert
  See Hamilton, Edmond
Werfel, Franz (Viktor) 1890-1945 ... **TCLC 8**
  See also CA 104; 161; DLB 81, 124; RGWL 2
Wergeland, Henrik Arnold
  1808-1845 .... **NCLC 5**
Wersba, Barbara 1932- .... **CLC 30**
  See also AAYA 2, 30; BYA 6, 12, 13; CA 29-32R, 182; CAAE 182; CANR 16, 38; CLR 3, 78; DLB 52; JRDA; MAICYA 1, 2; SAAS 2; SATA 1, 58; SATA-Essay 103; WYA; YAW
Wertmueller, Lina 1928- .... **CLC 16**
  See also CA 97-100; CANR 39, 78
Wescott, Glenway 1901-1987 .. **CLC 13; SSC 35**
  See also CA 13-16R; 121; CANR 23, 70; DLB 4, 9, 102; RGAL 4
Wesker, Arnold 1932- .... **CLC 3, 5, 42**
  See also CA 1-4R; CAAS 7; CANR 1, 33; CBD; CD 5; CDBLB 1960 to Present; DAB; DAM DRAM; DLB 13; MTCW 1; RGEL 2; TEA
Wesley, Richard (Errol) 1945- .... **CLC 7**
  See also BW 1; CA 57-60; CAD; CANR 27; CD 5; DLB 38
Wessel, Johan Herman 1742-1785 .... **LC 7**
West, Anthony (Panther)
  1914-1987 .... **CLC 50**
  See also CA 45-48; 124; CANR 3, 19; DLB 15
West, C. P.
  See Wodehouse, P(elham) G(renville)
West, Cornel (Ronald) 1953- .... **CLC 134; BLCS**
  See also CA 144; CANR 91; DLB 246
West, Delno C(loyde), Jr. 1936- .... **CLC 70**
  See also CA 57-60
West, Dorothy 1907-1998 .... **TCLC 108**
  See also BW 2; CA 143; 169; DLB 76
West, (Mary) Jessamyn 1902-1984 ... **CLC 7, 17**
  See also CA 9-12R; 112; CANR 27; DLB 6; DLBY 1984; MTCW 1, 2; RHW; SATA-Obit 37; TUS; YAW

West, Morris L(anglo) 1916-1999 ..... **CLC 6, 33**
  See also BPFB 3; CA 5-8R; 187; CANR 24, 49, 64; CN 7; CPW; MTCW 1, 2
West, Nathanael 1903-1940 .... **TCLC 1, 14, 44; SSC 16**
  See also AMW; BPFB 3; CA 104; 125; CDALB 1929-1941; DA3; DLB 4, 9, 28; MTCW 1, 2; RGAL 4; TUS
West, Owen
  See Koontz, Dean R(ay)
West, Paul 1930- .... **CLC 7, 14, 96**
  See also CA 13-16R; CAAS 7; CANR 22, 53, 76, 89; CN 7; DLB 14; INT CANR-22; MTCW 2
West, Rebecca 1892-1983 ... **CLC 7, 9, 31, 50**
  See also BPFB 3; BRWS 3; CA 5-8R; 109; CANR 19; DLB 36; DLBY 1983; FW; MTCW 1, 2; NCFS 4; RGEL 2; TEA
Westall, Robert (Atkinson)
  1929-1993 .... **CLC 17**
  See also AAYA 12; BYA 2, 6, 7, 8, 9; CA 69-72; 141; CANR 18, 68; CLR 13; FANT; JRDA; MAICYA 1, 2; MAICYAS 1; SAAS 2; SATA 23, 69; SATA-Obit 75; WYA; YAW
Westermarck, Edward 1862-1939 . **TCLC 87**
Westlake, Donald E(dwin) 1933- . **CLC 7, 33**
  See also BPFB 3; CA 17-20R; CAAS 13; CANR 16, 44, 65, 94; CMW 4; CPW; DAM POP; INT CANR-16; MSW; MTCW 2
Westmacott, Mary
  See Christie, Agatha (Mary Clarissa)
Weston, Allen
  See Norton, Andre
Wetcheek, J. L.
  See Feuchtwanger, Lion
Wetering, Janwillem van de
  See van de Wetering, Janwillem
Wetherald, Agnes Ethelwyn
  1857-1940 .... **TCLC 81**
  See also CA 202; DLB 99
Wetherell, Elizabeth
  See Warner, Susan (Bogert)
Whale, James 1889-1957 .... **TCLC 63**
Whalen, Philip 1923- .... **CLC 6, 29**
  See also CA 9-12R; CANR 5, 39; CP 7; DLB 16; WP
Wharton, Edith (Newbold Jones)
  1862-1937 ... **TCLC 3, 9, 27, 53; SSC 6; WLC**
  See also AAYA 25; AMW; AMWR 1; BPFB 3; CA 104; 132; CDALB 1865-1917; DA; DA3; DAB; DAC; DAM MST, NOV; DLB 4, 9, 12, 78, 189; DLBD 13; EXPS; HGG; LAIT 2, 3; MAWW; MTCW 1, 2; NFS 5, 11, 15; RGAL 4; RGSF 2; RHW; SSFS 6, 7; SUFW; TUS
Wharton, James
  See Mencken, H(enry) L(ouis)
Wharton, William (a pseudonym) . **CLC 18, 37**
  See also CA 93-96; DLBY 1980; INT 93-96
Wheatley (Peters), Phillis
  1753(?)-1784 ... **LC 3, 50; BLC 3; PC 3; WLC**
  See also AFAW 1, 2; CDALB 1640-1865; DA; DA3; DAC; DAM MST, MULT, POET; DLB 31, 50; EXPP; PFS 13; RGAL 4
Wheelock, John Hall 1886-1978 .... **CLC 14**
  See also CA 13-16R; 77-80; CANR 14; DLB 45
White, Babington
  See Braddon, Mary Elizabeth

DLB 36, 100, 162; DLBD 10; EXPS; FW;
LAIT 3; MTCW 1, 2; NCFS 2; NFS 8,
12; RGEL 2; RGSF 2; SSFS 4, 12; TEA;
WLIT 4

Woollcott, Alexander (Humphreys)
1887-1943 .... **TCLC 5**
See also CA 105; 161; DLB 29

Woolrich, Cornell .... **CLC 77**
See also Hopley-Woolrich, Cornell George
See also MSW

Woolson, Constance Fenimore
1840-1894 .... **NCLC 82**
See also DLB 12, 74, 189, 221; RGAL 4

Wordsworth, Dorothy 1771-1855 .. **NCLC 25**
See also DLB 107

Wordsworth, William 1770-1850 .. **NCLC 12,
38, 111; PC 4; WLC**
See also BRW 4; CDBLB 1789-1832; DA;
DA3; DAB; DAC; DAM MST, POET;
DLB 93, 107; EXPP; PAB; PFS 2; RGEL
2; TEA; WLIT 3; WP

Wotton, Sir Henry 1568-1639 .... **LC 68**
See also DLB 121; RGEL 2

Wouk, Herman 1915- .... **CLC 1, 9, 38**
See also BPFB 2, 3; CA 5-8R; CANR 6,
33, 67; CDALBS; CN 7; CPW; DA3;
DAM NOV, POP; DLBY 1982; INT
CANR-6; LAIT 4; MTCW 1, 2; NFS 7;
TUS

Wright, Charles (Penzel, Jr.) 1935- .. **CLC 6,
13, 28, 119, 146**
See also AMWS 5; CA 29-32R; CAAS 7;
CANR 23, 36, 62, 88; CP 7; DLB 165;
DLBY 1982; MTCW 1, 2; PFS 10

Wright, Charles Stevenson 1932- ... **CLC 49;
BLC 3**
See also BW 1; CA 9-12R; CANR 26; CN
7; DAM MULT, POET; DLB 33

Wright, Frances 1795-1852 .... **NCLC 74**
See also DLB 73

Wright, Frank Lloyd 1867-1959 .... **TCLC 95**
See also AAYA 33; CA 174

Wright, Jack R.
See Harris, Mark

Wright, James (Arlington)
1927-1980 .... **CLC 3, 5, 10, 28; PC 36**
See also AITN 2; AMWS 3; CA 49-52; 97-
100; CANR 4, 34, 64; CDALBS; DAM
POET; DLB 5, 169; EXPP; MTCW 1, 2;
PFS 7, 8; RGAL 4; TUS; WP

Wright, Judith (Arundell)
1915-2000 .... **CLC 11, 53; PC 14**
See also CA 13-16R; 188; CANR 31, 76,
93; CP 7; CWP; DLB 260; MTCW 1, 2;
PFS 8; RGEL 2; SATA 14; SATA-Obit
121

Wright, L(auraii) R. 1939- .... **CLC 44**
See also CA 138; CMW 4

Wright, Richard (Nathaniel)
1908-1960 .... **CLC 1, 3, 4, 9, 14, 21, 48,
74; BLC 3; SSC 2; WLC**
See also AAYA 5, 42; AFAW 1, 2; AMW;
BPFB 3; BW 1; BYA 2; CA 108; CANR
64; CDALB 1929-1941; DA; DA3; DAB;
DAC; DAM MST, MULT, NOV; DLB 76,
102; DLBD 2; EXPN; LAIT 3, 4; MTCW
1, 2; NCFS 1; NFS 1, 7; RGAL 4; RGSF
2; SSFS 3, 9, 15; TUS; YAW

Wright, Richard B(ruce) 1937- .... **CLC 6**
See also CA 85-88; DLB 53

Wright, Rick 1945- .... **CLC 35**

Wright, Rowland
See Wells, Carolyn

Wright, Stephen 1946- .... **CLC 33**

Wright, Willard Huntington 1888-1939
See Van Dine, S. S.
See also CA 115; 189; CMW 4; DLBD 16

Wright, William 1930- .... **CLC 44**
See also CA 53-56; CANR 7, 23

Wroth, Lady Mary 1587-1653(?) .... **LC 30;
PC 38**
See also DLB 121

Wu Ch'eng-en 1500(?)-1582(?) .... **LC 7**

Wu Ching-tzu 1701-1754 .... **LC 2**

Wurlitzer, Rudolph 1938(?)- .... **CLC 2, 4, 15**
See also CA 85-88; CN 7; DLB 173

Wyatt, Sir Thomas c. 1503-1542 . **LC 70; PC
27**
See also BRW 1; DLB 132; EXPP; RGEL
2; TEA

Wycherley, William 1640-1716 .... **LC 8, 21**
See also BRW 2; CDBLB 1660-1789; DAM
DRAM; DLB 80; RGEL 2

Wylie, Elinor (Morton Hoyt)
1885-1928 .... **TCLC 8; PC 23**
See also AMWS 1; CA 105; 162; DLB 9,
45; EXPP; RGAL 4

Wylie, Philip (Gordon) 1902-1971 ... **CLC 43**
See also CA 21-22; 33-36R; CAP 2; DLB
9; SFW 4

Wyndham, John .... **CLC 19**
See also Harris, John (Wyndham Parkes
Lucas) Beynon
See also DLB 255; SCFW 2

Wyss, Johann David Von
1743-1818 .... **NCLC 10**
See also JRDA; MAICYA 1, 2; SATA 29;
SATA-Brief 27

Xenophon c. 430 B.C.-c. 354
B.C. .... **CMLC 17**
See also AW 1; DLB 176; RGWL 2

Yakumo Koizumi
See Hearn, (Patricio) Lafcadio (Tessima
Carlos)

Yamamoto, Hisaye 1921- .... **SSC 34; AAL**
See also DAM MULT; LAIT 4; SSFS 14

Yanez, Jose Donoso
See Donoso (Yanez), Jose

Yanovsky, Basile S.
See Yanovsky, V(assily) S(emenovich)

Yanovsky, V(assily) S(emenovich)
1906-1989 .... **CLC 2, 18**
See also CA 97-100; 129

Yates, Richard 1926-1992 .... **CLC 7, 8, 23**
See also AMWS 11; CA 5-8R; 139; CANR
10, 43; DLB 2, 234; DLBY 1981, 1992;
INT CANR-10

Yeats, W. B.
See Yeats, William Butler

Yeats, William Butler 1865-1939 .... **TCLC 1,
11, 18, 31, 93, 116; PC 20; WLC**
See also BRW 6; BRWR 1; CA 104; 127;
CANR 45; CDBLB 1890-1914; DA; DA3;
DAB; DAC; DAM DRAM, MST, POET;
DLB 10, 19, 98, 156; EXPP; MTCW 1,
2; NCFS 3; PAB; PFS 1, 2, 5, 7, 13, 15;
RGEL 2; TEA; WLIT 4; WP

Yehoshua, A(braham) B. 1936- .. **CLC 13, 31**
See also CA 33-36R; CANR 43, 90; RGSF
2

Yellow Bird
See Ridge, John Rollin

Yep, Laurence Michael 1948- .... **CLC 35**
See also AAYA 5, 31; BYA 7; CA 49-52;
CANR 1, 46, 92; CLR 3, 17, 54; DLB 52;
FANT; JRDA; MAICYA 1, 2; MAICYAS
1; SATA 7, 69, 123; WYA; YAW

Yerby, Frank G(arvin) 1916-1991 . **CLC 1, 7,
22; BLC 3**
See also BPFB 3; BW 1, 3; CA 9-12R; 136;
CANR 16, 52; DAM MULT; DLB 76;
INT CANR-16; MTCW 1; RGAL 4; RHW

Yesenin, Sergei Alexandrovich
See Esenin, Sergei (Alexandrovich)

Yevtushenko, Yevgeny (Alexandrovich)
1933- ...... **CLC 1, 3, 13, 26, 51, 126; PC
40**
See also Evtushenko, Evgenii Aleksandrovich
See also CA 81-84; CANR 33, 54; CWW
2; DAM POET; MTCW 1

Yezierska, Anzia 1885(?)-1970 .... **CLC 46**
See also CA 126; 89-92; DLB 28, 221; FW;
MTCW 1; RGAL 4; SSFS 15

Yglesias, Helen 1915- .... **CLC 7, 22**
See also CA 37-40R; CAAS 20; CANR 15,
65, 95; CN 7; INT CANR-15; MTCW 1

Yokomitsu, Riichi 1898-1947 .... **TCLC 47**
See also CA 170

Yonge, Charlotte (Mary)
1823-1901 .... **TCLC 48**
See also CA 109; 163; DLB 18, 163; RGEL
2; SATA 17; WCH

York, Jeremy
See Creasey, John

York, Simon
See Heinlein, Robert A(nson)

Yorke, Henry Vincent 1905-1974 ..... **CLC 13**
See also Green, Henry
See also CA 85-88; 49-52

Yosano Akiko 1878-1942 .... **TCLC 59; PC 11**
See also CA 161

Yoshimoto, Banana .... **CLC 84**
See also Yoshimoto, Mahoko
See also NFS 7

Yoshimoto, Mahoko 1964-
See Yoshimoto, Banana
See also CA 144; CANR 98

Young, Al(bert James) 1939- . **CLC 19; BLC
3**
See also BW 2, 3; CA 29-32R; CANR 26,
65, 109; CN 7; CP 7; DAM MULT; DLB
33

Young, Andrew (John) 1885-1971 ...... **CLC 5**
See also CA 5-8R; CANR 7, 29; RGEL 2

Young, Collier
See Bloch, Robert (Albert)

Young, Edward 1683-1765 .... **LC 3, 40**
See also DLB 95; RGEL 2

Young, Marguerite (Vivian)
1909-1995 .... **CLC 82**
See also CA 13-16; 150; CAP 1; CN 7

Young, Neil 1945- .... **CLC 17**
See also CA 110; CCA 1

Young Bear, Ray A. 1950- .... **CLC 94**
See also CA 146; DAM MULT; DLB 175;
NNAL

Yourcenar, Marguerite 1903-1987 ... **CLC 19,
38, 50, 87**
See also BPFB 3; CA 69-72; CANR 23, 60,
93; DAM NOV; DLB 72; DLBY 1988;
EW 12; GFL 1789 to the Present; GLL 1;
MTCW 1, 2; RGWL 2

Yuan, Chu 340(?) B.C.-278(?)
B.C. .... **CMLC 36**

Yurick, Sol 1925- .... **CLC 6**
See also CA 13-16R; CANR 25; CN 7

Zabolotsky, Nikolai Alekseevich
1903-1958 .... **TCLC 52**
See also CA 116; 164

Zagajewski, Adam 1945- .... **PC 27**
See also CA 186; DLB 232

Zalygin, Sergei -2000 .... **CLC 59**

Zamiatin, Evgenii
See Zamyatin, Evgeny Ivanovich
See also RGSF 2; RGWL 2

Zamiatin, Yevgenii
See Zamyatin, Evgeny Ivanovich

Zamora, Bernice (B. Ortiz) 1938- .. **CLC 89;
HLC 2**
See also CA 151; CANR 80; DAM MULT;
DLB 82; HW 1, 2

SSC Cumulative Nationality Index

Nationality Index

SSC-55 Title Index

ISBN 0-7876-5955-X

90000

9 780787 659554